Introduction to
Advertising & Promotion

···

An Integrated
Marketing Communications Perspective

Second Edition

Introduction to
Advertising & Promotion

*An Integrated
Marketing Communications Perspective*

George E. Belch

Michael A. Belch
both of San Diego State University

IRWIN

Homewood, IL 60430

Boston, MA 02116

© RICHARD D. IRWIN, INC., 1990 and 1993

Executive editor: Rob Zwettler
Developmental editor: Eleanore Snow
Marketing manager: Scott J. Timian
Project editor: Paula M. Buschman
Production manager: Bette K. Ittersagen
Designer: Kay Fulton/Keith McPherson
Art manager: Kim Meriwether
Photo research coordinator: Patricia A. Seefelt
Compositor: Carlisle Communications, Ltd.
Typeface: 10/12 Sabon
Printer: Von Hoffmann

Library of Congress Cataloging-in-Publication Data

Belch, George E. (George Eugene)
    Introduction to advertising and promotion : an integrated
marketing communications perspective / George E. Belch, Michael A.
Belch—2nd ed.
        p.   cm.
    ISBN 0-256-10516-2.—ISBN 0-256-10825-0 (International ed.)
    1. Advertising.   2. Sales promotion.   3. Communication in
marketing.   I. Belch, Michael A.   II. Title.
HF5823.B387   1993
659.1—dc20

92–22766

Printed in the United States of America
1 2 3 4 5 6 7 8 9 0   VH   9 8 7 6 5 4 3 2

THE IRWIN SERIES IN MARKETING

Consulting Editor
Gilbert A. Churchill, Jr.
University of Wisconsin—Madison

Alreck & Settle
The Survey Research Handbook
Second Edition

Belch & Belch
Introduction to Advertising and Promotion
Second Edition

Berkowitz, Kerin, Hartley & Rudelius
Marketing
Third Edition

Bernhardt & Kinnear
Cases in Marketing Management
Fifth Edition

Bingham & Raffield
Business to Business Marketing Management
First Edition

Bovee & Arens
Contemporary Advertising
Fourth Edition

Boyd & Walker
Marketing Management: A Strategic Approach
First Edition

Boyd, Westfall & Stasch
Marketing Research: Test and Cases
Seventh Edition

Burstiner
Basic Retailing
Second Edition

Cadotte
The Market Place: A Strategic Marketing Simulation
First Edition

Cateora
International Marketing
Eighth Edition

Churchill, Ford & Walker
Sales Force Management
Fourth Edition

Cole
Consumer and Commercial Credit Management
Ninth Edition

Cravens
Strategic Marketing
Third Edition

Cravens & Lamb
Strategic Marketing Management Cases
Fourth Edition

Crawford
New Products Management
Third Edition

Dillon, Madden & Firtle
Essentials of Marketing Research
First Edition

Dillon, Madden & Firtle
Marketing Research in a Marketing Environment
Second Edition

Engel, Warshaw & Kinnear
Promotional Strategy
Seventh Edition

Faria, Nulsen & Roussos
Compete
Fourth Edition

Futrell
ABC's of Selling
Third Edition

Futrell
Fundamentals of Selling
Fourth Edition

Hawkins, Best & Coney
Consumer Behavior
Fifth Edition

Kurtz & Dodge
Professional Selling
Sixth Edition

Lambert & Stock
Strategic Logistics Management
Third Edition

Lehmann & Winer
Analysis for Marketing Planning
Second Edition

Lehmann
Marketing Research and Analysis
Fourth Edition

Levy & Weitz
Retailing Management
First Edition

Mason, Mayer & Wilkinson
Modern Retailing
Sixth Edition

Mason, Mayer & Ezell
Retailing
Fourth Edition

Mason & Perreault
The Marketing Game
Second Edition

McCarthy & Perreault
Basic Marketing: A Global-Managerial Approach
Eleventh Edition

McCarthy & Perreault
Essentials of Marketing
Fifth Edition

Peter & Olson
Consumer Behavior and Marketing Strategy
Third Edition

Peter & Donnelly
A Preface to Marketing Management
Fifth Edition

Peter & Donnelly
Marketing Management: Knowledge and Skills
Third Edition

Quelch & Farris
Cases in Advertising and Promotion Management
Third Edition

Quelch, Dolan & Kosnik
Marketing Management: Text and Cases
First Edition

Smith & Quelch
Ethics in Marketing
First Edition

Stanton, Spiro & Buskirk
Management of a Sales Force
Eighth Edition

Thompson & Strappenbeck
The Marketing Strategy Game
First Edition

Walker, Boyd & Larréché
Marketing Strategy: Planning and Implementation
First Edition

Weitz, Castleberry & Tanner
Selling: Building Partnerships
First Edition

Preface

There is probably no more dynamic and fascinating a field to either practice or study than that of advertising and promotion. In our increasingly complex world, organizations in both the private and public sector have learned that their ability to create and disseminate effective advertising and promotional messages to their target audiences is often critical to their success. Advertising messages are used to sell products and services as well as to promote causes, market political candidates, and deal with societal problems such as the AIDS crisis or drug abuse. Advertising has become a prestigious profession and a major course of study in many universities as more and more students choose careers in advertising or a related area of marketing and promotion.

This text serves as an introduction to the field of advertising and promotion. While advertising is its major focus, it is more than just a book on advertising, however. This is because there is more to an organization's marketing communications efforts than simply advertising. In recent years, the role of advertising and promotion in the overall marketing process has changed considerably. The audiences that marketers seek, along with the media and methods for reaching them, have become increasingly fragmented. Advertising and promotional efforts have become more regionalized and targeted to specific audiences. Spending on sales promotion activities targeted at both consumers and the trade has surpassed advertising media expenditures. Many marketers coordinate all their communications efforts so they can send cohesive and effective messages to their customers. Many advertising agencies have acquired, started, or become affiliated with sales promotion, direct marketing, and public relations companies to better serve their clients' marketing communications and promotional needs.

In the 1990s, many companies are approaching advertising and promotion from an integrated marketing communications perspective, which involves coordinating the various promotional mix elements along with other marketing activities that communicate with a firm's customers. Integrated marketing communications calls for a "big picture" approach to planning marketing and promotion programs and coordinating the various communication functions. This test examines advertising and promotion from an integrated marketing communications perspective. The text is built around an integrated marketing communications planning model and recognizes the importance of coordinating all of the promotional mix elements to develop an effective communications program. Although media advertising is often the most visible part of a film's promotional program, attention must also be given to other promotional areas such as direct marketing, sales promotion, public relations, and personal selling to understand advertising's role in contemporary marketing.

This text takes a broad view in examining the field of advertising and promotion and the world of marketing communications. To effectively plan, implement, and evaluate advertising and promotional programs requires an understanding of the overall marketing process, consumer behavior, and communications theory. We have attempted to present a balance of theoretical and practical perspectives and to integrate the two. We draw from the extensive research and theorizing in fields such as advertising, consumer behavior, communications, marketing, sales promotion, and other areas to give the reader a basis for understanding the marketing communications process and how it influences consumer decision making.

A particular strength of this text is the integration of the various concepts, theories, and ideas with practical application. Nearly every day an article or example of advertising and promotion in practice is reported in the media. We have used a variety of sources such as *The Wall Street Journal, Business Week, Fortune, Marketing & Media Decisions, Advertising Age, Adweek, Business Marketing,* and many others to find practical examples that are integrated throughout the text. Each chapter begins with a vignette that presents a practical example of effective (or sometimes ineffective) advertising and promotion or other interesting insights. Each chapter also contains a number of boxed items, Promotional Perspectives, that present in-depth discussions of particular issues related to the chapter material. **Global Perspectives** are presented throughout the text in recognition of the increasing importance of international marketing and the need to understand how the text material might apply to the practice of international advertising and promotion. **Ethical Perspectives** are also included to focus attention on important social issues and to show how ethical considerations must be taken into account when planning or implementing advertising and promotional programs. We have included more than 400 advertisements and illustrations, all of which were carefully chosen and keyed to the topic material to illustrate a particular idea, concept, theory, or practical application.

To the Student

As professors we were, of course, once students ourselves. In many ways we are perpetual students in that we are constantly striving to learn about, understand, and explain how advertising and promotion work. We share many of the interests and concerns that you do, and are often excited (and bored) by the same things. Having taught in the advertising and promotion area for a combined 30-plus years, we believe we have developed an understanding of what makes a book in this field interesting to students.

In writing this book we tried to remember how we felt about the various texts we have used throughout the years. We have tried to incorporate the good things and minimize those we felt were of little use. We have strived not to make this a book of terms or overburden you with definitions, although we do call out those we feel are especially important to your understanding of the material. We also remember that, as students, we were often not really into theory—that was something for the professor to get excited about. It is our belief, however, that to fully understand how advertising and promotion works, it is necessary to establish some theoretical basis. The more you can understand about how things are supposed to work, the easier it will be for you to understand and explain why they do or do not work as planned.

Perhaps the one question that students most often ask is, "How do I use this in the 'real' world?" To answer this question, we have provided numerous examples of how the various theories, concepts, principles, and so on can be used in practice. As you will see, these examples are from actual companies. Some are older, classic examples, while most are current, and they cover a variety of products, services, markets, and topics. Please take time to read the chapter openings and Promotional, Global, and Ethical Perspectives and study the diverse ads and illustrations. We think you will find they stimulate your interest and are not far removed from events you deal with in your daily life as a consumer and as a target of advertising and promotion.

To the Instructor

This text approaches advertising and promotion from an integrated marketing communications perspective that integrates theory with planning, management, and strategy. While we consider this an introductory text, we do treat each topic in some depth. We believe the marketing and advertising student of today needs a text that provides more than just an introduction to terms, definitions, and topics.

The book is positioned primarily for the introductory advertising, marketing communications, or promotions course as taught in the business/marketing curriculum. It can also be used in journalism/communications courses when there is an emphasis on a marketing and promotional planning perspective. In addition to its coverage of advertising, this text has chapters on sales promotion, direct marketing, personal selling, and publicity/public relations. These chapters stress the integration of advertising with other promotional mix elements and the need to understand their role in the overall marketing program.

Organization of This Text

This text is divided into seven major parts. In Part I we examine the role of advertising and promotion in marketing and introduce the concept of integrated marketing communications. Chapter 1 provides an overview of the various promotional mix elements and discusses their advantages and limitations. An integrated marketing communications planning model is presented that shows the various steps in the promotional process and how the various promotional mix elements are combined to help achieve an organization's marketing and communication objectives. This model presents a framework for developing the integrated marketing communications program and is followed throughout the text. In Chapter 2 we examine the marketing process and the role of advertising and promotion in the overall marketing program. Attention is given to the various elements of the marketing mix and how they both influence and interact with advertising and promotional strategy.

In Part II of the text we cover topic areas relevant to the promotion program situation analysis. In Chapter 3 we examine how firms organize for advertising and promotion and the role of advertising agencies and other firms providing marketing and promotional services. We give particular attention to advertising agencies and the ways they are selected, evaluated, and compensated as well as the changes occurring in the agency business. Chapter 4 covers important perspectives on consumer behavior. We examine the stages of the consumer decision making process and the various internal psychological factors as well as external factors that influence consumer behavior. The main focus of this chapter is on how an understanding of buyer behavior can be used in the development of effective advertising and other forms of promotion. In Chapter 5 we discuss market segmentation and positioning and how they play an important role in the development of an advertising and promotional program.

Part III of the text analyzes the communications process. Chapter 6 presents a detailed examination of various communication theories and models of how consumers respond to advertising messages, while in Chapter 7 we consider specific areas of communication such as source, message, and channel factors. The purpose of these first three sections of the text is to provide the student with a solid background in various areas of marketing, consumer behavior, and communications that are important to promotional planners and against which specific advertising and promotional planning decisions can be made and evaluated.

In Part IV we consider how firms develop goals and objectives for their marketing communications programs and determine how much money should be spent trying to achieve them. Chapter 8 focuses on determining the objectives for the advertising program and stresses the importance of knowing what to expect from advertising, the differences between advertising versus communication objectives, characteristics of good objectives, and problems in setting objectives. Budgeting for advertising and promotion is discussed in Chapter 9, with attention given to various methods for determining and allocating the promotional budget.

Part V of the text examines the various promotional mix elements that form the basis of the integrated marketing communications program. We begin with advertising and focus first on the development of the advertising message. In Chapter 10 we discuss the planning and development of the creative strategy and advertising campaign and examine the creative process of advertising. In Chapter 11 we turn our attention to the various ways of implementing or executing the creative strategy and some guidelines or criteria for evaluating creative work.

Chapters 12 through 15 cover media strategy and planning and the various advertising media. Chapter 12 introduces the key concepts and principles of media planning and strategy and examines the various considerations involved in the development of a media plan. Chapter 13 discusses the advantages and disadvantages of the broadcast media of television and radio as well as issues regarding the purchase of radio and television time and audience measurement. Chapter 14 considers the same issues for the print media of magazines and newspapers. Chapter 15 examines the role of support media such as outdoor and transit advertising and some of the newly developing media alternatives.

In Chapters 16 through 19 we continue to focus on the development of the integrated marketing communications program by examining other areas of the promotional mix. Chapter 16 examines the rapidly growing area of direct marketing and how many companies are communicating directly with target customers to generate a response or transaction. Chapter 17 examines the role of sales promotion in the marketing and promotional program and focuses on consumer-oriented promotion as well as sales promotion programs targeted to the trade. Chapter 18 covers publicity and public relations and the role they play in an integrated marketing communications program as well as corporate advertising. Basic issues regarding personal selling and its role in promotional strategy are presented in Chapter 19.

Part VI of the text consists of Chapter 20 where we discuss ways to evaluate and measure the effectiveness of advertising and promotion. Various methods for pretesting and posttesting advertising messages and entire campaigns are discussed in this chapter. In Part VII we turn our attention to special markets, topics, and perspectives that are becoming increasingly important in contemporary marketing. Chapter 21 deals with business-to-business marketing and examines how advertising and other forms of promotion are used to help one company sell its products and/or services to another firm. In Chapter 22 we examine the global marketplace and the role of advertising and other promotional mix variables in international marketing.

The text concludes with a discussion of the regulatory, social, and economic environments in which advertising and promotion operate. Chapter 23 examines the area of advertising regulation, including industry self-regulation and regulation by governmental agencies such as the Federal Trade Commission. Attention is also given to the regulation of sales promotion and direct marketing. Advertising's role and influence in society is constantly changing, and our discussion would not be complete without considering the various criticisms that are often made against it. In Chapter 24 we consider the various criticisms regarding the social, ethical, and economic aspects of advertising and promotion.

Chapter Features

The following features are in each chapter to enhance students' learning and understanding of the material as well as their reading enjoyment.

Chapter Objectives

Provided at the beginning of each chapter to identify the major goals and indicate what should be learned from each chapter.

Opening Vignettes

Provide a practical example or application or discuss an interesting issue that is relevant to the chapter. These opening vignettes are designed to create interest in the material that is presented in the chapter.

Promotional Perspectives

Boxed items featuring in-depth discussions of interesting issues related to the chapter coverage. Each chapter contains several of these insights into the world of advertising and promotion.

Global Perspectives

Provide information similar to that in the Promotional Perspectives, with a specific focus on international aspects of advertising and promotion.

Ethical Perspectives

Discuss the moral and/or ethical issues regarding practices engaged in by marketers. These Ethical Perspectives are also tied specifically to the materials presented in the chapters.

Key Terms

Highlighted in boldface throughout the chapter, with a list at the end of each chapter. These terms help call students' attention to important ideas, concepts, and definitions.

Chapter Summaries

Written in detail to provide a synopsis and serve as a quick review of important topics covered.

Discussion Questions

Provided at the end of each chapter to give students an opportunity to test their understanding of the material and to apply it. These questions can also serve as a basis for class discussion as well as assignments.

Four-Color Visuals

Print advertisements, photoboards, and other examples appear throughout the book. More than 400 ads and illustrations are included.

Changes in the Second Edition

We have made a number of changes in the second edition that we feel have resulted in significant improvements in the text:

- **An Integrated Marketing Communications Perspective**
  The second edition approaches the field of advertising and promotion from an integrated marketing communications perspective. We examine how the various elements of an organization's promotional mix are combined to develop a total marketing communications program that sends a consistent message to its customer. An integrated marketing communications planning model is presented in the first chapter and is followed throughout the text.
- **New Chapters on Direct Marketing, Personal Selling, and Creative Strategy**
  Three new chapters have been added to the second edition. Direct marketing, viewed as a different element of the promotional mix, is now covered in a separate chapter (16). Coverage of personal selling has also been expanded to a full chapter (19). Attention is given to showing the role of these promotional mix elements in the overall marketing communications program. A second chapter (11) has also been added to expand the coverage

of creative strategy. This chapter includes a focus on various tactical issues of creating the advertising message.

- **Revised Chapter on Consumer Behavior**
  The consumer behavior chapter (4) has undergone significant revision. The new chapter follows the consumer decision process model approach and examines the role of various psychological concepts such as motivation, perception, attitudes, integration, and learning theories at each stage of the decision making process. Attention is given to how advertising and promotion planners can use various psychological theories and concepts in the design and implementation of marketing communications.

- **Expanded Coverage of Sales Promotion**
  The fast-growing field of sales promotion receives expanded coverage in the second edition. Both consumer and trade-oriented sales promotions are now covered in the same chapter (17). Coverage of sales promotion has also been expanded in the international chapter (22) and the chapter on regulation (23).

- **New and Updated Promotional Perspectives and Opening Vignettes**
  All of the chapter opening vignettes in the second edition are new, as are 80 percent of the Promotional Perspectives. Promotional Perspectives retained from the first edition have been updated.

- **Global and Ethical Perspectives**
  New boxed items focusing on global and ethical issues of advertising and promotion have been added to the second edition. The Global Perspectives offer interesting insights into the role of advertising and other promotional areas in international markets. The Ethical Perspectives discuss specific issues, developments, and problems that often result in concern or questioning of the ethics of marketers and their decisions, as they develop and implement their advertising and promotional programs.

- **Chapter Reorganization**
  The order of the chapters has been reorganized somewhat to provide a more logical flow that is consistent with the integrated marketing communications planning model framework. Market segmentation and positioning is now covered in Chapter 5 to better show the importance of these topics in the promotional situation analysis. Creative strategy and implementation, expanded to two chapters (10 and 11), is covered before the chapters on media strategy and evaluation of various media. The new chapter on direct marketing (16) follows the media chapters—and while viewed here as a distinct element of the promotional mix, is considered by some as another form of media available for reaching target customers.

- **Glossary of Key Terms**
  A glossary of key terms has been added to the second edition. The glossary contains a short definition of all of the key terms discussed in the text and provides students with a quick reference guide as well as a study tool.

- **Extensive Four-Color Illustration Program**
  The second edition is done using attractive four-color illustrations throughout the book. Most advertisements are in four color, which allows the student to appreciate the important visual aspects of advertising. The text is also heavily illustrated with charts, diagrams, tables, and graphs, all of which are done in color to enhance the appearance of the text and make it more enjoyable for students to read.

Support Material

A high-quality package of instructional supplements supports the second edition. All of the supplements have been developed by the authors to ensure their coordination with the text. We offer instructors a support package that facilitates the use of our text and enhances the learning experience of the student.

Instructor's Manual

The Instructor's Manual is a very valuable teaching resource that includes learning objectives, chapter and lecture outlines, answers to all of the end-of-chapter discussion questions, transparency masters, and additional insights and teaching suggestions. Additional discussion questions not included in the text are also presented for each chapter. These questions can be used for class discussion purposes or as short-answer essay questions for an exam.

Computerized Test Bank

A test bank of more than 1,500 multiple-choice questions has been developed to accompany the text. The questions provide thorough coverage of the chapter material, including the Promotional, Global, and Ethical Perspectives, and are categorized by level of learning (definitional, conceptual, or application). A computerized version of the test bank is available to adopters of the text.

Four-Color Transparencies

Each adopter may request a set of 75 four-color acetate transparencies. These acetates present additional print advertisements, photoboards, sales promotion offers, and other materials that do not appear in the text. A number of important models or charts appearing in the text are also provided as color transparencies. Slipsheets are included with each transparency to give the instructor useful background information about the illustration and how it can be integrated into the lecture.

Video

A video has been developed specifically for use with this text. The video contains nearly 100 commercials that are examples of creative advertising and can be used to help the instructor explain a particular concept of principle discussed in the text. Many of the commercials are also tied to the chapter openings or promotional perspectives as well as specific examples cited in the text. The video also contains several case studies dealing with strategies used in developing and implementing advertising and promotional programs. Interesting insights and/or background information about each commercial is provided in the Instructor's Manual along with discussion questions for the video cases.

Acknowledgments

The task of writing this second edition has proven to be enormous. While this project represents a tremendous amount of work on our part, it would not have become a reality without the assistance and support of many other people.

Most authors probably begin a project thinking that they have the best ideas, approach, examples, organization, and the like for writing a great book. However, you quickly learn that despite how good your ideas and efforts may be, there is always room for them to be improved on by others. A number of colleagues provided us with detailed, thoughtful reviews that were immensely helpful in making this a better book. We are very grateful to the following individuals who worked with us on the first edition. They include:

Lauranne Buchanan
University of Illinois

Lindell Chew
University of Missouri, St. Louis

Catherine Cole
University of Iowa

John Faier
Miami University

Raymond Fisk
Oklahoma State University

Donald Grambois
Indiana University

Stephen Grove
Clemson University

Ron Hill
American University

Paul Jackson
Ferris State College

Don Kirchner
California State University, Northridge

Paul Prahhaker
DePaul University, Chicago

Mary Ann Strutts
Southwest Texas State University

Terrence Witkowski
California State University, Long Beach

Robert Young
Northeastern University

We are particularly grateful to the individuals who helped us with the revision of the book and provided constructive comments on how to make the Second Edition a better book. Their comments and ideas were very valuable and gave us many excellent ideas on how to improve the book. The reviewers for the Second Edition were:

Dr. Roy Busby
University of North Texas

Professor Geoff Gordon
University of Kentucky

Professor Clark Leavitt
Ohio State University

Professor Charles Overstreet
Oklahoma State University

Professor Scott Roberts
Old Dominion University

Professor Harlan Spotts
Northeastern University

We also would like to acknowledge the assistance and cooperation we received from many people in the business, advertising, and media communities. This book contains several hundred ads, illustrations, charts, and tables that have been provided by advertisers and/or their agencies, various publications, and other advertising and industry organizations. Many individuals took time from their busy schedules to provide us with requested materials. The numerous ads, charts, graphs, and other visuals they have given us permission to use are extremely valuable to an advertising text.

Several advertising practitioners helped make this book more practical and realistic by sharing their insights and experiences. We would like to acknowledge the assistance of Richard Brooks and Ann Collins of Phillips-Ramsey, Inc., as well as Rebecca Holman and Bruce Goerlich of D'Arcy Masius Benton & Bowles, Inc. Kate Prescott of Della Femina McNamee, Inc. also provided valuable insights.

Obviously, a manuscript does not become a book without a great deal of work on the part of a publisher. Various individuals at Richard D. Irwin have been involved with this project over the past two years. Our editor Rob Zwettler provided valuable advice and guidance while Eleanore Snow kept us on track and gently (and sometimes not so gently!) prodded us to keep near schedule. Thanks also to Paula Buschman for managing the production process.

We acknowledge the support we have received from the College of Business at San Diego State University. Dean Allan Bailey has provided us with an excellent working environment and has been very supportive. Tori McCoy and Althea Channell have been a tremendous help with their secretarial support.

On a more personal note, a great deal of thanks goes to our families for putting up with us over the past few years while we were revising this book. Renee, Jessica, Gayle, Danny, and Derek have had to once again endure the deviation from our usually pleasant personalities and dispositions. We look forward to returning to normal. Finally, we would like to acknowledge each other for making it through this ordeal a second time. Our mother will be happy to know that we still get along after all of this, and, for now, still talk to each other.

George E. Belch
Michael A. Belch

Contents in Brief

Contents

chapter **2**

The Role of Advertising and Promotion in the Marketing Process 36

part II   ## Promotion Program Situation Analysis   75

chapter **3**

Organizing for Advertising and Promotion and the Role of Agencies   76

chapter **4**

Perspectives on Consumer Behavior   112

chapter **5**

Market Segmentation and Positioning   156

part IV   *Establishing Objectives and Budgeting for the Promotional Program*   **257**

chapter **8**

Determining Advertising and Promotional Objectives   258

chapter **9**

The Advertising and Promotions Budget   290

chapter

Media Planning and Strategy   386

chapter

Evaluation of Broadcast Media   428

chapter 14

Evaluation of Print Media: Magazines and Newspapers   474

chapter ⑱

Public Relations, Publicity, and Corporate Advertising   626

chapter **19**

Personal Selling 658

part VI   ## *Monitoring, Evaluation, and Control* 677

chapter **20**

Measuring the Effectiveness of the Promotional Program 678

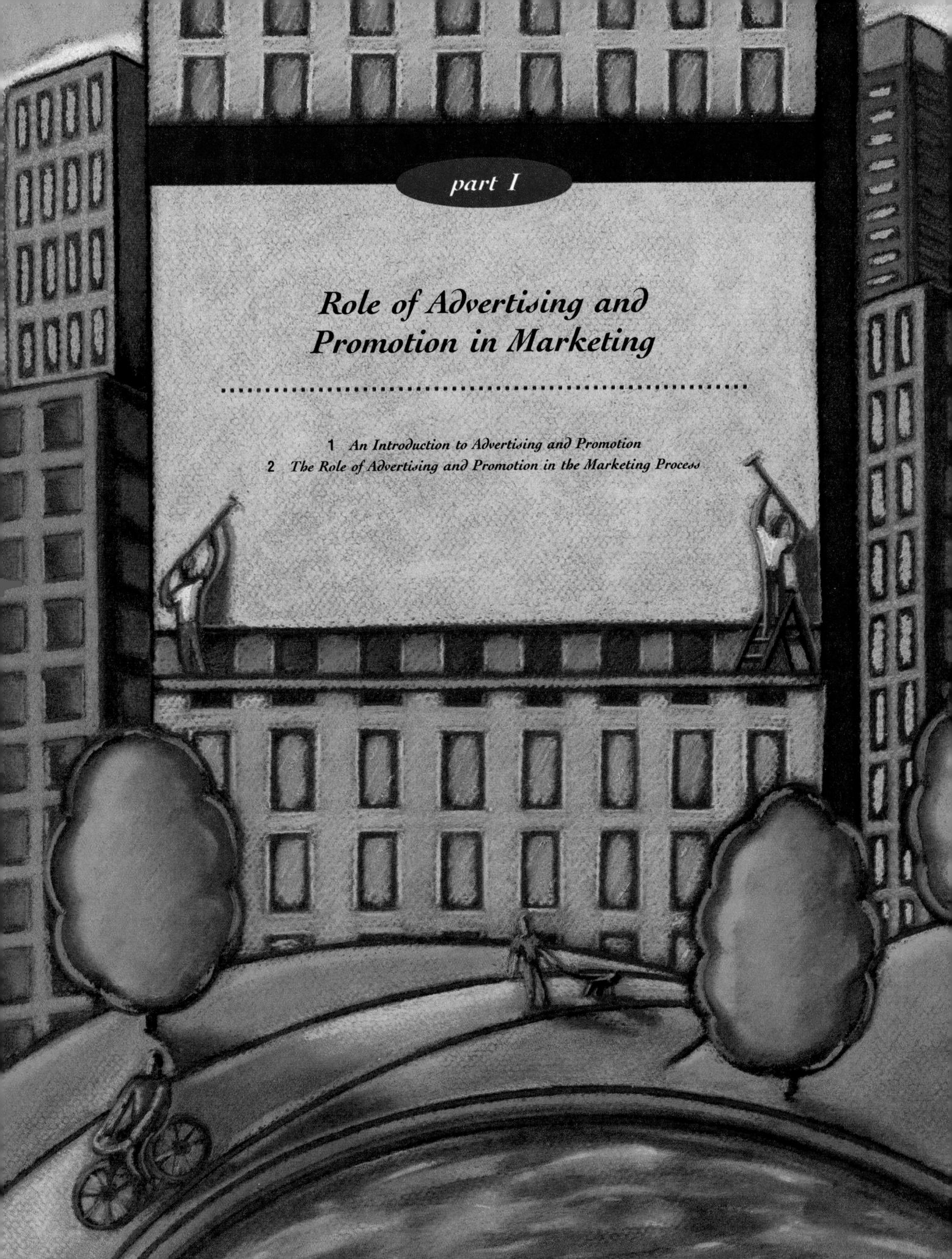

part I

Role of Advertising and Promotion in Marketing

chapter **1**

An Introduction to Advertising and Promotion

chapter objectives

➢ To examine the promotional function and the growing importance advertising and other promotional elements play in the marketing programs of domestic and foreign companies.

➢ To introduce the concept of integrated marketing communications and examine how the various marketing and promotional elements must be coordinated to communicate effectively.

➢ To introduce the various elements of the promotional mix and consider the advantages and limitations of each.

➢ To examine the various tasks and responsibilities involved in promotional management.

➢ To introduce a model of the integrated marketing communications planning process and examine the various steps in developing a marketing communications program.

A New Advertising Campaign Keeps Energizer Sales "Going and Going"

In 1986, the Ralston Purina Company purchased the Eveready Battery Co. from Union Carbide Corporation. For several years after the acquisition, Eveready struggled through market share declines, and its core Energizer brand battled to keep pace with Duracell, the market leader in the $2 billion a year U.S. alkaline battery market. Over a four-year period, Energizer had three different ad spokespersons—actor Robert Conrad, Olympic gold medal gymnast Mary Lou Retton, and the irreverent "Jacko" Jackson, a bombastic former Australian football player who screamed at consumers to buy Energizer batteries. Energizer had successfully used Jacko in its advertising in Australia and decided he might be effective in the United States as well. Although Jacko increased consumer awareness of the Energizer brand, the campaign was not well received by consumers and also hurt Eveready's credibility with its sales force and retailers.

After abandoning the irritating Jacko ads, Eveready's agency developed a new commercial aimed at Duracell's claim that its product outlasted "ordinary batteries." The objective of this ad was to neutralize Duracell's claim of product superiority. The commercial featured a group of mechanical bunnies, similar to those used in Duracell ads, having their drumming interrupted by the Energizer bunny as a voice-over complained Duracell had "never invited us to their party." This ad, however, was seen as a short-term solution to Energizer's advertising problem, and in 1988, Eveready put the Energizer's advertising business up for review. This meant other agencies were invited to present ideas for a new creative campaign for the Energizer.

One competitor in the review was the Chiat/Day/Mojo agency, known for its excellent creative work for clients such as Nike, Apple Computer, and Nissan. Chiat/Day/Mojo developed a creative idea that was so well received by Eveready the company cut short its usual agency review process and awarded Chiat/Day/Mojo the account. The creative execution called for the pink, drum-thumping Energizer bunny to barge across the screen interrupting ads for fictional products such as flavored instant coffee, pretentious wines, deodorant soaps, and nasal sprays. A key creative executional element is getting consumers interested and involved with ads before the bunny interrupts the commercial. As one agency executive noted, "The key element is surprise. Where will the bunny turn up next?"

Since launching the campaign in October 1989, the bunny has interrupted more than 20 parody commercials. Eveready increased its advertising budget significantly to support the bunny campaign—and with good reason. Awareness of the Energizer campaign and its "long-lasting" product message are up nearly 50 percent.

(continued)

Eveready has also used the successful ad campaign to improve its trade relations. The company has offered stuffed bunnies as retailer giveaways and provided point-of-purchase materials that prominently feature the bunny. Eveready's statistics show a 40 percent increase in the number of displays retailers use to merchandise Energizer batteries. To defuse the criticism that consumers were not sure whether the bunny spots advertised Energizer or Duracell and to increase the campaign's impact, a picture of the bunny was put on Energizer packages.

The bunny spots were named the Best TV Commercials of 1989 by the editors of *Advertising Age*, the lead-ing trade publication of the advertising industry. Of course, the ultimate measure of success is in the marketplace, and Eveready has indicated the bunny ads have halted Energizer's decline in market share and resulted in double-digit increases in sales. It is likely that the ads, along with Energizer sales, will "keep going and going and going."

Source: Julie Liesse, "How the bunny charged Eveready," Advertising Age, April 4, 1991, pp. 20, 55; "Advertising Age Best Advertising of 1989—Pink bunny romps through 'best' TV spot," Advertising Age, April 30, 1990, pp. 29–31; Julie Liesse, "Duracell ups lead over Energizer," Advertising Age, April 16, 1990, p. 4; Julie Liesse, "Bunny back to battle Duracell," Advertising Age, September 17, 1990, p. 4.

The success of the Energizer bunny parody ads illustrates the significant role advertising and promotional strategy plays in modern marketing. Advertising is especially important in influencing consumers' purchase decisions for batteries, as this is a commodity business in which competing products look the same and differentiating a brand is very difficult. Moreover, advertising and other forms of promotion help generate support from retailers in the form of shelf space, promotional displays, and other merchandising activities, all of which are very important because batteries are often an impulse purchase.

Eveready recognized the critical role advertising plays in the marketing of batteries and sought an agency that could deliver a strong creative execution in both television and print (Exhibit 1–1). However, the increase in Energizer sales is due to more than just a great advertising campaign. Eveready used the popularity of the Energizer campaign to improve its relations with retailers and the morale of its sales force. The advertising was supported by various forms of sales promotion such as couponing, premium offers, and point-of-purchase displays. The popularity of the bunny ads also resulted in publicity that contributed to awareness of the Energizer brand name. Interestingly, the Energizer campaign, which was itself based on a parody, fostered a number of parody ads by other advertisers.

The Energizer example demonstrates how a creative advertising campaign can be leveraged into a total advertising and promotional program. Eveready, along with thousands of other companies, recognizes the value of advertising and promotion and its importance in the marketing of products and services. By examining the size and growth of this industry, we can gain some appreciation for just how important advertising and promotion have become in modern marketing.

The Growth of Advertising and Promotion

Advertising and promotion are an integral part of our social and economic systems. In the complex society and economic system in which we live, advertising has evolved into a vital communication system for both consumers and businesses. The ability of advertising and other promotional methods to deliver carefully prepared messages to targeted audiences has given them a major role in the marketing programs of most organizations. Companies ranging from large multinational corporations to small retailers increasingly rely on advertising and promotion to help them market products and services. In market-based economies, consumers have learned to rely on advertising and other forms of promotion to provide them with information they can use in making purchase decisions.

Evidence of the increasing importance of the role of advertising and promotion comes from the growth in expenditures in these areas over the past decade. In 1980, advertising expenditures in the United States were $53 billion, and $49 billion was spent on sales promotion techniques such as product samples, coupons, contests, sweepstakes, premiums, rebates, and allowances and discounts to retailers. By 1990,

➤ *Exhibit 1–1*   **The Energizer parody ads have been very successful**

MONUMENT VALLEY, UTAH. 5:32 P.M. STILL GOING. NOTHING OUTLASTS THE ENERGIZER.

$130 billion was spent on advertising, while sales promotion expenditures increased to more than $140 billion! Companies bombarded the U.S consumer with messages and promotional offers, collectively spending more than $6 a week on every man, woman, and child in the country—nearly 50 percent more per capita than in any other nation.[1] While expenditures on advertising and promotion in the United States far exceed the rest of the world, promotional expenditures in international markets have grown as well. Advertising expenditures outside of the United States increased from $55 billion in 1980 to $265 billion by 1990.[2] In addition to the monies spent on advertising and sales promotion, both foreign and domestic companies spend billions more on personal selling and public relations, which are also important parts of a firm's marketing communications program.

The tremendous growth in expenditures for advertising and promotion is in part a reflection of the growth of the United States as well as the global economy.[3] For example, Global Perspective 1–1 discusses how expansion-minded marketers are turning their attention to global markets to take advantage of the growth opportunities in various regions of the world. The growth in promotional expenditures also reflects the fact that marketers around the world recognize the value and importance of advertising and promotion. Promotional strategies play an important role in the marketing programs of companies as they attempt to communicate with and sell their products to their customers. Advertising and promotion have become integral parts of this marketing process in most organizations. To understand the role advertising and promotion plays in the marketing process better, let us first examine the marketing function.

What Is Marketing?

Before reading on, stop for a moment and think about how you would define what marketing is and what it entails. Chances are that each student reading this book would come up with a somewhat different answer to this question, as marketing is often viewed in terms of individual activities that constitute the overall marketing

Global Perspective 1–1

The Whole World Is a Marketplace

In recent years, many companies have recognized that the U.S. market offers them limited opportunity for expanding their sales and profits. Reduced population growth, a stagnant economy, intense competition, and markets saturated with overproduction and over-choice are making it difficult for companies to meet growth objectives by focusing only on the U.S. market. While the U.S. market may offer limited growth potential, only the most myopic marketer would fail to recognize the opportunities available in international markets. The United States is perhaps the most prosperous nation in the world and has the largest economy; however, the fact is it accounts for less than 5 percent of the world's population. The nearly 5 billion people living outside of the United States represent a huge and, in many cases, untapped market. In many countries, disposable income is rising, demand for consumer products is increasing, and markets are becoming easier to reach. The enormous potential of global markets comes as no surprise to many of America's largest companies. For example, Procter & Gamble generates nearly 40 percent of its sales from its international business and has identified 24 of the 165 brands it sells in 140 countries as "world brands." Over the past three years, Coca-Cola has made more money in both Japan and Western Europe than in the United States, while its archrival, Pepsi, also markets its soft drinks around the world.

For many years, American companies have focused their international marketing efforts on the more industrialized and highly developed nations such as Japan and countries in Western Europe. For example, many marketers have been focusing their attention on how to deal with the Europe "1992" plan whereby 12 countries of Western Europe are creating a unified economic market representing 320 million people. However, the fall of communism in Eastern Europe and the Soviet Union means these countries will be opening their doors to western ideas and products. Many western companies are salivating at the huge, untapped market of nearly 400 million people in Eastern Europe and the Soviet Union. However, at the same time, they recognize that there are tremendous obstacles to marketing products in countries with moribund economies, massive bureaucracies, poor distribution systems, and an entire generation who has never experienced free market choice or purchased a product for any reason other than functional utility. Nevertheless, despite these obstacles, many companies are taking a long-term perspective and entering joint ventures or making other plans for entering the Eastern European market.

Expansion-minded global marketers are also turning their attention to other areas of the world such as China, South America, and the Pacific Rim market. For example, in Indonesia, more than half of the country's 168 million people are under the age of 20 and these young people are very enthusiastic purchasers of consumer products. An emerging and more affluent middle class in many Latin American countries will also present global marketers with many opportunities over the next decade.

Advances in technology, travel, and communications are turning the world into a global village. Television, motion pictures, and music have helped to create a shared world culture, particularly among the youth of the world. Entertainers such as Michael Jackson and Madonna, along with athletes such as Michael Jordan and Jack Nicklaus, enjoy worldwide recognition and popularity and can serve as effective advertising spokespersons all over the world. Global markets offer tremendous opportunities, and challenges, to marketers who recognize that the future lies in their ability to compete at a global level.

Source: "We Are the World," *Adweek's Marketing Week Superbrands 1990,* pp. 61–68; and "World of Change," *Adweek's Marketing Week Superbrands 1991,* pp. 34–41.

process. For example, one popular conception of marketing is that it primarily involves sales and the selling process. Other perspectives view marketing as consisting primarily of advertising or retailing activities. For some of you, activities such as market research, pricing, or product planning may have come to mind. While all these activities are a part of marketing, it is incorrect to limit your perspective to just these individual elements. The American Marketing Association, which represents marketing professions in the United States and Canada, defines **marketing** as

> the process of planning and executing the conception, pricing, promotion, and distribution of ideas, goods, and services to create exchanges that satisfy individual and organizational objectives.[4]

This definition reveals that marketing involves more than just an individual activity such as sales or promotion. Effective marketing requires that managers

RAY: "Uh huh, you got the right
  one baby. You know I just love
  this new Diet Pepsi song, but
  do you think it's caught on yet?"
CROWD IN CHINA SINGS: "Uh huh, Uh
  huh, you got the right one baby!"
  "Uh huh, Uh huh, Diet Pepsi."
AFRICAN TRIBE SINGS: "Uh huh, Uh huh,
  Uh huh, Uh huh."
MAN FROM BANGLADESH SAYS: "If it's
  irresistibly sippable. . ."

COWBOY SINGS: "Uncontestably
  tastable and eminently wonderful. . ."
ENGLISH WAITER: "You got the right one
  baby. Uh huh."
GOSPEL CHOIR SINGS: "You got the right
  one baby!"
GEISHA GIRLS SING: "Uh huh, Uh huh,
  You got the right one baby."

MONKS CHANT: "Uh huh, Uh huh, Uh huh,
  Uh huh."
UNITED NATIONS: "Uh huh, Uh huh. . ."
UNITED NATIONS: ". . .Diet Pepsi!"
RAY: "Do you think it's caught on yet?. . .
  Naaah!"
UH HUH GIRLS LAUGH.

recognize the interdependence of these various activities and how they can be combined to develop a marketing program.

Marketing Focuses on Exchange

The definition presented above, along with most contemporary perspectives of marketing, recognizes that exchange is a central concept in marketing. It has been suggested that **exchange** constitutes the core phenomenon or basic domain for study in marketing.[5] For exchange to occur, there must be two or more parties with something of value to one another, a desire and ability to give up their something of value to the other party, and a way for the parties to communicate with each other. Advertising and promotion play an important role in the exchange process by informing consumers of an organization's product or service and convincing them of its ability to satisfy their needs or wants.

The exchange process generally involves consumers exchanging money for a company's product or service. However, not all marketing transactions involve the exchange of money for a tangible product or service. Nonprofit organizations such as charities, religious organizations, the arts, and colleges and universities (probably including the one you are attending) seek and receive millions of dollars in donations every year. Charitable organizations often use ads such as the one shown in Exhibit 1–2 to solicit contributions from the public. Donors generally do not receive any material benefits for their contributions but donate in exchange for intangible social and psychological satisfactions such as feelings of goodwill or altruism.

The Marketing Mix

Marketing facilitates the exchange process by carefully examining the needs and wants of consumers, developing a product or service that satisfies these needs, offering it at a certain price, making it available through a particular place or channel of distribution, and developing a program of promotion or communication to create awareness and interest. These 4Ps—*product, price, place* (distribution), and *promotion*—are referred to as elements of the **marketing mix.** The basic task of marketing is one of combining these four elements into a marketing program to facilitate the potential for exchange with consumers in the marketplace.

Determining the proper marketing mix does not just happen. Marketers must be knowledgeable of the issues and options involved in decisions regarding each element of the mix. They must also be aware of how these elements interact and how they can be combined to provide an effective marketing program. Developing a marketing program requires that the market be analyzed through consumer research and that this information be utilized in developing an overall marketing strategy and mix.

The primary focus of this book is on one element of the marketing mix: the promotional variable. However, the promotional program must be part of a viable

➢ *Exhibit 1–2*
Nonprofit organizations use advertising to solicit contributions and support

marketing strategy and coordinated with other marketing activities. A firm can spend large sums of money on advertising or sales promotion, but it stands little chance of success if the product is of poor quality, is priced improperly, or does not have adequate distribution and availability to consumers. Marketers have long recognized the importance of combining and coordinating the elements of the marketing mix into a cohesive marketing strategy. Many companies also are recognizing the importance of integrating and coordinating their various marketing communication efforts such as media advertising, direct marketing, sales promotion, and public relations to achieve more efficient and effective marketing communication. This combining of elements is part of a movement toward what is being called integrated marketing communications.

Integrated Marketing Communications

In past decades, many marketers built strong barriers around the various marketing and promotional functions and planned and managed them separately with different budgets, different views of the market, and different goals and objectives. These companies failed to recognize that the wide range of marketing and promotional tools must be coordinated to communicate effectively and present a consistent image to target markets. In the 1990s, many companies are moving toward the concept of **integrated marketing communications,** which involves coordinating the various promotional elements along with other marketing activities that communicate with a firm's customers.[6]

Integrated marketing communications calls for a "big picture" approach to planning marketing and promotion programs and coordinating the various communication functions. It requires firms to develop a total marketing communications strategy that recognizes all of a firm's marketing activities, not just the promotional variable, communicate with its customers. Consumers' perceptions of a company

> *Exhibit 1–3*
A distinctive package and brand name help communicate a quality image for a product

➤ *Exhibit 1–4*
Elements of the promotional mix

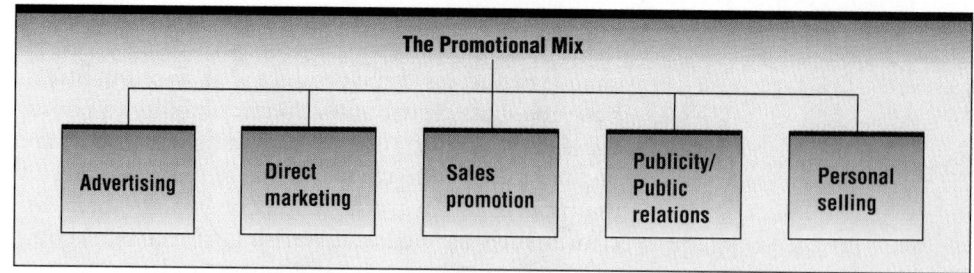

and/or its various brands is a synthesis of the "bundle" of messages they receive (such as media advertisements, price, direct marketing efforts, publicity, sales promotions, and type of store where a product is sold). For example, a high price may symbolize and communicate quality to customers, as may various other aspects of the marketing program such as the shape or design of a product, its packaging, brand name, or the image of the stores in which it is sold. Vanderbilt perfume is an example of a product that uses a distinctive package and brand name as well as a high price to connote a quality, upscale image that is reinforced by its advertising (see Exhibit 1–3 on page 9). The product is available only through upscale specialty or department stores that project an image consistent with the high-quality positioning of the brand.

Integrated marketing communications seeks to have all of a company's marketing and promotional activities project a consistent and unified image to the marketplace. By integrating and coordinating their marketing communication efforts, companies can avoid duplication, take advantage of the synergy among various communication tools, and develop more efficient and effective marketing communication programs. However, successful communication requires that a firm find the right combination of promotional tools and techniques, define their role and the extent to which they can or should be used, and coordinate their use. To accomplish this, those responsible for the company's communications efforts must understand the various ways a company can communicate with its customers and the role of promotion in the marketing program. Let us turn our attention to examining the role of promotion and its various components.

The Role of Promotion in Marketing

Promotion has been defined as *the coordination of all seller-initiated efforts to set up channels of information and persuasion to sell goods and services or promote an idea.*[7] As noted in the discussion of integrated marketing communications, implicit communication occurs through the various elements of the marketing mix. However, most of an organization's communications with the marketplace occur through a carefully planned and controlled promotional program. The basic tools or elements used to accomplish an organization's communication objectives are often referred to as the **promotional mix** and include advertising, personal selling, publicity/public relations, and sales promotion (Exhibit 1–4). In this text, we will also view direct marketing as a major promotional mix element that can be used by marketers to communicate with their target markets. Each of the promotional mix elements plays a distinctive role in an integrated marketing communications program and may take on a variety of forms, and each has certain advantages and limitations. We examine these promotional mix elements in more detail below.

The Promotional Mix

Advertising

Advertising is defined as any paid form of nonpersonal communication about an organization, product, service, or idea by an identified sponsor.[8] Several aspects of this definition should be noted. First, the *paid* aspect of this definition reflects the fact that the space or time for an advertising message generally must be bought. (An occasional exception to this is the public service announcement [PSA] where the advertising space or time is donated by the media.) The *nonpersonal* component

➤ *Exhibit 1–5(a)*
Marlboro became a leading brand of cigarettes by developing a masculine image for the product

indicates advertising involves mass media (e.g., television, radio, magazines, newspapers) whereby a message can be transmitted to large groups of individuals, often at the same time. The nonpersonal nature of advertising means there is generally no opportunity for immediate feedback from the message recipient (except in direct-response advertising). Therefore, before the message is sent, the advertiser must attempt to understand how the audience will interpret and respond to the message.

Advantages of advertising

There are several advantages to the use of advertising in the firm's promotional mix. Since the company pays for the advertising space, it can *control* what it wants to say, when it wants to say it, and to some extent, to whom the message is sent. Advertising can also represent a cost-effective method for communicating with large audiences, and cost per contact through advertising is often quite low. For example, during the 1990–91 prime-time television season, the average 30-second spot on network television reached nearly 12 million households. The cost-per-thousand houses reached was just $9.00, which shows how cost effective advertising can be for reaching large audiences.[9]

Advertising also can be used to create images and symbolic appeals for products and services, a capability that is very important to companies selling products and services that are difficult to differentiate. For example, many consumers cannot distinguish one brand of beer or cigarettes from another on the basis of taste. Thus, the image or psychological associations that consumers have of a brand become a very important part of their purchase decisions. Marlboro cigarettes is an example of a product that became a market leader as a result of an advertising campaign that took a lackluster brand targeted toward women and repositioned it by creating a masculine image for the brand (Exhibit 1–5(a)).

➤ *Exhibit 1–5(b)*   **The Dancing Raisins commercials helped boost sales of raisins**

(MUSIC UP)	I heard it through the grapevine.	SINGERS: Don't ya know
(SFX: Finger snaps)	Raised in the California sunshine.	I heard it through the grapevine.
SINGERS: Ooo, Ooo	ANNCR (VO): California Raisins from the California Vineyards.	ANNCR (VO): Sounds grape, doesn't it?
		(MUSIC OUT)

Another advantage of advertising is its value in creating and maintaining *brand equity.* Brand equity can be thought of as a type of intangible asset of added value or goodwill that results from the favorable image, impressions of differentiation, and/or the strength of consumer attachment to a company name, brand name, or trademark. The equity that results from a strong company or brand name is important because it allows a brand to earn greater sales volume and/or higher margins than it could without the name and also provides the company or brand with a competitive advantage.[10] In many cases, the strong equity position a company and/or its brand enjoys is established and reinforced through advertising that focuses on the image, product attributes, service, or other features of the company and its products or services. Companies such as Eastman Kodak, International Business Machines, Nike, and Coca-Cola, as well as popular brands such as Cheerios, Tide, Alka Seltzer, Campbell's soup, and Jello, enjoy strong brand equity that has been established and maintained, at least in part, through advertising.

Yet another advantage of advertising is its ability to strike a responsive chord with consumers when other elements of the marketing program have not been successful. For example, in 1986, the California Raisin Advisory Board's "I heard it through the grapevine" advertising campaign, which featured the colorful dancing raisins, helped boost raisin sales by 20 percent (Exhibit 1–5(b)). The raisin characters became popular figures as toys, in books, and were known by all ages. One of the most effective and long-running advertising campaigns of all time was that used for Miller Lite beer. The campaign used humorous commercials featuring famous (and not so famous) ex-athletes and show business personalities arguing whether the brand's main appeal was its great taste or the fact it was less filling (Exhibit 1–6). The ads

➤ *Exhibit 1–6* **Miller Lite's classic advertising compaign ran for more than 20 years**

BOOG: For years now we've been kidding Jim here about his eyesight.
The fact is that Jim has the eyes of an eagle.
JIM: Thanks, Boog.
BOOG: Why, he was one of the first guys to spot Lite Beer from Miller.

He saw right away that Lite tastes great... and is less filling.
JIM: Sure, all you have to do is read the label.
JIM: It says Lite has 1/3 less calories than their regular beer.
BOOG: I think you want this, Jim.

JIM: As I was saying, it's as plain as the nose on your face.
ANNCR: (VO) Lite Beer from Miller. Everything you always wanted in a beer. And less.
BOOG: I don't believe this!

helped make Miller Lite the second-best selling beer in the United States as well as created a new segment in the beer market. (The campaign also did wonders for the popularity and careers of Rodney Dangerfield and Bob Uecker.) Another example of the power of a creative ad to affect a product's sales is the "1984" ad used to introduce Apple's Macintosh personal computer, which is discussed in Promotional Perspective 1–1.

Disadvantages of advertising

Advertising has some disadvantages. The costs of producing and placing advertising can be very high. One study indicated the cost of producing a 30-second commercial for a national brand averages nearly $200,000 when all the costs, including those for development of material that is later rejected, are considered.[11] Media costs have also been increasing rapidly, particularly for television, as the cost of a 30-second spot on network TV during the evening averaged $122,000 in 1991 as compared with only $57,900 in 1980.[12] The lack of direct feedback of most advertising is also a drawback, as this makes it difficult for the advertiser to determine how well the message was received and whether it was effective.

Other problems with advertising include its credibility and the ease with which it can be ignored. Advertising is often treated with skepticism by consumers, many of whom perceive it to be very biased and are concerned by its intent to persuade. Not only are consumers skeptical about many of the advertising messages they see and

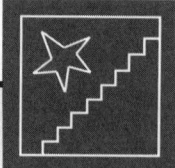

Promotional Perspective 1–1

One of the Most Successful Commercials of All Time—And Why We Almost Never Saw It

In 1983, Apple Computer was planning the introduction of its new line of Macintosh personal computers, which was designed to take on its main competitor and corporate giant IBM. Apple had just lost its lead in the PC market to IBM and its previous product introduction, the $10,000 Lisa, had not been very successful. Some analysts suggested that the survival of Apple might depend on the market's response to the "Mac."

Apple's marketing strategy called for the introduction of the Macintosh to be a major event that would generate immediate impact and support for the new product. The advertising agency, Chiat/Day (now Chiat/Day/Mojo), was given the creative challenge of coming up with a blockbuster idea that would result in a dramatic commercial to introduce the Macintosh. Chiat/Day's creative team created a commercial based on the concept of "Big Brother" from George Orwell's classic novel *1984*. The ad used stark images of Orwell's vision of Big Brother (which purportedly symbolized IBM) and contained a dramatic portrayal of a young woman throwing a sledgehammer through a movie screen to destroy the controlling force. More than $500,000 was spent to produce the "1984" commercial, which was filmed in London under the direction of well-known film director Ridley Scott and contained a cast of more than 200.

When the "1984" commercial was first shown at Apple's annual sales meeting in October 1983, there was stunned silence followed by a 15-minute standing ovation. The media plan for "1984" called for the airing of the 60-second spot during the 1984 Super Bowl at a cost of $500,000. However, buoyed by the rave reviews of the ad from its sales force, Apple approved the purchase of a second 60-second spot. Thus, Apple was ready to showcase its ad on the Super Bowl, which was expected to be the most widely watched program of the year with more than 100 million viewers. However, there was still one problem—getting approval from Apple's board of directors for the avant-garde ad and the million-dollar media purchase.

After viewing the commercial, the board thought it was too controversial and might be detrimental to Apple's image, particularly in the business market. The cost-conscious board also believed the Super Bowl rates were too expensive and directed the marketing department and agency to sell off the two 60-second spots. The agency began working to sell the media time but was simultaneously lobbying Apple not to cancel the ad. The agency did manage to sell two 30-second spots but could not attract a reasonable offer for the second 60-second slot. Two days before the game, the Apple board reluctantly approved the airing of "1984" during the Super Bowl.

The Super Bowl showing of "1984" was the only time it ever appeared as a commercial spot on network television. However, the impact of the ad was tremendous. Following the Super Bowl, the "1984" spot was the focus of attention on national and local newscasts and was the talk of the advertising and marketing industry. Perhaps most important, the ad helped Apple exceed what was considered a very ambitious sales goal. Apple projected sales of 50,000 Macs in the first 100 days, and actual sales surpassed 72,000 units. Over time, the "1984" spot became one of the most talked about commercials ever, and in 1990 was chosen by *Advertising Age*, the ad industry's leading trade publication, as the Commercial of the Decade. And to think the ad came close to never running!

Source: Cleveland Horton, "Apple's Bold '1984' Scores on All Fronts," *Advertising Age*, January 1, 1990, p. 12.

Apple Computer's famous "1984" ad is considered one of the most successful commercials ever made

hear, but also it is relatively easy for them to process selectively only those ads of interest to them. Actually, with so many messages competing for our attention every day, it is out of necessity that we must ignore the vast majority of them. The high level of "clutter" is a major problem in advertising. The numerous commercials we see on television or hear on the radio, as well as the many ads that appear in most magazines and newspapers, make it very difficult for advertisers to get their messages noticed and attended to by consumers.

Direct Marketing

Direct marketing refers to a system of marketing by which organizations communicate directly with target customers to generate a response and/or a transaction. Traditionally, direct marketing has not been considered an element of the promotional mix. However, because it has become such an integral part of the integrated marketing communications program of many organizations and often involves separate objectives, budgets, and strategies, we view direct marketing as a component of the promotional mix.

While there is often a tendency to equate direct marketing with direct mail and the use of mail-order catalogs, there is much more to this form of promotion. It involves the use of a variety of activities, including direct selling, telemarketing, and direct-response advertisements through direct mail and various broadcast and print media. There are direct-selling companies, such as Tupperware, Discovery Toys, and Encyclopaedia Britannica, that do not use any other marketing distribution channels, relying on independent sales contractors to sell their products directly to consumers. Companies such as L. L. Bean, Lands' End, and The Sharper Image, while utilizing other distribution channels, rely heavily on direct marketing and have been very successful through their direct-mail and phone-order business. Firms such as Soloflex rely on direct-response television and print ads to market exercise equipment (Exhibit 1–7).

Direct-selling and marketing companies often rely solely on direct marketing to sell their products and services. However, direct-marketing tools and techniques are

➤ *Exhibit 1–7*
Soloflex relies on direct response advertising to market its exercise equipment

To unlock your body's potential, we proudly offer Soloflex. Twenty-four traditional iron pumping exercises, each correct in form and balance. All on a simple machine that fits in a corner of your home.
For a free Soloflex brochure, call anytime 1·800·453·9000. In Canada, 1·800·543·1005.
VHS Video Brochure™ available upon request.

BODY BY SOLOFLEX

also being used by companies that distribute their products through traditional distribution channels or have their own sales force. Direct marketing plays a very big role in the integrated marketing communication programs of consumer products companies and business-to-business marketers. These companies spend billions of dollars each year to call customers directly and attempt to sell them products and services or to qualify them as sales leads. Marketers send out direct-mail pieces ranging from simple letters and fliers to detailed brochures and videotapes to communicate with potential customers and provide them with information about their products or services. Direct-marketing techniques are used by companies to distribute product samples or to target users of a competitive brand of a product or service.

Advantages of direct marketing

Direct marketing has become so popular and is being integrated into companies' promotional programs for a number of reasons. First, changes in society (two-income households, greater use of credit) have made consumers more receptive to the convenience of direct-marketed products. Direct marketing allows a company to be more selective and target its marketing communications to specific customer segments. Messages can also be customized to fit the needs of the segment and, with new technologies, can even be personalized for individual customers. The success or failure of direct-marketing efforts are also often easier to assess since the outcomes are measured through specific criteria such as number and size of orders, leads generated, or requests for more information.

Disadvantages of direct marketing

Direct marketing also has its problems. For example, consumers and business customers are being bombarded with unsolicited mail and phone calls. This makes them less receptive to direct-marketing efforts and also has created image problems for products and services marketed this way. Like other forms of communication, direct marketing must deal with the problem of clutter, where too many messages compete for consumers' attention.

Sales Promotion

The next variable in the promotional mix is **sales promotion,** which is generally defined as those marketing activities that provide *extra value or incentives* to the sales force, distributors, or the ultimate consumer and can stimulate immediate sales. Sales promotion is generally broken into two major categories: *consumer-oriented* and *trade-oriented* activities. Consumer-oriented sales promotion is targeted to the ultimate user of a product or service and includes a variety of tools such as couponing, sampling, premiums, rebates, contests, sweepstakes, and various point-of-purchase materials (Exhibit 1–8). Trade-oriented sales promotion techniques are targeted toward marketing intermediaries such as wholesalers, distributors, and retailers. Promotional and merchandising allowances, price deals, sales contests, and trade shows are examples of some of the promotional tools used to encourage the trade to stock and promote a company's products.

Sales promotion expenditures in the United States exceeded $140 billion in 1991 and accounted for more promotional dollars than advertising. Among many consumer package-goods companies, sales promotion often accounts for between 60 and 70 percent of the promotional budget.[13] Some companies have switched the emphasis of their promotional strategy from advertising to sales promotion. For example, a few years ago the Scott Paper Company reduced its advertising budget significantly so that more monies could be allocated to price promotions. Scott also terminated its relationships with its two long-term advertising agencies in favor of a smaller agency with direct-marketing and sales promotion expertise.[14] Over the past several years, the H. J. Heinz Co. cut its advertising expenditures by nearly 43 percent while nearly all of its increased marketing spending in 1992 was allocated to trade promotions.[15]

> *Exhibit 1–8*
Coupons are a popular
consumer-oriented sales
promotion tool

Advantages of sales promotions

Several factors underlie the rapid growth and use of sales promotion by marketers. Trade-oriented promotions provide marketing intermediaries with a financial incentive to stock and promote a company's products. Retailers often demand price deals or discounts from manufacturers in exchange for shelf space or promotional displays. Consumer-oriented sales promotion encourages consumers to make an immediate purchase and thus can stimulate short-term sales. For example, samples, coupons, price reductions, or premium offers can induce trial of a new brand or maintain loyalty to an existing brand. Contests and sweepstakes create interest or excitement in a company's product or service and serve as "insurance" to help increase the likelihood that an advertisement or promotional display gets attention. Sales promotion also provides marketers with a way of responding to price-sensitive consumers who prefer to use coupons or purchase products offered at a discount.

Disadvantages of sales promotions

The ability of consumer- and trade-oriented promotions to generate immediate sales has made sales promotion a popular promotional tool among marketing managers, particularly those concerned with short-term performance. However, problems are also associated with sales promotion techniques. Many firms are concerned about becoming too reliant on sales promotion and focusing too much attention on short-run marketing planning and performance. Critics of sales promotion argue that the sales gains resulting from these programs are often temporary and the short-term sales goals are often achieved at the expense of long-term brand equity. The rapid growth of sales promotion has also created *promotional clutter*, as consumers are bombarded with too many coupons, contests, sweepstakes, and other promotional offers.

Before ending our discussion of sales promotion, we would like to address a potential terminology problem. *Promotion* and *sales promotion* are two terms that often create confusion in the advertising and marketing fields. As previously noted, the term *promotion* represents an element of the marketing mix by which firms communicate with their customers and includes the various promotional mix elements we have just discussed. However, among many marketing and advertising practitioners, the term *promotion* is used more narrowly to refer to *sales promotion* activities to either consumers or the trade (retailers, wholesalers). In this book, *promotion* is used in the broader sense and refers to the various marketing communication activities of an organization. When discussing sales promotion activities, we are referring to this one specific element of the promotional mix.

**Publicity/Public
Relations**

Another important component of an organization's promotional mix is that of publicity/public relations. **Publicity** refers to nonpersonal communications regarding an organization, product, service, or idea that is not directly paid for nor run under identified sponsorship, usually coming in the form of a news story, editorial, or announcement about an organization and/or its products and services. Like advertising, publicity involves nonpersonal communication to a mass audience, but unlike advertising, publicity is not directly paid for by the company. The company or organization will attempt to get the media to provide coverage of or run a favorable story on a product, service, cause, or event to affect awareness, knowledge, opinions, and/or behavior. The various techniques used to gain publicity include news releases, press conferences, feature articles, photographs, films, and tapes.

Advantages of publicity

An advantage of publicity over other forms of promotion is its credibility. Consumers generally tend to be less skeptical toward favorable information about a product or service when it comes from a source they perceive to be unbiased and objective. For example, the success (or failure) of a new movie is often determined by the reviews it receives from film critics, who are viewed as objective evaluators by many moviegoers.

Another advantage of publicity is its low cost, as the company is not paying for time or space in a mass medium such as television, radio, or newspaper. While an organization may incur some costs in developing publicity items or in maintaining a staff to execute this function, these expenses will be far less than for the other promotional programs.

Disadvantages of publicity

While the low cost and credibility associated with publicity are advantages of this promotional element, a major disadvantage is the lack of control afforded the company. An organization can issue press releases or invite the media to preview its new, innovative product and hope for favorable coverage in the newspaper or on the evening news. However, there is no guarantee that a story about the product will appear in the paper or be aired when the company's key target audience is watching. Moreover, information about the product might be improperly presented or some critical details omitted. It should also be noted that publicity is not always favorable and can be very damaging to an organization. Promotional Perspective 1–2 discusses the problems American Suzuki Motor Corporation encountered as a result of negative publicity from allegations over the safety of the Suzuki Samurai.

Public relations

It is important to recognize the distinction between publicity and public relations. When an organization systematically plans and distributes information in an attempt to control and manage the nature of the publicity it receives and its image, it is really engaging in a function known as public relations. **Public relations (PR)** is defined as "the management function which evaluates public attitudes, identifies the policies and procedures of an individual or organization with the public interest, and executes a program of action to earn public understanding and acceptance."[16] Public relations generally has a broader objective than publicity, as its purpose is to establish and maintain a positive image of the company among its various publics.

Publicity is one of the most important communication techniques used in public relations. However, the public relations function uses a variety of other tools to manage an organization's image, including special publications, participation in community activities, fund-raising, sponsorship of special events, and various public affairs activities. Organizations also use advertising as a public relations tool to

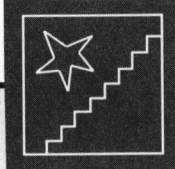

Promotional Perspective 1-2

Suzuki Survives Negative Publicity

Marketers fear few things as much as a wave of negative publicity concerning their products' safety. The American Suzuki Motor Corporation is seeing firsthand how damaging negative publicity can be as it struggles to survive a controversy concerning the safety of its Samurai sports utility vehicle. The controversy began in June 1988 when Consumers Union, publisher of *Consumer Reports* magazine, held a press conference announcing it would give the Samurai the first "not acceptable" rating it had issued for a car in a decade. Consumers Union argued that basic design flaws tended to make the Samurai prone to roll over when cornered hard and thus dangerously unsafe. It also called on Suzuki to recall all 160,000 Samurais that had been sold in the United States, to take the vehicle off the market, and to give full refunds to Samurai owners.

The attack on the safety of the Samurai became front-page stories in newspapers across the country and was featured on both national and local television news. The vehicle was quickly in danger of becoming a national joke as comedians incorporated the rollover claims into their routines and consumers joked about it. Within a few weeks of the Consumers Union announcement, sales of the Samurai plummeted, dropping 71 percent in one month.

Suzuki immediately began an advertising and public relations program to address the safety controversy and Consumers Union charges. The company held a press conference within a week criticizing Consumers Union for using shoddy and biased testing procedures and provided videotapes of the Samurai safely performing the turning maneuvers that led to the alleged rollover problem. In the 10 days following the Consumers Union press conference, Suzuki spent $1.5 million over and above its normal advertising budget to run ads quoting positive reviews of the Samurai in automotive trade publications. The company also provided dealers with material disputing the charges to help them handle the controversy, and a toll-free number was set up for customers to call with any questions.

In September 1988, the National Transportation Safety Board denied a petition by the Center for Auto Safety calling for a government recall of the Samurai. The government agency later dismissed the Consumers Union study and said the Samurai was no more likely to roll over than any other sports utility vehicle. However, the government report never received the same publicity as the Consumers Union study, and Samurai sales plunged from 81,349 vehicles in 1987 to 5,038 units in 1989, and 1991 sales were projected to be only 4,308.

The impact of the rollover controversy was particularly damaging to Suzuki as the Samurai was the only vehicle it sold in the U.S. market at the time. In 1989, Suzuki introduced two new vehicles, the Swift subcompact car line and the Sidekick, a sport utility vehicle similar to the Samurai but with a wider wheelbase. However, the loss in consumer confidence along with the recession and the overall decline in auto sales have made it difficult for the company to recover. American Suzuki expected to sell only 22,000 total vehicles in 1991—a far cry from the 300,000 figure it had predicted in 1985 when it launched its automotive line in the United States.

The decline in American Suzuki's sales base has changed the way it markets its products in the United States. The advertising budget was slashed from more than $30 million in 1987 to about $12 million in 1991. Suzuki practices what it calls "laser marketing," which involves carefully defining the demographic and psychographic characteristics of its customers and targeting ads to them, mostly in magazines and occasionally on cable television. Suzuki ads play on the favorable reviews its products have received by various enthusiast magazines such as *Road & Track* and *4WD Sport Utility Magazine*. The Sidekick and the Swift receive the marketing attention, and the company has recently launched a campaign aimed at increasing corporate brand awareness.

Suzuki still makes the Samurai, although it doesn't promote it, and some industry analysts are critical of the company for hanging on to the vehicle that nearly destroyed the company. However, the company believes the Samurai is a valuable part of the product line, as it gives Suzuki dealers the lowest-priced sports utility vehicle on the market. American Suzuki believes its Samurai problems are behind it, and the company hopes to provide the industry with a textbook example of what must be done to bounce back from the disaster created by the rollover controversy. However, one thing is certain—Suzuki is unlikely to forget just how devastating the impact of negative publicity can be.

Source: James Risen, "Suzuki Calls Consumer Group's Safety Test on Samurai 'Flawed,'" *Los Angeles Times*, June 10, 1988, part IV, p. 1.; James Risen, "Suzuki Shifted into High Gear When Crisis Hit," *Los Angeles Times*, June 27, 1988, part IV, p. 1; Bradley A. Stertz, "Suzuki Takes Extraordinary Measures to Halt Sales Plunge of Samurai Model," *The Wall Street Journal*, July 15, 1988, p. 22; and John O'Dell, "Suzuki on Road of Return from a Near Disaster," *Los Angeles Times*, September 1, 1991, pp. D1, 16.

---

enhance their image. For example, Exhibit 1–9 shows an example of a corporate ad for State Farm Insurance Companies.

Traditionally, publicity and public relations have been assigned more of a supportive role rather than considered a primary part of the marketing and promotional process. However, over the past five years, many firms have begun making public relations an integral part of their predetermined marketing and promotional strategies.[17] PR firms are increasingly touting public relations as a communications tool that can take over many of the functions of conventional advertising and marketing.

➤ *Exhibit 1–9*
Advertising is often used by companies to enhance their corporate image

Personal Selling

The final element of an organization's promotional mix is **personal selling**—a form of person-to-person communication in which a seller attempts to assist and/or persuade prospective buyers to purchase the company's product or service or to act on an idea.

Advantages

Unlike advertising, personal selling involves direct contact between the buyer and seller, either face-to-face or through some form of telecommunications such as telephone sales. This interaction gives the marketer communication flexibility, as the seller can see or hear the potential buyer's reactions to the message and modify the message accordingly. The personal, individualized communication that occurs through personal selling allows the seller to tailor and adapt the message to the specific needs or situation of the customer. Personal selling also involves more immediate and precise feedback because the impact of the sales presentation can generally be assessed by the reactions of the customer. If the feedback is unfavorable, the salesperson can modify the message. Personal selling efforts can also be targeted to specific markets and customer types who are the best prospects for the company's product or service.

Disadvantages

Personal selling also has some disadvantages. A major problem with personal selling lies in the high cost per contact. In 1990, the average cost of a sales call was estimated to range from $196 to $225, depending on the industry.[18] Thus, it can be very expensive to reach large audiences through this means. In addition, different salespeople may not deliver the same message, which makes it difficult to deliver a consistent and uniform message to all customers.

Promotional Management

In the previous pages, we examined the elements that constitute the promotional mix and considered the advantages and disadvantages associated with each. In the actual development of a promotional strategy, these promotional mix elements must be combined, balancing the strengths and weaknesses of each, to produce an effective promotional campaign. **Promotional management** involves the process of coordinating the promotional mix elements to develop a controlled and integrated program of effective marketing communication.

In assembling the proper promotional mix, the marketer must consider which promotional tools to use and how to combine them to achieve the organization's marketing and promotional objectives. Advertising campaigns, sales promotion techniques, publicity and public relations, personal selling, and direct-marketing efforts must be coordinated and integrated into the overall marketing strategy to generate an effective communications program.

Companies also face the task of distributing the total promotional budget across the promotional mix elements. For example, a decision has to be made as to the roles of advertising, sales promotion, direct marketing, and personal selling and what percentage of the promotional budget to allocate to each. For most companies, the decision is not whether to use a promotional mix variable but rather how to combine variables to communicate with the target audience effectively.

Companies consider many factors in developing their promotional mix, including the type of product, the target market, the decision process of the buyer, the stage of the product life cycle, and its channels of distribution. For example, companies selling consumer products and services generally rely on advertising through mass media to communicate with ultimate consumers, whereas business-to-business marketers, who generally sell expensive, risky, and often complex products and services, more often tend to use personal selling. However, while advertising may receive less emphasis than personal selling in business-to-business marketing, it still is used to perform important functions such as building awareness of the company and its products, generating leads for the sales force, and reassuring customers about the purchase they have made. Conversely, personal selling also plays an important role in consumer product marketing. A consumer goods company retains a sales force to call on marketing intermediaries (wholesalers and retailers) that distribute the product or service to the final consumer. While the company sales rep does not communicate with the ultimate consumer, that rep makes an important contribution to the marketing effort by gaining new distribution outlets for the company's product, securing shelf position and space for the brand, informing retailers about advertising and promotion efforts to ultimate users, and encouraging dealers to merchandise and promote the brand at the local market level.

While advertising and personal selling efforts may vary depending on the type of market being sought, even firms in the same industry may differ in the allocation of their promotional efforts. For example, in the cosmetics industry, Avon and Mary Kay Cosmetics concentrate their promotional efforts on direct selling, whereas companies such as Revlon and Max Factor rely heavily on consumer advertising. Firms also differ in the relative emphasis they place on advertising and sales promotion. Companies selling high-quality brands will rely on advertising to convince consumers of their superiority, to justify their higher prices, and to maintain their "image" in the minds of consumers. Brands of lower quality, or those that are difficult to differentiate, often compete more on a price or "value-for-the-money" basis rather than on image and may rely more on sales promotion to the trade and/or consumers.

The marketing communications program of an organization is generally developed with a specific purpose or objective in mind and is the end product of a detailed marketing and promotional planning process. We will now turn our attention to a model of the promotional planning process that presents the sequence of decisions that must be made in developing and implementing the marketing communications program.

The Promotional Planning Process

As with any business function, planning plays a fundamental role in the development and implementation of an effective promotional program. Those individuals involved in the promotional management must develop a **promotional plan** that provides the framework for developing, implementing, and controlling the organization's integrated marketing communication program and activities. Promotional planning is best viewed as a dynamic process, as it generally evolves over a period of time and involves interactions among company personnel as well as with external parties such as advertising agencies, public relations and marketing research firms, and consultants.

➢ *Exhibit 1–10*
**An integrated marketing
communications planning model**

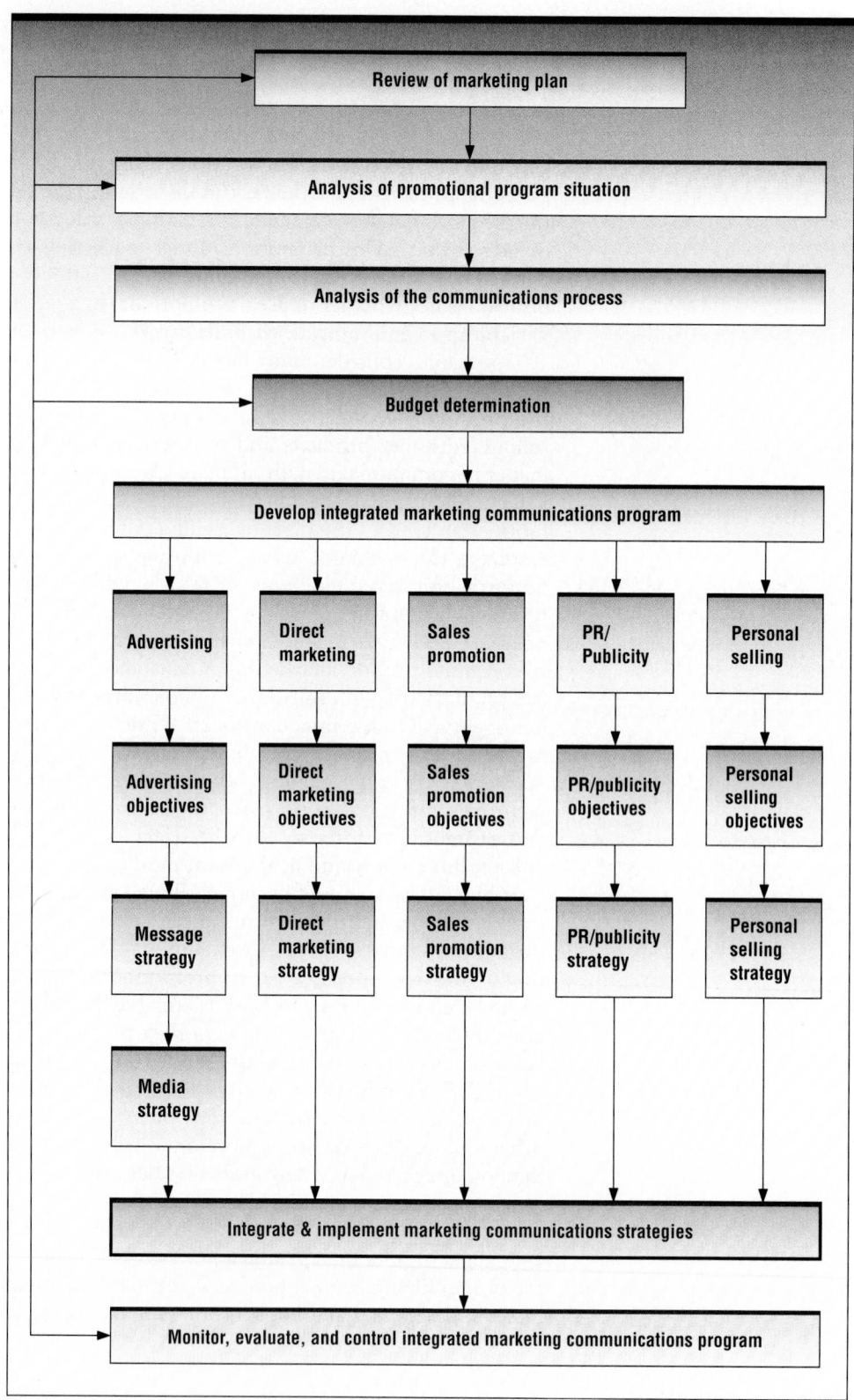

As was noted earlier, the goal of the promotional program is to develop an effective program of integrated marketing communication that will help an organization achieve its marketing objectives. To accomplish this, the promotional planners must make decisions regarding the role and function of the specific elements of the promotional mix, develop strategies for each element, and implement the plan. In planning and executing

➤ *Exhibit 1–10*
Concluded

Review of marketing plan
    Examine overall marketing plan and objectives
    Role of advertising and promotions
    Competitive analysis
    Assess environmental influences

Analysis of promotional program situation
    Internal analysis
        Promotional department organization
        Firm's ability to implement promotional program
        Agency evaluation and selection
        Review of previous program results

    External analysis
        Consumer behavior analysis
        Market segmentation and target marketing
        Market positioning

Analysis of communications process
    Analyze receiver's response processes
    Analyze source, message, channel factors
    Establish communications goals and objectives

Budget determination
    Set tentative marketing communications budget
    Allocate tentative budget

Develop integrated marketing communications program
    Advertising
        Set advertising objectives
        Determine advertising budget
        Develop message strategies
        Develop media strategies
    Direct marketing
        Set direct marketing objectives
        Determine direct marketing budget
        Develop direct marketing strategies

    Sales promotion
        Set sales promotion objectives
        Determine sales promotion budget
        Develop sales promotion strategies
    Public relations/publicity
        Set PR/publicity objectives
        Determine PR/publicity budget
        Develop PR/publicity functions
    Personal selling
        Set personal selling objectives
        Determine personal selling budget
        Develop selling roles and responsibilities

Integrate and implement marketing communications strategies
    Integrate promotional mix strategies
    Create and produce ads
    Purchase media time, space, etc.
    Design and implement direct marketing programs
    Design and distribute sales promotion materials
    Design and implement public relations/publicity programs

Monitor, evaluate, and control integrated marketing communications program
    Evaluate promotional program results/effectiveness
    Take measures to control and adjust promotional strategies

the promotional plan and strategies, it must be remembered that promotion is but one part of, and must be integrated into, the overall marketing plan and program.

A model of the integrated marketing communication planning process is shown in Exhibit 1–10. The remainder of this chapter presents a brief overview of the various steps involved in this process.

Review of the Marketing Plan

The first step in the promotional planning process is a review of the marketing plan and objectives. Before developing a promotional plan, it is important to understand where the company (or the brand) has been, its current position in the market, where it intends to go, and how it plans to get there. Most of this information should be contained in the **marketing plan**, a written document that describes the overall marketing strategy and programs developed for an organization, a particular product line, or a brand. Marketing plans can take a variety of forms but generally include five basic elements:

1. A detailed situation analysis that consists of an internal marketing audit and review and an external analysis of the market competition and environmental factors.
2. The establishment of specific marketing objectives that provide direction, a time frame for marketing activities, and a mechanism for measuring performance.
3. The formulation of a marketing strategy and program that includes selection of the target market(s) and decisions and plans for the four elements of the marketing mix.
4. A program for implementing the marketing strategy, including determining specific tasks to be performed and responsibilities.
5. A process for monitoring and evaluating performance and providing feedback so proper control can be maintained and any necessary changes made in the overall marketing strategy or tactics.

It is important for individuals involved in the promotional planning process to begin by carefully reviewing the marketing plan. For most firms, the promotional plan is an integral part of the marketing strategy. Thus, the promotional planners must know the role advertising and other promotional mix elements will play in the overall marketing program. Also, development of the promotional plan follows a procedure very similar to that used in the marketing plan and often uses the detailed information contained in this document. Promotional planners will want to focus on information in the marketing plan that is relevant to the development of the promotional strategy and its implementation.

Promotional Program Situation Analysis

Having reviewed the overall marketing plan, the next step in the development of a promotional plan is to conduct the promotional program situation analysis. The situation analysis in the integrated marketing communications program focuses on those factors that influence or are relevant to development of a promotional strategy. As with the overall marketing situation analysis, the promotional program situation analysis will include both an **internal analysis** and an **external analysis.**

Internal analysis

The internal analysis assesses relevant areas involving the product/service offering and the firm itself. The capabilities of the firm and its ability to develop and implement a successful promotional program, the organization of the promotional department, and a review of the successes and failures of past programs should be considered. In addition, the analysis should study the relative advantages and disadvantages of performing the promotional functions in-house as opposed to hiring an external agency (or agencies). For example, the internal analysis may indicate the firm is not capable of planning, implementing, and managing certain areas of the promotional program. If this is the case, it would be advantageous to look externally for assistance from an advertising agency or some other promotional facilitator. In many situations, the organization may already be using an advertising agency, and the focus will be on the quality of the agency's work and the results achieved by past and/or current campaigns.

➤ *Exhibit 1–11*
This ad for the Adolph Coors Company is designed to improve the company's image

In this text, we will examine advertising agencies and discuss the role they play, the functions they perform for their clients, the agency selection process, compensation, and considerations in evaluating agency performance. We will also discuss the role and function of other promotional facilitators such as sales promotion firms, public relations agencies, and marketing research firms.

Another aspect of the internal analysis is assessing the strengths and weaknesses of the firm or the brand from an image perspective. Often, the image the firm brings to the market will have a significant impact on its promotional program. A firm with a strong corporate image, such as IBM, American Airlines, McDonald's, or Sony, is already a step ahead when it comes to marketing its products or services owing to its reputation for quality service, and so on. Companies or brands that are new to the market, and thus without an established image, or those with a negative image may have to concentrate on their image as well as on the benefits or attributes of the specific product. For example, the Adolph Coors Company is well known but not well liked by some groups that have made its products the target of numerous boycotts. Thus, the company has spent a considerable amount of money on corporate image advertising in addition to its basic product-oriented ads (Exhibit 1–11).[19]

Another aspect of the internal analysis is the assessment of the relative strengths and weaknesses of the product or service. Consideration must be given to the relative advantages and disadvantages of the product/service; any unique selling points or benefits it may have; its packaging, price, and design; and so on. This information is particularly important to the creative personnel who must develop the advertising message for the brand.

Exhibit 1–12 shows a checklist of some of the areas that might be considered when performing an internal analysis for promotional planning purposes. However,

➤ *Exhibit 1–12* **Checklist of areas covered in the situation analysis**

Internal Factors	External Factors

Assessment of firm's promotional organization and capabilities
    Organization of promotional department
    Capability of firm to develop and execute promotional
      programs
    Determination of role and function of advertising agency
      and other promotional facilitators
Review of firm's previous promotional programs and results
    Review previous promotional objectives
    Review previous promotional budgets and allocations
    Review previous promotional mix strategies and programs
    Review results of previous promotional programs
Assessment of firm or brand image and implications for
  promotion
Assessment of relative strengths and weaknesses of
  product/service
    What are the strengths and weaknesses of product or
      service?
    What are the product's/service's key benefits?
    Does the product/service have any unique selling points?
    Assessment of packaging/labeling/brand image
    How does our product/service compare with competition?
	Customer analysis
	    Who buys our product or service?
	    Who makes the decision to buy the product?
	    Who influences the decision to buy the product?
	    How is the purchase decision made? Who assumes what
	      role?
	    What does the customer buy? What needs must be satisfied?
	    Why do customers buy a particular brand?
	    Where do they go or look to buy the product or service?
	    When do they buy? Any seasonality factors?
	    What are the customers' attitudes toward our product or
	      service?
	    What social factors might influence the purchase decision?
	    Does the customers' lifestyle influence their decisions?
	    How is our product/service perceived by the customers?
	    How do demographic factors influence the purchase
	      decision?
	Competitive analysis
	    Who are our direct and indirect competitors?
	    What key benefits and positioning are used by our
	      competitors?
	    What is our position relative to the competition?
	    What is the size of the competitors ad budgets?
	    What message and media strategies are competitors using?
	Environmental analysis
	    Are there any current trends or developments that might
	      affect the promotional program?

addressing these areas may require information the company does not have available internally and must be gathered as part of the external analysis.

External analysis

The external analysis focuses on factors such as characteristics of the firm's customers, market segments, positioning strategies, and competitors, as is shown in Exhibit 1–12. An important part of the external analysis is a detailed consideration of the customers in terms of their characteristics and buying patterns, their decision processes, and factors influencing their purchase decisions. Attention must also be given to areas such as consumers' perceptions and attitudes, lifestyles, and criteria used in making purchase decisions. Often, marketing research studies are necessary to answer some of these questions.

A key element of the external analysis involves an assessment of the market. The attractiveness of various market segments must be evaluated, and the decision as to which segments to target must be made. Once the decision has been made in respect to which target markets will be pursued, the emphasis will be on determining how the product should be positioned—that is, what image or place the product will occupy in consumers' minds.

The external phase of the promotional program situation analysis will also include an in-depth examination of the competition, including both direct and indirect competitors. While an in-depth analysis of competitors would have been conducted in the overall marketing situation analysis, even more attention is devoted to promotional aspects at this phase. Attention will be focused on the firm's primary competitors with respect to their specific strengths and weaknesses, their segmentation, targeting and positioning strategies, and the promotional strategies they have employed. The size and allocation of their promotional budgets, their media strategies, and the messages they are sending to the marketplace should all be considered.

Analysis of the Communications Process

At this stage of the promotional planning process, consideration is given to how the company can effectively communicate with consumers in its target markets. The promotional planner must think about the type of response process consumers will go through in responding to marketing communications. For example, the response process for products or services where the consumer decision-making process is characterized by a high level of interest and involvement is often different from that for low-involvement or routine purchase decisions as are the promotional strategy implications.

Communication decisions regarding the use of various source, message, and channel factors must also be considered. For example, the promotional planner should recognize the different effects various types of advertising messages might have on consumers and whether they are appropriate for the product or brand. Issues such as whether a celebrity spokesperson should be used and at what cost may also be studied. Preliminary discussion of various media mix options (print, television, radio, newspaper, direct marketing) and their cost implications might also be considered at this stage.

A very important part of this stage of the promotional planning process is establishing communication goals and objectives. In this text, we stress the importance of distinguishing between communications and marketing objectives. **Marketing objectives** refer to what is to be accomplished by the overall marketing program and are often stated in terms of criteria such as sales, market share, or profitability. **Communication objectives** refer to what the firm seeks to accomplish with its promotional program and are often stated in terms of the nature of the message to be communicated or what is to be accomplished in terms of specific communication effects. Communication objectives may include creating awareness or knowledge about a product and its attributes or benefits, creating an image, or developing favorable attitudes, preferences, or purchase intentions. Communication objectives should be the guiding force for the development of the overall marketing communications strategy and will also guide the development of objectives for each of the promotional mix areas.

Budget Determination

After determining the communications objectives to be accomplished, attention turns to determining the promotional budget. The basic questions being asked at this point are: What will the promotional program cost? and How will these monies be allocated? The amount of money a firm needs to spend on promotion should be determined by what must be done to accomplish its communications objectives and what it will cost to perform these tasks. However, in reality, promotional budgets are often determined using a more simplistic approach such as determining how much money is available or basing promotional expenditures on a percentage of a company's or brand's sales revenue. At this stage, the budget is often only tentative and may not be finalized until specific promotional mix strategies are developed.

Developing the Integrated Marketing Communications Program

This step of the promotional planning process is generally the most involved and detailed. As discussed earlier, each of the promotional mix elements has certain advantages and limitations. At this stage of the planning process, decisions have to be made regarding the role and importance of each promotional mix element and their coordination with one another. As can be seen in Exhibit 1–10, each promotional mix element will have its own set of objectives and a budget and strategy for meeting these objectives. Decisions must be made and activities performed to implement the promotional programs and procedures developed for monitoring and evaluating performance and making any necessary changes.

Let us examine the advertising program as an example. This element of the promotional program will have its own set of objectives—usually involving the communication of some message or appeal to a target audience. A budget will be determined, providing the advertising manager and the agency with a sense of how much money is available for developing the advertising campaign and purchasing media to disseminate the advertising message. Two very important aspects of the advertising program are the development of the message and media strategy. Message development, often referred to as creative strategy, involves determining the basic appeal and message the advertiser wishes to convey to the target audience. This process, along with the advertisements that result, is to many students the most fascinating aspect of promotion. Media strategy involves determining the communications channels that will be used to deliver the advertising message to the target audience. Decisions must be made regarding the various types of media that will be used (e.g., newspapers, magazines, radio, television, billboards) as well as specific media selections such as a particular magazine or TV program. This task requires careful evaluation of the media options including their advantages and limitations, costs, and ability to deliver the message effectively to the target market.

Once the message and media strategies have been determined, steps must be taken to implement them. Most large companies hire advertising agencies to plan and produce their messages and to evaluate and purchase the media that will carry their advertisements. However, most agencies work very closely with their clients as they develop the ads and make media selection decisions, because it is the advertiser that must ultimately approve the creative work and media plan.

Monitoring, Evaluation, and Control

The final stage of the promotional planning process shown is that of monitoring, evaluating, and controlling the promotional program. It is important to determine how well the promotional program is doing in meeting communications objectives and helping the firm accomplish its overall marketing goals and objectives. The promotional planner wants to know not only how well the promotional program is doing but also why. For example, problems with the advertising program may lie in the nature of the message or with a media plan that does not reach the target market effectively. By knowing the reasons for the results, the manager can take the appropriate steps to correct the program.

This final stage of the process is designed to provide managers with continual feedback concerning the effectiveness of the promotional program, which in turn can be used as input into the planning process. As Exhibit 1–10 shows, information on the results or outcomes achieved by the promotional program serves as an input to subsequent promotional planning and strategy development.

An Example of an Integrated Marketing Communications Program

The promotional planning process presented above provides a sequence of steps for managers to follow in planning, implementing, and evaluating the promotional program. To further explore what is involved in planning, developing, and implementing promotional strategy, we will examine the integrated marketing communications program used in the marketing of the San Diego Zoological Society and its two main attractions—the San Diego Zoo and Wild Animal Park.

Situation Analysis

Organizational background

One of the most popular tourist attractions in the United States is the world-famous San Diego Zoo. The zoo contains more than 800 species of animals from throughout the world living in enclosures as similar to their native habitat as possible. The zoo is owned by the San Diego Zoological Society, which also operates the San Diego Wild Animal Park. This is an 1,800-acre preserve where a 50-minute safari aboard a monorail allows visitors to view 2,500 animals living together in their re-created African and Asian habitats.

Competition

The southern California market is one of the most competitive entertainment attraction battlegrounds in the country. The obvious competitors to the San Diego Zoo and Wild Animal Park include Sea World, which is also in San Diego; Disneyland and Knott's Berry Farm in nearby Orange County; and Universal Studios and Magic Mountain Amusement Park in the Los Angeles area. The zoo's marketing department also defines competition in a more generic sense as including any discretionary spending opportunity for a family entertainment or educational experience.

Customer analysis and target market

The San Diego Zoo defines its target audiences in geographic, demographic, and psychographic dimensions. For example, in terms of geography, 40 percent of the visitors to the zoo and wild animal park come from San Diego County, 14 percent from other parts of southern California, 6 percent from other parts of California, 35 percent from the rest of the United States, and 5 percent from foreign countries. The zoo also uses a variety of demographic variables to identify its target markets including age, gender, education level, household income, occupation, and ethnicity. In terms of psychographics, research shows zoo visitors to be societally conscious and more likely to be the conforming and traditional family-oriented type. In addition to providing detailed demographic, geographic, and psychographic information on visitors and nonvisitors, marketing research is used to identify visitors' likes and dislikes, evaluations and ratings of various attractions, areas needing improvement, and new opportunities. Research information is gathered through telephone tracking surveys, exit gate intercept surveys, mail surveys, and focus group studies.

Communication Objectives

The marketing communications program for the San Diego Zoological Society has a number of objectives. First, it must provide funding for the society's programs and maintain a large and powerful base of supporters for financial and political strength. The communications program must educate the public about the society's various programs and maintain a favorable image on a local, regional, national, and even international level. A major objective of the integrated marketing communications program is drawing visitors to the two attractions.

Integrated Marketing Communications

To achieve these objectives, the San Diego Zoological Society uses an integrated marketing communications program that employs a variety of promotional tools including advertising, sales promotion, direct marketing, public relations, personal selling, and other methods. An advertising agency assists in the marketing communications efforts. The agency's responsibilities include working with the zoo's marketing department and planning and executing the advertising program. Some examples of ads developed by the agency are shown in Exhibit 1–13. The agency also works with the zoo's marketing department on public relations and publicity matters. Exhibit 1–14 shows how various promotional tools are used in the San Diego Zoological Society's integrated marketing communications program.

Perspective and Organization of This Text

Traditional approaches taken in teaching advertising, promotional strategy, or marketing communication courses have often treated the various elements of the promotional mix as separate communication functions. As a result, many of those who work in areas such as advertising, sales promotion, direct marketing, or public relations tend to approach marketing communication problems from the perspective of their particular communication specialty. For example, an advertising person may believe marketing communication objectives are best met through the use of media advertising; a promotional specialist argues for the use of a sales promotion program to motivate consumer response; while a public relations person advocates the use of a PR campaign to tackle the problem. These orientations are not surprising since each person has been trained and conditioned to view marketing communications problems primarily from one perspective, which usually happens to be that of their area of expertise.

➤ *Exhibit 1–13* **Outdoor advertising is part of the marketing communications program for the San Diego Zoo**

In the contemporary business world, however, individuals working in marketing, advertising, and other promotional areas are expected to understand and use a variety of marketing communications tools, not just the one in which they specialize. Advertising agencies no longer confine their services to the advertising area. Many are involved in sales promotion, public relations, direct marketing, event sponsorship, and other marketing communication areas. Individuals working on the client or advertiser side of the business, such as brand, product, or promotional managers, are developing marketing programs that use a variety of marketing communication methods.

This text views advertising and promotion from an integrated marketing communications perspective. We will examine all of the promotional mix elements and their role in an organization's integrated marketing communications efforts. Although media advertising may be the most visible part of the communications program, to understand its role in contemporary marketing, attention must be given to other promotional areas such as direct marketing, sales promotion, public relations, and personal selling. Not all the promotional mix areas are under the direct control of the advertising or marketing communications manager. For example, personal selling is typically a specialized marketing function outside of the control of the advertising or promotional department. Likewise, publicity/public relations is often assigned to a separate department. There should, however, be communication among all of these departments as all of an organization's marketing communication tools need to be integrated and coordinated.

The purpose of this book is to provide you with a thorough understanding of the field of advertising and other elements of a firm's promotional mix and show how they are combined to form an integrated marketing communications program. To plan, develop, and implement an effective integrated marketing communications

> *Exhibit 1–14*
The integrated marketing communications program for the San Diego Zoo

Advertising

Objectives: Drive attendance to Zoo and Wild Animal Park. Uphold image and educate target audience and inform them of new attractions and special events and promotions.

Audience: Members and non members of Zoological Society. Households in primary and secondary geographic markets consisting of San Diego County and 5 other counties in southern California. Tertiary markets of 7 western states. Tourist and group sales markets.

Timing: As allowed and determined by budget. Mostly timed to coincide with promotional efforts.

Tools/media: Television, radio, newspaper, magazines, direct mail, outdoor, tourist media (television and magazine).

Sales Promotions

Objectives: Use price, product, and other variables to drive attendance when it might not otherwise come.

Audience: Targeted, depending on co-op partner, mostly to southern California market.

Timing: To fit needs of Zoo and Wild Animal Park and co-sponsoring partner.

Tools/media: Coupons, sweepstakes, tours, broadcast tradeouts, direct mail: statement stuffers, fliers, postcards.

Public Relations

Objectives: Inform, educate, create, and maintain image for Zoological Society and major attractions, reinforce advertising message.

Audience: From local to international, depending on subject, scope, and timing.

Timing: Ongoing, although often timed to coincide with promotions and other special events. Spur-of-the moment animal news and information such as acquisitions, births, etc.

Tools/media: Coverage by major news media, articles in local, regional, national and international newspapers, magazines and other publications such as visitors guides, tour books and guides, appearances by Zoo spokesperson Joanne Emery on talk shows (such as "The Tonight Show").

program, those involved must understand marketing, consumer behavior, and the communications process. The first part of this book is designed to provide this foundation by examining the role of advertising and other forms of promotion in the marketing process, and how firms organize for advertising and promotion and make decisions regarding advertising agencies and other firms providing marketing and promotional services.

32   part I   *Role of Advertising and Promotion in Marketing*

➤ *Exhibit 1–14*
Concluded

Cause Marketing/Corporate Sponsorships/Events Underwriting

Objectives: To provide funding for Zoological Society programs and promote special programs and events done in cooperation with corporate sponsor. Must be win-win business partnership for Society and partner.

Audience: Supporters of both the Zoological Society and the corporate or product/service partner.

Timing: Coincides with needs of both partners, and seasonal attendance generation needs of Zoo and Wild Animal Park.

Tools: May involve advertising, publicity, discount co-op promotions, ticket trades, hospitality centers. Exposure is directly proportional to amount of underwriting by corporate sponsor, both in scope and duration.

Direct Marketing

Objectives: Maintain large powerful base of supporters for financial and political strength.

Audience: Local, regional, national and international. Includes children's program (Koala Club), seniors (60+), couples, single memberships, and incremental donor levels.

Timing: On-going, year-round promotion of memberships.

Tools: Direct mail and on-grounds visibility.

Group Sales

Objectives: Maximize group traffic and revenue by selling group tours to Zoo and Wild Animal Park.

Audience: Conventions, incentive groups, bus tours, associations, youth, scouts, schools, camps, seniors, clubs, military, organizations, domestic and foreign travel groups.

Timing: Targeted to drive attendance in peak seasons or at most probable times such as convention season.

Tools: Travel and tourism trade shows, telemarketing, direct mail, trade publication advertising.

We then focus on consumer behavior and market segmentation and positioning and see how an understanding of these important areas can be helpful in developing promotional strategies and programs. We also analyze the communications process and consider various models of value to promotional planners in developing strategies and establishing goals and objectives for advertising and other forms of promotion. We also consider how firms determine and allocate the marketing communications budget.

After laying the foundation for the development of a promotional program, this text will follow the integrated marketing communications planning model presented in Exhibit 1–10. We examine each of the promotional mix variables beginning with advertising. Our detailed examination of advertising includes a discussion of creative strategy and the process of developing the advertising message, an overview of media strategy, and an evaluation of the various media (print, broadcast, and support media). The discussion then turns to the other areas of the promotional mix—direct marketing, sales promotion, public relations/publicity, and personal selling. Our examination of the integrated marketing communications planning process concludes with a discussion of how the promotional program is monitored, evaluated, and controlled. Particular attention is given to measuring the effectiveness of advertising and other forms of promotion.

In the final part of the text, attention is given to special topic areas and perspectives that are becoming increasingly important in contemporary marketing including business-to-business communications and international advertising and promotion. The text concludes with an examination of the environment in which advertising and promotion operates, including the regulatory, social, and economic factors that influence, and are in turn influenced by, a firm's promotional program.

SUMMARY

Advertising and other forms of promotion are an integral part of the marketing process in most organizations. Over the past decade, the amount of money spent on advertising, sales promotion, and other forms of marketing communication has increased tremendously, both in the United States and in foreign markets. To understand the role of advertising and promotion in a marketing program, it is necessary to understand first what marketing's role and function are in an organization. The basic task of marketing is that of combining the four controllable elements, known as the marketing mix, into a comprehensive program that facilitates exchange with a target market. The elements of the marketing mix include the product or service, price, place or distribution, and promotion. Many companies are recognizing the importance of integrated marketing communications whereby the various marketing and promotional elements are coordinated to achieve more efficient and effective communication programs.

Promotion is best viewed as the communication function of marketing and is accomplished through a promotional mix that includes advertising, personal selling, publicity/public relations, sales promotion, and direct marketing. Each of these promotional mix elements has inherent advantages and disadvantages that influence the role they play in the overall marketing program. In developing the promotional program, the marketer must consider what particular tools to use and how to combine them to achieve the organization's marketing and communication objectives.

Promotional management involves coordinating the promotional mix elements to develop an integrated program of effective marketing communication. A model of the integrated marketing communications planning process was presented that contains a number of steps—a review of the marketing plan; promotional program situation analysis; analysis of the communications process; budget determination; development of an integrated marketing communications program; integration and implementation of marketing communication strategies; and monitoring, evaluating, and control of the promotional program.

KEY TERMS

marketing	advertising	promotional plan
exchange	direct marketing	marketing plan
marketing mix	sales promotion	internal analysis
integrated marketing communications	publicity	external analysis
promotion	public relations	marketing objectives
promotional mix	personal selling	communication objectives
	promotional management	

DISCUSSION QUESTIONS

1. Why do you think there has been such tremendous growth in the amount of monies spent on advertising and promotion in the past decade both in the United States and throughout the world?

2. Discuss the role advertising and promotion play in facilitating the exchange process between an organization and its customers. Choose a specific company and discuss how it uses marketing, and promotion in particular, in the development and maintenance of exchange relationships with its customers.

3. What is meant by the concept of integrated marketing communications? How might a firm that is using integrated marketing communications differ from one that looks at advertising and promotion in a more traditional way?

4. It has been argued that the way an organization communicates with its customers is not limited to promotion, as all marketing activities send a message. Discuss how an organization communicates with its customers through marketing activities other than promotion. Cite several examples.

5. Discuss the differences between a company's marketing mix and its promotional mix. How might the nature of the promotional mix be influenced by the marketing program?

6. Analyze the five elements of the promotional mix and their role in an integrated marketing communications program for each of the following:
   a. a manufacturer of consumer products such as Quaker Oats
   b. a nonprofit organization such as a symphony orchestra in a major city
   c. a major league baseball or basketball franchise

7. What are the advantages and disadvantages of the five elements of the promotional mix? Identify the types of situations where a firm might rely heavily on a particular element.

8. Identify a product, service, or cause that has been positively or negatively affected by publicity in recent years. Analyze any responses the company or organization took to deal with the problems or opportunity created by the publicity.

9. What is the difference between the internal and external phases of the promotional program situation analysis? Describe the various factors considered in each.

10. Why is it important for those who work in the field of promotion to have an appreciation for and understanding of all elements of the promotional mix and not just the one in which they specialize?

chapter **2**

The Role of Advertising and Promotion in the Marketing Process

➤ To examine the marketing process and the role of advertising and promotion in an organization's marketing program.

➤ To examine the various decision areas under each element of the marketing mix and how they influence and interact with advertising and promotional strategy.

➤ To examine classifications of various types of advertising targeted to both the consumer and business and professional markets.

➤ To examine the macroenvironment of marketing and the impact of various environmental influences on marketing and promotional strategy.

Smart Marketing for Smartfoods

One of the hottest new food products in years is a white cheddar cheese popcorn called *Smartfood* brand popcorn. Unlike most new snack products, Smartfood popcorn did not come out of the research and development department of a major company. It was born eight years ago when three friends in Boston went into business together to manufacture and market a reclosable snack bag. They decided the best way to demonstrate the bag's effectiveness was to put something in it, so they came up with their own brand of cheddar cheese popcorn. However, on further analysis, they decided the real potential for a successful new product lay not in the bag, but rather what was inside. The trio thought it would make a very smart idea for an all-natural snack food—so smart, they decided to call it Smartfood popcorn.

Like most entrepreneurs, the founders of Smartfoods, the company, had little money to promote their new product. Company President Ken Meyers thought he could reach consumers with a standard marketing campaign relying heavily on local advertising in New England. He soon learned, however, that a $100,000 advertising budget would not go far. So, lacking the funds for a traditional marketing effort, Meyers came up with a new approach he called "guerrilla marketing" that was designed to get people to try the popcorn.

The new marketing approach relied on a variety of irreverent techniques such as having a "Wacky Attacky Team" show up in various places to distribute product samples. One of the first marketing efforts was the Smartfood popcorn "air show." Meyers and some friends sewed three bedsheets together with the words "Smartfood popcorn" painted on them. He then hired an airplane to tow the banner up the New England coast. As the plane passed over the beaches, Meyers and others passed out samples of the popcorn. The team also dressed in giant popcorn bags and skied down the slopes, passing out samples, at a number of New England ski resorts. The guerrilla marketing approach began to pay, and sales grew to a point where Smartfoods could start advertising in more conventional ways. However, the company stuck to its offbeat approach as it began developing a media advertising campaign.

By 1988, Smartfoods had grown from a $35,000 startup operation to a business with nearly $10 million in annual sales. However, the company faced problems gaining distribution outside of the New England area, and competitors began to discover the new market. Major companies such as Keebler, Borden, and Anheuser-Busch's Eagle Snack Foods division, along with a number of regional firms, brought out various types of cheddar cheese popcorn. In January 1989, Smartfoods was

(continued)

acquired by snack-food leader Frito-Lay, Inc., for an estimated $14 million.

Frito-Lay provides Smartfoods with the distribution network needed to make it a successful national brand. There was initially some concern over how the Smartfoods guerrilla marketing approach would be perceived by the more traditional Frito-Lay. However, Frito-Lay operates the company as a wholly owned subsidiary and has allowed Smartfoods to continue the offbeat and irreverent approach to marketing that has made the company so successful. As Meyers noted, "This is not just popcorn; it's Smartfood popcorn, a snack with an irreverent personality and a sense of humor. . . . We're selling more than just a product. We are selling an experience."

Thus far, Frito-Lay seems happy to let Smartfoods continue its unique, guerrilla marketing techniques. The "Wacky Attacky Team" continues to show up in unusual places, such as busy downtown intersections or outside city hall in Chicago, distributing free samples. The crew distributes an average of 6,000 samples a day at these "ambush samplings" and also makes the occasion a happening or event that receives press coverage and strong crowd participation. Frito-Lay expects sales of Smartfood popcorn to reach $100 million in two years, making it a strong addition to its other successful snack products such as the Ruffles potato chips, Cheetos cheese-flavored snacks, Fritos corn chips, and Doritos tortilla chips. Thus, what started out as a mere bag filler for a new snack-food packaging concept has gone on to become one of the most successful new products ever introduced.

Source: "Kernels of Wisdom from Ken Meyers," Sales & Marketing Management, *March 1991, pp. 24–25; Jane Wuerthner, "Taking It to the Street,"* Snack World, *May 1990, pp. 30–31; Joseph P. Kahn, "The Snack Food That's Eating America,"* Inc., *August 1988, pp. 34–39; and Cyndee Miller, "Consumers Ambushed by Life-Size Popcorn Bags!"* Marketing News, *August 20, 1990, p. 2.*

The success of Smartfoods is an interesting example of how a small company used a creative, and irreverent, approach to marketing a new product. The guerrilla marketing approach was instrumental to the successful introduction and sales growth of the product. However, there is much more to the ongoing success of Smartfood popcorn than just the unconventional marketing tactics. First, Smartfood popcorn is a premium-quality popcorn that is wholesome, natural, has no artificial preservatives or coloring, and has a taste that consumers of all ages seem to like. The product comes in a very clever package—a shiny black bag with cute little messages from the company all over it. The product ingredients, the name, and the packaging have helped position Smartfood popcorn as a nutritious snack product, as opposed to junk food. Thus, the product seized a *marketing opportunity* by coming up with a tasty and natural snack food that would appeal to the ever-growing number of nutrition-conscious consumers. Smartfoods' unique advertising and promotional approach has given the product a certain mystique and *competitive advantage* that competitors have been unable to capture (see Exhibit 2–1). Finally, the acquisition of Smartfoods by Frito-Lay, Inc., gave the company access to a national distribution system and the resources to compete with other national brands in the highly competitive snack-food industry.

Advertising and promotion have played an integral role in the explosive sales growth of Smartfoods. The company has used an integrated marketing communications program. Various marketing techniques, including media advertising, direct mail, publicity, sales promotion, and even the packaging concept, have been coordinated to create and maintain a unique image and position for the product. The promotional program continues to be successful because the other elements of the marketing program—product, pricing, and distribution strategies—are in place. Promotion is only one part of the marketing program and is successful only when it is part of a sound marketing strategy and plan.

In this chapter, we take a closer look at how marketing influences the role of promotion and how promotional decisions must be coordinated with other areas of the marketing mix. We use the model in Exhibit 2–2 (on page 40) as a framework for analyzing how promotion fits into an organization's marketing strategy and programs.

This model consists of three major components—the organization's marketing strategy and plan, the marketing program development (which includes the promotional mix), and the target market. As can be seen in this model, the marketing

➤ *Exhibit 2–1*
Irreverent advertising is part of the unique marketing used by Smartfoods

YOU CAN'T GET IT OFF YOUR MIND

Totally natural SMARTFOOD©. Air-popped popcorn smothered in white cheddar cheese.

process begins with the development of a marketing strategy whereby the company decides the product or service areas and particular markets in which it wants to compete. The company must then coordinate the various elements of the marketing mix into a cohesive marketing program that will reach the target market effectively. Note in Exhibit 2–2 that a firm's promotion program is directed not only to the final buyer but also to the channel or "trade" members that distribute its products to the ultimate consumer. These channel members must be convinced there is a demand for the company's products so they will carry them and will also aggressively merchandise and promote them to the consumer. Thus, we will consider promotion's role in the marketing program for building and maintaining demand not only among final consumers but among the trade as well.

The second part of this chapter considers the environment in which marketing decisions are made, giving particular attention to the way it affects a company's promotional strategies and programs. Marketing is a very dynamic field that must constantly monitor and react to changing environmental trends and conditions. These changes create marketing opportunities for some organizations but pose threats to others. They also have a direct influence on a firm's advertising and promotional strategy and programs.

Marketing Strategy and Plan

Any organization that wants to exchange its products or services in the marketplace successfully should have in place a strategic marketing plan to guide the allocation of its resources. A **strategic marketing plan** usually evolves from an organization's overall corporate strategy and serves as a guide for specific marketing programs and policies. As we noted in the first chapter, the development of marketing strategy is based on a situation analysis—a detailed assessment of the current marketing

➤ *Exhibit 2–2*   **Marketing and promotions process model**

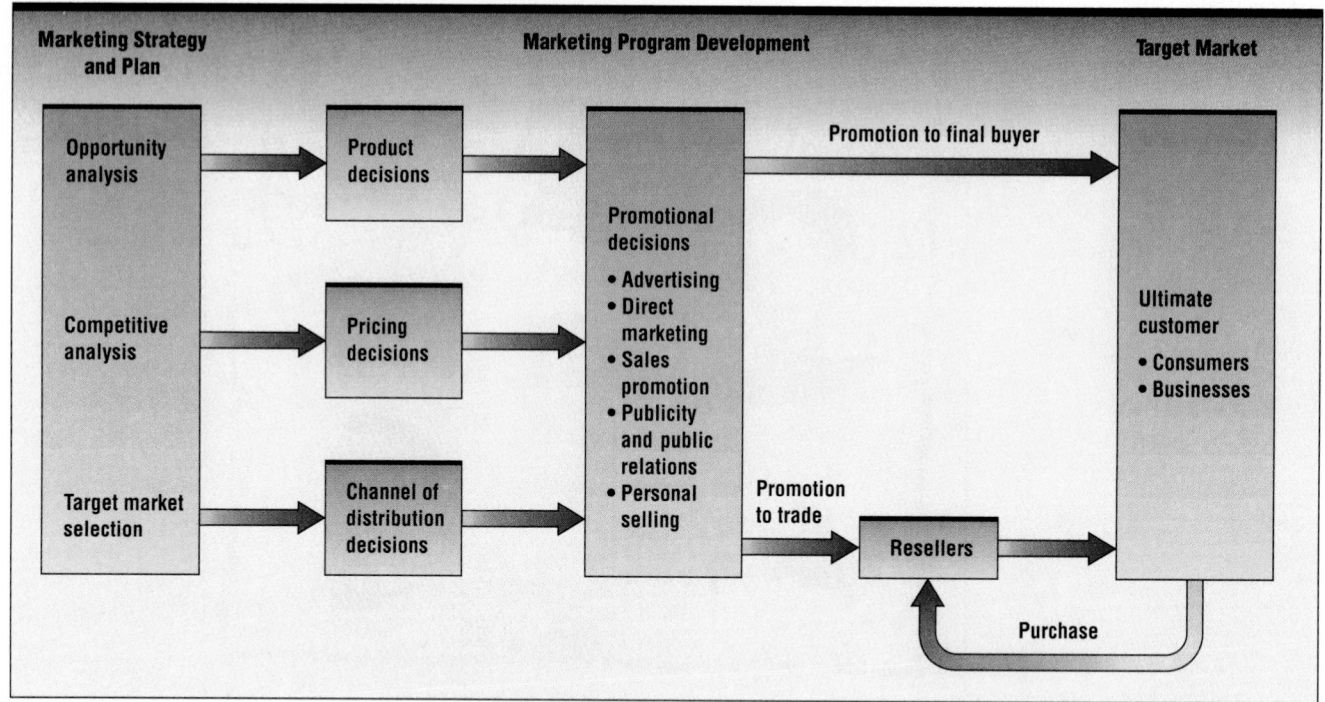

conditions facing the company, its product lines, or its individual brands. From this situation analysis, a firm develops an understanding of the market and the various opportunities it offers, the competition, and the market segments or target markets the company may wish to pursue. We examine each step of the marketing strategy phase in more detail.

Opportunity Analysis   A careful analysis of the marketplace should lead to alternative market opportunities the company might consider pursuing. This can include opportunities for existing product lines in current or new markets, developing new products for current markets, or entering new markets with new products. **Market opportunities** represent areas where there are favorable demand trends, where the company believes customer needs and opportunities are not being satisfied, and where it can compete effectively. For example, in recent years, the number of people who have taken up walking for exercise has increased tremendously, and the market for walking shoes has reached nearly $100 million. Athletic shoe companies such as Nike and Reebok see the walking shoe market as an opportunity to broaden their traditionally younger customer base to include an older market. To capitalize on this opportunity, Nike brought out a line of walking shoes and Reebok acquired Rockport Company, one of the largest manufacturers of walking shoes.

Another example of a market opportunity is the resurgence in the bicycle market brought on by the growing popularity of mountain bikes, also known as all-terrain bikes.[1] The sales of mountain bikes have helped transform the bicycle industry over the past decade from a stagnant market to a high-growth $3.5 billion industry. In 1991, mountain bikes accounted for more than half of the 10.7 million bicycles sold in the United States, with over 125 domestic and foreign brands competing for a share of this market.[2] Companies such as Specialized Bicycle Components, Trek, and Cannondale compete against industry leader Schwinn Bicycle Company (Exhibit 2–3). The popularity of mountain bikes has also resulted in a global market

> *Exhibit 2–3*
Companies such as Schwinn are pursuing the market opportunities for mountain bikes

opportunity for these companies as American-made all-terrain bikes are leading sellers in many European countries as well as Japan.

Market opportunities are generally identified by carefully examining the marketplace and noting demand trends and competition in various **market segments.** A market can rarely be viewed as a large homogeneous group of customers, but rather consists of many heterogeneous groups of segments. In recent years, many companies have recognized the importance of tailoring their marketing to meet the needs, requirements, and demand trends of different market segments.[3]

For example, different market segments in the personal computer industry include the home, education, science, and business markets. These segments can be even further divided. The business market consists of both small companies and large corporations, while the education market can range from elementary schools to colleges and universities. Thus, a company that is marketing its products in the personal computer industry must decide on the particular market segment or segments in which it wishes to compete. This decision will depend on the amount and nature of competition the brand will face in a particular market. For example, Apple Computer is very firmly entrenched in the education market but is also targeting the business segment where IBM and Compaq are strong competitors. A competitive analysis is an important part of marketing strategy development and warrants further consideration.

Competitive Analysis

In developing the firm's marketing strategies and plans for its products, the manager must carefully analyze the competition the brand will face in the marketplace. Every organization faces competition of one form or another. It may range from direct brand competition (which can also include its own brands) to more indirect forms of competition such as product substitutes. For example, General Foods markets Maxwell House coffee as its flagship brand in the regular ground coffee segment of the market. However, several years ago, the company introduced Master Blend, a high-yield brand that gives more cups per pound than regular coffee. The new product ended up taking away sales from Maxwell House. However, the combined sales of the two brands gave General Foods a net gain in its share of the ground market, as Master Blend helped slow the sales of competing brands such as Procter & Gamble's Folgers, Nestlé's Hills Brothers, and various regional brands.

In addition to these direct competitors, Maxwell House faces competition from other product forms such as instant and decaffeinated coffee. Also, many consumers have been switching to other beverages such as tea and soft drinks. Thus, competition is not only found in directly competing brands but also comes from other products that satisfy consumers' needs for a beverage.

At a more general level, marketers must recognize they are competing for the consumer's discretionary income, which requires that they understand the various ways potential customers choose to spend their money. For example, sales of motorcycles in the United States declined from 1.3 million bikes in 1984 to only 700,000 in 1990. This decline in sales reflects shifting demographic patterns—aging baby boomers are less inclined to ride motorcycles and the number of 18-to-34-year-old males has been declining. The drop in sales can also be attributed to the number of other options consumers can spend their discretionary income on, including jet skis, personal computers, home fitness equipment, Jacuzzis, and home entertainment systems such as large-screen television sets and stereos. Thus, motorcycle marketers such as Honda and Kawasaki must convince potential buyers that a motorcycle is worth a sizable portion of their disposable income in comparison to other purchase options.

An important aspect of marketing strategy development is the search for competitive edge or advantage over the competition. A **competitive advantage** refers to something unique or special a firm does or possesses that gives it an edge over competitors. Competitive advantage can be achieved in a variety of ways, including having quality products that command a premium price, providing superior customer service, having the lowest production costs and lower prices, or dominating channels of distribution. Competitive advantage can also be achieved through excellent advertising that creates and maintains product differentiation and brand equity. For example, the strong brand images of products such as Colgate toothpaste, Campbell soup, Apple computers, and Budweiser beer provide them with a competitive advantage in their respective markets.

Recently, there has been concern that some marketers have not been spending enough money on advertising to allow leading brands to sustain their competitive edge.[4] Advertising proponents have been calling for companies to protect their brand equity and franchises by investing more money in advertising and spending less on costly trade promotions. Some companies are recognizing the important competitive advantage strong brands provide and have been increasing their advertising investment in them. For example, in 1991, Campbell Soup Company announced it would increase its advertising spending by 30 percent to "restore brand power."[5] Colgate-Palmolive also recently boosted its marketing and advertising spending to increase support for major brands.[6]

In the development of marketing programs, companies must be concerned with the ever-changing competitive environment. Competitors' marketing programs will have a major impact on the firm's marketing strategy and must be analyzed and monitored. The reactions of competitors to a company's marketing and promotional strategy are also very important. Competitors may cut price, increase promotional spending, develop new brands, or attack one another through comparative advertising. One of the more intense competitive rivalries is the battle Coca-Cola and Pepsi-Cola have been waging against one another for more than a decade. The latest round of the "cola wars" is discussed in Promotional Perspective 2–1.

A final aspect of competition that should be noted is the growing number of foreign companies penetrating the U.S. market and taking business from domestic firms. In products ranging from electronics to automobiles to beer, imports are becoming an increasingly strong form of competition with which U.S. firms must contend. As we move from a national to a more global economy, U.S. companies not only must defend their domestic markets but also must learn how to compete effectively in the international marketplace. We examine the role of advertising and promotion in international markets in Chapter 22.

Target Market Selection

After evaluating the marketing opportunities presented by the various segments, including a detailed competitive analysis, the company may select one or more as a target market. This target market becomes the focus of the firm's marketing effort, and goals and objectives are set according to where the company wants to be and what it hopes to accomplish in this market. As noted in Chapter 1, these goals and objectives are set in terms of specific performance variables such as sales, market share, and profitability. The selection of the target market (or markets) in which the firm will compete not only is a very important part of its marketing strategy but also has direct implications for its advertising and promotional efforts. Segmenting a market, choosing target markets, and positioning the product or service within the market are discussed in detail in Chapter 5.

Developing the Marketing Program

The development of the marketing strategy and selection of a target market(s) tell the marketing department which customers to focus on and what needs to attempt to satisfy. The next stage of the marketing process involves combining the various elements of the marketing mix into a cohesive and effective marketing program. The challenge facing the marketing manager at this point is somewhat analogous to that of a chef. In blending different combinations of ingredients to produce the meal, the chef does not always follow a recipe but rather uses his or her own creativity or insight. In a similar manner, the marketing manager must blend the various elements of the marketing mix to develop an effective marketing program. In marketing, there is no standard formula to follow for a successful combination of marketing elements, as marketing mix strategies vary from company to company and across various situations. Experienced managers, like expert chefs, apply their skill, experience, and creativity to develop an effective and successful marketing program.

As was noted earlier, development of a successful marketing program requires combining all elements of the marketing mix. The product or service must offer a benefit that satisfies a need at a price the customer is willing to pay and must be available where and when the consumer wants to purchase it. Promotion makes the customer aware of the product, the benefits it offers, and where it can be purchased. In Chapter 1, we saw how promotion includes a number of elements such as advertising, direct marketing, personal selling, sales promotion, and publicity/public relations. Actually, each marketing mix element is multidimensional and includes a number of decision areas. We now examine these elements of the marketing mix and how each influences and interacts with promotion.

Product

An organization exists because it has some product, service, or idea to offer consumers, generally in exchange for money. This offering may come in the form of a physical product (such as a soft drink, pair of jeans, automobile), a service (a bank,

Promotional Perspective 2–1

The Cola Wars Continue

For nearly two decades, the Coca-Cola Company and its arch-rival, Pepsi-Cola, have been battling for leadership of the soft-drink market. It's not difficult to understand why the two soft-drink superpowers, which between them account for 70 percent of industry sales, spend hundreds of millions of advertising dollars each year to convince consumers whose brands are the "real thing" or "the right one." Every percentage point of the soft-drink market is worth $460 million in retail sales.

While Coke and Pepsi have been competing against each other for decades, the battle became very intense in 1975 when Pepsi launched its "Pepsi Challenge" advertising and promotional campaign, which showed consumers preferring the taste of Pepsi in blind taste tests. The Challenge campaign convinced many consumers that Pepsi had a superior taste and induced them to switch brands. By 1984, Pepsi had achieved a 2 percent market share lead over Coke in supermarket sales. Pepsi's success was a major factor in Coca-Cola's controversial decision to change the formula of its 99-year-old flagship brand and launch New Coke in April 1985. The introduction of New Coke resulted in strong protest from consumers loyal to the old formula and led to the subsequent reintroduction of original Coke as Coca-Cola Classic a few months later.

In 1988, the battle shifted to the sugar-free or diet segment, which represented nearly 25 percent of the soft-drink market and where sales were growing four to five times faster than those of sugared products. Pepsi began a new round in the cola wars with another taste-test challenge campaign claiming, "Americans preferred the taste of Diet Pepsi over diet Coke 55 percent to 45 percent." Coke countered by filing a protest with the television networks over Pepsi's test results, asking them not to air Pepsi's commercials. Coke also produced its own taste-test commercials and print ads claiming taste superiority. Pepsi in turn filed a complaint with the major networks charging the diet Coke ad was "misleading and factually inaccurate and should be withdrawn immediately." The three major networks found no flaws or problems with the research studies used by either company and ruled they would air both firms' commercials, despite the conflicting claims over taste superiority. However, in early 1991, after three years of the contradictory comparisons, the cola giants abandoned the taste-test claims.

The advertising battle has shifted strategies recently with both companies using celebrities to pitch their products. Coke has used Randy Travis, Anita Baker, Wayne Gretzky, Paula Abdul,

and C+C Music factory. Coke had an endorsement deal with basketball star Michael Jordan but terminated it when he asked for a long-term contract and more money. (Jordan ended up signing on as the spokesperson for Gatorade in a deal reportedly worth $18 million over 10 years.) Pepsi has used Jimmy Connors, Michael Jackson, Bo Jackson, and Bert Parks, among others. The company's ads for Diet Pepsi featuring singer Ray Charles performing the "You've got the right one, baby, uh huh" refrain have proved to be particularly popular. Pepsi's use of hot celebrities, superstars, and elaborate productions has given it the edge in advertising, according to Video Storyboard Tests Inc., a New York company that surveys consumers' opinions about commercials. In 1992, Pepsi changed the advertising for its flagship brand to the "Gotta Have It" theme to broaden the appeal of Pepsi across all age groups. However, in international markets, Pepsi uses the "Choice of a New Generation" theme to target young people who represent the key market segment.

Coke has apparently recognized it is falling behind in the advertising war with Pepsi. In 1991, the company signed an agreement with Hollywood super agent Michael Ovitz and the Creative Artists Agency (CAA), which manages the careers of actors such as Kevin Costner, Dustin Hoffman, and Tom Cruise. CAA is expected to negotiate everything from celebrity endorsements to product tie-ins for promotions on behalf of Coke. Coke has also made changes in its advertising and marketing personnel and plans a worldwide advertising campaign to stress Coca-Cola's ubiquity and heritage with a blend of ads using old and new footage that harkens back to its "real-thing" positioning. The company also plans to boost its advertising spending, particularly for diet Coke.

It appears that the current cola wars battle is being won by Pepsi. However, the war is ongoing, and it is likely that Coke will use the resources of CAA and other tactics to attack Pepsi on all fronts and battle to retain its position as the leading soft-drink company.

Source: John Lippman, "Coca-Cola Pours More Energy into Ads," *Los Angeles Times,* September 5, 1991, pp. D1,7; Alison Fahey and Gary Levin, "Coke Plans 'Real Thing' Global Attack," *Advertising Age,* August 5, 1991, pp. 1, 36; Alison Fahey, "Coke Keeps Share Lead Despite Pepsi's Charge," *Advertising Age,* October 7, 1991, pp. 1, 70; and Alison Fahey, "Pepsi's Concerts versus Coke's Games," *Advertising Age,* February 10, 1992, p. 47.

airline, or legal assistance), a cause (United Way, March of Dimes), or even a person (a political candidate). In the broadest sense, the product consists of anything that can be marketed and that, when used or supported, gives satisfaction to the individual.

A product is not just a physical object; rather, a product should be viewed as a bundle of benefits or values that satisfies the needs of consumers. The needs may be

RAY: "You got the right one baby!"
CHORUS: "Uh huh!"
RAY: "These days as soon as you get a hit song, everybody thinks they can sing it better."
JERRY LEWIS: "You got the right one baby, Uh huh, oh-ho, eeh-hee."
OPERA SINGER: "You got the right one baby, Uh huh, Uh huh, Uh huh."
PUNK SINGER: "You got the right thing, Uh huh, Uh huh."
VIC DAMONE: "You got the right one, Uh huh, Uh huh."

FLAMENCO DANCER: "Diet, Diet Pepsi."
ACCORDION PLAYER: "You got the right one, everybody!"
RAGA MAN: "Infinitely blissful, spiritually wonderful, Diet Pepsi Uh huh."
ROGER MILLER: "Do do do do do do!"
GUY WITH DOG: "He can do it, he really can!"
BO JACKSON: "Uh huh!"
DOG CROONS
JERRY LEWIS: "Aaah!"
TINY TIM: "Oooh, oooh, Diet Pepsi."

COUNTRY TRIO: "You got the right one baby!"
CHARO: "Baby you got the right one."
PUNK SINGER: "Uh huh!"
REGGAE SINGER: "Uh huh"
BO JACKSON: "Uh huh!"
VIC DAMONE: " I thought I was great."
TINY TIM: "I hope you liked it."
JERRY LEWIS: " Do I get a call back?"
BO JACKSON: "How's that!?"
RAY: "There's only one right one baby! You got the right one baby, Uh huh!"

functional and may include social and psychological benefits as well. For example, the ad for Michelin tires in Exhibit 2–4 stresses the quality built into Michelin tires (value) as well as their performance and durability (functional). The term **product symbolism** is used to refer to what a product or brand means to consumers and what they experience in purchasing and using it.[7] For many products, strong symbolic features and social and psychological meaning may be more important than func-

> *Exhibit 2–4*
Advertising for Michelin tires stresses security as well as performance

> *Exhibit 2–5*
Advertising for designer jeans helps create symbolism and image to consumers

tional utility.[8] For example, designer jeans such as Guess?, Calvin Klein, Jordache, and Lawman are often purchased on the basis of their symbolic meaning and image, particularly by teenagers and young adults. Advertising plays an important role in developing and maintaining the image of these brands (Exhibit 2–5).

Product planning involves decisions not only about the item itself, such as design and quality, but also about other aspects such as service and warranties that go along

➤ *Exhibit 2–6*
The Michelob brand name has been extended to light, dark, and dry versions of beer

with it, as well as the selection of a brand name and package design. The branding and packaging decisions are particularly important as communication devices and warrant further discussion.

Branding

Choosing a brand name for a product is important from a promotional perspective because brand names communicate attributes and meaning. Marketers search for brand names that can effectively communicate product concepts and help position the product in the mind of the customer. Names such as Safeguard (soap), I Can't Believe It's Not Butter! (margarine), Easy Off (oven cleaner), Arrid (antiperspirant deodorant), and Spic and Span (floor cleaner) all clearly communicate the value and benefits of using these products.

Many companies use individual brand names for each of their products because they want each brand to have a unique and distinct image and not be influenced by association to a company, family, or product line name. However, promotional costs for new products are generally higher when individual brand names are used, as the company must create awareness among both consumers and retailers without the benefit of these same prior associations.

In recent years, the high costs of introducing products and establishing an identity for a new brand have prompted many companies to use a **brand extension strategy** whereby a firm extends an existing brand name to a new product. There are two types of brand extensions.[9] A **line extension** applies an existing brand name to a product in one of the existing product categories. For example, the Coca-Cola brand name has been extended to a number of other soft drinks including Classic Coke, diet Coke, caffeine-free Coke, and Cherry Coke. Anheuser-Busch has also extended the Michelob name to several brands including Michelob Light, Michelob Dark, and its newest brand, Michelob Dry (Exhibit 2–6). A **category extension** applies an existing brand name to a new product category. Examples of category extensions include Jell-O pudding pops, Bic disposable lighters, Woolite rug cleaner, and Tropicana Twister Light fruit juices.

The use of brand extension strategies has almost become the norm among marketers introducing new package goods. For example, of the 6,125 new products placed on shelves in the first five months of 1991, only 5 percent carried new brand names.[10] Marketers are relying on line extensions for several reasons. Many firms believe they can borrow on the equity in their established brand names and achieve immediate name recognition and some "affect transfer" whereby the positive feelings and benefits associated with a familiar brand are extended to the brand. Line extensions can also reduce the advertising and promotional expenditures required to introduce a new brand and make it easier to gain distribution and shelf space in stores.[11]

The use of brand line and category extensions has been criticized by some advertising experts on the grounds that excessive use of a brand name can erode brand image and create confusion among consumers.[12] Line extensions can weaken the core brand and may even hurt its sales. For example, Miller High Life was the number two beer brand in 1979, selling more than 23 million barrels a year. However, several line extensions including Miller Lite and Miller Genuine Draft cannibalized Miller High Life sales, which sold only 6.4 million barrels in 1990. Brand extensions may also be risky if a new product does not live up to consumer expectations, as this may hurt consumers' perceptions of other products using the name.

It has been argued that the decision to use a brand extension strategy is a compromise between dilution of brand image and possible consumer confusion, on one hand, and advertising efficiency, on the other.[13] As media costs escalate and shelf space becomes increasingly scarce, companies with strong brand names are likely to continue to use brand extension strategies to reduce costs and increase awareness and, it is hoped, acceptance of their new products among both consumers and retailers.

➤ *Exhibit 2–7*
Procter & Gamble introduces a neat way to squeeze its Crest toothpaste out of the container

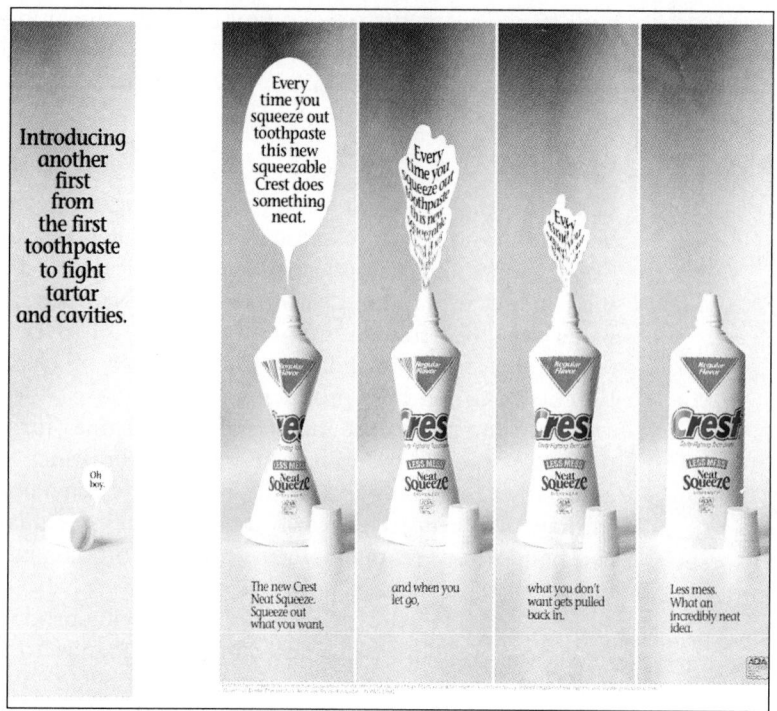

Packaging

Packaging is another aspect of product strategy that has become increasingly important. Traditionally, the package provided functional benefits such as economy, protection, and storage. However, the role and function of the package have changed because of the self-service emphasis of many stores and the fact that more and more purchase decisions are being made at the point of purchase. One study estimated that as many as two thirds of all supermarket purchases are unplanned and made in the store.[14] The package is often the consumer's first exposure to the product and must make a favorable first impression. For example, a typical supermarket has more than 20,000 items competing for a consumer's attention. Not only must a package attract and hold the consumer's attention, but it must also communicate information such as how to use the product, divulge its composition and content, and satisfy any legal requirements regarding disclosure. Moreover, many firms design a package to carry a sales promotion message such as a contest, sweepstakes, or premium offer.

Many companies view the package as an important way of both communicating with consumers and also of creating an impression of the brand in their minds. Design factors such as size, shape, color, and lettering all contribute to the appeal of a package and can be as important as a commercial in determining what goes from the store shelf to the consumer's shopping cart. Many products have used packaging to create a distinctive brand image and identity such as Michelob beer with its unusually shaped bottle and distinctive label (Exhibit 2–6). Packaging can also be used to make a product more convenient to use. For example, Procter & Gamble introduced its Crest Neat Squeeze dispenser that sucks the extra, unused toothpaste back into the container when you let go (Exhibit 2–7).

Many companies are also recognizing the importance of redesigning their packages and corporate logos to improve their images and to make their products more environmentally sensitive, as discussed in Promotional Perspective 2–2.

Promotional Perspective 2–2

Packaging Takes on New Looks and Form for the '90s

In December 1991, a new Pepsi logo and package design began appearing on cans. The new logo removed the word *Pepsi* from its old position inside a red-and-blue bull's-eye swirl and runs it vertically along cans and horizontally along bottles. The changes, which were made to make Pepsi look more modern and upbeat, may seem simple and small. However, there was nothing simple about the process. It took the company four years, five design firms, and millions of dollars to make the changes. Pepsi conducted research studies where consumers viewed screens that projected lightning-fast flashes of newly designed cans on store shelves. The consumers were then asked if they remembered, or even recognized, the Pepsi cans.

Why would a company spend so much money and effort changing a logo and redesigning a package? PepsiCo, like many other consumer package-goods companies, recognizes the important role packaging plays in today's shopping environment. One packaging design expert cites three numbers in noting the importance of packaging: 25,000, or the number of items in a typical grocery store; 20, or the average number of minutes a consumer spends shopping in a grocery store; and 80, or the percentage of shoppers who make their final purchase decision while in the store. Another notes, "Your package is your delivery . . . your total company" and must make a statement to the consumer.

The trend toward package and logo redesign is expected to be very strong in the 1990s. Many companies want their products and corporate images to look more modern. Others, such as Coke, Pepsi, and Procter & Gamble, want global images that will communicate the same thing wherever their products are sold. For international marketing, many companies plan to use pictographs on packages to convey important product information, rather than cluttering the package with numerous languages.

Many marketers are also changing their package designs in response to environmental concerns. For example, McDonald's made its packaging more environmentally sensitive by eliminating Styrofoam containers for most of its products and wrapping them in paper. The makers of L'Eggs hosiery also redesigned its packaging to make it more environmentally sensitive. Many companies now use recyclable or biodegradable materials in their packaging and are more careful not to overpackage products. For example, Procter & Gamble eliminated cardboard boxes in the packaging of its deodorant products. As one packaging expert noted, "For packaging, the environment will be to the '90s what convenience was to the '80s."

New Pepsi Logo

Old Pepsi Logo

Source: Bruce Horowitz, "Firms Focus on Logos to Project Right Image," *Los Angeles Times*, October 1,1991, p. D6; Howard Schlossberg, "Effective Packaging 'Talks' to Consumers," *Marketing News*, August 6, 1990, p. 6; and Howard Schlossberg, "Designers Feel the Squeeze as Environmental Concern Grows," *Marketing News*, August 6, 1990, p. 6.

Price

The *price variable* refers to what the consumer must give up to purchase a product or service. While price will be discussed in terms of the dollar amount exchanged for an item, it has also been argued that the cost of a product to the consumer includes time, mental or cognitive activity, and behavioral effort.[15] The marketing manager is usually concerned with establishing a price level, developing pricing policies, and monitoring competitors' and consumers' reactions to prices in the marketplace. A

➤ *Exhibit 2–8*
**The goal of advertising under
nonprice competition is to move
the demand curve up and to the
right**

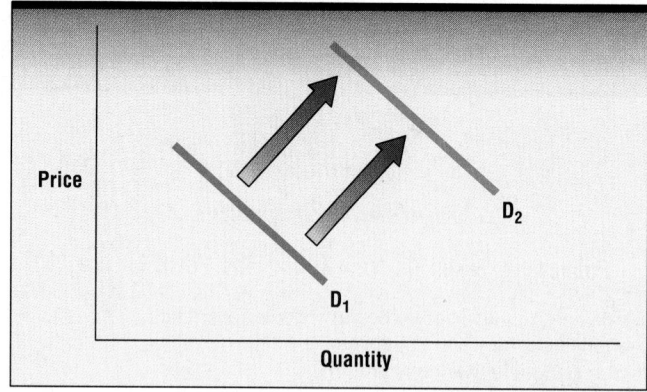

firm must consider a number of factors in determining the price it charges for its
product or service, including costs, demand factors, competition, and perceived value.

Costs

Costs are a basic determinant of price, as the firm will generally set a price that
covers the costs of producing, distributing, and promoting its product or service and
includes a profit figure that yields a certain return on its investment. While promotional expenses such as advertising, personal selling, and sales promotion must be
covered in a firm's pricing structure, they also reduce costs by creating demand for
the product that results in more sales and economies of scale in production and
distribution.

Demand Factors

Another important consideration in setting price is the demand for the product or
service that will be generated at various price levels. The relationship between price
and demand is generally an inverse one, meaning that as price declines, demand will
increase, and vice versa. However, in some situations, the relationship between price
and demand may be positive if the consumer perceives price as an indicator of
quality.[16] Thus, a higher price may result in more sales for a product (up to a point).

An important consideration in setting price is the concept of **price elasticity,** or the
responsiveness of the market to changes in price. Elastic demand exists when the
market is price sensitive such that a small decrease (increase) in price produces a
larger increase (decrease) in demand. Inelastic demand exists when the market is
price insensitive, and a small decrease (increase) in price results in a smaller increase
(decrease) in demand. When a firm competes on the basis of price, a change in price
will usually result in a change in demand, depending on the degree of elasticity.

However, many firms try to increase demand through **nonprice competition** by
using product differentiation, advertising, and other nonprice factors to influence
demand. Under nonprice competition, the firm seeks to shift its demand curve upward and to the right, as shown in Exhibit 2–8, which makes demand more inelastic
and less price sensitive and results in greater sales at a given price. For example, many
premium products such as Häagen-Dazs ice cream or Godiva chocolates are made
from more expensive ingredients and perceived by consumers as being of superior
quality and value. This perception is reinforced through their advertising, which
helps these brands command premium prices from consumers willing to pay more
for the best quality (Exhibit 2–9).

Competition

Another fundamental consideration in setting price is competition. Price is the one
element of the marketing mix that is easiest to change, at least in the short run, and

➤ *Exhibit 2–9*
Some products compete on the basis of quality rather than price

is often used as a competitive tool. Many companies use **competition-oriented pricing** whereby prices are set based primarily on what competitors are charging. Prices may be set to achieve competitive parity, or a firm may seek to keep its prices lower or higher than the competition. When competition-oriented pricing is used, prices are subject to rapid change and are often lowered to meet competition in specific markets. Competition-oriented pricing is very common in the retailing area, particularly among grocery stores, and in the marketing of services, such as in the airline industry. Extremely intense competition can sometimes lead to "price wars," such as in the airline industry where carriers are often forced to cut prices to remain competitive on certain routes.

Perceived value

Most marketers recognize that price levels for a product or service must be in line with the perceived value of the offering. Consumers often use price to determine a product's value, suggesting a relationship between price and perceived quality. For example, Curtis Mathes has used the advertising slogan "The Most Expensive Television Sets Money Can Buy" for many years to promote its products as being of extremely high quality. Marketers often use non-price variables such as superior product quality, service, warranties, and brand image to build perceived value in the consumer's mind and then price their products accordingly. In the ad shown in Exhibit 2–10, Yonex Corporation explains how the advanced technology behind its golf clubs leads to superior performance that is worth paying for even if it costs twice as much.

Relating price to advertising

As we have seen in our discussion of price determination, factors such as product quality, competition, and advertising all interact in determining what price a firm can

> *Exhibit 2–10*
Yonex explains why its golf clubs cost much more than competitors' clubs

and should charge. The relationship between price, product quality, and advertising was examined in one study using information on 227 consumer businesses from the PIMS (Profit Impact of Marketing Strategies) project of the Strategic Planning Institute.[17] Several interesting findings concerning the interaction of these variables emerged from this study:

- Brands with high relative advertising budgets were able to charge premium prices, whereas brands spending less than their competitors on advertising charged lower prices.
- Companies with high-quality products charged high relative prices for the extra quality, but businesses with high quality *and* high advertising levels obtained the highest prices. Conversely, businesses with low quality and low advertising charged the lowest prices.
- The positive relationship between high relative advertising and price levels was stronger for products in the late stage of the product life cycle, for market leaders, and low-cost products (under $10).
- Companies with relatively high prices and high advertising expenditures showed a higher return on investment than companies with relatively low prices and high advertising budgets.

Another interesting finding was that companies with high-quality products were hurt the most, in terms of return on investment, by inconsistent advertising and pricing strategies. The researchers concluded pricing and advertising strategies go together, as high relative ad expenditures should accompany premium prices and low relative ad expenditures should be tailored to low prices.

Channels of Distribution   As consumers, we generally take for granted the role of marketing intermediaries or channel members. If we want a six-pack of soda or a box of detergent, we can buy them at a supermarket, a convenience store, or even a drugstore. However, manufacturers understand the value and importance of these intermediaries.

One of the most important marketing decisions a firm must make involves the way its products and services are made available for purchase. A firm can have an excellent product at a great price, but it will be of little value unless it is available where the customer wants it, when the customer wants it, and with the proper support and service. **Marketing channels,** or the place element of the marketing mix, refers to "sets of interdependent organizations involved in the process of making a product or service available for use or consumption."[18]

Channel decisions involve the selection, management, and motivation of intermediaries such as wholesalers, distributors, brokers, retailers, and other parties that help a firm make a product or service available to customers. These intermediaries are sometimes called **resellers** and are very critical to the success of a company's marketing program.

A company can choose not to use any channel intermediaries and sell to its customers through **direct channels.** This type of channel arrangement is sometimes used in the consumer market by firms using direct-selling programs, such as Avon, Tupperware, or Fuller Brush, or those firms that use direct-response advertising or telemarketing to sell their products. Direct channels are also frequently used by manufacturers of industrial products and services, as they often are selling expensive and complex products that require extensive negotiations and sales efforts, as well as service and follow-up calls after a sale is made. Most consumer product companies distribute through **indirect channels** usually using a network of wholesalers or institutions that sell to other resellers and/or retailers—institutions that sell primarily to the final consumer.

Developing Promotional Strategies—Push versus Pull

Most of you are aware of advertising and other forms of promotion directed toward ultimate consumers or business customers. We see these ads in the media and are often part of the target audience for the promotions. However, in addition to developing a consumer marketing mix, a company must also have a program to encourage the channel members to stock and promote its products. Programs designed to persuade the trade to stock, merchandise, and promote a manufacturer's products are part of what is known as a **promotional push strategy.** The goal of this type of strategy is to "push" the product through the channels of distribution by aggressively selling and promoting the item to the resellers or trade.

As shown earlier in Exhibit 2–2, promotion to the trade includes all the elements of the promotional mix. Company sales representatives will call on resellers to explain the product, to discuss the firm's plans for building demand among ultimate consumers, and to describe special programs being offered to the trade, such as introductory discounts, promotional allowances, and cooperative ad programs. **Trade advertising** may be used by the company to interest wholesalers and retailers and motivate them to purchase its products for resale to their customers. Trade advertising usually appears in publications that serve the particular industry. For example, buyers in the grocery industry read *Progressive Grocer,* whereas a drugstore manager or buyer will read *Drug Store News.* An example of a trade ad for Ames Tools that appeared in a publication targeted to home improvement retailers is shown in Exhibit 2–11.

The goal of a push strategy is to convince resellers they can make a profit on a manufacturer's product and to encourage them to order the merchandise and push it through to their customers. However, in some situations, manufacturers may face resistance from channel members because they may not want to take on an additional product line or brand. In these instances, companies may turn to a **promotional pull strategy** whereby monies are spent on advertising and sales promotional efforts directed toward the ultimate consumer. The goal of a pull strategy is to create demand on the consumer end and encourage them to request the product from the retailer. Seeing the favorable demand from consumers, retailers will order the product

➤ *Exhibit 2–11*
Trade advertising is used to interest resellers in a manufacturer's product

from wholesalers (if they are used), which in turn will request it from the manufacturer. Thus, the product is "pulled" through the channels of distribution by stimulating demand at the end-user level.

Whether to emphasize a push or a pull strategy depends on a number of factors including the company's relations with the trade, its promotional budget, and demand for the firm's products. Companies that have very favorable channel relationships may prefer to use a push strategy and work closely with channel members to encourage them to stock and promote their products. A firm with a limited promotional budget may not have the funds for advertising and sales promotion that a pull strategy requires and may find it more cost-effective to build distribution and demand by working closely with resellers. When the demand outlook for a product is very favorable because it has unique benefits, is superior to competing brands, or is very popular among consumers, a pull strategy may be more appropriate. Actually, companies often use a combination of both push and pull strategies, with the emphasis often changing as the product moves through the life cycle.

Promotion to the Final Buyer

As is shown in the marketing model in Exhibit 2–2, the marketing program includes promotion both to the trade or channel members and to the company's ultimate customers as well. Marketers use the various promotional mix elements—advertising, personal selling, sales promotion, direct marketing and publicity/public relations—to inform consumers about their products, prices, and places where they are available. As was discussed in Chapter 1, each of these promotional mix variables helps marketers achieve their promotional objectives. However, advertising is generally relied on for communicating information about products and services to the consumer market and is becoming increasingly important in communicating with business customers as well. Thus, we will now examine the different forms of advertising used to communicate with the ultimate buyers of a product or service.

Classifications of Advertising

The nature and purpose of advertising differ from one industry to another and/or across situations. The target of an organization's advertising efforts often varies, as does its role and function in the marketing program. One advertiser may seek to

generate immediate response or action from the customer, whereas another may be interested in developing awareness or a positive image for its products over a longer period. To better understand the nature and purpose of advertising to the final buyer, it is useful to examine some classifications of the various types of advertising.

Advertising to the Consumer Market

National advertising

Advertising done by a company on a nationwide basis or in most regions of the country and targeted to the ultimate consumer market is known as **national advertising**. The companies that sponsor these ads are generally referred to as **national advertisers**. Most of the ads for well-known brands that we see on prime-time television or in other major national or regional media are examples of national advertising. This form of advertising is usually very general, as it rarely includes specific prices, directions for buying the product, or special services associated with the purchase. This type of advertising makes known or reminds consumers of the brand and its features, benefits, advantages, and uses or reinforces its image so consumers will be predisposed to purchasing it, wherever and whenever it is needed and convenient to do so. The ad for Jell-O in Exhibit 2–12 is an example of national advertising.

National advertising is the best-known and most widely discussed form of promotion, probably because of its pervasiveness. Exhibit 2–13 shows the advertising expenditures of the 25 leading national advertisers for 1990. These figures reflect money spent in measured media as well as unmeasured media spending. Measured media include network and spot (local) television and radio, network cable TV, magazines, newspapers, and outdoor advertising. Unmeasured media spending

➤ *Exhibit 2–13*
25 leading advertisers in 1991

| Rank | | Advertisers | Ad Spending |
'91	'90		in 1991
1	1	Procter & Gamble Co.	$2,149.0
2	2	Philip Morris Cos.	2,045.6
3	4	General Motors Corp.	1,442.1
4	3	Sears, Roebuck & Co.	1,179.4
5	6	PepsiCo	903.4
6	5	Grand Metropolitan	744.7
7	15	Johnson & Johnson	733.0
8	8	McDonald's Corp.	694.8
9	14	Ford Motor Co.	676.6
10	13	Eastman Kodak Co.	661.4
11	12	Warner-Lambert Co.	656.5
12	16	Toyota Motor Corp.	632.2
13	7	AT&T Co.	617.3
14	10	Nestlé SA	600.5
15	18	Unilever NV	593.7
16	9	Time Warner	587.5
17	17	Kellogg Co.	577.7
18	11	RJR Nabisco	571.0
19	20	General Mills	555.6
20	21	Chrysler Corp.	531.1
21	19	Kmart Corp.	527.2
22	22	Anheuser-Busch Cos.	508.4
23	23	Walt Disney Co.	489.1
24	25	American Home Products Corp.	447.1
25	26	Sony Corp.	438.6

represents money that went into support services such as direct-mail, sales promotion, and co-op advertising programs.

Retail (local) advertising

Another prevalent type of advertising directed at the consumer market is classified as **retail/local advertising.** This type of advertising is done by retailers or local merchants to encourage consumers to shop at a specific store or to use a local service such as a bank, fitness club, or restaurant. Whereas the national advertisers are concerned with selling their products at any location, retail or local advertisers must give the consumer a reason to patronize their establishment. Retail advertising tends to emphasize specific customer benefits such as store hours, credit policies, service, store atmosphere, merchandise assortments, or other distinguishing attributes. In addition, product availability and price are important advertising themes, often used in conjunction with a sale or special event. Retailers are concerned with building store traffic, and often their promotions take the form of **direct-action advertising** designed to produce immediate store traffic or sales. A direct-action retail advertisement for The Broadway department store is shown in Exhibit 2–14.

In addition to their product- and price-oriented advertising, many retailers use image advertising to influence consumers' perceptions of their stores.[19] Exhibit 2–15 shows how The Broadway uses image advertising.

Direct-response advertising

One of the fastest-growing sectors of the U.S. economy is that of direct marketing. **Direct-response advertising** is a method of direct marketing whereby a product is promoted through an advertisement that offers the customer the opportunity to purchase directly from the manufacturer. Traditionally, direct mail has been the

➤ *Exhibit 2–14*
**Retail advertising often
encourages consumers to take
immediate action (left)**

➤ *Exhibit 2–15*
**Retailers attempt to project
certain images for their stores
through advertising (right)**

primary medium for direct-response advertising, although television is becoming an increasingly important medium.

Direct-response advertising has become very popular in recent years owing primarily to changing lifestyles, particularly the increase in two-income households. This has meant more discretionary income but less time for in-store shopping. Thus, the convenience of shopping through the mail or by telephone has led to the tremendous increase in direct-response advertising. Credit cards and "800" or toll-free telephone numbers have also facilitated the purchase of products from direct-response advertisements.

Primary and selective demand advertising

Another way of viewing advertising to the ultimate customer is in terms of whether the message is designed to stimulate either primary or selective demand. **Primary demand advertising** is designed to stimulate demand for the general product class or entire industry, whereas **selective demand advertising** focuses on creating demand for a particular manufacturer's brands. Most of the advertising for various products and services is concerned with stimulating selective demand and emphasizes reasons for buying a particular brand. Advertisers generally assume there is a favorable level of primary demand for the product class and focus attention on increasing their market share. Thus, their advertising attempts to give consumers a reason to buy their brand.

Advertisers might concentrate on stimulating primary demand in several situations. When a company's brand dominates a market, advertising may focus on creating demand for the product class, as it will benefit the most from market growth. For example, Campbell Soup has over a 70 percent share of the condensed soup market, and the company's advertising objective is to encourage consumers to eat more soup. Notice the "Campbell's soup is good food" ad (Exhibit 2–16) emphasizes the benefits of eating soup more than the brand.

Primary demand advertising is often used as part of a promotional strategy for a new product to help it gain acceptance among customers. Products in the introductory or growth stages of their life cycles often have primary demand stimulation as a promotional objective because the challenge is to sell customers on the product as much as it is to sell a particular brand. Selective demand stimulation is not ignored,

➤ *Exhibit 2–16*
This ad by market leader Campbell's is designed to stimulate overall demand for soup

but the major concern is getting consumers to consider using the product. For example, when Sony introduced the videocassette recorder (VCR) to the market in the mid-1970s, much of its advertising stressed the benefits of video recorders in general. As competition entered the market, its advertising strategy shifted to a selective demand stimulation strategy whereby benefits of the Sony VCR over other brands were emphasized.

Industry trade associations such as the American Dairy Association, the Florida Citrus Growers, or the Potato Board also seek to stimulate primary demand. These associations will assess their members for funds to be used in promotional efforts to encourage the use of their product or services or to overcome declining primary demand trends. For example, the Beef Industry Council has been sponsoring an advertising campaign to help counter a decline in red meat consumption. Ads such as the one in Exhibit 2–17 have been used to convince consumers that beef belongs in a normal diet and is low in calories and fat content. Sometimes major competitors may even join to help stimulate sluggish or declining demand for their product class. Promotional Perspective 2–3 (on page 60) discusses how the pork industry used primary demand advertising to stimulate consumption of "the other white meat."

Advertising to the Business and Professional Markets

For many companies, the ultimate customer is not the mass consumer market but rather another business, industry, or profession. **Business-to-business advertising** is used by one business to advertise its products or services to another. The target for business advertising is individuals who either use a product or service or influence a firm's decision to purchase another company's product or service. Three basic categories of business-to-business advertising are industrial, professional, and trade advertising. (Trade advertising was discussed earlier in the chapter under promotional pull strategies.)

Industrial advertising

Advertising targeted at individuals who buy or influence the purchase of industrial goods or other services is known as **industrial advertising.** Industrial goods are those products that either become a physical part of another product (raw material, component parts), are used in the manufacture of other goods (machinery, equipment), or are used to help the manufacturer conduct business (office supplies, computers, copy machines, etc.). Business services, such as insurance, financial services, and health care, are also included in this category. Industrial advertising is usually found in general business publications (such as *Fortune, Business Week,* and *The Wall Street Journal*) or in publications targeted to the particular industry. However, in recent years, advertisements for industrial products and services have become more common in mass media such as television. Exhibit 2–18 (p. 61) shows a storyboard of a commercial for Ricoh copiers that stresses the reliability of its products.

Industrial advertising is often not designed to sell a product or service directly, as the purchase of industrial goods is often a complex process involving a number of individuals. An industrial ad helps make the company and its product or service better known by the industrial customer, assists in developing an image for the firm, and perhaps most important, opens doors for the company's sales representatives when they call on these customers. Exhibit 2–19(a) on page 62 shows an example of a classic ad run by McGraw-Hill Magazines for its business publications that addresses the reasons a business-to-business marketer would want to advertise.

Professional advertising

Advertising that is targeted to professional groups—such as doctors, lawyers, dentists, engineers, or professors—to encourage them to use or specify the advertiser's

Promotional Perspective 2–3

Stimulating Demand for "The Other White Meat"

In recent years, a number of industries have invested heavily in advertising and promotional campaigns to stimulate primary demand for their product categories. Primary demand advertising programs have been used successfully by the American Dairy Association, the Beef Industry Council, and Florida Citrus Growers. These advertising campaigns seek to position or reposition the product, disseminate information, and increase sales. Over the past several years, one of the more interesting, and effective, industrywide advertising campaigns has been that used by the National Pork Producers Council.

In 1987, the council embarked on an advertising and promotional campaign designed to change consumers' attitudes toward pork. The objective of the campaign was to position pork as "The Other White Meat" by portraying it as a healthy, versatile, and new alternative that is appropriate for any meal. The council believed that if it could change consumers' attitudes, it would ultimately increase pork sales. The campaign has used television commercials that show tantalizing close-ups of pork and describe how pork fits today's active, healthy lifestyles. Print ads were placed in leading national magazines, many of which contained recipes for tasty, easy-to-prepare pork dishes. Radio spots were also used to spread the good word about pork.

In 1990, the target markets for the campaign were expanded to include restaurants and other food-service markets. Educa-

tional material, sales force seminars, and training programs were conducted to aid the marketing effort. Retailers were also targeted and encouraged to use in-store posters, display materials, and recipe stickers at the point of sale. A Pork Information Bureau was established to answer questions and disseminate information to professional food communicators. Plans call for the use of outdoor posters, fact sheets, and videotapes in addition to those programs already in operation.

There is plenty of evidence that the campaign has changed the way consumers perceive pork. Unaided awareness of pork as a white meat increased in all markets—in some cases by as much as 61 percent. The percentage of consumers who have an awareness of or associate pork with white meat increased from less than 20 percent to nearly 82 percent in just two years. The white meat reference to pork has had a positive impact on 53 percent of the consumers who recall the reference or think of pork as a white meat. And, most important to those who sell pork, the total retail value of pork increased by nearly $4 billion from 1987 to 1990. One would have to conclude that "The Other White Meat" campaign has been very successful in changing attitudes toward pork and increasing sales.

Source: "The Other News," Pork Industry Promotion Summary, National Pork Producers Council, Des Moines, Iowa, 1990.

Ads such as this have helped reposition pork as "The Other White Meat" and increase sales

product for others' use is known as **professional advertising.** Professional groups are important because they constitute a market for products and services they use in their businesses. Also, their advice, recommendation, or specification of a product or service often influences many consumer purchase decisions. For example, Vipont Pharmaceutical initially targeted advertising for Viadent plaque-fighting toothpaste and oral rinse to dentists to encourage them to recommend these products to their patients (Exhibit 2–19(b), page 62).

Professional advertising should not be confused with advertising done *by* professionals. In recent years, advertising by professionals such as dentists, lawyers, and doctors has been increasing in popularity as legal restrictions have been removed and competition has increased.

➤ *Exhibit 2–18*   **Television commercials are being used more frequently to advertise business products**

 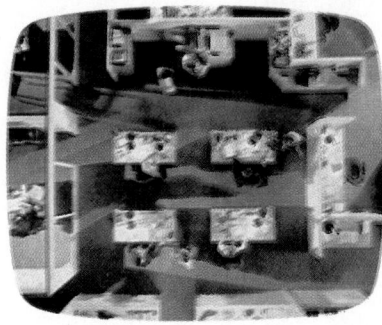 

24,000! 36,000! 48,000 a year!
  Where is everybody?
At the copier.
Which is why Ricoh created a super
  efficient copier

that automatically feeds, copies, sorts,
covers and staples reports
for about fifteen dollars a day.

So your employees can get back to work
  on the things you hired them to do.
Like putting your company on top.
Improve your productivity with a Ricoh
  copier. Call 1-800-63-RICOH.

These classifications of the various types of advertising demonstrate that this promotional element is used in a variety of ways and by a number of different organizations. Advertising is a very flexible promotional tool whose role in a marketing program will vary depending on the situation facing the organization and what information needs to be communicated.

Environmental Influences on Marketing and Promotion

The three components of the marketing model we have just examined represent "controllable factors" that are determined by the organization. A firm's marketing strategy, selection of a target market, and development, implementation, and control of its marketing program are all directed by management. However, a number of factors cannot be controlled or directed by the firm or organization. These uncontrollable forces constitute what is often referred to as the **macroenvironment** of marketing and include demographic, economic, technological, natural/physical, sociocultural, and regulatory factors (Exhibit 2–20, page 63). These environmental forces or influences can have a significant impact on a firm's marketing strategy and programs both in the short and long term and must be continually monitored and responded to. In this section, we examine these environmental influences, giving particular attention to the impact each has on the promotional element of an organization's marketing program.

Demographic Environment

Demographics deals with the practice of analyzing and describing the distribution of the population according to selected characteristics such as age, sex, income, education, occupation, and geographic dispersion. Major demographic developments in the United States are affecting firms' marketing and promotional programs. These

> *Exhibit 2–19(a)*
This ad shows why industrial marketers need to advertise

> *Exhibit 2–19(b)*
Vipont uses ads targeted to dentists to encourage them to recommend Viadent products to their patients

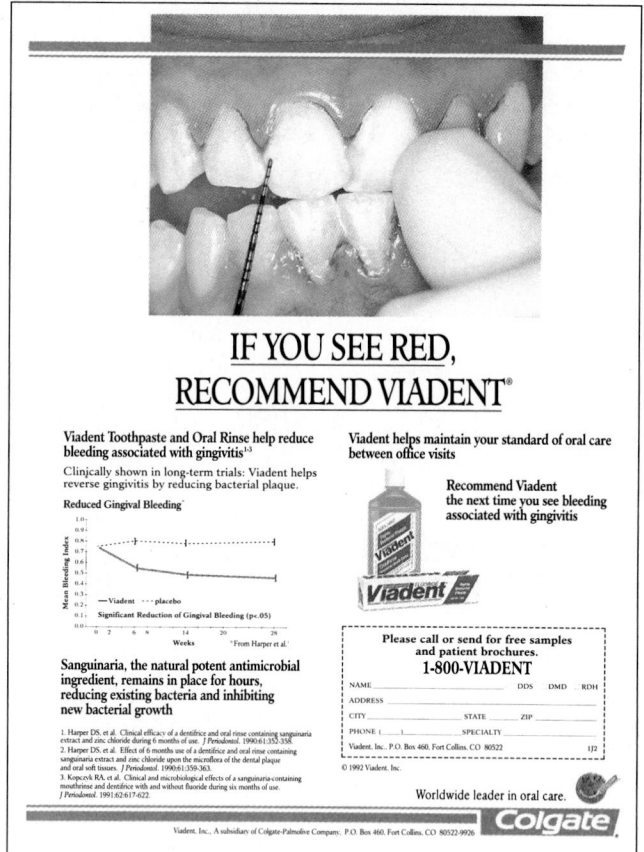

include the aging of the U.S. population, the increasing number of women in the labor force, and changing ethnic compositions. Some of the effects of each of these are discussed in the following pages.

Aging of the population

Perhaps one of the most notable characteristics of the U.S. population is the fact that it is aging as birthrates decline, life expectancies increase, and the baby boom generation gets older. A large reason for the graying of America is that the **baby boomers,** the 74 million Americans born between 1946 and 1964, are entering middle age. As this age cohort has grown older, they have represented a significant opportunity to marketers because of their size and purchasing power. In the 1970s and 1980s, the baby boomers made the 18-to-34-year-old age group the fastest-growing segment of the population. Between 1990 and the year 2000, as the baby boomers enter middle age, the number of people in the 35-to-44 age segment will grow 23 percent and the 45-to-54 age segment will increase by 45 percent.[20]

The aging of the baby boomers means the middle-age market segment will be especially large and lucrative during the 1990s. However, baby boomers have a distinct profile compared with people of the same age in previous generations. They differ in terms of their values, lifestyles, education level, women's roles, tastes, buying habits, and affluence. For example, in recent years, many marketers focused attention on a segment of the baby boomers known as "yuppies," or young, urban professionals. This segment represents the better-educated, more affluent, and

➤ *Exhibit 2–20* **Forces in the marketing environment**

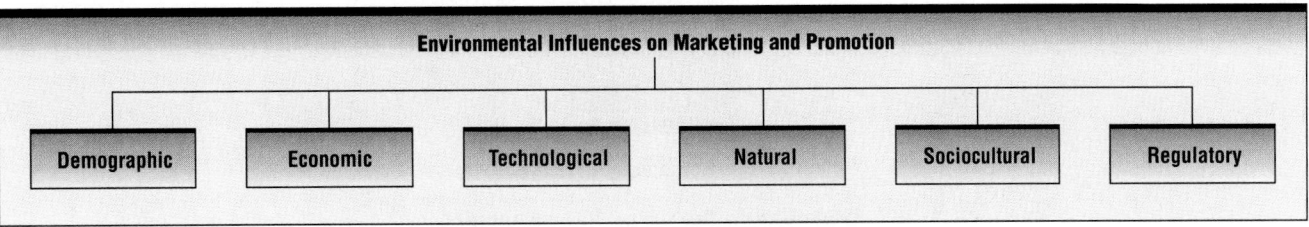

according to many critics, more materialistic group of baby boomers.[21] Interest in yuppies has decreased somewhat in recent years as many baby boomers rebelled against the stereotypic lifestyle and values of this group, and many marketers became concerned about having their brands categorized as a "yuppie product." For example, BMW automobiles, which have been described as the quintessential product of the "yuppie" movement of the 1980s, recently launched a new advertising campaign to position the cars as sensitive to concerns such as safety and value and move away from the yuppie image.[22] As the baby boomers enter middle age, they will present marketers with new problems and opportunities, as is discussed in Promotional Perspective 2–4.

The baby boomers will continue to have a major impact on the market for consumer products and services in other ways. For example, the original baby boomers are creating a mini baby boom in the United States. Nearly 4.2 million babies were born in the United States in 1990, more than at any time in the last 30 years and approaching the baby boom peak of 4.3 million births recorded in 1957.[23] This mini baby boom is creating strong sales growth for companies marketing products for babies and young children such as clothing, toys, diapers, and furniture as well as for the retailers that carry these products. Many companies are developing promotional strategies to compete for this growing market segment. For example, Sears recently introduced a "KidVantage" frequent-buyer and warranty program. This program promises that for as long as your child wears the original garment's size, Sears will replace it if it wears out. The program also offers discounts based on cumulative purchases of children's apparel.[24]

While marketers that make products and services that appeal to the baby boom market have prospered and should continue to do so, those companies whose primary target market consists of consumers in other age groups face potential problems. During the 1990s, the number of people 18 to 34 years old will decrease by 11 percent from 70 million in 1990 to 62.4 million in 2000.[25] For marketers that have traditionally targeted their products and services to this age group, such as soft-drink, snack-food, and beer companies, this decline in market size will create a new marketing challenge.

Marketers must continually adapt their marketing strategies to account for shifts in consumer demographics. For example, cereal companies prospered for several decades when the baby boom generation was at the prime cereal-consuming age. However, as the baby boomers grew up and birthrates declined, the number of children declined significantly. Companies such as Kellogg, General Mills, and General Foods have had to refocus their marketing efforts to persuade the aging baby boomers to eat more cereal. They have been introducing more adult-oriented cereals such as high-grain and fiber products. The selection of media has also become more adult oriented. Cereal ads often appear on adult-oriented television programs and sporting events and in magazines that appeal to fitness- and nutrition-conscious consumers such as *Self, Runner's World,* and *Sports Illustrated.* These companies also seek new growth by expanding into international markets such as in Europe where cereal sales are growing much faster than in the United States.[26]

Promotional Perspective 2–4

Marketing to the Aging Baby Boomers

For years, baby boomers have been one of the most coveted market segments in marketing history. Over the past three decades, many companies enjoyed unparalleled growth as they targeted products and services such as soft drinks, beer, credit cards, blue jeans, stereo equipment, luxury sports sedans, and fast food to the "Pepsi generation." However, the baby boomers are leaving their youth and migrating into middle age. By the end of this decade, they will have filled the 35-to-54-year-old age bracket.

The aging of the baby boom cohort can be another tremendous marketing opportunity to many companies since consumer spending peaks between the ages of 35 and 44. Consumers in this age group spend more on housing, apparel, automobiles, life insurance, entertainment, and other products and services than any other 10-year age group. The increase in their spending revolves around expenses associated with owning a home, raising children, and maintaining and protecting both.

The eventual success or failure of many businesses will depend on their ability to market their products and services to the aging baby boomer. The astute marketer will recognize that these boomers will not behave the same as their parents did when they reached middle age. Marketers must recognize that the aging baby boomers are a group in transition. They want to hang onto their youth as long as possible, yet they are distracted by the expenses and time demands of working and raising children. Many baby boomers have relatively high incomes, yet are not as well off as their parents. Approximately 20 percent have very low household incomes (under $20,000 annually). Many are just starting families and/or switching careers, while 25 percent of the baby boomers are single.

Marketers will have to adapt their products and services as well as marketing and promotional strategies to take advantage of the opportunities afforded by, as well as meet the needs and demands of, the aging baby boom market. For example, convenience and comfort will become increasingly important demands of the aging boomers, and they will be willing to pay for products and services that save time or make life easier. Because they are the most highly educated generation in our history, they will increase the market potential for products such as personal computers and educational toys, videos, and tutoring services. However, their high level of education will result in greater demands for product information, increased skepticism, less brand loyalty, and more rational purchase decisions. As seasoned consumers, they will be more thoughtful and critical purchasers who base their choices on years of consumer experience and product trials. Product quality will be extremely important.

From an advertising perspective, many changes will be occurring as well. Marketers will have to change not only their products, but also their advertising campaigns to appeal to the aging baby boomers. For example, Lee's jeans began a multimillion-dollar advertising campaign aimed at older jeans wearers with youthful hearts but expanding behinds. One of the most successful efforts at targeting the aging baby boomers is Levi Strauss & Co.'s Dockers apparel line. Introduced just five years ago, sales of the Dockers line reached more than $600 million in 1991, about 20 percent of the company's total sales.

As middle age becomes more acceptable, advertisers will be more likely to use middle-aged models such as Lauren Hutton or Cheryl Tiegs in their ads. Auto manufacturers are rethinking the images they portray for their cars. For example, Cadillac has

The aging of the population has led marketers to put more emphasis on older consumers. In 1960, only 9 percent of the U.S. population was over 65 years of age, but by the year 2000, the number of people over 65 is expected to be close to 22 percent of the population.[27] Older Americans, variously referred to as the "mature market," "welderly" (well-to-do elderly), and "gray powers," have become and will continue to be a prime target for marketers. Americans over age 50 constitute 25 percent of the population but have 50 percent of the nation's disposable income buying $800 million worth of goods and services each year.[28] Exhibit 2–21(a) on page 66 shows an advertisement for Choice Hotels International, which offers a discount on rooms to anyone over 60.

The aging of the population is also resulting in an increased demand for media to reach older consumers. For example, *Modern Maturity,* which is provided as part of the American Association of Retired Person's (AARP) annual membership, has the largest paid circulation of any magazine in the United States with over 22.5 million subscribers.[29] This magazine has become a popular media vehicle for reaching active senior citizens (Exhibit 2–21(b), page 66).

targeted the aging baby boomer segment for advertising and direct-mail programs in an attempt to woo the more affluent boomers away from German and Japanese luxury cars and into Cadillacs.

As the baby boomers migrate out of youth and into middle age, marketers must adapt their marketing and promotional programs to follow them. The complex and diverse experiences, background, and lifestyles of the aging baby boomers will make marketing and advertising to them very challenging. However, those companies that respond to the changes will enjoy tremendous growth opportunities in the 1990s.

Source: "Those Aging Baby Boomers," *Business Week*," May 20, 1991, pp. 106–11; Gary Levin, "Boomers Leave a Challenge," *Advertising Age*, July 8, 1991, pp. 1, 14; and Ken Dychtwald and Greg Gable, "Portrait of a Changing Consumer," *Business Horizons*, January–February 1990, pp. 62–73.

Levi Strauss & Co. has been very successful in reaching baby boomers with its Dockers line

The changing role of women

One of the most significant changes in American society over the past two decades has been the increase in the number of working women. The percentage of adult women in the labor force rose from 36.7 percent in 1965 to 56.4 percent in 1988, and projections are that by the year 2000 nearly two thirds of all women will be working outside the home.[30] The increase in working women has had a dramatic effect on the demand for a wide variety of products and services such as child-care services, microwave ovens, easy-to-prepare foods, restaurant meals, and women's clothing.

Another important effect of the increase in working women is the greater amount of disposable income in the dual-earner household. In 1980, the median income of a family with a working wife was nearly $27,000, as compared with $19,000 for families with a nonworking wife. By 1988, the median income grew to $42,709 for households with working wives, compared with only $27,220 for those where the wife did not work outside the home.[31] This additional income affords the family greater opportunity to purchase more products and services, to take more trips and vacations, to eat out more often, and basically to enjoy a higher standard of living.

➢ *Exhibit 2–21(a)*
Choice Hotels International targets senior citizens with its discount program

➢ *Exhibit 2–21(b)*
***Modern Maturity* has the largest circulation of any U.S. magazine**

The increase in the number of working women has many implications for marketing and promotional strategy. Many marketers are directing more of their advertising to working women, as they not only constitute an important market segment but also are more likely to be involved in purchase decisions that have traditionally been the domain of men. A study by the Young and Rubicam advertising agency found that working women are more likely to be concerned with decisions regarding financial services, travel, and the selection of an automobile than are nonworking women.[32]

Advertisers have also had to change their media strategies to reach working women, as they are less likely to be around the house watching television or reading traditional women's magazines such as *Good Housekeeping* and *Ladies Home Journal.* Over the past decade, a number of new magazines have been introduced to respond to the needs and interests of the working woman such as *Working Woman, Working Mother, Self, New Woman,* and *Savvy* (Exhibit 2–22).

Changing ethnic and racial profile

The racial and ethnic profile of the U.S. population is changing rapidly. One in five Americans today is black, Hispanic, Asian, or a member of some other minority group. Blacks are the largest minority group, numbering nearly 28 million and having an estimated purchasing power of nearly $200 billion. However, the fastest-growing of all minority groups is the Hispanic, which comprises a number of different Spanish-speaking nationalities such as Mexican, Puerto Rican, and Cuban.

The more than 20 million Hispanics account for 10 percent of the U.S. population and have an estimated purchasing power of over $170 billion. As a result of high

➤ *Exhibit 2–22*
Many magazines are targeted to women in the work force

immigration and birthrates, Hispanics are growing five times faster than the general population and will soon constitute the country's largest minority group.[33] Some 90 percent of all Hispanics are concentrated in only 10 states, with 71 percent living in four major markets—New York, California, Florida, and Texas. The increase in the Hispanic population has led to the introduction of three Spanish television networks, numerous television and radio stations, and a number of Hispanic-oriented newspapers and magazines. Over the past 10 years, nearly every segment of the Hispanic market has doubled its income, making this ethnic market very important and attractive to marketers.

The Asian population has also burgeoned as the number of Chinese, Japanese, Filipinos, Koreans, Asian Indians, and Vietnamese has increased over the past decade. In 1990, the Asian population in the United States was estimated to be about 5.6 million.[34] This number is expected to increase to nearly 10 million by the end of the decade, with most of the Asians living in California, New York, Texas, and Hawaii. The fast-growing Asian-American market has been described as younger, more affluent, and more quality conscious than the U.S. market as a whole. However, many companies have found this market difficult to reach because of its diversity and the potential for embarrassing cultural faux pas. Many marketers also believe the Asian-Americans tend to be well assimilated and more attracted by an appeal to lifestyle than ethnicity. Thus, many marketers think this market is best reached by ads in regular media such as magazines and television. However, some companies, such as Anheuser-Busch, have been developing campaigns targeted to Asian-Americans in areas such as California where Asians account for 8 percent of the population.[35]

The size of these minority groups, as well as their diverse cultures, needs, and buying habits, makes them important market segments for many companies. However, advertisers are finding that the Hispanic and Asian minorities in particular cannot be reached effectively through the general media with traditional English-language appeals. Thus, many companies are developing products and advertising appeals specifically for these markets. Advertising for ethnic subcultures is discussed in more detail in Chapter 4.

Other trends

The demographic trends discussed above are some of the more notable and significant changes occurring in the United States. Other demographic changes also taking place are geographic shifts in the population, rising education levels, and changes in the structure of American households, such as more one-parent families and the increase in single-person households. The decline of the traditional American household—married parents and one to three children—has been cited as a prime motivator of marketing innovations over the past two decades.[36] For example, the 1990 census revealed approximately 23 million Americans live by themselves—a 91 percent increase for women and a 156 percent increase for men since 1970. These single Americans represent $660 billion in earning power and have their own needs for products and services. They tend to spend more on travel, convenience foods, and restaurants than do married adults and may require special advertising appeals and media to be targeted effectively.[37]

It is important for marketers to monitor changes in the demographic environment and identify their implications for their industry and individual products and services. Fortunately, demographic changes are the most predictable of all the forces that constitute the macroenvironment. A wealth of demographic information is available from both government and commercial sources.[38] Thus, companies should be well aware of relevant demographic trends and developments and how they might influence their marketing and promotional strategies.

Economic Environment

Marketing activity is influenced very heavily by the state of the economy. Thus, economic conditions and trends and their potential impact on the demand for various products and services must be studied. Attention must be given to **macroeconomic conditions** that influence the state of the economy such as changes in gross national product (GNP), whether the economy is in an inflationary or recessionary period, interest rates, and unemployment levels. **Microeconomic trends** such as consumer income, savings, debt, and expenditure patterns are also important, as consumers' ability to buy is a function of many factors including changes in real income, disposable and discretionary income, savings, and debt levels. An interesting characteristic of the younger generation of American consumers is their willingness to use credit to finance many of their purchases. In recent years, competition among the major credit card companies has intensified as they promote their cards to consumers (Exhibit 2–23).

Changes in economic conditions may have a significant impact on marketing and advertising strategies. For example, during a recession companies will often cut back on marketing and advertising expenditures to meet budgets and/or profit plans. Advertising expenditures may be a prime candidate for cutbacks since many executives question the need to spend large sums of money in this area. Also, advertising, unlike other areas such as interest expenses or capital costs, is one of the easiest expenses to cut when profits (or profit projections) fall because the savings go straight to the bottom line.

The recession of the early 1990s had a particularly hard impact on the advertising industry. As consumer spending slowed, many companies experienced declines in their sales and/or profits, which resulted in cuts in their advertising. Forty-three of the top 100 advertisers spent less money on advertising in 1990 than they did in 1989.[39] The recession also changed the way many companies promote their products and services. Many shifted spending away from advertising and into short-term promotions such as coupons, price deals, contests, and sweepstakes.[40] Many companies switched from image-oriented ads to appeals that focused on economy, value, and savings. For example, Volkswagen of America began a program called Payment Protection Plus, whereby the company would take over the car and insurance payments of anyone who bought or leased a new VW in the event they were laid-off from their job within three years of purchase (see Exhibit 2–24, page 70).[41] The decline in advertising expenditures and shift in promotional strategies by many companies during a recession affects other participants in the advertising industry. Lower advertising budgets mean decreased billings for advertising agencies and less media spending.[42]

➤ *Exhibit 2–23*
**Advertising often encourages
consumers to use payment cards**

**You don't have to go to
extremes to pull for the team.**

Kris Feddersen, U.S. Ski Team

Using Visa® Is All It Takes To Support The U.S. Olympic Team.

You don't have to set a new record in the down-hill. Hit three triple axels in a row. Or score a hat trick to support our Olympic athletes. Just use your Visa Card or buy a Visa Travelers Cheque.

VISA
WORLDWIDE SPONSOR
1992 OLYMPIC GAMES
⬠⬠⬠⬠⬠

Because every time you do, Visa will make a donation to the 1992 U.S. Olympic Team. Giving our athletes their best chance for Olympic gold. And you the great feeling of having helped them.

Visa has guaranteed a minimum total contribution of $2,000,000 in relation to sales through July 31, 1992. Void where prohibited or restricted. © Visa U.S.A. Inc. 1991. 36 USC 380.

**Technological
Environment**

Perhaps the most dramatic of the macroenvironmental forces that affect marketing is that of technology. Changes in technology can affect an industry in several ways. Technology can result in the emergence of a new industry. For example, the PC industry started in the 1970s and is already a multibillion-dollar industry spending several hundred million dollars a year on advertising.

Technology can also radically alter or even destroy an existing industry. Consider the growth of the VCR industry. Over two thirds of U.S. households now own videocassette recorders.[43] This growth in the VCR market has created tremendous opportunities for manufacturers of the players and tapes, the movie industry, and the video stores that rent tapes to consumers. The growth of this industry, however, has also posed a threat to other markets such as movie theaters and pay-TV companies. Attendance at movie theaters declined in the late 1980s and early 1990s as more people rented movies to watch at home. Likewise, fewer households were subscribing to pay television, such as Home Box Office (HBO), since they were able to rent the movies before they were shown on the pay channels.

Technology can also stimulate new markets in related industries. For example, the penetration of the microwave oven into nearly 70 percent of American homes has resulted in a resurgence of the frozen-dinner market. Products such as Le Menu, Stouffer's Entrees, and Lean Cuisine have enjoyed tremendous growth, partly as a result of the microwave convenience of preparing these dishes as well as improvements in product quality (Exhibit 2–25, page 71).

Changes in technology are also affecting the marketing and advertising process. Computerized checkout lanes provide supermarkets with information concerning consumer demand for products on a daily basis. Home-shopping channels are already proving to be successful, whereas shopping through computers for banking services, airline tickets, stocks brokerage services, and even new cars is common in some areas.

➤ *Exhibit 2–24*
Volkswagen developed the Payment Protection Plus program to encourage consumers to purchase cars during the recession

Natural Environment

Perhaps the most difficult environmental influence to forecast or predict is change in the physical or natural environment. The natural environment includes the forces of nature as well as the availability of natural resources that influence a company's business and marketing strategy. Forces of nature such as weather patterns can influence demand for many products and services. For example, many ski resorts suffered severe losses in the early 1980s owing to a lack of snow. To respond to this problem, many resorts installed snowmaking equipment and began running ads guaranteeing consumers skiable conditions, particularly early in the season.

The natural environment also provides companies with resources for producing goods and services. Changes in the availability and prices of raw materials have had a significant impact on the companies that use them and on consumers. For example, the drought of the summer of 1991 created havoc for farmers and their crops and resulted in a significant increase in the costs of many consumer products. Shortages in raw materials, increasing costs of energy, concern over increased levels of pollution, and increased intervention in resource management by governments and other agencies have resulted in both threats and opportunities to many companies.

Sociocultural Environment

Marketing, and advertising in particular, is influenced by the basic beliefs, values, norms, customs, and lifestyle patterns of a society. Marketers must consider the core cultural beliefs and values that exist in the countries that compose their marketplace. Many U.S. firms are increasingly looking to international markets as the domestic market becomes more saturated. While understanding the cultural

➤ *Exhibit 2–25*
Microwave dinners have become very popular

values and customs of foreign markets is important to multinational companies, many marketers have their hands full tracking changes in the values, norms, and lifestyles of American consumers. Marketers must constantly monitor the sociocultural environment of the American public to spot new opportunities or to identify new threats. They must monitor social trends and changes in consumer values and respond to them through their marketing and promotional programs.

In recent years, marketers have identified and responded to a number of changes in consumers' values and lifestyles. Consumers have become more concerned with physical fitness, health, and nutrition, which is reflected in the avalanche of new products and advertising that make or use health claims and appeals. Many consumers have become more societally conscious and concerned with issues such as the environment and less sensitive to status and image. Many companies have introduced new products or repositioned their brands to capitalize on these trends. For example, consumption of bottled water has experienced tremendous growth in the United States over the past few years. The popularity of products such as Evian bottled water (Exhibit 2–26) reflects the increasing emphasis on health and fitness, concerns with the purity of water supplies in many areas, and the trend away from alcoholic beverages and high-calorie soft drinks. Many marketers have also sought a competitive edge by using **green marketing** techniques.[44] These include making and promoting products that are environmentally safe or friendly such as phosphate-free detergents, recycled paper products, cloth diapers, or dolphin-safe tuna.

We should also recognize that marketing and advertising are often major contributors to social trends and changes in consumers' lifestyles and values. We will consider how sociocultural factors influence consumer behavior in more detail in Chapter 4, while the impact of advertising on society is discussed in Chapter 24.

➤ *Exhibit 2–26*
This Evian ad touts the purity of the product

Regulatory Environment

The final, and in many ways most frustrating, component of the external environment is composed of the regulatory influences. Marketing decisions are constrained, directed, and influenced by the practices and policies of federal, state, and local governments. These policies are expressed through laws and regulations. Virtually every element of the marketing mix is influenced by some type of government regulation. Numerous laws exist to ensure product safety and to protect the health and well-being of consumers. The pricing variable is the focus of laws dealing with areas such as price fixing, price discrimination, discounts, and resale price maintenance. Distribution decisions and arrangements are also subject to a number of restrictions and regulations.

Of particular interest in this text are laws and regulations that affect advertising and promotion. Advertising and promotional practices are closely monitored at both the state and federal levels. The Federal Trade Commission (FTC) and numerous other federal agencies scrutinize advertising to protect consumers from false or misleading ads and to prevent a firm from gaining any competitive edge through unfair or deceptive advertising. Policing of the advertising industry is also undertaken by advertisers and other groups such as the media through various self-regulatory programs. Chapter 23 examines the regulatory environment of advertising and promotion.

SUMMARY

Promotion plays an important role in an organization's efforts to market its product, service, or ideas to its customers. A model consisting of three components was presented for analyzing how promotion fits into a company's marketing program—the marketing strategy and plan, the marketing program development, and the target market. The marketing process begins with determining a marketing strategy that is based on a detailed situation analysis and serves as the guide for target market selection and development of the firm's marketing program.

The various elements of the marketing mix must be coordinated to develop an effective and successful marketing program. Each marketing mix variable is multidimensional and includes a number of decision areas. Product planning involves decisions regarding the basic product as well as selection of a brand name and packaging, all of which are important from a communications perspective. Price levels and pricing policies must consider cost and demand factors as well as competition and the consumers' perceived value of the product or service offering.

One of the most important marketing decisions a firm must make is the selection of marketing channels by which the product is made available to the customer. While some firms sell directly to the customer, most use marketing intermediaries or resellers such as wholesalers and/or retailers. Marketing and promotional programs must be developed for these intermediaries to encourage them to stock, merchandise, and promote the manufacturer's product. Programs geared to the resellers or trade are part of a promotional push strategy, whereas monies spent on advertising and sales promotion to create demand among ultimate consumers constitutes a promotional pull strategy. Promotion to the final buyer occurs through the various promotional mix elements, although advertising is most often relied on to communicate information to both consumer and business markets. Various classifications of advertising to final customers were examined including national, retail or local, and business-to-business advertising, which includes industrial, trade, and professional advertising.

A number of factors cannot be controlled or directed by the organization and make up the macroenvironment of marketing, including demographic, economic, technological, natural/physical, sociocultural, and regulatory influences. These uncontrollable forces can have a significant impact on a firm's marketing strategy and programs, both in the short and long terms.

KEY TERMS

strategic marketing plan
market opportunities
market segments
competitive advantage
product symbolism
brand extension strategy
line extension
category extension
price elasticity
nonprice competition
competition-oriented
  pricing
marketing channels
resellers

direct channels
indirect channels
promotional push
  strategy
trade advertising
promotional pull strategy
national advertising
national advertisers
retail/local advertising
direct-action advertising
direct-response
  advertising
primary demand
  advertising

selective demand
  advertising
business-to-business
  advertising
industrial advertising
professional advertising
macroenvironment
demographics
baby boomers
macroeconomic
  conditions
microeconomic trends
green marketing

DISCUSSION QUESTIONS

1. What is meant by a marketing opportunity? Discuss several examples of market opportunities that companies have taken advantage of in recent years.

2. In 1990 Pepsi-Cola test marketed a new product called "Pepsi A.M.," which was a cola drink with more caffeine and lower carbonation and was positioned as a morning beverage. Discuss the competitive factors that might have been considered in deciding to introduce this product. Do you think a soft-drink cola product can be marketed successfully as an alternative to coffee? Why or why not?

3. Find an example of a situation where a new product was recently introduced using a brand-extension strategy. Discuss the advantages and disadvantages of using this strategy. Do you think a brand extension was appropriate in this situation? Why or why not?

4. Discuss the relationship of pricing strategies and tactics to advertising. What are some of the price-related factors that must be considered in developing the promotional program?

5. Discuss the differences between a promotional push strategy and a promotional pull strategy. What factors influence a firm's decision to use either a push or a pull strategy?

6. What are the differences between primary and selective demand advertising? When would a company or organization use each?

7. Discuss the role of advertising in business-to-business firms who sell directly to other companies. Given that these companies rely heavily on personal selling, who do they need to advertise?

8. Discuss the implications of the aging of the U.S. population for marketers, giving particular attention to advertising and promotion.

9. How has the recent recession the U.S. has gone through in the early 1990s impacted advertising? Do you think it will be business as usual for advertisers when the recession ends—or have fundamental changes occurred in the way companies will market their products and services?

10. What is meant by "green marketing"? Why do companies use green marketing techniques? Discuss how marketers might misuse or even abuse green marketing.

part II

Promotion Program Situation Analysis

chapter 3

Organizing for Advertising and Promotion and the Role of Agencies

chapter objectives

➢ To examine the structure of the advertising and promotions industry.

➢ To understand how companies organize for the advertising and promotions function.

➢ To explain the role and functions of each of the participants in the promotions process.

➢ To present methods for compensating and evaluating advertising agencies.

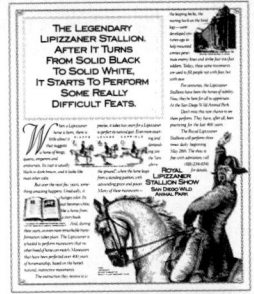
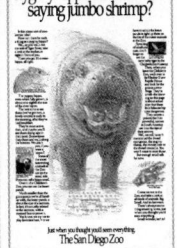

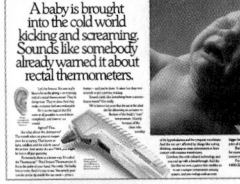

Tough Times on Madison Avenue

During the 1970s and 1980s, the U.S. advertising business was one of the economy's fastest-growing and most buoyant industries and had become accustomed to a seemingly limitless boom. From 1976 to 1988, total U.S. ad spending consistently grew faster than the overall economy. Even during the recession years of 1981 and 1982, the advertising business enjoyed growth rates of 12.8 percent and 10.2 percent, respectively.

During the late 1970s and 1980s, new product categories such as personal computers, videocassette players, video cameras, and compact disk players were introduced and required large amounts of advertising. Airline deregulation resulted in ad-intensive fare wars. Growth returned to the automobile industry; and as competition intensified, advertising budgets of both domestic and foreign automakers soared. Advertising for financial services followed along with the bullish stock market. As advertising budgets increased, so did demand for media time and space, which resulted in double-digit rate hikes every year. As ad revenues soared, agencies reaped millions of dollars from their standard 15 percent commission on media billings (the amount of the client's media spending, on which the agency earns a commission). It is little wonder that Madison Avenue* was always said to be a street with just one side: sunny.

As we enter the 1990s, Madison Avenue is finding that it does have a shady, or perhaps even a dark, side. The advertising business is suffering through its deepest and most prolonged downturn in decades. The problems began as the 1980s drew to a close. As consumer spending slowed and corporate profits declined, marketers began cutting back on advertising expenditures. Total ad spending grew only 5 percent in 1989, 3.8 percent in 1990, and 3 percent in 1991. While the recession is responsible for some of the cutbacks in ad expenditures, other forces are giving advertising a diminished role in the marketing process. Many companies are relying less on mass media advertising and are targeting their ads more carefully with direct mail and other specialized media. Marketers are also turning to trade and consumer-oriented sales promotion techniques as they scramble to boost short-term sales instead of investing in the more long-term and image-building value of national advertising.

The changes and instability in the advertising industry have had a major impact on advertising agencies. Longtime clients feel little or no loyalty to their agencies. They see a new campaign that they like from one of their

*Madison Avenue is a term used to refer to the advertising agency business in recognition of the street in New York City where many of the large agencies are, or used to be, headquartered.

(continued)

competitors and then call an account review in which they invite other agencies to make presentations showing how they would handle the account. While the incumbent agency may also be invited to participate, nearly 90 percent of the time it loses the account. The intense competition has also led many agencies to raid one another for business, and agency jumping has become more common. For example, in 1990, athletic shoe maker Reebok moved its advertising from Chiat/Day/Mojo in Los Angeles to the Hill, Holliday, Connors & Cosmopulos agency in Boston. By early 1991, Reebok left the Boston agency and gave part of the $40 million account back to Chiat. From July 1990 to July 1991, more than $800 million worth of U.S. advertising billings switched agencies.

When not switching agencies, advertisers now demand more accountability from their agencies and put more pressure on them to prove the advertising program delivers sales and market-share results. Advertisers are taking a close look at the tone and effectiveness of ads along with the media strategies used to deliver the messages to consumers. Many companies have tied agency compensation to sales performance. Others have found agencies willing to work from commissions as low as 5 percent versus the traditional 15 percent. In his book *Whatever Happened To Madison Avenue?* Martin Mayer

noted, "Agencies are in danger of turning into little more than vendors competing on price."

Many advertising analysts argue that agencies are responding to the instability of the industry and pressures from clients by retreating to safe ideas and campaigns rather than trying newer and more creative approaches that will attract consumer attention. In 1990, *Advertising Age* failed to bestow its prestigious "Agency of the Year" award for the first time since it began the practice in 1973. In defending the decision, the editors noted, "While there was a goodly amount of clever recycling around, conceptual innovations were in short supply." The editors concluded the main reason for the lack of creative advertising by agencies was that clients had been harassing them so much during a tough business cycle.

Many experts argue it will be a long time, if ever, before the advertising industry experiences the growth and free spending it enjoyed during the past two decades. It has been argued that agencies must return to the fundamentals of their business—coming up with good ideas and creative ads that sell their clients' products and services. If they do not, another agency will be waiting to make a pitch for the account.

Source: "What Happened to Advertising?" Business Week, *September 23, 1991, pp. 66–72; "Feeling a Little Jumpy,"* Time, *July 8, 1991, pp. 42–44; and Fred Danzig, "The Winner is _____ !"* Advertising Age, *March 25, 1991, p. S-3.*

The development and implementation of a promotional program usually constitute a complex and detailed process involving the efforts of many persons. As consumers, we generally give little thought to the individuals or organizations that create the clever advertisements that capture our attention and interest or the contest or sweepstakes that we enter and hope to win. However, to those involved in marketing, it is important to understand the nature of the industry and the structure and functions of the organizations involved. As you can see in the opening to this chapter, the advertising and promotions business is a dynamic one, with money, reputations, and jobs hinging on every decision as to which agency will be employed.

This chapter examines the structure of the promotions industry and the responsibilities of the participants involved. Attention is focused on how the promotions function is organized and operates, as well as the roles of other participants—particularly the role of the advertising agency.

Participants in the Promotions Process—An Overview

Before we discuss the specifics of the industry, it may be helpful to provide an overview of the entire system and to identify some of the players involved. As shown in Exhibit 3–1, four groups participate in the industry—the advertiser (or client), advertising agencies, media organizations, and collateral services. Each of these groups has specific roles to perform in the promotional process.

The advertisers, or **clients,** are the key participants in the process, as they have the products, services, or causes to be marketed, and they provide the funds that pay for the advertising and promotions efforts. The advertiser also assumes the major responsibility for developing the marketing program and for making the final decisions regarding the advertising and promotional program that will be employed. (Though, in many cases, advertising agencies are assuming more of this responsibility, acting as "partners" with the advertisers in this process.) The organization itself may

> *Exhibit 3–1*

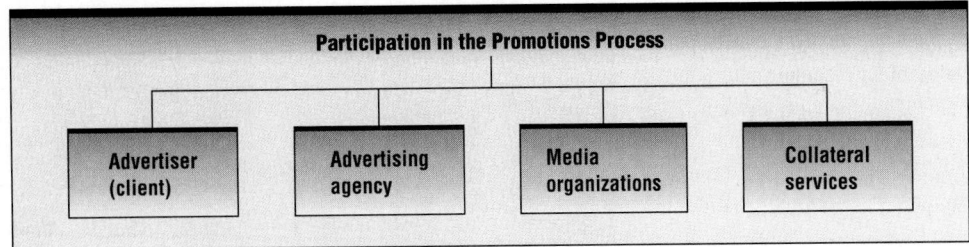

perform most of these efforts, either through its own advertising department or by setting up an in-house agency. However, many organizations choose to use an **advertising agency,** which is an outside firm that specializes in the creation, production and/or placement of the communications message and that may provide other services that facilitate the marketing and promotions process. Many large advertisers retain the services of a number of agencies, particularly when they market a number of products. For example, Kraft/GF uses as many as 10 advertising agencies, while Procter & Gamble uses as many as 10 promotional agencies for its Canadian business alone.[1]

Media organizations are another major participant in the advertising and promotions process. The primary function of most media is to provide information or entertainment to its subscribers—the viewers or readers. However, from the perspective of the promotions planner, the purpose of the media is to provide an environment for the firm's marketing communications message. The media must have editorial or program content that attracts consumers so the media vehicle can sell the advertisers and their agencies on the viability of buying time or space with them. An example of one publication's attempt to convince buyers of the attractiveness of their medium is shown in Exhibit 3–2. While the media perform many other functions for advertisers that help them understand their markets and their customers, the primary objective of the medium is to sell itself as a way for companies to reach their target markets with their messages effectively.

The final participants shown in the promotions process of Exhibit 3–1 are those that provide **collateral services,** or the wide range of specialized functions used by advertisers, agencies, and media organizations. Collateral services include organizations such as package design firms, sales promotions firms, media buying services, research organizations, and production firms. The function of these services varies depending on the need and situation of the advertiser. For example, a sales promotion firm may be utilized to develop a contest or sweepstakes that will be used as part of the firm's promotions campaign, whereas research organizations may provide input into, or evaluations of, the promotional program. We will now examine the role of each of these participants in more detail.

Organizing for Advertising and Promotion in the Firm—the Role of the Client

Virtually every business organization uses some form of advertising and promotion. However, the way the firm organizes for these efforts depends on several factors including the size of the company, the number of products it markets, the role of advertising and promotion in the company's marketing mix, the advertising and promotions budget, and the marketing organization structure of the firm. Many individuals throughout the organization may be involved in the promotions decision-making process. Marketing personnel have the most direct relationship with advertising and will often become involved in many aspects of the decision process, such as providing input to the campaign planning process, agency selection, and evaluation of proposed programs. Top management is usually interested in how the advertising program represents the firm, which may also mean being involved in advertising decisions, even though these decisions may not be included in their day-to-day responsibilities.

While many people, both inside and outside the organization, are interested in, or have some input into, the advertising and promotions process, the direct responsibility

➤ *Exhibit 3–2*
Soap Opera Digest advertises the value of its medium

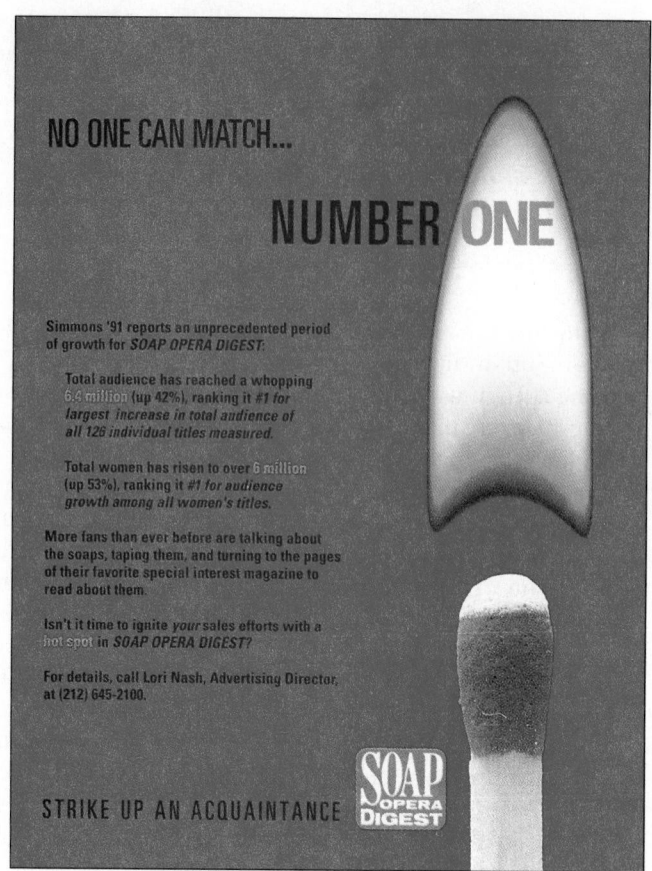

for administering the program must be assumed by someone within the firm. For many companies, this responsibility is assumed by an advertising department headed by an advertising or communications manager operating under a marketing director. An alternative, used by many large multiproduct firms, is to use a *decentralized marketing* or *brand management system*. Still a third option is to form a separate agency within the firm—or an *in-house agency*. Each of these alternatives is examined in more detail in the following sections.

The Centralized System

In many organizations, marketing activities are divided along functional lines, with advertising placed alongside other marketing functions such as sales, marketing research, and product planning, as shown in Exhibit 3–3. Under this arrangement, the **advertising manager** is responsible for all promotions activities except sales, with all advertising and promotions matters channeled through this department. The most common example of a **centralized system** is the advertising department wherein the advertising manager controls the entire promotions operation, including budgeting, coordinating creation and production of advertisements, planning media schedules, and monitoring and administering the sales promotions programs for all the company's products or services.

The specific duties of the advertising manager depend on the size of the firm and the importance placed on promotional programs. Some of the basic functions the manager and staff must perform include the following:

Planning and budgeting   The department is responsible for developing advertising and promotions plans that will be approved by management and recommending a promotions program based on the overall marketing plan, objectives, and budget. Formal plans are submitted on an annual basis or when a program is being changed

➤ *Exhibit 3–3* **The advertising department under a functional organization**

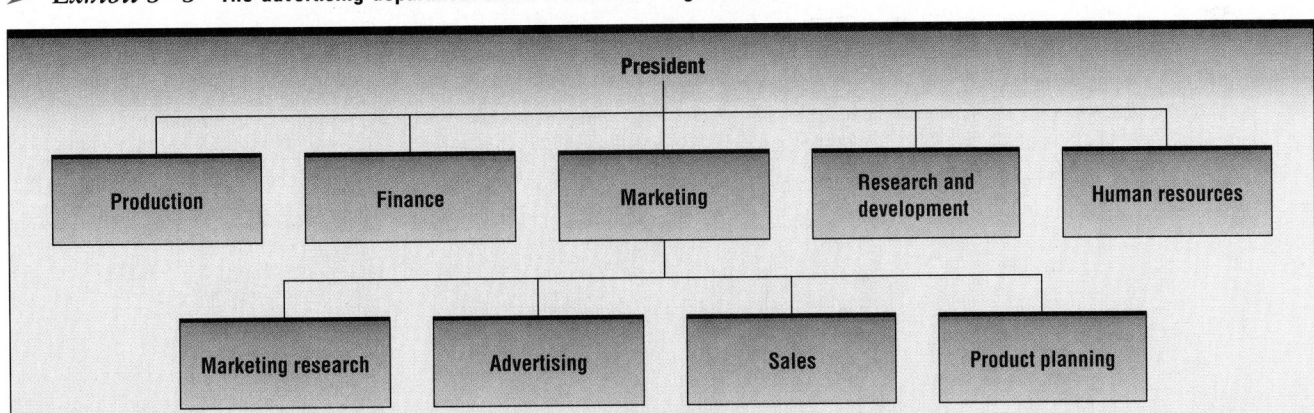

significantly, such as the development of a new campaign. While the advertising department assumes the responsibility for developing the promotional budget, the final decision on the allocation of funds is usually made by top management.

Administration and execution The manager must organize the advertising department and supervise and control its activities. The manager is also responsible for supervising the execution of the plan by subordinates and/or the advertising agency. This requires working with various departments such as production, media, art, copy, and sales promotion. If an outside agency is used, the advertising department is relieved of much of the executional responsibilities; however, plans of the agency must be reviewed and approved.

Coordination with other departments The manager must coordinate the advertising department's activities with those of other departments—particularly those involving other marketing functions. For example, the advertising department must communicate with marketing research and/or sales to determine which product features are important to customers and should be emphasized in the company's communications. Research may also provide profiles of users and nonusers for the media department to use in selecting broadcast or print media. The advertising department may also be responsible for preparing material that can be used by the sales force when calling on customers, such as sales promotions tools, advertising materials, and point-of-purchase displays.

Coordination with outside agencies and services Many companies have an advertising department but still utilize many outside services. For example, companies may develop their advertising programs in-house, while employing media buying services to place their ads, and/or use collateral services agencies to develop brochures, point-of-purchase materials, and so on. The department serves as liaison between the company and any outside service providers and also determines which ones to use. Once outside services are retained, the manager will work with other marketing managers to coordinate their efforts and evaluate their performances.

The Decentralized System

The centralized advertising department structure was the most commonly employed organization system for many years. However, many firms developed problems with the traditional functional organization, particularly as the company grew and developed more products and brands. The major problem with the centralized structure concerns coordination and responsibility requirements. Under this arrangement,

➤ *Exhibit 3–4* **The product manager organizational chart**

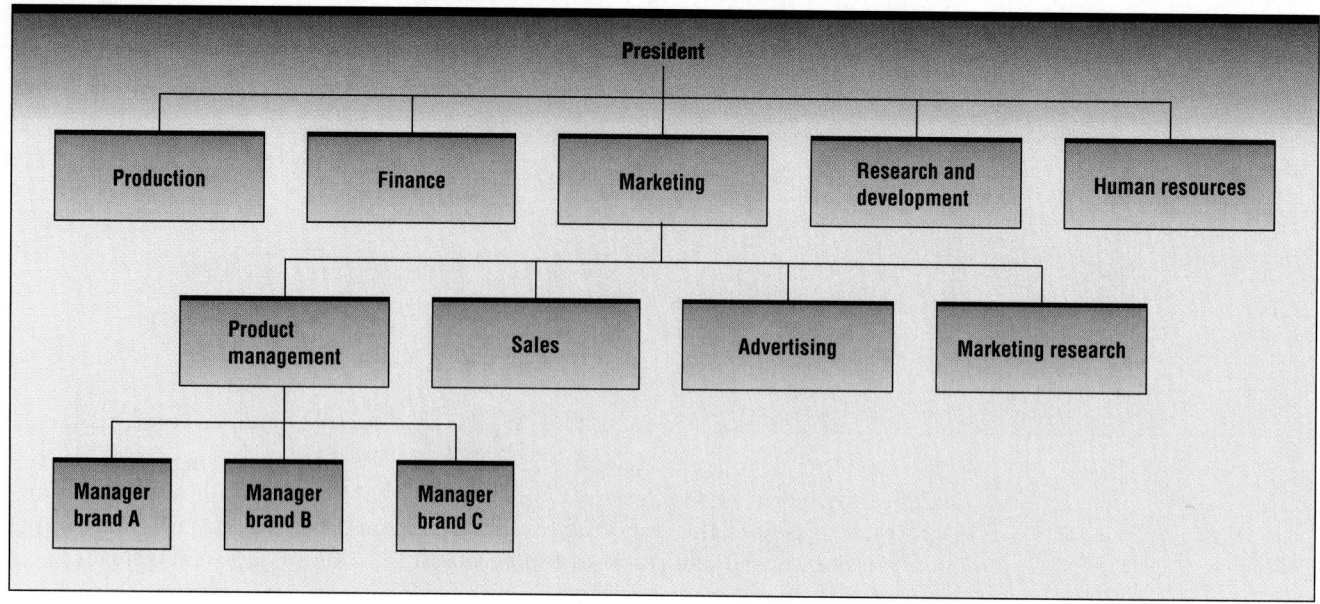

marketing decisions are made by several functional managers and must be coordinated by someone in the marketing department. Moreover, no one department has specific responsibility for the welfare or problems of individual products or brands. Because of these problems, many companies developed **decentralized systems** such as the product or brand manager organization (this organizational system is now the most dominant structure in large consumer and industrial products companies).[2]

In this system, a **product manager,** or management team, has the responsibility for the planning, implementation, and control of the marketing program for an individual brand. The product manager is also responsible for sales projections and profit performance of the brand and must develop and coordinate the budget. Companies utilizing this form of organization will generally support product managers with a structure of marketing services including sales, marketing research, and advertising departments, as shown in Exhibit 3–4. The product manager will utilize these services in gathering information on customers, middlemen, competitors, product performance, and specific marketing problems and opportunities. (The terms *brand manager* and *product manager* are both used to describe this position in various organizations).

In a product management system, the responsibilities and functions associated with advertising and promotions are often transferred to the brand manager. The brand manager becomes the liaison between the outside service agencies and is involved with the agency in the development of the promotional program.

Some companies may have an additional layer of management above the brand managers to improve and coordinate efforts among groups of product categories. An example is the organizational structure of Procter & Gamble as shown in Exhibit 3–5. This system—generally referred to as a **category management** system—includes category managers as well as brand and advertising managers.

In a multiproduct firm, each brand may have its own advertising agency and, while positioned differently, may compete against other brands within the company as well as with outside competitors. For example, the brands shown in Exhibit 3–6 are all products of Procter & Gamble, with each competing for its own share of the market.

In a product management organization, the advertising department provides advertising and promotions support for the brand manager. The department may assist the manager in coordinating the advertising and sales promotions programs and may provide research and other support services. The advertising manager may review

➤ *Exhibit 3–5*
A Procter & Gamble division using the category management system of organization

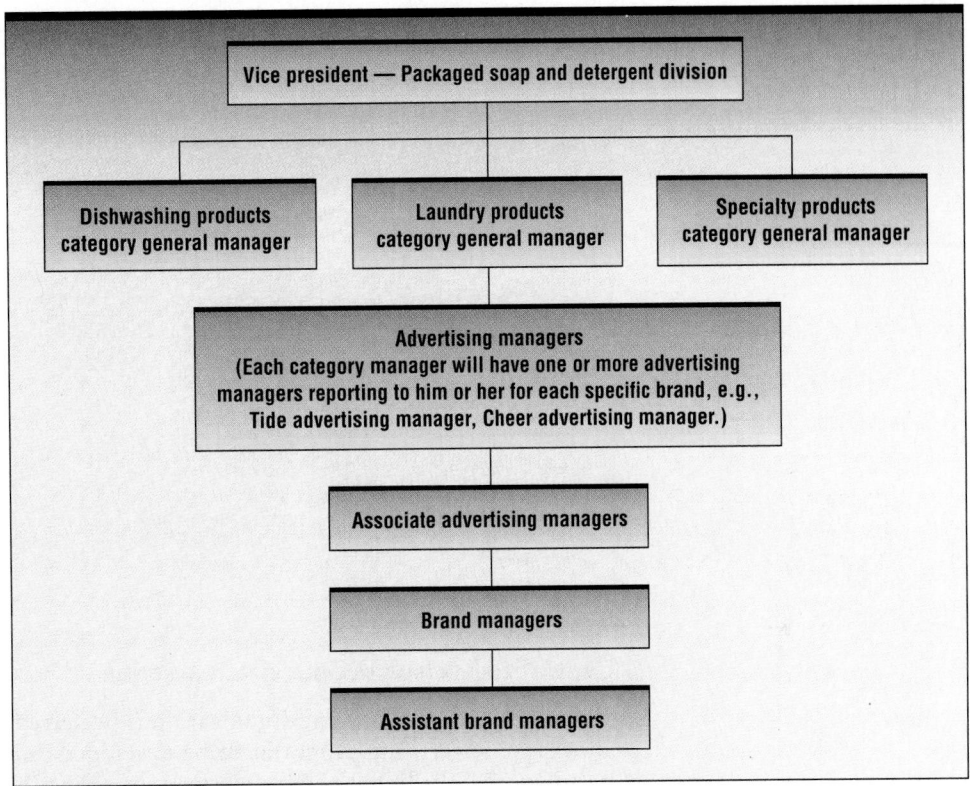

➤ *Exhibit 3–6*
Many of Procter & Gamble's brands compete against each other

and evaluate the various parts of the program and serve as consultant and adviser. This person may have the authority to override the product manager's decisions on promotions. In some multiproduct firms in which many dollars are spent on advertising, the advertising manager may coordinate the work of the various agencies to obtain media discounts as a result of the large volume of media purchases made by the firm. For example, before 1991, Nestlé had as many as 11 agencies purchasing media time for its products. Likewise, Eastman Kodak and its subsidiary Sterling Drug each had their own agencies purchasing over $100 million in television time. In 1991, Nestlé consolidated its $250 to $300 million media buying into one agency—McCann AOR—while Kodak and Sterling's buys became the responsibility of Lintas: USA. These consolidations were designed to afford them more clout in the media buying market, as well as to improve control over the management and administrative process. (In addition, the companies saved an estimated $5 to $10 million in agency fees.)[3]

Some companies, in an effort to reduce costs and have greater control over agency activities, have set up their own advertising agencies internally. An **in-house agency** is an advertising agency that is set up, owned, and operated by the advertiser. Some in-house agencies are little more than an advertising department, whereas in other companies they may be given a separate identity and be responsible for the expenditure of large sums of advertising dollars. Many companies use in-house agencies exclusively, whereas others may combine in-house efforts with those of outside agencies. (The specific roles performed by in-house agencies will become more clear once we have discussed the functions of outside agencies.)

Evaluations of Advertising Organization Systems

Each of the organizational designs just discussed has its advantages and disadvantages, as summarized in Exhibit 3–7. We will consider these by first comparing the centralized system versus the decentralized system and then considering the merits of the in-house agency.

➤ *Exhibit 3–7*
Comparison of advertising organization systems

Organizational System	Advantages	Disadvantages
Centralized	• Facilitated communications • Fewer personnel required • Continuity in staff • Allows for more top-management involvement	• Less involvement with and understanding of overall marketing goals • Longer response time • Inability to handle multiple product lines
Decentralized	• Concentrated managerial attention • Rapid response to problems and opportunities • Increased flexibility	• Ineffective decision making • Internal conflicts • Misallocation of funds • Lack of authority
In-house agencies	• Cost savings • More control • Increased coordination	• Less experience • Less objectivity • Less flexibility

Centralized versus decentralized systems

The advertising department organization is preferred by many companies because it allows the advertising programs to be developed and coordinated from one central location. This facilitates communication regarding the promotions program, making it easier for top management to participate in decision making. A centralized system may also result in a more efficient operation because fewer people are involved in the program decisions, and as their experience in making such decisions increases, the process will become easier.

At the same time, problems are inherent in a centralized operation. First, it is difficult for the advertising department to become involved with, and to understand, the overall marketing strategy for the brand. The department may also be slow in responding to specific needs and problems of a product or brand. Moreover, as companies become larger and develop or acquire new products, brands, or even divisions, the centralized system may become impractical. This may force the company to adopt a decentralized system.

An advantage of the decentralized system is that each brand will receive concentrated managerial attention, resulting in faster response to both problems and opportunities. The product manager system allows for increased flexibility in the advertising program, which means the campaign may be adjusted more easily.

There are also drawbacks to the decentralized approach. Product managers often lack training and experience in advertising and promotion. They may be concerned with short-run planning and administrative tasks rather than with the development of long-term programs. Also, individual product managers often end up competing for resources, which can lead to unproductive rivalries and potential misallocation of funds. The persuasiveness of the manager, rather than the long-run profit potential of the brands, may be the critical factor determining the budgets. Finally, the product manager system has been criticized for failing to provide the brand manager with the authority over the functions that are needed to implement and control the plans they develop.[4] Some companies have dealt with this problem by expanding the role and responsibility of the advertising manager and his or her staff of specialists. The staff specialists counsel the individual product managers, with the advertising decision-making process involving the ad manager, the product manager, and the marketing director.

Those who argue against the product management system cite recent changes at Procter & Gamble to support their position. Perhaps the most renowned practitioner of the product management system, Procter & Gamble has decided to reorganize along entire product category lines (for example, all laundry detergents).[5] Procter &

➤ *Exhibit 3–8*
Benetton uses an in-house agency to create its advertising appeals

Gamble has called this change the major management decision in the company in the past 30 years and believes the new organization will foster cooperation among the brand managers. Greater emphasis will be placed on how the products could work together—as opposed to having each compete for funding, plant capacity, and top managers' time and attention.

Evaluation of the in-house agency

A major reason for using an in-house agency is to reduce advertising and promotions costs. Companies with very large advertising budgets pay a substantial amount of money to outside agencies in the form of media commissions. With an internal structure, these commissions go to the in-house agency, resulting in substantial savings. An in-house agency can also provide related work such as preparing sales presentations and sales force materials, package design, and public relations efforts at a lower cost than outside agencies. Companies also prefer to have their advertising performed in-house to maintain tight control over the process, believing this arrangement makes it easier to coordinate the promotions with the firm's overall marketing program . . . and saves time. Some companies also use an in-house agency because they believe they can do a better job than an outside agency could.[6] (See Exhibit 3–8.)

Opponents of the in-house system argue they cannot give the advertiser the experience and objectivity of an outside agency, nor the range of services. They argue that outside agencies have more highly skilled specialists and attract the best creative talent, and that by using an external firm the company will have a more varied perspective to its advertising problems as well as greater flexibility. In-house personnel may become narrow or grow stale while working on the same product line, but outside agencies may have different people with a variety of backgrounds and ideas working on the account. Flexibility is greater, as an outside agency can be more easily dismissed if the company is not satisfied, whereas changes in an in-house agency could be slower and more disruptive.

Promotional Perspective 3–1

Taking the Advertising Business "in House"

Some companies believe the best advertising agency is no ad agency at all—that is, they think advertising should be handled "in house" (by the company itself). The idea of performing the advertising function is certainly not new; Procter & Gamble, Lever Brothers, and American Home Products all had in-house agencies at one time. But more companies appear to be considering the in-house alternative. Many companies split the responsibilities, going outside for some services, while performing others themselves.

A study conducted by M. Louise Ripley revealed that creative and media services were the most likely functions to be performed outside, while merchandising and sales promotion were the most likely to be performed in-house. Ripley also found that consumer products companies were most likely to use the services of outside agencies, while wholesale and service industries were least likely.

Why does a company go in-house? The most commonly assumed reason is to save the 15 percent commission paid to advertising agencies. For some companies, this could result in millions of dollars in savings. But not all companies cite this as the primary reason. Time savings, bad experiences with agencies, and the increased knowledge that comes from working with the products on a day-to-day basis are also reasons. Some companies, such as Buena Vista Pictures (the distributor of all Walt

Disney motion pictures) and Stash Teas among others, just believe they can do a better job themselves.

Then why do companies go outside? L. A. Gear was one company that believed it would be better off in-house. The company cited many of the reasons above for not using agencies. The company quickly became the number three athletic shoe maker—behind Nike and Reebok—saving about $2.5 million a year in advertising fees in the process. Unfortunately, L. A. Gear's good fortunes didn't last, and the company is using an outside agency to enhance its image and bolster its sagging sales. Likewise, Redken Laboratories moved its in-house work to an outside agency. Redken cited the need for "a fresh look" and objectivity as the reasons, noting that management gets too close to the product to come up with different ideas.

So, what is the answer? Based on these examples, it would appear both strategies have advantages and disadvantages. A company has to determine what works best for it given market conditions and internal strengths and weaknesses.

Source: M. Louise Ripley "What Kind of Companies Take Their Advertising In-House?" *Journal of Advertising Research,* October–November 1991, pp. 73–80; and Bruce Horovitz, "Some Companies Say the Best Ad Agency Is No Ad Agency at All," *Los Angeles Times,* July 4, 1989, Sec. IV, p. 5.

The cost savings of an in-house agency must be evaluated against these considerations. For many companies, high-quality advertising is critical to their marketing success and should be the major criterion in determining whether to use in-house services. Some of these considerations are discussed in Promotional Perspective 3–1.

The ultimate decision as to which advertising organization to use depends on which arrangement works best for the company. There are advantages and disadvantages to each system. Regardless of which system is chosen, an outside agency may still be useful. We now turn our attention to the functions of outside agencies and the roles they perform in the promotional process.

Advertising Agencies

Many major companies use an advertising agency to assist them in developing, preparing, and executing their promotional programs. An advertising agency is a service organization that specializes in the planning and execution of advertising programs for its clients. Over 7,000 agencies are listed in the *Standard Directory of Advertising Agencies;* however, the majority of the companies are individually owned small businesses employing fewer than five people. The U.S. advertising agency business is highly concentrated, with nearly half of the domestic **billings** (the amount of client money agencies spend on media purchases and other equivalent activities) handled by the top 500 agencies. In 1991, the U.S. gross income of the top 500 agencies totaled $7.7 billion on domestic billings of nearly $56 billion. Moreover, the top 10 U.S. agencies handle nearly 50 percent of the total volume of

➤ *Exhibit 3–9*   **The top 25 U.S.-based consolidated agencies in worldwide gross income (1991)**

Rank 1991	Rank 1990	Agency, headquarters	Worldwide Gross Income	Worldwide Billings
1	1	Young & Rubicam, New York	$980.8	$7,331.4
2	2	Saatchi & Saatchi Advertising Worldwide, New York	829.2	5,665.7
3	4	McCann-Erickson Worldwide, New York	811.6	5,413.5
4	3	Oglivy & Mather Worldwide, New York	794.9	5,520.7
5	6	BBDO Worldwide, New York	772.8	5,408.7
6	5	Lintas:Worldwide, New York	729.7	4,887.2
7	7	J. Walter Thompson Co., New York	727.0	5,048.8
8	8	DDB Needham Worldwide, New York	698.4	5,034.3
9	9	Backer Spielvogel Bates Worldwide, New York	630.4	4,266.3
10	11	Foote, Cone & Belding Communications, Chicago	616.0	4,651.0
11	10	Grey Advertising, New York	615.1	4,142.7
12	13	Leo Burnett Co., Chicago	576.6	3,890.6
13	12	D'Arcy Masius Benton & Bowles, New York	534.6	4,509.3
14	14	Bozell, New York	221.0	1,660.0
15	15	Lowe Group, New York	220.4	1,551.4
16	16	N W. Ayer, New York	171.3	1,361.1
17	19	TBWA Advertising, New York	144.8	1,001.9
18	17	Chiat/Day/Mojo, Venice, Calif.	137.7	999.9
19	18	Ketchum Communications, Pittsburgh	127.2	978.8
20	20	Campbell-Mithun-Esty, Minneapolis	122.2	906.8
21	21	Ross Roy Group, Bloomfield Hills, Mich.	105.1	700.5
22	22	Wells Rich Greene BDDP, New York	105.0	923.7
23	23	Scali McCabe, Sloves, New York	91.1	631.1
24	24	Della Femina, McNamee, New York	85.6	713.0
25	25	TMP Worldwide, New York	65.3	435.3

business done by the top 500 agencies in the United States. The top agencies also have foreign operations that generate a substantial amount of billings and income. The top 25 U.S.-based consolidated agencies ranked by their worldwide gross income are shown in Exhibit 3–9.

As can be seen in Exhibit 3–9, the advertising business is also geographically concentrated with 19 of the top 25 agencies headquartered in New York City. New York City-based agencies dominate ad spending; 43 percent of total U.S. billings in 1990, or $24.1 billion, was handled by agencies in the Big Apple. Chicago finished a distant second, followed by Los Angeles. On a worldwide basis, Tokyo, which is home to 12 of the world's top 50 advertising organizations, moved ahead of New York City to claim the title of world advertising capital in 1991. Billings by Tokyo agencies totaled $24.5 billion.

During the latter half of the 1980s, the advertising industry became even more concentrated as large agencies merged or acquired other agencies and support organizations to form large advertising organizations, or **superagencies.** These superagencies were formed so that agencies could provide clients with integrated marketing communication services on a worldwide basis. Exhibit 3–10 lists the 25 top agencies worldwide. Global Perspective 3–1 (page 89) discusses how some agencies have turned to megamergers to form large advertising organizations that can provide clients with integrated marketing services. Later in this chapter, we examine the advantages and disadvantages of these superagencies.

The Role of the Advertising Agency

The functions performed by advertising agencies might be conducted by the clients themselves through one of the designs discussed earlier in this chapter, yet most large companies use outside firms. This section discusses some reasons advertisers use these external agencies.

➤ *Exhibit 3–10* **World's top 25 advertising organizations (ranked by equity gross income, 1991)**

Rank 1991	Advertising Organization, Headquarters	U.S.-Based Agencies Included	Worldwide Gross Income (in millions)	Worldwide Capitalized Volume (in millions)
1	WPP Group, London	Ogilvy & Mather Worldwide, J. Walter Thompson Co, Scali, McCabe, Sloves	$2,661.8	$17,915.8
2	Interpublic Group of Cos., New York	McCann-Erickson Worldwide, Lintus: Worldwide Lowe Group	1,798.9	12,100.8
3	Saatchi & Saatchi Co., New York/London	Saatchi & Saatchi Advertising Worldwide, Backer Spielvogel Bates Worldwide, Campbell-Mithun-Esty	1,705.5	11,663.4
4	Omnicom Group, New York	BBDO Worldwide, DDB Needham Worldwide	1,471.2	10,442.9
5	Dentsu Inc., Tokyo	Dentsu America	1,451.0	10,680.1
6	Young & Rubicam, New York	Young & Rubicam	1,057.1	7,840.1
7	Euro RSCG, Paris	Della Femina, McNamee	1,016.3	6,955.7
8	Grey Advertising, New York	Grey Advertising	659.3	4,437.4
9	Hakuhodo, Tokyo	Hakuhodo Advertising America	655.6	4,686.7
10	Foote, Cone & Belding Communications, Chicago	Foote, Cone & Belding Communications	616.0	4,651.0
11	Leo Burnett Co., Chicago	Leo Burnett Co.	576.6	3,890.6
12	D'Arcy Masius Benton & Bowles, New York	D'Arcy Masius Benton & Bowles	534.6	4,509.3
13	Publicis-FCB Communications, Paris	Publicis	512.8	3,433.7
14	BDDP Worldwide, Boulogne, France	Wells Rich Greene BDDP	277.0	1,941.3
15	Bozell, Jacobs, Kenyon & Eckhardt, New York	Bozell	221.0	1,660.0
16	Tokyu Agency, Tokyo	NA	176.9	1,482.4
17	Daiko Advertising, Osaka, Japan	NA	174.3	1,278.1
18	N W Ayer, New York	N W Ayer	171.3	1,361.1
19	Asatsu, Tokyo	Asatsu America	166.2	1,194.0
20	Dai-Ichi Kikaku Co., Tokyo	Kresser Craig D. I. K.	159.9	1,113.1
21	TBWA Advertising, New York	TBWA Advertising	144.8	1,001.9
22	Chiat/Day/Mojo, Venice, Calif.	Chiat/Day/Mojo	141.1	1,022.6
23	Dentsu, Young & Rubicam Partnerships, New York	Lord, Dentsu & Partners	129.2	935.9
24	Ketchum Communications, Pittsburgh	Ketchum Communications	127.2	978.8
25	Lopex, London	Warwick Baker & Fiore	124.0	818.4

Reasons for using an agency

Probably the main reason outside agencies are used is that they provide the client with the services of highly skilled individuals who are specialists in their chosen fields. An advertising agency staff may include artists, writers, media analysts, researchers, and others with specific skills, knowledge, and experience that can be used to help market the client's products or services. Many agencies specialize in a particular type of business—for example, business-to-business advertising—and use their knowledge of the industry to assist their clients.

Another reason for using an advertising agency is that an outside agency can provide an objective viewpoint of the market and its business that is not subject to internal company policies, biases, or other limitations. The agency can also draw on the broad range of experience it has gained while working on a diverse set of marketing problems for its various clients. For example, an advertising agency that is handling a travel-related account may have individuals who have worked with the airlines, cruise ship companies, travel agencies, hotels, and other travel-related industries, or the agency may have worked in this area. Sometimes the agency may have previously worked on the advertising account of the client's competitors. Thus,

Global Perspective 3–1

Agencies Turn to Megamergers to Serve Global Marketers

The 1980s was the decade of merger mania in the business world as a record number of mergers and acquisitions occurred. Several megacorporations evolved with multibillion-dollar advertising and promotion budgets. For example, the Philip Morris Cos.' 1988 acquisition of Kraft Foods and 1985 purchase of General Foods had made it the nation's largest food company. Other megadeals included Procter & Gamble's acquisition of Richardson Vicks and R. J. Reynolds' purchase of Nabisco.

As we enter the 1990s, mergers, acquisitions, and strategic alliances are continuing to concentrate vast market power in the hands of fewer and fewer companies in many industries, including financial services, airlines, tires, and appliances. Proponents of these megamergers argue that they are necessary if U.S. companies are to remain competitive in the global market where they compete against larger foreign competitors. They point to the European consortiums such as Airbus Industrie and Japanese firms that belong to huge industrial combines known as *keiretsus* as reasons for pumping up the size of American companies.

Merger mania has not been confined to the client side of the business. Many of the largest agencies in the United States have either merged with or been acquired by other agencies. The trend started in April 1987 when three of the country's largest agencies—Batten, Barton, Durstine and Osborne (BBDO); Doyle Dane Bernbach; and Needham Harper Worldwide—merged in what was called the "Big Bang" and formed Omnicom Group, Inc. Shortly thereafter, London-based Saatchi & Saatchi PLC acquired the Ted Bates agency, along with other agencies and firms in related communication fields, including the major market research firms of Yankelovich, Skelly and White and Clancey Shulman, to form the world's largest advertising organization. Saatchi & Saatchi Co.'s reign at the top did not last long. In 1990, another London-based organization, WPP Group, acquired Ogilvy & Mather Worldwide in a hostile takeover and added it to its group, which also included another large New York agency, J. Walter Thompson, which WPP acquired in 1987. (The world's top 25 advertising organizations are shown in Exhibit 3–10.)

Several reasons underlie the megamergers that have hit Madison Avenue. First, the advertising business became somewhat stagnant in the late 1980s with the cutbacks in media spending that resulted from the recession, prompting agencies to turn to mergers and acquisitions to seek growth. A second factor is the increased merger and acquisition activity among name-brand consumer product companies. The resulting megacompanies with strong, established brands and huge advertising and promotion budgets have the marketing power to dominate and expand their presence in the various markets they serve. These companies generally seek agencies with top creative and marketing talent, which is often found in the largest and most sophisticated agencies.

Also, the new superagencies consist of ad agencies as well as other communication organizations such as public relations, market research, sales promotion, and direct-marketing companies. Thus, they can offer clients the ability to design and implement integrated marketing communications programs through one organization. Finally, the superagencies argue that they can offer greater global marketing capabilities and synergies to their clients. This means they can better serve the megacorporations competing in the new global marketplace by helping them plan and implement worldwide promotional plans and programs.

The creation of the new superagencies has received mixed reactions as not everyone believes big companies need big ad agencies. Many small to midsized agencies have seized this opportunity to pursue larger accounts by offering them special attention and service that might not be available from the new superagencies. The agency mergers and acquisitions have also created problems with client conflicts as many companies have refused to remain with an agency that handles a competitor anywhere in the holding company.

The consolidation of many agencies and other support companies into one organization has also created personnel and other management problems. The superagencies are facing challenges such as how to foster creativity and maintain close agency/client relationships in their large organizational structures. Some, such as WPP Group and Saatchi & Saatchi, are also dealing with financial problems resulting from the large debt they incurred for their acquisitions. Others such as Omnicom Group have merged or sold many of their unprofitable or overlapping agencies.

It is probably too soon to tell if the creation of the superagency groups will make it possible for these agencies to effectively deliver integrated marketing communication services to their clients on a worldwide basis. The fate of the superagencies will probably depend on how well they are managed *and* how well they serve the needs of their clients.

Source: "Advertising's 'Big Bang' Is Making Noise At Last," *Business Week*, April 1, 1991, pp. 62–63; R. Craig Endicott, "WPP Biggest Ad Group; Burnett Top U.S. 'Brand'," *Advertising Age*, March 25, 1991, pp. S1,4; and "The Age of Consolidation," *Business Week*, October 14, 1991, pp. 86–93.

the agency can provide the client with experience and insight into the industry (and in some cases, the competition).

Exhibit 3–11 shows a poster used as a promotional piece for Phillips-Ramsey to demonstrate the variety of accounts the agency has served. As you can see, many of the clients may benefit from experiences of other products and services the agency has worked with.

➤ *Exhibit 3–11* **Phillips-Ramsey demonstrates the variety of clients it serves**

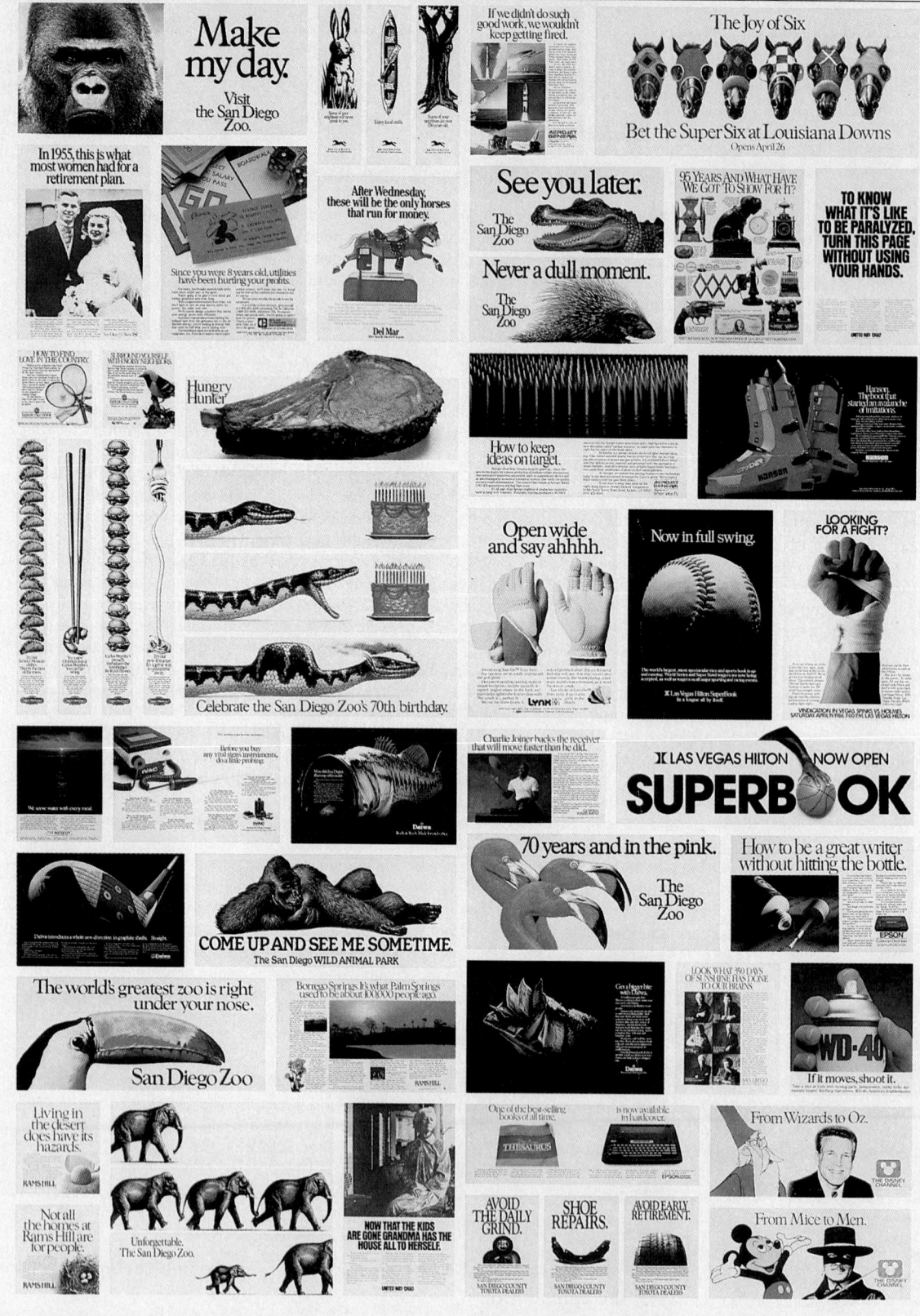

85% of all advertising never gets noticed. You're looking at the other 15%. Phillips-Ramsey. Call our President Dick Brooks at (619) 574-0808.

➤ *Exhibit 3–12* **Full-service agency organizational chart**

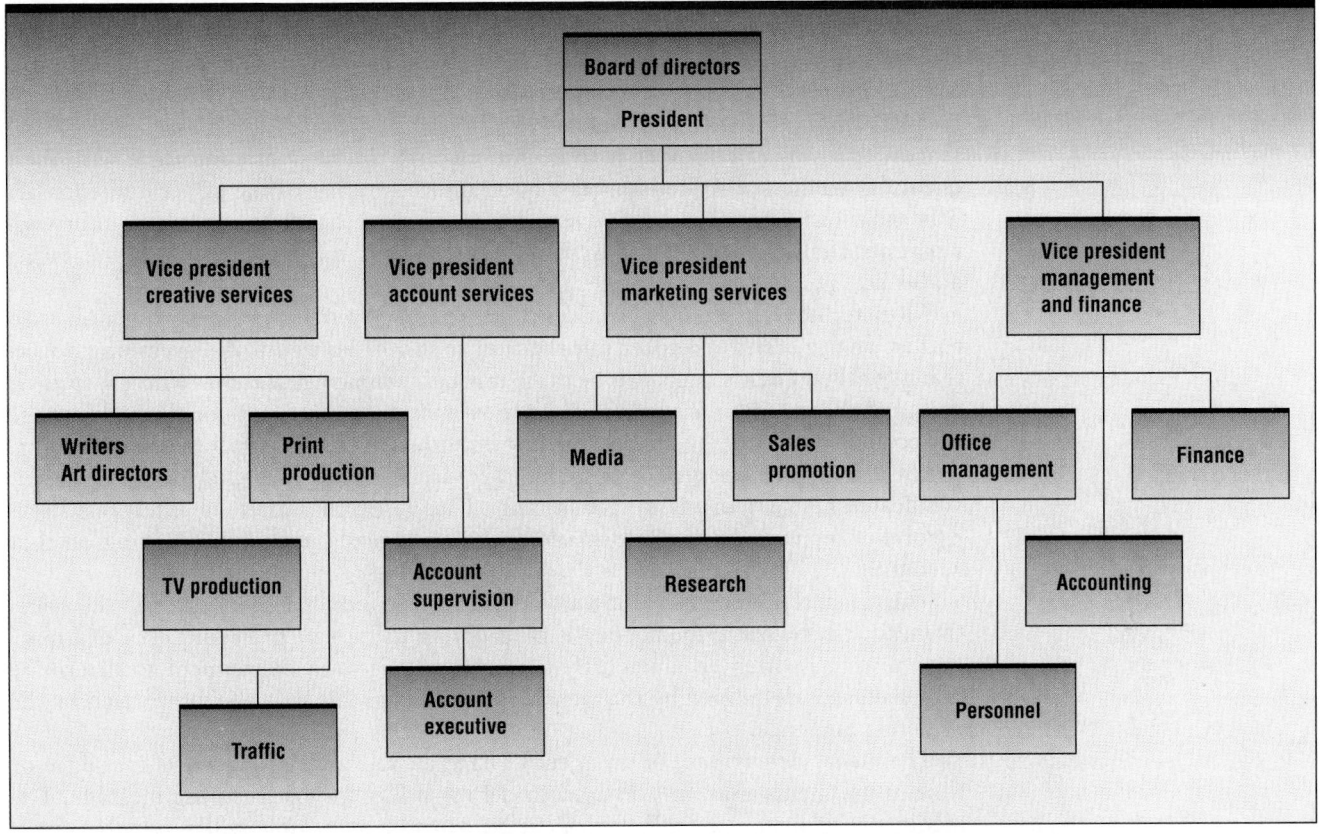

Types of Advertising Agencies

As you learned earlier, advertising agencies can range in size from a one- or two-person operation to large organizations with over 1,000 employees. Given this variation in size, the services offered and functions performed by an agency will vary. In this section, we examine the different types of agencies, the services they perform for their clients, and how they are organized.

Full-service agencies

Many companies employ what is known as a **full-service agency.** A full-service agency offers its clients a full range of marketing, communications, and promotions services, including planning, creating, and producing the advertising, performing research, and selecting media. A full-service agency may also offer nonadvertising services such as strategic market planning; production of sales promotions, sales training, and trade show materials; package design; and public relations and publicity.

The full-service agency is made up of departments that provide the activities needed to perform the various advertising functions and serve the client, as shown in Exhibit 3–12 and discussed below.

Account services   Account services, or account management, is the link between the advertising agency and its clients. Depending on the size of the client and its advertising budget, one or more account executives serve as a liaison between the two entities. The **account executive** is responsible for understanding the advertiser's marketing and promotions needs and interpreting them to agency personnel. He or she is responsible for working with the agency and coordinating efforts in planning, creating, and producing ads. The account executive must also present and obtain client approval for agency recommendations.

As the focal point of agency-client relationships, the account executive must know a great deal about the client's business and be able to communicate this to specialists in the agency working on the account. The ideal account executive has a strong marketing background as well as a thorough understanding of all the phases of the advertising process.

Marketing services Over the past two decades, use of marketing services has increased dramatically. One of the services gaining increased attention is that of research, as agencies realize that to do an effective job of communicating with their clients' customers, they must have a good understanding of the target audience. As was shown in Chapter 1, the advertising planning process begins with a thorough situation analysis, which is based on research and information about the target audience.

Most full-service agencies maintain a *research department* whose function is to gather, analyze, and interpret information that will be useful in developing advertising for their clients. This can be done through primary research—where a study is designed, executed, and interpreted by the research department—or through the use of secondary or existing sources of information previously published. In some situations, the research department may acquire studies conducted by independent syndicated research firms or consultants. The research staff then interprets these reports and passes on the information to other agency personnel working on that account.

The research department may also design and conduct research to test the effectiveness of advertising the agency is considering using—or pretesting. For example, copy testing is often conducted by the agency's research department to determine how messages developed by the creative specialists are likely to be interpreted by the receiving audience.

The *media department* of an agency analyzes, selects, and contracts for space or time in the media that will be used to deliver the client's advertising message. The media department is expected to develop a media plan that will reach the target market and effectively communicate the message. Since most of the client's ad budget is spent on media time and/or space, this department must develop a plan that both communicates with the right audience and is cost-effective.

Media specialists must be knowledgeable of all the alternative media including the audience they reach, their rates, and how well they match the client's target market. Media departments must review information on demographics, magazine and newspaper readership, radio listenership, and television viewing patterns of consumers to be able to develop an effective media plan. The media buyer assumes responsibility for implementing the media plan by purchasing the actual time and space.

Interestingly, the members of the media department also constitute a target market themselves. As you can see by the ad in Exhibit 3–13, these individuals are the target of advertising as well as sales promotions and personal selling efforts by representatives of various media who seek advertisements for their vehicles.

The departments discussed above perform most of the functions that full-service agencies need to plan and execute their client's advertising programs. Some agencies also offer additional marketing services to their clients to assist in other promotional areas. For example, an agency may have a *sales promotion department,* or merchandising department, that specializes in developing contests, premiums, promotions, point-of-sale materials, and other sales materials. Agencies may also have direct-marketing specialists and package designers available, and a number of firms may have public relations/ publicity departments as well. Generally, these services are not included as part of the regular advertising process and are available to clients on a separate-fee basis. However, the development of superagencies has led to an increase in *integrated marketing,* and many of these services are now being offered under the agency's umbrella.[7]

Creative services The creative services department is responsible for the creation and execution of the advertisements. The individuals who conceive the ideas for the ads and write the headlines, subheads, and body copy (the words constituting the

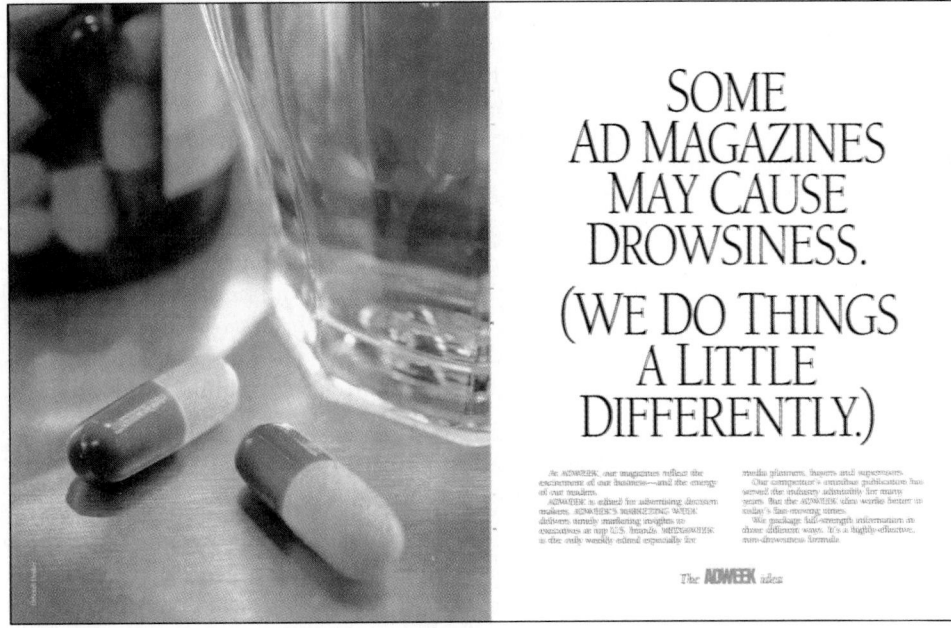

message of the ad) are known as **copywriters.** Copywriters may also be involved in determining the basic appeal or theme of the ad campaign and often prepare a rough initial visual layout of the print ad or television commercial.

While copywriters are responsible for what the communication message says, the *art department* consists of art directors who are responsible for how the advertisement will look. For print ads, the art director and graphics designers prepare *layouts,* which are drawings that show what the ad will look like and from which the final artwork will be produced. In the case of television commercials, the layout is known as a *storyboard,* or a sequence of frames or panels that depict the commercial in still form.

Members of the creative department work together to develop advertisements that will communicate the key points determined to be the basis of the creative strategy for the client's product or service. Writers and artists generally work under the direction of the agency's creative director, who oversees all the advertising produced by the organization. The director sets the creative philosophy of the department and may even become directly involved in the creation of ads for the agency's largest clients.

Once the copy, layout, illustrations, and mechanical specifications of the advertisement have been completed and approved, the ad is turned over to the *production department.* Most agencies do not actually produce finished ads but rather maintain relationships with printers, engravers, photographers, typographers, and other suppliers whose services are needed to complete the finished product. For broadcast production, the approved storyboard must be turned into a finished commercial. The production department's role may be to supervise the selection of people to appear in the ad and the setting for the scenes as well as to choose an independent production studio. The department may hire an outside director to turn the creative idea or concept into a commercial. For example, the famous "1984" ad for Apple Computer discussed in Chapter 1 was directed by Ridley Scott, the director of many movies including the science-fiction film *Aliens.* Nike has used film director Spike Lee to direct a number of its commercials. Copywriters, art directors, account managers, people from research and planning, and representatives from the client side may all participate in production decisions, particularly when large sums of money are involved.

Creating an advertisement often involves many people and may take several months. In large agencies with many clients, coordinating the creative and production processes can be a major problem. To ensure that the development of the advertising progresses properly, a *traffic department* is used in agencies to coordinate all phases of production, to see that the ads are completed on time and that all deadlines for submitting the ads to the media are met. The traffic department may be located in the creative services area of the agency, as part of media or account management, or it may be separate.

Management and finance   Like any other business, an advertising agency must be managed and perform basic operating and administrative functions such as accounting, finance, and personnel management as well as attempt to generate new business. A large agency will employ administrative, managerial, and clerical people to perform these functions. The bulk of an agency's income (approximately 64 percent) goes to salary and benefits for its employees. Thus, an agency must manage its personnel carefully and get maximum productivity from them.

Agency organization and structure

Full-function advertising agencies must develop an organizational structure that will meet the needs of their clients as well as serve the agency's own internal requirements. Most medium- and large-sized agencies are structured under either a departmental or group system. Under the **departmental system,** each of the agency functions shown in Exhibit 3–12 is set up as a separate department and is called on as needed to perform its specialty and serve all of the agency's clients. Thus, the ad layout, writing, and production is done by the creative department, while marketing services is responsible for any research or media selection and purchases, and the account services department handles the client contact. Some agencies prefer the departmental system because it gives employees the opportunity to become involved with, and develop expertise in servicing, a variety of accounts.

Many large agencies use the **group system,** in which individuals from each department work together in groups to service particular accounts. Each group is headed by an account executive or supervisor and has one or more media people, including media planners and buyers; a creative team, which includes copywriters, art directors, artists, and production personnel; and one or more account executives. The group may also include individuals from other departments such as marketing research, direct marketing, or sales promotion. The size and composition of the group varies depending on the client's billings and the importance of the account to the agency. For very important accounts, the group members may be assigned exclusively to one client. But in some agencies, they may serve a number of smaller clients. Many agencies prefer structuring under a group system because this makes individuals very knowledgeable in the client's business and ensures continuity in servicing the account.

Other types of agencies and services

Not every agency is a full-service agency, nor is every one a large organization. Many smaller agencies expect their employees to handle a variety of jobs. For example, account executives may do their own research, work out their own media schedule, and coordinate the production of advertisements written and designed by the creative department.

Many advertisers, including some large companies, are not always interested in paying for the services of a full-service agency but may be interested in some of the specific services agencies have to offer. Over the past few decades, several alternatives to full-service agencies have evolved, including the following.

Creative boutiques

A **creative boutique** is an agency that specializes in and provides only creative services. These specialists have developed in response to some clients' desires to utilize only the creative talent of an outside provider while maintaining the other functions internally. The client may seek outside creative talent because it believes an extra creative effort is required or those internal to the organization do not have sufficient skills in this regard.

Creative boutiques are usually founded by members of the creative department of full-service agencies who have left the firm and taken with them clients primarily interested in maintaining their creative talents. These boutiques usually perform the creative function under a fee basis.

Media buying services

Another type of specialized service was developed in the 1960s to provide assistance for smaller agencies and creative boutiques. **Media buying services** are independent companies that specialize in the buying of media, particularly radio and television time. As the task of purchasing advertising media has grown more complex—owing to the proliferation of specialized media—media buying services have found a niche by specializing in the analysis and purchase of advertising time and space. Both agencies and clients utilize their services, usually developing their own media strategies and using the buying service to execute them. Because media buying services purchase such large amounts of time and space, they receive large discounts and can save the small agency or client money on media purchases. Media buying services are paid a fee or commission for their work.

Agency Compensation

As you have seen in the previous sections, the type and amount of services an agency performs can vary from one client to another. As a result, agencies use a variety of methods to receive compensation for their services. Agencies are typically compensated in three ways: through commissions, through percentage charges or markups, and through fees.

Commissions from Media

The traditional method of compensating agencies has been through a **commission system.** In this system, the agency receives a specified percent (usually 15) commission from the media on any advertising time or space it purchases for its client (outdoor advertising provides a 16⅔ percent commission). This system provides a very simple method of determining payments, as shown in the following example.

Assume an agency prepares a full-page magazine ad and arranges to place the ad on the back cover of a magazine at a cost of $100,000. The agency will place the order for the space and deliver the ad to the magazine. Once the ad is run, the magazine will bill the agency for $100,000 less the 15 percent ($15,000) commission. The media will also offer a 2 percent cash discount for early payment, which the agency may also pass along to the client. The agency will bill the client $100,000 less the 2 percent cash discount on the net amount, or a total of $98,300, as shown in Exhibit 3–14. The $15,000 commission represents the agency's compensation for its services.

Appraisal of the commission system

Use of the commission system to compensate agencies has been the target of considerable controversy for many years. A major problem centers around whether the

> *Exhibit 3–14*
Example of commission system payment

Media Bills Agency		Agency Bills Advertiser	
Costs for magazine space	$100,000	Costs for magazine space	$100,000
Less 15% commission	−15,000	Less 2% cash discount	−1,700
Cost of media space	85,000	Advertiser pays agency	98,300
Less 2% cash discount	−1,700		
Agency pays media	83,300	Agency income	15,000

15 percent commission represents equitable compensation for services performed. For example, two agencies may require the same amount of effort to create and produce an ad. However, one client may spend $200,000 in commissionable media, which results in $30,000 in agency income, whereas the other may spend $2 million, thus generating $300,000 in commissions. Critics argue that the commission system can encourage agencies to recommend high media expenditures so as to increase their commission level.

Another criticism of the commission system is that it ties agency compensation to media costs. In periods of media cost inflation, the agency is (according to the client) disproportionately rewarded. For example, in the latter half of the 1980s, media costs increased over 5.7 percent, whereas the overall inflation level of the U.S. economy averaged only 2 to 4 percent.[8] On the other hand, when media costs decrease—as they did throughout most of 1991—the agency receives less.

The commission system has also been criticized for encouraging agencies to ignore cost accounting systems to justify the expenses attributable to work on a particular account. Still others charge that this system tempts the agency to avoid noncommissionable media such as direct-mail, sales promotions, or advertising specialties, unless they are requested by the client.

Defenders of the commission system argue that it should be retained because it is simple and easy to administer and because it keeps the emphasis in agency competition on nonprice factors such as the quality of the advertising developed. Proponents argue that agency services are proportional to the size of the commission, as more time and effort are devoted to the large accounts that generate the high revenue for the agency. It has also been argued that the system is more flexible than it appears because agencies can often perform other services for large clients at no extra charge, justifying such actions through the large commission to be received.

Overall, the commission system has become a heated topic among advertisers. Opponents of the system have been designated as "traitors" and "public enemy number one" by their colleagues, who argue that their lack of support costs everyone in the agency business money and that their opposition is nothing more than a competitive strategy designed to gain accounts.[9] Those in support of an alternative system contend that the old system is outdated. The American Association of Advertising Agencies (AAAA) estimates that 40 percent of advertising agencies' income now comes from the fixed commission, with the balance coming from a mix of fees and other variable charges.[10]

As you can see in Exhibit 3–15, some clients have gone to a **negotiated commission.** This commission structure can take the form of reduced percentage rates, variable commission rates, and commissions with minimum and maximum profit rates. Negotiated commissions are designed to consider the needs of the client as well as the amount of time and effort exerted by the agency, thereby avoiding some of the problems inherent in the traditional system.

For example, in the Quaker plan listed in Exhibit 3–15, the company guarantees the agency will receive a commission based on 90 percent of the original budget.

➤ *Exhibit 3–15*
Clients who have negotiated commissions

Company	1990 Billings (in millions)	Agency Compensation
Kraft/General Foods	$ 500	• 13–14% based on goal attainment
Quaker Oats Co.	329.3	• Guarantee based on 90% of budget; sliding scale
Campbell Soup Co.	175.3	• Sliding scale bonus based on performance
Carnation Co.	—	• Sliding scale bonus based on performance
Sears, Roebuck & Co.	1,502.8	• Sliding scale bonus based on performance
Nissan	410.2	• Negotiated fee based on costs

Additional commissions will be achieved on a sliding scale in which the agency will get 15 percent for the first $10 million of the account's billings, 13 percent for each dollar between $10 million and $20 million, and 10 percent on all dollar amounts over $20 million.

Percentage Charges

Another way an agency is compensated is by adding a markup of **percentage charges** to various services the agency purchases from outside providers. These may include market research, artwork, printing, photography, and other services or materials. *Markup charges* usually range from 17.65 to 20 percent and are added to the client's overall bill. The logic of markups stems from the fact that the suppliers of these services do not allow the agency a commission, and the percentage charges cover administrative costs while allowing for a reasonable profit for the agency's efforts. (A markup of 17.65 percent of the costs added to the cost would yield a 15 percent commission. For example, research costs of $100,000 + 17,650 (17.65%) = $117,650. $17,650 as a percentage of $117,650 yields approximately 15 percent.)

Fee- and Cost-Based Systems

As previously noted, many believe the standard 15 percent commission system is not equitable to all parties. As a result, many agencies and their clients have developed fixed-fee arrangements or cost-plus agreements.

Fixed-fee arrangement Under this arrangement, the agency and client agree on the specific work to be done and the amount of money the agency will be paid for its services. The arrangement requires the agency to make a careful assessment of its costs of serving the client for the specified period, or for the project, plus determining a desired profit margin. **Fixed-fee agreements** should specify exactly what services the agency is expected to perform for the client to avoid any later disagreement.

Cost-plus agreement Under a **cost-plus system,** the client agrees to pay the agency a fee based on the costs of its work plus some agreed-on profit margin (which is often a percentage of total costs). This system requires the agency to keep detailed records of the costs it incurs in working on the client's account. Direct costs (personnel time and out-of-pocket expenses) plus an allocation for overhead and a markup for profits determine the amount the agency bills the client.

In some situations, agencies are compensated through a fee-commission combination in which the media commissions received by the agency are credited against the fee. If the commissions received by the agency are less than the agreed-on fee, the client must make up the difference to the agency. If the agency does much work for the client in noncommissionable media, the fee may be charged over and above the commissions received.

Fee agreements and cost-plus systems are commonly used in conjunction with a commission system arrangement. The fee-based system can be advantageous to both the client and the agency, depending on the size of the client, advertising budget, media used, and services required. Many clients prefer fee or cost-plus systems because they are provided with a detailed breakdown of where and how their advertising and promotions dollars are being spent. However, these arrangements can be difficult for the agency, as they require careful cost accounting and may also be difficult to estimate when bidding for an advertiser's business. Agencies are also reluctant to have clients involved in their internal cost figures.

As you can see from the preceding discussion of how agencies are compensated, there is no fixed method to which everyone subscribes. Usually, an agreement will be established in which a combination of methods of payment is used—a trend that will likely be even more common in the future.

➤ *Exhibit 3–16*   **Borden's ad agency report card**

	SECTION	PAGE		
	12.00.0	15 of 22		
	DATE ISSUED	DATE REVISED		
	4/85			

Agency: _____
Product(s): _____

ACCOUNT REPRESENTATION AND SERVICE

	Excellent	Good	Average	Fair	Poor	Not Observed (Unknown)
1. Account Executives have *frequent personal contact* with product group.	( )	( )	( )	( )	( )	( )
2. Account persons act with *personal initiative.*	( )	( )	( )	( )	( )	( )
3. Account representatives *anticipate needs* in advance of direction by product group.	( )	( )	( )	( )	( )	( )
4. Account group *takes direction* well.	( )	( )	( )	( )	( )	( )
5. Agency readily *adapts to changes* in client's organization or needs.	( )	( )	( )	( )	( )	( )
6. Agency makes reasonable *recommendations* on allocation of budgets.	( )	( )	( )	( )	( )	( )
7. Account representatives function as *marketing advisors* rather than creative/media advisors only.	( )	( )	( )	( )	( )	( )
8. Account representatives *contribute effectively* to the development of new programs.	( )	( )	( )	( )	( )	( )
9. Account representatives respond to *client requests* in a timely fashion.	( )	( )	( )	( )	( )	( )
10. Agency recommendations are *founded on sound reasoning* and supported factually.	( )	( )	( )	( )	( )	( )
11. Account persons submit *alternative plans*, vs. a single plan/campaign/ad for brand review.	( )	( )	( )	( )	( )	( )
12. Account persons have a *firm point of view* and "sell" their recommendation.	( )	( )	( )	( )	( )	( )
13. Senior account management *is involved*, where appropriate.	( )	( )	( )	( )	( )	( )
14. Other areas not mentioned: _____ _____ _____	( ) ( ) ( )	( ) ( ) ( )	( ) ( ) ( )	( ) ( ) ( )	( ) ( ) ( )	( ) ( ) ( )

	Excellent	Good	Average	Fair	Poor
Overall evaluation of Account Representation and Service	( )	( )	( )	( )	( )

General Comments on Account Representation and Service: _____

	SECTION	PAGE		
	12.00.0	16 of 22		
	DATE ISSUED	DATE REVISED		
	4/85			

Agency: _____
Product(s): _____

CREATIVE SERVICES

	Excellent	Good	Average	Fair	Poor	Not Observed (Unknown)
1. Agency produces *fresh ideas* and original approaches.	( )	( )	( )	( )	( )	( )
2. Agency *accurately interprets* facts, strategies and objectives into usable advertisements and plans.	( )	( )	( )	( )	( )	( )
3. Creative group is *knowledgeable* about Consumer Products Division's products, markets and strategies.	( )	( )	( )	( )	( )	( )
4. Creative personnel are concerned with *good advertising communications* and develops campaigns/ads that exhibit this concern.	( )	( )	( )	( )	( )	( )
5. Creative group *produces on time.*	( )	( )	( )	( )	( )	( )
6. Creative team *performs well* under pressure.	( )	( )	( )	( )	( )	( )
7. Agency presentations are well organized with sufficient *examples of proposed executions.*	( )	( )	( )	( )	( )	( )
8. Creative team *participates* in major campaign presentations.	( )	( )	( )	( )	( )	( )
9. Agency presents *ideas and executions* not requested but felt to be good *opportunities.*	( )	( )	( )	( )	( )	( )
10. Overall *quality of agency's television* creative ideas and executions.	( )	( )	( )	( )	( )	( )
11. Overall *quality of agency's radio* creative ideas and executions.	( )	( )	( )	( )	( )	( )
12. Overall *quality of agency's print* creative ideas and executions.	( )	( )	( )	( )	( )	( )
13. Other ares not mentioned: _____ _____ _____	( ) ( ) ( )	( ) ( ) ( )	( ) ( ) ( )	( ) ( ) ( )	( ) ( ) ( )	( ) ( ) ( )

	Excellent	Good	Average	Fair	Poor
Overall evaluation of Creative Services:	( )	( )	( )	( )	( )

General Comments on Creative Services: _____

Evaluating Agencies

Given the substantial amounts of monies being spent on advertising and promotion, demand for accountability of the expenditures has increased. This accountability must extend to the agency as well as the client, and regular reviews of the agency's performance are necessary.

The **agency evaluation process** usually involves two types of assessments, one of which is financial and operational and the other is more qualitative. The **financial audit** focuses on how the agency conducts its business. It is designed to verify costs and expenses, the number of personnel hours charged to an account, and analyses of payments to media and outside suppliers. The **qualitative audit** focuses on the agency's efforts in planning, developing, and implementing the client's advertising and promotions programs and considers the results achieved by the same.

In many situations, the agency evaluation is done on a subjective, informal basis, particularly in smaller companies where advertising budgets are low or advertising is not seen as the most critical factor in the firm's marketing performance. In some companies, formal systematic evaluation systems have been developed—particularly when budgets are large and the advertising function receives much emphasis. As advertising costs continue to rise, the top management of these companies wants to be sure money is being spent efficiently and effectively.

One example of a formal agency evaluation system is that used by Borden, Inc., a marketer of a variety of consumer products.[11] Borden's top executives meet twice a year with the company's various agencies to review their performances. Division presidents and other marketing executives complete the "Advertising Agency Per-

➤ *Exhibit 3–16* **(concluded)**

PRODUCTION SERVICES

SECTION 12.00.0 PAGE 17 of 22
DATE ISSUED 4/85 DATE REVISED

Agency: _____
Product(s): _____

	Excellent	Good	Average	Fair	Poor	Not Observed (Unknown)
1. Account group, creative group and production team operate in a business-like manner to *control production costs* and other creative costs charges/services.	( )	( )	( )	( )	( )	( )
2. Agency obtains *three (3) bids on work* performed by outside suppliers/vendors.	( )	( )	( )	( )	( )	( )
3. Production personnel accurately *integrate creative plans and ideas* into usable finished advertising units.	( )	( )	( )	( )	( )	( )
4. Agency production group controls *mechanical production* (photographs, photostats, typesetting/proofs, engraving, electro-types, mats, printing and similar items) in a cost efficient manner.	( )	( )	( )	( )	( )	( )
5. Production group provides *cost efficient talent, testimonial and residual services* for television, radio and print commercial units.	( )	( )	( )	( )	( )	( )
6. *Jingles, musical arrangements and production,* recordings, etc. are completed in a cost efficient manner.	( )	( )	( )	( )	( )	( )
7. Other areas not mentioned: _____ _____ _____	( ) ( ) ( )	( ) ( ) ( )	( ) ( ) ( )	( ) ( ) ( )	( ) ( ) ( )	( ) ( ) ( )

	Excellent	Good	Average	Fair	Poor
Overall rating of production services	( )	( )	( )	( )	( )
Overall evaluation of agency's production cost controls (i.e. are advertising creative units being produced within generally accepted national cost ranges?)	( )	( )	( )	( )	( )

General comments on production services/costs: _____

MEDIA SERVICES

Agency: _____
Product(s): _____

SECTION 12.00.0 PAGE 18 of 22
DATE ISSUED 4/85 DATE REVISED

	PRODUCT GROUP EVALUATION						ADVERTISING SERVICES EVALUATION					
	Excellent	Good	Average	Fair	Poor	Not Observed (Unknown)	Excellent	Good	Average	Fair	Poor	Not Observed (Unknown)
1. Media group activity explores creative uses of the various media available.	( )	( )	( )	( )	( )	( )	( )	( )	( )	( )	( )	( )
2. Senior media personnel are appropriately involved in media planning/execution.	( )	( )	( )	( )	( )	( )	( )	( )	( )	( )	( )	( )
3. Agency media group presents alternative plans to the recommended plan.	( )	( )	( )	( )	( )	( )	( )	( )	( )	( )	( )	( )
4. Agency media recommendations reflect sufficient knowledge of Consumer Products Division's markets, audiences, products and objectives.	( )	( )	( )	( )	( )	( )	( )	( )	( )	( )	( )	( )
5. Agency keeps client up to date on trends and developments in the field of media.	( )	( )	( )	( )	( )	( )	( )	( )	( )	( )	( )	( )
6. Agency subscribes to and makes use of available and applicable *syndicated marketing and media services.*	( )	( )	( )	( )	( )	( )	( )	( )	( )	( )	( )	( )
7. Agency utilizes *marketing and media research* in relating to the selection and use of media.	( )	( )	( )	( )	( )	( )	( )	( )	( )	( )	( )	( )
8. Agency provides client with a regular review and analysis of *competition's media usage/spending.*	( )	( )	( )	( )	( )	( )	( )	( )	( )	( )	( )	( )
9. Agency media administrative practices are adequate, including coordination of media schedules, contracts, checking media to verify advertising has run, etc.	( )	( )	( )	( )	( )	( )	( )	( )	( )	( )	( )	( )
10. Agency is effective in media negotiations for *best possible position* for brand advertising.	( )	( )	( )	( )	( )	( )	( )	( )	( )	( )	( )	( )
11. Agency has proven to be an *"efficient bargainer"* in cases where negotiated purchases of media are possible.	( )	( )	( )	( )	( )	( )	( )	( )	( )	( )	( )	( )
12. Other areas not mentioned: _____ _____	( ) ( )	( ) ( )	( ) ( )	( ) ( )	( ) ( )	( ) ( )	( ) ( )	( ) ( )	( ) ( )	( ) ( )	( ) ( )	( ) ( )

	Excellent	Good	Average	Fair	Poor		Excellent	Good	Average	Fair	Poor
Overall evaluation of Media Services.	( )	( )	( )	( )	( )		( )	( )	( )	( )	( )

General Comments on Media Services: _____

---

formance Evaluation" report, part of which is shown in Exhibit 3–16. These reports are compiled and reviewed with the agency at each semiannual meeting. Borden's evaluation process consists of three areas of performance—share of market performance, creativity, and cooperation. Each area is weighted differently, with agency performance in achieving market share goals accounting for 60 percent of the total score and creativity and cooperation each constituting 20 percent.

While many question the assumption that the sales effectiveness of advertising can be quantified, Borden believes agencies are warned that the evaluation will be tied to market performance. The company has dropped agencies that have not scored well after two semiannual evaluations.

Others more critical of the attempt to relate advertising effectiveness directly to sales have developed their own evaluation procedures. For example, R. J. Reynolds emphasizes creative development and execution, marketing counsel and ideas, promotion support, and cost controls, without any mention of sales figures. Sears' approach focuses on the performance of the agency as a whole, arguing that a "partnership" between the agency and the client is established with this method.

These evaluation forms, as well as others employed by a variety of clients, are being adopted more regularly in the advertising community. As fiscal controls tighten, clients will increase the accountability requirements placed on their providers.

Gaining and Losing Clients

The evaluation process often results in outcomes that are not favorable to the agency. As you can see in Exhibit 3–17, switching agencies is not uncommon. A number of

➤ *Exhibit 3–17* **A rash of advertisers switch agencies**

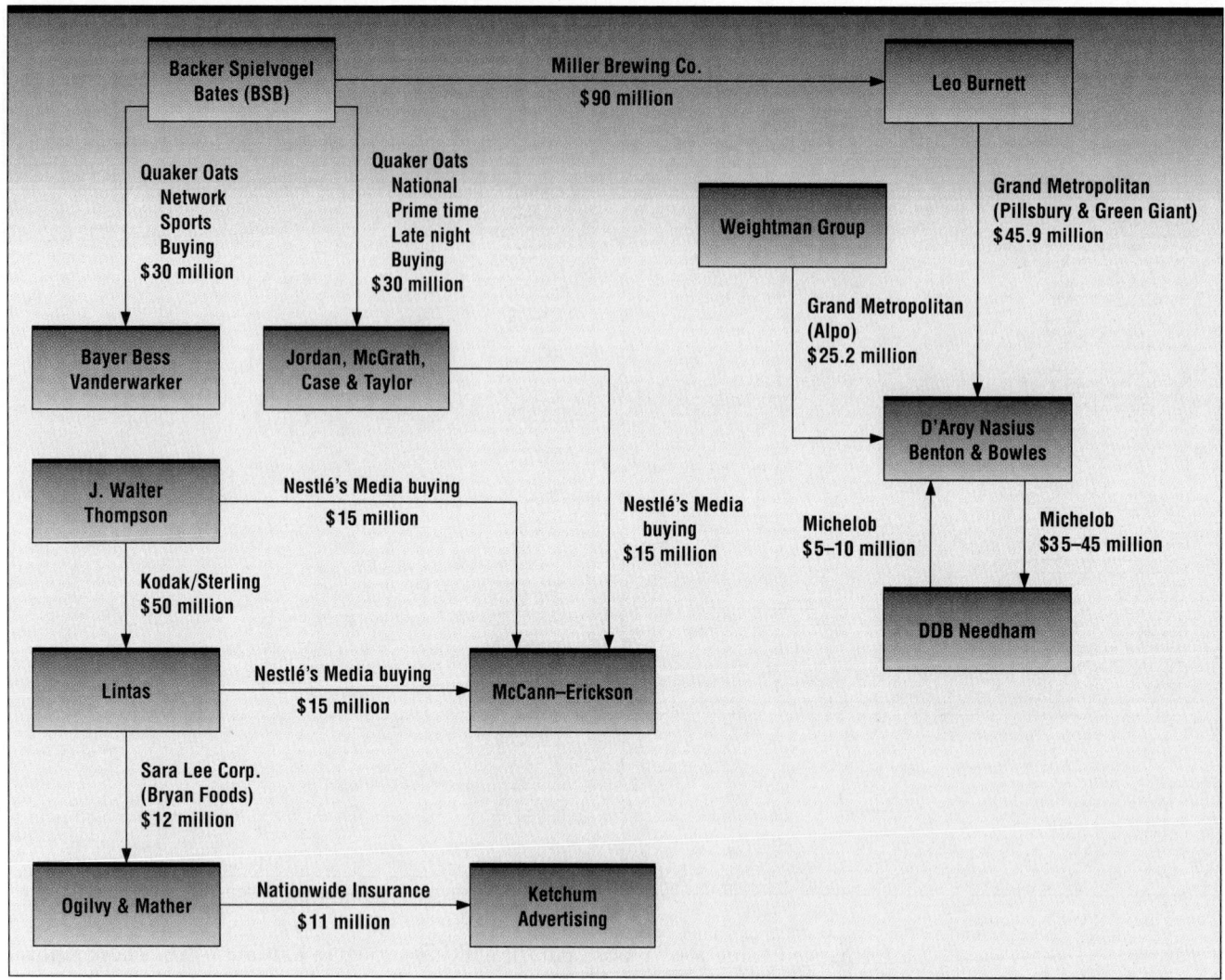

reasons can be cited as causes for switching agencies. Understanding these potential problems decreases the likelihood they will occur.[12] In addition, it is important to understand the process agencies go through in trying to gain new clients. Let us first examine some of the most commonly cited reasons for losing clients.

Why agencies lose clients

Some of the more well-known and cited reasons as to why agencies lose clients are:

- **Poor performance or service by the agency.** The client becomes dissatisfied with the quality of the advertising provided by the agency and/or the service provided.
- **Poor communication.** The client and agency personnel fail to develop or maintain a proper level of communication necessary to sustain a favorable working relationship.
- **Unrealistic demands by the client.** The client places demands on the agency that exceed the amount of compensation received and reduces the profitability of the account.
- **Personality conflicts.** Personnel working on the account on either the client or agency side do not have rapport or do not work well together.

TUMBLEWEEDS by **TOM K. RYAN**

- **Personnel changes.** A change in personnel either at the agency or with the advertiser can create problems. New managers may wish to use an agency they have previously used or with whom they have established previous ties. Agency personnel often take accounts with them when they switch agencies or start their own.
- **Changes in size of the client or agency.** The client may outgrow the agency or decide it needs a larger agency to handle its business. If the agency gets too large, the client may represent too small a percentage of the agency's business to command attention.
- **Conflicts of interest.** A conflict may develop when an agency merges with another agency or when an acquisition or merger occurs between two clients. In the United States, an agency cannot handle two accounts that are in direct competition with each other. In some cases, even indirect competition will not be tolerated. For example, Lintas lost its $60 million Noxell assignment when P&G bought Noxell, because of Lintas' extensive work for P&G arch-rival Haileve.[13]
- **Changes in the client's marketing strategy.** A client may decide to switch agencies when a change in marketing strategy occurs and the advertiser thinks a new agency is needed to carry out the firm's marketing program.
- **Declining sales.** When sales of the client's product or service are stagnant or declining, advertising may be seen as contributing to the problem, and a new agency may be sought to seek a new approach.
- **Conflicting compensation philosophies.** When conflicting compensation philosophies emerge, disagreement develops over the level or method of compensation.
- **Changes in policies.** Changes in policies on either the agency or client side are often seen as reasons for change. Such policy changes may result from reevaluating the importance of the relationship, acquisition of a new (and larger) client by the agency, and/or mergers and acquisitions by either side.

If the agency recognizes these warning signals, it will be more able to adapt its programs and policies to ensure the client is satisfied. Some of the situations discussed here are unavoidable, and others may be beyond the control of the agency. Those within the agency's control must be addressed to ensure maintenance of the account.

The time may come when the agency decides it is no longer in its best interest to continue to work with the client. Personnel conflicts, changes in management philosophy, and/or insufficient financial incentives are just a few of the reasons for such a decision. Then the agency may terminate the account relationship.

How agencies gain clients

Competition for accounts in the agency business is intense, as most companies already have organized for the advertising function, and only a limited number of new businesses require such services each year. While small agencies may be willing to work with a new company and grow along with it, larger agencies often do not become interested in these firms until they are able to spend a minimum of $1 million per year on advertising. Many of the top 15 agencies wouldn't accept an account that spends less than $5 million per year. Once that expenditure level is reached, the competition for the account intensifies.

In large agencies, most new business results from clients that already have an agency but have decided to change their relationships. Thus, agencies must constantly search and compete for new clients. Some of the ways in which this is done are discussed below.

Referrals   Many good agencies obtain new clients as a result of referrals from existing clients, media representatives, and even other agencies. These agencies must maintain good working relationships with their clients, the media, and outside parties that might provide potential business to them.

Solicitations   One of the more common ways of gaining new business is through direct solicitation. In smaller agencies, the president may solicit new accounts. In most large agencies, a new business development group will search for and establish contact with new clients. The group is responsible for writing solicitation letters, conducting "cold calling," and following up on leads.

Presentations   One of the basic goals of the new business development group is to receive an invitation from a company to make a presentation. In this presentation, the agency has the opportunity to present information about itself, including its experience, personnel, capabilities, and operating procedures, as well as to demonstrate its previous work.

In many situations, the agency might be asked to make a speculative presentation, in which it is asked to examine the client's marketing situation and then propose a tentative communications campaign. Because speculative presentations may require a great deal of time and preparation and may cost the agency money without a guarantee of gaining the business, many firms refuse to participate in what they consider to be "creative shootouts." They argue that agencies should be selected based on their experience and the services and programs they have provided for previous clients.[14] Nevertheless, most agencies do participate in this form of solicitation, either by choice or because they are required to do so to gain accounts. An example of what may be involved in a speculative presentation is discussed in Promotional Perspective 3–2 (page 104).

Due in part to the emphasis placed on speculative presentations, a new and very important role has developed for the presentation consultant. These consultants specialize in helping clients choose advertising agencies. Because their opinions are respected by clients, the entire agency review process may be structured according to their guidelines. As you might imagine, these consultants yield a great deal of power and receive the respect of both the client and the agency.

Public relations   Agencies also seek business through publicity/public relations efforts. These agencies often participate in civic and social groups and work with charitable organizations pro bono (for costs covered only, with no profits) to help the agency become respected in the community. Participation in professional associations, such as the AAAA, the Advertising Education Foundation, and so on, will also assist in cultivating new contacts. Successful agencies often receive free publicity for their work throughout the industry, as well as by the mass media.

Image and reputation   Perhaps the most effective manner in which an agency can gain new business is through its reputation. Agencies that consistently develop excellent campaigns acquire favorable reputations and images and are often approached by

➤ *Exhibit 3–18*
**Agencies often advertise
themselves to gain new business**

SOME HOME RUNS CLEAR THE BENCHES, OURS CLEAR THE SHELVES. From a pin drop heard round the world for Sprint® to six words that taught consumers to butter their bread with Philly® instead. From the Few, the Proud, the Marines to a question asked by our consumer research that helped make Ford Escort the best-selling small car and Ford Taurus the best-selling wagon in the U.S.A. From candid testimonials that helped Jenny Craig™ grow from 200,000 clients to over a million to a slogan that became a battle cry, "Nupe It.™" We hit home runs-we're J.Walter Thompson. Winning 50 EFFIES for effective advertising, 1987-1991. More EFFIES, for more clients, than any other agency. Need a home run? Call Ron Burns or Jim Patterson at (212) 210-7000. Give us the chance to go to bat for you.

clients. Agencies may enter their work in award competitions or advertise themselves to enhance their reputation and image in the marketing community (see Exhibit 3–18).

Collateral Services

For many companies, the development and implementation of their promotional programs become the responsibility of an agency. However, several other types of providers' specialized services complement the efforts of ad agencies, including direct-marketing firms, sales promotion specialists, marketing research companies, and public relations/publicity agencies. Let us examine the role that these firms play and the functions they perform.

Direct-Marketing Companies

One of the fastest-growing areas in promotions is that of **direct marketing,** in which companies directly communicate with consumers through telemarketing, direct-response advertising, and direct mail. As this industry has grown, numerous direct-

Promotional Perspective 3–2

Wooing Subaru—How Ad Agencies Pitched the $70 Million Account

One way agencies acquire accounts is through the speculative presentation—or "pitch." In this process, the advertising agency is invited to show the client how it would handle the advertising. While the incumbent agency is usually invited to participate, in most cases it is not likely to come out the winner.

One client in need of a new agency in 1991 was the Japanese automaker Subaru. Because of a lack of a distinct image, Subaru sales had dropped from a high of 186,000 cars a year sold in the United States in 1986 to only 108,000 in 1990. In addition, the company planned to introduce in 1991 a new sports car—the SVX—costing about $25,000. Without a distinct image, the company knew it was in trouble. Subaru asked agencies to apply for the $70 million advertising account—an amount that would put about $10 million in the agency's pocket at the standard 15 percent commission rate.

The *New York Times Magazine* reported on the review process as follows:

"The process began in April with a statistical evaluation of 35 agencies on Subaru's initial contact list. Mark Dunn developed a computer spreadsheet analysis that ranked each agency on the basis of their answers to a 17-question survey. Twelve agencies made the semifinals and were rewarded with a visit from Subaru".

"At that point the procedure began to take on elements of a beauty pageant. W. B. Doner covered itself with expensive baubles for the Subaru visit, trotting out current clients to give testimony to the agency's prowess and revealing, via live satellite transmission, the scene inside a Subaru dealership in Troy, Michigan, to which some 30 car shoppers had been drawn by a direct-mail solicitation the agency had put together. In Doner's garage, every parking space was taken up by a new (albeit rented) Subaru Legacy.

"Of the 12 semifinalists, 6 were invited by Subaru to pitch for its account." Each had a specialty; each had something to prove.

"The six finalists had one month to gather existing market studies, conduct original research, comprehend Subaru's problems, visit dealers and salesmen, rank the psychodemographic characteristics of Subaru's target consumers, develop a media plan to reach them, assemble an account team, devise and discard ideas, create campaigns for the Legacy and SVX, compose camera-ready print ads, record radio spots, draw storyboards for the television commercials, and, if time permitted, produce finished television ads.

"The decision was far from easy. Each afternoon the Subaru executives had gathered in the dark, empty bar of the Hyatt to debate: Should they pick a traditional agency whose work would please dealers? Or should they go for an unconventional agency that might inspire a sales burst but whose ads could backfire? Or should Subaru select a single campaign that could lead to immediately increased sales, possibly at the expense of long-term image-building?"

The winner was Wieden & Kennedy. The agency won the battle with an off-the-wall campaign featuring ads such as the one shown here, as well as others showing that a Subaru moves just as fast as other cars in bumper-to-bumper traffic. Their "what to drive" campaign was considered the most unique (and most risky!).

For the agencies that lost, it meant back to pitch another account. To one of the losers, it meant the firing of 40 percent of the agency staff. Pitching big accounts means big rewards and losses.

Source: Randall Rothenberg, "Seducing These Men," *New York Times Magazine,* October 20, 1991, pp. 30+.

marketing firms have evolved offering companies their specialized skills in both the consumer and business markets. These companies provide research, media services, and creative and production capabilities. A more extensive discussion of their role is reserved until Chapter 16.

Sales Promotion Specialists

The fastest-growing component of consumer products companies' promotional mix is that of sales promotion, with nearly $140 billion spent in this area in 1991. The development and management of sales promotion programs such as contests, sweepstakes, refund and rebate offers, and sampling and incentive programs constitute a very complex task. Thus, most companies use a sales promotion agency to develop and administer these programs. Sales promotion specialists often work in conjunction with the company's advertising agency to coordinate their efforts with the advertising program and, as shown in Exhibit 3–19 on page 106, tout their service

Wieden & Kennedy won the Subaru account with the "What to drive" car theme

The Subaru SVX

A sports car for both sides of your brain. The half that's seventeen, and the half that's retired and living in Miami.

THERE YOU ARE, both of you, considering a Subaru SVX. The younger, more adventurous you is taken aback by the Italian styling. And the SVX engine! A 6-cylinder, 230-horsepower monster capable of blasting from 0 to 60 in just over 7 seconds. The wilder you also goes on about the absurd top speed of 140 miles an hour and the fact the special window design allows you to drive in a rainstorm with the windows down without getting drenched. The windows down in a rainstorm without getting drenched, the crazy you shouts again.

And right then and there the conservative you, the joyless voice of reason, gets ready to reprimand such reckless thoughts, but then you pause and think—Hey, this is a practical car. It's a Subaru, and that means reliable, dependable transportation. Furthermore, the SVX has room for four beefy adults, and it comes with sensible All-Wheel Drive traction, 4-channel anti-lock brakes, a driver's-side air bag and a fully-independent suspension. Now both of you are smiling. Everything is beautiful. Until you're driving home. What to listen to on the optional 6-speaker CD player? Big band or heavy metal?

Subaru SVX

Subaru. What to drive.™

©1992, Subaru of America, Inc.

offerings to these organizations. Some agencies have also created their own sales promotion subsidiaries or have acquired such a firm. More insight into the roles and functions of these companies is provided later in this text.

Marketing Research Companies

Companies are increasingly turning to marketing research to assist them in understanding their target audiences and to gather information that will be of value in designing their advertising and promotions programs and evaluating these programs. While some advertisers have their own marketing research departments and the capabilities to conduct research, many do not. Even companies with marketing research departments will often use outside research agencies to perform some services. Many research companies are used because of the specialized services they offer and their capabilities to gather objective information that is valuable to the advertiser's promotional programs. (See Exhibit 3–20 on page 107.)

➤ *Exhibit 3–19*
Advertising for a sales promotion firm

Public Relations/ Publicity Agencies

Many large companies will use both an advertising agency and a public relations firm. The public relations firm develops and implements programs to manage the organization's publicity and affairs with consumers and other relevant public. Public relations and publicity activities should also be coordinated with the other elements of the promotional program. As we will discuss the public relations function in more detail in Chapter 19, we will just note here that such collateral services are offered.

Integrated Services

As mentioned earlier, one of the trends in the advertising and promotions industry is that of integrated marketing communications, whereby ad agencies offer a variety of promotional services under one roof. In addition to advertising, the agency may offer direct-marketing, public relations, sales promotion, and/or marketing research services through subsidiary organizations.

Many of the large superagency organizations discussed earlier in this chapter have been leaders in the move toward integrated marketing communications, such as Lintas: USA, a member of the Interpublic Group, and DDB Needham, which is part of the Omnicom Group. Lintas, in conjunction with the University of Chicago, developed an intensive training program to teach its employees how to handle a broad range of communication tools ranging from Yellow Pages to telemarketing. Over the past five years, the Leo Burnett agency recruited 80 specialists in direct mail, retail marketing, sales promotion, and public relations to make the agency a star in integrated marketing communications (see Exhibit 3–21).[15] The WTT Group consists of three ad agencies, J. Walter Thompson Company, Ogilvy and Mather Worldwide, and Scali, McCabe, Sloves, and a huge public relations arm that includes Hill & Knowlton, Carl Byoir & Associates, and Ogilvy Public Relations Group, among others. WTT also has market research companies, including the MRB Group, and several sales promotion and specialist communication firms.

Proponents of the integrated marketing or one-stop services agency argue that by maintaining control of the entire promotional process, greater synergy among each

> *Exhibit 3–20*
Marketing research companies offer specialized services

of the communication program elements is achieved. They also note that it is more convenient for the client to coordinate all of its marketing efforts, such as media advertising, direct mail, special events, sales promotion, and public relations, through one agency. An agency with integrated marketing capabilities can create a single image for the product or service and address everyone, from the wholesaler to the consumer, with one voice.

Not everyone accepts the integrated marketing communications concept and the idea of turning the entire promotional program over to one agency. Opponents contend all the providers become involved in political wrangling over budgets, do not communicate with each other as well and as often as they should, and do not achieve synergy. Many advertisers prefer to orchestrate their own coordinated communication programs. Several surveys of leading advertisers found that while most companies support the concept of integrated marketing, company executives believe they are better suited than agencies to coordinate diversified communication programs. Large advertisers (those with advertising and promotion budgets of more than $50 million) were less likely to want to use one agency for all their communications needs than smaller agencies. Agency egos, fear of budget loss, and lack of knowledge by agencies in multiple areas were seen as the biggest barriers to an integrated marketing communications program through one agency.[16]

Opponents of the single agency concept also claim the efforts by agencies to control all aspects of the promotional program are nothing more than an attempt to hold on to business that might otherwise be lost to independent providers. They note that synergy and economies, while nice in theory, have been very difficult to achieve, and competition and conflict among the agency subsidiaries has been a major problem.[17] Many companies, such as Miller Brewing and Reebok, use a variety of vendors for various communication functions, choosing the specialist they believe is best-suited for the promotional task such as advertising, sales promotion, or public

> *Exhibit 3–21* **The Leo Burnett Agency developed an integrated campaign for United Airlines that included print, direct mail, and television advertising**

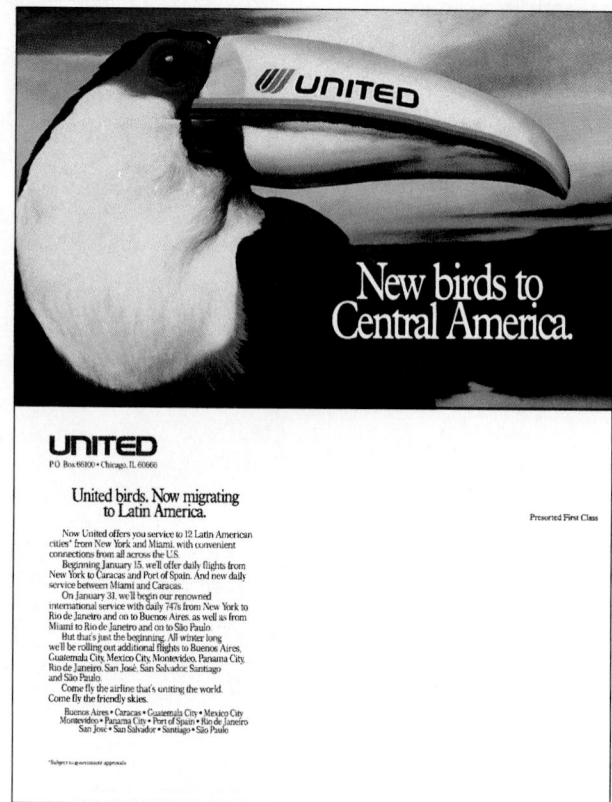

relations. Many marketers share the feelings of the vice president of advertising at Reebok who noted, "Why should I limit myself to one resource when there is a tremendous pool of fresh ideas available?"[18]

It has been argued that the concept of integrated marketing is nothing new; agencies have been trying to gain more of their clients' promotional business for over 20 years. However, in the past, the ancillary services were run as separate profit centers and each was motivated to push its own expertise and pursue its own goals rather than develop truly integrated marketing programs. Moreover, the creative specialists in many agencies resisted becoming involved in sales promotion or direct marketing. They preferred to concentrate on developing magazine ads or television commercials rather than designing coupons or direct-mail pieces. Proponents of integrated marketing contend past problems are being solved, and the various individuals in the agencies and subsidiaries are learning to work together to deliver a consistent message to the client's customers.

Both successes and failures have been reported regarding integrated marketing communications, and the debate continues about its merits. One thing is certain, however: as companies continue to shift their promotional dollars away from media advertising to sales promotion, direct marketing, and other nonmedia forms of promotion, agencies will continue to explore ways to keep these monies under their roofs.

SUMMARY

The development, execution, and administration of an advertising and promotions program involve the efforts of many individuals, both within the company and outside the organization. A number of organizational designs may be considered for this purpose.

Centralized systems offer the advantages of facilitated communications, lower personnel requirements, continuity in staff, and more top management involvement. Disadvantages include a lower involvement with overall marketing goals, longer response times, and difficulties in handling multiple product lines. Decentralized systems offer the advantages of concentrated managerial attention, more rapid responses to problems, and increased flexibility, though they may be limited by ineffective decision making, internal conflicts, misallocation of funds, and a lack of authority. In-house agencies, while offering the advantages of cost savings, control, and increased coordination, also have the disadvantage of less experience, objectivity, and flexibility.

Many firms use advertising agencies to assist them in developing and executing their programs. These agencies may take on a variety of forms, including full-service agencies, creative boutiques, and media buying services. The first of these offers the client a full range of services including creative, account, marketing, and financial and management services, while the other two specialize in creative and media buying, respectively. Agencies are compensated through commission systems, percentage charges, and fee- and cost-based systems.

Recently, the emphasis on agency evaluations has increased. Agencies are being evaluated on both financial and qualitative aspects, and some clients are basing the agencies' compensations on their performances.

Finally, a number of superagencies have developed. These large agencies are formed through the combination of separate agencies or agencies offering other marketing-related services such as direct marketing, sales promotion, marketing research, and public relations. These agencies offer one-stop integrated marketing services and have been both supported and criticized by clients.

KEY TERMS

clients	billings	commission system
advertising agency	superagencies	negotiated commission
media organizations	full-service agency	percentage charges
collateral services	account executive	fixed-fee agreements
advertising manager	copywriters	cost-plus system
centralized system	departmental system	agency evaluation process
decentralized system	group system	financial audit
category management	creative boutique	qualitative audit
in-house agency	media buying services	direct marketing

DISCUSSION QUESTIONS

1. Discuss the role of the four participant groups in the advertising and promotions process.

2. What are some of the specific responsibilities and duties of the advertising manager under a centralized advertising department

structure? Is an advertising manager needed if a company uses an outside agency?

3. What are the advantages of using a decentralized system? Discuss the responsibilities of a product manager with respect to advertising and promotions.

4. Discuss the pros and cons of using an in-house agency. When is a company likely to use this structure?

5. Discuss the reasons companies use outside agencies. Analyze the importance of the various services provided by a full-service agency.

6. Describe the functions and responsibilities of full-service advertising agencies. For what type of companies would a full-service agency be most appropriate?

7. Discuss some of the reasons agencies lose clients. What might an agency do to reduce the likelihood of client turnover?

8. A number of companies have developed new systems in which agency compensation is based on brand performance in the marketplace. Do you believe this system is fair? Would you accept such a system if you were an agency?

9. What are some of the criteria that should be used by a client in evaluating its agency? Describe how the importance of these criteria might vary among different firms.

10. Discuss the advantages and disadvantages associated with the use of superagencies. For what type of company or product/service would a superagency be best suited?

11. If you were the president of a medium-sized or large advertising agency, would you be expanding your capabilities to include nontraditional advertising services such as direct marketing, marketing research, and publicity/public relations? Why or why not?

4

Perspectives on Consumer Behavior

chapter objectives

➤ To examine the role consumer behavior plays in the development and implementation of advertising and promotional programs.

➤ To examine the consumer decision-making process and how it varies for different types of purchases.

➤ To examine various internal psychological processes, their influence on consumer decision making, and implications for advertising and promotion.

➤ To examine various approaches to studying the consumer learning process and their implications for advertising and promotion.

➤ To examine external factors such as culture, social class, group influences, and situational determinants and how they affect consumer behavior.

The Consumer of the 90s

Reaching consumers and persuading them to buy products and services has been the goal of marketers for decades. Many companies may find achieving this goal to be more challenging in the 1990s than in previous decades. During the 80s, marketers capitalized on a strong economy and a generation of consumers who wanted quality products, were willing to pay the high prices, and even flaunted them as symbols of prestige and achievement. Their free spending buoyed the sales of many expensive products and brands such as BMW automobiles, Louis Vuitton bags and luggage, Moet and Chandon champagne, and Rolex watches.

The 1990s, however, find consumers in a different mood. Many are denouncing the conspicuous consumption and wretched excess of the 80s and are searching for more traditional values of home and family. They are becoming more practical and taking a cautious approach to discretionary spending. They recognize that quality is not limited to national brands sold at premium prices, and factors such as image and prestige or the store where a product is purchased are becoming less important. The percentage of consumers who associate wearing designer clothing, driving fancy cars, and staying at luxury hotels as symbols of achievement and success has declined significantly since the late 1980s. Economic and demographic developments have led to fundamental shifts in consumer attitudes. Many aging baby boomers are assuming more family burdens and facing more financial concerns, such as college tuition and saving for retirement, while seeing their income grow very slowly.

In the 90s, consumers are cutting back and looking for ways to buy more for less, yet are becoming more demanding in the process. The marketing watchword for the 90s is *value* as consumers are demanding the right combination of product quality, fair prices, and good service. However, marketers are recognizing that value is not just a buzzword that can be slapped on packages or trumpeted in ads. Value marketing means giving consumers more, such as improved products with added features and enhanced service, and at a better price. It also means marketing must become part of the system for delivering value to consumers. This means more informational advertising that informs rather than just hypes products. It means better guarantees and longer warranties. It means making improvements in packaging that aren't merely intended to catch the shopper's eye but to make the product easier to use and more friendly to the environment. It means more customer service after the sale and more efforts to build customer satisfaction and loyalty such as through the use of toll-free telephone numbers to handle customer problems and complaints.

113

(continued)

The emphasis on value may put pressure on marketers to lower costs and prices, and only the leanest and most efficient will be able to compete. However, some marketers believe that in the long run, this trend may offer a way of returning value to brand names and getting marketers of national brands out of the discounting trap. After years of offering price cuts, coupons, and other promotional deals, marketers may be able to command higher prices for products and services that have real value.

While value may be the key to successful marketing in the 90s, marketers may find that reaching consumers and telling them about what they have to offer will be increasingly difficult. The consumer of the 90s is better educated, sophisticated, skeptical of advertising, and more difficult to reach than consumers of previous generations. The three major television networks have seen their share of the prime-time television audience decline to about 60 percent from 87 percent 10 years ago, and the average prime-time television show attracts only 15.8 million viewers instead of 24.1 million. Moreover, many consumers are becoming brain dead to commercials and cannot recall the ads they see. Marketers recognize that new approaches are needed to reach consumers and are promoting their products in a variety of ways. For example, many companies are promoting their brands in the store—on shopping carts, on electronic ads shown above the aisles, and through coupon dispensers attached to store shelves.

In the 1990s, marketers will find it more important than ever to monitor consumer needs and offer products and services that truly satisfy them. They must also continue to find ways to communicate and deliver the value, quality, and service customers demand. Marketers who figure out how to do this will survive the challenging decade of the 90s and prosper. Those who fail to meet this challenge may wish they were still back in the 80s.

Source: Patricia Sellers, "Winning Over the New Consumer," Fortune, July 29, 1991, pp. 113–124; and "Value Marketing," Business Week, November 11, 1991, pp. 132–40.

The development of successful marketing communication programs begins with understanding why consumers behave as they do. Those who develop advertising and other promotional strategies begin by identifying relevant markets and then analyzing the relationship between target consumers and the product/service or brand. As was discussed in the opening vignette, the way many consumers relate to products and services, along with the goals and motives they seek to achieve or satisfy, has been changing in recent years. The move toward more practical and value-focused consumption patterns is an important development to which many marketers have responded (Exhibit 4–1). However, this is just one aspect of consumer behavior promotional planners must consider in developing integrated marketing communication programs. Consumer choice behavior is influenced by a variety of factors.

➤ *Exhibit 4–1*
Many marketers are emphasizing value in their advertising campaigns

Here's one Bill you won't have to pay.

The New Elantra.

Because for two years we'll be taking care of your new Elantra for you. For nothing.
Imagine that. A car so well-built and backed, about all you'll pay for is gas.* Because whatever needs to be done, we'll do. Just pick up your car. We'll pick up the tab. Of course, this is over and above our three year bumper-to-bumper warranty as well as our five year powertrain warranty.†
Now knowing all that, don't you think it would pay to find out more about the new Elantra? Call 800-826-CARS for a brochure. Naturally, we're giving them away, too.

HYUNDAI

Hyundai. Yes, Hyundai.

This chapter provides a fundamental understanding of consumer behavior. It is beyond the scope of this text to examine this area in depth. However, promotional planners need a basic understanding of consumer decision making, factors that influence this process, and how this knowledge can be used in developing promotional strategies and programs. We begin with an overview of consumer behavior.

An Overview of Consumer Behavior

A common challenge faced by all marketers is their desire to influence the purchase behavior of the consumer in favor of the product or service they offer. For companies such as American Express this means getting consumers to charge more purchases on their American Express cards. For Frito-Lay, it means getting them to purchase and consume more of its snack-food products, while for business-to-business marketers such as Canon or Ricoh it means getting organizational buyers to purchase more of their copiers or fax machines. While the ultimate goal of marketers is to influence purchase behavior of customers, most marketers understand that the actual purchase is only part of an overall process.

Consumer behavior can be defined as the process and activities that people engage in when searching for, selecting, purchasing, using, evaluating, and disposing of products and services so as to satisfy their needs and desires. For many products and services, purchase decisions are the result of a long and detailed process that might include extensive information search, brand comparisons and evaluations, and other activities. Some purchase decisions are more incidental and may result from little more than seeing a product prominently displayed at a discount price in a store. Think of how many times you have made impulse purchases in stores with little thought or deliberation.

Marketers' success in influencing purchase behavior depends in large part on how well they understand consumer behavior. Marketers need to know the specific needs and motives customers are attempting to satisfy and how they translate into purchase criteria. They need to understand how consumers gather information regarding various alternatives and use this information to evaluate and select from a set of alternative brands. They need to understand how customers make purchase decisions. For example, where do they prefer to buy a product? How are they influenced by marketing stimuli at the point of purchase? Marketers also need to understand how the consumer decision process and reasons for purchase vary among different types of customers. Purchase decisions may be influenced by the personality or lifestyle characteristics of the consumer.[1] For example, notice how the ad for the Mazda MX-3 Gs, shown in Exhibit 4–2, suggests that this new sports car offers consumers a way to express their individuality.

Promotional Perspective 4–1 discusses how Frito-Lay Inc. has made understanding the consumer an obsession and used this information to become the market leader in the $4 billion snack-foods market.

The conceptual model shown in Exhibit 4–3 will be utilized as a framework for analyzing the consumer decision process. We will take you through the various stages of this model and discuss what occurs at each and how advertising and promotion can be used to influence decision making. We will also examine the influence of various psychological concepts or influences such as motivation, perception, attitudes, and integration processes. Variations in the consumer decision-making process will be examined as will alternative perspectives regarding consumer learning. The chapter concludes with a consideration of external influences on the consumer decision process, which include sociocultural and situational factors.

The Consumer Decision-Making Process

As can be seen in Exhibit 4–3, the consumer's purchase decision process is generally viewed as consisting of sequential steps or stages through which the buyer passes in purchasing a product or service. This model shows that the decision-making process also involves a number of internal psychological processes. These personal processes such as motivation, perception, attitude formation, integration, and learning are

> *Exhibit 4–2*
Marketers may appeal to personality traits such as individuality

important to advertising and promotional planners as they influence the general decision-making process of the consumer. We will examine each stage of the purchase decision model and discuss how the various subprocesses can influence what occurs at this step of the consumer behavior process. As we examine each of these stages, we will also discuss how promotional planners can influence this process.

Problem Recognition

As shown in Exhibit 4–3, the first stage in the consumer decision-making process is that of **problem recognition**. At this stage, the consumer perceives a need and becomes motivated to solve the problem. The problem recognition stage initiates the subsequent decision processes.

Problem recognition is caused by a difference between the consumer's *ideal state* and *actual state*. In other words, a discrepancy exists between what the consumer wants the situation to be like and what the situation is really like. (Note that *problem* does not always imply a negative state. It should be thought of more in the sense that a goal exists for the consumer, and this goal could be the attainment of a more positive situation.)

Sources of problem recognition

The causes of problem recognition may range from very simple to very complex and may result from changes in the consumer's current and/or desired state. In addition, these causes may be influenced by internal as well as external factors.

Out of stock   One of the simplest and most common sources of problem recognition occurs when consumers use their existing supply of a product and must replenish their stock. Most routine purchases for consumer products such as milk, cereal, soft drinks, and the like are made to replace products that have been used up. These

➤ *Exhibit 4–3*   **A basic model of consumer decision making**

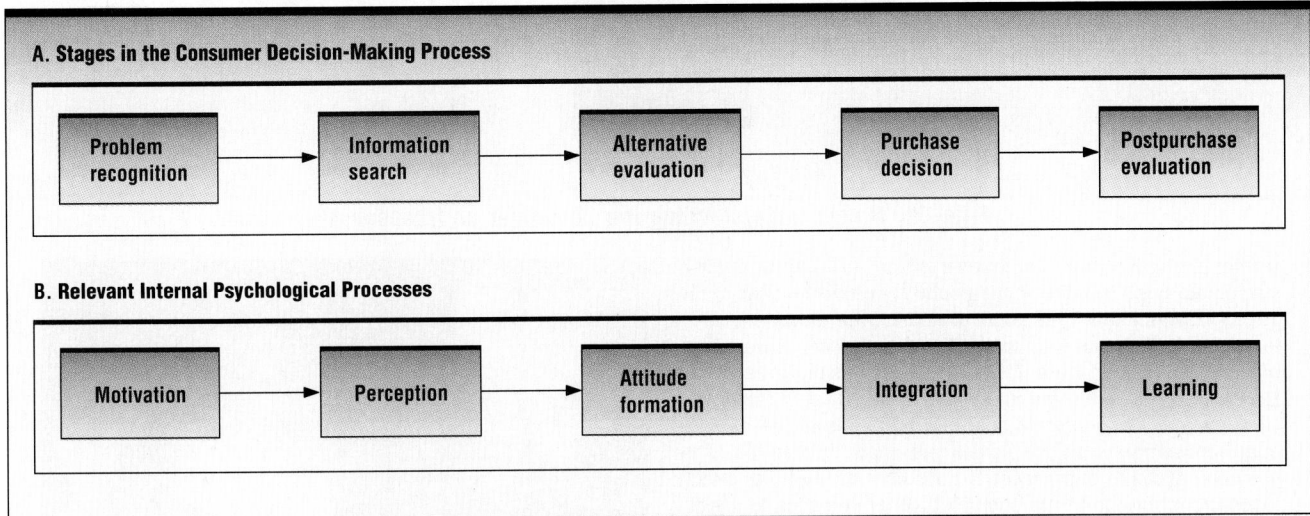

types of consumption problems are often resolved by choosing a familiar brand or one to which the consumer may be loyal.

Dissatisfaction   A second cause of problem recognition is created by the consumer's dissatisfaction with the current state of affairs and/or the product or service being used. For example, a consumer may think her ski boots are no longer comfortable or as stylish as she might prefer. In some cases, advertising may be used to help consumers recognize when they might have a problem and/or need to make a purchase. For example, Oral-B added a feature to its toothbrush to help consumers recognize when it is time to buy a new brush (Exhibit 4–4).

New needs/wants   Changes in consumers' lives often result in new needs and thus trigger problem recognition. Changes in one's financial situation, employment status, or lifestyle may lead to the creation of new needs and trigger problem recognition. For example, when you graduate from college and begin your professional career, your new job may necessitate a change in your wardrobe (good-bye blue jeans and T-shirts, hello suits and ties). Changes within the family can also create new needs. The birth of a child (particularly the first one) creates a variety of new needs for items such as baby clothes, diapers, strollers, toys, and the like.

Not all product purchases are based on needs. Some products or services sought by consumers are not essential, but nevertheless are desired. A **want** has been defined as a felt need that is shaped by a person's knowledge, culture, and personality.[2] It has been argued that many products sold to consumers reflect ways of satisfying their wants rather than basic needs. A very basic criticism of marketing, and advertising in particular, is that it encourages consumers to buy things based on wants rather than needs. We examine this issue in more detail in Chapter 24.

Related products/purchases   Problem recognition can also be stimulated by the purchase of a product. For example, the purchase of a new camera may lead to the recognition of a need for accessories such as additional lenses or a carrying case. The purchase of a personal computer may prompt the need for software programs or upgrades. Marketers often try to identify consumers who have purchased a new home because they will be good candidates for purchasing additional products such as furniture, window coverings, landscaping, and the like.

Marketer-induced problem recognition   Another source of problem recognition among consumers comes from the actions of marketers that encourage consumers not to be content or satisfied with their current state or situation. Ads for personal

Promotional Perspective 4–1

Frito-Lay Makes Understanding the Consumer an Obsession

In the 1930s, Herman Lay, founder of the Frito-Lay Company, sold potato chips by toting them around in one-ounce bags in his 1929 Model A. He learned about customer preferences primarily through informal conversations with a few grocery store clerks and gas station managers. The informal conversations begun by Herman Lay have evolved into nearly 500,000 consumer interviews a year. An important goal of Frito-Lay is knowing more about consumers than the consumers know themselves. The company explores every facet of consumer behavior for snack foods, from obvious things such as taste preferences to understanding more subtle psychological feelings and desires.

Chemists, engineers, and psychologists work in Frito-Lay's "Potato Chip Pentagon," a guarded building near Dallas, developing and testing new products and working to enhance the company's understanding of consumer preferences. They use a simulated human mouth made of aluminum to measure the jaw power required to crunch single chips. By comparing consumer preferences in taste tests with results from the aluminum mouth, Frito-Lay researchers know that most people prefer chips that break under 4 pounds of pressure per square inch. The company tests a few chips from every batch it makes at its factories to ensure the standard is met. Quality control engineers measure the thickness of chips because consumers have complained about chips that were cut 8/1,000ths of an inch too thick or thin. Other engineers test the chemical reactions of single chips on a computer screen that shows flavor patterns in eight colors. Computer printouts show results of the roughly 50 chemical components in a chip and are helpful to scientists in developing new products such as barbecue- or vinegar-flavored chips.

Frito-Lay also understands a great deal about the way consumers eat snack foods. Its research has shown that 65 percent of all potato chips are eaten in private. Under ideal psychological conditions—relaxing at a movie with a soft drink—a typical adult eats about 72 chips, or 4 ounces, at a sitting. The company arrived at this figure by renting movie theaters and offering thousands of consumers free tickets and unmarked bags of chips. Researchers collected the bags as consumers left and counted the uneaten chips. The test results showed that consumers eat about one-third more chips at a sitting than they admit to in interviews, which prompted Frito-Lay to push bigger package sizes.

Consumer research has also shown that consumers are very persnickety when it comes to potato chips. They expect their chips to reach a certain level of excellence in appearance, size, shape, and taste. The company's vice president of marketing research believes consumers expect more from potato chips than certain foods because they figure that if they are going to eat snack foods, they better get a lot of pleasure from it. Consumers

also tend to be very intolerant of broken chips and do not like chips that are too big or small.

Frito-Lay also knows a great deal about the psychological profiles and personality differences among eaters of various snack foods. Researchers at Tracy-Locke, promotions agency for Frito-Lay, have prepared videotapes depicting the types of people they think eat the company's various products. The videos were created based on interviews with more than a 1,000 Frito-Lay consumers in which they were shown photographs of consumers in various situations and asked whether these people are likely to eat certain snack foods. The videos reflect distinct personality differences among eaters of various snack foods. For example, the users of Ruffles potato chips are depicted as "expressive, aware, and confident enough to make a personal statement." Scenes in the video show people getting into a BMW and other cars, a man opening champagne, wind surfers, and a woman working out in a fashionable outfit.

Frito-Lay's obsession with understanding customers is paying off. Its share of the $4 billion snack food market has risen to 33 percent from 25 percent just a decade ago and is more than double its largest competitor. Pretax profit margins approach nearly 20 cents on every dollar. The company is also the leader in a variety of other snack-food categories such as tortilla and corn chips. Consumer research at Frito-Lay has come a long way since Herman Lay's days. However, the company knows consumers have changed a great deal as well, and its success comes from understanding consumers and developing products that meet their needs.

Source: Robert Johnson, "In the Chips," *The Wall Street Journal,* March 22, 1991, pp. B1,2.

➤ *Exhibit 4–4*
The new Oral-B toothbrush helps consumers recognize when they need to replace it

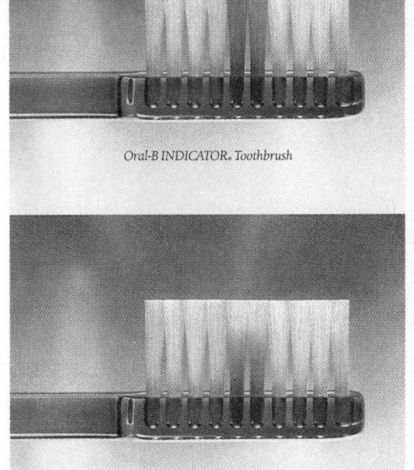

Your dentist can't remind you when to replace your toothbrush. That's our job.

Although dentists advise you to replace your brush, they really can't be there to tell you when. But the Oral-B Indicator can.

You see, the American Dental Association recommends you replace your toothbrush every three months. They believe strongly that a worn toothbrush is less effective at removing plaque. That's why most dentists tell you to change your toothbrush. And the very reason Oral-B developed the INDICATOR Toothbrush. The blue band fades with brushing, so you can see when it's time for a new Indicator. It's that simple.

But developing the Indicator was anything but. It's been thoroughly researched over an extensive period with more than 1,500 patients and 300 dentists and hygienists.

Also, like all Oral-B brushes, the Indicator was clinically shown to be unsurpassed at removing plaque versus the other leading brands. Without any sign of gingival irritation or abrasion. No wonder Oral-B is the toothbrush more dentists use.

All in all, the Indicator is another fine example of Oral-B's ongoing commitment to serious dental care.

So listen to your dentist. Replace your brush with the Indicator from Oral-B. It's the ultimate gentle reminder.

The Brand More Dentists Use.

Oral-B INDICATOR Toothbrush

*About 3 months later
(when dentists recommend replacing your toothbrush)*

hygiene products such as mouthwash, deodorant, and foot sprays may be designed to create insecurities among consumers that can be resolved through the use of these products. Marketers change fashions and clothing designs and create perceptions among consumers that their wardrobes may be "out of style."

Marketers also take advantage of consumers' tendency toward *novelty-seeking behavior*, which leads them to try new and/or different brands. Consumers often try new products or brands even though they are basically satisfied with their regular brand. Marketers encourage brand switching by introducing new brands into markets that are already saturated and by using advertising and sales promotion techniques such as free samples, introductory price offers, and coupons to induce trial.

New products   Problem recognition can also occur when innovative products are introduced and brought to the attention of consumers. Marketers are constantly introducing innovative products and services and telling consumers about the types of problems they solve. For example, marketers of cellular phones tell us why we need telephones in our cars and stress the time savings and convenience offered by this innovation. Communicating by way of fax machines is becoming so prevalent that nearly every businesses recognizes the need to have them. Even consumers who work at home are finding it necessary to have fax capabilities in their home offices (Exhibit 4–5).

Marketers' attempts to create problem recognition among consumers are not always successful, however. Consumers may not see a problem or need for the product the marketer is selling. For example, a main reason many consumers have been reluctant to purchase home computers is that they fail to see the problems that will be solved by owning one. One way home computer manufacturers have attempted to activate problem recognition is by stressing the importance of having a computer for children to improve their academic skills and do better in school.

Examining Consumer Motivations

Marketers recognize that while problem recognition is often a very basic and simple process, the way a consumer perceives a need and becomes motivated to solve the problem will influence the remainder of the decision process. For example, one consumer may perceive the need to purchase a new watch from a functional perspective and focus on reliable, low-priced alternatives. However, another consumer may see the purchase of a watch as more of a fashion statement and focus on the design and image of various brands. To better understand the reasons underlying consumer purchases, marketers devote considerable attention to examining **motives**— that is, those factors that compel or drive a consumer to take a particular action.

Hierarchy of needs

One of the most basic and popular approaches to understanding consumer motivations is based on the classic theory of human motivation popularized many years ago by psychologist Abraham Maslow.[3] His **hierarchy of needs** theory postulates five basic levels of human needs arranged in a hierarchy based on their importance. As can be seen in Exhibit 4–6, the five needs include: (1) *physiological needs*—the basic level of primary needs for things required to sustain life such as food, shelter, clothing, and sex; (2) *safety needs*—the need for security and safety from physical harm; (3) *social/love and belonging needs*—the desire to have satisfying relationships with others and have a sense of love, affection, belonging, and acceptance; (4) *esteem needs*—the need to feel a sense of achievement or accomplishment and gain a sense of recognition, status, and respect from others; and (5) *self-actualization needs*—the need for self-fulfillment and a desire to realize one's own potential.

According to Maslow's theory, the lower-level physiological and safety needs have to be satisfied before the higher-order needs would become meaningful. Once these

> *Exhibit 4–6*
Maslow's hierarchy of needs

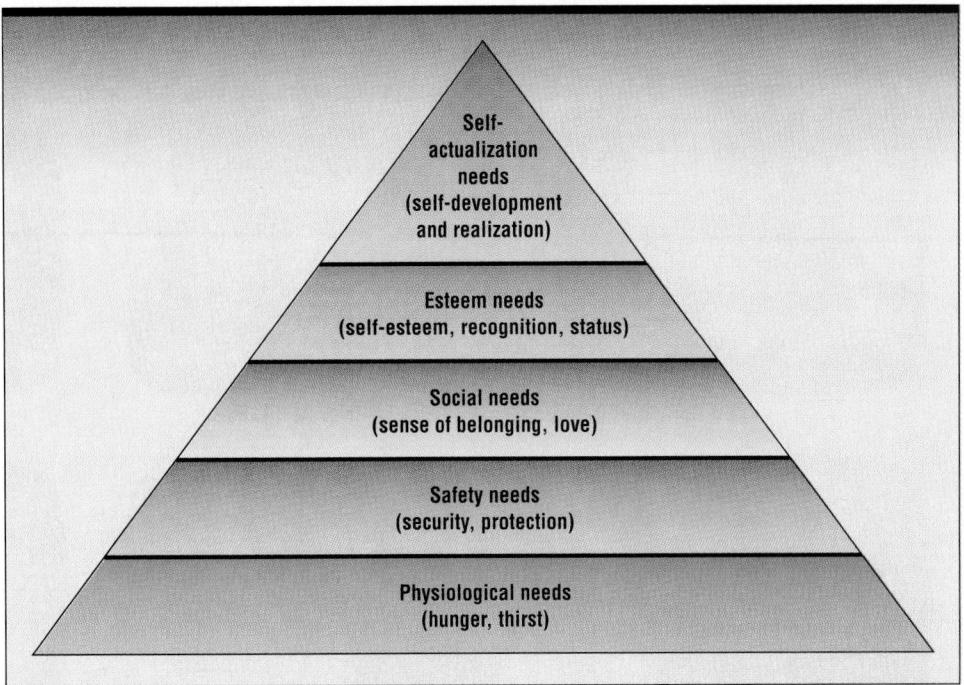

basic needs are satisfied, the individual moves on to attempting to satisfy higher-order needs such as self-esteem and self-actualization. In reality, it is unlikely that individuals move through the need hierarchy in a stair-step manner whereby they satisfy all lower-level needs and then move on to higher-level needs. Lower-level needs are an ongoing source of motivation for consumer purchase behavior. However, since basic physiological needs are met in most developed countries, marketers recognize they often must sell products that appeal to basic physiological needs by appealing to consumers' higher-level needs. For example, in marketing its condensed soups, Campbell Soup Co. focuses on the love between a parent and child (social needs) in additional to the nutritional value of the product (Exhibit 4–7).

While problems have been noted with Maslow's need hierarchy, it offers a framework for marketers to use in determining what needs they want to show their products and services as satisfying. Advertising campaigns can then be designed to show how a brand can fulfill these needs. Marketers also recognize that different market segments may place greater emphasis on certain need levels. For example, a young, single person may be attempting to satisfy social or self-esteem needs in purchasing a car while a family with children will focus more on safety needs. Volvo has used ads such as the one shown in Exhibit 4–8 to position its cars as meeting the safety needs of consumers with children.

Psychoanalytic theory

A very interesting and somewhat more controversial approach to the study of consumer motives is the **psychoanalytic theory** pioneered by Sigmund Freud.[4] Although Freud's work dealt with the structure and development of personality, he also focused on the underlying motivations for human behavior. Psychoanalytic theory had a very strong influence on the development of modern psychology and has been widely studied by psychologists interested in motivation and personality. It has also been applied to the study of consumer behavior by marketers interested in probing into deeply rooted motives that might underlie purchase decisions.

> *Exhibit 4–7* **Campbell appeals to love and belonging needs in this ad**

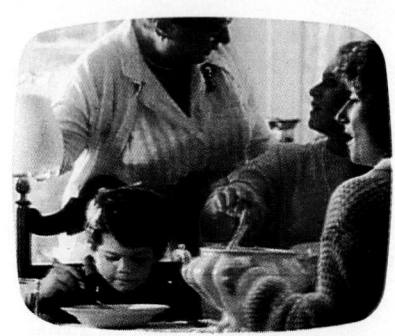

BOY SINGS: (VO) There's nothing like
getting
to the bottom of a bowl of soup.
Puts me in a real good mood.
There's nothing like getting

to the bottom of a bowl of soup.
ANNCR: (VO) Campbell's Chicken
Noodle Soup.
So good, and like most of Campbell's
soups

so low in cholesterol.
BOY SINGS: (VO) Cause at the
bottom of it all
soup is good food.
BOY: (VO) Campbell's!

Those who attempt to relate psychoanalytic theory to consumer behavior believe consumers' motivations for purchasing are often very complex and would not be obvious to the casual observer—or to the consumers themselves. Thus, many of the motives for purchase and/or consumption might be driven by deeply rooted motives that could be determined only by probing the subconscious. An excellent example is given in Promotional Perspective 4–2.

Two of the first to conduct this type of research in marketing—Ernest Dichter and James Vicary—were employed by a number of major corporations to use psychoanalytic techniques to determine consumers' purchase motivations. The work of these researchers, and others who continue to use this approach, assumed the title of **motivation research.**

Motivation research in marketing

Motivation researchers use a variety of methodologies to gain insight into the "true" underlying causes of consumer behavior. Some of the methods employed include in-depth interviews, projective techniques, association tests, and focus groups (see Exhibit 4–9) in which consumers are encouraged to bring out associations related to products and brands. As one might expect, such associations often lead to interesting insights and conclusions as to why people purchase, for example:

- A man buys a convertible as a substitute mistress.
- Women like to bake cakes because they feel like they are giving birth to a baby.

➤ *Exhibit 4–8*
Volvo appeals to consumers' safety needs

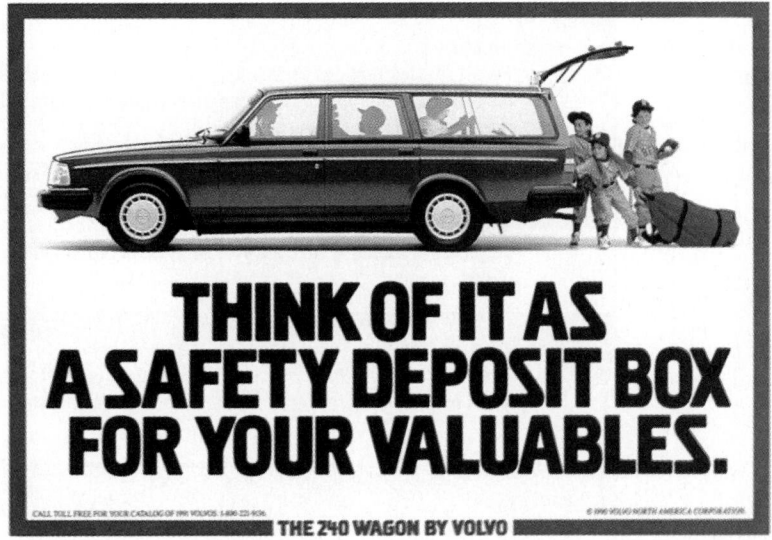

- Women wear perfume to "attract a man" and to "glorify their existence."
- Men like frankfurters better than women because cooking them (frankfurters, not men!) makes women feel guilty—it's an admission of laziness.
- When people shower, their sins go down the drain with the soap as they rinse.[5]

As you can see from these examples, motivation research has led to some very interesting, albeit controversial, findings and to much skepticism from marketing managers. At the same time, however, major corporations and advertising agencies continue to use motivation research to help them market their products.

Problems and contributions of psychoanalytic theory and motivation research

Psychoanalytic theory has been criticized as being too vague, unresponsive to the external environment, too reliant on the early development of the individual, and using too small a sample for drawing conclusions. Because of the emphasis on the unconscious, results are difficult, if not impossible, to verify, leading motivation research to be criticized both for the conclusions drawn as well as its lack of experimental validation. Since motivation research studies typically employ a small number of participants, there is also concern that what is really being discovered are the idiosyncrasies of a few individuals and that these findings are not generalizable to the whole population.

Still, it is difficult to ignore the psychoanalytic approach in furthering our understanding of consumer behavior. These insights can often be used as a basis for advertising messages aimed at the buyers' deeply rooted feelings, hopes, aspirations, and fears. In many instances, these strategies may be more effective than rationally based appeals.

While often criticized, motivation research has also contributed to the marketing discipline. The qualitative nature of the research is considered important in assessing how and why consumers buy. Focus groups and in-depth interviews are valuable methods for gaining insights into consumers' feelings, and projective techniques are often the only means of getting around stereotypical or socially desirable responses. In addition, motivation research is the forerunner of "psychographics"—or lifestyle research—a popular basis for segmenting markets and developing consumer profiles, which will be discussed in Chapter 5.

➤ *Exhibit 4–9*
Some of the marketing research
methods employed to probe the
mind of the consumer

In-depth interviews
Face-to-face situations in which an interviewer asks a consumer to talk freely in an
unstructured interview using specific questions designed to obtain insights into his or her
motives, ideas, or opinions.

Projective techniques
Efforts designed to gain insights into consumers' values, motives, attitudes, or needs that are
difficult to express or identify by having them project these internal states upon some external
object.

Association tests
A technique in which an individual is asked to respond as to the first thing that comes to mind
when he or she is presented with a stimulus; the stimulus may be a word, picture, ad, and so
on.

Focus groups
A small number of people with similar backgrounds and/or interests are brought together to
discuss a particular product, idea, or issue.

Finally, we know that buyers are sometimes motivated by symbolic as well as functional drives in their purchase decisions. (Thus, we see the use of sexual appeals and symbols in ads such as those shown in Exhibit 4–10.)

Information Search

The second step in the consumer decision-making process is *information search.* Once consumers perceive a problem or need that can be satisfied by the purchase of a product or service, they begin to search for information needed to make a purchase decision. The initial search effort often consists of an attempt to scan information stored in *memory* to recall past experiences and/or knowledge regarding various purchase alternatives.[6] This information retrieval is referred to as **internal search.** For many routine and repetitive purchases, previously acquired information that is stored in memory (such as past performance or outcomes from using a brand) may be sufficient for comparing alternatives and making a choice. If the internal search does not yield enough information, the consumer will seek additional information by engaging in **external search.**

In external search, consumers are required to go outside the confines of their mind to acquire information. External sources of information include:

- *Personal sources* such as friends, relatives, or co-workers.
- Commercial or *marketer controlled* sources such as information from advertising, salespersons, or point-of-purchase displays and materials.
- *Public sources,* including articles in mass media publications such as magazines or newspapers or reports on television programs.
- *Personal experience* such as actually handling, examining, or testing the product.

Determining how much and which sources of external information to use is a function of several factors, including the importance of the purchase decision, the effort needed to acquire information, the amount of past experience relevant to the purchase decision, the degree of perceived risk associated with the purchase, and the time available. For example, the selection of a movie to see on a Friday night might entail talking to a friend or reviewing the movie guide in the daily newspaper. A more complex purchase, such as a new car, might use a number of information sources. A review of *Road & Track, Motortrend,* or *Consumer Reports;* discussion

Promotional Perspective 4–2

Using Motivation Research in Advertising—Probing the Mind of the Consumer

A few years ago, researchers at the McCann-Erickson advertising agency were baffled about how southern women selected a brand of insecticide. The women thought a new brand sold in little plastic trays was less messy and more effective than traditional bug sprays, yet they never switched to the new product.

To find out why the women didn't change, the agency's researchers used a technique often used in psychological research. They had the women draw pictures of roaches and then write stories about them. Some of their drawings and accompanying explanations are shown here.

McCann Erickson is not the only agency employing Freudian techniques. For example:

- N W Ayer asked consumers to draw shapes with their left hands in response to questions regarding new product ideas, in the belief that the right side of the brain (which controls the left side of the body) is more visual, symbolic, and emotional and therefore would be better for expressing images.
- Foote, Cone & Belding gave consumers stacks of photographs of people's faces, asking them to associate the faces with the kind of person who might use particular products.
- McCann-Erickson Worldwide had consumers draw stick figures of American Express gold and green card users. The gold card user was portrayed as more active than the "couch potato in front of a TV set" green card user.
- Saatchi & Saatchi Advertising WW used psychological probes to conclude that Ronald McDonald created a more nurturing mood than did the Burger King, who was perceived as "more aggressive, masculine and distant."

As you can see from these examples, motivation research is alive and well in the advertising agency business!

The Mind of a Roach Killer

The McCann-Erickson ad agency asked women to draw and describe how they felt about roaches. The agency concluded from the drawings that the women identified the roaches with men who had abandoned them and thus enjoyed watching the roaches-men squirm and die. That's why, the agency figured, that women prefer spray roach killers to products that don't allow the user to see the roach die.

"ONE NIGHT I just couldn't take the horror of these bugs sneaking around in the dark. They are always crawling when you can't see them. I had to do something. I thought wouldn't it be wonderful if when I switched on the light the roaches would shrink up and die like vampires to sunlight. So I did, but they just all scattered. But I was ready with my spray so it wasn't a total loss. I got quite a few...continued tomorrow night when night time falls."

"I TIPTOED quietly into the kitchen perhaps he wasn't around. I stretched my arm up to the light. I hoped I'd be alone when the light went on. Perhaps he is sitting on the table I thought. You think that's impossible? Nothing is impossible with that guy. He might not even be alone. He'll run when the light goes on I thought. But what's worse is for him to slip out of sight. No, it would be better to confront him before he takes control and 'invites a companion'."

"A MAN LIKES a free meal you cook for him, as long as there is food he will stay."

Source: Ronald Alsop, "Advertisers Put Consumers on the Couch," *The Wall Street Journal,* May 13, 1988, p. 19.

with family members and friends; and test-driving cars might all occur in an attempt to acquire information. At this point in the purchase decision, the information-providing aspects of advertising are extremely important.

Perception

Knowledge of how the consumer acquires and uses the information from external sources is very important to marketers in formulating communication strategies. Marketers are particularly interested in (1) how consumers sense external information, (2) how they select and attend to various sources of information, and (3) how this information is interpreted and given meaning. These processes are all part of **perception**—the process by which an individual receives, selects, organizes, and interprets information to create a meaningful picture of the world.[7] As this definition suggests, perception is an individualized process; it depends on internal factors such as a person's beliefs, experiences, needs, moods, and expectations. The perceptual

➤ *Exhibit 4–10*   **The use of sexual appeals and symbols in ads**

A. Obsession ads employ the use of sex appeals

B. After Six uses symbolism in its ad for clothing

process is also influenced, however, by the characteristics of a stimulus such as its size, color, intensity, and the context in which it is seen or heard.

Sensation

As noted above, perception involves three distinct processes. **Sensation** is the immediate and direct response of the senses (taste, smell, sight, touch, and hearing) to a stimulus such as an advertisement, a package, a brand name, or a point-of-purchase display. Perception involves using these senses to create a representation of the stimulus. Marketers recognize that it is important to understand consumers' physiological reactions to marketing stimuli. For example, the visual elements of an ad or package design must attract consumers' attention and be evaluated favorably. Marketers sometimes try to increase the level of sensory input so that their advertising messages will get noticed. For example, marketers of colognes and perfumes often use strong visuals as well as "scent strips" to appeal to multiple senses and attract the attention of magazine readers. Some advertisers have even begun inserting microcomputer chips in their print ads that play a song or deliver a message.

Selecting information

Sensory inputs are important but serve as only one part of the perceptual process. The other determinants of whether marketing stimuli will be attended to and how they will be interpreted include internal psychological factors such as the consumer's personality, needs, motives, expectations, and experiences. These psychological

> *Exhibit 4–11*
This ad reminds consumers of how advertising responds to their needs

ISN'T IT FUNNY HOW
STEREO ADS ARE BORING
UNTIL YOU WANT A STEREO?

We admit it. There are times when advertising isn't especially interesting.
For instance, stereo ads when you're not looking for a new stereo. Or insurance ads when you're not looking for a new insurance company. Or detergent ads when you're not looking for a new detergent.
But suppose your stereo breaks down. Or your insurance rates go up. Or your laundry comes out gray.
All of a sudden, stereo ads, insurance ads and detergent ads start looking a lot more interesting.
It's one of the basic truths of advertising. We try to be entertaining, but that's not really our job. Our job is to help you make the right choices when you're in the market for any kind of product or service.
Of course, when you're not in the market, we recognize that advertising may seem beside the point. In that case, you're free to pretend it isn't there.
In fact, you're free to ignore advertising for as long as you choose.
Right up until your stereo breaks down.

ADVERTISING.
ANOTHER WORD FOR FREEDOM OF CHOICE.
American Association of Advertising Agencies

inputs explain why people focus attention on some things and ignore others and how two people may perceive the same stimuli in very different ways because they select, attend, and comprehend differently. An individual's perceptual processes are most likely to focus on elements of the environment important to that person. Individuals are more likely to expose themselves and attend to stimuli that are relevant to their needs and interests and tune out irrelevant stimuli. For example, think about how much more attentive you might be to advertising for personal computers, tires, or stereos if you are in the market for one of these products, a point which is made by the message from the American Association of Advertising Agencies in Exhibit 4–11.

Interpreting the information

Once a consumer selects and attends to a stimulus, the perceptual process focuses on organizing, categorizing, and interpreting the incoming information. This stage of the perceptual process is very individualized and is influenced by internal psychological factors. The interpretation and meaning an individual assigns to an incoming stimulus is also a function of the nature or characteristics of the stimulus. For example, most advertisements are very objective, and the message and meaning they attempt to communicate are very clear and straightforward. Some ads, however, are more ambiguous, and their message and meaning will be strongly influenced by the consumer's individual interpretation.

As can be seen from the preceding discussion, selectivity occurs throughout the various stages of the consumer's perceptual process. Perception may be viewed as a filtering process as these internal and external factors influence what is received and how it is processed and interpreted. The sheer number and complexity of the

➢ *Exhibit 4–12*
The selective perception process

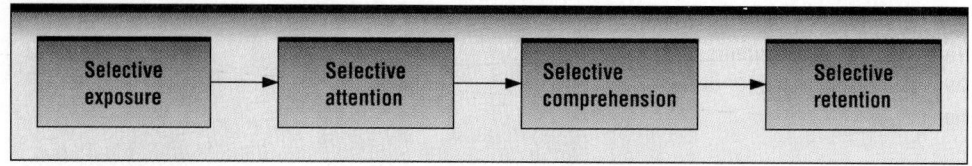

marketing stimuli a person is exposed to in any given day require that this filtering occur. **Selective perception,** which refers to a filtering or screening of exposure, attention, comprehension, and retention, may occur at a number of perceptual stages as shown in Exhibit 4–12.

Selective perception

Selective exposure may occur as consumers choose whether or not to make themselves available to information. For example, a viewer of a television show may change channels or leave the room during commercial breaks to avoid exposure to the advertisements. **Selective attention** occurs when the consumer chooses to focus attention on certain stimuli while excluding others. One study of selective attention estimates the consumer is potentially exposed to nearly 1,500 ads per day yet perceives only 76 of these messages.[8] This means advertisers must take considerable effort to attract the attention of consumers and have their messages noticed. To gain the consumer's attention, advertisers often focus on the creative aspects of their ads. For example, some advertisers have tried to set their ads off from others and gain readers' attention by showing their products in color against a black-and-white background (Exhibit 4–13). This creative tactic has been used in advertising for a number of products such as Cherry 7-Up, Nuprin, and Pepto-Bismo.[9]

Even if the consumer does give attention to the advertiser's message, there is no guarantee it will be interpreted in the intended manner. Consumers may engage in **selective comprehension** in which they interpret information based on their own attitudes, beliefs, motives, and experiences. In selective comprehension, consumers often interpret information in a manner that will support their own position. For example, an advertisement that disparages a consumer's favorite brand may be seen as biased or untruthful, and the claims may not be accepted.

The final screening process shown in Exhibit 4–12 —**selective retention**—means consumers do not remember all the information they see, hear, or read even after attending and comprehending it. Advertisers must attempt to ensure that information will be retained in the consumer's memory so as to be available when it is time to make a purchase. **Mnemonics** such as symbols, rhymes, associations, and images that assist in the learning and memory process are helpful. For example, many advertisers use telephone numbers that spell out the company name and are easy to remember. Eveready put pictures of its pink bunny on packages to remind consumers at the point of purchase of its creative advertising executions.

Subliminal perception

Advertisers are aware consumers use selective perception to filter out irrelevant or unwanted advertising messages, so they employ various creative tactics to get their messages noticed. One controversial tactic advertisers have been accused of using is that of appealing to the consumers subconscious. **Subliminal perception** refers to the ability of an individual to perceive a stimulus that is below the level of conscious awareness. Psychologists generally agree it is possible to perceive things without being consciously aware of them. As you might imagine, the possibility of using "hidden persuaders" such as subliminal audio messages or visual cues to influence consumers might be intriguing to advertisers but would not be welcome by consumers. The possibility that marketers could influence consumers at a subconscious level

➤ *Exhibit 4–13*
Splash of color ads help attract attention

has very strong ethical implications and has prompted researchers in a variety of disciplines to examine whether subliminal messages might be effective. As discussed in Ethical Perspective 4–1, those who have examined the research believe subliminal messages are not likely to be effective in influencing consumer behavior. The use of subliminal techniques is not a creative tactic we believe in or would recommend to advertisers!

Alternative Evaluation

The evoked set

After acquiring information during the information search stage of the decision process, the consumer moves to alternative evaluation. In this stage, the consumer compares the various brands or products and services that have been identified as being capable of solving the consumption problem and satisfying the needs or motives that initiated the decision process. The various brands identified as purchase options to be considered during the alternative evaluation process are referred to as the consumer's *evoked set*. The evoked set is generally only a subset of all the brands of which the consumer is aware. The consumer reduces the number of brands to be reviewed during the alternative evaluation stage to a manageable level. The exact size of the evoked set varies from one consumer to another and depends on factors such as the importance of the purchase and the amount of time and energy the consumer wants to devote to comparing alternatives.

It is important for marketers to ensure that their brands are included in the evoked sets of at least some consumers. And the goal of most advertising and promotional strategies is to increase the likelihood that a brand will be included in the consumer's evoked set and considered during alternative evaluation. For example, marketers use advertising to create *top-of-mind awareness* among consumers so their brands are included in the evoked set of their target audiences. Popular brands with large advertising budgets use *reminder advertising* to maintain high awareness levels and increase the likelihood they will be considered by consumers when they are in the market for the product. Marketers of new brands or those with a low market share need to gain awareness among consumers and break into their evoked sets. They can do this through methods such as comparative advertising whereby a brand is compared to market leaders, thus encouraging the customer to consider it when making a purchase. The ad for the new Audi 100 (Exhibit 4–14, page 131) is an example of this strategy. This ad encourages prospective car buyers who might be

Ethical Perspective 4–1

Subliminal Perception—Fact or Fiction?

One of the most interesting and controversial topic areas in all of advertising is that of subliminal advertising. Rooted in psychoanalytic theory, subliminal advertising supposedly influences consumer behaviors by subconsciously altering perceptions or attitudes toward products without the knowledge—or consent—of the consumer.

The concept of subliminal advertising was introduced in 1957 when a marketing research group reported it increased the sales of popcorn and Coke by subliminally flashing "Eat popcorn" and "Drink Coca-Cola" across the screen during a movie in New Jersey. Since then, numerous books and research studies have been published regarding the existence and effectiveness of this advertising form. In 1982, Timothy Moore, publishing in the *Journal of Marketing,* reviewed the vast literature on subliminal perception. He concluded

> while subliminal perception is a bona fide phenomenon, the effects obtained are subtle and obtaining them typically requires a carefully structured context. Subliminal stimuli are usually so weak that the recipient is not just unaware of the stimulus but is also oblivious to the fact that he/she is being stimulated. . . . These factors pose serious difficulties for any marketing application. . . .
>
> The point is simply that subliminal directives have not been shown to have the power ascribed to them by advocates of subliminal advertising. In general, the literature on subliminal perception shows that the most clearly documented effects are obtained only in highly contrived and artificial situations. These effects, when present, are brief and of small magnitude. . . . These processes have no apparent relevance to the goals of advertising. [P. 46]

In 1988, after additional research in this area, Moore concluded, "There continues to be no evidence that subliminal messages can influence motivation or complex behavior." In addition to Moore's conclusions, a review of the literature by Joel Saegert and a study by Jack Haberstroh further discount this strategy. In the latter study, Haberstroh asked advertising agency executives if they had ever deliberately used subliminal advertising; 96 percent said no, 94 percent said they never supervised the use of implants, and 91 percent denied knowing anyone who had ever used this technique. Thus, it seems few people think subliminal advertising works and even fewer claim to use it.

The advertising industry states its position on subliminal messages

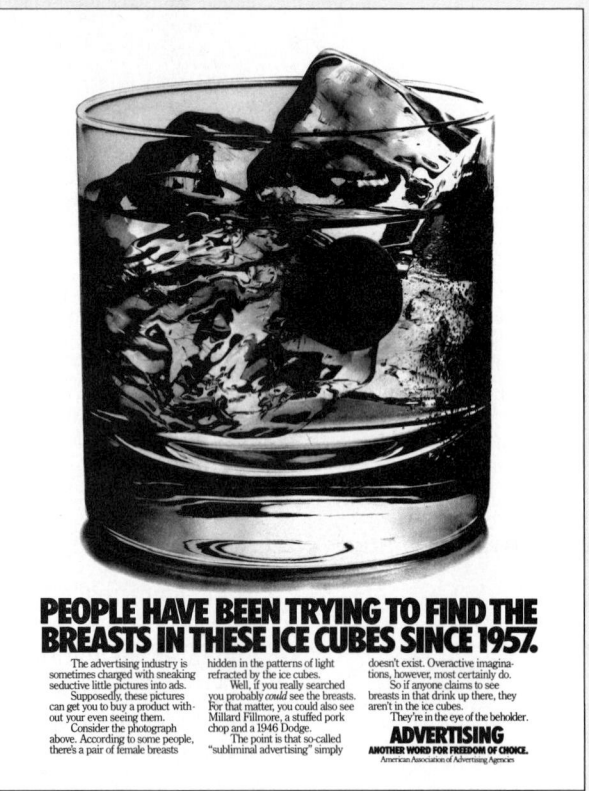

PEOPLE HAVE BEEN TRYING TO FIND THE BREASTS IN THESE ICE CUBES SINCE 1957.

The advertising industry is sometimes charged with sneaking seductive little pictures into ads.

Supposedly, these pictures can get you to buy a product without your even seeing them.

Consider the photograph above. According to some people, there's a pair of female breasts hidden in the patterns of light refracted by the ice cubes.

Well, if you really searched you probably *could* see the breasts. For that matter, you could also see Millard Fillmore, a stuffed pork chop and a 1946 Dodge.

The point is that so-called "subliminal advertising" simply doesn't exist. Overactive imaginations, however, most certainly do.

So if anyone claims to see breasts in that drink up there, they aren't in the ice cubes.

They're in the eye of the beholder.

ADVERTISING
ANOTHER WORD FOR FREEDOM OF CHOICE.
American Association of Advertising Agencies

Source: Jack Haberstroh, "Can't Ignore Subliminal Ad Charges," *Advertising Age,* September 17, 1984, pp. 3, 42–44; Timothy Moore, "Subliminal Advertising: What You See Is What You Get," *Journal of Marketing* 46, no. 2 (Spring 1982), pp. 38–47; idem, "The Case against Subliminal Manipulation," *Psychology and Marketing* 5, no. 4 (Winter 1988), pp. 297–316; and Joel Saegert, "Why Marketing Should Quit Giving Subliminal Advertising the Benefit of the Doubt," *Psychology and Marketing* 4, pp. 107–120.

considering a German sports sedan such as a Mercedes or BMW to include the Audi 100 in their evoked set.

Advertising is a very valuable promotional tool for creating and maintaining brand awareness and ensuring a brand is included in the evoked set. However, marketers also work to promote their brands in the actual purchase environment where decisions are made. Point-of-purchase materials and promotional techniques such as in-store sampling, end-aisle displays, or shelf tags touting special prices are

➤ *Exhibit 4–14*
Audi makes effective use of comparative advertising to enter the evoked set

NEW AUDI TAKES AIM AT LEXUS AND ACURA.

In order to stand out in the highly competitive American car market, Audi has invested millions of dollars in redesigning and rethinking every automobile in its line-up, starting with the all-new Audi 100 V-6. At a base price of only $29,900,* it's clear Audi is not content to let Lexus and Acura corner the market. Indeed, Audi believes the new 100 will break from the pack, being the first new automobile in its class to offer German engineering with Japanese pricing. With front-wheel drive, driver's side air bag, and ABS standard on every Audi 100, Japanese car buyers may find the new Audi too good a value to ignore.
—KARL TREUTLER, DETROIT

*Manufacturer's suggested retail price, excluding taxes, license, freight, dealer charges and options. Price subject to change. 100 S shown with $470 optional metallic paint.

often used to encourage consumers to consider brands that may not have initially been in their evoked set.

Evaluative criteria and consequences

Once consumers have identified an evoked set and have a list of alternatives from which they plan to make their selection, they must evaluate the various brands. This involves an evaluation or comparison of the choice alternatives on specific criteria important to the consumer. **Evaluative criteria** are the dimensions or attributes of a product or service that are used to compare different alternatives. Evaluative criteria are generally thought of in terms of product or service attributes and can be objective or subjective. For example, in buying an automobile, consumers use objective attributes such as price, warranty, and fuel economy ratings as well as subjective factors such as image, styling, quality, and performance.

Evaluative criteria are usually viewed as product or service attributes. Many marketers view their products or services as *bundles of attributes*. However, consumers often tend to think about products or services in terms of their *consequences* rather than their attributes. J. Paul Peter and Jerry Olson refer to consequences as specific events or outcomes that consumers experience when a product or service is purchased and/or consumed.[10] They distinguish between two broad types or levels of consequences. **Functional consequences** are concrete outcomes of product or service usage that are tangible and directly experienced by consumers. The taste of a soft drink or potato chip, the acceleration of an automobile, or the clarity of a facsimile transmission are examples of functional consequences. **Psychosocial consequences** refer to abstract outcomes that are more intangible, subjective, and personal, such as how a product makes you feel or how you think others will view you for purchasing or using it.

Marketers should distinguish between product/service attributes and consequences because the importance and/or meaning consumers assign to an attribute is usually determined by the consequences it has for them. Moreover, advertisers must be sure consumers understand the linkage between a particular attribute and a consequence. For example, the Nikon ad in Exhibit 4–15 discusses the attributes of the N5005 camera but emphasizes the consequences or outcomes of using it—the ability to take great pictures.

Product/service attributes and the consequences or outcomes consumers think they will experience from using a particular brand are very important, for they are often the basis on which consumers form attitudes and purchase intentions and

> *Exhibit 4–15*
This ad emphasizes the great pictures that can be taken with a Nikon camera

decide among various choice alternatives. Two subprocesses are very important during the alternative evaluation stage—the process by which consumer attitudes are created, reinforced, and changed and the consumer decision rules or integration strategies consumers use to compare brands and make purchase decisions. We will examine each of these processes in more detail.

Attitudes

Attitudes represent one of the most heavily studied concepts in consumer behavior. According to Gordon Allport's classic definition, "attitudes are learned predispositions to respond to an object."[11] More recent perspectives view attitudes as a summary construct that represents an individual's overall feelings or evaluation of an object.[12] Consumers hold attitudes toward a variety of objects that are important to marketers including individuals (celebrity endorsers such as Joe Montana or Bill Cosby), brands (Cheerios, Kix), companies (Exxon, IBM), product categories (beef, pork, tuna), retail stores (Kmart, Sears), or even advertisements (the Energizer bunny ads).

Attitudes are important to marketers because they theoretically summarize a consumer's evaluation of an object (brand, company) and represent positive or negative feelings and behavioral tendencies. Marketers' keen interest in attitudes is based on the assumption that they are related to consumers' purchase behavior. A considerable amount of evidence supports the basic assumption of a relationship between attitudes and behavior.[13] However, the attitude-behavior link does not always hold; many other factors in addition to attitude can affect behavior.[14] Nevertheless, attitudes are considered very important to marketers and are particularly relevant to advertising and promotion planners. Advertising and promotion are used to create favorable attitudes toward new products/services or brands, reinforce or maintain existing favorable attitudes, and/or change negative attitudes. An approach to studying and measuring attitudes that is particularly relevant to advertising is that of multiattribute attitude models.

Multiattribute attitude models   Consumer researchers, as well as marketing practitioners, have been using multiattribute attitude models to study consumer attitudes over the past two decades.[15] A **multiattribute attitude model** views an attitude object, such as a product or brand, as possessing a number of attributes that provide the basis on which consumers form their attitudes. According to this model, consumers have beliefs about specific brand attributes and attach different levels of importance to these attributes. Using this approach, an attitude toward a particular brand can be represented as

$$A_B = \sum_{i=1}^{n} B_i \times E_i$$

where

A_B = attitude toward a brand
B_i = beliefs about the brand's performance on attribute i
E_i = importance attached to attribute i
n = number of attributes considered

For example, a consumer may have beliefs (B_i) about various brands of toothpaste on certain attributes. One brand may be perceived as having fluoride and thus preventing cavities, tasting good, and helping control tartar buildup. Another brand may not be perceived as being as good on these attributes, but consumers may believe it performs well on other attributes such as freshening breath and whitening teeth.

To predict attitudes, it is necessary to know how much importance consumers attach to each of these attributes (E_i). For example, parents purchasing a brand for their children may prefer a brand that performs well on cavity prevention, which would lead to a more favorable attitude toward the first brand. Teenagers and young adults may prefer a brand that freshens their breath and makes their teeth white and thus prefer the second brand.

Consumers may hold a number of different beliefs about brands in any product or service category. However, not all of these beliefs are activated in forming an attitude. Beliefs concerning specific attributes or consequences that are activated and form the basis of an attitude are referred to as **salient beliefs.** Marketers should identify and understand these salient beliefs. They must also recognize that the saliency of beliefs may vary among different market segments, over time, and across different consumption situations.

Attitude change strategies Multiattribute models allow marketers to better understand and diagnose the underlying structure or basis of consumers' attitudes. By understanding the beliefs that underlie consumers' evaluations of a brand and the importance of various attributes or consequences, the marketer is better able to develop communication strategies for creating, changing, or reinforcing brand attitudes. The multiattribute model provides insight into several ways marketers can influence consumer attitudes, including:

- Increasing or changing the strength or belief rating of a brand on an important attribute.
- Changing consumers' perceptions of the importance or value of an attribute.
- Adding a new attribute to the attitude formation process.
- Changing perceptions of belief ratings for a competing brand.

The first strategy is probably one of the most commonly used by advertisers. They identify an attribute or consequence that is important and remind consumers how well their brand performs on this attribute. In situations where consumers do not perceive the marketer's brand as possessing an important attribute or the belief strength is low, advertising strategies may be targeted at changing the belief rating. Even in situations where belief strength is high, advertising may be used to increase or reinforce the rating of a brand on an important attribute.

The Penn campaign used this strategy effectively to promote the quality of its tennis balls. In 1986, Penn was the number two manufacturer of tennis balls, behind Wilson, even though its product better satisfied the United States Tennis Association

➤ *Exhibit 4−16*
Penn focused on the consistent quality of its product to become the leading brand of tennis balls

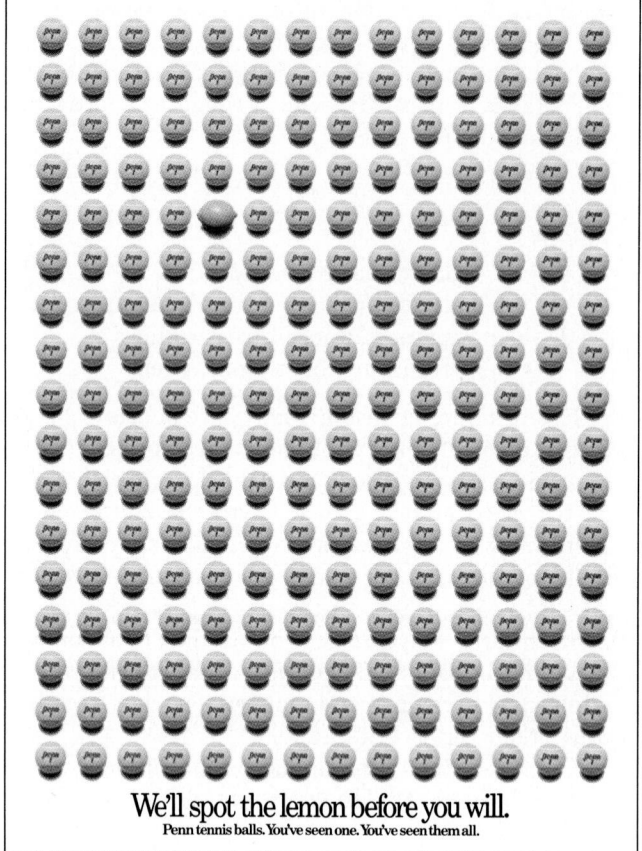

We'll spot the lemon before you will.
Penn tennis balls. You've seen one. You've seen them all.

specifications for weight and bounce. Penn's ad agency leveraged the company's superior manufacturing to position the Penn tennis balls as the most consistent in quality. The advertising theme developed to communicate the consistency attribute—"Penn tennis balls. You've seen one. You've seen them all"—was incorporated into ads such as that shown in Exhibit 4−16. The campaign helped Penn become the leading brand of tennis balls, enjoying a brand loyalty level almost twice that of its competitors.

Marketers often attempt to influence consumer attitudes via the second strategy of changing the relative importance of a particular attribute. This strategy involves getting consumers to attach more importance to the attribute in forming their attitude toward the brand. Marketers using this strategy want to increase the importance of an attribute where their particular brand performs very well.

The third strategy for influencing consumer attitudes is to add or emphasize a new attribute that can be used by consumers in evaluating a brand. Marketers often do this by improving their products or focusing on additional benefits or consequences associated with using the brand. Exhibit 4−17 shows how Listerine influences consumer attitudes by showing how the brand can help prevent gingivitis. The objective of this type of advertising is to persuade consumers to consider this attribute in forming attitudes toward mouthwashes and thus make evaluations of Listerine more favorable.

A final strategy marketers might consider is changing consumer beliefs about the attributes of competitive brands or product categories. This strategy has become much more common with the increase in comparative advertising as marketers compare their brands to competitors on specific product attributes. An example of this is the Geze ad shown in Exhibit 4−18 where the company compares a number of important attributes of its ski bindings to those of competitors.

> *Exhibit 4–17*
Listerine attempts to influence consumers' attitudes by adding a new attribute for consideration

> *Exhibit 4–18*
Geze compares its ski bindings to competing brands on specific attributes

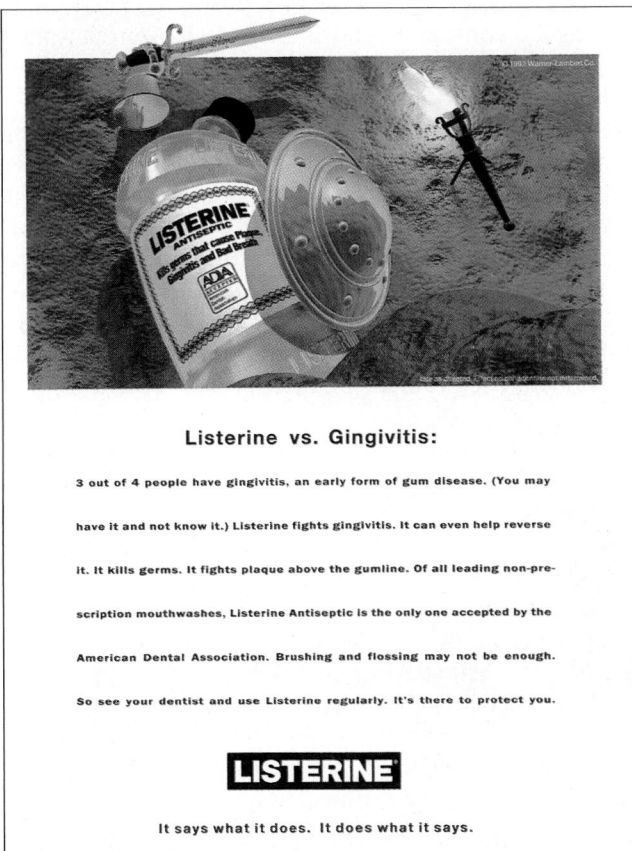

Listerine vs. Gingivitis:

3 out of 4 people have gingivitis, an early form of gum disease. (You may have it and not know it.) Listerine fights gingivitis. It can even help reverse it. It kills germs. It fights plaque above the gumline. Of all leading non-prescription mouthwashes, Listerine Antiseptic is the only one accepted by the American Dental Association. Brushing and flossing may not be enough. So see your dentist and use Listerine regularly. It's there to protect you.

LISTERINE

It says what it does. It does what it says.

Integration processes and decision rules

Another important aspect of the alternative evaluation stage is the way consumers integrate or combine information they have about the characteristics of brands to arrive at a purchase decision. **Integration processes** involve the way information such as product knowledge, meanings, and beliefs is combined to evaluate two or more alternatives.[16] To understand the integration process, attention has focused on the different types of *decision rules* or strategies consumers use to decide among purchase alternatives. These decision rules can represent very detailed and formal integration processes or more simple procedures commonly referred to as heuristics. We will briefly examine some of the various decision rules that consumers might use and discuss their implications for promotional planners.

Formal integration rules   Consumers often make purchase selections by using formal integration strategies or decision rules that require examination and comparison of alternatives on specific attributes. The compensatory rule is a decision rule that involves a more formal integration strategy. Consumers using a **compensatory decision rule** evaluate each brand under consideration with respect to how it performs on the relevant or salient attributes used as evaluative criteria. Consideration is also given to the weighting or importance of each attribute to the consumer. This decision rule suggests that consumers will arrive at an evaluation or summary score for each alternative by considering how well it performs across all of the attributes, taking into account varying levels of attribute importance. The multiattribute attitude model discussed earlier is an example of a compensatory integration process or decision rule.

The compensatory decision rule allows for a negative evaluation or performance on one attribute to be balanced out or *compensated* for by a positive evaluation on some other attribute. For example, a consumer who is considering purchasing a luxury automobile may allow attributes such as size, safety, comfort, and performance to compensate for its poor fuel economy.

Compensatory decision rules are likely to be used when alternatives are being compared on a number of evaluative criteria that are important and none of the alternatives is clearly superior. This type of decision rule requires consumers to make *trade-offs* because strong performance on an attribute may mean less favorable performance on another (e.g., more comfort, safety, and performance may mean sacrificing some fuel economy). Advertisers that know their product is weak on a particular attribute but strong on others may want to encourage consumers to use a compensatory decision rule. The various attitude change strategies discussed under multiattribute attitude models are also relevant to influencing consumers using a compensatory decision rule.

In addition to compensatory decision rules, consumers also use **noncompensatory integration strategies,** which do not allow negative evaluation or performance on a particular attribute to be compensated for by a positive evaluation on some other attribute. Two interesting examples of noncompensatory integration strategies are the lexicographic and conjunctive decision rules.

Consumers using a **lexicographic decision rule** will first rank their choice criteria in terms of relative importance. Brands are then evaluated on each attribute starting with the most important one. If one of the brands is seen as being significantly better on the most important attribute, it is chosen and the decision process ends. If two or more alternatives are rated similarly on this attribute, the consumer will compare them on the next most important attribute (and so on), repeating the comparison until an alternative is found to be better than the others on a particular attribute.

Because a lexicographic decision rule is noncompensatory, a brand that is rated low on a very important attribute will be eliminated from consideration. Strong performance on a number of other attributes cannot compensate for weakness on evaluative criteria that are most important to consumers. Consumers may use a lexicographic decision rule when there are only one or a few particular attributes on which their purchase decision is based. For example, many golfers decide which type of ball to use on the basis of one factor—distance. Thus, it is very common to see ads for certain brands of golf balls where the only claim is that of superior performance on the distance attribute (Exhibit 4–19).

➣ *Exhibit 4–19*
This ad for ULTRA 270 golf balls focuses on the product's distance superiority

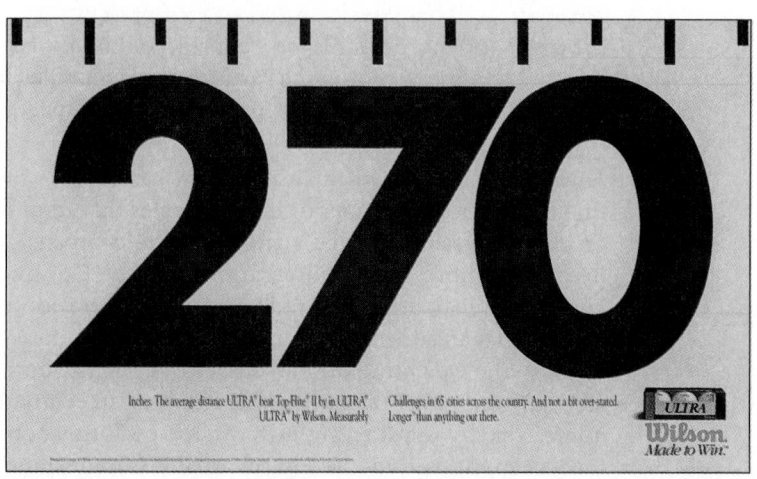

If a **conjunctive decision rule** is used, the consumer will establish cutoffs or minimally acceptable levels of performance for each important attribute. Any alternative failing to meet the cutoff levels for any of the attributes will be eliminated. For many decisions, the use of a conjunctive strategy may result in several acceptable alternatives, and the consumer will have to apply another decision rule to make a final selection. The conjunctive rule may be used as part of a **phased processing strategy** where more than one decision rule is applied during the purchasing process.[17] For example, a conjunctive rule may be used to reduce the number of alternatives, while another rule such as the compensatory or lexicographic may be applied to arrive at a final purchase decision.

Informal decision rules In some situations, consumers may make their purchase decision using more simplified or basic decision rules known as **heuristics.** Peter and Olson note that heuristics are easy to use and are highly adaptive to specific environmental situations (such as in a retail store).[18] For familiar products that are purchased frequently, consumers may use heuristics such as price-based decision rules (buy the least expensive brand) or promotion-based heuristics (choose the brand for which I can get a price reduction through use of a coupon, rebate, special deal, and the like).

Another type of heuristic is the **affect referral decision rule.**[19] Consumers using this decision rule make a selection on the basis of an overall impression or summary evaluation of the various alternatives under consideration. The use of this decision rule suggests that consumers have affective impressions of brands stored in memory that can be accessed at the time of purchase. Think about how many times you have gone into a store and purchased various products based on your overall impressions or evaluations of the brands rather than going through any type of detailed comparisons of the alternatives on specific attributes.

Marketers selling familiar and popular brands may want to appeal to an affect referral rule by stressing overall affective feelings or impressions about their products. For example, market leaders, whose products enjoy strong overall brand images, often use ads that promote the brand as the best overall. For example, Coke is the "Real Thing," Diet Pepsi tells consumers "You've Got The Right One Baby. Uh Huh!" Miller Lite beer says, "It's it and that's that," while Budweiser is the "King of Beers (Exhibit 4–20).

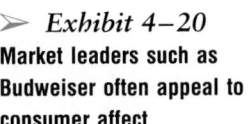

➤ *Exhibit 4–20*
Market leaders such as Budweiser often appeal to consumer affect

Implications of integration strategies Promotional planners should understand consumers' integration processes and the types of decision rules they might use in selecting a product or service. If a marketer knows a particular decision rule is likely to be used for certain products or services or in certain situations, an advertisement can be designed in a format consistent with the decision rule. Alternatively, an advertising message may be designed to suggest how consumers might make the purchase decision.[20] (Naturally, the ad will be designed to move the consumer toward purchasing the advertiser's brand!)

Marketers also must recognize that some purchase decisions are the result of a *constructive* process that occurs at the time of purchase.[21] Thus, it may be important for marketers to use packaging and other promotional techniques that will motivate consumers to choose their brands at the point of purchase.

Purchase Decision

At some point in the buying process, the consumer must stop searching for and evaluating information about alternative brands in the evoked set and make a *purchase decision*. As an outcome of the alternative evaluation stage, the consumer may develop a **purchase intention** or predisposition to buy a certain brand. Purchase intentions are generally based on a matching of purchase motives with attributes or characteristics of brands under consideration. Their formation involves many of the personal subprocesses discussed in this chapter including motivation, perception, attitude formation, and integration.

A purchase decision is not the same as an actual purchase. Once a choice is made as to which brand to buy, the consumer must still implement the decision and make the actual purchase. Additional decisions may need to be made such as when to buy, where to buy, and how much money to spend. Often, there is a time delay between the formation of a purchase intention or decision and the actual purchase, particularly for highly involved and complex purchases such as automobiles, personal computers, or consumer durables.

For nondurable products, which include many low involvement items such as consumer package goods, the time between the decision and actual purchase may be short. For many of these products, the purchase decision may occur before the actual purchase. For example, before leaving home, the consumer may make a shopping list that includes specific brand names. Brands may be included on this list because the consumer has developed **brand loyalty**—a preference for a particular brand—that results in its repeated purchase. Marketers strive to develop and maintain brand loyalty among consumers. They use reminder advertising to keep their brand names in front of consumers, maintain prominent shelf positions and displays in stores, and run periodic promotions to deter consumers from switching brands. Maintaining consumers' brand loyalty is not easy. Competitors use a variety of techniques to encourage consumers to try their brands such as new product introductions, free samples, and other promotional offers. As can be seen from Exhibit 4–21, the percentage of consumers who are loyal to one brand is less than 50 percent for many products. Thus, marketers must continually battle to maintain their loyal consumers, while at the same time replacing those who switch brands.

While purchase decisions for nondurable, convenience items may occur before actual purchase, these decisions sometimes take place in the store, as decision and purchase occur almost simultaneously. For these types of decisions, marketers must ensure that consumers have top-of-mind awareness of their brands so they are quickly recognized and considered. Marketers must also recognize that these types of decisions are influenced at the actual point of purchase. As noted previously, packaging, shelf displays, point-of-purchase-materials, and promotional tools such as on-package coupons or premium offers may be helpful in influencing decisions made through constructive processes at the time of purchase. These promotional tools can supplement or reinforce the awareness or brand identity created by the advertising program.

➤ *Exhibit 4–21* **Percentage of users of these products who are loyal to one brand**

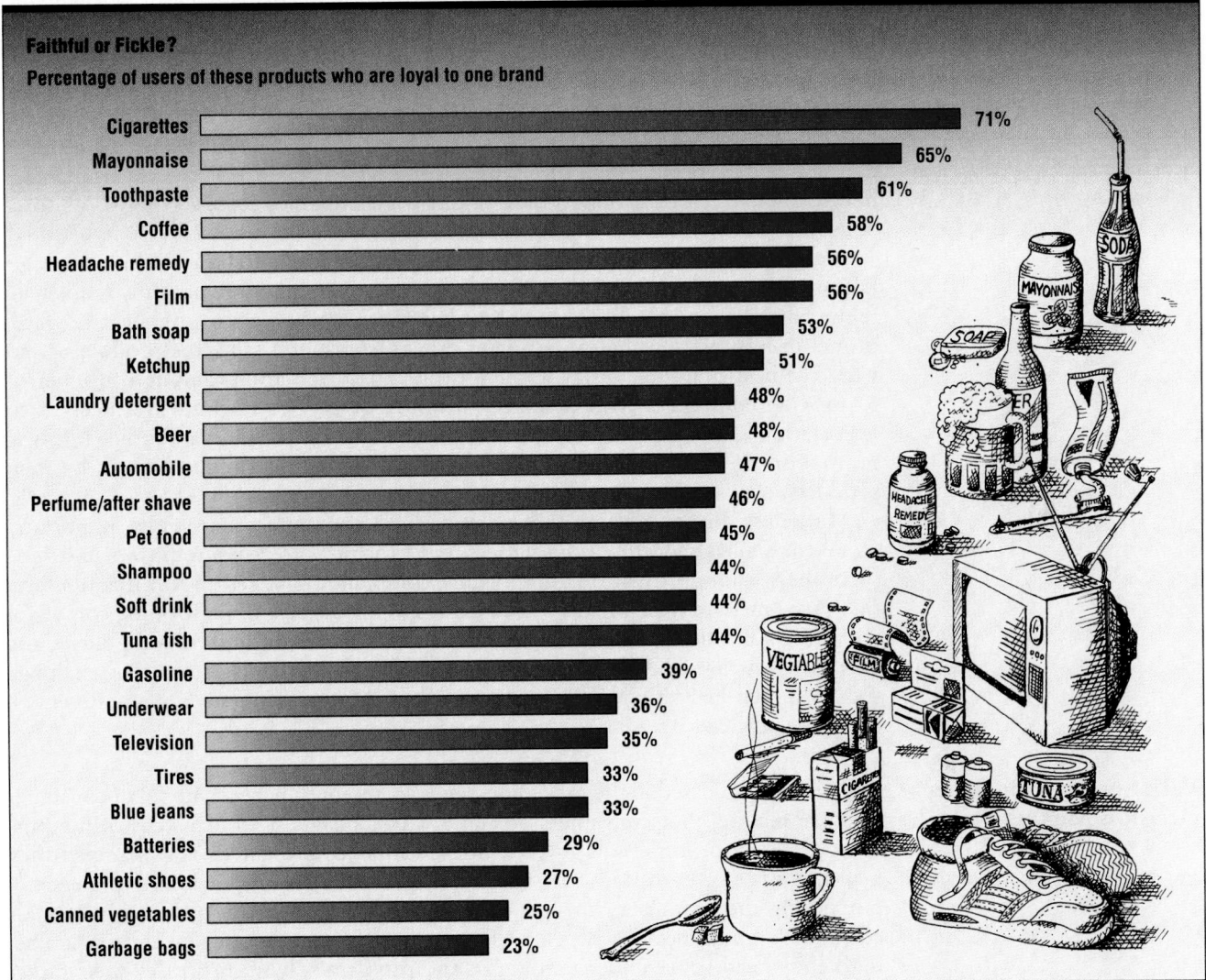

Faithful or Fickle?
Percentage of users of these products who are loyal to one brand

Product	Percentage
Cigarettes	71%
Mayonnaise	65%
Toothpaste	61%
Coffee	58%
Headache remedy	56%
Film	56%
Bath soap	53%
Ketchup	51%
Laundry detergent	48%
Beer	48%
Automobile	47%
Perfume/after shave	46%
Pet food	45%
Shampoo	44%
Soft drink	44%
Tuna fish	44%
Gasoline	39%
Underwear	36%
Television	35%
Tires	33%
Blue jeans	33%
Batteries	29%
Athletic shoes	27%
Canned vegetables	25%
Garbage bags	23%

Postpurchase Evaluation

The consumer decision process does not end once the product or service has been purchased. After using the product or service, the consumer compares the level of performance with expectations and is either satisfied or dissatisfied. *Satisfaction* occurs when the consumer's expectations are either met or exceeded, while *dissatisfaction* results when performance is below expectations. The postpurchase evaluation process is very important because the information acquired from actual use of a product serves as feedback that will influence the likelihood of future purchases. Positive performance or consequences resulting from use of the brand means the brand is retained in the evoked set and increases the likelihood it will be purchased again. Unfavorable outcomes may lead to the formation of negative attitudes toward the brand and lessen the likelihood it will be purchased again or even result in elimination from the consumer's evoked set.

Another possible outcome of purchase is **cognitive dissonance,** which refers to a feeling of psychological tension or postpurchase doubt that a consumer experiences after making a difficult purchase choice. Dissonance results in a feeling of anxiety or uneasiness and is more likely to occur for important decisions where the consumer must choose among close alternatives (for example, the unchosen alternative has unique or desirable features that the selected alternative does not have). Consumers experiencing cognitive dissonance may use a number of strategies to attempt to reduce it. They may seek out reassurance and opinions from others to confirm the wisdom of their purchase decision; they may lower their attitudes or opinions of the unchosen alternative; they may deny or distort any information that does not support the choice they made; or they may look for information that is supportive of their choice. An important source of this supportive information is advertising; consumers have been shown to be more attentive to advertising for the brand they have chosen.[22] Thus, it may be important for companies to advertise to reinforce consumer decisions to purchase their brands.

Marketers must recognize the importance of the postpurchase evaluation stage. Dissatisfied consumers who are still experiencing dissonance are not only unlikely to repurchase the marketer's product, but they may also be a source of negative word-of-mouth information that might deter others from purchasing the product or service. The best guarantee of favorable postpurchase evaluations among consumers is to provide consumers with a quality product or service that always meets their expectations. However, marketers must be sure their advertising and other forms of promotion do not create unreasonable expectations that cannot be met by their products.

Marketers are recognizing that postpurchase communication is also important. Some companies send follow-up letters and brochures to reassure buyers and reinforce the wisdom of their decision. Many companies have set up toll-free numbers that consumers may call if they need information or have a question or complaint regarding a product. Marketers also offer liberalized return and refund policies and extended warranties and guarantees to ensure customer satisfaction. For example, the ad shown in Exhibit 4–22 promotes Ford Motor Company's commitment to customer service.

Variations in Consumer Decision Making

The process discussed in the preceding pages represents a general model of consumer decision making. But consumers do not always engage in all five steps of the purchase decision process, nor proceed in the sequence presented. For example, they may minimize or even skip one or more stages if they have previous experience in purchasing the product or service or if the decision is of low personal, social, or economic significance. To develop effective promotional strategies and programs, marketers need some understanding of the problem-solving processes their target consumers use to make purchase decisions. We will briefly examine three major variations of the consumer decision-making process: routine response behavior, limited problem solving, and extended problem solving.[23]

Routine response behavior

Many of the purchase decisions we make as consumers are based on a habitual or routine choice process. For many low-priced, frequently purchased products, the decision process consists of little more than recognizing the problem, engaging in a quick internal search, and making the purchase. The consumer spends little or no effort engaging in external search or alternative evaluation. Think about your own decision-making process for products such as milk, soda, or toothpaste. How much time do you spend searching for different brands or evaluating alternatives? For most consumers, the purchase process for such products is relatively automatic as it involves little more than implementing a learned or programmed decision plan.

Marketers of products characterized by a routine response purchase process should attempt to get and/or maintain their brands in the consumer's evoked set and to avoid anything that may result in their removal from consideration. Established brands that have strong market share position are likely to be in the evoked set of most consumers. Marketers of these brands will want consumers to follow a routine

choice process and continue to purchase their products. This means maintaining high levels of brand awareness through reminder advertising, running periodic promotions, and maintaining prominent shelf positions in retail stores. Promotional Perspective 4–3 discusses how General Mills has done an excellent job of maintaining consumer demand for many of its established brands.

Marketers of new brands or those with a low market share face a different challenge because they must find ways to disrupt consumers' routine choice process and get them to consider different alternatives. High levels of advertising may be used to encourage trial or brand switching along with sales promotion efforts in the form of free samples, special price offers, high value coupons, and the like.

Limited problem solving

A more complicated decision-making process may occur when the consumer has a limited amount of experience in purchasing a particular product or service and is only somewhat aware or knowledgeable of the brands available and/or the criteria to use in making a purchase decision. For limited problem solving, consumers will engage in a moderate amount of search behavior and alternative evaluation. They may have to learn what attributes or criteria should be used in making a purchase decision and how the various alternatives perform on these dimensions. Think about your last purchase of clothing or even the selection of a restaurant for a nice Saturday night dinner date. While you may not have become involved in a major decision process, you may have spent some time acquiring information and discussing and evaluating various alternatives.

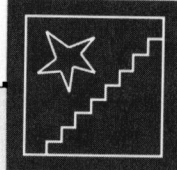

Promotional Perspective 4–3

Building Excitement for Older Brands

In recent years, many consumer package-goods companies have turned to new products to achieve their growth objectives. However, brand managers at General Mills have shown that sales and profit growth can be achieved by rejuvenating established products as well. While the U.S. food industry parallels population growth and expands at only about 1 percent a year, General Mills' sales increased 8 percent in the 1991 fiscal year, and net earnings have risen 20 percent annually over the past five years. Much of the company's growth has come from its existing brands, including Betty Crocker products such as the Hamburger Helper and Nature Valley granola snack lines, along with its ancient and plain-tasting cereals such as Kix, Wheaties, and Cheerios.

Many companies abandon older brands when they reach the late maturity stage of the product life cycle and turn their attention to new products. At General Mills, however, marketing and brand managers work hard to prove that older brands are not washed up and ready for the marketing graveyard. They use a variety of marketing and promotional techniques to not only keep these brands alive, but to keep them growing as well. For example, Kix cereal, a 54-year old brand, has been performing more like a hot new product recently as sales increased 30 percent in fiscal 1991 and 13 percent the previous year. A few years ago, the manufacturing people gave Kix a sweeter taste by putting sugar on the coating of the cereal instead of in the batter. The sugar content stayed the same, and General Mills has been promoting Kix as low in sugar using the "kid-tested, mother-approved" advertising theme.

To perk up sales of Wheaties, its oldest brand, General Mills has focused attention on the packaging. The package for the "breakfast of champions" has long featured pictures of popular athletes. In 1987, the company began using limited edition boxes featuring pictures of championship sports teams (the New York Giants, the Chicago Bulls, the Pittsburgh Penguins, the Minnesota Twins). In 1991, Wheaties scored big with a package featuring basketball star Michael Jordan on the front and a basketball game that popped out from the back of the box. A box featuring a Joe Montana football game on the back panel is being planned.

General Mills has also kept Cheerios growing by increasing advertising spending and touting its oat bran content and that the product is low in sugar and fat. Basic yellow box Cheerios became the leading brand of cereal (in dollar volume) in 1989 and continues to fight for the top spot with Kellogg's Frosted Flakes. The company also extended the Cheerios brand by bringing out two new variations—Honey Nut in 1979 and Apple Cinnamon in 1988—to create a megabrand that accounts for nearly 8 percent of corporate revenue and an even greater portion of its profits.

General Mills stays in close touch with cereal consumers, calling almost 300 households every weekday to ask people what they ate for breakfast and how it tasted. In addition to extensive consumer research, the marketing director encourages the R&D and manufacturing departments to be more creative and meet with the advertising agencies for the company's various brands. The marketers at General Mills continue to show that through creative and innovative marketing, it can build excitement, along with sales and profits, for old, established products better than anyone in the food business.

Source: Patricia Sellers, "A Boring Brand Can Be Beautiful," from *Fortune,* November 18, 1991, pp. 169–79. © 1991 Time, Inc. All rights reserved.

When consumers are likely to purchase a product through limited problem solving, marketers should make information available to consumers that will be helpful to them in making their decision. Advertising that provides consumers with detailed information about a brand and how it can satisfy their purchase motives and goals is important. Marketers may also want to provide consumers with information at the point of purchase, either through displays or brochures. Distribution channels should have knowledgeable sales personnel available to explain the features and benefits of the company's product or service and why it is superior to competing products.

Extended problem solving

Extended problem solving represents the most complex and detailed of the three types of decision-making processes. When consumers engage in extensive problem solving, they will go through each stage of the consumer decision-making process and are likely to spend considerable time and effort on external information search and in identifying and evaluating alternatives.

They may have little, if any, knowledge regarding the criteria that should be used in making the purchase decision or the various brands available. For example, consider a student who knows very little about personal computers and wants to purchase one for college. She may spend a great deal of time learning about what criteria are important and how the various brands compare on these attributes. She may spend time acquiring information by talking to friends, reading magazine reviews, visiting dealers, and/or reading the advertising and other promotional information supplied by various manufacturers. This information may be used to reduce the number of brands to a level that can be carefully compared and evaluated. The whole process will be very involving and may take some time before she arrives at a decision and makes the purchase.

As with limited problem solving, marketers of products characterized by an extensive problem-solving process will want to provide consumers with detailed information that can be used to evaluate their brand. The various techniques discussed under limited problem solving are also relevant for consumers engaging in extensive problem solving. The Epson ad shown in Exhibit 4–23 is a good example of how advertising can appeal to consumers who might be engaging in extended problem solving when purchasing a laser printer. Notice how the ad communicates with consumers who might know little, if anything, about how to purchase this product. The ad also makes more detailed information available by offering a free booklet designed to help first-time buyers.

Alternative Perspectives on Consumer Behavior

The discussion of the decision process shows that the way consumers make a purchase varies depending on a number of factors, including the nature of the product or service, the amount of experience the consumer has with the product, and the importance of the purchase. One factor that determines the level of problem solving to be employed is the consumer's *involvement* with the product or brand. Chapter 6 examines the meaning of involvement, the difference between low and high involvement decision making, and the implications of involvement for developing advertising and promotional strategies.

Our examination of consumer behavior thus far has looked at the decision-making process from a *cognitive orientation*. The five-stage decision process model views the consumer as a problem solver and information processor who engages in a variety of mental processes in evaluating various alternatives and determining the degree to which they might satisfy needs or purchase motives. Note, however, there are alternative perspectives regarding how consumers acquire the knowledge and experience they use in making purchase decisions. To understand these

➤ *Exhibit 4–23*
This ad for Epson laser printer shows how marketers can appeal to consumers engaging in extended problem solving

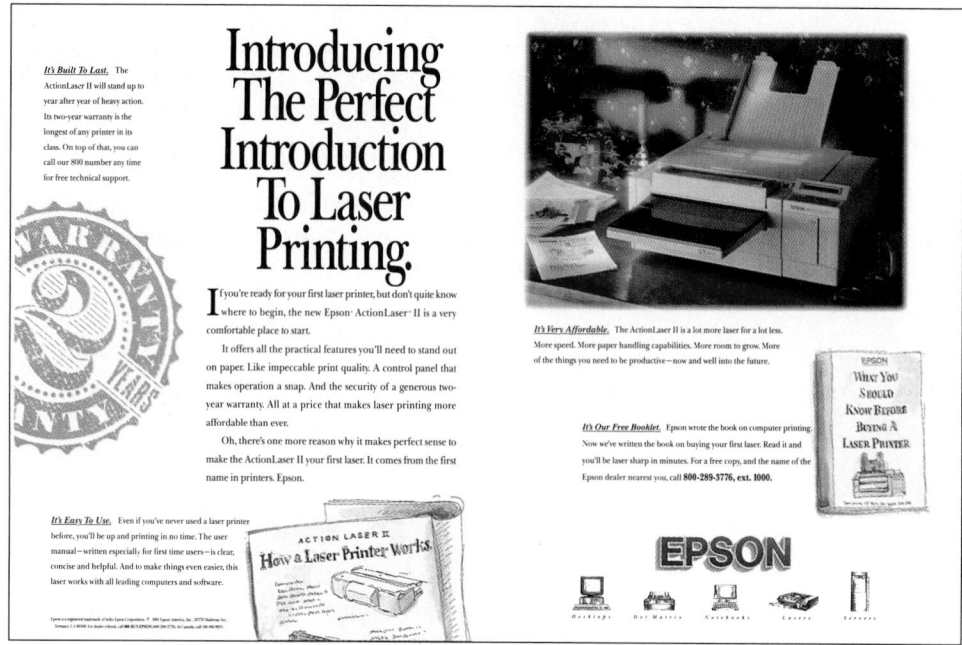

alternative perspectives, we turn our attention to the consumer learning process and examine various approaches to learning and their implications for advertising and promotion.

The Consumer Learning Process

Consumer learning has been defined as "the process by which individuals acquire the purchase and consumption knowledge and experience they apply to future related behavior."[24] Two basic approaches to learning are the behavioral approach and cognitive learning theory. We begin by examining the basic principles and implications of behavioral learning.

Behavioral Learning Theory

Behavioral learning theories emphasize the role of external or environmental stimuli in causing behavior while minimizing the significance of internal psychological processes. Behavioral learning theories are characterized by the "S-R" or *stimulus response orientation* because they are based on the premise that learning occurs as the result of responses to external stimuli in the environment. Behavioral learning theorists believe learning occurs through the connection between a stimulus and a response. We will examine the basic principles of two behavioral learning theory approaches: classical conditioning and operant conditioning.

Classical conditioning

Classical conditioning assumes that learning is essentially an *associative process* with an already existing relationship between a stimulus and a response. Probably the best-known example of this type of learning comes from the well-known studies done with animals by the Russian psychologist Pavlov.[25] Pavlov noticed that at feeding times, his dogs would salivate at the sight of food. The connection between food and salivation is not taught but is an innate reflex reaction. Because this relationship exists before the conditioning process, the food is referred to as an *unconditioned stimulus* and salivation is an *unconditioned response*. To see if salivation could be conditioned to occur in response to another neutral stimulus, Pavlov paired the ringing of a bell with the presentation of the food, and after a number of trials, the dogs learned to salivate at the sound of the bell alone. Thus, the bell

➤ *Exhibit 4–24*
The classical conditioning process

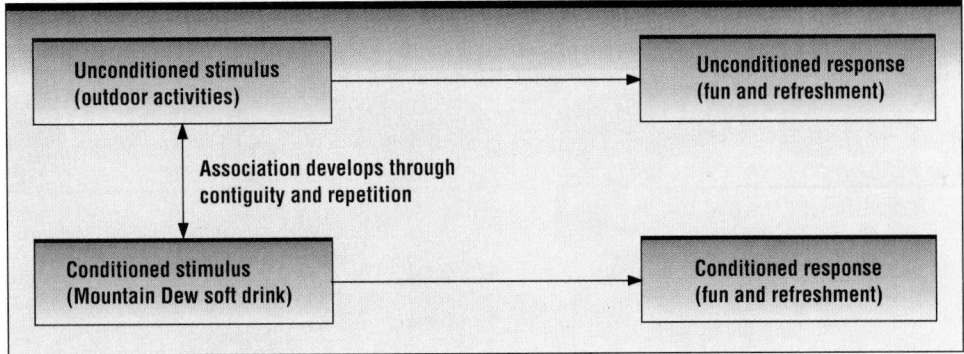

became a **conditioned stimulus** that elicited a **conditioned response** resembling the original unconditioned reaction.

Two factors are important for learning to occur through the associative process. The first is *contiguity*, which means the unconditioned stimulus and conditioned stimulus must occur in proximity in time and space. In Pavlov's experiment, the dog learns to associate the ringing of the bell with food because of the contiguous presentation of the two stimuli. The other important principle is *repetition*, or frequency, of the association. The more often the unconditioned and conditioned stimuli occur together, the stronger the association between them will be.

Applying classical conditioning   Learning through classical conditioning plays an important role in marketing, as buyers can be conditioned to form favorable impressions and images of various brands through the associative process. Advertisers strive to associate their products and services with perceptions, images, and emotions known to evoke positive reactions from consumers. Many products are promoted through image advertising in which the brand is shown with an unconditioned stimulus that is known to elicit pleasant and favorable feelings. Through the simultaneous presentation of the brand with this unconditioned stimulus, the brand itself becomes a conditioned stimulus that elicits the same favorable response. Exhibit 4–24 provides a diagram of this process, whereas the ad for Mountain Dew shown in Exhibit 4–25 is an example of an application of this strategy. Notice how this commercial associates Mountain Dew with fun and refreshment by showing people drinking it at a summertime party.

Classical conditioning can also be used by associating a product or service with a favorable emotional state. A study by Gerald Gorn used this approach to examine how background music in advertisements influenced product choice.[26] He found that subjects were more likely to choose a product when it was presented against a background of music they liked rather than music they disliked. These results suggest the emotions generated by a commercial are important because they may become associated with the advertised product through classical conditioning. Advertisers will often attempt to pair a previously neutral product or service stimulus with an event or situation that arouses positive feelings such as humor, an exciting sports event, or popular music.

Operant conditioning

Classical conditioning views the individual as a passive participant in the learning process who is simply a receiver of stimuli. Conditioning occurs as a result of exposure to a stimulus that occurs before the response. In the **operant conditioning** approach, the individual must actively *operate* or act on some aspect of the environment for learning to occur. Operant conditioning is sometimes referred to as *instrumental conditioning* because the response of the individual is instrumental in

➤ *Exhibit 4–25* **This commercial uses classical conditioning by associating Mountain Dew with summertime fun and refreshment**

(MUSIC STARTS)
BEING COOL YOU'LL FIND
IS A STATE OF MIND, A REFRESHING
   ATTITUDE
WHEN THINGS GET HOT

COOL IS ALL YOU GOT
DOING IT COUNTRY COOL
MOUNTAIN DEW
SO CHILL ON OUT WHEN THE HEAT
   COMES ON

WITH THE COOL SMOOTH
MOUNTAIN DEW
DOING IT COUNTRY COOL.
MOUNTAIN DEW, DOING IT COUNTRY
   COOL, (FADING OUT) MOUNTAIN DEW.

getting a positive reinforcement (reward) or negative reinforcement (punishment). **Reinforcement** refers to the reward or favorable consequences associated with a particular response and is an important element of instrumental conditioning. Behavior that is reinforced strengthens the bond between a stimulus and a response. Thus, if a consumer buys a product in response to an advertisement and the outcomes resulting from the use of the product are positive, the likelihood of the consumer using this product again is increased. If the outcomes are not favorable, the likelihood of buying the product again decreases.

The principles of operant conditioning can be applied to marketing, as shown by Exhibit 4–26. Companies attempt to provide their customers with products and services that satisfy their needs and reward them to reinforce the probability of repeat purchase. Reinforcement can also be implied in advertising, as many ads emphasize the benefits or rewards a consumer will receive from using a product or service. Reinforcement can also be applied to advertising by encouraging consumers to use a particular product or brand to avoid unpleasant consequences. For example, the ad for Dixie bathroom cups shown in Exhibit 4–27 focuses on the negative consequence of family members drinking from the same cup.

Two concepts that are particularly relevant to marketers in their use of reinforcement through promotional strategies are *schedules of reinforcement* and *shaping*. Different **schedules of reinforcement** result in varying patterns of learning and behavior. Learning occurs most rapidly under a *continuous* reinforcement schedule whereby every response is rewarded, but the behavior is likely to cease when the

➤ *Exhibit 4–26*
Instrumental conditioning in marketing

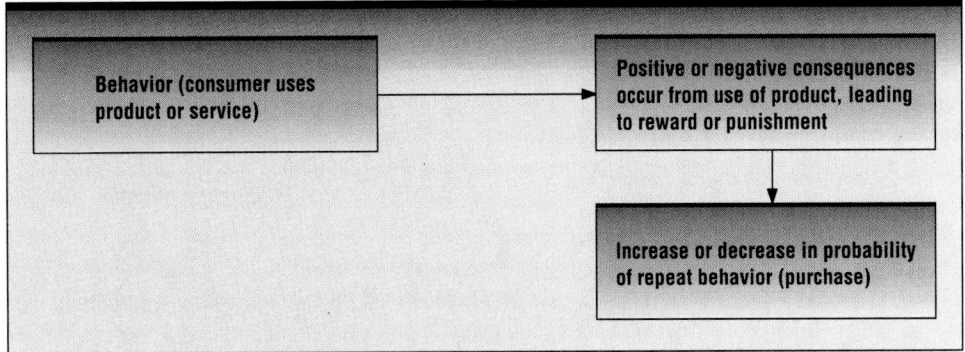

reinforcement stops. Marketers must provide continuous reinforcement to consumers or risk having them switch to brands that will provide satisfaction.

Learning occurs more slowly but lasts longer when a *partial* or *intermittent* reinforcement schedule is used and only some of the individual's responses are rewarded. An example of partial reinforcement schedules can be seen in the designing of promotional programs. A firm may want to periodically offer consumers an incentive to use the company's product. However, the firm would not want to offer the incentive every time (continuous reinforcement) because consumers might become dependent on it and stop buying the brand when the incentive is withdrawn. An example of this approach comes from a study that examined the use of a continuous versus partial reinforcement on bus ridership.[27] It was found that discount coupons given as rewards for riding the bus were equally effective when given on a partial schedule as when given on a continuous schedule. The cost of giving the discount coupons under the partial schedule, however, was considerably less.

Reinforcement schedules can also be used to influence consumer learning and behavior through a process known as **shaping.** Shaping refers to the reinforcement of successive acts that lead to a desired behavior pattern or response. Rothschild and Gaidis argue that shaping is a very useful concept for marketers and provide the following rationale for its use.[28]

> Shaping is an essential process in deriving new and complex behavior because a behavior cannot be rewarded unless it first occurs; a stimulus can only reinforce acts that already occur. New, complex behaviors rarely occur by chance in nature. If the only behavior to be rewarded were the final complex sought behavior, one would probably have to wait a long time for this to occur by chance. Instead, one can reward simpler existing behaviors; over time, more complex patterns evolve and these are rewarded. Thus the shaping process occurs by a method of successive approximations.

In a promotional context, shaping procedures are used as part of the introductory program for new products. Exhibit 4–28 provides an example of how samples and discount coupons could be used to introduce a new product and take a consumer from trial to repeat purchase. Marketers must be careful in their use of shaping procedures because dropping the use of incentives too soon may result in the consumer failing to establish the desired behavior, while overusing them may result in the consumer's purchase becoming contingent on the presence of the promotional incentive rather than the product or service.

Cognitive Learning

Behavioral learning theories have been criticized for assuming a mechanistic view of the consumer that puts too much emphasis on external stimulus factors. Internal psychological processes such as motivation, thinking, and perception are ignored under the assumption that the external stimulus environment will elicit fairly predictable responses. However, many consumer researchers and marketers disagree with the simplified explanations of behavior offered by behavioral learning theories

➤ *Exhibit 4–27*
This ad shows how Dixie bathroom cups can help consumers avoid negative consequences

and are more interested in examining the complex mental processes that might underlie consumer decision making. As a result, the cognitive approach to studying learning and decision making has dominated the field of consumer behavior in recent years.

Cognitive learning theory has as its basis a problem-solving, information-processing, reasoning approach to human behavior. In contrast to the behavioral learning theory perspectives, cognitive orientations emphasize *internal processing*—or thinking. **Cognitive processing** concerns the individual's transformation of external information into meaning or patterns of thought and how these meanings are combined to form judgments about behavior.[29] This approach is quite different from the behaviorists' perspective, as can be seen in the following comparison:

> The basic concept contends that consumers do not respond simply to stimuli but instead act on beliefs, express attitudes and strive toward goals. The cognitivist is thus concerned with this entire range of conscious experience and not just objective behavior. . . . The human being is viewed as a highly complex sensory processing and data gathering organism . . . . pulled to acts of choice by his goals and aspirations.[30]

While recognizing the behaviorists' perspective that some learning involves the simple process of association between stimulus and response, cognitive learning theory considers the consumer to be an adaptive problem solver who utilizes various processes in reasoning, forming concepts, and acquiring knowledge. Exhibit 4–29 shows how cognitive theorists view the learning process.

As consumer behavior typically involves choices and decision making, the cognitive perspective has particular appeal to those studying this discipline. Cognitive learning theory is seen as particularly relevant for important and involved purchase decisions. Cognitive processes such as perception, formation of beliefs about brands,

> *Exhibit 4–28*
Application of shaping procedures in marketing

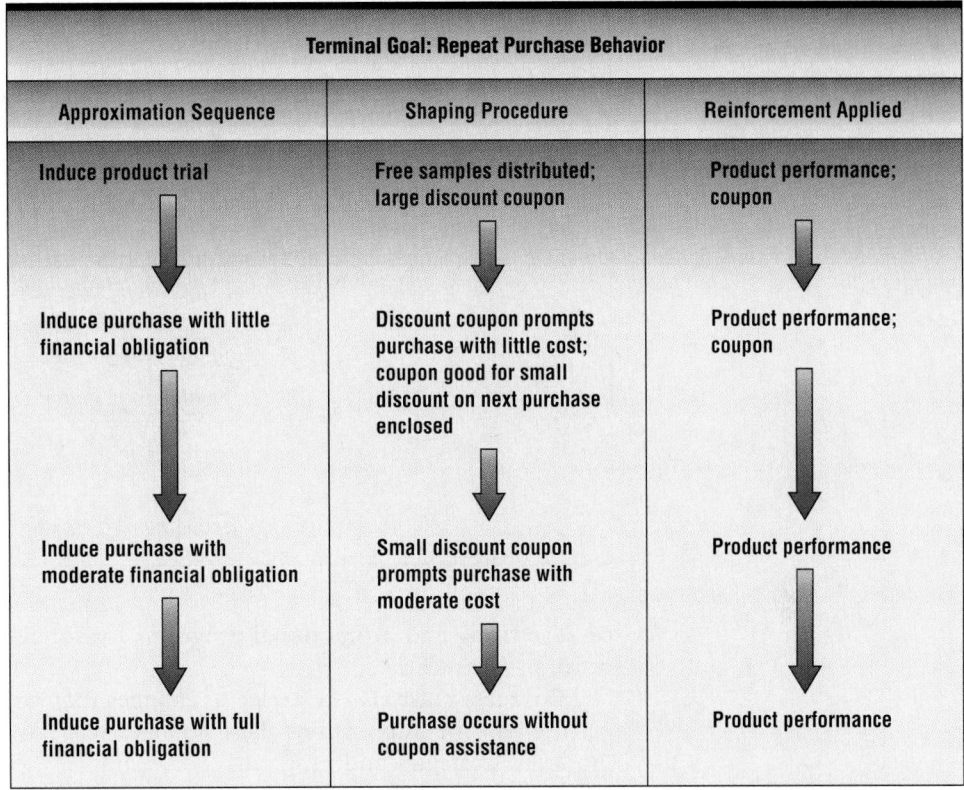

Terminal Goal: Repeat Purchase Behavior		
Approximation Sequence	**Shaping Procedure**	**Reinforcement Applied**
Induce product trial	Free samples distributed; large discount coupon	Product performance; coupon
Induce purchase with little financial obligation	Discount coupon prompts purchase with little cost; coupon good for small discount on next purchase enclosed	Product performance; coupon
Induce purchase with moderate financial obligation	Small discount coupon prompts purchase with moderate cost	Product performance
Induce purchase with full financial obligation	Purchase occurs without coupon assistance	Product performance

> *Exhibit 4–29*
The cognitive learning process

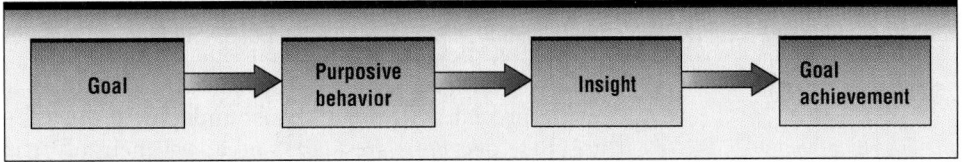

Goal → Purposive behavior → Insight → Goal achievement

attitude development and change, and integration processes are seen as very important and relevant to understanding the decision-making process for many types of purchases. The various subprocesses examined during our discussion of the five-stage decision process model are all relevant to a cognitive learning approach to consumer behavior.

Environmental Influences on Consumer Behavior

The consumer does not make purchase decisions in isolation. A number of external factors have been identified that may influence consumer decision making. Exhibit 4–30 shows various external factors that influence the consumer decision-making process. The remainder of this chapter examines some of these factors.

Culture

The broadest and most abstract of the various external factors that influence consumer behavior is culture. **Culture** refers to the complexity of learned meanings, values, norms, and customs shared by members of a society. Cultural norms and values offer direction and guidance to members of a society in all aspects of their lives including their consumption behavior. The need to understand the impact culture has on consumer behavior has become increasingly important as marketers expand their international marketing efforts. Each country has certain cultural traditions, customs, and values that must be understood by marketers in the development of marketing programs. The importance of cultural values in the development

> *Exhibit 4–30*
External influences on consumer behavior

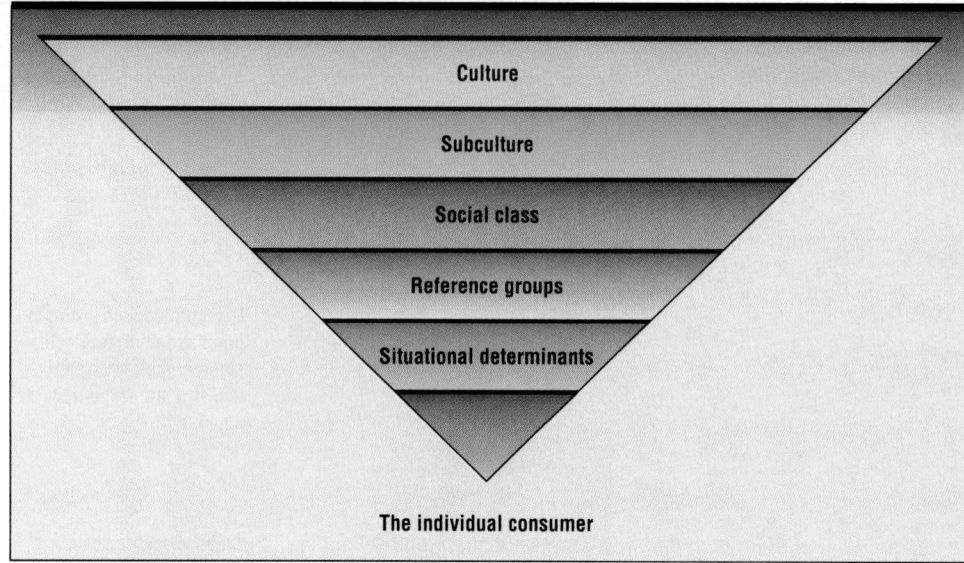

of advertising and promotional programs for foreign markets is examined in more detail in Chapter 22.

Marketers must also be aware of changes that might be occurring in a particular culture and the implications these changes will have on their advertising and promotional strategies and programs. For example, the American culture continues to go through a number of changes, many of which have direct implications for advertising. Marketing researchers continually monitor these changes and the impact they will have on the ways companies market their products and services.

While marketers recognize that culture exerts a demonstrable influence on the consumer, they often find it difficult to respond to cultural differences that exist in various markets. The subtleties of various cultures are often difficult to understand and appreciate. Marketers must understand the cultural context in which consumer purchase decisions are made and adapt their advertising and promotional programs accordingly.

Subcultures

Within a given culture are generally found smaller groups or segments that possess similar beliefs, values, norms, and patterns of behavior that set them apart from the larger cultural mainstream. These groups are referred to as **subcultures** and may be based on age, geography, race, religious, racial, and/or ethnic differences. A number of subcultures exist within the United States. The three largest racial/ethnic subcultures are blacks, Hispanics, and various Asian groups. As was noted in Chapter 2, these racial/ethnic subcultures are important because of their size, growth, purchasing power, and distinct purchasing patterns. Marketers recognize the importance of these subcultures as target markets for various products and services that can be reached through their own media (Exhibit 4–31).

Social Class

Virtually all societies exhibit some form of social stratification whereby individuals can be assigned to a specific strata or social class category based on criteria important to members of that society. **Social class** refers to relatively homogeneous divisions in a society into which people sharing similar lifestyles, values, norms, interests, and behaviors can be grouped. While a number of methods for determining social class exist, class structures in the United States are generally based on occupational status, educational attainment, and source of income. Sociologists generally agree there are three broad levels of social class groups in the United States—the upper (14 percent), middle (70 percent), and lower (16 percent) classes.[31]

➤ *Exhibit 4–31*
An example of a magazine targeted to blacks

➤ *Exhibit 4–32*
This ad is targeted to consumers in the upper social classes

Social class is an important concept to marketers as consumers within each social stratum often exhibit similar values, lifestyles, and buying behavior. Thus, the various social class groups provide a natural basis for market segmentation. Consumers in the various social classes differ in the degree to which they use various products and services, their leisure activities, shopping patterns, and media habits. Marketers respond to these differences through the positioning of their products and services, the media strategies they use to reach different social classes, and the types of advertising appeals they develop. The ad for Chubb Insurance in Exhibit 4–32 shows how a service targeted to the upper classes attempts to appeal to the characteristics of this group in both the copy and illustration.

Reference Groups

Think about the last time you attended a party. As you thought about dressing for the party, you probably asked yourself (or someone else) what others would be wearing. As a result, your selection of attire may have been influenced by those likely to be present. This simple example reflects one form of impact that groups may exert on your behavior.

A *group* has been defined as "two or more individuals who share a set of norms, values, or beliefs and have certain implicitly or explicitly defined relationships to one another such that their behavior is interdependent."[32] Groups are one of the primary factors influencing learning and socialization, and group situations constitute many of our purchase decisions. **Reference groups**—"a group whose presumed perspectives or values are being used by an individual as the basis for his or her judgments, opinions, and actions"—are used by consumers as a guide to specific behaviors, even

➤ *Exhibit 4–33*   The use of aspirational and disassociative groups in ads

A. This ad portrays the Air Force as an aspirational reference group

B. This ad attempts to portray teenage parents as a disassociative reference group

IF CLIMBING THE LADDER OF SUCCESS ISN'T STIMULATING, WHAT'S THE POINT?

Getting to the top of most fields requires concentration, dedication and determination.

We think anyone willing to summon that kind of effort deserves a little exhilaration along the way. A commodity that's in plentiful supply in today's Air Force.

We can take a person as high and as fast as they want to go. In over 200 of today's most sought-after fields.

With top-quality training and every opportunity to put what they've learned to use. That's guaranteed.

Along with the chance to continue their education.

So, not only do we help get careers off the ground. Quite often we do it in supersonic fashion.

For more information, call 1-800-423-USAF.   **AIM HIGH.**

DON'T LET A HOT DATE TURN INTO A DUE DATE.

Just a reminder that one night with your girlfriend could last a lifetime.
THE CHILDREN'S DEFENSE FUND

though they might not be present at the time.[33] In the party example, your peers—while not present—provided a standard of dress that you referred to in your clothing selection. Likewise, your college classmates, family, co-workers, or even a group to which we might aspire might serve as a referent, and your consumption patterns will typically conform to the expectations of these groups.

Marketers utilize reference group influences in developing advertisements and promotional strategies. The ads shown in Exhibit 4–33 reflect examples of the use of *aspirational reference groups* (groups to which one might like to belong) and *disassociative groups* (groups to which we do not wish to belong or use as referents), respectively.

Family decision making—an example of group influences

In some instances, the group may be involved more directly than just as a referent. In the family group, the family members may serve as referents to each other, or they may actually be involved in the purchase decision process itself—acting as an individual buying unit. As shown in Exhibit 4–34, a variety of roles may be assumed in the family decision-making process, with each having implications for marketers.[34]

The implications of family decision making for advertising are many. First, the advertiser must determine who is responsible for the various roles in the decision-making process so messages might be targeted at that person or persons. These roles

➤ *Exhibit 4–34*
**Roles in the family
decision-making process**

The initiator. The person responsible for initiating the purchase decision process; for example, the mother who determines she needs a new car.

The information provider. The individual responsible for gathering information to be used in making the decision; the teenage "car buff" who knows where to find product information in specific magazines or collects it from dealers; and so on.

The influencer. The person who exerts influence as to what criteria will be used in the selection process. All members of the family may be involved. The wife may have her criteria, whereas others may each have their own input.

The decision maker(s). That person(s) who actually makes the decision. In our example, it may be the wife alone or in combination with another family member.

The purchasing agent. That individual who performs the physical act of making the purchase. In the case of an auto, both the husband and wife may decide to pick a car together and sign the purchase agreement.

The consumer. The actual user of the product. In the case of a family car, all family members are consumers. If a private auto, only the wife might be the consumer.

will also dictate media strategies, as the appropriate magazine, newspaper, or television or radio stations must be used. Second, understanding the decision-making process and the use of information by individual family members is critical to the design of messages and choice of promotional program elements. In sum, an overall understanding of how the decision process works and the role that each family member plays is necessary to develop an effective promotional program.

Situational Determinants

The final external factor is that of the purchase and usage situation. The specific situation in which consumers are to use the product or brand directly affects their perceptions, preferences, and purchasing behaviors.[35] Three types of **situational determinants** may have an effect—the specific *usage* situation, the *purchase* situation, and the *communications* situation. Usage refers to the situations in which the product will be used. For example, purchases made for private consumption may be thought of differently than those in which the purchase will be obvious to the public. The purchase situation more directly involves the environment operating at the time of the purchase. Time constraints, store environments, and other factors may all have an impact. The last of these—the conditions in which an advertising exposure occurs (in a car listening to the radio, with friends, etc.)—may be of the most relevance to the development of promotional strategies because the impact on the consumer will vary according to the particular situation. For example, the ability for a commercial to be attended to may be greater when it is heard alone while driving in a car than it would in the presence of friends, at work, and so on, where a number of distractions may be present, all competing for the listener's attention. If advertisers can isolate a particular time in which the listener is more likely to be attentive—for example, driving time—they will be more likely to have the undivided attention of the listener.

In sum, situational determinants may either enhance or detract from the potential success of a message. To the degree that advertisers can assess situational influences that may be operating, they will increase the likelihood of successfully communicating with their target audiences.

SUMMARY

This chapter introduced you to the field of consumer behavior and examined its relevance to promotional strategy. Consumer behavior is best viewed as the process and activities that people engage in when searching for, selecting, purchasing, using, evaluating, and disposing of products and services to satisfy their needs and desires. A five-stage model of the consumer decision-making process is made up of problem recognition, search, alternative evaluation, purchase, and postpurchase evaluation. Various internal psychological processes influence the consumer decision-making process, including motivation, perception, attitude formation and change, and integration processes.

Three variations in the consumer decision-making process are routine response behavior, limited problem solving, and extended problem solving. The decision process model views consumer behavior primarily from a cognitive orientation. The chapter considered alternative perspectives by examining various approaches to consumer learning and their implications for advertising and promotion. Behavioral learning theories such as classical conditioning and operant or instrumental conditioning were discussed. Problems with behavioral learning theories were noted, and the alternative perspective of cognitive learning was discussed.

The chapter concluded with an examination of relevant external factors that influence consumer decision making. Culture, subculture, social class, group processes and influences, and situational determinants were discussed along with their implications for the development of promotional strategies and programs.

KEY TERMS

consumer behavior
problem recognition
want
motives
hierarchy of needs
psychoanalytic theory
motivation research
internal search
external search
perception
sensation
selective perception
selective exposure
selective attention
selective comprehension
selective retention
mnemonics
subliminal perception
evaluative criteria

functional consequences
psychosocial
   consequences
multiattribute attitude
   model
salient beliefs
integration processes
compensatory decision
   rule
noncompensatory
   integration strategies
lexicographic decision
   rule
conjunctive decision rule
phased processing
   strategy
heuristics
affect referral decision
   rule

purchase intention
brand loyalty
cognitive dissonance
classical conditioning
conditioned stimulus
conditioned response
operant conditioning
reinforcement
schedules of
   reinforcement
shaping
cognitive processing
culture
subcultures
social class
reference groups
situational determinants

DISCUSSION QUESTIONS

1. Why is it important for promotional planners to have an understanding of consumer behavior? What are some of the aspects of consumer behavior that need to be understood by those planning advertising and promotion programs?

2. Use the basic model of consumer decision making to analyze the purchase process a consumer would go through in purchasing a laundry detergent versus a new computer. Discuss the role advertising and other forms of promotion would play at each stage of the decision process.

3. Discuss the various sources of problem recognition. Discuss how marketers can influence problem recognition. Find an example of an advertisement that is designed to create or appeal to problem recognition.

4. Marketing has often been criticized for appealing to consumer wants rather than their needs. Do you feel that it is ethical for marketers to encourage consumers to purchase products and services on the basis of wants rather than needs? Defend your position.

5. Discuss how psychoanalytic theory can be applied to marketing and

advertising. Find three ads that may be applying psychoanalytic theory techniques and explain why.

6. What are the five levels of needs recognized in Maslow's hierarchy? Discuss the implications of the hierarchy of needs for advertising.

7. What problems does the selective perception process create for advertisers? How might they overcome some of these problems?

8. Discuss the various attitude change strategies recognized by the multiattribute model. Discuss how an airline could use some of these attitude change strategies in its marketing and advertising programs.

9. Discuss how promotional planners can use the principles of various behavioral learning theories such as classical and operant conditioning and modeling in the design of advertising and promotional strategies.

10. Analyze the purchase of a cereal from a family decision making perspective. Discuss the roles various family members would play in the decision process and how advertising and promotion could be used to influence them.

chapter **5**

Market Segmentation and Positioning

chapter objectives

➢ To review the strategies available to the marketer for selecting and entering a market.

➢ To provide an understanding of the concept of target marketing and its use in advertising and promotion.

➢ To provide an understanding of the concept of market segmentation and its use in advertising and promotion.

➢ To understand the use of positioning and repositioning strategies in advertising and promotion.

➢ To examine the factors to be considered in developing a positioning strategy.

Cadillac Rolls into the Fast Lane

In 1908, when the company was only six years old, Cadillac won the Dewar Trophy for engineering expertise. For almost eight decades thereafter, the Cadillac name was synonymous with the best throughout the world. The company led other automakers in new product developments including the V-8 and V-16 engines, power steering, and cruise control. To America and the world, Cadillac was quality. Then something happened.

While the sale of luxury cars boomed in the 1980s, Cadillac's sales headed the other direction. By 1987, the company had only 2.5 percent of the luxury market, and customers were staying away in droves. Lost sales were costing the company an estimated $500 million a year.

It was in 1987 that Cadillac initiated plans for the 1992 cars. The emphasis was on redoing the Seville and Eldorado models to make them more competitive with foreign imports, which along with the Lincoln Continental were taking control of the market.

The new Cadillacs were to be targeted to "well-heeled" car buyers between the ages of 35 and 50, as the $32,000 and up price tags required affluence. The Eldorado would be targeted to traditional Cadillac owners who had purchased the car in the past, while the Seville would attempt to reach younger affluent buyers who might be interested in the Mercedes 300E or the 5 series BMW.

After researching the attitudes of affluent buyers under the age of 45, Cadillac and its ad agency launched a campaign designed to address these attitudes head on.

In the TV spots, young, professional-looking people voice these attitudes with statements such as "The luxury sedans of Europe and Japan seem to fit my lifestyle better." The ad goes on to say, "Until now," and then show how Cadillac can do the job even better. The ads appeared on shows such as "Northern Exposure" and "L.A. Law," and print versions stressing "Cadillac Style" were placed in upscale magazines such as *Atlantic, Tennis,* and the *Harvard Business Review.* In addition to the ads, a direct-marketing effort targeted to 170,000 key prospects included a beautiful mailer and an eight-minute videocassette on each new model.

How did this strategy of targeting boomers work? Consider the following: (1) 45 percent of those visiting dealerships in October were classified as "young affluents," meaning they were under age 50 and had a household income of $75,000 plus; (2) their average age was 42 with an average household income of $106,000; (3) the two new models account for as much as 60 percent of Cadillac sales in some regions; (4) by October 1, Cadillac had 27,000 dealer orders; and (5) the company hopes to sell 60,000 Eldorados and Sevilles in the 1992 model year. Based on these numbers, it would appear that the targeting strategy was a success!

Source: Raymond Serafin, "Cadillac Winning over Boomers," Advertising Age, December 2, 1991, p. 2; David Kiley, "A Bold Push for Cadillac's New Models," Adweek's Marketing Week, August 26, 1991; and Michelle Krebs, "Cadillac's Rolling Revival," Spirit, November 1991, pp. 48–61.

As the Cadillac example demonstrates, companies often pursue a strategy of "targeting" a specific market or market. In the case of Cadillac, the best potential for sales rested in the younger, more affluent markets that currently bought luxury imports. Because of the diversity of consumers' needs and wants, and the increase in competitive offerings that has occurred in the past few decades, marketers have segmented their markets and concentrated on marketing their products to specific groups rather than to the whole market. This means specific advertising and promotions strategies will be developed for each of these markets, as was demonstrated by Cadillac's overall promotional program. In this chapter, we examine the concepts of market segmentation, target marketing, and market positioning and their relevance to the promotional planning process.

Recall from our discussion of the integrated marketing communications planning program that the situation analysis is conducted at the beginning of the promotional planning process. You should also recall that the establishment of specific objectives—both marketing and communication—is derived from the situation analysis, and the promotional mix strategies are developed to achieve these objectives. Marketers rarely go after the entire market with one product, brand, or service offering; rather, a number of different strategies may be assumed, in which the market is broken into *segments*, and one or more of these segments is targeted for marketing and promotional efforts. This means different objectives may be established, different budgets may be used, and the promotional mix strategies may vary, depending on the market approach used. Focusing on one or more segments of the market involves a process referred to as *target marketing*. A discussion of this process follows.

The Concept of Target Marketing

Because few, if any, products can satisfy the needs of all consumers, companies often develop different marketing strategies to satisfy different consumer needs. The process by which marketers do this (presented in Exhibit 5–1) is referred to as *target marketing* and involves four basic steps—identifying markets with unfulfilled needs, market segmentation, targeting specific segments, and positioning one's product or service through marketing strategies.

Identifying Markets

As noted, marketers develop various strategies in an attempt to satisfy the needs of consumers. One approach used for accomplishing this objective is **product differentiation**, whereby the manufacturer produces a variety of products from which the consumer can choose, as demonstrated by the Coca-Cola product line shown in Exhibit 5–2. A second approach is **target marketing**, in which the marketer identifies the specific needs of groups of people (or segments), selects one or more of these segments as a target, and develops marketing programs directed to each. This latter approach has found increased applicability in marketing for a number of reasons, including changes in the market (consumers are becoming much more diverse in their needs, attitudes, lifestyles, etc.); increased use of segmentation by competitors; and more managers trained in segmentation, realizing the advantages associated with this strategy. Perhaps the best explanation, however, comes back to the basic premise that it is necessary to understand as much as possible about consumers to design marketing programs to meet their needs more effectively. In this regard, segmenting makes it possible to isolate consumers with similar lifestyles, needs, and

> *Exhibit 5–1* **The target marketing process**

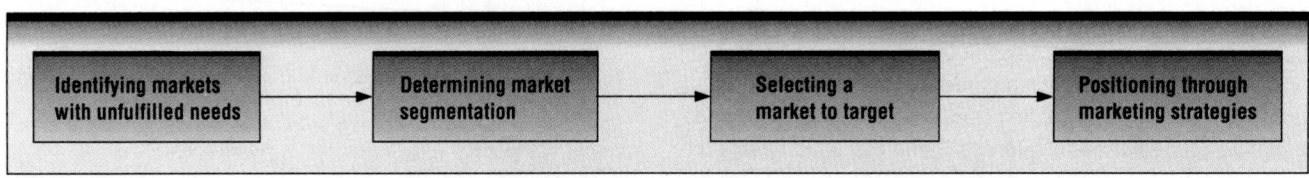

Identifying markets with unfulfilled needs → Determining market segmentation → Selecting a market to target → Positioning through marketing strategies

the like, and increase our knowledge of their specific requirements. The more marketers are able to establish this "common ground" with consumers, the more effective they will be in addressing these requirements in their communications programs and informing and/or persuading potential consumers that the product or service offering will meet their needs.

We will use the beer industry as an example. Many years ago, one might have considered beer as beer—very little differentiation, many local distributors, few truly national brands. The industry then began consolidating, with many brands either being assumed by the larger brewers or ceasing to exist. As the number of competitors decreased, the competition among the major brewers increased. To compete more effectively, brewers began to look at different tastes, lifestyles, and so on, of beer drinkers and used this information as input into their marketing strategies. A direct result of this process was a segmentation of the marketplace.

As you can see by examining Exhibit 5–3, the beer market has become quite segmented, with super premiums, premiums, populars (low price), imports, lights (low calorie), and malts being offered. Low-alcohol and nonalcoholic brands have also been introduced, as has draft beer in bottles and cans. And there are now imported lights, super premium drafts, dry beers, and on and on. Given that most of these product groups are thriving, it must be assumed each has its own set of needs that it satisfies. While taste is certainly one factor, others are also operating—some of which may include image, costs, and the size of one's waistline. A variety of reasons for purchasing are also operating, including social class, lifestyle, and economic considerations, any of which might be reflected in the brand's image.

The market has been segmented into a number of individual markets, each with its own specific characteristics and each requiring a separate marketing and promotions effort. The remainder of this chapter discusses some of the ways of approaching this task.

Market Segmentation

It is not possible to develop marketing strategies for every consumer. Rather, the marketer will attempt to identify broad classes of buyers who have the same needs and who will respond similarly to marketing actions. As noted by Eric N. Berkowitz, Roger A. Kerin, and William Rudelius, **market segmentation** is "dividing up a market

> *Exhibit 5–2*
Coca-Cola's approach to product differentiation

➢ *Exhibit 5–3*
Beer market breakdown by product (percent share)

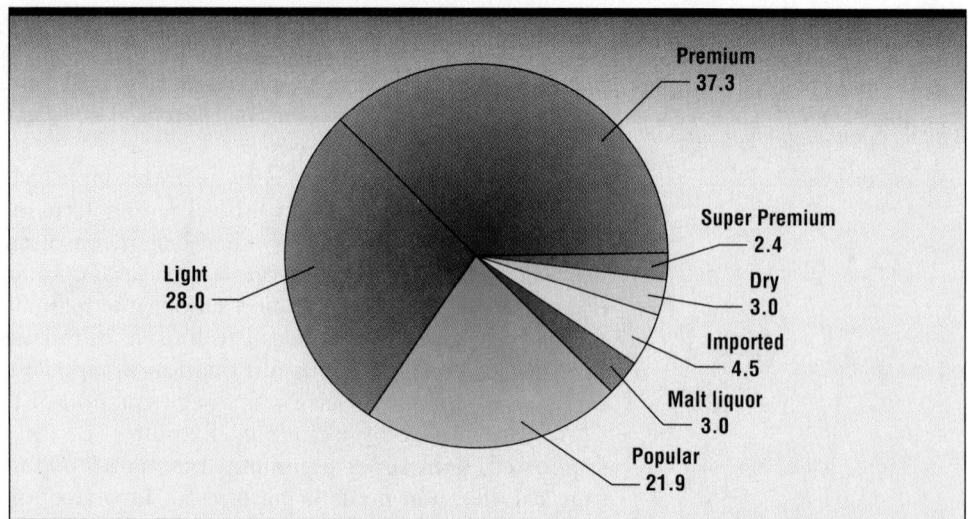

into distinct groups that (1) have common needs and (2) will respond similarly to a marketing action."[1] The segmentation process involves five distinct steps:

1. Finding ways to group consumers according to their needs.
2. Finding ways to group the marketing actions—usually the products offered—available to the organization.
3. Developing a market-product grid to relate the market segments to the firm's products or actions.
4. Selecting the target segments toward which the firm directs its marketing actions.
5. Taking marketing actions to reach target segments.

The more marketers segment the market, the more precise will be their understanding of it. At the same time, the more the market becomes divided, the less the number of consumers constituting each segment. Thus, a key decision to be made is, how far should one go in the segmentation process? That is, where does the process stop? As you can see by the strategy taken in the beer industry, it can go far!

In planning the promotional effort, managers must consider whether the target segment will support individualized strategies. More specifically, they must consider whether this group is *accessible* or can be reached with a communications program. For example, you will see in a later chapter that in some instances no media can be used to reach a targeted group. Or the promotions manager may identify a number of segments but will be unable to develop the required programs to reach them. In this latter case, the firm may have insufficient funds to develop the required advertising campaign, inadequate sales staff to cover all areas, or other promotional deficiencies. Having determined that a segmentation strategy is in order, the marketer must then establish the *basis* on which the market will be addressed. The following section discusses some of the bases for segmenting markets and demonstrates advertising and promotions applications.

Bases for segmentation

As shown in Exhibit 5–4, a variety of methods are available for segmenting markets. Marketers may use one of the segmentation variables shown in Exhibit 5–4 as the sole basis of their strategy, or a combination of approaches may be required. For example, consider the market segmentation strategy that might be employed to market snow skis. While the consumer's lifestyle—that is, active, fun-loving, enjoys outdoor sports—would certainly be important, so too would other factors, such as

➤ *Exhibit 5—4* **Bases for market segmentation**

A. Segmentation variables and breakdowns for consumer markets

Main Dimension	Segmentation Variable	Typical Breakdowns
Customer Characteristics		
Geographic	Region	Pacific; Mountain; West North Central; West South Central; East North Central; East South Central; South Atlantic; Middle Atlantic; New England
	City or metropolitan statistical area (MSA) size	Under 5,000; 5,000 to 19,999; 20,000 to 49,999; 50,000 to 99,999; 100,000 to 249,999; 250,000 to 499,999; 500,000 to 999,999; 1,000,000 to 3,999,999; 4,000,000 or over
	Density	Urban; suburban; rural
	Climate	Northern; southern
Demographic	Age	Infant, under 6; 6 to 11; 12 to 17; 18 to 24; 25 to 34; 35 to 49; 50 to 64; 65 or over
	Sex	Male; female
	Family size	1 to 2; 3 to 4; 5 or over
	Stage of family life cycle	Young single; young married, no children; young married, youngest child under 6; young married, youngest child 6 or older; older married, with children; older married, no children under 18; older single; other older married, no children under 18
	Ages of children	No child under 18; youngest child 6 to 17; youngest child under 6
	Children under 18	0; 1; more than 1
	Income	Under $5,000; $5,000 to $14,999; $15,000 to $24,999; $25,000 to $34,999; $35,000 to $49,999; $50,000 or over
	Education	Grade school or less; some high school; high school graduate; some college; college graduate
	Race	Asian; black; Hispanic; white; other
	Home ownership	Own home; rent home
Psychographic	Personality	Gregarious; compulsive; extroverted; aggressive; ambitious
	Lifestyle	Use of one's time; values and importance; beliefs
Buying Situations		
Benefits sought	Product features	Situation specific; general
	Needs	Quality; service; economy
Usage	Rate of use	Light user; medium user; heavy user
	User states	Nonuser; ex-user; prospect; first-time user; regular user
Awareness and intentions	Readiness to buy	Unaware; aware; informed; interested; intending to buy
	Brand familiarity	Insistence; preference; recognition; nonrecognition; rejection
Buying condition	Type of buying activity	Minimum effort buying; comparison buying; special effort buying
	Kind of store	Convenience; wide breadth; specialty

B. Segmentation variables and breakdowns for industrial markets

Customer Characteristics		
Geographical	Region	Pacific; Mountain; West North Central; West South Central; East North Central; East South Central; South Atlantic; Middle Atlantic; New England
	Location	In MSA; not in MSA
Demographic	SIC code	2-digit; 3-digit; 4-digit categories
	Number of employees	1 to 19; 20 to 99; 100 to 249; 250 or over
	Number of production workers	1 to 19; 20 to 99; 100 to 249; 250 or over
	Annual sales volume	Less than $1 million; $1 million to $10 million; $10 million to $100 million; over $100 million
	Number of establishments	With 1 to 19 employees; with 20 or more employees
Buying Situations		
Nature of good	Kind	Product or service
	Where used	Installation; component of final product; supplies
	Application	Office use; limited production use; heavy production use
Buying condition	Purchase location	Centralized; decentralized
	Who buys	Individual buyer; group
	Type of buy	New buy; modified rebuy; straight rebuy

age (participation in downhill skiing drops off significantly at about age 30) and/ or income (Have you seen the price of a lift ticket lately?). Let us review the bases for segmentation and examine examples of promotional strategies employed in each.

Geographic segmentation In the **geographic segmentation** approach, markets are divided into different geographic units. These units may include nations, states, counties, or even neighborhoods. For example, *USA Weekend,* a publication of the Roper Organization, provides marketplace portraits of the "9 Nations of the USA," in which profiles of consumer habits in each area are discussed (see Exhibit 5–5). Based on a number of economic and sociological factors, these reports have shown geographical differences with respect to

- **Weekend activities.** Differences exist in the amount of time devoted to leisure activities on the weekends, as well as to the type of activities engaged in. Gulf Coast dwellers are the most likely to have guests over for dinner; Heartlanders are most inclined to go out of town; and Multicultures and Western Horizon consumers are most likely to have guests over for brunch. Those in the Western Horizons are also most likely to perform chores on the weekends while others have fun.[2]
- **Ownership of convenience items.** Those living in the Western Horizons are the most likely to own convenience items such as time-saving appliances. Those in the New South are least likely.[3]
- **Television viewing.** Westerners are more likely to watch news and classic old movies on cable TV. In the Midwest, sports events are the top choice. Pay

➤ *Exhibit 5–5* *The 9 Nations of USA Weekend* **profile**

The 9 Nations of USA Weekend, a newsletter published by the Roper Organization, reports on nine geographic segments of the United States. These geographic segments typically demonstrate differences with respect to attitudes, lifestyles, and consumer behaviors. These differences may have significant implications for marketers and advertisers and may serve as a basis for geographic segmentation strategies.

The nine USA nations, according to the Roper Organization, are characterized as follows:

- **New New England** Those living in New England comprise only 5 percent of the households in the *USA* marketplace yet rank first with respect to household income, percentage of married couples, proportion of working women, median age, and proportion of executives and professionals in the workplace.
- **The Heartland** The Heartland segment resides in the midwestern "Bread Basket" and has a low household income, a lower level of education, and a high concentration of agricultural and blue-collar workers. The Heartland is the home of traditional American values.
- **Atlantic Expanse** Those living in the Mid-Atlantic states of New York south to Delaware and west to Pennsylvania and West Virginia constitute the largest of the nine nations. Their median age is just below the national norm, median income is slightly higher, and education levels are "smack in the middle." It has the largest proportion of full-time working persons and the highest level of white-collar workers.
- **New South and Traditional South** The New South is the area ranging along the Atlantic coast from Virginia to Florida, whereas the Traditional South is the center of the Cotton Belt—that is, Kentucky to Mississippi and west to Arkansas. The New South is characterized by slightly higher

than median incomes, strong educational backgrounds, a work force reflecting the national average, and a high proportion of widowed, divorced, or separated individuals. The Traditional South is characterized by a median income that is the lowest in the United States, the worst educational record, the lowest percentage of managerial and professional workers, and a higher-than-average married rate and family size.

- **Gulf Coast** The area including Louisiana, parts of Texas, and Oklahoma is considered the bridge between the South and the West. Education levels are high, although median income is below the national average. This area has the lowest level of full-time working persons, two-income households, and working women.
- **Made in the USA** The second largest of the nine nations comprises 17 percent of all households and is most closely a reflection of the norms of America with respect to median age and income. Located in the Great Lakes area, the residents are more likely to be married, have children, and have both spouses working than are other Americans.
- **Western Horizons** Physically the largest of the segments, this area ranges from Alaska to the Dakotas to Nebraska and Nevada. It has the least number of households, the most families with children under age 18, and lower household incomes. Only 17 percent of the population live in cities.
- **Multicultures** Extending from California to western Texas, this area has the second highest median income and is characterized by young, affluent, highly educated trendsetters. The number of marrieds is lowest, as is the number of families with children. The workers are very career minded.

cable subscriptions are highest in the Northeast, while all other regions tend to prefer recent pay-cable movies.[4]

In addition to those mentioned above, *USA Weekend* has reported on geographic differences with respect to the popularity of self-service, travel plans, personal interests, eating habits, and many other consumer behaviors.

While this segmentation profile involves regions of the country, others have developed programs targeted at specific states. The storyboard in Exhibit 5–6 is an excellent example of this latter approach, as Blue Cross has seemingly determined that those living in California may require a different health-care plan than those in other areas. Still other companies have found they may need to develop alternative strategies for areas as small as neighborhoods within a city, owing to differences in these areas.

Demographic segmentation   **Demographic segmentation** involves dividing the market on the basis of demographic variables such as age, sex, family size, income, and social class. Secret Deodorant is an example of a product that has met with a great deal of success by using the demographic variable sex as a basis for segmentation. (See Exhibit 5–7.)

Although market segmentation on the basis of demographics may appear to be obvious, companies sometimes discover that they need to focus more attention on a specific demographic group. For example, Levi Strauss & Co. recently conducted

➤ *Exhibit 5–6*   **Blue Cross employs geographic segmentation**

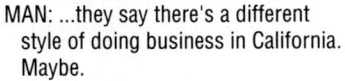

MAN: ...they say there's a different style of doing business in California. Maybe.
(MUSIC STARTS)
  WOMAN: Jo, phone.
MAN (VO): I mean, my friend... would have found it more difficult back East....

(OFFICE NOISES & VOICES IN BACKGROUND)
  MAN (VO): ...the "Establishment," you know.
MAN (VO): But out here, it's not what your father did...
  WOMAN (ON PHONE): ...we'll get on it right away...
WOMAN: Kim, we've had another call...
  MAN (VO): It's what you can do.

MAN: She always dreamt she'd be president.
ANNCR (VO): Here in California, businesses come in all types and sizes. And now Blue Cross is introducing a health plan that understands this.
CaliforniaCare. Keeping you in a healthy state.

> *Exhibit 5–7*
Secret deodorant—segmenting the market by sex

research that showed that 70 percent of the women surveyed were not sure if the company made jeans for women. These results were not surprising to the company since it had traditionally downplayed the Levi's name on the jeans it marketed to women and rarely advertised directly to them. In 1991, the company unleashed a $15 million print and outdoor advertising campaign targeted to women in order to help bolster awareness of Levis (Exhibit 5–8). The ultimate goal of the campaign is to grab a larger share of the $2.1 billion women's jeans market.

Other products that have successfully employed demographic segmentation include Virginia Slims cigarettes (sex), Affinity shampoo (age), automobiles (income), prepackaged dinners (family size), and many others.

While demographics may still be the most commonly used method of segmenting markets, it is important to recognize that factors other than age, sex, income, and education may be the underlying basis for homogeneity and/or consumer behaviors. For example, as noted by Rueff, "Consumer attitudes and behaviors are not demographically driven and, in many cases, are not even demographically related."[5] In addition, broad demographic segments (such as the commonly used age breakdowns 18–34 and 25–49) may include consumers who behave very differently. Eighteen-year-olds may assume very different lifestyles than those who are 34 and may have different needs and wants as well. The astute marketer will attempt to identify additional bases for segmenting and will recognize the limitations of demographics and use this segmentation basis accordingly.

Psychographic segmentation   Dividing the market on the basis of personality and/or lifestyles is referred to as **psychographic segmentation.** While there has been some disagreement as to whether personality is useful as a basis for segmentation, lifestyle factors have been proved to be used effectively. Many consider lifestyles the most effective criterion for segmentation.

The determination of lifestyles is usually based on an analysis of the activities, interests, and opinions (AIOs) of the consumer. These lifestyles are then correlated

> *Exhibit 5–8*
Levi Strauss initiated a major print and outdoor advertising campaign to increase sales of its jeans to women

with the consumer's product, brand, and/or media usage. For many products and/or services, lifestyles may be the best discriminator between use and nonuse, accounting for differences in food consumption, clothing apparel, and automobile selections, among numerous other consumer behaviors.[6]

Psychographic segmentation has met with increasing acceptance and utilization with the advent of the **values and lifestyles program** (VALS) (although marketers employed lifestyle segmentation long before the popularity of VALS). Developed by the Stanford Research Institute (SRI), VALS has become one of the more popular and widely used methods for applying lifestyle segmentation. In the VALS typology, consumers are classified according to the values and lifestyles they exhibit. VALS divides Americans into nine lifestyles, which are grouped in four categories based on their self-images, their aspirations, and the products they use.

While VALS has been widely adopted since its inception in 1978, in 1989 SRI International overhauled the system and introduced VALS 2.[7] According to SRI, the initial typology focused on the *differences* between inner-directed and outer-directed consumers, grouping people into nine clusters. In VALS 2, only three orientations are used, based on principle-oriented, status-oriented, and action-oriented characteristics (Exhibit 5–9). These groupings result in eight segments that exhibit distinctive attitudes, behaviors, and decision-making patterns. When combined with an estimate of the resources the consumer can draw on (education, income, health, energy level, self-confidence, and degree of consumerism), SRI believes the new system is more current and a better predictor of consumer behaviors. A variety of users of the VALS program have switched to VALS 2, including Chevron, Mercedes-Benz, and Eastman Kodak.

The VALS programs are not the only lifestyle systems available to marketers. While it is not possible here to detail all the alternatives, we will mention a few:

- **ClusterPlus.** This market segmentation system uses as its basis 47 lifestyle clusters. The Donnelley Marketing Information Services assigns each neighborhood in the country to one of the lifestyle clusters, representing groups of people with similar demographic characteristics and consumer behavior patterns.
- **Prism.** Claritas' system classifies 540,000 neighborhoods by demographic characteristics, consumer behavior patterns, and 40 basic lifestyle clusters.
- **MicroVision.** National Decision System clusters consumers into 50 lifestyle groupings and provides demographic, socioeconomic, and credit information on each.

Behavioristic segmentation **Behavioristic segmentation** divides consumers into groups according to their usage, loyalties, or buying responses to a product. For example, segmentation may be based on product or brand usage, degree (heavy versus light) of use, and/or brand loyalty. These characteristics are then combined with demographic and/or psychographic criteria to develop profiles of market segments. In the first case—usage—an assumption is made that nonpurchasers of a brand or product who have the same characteristics as purchasers will hold greater

➤ *Exhibit 5–9*   Lifestyle characteristics of the VALS 2 segments

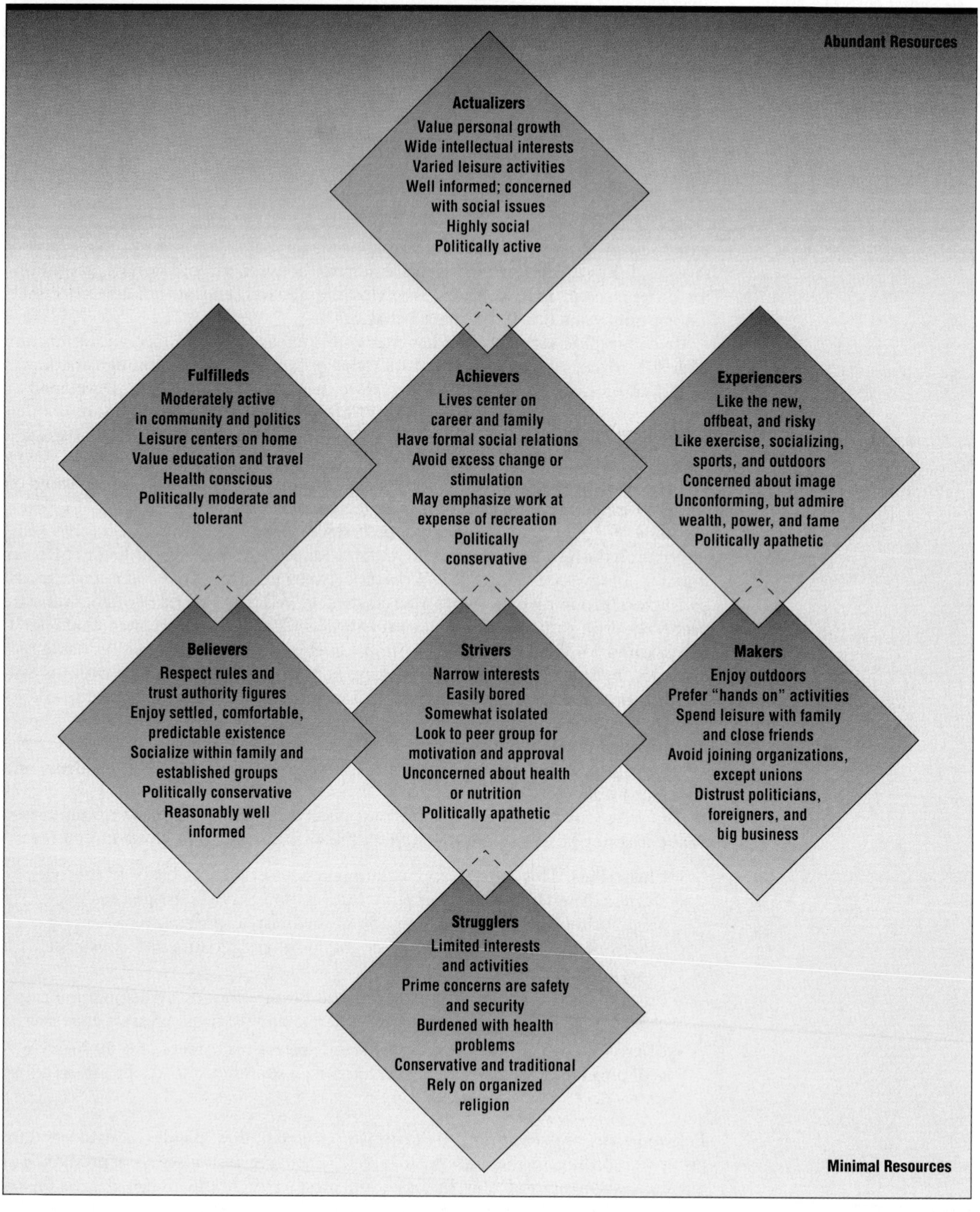

Abundant Resources

Actualizers
Value personal growth
Wide intellectual interests
Varied leisure activities
Well informed; concerned
with social issues
Highly social
Politically active

Fulfilleds
Moderately active
in community and politics
Leisure centers on home
Value education and travel
Health conscious
Politically moderate and
tolerant

Achievers
Lives center on
career and family
Have formal social relations
Avoid excess change or
stimulation
May emphasize work at
expense of recreation
Politically
conservative

Experiencers
Like the new,
offbeat, and risky
Like exercise, socializing,
sports, and outdoors
Concerned about image
Unconforming, but admire
wealth, power, and fame
Politically apathetic

Believers
Respect rules and
trust authority figures
Enjoy settled, comfortable,
predictable existence
Socialize within family and
established groups
Politically conservative
Reasonably well
informed

Strivers
Narrow interests
Easily bored
Somewhat isolated
Look to peer group for
motivation and approval
Unconcerned about health
or nutrition
Politically apathetic

Makers
Enjoy outdoors
Prefer "hands on" activities
Spend leisure with family
and close friends
Avoid joining organizations,
except unions
Distrust politicians,
foreigners, and
big business

Strugglers
Limited interests
and activities
Prime concerns are safety
and security
Burdened with health
problems
Conservative and traditional
Rely on organized
religion

Minimal Resources

➤ *Exhibit 5–10*
Heavy and light users of consumer products

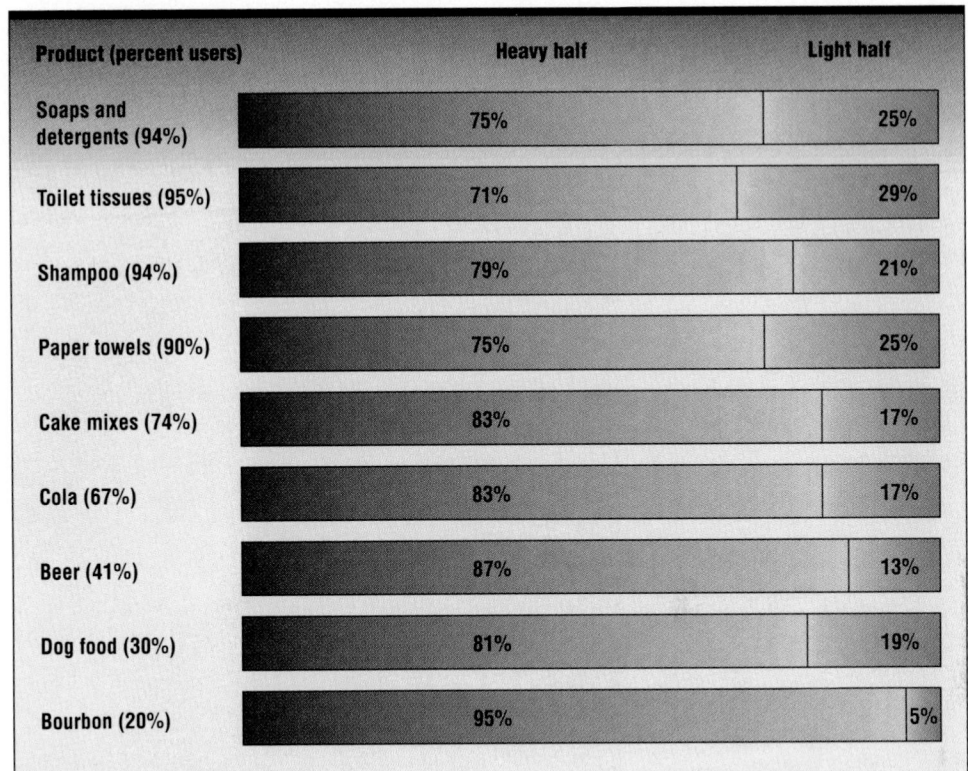

Product (percent users)	Heavy half	Light half
Soaps and detergents (94%)	75%	25%
Toilet tissues (95%)	71%	29%
Shampoo (94%)	79%	21%
Paper towels (90%)	75%	25%
Cake mixes (74%)	83%	17%
Cola (67%)	83%	17%
Beer (41%)	87%	13%
Dog food (30%)	81%	19%
Bourbon (20%)	95%	5%

potential for adoption than those with different characteristics. A profile (demographic or psychographic) of the user is developed, which serves as the basis for the development of promotional strategies designed to attract new users. For example, it might be expected that Yuppies—who share certain similarities in their consumption behaviors—who do not currently own a foreign car might be more likely to be potential buyers than those demonstrating different characteristics.

Degree of usage relates to the fact that a few consumers may account for a disproportionate amount of the share of purchase for many products or brands. For example, in industrial markets, many marketers refer to what they call the **80–20 rule,** meaning 20 percent of their buyers account for 80 percent of their sales volume. Once again, upon identifying the characteristics of these users, targeting them would allow for a much greater concentration of efforts and much less wasted time and monies. The same "heavy-half" strategy is possible in the consumer market as well, as the majority of purchases of many products (for example, soaps and detergents, shampoos, cake mixes, beer, dog food, colas, bourbon, and toilet tissue—yes, toilet tissue!) is accounted for by a small proportion of the population (Exhibit 5–10).[8] Perhaps you can think of some additional examples where this may be the case.

Benefit segmentation In purchasing products, consumers are generally trying to satisfy specific needs and/or wants. As a result, these consumers are looking for specific benefits that products might provide in satisfying these needs. The grouping of consumers on the basis of attributes sought in a product is known as **benefit segmentation**—a widely utilized basis for many firms.

Consider the purchase of a wristwatch. While you might consider buying a watch for particular benefits such as accuracy, water resistance, or stylishness, others may be seeking a different set of benefits. Watches are commonly given as gifts for birthdays, Christmas, and graduation. Certainly some of the same benefits are considered in the purchase of a gift, but at the same time, the benefits to be derived by the purchaser are different from those that will be obtained by the user. The appeals used in advertisements that portray watches as good gifts stress a different set of

➤ *Exhibit 5–11*
Rembrandt toothpaste stresses the benefit of its superior whitening ability

criteria to be considered in the purchase decision. The next time you see an advertisement or commercial for a watch, think about the basic appeal and the benefits offered in that ad.

Another example of benefit segmentation can be seen in the toothpaste market. In selecting a toothpaste, some consumers want a product with fluoride (Crest, Colgate), whereas others prefer one that freshens their breath (Close●Up, Aqua-fresh). More recent benefit segments are those offering tartar control (Crest) and assistance with plaque problems (Viadent). The Den Mal Corp. recently introduced Rembrandt Whitening toothpaste for consumers who are interested in having whiter teeth (Exhibit 5–11).

The process of segmenting a market

The segmentation process is exactly that—a process. This process develops over time and is an integral part of the situation analysis. It is in this stage that marketers are attempting to determine as much as they can about the market—that is, what needs are not being fulfilled, what benefits are being sought, and what characteristics distinguish between the various groups in seeking these products and services. Thus, a number of alternative segmentation strategies may be considered and employed. Each time a specific segment is identified, additional information is gathered to assist in the understanding of this group.

For example, once a specific segment is identified based on benefits sought, lifestyle characteristics and demographics will be examined to help characterize this group and to further the marketer's understanding of this market. In addition, behavioristic segmentation criteria will also be examined. To take the skiing example cited earlier one step further, specific benefits may be sought in the product—flexibility or stiffness, for example—because of the type of skiing that is done. This information will be combined with that discussed earlier to provide a complete profile of the skier.

➤ *Exhibit 5–12*

The 50 market segments of MicroVision are organized into one of nine groups.* Since each group comprises segments that have similar characteristics or habits, you can easily target several market segments that share common lifestyles and purchasing behaviors.

*Segments 49 and 50 were not placed in a group due to their nonhomogeneous nature.

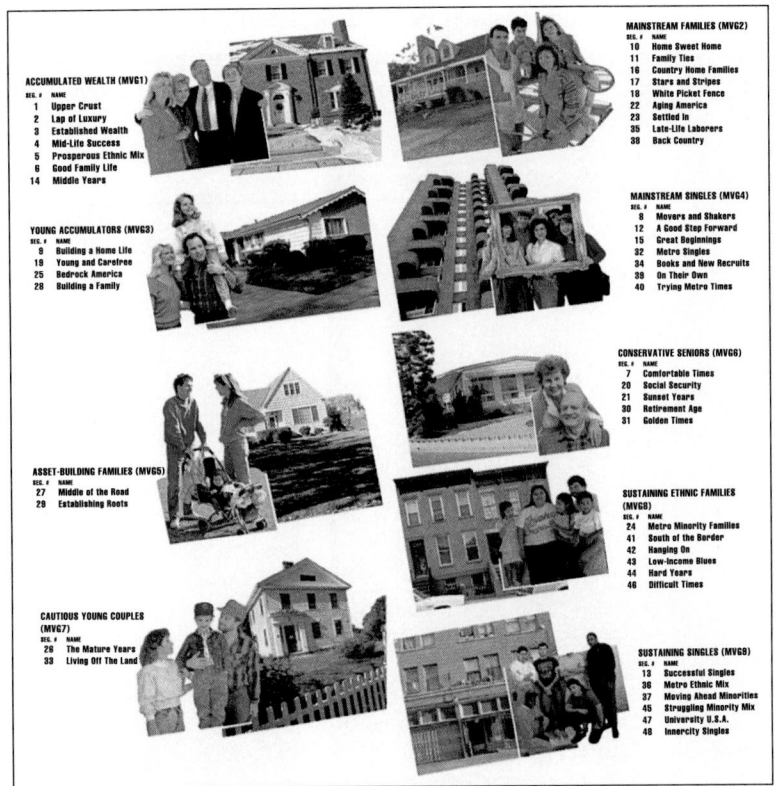

ACCUMULATED WEALTH (MVG1)
SEG. #   NAME
1   Upper Crust
2   Lap of Luxury
3   Established Wealth
4   Mid-Life Success
5   Prosperous Ethnic Mix
6   Good Family Life
14   Middle Years

YOUNG ACCUMULATORS (MVG3)
SEG. #   NAME
9   Building a Home Life
19   Young and Carefree
25   Bedrock America
28   Building a Family

ASSET-BUILDING FAMILIES (MVG5)
SEG. #   NAME
27   Middle of the Road
29   Establishing Roots

CAUTIOUS YOUNG COUPLES (MVG7)
SEG. #   NAME
26   The Mature Years
33   Living Off The Land

MAINSTREAM FAMILIES (MVG2)
SEG. #   NAME
10   Home Sweet Home
11   Family Ties
16   Country Home Families
17   Stars and Stripes
18   White Picket Fence
22   Aging America
23   Settled In
35   Late-Life Laborers
38   Back Country

MAINSTREAM SINGLES (MVG4)
SEG. #   NAME
8   Movers and Shakers
12   A Good Step Forward
15   Great Beginnings
32   Metro Singles
34   Books and New Recruits
39   On Their Own
40   Trying Metro Times

CONSERVATIVE SENIORS (MVG6)
SEG. #   NAME
7   Comfortable Times
20   Social Security
21   Sunset Years
30   Retirement Age
31   Golden Times

SUSTAINING ETHNIC FAMILIES (MVG8)
SEG. #   NAME
24   Metro Minority Families
41   South of the Border
42   Hanging On
43   Low-Income Blues
44   Hard Years
46   Difficult Times

SUSTAINING SINGLES (MVG8)
SEG. #   NAME
13   Successful Singles
36   Metro Ethnic Mix
37   Moving Ahead Minorities
45   Struggling Minority Mix
47   University U.S.A.
48   Innercity Singles

A number of companies now offer research services to assist marketing managers to define their markets and to develop strategies targeted to these groups. The VALS, MicroVision, and ClusterPlus systems discussed earlier are just a few of the services offered. As you can see by examining the clusters shown in Exhibit 5–12, Micro-Vision uses demographic, psychographic, and geographic bases to break down the market into "microgeographic" units. These segments get as specific as postal carrier routes and census block groupings, each of which has specific identifiable demographic and lifestyle characteristics. Whether these microunits meet the criteria considered necessary for useful segmentation will be determined by the user of the system. While it may be too specific for a national company to attempt to define such small segments, it may be much more applicable for companies operating within one specific city or geographical area. The same data are often provided by smaller companies for organizations requiring such information on a countywide basis.

Having completed the segmentation analysis, the marketer now moves to the third phase shown in Exhibit 5–1: targeting a specific market.

Selecting a Target Market

The outcome of the segmentation analysis will indicate to the firm the market opportunities available. The next phase in the target marketing process involves two steps: (1) determining how many segments to enter and (2) determining which segments will offer the most potential.

Determining how many segments to enter

Three market coverage alternatives are available to the firm. **Undifferentiated marketing** involves a decision to ignore the segment differences and to offer one product or service to the entire market. For example, many years ago when Henry Ford brought out the first assembly-line automobile, all potential consumers were offered the same basic product—a black Ford. For many years, Coca-Cola offered only one product version. While this standardized strategy allowed for cost savings to the company, it did not allow the opportunity to offer different versions of the product.

➤ *Exhibit 5–13* **Dewar's uses different appeals for the same product**

Differentiated marketing involves the decision to market in a number of segments, developing separate marketing strategies for each. The Dewar's ads shown in Exhibit 5–13 reflect a good example of this strategy. The "profile" ad appears to be targeting a specific group (perhaps upwardly mobile, young to middle-aged?), whereas the second example might appeal more to older (perhaps more traditional?) individuals.

While an undifferentiated strategy offers the opportunity to reduce costs through increased production, it does not allow for variety or tailoring to specific needs. Through differentiation, products—or in the case of Dewar's, advertising appeals— may be developed for the various segments, allowing for an increased opportunity to satisfy the needs and wants of various groups.

The third alternative, **concentrated marketing,** is used when the firm selects one specific segment and attempts to capture a large share of this market. An example of this strategy was that employed by Volkswagen in the 1950s when it was the only major automobile company competing in the economy car segment of the United States. While Volkswagen has now assumed a more differentiated strategy, other companies have found the concentrated strategy to be an effective one. For example, Above the Rim markets only basketball clothing and accessories. The company has built a loyal following among young consumers who like its functional features (Exhibit 5–14).

Determining which segments will offer the most potential

The second step in selecting a market involves determining the most attractive segment. The firm must examine the sales potential of the segment, the opportunities for growth, the competition, and its ability to compete.

➤ *Exhibit 5–14*
Above the Rim pursues a concentrated marketing strategy

Having determined the most attractive segment, the firm must then decide whether it can market to this group. Numerous stories abound of companies that have entered new markets only to find their lack of resources or expertise would not allow them to compete successfully. For example, Royal Crown Cola (RC Cola) has often been quite successful in identifying new segment opportunities but because of limited resources has been less able to capitalize on them. RC has been credited with being first to bring to market diet colas and caffeine-free colas but has not been able to establish itself as a market leader in either market.

Target marketing has recently come under fire from a variety of nonmarketing groups. Ethical Perspectives 5–1 examines a few of the reasons for the controversy and arguments on both sides of the issue.

Having selected the segments to target and having determined it is able to compete, the firm now proceeds to the final step in Exhibit 5–1—the market positioning phase.

Market Positioning

Positioning has been defined as "the art and science of fitting the product or service to one or more segments of the broad market in such a way as to set it meaningfully apart from competition."[9] As you can see by this definition, the position of the product, service, or even store is the image that comes to the mind of the consumer and the attributes he or she perceives as related to it. This communication occurs through the message itself—which explains these benefits—as well as the media strategy employed to reach the target group. Take a few moments to think about how some products are positioned and how this position is conveyed to you. For example, what comes to mind when we mention Mercedes, Dr. Pepper, or United Airlines? What about department stores such as Neiman-Marcus, Sears, and J. C. Penney? Now think of the advertisements, and when and where these ads are shown, for each of these products and companies. Are their approaches different from their competitors?

Approaches to positioning

Positioning strategies generally assume one of two approaches—one focusing on the consumer, the other on the competition. While both approaches involve the association of product benefits with consumer needs, the former does so by specifically linking the product with the benefits to be derived by the consumer or creating a favorable brand image, as shown in Exhibit 5–15 (page 173). The latter approach positions the product by comparing it, and the benefit it offers, to the competition,

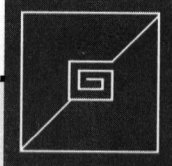

Ethical Perspective 5–1

Segmentation and Target Marketing on Trial

Ever hear of the brands Uptown, Dakota, and Powermaster? If you haven't already been exposed to these products, you probably never will be. Each of the brands was withdrawn from the market before it hit national distribution because of public outcry over the segmentation and targeting strategies to be employed.

Uptown, an R. J. Reynolds Tobacco Co. cigarette, and Powermaster, a G. Heileman Brewing Co. malt liquor, were both to be targeted to blacks. Dakota, another Reynold's cigarette, was to be targeted to young, poorly educated white women whose favorite pastimes include "cruising," "partying," and attending "hot rod shows" and "tractor pulls".

Public interest groups, consumer organizations, and government agencies all joined in the protest against the companies' new product introductions and some have taken the argument a step further. These groups question the ethics of the basic premise of the strategies of segmenting and targeting markets—particularly when the segments targeted are minorities. Both sides are armed with reasons these strategies should or should not be permitted. Let's examine these:

Pros:

1. All marketing is targeted. Different people have very different needs and wants and marketers cannot attempt to sell their products to everyone.
2. By definition, all target markets are minorities. Market segmentation requires the determination of smaller niches of society with similar needs and wants. As such, any small group could be called a minority of the population.
3. Targeting leads to better products/services. The strategy requires a better understanding of the segments sought. As such, the marketer can develop better products and services to satisfy these consumers.
4. Targeting leads to more efficient and effective marketing programs. By appealing only to those groups with an inter-

est, marketers develop more effective strategies, eliminate waste, and are more efficient. The cost savings are passed on to the consumer in the form of lower prices, better information, and so on.

Cons:

1. Minorities are often the target for detrimental products. Because of their lower educational and socioeconomic statuses, minorities are often selected as target markets for harmful products. They are considered easy game for more sophisticated marketers.
2. Targeting acerbates a larger social problem. Because of its effectiveness, targeting can lead to increased consumption of products such as cigarettes and alcohol and other harmful products.
3. Targeting leads to control. Because of the power of large marketers, they can control certain segments of the population, leading them to desire products they do not need but think they must have.
4. Target marketing is greedy. The only reason for targeting is to maximize profits and to capitalize on the marketplace—this is greed.

As you can tell from these arguments, targeting has become controversial. On the one hand, marketers consider targeting an important and necessary strategy for successful marketing. On the other, opponents consider it to be exploitative and unfair to those being targeted. The battle may have ended for now, but the war has not!

Source: John E. Calfee, "Targeting the Problem," *Advertising Age*, July 22, 1991, p. 16; "Target: Minorities," *Marketing & Media Decisions*, October 1990, pp. 70–71.

---

as shown in the example provided in Exhibit 5–16 (page 174). Other products such as Scope mouthwash (positioning itself as better tasting than Listerine) and Now cigarettes (comparing itself to a number of other cigarette brands on the amount of nicotine) have also employed this strategy successfully.

Market positioning has been considered by many advertising practitioners to be the most important factor in establishing a brand in the marketplace. As noted by David Aaker and John Myers, the term *position* or *positioning* has recently been used to indicate the brand's or product's image in the marketplace.[10] Jack Trout and Al Ries have suggested that to have a position in the marketplace, this brand image must be in respect to competitors'. These authors note, "In today's marketplace, the competitors' image is just as important as your own. Sometimes more important."[11] Thus, *positioning*—as used in this text—will relate to the image of the product and or brand relative to competitive products or brands. As noted in the examples previously provided, the position of the product or brand is the key factor

➤ *Exhibit 5–15* **Positioning that focuses on the consumer**

A. Timex stresses benefits to position its product

B. Gucci effectively creates a brand image

in communicating the benefits offered and in differentiating it from the competition. Let us now turn our attention to various strategies that might be employed to position a product.

Developing a positioning strategy

To create a position for a product or service, Trout and Ries suggest that managers ask themselves six basic questions:[12]

1. What position, if any, do we already have in the prospect's mind? (This information must come from the marketplace and not the managers' perceptions.)
2. What position do we want to own?
3. What companies must be outgunned if we are to establish that position?
4. Do we have enough marketing money to occupy and hold the position?
5. Do we have the guts to stick with one consistent positioning strategy?
6. Does our creative approach match our positioning strategy?

A number of positioning strategies exist that might be employed in the development of a promotional program. David Aaker and J. Gary Shansby[13] discuss six such strategies, whereas Aaker and Myers[14] add one additional approach. A discussion of each follows.

Using product attributes (characteristics)   One of the more common approaches to positioning is that of setting the brand apart from competitors' based on specific characteristics or benefits offered. Sometimes a product may be positioned on more

➤ *Exhibit 5–16*
Hewlett-Packard positions itself relative to its competition

➤ *Exhibit 5–17*
An example of positioning on numerous product benefits

than one product benefit. A good example of this is demonstrated in the advertisement shown in Exhibit 5–17.

Positioning by price/quality   Exhibit 5–18 reflects examples of brands that have been positioned on the price/quality dimension. The Discman approach reflects the image of a high-quality brand in which cost—while not irrelevant—should be considered secondary to the quality benefits to be derived. The Oneida ad suggests that quality need not be unaffordable. An important factor must be remembered in the latter approach and is demonstrated quite well by the Oneida ad: that is, that even if one attempts to position on the basis of price, quality is still important. Thus, while price may be the primary consideration, the product quality must be shown to be at least adequate—if not equal—to other competitive brands.

> *Exhibit 5–18* **Brands positioned on the price/quality dimension**
A. Discman positions itself on quality

OUR NEWEST
DISCMAN
MAY HAVE
AN EQUAL,
BUT
NOT IN THIS
WORLD.

Come to where the horns are mellower, the flutes purer and the voices sweeter. We refer, of course, to our newest Discman® CD player, the D-303. It's the world's first to bring the accuracy of 1-bit technology to a CD player you can bring anywhere. With superlative low-level linearity, the 1-bit system captures even the softest, subtlest sounds. Taking music to a higher plane of existence.

B. Oneida positions its brand on quality for the right price

For those who thought they couldn't afford exquisite stainless on a shoestring.

ONEIDA

Shown: Anticipation in stainless.

Positioning by use or application In this approach, the company attempts to position the product with a specific *use* or *application*. For example, in the ads shown in Exhibit 5–19, Nike is positioned for cross training (useful for the court or running), and New Balance is positioned exclusively as a running shoe.

While this strategy is often used to enter a market based on a particular use, it has also been demonstrated to be an effective way to expand into different markets. The WD-40 ad shown in Exhibit 5–20 (page 177) is an excellent example of a success story based on the ability of the product to satisfy a variety of needs. Likewise, Arm & Hammer pure baking soda has been promoted as being effective for everything from baking to relieving heartburn to eliminating odors in carpets, ashtrays, and refrigerators.

Positioning by product class Often the competition for a product may come from outside the product class. For example, those involved in the airline industry know that while they compete with other airline carriers, trains and buses also constitute viable alternatives. Amtrak has positioned itself as an alternative to taking the airplane, citing cost savings, enjoyment, and other advantages. Manufacturers of record albums must compete with those in the cassette and compact disc industries, whereas many margarines position themselves against butter. Thus, rather than positioning against another brand, an alternative strategy would be to position oneself against another product category, as shown by the advertisement for yogurt in Exhibit 5–21 (page 178).

Positioning by product user Positioning a product by associating it with a particular user or group of users is yet another approach utilized by marketers. The "273" ad (a perfume for the sexiest women around), shown in Exhibit 5–22 (page 178) is

➤ *Exhibit 5–19* **Positioning strategies for athletic shoes**

A. New Balance running shoes are designed specifically for runners

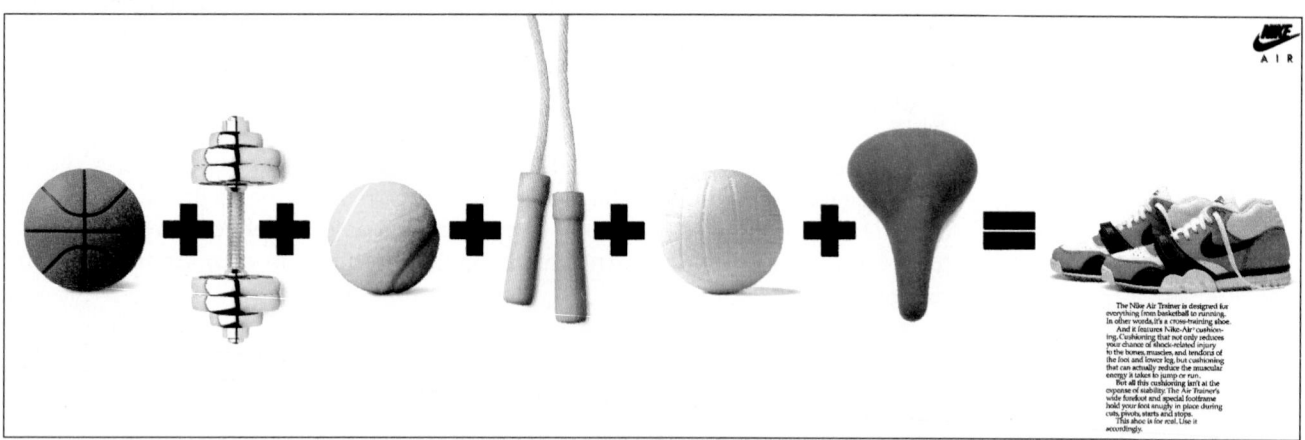

B. Nike cross trainers can be used for a variety of sports

one such example of this approach as were the Dewar's ads shown earlier. In both of these campaigns, identification or association with a specific group is evident.

Positioning by competitor   As we stated earlier in this chapter, competitors may be as important to positioning strategy as a firm's own product or services offering. As stated by Trout and Ries, the old strategy of ignoring one's competition will no longer work in today's marketplace.[15] (Advertisers used to think it was a cardinal sin to mention a competitor in their advertising!) In today's market, an effective

➤ *Exhibit 5–20*
WD-40 demonstrates numerous product uses

positioning strategy for a product or brand may be derived by focusing on specific competitors. This approach is very similar to that discussed in positioning by product class, although in this case the competition is within the same product category. Perhaps the most well known example of this strategy is that assumed by Avis, which positioned itself against the leader Hertz by stating, "We're number two, so we try harder." The Advil ad shown in Exhibit 5–23 (page 179) is an example of positioning a brand against the competition by emphasizing a specific use or application. In this ad, Advil is positioned as being more effective than competing brands for relieving menstrual pain. When positioning by competitor, it is often necessary to employ another positioning strategy as well to differentiate oneself.

Positioning by cultural symbols As earlier noted, Aaker and Myers include one additional positioning strategy in which *cultural symbols* are utilized to differentiate brands; for example, the Jolly Green Giant, the Keebler Elves, Speedy Alka-Seltzer, Bud Man, Buster Brown, Ronald McDonald, Chiquita Banana, and Mr. Peanut. Each of these companies—as well as others—has successfully differentiated its product from competitors' by identifying symbols that represent it (Exhibit 5–24, page 179).

> *Exhibit 5–21*
An example of positioning by product class

> *Exhibit 5–22*
273 is positioned as the perfume for women who want to feel sexy

Interestingly, the use of cultural symbols has become so common in our society that psychologists and sociologists have examined the mythological foundations underlying many of the characters and have expressed their own opinions as to the inherent meanings ascribed to them by consumers. A museum of modern mythology—featuring 20th-century cultural symbols of advertising—has been started in San Francisco. Part of the attraction of this museum is its tracing of the evolution of the characters over time, considering the changing culture of the United States and the impact it has had on such symbols.

Repositioning

One final strategy involving positioning involves the altering or changing of a product's or brand's position. **Repositioning** a product usually occurs because of declining or stagnant sales or because of anticipated opportunities in other market positions. Repositioning is often difficult to accomplish because of previously entrenched perceptions about and attitudes toward the product or brand. Many companies' attempts to change their positions have met with little or no success. (For example, Sears attempted to reposition itself as a store of higher quality, appealing to more well-to-do customers. The strategy was unsuccessful and subsequently abandoned. In 1989, Sears once again attempted a repositioning strategy—this time to a "lower-price store," and again with limited success.) Penney's decade-long attempt to reposition itself from a middle-class merchant into a more upscale department store has also met with limited success as both sales and profits are down.[16] One such effort

➤ *Exhibit 5–23*
Advil positions itself against the competition

➤ *Exhibit 5–24*
Brands that have become cultural symbols

at repositioning that has been extremely successful was that employed by *Rolling Stone* magazine. In an attempt to change the image held by advertisers of the type of person who reads *Rolling Stone*, the company embarked on an extensive advertising campaign to reposition the magazine in the minds of potential advertisers. The ad shown in Exhibit 5–25 is just one example of how this strategy was successfully implemented.

Other companies have also been successful in attempts to reposition. For example, Pontiac effectively repositioned its product as a sportier car that adds "excitement" whereas Dutch Boy paints was able to change its image to reach upscale, fashion-

➤ *Exhibit 5–25*
This ad is one of a series used in the campaign to reposition *Rolling Stone* **magazine**

oriented consumers. Promotional Perspective 5–1 discusses how Geritol was successful in its repositioning efforts.

Determining and developing the positioning strategy

Having explored the alternative positioning strategies available, the marketer must determine which strategy is best suited for the firm or product and begin developing the positioning platform. As can be seen by referring to the promotional planning process shown in Chapter 1, the input into this stage will be derived from the situation analysis—more specifically, the marketing research conducted therein. Essentially, the development of a positioning platform can be broken into a six-step process:[17]

1. **Identification of competitors.** As previously mentioned, this process requires broad thinking. Competitors may not be just those products and/or brands that fall into your product class or with which you directly compete. Consider wine as an example. A red wine competes with other red wines of various positions. At the same time, competition may also include white wines, champagnes, and nonalcoholic wines. Likewise, wine coolers provide an alternative, as do beer and other alcoholic drinks. To take the case further, other nonalcoholic drinks may come into consideration at various times and/or situations. Thus, the marketer must consider any and all likely competitors, as well as the various effects that use and situations may have on the consumer.

2. **Assessing consumers' perceptions of competitors.** Once we have been able to define the competition, it is necessary to determine how they are perceived and evaluated by consumers. This process involves determining which attributes are considered important to consumers in evaluating a product and/or brand. As you might expect, for many products, a wide variety of attributes, or product benefits, may be considered—most, if not all, of which are important. Much of the research conducted by marketing firms is directed at making such determinations. Consumers are asked to take part in focus groups and/or complete surveys indicating which attributes are important to them in their purchase decisions. For example, attributes considered important in the selection of a bank may include convenience, friendliness of the tellers, financial security, and a host of other factors. This process establishes the basis for the determination of competitive positions, or step three.

Promotional Perspective 5-1

Repositioning Geritol's "Iron-Poor Image"

The strategy of repositioning has been attempted by numerous firms—sometimes successfully, sometimes not. In recent years, a variety of old brands have repositioned themselves.

In the 1950s and 1960s, Geritol was pitched as a cure for "iron-poor blood." It was the kind of brand that older people (the target market) kept in the medicine cabinet and never talked about. As you can imagine, it was not one of your most exciting products! When SmithKline Beecham acquired the product in 1984, it reformulated it into a multivitamin—unsuccessfully. Sales went nowhere until 1989—the year of Geritol's rebirth.

Because many older consumers' cognitive age is younger than their chronological age (that is, they think they are younger than they really are), they were unwilling to adopt a product they perceived as being for "old age" people. When the brand was repositioned as Geritol Complete and targeted to middle-aged consumers, it was extremely successful—almost too successful as the average age of buyers had fallen into the mid-30s, and 7 out of 10 users were now under the age of 50. The problem was that with the aging of America, roughly 35 percent of all adults were now over the age of 50, a group that controls 50 percent of the discretionary income in the United States—and they were no longer buying Geritol or Geritol Complete.

SmithKline Beecham decided the best way to recapture the market was to design a new product for the over-50 group. The new product was called Geritol Extend. Unfortunately, the first few campaigns for Geritol Extend met with little success, and it was decided something radically different was needed.

Three versions of a new "motorcycle" campaign were tested with focus groups. Each used different background music ranging from Steppenwolf's "Born to be Wild" to the Beach Boys' "I get Around" to Glenn Miller's "In the Mood." While the first two generated little or no response, the Glenn Miller tune "got them out of their chairs." In the "Motorcycle" ad, a silver-haired Barbara Bush look-alike and her dapper companion roared down a country road on a motorcycle. An $8 million advertising campaign, a nine-month series of swing dance contests highlighting Geritol Extend, direct mail, and couponing came next.

How did it work? Geritol brands notched a 19 percent increase within the next year, and Geritol Complete gained 3 percent—an indication that Extend was not cannibalizing its own brand. In this case, repositioning worked!

Source: "Geritol Overcomes Its 'Iron-Poor' Image," *Adweek's Marketing Week,* November 12, 1990, p. 32–36.

3. **Determining competitors' positions.** Having determined the relevant attributes, and their relative importance to the consumer, the next step is to determine how each of the competitors (including your own entry) is positioned with respect to each attribute. This will also indicate how the competitors are positioned relative to each other. One such tool for making this determination is *multidimensional scaling* (MDS), a research methodology that leads to the development of a **perceptual map** of the positions of the various products and/or brands as perceived by the consumer. A number of companies have used perceptual mapping to gain insights into consumers' perceptions. For example, several years ago, Pontiac discovered that the Japanese imports by Nissan, Toyota, Honda, and Mazda and the German-made VW were perceived as more sporty and practical than the GM models (as is shown in the perceptual map in Exhibit 5–26). Based on this information, Pontiac repositioned itself as a more youthful, sporty auto with a more stylish and sporty body line and the "We Build Excitement" advertising campaign was developed to move Pontiac in the direction shown by the arrow in Exhibit 5–26. General Foods (coffee) and Quaker State (motor oil) have also successfully employed this strategy.

4. **Analyzing the consumers' preferences.** Our discussion of segmentation noted various factors that may distinguish between groups of consumers, including lifestyles, purchase motivations, demographic differences, and so on. Each of these various segments may have different purchase motivations and different attribute importance ratings. As such, it becomes necessary to understand such differences. One method for making this determination is by considering the "ideal" in the multidimensional scaling task. The *ideal* would be defined as the object the consumer

➤ *Exhibit 5–26*   **Pontiac division perceptual map, 1981, and "We Build Excitement" ad**

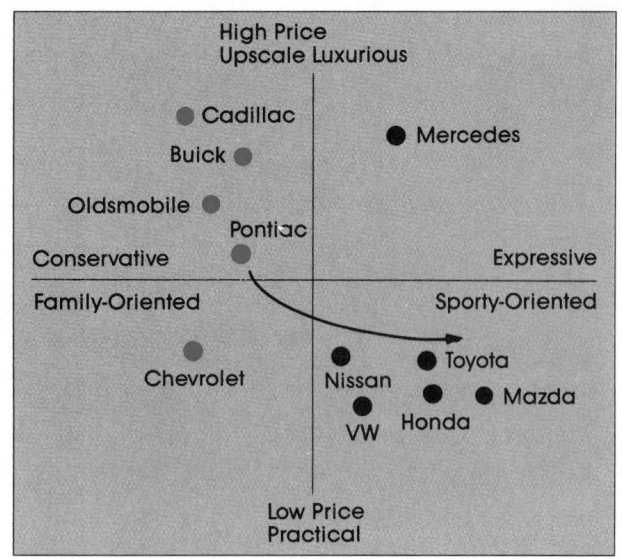

would prefer over all others, including objects that can be conceptualized but that do not exist. Identification of the ideal product may be useful for two purposes—either identifying different ideals among segments or identifying segments with similar or the same ideal points.

5. **Making the positioning decision.** Going through the previous four steps should allow for the decision on which position to assume in the marketplace. Such a decision is not always clear and well defined, however, and conducting the research just described may provide only limited input. In that case, it becomes necessary for the marketing manager—or groups of managers—to make some subjective judgments. To make these judgments a number of questions should be raised:

- **Is the segmentation strategy appropriate?** Positioning usually entails a decision to segment the market. Consideration must be given as to whether the market segment sought will support an entry and whether it is in the best interests of the company to deemphasize the remaining market. When a specific position is chosen, consumers may believe this is what the product is for. As such, those not looking for that specific benefit may not consider the brand as their first choice, assuming it is for some other purpose. Should the marketer decide on an undifferentiated strategy, it may be possible to deemphasize a specific positioning approach, being much more general in the positioning platform. For example, Toyota's campaign of "You asked for it, you got it—Toyota" emphasizes a variety of product attributes and allows consumers to assume they will get whatever they are looking for in the brand.

- **Are there sufficient resources available to communicate the position effectively?** It is very expensive to establish a position. One ad, or even a series of ads, is not likely to be enough to engrain the position. Thus, the marketer must commit to a long-range effort—in all aspects of the marketing campaign—to ensure the objectives sought are obtained. Too often, the firm abandons a position and/or advertising campaign long before it has had an opportunity to establish a position successfully. The *Rolling Stone* campaign discussed earlier is an excellent example of sticking with a campaign: The basic theme has now been running for a number of years. On the other hand, both Wendy's and Burger King have switched agencies and/or campaigns so often over the past few years it has been impossible for them to establish a distinct position in the consumer's mind. Further, once a successful position has been attained, it is likely to attract competitors.

Again, it may become expensive to ward off those attempting to become "me-too" brands—brands that attempt to assume the same position as the leader—and to continue to hold on to the brand distinction.

- **How strong is the competition?** The marketing manager must ask whether a position sought is likely to be maintained, given the strengths of the competition. For example, General Foods Corporation would often make it a practice not to be the first entry into a market, relying on the fact that it could make a better product. Thus, when competitors developed new markets with their entries, General Foods would simply improve on the product and capture a large percentage of the market share. This leads to two basic questions: First, if our firm is first into the market, will we be able to maintain the position (quality wise, price wise, etc.)? Second, if someone else is already in the market position we seek, will we be able to demonstrate specific advantages allowing us to capture our share? This brings up whether the product can live up to its claims. If it is positioned as finest quality, it must be. If it is positioned as lowest cost, then it has to be. Otherwise, the position claimed is sure to be lost.

- **Is the current positioning strategy working?** There is an old saying, "If it ain't broke, don't fix it." If one's current efforts are not working, then it may be time to consider an alternative positioning strategy. If they are working, such a change is usually unnecessary and unwarranted. Sometimes executives become bored with a theme or grow tired of it and decide it is time for a change. Often this change causes confusion in the marketplace and weakens a previously established position as a result. Unless there is strong reason to believe a change in positioning is necessary, one should stick with the current strategy.

6. **Can we monitor the position?** Once a position has been established, it is necessary to monitor how well this position is being maintained in the marketplace. At the same time, the impact of competitors must be determined.

One method of monitoring is utilizing tracking studies. Tracking studies are designed to measure the image of the product or firm over time. Thus, changes in consumers' perceptions can be determined, with any slippage immediately noted and reacted to. At the same time, the impact of competitors can be determined.

Before leaving this chapter, you might stop to think for a moment about the positioning (and repositioning) strategies pursued by different companies. We are sure you will quickly realize that almost any successful product that comes to your mind occupies a distinct market position.

SUMMARY

In the planning process, the situation analysis requires determining the marketing strategy to be assumed. The promotional program will be developed with this strategy as a guide. One of the key decisions to be made is that of target marketing—a process involving market segmentation, market targeting, and market positioning strategies.

Market segmentation—or dividing the market into smaller groups—is a process that allows for the development of specifically targeted marketing strategies. A number of bases for segmentation were discussed, including geographic segmentation, demographic segmentation, psychographic segmentation, behavioristic segmentation, and benefit segmentation. More than one basis for segmentation may be employed at a time. For example, a market may be segmented on the lifestyles of consumers while at the same time considering the demographic groups or income groups engaging in such lifestyles.

Upon determination of the best segmentation strategy, market targeting is considered. Determining the number of markets to enter and the most attractive segment—that is, the one with the greatest potential—is required. Having made these decisions, the next step is that of positioning, or creating an image of the product in the mind of the consumer. A number of positioning strategies were discussed—for example, positioning by product attributes, price/quality, use or application, product class, product user, competitor, and cultural symbol.

Sometimes it may be necessary to reposition—or change—the positioning of a product or brand. Sears, *Rolling Stone,* and Pontiac, among others, have at one time or another pursued a repositioning strategy.

Finally, it is important to remember that the process of target marketing is indeed that—a process. Market segmentation and target marketing and positioning do not just happen; rather, a series of steps are required, ultimately leading to a strategy to be pursued. Having gone through this process in the situation analysis, the manager is now ready to establish specific objectives to be sought.

KEY TERMS

product differentiation
target marketing
market segmentation
geographic segmentation
demographic
    segmentation
psychographic
    segmentation

values and lifestyles
    program (VALS)
behavioristic
    segmentation
80–20 rule
benefit segmentation
undifferentiated
    marketing

differentiated marketing
concentrated marketing
positioning
positioning strategies
repositioning
perceptual map

DISCUSSION QUESTIONS

1. Discuss the concept of target marketing and why it is so important to marketers.

2. Over the past two decades, market segmentation has become very prevalent in nearly every industry ranging from beer to soft-drinks to computers. Discuss the reasons underlying the increased use of market segmentation.
   Do you feel that it is possible for a mass marketed product to be successful in today's marketplace?

3. Discuss the process involved in segmenting a market. What are some factors that must be considered in determining how to segment the market?

4. Analyze the personal computer industry from a market segmentation perspective. Discuss the various market segments and how competitors position themselves to compete in this market.

5. What is meant by benefit segmentation? Find examples of three ads that are designed to appeal to specific benefits segments.

6. Many companies spend $30,000 or more to be part of the VALS program.

Discuss how promotional planners could use the information provided by VALS in developing marketing and promotional strategies.

7. What is meant by positioning? Discuss the various approaches to positioning and give examples of companies or brands using each approach.

8. What factors would lead a marketer to the use of a repositioning strategy? Find an example of a product or service that has been repositioned recently and analyze the strategy.

9. What are some of the factors that must be taken into consideration in developing a positioning strategy for a product or service?

10. Ethical Perspective 5–1 discusses how several tobacco and liquor companies have been criticized recently for targeting specific market segments. Evaluate the arguments for and against each company's rights to target certain market segments such as minorities, young people, or those with a lower education level.

part III

Analyzing the Communications Process

....

chapter **6**

The Communications Process

chapter objectives

➢ To examine the basic elements of the communications process and the role of communications in marketing.

➢ To examine various models of the communications process.

➢ To analyze the response processes of receivers of marketing communications, including alternative response hierarchies and their implications for promotional planning and strategy.

➢ To examine the nature of consumers' cognitive processing of marketing communications.

In Search of the Holy Grail

On any given day, the average American is exposed to about 300 advertising messages—which translates into more than 9,000 a month and nearly 110,000 a year. Obviously, consumers cannot attend to all the ads marketers bombard them with or, as one advertising researcher notes, "We'd all be in rubber rooms." While marketers do not expect consumers to attend to all of these messages, they are concerned that consumers have become too good at screening out most of them. According to Maples & Ross, a company that measures advertising effectiveness, some 80 percent of Americans cannot remember a typical commercial one day after they have seen it. Advertising has become so common that consumers effectively "zap" most commercials mentally, even without the use of a remote control device.

The mental zapping of most advertising messages by consumers has inspired researchers to continually search for an answer to a fundamental question, "What is the secret of making commercials memorable and effective?" There is some consensus among advertising researchers that consumers use a process of perceptual screening of which ads to attend to and remember. They constantly scan their environment, and when they see or hear something of relevance, they tune in to learn more. This still leaves researchers wondering what it is that gets consumers to tune in or out on some ads but not others.

Conventional research techniques have shown that some types of commercials are more effective than others at attracting attention and, ultimately, persuading consumers to change brands. Among the winners, according to Maples & Ross, are candid camera testimonials, ads that offer solutions to problems, and product demonstrations. These approaches are believed to be appealing because they present information in a way that doesn't tax a viewer's brain. Humorous ads and the use of celebrities are also appealing and memorable, but they may not be persuasive since they distract the viewers' attention away from the product.

In their quest to unlock the secret of what works best, companies are turning to a variety of research techniques. Inner Response Inc. uses machines that monitor the brain's reactions to commercials by measuring physiological changes such as electrical impulses in viewers' palms. The company believes this type of monitoring can show precisely what parts of a commercial a viewer is most attentive to and offer a series of second-by-second snapshots of how the brain is responding to an ad. Tracing interest and attention levels helps advertisers separate strong scenes in commercials from the weak.

Some companies use more complex measures such as electroencephalograms (or EEGs), which trace electrical activity within the brain. Scientists believe the brain's

(continued)

right hemisphere handles creative and spatial tasks while the left side handles more analytical tasks such as verbal and mathematical skills. For example, brain-wave research has shown that emotional slice-of-life commercials tend to be processed mostly by the right side of the brain. More logical ads, such as product demonstrations, are handled predominantly by the left side. Companies such as Neuro-Communication Research Laboratories suggest they can use brain-wave analysis to evaluate commercials and help spot problems. The company cites a commercial in which a father and daughter were speaking. The father's affection produced a high level of processing activity in the right side of the brain. However, just as the viewer was being drawn into the emotional scene, the commercial quickly cut to product information. The EEG measures showed the right hemisphere was

still highly active, making it difficult for the brain to process the information. Since linguistic processing usually requires roughly equal activity in both the left and right hemispheres, the timing may have interfered with the consumers' ability to process the message. Some researchers, however, are skeptical of brain-wave research and argue it is too complex and mysterious to offer insight into how to create better ads.

Advertisers are likely to continue their barrage of advertising messages, and consumers will probably continue to ignore most of them. However, researchers will find new ways to probe into the brains of consumers on a quest for the Holy Grail of Advertising: The secrets to making commercials memorable and effective.

Source: Michael J. McCarthy, "Mind Probe," The Wall Street Journal, *March 22, 1991, p. B3.*

The basic commonality shared by all elements of the promotional mix is that their function is to communicate. An organization's advertising and promotional strategy is implemented through the communications it sends to its current or prospective customers. Thus, advertising and promotional planners need to understand the communications process. As was noted in the introduction, the way consumers interpret, react, and respond to advertising can often be a very subtle and complex process. Creating an effective marketing communications program is far more complicated than just choosing a product feature or attribute to emphasize. Marketers must understand how their messages will be perceived and interpreted by consumers and how these reactions will shape their responses toward the product or service. This chapter reviews the fundamentals of communications and examines various perspectives regarding how consumers respond to promotional messages. Our ultimate goal is to demonstrate how an understanding of the communications process can be of value in planning, implementing, and evaluating the marketing communications program.

The Nature of Communication

Communication has been variously defined as "the passing of information," "the exchange of ideas," or as the process of establishing a commonness or oneness of thought between a sender and a receiver.[1] These definitions suggest that for communications to occur, there must be some common thinking between two parties and this information must be passed from one person to another (or from one group to another). As you will see in this chapter, the ability to establish this commonality in thinking is not always as easy as it might seem to be; many attempts to communicate are unsuccessful.

The communications process is often very complex, with success depending on many factors such as the nature of the message, the audience's interpretation of it, and the environment in which it is received. In addition, the receiver's perception of the source and the medium used to transmit the message may also affect the ability to communicate, as will many other factors. Words, pictures, sounds, and colors may have different meanings to different audiences, and people will vary in their perceptions and interpretations of them. For example, the word *soda* takes on different meanings in various parts of the country. If you were on the East Coast or West Coast and asked for a soda, you would receive a soft drink such as a Coke or Pepsi. However, in parts of the Midwest and South, a soft drink is referred to as a "pop." Asking for a soda may result in receiving a glass of pop with ice cream in it,

Global Perspective 6–1

Communication Problems in International Marketing

Communication is a major problem facing U.S. companies that market their products in foreign countries. International marketers must be aware of the connotation of the words, signs, symbols, and expressions used as brand names, logos, or in various forms of promotion. Advertising copy and slogans often do not transfer well into other languages. This not only creates communication problems but also sometimes results in embarrassing blunders that can damage a company's or brand's credibility or image as well as cost it customers.

There are numerous examples of mistranslations and faulty word choices that have created problems for firms engaging in international marketing. For example, an advertising campaign used by Pepsi-Cola—"Come Alive With Pepsi"—translated too literally in some countries. The German translation of "come alive" became "come out of the grave," while in Chinese it read "Pepsi brings your ancestors back from the dead." Another classic blunder occurred when General Motors tried to sell a Chevrolet model in Mexico and Latin America with the name Nova—which in Spanish means "it won't go." And an American airline competing in Brazil advertised "rendezvous lounges" in its jets until it discovered that in the Brazilian dialect of Portuguese this meant a place to make love.

International marketers can also have linguistic problems with brand names and their meaning or pronunciation, as when Coca-Cola introduced its product to China. The Chinese translated the name into Chinese characters that sounded like "Coca-Cola" but meant "bite the wax tadpole." With the help of a language spe-

cialist, the company substituted four Mandarin characters that sound like Coca-Cola but mean "Can Happy, Mouth Happy."

Mars Company encountered a problem in France with making the M&M's name pronounceable as neither the ampersand nor the apostrophe s plural exists in the French language. The company handled the problem by explaining to the French that M&M's should be pronounced "aim-ainaimze." Honda Motor Company also faced a communications dilemma when choosing a name for its new Acura automobile a few years ago. The brand-naming firm that created the name noted it would have been better to spell it with two Cs instead of one. With a double C more people would have made the connection to "accurate" and pronounced it correctly. However, Honda wanted a name that could be used around the world, and a double C is difficult to pronounce in some languages.

Many multinational companies are trying to develop "world brands" that can be marketed internationally using the same brand name and with a global advertising campaign. However, as these examples show, marketers must be careful to ensure that brand names, advertising slogans, and other forms of marketing communication translate properly into foreign languages.

Source: Ron Alsop, "Firms Create Unique Names, But Are They Pronounceable?" *The Wall Street Journal*, April 2, 1987, p. 29; "We Are the World," *Adweek's Marketing Week*, September 1990, pp. 61–68; David A. Ricks, *Big Business Blunders: Mistakes in Multinational Marketing* (Homewood, Ill.: Dow Jones-Irwin, 1983); and Laurel Wentz, "M&M Continues Global Roll," *Advertising Age*, September 14, 1987, p. 90.

as that is what is meant by a soda in these areas. Marketers must understand the meanings various words and symbols take on and how this might influence the consumers' interpretation of their products and messages. This can be particularly challenging to companies marketing their products in foreign countries as is discussed in Global Perspective 6–1.

A Basic Model of Communications

Over the years, a basic model of communications has evolved that represents the various elements of the communications process, as shown in Exhibit 6–1.[2] Two elements represent the major participants in the communications process—the sender and receiver; another two, the major communications tools—message and channel; and four others, major communications functions and processes— encoding, decoding, response, and feedback. The last element, noise, refers to any extraneous factors in the system that can interfere with the process and work against effective communication.

Source Encoding

The sender or **source** of a communication is the person or organization who has information to share with another person or group of people. The source may be an individual (for example, a salesperson or hired spokesperson, such as a celebrity, who appears in a company's advertisements) or a nonpersonal entity (such as the

➤ *Exhibit 6–1*
A model of the communications process

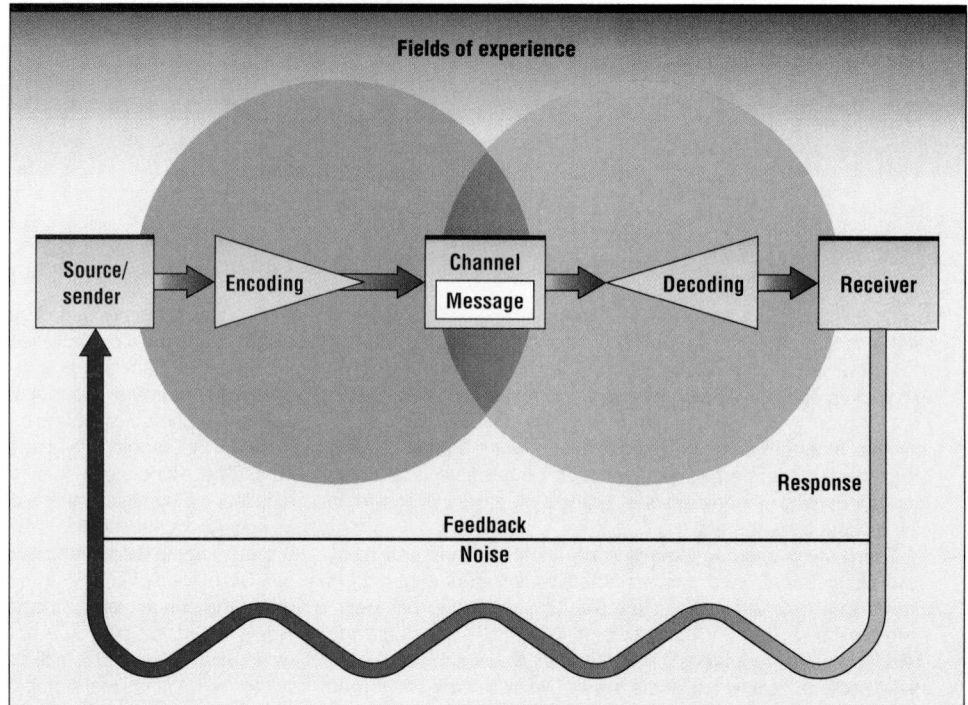

corporation or organization itself). For example, the source of the ad shown in Exhibit 6–2 is Motorola, Inc., as no specific spokesperson or source is shown. However, in Exhibit 6–3, Motorola uses golfer Lee Trevino as an advertising spokesperson.

Because the receiver's perceptions of the source will influence the manner in which the communication is received, marketers must be careful to select a communicator the receiver believes is knowledgeable and trustworthy or with whom the receiver can identify or relate in some manner. (Further discussion of how these characteristics will influence the receiver's responses is provided in Chapter 7.)

The communications process begins when the source selects words, symbols, pictures, and the like to represent the message that will be delivered to the receiver(s). The process known as **encoding** refers to putting thoughts, ideas, or information into a symbolic form. The sender's goal is to encode the message in such a way so as to ensure it will be understood by the receiver. This means using words, signs, or symbols that are familiar to and understood by the target audience. For example, many symbols have universal meaning such as the familiar circle with a line through it to denote no parking, no smoking, and so forth. Many companies also have highly recognizable universal symbols such as McDonald's golden arches or the Coca-Cola trademark.

Message

The encoding process leads to development of a *message* that contains the information or meaning the source hopes to convey. The message may be verbal or nonverbal, an oral or written statement, or a symbolic form or sign. Messages must be put into a transmittable form that is appropriate for the channel of communication being used. In advertising, this may range from simply writing some words or copy that will be read as a radio message to the expensive production of a television commercial. For many products, it is not the actual words contained in the message that determine its communication effectiveness but rather the impression or image the advertisement creates. Notice how Spellbound perfume shown in Exhibit 6–4 uses only a picture to deliver its message. However, the product name and picture help communicate a feeling of entrancement and fascination between the couple shown in the ad.

➤ *Exhibit 6–2*
The source of this ad is Motorola, Inc.

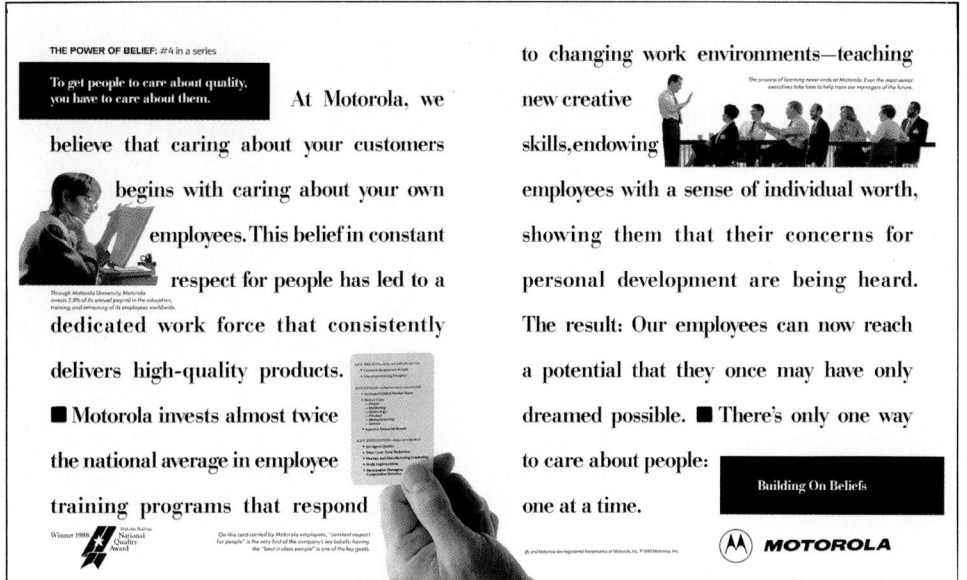

➤ *Exhibit 6–3*
Motorola uses Lee Trevino as a spokesperson in this ad

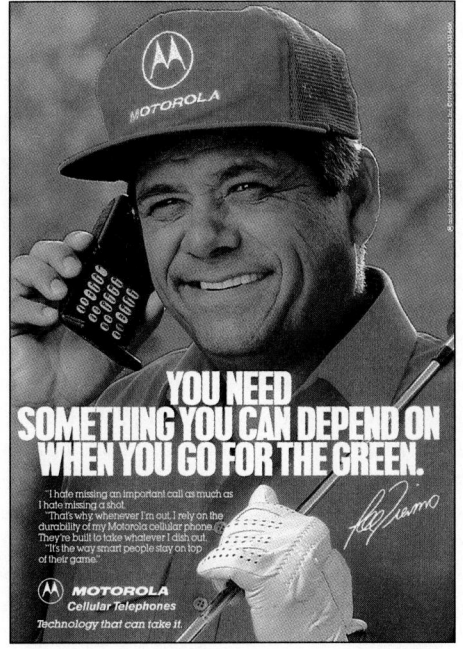

To better understand the symbolic meaning that might be conveyed in a communication, advertising and marketing researchers have begun focusing attention on semiotics. **Semiotics** involves the study of the nature of meaning and asks how our reality—words, gestures, myths, products/services, theories—acquire meaning.[3] Marketers are using individuals trained in semiotics to better understand the conscious and subconscious meaning and messages the nonverbal signs and symbols used in their advertisements transmit to consumers.

Look at the ad for Snuggle fabric softener shown in Exhibit 6–5 and think about what the teddy bear might symbolize. Lever Brothers Co. conducted a semiotic analysis to help understand the meaning of the huggable teddy bear (Snuggle) that has become such a successful advertising symbol. The semiologist concluded Snuggle is a "symbol of tamed aggression" and a perfect symbol for a fabric softener that "tames" the rough texture of clothing.[4]

➤ *Exhibit 6–4*
The image projected by an advertisement often communicates more than words

Some advertising and marketing people are skeptical about the value of semiotics. They question whether social scientists read too much into advertising messages and are overly intellectual in interpreting them. However, the meaning of an advertising message or other form of marketing communication lies not in the message, but with the people who see and interpret it. Moreover, consumers behave based on the meanings they ascribe to marketplace stimuli. Thus, marketers must consider the meaning consumers attach to the various signs and symbols. Semiotics may be helpful in analyzing how various aspects of the marketing program such as advertising messages, packaging, brand names, or even the nonverbal communications of salespeople (gestures, mode of dress) are interpreted by receivers.[5]

Channel

The **channel** is the method or medium by which the communication travels from the source or sender to the receiver. At the broadest level, channels of communication are of two types, personal and nonpersonal. **Personal channels** of communication are means of direct interpersonal (face-to-face) contact with target individuals or groups. Salespeople serve as personal channels of communication when delivering their sales message to a buyer or potential customer, whereas social channels of communication such as friends, neighbors, associates, co-workers, or family members are also examples. The latter often represent **word-of-mouth communications**, which are often a very powerful and influential source of information for consumers.[6]

Nonpersonal channels of communication are those that carry a message without involving interpersonal contact between sender and receiver. Nonpersonal channels are generally referred to as the **mass media** or mass communications, as the message is sent to many individuals at one time—for example, a television commercial broadcast on a prime-time show may be seen by 20 million households in a given evening. Nonpersonal channels of communication consist of two major types, print and broadcast, with several subtypes within each category. Print media include newspapers, magazines, direct mail, and billboards, whereas the broadcast media include radio and television.

Receiver/Decoding

The **receiver** is the person or persons with whom the sender shares thoughts or information. Generally, the receivers are the consumers in the audience or market targeted by a company who read, hear, and/or see the marketer's message and decode it. **Decoding** is the process of transforming and interpreting the sender's message back into thought. This process is heavily influenced by the receiver's frame

➢ *Exhibit 6–5*
Semiotic research suggests that the Snuggle bear symbolizes tamed aggression

of reference or **field of experience,** which refers to the experiences, perceptions, attitudes, and values carried into the communications situation.

For effective communication to occur, the message decoding process of the receiver must match the encoding of the sender. Simply put, this means the receiver understands and correctly interprets what the source is trying to communicate. As can be seen in Exhibit 6–1, both the source and the receiver have a frame of reference they bring to the communications situation. Effective communication is more likely when there is some *common ground* between the two parties. (This is represented by the overlapping of the two circles representing the fields of experience.) The more knowledgeable the sender is of the receivers, the greater the likelihood of understanding their needs, empathizing with them, and communicating effectively.

While this notion of common ground between sender and receiver may sound very basic, it often causes great difficulty in the advertising communications process. Marketing and advertising people often have a very different background and field of experience than the consumers who constitute the mass markets with whom they must communicate. For example, most advertising and marketing people are college educated and work and/or reside in large urban areas such as New York, Chicago, or Los Angeles. However, these advertisers are attempting to develop commercials that will effectively communicate with millions of consumers who have never attended college, who work in blue-collar occupations, and who live in rural areas or small towns. A quote from the executive creative director of a large advertising agency, commenting on how advertising executives become isolated from the cultural mainstream, describes this problem:

> We pull them in and work them to death. And then they begin moving in sushi circles and lose touch with Velveeta and the people who eat it.[7]

Promotional Perspective 6–1

Are Advertising People Different?

It has often been argued that people who work in advertising are different from the typical consumers who represent the target market for their clients' products and services. A study conducted by the DDB Needham Worldwide advertising agency suggests there are some significant differences between advertising people and consumers. The agency's Chicago office ran an abridged version of its annual Life Style Study questionnaire in an in-house publication and received about 200 responses from its employees. Martin Horn, the agency vice president who presides over the Life Style Study, compared the responses of the agency personnel with the sample of average Americans who participate in the full study and found big differences between the two groups.

The sample of DDB Needham agency personnel is not representative of all people working in ad agencies. There were, however, some major differences between agency people and the general public in their level of agreement with various activities, interests, and opinions statements. Some of the more striking differences were for the following:

	Agency	Public
• I want to look different from others.	82%	62%
• There's too much sex on prime-time TV.	50	78
• TV is my primary form of entertainment.	28	53
• I went to a bar or tavern in the past year.	91	50
• I like the feeling of speed.	66	35
• There should be a gun in every home.	9	32
• I hate to lose even friendly competition.	58	44
• My favorite music is classic rock.	64	35
• My favorite music is easy listening.	27	51
• Couples should live together before getting married.	50	33
• My greatest achievements are still ahead of me.	89	65
• Job security is more important than money.	52	75
• I bought a lottery ticket in the previous year.	75	61

Horn noted that the implication of these findings is clear. "Assuming the target customer to be just like us, we may end up with advertising that talks to no one—other than ourselves." The title of the article in which Horn summarized the results of this study provides probably the best message to those working in advertising: "I Have Met the Customer & He Ain't Me."

Source: Joseph M. Winski, "Study: 'The Customer Ain't Me,'" *Advertising Age,* January 20, 1992, p. 18.

Promotional Perspective 6–1 discusses some interesting findings from a study comparing individuals who work in advertising agencies with the general public.

To avoid these problems, advertisers spend millions of dollars every year to research their target markets to understand better the frame of reference of the consumers who receive their messages. In addition, much time and money is spent pretesting messages to ensure they are understood by the consumer and decoded in the manner in which the advertiser intended.

Noise

Throughout the communications process, the message is subject to extraneous factors that can distort or interfere with its reception. This unplanned distortion or interference in the communications process is known as **noise**. Errors or problems that occur in the encoding of the message, distortion in a radio or television signal, or distractions at the point of reception are examples of noise. A simple example of noise would be a situation where you are watching your favorite commercial on television and a problem occurs in the signal transmission. This would obviously interfere with your reception, and the impact of the commercial may be lessened.

Noise may also occur because the fields of experience of the sender and receiver have nothing in common. Lack of common ground may result in improper encoding of the message such as using a sign, symbol, or words that are unfamiliar to the receiver or have different meaning. As noted earlier, the more common ground there is between the sender and the receiver, the less likely this type of noise will occur.

Response/Feedback

The set of reactions the receiver has after seeing, hearing, or reading the message is known as a **response.** The responses of the receiver can range from nonobservable actions such as storing information in memory to taking immediate action such as dialing an 800 number to order a product advertised on television. Marketers are very interested in **feedback,** which is that part of the receiver's response that is communicated back to the sender. Feedback, which may take a variety of forms, closes the loop in the communications flow and provides the sender with a way of monitoring how the intended message is being decoded and received.

For example, in a personal selling situation, customers may pose questions, comments, or objections or indicate their reactions through nonverbal responses such as gestures and frowns.[8] While a salesperson has the advantage of receiving instantaneous feedback through the reactions of the customer, this is generally not the case when mass media are used. Because advertisers are not in direct contact with the customers, they must use other means of determining how their messages have been received. While the ultimate form of feedback occurs through sales, there are often problems in attempting to show a direct relationship between advertising and purchase behavior. Thus, marketers use other methods to obtain feedback, such as customer inquiries, store visits, coupon redemptions, and reply cards. Research-based feedback to analyze readership and recall of ads, message comprehension, attitude change, and other forms of response is also used. With this information, the advertiser can analyze reasons for success or failure in the communications process and make adjustments.

The 5-Ws Model of Communication

Another popular conceptualization of the communications process is the basic model developed by Lasswell a number of years ago.[9] This approach, which is often referred to as the **5-Ws model of communication,** says a communications model must deal with five basic elements or questions. As can be seen below, each of these questions corresponds to an element in the basic communications model discussed earlier.

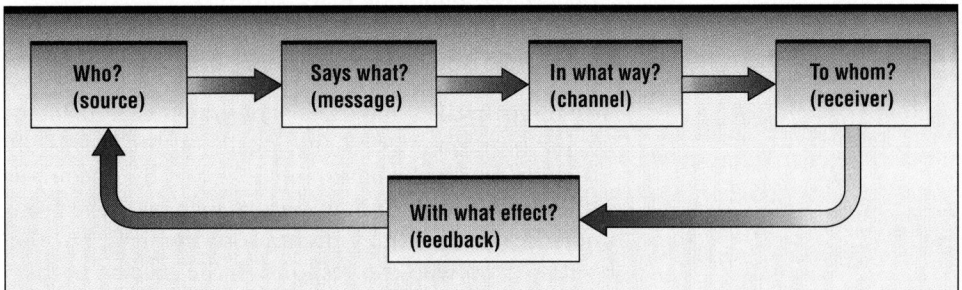

The basis of this model is a *message flow* whereby the communication initiates with the source, is formulated into a message, and is transmitted through a medium or channel to receivers constituting a target audience. The impact of the message is measured in terms of feedback, in which the receiver's reaction to the message is communicated back to the source. However, in the development of a communications plan, the marketer employs a *planning flow* in which this model is approached in reverse; that is, the receiver is the starting point since the success of a promotional program is affected by the nature of the consumers who receive it. The medium, message, and source are selected based on the characteristics of the receiver or target audience. This process recognizes that promotional planning logically begins with the receivers who make up the firm's target market, as it is this desired audience that should influence decisions as to what is to be said; how, when, and where it is to be said; and who is best suited to say it.

The receivers are considered to be an uncontrollable variable in that the marketer cannot really control the actions of these persons. Marketers can choose a target audience and attempt to influence their actions, but actual control of the receiver is beyond their capabilities. However, the marketer can control and change certain factors. These controllable variables include the source, message, and channel or media that will be utilized.

Successful communications are accomplished when the marketer selects an appropriate source, develops an effective appeal, and then selects the media that will best reach the target audience and effectively deliver the message. In Chapter 7, we will examine the source, message, and channel decisions and see how promotional planners work with these controllable variables to develop communications strategies. However, decisions in these areas must consider the target audience and how it will respond to the promotional message. Thus, in the remainder of this chapter, we examine the receiver in more detail and the process by which consumers respond to advertising and other forms of marketing communications.

Analyzing the Receiver

To communicate effectively with their customers, marketers must understand who the target audience is, what (if anything) the market knows or feels about the company's product or service, and how the audience needs to be communicated with to influence its decision-making process. In addition, marketers need to know how the market is likely to respond to various sources of communications or different types of messages. Before decisions are made regarding source, message, and channel variables, promotional planners must understand the potential effects associated with each of these factors. In this section, we focus on the receiver of the marketing communication and examine how the audience is identified and the process it may go through in responding to a promotional message. This information serves as a foundation for evaluating the controllable communications variable decisions covered in the next chapter.

Identifying the Target Audience

The marketing communications process really begins with identifying the audience that will be the focus of the firm's advertising and promotions efforts. One way of viewing the target audience is to recognize that it may consist of individuals, groups, or a general public or mass audience.

Individual and group audiences

The target market may consist of individuals having specific needs and for whom the communication must be specifically tailored. This often requires communication on a person-to-person basis and is generally accomplished through personal selling. Other forms of communication such as advertising may be used to attract the audience's interest and attention to the firm, but the detailed message is carried by a salesperson who can respond to the specific needs of the individual customer. Life insurance, financial services, and real estate are examples of products and services promoted this way.

A second level of audience aggregation is represented by the group. Marketers often must communicate with a group of people who influence or make the purchase decision. For example, organizational purchasing often involves **buying centers** or committees that vary in size and composition. Companies marketing their products and services to industrial users or other organizations must understand who is on the purchase committee, what aspect of the decision each individual influences, and the criteria each member is using in evaluating a product. Advertising might be directed to each member of the buying center, and multilevel personal selling may be necessary to reach those individuals who influence the decision-making process or actually make the decision. Promotional Perspective 6–2 shows one example of how advertising and promotion might operate when a buying committee or group is involved.

As you may recall from Chapter 4, decision making in the consumer market can also include a group when various family members become involved in the purchase of a product or service such as an automobile, furniture, or the family vacation. Thus, to develop an effective communications program in either of these markets, advertisers need to know who is involved in the decision-making process, what role they play, and how best to reach them.

Mass audiences

Many advertisers must communicate with large numbers of consumers or mass audiences. Marketers of most consumer products attempt to attract the attention of large numbers of present or potential customers through mass communications. Mass communications represent a one-way flow of information as the message flows from the marketer to the consumer, whereas feedback concerning the audience's reactions to the message is generally indirect and often difficult to measure.

Communicating with the general public or mass audiences generally requires that the marketer use some form of mass communication such as advertising or publicity. Using television advertising, for example, offers the marketer the opportunity to send a message to millions of consumers at the same time. However, this does not mean effective communication has occurred, as this may be only one of several hundred messages the consumer was exposed to that day. There is no guarantee the information was attended to, processed, comprehended, or stored in memory for later retrieval. Even if the advertising message is processed, it may be misunderstood or misinterpreted by consumers or be of little interest to them. Studies by Jacob Jacoby and Wayne D. Hoyer have shown that nearly 20 percent of all print ads are miscomprehended by readers. Television commercials are miscomprehended at an even higher rate.[10]

Unlike the personal or face-to-face communication situation, the marketer has no opportunity to explain or clarify the message to make it more effective when mass communication is being used. Thus, the marketer must enter the communication situation with knowledge of the target audience and how it is likely to react and be influenced by the message. This means the response process of the receiver must be understood along with its implications for promotional planning and strategy.

The Response Process

Perhaps the most important aspect of developing effective communications programs involves understanding the *response process* the receiver may go through in moving toward a specific behavior (like purchasing a product) and how the promotional efforts of the marketer might influence these responses. In many instances, the marketer may have only the objective of creating awareness of the company or brand name, as this may trigger interest in the product. In other situations, the marketer may want to convey detailed information so as to change consumers' level of knowledge and attitudes toward the brand and ultimately their behavior.

Traditional Response Hierarchy Models

A number of models have been developed to depict the response process or stages a consumer might pass through in moving from a state of not being aware of a company, product, or brand to actual purchase behavior. Exhibit 6–6 (page 199) shows four of the best-known response hierarchy models. While these response models may appear to be similar, they were developed for different reasons. Promotional planners may find a particular model relevant to certain marketing communication situations and thus should have a basic understanding of each.

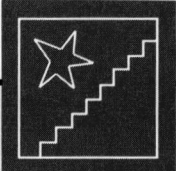

Promotional Perspective 6–2

Promoting to a Hospital

IVAC Corporation, one of the leading companies in the U.S. medical products industry, manufactures and sells a number of products including electronic thermometers, vital sign measurement systems, and intravenous (IV) infusion instruments and sets. To market these products to hospitals, IVAC must communicate with a variety of personnel involved in the decision-making process, including nurses, hospital pharmacists, purchasing agents, biomedical engineers, and administrators.

Each of these parties plays a different role in the purchase decision for IVAC products. For example, nurses are the actual users of the company's products and must be convinced they are reliable, easy to use, and time saving. Their opinions and input are important not only because they are users but also because they often serve as strong influencers on the hospital's purchase decision. Pharmacists have the responsibility of preparing the medicines that are delivered through the IVAC systems and are interested in efficient and cost-effective ways to administer the drugs. Thus, they are both *users* and *influencers* in the decision-making process. Purchasing agents and hospital administrators are, of course, concerned with controlling expenses and keeping operating costs down. They serve as *deciders* who have the power to select or approve final suppliers and also as *buyers* with formal authority for choosing the actual supplier and arranging the terms of purchase.

IVAC's promotional program is designed to reach these different personnel, as they all have some type of influence and input into the decision-making process. The company's highly trained and specialized sales force calls on the various hospital personnel to discuss their specific needs and concerns.

IVAC also uses a variety of advertising messages in various media to reach each group. For example, the company's ads appear in publications targeted to nurses such as *Nursing Management* and *Nursing 91* as well as publications read by hospital pharmacists such as *The American Journal of Hospital Pharmacy*. Advertisements that address factors of concern to purchasing agents and hospital administrators, such as cost-effectiveness, operating expenses, and other financial issues, appear in publications targeted to these individuals such as *Hospitals* and *Hospital Purchasing News*. The ad shown below, which is targeted at hospital administrators, discusses IVAC's consultative selling approach and how the company works with hospitals in analyzing their vital signs instrumentation needs.

IVAC targets advertising to hospital administrators

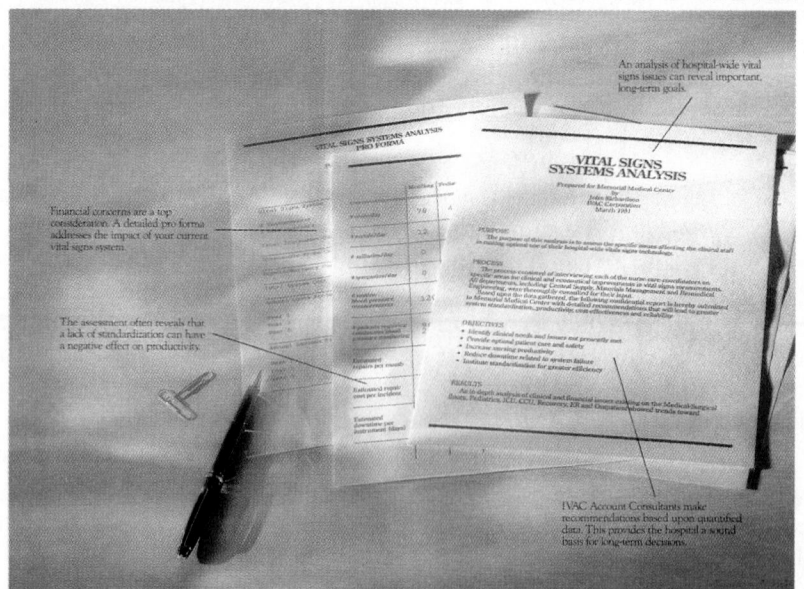

➤ *Exhibit 6−6* **Models of the response process**

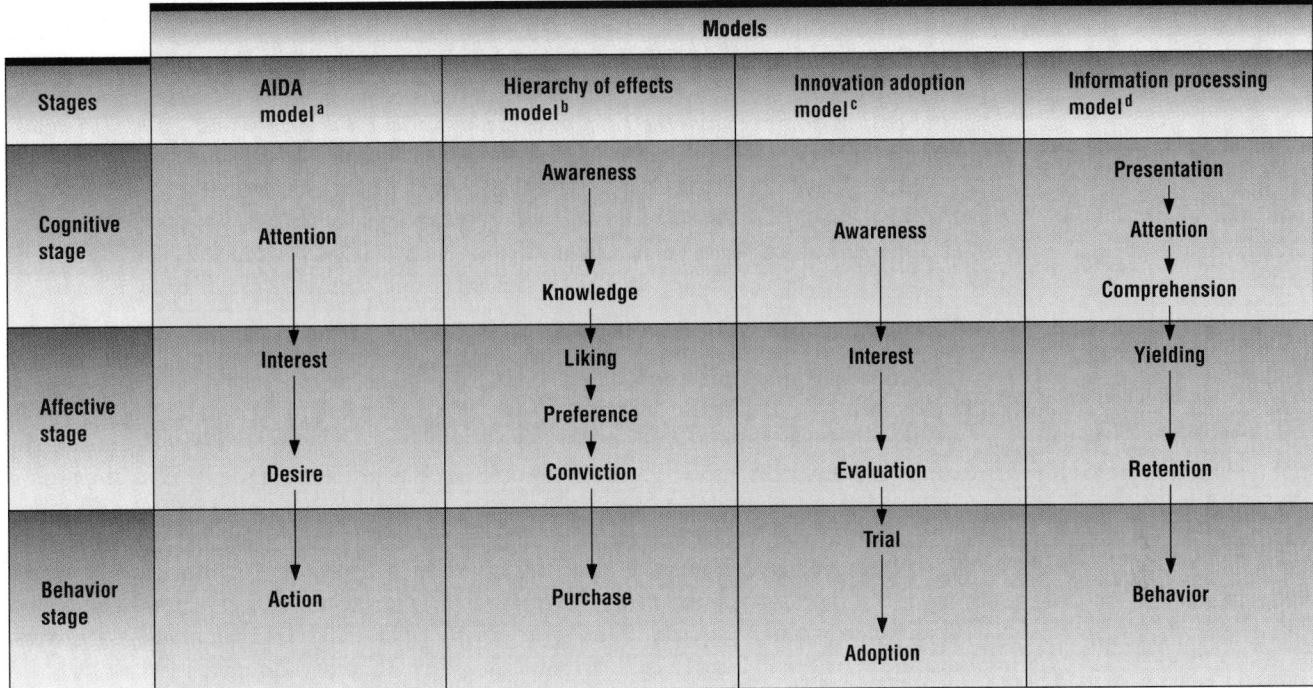

	Models			
Stages	**AIDA model**[a]	**Hierarchy of effects model**[b]	**Innovation adoption model**[c]	**Information processing model**[d]
Cognitive stage	Attention	Awareness ↓ Knowledge	Awareness	Presentation ↓ Attention ↓ Comprehension
Affective stage	Interest ↓ Desire	Liking ↓ Preference ↓ Conviction	Interest ↓ Evaluation	Yielding ↓ Retention
Behavior stage	Action	Purchase	Trial ↓ Adoption	Behavior

The AIDA model

The first of these hierarchical models was developed to represent the stages a salesperson must take a customer through in the personal selling process.[11] This model depicts the buyer as passing through successive stages of attention, interest, desire, and action (**AIDA model**). The salesperson must first get the attention of the customer and then arouse some level of interest in the company's product or service. This may be done by understanding the needs of the customer and showing the attributes or features of the product or service and emphasizing how they translate into benefits for the individual. Strong levels of interest it is hoped will create desire by the customer to own or use the product. The action stage in the AIDA model involves getting the customer to make a purchase commitment and closing the sale. To the marketer, this is the most important stage in the selling process, but it can also be the most difficult. Companies train their sales representatives in a variety of closing techniques to help them complete the selling process.

The hierarchy of effects model

Perhaps the best known of these response hierarchies is the model developed by Robert Lavidge and Gary Steiner as a paradigm for setting and measuring advertising objectives.[12] Their **hierarchy of effects model** represents the process by which advertising works and assumes a consumer must pass through a series of steps in sequential order from initial awareness of a product or service to actual purchase. A basic premise of this model is that advertising effects occur over a period of time, rather than being instantaneous. Thus, advertising communication may not lead to immediate behavioral response or action; rather, a series of effects must occur, with fulfillment of each step necessary before movement to the next stage in the hierarchy is possible.

As shown in Exhibit 6−6, the receiver must first become *aware* of the brand of product or service. Once awareness has occurred, the receiver must be provided with *knowledge* or information about the features, attributes, and so on, of the product. The information and knowledge the consumer acquires may lead to *liking*—a positive feeling or attitude toward the brand. These positive feelings may subsequently lead to *preference* whereby the brand is preferred over alternative brands. *Conviction* occurs when the consumer becomes convinced he or she should buy the brand and forms a purchase intention. The final step that translates these feelings and convictions into behavior is *purchase,* the ultimate goal sought by the marketer.

As we will see in Chapter 8, the hierarchy of effects model has become the foundation for objective setting and measurement of advertising effects in many companies. However, this model has also been criticized, particularly for the assumption that a consumer must pass through all the stages before purchasing a product.[13] Since alternative models will be examined later in this section, we reserve our discussion of these criticisms until that time.

The innovation-adoption model

The **innovation-adoption model** evolved from work in the area of the diffusion of innovations.[14] The innovation-adoption model represents the stages a consumer would pass through in the adoption of an innovation such as a new product. Like the other models, this model contends potential adopters must be moved through a series of steps including awareness, interest, evaluation, and trial before adoption.

In the *awareness* stage, potential adopters become aware the new product exists. At this stage, they know very little else about it and may not be motivated to learn any more unless they think the innovation is of interest to them. The marketer's next challenge is to move potential adopters to the *interest* stage, where they will learn more about the product such as its features, benefits, advantages, price, and availability. In the *evaluation* stage, consumers will decide whether the new product meets their needs and satisfies specific purchase criteria and goals. The best way to evaluate a new product is through actual usage or trial, so that performance can be experienced and judged. Marketers often encourage trial by using sales promotion techniques such as demonstrations, providing sampling programs, or making small sizes of a product available. After *trial,* consumers may move to the *adoption* stage if they decide to purchase the product or continue to use it. However, the outcome of trial may be rejection if the consumer decides against purchasing the new product or brand or using it in the future.

An excellent application of this model can be seen in the strategy used by Apple in the introduction of the Macintosh personal computer a few years ago. The stunning "1984" ad (discussed in Chapter 1) introduced the "computer for the rest of us" during the Super Bowl in January 1984. This ad attracted media attention also and helped create awareness and interest in the Macintosh. The advertising campaign then turned to other television and print ads, which provided extensive detail and information that could be used to make a more detailed evaluation of the Macintosh. In addition to the advertising campaign, a sales promotional program offered potential adopters the opportunity to "test-drive" the Macintosh at a local dealership by taking it home overnight or for a weekend (see Promotional Perspective 6–3). Awareness, interest, evaluation, and trial were all created through a well-planned and -coordinated promotional program. The result was a very successful product introduction that resulted in the adoption of the Macintosh by millions of consumers and businesses.

The information-processing model

The final of the four hierarchy models shown in Exhibit 6–6 is the **information-processing model** of advertising effects developed by William McGuire.[15] McGuire contends the appropriate view of a receiver in a persuasive communication situation like advertising is as an *information processor* or *problem solver.* He suggests the series of steps a receiver goes through in being persuaded constitute a *response hierarchy* consisting of a series of stages including (1) message presentation or exposure, (2) attention, (3) comprehension, (4) message acceptance or yielding, (5) retention, and

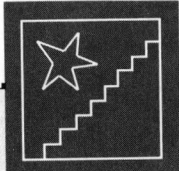

Promotional Perspective 6–3

Test-Drive a Macintosh

When Apple Computer introduced the Macintosh, it was reputed to be one of the most innovative personal computers ever developed and also one of the most user-friendly. However, before Apple could expect consumers to pay several thousand dollars for a Mac, it had to convince them the product was worth the money. To address this problem, Apple and its advertising agency, Chiat Day, borrowed a concept from the automobile industry by challenging consumers to "test-drive" a Macintosh. Apple was confident that once users had the chance to try its new computer, it would be difficult for them to resist purchasing it.

Under the test-drive program, interested consumers were actually permitted to take one of the computers home and use it for 24 hours. Apple developed software specifically for the trial that explained the unique benefits of the Mac. The promotion was supported with a television and print advertising campaign, and a variety of point-of-purchase material was developed to call attention to the promotion in computer stores. Also, to encourage retail support of the promotion, a 12-region sweepstakes was run awarding winners the use of a Porsche automobile for a year. The promotion was very successful, as more than 200,000 Macintoshes were "test-driven," and 40 percent of store sales were attributed to the promotion.

Source: Based on Jeffrey K. McElnea and Michael J. Enzer, "Building Brand Franchises," *Marketing Communications*, April 1986, p. 42.

Apple's "Test-Drive a Mac" promotion allowed consumers to sample a Macintosh

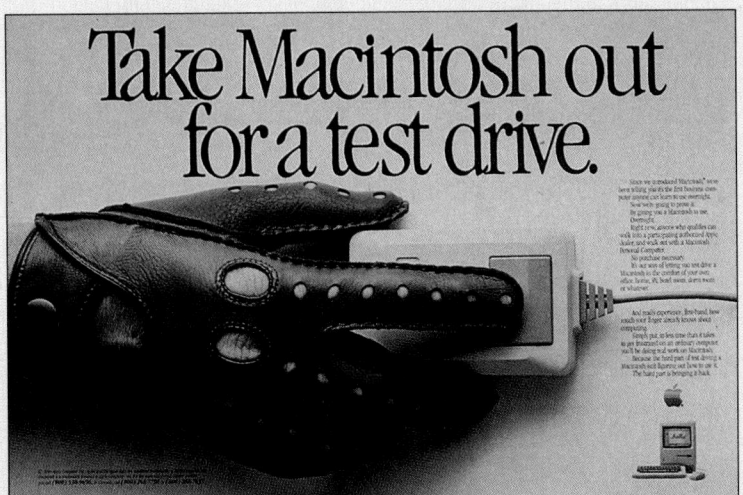

(6) behavior. The stages of this model are similar to those of the hierarchy of effects sequence, as *attention* and *comprehension* are similar to *awareness* and *knowledge*, whereas *acceptance* or *yielding* is synonymous with *liking*. McGuire's model includes a stage not found in the other models: retention. The *retention* stage refers to the receiver's ability to retain that portion of the comprehended information that is accepted as valid or relevant. The retention stage is important since most promotional campaigns are not designed to motivate consumers to take immediate action but rather are providing information that will be used when a purchase decision is being made at some subsequent time.

Each stage of the response hierarchy can be considered as a dependent variable that must be attained and that may serve as an objective of the communications process. As shown in Exhibit 6–7, each of these stages is measurable and thus capable of providing the advertiser with feedback regarding the effectiveness of various strategies designed to move the consumer to purchase. As such, the model

➤ *Exhibit 6–7*
Methods of obtaining feedback in the response hierarchy

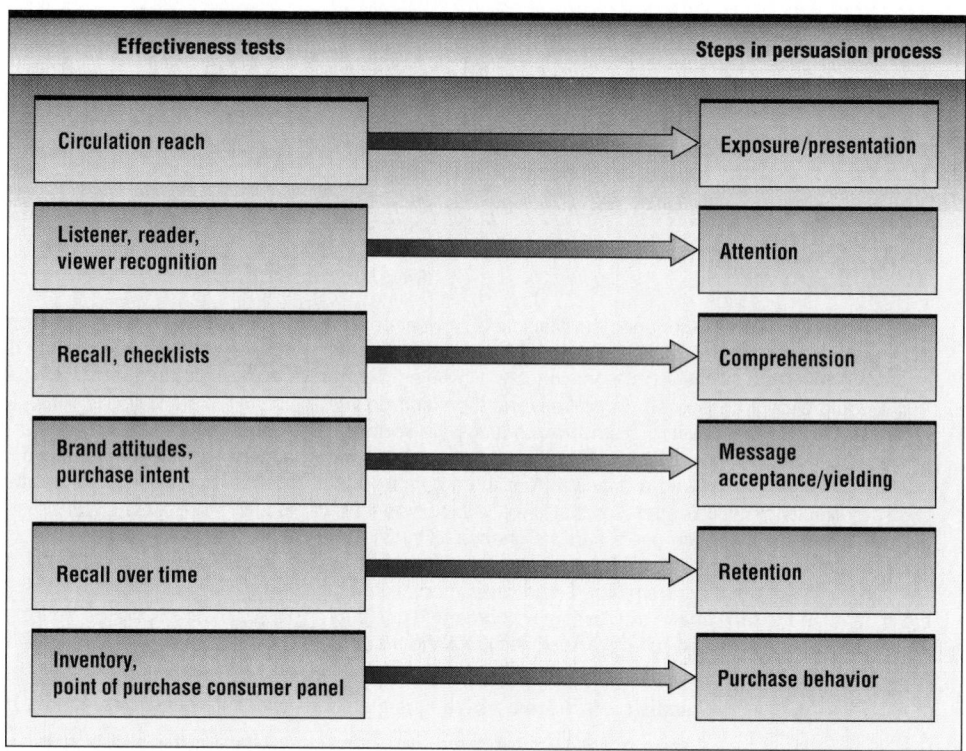

Effectiveness tests	Steps in persuasion process
Circulation reach	Exposure/presentation
Listener, reader, viewer recognition	Attention
Recall, checklists	Comprehension
Brand attitudes, purchase intent	Message acceptance/yielding
Recall over time	Retention
Inventory, point of purchase consumer panel	Purchase behavior

may serve as an effective framework for planning and evaluating the effects of a promotional campaign.

Implications of the Traditional Hierarchy Models

The hierarchy models of communication response are useful to promotional planners from several perspectives. First, they delineate the series of steps or stages potential purchasers must be taken through to move them from a state where they are unaware of the existence of a product or service to the point where they are ready to purchase it. Second, potential buyers may be at different stages in the hierarchy, and thus the advertiser will face different sets of communication problems. For example, the marketer of innovative products, such as a compact disc player or big-screen television, may need to devote considerable effort to making people aware of the product, explaining how it works and what its benefits are, and convincing consumers they should consider purchasing it (Exhibit 6–8). Marketers of a mature brand that enjoys a high level of customer loyalty may need to engage only in supportive or *reminder* advertising to reinforce positive perceptions and maintain the awareness level for the brand.

The hierarchy models can also be useful as "intermediate" measures of communication effectiveness. The marketer needs to know where audience members are with respect to the various stages of the response hierarchy. For example, research may reveal that one target segment has low awareness of the advertiser's brand, whereas another is aware of the brand and its various attributes but has a low level of liking or brand preference.

In the first segment, the communications task would involve increasing the awareness level for the brand. The number of ads might be increased to gain exposure, or a product sampling program could be used to help increase brand awareness. However, in the second segment, where awareness is already high but liking and preference are low, the advertiser would have to determine the reason for the negative feelings and then attempt to address this problem in future advertising. For example, business fliers may be aware of the fact that an airline offers service between various cities but avoid flying the airline because they think the flights rarely are on time. The

➤ *Exhibit 6–8*
Advertising for a new product explains features and benefits to get consumers' interest

➤ *Exhibit 6–8*
Advertising for a new product explains features and benefits to get consumers' interest

airline would have to correct this perception, perhaps by using advertising stressing the company's on-time-arrival record (assuming it *is* good!).

In situations where research or other evidence reveals a company is perceived favorably on a particular attribute or performance criterion, the company may want to take advantage of this in its advertising. For example, Alaska Airlines has established a reputation for excellent service, which it emphasizes with ads such as the one shown in Exhibit 6–9.

Evaluating Traditional Response Hierarchy Models

As can be seen in Exhibit 6–6, the four models presented all view the response process as consisting of movement through a sequence of three basic stages. The *cognitive stage* represents what the receiver knows or perceives about the particular product or brand. This state includes awareness that the brand exists and knowledge, information, or comprehension about specific aspects of it such as its attributes, characteristics, or benefits. The *affective stage* refers to the receiver's feelings or affect level (liking or disliking) for the particular brand. This stage also includes stronger levels of affect such as desire, preference, or conviction. The *behavioral stage* refers to the consumer's action toward the brand such as trial, purchase, or adoption.

These models are also similar in that they assume a similar ordering of these three stages whereby cognitive development precedes affective reactions, which in turn precede behavior. One might assume from the ordering shown in these models that consumers become aware and knowledgeable of a brand, develop interest and feelings toward it, form a desire or preference, and then make a purchase. While this is a logical progression that may be accurate in many situations, the response sequence may not always operate this way.

Over the past two decades, considerable research in the marketing, social psychology, and communications areas has resulted in questioning the traditional notion of a cognitive → affective → behavioral sequence of response. This has led to the development of several possible configurations of the response hierarchy. Michael Ray has developed a three-orders model of information processing that identifies three alternative orderings of these three stages based on perceived product differentiation and product involvement level.[16] (See Exhibit 6–10, page 205.) We now turn our attention to examining these three models and their implications.

➤ *Exhibit 6–9*

Alaska Airlines has developed a reputation for excellent service, which it emphasizes in ads like this

Alternative Response Hierarchies

Three alternative response hierarchies are standard learning, dissonance/attribution, and low-involvement.

The standard learning hierarchy

In many purchase situations, the consumer will go through the response process in the sequence depicted by the communications models just reviewed. Ray has termed this a **standard learning model,** which consists of a "learn → feel → do" sequence or hierarchy. Information and knowledge acquired or *learned* about the various brands become the basis for the development of affect or *feelings* that guide what the consumer will *do* (e.g., actual trial or purchase). Under this hierarchy, the consumer is viewed as an active participant in the communications process who actively seeks or gathers information through "active learning."

Ray suggests the standard learning hierarchy is likely to occur when the consumer is highly involved in the purchase process and when there is a high amount of differentiation among competing brands. High-involvement purchase decisions such as those for industrial products and services and consumer durables such as personal computers, videocassette recorders, and automobiles are examples of areas where a standard learning hierarchy response process would be likely. Advertisements for products and services in these areas are usually very detailed and informative and attempt to provide the consumer with a great deal of information about the brand.

The dissonance/attribution hierarchy

A second response hierarchy proposed by Ray involves situations where consumers first behave, then develop attitudes or feelings as a result of that behavior, and then

➤ *Exhibit 6–10*
Alternative response hierarchies: the three-orders model of information processing

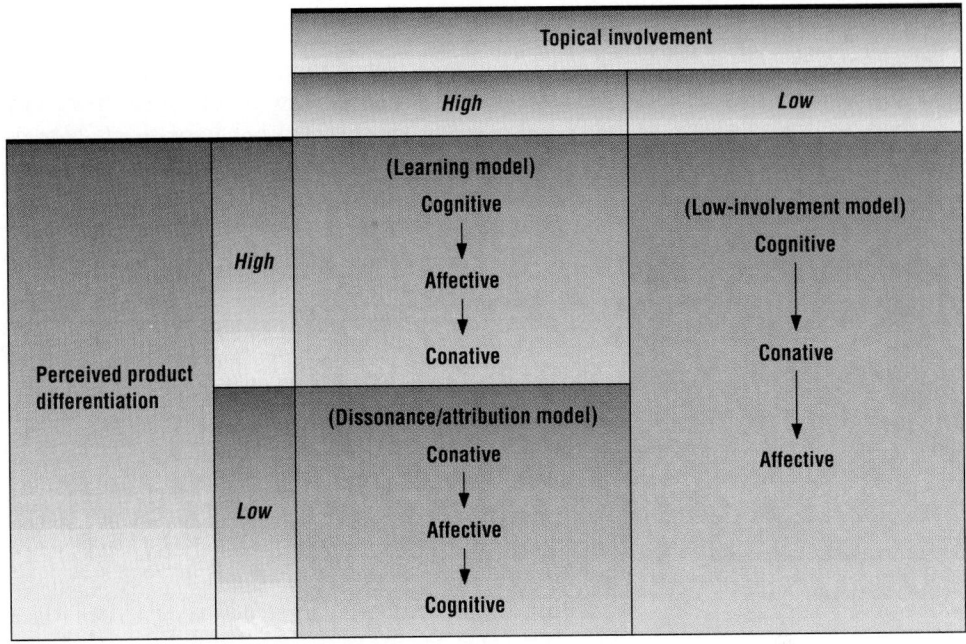

learn or process information that supports the earlier behavior. This dissonance/attributional, or "do → feel → learn," may occur in situations where consumers must choose between two alternatives that are similar in quality but are complex and may have hidden or unknown attributes. The consumer may purchase the product based on the recommendation of some nonmedia source and may then attempt to support or rationalize the decision by developing a positive attitude toward the brand and perhaps even developing negative feelings toward the rejected alternative(s). This might be done as a way of reducing *postpurchase dissonance* or anxiety the consumer may experience resulting from doubt or concern over the purchase, as was discussed in Chapter 4. This dissonance reduction process involves *selective learning* whereby the consumer seeks information that supports the choice made and avoids information that fails to bolster the wisdom of the decision.

According to this model, marketers need to recognize that in some situations, attitudes develop *after* purchase, as does learning from the mass media. Ray suggests that in these situations the main effect of the mass media is not so much in promoting original choice behavior and attitude change but rather in reducing dissonance by reinforcing the wisdom of the purchase or providing supportive information.

As with the standard learning model, this response hierarchy is likely to occur when the consumer is involved in the purchase situation, and it is particularly relevant for postpurchase situations. For example, a consumer may purchase a life insurance policy through the recommendation of a general agent and then develop a favorable attitude toward the company and/or pay close attention to advertisements to reduce dissonance.

Perhaps the major problem with this view of the response hierarchy is accepting the notion of the mass media's not having any effect on the consumer's initial purchase decision. However, the rationale for this hierarchy is not that the mass media have no effect on the original choice decision but rather that the major impact of the mass media occurs *after* the purchase has been made. Thus, marketing communications planners must be aware of the need for advertising and promotion efforts both to encourage brand selection and to reinforce choices and ensure that a purchase pattern will continue.

The low-involvement hierarchy

Perhaps the most intriguing of the three response hierarchies proposed by Ray is what has been termed the **low-involvement hierarchy** in which the receiver is viewed as passing from cognition to behavior to attitude change. This "learn → do → feel" sequence is thought to characterize situations of low consumer involvement in the purchase process. Ray suggests this hierarchy tends to occur when involvement in the purchase decision is low, when there are minimal differences between brand alternatives, and when mass media advertising, particularly through broadcast media, is important.

The notion of a low-involvement hierarchy is based in large part on the work of Herbert Krugman's theory explaining the effects of television advertising.[17] Krugman was interested in determining why television advertising produced a strong effect on brand awareness and recall yet little change in consumers' attitudes toward the product. He hypothesized that television was basically a low-involvement medium and the viewer's perceptual defenses are reduced or even absent when watching commercials. In a low-involvement situation, the consumer does not compare the message with previously acquired beliefs, needs, or past experiences as the individual might in a high-involvement situation. The commercial results in subtle changes in the consumer's knowledge structure, particularly with repeated exposure to the message. This change in the consumer's knowledge does not result in attitude change but is related to the learning of something about the advertised brand such as the ability to recall a brand name, ad theme, or slogan. According to Krugman, when the consumer enters a purchase situation, this information may be sufficient to trigger a purchase. The consumer will then form an attitude toward the purchased brand as a result of experience with it. Thus, in the low-involvement situation the response sequence is as follows:

Message exposure under low involvement →

Shift in cognitive structure → Purchase →

Positive or negative experience → Attitude formation

Under the low-involvement hierarchy, the consumer is viewed as engaging in *passive learning* and *random information catching* rather than active information seeking. Thus, if the consumer is passive and disinterested, the advertiser must recognize that the consumer is less likely to give attention to actual message content but may focus more on nonmessage elements such as music, characters, symbols, and slogans or jingles. The advertiser might capitalize on this situation by developing advertising that uses a catchy slogan or jingle that is stored in the consumer's mind without any active cognitive processing and that becomes salient when he or she enters the actual purchase situation.

Examples of low-involvement advertising appeals are prevalent in much of the advertising we see for frequently purchased consumer products: Ads for Charmin toilet paper show Mr. Whipple imploring buyers, "Please, don't squeeze the Charmin!"; Bic disposable lighters are promoted by the theme "Flick my Bic"; Wrigley's Doublemint gum invites consumers to "Double your pleasure"; Bounty paper towels claim to be the "Quicker picker upper." Each of these appeals is designed to assist the consumer in making an association without really attempting to formulate an attitude or create attitude change.

Another popular creative strategy used by advertisers of low-involvement products is what advertising analyst Harry McMahan calls VIP, or visual image personality.[18] Advertisers often use symbols such as the Pillsbury Doughboy, Charlie the Tuna, Morris the Cat, Tony the Tiger, Speedy Alka-Seltzer, and Mr. Clean to develop visual images that will lead to identification and retention of advertisements. The campaign featuring Morris the Cat has helped make 9-Lives a leading brand of cat food, and the feline has become so popular that he even has his own fan club (Exhibit 6–11)!

➤ *Exhibit 6–11*

Morris the cat has been a very effective VIP for 9-Lives cat food

The Integrated Information Response Model

Advertising and consumer researchers recognize that there are response sequences and behaviors that are not explained adequately by either the traditional standard learning or low-involvement response hierarchies. Advertising is just one source of information consumers use in forming attitudes and/or making purchase decisions. Moreover, for many consumers, purchase does not reflect commitment or loyalty to a brand but rather serves as a way of obtaining first-hand information from trial use of a product.

Robert Smith and William Swinyard developed a revised interpretation of the advertising response sequence, which they call the integrated information response model.[19] This model, shown in Exhibit 6–12, integrates concepts from both the traditional and low-involvement response hierarchy perspectives. It also accounts for the effects of direct experience and recognizes that different levels of belief strength result from advertising versus personal experience with a product.

The integrated information response model suggests several different response patterns that can result from advertising. For low-involvement purchases a cognition → trial → affect → commitment response sequence may be operating. This can be seen in the top line of the detailed sequence in Exhibit 6–12. According to this sequence, in general, advertising leads to low information acceptance, lower order beliefs, and low order affect. However, as repetitive advertising builds awareness, consumers become more likely to engage in a trial purchase to gather information. The subsequent direct experience that results from trial leads to high information acceptance and higher order beliefs and affect, which can result in commitment or brand loyalty.

Advertising generally leads only to lower order beliefs and affect because it is seen as a biased or vested source of interest and is subject to high levels of source and message discounting and/or rejection. However, in some situations, such as where perceived risk and involvement are low, advertising may move consumers directly to purchase.

If consumers are involved with the product, they may seek additional information from other external sources (for example, more advertising, word of mouth, salespeople) and/or from direct experience. This means a response sequence similar to the traditional hierarchy of effect model (cognition → affect → commitment) will be

➤ *Exhibit 6–12*
Integrated information response model

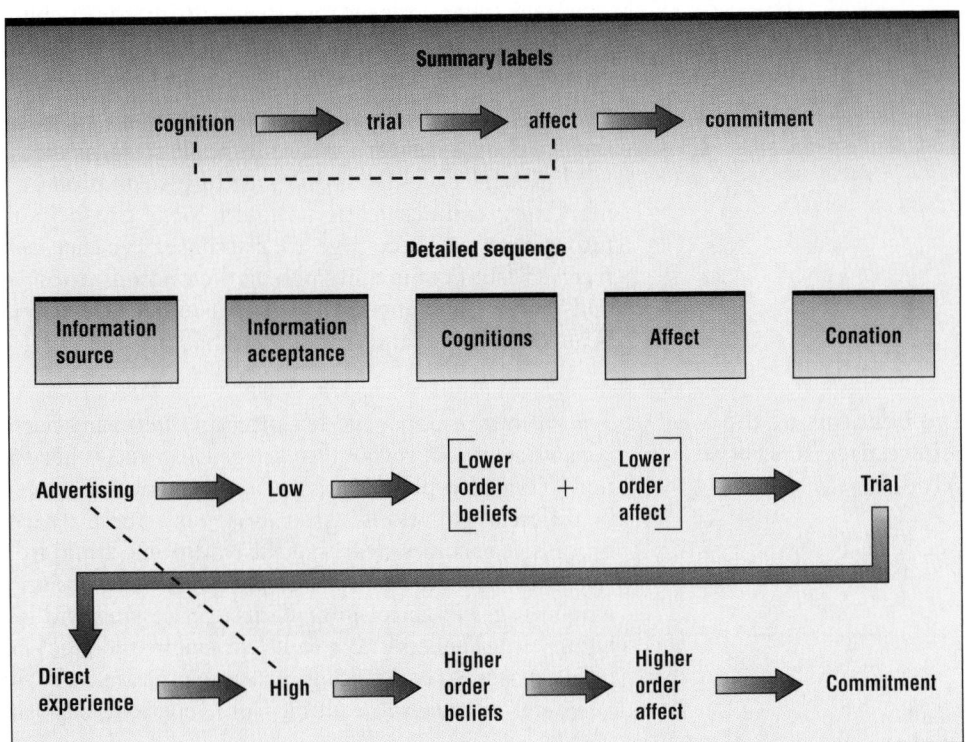

operating. The higher order response path (bottom line of the detailed response sequence shown in Exhibit 6–12) shows that direct experience, or in some cases advertising, is accepted at higher order magnitudes, which results in higher order beliefs and affect. This strong affect is more likely to result in preferences and committed purchases.

Smith and Swinyard discuss the implications of the integrated response model regarding promotional strategy for low- versus high-involvement products. For example, they recommend less enthusiastic promotional goals for low-involvement products, because advertising has limited ability to form or change higher order beliefs and affect:

> Low-involvement products, for example, could benefit from advertisements oriented to inducing trial by creating generally favorable lower order beliefs. This could be accomplished with campaigns designed to reduce perceived risk through repetition and familiarity, or those directly advocating a trial purchase. In addition, the integrated response model suggests that other marketing strategies designed to facilitate trial should be coupled with the advertising campaign. Free samples, coupons, price-cuts, or effective point-of-purchase displays could all be integrated with media advertising to produce an environment highly conducive to trial. So too, because low-involvement products are frequently homogeneous, subsequent advertisements might be designed to reaffirm the positive aspects of trial. If successful, these efforts might generate brand loyalty based upon higher order beliefs and affect. This could be a major advantage for advertisers of low-involvement products where frequent brand switching may be based on the absence of antecedents for commitment (i.e., higher order beliefs and affect).[20]

For high-involvement products, Smith and Swinyard note that more basic attitude change strategies are warranted. However, they note that the higher order response sequence focuses attention on message acceptance as a prerequisite for affective development, which has certain implications:

> In this instance, the advertising manager should attempt to isolate the conditions facilitating the formation of higher order beliefs. Factors influential in this process could include whether the message claims are easily verifiable/(e.g., price) and/or demonstrable (e.g., styling), whether the individual knows the sponsoring company and its reputation/credibility, selection of a credible spokesperson to deliver the message, whether the message is consistent with already established beliefs, etc. It also is likely that interactions could exist between acceptance factors, and that certain message configurations would be much more successful than others.[21]

Smith and Swinyard point out that communication strategies for high-involvement products may be difficult to implement since media advertising often has little effect on higher order attitude formation or change. Thus, they suggest that marketing communication should focus on facilitating a product demonstration rather than a direct urge to purchase. Product demonstrations and information received from compelling personal communication sources, such as knowledgeable and well-trained in-store sales personnel, are more likely to affect higher order beliefs and affect and lead to purchase.

Implications of the Alternative Response Models

The various response models offer an interesting perspective of the process by which consumers might respond to advertising and other forms of marketing communication. They also provide insight into promotional strategies marketers might pursue in different situations. After reviewing these alternative models of the response process, it becomes clear that the traditional standard learning model of the response sequence may not always be applicable. The notion of a highly involved consumer who engages in active information processing and learning and acts on the basis of higher order beliefs and a well-formed attitude may be inappropriate for some types of purchases. In some situations, consumers may make a purchase decision based on a general awareness resulting from repetitive exposure to advertising, and attitude development occurs after the purchase, if at all. As was suggested by the integrated information response model, the role of advertising and other forms of promotion may be to induce trial—and consumers will develop brand preferences and loyalties primarily on the basis of their direct experience with the product.

From a promotional planning perspective, it is important that marketers examine the communications situation for their product or service and determine which type of response process is most likely to occur. This may be determined by analyzing involvement levels and product/service differentiation as well as consumers' use of various information sources and their levels of experience with the product or service. Once the manager has determined which response sequence is most likely to operate, the integrated marketing communications program can be designed to influence the response process in favor of the advertiser's product or service. However, all of this requires that marketers be able to determine the involvement level of consumers in their target markets. Thus, we examine the concept of involvement in more detail.

Understanding Involvement

Over the past two decades, consumer behavior and advertising researchers have extensively studied the concept of involvement.[22] Involvement is viewed as a variable that can help explain the way consumers might process advertising information and how this information might affect message recipients. However, one problem that has plagued the study of involvement has been agreeing on how to define and measure it. Advertising managers must be able to determine targeted consumers' involvement levels with their products.

Some of the problems in conceptualizing and measuring involvement have been addressed in research by Judith Zaichkowsky. Based on an extensive review, she has noted that although there is not a single precise definition of involvement, there is an underlying theme focusing on *personal relevance*.[23] Zaichkowsky developed a conceptualization of the involvement construct (shown in Exhibit 6–13) that includes three antecedents or variables proposed to precede involvement. The first is characteristics of the person (value system, unique experiences, needs). The second factor relates to the characteristics of the stimulus that might pertain to differences in type of media (television, radio, or print), content of the communication, or product class variations. The third antecedent factor is situational factors such as whether one is, or is not, in the market for a particular product.

The various antecedent factors can influence the consumer's level of involvement in several ways, including the way the consumer responds to the advertising, the products being advertised, and the actual purchase decision. This conceptualization of involvement shows that a variety of outcomes or behaviors can result from involvement with advertising, products, or purchase decisions.

In recent years, several advertising planning models or "grids" have been developed that consider involvement levels as well as several other factors, including response processes, and motives that underlie attitude formation and subsequent brand choice. We now examine these models and their implications for communication strategies.

The FCB Planning Model

An interesting approach to analyzing the communications situation comes from the work of Richard Vaughn of the Foote, Cone & Belding advertising agency. Vaughn and his associates developed an advertising planning model by building on traditional response theories such as the hierarchy of effects model and its variants and research on high and low involvement.[24] They also added the dimension of thinking versus feeling processing at each involvement level by bringing in theories regarding brain specialization. The right/left brain theory suggests the left side of the brain is more capable of rational, cognitive thinking, whereas the right side is more visual and emotional and engages more in the affective or feeling functions. Their model,

➤ *Exhibit 6–13* **Conceptualizing involvement**

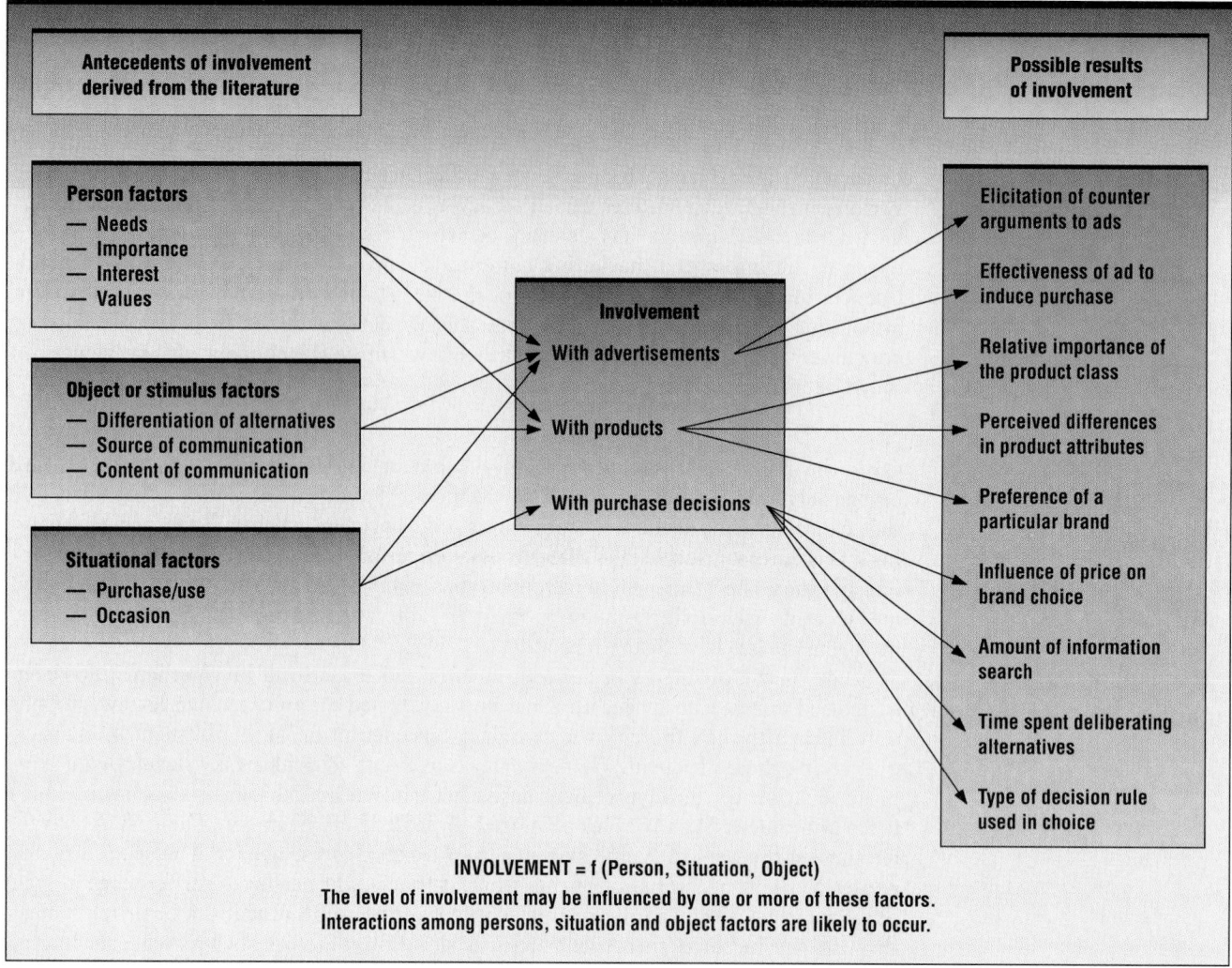

Involvement with advertisements

Involvement with products

Involvement with purchase decisions

Antecedents of involvement derived from the literature

Person factors
— Needs
— Importance
— Interest
— Values

Object or stimulus factors
— Differentiation of alternatives
— Source of communication
— Content of communication

Situational factors
— Purchase/use
— Occasion

Involvement

With advertisements

With products

With purchase decisions

Possible results of involvement

Elicitation of counter arguments to ads

Effectiveness of ad to induce purchase

Relative importance of the product class

Perceived differences in product attributes

Preference of a particular brand

Influence of price on brand choice

Amount of information search

Time spent deliberating alternatives

Type of decision rule used in choice

INVOLVEMENT = f (Person, Situation, Object)
The level of involvement may be influenced by one or more of these factors.
Interactions among persons, situation and object factors are likely to occur.

which became known as the "FCB grid," delineates four primary advertising planning strategies—informative, affective, habitual, and satisfaction—along with the most appropriate variant of the alternative response hierarchies (Exhibit 6–14).

Vaughn suggests that the *informative strategy* is for highly involving products/services where rational thinking and economic considerations prevail, and the standard learning hierarchy is the appropriate response model. The *affective strategy* is for highly involving and feeling purchases. For these types of products, psychological and emotional motives such as fulfilling self-esteem or enhancing one's ego or self-image would be stressed in the advertising. The ad for Lady Stetson cologne shown in Exhibit 6–15 appeals to these types of motives.

The *habitual strategy* is for low-involvement and thinking products with such routinized behavior patterns that learning occurs most often after a trial purchase. The response process for these products is consistent with a behavioristic learning-by-doing model (remember our discussion of instrumental conditioning in Chapter 4?). The *self-satisfaction strategy* is for low-involvement/feeling products where appeals to sensory pleasures and social motives would be important. Again, the "do" before "feel" or "learn" hierarchy is seen as operating, since product experience is an important part of the learning process. Vaughn acknowledges that some minimal level of awareness (passive learning) may precede purchase of both types of low-involvement products, although deeper, active learning is not necessary. This

> *Exhibit 6–14*
> **The Foote, Cone & Belding (FCB) grid**

	Thinking	Feeling
High involvement	**1. Informative (thinker)** Car–house–furnishings– new products model: Learn–feel–do (economic?) **Possible implications** Test: Recall Diagnostics Media: Long copy format Reflective vehicles Creative: Specific information Demonstration	**2. Affective (feeler)** Jewelry–cosmetics– fashion apparel–motorcycles model: Feel–learn–do (psychological?) **Possible implications** Test: Attitude change Emotional arousal Media: Large space Image specials Creative: Executional Impact
Low involvement	**3. Habit formation (doer)** Food–household items model: Do–learn–feel (responsive?) **Possible implications** Test: Sales Media: Small space ads 10 second I.D.'s Radio; POS Creative: Reminder	**4. Self-satisfaction (reactor)** Cigarettes–liquor–candy model: Do–feel–learn (social?) **Possible implications** Test: Sales Media: Billboards Newspapers POS Creative: Attention

suggests the low-involvement hierarchy discussed above (learn → do → feel) would be consistent with the FCB grid.

The FCB grid provides a useful way for those involved in the advertising planning process, such as creative specialists, to analyze consumer/product relationships and to develop appropriate promotional strategies. Consumer research can be used to determine how consumers perceive products or brands on the involvement and thinking/feeling dimensions.[25] This information can then be used to develop effective creative options such as using rational versus emotional appeals, increasing involvement levels, or even getting consumers to evaluate a think-type product more on the basis of feelings. The ad for kitchen appliances shown in Exhibit 6–16 is an example of this latter strategy, as it emphasizes psychological and emotional motives such as style and appearance. Appliances have traditionally been sold on the basis of more rational, functional motives.

The Rossiter-Percy Grid

An alternative grid approach to advertising planning has been developed recently by John R. Rossiter and Larry Percy.[26] The Rossiter-Percy Grid is similar to the FCB planning model in that it attempts to represent how consumers evaluate products or brands and form attitudes using two dimensions. Like the FCB model, Rossiter and Percy use involvement as one of the dimensions. However, their model uses "type of motivation" as the second dimension, which differs from the thinking versus feeling notion used in the FCB model. The Rossiter-Percy grid also differs in that it incorporates brand awareness as a necessary precursor to brand attitudes, while the FCB grid focuses only on the actual attitude formation process.

Cognitive Processing of Communications

The hierarchical response models discussed above were for many years the primary focus of approaches to study the receivers' responses to marketing communications. Attention centered on identifying relationships between specific controllable variables—such as source and message factors—and outcome or response variables—such as attention, comprehension, attitudes, and purchase intentions. This approach

➤ *Exhibit 6–15*
Cosmetic ads appeal to emotional motives

➤ *Exhibit 6–16*
A think-type product is advertised by appealing to feelings

We've never been so pleased

to fade into the woodwork.

Or to keep such a low profile. GE's remarkably sleek flush wall oven and down-draft cooktop are designed to create a smooth, integrated look with your kitchen cabinets.
  Installed in place of your old appliances, they can fit perfectly, with no jutting or over-hanging. Plus, on top of those clean, contemporary lines, you get the beauty of GE advanced electronics. Precise temperature controls. Self-cleaning interiors. And

a superb downdraft exhaust system that actually retracts when not in use.
  We might also add that, while our beautiful flush wall oven and gas downdraft cooktop don't stand out, our people do. So call the GE Answer Center® service for information, anytime, at 800.626.2000.
  We're sure you'll be pleased by the results.

We bring good things to life.

has been criticized on a number of fronts and has been referred to as being "black box" in nature owing to its inability to explain what might be causing or determining these reactions.[27] In response to these concerns, researchers began trying to understand the nature of *cognitive* reactions to persuasive messages. Several approaches and models have been developed to examine the nature of consumers' cognitive processing of advertising messages.

The Cognitive Response Approach

One of the most widely used methods for examining consumers' cognitive processing of advertising messages is through the assessment of their **cognitive responses** or the thoughts that occur to them while reading, viewing, and/or hearing a communication.[28] These thoughts are generally measured by having consumers write down or verbally report the thoughts they have in response to a message. The basic assumption is that these thoughts reflect the recipient's cognitive processes or reactions and help shape and determine ultimate acceptance or rejection of the message. The cognitive response approach has been widely used in advertising research, both by academicians and advertising practitioners. The focus of this research has been to determine the types of thought processes or responses evoked by an advertising

➤ *Exhibit 6–17* **A model of cognitive response**

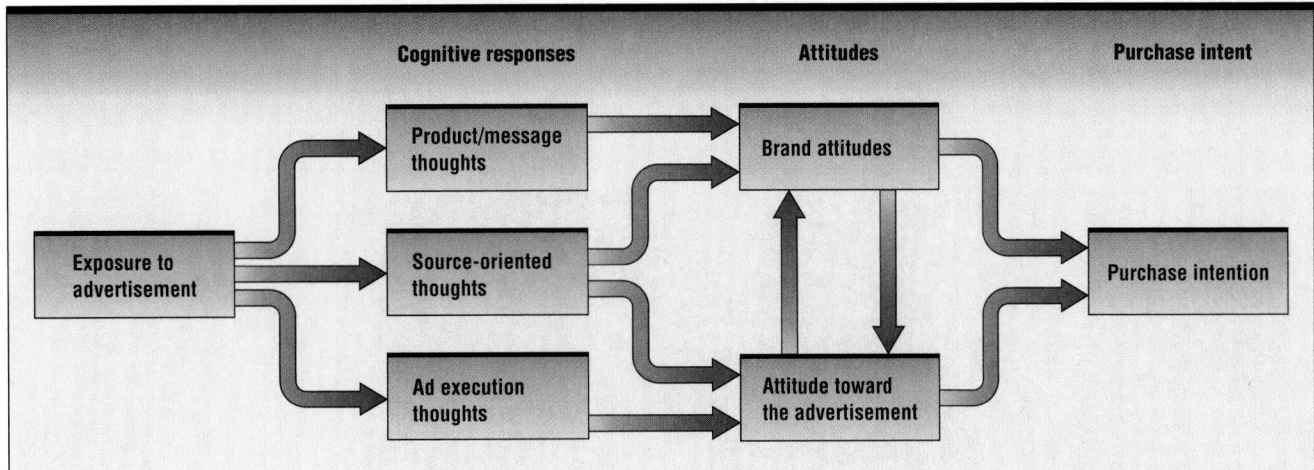

message and how these responses relate to measures such as attitudes toward the ad, brand attitudes, and purchase intentions. The model shown in Exhibit 6–17 depicts the three basic categories of cognitive responses researchers have identified and how they might relate to attitudes and intentions.

Product message thoughts

The first category of thoughts are those directed at the product or service and/or the claims being made in the communication. Much of the attention has focused on two particular types of responses—counterarguments and support arguments.

Counterarguments are thoughts the recipient has that are counter or opposed to the position taken in the message. For example, consider the ad for Ultra-Tide shown in Exhibit 6–18. A consumer may express disbelief or disapproval of a claim made in an ad ("I don't believe that any detergent could get that stain out!"). However other consumers who see this ad may generate **support arguments** or thoughts that support or affirm the claims being made in the message ("Ultra Tide looks like a really good product—I think I'll try it").

The likelihood of counterarguing is greater when the message makes claims that oppose the beliefs or perceptions held by the receiver. For example, a consumer viewing a commercial that attacks a favorite brand is likely to engage in counterarguing. Counterarguments have been shown to be negatively related to message acceptance, as the more the receiver counterargues, the less likely he or she is to accept the position advocated in the message.[29] Support arguments, on the other hand, are positively related to message acceptance. Thus, the marketer should develop advertisements or other promotional messages that minimize the likelihood of counterarguing and encourage the generation of support arguments.

Source-oriented thoughts

A second category of cognitive responses are those directed at the source of the communication. One of the most important responses in this category is that of **source derogations**, or negative thoughts about the spokesperson or organization making the claims, as it has been determined that such thoughts generally lead to a reduction in message acceptance. If consumers find a particular spokesperson annoying or distrustful, this may result in a lower likelihood of their accepting what these sources have to say.

An example of this occurred a few years ago when Dreyer's ice cream developed an advertising campaign for its new Grand Light product, which centered around the

use of spokespersons whose credibility was known to be suspect. The theme of the campaign was "An unbelievable spokesperson for an unbelievable product," which intended to be lighthearted and to acknowledge the dubious character of the spokespersons. However, many consumers became upset when convicted Watergate conspirator John Ehrlichman appeared in one of the commercials. Reactions against the company's use of Ehrlichman were so strong that the ad had to be withdrawn—obviously, a strong indication of the effects of source derogation.

Of course, source-related thoughts are not always negative. Receivers may react favorably to the source and generate favorable thoughts or **source bolsters.** As you would expect, most advertisers attempt to hire spokespersons to whom their target audience will react favorably so as to carry this effect over to the message.

Ad execution thoughts

The third category of cognitive responses shown in Exhibit 6–17 is thoughts the individual has toward the ad itself. Many of the thoughts receivers have when reading or viewing an ad do not directly concern the product and/or message claims per se but rather are affective reactions representing their feelings toward the ad. These thoughts may include reactions to ad execution factors such as the creativity of the ad, the quality of the visual effects, colors, and voice tones. Execution-related thoughts can be either favorable or unfavorable and are important because of their effect on attitudes toward the advertisement as well as the brand.

In recent years, much attention has been focused on consumers' affective reactions to advertisements—particularly television commercials.[30] **Attitude toward the ad** (A → ad) represents the receivers' feelings of favorability or unfavorability toward the ad. Interest in consumers' reactions to the ad reflects the advertisers' acceptance of the fact that affective reactions are an important determinant of advertising effectiveness, as these reactions may be transformed to the brand itself, directly influencing purchase behaviors. For example, one study found that people who enjoy a commercial are two times more likely than those who are neutral toward the ad to be convinced that the brand is the best.[31]

The above discussion suggests that consumers' feelings toward the ad may be just as important as attitudes toward the brand (if not more so) in determining an advertisement's effectiveness.[32] However, the importance of affective reactions and feelings generated by the ad depend on several factors such as the nature of the advertisement and the type of processing engaged in by the receiver.[33] Many advertisers have begun to use emotional ads designed to evoke feelings and affective reactions, as the basis of their creative strategy. The success of this strategy depends, in part, on the consumers' involvement with the brand and their likelihood of attending to and processing the message. We end our analysis of the receiver by briefly examining a model that integrates some of the factors that may account for different types and levels of cognitive processing of a message.

The Elaboration Likelihood Model (ELM)

Differences in the ways consumers process and respond to persuasive messages have been addressed in the elaboration likelihood model (ELM) developed by Richard Petty and John Cacioppo, which is shown in Exhibit 6–19.[34] The ELM was developed to explain the process by which persuasive communications (such as advertisements) lead to persuasion by influencing *attitudes*. According to this model, the attitude formation or change process depends on the amount and nature of **elaboration** or processing of relevant information that occurs in response to a persuasive message. High elaboration means the receiver engages in careful consideration, thinking, and evaluation of the information or arguments contained in the message. Low levels of elaboration occur when the receiver does not engage in active information processing or thinking, but rather makes inferences about the position being advocated in the message based on simple positive or negative "cues" that are present.

The ELM shows that *elaboration likelihood* is a function of two elements—*motivation to process* and *ability to process* the message. Motivation to process the message is a function of factors such as involvement, personal relevance, and individuals needs and arousal levels. Ability to process is a function of factors such as whether the individual has the knowledge, intellectual capacity, or opportunity to process the message. For example, an individual viewing a humorous commercial or one containing an attractive model may be *distracted* from processing the information presented about the product.

According to the ELM, there are two basic processes or *routes to persuasion* or attitude change. Under the **central route to persuasion,** the receiver is viewed as a very active and involved participant in the communications process whose ability and motivation to attend, comprehend, and evaluate messages are very high. When central processing of an advertising message occurs, the consumer pays close attention to message content and scrutinizes the message arguments. A high level of cognitive response activity or processing occurs, and the ability of the ad to persuade the receiver depends primarily on the receiver's evaluation of the quality of the arguments presented. Predominantly favorable cognitive responses (support arguments and source bolsters) lead to favorable changes in cognitive structure such as the formation of positive beliefs. This leads to positive attitude change or persuasion. Conversely, if the cognitive processing is predominantly unfavorable and results in counterarguments and/or source derogations, the changes in cognitive structure are unfavorable and *boomerang* or result in negative attitude change. Attitude change that occurs through central processing is relatively *enduring* and should resist subsequent efforts to change it.

➤ *Exhibit 6–19*
The elaboration likelihood model of persuasion

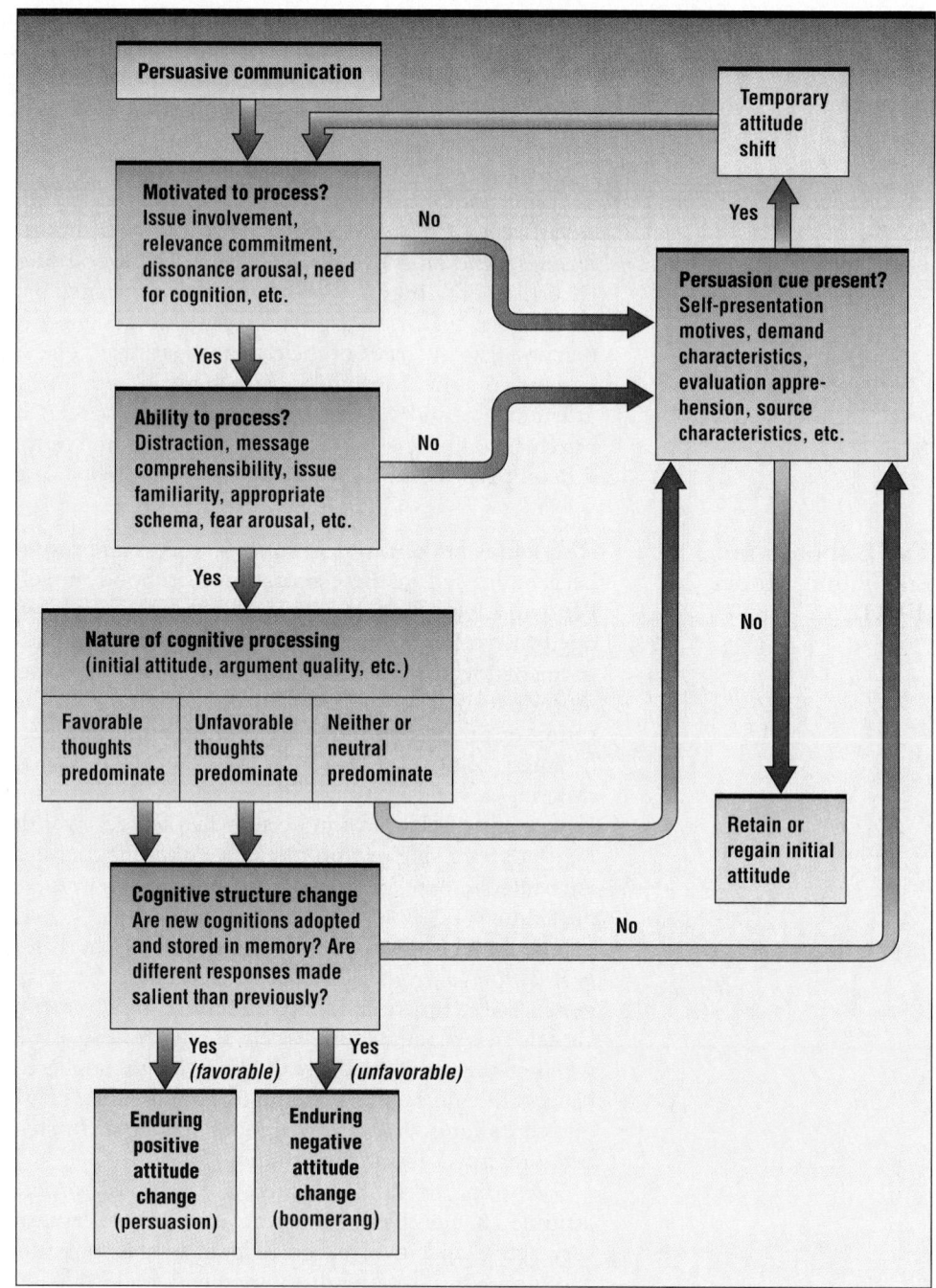

Under the **peripheral route to persuasion,** which is shown on the right side of Exhibit 6–19, the receiver is viewed as lacking the motivation or ability to process information and is not likely to engage in detailed cognitive processing. Rather than thinking about and evaluating the information presented in the message, the receiver relies on "peripheral cues" that may be incidental to the main arguments or position being advocated. The receiver's reactions to the message or attitude change depend on how the receiver evaluates these peripheral cues.

The consumer might use several types of peripheral cues or cognitive "shortcuts" rather than carefully evaluating the message arguments presented in an advertisement.[35] Favorable attitudes may be formed if the endorser in the ad is viewed as an expert or is attractive and/or likable, or if the consumer likes certain executional aspects of the ad such as the way it is made, the music, or imagery used. Notice how

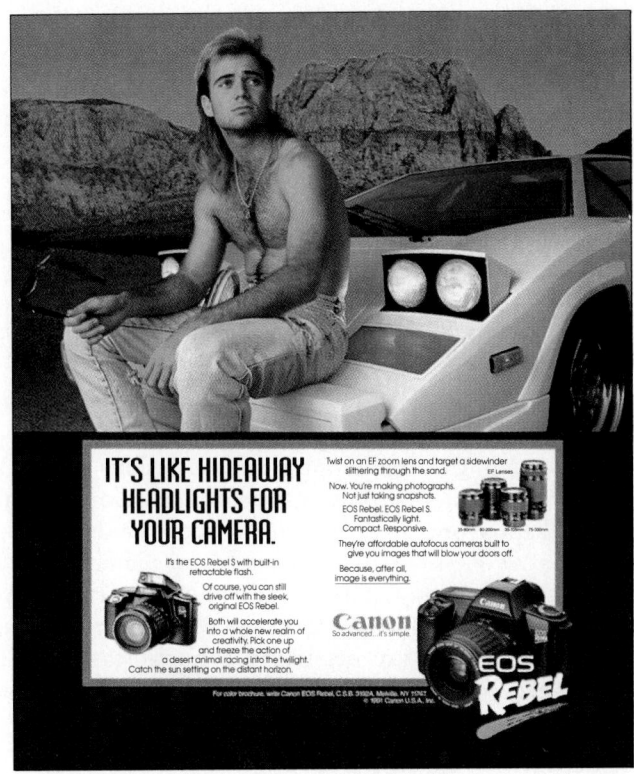

the ad in Exhibit 6–20 for the Canon EOS Rebel camera contains a number of positive peripheral cues such as an attractive and popular celebrity endorser (tennis star Andre Agassi), a sports car, and excellent visual imagery.

Peripheral cues can also lead to rejection of a message. For example, ads that advocate extreme positions, use endorsers who are not well liked or have credibility problems, or are not executed well (such as many low-budget ads for local retailers) may be rejected without any consideration of their information or message arguments. As can be seen in Exhibit 6–19, according to the ELM, attitudes resulting from peripheral processing are viewed as temporary. Thus, continual exposure to the peripheral cues, such as through repetitive advertising, is needed to maintain favorable attitudes created through this route.

Implications of the ELM

The elaboration likelihood model has important implications for marketing communication, particularly with respect to involvement. For example, if the involvement level of consumers in the target audience is high, an advertisement or sales presentation should contain strong arguments that are difficult for the message recipient to refute or counterargue. However, if the involvement level of the target audience is low, peripheral cues may be more important than detailed message arguments.

An interesting test of the ELM showed that the effectiveness of a celebrity endorser in an advertisement depends on the receiver's involvement level.[36] When involvement was low, an advertisement with a celebrity endorser had a significant effect on attitudes. When the receiver's involvement level was high, however, the use of a celebrity had no effect on brand attitudes; rather, the *quality* of the arguments used in the ad was more important.

The explanation given for these findings was that a celebrity may serve as a peripheral cue in the low-involvement situation, which allows the receiver to develop favorable attitudes based on feelings toward the source rather than engaging in extensive processing of the message. Under high involvement, however, the consumer engages in more detailed central processing of the message content. Thus, the quality of the message claims becomes more important than the celebrity status of the endorser.

The ELM suggests the type of message that is most effective depends on the route to persuasion the consumer follows. Many marketers recognize that involvement levels are low for their product categories and consumers are not motivated to process advertising messages in any detail. Thus, marketers of low-involvement products often rely on creative tactics that emphasize peripheral cues and use repetitive advertising to create and maintain favorable attitudes toward their brand.

A Final Word on the Response Process

As can be seen from our analysis of the receiver, the process consumers go through in responding to marketing communications can be viewed from a number of perspectives. We hope the discussion of the various communication models presented in this chapter provides you with a better understanding of how consumers process persuasive messages. The promotional planner needs to learn as much as possible about the company's target market and how it might respond to the firm's marketing communication efforts. Marketers who understand the process by which their target audience responds to persuasive communications will be able to make better decisions regarding various aspects of the promotional program.

SUMMARY

The common factor shared by all elements of the promotional mix is that their function is to communicate. Promotional planners must understand the communications process. This process can be very complex, with successful marketing communication depending on a number of factors including the nature of the message, the audience's interpretation of it, and the environment in which it is received. A basic model of communication shows the key elements of the communications process. For effective communication to occur, the sender must encode a message in such a way that it will be decoded by the receiver in the intended manner. Feedback from the receiver helps the sender determine whether proper decoding has occurred or whether noise may have interfered with the communications process.

Promotional planning begins with the receiver or target audience, as marketers must understand how the audience is likely to respond to various sources of communication or types of messages. The receiver can be analyzed for promotional planning purposes both with respect to the composition of the target audience (i.e., individual, group, or mass audiences) and the response process the message recipient goes through. Different orderings of the traditional response hierarchy include the standard learning, dissonance, and low-involvement models. The information response model integrates concepts from both the high- and low-involvement response hierarchy perspectives and recognizes the effects of direct experience with a product.

The cognitive response approach examines the thoughts evoked by a message and how they shape and determine the receiver's ultimate acceptance or rejection of the communication. The elaboration likelihood model of attitude formation and change recognizes two forms of message processing—the central and peripheral routes to persuasion, which are a function of the receiver's motivation and ability to process a message.

KEY TERMS

communication	channel	nonpersonal channels
source	personal channels	mass media
encoding	word-of-mouth	receiver
semiotics	communications	decoding

field of experience
noise
response
feedback
5-Ws model of
   communication
buying centers
AIDA model
hierarchy of effects model

innovation-adoption
   model
information-processing
   model
standard learning model
low-involvement
   hierarchy
cognitive responses
counterarguments

support argument
source derogations
source bolsters
attitude toward the ad
elaboration
central route to
   persuasion
peripheral route to
   persuasion

DISCUSSION QUESTIONS

1. What is necessary for effective communication to occur? Discuss some of the barriers to effective communication in advertising.

2. Why are personal channels of communication often more effective than nonpersonal channels?

3. What is meant by *noise* in the communications process? What can be done to reduce noise in marketing communications?

4. Discuss the various forms feedback might take in the following situations:
   - An office copier salesperson has just made a sales presentation to a potential account.
   - A consumer has just seen a direct-response ad run on late-night television for an exercise machine.
   - Millions of consumers are exposed to an ad for a sports car during a Sunday afternoon football game.

5. Use the 5-Ws model to outline a promotional program for a company attempting to sell a new soft drink to the 18- to 24-year-old market.

6. Explain how the promotional process would differ for a personal computer company promoting its products to each of the following:
   - Individual consumers purchasing a computer for home use.
   - A corporation considering buying a number of personal computers for use by its employees.

7. Explain how the various response models discussed in this chapter would be useful in the following situations:
   - For a company introducing a new innovation such as a compact disc player.
   - For a manufacturer of electronic components training new sales representatives.
   - For a marketer of a consumer product such as paper towels.

8. Find examples of ads for a product or service that fit into particular cells of the FCB model. Discuss how and whether the ads fit the creative recommendations at these planning models.

9. Have three friends read a print ad or watch a television commercial and write down their reactions to it. Use the cognitive response model discussed in this chapter to analyze their reactions. How do their responses relate to their overall evaluation of the ad as well as the product or service?

10. Compare the central and peripheral routes to persuasion. Provide examples of an ad you think would be processed by a central route and one where you think peripheral processing would occur.

chapter 7

Source, Message, and Channel Factors

➤ To examine the major variables in the communications system and how they influence consumers' processing of promotional messages.

➤ To examine the various options and considerations involved in the selection of a source or communicator of a promotional message.

➤ To examine various factors concerning the development of the promotional message including the effects of different types of message structures and appeals.

➤ To consider how the channel or medium used to deliver a promotional message influences the communications process.

Cliff, Candice, and Friends

One of the fiercest advertising and marketing battles in recent memory is being waged by the three major long-distance carriers—American Telephone & Telegraph (AT&T), Sprint, and MCI Telecommunications Corporation. The advertising battle began in March 1980 when MCI began marketing its long-distance services to small businesses and residential customers and ran its first TV commercial telling consumers they could save money by switching from AT&T. Since then, the three carriers have spent billions of dollars on advertising to convince consumers they are the most reliable, least expensive, have the most advanced equipment, or offer the best service. AT&T spent $797 million on advertising in 1990, which is more than Coca-Cola and Pepsi Cola combined, to hold onto its 65 percent share of the $56 billion long-distance market.

The marketing and advertising campaigns used by the three competitors have been very different as has their choice of advertising spokespersons and how they have chosen them. For the past 10 years, AT&T has relied on the trusted image of actor Cliff Robertson to deliver many of its advertising messages, while Sprint recently chose actress Candice Bergen as its spokesperson. MCI has taken a different approach recently by encouraging its new and existing customers to recommend friends and family members who can become

part of "calling circles" and save money when they call each other.

AT&T's choice of Cliff Robertson was the result of an extensive and deliberate search for a celebrity spokesperson. In 1983, the company conducted a marketing survey and found that only 4 percent of consumers knew AT&T provided long-distance service. It was decided the company had to make itself better known to consumers as a long-distance carrier and in the process downplay price by advertising that only AT&T could be trusted to provide consistent quality and reliable service. AT&T began a secret search for a celebrity who had the right image to serve as its spokesperson and communicate the quality and trust message to consumers. The company surveyed thousands of consumers about celebrities they liked and disliked and conducted extensive background checks on those who were rated the highest. The celebrity search was so secretive that Robertson and the other finalists who were brought in for auditions were not told the name of the company they would be representing.

Although Robertson says he still does not know why he was chosen as AT&T's spokesperson, company officials know precisely why. According to AT&T's advertising director, the company chose him because he represented integrity and confidence and "people just trust him." Robertson was a highly respected, Academy Award-winning

221

(continued)

actor and in one of his roles played John F. Kennedy in the movie *PT 109,* which portrayed the former president's heroics as a naval officer during World War II. The company decided his squeaky-clean image was perfect for representing AT&T as the company that stood for all things good in its battle against the two smaller competitors. Robertson does not appear often in AT&T's ads now, but the company still relies on his distinctive and comforting voice. AT&T sends engineers all over the world to catch up with Robertson and record his voice-over for its commercials.

In 1990, Sprint also decided to peg its image on a celebrity. According to an executive from its advertising agency, Sprint was looking for a personality figure — preferably a woman — who could make sort of a counterpoint to Cliff Robertson. However, the process by which Sprint chose its celebrity spokesperson was quite different from the extensive procedure used by AT&T. Sprint's marketing executives met to discuss possible celebrity spokespersons. While talking about popular TV shows, the president of Sprint's consumer services group blurted out the name of Candice Bergen, star of the popular TV show "Murphy Brown." Sprint's decision to use Bergen was not based on extensive consumer research but rather on gut feelings. Some marketing experts have speculated it was not so much Candice Bergen that Sprint hired as its spokesperson but the quirky newscaster she plays on the show. Murphy Brown's character embodies the irreverent, alternative image Sprint wants to project, and it comes across when Bergen delivers sarcastic little zingers at AT&T.

MCI's latest advertising campaign does not use any well-known celebrities but relies on the close relationships that friends and family members have with each other. The idea for MCI's current "Friends & Family" campaign came from focus group studies which found that a 20 percent savings on long distance calls would motivate consumers to switch to MCI. With "Friends & Family," customers save 20 percent on long distance calls to other MCI customers in their "Calling Circle" of up to 20 people. The program relies on personal referrals — as those who join provide names and addresses of friends or family members they nominate for their Calling Circle. MCI then contacts the individuals and invites them to join "Friends & Family" and start "Calling Circles" of their own. The campaign began in March 1991, and MCI says it signed up nearly 7 million new customers in the first year.

Source: Bruce Horowitz, "Long-Distance Overload," Los Angeles Times, January 19, 1992, pp. D1, 9, 17; and Barbara Lipert, "Sprint's New Spots Lighten Up the Phone Ad Wars," Adweek, October 22, 1990, p. 21.

T he advertising campaigns of AT&T, Sprint, and MCI are examples of the different approaches advertisers take in attempting to communicate with consumers. In all three campaigns, decisions had to be made regarding the source or spokesperson who would deliver the message as well as the type of appeal that would be used. AT&T and Sprint chose well-known celebrities to serve as their advertising spokespersons, while MCI tries to take advantage of the ability of friends and family members to influence one another (Exhibit 7–1). The three campaigns probably communicate most effectively through the channel or medium of television, although print ads are also a part of the media mix for each company.

In this chapter, we analyze the major variables in the communications system — the source, the message, and the channel. We examine the characteristics of sources of a message, explore how they affect cognitive processing, and consider some of the reasons one type of communicator might be more effective than another. We then focus on the message itself and how structure and type of appeal might influence the effectiveness of the communication. Finally, we consider how factors related to the channel or medium by which the message is sent affects the communications process. Before examining each of these communications variables, however, we should examine how they interact with the receiver's response process.

Promotional Planning through the Persuasion Matrix

The development of an effective advertising and promotional campaign requires that the firm select the right spokespersons to deliver compelling messages through appropriate channels or media. Source, message, and channel factors were introduced in the previous chapter as controllable elements in a communications model. It was noted that in making decisions regarding each of these communications components, consideration must be given to how they interact with the response process. A useful approach combining the communications components and the stages of the

➢ *Exhibit 7–1*
MCI's "Friends & Family" campaign relies on interpersonal influence

FRIENDS & FAMILY™ CALLING CIRCLES® HAVE CHANGED THE WAY PEOPLE TALK. AND FEEL. AND SAVE.

ADD TO YOUR CIRCLE. ADD TO YOUR SAVINGS
1-800-695-4040
MCI Friends & Family

response process has been suggested by William McGuire and is termed the **persuasion matrix**[1] (Exhibit 7–2).

The persuasion matrix has two sets of variables of interest—independent variables, which represent the components of the 5-Ws model of communication outlined in Chapter 6, and dependent variables, which represent the response hierarchy or the steps a receiver goes through in being persuaded. The independent variables represent the controllable components of the promotional program, as the marketer can choose the person who delivers the message, the type of appeal used, and the channel or medium. Marketers cannot really exert any control over the receiver, but they can choose the target audience to whom their promotional messages will be directed. The destination variable is included because the initial message recipient might pass information to others, such as friends or associates, through word-of-mouth communication.

A major consideration facing the promotional planner is how decisions regarding each independent variable will influence the various stages of the response hierarchy. For example, the use of a well-known celebrity or a sexy model as a spokesperson may enhance the attention given to the ad. However, the problem of enhancing one level of the hierarchy at the expense of another must also be considered. A humorous message may gain attention but may result in decreased comprehension if consumers fail to process its content. Many ad campaigns using techniques such as humor, explicit sexual appeals, or celebrities have captured consumers' attention but resulted in poor recall of the brand name or copy points of the message.

McGuire suggests that the persuasion matrix can be of value in advertising planning by considering how each component of the campaign influences the steps in the response hierarchy. The following examples, which correspond to the numbers shown in the cells in Exhibit 7–2, reflect a few of the decisions that can be evaluated using the persuasion matrix.

(1) Receiver/Comprehension: Will the receiver be able to comprehend the ad? Throughout the previous chapters, we have emphasized the importance of understanding the consumer. One important question to be addressed is, At what level is the consumer able to comprehend the message? For example, a less-educated person might have more difficulty than one with a higher education level interpreting a message. Jargon commonly referred to in one person's world may be unheard of in another's. Do you think everyone knows what a "BYTE" is? The more marketers know about the consumer, the more they will understand which words, symbols, expressions, and the like, they understand.

> *Exhibit 7–2*
The persuasion matrix

Dependent variables: Steps in being persuaded	Independent variables: The communication components				
	Source	Message	Channel	Receiver	Destination
Message presentation			(2)		
Attention	(4)				
Comprehension				(1)	
Yielding		(3)			
Retention					
Behavior					

(2) **Channel/Presentation: Which media will increase presentation?** A top-rated television program in prime time will be seen by nearly 30 million households each week, whereas the 60th-rated program will reach approximately 5 million homes. *TV Guide* and *Reader's Digest* are two of the leading magazines in terms of circulation, reaching nearly 16 million homes each week. The opportunity to have your ad presented to potential consumers is largely determined by the medium used. While the media noted above may reach large numbers of consumers, the important issue is how well they reach members of the marketer's target audience. Weekly telecasts of golf tournaments reach only 3 to 4 million viewers, but this audience consists mostly of upscale businesspeople who are prime prospects for expensive cars, financial services, or business-related products.

(3) **Message/Yielding: What type of message should be used to create favorable attitudes or feelings?** Marketers generally try to create advertising messages that consumers will find agreeable and will result in positive affect toward the product or service. Humorous messages may be used to put consumers in a good mood and evoke positive feelings that might become associated with the brand being advertised. Advertisers often integrate music into their commercials to add emotion and feelings that will make consumers more receptive to the message. In recent years, many advertisers have turned to explicit sexual appeals designed to arouse consumers or suggest they can enhance their appearance and/or appeal to the opposite sex by using a product. Some marketers prefer to use comparative messages whereby they make specific comparisons of their brand with the competition.

(4) **Source/Attention: Who will be effective in getting consumers to pay attention to our ad?** The large number of ads we are bombarded with every day makes it very difficult for advertisers to break through the "clutter" and get us to attend to their messages. One way marketers deal with this problem is by using as a communicator or source someone who will attract the attention of the target audience. For example, companies hire well-known celebrities such as actors, athletes, or rock stars to appear in their ads to get the viewers' or readers' attention. Attractive models are also used to get consumers to attend to an advertising message.

Each year, *Advertising Age* gives a Star Presenter award to the individual it believes has been most effective as an advertising spokesperson. The winners for the past 15 years are shown in Exhibit 7–3. Note that these star presenters are chosen

1991	John Cleese
1990	Ray Charles
1989	Bo Jackson
1988	Wilford Brimley
1987	Michael J. Fox
1986	Paul Hogan
1985	William Perry
1984	Cliff Robertson
1983	John Cleese
1982	Rodney Dangerfield
1981	John Houseman
1980	Brooke Shields
1979	Robert Morley
1978	James Garner/ Mariette Hartley
1977	Bill Cosby
1976	O. J. Simpson
1975	Karl Malden

> *Exhibit 7–3*
***Advertising Age* star presenters**

➤ *Exhibit 7–4*
Actor Wilfred Brimley serves as a spokesperson for Quaker Oats

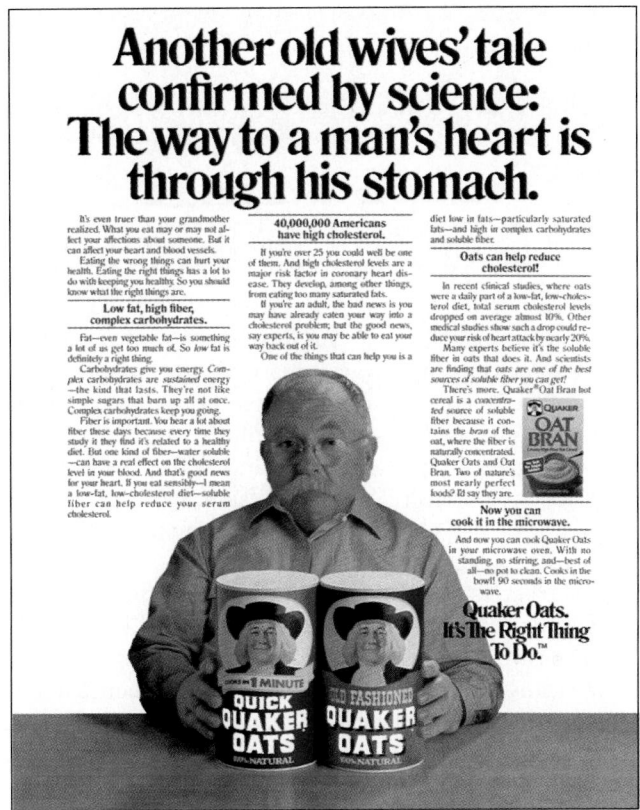

not just for their ability to attract attention. Consideration is also given to how well they communicate the advertising message and influence other steps in the response hierarchy, including what most consider the most important—behavior as reflected in sales.

We now turn our attention to a more in-depth examination of the various considerations involved in making decisions regarding each of these communication components.

Source Factors

The source component of the marketing communications process can be viewed as a multifaceted concept since many types of sources can be involved in a promotional situation. For example, when Michael Jordan appears in a commercial as a spokesperson for Wheaties, is the source Jordan himself, the company (General Mills), or some combination of the two? When you read a favorable article on a new automobile in *Road & Track,* the magazine is probably viewed as the source. As consumers, we often receive information from personal sources such as friends, relatives, or neighbors. These personal sources are often the most important influences on our purchase decisions.

While there are many alternative ways the receiver may view the source of communications, we use the term **source** to mean the person involved in the communication of a marketing message in either a direct or an indirect manner. A direct source would be a spokesperson or endorser who delivers a message and/or demonstrates the product or service. For example, actor Wilfred Brimley has been a very effective spokesperson for Quaker Oats for many years (Exhibit 7–4). In contrast an indirect source does not actually deliver a message but appears as more of a "decorative model" whose role is to draw attention to and/or enhance the appearance of the ad. Most theory and research in the study of source factors deal with the characteristics of individuals as a message source and how they influence communication effectiveness. Our examination of source factors follows this approach.

➤ *Exhibit 7–5*
Source attributes and receiver processing modes

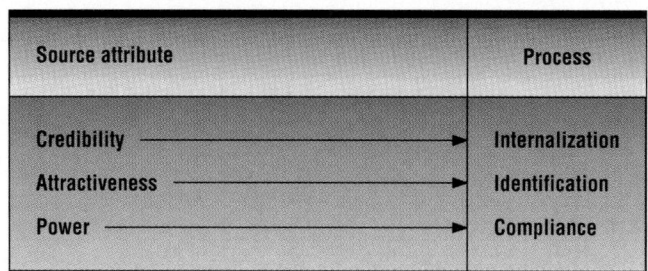

Source attribute	Process
Credibility ————————➤	Internalization
Attractiveness ————————➤	Identification
Power ————————➤	Compliance

Source Characteristics

Companies are very careful in selecting individuals to deliver their selling messages. Many firms spend large sums of money to have certain individuals endorse their products, serve as spokespeople, or simply appear in their ads. In addition, companies spend millions of dollars on the recruitment, selection, and training of salespeople to represent them and deliver sales presentations for their products or services. The reason for all this concern is marketers' recognition that the characteristics of the source often have a significant impact on the effectiveness of their sales and advertising messages.

Marketers select as communicators individuals who have characteristics that will maximize message influence. The source's influence may stem from the fact that he or she is very knowledgeable and qualified in a particular area, is very popular and/or physically attractive, typifies the target audience and is seen as similar to the receiver, or can reward or punish the receiver in some manner.

A very useful framework for examining source attributes or characteristics is the classification scheme developed by Herbert Kelman.[2] According to this scheme, there are three basic categories of source attributes—credibility, attractiveness, and power. Each attribute involves a different "process" by which the source influences attitudinal or behavioral change in the message recipient. Exhibit 7–5 shows the three categories of source attributes and the psychological processes through which they operate. The following sections examine these attributes and their importance in selecting the source of a marketing communication.

Source Credibility

Credibility refers to the extent to which the source is perceived as having knowledge, skill, or experience relevant to the communication topic and can be trusted to give an unbiased opinion or present objective information on the issue. There are two important dimensions to credibility—expertise and trustworthiness.

Expertise is a very important aspect of credibility, as a communicator who is perceived as being knowledgeable in a given area will be more persuasive than one with less expertise. **Trustworthiness** refers to the honesty, integrity, and believability of the source and is also an important aspect of credibility. A source may be perceived as being very knowledgeable, but his or her influence will be lessened if the audience members perceive the source as being biased or having underlying personal motives for advocating a particular position (such as being paid to endorse a product).

One of the most reliable effects found in communications research is that expert and/or trustworthy sources are more persuasive than sources who have less expertise or trustworthiness.[3] Information from a credible source can influence beliefs, opinions, attitudes, and/or behavior through a process known as **internalization.** Internalization occurs when the receiver is motivated to have an objectively correct or "right" position on an issue. The receiver will learn and adopt the opinion or attitude of the credible communicator since he or she believes information from this source represents an accurate position on the issue. Once the receiver internalizes an opinion or attitude, it becomes integrated into his or her belief system and may be maintained even if the source of the message is forgotten.

The use of a highly credible communicator is particularly important when message recipients have a negative position toward the product, service, company, or issue being promoted, as the credible source is more likely to inhibit counterarguments than are those of moderate or low credibility. As discussed in Chapter 6, reduced counterarguing should result in greater message acceptance and persuasion.

Applying expertise

Because attitudes and opinions developed through an internalization process become part of the individual's belief system, it is desirable for marketers to use communicators who are high in credibility. Companies use a variety of techniques to convey source expertise. For example, millions of dollars are spent to train sales personnel to make them knowledgeable of the product line and thus increase their level of expertise in the eyes of the customer. Marketers of highly technical products recruit sales representatives with specialized technical backgrounds in engineering, computer science, and other areas to ensure their expertise.

Advertisers also go to great lengths, and often great expense, to achieve source credibility. Spokespersons are often chosen because of their knowledge, experience, and expertise in a particular product or service area. For example, former test pilot Chuck Yeager appears in ads for Delco auto parts (Exhibit 7–6). Endorsements from individuals or groups recognized as experts such as doctors or dentists are also common in advertising.

Applying trustworthiness

While finding spokespersons who have expertise is important, it is also important that the message recipients find the source believable. Finding celebrities or other figures with a trustworthy image is often difficult. Many trustworthy public figures hesitate to endorse products because of the impact it could have on their reputation and image. It has been suggested that former CBS news anchorman Walter Cronkite, who has repeatedly been rated as one of the most trusted people in America, could command millions of dollars as a product spokesperson. Consumer advocate Ralph Nader also has a very trustworthy image and would probably be a very credible endorser. However, it is unlikely either would agree to appear in advertisements.

Advertisers use other techniques to increase perceptions of the trustworthiness of the communicators in their messages. Hidden-camera techniques are often used to show that the consumer is not a paid spokesperson and is making an objective

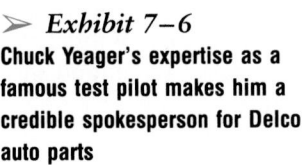

➤ *Exhibit 7–6*
Chuck Yeager's expertise as a famous test pilot makes him a credible spokesperson for Delco auto parts

➤ *Exhibit 7–7* Lee Iacocca has been a very effective corporate spokesperson for Chrysler and has become a business celebrity in the process

LEE IACOCCA: It's no secret that foreign competitors
have been giving American car makers a real beating.
About five years ago, we decided "enough is enough. This is where it stops."
The first thing we did was to take a good hard look at our own company.
(SFX: BLAST)
If we found something that slowed things

down, or didn't add value or improve quality, we dumped it.
Then we reorganized the whole place into four platform teams. Large car. Small car. Truck. And minivan.
We spent a billion dollars on a new Technology Center.
Now, this new way of doing business means we'll be putting our concepts in your garage while the competition is still sharpening their pencils.

And if you want proof, we've got proof.
The Dodge Viper, a Jeep Grand Cherokee and this fall, a whole new line of family sedans.
At Chrysler, we believe that standing still is a great way to get run over. In this business, you lead, follow or get out of the way.
(SFX)

evaluation of the product. Advertisers also use disguised comparisons in which their brand is compared with another by a consumer who is unaware of the brand identities. (Of course, the sponsor's brand *always* performs better than the consumer's regular brand, and he or she acts surprised on learning this outcome!) While these techniques may be of some value, most consumers are skeptical of them, and they may have limited value in enhancing perceptions of credibility.

Using corporate leaders as spokespersons

Another popular approach to enhancing source credibility is the use of the company president or chief executive officer (CEO) as a spokesperson in the firm's advertising. Many companies believe the use of a president or CEO is the ultimate expression of the company's commitment to quality, service, and meeting the needs of the customer. Many companies have used their leaders to advertise their products and services; and in some cases, the ads have not only been successful but also have helped turn these individuals into celebrities.[4] (Exhibit 7–7).

Some research evidence suggests the use of a company president or CEO can have a positive effect on attitudes and consumer likelihood of inquiring about the company's product or service.[5] It is also becoming common to see local companies such as retailers use the owner or president in their ads. It is likely that many companies will continue to use their top executives in their advertising, particularly when they have celebrity value that helps enhance the firms' image. However, as discussed in Promotional Perspective 7–1, there can be problems when companies rely on their leaders as advertising spokespersons.

Limitations of credible sources

Several studies have shown that a high-credibility source is not always an asset, nor is a low-credibility source a persuasive liability. For example, high- and low-credibility sources have been found to be about equal in effectiveness when the source is arguing for a position opposing his or her own best interest.[6] A high-credibility source is more effective when message recipients are not in favor of the position advocated in the message.[7] However, the use of a high-credibility source is less important when the audience has a neutral position and may even be less effective than a moderately credible source when the receiver has a favorable initial attitude or position.[8]

Another reason a low-credibility source may be as effective as a high-credibility source is the **sleeper effect** phenomenon, whereby the persuasiveness of a message increases with the passage of time. The immediate impact of a persuasive message may be inhibited because of its association with a low-credibility source. However, with the passage of time, the association of the message with the low-credibility source diminishes, and the receiver's attention focuses more on favorable information in the message, which results in more support arguing. However, many studies have failed to demonstrate the presence of a sleeper effect.[9] Many advertisers question the strategy of relying on the sleeper effect, suggesting that a more reliable strategy would be to use repeated exposure to a communication attributed to a credible source.[10]

Source Attractiveness

The source characteristic used most by advertisers is probably that of **attractiveness.** Just as there are several components to source credibility, source attractiveness also consists of various subcomponents including similarity, familiarity, and likability.[11] *Similarity* refers to a supposed resemblance between the source and the receiver of the message, while *familiarity* refers to knowledge of the source through exposure. *Likability* refers to affection for the source as a result of the source's physical appearance, behavior, or other personal characteristics. For example, even though they have no similarity to celebrities such as athletes or movie stars, consumers often find them likable because they admire their physical appearance, talent, and/or personality.

When a receiver considers a source attractive, persuasion may occur through a process known as **identification.** Identification occurs when the receiver is motivated to seek some type of relationship with the source and thus adopts a similar position in terms of beliefs, attitudes, opinions, preferences, or behavior. Maintaining this position depends on the source's continued support for the position as well as the receiver's continued identification with the source. If the source changes position, the receiver may also change. Note that unlike internalization, information from an attractive source does not usually become integrated into the receiver's belief system. Thus, the receiver may maintain the attitudinal position or behavior only so long as it is supported by the source or so long as the source remains attractive.

Marketers recognize that receivers of persuasive communications are more likely to attend to and identify with people they find likable or similar to themselves. Similarity and likability are the two source characteristics often sought by marketers when choosing a communicator.

Promotional Perspective 7–1

Do CEOs Make Good Spokespeople?

In 1971, the advertising agency for Perdue Farms, Inc., of Salisbury, Maryland, was developing a new ad campaign that would focus on the quality of Perdue chickens. The creative director suggested a novel strategy of featuring Frank Perdue, the tough-minded president of Perdue Farms, as the spokesperson for the company's advertising using a "tough man/tender chicken" theme. The company's sales soared as a result of the campaign, and Frank Perdue has continued to pitch Perdue chicken ads for more than 20 years, becoming a folk hero throughout the East in the process. Moreover, this campaign set the stage for a new advertising genre—the use of a company president or chief executive officer as advertising spokesperson.

Over the past two decades, a number of companies have relied on their chief executive as an advertising spokesperson. Victor Kiam was a very effective spokesman for Remington Products for many years with his well-known pitch "I liked the razor so much I bought the company." Perhaps the best known of the corporate spokespersons is Lee Iacocca, who became a national business hero for his turnaround of the nearly bankrupt Chrysler Corporation in the early 1980s.

Many marketing experts question the strategy of featuring CEOs and think it is often egos rather than logic that result in their use. The chairman of one agency noted that most agencies only put CEOs in ads because they want to be in them. Critics argue that consumers may not understand why the corporate leaders are being used or may not believe them, since they have so much at stake in the company.

Problems can occur even with well-known and credible CEO spokespersons. Sometimes they become celebrities who receive more attention than their company's products or advertising message. A company's image can also become tied too closely to a popular CEO spokesperson, which creates problems if that person leaves the firm or retires. For example, Frank Perdue is now in his 70s, and it is speculated he will soon step down as the company's chairman and pitchman. To prepare, the company has created and test marketed a campaign that does not use him. It is also questionable as to how long Orville Redenbacher will be able to pitch his popcorn, and the company has already begun working his grandson into some of its ads.

Yet another problem can occur when the executive spokesperson falls from grace with the public. For example, Leona Helmsley was the self-styled "queen" of the Helmsley hotel chain and insisted on appearing in corporate ads while on trial for tax evasion. Even after she was convicted, it took the advertising agency months to persuade her to remove herself from the ads.

Victor Kiam's credibility was also damaged when members of his New England Patriots football team were charged with sexual harassment of a female reporter in the locker room. Kiam initially stood up for his players and was quoted as calling the female writer a "classic bitch" and joking about the incident a few months later when speaking at a sports banquet. The writer sued Kiam and the team for harassment, civil rights violations, and emotional distress; and the National Organization for Women called for a boycott of the company. Female consumers are very important to the company, as they buy gifts for men, and the Lady Remington brand has 40 percent of the women's electric shaver market. Although Remington's 1990 sales dropped an estimated $50 million, Kiam continued as the advertising spokesperson.

Despite the many potential problems with using corporate chieftains as advertising spokespeople, the practice is likely to continue. As one advertising executive noted, "It's a perk that's tougher to walk away from than a corporate jet."

Source: Joanne Lipman, "Chairmen Starring as Spokesmen May Eventually Lose Their Luster," *The Wall Street Journal*, February 12, 1992, p. B6; Bruce Horowitz, " 'Boss as Star' Campaigns Can Backfire if the Executive Falls from Grace," *Los Angeles Times*, October 16, 1990, D6; and Roy Furchgott, "Where Have All The Spokesmen Gone?" *Adweek's Marketing Week*, May 6, 1991, pp. 20–21.

Applying similarity

Most marketers recognize that people are more likely to be influenced by a persuasive appeal if it is perceived as coming from someone with whom they feel a sense of similarity.[12] If the receiver shares similar interests, lifestyles, opinions, and the like, with the communicator, he or she is more likely to share the same needs, desires, or goals, and the position advocated by the source would be better understood and received.

Similarity is used in various ways in marketing communications. For example, companies select salespersons who have characteristics that match well with their customers. A sales position for a particular region of the country may be staffed by someone from the local area to ensure the rep has a common background and interest with the customers. Imagine the problems a person from a large urban area

Frank Perdue has helped convince consumers of the quality of Perdue chickens

FRANK: When it comes to raising my chickens, I'm a real mother hen.

From the healthy natural feed they eat to the way they drink.

I've even given them their own water fountains they just reach up and peck.

So they never share the same water. Which means

their water isn't just cleaner, it's healthier, too.

These inventions are called nipple drinkers.

(SFX: BABY CRIES)

It's not really a new idea.

You may have even used one yourself.

(FRANK TALKS TO BABY UNDER)

such as New York City or Los Angeles might have in trying to sell to customers in rural areas such as Wyoming and Montana!

Companies may also try to recruit salespersons with a particular background to sell to customers to establish a common interest. Former athletes are often recruited to sell sporting goods equipment or to act as sales reps for beer companies, since their customers usually have a strong interest in sports. Several studies have shown that customers who perceive a salesperson as similar to themselves are more likely to accept or be influenced by his or her message.[13]

Similarity is also used by advertisers who will try to create a situation whereby the consumer has empathy for the person shown in the commercial. For example, in a "slice-of-life" commercial, the advertiser usually starts by presenting a predicament or problem situation with the hope of getting the consumer to think: "I can see myself in that situation." This can help establish a bond of similarity

➤ *Exhibit 7–8*
Michael Jordan endorses Gatorade

between the communicator and the receiver and thus increase the source's level of persuasiveness.

Applying likability: using celebrities

Advertisers have long recognized the value of using spokespersons who are well liked and often admired, such as television and movie stars, athletes, musicians, or other popular figures. The use of celebrities from the sports and entertainment fields to promote products and services has become very popular among advertisers. It is estimated that more than 20 percent of all TV commercials feature celebrities, with advertisers paying more than $500 million per year for their services. For example, Pepsi has paid Michael Jackson an estimated $25 million over the span of three endorsement deals to promote its soft drinks worldwide.[14] Quaker Oats signed a long-term contract with basketball superstar Michael Jordan to endorse its Gatorade sports drink (Exhibit 7–8). Jordan agreed to an exclusive endorsement deal whereby Gatorade would be the only beverage product he endorses and terminated his contract with Coca-Cola. Quaker Oats executives think basketball is a global sport, and Jordan is a global personality who can promote Gatorade all over the world.[15] Jordan also makes millions more from his endorsement deals with Nike, General Mills, and Hanes.

Why are companies willing to spend huge sums of money to have celebrities appear in their ads and endorse their products? They view a celebrity as having "stopping power" and as a way of drawing attention to their advertising messages in a very cluttered media environment. Another reason is the expectation that the respect, popularity, and/or admiration the celebrity enjoys will favorably influence consumers' feelings, attitudes, and ultimately their purchase behavior. Celebrities also can enhance the target audience's perceptions of the product in terms of image and/or performance. For example, when a well-known athlete endorses a product he or she can not only attract attention to the ad but also may help convince potential buyers that the product helps their own performance (Exhibit 7–9).

Issues in using celebrities

A number of factors must be considered in the decision to use a celebrity as an endorser or spokesperson.

Overshadowing the product   How will the celebrity affect the target audience's processing of the advertising message? While a celebrity may draw attention to the ad effectively, his or her impact on other response variables such as brand awareness, recall of copy points and message arguments, brand attitudes, and purchase intentions must also be considered. A common concern is that consumers will focus their attention on the celebrity and fail to note the brand being promoted. This problem

reportedly occurred when comedian Rich Little was used in ads for Pizza Hut restaurants and Rodney Dangerfield appeared in commercials for Lo-Sal antacid tablets. And Mazda dropped actor James Garner as its spokesperson after four years so its ads could focus exclusively on the cars. Mazda's vice president of advertising stated, "We want the cars to be the stars."[16]

Overexposure   Consumers, recognizing that celebrities endorse a product or service because they are being paid to do so, may become skeptical of the endorsements.[17] This problem can become particularly pronounced when a celebrity endorses multiple products or companies and becomes "overexposed." For example, many people thought actor Bill Cosby was overexposed a few years ago in doing ads for Jell-O, Coca-Cola, Texas Instruments, Kodak, and E. F. Hutton.[18] Basketball superstar Michael Jordan and CBS sportscaster John Madden are other celebrities who endorse numerous products and thus may risk overexposure.[19]

Some advertisers protect themselves from celebrity overexposure by using an exclusivity clause that limits the number of products a celebrity can endorse. Clauses limiting the total number of a celebrity's endorsements are usually expensive and so are not used by many companies. However, most celebrities agree not to endorse products in the same or a related product category. Many celebrities recognize that their fame and popularity will last only for a limited time and thus try to earn as much endorsement money as possible. However, a celebrity must also be aware of the importance of credibility as an advertising spokesperson and be careful not to damage it by endorsing too many products.

Target audiences   Attention must also be given to the audience toward whom the advertising campaign will be targeted. Consumers who are particularly knowledgeable about a product or service or have strongly established attitudes may be less impressed or influenced by a celebrity than those with little knowledge or neutral attitudes. For example, one study found that college-age students were more likely to have a positive attitude toward a product endorsed by a celebrity than were older consumers.[20] The teenage market segment is very receptive to celebrity endorsers, as evidenced by the prevalent use of entertainers and athletes that appear in ads targeted to this group for products such as soft drinks, apparel, and cosmetics.

Risk to the advertiser   Another important factor marketers must consider when contemplating using a celebrity is whether there is any risk associated with having that person represent your company or products because of image or behavior. Several well-known entertainers and athletes have been arrested for drug abuse or have been involved in other activities that were potentially embarrassing to the companies whose products they were endorsing.[21] For example, Pepsi dropped a television ad featuring pop singer Madonna and canceled its sponsorship of her concert tour when a controversy arose over one of her music videos. Several religious groups and many consumers found Madonna's "Like a Prayer" video objectionable on religious grounds and threatened a boycott of Pepsi products if the company continued to use her in its advertising.[22] Pepsi had also used former heavyweight boxing champion Mike Tyson a few years ago to endorse Diet Pepsi. However, the company distanced itself from the troubled athlete when he began having personal problems. The Beef Industry Council suffered some embarrassing moments a few years ago when actress Cybil Shepherd, who was appearing in ads encouraging consumers to eat beef, was quoted as saying she did not eat red meat.[23] To avoid these problems, companies often carefully research the personal life and background of celebrities before using them. Many firms also include a moral clause in the contract, allowing them to terminate a celebrity should any controversy arise involving that individual.

Matching product, target market, and celebrity   One of the most important considerations in attempting to use a celebrity to influence consumers is making sure the image of the product and characteristics of the target market are carefully matched with the personality of the celebrity.[24] A study by Roobina Ohanian examined consumers' perceptions of the various characteristics of celebrity endorsers and how this influenced their intentions to purchase a product endorsed by the celebrity.[25] She found that the perceived expertise of celebrity endorsers was more important in explaining purchase intentions than their attractiveness or trustworthiness. Ohanian suggests that celebrity spokespersons are most likely to be effective when they are knowledgeable, experienced, and qualified to talk about the product they are endorsing.

Many advertisers attempt to use celebrities who are connected in some way to the products they are endorsing. An excellent example of this is the campaign for Nuprin ibuprofen pain reliever that features the aging, but still competitive, tennis star Jimmy Connors. The campaign has resulted in a significant increase in Nuprin sales.[26] Likewise, Duracell chose seemingly ageless baseball pitcher Nolan Ryan to deliver the message that nothing lasts longer than Duracell (see Exhibit 7–10).

Understanding the meaning of celebrity endorsers

The image and meaning celebrities project to consumers can be just as important as their ability to attract attention to the ads in which they appear. The traditional explanation for the communication effectiveness of celebrity endorsers has been based on the source credibility and source attractiveness characteristics discussed above. However, a new perspective on celebrity endorsement has been developed recently by Grant McCracken.[27] He argues that these source characteristic models do not offer a sufficient explanation for how and why celebrity endorsements work. McCracken offers a model of the celebrity endorsement process based on *meaning transfer* (Exhibit 7–11).

➤ *Exhibit 7–10a*
Jimmy Connors matches up very well with Nuprin (left)

➤ *Exhibit 7–10b*
Nolan Ryan's image fits very well with the message Duracell wants to communicate (right)

According to this model, a celebrity's effectiveness as an endorser depends on the culturally acquired meanings he or she brings to the endorsement process. The number and variety of the meanings contained in celebrities are very large and include status, class, gender, and age as well as personality and lifestyle type. In explaining Stage 1 of the meaning transfer process, McCracken notes:

> Celebrities draw these powerful meanings from the roles they assume in their television, movie, military, athletic, and other careers . . . . Each new dramatic role brings the celebrity into contact with a range of objects, persons and contexts. Out of these objects, persons and contexts are transferred meanings that then reside in the celebrity.[28]

Examples of meanings that have been acquired by celebrities include Bill Cosby and Michael Gross as the perfect fathers (from their roles on "The Cosby Show" and "Family Ties" respectively), Bo Jackson as the ultimate athlete (based on his ability to excel in both professional football and baseball), or General Norman Schwartzkof as the great leader and military hero (based on his role as the commander of Operation Desert Storm during the Persian Gulf War).

McCracken suggests celebrity endorsers bring their meanings into the advertisement and transfer them to the products they are endorsing (Stage 2 of the model in Exhibit 7–11). Thus, some of the meaning of the celebrity become meanings of the product. Of course, marketers that use a celebrity endorser try to ensure that the exact set of meanings being sought from the celebrity are captured in the advertising campaign and that unwanted meaning is not transferred. For example, as noted above, Nuprin has done an excellent job of using Jimmy Connors as an endorser by focusing on his appeal as an aging, yet defiant tennis star who is still capable of competing against younger players, but "hurts all over" when he is done playing. This meaning was reinforced when Connors captivated tennis fans by reaching the semifinals of the 1991 U.S. Open Tennis Tournament at the age of 39.

In the final stage of McCracken's model, the meanings the celebrity has given to the product are transferred to the consumer. For example, Jimmy Connors' endorsement helps in positioning the brand as the "body pain medicine" and is effective in encouraging consumers to use the product to relieve their aches and pains. McCracken notes that this final stage is very complicated and sometimes difficult to achieve because there is no automatic transfer of meaning nor transformation of the consumers' self-concept. The way consumers take possession of the meaning the celebrity may have transferred to a product is probably the least understood part of this process.

➤ *Exhibit 7–11* **Meaning movement and the endorsement process**

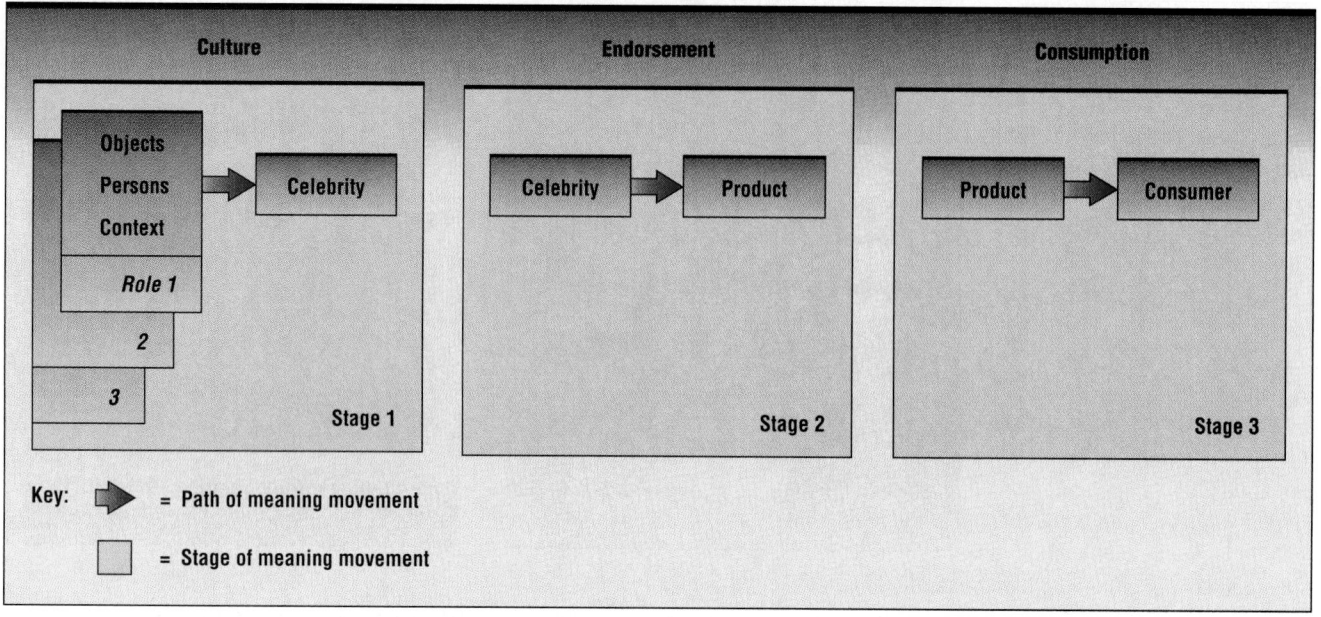

The meaning transfer model has some important implications for companies that use celebrity endorsers. Marketers must first decide on the image or symbolic meanings important to their target audience for this particular product. They must then determine the celebrity who best represents the meaning or image to be projected for the product or the company. An advertising campaign must then be designed that captures the meanings of the celebrity in the product and moves this meaning from the product to the consumer. Marketing and advertising personnel often rely on their judgments and intuition in choosing celebrity endorsers for their companies or products. However, some companies conduct research studies to determine consumers' perceptions of the meaning or image of celebrities. Examples of intuitive versus more formal ways of choosing a celebrity were evident in the processes by which Sprint and AT&T chose Candice Bergen and Cliff Robertson as their advertising spokespersons, as discussed at the beginning of the chapter.

Pretesting of advertisements may also be needed to determine whether an ad utilizing a celebrity endorser is successful in transferring the proper meaning to the product. When celebrity endorsers are used, the marketer should track the campaign's effectiveness and determine whether the celebrity continues to be effective in communicating the proper meaning to the target audience. Many actors or athletes who are no longer in the limelight may lose their appeal and ability to transfer any significant meanings to the product.

Also, the image of the celebrity can change due to unforeseen events and affect his or her appropriateness as an endorser for certain companies or brands. For example, the Beef Industry Council encountered such a problem a few years ago when its spokesperson, actor James Garner, underwent heart bypass surgery, bringing to attention the possible link between red meat and cholesterol. More recently, companies using basketball star Earvin "Magic" Johnson as an endorser encountered a serious problem when he announced he was retiring from the Los Angeles Lakers after testing positive for the HIV virus, which has been linked to AIDS. Companies such as Pepsi-Cola, Converse, and Kentucky Fried Chicken were faced with a very difficult situation: they did not want to abandon Magic yet had to consider the impact the revelation would have on his image and appeal as their advertising spokesman.[29]

CROCK By Bill Rechin and Don Wilder

As we have seen, marketers must consider many factors when choosing a celebrity to serve as an advertising spokesperson for the company or a particular brand. Promotional Perspective 7–2 discusses some interesting issues regarding the choice of celebrity endorsers and why some are more effective, and are paid more, than others.

Applying likability: decorative and physically attractive models

A common technique employed by advertisers to draw attention to an ad and enhance its effectiveness is to use a physically attractive model. Often, the attractive model is used as a passive or "decorative" model rather than as an active communicator. Research suggests that physically attractive communicators generally have a positive impact, as they result in more favorable evaluations of the ad and the product than do less attractive models.[30] However, it has also been shown that the gender appropriateness of the model for the product being advertised and the relevancy of the model to the product are also important considerations.[31] Products such as cosmetics or fashionable clothing are likely to benefit from the use of an attractive model, since physical appearance is very relevant in marketing these items.

Consideration must also be given to whether the model will draw attention to the ad but not to the product or message. The presence of an attractive or decorative model facilitates recognition of the ad but does not enhance copy readership or message recall.[32] Thus, advertisers must take steps to ensure that the consumer's attention will go beyond the model and get the individual to devote some attention to the product and advertising message.

Source Power

The final source characteristic in Kelman's classification scheme is that of **source power.** A source may have power when he or she can actually administer rewards and punishments to the receiver. As a result of this power, the source may be able to induce another person(s) to respond to the request or position he or she is advocating. However, the perceived power of the source depends on several factors. First, the source must be perceived as being able to administer positive or negative sanctions to the receiver *(perceived control).* Also, the receiver must think the source cares about whether or not the receiver conforms *(perceived concern).* Finally, the receiver's estimate of the source's ability to observe the source's conformity is important *(perceived scrutiny).*

When a source is perceived by the receiver as having power, the influence process occurs through a process known as **compliance.** Compliance results when the receiver accepts the persuasive influence of the source and acquiesces to his or her advocated position in hopes of obtaining favorable reaction or avoiding punishment. The receiver may show an outward or public acquiescence to the source's position but may not have an internal or private commitment to this position. Thus, persuasion

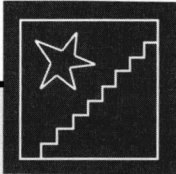

Promotional Perspective 7-2

Choosing a Celebrity Endorser

It has become very common for star entertainers and athletes to make almost as much money, or even more, off the stage, screen, field, or court than they do on it by appearing as advertising spokespersons. Corporations are always looking for a celebrity whose presence in their ads will attract the viewers' or readers' attention and enhance the image of the company or brand they are endorsing. This requires that marketers have some idea of whether a celebrity will be an effective spokesperson for the company or one of its brands.

Advertisers often rely on surveys that measure a celebrity's appeal to help them choose an endorser. One of the more popular measures is the "Q" rating derived from research by Marketing Evaluations Inc.'s TVQ Services. The company surveys more than 7,000 people each year to come up with recognizability scores and its "Q" rating for television and movie actors, athletes, authors, businesspeople, and other personalities. The recognizability score indicates what percentage of people recognize the celebrity. The Q score tells the percent of people recognizing the celebrity who rate him or her as one of their favorite performers. For example, Bill Cosby set a record a few years ago when 96 percent of those surveyed recognized him and he had a Q score of 71 (i.e., 71 percent of those who recognized him said he was one of their favorite performers). The average Q score for performers is 18. Marketing Evaluations' celebrity ratings are also broken down by various demographic groups such as age, income, occupation, education, and race. Thus, marketers have some idea of how a celebrity's popularity might vary among different groups of consumers.

Other studies of celebrity appeal also may help advertisers choose a spokesperson. For example, Video Storyboard Tests, Inc., conducts an annual survey of more than 1,000 adult TV viewers to measure their attitudes toward celebrities as endorsers, their persuasiveness, and credibility. The accompanying table shows consumers' ratings of the most popular entertainer and athlete television endorsers for 1991.

There are many other factors to consider in signing celebrities to endorsement contracts, such as their visibility and personalities. For example, among athletes, the biggest endorsement money goes to basketball players, followed by golfers and tennis players. The reason is that the public buys the footwear, clubs, balls, rackets, and clothing that these highly visible athletes wear or use. Even though basketball, football, and baseball players have the highest level of mass-market appeal, three of the top four athletes in endorsement income are golfers—Arnold Palmer, Jack Nicklaus, and Greg Norman. Golfers make large sums of money on endorsements since the sport is popular among chief executive officers, who often help decide where sponsorship dollars are spent.

Fame and athletic prowess alone don't always lead to large endorsement contracts, however. For example, tennis star Ivan Lendl has never been popular among advertisers, which many attribute to his craggy personality and tendency to frown during matches. In fact, personality and image is sometimes more important than athletic achievements. For example, Bob Uecker has used his self-proclaimed athletic mediocrity and the nonhero image that made him so popular in Miller Lite ads as a springboard to endorsements for many other products. For some athletes such as Uecker, their commercials have brought them more celebrity status than their sports careers did.

Source: Joanne Lipman, "Celebrities Are Popular Again," *The Wall Street Journal,* September 4, 1991, R5; Roger Lowenstein, "Many Athletes Have a Tough Time Playing the Endorsement Game," *The Wall Street Journal,* August 29, 1986, p. 32; Joanne Lipman, "For Endorsers, One Win Is Not Enough," *The Wall Street Journal,* August 14, 1991, B4; Dan Hurley, "Those Hush-Hush Q Ratings—Fair or Foul?" *TV Guide,* December 10, 1988, pp. 3-6; and Christy Marshall, "It Seemed Like a Good Deal at the Time," *Forbes,* February 28, 1987, p. 98.

Most popular promoters and their products, 1991

Bill Cosby: Jell-O, Kodak Colorwatch	Michael Jordan: Nike, McDonald's, Hanes, Wheaties, Gatorade
Ray Charles: Diet Pepsi	Bo Jackson: Nike
Paula Abdul: diet Coke	Tommy Lasorda: Ultra Slimfast
Candice Bergen: Sprint	Earvin "Magic" Johnson: Converse, Pepsi, Kentucky Fried Chicken
Linda Evans: Clairol, LensCrafters	
Ed McMahon: American Family Publishers, Colonial Penn Insurance	Joe Namath: Flex-All, The Wiz
	Bob Uecker: Miller Lite
Angela Lansbury: Bufferin	Joe Montana: Diet Pepsi
Kathie Lee Gifford: Carnival Cruise Lines, Ultra Slimfast	Nolan Ryan: Advil
Hammer: Pepsi, British Knights	Hulk Hogan: Right Guard
Lynn Redgrave: Weight Watchers	Arnold Palmer: Jiffy Lube, Hertz, Sears

induced through the use of a communicator who relies on power may be superficial and last only as long as the receiver perceives that the source can administer some reward or punishment. This is quite different from the influence process, which occurs in reaction to a credible source, as previously discussed.

The use of power as a source characteristic is very difficult to apply through a nonpersonal influence situation such as that found in advertising. A communicator in an ad generally cannot apply any sanctions to the receiver or determine whether compliance actually occurs. An indirect way of using power may be to use an individual with a very authoritative personality or appearance as a spokesperson. For example, actor Charles Bronson, who typifies this type of image, has appeared in public service campaigns commanding people not to pollute or damage our natural parks (Exhibit 7–12).

The use of source power has greater applicability to situations involving personal communication and influence. For example, in a personal selling situation, the sales rep may have some power over a buyer if the latter anticipates receiving special rewards or favors for complying with the salesperson's requests. Some companies provide their sales reps with large expense accounts to spend on customers for this very purpose. Representatives of companies in a dominant position, where demand for their product exceeds supply, are often in a position of power, as buyers may comply with their requests to ensure an adequate supply of the seller's product.

Sales reps must be very careful in their use of a power position, as long-term relationships with a customer may be damaged if a power base is abused to maximize short-term gains. For example, several years ago Procter & Gamble had developed a very negative image among retailers who thought that because of the strength the company had developed with its dominant brands, P&G and its sales force had become very rigid and arrogant in its procedures and policies toward the trade. However, many of P&G's markets began to mature and become more competitive, and the major retailers' clout began to increase as a result of mergers and smaller stores going out of business. Thus, P&G and its sales reps had to develop a much more conciliatory attitude and policies to maintain its sales growth.[33]

Message Factors

The manner in which marketing communications are presented is very important in determining their effectiveness. Promotional managers must consider not only what the content of their persuasive messages will be but also how this information will be structured for presentation and the type of message appeal that will be utilized. Advertising, in all media except radio, relies heavily on visual as well as verbal information. A considerable number of options are available with respect to the design and presentation of a message. In this section, we examine various issues in designing the structure of a message and also consider what is known about the effects of different types of appeals used in advertising.

Message Structure

Marketing communications usually consists of a number of elements or message points that the communicator wants to get across. An important aspect of message strategy is knowing the best way to communicate these points and overcome any opposing viewpoints or attitudes audience members might hold. Extensive research has been conducted on how the structure of a persuasive message can influence its effectiveness, including order of presentation, conclusion drawing, message sidedness, refutation, and verbal versus nonverbal message characteristics.

Order of presentation

A basic consideration in the design of a persuasive message concerns the order of presentation of the message arguments. Should the most important message points be placed at the beginning of the message, in the middle, or at the end? Research on

➤ *Exhibit 7–13*

Ad message recall as a function of order of presentation

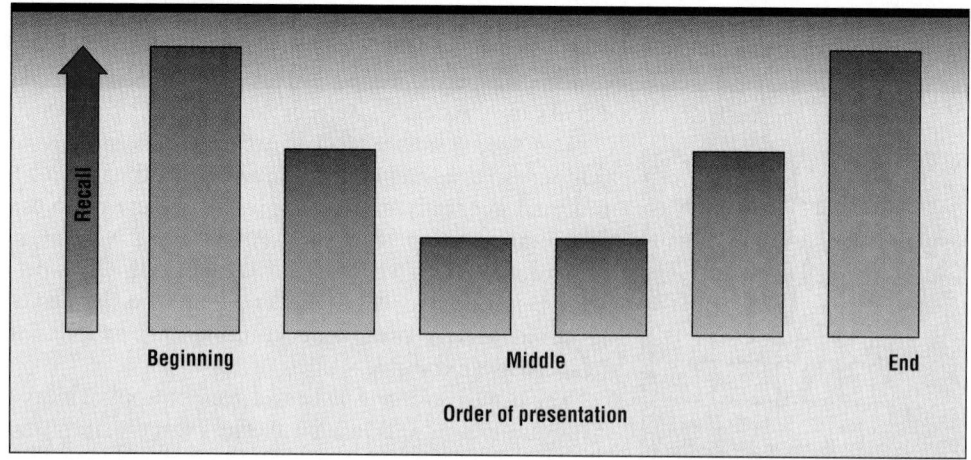

Recall

Beginning   Middle   End

Order of presentation

learning and memory generally indicates that, given a series of things to remember, those presented first and last are remembered better than those presented in the middle (see Exhibit 7–13).[34] This would suggest that a communicator's strongest arguments should be presented early or late in the message but never in the middle.

Presenting the strongest arguments at the beginning of the message assumes a **primacy effect** is operating whereby information presented first is most effective. Putting the strong points at the end of the communication would assume a **recency effect** will occur whereby the arguments presented at the end of the message are the most persuasive.

The decision whether to place the strongest selling points at the beginning or the end of the message depends on several factors. If the target audience is opposed to the communicator's position, it may be necessary to present strong points first to reduce the counterarguing the receiver would engage in. Putting weak arguments first might lead to such a high level of counterarguing that strong arguments will not be attended to or believed. Putting strong arguments at the beginning of the message may also be necessary if the audience has a low level of interest in the topic, as they may be needed to arouse attention and interest in the message. When the target audience is favorably predisposed toward the communicator's position or has a high level of interest in the issue or product, strong arguments can be saved for the end of the message. This should not only result in the audience members' leaving with a favorable opinion but should also result in better retention of the information. Decisions regarding the order of presentation of message arguments depend on the situation facing the communicator. The order of presentation of message arguments can be particularly critical when a long, detailed message with many arguments is being presented, such as a sales presentation. Most effective sales presentations open and close with strong selling points, whereas weaker arguments are buried in the middle of the presentation. For short communications, such as a 15- or 30-second television or radio commercial, the order of argument presentation would appear to be less critical. However, many products and services are received by consumers with a low level of involvement, and consumer interest is minimal. Thus, an advertiser may want to present information such as the brand name and key selling points early in the message as well as at the end to enhance recall and retention.

Conclusion drawing

Another issue facing marketing communicators is whether their messages should explicitly draw a firm conclusion for the audience or allow them to draw their own conclusions. Research suggests that, in general, messages with explicit conclusions are more easily understood and effective in influencing attitudes. However, other studies have shown that the effectiveness of conclusion drawing may depend on the target audience, the type of issue or topic, and the nature of the situation.[35]

For example, more highly educated people prefer to draw their own conclusions and may be annoyed at an attempt to explain the obvious or to draw an inference for them. However, a less educated audience may need to have the conclusion stated for them, as they may never draw a conclusion or may make an incorrect inference from the message. Marketers must also consider the audience's level of involvement in the topic or issue. For highly personal or ego-involving issues, message recipients may want to make up their own minds and may resent any attempts by the communicator to draw a conclusion. A recent advertising study by Alan Sawyer and Daniel Howard found that open-ended ads without explicit conclusions were more effective than close-ended arguments that did include a specific conclusion—but only for involved audiences.[36]

The decision as to whether to draw a conclusion for the audience also depends on the complexity of the topic or issue. While a less intelligent audience may not understand the conclusions to be drawn on a complex issue, even a highly educated audience may need assistance if its knowledge level in a particular area is low. Consideration must also be given to whether the marketer wants the message to trigger immediate action or whether a more long-term effect is desired. If immediate action is an objective, the message should draw a definitive conclusion for the target audience. This is a very common strategy in political advertising, particularly for ads run close to election day. When immediate impact is not the objective and repeated exposure will give the audience opportunities to draw a conclusion, an open-ended message might be used.

Drawing a conclusion in a message may be a way of ensuring the target audience gets the point the marketer intended. However, assuming the audience will do so, many advertisers believe it is beneficial for customers to draw their own conclusions and thereby reinforce the points being made in the message. For example, a health services agency in Kentucky found that open-ended ads were more likely to be remembered and were more effective in getting consumers to use health services than ads stating a conclusion. Ads that posed questions about alcohol and drug abuse and left them unanswered resulted in more calls by teenagers to a help line for information than when a message offering a resolution to the problem was used.[37]

Some advertisers prefer to use a somewhat ambiguous message, hoping consumers will become involved in interpreting the message in a manner that is personally relevant to them. Promotional Perspective 7–3 discusses how an ambiguous ad for Benson & Hedges cigarettes resulted in one of the most talked about ad campaigns in recent years.

Message sidedness

Another message structure decision facing the marketer is whether advertisements and sales presentations should use a **one-sided message,** and mention only positive attributes or benefits of a product or service, or a **two-sided message,** whereby good and bad points are presented. Research has shown that one-sided messages are most effective when the target audience already holds a favorable opinion toward the topic and will not hear opposing arguments. One-sided messages also have been found to work better than two-sided messages with a less educated audience.

Two-sided messages have been shown to be more effective when the target audience's initial opinion opposes that of the communicator and when the audience is highly educated. Two-sided messages may be more effective because they enhance the credibility of the source and thus the message. By presenting both sides of an issue or acknowledging opposing viewpoints, the communicator is likely to be seen as less biased and more objective than when a one-sided message is used. Also, a better-educated audience is more likely to know there are opposing arguments to the issue. Thus, by acknowledging the other viewpoint or admitting a weakness in his or her position, the communicator can improve credibility with this group.

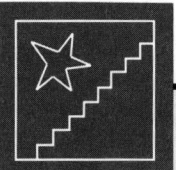

Promotional Perspective 7–3

What's Going On in These Ads?

One of the most talked about cigarette advertising campaigns in recent years was a series of ads that Philip Morris Company used for Benson & Hedges cigarettes in its "For people who like to smoke" campaign. The campaign consisted of a series of ads showing people in various social settings enjoying a cigarette. According to the president of the agency that created the campaign, the appeal of the ads was that people create their own stories behind the pictures, and there was no strict interpretation to them.

The ad in the campaign that drew the most attention showed a mysterious man in pajamas talking to a group of five women and one man. The photographer and director who shot the picture said that his interpretation of the ad was that someone sick at home comes from his bedroom, curious about the noise in another room, and discovers his family and friends having brunch. However, the agency itself vowed silence on what the ad was supposed to mean or what the jammie man was doing, leaving many people to come up with their own interpretation. *Advertising Age,* the ad industry's leading trade publication, asked its readers to send in their interpretation of the ad and got more than 400 responses, many noting that "everyone in the office has been wondering about it, too."

The interest in the ad was so great it prompted Philip Morris to run its own contest asking consumers to provide their opinion of what was going on in the ad. Entrants received a free coupon for Benson & Hedges, and the most original entries received a pair of designer pajamas—bottoms *and* tops.

The goal of the campaign, which consisted of 35 different ads, was to attract attention to Benson & Hedges among younger, upscale smokers. The brand's sales had declined since 1986 owing to an image problem created by an aging consumer base and declining sales in the high-quality cigarette segment in which it competed. Although Philip Morris officials would not discuss the specific results of the campaign, observers believe it helped meet this goal. Philip Morris has since moved on to a new ad campaign for Benson & Hedges—sans the jammie man.

What is your explanation of what is going on in this ad?

Source: Judann Dagnoli, "B & H Ads to Change?" *Advertising Age,* April 25, 1988, p. 4; Lenore Skenazy, "B & H Bedtime Stories," *Advertising Age,* May 9, 1988, p. 102.

Marketers generally present only favorable benefits of their products or services without mentioning any negative characteristics of their products or acknowledging an advantage a competitor might have. However, it has been shown that the use of a two-sided advertising message results in more positive perceptions of a source than does a one-sided message.[38]

The evidence noted above suggests there are situations in which companies might benefit from the use of a two-sided message rather than the traditional one-sided appeal. However, most advertisers refuse to use two-sided messages, as they are concerned over negative effects of acknowledging a weakness in their brand or do not want to say anything positive about their competitors'. There are exceptions, however, as advertisers will sometimes compare brands on various attributes and do not always show their product as being the best on every one.

Refutation

A special type of two-sided message known as a **refutational appeal** is sometimes used whereby the communicator presents both sides of an issue and then offers arguments to refute the opposing viewpoint. Refutational appeals may be effective because they "inoculate" the target audience against potential counterclaims that might be raised by a competitor. Thus, the receiver will not be surprised by subsequent counterarguments and might be better able to resist these claims by arguing against them. Several marketing studies have shown that two-sided refutational ads are more effective than one-sided messages in making consumers resistant to a message presenting an opposing viewpoint.[39]

Refutational messages may be useful in situations where marketers wish to build attitudes that are resistant to change and must defend against attacks or criticism of their products. Exhibit 7–14 shows an example of a refutational ad used by Quaker Oats to refute arguments that rice cakes taste bland. Market leaders, who are often the target of comparative messages, may find it advantageous to acknowledge the claims made by their competitors and then refute them to help build resistant attitudes and loyalty among their customers.

Verbal versus nonverbal messages

The various message structure issues discussed thus far have focused primarily on the information or verbal portion of the promotional message. Advertising copy is obviously an important component of an advertisement; however, the nonverbal or visual elements of an ad are also very important. As was noted in the previous chapter, many advertisements provide little product attribute information; instead, they rely on visual elements to communicate by portraying the type of person who uses the brand or evoking some type of emotional reaction from the receiver. Non-

➤ *Exhibit 7–15*
Visual images are often designed to support verbal appeals

verbal elements such as pictures and illustrations are commonly used in advertising to convey information or reinforce copy or message claims.

Both the verbal and visual portions of an advertisement influence the way an advertising message is processed.[40] Consumers may develop images or inferences about a brand based on the visual elements of an ad such as a picture or illustration or the scenes in a television commercial. In some cases, the visual portion of an ad may reduce the persuasiveness of the ad because the processing stimulated by the picture may be less controlled and consequently less favorable than that stimulated by words.[41]

Marketers must understand how nonverbal elements such as pictures affect the processing of accompanying verbal information such as advertising copy. For example, a recent study compared print ads where the verbal attribute information was low in imagery and unlikely to evoke images in consumers' minds versus ads where the verbal information was high in imagery-provoking ability.[42] The findings showed that when verbal information was low in imagery value, the use of pictures providing examples of that information increased both immediate and delayed recall of product attributes. However, when the verbal information was already high in imagery value, the addition of pictures did not increase the recall of product attribute information. These findings suggest that providing pictures that exemplify verbal claims is more important for advertising copy that is low in imagery value than for high imagery copy. Advertisers often design ads whereby the visual image supports the verbal appeal so as to generate a compelling impression in the consumer's mind. Notice how the ad for Ortega taco salsa uses visual elements to demonstrate the product's ingredients and reinforce the claims made in the advertising copy (Exhibit 7–15).

Message Appeals

One of the most important creative strategy decisions facing the advertiser involves the choice of an appropriate appeal. Some ads contain a great deal of information and are designed to appeal to the rational or logical aspect of the consumer's decision-making process, whereas others rely more on visual elements and appeal to feelings in an attempt to evoke some type of emotional reaction. Many believe that effective advertising combines the practical reasons for purchasing a product with emotional values.

Rational appeals

Many promotional messages are based on **rational appeals,** which attempt to communicate directly information regarding the product or service such as its features and/or the benefits of owning or using it. The content of the rational appeal message is usually presented in a direct or logical manner and often relies on explanations and comparisons. Rational appeals require a certain level of interest or involvement and information processing on the part of the message receiver to be effective. As was noted in the discussion of the elaboration likelihood model in Chapter 6, when motivation and ability to process the message are high, persuasion will occur through central processing of message content, and advertisements will be most effective if they contain strong and logical arguments for purchasing the product.

Rational appeals are often used for highly involving or complex consumer products, such as appliances, electronic products, or automobiles, where consumers have a high need for information and are likely to engage in evaluation and comparison of alternative brands. They are also very common in business-to-business marketing, both in advertising and in the development of sales presentations. Organizational buyers are usually very knowledgeable about the product or service they are purchasing and must be informed and convinced in a logical manner of the specifications, performance, value, quality, and so on, of an item before making a purchase (Exhibit 7–16).

Rational appeals are also used for many nondurable products, particularly when functional performance or efficacy is important to the consumer. Many consumer products companies use a particular type of rational appeal known as comparative advertising as the basis for their advertising messages.

Comparative advertising

Comparative advertising refers to the practice of either directly or indirectly naming one or more competitors in an ad and usually making a comparison on one or more specific attributes or characteristics.[43] This form of advertising became a legitimate and popular practice after the Federal Trade Commission (FTC) began advocating its use in 1972. The FTC reasoned that the direct comparison of brands would provide more pertinent product information to consumers and thus a more rational basis for making purchase decisions. Television networks cooperated with the FTC by lifting their ban on comparative ads, and the result has been a flurry of comparative commercials. It has been estimated that nearly 35 percent of all television ads are comparative messages.[44]

The decision to use a comparative message involves a number of considerations including consumers' response to the ad, perceptions of credibility, characteristics of the target audience, and the company's position in the market. An initial reason offered for using a comparative ad was that consumers would be more likely to pay attention to this type of message because of its novelty. However, since comparative ads have become so common, their attention-getting value has probably declined.

It has been shown that viewers of comparative messages demonstrate higher recall of message content than viewers of noncomparative messages. However, comparative ads have generally not been shown to be more effective than noncomparative

➤ *Exhibit 7–16*   **Rational appeals are often used in selling products to organizations such as hospitals**

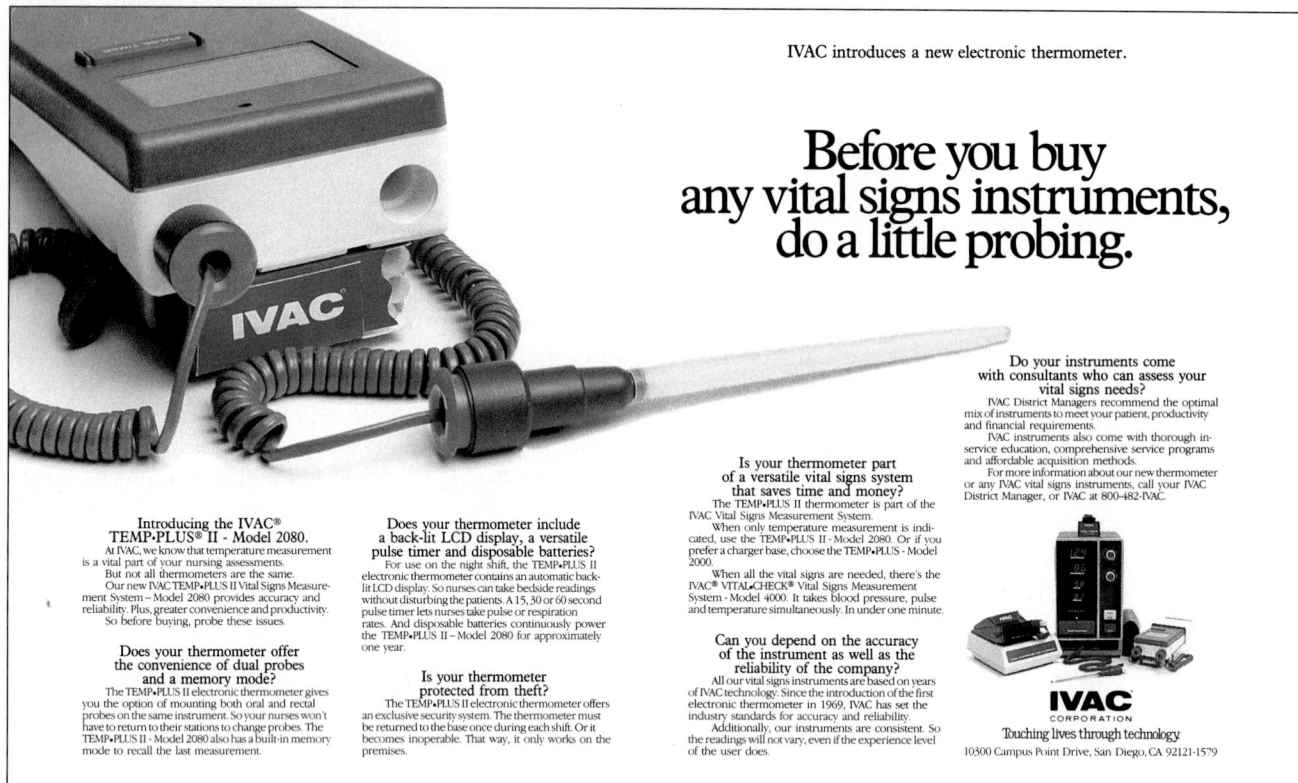

messages with respect to response variables such as brand attitudes or purchase intentions.[45] The advertiser must also consider how comparative messages might impact the credibility of the message. Consumers may perceive comparative ads as less believable and more offensive than noncomparative messages. Users of the brand that is attacked in the comparative message may be particularly skeptical about the credibility of the advertiser's claims.

Comparative advertising may be particularly useful for new brands. Comparative advertising allows a new market entrant to position itself directly against the more established brands and to promote its distinctive advantages relative to these competitors. Direct comparisons provide a new brand with a way of positioning itself in the "evoked" or choice set of brands the customer might be considering. For example, Ricoh Copiers used comparative messages when first introduced to position itself in the market with large companies such as IBM and Xerox. In the comparative ad shown in Exhibit 7–17, California Slim compares its brand to Ultra Slim-Fast, the leading brand in the nutrition meal replacement drink market.

Generally, comparative advertising is used the most by brands with the least to lose, which are those with the smallest market share. These brands will often compare themselves with the market leader, hoping to create an association with the established brand and to tap into the market segment the leader has carved out. Market leaders, on the other hand, are often hesitant to use comparison ads, as most believe they have little to gain by featuring competitors' products in their ads. There are exceptions, of course, such as when Coca-Cola resorted to comparative advertising in response to challenges made by Pepsi that were reducing Coke's market share.

Emotional appeals

While rational appeals attempt to present useful information and influence consumers' logical, cognitive thought processes, advertisers often attempt to appeal to their

> *Exhibit 7–17*
California Slim uses a comparative message to position itself against Ultra Slim-Fast

> *Exhibit 7–18*
General Foods uses an emotional appeal for its International Coffees

feelings and emotions. The use of **emotional appeals** in advertising is really nothing new; companies such as AT&T, Hallmark, Kodak, and various life insurance companies have been utilizing this form of advertising for years. What is relatively new, however, is the number of companies in a variety of product/service areas that have turned to emotionally based advertising appeals. During the 1980s, many packaged-goods advertisers, which traditionally relied on rational arguments to sell their brands, began to recognize that emotional advertising can work effectively for them.[46] Marketers of products such as orange juice, toilet paper, bath towels, and coffee have turned to emotional appeals to differentiate their brands (Exhibit 7–18).

The increase in the use of emotional advertising appeals is due to several factors. First, the increased competition and similarity among brands that occur in the maturity stage of the product life cycle make it very difficult to differentiate a product using rational appeals. As one marketer noted:

Many advertisers have turned to sentiment because they've run out of compelling appeals to logic. Their own sales pitches have lost their punch and for the increasing number of products that don't differ markedly from their competitors, new arguments are hard to find.[47]

A second reason for using emotional appeals is that they can have a positive effect on consumers' reactions to the ad. Emotional arousal can enhance communication by increasing consumers' attention and their involvement with the ad and/or the brand. As we discussed in Chapter 6, the feelings generated by an ad have been shown to influence the nature of message processing and affect attitudes toward the ad itself as well as brand attitudes.[48]

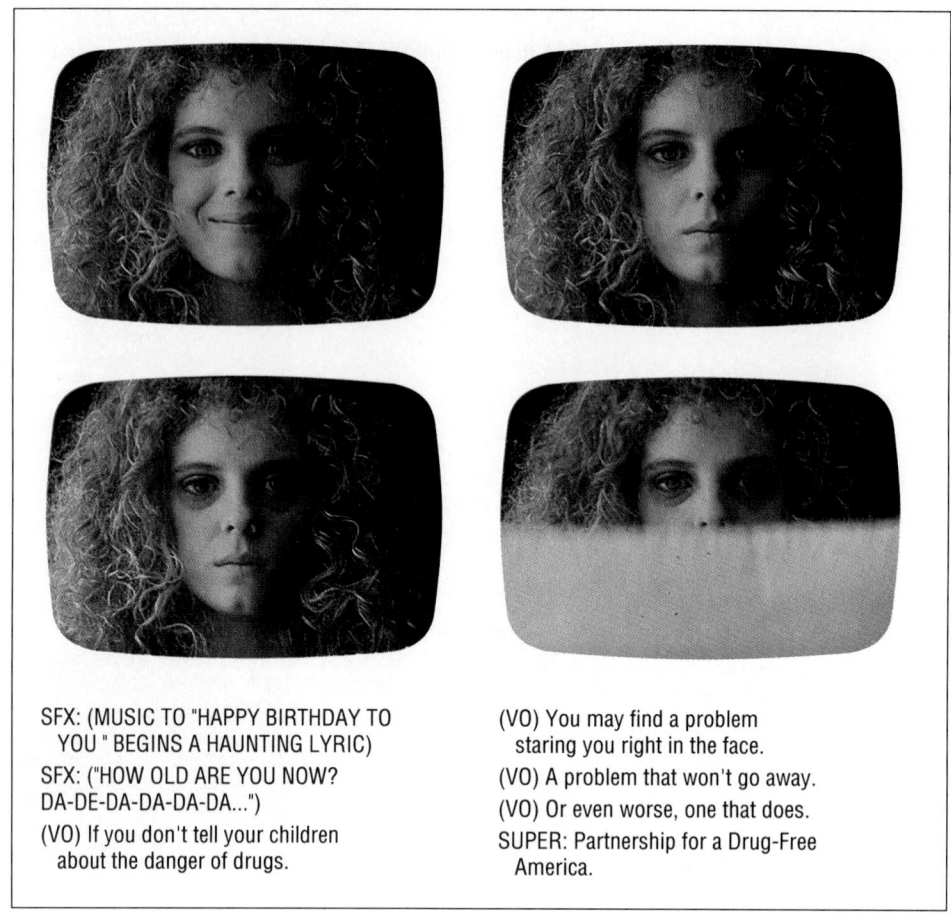

SFX: (MUSIC TO "HAPPY BIRTHDAY TO YOU " BEGINS A HAUNTING LYRIC)
SFX: ("HOW OLD ARE YOU NOW? DA-DE-DA-DA-DA-DA...")
(VO) If you don't tell your children about the danger of drugs.

(VO) You may find a problem staring you right in the face.
(VO) A problem that won't go away.
(VO) Or even worse, one that does.
SUPER: Partnership for a Drug-Free America.

Advertisers use a number of emotion-based appeals, as will be seen later in the book in our discussion of creative strategy (Chapters 10 and 11). However, two of the more prevalent and interesting emotional appeals are those that use fear and humor.

Fear appeals   Marketers sometimes use **fear appeals** in their messages to create anxiety in the audience and arouse individuals to act. Fear can be implemented in several ways. Some ads stress the physical danger or other negative consequences that can occur if attitudes or behaviors are not altered. For example, the American Cancer Society's anti-smoking ads stress that cigarette smoking is linked to lung cancer and other diseases and encourage consumers to stop smoking to protect their health. The negative consequences that can result from particular behaviors such as drunken driving or drug abuse are often shown in ads dealing with these problems (Exhibit 7–19). Fear appeals are also used to demonstrate negative consequences that may result if one does not engage in a particular behavior such as using a sunscreen or practicing regular dental hygiene.

Fear is also used through the threat of social disapproval or rejection that the individual might suffer if he or she does not use a particular product or service. Products such as deodorants, mouthwashes, and dandruff shampoos often appeal to the individual's need for approval and point out the embarrassment one might be saved from by using these products.

How fear operates   Before deciding to use a fear appeal-based message strategy, the advertiser should consider how fear operates, what level to use, and how different target audiences might respond to it. The relationship between the level of fear in a message and acceptance or persuasion has been shown to be *nonmonotonic* or

➤ *Exhibit 7–20*
Relationship between fear levels and message acceptance

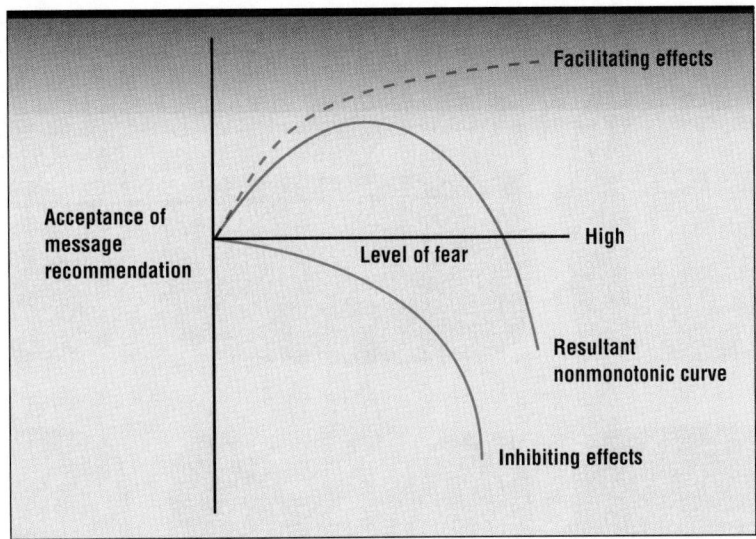

curvilinear, as shown in Exhibit 7–20. This means that with low levels of fear, message acceptance or persuasion increases as the amount of fear used rises. This increase in message acceptance does not continue, however, and beyond a certain point, acceptance or persuasion decreases as the level of fear rises.

This relationship between fear and persuasion can be explained by the fact that fear appeals have both facilitating and inhibiting effects.[49] A low level of fear can have *facilitating effects,* as it attracts attention and interest in the message and may motivate the receiver to act to resolve the problem presented in the ad. Thus, increasing the level of fear in a message from low to moderate can result in increased persuasion. High levels of fear, however, can produce *inhibiting effects* whereby the receiver may emotionally block out the message by tuning it out, selectively perceiving it, or denying the message arguments outright. Exhibit 7–20 illustrates how these two countereffects operate to produce the curvilinear relationship between fear and persuasion. For fear appeals to be successful, the level of fear utilized must be high enough to get the audience's interest and attention but not so high as to cause the consumer to reject or distort the message.

It is also important to consider the audience the message is targeted toward and how individuals might respond to fear appeals. Fear appeals are more effective when the message recipient is self-confident and less subject to anxieties and prefers to cope with dangers rather than avoid them.[50] They are also more effective among nonusers of a product than among users. Thus, a fear appeal may be more useful in refraining nonsmokers from starting than in persuading smokers to stop.

It has been suggested that fear appeals work best when the message provides the receiver with specific recommendations or actions to deal with the problem presented in the message. For example, ads for American Express Travelers Cheques show how a vacation can be ruined if you lose all your cash. However, the anxiety created is reduced by offering a solution to the problem—using the company's travelers checks and getting an immediate refund if they are lost or stolen.

Humor appeals At the opposite end of the emotional spectrum from fear appeals are messages that utilize humor. Humorous ads are often among the best known and remembered of all the advertising messages we see and/or hear and are also generally the most talked about. For example, as discussed in Chapter 1, the humorous commercials for Miller Lite beer were the basis of one of the most effective and longest-running ad campaigns ever developed. Many other advertisers have also used humor appeals very effectively. For example, Alaska Airlines uses humorous ads such as the

➤ *Exhibit 7–21*   Alaska Airlines uses humorous ads to poke fun at other airlines' service and treatment of customers

ANNCR: Many airlines offer reduced rate fares. Unfortunately, that's not all they've reduced. It makes you wonder . . . what's next?

MAN (addressing other passengers): I'd appreciate it. Do you

have four quarters for a dollar? Anybody have two quarters for a dollar? Yes, miss. Do you have two quarters for two dollars? Two quarters for five dollars, please? Oh, boy, I'd appreciate it. Any-

body have two quarters for five dollars?

ANNCR: On Alaska Airlines, we have low fares, too. But you'd never know it by the way we treat you.

one shown in Exhibit 7–21 to poke fun at the level of service on some airlines and the way they treat their customers.

An advertiser might choose to use a humorous message for many reasons. Humorous messages are often more effective in attracting and holding consumers' attention and interest than are serious advertisements. Humor can also enhance the effectiveness of a message by putting the consumer in a positive mood. Positive moods not only may result in increased affect or liking of the ad itself but might also enhance the receiver's feeling toward the product or service. It has also been suggested that humorous commercials are effective because the humor can act as a distraction and thereby reduce the likelihood of the receiver's counterarguing against the message.[51]

While the factors noted above provide good reasons for using humor, not all marketing and advertising executives believe humorous appeals are the best way to spend their advertising dollars. Many think that while humor may be effective in drawing attention to the ad, it is often done at the expense of the message content. There is concern that humor can distract attention from the brand and its attributes and toward the humorous situation or person depicted in the ad. Also, effective humor can be very difficult to produce, and the end result is often a message that is too subtle to be understood by mass audiences. Thus, many advertisers prefer to use hard-sell, rational appeals that emphasize product attributes and key selling points rather than attempting to induce persuasion through a humorous appeal.

Obviously, there are valid reasons both for and against the use of humor in advertising, and not every product or service will lend itself to the use of a humorous appeal. An interesting study examined the viewpoints of advertising executives concerning the communication effectiveness of humor by surveying the research and

➤ *Exhibit 7–22*
Summary of study of top advertising agency research and creative directors' opinions regarding use of humor

---

Humor does aid awareness and attention, which are the objectives best achieved by its use.
Humor may harm recall and comprehension in general.
  Humor may aid name and simple copy registration.
  Humor may harm complex copy registration.
  Humor may aid retention.
Persuasion in general is not aided by humor.
  Humor may aid persuasion to switch brands.
  Humor creates a positive mood that enhances persuasion.
Source credibility is not aided by humor.
Humor is generally not very effective in bringing about action/sales.
Creatives are more positive on the use of humor to fulfill all the above objectives than the research director.
Radio and TV are the best media to use humor, whereas direct mail and newspaper are least suited.
Consumer nondurables and business services are best suited to humor, whereas corporate advertising and industrial products are least suited.
Humor should be related to the product.
Humor should not be used with sensitive goods or services.
Audiences that are younger, better educated, upscale, male, and professional are best suited to humor; older, less educated, and downscale groups are least suited to humor appeals.

---

creative directors of the top 150 advertising agencies. The directors were asked questions regarding which communications objectives are facilitated through the use of humor and the appropriate situational use of humor in terms of media, product, and audience factors. The general conclusions of this study are shown in Exhibit 7–22.

Channel Factors

Thus far, our discussion of variables affecting the communications process has examined characteristics of the source or communicator and options regarding message structure and appeals. We have seen that effective communication often depends on the type of message employed and the person utilized to deliver this message. The final controllable variable of the communications process to be considered is the *channel* or *medium* used to deliver the message to the target audience. While a variety of methods are available to transmit marketing communications, as noted in Chapter 6, they can be classified into two broad categories, *personal* and *nonpersonal* media. Let us consider some of the differences between these two communications modalities.

Personal versus Nonpersonal Channels

There are a number of basic differences between personal and nonpersonal communications channels. Information received from personal influence channels is generally more persuasive than is information received via the mass media. Reasons for the differences in the persuasive impact of personal versus mass media are summarized quite well in the following comparison of advertising versus personal selling:

> From the standpoint of persuasion, a sales message is far more flexible, personal and powerful than an advertisement. An advertisement is normally prepared by persons having minimal personal contact with customers. The message is designed to appeal to a large number of persons. By contrast, the message in a good sales presentation is not determined in advance. The salesman has a tremendous store of knowledge about his product or service and selects appropriate items as the interview progresses. Thus the salesman can adapt this to the thinking and needs of the customer or prospect at the time of the sales call. Furthermore, as objections arise and are voiced by the buyer, the salesman can treat the objections in an appropriate manner. This is not possible in advertising.[52]

Effects of Alternative Mass Media

The various mass media that advertisers use to transmit their persuasive messages differ in many ways including the number and type of people they reach, their costs, and their information-processing requirements and qualitative factors. Evaluation of mass media in terms of how efficiently they expose a target audience to a communication is important, as we will see in the media chapters. However, we should also recognize there are important differences in advertising media with respect to the effect they have on information processing and communications are also influenced by the context or environment in which they appear.

Differences in information processing

Very basic differences among alternative mass media are the manner and rate at which information is transmitted and can be processed by the message recipient. Information from ads in print media, such as newspapers, magazines, or direct mail, is *self-paced media.* An individual reading a print ad processes the information at his or her own rate and can read or study the ad as long as is desired. In contrast, information from the broadcast media of radio and television is *externally paced media,* as the information transmission rate is controlled by the medium rather than by the message recipient.

The difference in the processing rate for print and broadcast media has some obvious implications for advertisers. Self-paced print media make it easier for the message recipient to process a long, complex message that may be difficult to understand. Thus, advertisers often use print ads when they want to present a detailed message with a lot of information. The ad for Apple's Macintosh Quadra personal computer shown in Exhibit 7–23 is an example. When broadcast media are used, however, the advertiser cannot use a detailed or complex message and must be careful to ensure that the information that is transmitted is understood. Thus, broadcast media may be more effective for transmitting shorter messages or, in the case of television, for presenting pictorial information along with a verbal message.

While there are limitations to the length and complexity that can be used in broadcast messages, advertisers can deal with this problem. One strategy is to use a radio or television ad to get consumers' attention and direct them to specific print media for a more detailed message. For example, a real estate developer may use radio ads to draw attention to a housing development and direct the listener to the real estate section of the newspaper for more details. Or advertisers can develop a broadcast and print version of the same message. The copy portion of the message will be similar in both media, but the print version of the ad can be processed at a rate that is comfortable to the individual receiver.

Effects of Context and Environment

Reactions to and interpretation of an advertising message can be a function of not only the message content but also the context or environment in which the ad appears. The famous communication theorist Marshall McLuhan's thesis "the medium is the message" implies that the medium communicates an image that is independent of any message it contains.[53] The notion of a **qualitative media effect** refers to the positive or negative influence the medium may contribute to the message. The medium may affect reactions to the message either through the image of the media vehicle itself or through the reception environment that is created.

For example, an advertisement for a high-quality men's clothing line might have more of a significant impact in a prestigious magazine such as *The New Yorker* or *Esquire* than in *Sports Afield* or *National Lampoon.* The former two magazines create a more appropriate reception environment for this type of advertising than the latter two. Advertisements can draw qualitative value from certain media because of the editorial content of the publication and the type of people attracted to it and the meaning or role the medium plays in the lives of consumers. An avid skier may respond very positively to an ad for ski boots in *Skiing* magazine partly because the articles, pictures, and other ads have gotten the reader excited over the upcoming ski season.

Media environments can also be created by the nature of the program in which a commercial appears. For example, a study of consumers' reactions to commercials shown during a happy-mood television program versus a sad-mood program found

➤ *Exhibit 7–23*
Messages containing a great deal of information are best suited to print media

that the happy program not only created a more positive mood state but also resulted in greater perceived commercial effectiveness, more favorable cognitive responses, and better recall relative to the sad program.[54]

Advertisers may pay premium dollars to advertise on programs that are popular and create very positive moods. For example, the Olympics is a very popular media purchase among television advertisers as they seek to become a part of the excitement and festivities associated with the event (Exhibit 7–24). Christmas specials are another example of programs that can create favorable moods.

Sometimes advertisers avoid certain media environments if they think the program might create a negative mood among viewers, or if they believe association with a program may be detrimental to the company or its products. For example, many companies have ceased advertising on programs that have excessive violence or sex in them. A few years ago, Chrysler withdrew its advertising from the ABC network miniseries *Amerika*, which was about life in the United States after a Soviet takeover. The company indicated the subject matter and its portrayal were too intense and emotional and its upbeat product commercials would be both inappropriate and of limited effectiveness in that viewing environment.[55] Coca-Cola has a corporate policy not to advertise on television news programs because it thinks bad news is inconsistent with the image of Coke as an upbeat, fun product. General Foods advertises coffee on news programs but not food products. A company spokesperson noted, "When a food commercial arrives after the reporting of hard news, you may have destroyed that feeling about food."[56]

Clutter

Another aspect of the media environment that is important to advertisers is the problem of **clutter,** which refers to all the nonprogram material that appears in the broadcast environment, including commercials, promotional messages for shows, public service announcements, and the like. Clutter has become an increasing concern to advertisers, as there are simply too many messages competing for the consumer's attention, and it has become very difficult for the advertising for any one brand to get noticed.[57] The clutter problem has become compounded in television advertising by increases in nonprogram time and the trend toward shorter commercials. The 30-second commercial, which became the industry standard in the 1970s,

➤ *Exhibit 7–24*   **The Olympic Games are a very favorable advertising environment**

(MUSIC THROUGHOUT)
ANNCR: (VO) This neighborhood produces most of our Olympic team stars.
It's where you'll find the Emerson Flag Company.

They send thousands of flags to the Olympic Games
and for rush orders they use
Express Mail from the Postal Service.
It offers convenient pick up service,

guaranteed overnight delivery,
plus great low prices
which could help a small company like this have a banner year.
SINGERS: WE DELIVER FOR YOU.
(MUSIC OUT)

replacing 60-second spots, is giving way to 15-second commercials. Many advertisers are requesting 15-second spots, which is causing concern among the networks because of the clutter problem.

The advertising industry continues to express concern over the highly cluttered commercial viewing environment. Advertisers are increasingly turning to techniques such as humor, use of celebrity spokespersons, or other novel and/or unique, creative approaches as ways of breaking through the clutter and drawing attention to their messages. Promotional Perspective 7–4 discusses some recent concerns over the problem of increasing clutter.

Obviously, there are numerous other characteristics regarding source, message, and channel factors that must be considered in developing an advertising and promotional program.[58] Our goal in this chapter has been to provide a broad overview of some of the factors that must be considered regarding these communications variables and how they influence the response process of the message recipient. We consider these communications variables again later in the text. In Chapters 12 through 14, specific characteristics of the print and broadcast media are discussed along with media strategy, whereas in Chapter 10 we examine creative strategy and the development of advertising messages and campaigns.

SUMMARY

This chapter focused on the controllable variables that are part of the communications process, including source, message, and channel factors. Decisions regarding each of these variables should consider the impact on the various stages or steps of

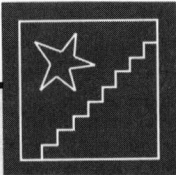

Promotional Perspective 7–4

Too Many Commercials in Prime Time

How many minutes of commercials do you think there are per hour of prime-time programming on the three major television networks (ABC, CBS, NBC)? If you are like most people, your answer is probably "too many!" TV viewers are not the only ones annoyed by all of the commercials and other clutter during prime time such as public service announcements and promotional spots for upcoming shows. Advertisers and the major agencies have complained to the networks for years about the clutter problem. They argue that it annoys the consumer, and too many commercials compete for attention and remembrance, which makes it difficult to communicate effectively.

A new study by the Association of National Advertisers and the American Association of Advertising Agencies shows that these concerns are justified. The study found that the amount of clutter increased as much as 14 percent between 1983 and 1991. Nonprogram time at CBS jumped from 9 minutes and 46 seconds per prime-time hour in 1983 to 11 minutes and 6 seconds per hour in 1991, a 14 percent increase. NBC had a total of 11 minutes of nonprogram time per hour in 1991, a 13 percent increase over the 9 minutes and 45 seconds the network ran in 1983. The smallest increase was the 5 percent at ABC, which ran only 10 minutes and 16 seconds of ads in 1991 compared to 9 minutes and 45 seconds in 1983.

Compounding the problem is that many prime-time shows have even higher clutter levels. The study found that popular shows such as NBC's *"Seinfeld"* had the equivalent of 16 minutes and 24 seconds of nonprogramming time per hour, and ABC's *"Full House"* contained the one-hour equivalent of 15 minutes and 12 seconds (in this study, clutter times in half-hour shows were doubled). The networks add more commercials to hit shows because they can charge more for the spots. However, it has also been argued that advertisers and their agencies perpetuate this problem because they pressure the networks to squeeze their ads into top-rated shows with the largest audi-

ences. Yet another part of the problem of "competitive clutter" is showing ads for competing products during the same program. A study by Robert Kent, a marketing professor at Drexel University, found that airing competing ads in the same program can reduce memorability by 25 to 40 percent.

Advertisers and the major agencies are concerned over the clutter problem and the fact that the networks have been adding commercial time to the more popular shows without telling them. Many agencies are asking the networks to renegotiate the upfront deals they have made for their clients. They argue that compensation is due if the number of actual commercial minutes in a program exceeds what they were told during negotiations. Agency media buyers are asking the networks to commit to a minimum amount of program time and then manage the nonprogram portion however they see fit. Thus, if the networks want to add more commercials, it would come out of their promos, public service announcements, or program credit time.

The networks may not acquiesce to the requests to cut back on the number of commercials and other forms of clutter. All three networks have been experiencing financial difficulties in recent years and need the revenue that commercials generate. They also note that the three major networks devote less time to commercials than Fox, cable networks, or syndicated programs. Ultimately, the viewers may determine when clutter has gotten out of control. Unless consumers complain about being bombarded with too many messages, the networks are unlikely to cut back on commercial time that can bring in more than $5,000 or more per second.

Source: Joanne Lipman, "Prime-Time Commercial Loads Grow," *The Wall Street Journal*, February 10, 1992, B6; Joe Mandese, "Study Finds Shows with Worst Clutter," *Advertising Age*, February 17, 1992, pp. 3, 61; and Joe Mandese, "Fight Looms over TV Clutter," *Advertising Age*, September 23, 1991, pp. 1, 42.

---

the response hierarchy the message receiver passes through. The persuasion matrix was presented for use in assessing the effect of controllable communication decisions on the response process.

Selection of the appropriate source or communicator to deliver a message is an important aspect of communication strategy. Three important attributes or characteristics were examined, including source credibility, attractiveness, and power, along with the process by which they might induce attitude or opinion change. Marketers utilize source characteristics to enhance message effectiveness by hiring communicators who are experts in a particular area and/or have a very trustworthy image. The use of attractive communicators such as celebrities to deliver advertising messages has become very popular; advertisers hope they will catch the receivers' attention and influence their attitudes or behavior through an identification process. Attention was given to the meaning a celebrity brings to the endorsement process and the importance of matching the meaning or image of the celebrity with that of the company or brand.

The design of the advertising message is a critical part of the communications process. Attention was given to various options regarding message structure, including order of presentation of message arguments, conclusion drawing, message sidedness, and use of refutational appeals. The advantages and disadvantages of different message appeal strategies were considered including rational appeals, such as comparative messages, and emotional appeals, such as fear and humor.

Finally, attention was focused on the channel or medium used to deliver the message. Differences in personal and nonpersonal channels of communication were discussed. Alternative mass media can have an effect on the communications process as a result of information processing and qualitative factors. The context in which an ad appears and the reception environment are important factors to consider in the selection of mass media. Clutter has become a serious problem for advertisers, particularly on television where commercials have become shorter and more numerous.

KEY TERMS

persuasion matrix
source
credibility
expertise
trustworthiness
internalization
sleeper effect
attractiveness

identification
source power
compliance
primacy effect
recency effect
one-sided message
two-sided message

refutational appeal
rational appeals
comparative advertising
emotional appeals
fear appeals
qualitative media effect
clutter

DISCUSSION QUESTIONS

1. Choose a particular print ad or television commercial currently being used by a company and use the persuasion matrix to analyze how it might influence the consumer's response process.
2. What are the basic components of source credibility? Discuss how these credibility components are utilized in marketing communications.
3. Discuss the various components of source attractiveness. Provide examples of how attractiveness is used in advertising.
4. Choose three celebrities currently being used as advertising spokespersons and analyze their endorsement, using the meaning transfer model presented in Exhibit 7–11.
5. Discuss the pros and cons of using celebrities as advertising spokespersons. Provide examples of two celebrities who you believe are very appropriate (or inappropriate) for the brands they are endorsing and explain why.
6. Do you think companies such as Pepsi-Cola and Quaker Oats can

justify paying celebrities such as Michael Jackson or Michael Jordan and others millions of dollars to appear in their commercials? Support your position.
7. Discuss the pros and cons of using the following types of message structures or appeals:
   • One- and two-sided messages.
   • Messages that do or do not use a specific conclusion.
   • Comparative advertisements.
   • Fear appeals.
   • Humorous advertisements.
8. Analyze the use of fear appeal messages, such as the one shown in Exhibit 7–19, to deter drug abuse among teenagers and young adults. Do you think these ads are effective? Why or why not?
9. What is meant by a qualitative media effect? Choose several examples of media and analyze their qualitative factors.
10. What is meant by advertising clutter? What can advertisers and the media do to deal with the clutter problem?

chapter 8

Determining Advertising and Promotional Objectives

chapter objectives

> To analyze the importance and value of setting specific objectives for advertising and promotion.

> To examine the role objectives play in the promotional planning process and the relationship of promotional objectives to marketing objectives.

> To consider the differences between sales and communications objectives and issues regarding the use of each.

> To examine the DAGMAR approach to setting advertising objectives and its value and limitations.

> To examine some problems advertisers encounter in setting objectives and measuring their accomplishment.

I N F I N I T I.

A Shade, a Smell, a Sound, a Feeling: The Nissan Infiniti Campaign

In 1989, Nissan Motor Company's Infiniti division was about to introduce its two new luxury automobiles to the U.S. market. The Infiniti division was formed to manufacture and market cars to compete in the luxury sports sedan segment. This market included the established European imports such as BMW, Mercedes, Volvo, and Jaguar as well as two recently introduced Japanese luxury cars—the Acura (a division of Honda Motors) and the Lexus (a division of Toyota).

Many advertising agencies introduce new automobiles by immediately focusing on the cars and saying great things about them. However, Hill, Holliday, Connors, Cosmopulos, the agency for Infiniti, decided to take an unconventional approach by creating commercials and print ads that showed scenes of rocks, trees, clouds, the ocean, and even flying geese but never the cars. The ads' goal was to explain the philosophy behind the design of the new cars and to suggest the Infiniti be a new kind of luxury car—a "Japanese sense of luxury." The "Zenlike" advertising campaign began several months before the cars went on sale and kept the public in suspense by never showing the cars. The cars finally appeared in some ads just before their November debut, but only as a brief, blurred image flashing in the background. The abstract ad campaign continued for several months after the two new Infiniti models were available in dealer showrooms.

The teaser campaign used to launch the new Infiniti appeared to be very successful from a number of perspectives. The ads scored extremely high in surveys of advertising awareness; a monthly survey conducted for *Advertising Age* showed that after two months of running the campaign, Infiniti had the highest recall of any advertiser. Moreover, tracking studies showed that 80 percent of the consumers in the target audience could identify the car's logo just six weeks into the campaign. Even more important, the ads were very effective in generating requests for information about the cars and visits to dealer showrooms. For example, the company stated that more than 60,000 people called for information and 35,000 visited dealer showrooms during the first two months following the introduction of the Infiniti.

Despite the apparent success of the advertising campaign, initial sales of the Infiniti were well below forecasts; only 1,700 cars were sold in the first two months. Some automotive industry analysts argued that the sluggish sales prompted the company to accelerate its move out of the image-oriented, launch campaign and respond to dealer demands for more product-oriented advertising. By spring 1990, a new campaign was launched that relied on pictures of cars and highlighted specific features and benefits of the Infiniti (Exhibit 8–1).

The unconventional ads used to introduce the Infiniti became one of the most talked about and controversial advertising campaigns in recent memory. The campaign also triggered a debate over the role of advertising in the

> *Exhibit 8–1*
A few months after launch Infiniti switched to product-oriented advertising

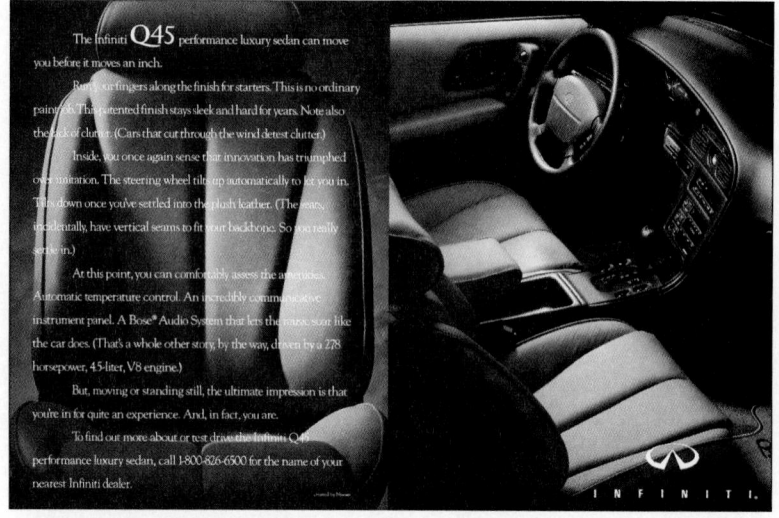

> *Exhibit 8–2*
The 1992 campaign for the Infiniti focuses on the personality of the car and those who drive it

(*continued*)

marketing of automobiles. Many advertising and marketing experts criticized the campaign for not focusing sooner on the cars and their features. They argued that while the "rocks and trees" approach to advertising may have raised awareness and curiosity levels, it failed to develop a distinct image and position for the Infiniti that would motivate consumers to choose the car over competing luxury sports sedans. However, others thought the campaign represented a bold and different creative move that was very successful in breaking through the clutter and grabbing the consumers' attention. They argued that the function of automobile advertising is to capture the consumers' interest and attention and get them into the showroom. From there the dealer and the product have to take over and complete the sale.

So what does Infiniti think about all of this? The company has argued from the beginning that it was primarily interested in long-term sales and performance and that the nature campaign successfully outlined its corpo-

rate philosophy. Once this was accomplished, the company was ready to move on to a more product-oriented advertising approach. By the end of 1991, Infiniti was selling more than 33,000 cars a year, which the company says is consistent with the objectives set in 1989.

And what about the advertising? After two years of traditional product-oriented ads, Infiniti returned to a somewhat riskier approach in 1992 that tries to promote the personality of the cars, the company, and its customers. The new ad campaign focuses on the enjoyment of owning and driving an Infiniti and is designed to appeal to the self-assured individual not seeking peer approval. And in case you were wondering, the 1992 ads do show the car, as can be seen in Exhibit 8–2.

Source: Bradley A. Stertz, "Nissan's Infiniti Gets Off to Slow Start," The Wall Street Journal, January 8, 1990, p. B6; Cleveland Horton, "Infiniti Finally Shows its Cars," Advertising Age, February 12, 1990, pp. 1, 56; "Infiniti Ads Trigger Auto Debate," Advertising Age, January 22, 1990, p. 49; and Cleveland Horton, "Infiniti Drives Back to Edge," Advertising Age, December 16, 1991, pp. 1, 30.

The introductory advertising campaign for the Infiniti illustrates the importance often assigned to a company's advertising and promotional program. The unconventional, teaser ad campaign that introduced the Infiniti generated much attention and discussion. However, the advertising campaign was only part of a well-planned and executed marketing strategy developed by Nissan. This strategy called for the formation of the Infiniti division as a way for Nissan to compete in the upscale, luxury sports sedan segment of the U.S. automobile market. It included establishing a separate dealership network, designing dealer showrooms in an Oriental decor, and training dealers and their employees in the Japanese way of doing business. The marketing strategy called for Infiniti to create a "Japanese sense of luxury" and not simply to sell a car but to promote the environment in which the cars would be sold and serviced. The marketing plan called for 2,500 cars to be sold each month by the end of 1990.[1]

The introductory advertising campaign was developed with Nissan's marketing strategy for the Infiniti in mind. Nissan allocated more than $60 million to the launch campaign so communication objectives, such as creating high levels of awareness and interest among consumers identified as prospects for buying a luxury sports sedan, could be achieved. According to the Infiniti advertising director, the campaign was also designed to create a Japanese aura and communicate to consumers that "the Infiniti would offer a different kind of luxury because it conforms to the Japanese concept of luxury."[2] Measures of advertising awareness, brand logo identification, and showroom visits helped Infiniti determine that the awareness and interest objectives were being met.

Many critics argue that while "the Japanese sense of luxury" positioning concept may have been communicated effectively, the low level of initial sales suggests Infiniti was not sending the right message to the luxury car buyer. The issue here, however, is not whether Infiniti's advertising campaign positioned the car properly, but rather to demonstrate the role objectives play in developing a marketing communications program. And we want to stress that communication objectives are derived from the role advertising and other forms of promotion play in the marketing strategy and program.

Unfortunately, many companies have difficulty with what many view as the most critical step in the promotional planning process—the setting of realistic objectives that will guide the development of the integrated marketing communications program. Complex marketing situations, conflicting perspectives regarding the role and function of advertising and other promotional mix elements and what they are expected to accomplish, and uncertainty over resources make the setting of marketing communication objectives "a job of creating order out of chaos."[3] While the task of setting objectives can be complex and difficult, this must be done properly because specific goals and objectives are the foundation on which all other promotional decisions are made. Budgeting for advertising and other promotional areas, as well as creative and media strategies and tactics, evolves from the objectives that have been set and what must be done to attain them. Clearly stated objectives also provide a goal or standard against which performance can be measured and evaluated.

Although setting specific advertising and promotional objectives should be an integral part of the planning process, many companies either fail to set objectives for their promotional program or set them so they are inappropriate or inadequate for guiding the development of the promotional plan or guiding its effectiveness. Many marketers are uncertain as to what advertising and promotion can, or should be expected to, contribute to the marketing program. To many managers, the goal of their company's advertising and promotional program is quite simple: to generate sales. They fail to recognize what is required in preparing customers to buy a particular product or service and the specific tasks that advertising and other promotional mix variables must perform before a sale results.

As we know, advertising and promotion are not the only marketing activities involved in generating sales. Moreover, it is not always possible to measure the effects of advertising in terms of sales. For example, the Dow Chemical ad shown in

"When I was growin' up, Mom and Dad taught me that we've only got one planet, and we'd better take care of it. Now I'm about to join a company that's committed itself to helping people preserve our wildlife...and to finding new ways to protect the earth.

I can't wait."

Dow lets you do great things.
DOW.

Exhibit 8–3 is designed to promote the company as a desirable place to work among prospective employees such as college students. Consider for a moment the ad shown in Exhibit 8–4 for beta carotene's ability to reduce cancer risks. What objectives might the sponsor, Hoffmann-LaRoche Inc., have for this ad and how might the company determine its effectiveness?

In this chapter, we examine the nature and purpose of advertising and promotional objectives and the role they play in guiding and controlling promotional decision making. Attention is given to the various types of objectives appropriate for different situations. We also examine a specific model that has been used effectively for many years as a method for setting advertising objectives.

The Value of Objectives

Perhaps one of the reasons many companies fail to set specific objectives for their advertising and promotional programs is that they fail to recognize the value of doing so. Advertising and promotional objectives are needed for several reasons, including the functions they serve in communication, planning and decision making, and measurement and evaluation.

Communications

Specific objectives for the promotional program serve as communications devices and facilitate coordination of the various groups working on the campaign. Many people are involved in the planning and development of an advertising campaign on the side of both the client and the agency. All the parties involved in the promotional campaign development and approval process must understand the roles advertising and other promotional mix elements are expected to play in the marketing plan and what is expected from these elements of the marketing program.

Coordination of the advertising and promotional program must occur within both the company and the agency, as well as between the two. Any other parties involved in the promotional campaign, such as public relations and/or sales promotion

➤ *Exhibit 8–4*
What do you think the objectives of this ad might be?

RESEARCH SHOWS SIX OF THE WAYS TO HELP REDUCE YOUR RISK OF CANCER. INCLUDING ONE WAY YOU MAY NOT KNOW.

1. Stop smoking now.
Your risk of getting lung cancer is much higher if you smoke. And the risk applies to cigars and pipes, as well as cigarettes.

2. Include fiber in your diet.
Eat foods that have a high fiber content, such as whole grain breads and cereals. Raw fruits, nuts and vegetables such as beans and peas are also good sources.

3. Cut down on fats.
Eat more fish and poultry, less red meats and other fatty foods. Broil, bake or roast, instead of frying.

4. Eat foods high in vitamins C and E.
There is scientific evidence that eating foods high in these "protective vitamins" may help reduce cancer risk and studies are continuing to identify their roles more clearly. You'll find vitamin C in citrus fruits and green leafy vegetables and vitamin E in whole grains and nuts.

5. Have regular medical check-ups.
At least once a year, unless your physician believes that you should be checked more frequently because of any particular health problem or family history.

6. Eat foods rich in Beta Carotene.
There is increasing evidence from research that including foods rich in Beta Carotene in your diet may help reduce your risk of certain cancers, particularly lung cancer. For example, *The New England Journal of Medicine** recently published a study done at Johns Hopkins University which showed a significantly lower occurrence of lung cancer in a group of people who had high blood levels of Beta Carotene.
   Where will you find Beta Carotene? In dark green leafy vegetables like broccoli, spinach and kale. Also carrots, pumpkins and sweet potatoes. Plus fruits, such as apricots, peaches, papayas, cantaloupe and similar melons.

*"Serum Beta Carotene, Vitamins A and E, Selenium and the Risk of Lung Cancer" New England Journal of Medicine, Nov. 13, 1986.

A health message from Hoffmann-La Roche Inc.

ROCHE

firms, research specialists, or media buying services, must also be aware of what the company hopes to accomplish through its marketing communications program. Many problems can be avoided if all parties involved have a set of written and approved objectives to guide their actions. The objectives can then serve as a common base for discussing issues related to the promotional program.

Planning and Decision Making

Specific promotional objectives also serve as a guide to the development of the advertising and promotional plan. As was noted earlier, all phases of a firm's promotional strategy will be developed and based on the established objectives, including budgeting, creative, and media decisions as well as the role of supportive programs such as public relations/publicity, sales promotion, and/or reseller support.

Specific and meaningful objectives can also be useful as a guide for decision making. Promotional planners are often faced with a number of strategy and tactic options in terms of choosing among various creative options, media selection, and allocation of the budget among various elements of the promotional mix. Choices among these options should be made on the basis of how well a particular strategy matches the firm's promotional objectives.

Measurement and Evaluation of Results

A very important reason for setting specific objectives is that they provide a benchmark or standard against which the success or failure of the promotional campaign can be measured. If specific objectives have not been set, it becomes extremely difficult to determine what was accomplished by the firm's advertising and promotion efforts. As we will see later in this chapter, one of the characteristics of good objectives is that they are *measurable;* that is, they include a specification of a method and criteria for determining how well the promotional program worked. By setting specific and meaningful objectives, the promotional planner is essentially providing a measure(s) that can be used to evaluate the effectiveness of the advertising campaign. Most organizations are concerned over the returns they get for their promotional investment, and a comparison of actual performance against measurable objectives is the best way to determine if the return on the advertising and promotion investment justifies the expense.

Determining Promotional Objectives

The determination of objectives for advertising and promotion occurs after a thorough situation analysis has been conducted and the marketing and promotional issues facing the company or a brand have been identified. A thorough situation analysis is critical to the marketing and promotional planning process, as this review becomes the foundation on which marketing objectives are determined and the marketing plan is developed. Promotional objectives evolve from the company's overall marketing plan and are rooted in the firm's marketing objectives. While advertising and promotion objectives are not the same as marketing objectives, many firms tend to treat the two as synonymous. Thus, a discussion of the differences between the two is in order.

Marketing versus Communications Objectives

Marketing objectives are generally stated in the firm's marketing plan and are statements of what is to be accomplished by the overall marketing program within a given time period. Marketing objectives are usually defined in terms of specific, measurable outcomes such as sales volume, market share, profits, or return on investment. Good marketing objectives should be quantified, include a delineation of the target market, and note the time frame for accomplishing the goal (often this is one year since this is the planning period used by most marketers). For example, a personal computer company may have as its marketing objective: "to increase sales by 10 percent in the small-business segment of the market during the next 12 months."

A company with a very high market share may seek to increase its sales volume by stimulating growth in the product category. This might be accomplished by increasing consumption by current users or encouraging nonusers to use the product. Some firms have as their marketing objectives increasing sales by expanding distribution of their product in certain market areas. Companies often have secondary marketing objectives that are related to actions they must take to solve specific problems and thus achieve their primary objectives. For example, ways to increase sales or market share may be to enhance product quality, improve trade relations, lower prices, or increase advertising.

As was noted earlier, objectives for advertising and promotion are derived from marketing objectives, as the planning of promotional strategy must consider what the firm hopes to achieve in terms of sales volume, market share, or other criteria and the secondary objectives related to these goals. Once the advertising or promotional manager has reviewed the marketing plan, he or she should have an understanding of where the company hopes to go with its marketing program, how it intends to get there, and the role advertising and promotion will play.

It should be recognized, however, that marketing goals defined in terms of criteria such as sales, profit, or market share increases are usually not appropriate as promotional objectives. These are objectives for the entire marketing program, and their achievement will depend on having the proper coordination and execution of all the marketing mix elements including product planning and production, pricing, and distribution, in addition to promotion.

Advertising objectives should be based on the particular communications tasks required to deliver the appropriate message to the target audience. This requires that the advertising manager be able to translate general marketing goals into communications goals and specific promotional objectives. Some guidance in doing this may be available from the marketing plan, as the situation analysis should provide the promotional planner with important information on factors such as

- The market segments the firm wants to target and information on the target audience such as demographics, psychographics, and purchase motives.
- Information on the product and its main features, advantages, benefits, uses, and applications.
- Information on the company's as well as competitors' brands such as sales and market share in various segments, positioning, competitive strategies, promotional expenditures, creative and media strategies, and tactics.
- Ideas on how the brand should be positioned and specific behavioral responses being sought such as trial, repurchase, brand switching, and increased usage.

For example, the ads for Del Monte stewed tomatoes and Snack Cups shown in Exhibit 8–5 were part of the company's marketing strategy to increase sales and market share for its various food products by targeting existing or lapsed users as well as new, younger customers. The 12-month, $20 million advertising campaign used a series of four-color ads featuring new recipe ideas or serving suggestions. All of the ads in the campaign used the same graphic format to help build the overall franchise for Del Monte brands while promoting individual products. The campaign resulted in increases in market share for all four of the advertised categories.

In some situations, the company may not have a formal marketing plan, and the information noted above may not be readily available. If this is the case, the promotional planner must attempt to gather as much information as possible about the product and its markets from sources both inside and outside the company.

After reviewing the information in the marketing plan or that gathered on his or her own, the promotional planner should have an understanding of how promotion fits into the marketing program and what the firm hopes to achieve through advertising and other promotional elements. The next step is to set specific objectives for advertising and other promotional mix variables in terms of communications goals or tasks.

Many promotional planners approach promotion from a communications perspective and agree that the objective of advertising is usually to communicate information or a selling message about a product or service. However, many managers view their promotional programs from a sales perspective and argue that sales or some related measure, such as market share, is the only meaningful goal for advertising and

➤ *Exhibit 8–5*
Ads for Del Monte food products were part of a marketing strategy designed to increase sales and market share

promotion and thus should be the basis for setting objectives. These two perspectives have been the topic of considerable debate and are worth examining further.

Sales versus Communications Objectives

Sales-Oriented Objectives

To many managers, the only meaningful objective for their promotional program is sales. They take the position that the basic reason a firm spends money on advertising and promotion is to sell its product or service. Spending on advertising and promotion represents an investment and allocation of a firm's scarce resources that require an economic justification. Rational managers generally evaluate and compare investment options on a common financial basis such as return on investment (ROI). As will be discussed in Chapter 9, determining the specific return on advertising and promotional dollars is often quite difficult. However, many managers believe that monies spent on advertising and other forms of promotion should produce measurable results such as increasing sales volume by a certain percentage or dollar amount or increasing the brand's market share. Thus, they argue that objectives (as well as the success or failure of the campaign) should be based on the achievement of sales results.

Some managers also prefer *sales-oriented objectives* since they think this makes the individuals involved in the advertising and promotional process think in terms of how the promotional program will influence sales. Another reason is that managers often tend to confuse marketing objectives with advertising and promotion objectives. For example, a firm's marketing goal may be to increase its sales level to $200 million. This goal not only becomes the basis of the marketing plan but also carries over as the primary objective of the promotional program as well. Thus, when the advertising and promotional campaign is being planned, the only guiding objective is the $200 million sales goal figure, and the success of the campaign is judged against attainment of this target.

Problems with sales objectives

Think about the situation described above. If the company failed to achieve its target sales level of $200 million, does this mean the advertising and promotional program was ineffective? Before answering this question, it might be helpful to compare this situation to that of a football game and think of the role of advertising as being

➢ *Exhibit 8–6*
Factors influencing sales

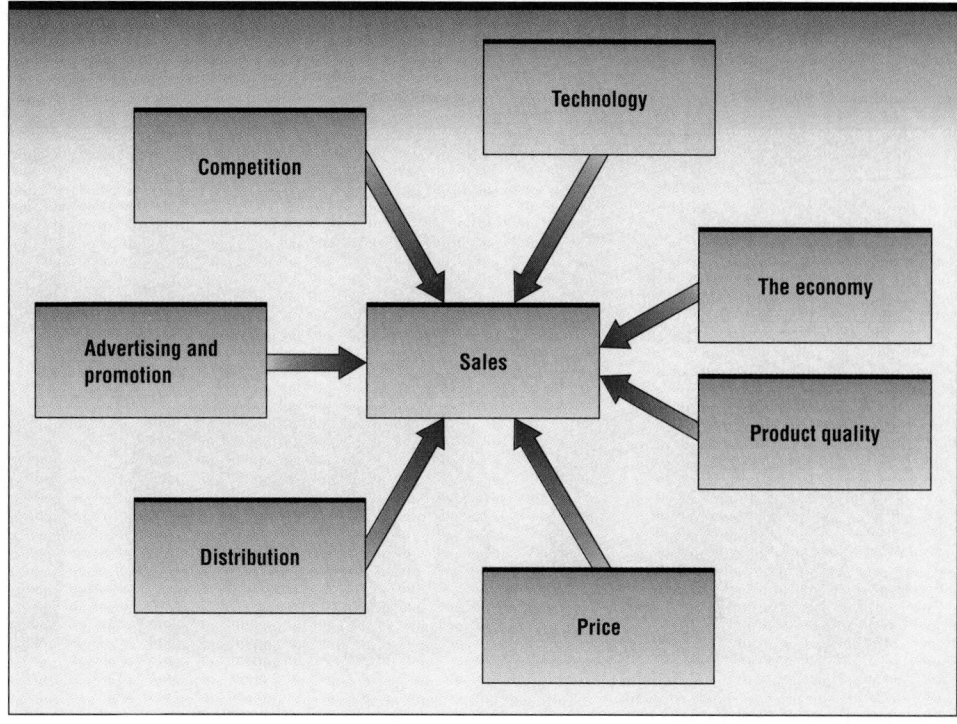

similar to that of a quarterback. The quarterback is often one of the most important players on the team but is only effective if the individual gets support from the other players. If the team loses, is it fair to blame the loss entirely on the quarterback? The answer to both questions is no. Just as the quarterback is but one of the players on the football team, promotion is but one element of the marketing program and there are many other explanations as to why the targeted sales level was not reached. In the football game, the quarterback is going to lead the team to victory only if the linemen block, the receivers catch the quarterback's passes, and the running backs help the offense establish a balanced attack of running and passing. The quarterback can play an outstanding game and the team can still lose if the defense gives up too many points.

In the business world, problems in achieving sales results could lie with any of the other marketing mix variables, including product design or quality, packaging, distribution, or pricing. The advertising program can be effective in making consumers aware of and interested in the brand, but this does not mean they will buy it, particularly if it is not readily available or is priced higher than a competing brand. As shown in Exhibit 8–6, sales are a function of many factors, not just advertising and promotion.

The Infiniti situation illustrates this problem well. Some automotive analysts argued that the reason for Infiniti's sluggish sales may have been due to product and competitive factors. For example, Toyota Motor Corporation had introduced its own luxury sports sedan line, the Lexus, just two months before the Infiniti hit the market. It has also been suggested that Nissan underestimated the competition it would face in the luxury car market from companies such as BMW, Mercedes, Volvo, Cadillac, and Ford's Lincoln line.[4]

There are other examples of situations where companies have experienced declining sales even though their campaigns were very effective in generating awareness and interest among consumers. For example, General Motors developed the "New Generation" campaign a few years ago to reposition its Oldsmobile line to appeal to baby boomers in their late 30s and early 40s. The campaign's TV commercials featured celebrities from the 1950s and 1960s being introduced to the new Oldsmobile cars

➤ *Exhibit 8–7*   The "New Generation" campaign increased awareness of Oldsmobile's advertising but did not help sell more cars

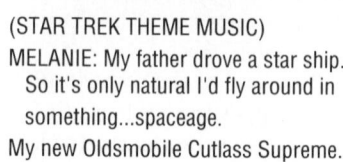

(STAR TREK THEME MUSIC)
MELANIE: My father drove a star ship.
  So it's only natural I'd fly around in
  something...spaceage.
My new Oldsmobile Cutlass Supreme...
totally redesigned for the future.
It's powered by a fuel injected V-6.

Monitored by an on-board computer.
I guess some things were just meant
  for the next generation.
(MUSIC: UP AND UNDER)
  SINGERS: THIS IS NOT...
YOUR FATHER'S OLDSMOBILE.
(SFX)

MELANIE: Ready Dad?
WILLIAM: I'm ready. You ready?
MELANIE: I'm ready .
WILLIAM: Steady as she goes.
SINGERS: THIS IS...
THE NEW GENERATION...
OF OLDS.

by their children (Exhibit 8–7). The campaign received critical acclaim and raised awareness of Oldsmobile advertising to an all-time high. However, despite the great ad campaign and a $120 million budget, Oldsmobile sales declined. The problem was believed to lie with the cars, as most of the Oldsmobile models were considered too bland to appeal to the younger automobile buyers targeted in the ads.[5]

Another problem with sales objectives is that the effects of advertising are not always immediate and often occur over an extended period. Many experts recognize that advertising has a lagged or **carryover effect** such that monies spent on advertising do not necessarily have an immediate impact on sales.[6] Advertising may create awareness, interest, and/or favorable attitudes toward a brand, but these feelings may not result in an actual purchase until the consumer enters the market for the product, which may occur later. A review of econometric studies that examined the duration of cumulative advertising effects found that for mature, frequently purchased, low-priced products, advertising's effect on sales lasts for up to nine months.[7]

When sales are used as a measure of promotional effectiveness, consideration must be given to the fact that the influence of advertising may not be evident during the period it occurs. Thus, sales results gathered either during or immediately after an advertising campaign will not always reflect its full impact. Models have been developed to account for the carryover effect of advertising and to help determine the long-term effect of advertising on sales.[8] However, the carryover effect adds to the difficulty of determining the precise relationship between advertising and sales.

Yet another problem with using sales objectives is that they offer little guidance or direction to those responsible for planning and developing the promotional program. The creative and media people working on the account need some direction as to the nature of the advertising message the company hopes to communicate, the

> *Exhibit 8–8*
Sales results are an appropriate objective for direct-response advertising

intended audience, and the particular effect or response sought. As we see later in this chapter, communications objectives are recommended because they provide operational guidelines for those involved in planning, developing, and executing the advertising and promotional program.

Where sales objectives are appropriate

As the preceding discussion reveals, there can be many problems in attempting to use sales as objectives for a promotional campaign. However, there are situations where sales objectives are appropriate. Certain types of advertising and promotion efforts are *direct action* in nature, as they attempt to induce the prospective customer to take immediate action in the form of some overt behavioral response. Direct-response advertising is an example of a type of advertising that evaluates its effectiveness on the basis of sales. Under this form of advertising, merchandise is advertised in material mailed to customers, in newspapers and magazines, or on television. The consumer purchases the merchandise through the mail or by calling an 800 number. The ad for the Escort radar detector shown in Exhibit 8–8 is an example of a product sold through direct-response advertising.

The direct-response advertiser generally sets objectives and measures success in terms of the level of sales response generated by the ad. For example, objectives for and the evaluation of a direct-response ad run on television are based on the number of orders received each time a station broadcasts one of the commercials. Because advertising is really the only form of communication and promotion used in this situation and response is generally immediate, setting objectives in terms of sales is appropriate.

Retail advertising, which accounts for a significant percentage of all advertising expenditures, is another area where the advertiser is often seeking a direct response,

➤ *Exhibit 8–9*
Retail advertising often has as an objective the generation of immediate sales

SAVE 34%
ALL MEN'S DESIGNER SUITS,
SPORTCOATS AND DRESS SLACKS
SIX DAYS ONLY!
WEDNESDAY, MAY 20, THROUGH
MONDAY, MAY 25
MAKE NO PAYMENT
UNTIL SEPTEMBER, 1992!
SEE REVERSE SIDE FOR DETAILS.

THE BROADWAY

particularly when sales or special events are being promoted. The ad for the Broadway's men's sale shown in Exhibit 8–9 is designed to attract consumers to stores during the sales period (and to generate sales volume). Broadway management can determine the effectiveness of its promotional effort by analyzing store traffic and sales volume during sale days and comparing them to figures for normal, nonsale days. As we saw in Chapter 2, retailers may also want to allocate advertising and promotional dollars to "image building" campaigns designed to create and enhance favorable impressions and perceptions about their stores. In this case, sales-oriented objectives would not be appropriate because the effectiveness of the campaign would be based on its ability to create or change consumers' perceptions or images of the store.

Sales-oriented objectives are also used when advertising plays a dominant role in a firm's marketing program and other factors are relatively stable. For example, many packaged-goods products compete in mature markets with established channels of distribution, stable competitive prices, and promotional budgets and sell products of similar quality. In this situation, advertising and sales promotion in particular are viewed as the key determinants of a brand's sales or market share, and thus it may be possible to isolate the effects of these promotional mix variables.[9] Many companies have accumulated enough market knowledge and experience with their advertising, sales promotion, and direct-marketing programs so as to have considerable insight into the sales levels that should be expected to result from their promotional efforts. Thus, they believe it is reasonable to set objectives and to evaluate the success of their promotional efforts in terms of sales results. The repositioning of established brands (discussed in Chapter 5) is often done with the goal of improving their sales or relative market share.

Advertising and promotional programs are prone to be evaluated in terms of sales, particularly when expectations are not being met. Marketing and brand managers are often under pressure to show sales results and often take a short-term

➤ *Exhibit 8–10*
Some ads have an objective of creating favorable attitudes

No one on earth has had as long and as loving a relationship with television as Americans. Because we're its most **RCA. NUMBER ONE WITH THE TOUGHEST CRITICS IN THE WORLD.** adoring fans and its most knowledgeable critics. After all, over time we've developed quite a keen and discriminating eye.

So it's not at all surprising that in a nation of experts, the camcorders, televisions and VCR's of choice come from the people who are responsible for nothing less than the most technological innovations in the industry. RCA.

Something that you'll find immediately apparent upon viewing one of our ColorTrak Monitor-Receivers. Perhaps that's why every major manufacturer of televisions, VCR's and camcorders in the world uses technology patented by RCA.

And it's technological superiority like this that has led more Americans to choose RCA video equipment than any other.

A fact we're quite proud of. After all, you can't receive higher critical acclaim than that. **RCA**

perspective in their evaluation of advertising and sales promotion programs. They are often looking for an explanation or a "quick fix" for declining sales or loss of market share, and advertising and/or sales promotion are often the first areas examined. The problems of making direct links between advertising and sales are ignored, and campaigns, as well as advertising agencies, may be changed if sales expectations are not being met. As was discussed in Chapter 3, many companies are asking their agencies to accept incentive-based compensation systems tied to actual sales performance. Thus, while sales may not be an appropriate objective in many advertising and promotional situations, many managers are inclined to keep a close eye on sales and market share figures and make changes in the promotional program when these numbers become stagnant or begin to decline.

Communications Objectives

While some marketers argue that promotional objectives should be based on sales, many recognize the problems associated with attempting to use sales-oriented objectives. In certain situations, the goal of advertising is not really sales oriented but rather is designed to enhance the image or reputation of the company or achieve some other nonbehavioral effect.

Given the problems inherent in the use of sales-oriented objectives, many marketers take the perspective that the primary role of promotional elements such as advertising is to communicate and thus efforts should be based on **communications objectives.** Advertising and other promotional efforts are viewed as being designed to accomplish various communications tasks such as creating awareness, brand knowledge and interest, favorable attitudes and image, and purchase intentions. The consumer is generally not expected to respond immediately after seeing an ad; rather, there is a realization that advertisers often have to provide the consumer with relevant information and create favorable predispositions toward the brand before purchase behavior will occur.

For example, the ad for RCA ColorTrak Monitor-Receivers shown in Exhibit 8–10 is designed to convince consumers of the product's technological superiority

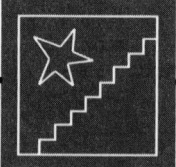

Promotional Perspective 8–1

For Some Companies the Objective Is Awareness

For most consumers, brand names of athletic shoe and apparel companies such as Nike and Reebok are household words. This is no accident. These industry leaders spend more than $100 million annually to advertise their products and keep their names in front of consumers. However, not all athletic shoe companies enjoy such high levels of name recognition, which makes competing against these well-known competitors all the more difficult. One such company is Avia Athletic Footwear, which began as a manufacturer of a high-quality line of aerobic shoes and then expanded its product line to include tennis, walking, cross-training, and running shoes.

In 1987, Avia was purchased by Reebok International, which decided to operate the company as an independent subsidiary. Avia has found that it can be quite difficult trying to compete against its parent company and Nike, which have advertising budgets more than 10 times larger than Avia's and a whole stable of star athletes to serve as endorsers and advertising spokespersons. A major challenge facing Avia has been making its name known to consumers. A 1991 survey found that only 4 percent of U.S. consumers knew Avia makes athletic shoes and sports apparel. As one brand-image consultant noted, selling an unknown product "is like rowing a boat upstream, movement is mostly backwards."

Avia has recognized the importance of capturing the public's attention and increasing its level of brand name recognition. Part of Avia's strategy has been to acknowledge that its name is not well known and turn its disadvantage into an advantage. In a recent campaign, Avia has been acknowledging, and even poking fun at, the fact that many consumers are unaware of its shoes. For example, Avia's ad agency produced a 60-second radio spot in which people at New York's Time Square, Boston's Faneuil Hall, Dallas-Fort Worth Airport, and other places are asked what they think the Avia name suggests. The answers range from "an Arab head covering like Arafat wears" to "a natural spring water" to "bathroom tissue, the two-ply kind they have out." The ads conclude with comments from those who have heard of Avia such as health club members and other fitness fanatics. Avia has also used print ads such as the accompanying one to acknowledge that its shoes are not for everyone and to position them as footwear for the serious athlete.

Avia isn't the only company that has faced brand awareness problems. Royal Crown Cola spends more than $40 million a year to ensure its name is not forgotten amid the barrage of advertising from Coca-Cola and PepsiCo, each of which spends over $400 million a year on advertising. While Coca-Cola's and Pepsi's ad spending is just 4 percent of annual sales, Royal Crown's budget is nearly 40 percent of sales. However, Royal Crown's communications director acknowledges the company has little choice but to advertise if it wants to compete against two of the most recognized brand names in the world.

Some companies that cannot afford to spend large sums of money on advertising have found creative ways to get their name in front of consumers. For example, Franklin Sports Industries was a small sports equipment manufacturer in 1980 with sales of about $15 million when it signed Philadelphia Phillies star third baseman Mike Schmidt to endorse its baseballs and gloves. Schmidt convinced President Irving Franklin that batting gloves were an unexploited opportunity for baseball. Franklin designed a glove that was contoured to fit around a bat and started handing them out to every major league ballplayer. The gloves, which sport the Franklin name in inch-high letters on the back of the hand, show up often on television when the camera focuses on a batter and have appeared on batters shown on the cover of major sports publications such as *Sports Illustrated*. Young baseball players are strongly influenced by major league players, and the exposure has helped make batting gloves a very profitable business for Franklin. Also, the name recognition created by its batting gloves has improved Franklin's credibility among sporting goods retailers where it was overshadowed by large competitors such as Spalding. By 1991, Franklin's annual sales had increased to about $65 million, despite spending only $1 million a year on advertising.

Nevica USA, a distributor of a British skiwear line, also used some ingenuity to get its name recognized when it entered the U.S. market in 1988 and lacked the money to run full-color ads in major skiing publications. The company president instructed her staff to find the photographers whose pictures appeared most frequently in ski magazines such as *Ski* and *Skiing*. The photographers were promised free skiwear and a fee each time one of their pictures featuring a skier wearing Nevica skiwear appeared

---

and create favorable attitudes toward the brand. While there is no call for immediate action in the ad, it is designed to create favorable impressions about the product such that consumers will consider this brand when they enter the market for video equipment.

Many marketers recognize that one of the biggest problems they face is that of creating and maintaining brand awareness, as is discussed in Promotional Perspective 8–1.

Advocates of communications-based objectives generally use some form of the hierarchical models discussed in Chapter 6 as a basis for setting advertising and

in one of the skiing magazines. The strategy helped Nevica get its name in front of skiers and retailers and now the company can afford to advertise in ski magazines.

Many companies and products fail because they never achieve, or cannot sustain, a proper level of awareness or recognition among consumers and retailers. These companies face a classic marketing paradox, however. They cannot generate sales without name recognition, but they do not have the money needed to create the brand or company recognition that produces sales. As can be seen from the examples discussed here, creativity is often necessary to get an unfamiliar brand noticed.

Source: Joseph Pereira, "Name of the Game: Brand Awareness," *The Wall Street Journal*, February 14, 1991, pp. B1, 5; and William M. Bulkeley, "It Needn't Always Cost a Bundle to Get Consumers to Notice Unfamiliar Brands," *The Wall Street Journal*, February 14, 1991, pp. B1, 5.

Avia's advertising acknowledges its low level of brand awareness

It doesn't bother us that most of them don't wear our shoes.

The Meg Millers of the world do.

Apparel product manager, wife, Yoga practitioner, chocolate nut, theatre goer and semi-fanatic walker. Meg Miller, Portland, Oregon. She's who we build shoes for. *AVIA*

promotion objectives. These hierarchy models vary somewhat in terms of the intermediate steps they use but essentially view the consumer as having to pass through three successive stages including a cognitive, affective, and conative sequence. The underlying logic of these models is that as consumers proceed through the successive stages, they move closer to making a purchase. Exhibit 8–11 shows the various steps in the Lavidge and Steiner hierarchy of effects model the consumer passes through in moving from awareness to purchase, along with examples of types of advertising or promotion relevant to each step.

➤ *Exhibit 8–11*
Effect of advertising on consumers: movement from awareness to action

Related behavioral dimensions	Movement toward purchase	Example of types of promotion or advertising relevant to various steps
Conative: The realm of motives. Ads stimulate or direct desires.	Purchase ⬆ Conviction ⬆	Point-of-purchase Retail store ads Deals "Last-chance" offers Price appeals Testimonials
Affective: The realm of emotions. Ads change attitudes and feelings.	Preference ⬆ Liking ⬆	Competitive ads Argumentative copy "Image" copy Status, glamour appeals
Cognitive: The realm of thoughts. Ads provide information and facts.	Knowledge ⬆ Awareness	Announcements Descriptive copy Classified ads Slogans Jingles Skywriting Teaser campaigns

Communications effects pyramid

A way of understanding communications tasks to be performed by advertising and promotion is to view them as being analogous to building a pyramid by accomplishing lower-level objectives such as awareness and knowledge or comprehension.[10] Subsequent tasks involve moving consumers who are aware of or knowledgeable about the product or service to higher levels in the pyramid. The initial stages, at the base of the pyramid, will be easier to accomplish than those toward the top, such as trial and repurchase or regular use. Thus, the percentage of prospective customers moved to each level will decline as they move up the pyramid. We use the communications effects pyramid presented in Exhibit 8–12 to show how a company introducing a new brand of shampoo targeted at 18- to 34-year-old females might set its advertising and promotion objectives.

The first task of the promotional program for a new product is to create a broad level of awareness among the target audience. This can be done through repetitive advertising in a variety of media that reach 18- to 34-year-old females such as magazines, television, and radio. Thus, the specific objective would be:

> To create a 90 percent awareness of Backstage shampoo among 18- to 34-year-old females during the first six weeks of the campaign.

The next step in the pyramid process is to communicate information so a certain percentage of the target audience will not only be aware of the new product but will

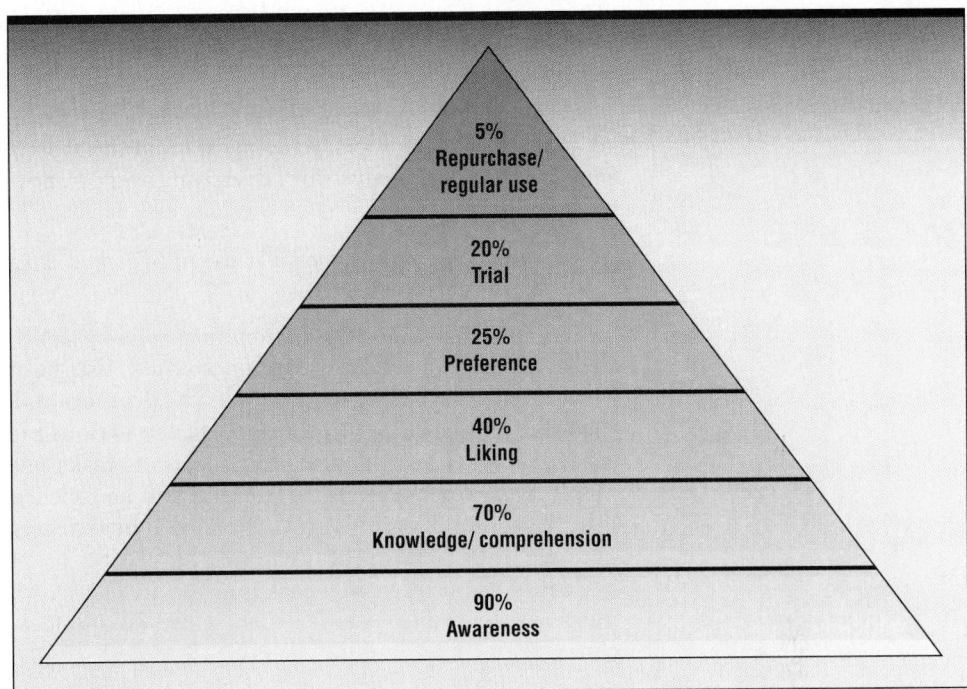

also understand its features and benefits. Let us assume the new Backstage brand is being positioned as a milder shampoo that contains no soap and improves the texture and shine of the hair. The specific objective for the second stage would be as follows:

> To communicate the specific benefits of Backstage shampoo—that it contains no soap and improves the texture and shine of the hair—among 70 percent of the target audience to make them interested in the brand.

At the next level, the promotional campaign is designed to create positive feelings toward the new Backstage brand. A certain percentage of the consumers who have been made aware of the new brand must be moved to the affective stages of liking and preference. To accomplish this, the advertising must effectively communicate the benefits so as to create favorable attitudes toward the product. Only a certain percentage of the target audience will develop a liking or positive feelings for the brand, and an even smaller number will be moved to the preference block. The specific objective at this stage would be:

> To create positive feelings toward Backstage shampoo among 40 percent of the target audience and a preference for the brand among 25 percent.

Once the preceding steps have been accomplished, a certain percentage of the target audience will move to the action stage at the top of the pyramid. The promotional plan may be designed to create trial among consumers that will be influenced not only by advertising but also by sales promotion techniques such as couponing and sampling. The objective at this stage might be:

> To use sampling and cents-off coupons, along with advertising, to elicit trial of Backstage shampoo among 20 percent of 18- to 34-year-old females during the first three months.

The ultimate goal of the promotional program is to make consumers loyal to the new brand so they will repurchase it. Repurchase and regular use of Backstage shampoo will depend on the consumers' evaluations and feelings after using it. However, the promotional program may call for continued advertising and periodic sales promotions not only to retain those consumers who have tried Backstage shampoo but also to take new consumers through the pyramid and get them to try the brand. The shampoo market is extremely competitive, with only a few brands having more than a 10 percent market share. Thus, the ultimate goal may be to get a percentage of women who try the brand to become regular users and to continue to attract new customers. Keeping in mind the aforementioned problems of attempting to use sales objectives for advertising and promotion, the final objective would be as follows:

> To develop and maintain regular use of Backstage shampoo among 5 percent of the 18- to 34-year-old females.

While we have used the communications pyramid to show how objectives would be set for a new brand, this model could also be used to determine promotional objectives for an established brand. The promotional planner must determine where the target audience lies with respect to the various blocks in the pyramid, as this will provide insight into what communications tasks need to be accomplished. For example, if awareness levels for a brand and knowledge of its features and benefits are low, the communications objective should be to increase them. Or these blocks of the pyramid may already be in place, but liking or preference may be low. In this situation, the advertising goal may be to change the target markets' attitudes or image of the brand to make them more favorable and move them through to purchase.

Problems with communications objectives

Not all marketing and advertising managers accept the idea of using communications objectives. Accomplishing communications objectives is seen as being of value only if this results in sales for the product, and they argue it is too difficult to translate a sales goal into a specific communications objective. However, it should be recognized that at some point a sales goal must be transformed into a communications objective. For example, if the marketing plan for an established brand has as an objective increasing sales by 10 percent, the promotional planner will eventually have to think in terms of the message that will be communicated to the target audience to achieve this. Possible objectives in this situation might include the following:

- Increasing the percentage of consumers in the target market that associate specific features, benefits, or advantages with our brand.
- Increasing the number of consumers in the target audience who prefer our product over the competition's.
- Encouraging current users of the product to use the product more frequently or in more situations.

In attempting to translate sales goals into specific communications objectives, promotional planners often are not sure what constitutes adequate levels of awareness, knowledge, liking, preference, or conviction. There are no formulas, books, or specific sources that can provide this information. The promotional manager will have to use personal experience along with that of others such as the brand or product managers as well as the marketing history of this and similar brands. Consideration should be given to norms or average scores on various communications measures for this or similar products, as well as the levels achieved by competitor's products. This information can be related to the amount of money and time spent building these levels as well as the resulting sales or market share figures. Promotional Perspective 8–2 discusses an interesting study that identified five basic advertising communications objectives critical to the success of a commercial for a new product.

At some point, sales-oriented objectives must be translated into what the company hopes to communicate and to whom they hope to communicate it in order for the planning and implementation of the promotional strategy to proceed. Many

Promotional Perspective 8–2

Making Successful Commercials for New Products

Every year, thousands of new products are introduced to the consumer market, many of which are supported by multimillion-dollar television advertising campaigns. Unfortunately, nearly 80 percent of these products will fail for various reasons, including poor product quality, bad timing, lack of a significant difference from competing products, or poor execution of the marketing program—including advertising. With respect to advertising, the basic issue is whether these new products are being backed by commercials that help or hurt their chances for success. Some insight into this question was provided in a yearlong study conducted by Evalucom, Inc., a commercial testing company, in conjunction with major advertisers involved in new product introductions.

Evalucom evaluated 50 commercials used to introduce new products in 10 broad product categories. For each commercial, the advertiser had previously determined whether or not it had succeeded or failed in stimulating anticipated levels of trial, using ad tracking and sales results. Of the 50 commercials studied, 27 were judged to have been successful and 23 were deemed unsuccessful. Attempts were also made to control for problems from other areas of the marketing program such as promotion, pricing, distribution, and media spending.

The Evalucom analysis used a procedure whereby a diagnostic evaluation of the commercial is made using a method that identifies communications building blocks or "meaning segments." Trained analysts, assisted by a computer, systematically search each ad for the presence or absence of more than 2,000 criteria relating directly to the content, structure, and manner of presentation. Evalucom has found five basic advertising communications objectives that are critical to the success of any commercial. These include

- Capturing attention at the start of the commercial.
- Building interest and involvement.
- Communicating clearly.
- Creating awareness of the brand name.
- Meeting the advertiser's communications strategy.

The new product study, however, went beyond these basic communications requirements and considered factors that were related to the success or failure of commercials for new products. Evalucom's study pointed to the existence of four factors that made a difference as to whether a new product commercial was successful in generating sales. These included the following:

1. **Communicating that something is different about the product.** All the successful introductory commercials in the study communicated some point of difference for the new product.
2. **Positioning the brand difference in relation to the product category.** All 27 successful commercials positioned their brand's difference within a specific product category. For example, a new breakfast product was positioned as the "crispiest cereal" or a new beverage as the "smoothest soft drink."
3. **Communicating that the product difference is beneficial to consumers.** Some 93 percent of the successful commercials linked a benefit directly to the new product's difference.
4. **Supporting the idea that something about the product is different and/or beneficial to the consumer.** All the successful commercials communicated support for the product's difference claim or its relevance to consumers. Support took the form of demonstrations of performance, information supporting a uniqueness claim, endorsements, or testimonials.

The results of this study suggest that advertisers and their agencies can increase their odds of developing sales-effective new product commercials by incorporating these communications imperatives into their messages.

Source: Kirby Andrews, "Communications Imperatives for New Products," *Journal of Advertising Research* 26, no. 5 (October–November, 1986), pp. 29–32.

marketing and promotional managers recognize the value of setting specific communications objectives and the important role they play as operational guidelines to the planning, execution, and evaluation of the promotional program. Communications objectives are the criteria used in the DAGMAR approach to setting advertising goals and objectives, which has become one of the best known and most influential approaches to the advertising planning process. We now turn our attention to the DAGMAR model and the role communications objectives play in this approach.

DAGMAR—An Approach to Setting Objectives

In 1961, Russell Colley prepared a report for the Association of National Advertisers titled *Defining Advertising Goals for Measured Advertising Results*.[11] In it, Colley developed a model (that became known by the acronym **DAGMAR**) for setting advertising objectives and measuring the results of an advertising campaign against

➤ *Exhibit 8–13*   **Advertising task checklist**

| This checklist is a "thought starter" in developing specific advertising objectives. It can be applied to a single ad, a year's campaign for each product, or it can aid in developing a company's entire advertising philosophy among all those who create and approve advertising. |

Scale of Importance

Not important — Very important
0   1   2   3   4   5

- **To what extent does the advertising aim at closing an immediate sale?**
  1. Perform the complete selling function (take the product through all the necessary steps toward a sale)
  2. Close sales to prospects already partly sold through past advertising efforts ("Ask for the order" or "clincher" advertising)
  3. Announce a special reason for "buying now" (price, premium, etc.)
  4. Remind people to buy
  5. Tie in with some special buying event
  6. Stimulate impulse sales
- **Does the advertising aim at *near-term* sales by moving the prospect, step by step, closer to a sale (so that when confronted with a buying situation the customer will ask for, reach for, or accept the advertised brand)?**
  7. Create awareness of existence of product or brand
  8. Create "brand image" or favorable emotional disposition toward the brand
  9. Implant information or attitude regarding benefits and superior features of the brand
  10. Combat or offset competitive claims
  11. Correct false impressions, misinformation, and other obstacles to sales
  12. Build familiarity and easy recognition of package or trademark
- **Does the advertising aim at building a "long-range consumer franchise"?**
  13. Build confidence in company and brand that is expected to pay off in years to come
  14. Build customer demand, which places company in stronger position in relation to its distribution (not at the "mercy" of the marketplace)
  15. Place advertiser in position to select preferred distributors and dealers
  16. Secure universal distribution
  17. Establish a "reputation platform" for launching new brands or product lines
  18. Establish brand recognition and acceptance, which will enable the company to open new markets (geographic, price, age, sex)
- **Specifically, how can advertising contribute toward increased sales?**
  19. Hold present customers against the inroads of competition
  20. Convert competitive users to advertiser's brand
  21. Cause people to specify advertiser's brand instead of asking for product by generic name
  22. Convert nonusers of the product type to users of product and brand
  23. Make steady customers out of occasional or sporadic customers
  24. Advertise new uses of the product
  25. Persuade customers to buy larger sizes or multiple units
  26. Remind users to buy
  27. Encourage greater frequency or quantity of use

these objectives. The major thesis of the DAGMAR model is that communications effects are the logical basis for advertising goals and objectives and against which success or failure should be measured. Colley's rationale for communications-based objectives was as follows:

> Advertising's job, purely and simply, is to communicate to a defined audience information and a frame of mind that stimulates action. Advertising succeeds or fails depending on how well it communicates the desired information and attitudes to the right people at the right time and at the right cost.[12]

Under the DAGMAR approach, an advertising goal involves a communications task that is specific and measurable. A **communications task,** as opposed to a marketing task, involves something that can be performed by, and attributed to, advertising rather than requiring a combination of several marketing factors. Colley proposed that the communications task be based on a hierarchical model of the

➤ *Exhibit 8–13* (concluded)

	Scale of Importance
	Not important 0 1 2 3 4 5 Very important

- **Does the advertising aim at some specific step that leads to a sale?**
  28. Persuade prospect to write for descriptive literature, return a coupon, enter a contest
  29. Persuade prospect to visit a showroom, ask for a demonstration
  30. Induce prospect to sample the product (trial offer)
- **How important are "supplementary benefits" of end-use advertising?**
  31. Aid salespeople in opening new accounts
  32. Aid salespeople in getting larger orders from wholesalers and retailers
  33. Aid salespeople in getting preferred display space
  34. Give salespeople an entree
  35. Build morale of company sales force
  36. Impress the trade (causing recommendation to their customers and favorable treatment to salespeople)
- **Is it a task of advertising to impart information needed to consummate sales and build customer satisfaction?**
  37. "Where to buy it" advertising
  38. "How to use it" advertising
  39. New models, features, package
  40. New prices
  41. Special terms, trade-in offers, etcetera
  42. New policies (guarantees, etc.)
- **To what extent does the advertising aim at building confidence and goodwill for the corporation among:**
  43. Customers and potential customers?
  44. The trade (distributors, dealers, retailer people)?
  45. Employees and potential employees?
  46. The financial community?
  47. The public at large?
- **Specifically, what kind of images does the company wish to build?**
  48. Product quality, dependability
  49. Service
  50. Family resemblance of diversified products
  51. Corporate citizenship
  52. Growth, progressiveness, technical leadership

communications process. The four stages of commercial communication suggested by Colley include:

- *Awareness*—making the consumer aware of the existence of the brand or company.
- *Comprehension*—developing an understanding of what the product is and what it will do for the consumer.
- *Conviction*—developing a mental disposition or conviction in the consumer to buy the product.
- *Action*—getting the consumer to take some action and purchase the product.

As discussed previously, other hierarchical-type models of advertising effects can be used as a basis for analyzing the communications response process. Some advertising theorists have advocated using the Lavidge and Steiner hierarchy of effects model since it is more specific and provides a better method of establishing and measuring results.[13]

While the hierarchical model of advertising effects was the basic model of the communications response process used in DAGMAR, Colley also gave attention to other specific tasks that advertising might be expected to perform in leading to the ultimate objective of a sale. He developed an "advertising task checklist," shown in Exhibit 8–13, that consists of 52 tasks that might characterize the purpose and contribution of advertising. Colley advocated that all those individuals concerned with advertising go through this or a similar checklist and thoughtfully consider each item. The result would be establishment of realistic and agreed-upon goals. While Colley did not suggest this list was complete, it provides a number of considerations for campaign planners attempting to develop advertising objectives.

Characteristics of Objectives

A second major contribution of DAGMAR to the advertising planning process was Colley's specification of what constitutes a *good objective*. Colley argued that advertising objectives should be stated in terms of concrete and measurable communications tasks, specify a target audience, indicate a benchmark starting point and the degree of change sought, and specify a time period for accomplishing the objective(s). Each of these requirements is examined more closely.

Concrete and measurable

The communications task specified in the objective should be a precise statement of what appeal or message the advertiser wants to communicate to the target audience. Advertisers generally use a copy platform to describe the basic message they hope to communicate to their target audience. The objective or copy platform statement should be specific and clear enough to provide guidance and direction to creative specialists who must develop the actual advertising message. For example, for several years McDonald's has run advertising to neutralize the junk-food misconceptions about its foods and sell the nutritional value of the menu. The purpose of these ads is to respond to concerns and criticisms about the nutritional value of its food.[14]

According to DAGMAR, the objective must also be measurable and attention must be given to the method and criteria that can be used to determine if the intended message has been properly communicated. In the case of the McDonald's campaign, consumers' perceptions of the quality and nutritional value of its food could be used to determine if the communications objectives were being met.

Target audience

Another important characteristic of good objectives is that they include a well-defined target audience. Generally, the primary target audience for a company's product or service is identified and described in the situation analysis and may be based on descriptive variables such as geography, demographics, and psychographics as well as on behavioral variables such as usage rate or benefits sought. When variables such as usage rate or benefits sought are the basis for target audience selection, attention must still be given to describing their demographic and, if possible, psychographic characteristics since advertising media selection decisions are based on these variables. For example, Sonance, a company that makes architectural audio systems that include in-wall speakers and controls, defines its target audience as "affluent audio enthusiasts who are also design trendsetters." To reach this target market and communicate its message of "total audio ambiance," Sonance advertises in upscale, design-oriented magazines such as *Architectural Digest* (Exhibit 8–14).

Benchmark and degree of change sought

An important part of setting objectives is knowing the target audience's present status concerning response hierarchy variables such as awareness, knowledge, image, attitudes, and intentions and then determining the degree to which the consumers must be changed or moved by the advertising campaign. Determining the target market's present position regarding the various response stages requires that **benchmark measures** be taken. This often requires that a marketing research study be conducted to determine prevailing levels of the response hierarchy. In the case of

> *Exhibit 8–14*
Sonance's target audience is the affluent audio enthusiast

a new product or service, the starting conditions are generally at or near zero for all the variables, and no initial research would be needed.

Establishing benchmark measures is important, as this gives the promotional planner a basis for determining what communications tasks need to be accomplished and for specifying particular objectives. For example, a preliminary study for a brand may reveal that awareness is high, but knowledge of its specific benefits is low, as are consumer attitudes. Thus, the objective for the advertising campaign would not be concerned with increasing awareness but rather with improving the target audience's knowledge level of the brand and improving attitudes toward it. A good example of this is the marketing situation faced by Hush Puppies shoes. The company's market research showed the Hush Puppies brand name is very familiar to most consumers but suffered from an image problem. Many people were reluctant to admit to wearing Hush Puppies as they were perceived as low-priced shoes that are somewhat old-fashioned. To correct this image problem, a new campaign was developed to give Hush Puppies more personality and appeal. The campaign, targeted at both consumers and retailers, uses the company's basset hound mascot in a series of clever print ads designed to make Hush Puppies more acceptable to a variety of target audiences, including women and business executives (Exhibit 8–15).

The use of quantitative benchmarks not only is valuable in establishing communications goals and objectives but also is a prerequisite to determining if the campaign was successful. As noted earlier in this chapter, objectives provide the standard against which the success or failure of a campaign is measured. An ad campaign that results in a 90 percent awareness level for a brand among its target audience cannot really be judged to be effective unless one knows what percentage of the consumers were aware of the brand before the campaign began. A 70 percent precampaign awareness level would lead to a different interpretation of the campaign's success than would a 30 percent level.

➤ *Exhibit 8–15*
This ad for Hush Puppies is part of a campaign designed to give the brand more personality and appeal

Ventilated Hush Puppies.

Specified time period

A final consideration in setting advertising objectives is specifying the time period in which the objectives are to be accomplished. Appropriate time periods can range anywhere from a few days to a year or more. Most ad campaigns specify time periods ranging from a few months to a year. The length of the period depends on the situation facing the advertiser and the type of response being sought. For example, creating or increasing awareness levels for a brand can be accomplished fairly quickly through an intensive media schedule, which results in widespread and repetitive advertising to the target audience. Repositioning of a product requires a change in consumers' perceptions regarding the image of the brand and will require much more time. For example, the repositioning of Marlboro cigarettes from a feminine brand to one with a masculine image took several years.

Assessment of DAGMAR

The DAGMAR approach to setting advertising objectives has had a tremendous amount of influence on advertising. Many promotional planners have turned to this model as a basis for setting objectives and assessing the effectiveness of their promotional campaigns. DAGMAR also focused advertisers' attention on the value of using communications-based objectives, rather than sales-based, as measures of advertising effectiveness and encouraged the measurement of stages in the response hierarchy as a way of assessing a campaign's impact. Colley's work has led to improvements in the advertising and promotional planning process by providing those involved with a better understanding of the goals and objectives toward which their efforts should be directed. This usually results in less subjectivity and also leads to better communication and relationships between the client and its agency.

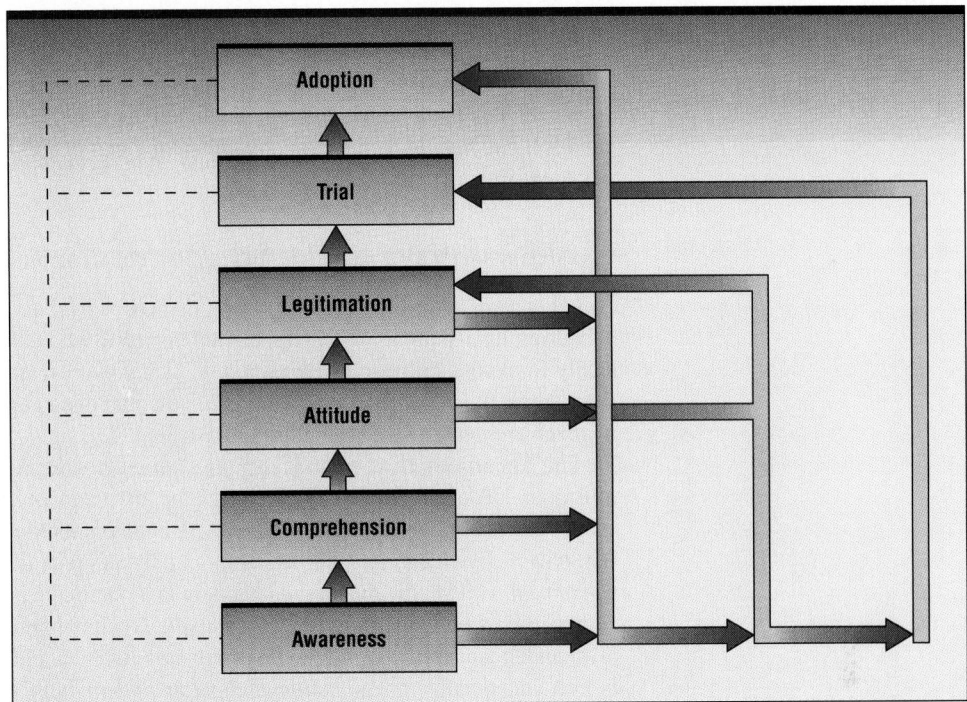

While DAGMAR has contributed to the advertising planning process, this approach has not been totally accepted by everyone in the advertising field. A number of problems have been noted with the DAGMAR model that have led to questions regarding its value as an advertising planning technique.[15]

Problems with the response hierarchy

A major criticism of the DAGMAR approach centers on the hierarchy of effects model on which it is based. Colley proposed that the communications task be based on a hierarchical-type response model and suggested that movement through the sequential steps such as awareness, comprehension, attitude, and conviction will ultimately lead to purchase. As discussed in Chapter 6, critics of the hierarchy of effects model argue that consumers do not always go through this sequence of communications effects before making a purchase. For example, a consumer may pass directly from awareness to purchase without learning about the product, forming an attitude toward it, or developing a conviction to buy it.

The problem concerning the assumption that consumers always proceed through the various levels of the response hierarchy in the specified order has been recognized, and alternative response models have been developed.[16] For example, an updated version of DAGMAR, known as DAGMAR MOD II, was developed.[17] This version recognizes that the appropriate response model will depend on the situation and emphasizes identifying the sequence of decision-making steps that are applicable in a buying situation.

In developing the Foote, Cone & Belding grid, which was discussed in Chapter 6, Richard Vaughn proposed using Thomas Robertson's adoption process model[18] as a modified hierarchy model. Vaughn's model (shown in Exhibit 8–16) proposes that

some consumers, under some conditions, for some products, might follow a sequential path. The dotted lines [in Exhibit 8–16] are feedbacks which can alter outcomes. Other decision patterns on the right track consumers as they violate the formal sequence of the hierarchy. Thus, consumers can learn from previous experience and swerve from the awareness to purchase pattern.[19]

Vaughn suggests this modified model preserves the "learn → feel → do" sequence of most hierarchy models but also adds more flexibility. Examination of this model shows it offers a way of integrating the three response hierarchies discussed in Chapter 6. Thus, promotional managers must determine which response sequence is relevant in the purchase process for the product or service being advertised and what role advertising and other promotional mix elements play in moving consumers through the applicable hierarchy. Appropriate objectives can then be set to guide the promotional program.

Problems with the attitude-behavior relationship

Another problem implicit in the DAGMAR model concerns the relationship between attitudes and behavior. Many critics contend that attitude change does not necessarily lead to a change in behavior.[20] Thus, even if advertising efforts do lead to the development of favorable affective states, there is no guarantee consumers will make a purchase on the basis of their attitude.

The argument that attitude change does not lead to behavior is not really damaging to DAGMAR. Problems with the attitude-behavior relationship often result from the fact that general attitudes are often used to attempt to measure specific behaviors. By using specific measures such as attitude toward purchasing or using a particular brand or intentions to buy a specific brand, the attitude-behavior relationship can be improved.[21] In extensive study of the relationship between attitudes and purchase behavior for consumer products, a clear relationship was shown between the two.[22] Thus, while the relationship between attitudes and purchase behavior may not always be high, attitude change is generally considered a valid advertising objective, particularly in high-involvement purchase situations.

Sales objectives

Another objection to DAGMAR comes from those who argue that the only relevant measure of advertising objectives is sales. Communications objectives are viewed as a "cop-out" and as ignoring the basic reason a firm spends money on advertising—to generate sales. They point out that advertising can accomplish communications objectives yet have little or no impact on sales and that advertising is effective only to the extent it induces consumers to make a purchase.[23] Thus, since a communications variable is only of interest if it can be shown to be related to sales, why not measure sales directly? The fallacy in this logic has been addressed in our discussion of reasons for using communications objectives and need not be repeated here.

Practicality and costs

A fourth problem often noted with DAGMAR concerns the difficulties involved in implementing this approach. A manager attempting to utilize DAGMAR has to determine what constructs or variables are relevant and how they should be measured. The establishment of quantitative benchmarks and the ultimate measurement of communications results require that money be spent on research. Not only is this costly, but it can also be time-consuming and can lead to considerable disagreement over method, criteria, measures, and so forth. As a result, many critics argue that DAGMAR is viable only for large companies with big advertising and research budgets and the capabilities of conducting the research needed to establish benchmarks and measure changes in the communications response hierarchy. Many firms do not want to spend the money on research that is needed to utilize the DAGMAR approach effectively or believe they cannot afford to do so.

Inhibits creativity

A final criticism of DAGMAR is that it inhibits advertising creativity by imposing too much influence and structure on the creative people responsible for developing the advertising. Creative people in advertising are often searching for the "great idea" that will result in a unique and, hopefully, effective campaign. Many creative personnel think that having to adhere to the rational and planned DAGMAR approach makes the creative department overly concerned with numbers and quantitative assessment of a campaign's impact in terms of measures such as awareness, brand name recall, or specific persuasion measures. The net effect is that the emphasis is on "passing the numbers test" rather than developing a message that is truly creative and adds to or enhances the product. The problems associated with the quantification of advertising and overresearching its effectiveness are examined in greater detail in Chapter 20.

There is little question that the DAGMAR approach makes the creative personnel more accountable and may inhibit their freedom to search for the great creative idea. On the other hand, spectacular advertising ideas are not easy to come by, and many advertisers are more concerned with avoiding ineffective advertising. Well-planned campaigns using a DAGMAR approach are viewed by many advertising and marketing managers as a way of avoiding ads with no specific direction or purpose, even if the result is some restriction on the creative department.

Problems in Setting Objectives

The DAGMAR approach specifies that advertising goals and objectives should include a statement of the basic message to be delivered, the target audience, the intended effect, and specific criteria to be used to measure the success of the campaign. Thus, when the time comes to determine whether the campaign was successful, the advertiser can evaluate it by comparing actual performance against intended results that were specified in the original objectives. The logic underlying DAGMAR is that the advertising or promotional manager should decide what the advertising and promotions campaign is expected to achieve and then make plans to test and determine how successful the outcome was, relative to expected results.

While this may sound like a logical process to the advertising and promotion planning process, most advertisers and their agencies fail to follow these basic principles. They often fail to set specific objectives for their campaigns and/or usually do not have the proper evidence to determine the success of their promotional programs. Promotional Perspective 8–3 discusses a classic study that examined the problems with how advertisers set objectives and measure their accomplishment.

The results of the study discussed in Promotional Perspective 8–3 suggest most advertising agencies did not state appropriate objectives for determining success and thus could not really demonstrate whether a supposedly successful campaign was a success. Even though these campaigns may have been doing something right, they generally were not aware of what it was. Although this study was conducted in 1969, the same problems may still be prevalent in advertising today.

A recent study examined the advertising practices of business-to-business marketers to determine whether their advertisements used advertising objectives that met the four DAGMAR criteria specified by Colley.[24] Entries from the annual Business/Professional Advertising Association Gold Key Awards competition, which solicits the best marketing communications efforts from business-to-business advertisers, were evaluated with respect to their statements of objectives and summary of results of their campaigns. The results of this study indicated these advertisers did not utilize the four components of good advertising objectives, specify objective tasks, measure results in terms of stages of a communications hierarchy of effects strategy, or match objectives to evaluation measures. The authors concluded

> Advertising practitioners have only partially adopted the concepts and standards of objective setting and evaluation set forth over 25 years ago.[25]

Improving Promotional Planners' Use of Objectives

As we have seen, it is very important that advertisers and their agencies pay close attention to the objectives they set for their campaigns. They should strive to set specific and measurable objectives that not only serve as a guide to promotional planning and decision making but also can be used as a standard against which

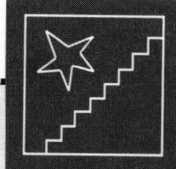

Promotional Perspective 8–3

Ad Campaigns Do Something Right, But What?

An interesting study was conducted some years ago by an advertising researcher in which the campaign objectives and "proofs of success" for 135 supposedly successful ad campaigns created by 40 agencies were analyzed. Two specific questions addressed in this study included:

1. Did the agency set specific objectives for the campaign, that is, objectives specific enough to be measured?
2. Did the agency attempt to measure the effectiveness of the campaign by clearly stating how the campaign fulfilled the previously set objectives?

As a basis for analysis relative to the first question, a *specific objective* was defined as one that made clear the four criteria set forth in DAGMAR: (1) what message was to be delivered (2) to what audience and (3) with what intended effect(s) and (4) what specific criteria were going to be used to measure the success of the campaign.

The analysis of the stated campaign objectives showed that 64 percent fulfilled the first three criteria, but only 2 of the 135, or less than 1 percent, met all four criteria. The major problems found in the objectives included a failure to state objectives in quantifiable terms, a failure to realize that the results of advertising could not be measured in sales, and a failure to specify the target audience. Relative to the first question, only 2 of the 135 campaigns used a quantified objective, which is needed to establish benchmarks and measurement criteria. Twenty-four percent of the campaigns stated objectives in terms of sales, thus ignoring the other factors that may have influenced sales results during the campaign; 16 percent of the objectives failed to specify a target audience.

In regard to the second question concerning evidence of how the campaign fulfilled the objectives, the study found that only in 31 percent of the campaigns were proofs of success related directly to the objectives the agency set. The major problems found were the following:

1. With an objective of awareness, success was stated in sales.
2. With an objective of new image, success was stated in terms of readership or inquiries.
3. With more than one objective set forth, success was stated only in relation to one of them.

An example of a campaign where the proof of success did not logically relate to the statement of campaign objectives was that for Welch's grape juice:

Objectives: To convince mothers that Welch's Grape Juice is the best fruit drink they can serve for their children:

- Because it is good for them.
- Because it is the best tasting of all fruit drinks.

Proof of success: Despite the aggressive competition from scores of competitive brands of fruit drinks, Welch's not only has held its position but also has shown consistent improvement in sales year after year.

The objective of this campaign was to convince mothers that this product was the best fruit drink for their children because of its nutritional value and good taste. However, the proof of success or advertising effectiveness was cited in terms of sales, and no mention was made of mothers' awareness or image of the brand's taste or nutritional value.

Source: Stewart H. Britt, "Are So-Called Successful Advertising Campaigns Really Successful?" *Journal of Advertising Research* 9, no. 2 (1969), pp. 3–9.

advertising and promotional performance can be evaluated. Unfortunately, as we have seen, many companies either do not understand how to set appropriate objectives for their advertising and promotional programs or fail to do so for some other reason.

Many companies lack the understanding of what the role and function of advertising are because top management has only an abstract idea of what the firm's advertising is supposed to be doing. A study by the American Business Press, which measured the attitudes of chairmen, presidents, and other senior managers of business-to-business advertising companies, found that more than 50 percent of the 427 respondents said they did not know whether their advertising was working, and less than 10 percent said they thought their advertising was working well.[26] This study showed overwhelmingly that top management did not even know what their company's advertising was supposed to do, much less how to measure it.

It is unlikely that most firms are going to set objectives meeting all the criteria set forth in DAGMAR. However, promotional planners should set objectives that are specific and measurable and go beyond basic sales goals. Even if steps are not always taken to measure specific communications response elements, meeting the other criteria will sharpen the focus and improve the quality of the advertising and promotions planning process.

Objectives for Other Promotional Elements

While the goal of this chapter has been to discuss and consider various issues regarding the determination of objectives for an organization's overall promotional program and strategy, much of the attention has focused on setting objectives for advertising. For example, DAGMAR is basically a model for setting objectives and planning the advertising program. One of the reasons so much attention is given to advertising objectives is that it is often the lead element in the promotional mix, particularly in consumer products marketing, and thus receives most of the attention in the planning process. Elements such as sales promotion and/or publicity/public relations often are used on an intermittent basis to support and complement the advertising program. However, advertising is used on a continual basis and is viewed as the key element in the firm's promotional strategy and its ability to meet communications objectives.

In some situations, advertising plays a subservient role to other elements of the promotional mix, as in business-to-business marketing where personal selling is the major promotional element. However, as will be discussed in Chapter 21, advertising can also play an important role in the promotional programs of these firms as well.

Many of the considerations discussed in determining advertising objectives are relevant when setting goals for other elements of the promotional mix. The promotional planner should determine what role elements such as various sales promotion techniques, publicity and public relations, direct marketing, and personal selling will play in the overall marketing program and how they will interact with advertising, as well as with one another. When setting objectives for these other promotional elements, consideration must be given to what the firm hopes to communicate or accomplish through the use of this element, among what target audience, and during what time period. As with advertising, results should be measured and evaluated against the original objectives, and attempts should be made to isolate the effects that each promotional element played. A more thorough discussion of objectives for other promotional elements is provided in the chapters devoted to each in the next section of the text.

SUMMARY

This chapter has examined the role of objectives in the planning and evaluation of the advertising and promotional program. Specific objectives are needed to guide the development of the promotional program as well as to provide a benchmark or standard against which performance can be measured and evaluated. Objectives serve important functions as communications devices, as a guide planning the promotional program and making decisions regarding various alternatives, and for the measurement and evaluation of the promotional program.

Advertising and promotional objectives evolve from the organization's overall marketing plan, and objectives are based on the role these elements play in the marketing program. The determination of promotional objectives occurs after a thorough situation analysis has been conducted and the marketing and promotional issues have been identified. Many managers view their advertising and promotional programs from a sales perspective and use sales or a related measure such as market share as the basis for setting objectives. However, because of the various problems associated with sales-based objectives, many promotional planners take the perspective that the role of advertising is to communicate. Thus, communications-based objectives such as those in the response hierarchy are used as the basis for setting advertising goals. A communication effects pyramid was discussed and used to illustrate what appropriate objectives might be for the various stages in the hierarchy.

The DAGMAR approach to setting objectives was examined in detail, along with the characteristics of good objectives specified by this advertising planning process. Good advertising objectives meet four basic criteria: They are set in concrete and measurable communications terms; they specify a target audience; they contain a benchmark and indicate the degree of change being sought; and they specify a time period for accomplishing the objectives. Many companies fail to meet these criteria in setting objectives for their advertising and promotional programs. Many of the principles used in setting advertising objectives can also be applied to other elements in the promotional mix.

KEY TERMS

marketing objectives
carryover effect

communications objectives
DAGMAR

communications task
benchmark measures

DISCUSSION QUESTIONS

1. Assume you are an outside marketing consultant and have been asked to evaluate the teaser campaign used to introduce the Infiniti. Based on the information provided in the chapter opening, how would you evaluate the success of this campaign? Defend your position.

2. Discuss the importance and value of setting objectives for advertising and other promotional mix elements and the role they play in the promotional planning process.

3. What are the differences between marketing objectives and communications objectives? Why do so many managers confuse the two?

4. You are in a meeting to discuss plans for a new advertising and promotional program for your company. The vice president of marketing opens the meeting by stating there is only one objective for the new campaign—to increase sales. How would you respond to this statement?

5. What is meant by an advertising carryover effect? Discuss the problems a carryover effect creates for managers who are trying to determine the impact their advertising has on sales.

6. You are the advertising manager for an established brand of laundry detergent and have just fought hard to have the promotional budget for the brand increased by 10 percent. You have just received a report for the latest quarter that shows sales did not change despite the increase in advertising spending. The marketing vice president is concerned about the lack of increase in sales and wants you to explain the problem. How might you respond?

7. One of the more controversial areas of marketing and promotion is whether sales are the most appropriate criteria for measuring advertising effectiveness or whether communications objectives should be used. Discuss the use of sales versus communications objectives, giving attention to the problems and advantages of each.

8. Discuss how the communication effects pyramid can be used in developing communications objectives for a new brand as well as an established brand. Find three examples of commercials used to introduce new products to the consumer market. Evaluate these commercials using the four communications imperatives for new products discussed in Promotional Perspective 8–2.

9. What are the four characteristics of good objectives suggested by DAGMAR? Do you think most advertisers set objectives that meet these criteria?

10. A criticism of DAGMAR is that it limits advertising creativity by imposing too much influence and structure on the creative specialists. Do you agree or disagree? Evaluate this criticism.

11. It has been suggested that most top managers of business-to-business firms are not aware of whether their advertising is working and what it is supposed to be doing. How would you explain the role and function of advertising to these managers?

chapter 9

The Advertising and Promotions Budget

chapter objectives

➤ To understand the process of advertising and promotions budget setting.

➤ To understand theoretical issues involved in budget setting.

➤ To examine the various methods for establishing an advertising budget.

➤ To examine factors influencing the size and process of allocating the advertising and promotions budget.

The Advertising Spending Drought

1991 ended, but the drought in advertising spending continues. According to most analysts, the advertising industry is experiencing its deepest and most prolonged ad drought in the past 20 years. Even worse, the end does not appear to be in sight. Some industry forecasters believe a real turnaround is not likely before 1995, and advertising spending is not likely to even keep pace with inflation during the next few years.

Many reasons are offered for the dismal forecast. Shifts in ad spending to other media, a loss of confidence in the power of advertising, and the sluggish economy are all seen as contributors. The biggest villain appears to be the economy, however. Advertisers slashed their budgets throughout 1991, and an expected boost after the Gulf War never materialized. The common strategy of increasing budgets during the Olympics also never occurred.

The United States is not experiencing the slump alone, thus compounding the problem. The United Kingdom saw an even steeper drop than the United States, and other European countries have reported declines as well.

The advertising industry is not just sitting back and watching these declines. The media are learning how to lure advertisers back to the marketplace. CBS, for example, enticed advertisers to buy advertising time with extras such as sweepstakes and promotions created around the ads. Time Warner offered packages for big advertisers that included magazine ads, home videos, books, and so on. *The Wall Street Journal* and the American Association of Advertising Agencies (AAAA) ran similar advertising campaigns to demonstrate reasons advertisers should maintain or increase budgets in recessionary periods.

The Wall Street Journal and AAAA campaign focused on the value associated with advertising in a recession. Citing McGraw-Hill studies conducted during previous economic downturns, the ad encouraged advertisers not to panic or to get defensive. Those who were brave, the ad continues, achieved a 3.2-to-1 sales advantage, while those who weren't lost ground they would never regain. The ad cites other reasons for advertising in a recession, noting "the natural inclination to cut spending in an effort to increase profits in a recession doesn't work."

So what does the future hold? Many observers forecasted even more gloom in 1992 and 1993, as companies do not heed the advice of the AAAA and *The Wall Street Journal* ads. As corporate profits fell in 1991, companies such as IBM, Adolph Coors, and Chrysler cut their ad budgets. As the recession continues, other companies are likely to do the same. Still others predict Madison

IN A RECESSION, THE BEST DEFENSE IS A GOOD OFFENSE.

It's a recession. Your instincts demand that you cut the ad budget. But, as the McGraw-Hill Research[1] analysis of business-to-business advertising expenditures during the 1981-82 recession shows, it's those with the courage to maintain or increase advertising in a recession who reap a major sales advantage over their competitors who panic and fall back into a defensive posture. And this advantage continues to expand long after the recession is over.

Effects of Advertising in a Recession on Sales (Indices)

Companies that Maintained or Increased Advertising in Both 1981 and 1982

Companies that Eliminated or Decreased Advertising in Both 1981 and 1982

Year	Maintained/Increased	Eliminated/Decreased
1980	100	100
1981	96	137
1982	88	159
1983	89	195
1984	106	283
1985	119	375

McGraw-Hill Research, 1986.

Recessions last an average of 11 months, but any advertising decision made during one can have permanent repercussions. The McGraw-Hill study demonstrates that nervous advertisers lose ground to the brave and can't gain it back. In 1980, according to the chart seen here, sales indices were identical, but by 1985 the brave had racked up a 3.2 to 1 sales advantage. A similar study done by McGraw-Hill during the 1974-75 recession corroborates the 1980's research.

A recession is the single greatest period in which to make short- and long-term gains. And, surprisingly, increasing advertising modestly during one has much the same effect on your profits as cutting advertising does. According to The Center for Research & Development's October 1990 study of consumer advertising during a recession, advertisers who yield "to the natural inclination to cut spending in an effort to increase profits in a recession find that it doesn't work."[2] This study, relying on the PIMS[3] database, also uncovered that aggressive recessionary advertisers picked up 4.5 *times* as much market share gain as their overcautious competitors, leaving them in a far better position to exploit the inevitable recovery and expansion.

Chevrolet countered its competitors during the 1974-75 recession by aggressively beefing up its ad spending and attained a two percent market share increase. Today, two share points in the automotive industry are worth over $4 billion. Delta Airlines and Revlon also boosted ad spending in the 1974-75 recession and achieved similar results.

Continuous advertising sustains market leadership. And it's far easier to sustain momentum than it is to start it up again. Consider this list of market category leaders: Campbell's, Coca-Cola, Ivory, Kellogg, Kodak, Lipton and Wrigley. This is the leadership list for 1925. And 1990. These marketers have maintained a relentless commitment to their brands in both good times and bad. Kellogg had the guts to pump up its ad spending during the Great Depression and cemented a market leadership it has yet to relinquish.

These are the success stories. Space and diplomacy don't allow the mention of the names of those who lacked gusto and chose to cut their ad spending in recessionary times.

But if you would like to learn more about how advertising can help make the worst of times the best of times, please write to Department C, American Association of Advertising Agencies, 666 Third Avenue, New York, New York 10017, enclosing a check for five dollars. You will receive a booklet covering the pertinent research done on all the U.S. recessions since 1923. Please allow 4 to 6 weeks for delivery.

[1] McGraw-Hill Research, 1986. [2] The Center for Research and Development ©1990.
[3] Profit Impact of Market Strategies, The Strategic Planning Institute, Cambridge, MA.

AAAA

(*continued*)
Avenue will never be the same—that is, it will never experience the ad spending growth of previous years. These "experts" believe advertising will no longer be the dominant promotional tool as it was in the past, as alternative media will receive more of the marketer's budget.

These two factors are likely to keep the advertising industry dry for some time.

Source: "What Happened to Advertising," Business Week, September 23, 1991, pp. 66–72; and Joanne Lipman, "Ad Spending Looks Unlikely to Revive Soon," The Wall Street Journal, December 9, 1991, pp. B1, B4.

Falling advertising budgets have created concern throughout the advertising world. The problems stem from two sources: falling budgets and allocations of advertising dollars to other communication tools. The budgeting decisions of advertisers have a significant impact not only on the firm itself, but also for numerous others involved either directly or indirectly. This chapter provides insight into some underlying theory with respect to budget setting, discusses how companies budget for promotional efforts, and demonstrates the inherent strengths and weaknesses associated with these approaches. Essentially, we focus on two primary budgeting decisions—the establishment of a budget amount and the budget allocation decision.

Establishing the Budget

The size of a firm's advertising and promotions budget can vary from a few thousand dollars to more than a billion. Regardless of its size, the budgeting decision is not a trivial matter. When companies like Procter & Gamble and McDonald's spend over a billion dollars per year to promote their products, they expect such expenditures to lead to the accomplishment of their stated objectives. The budget decision is no less critical to a firm spending only thousands of dollars, as its ultimate success or failure may often depend on the monies spent. Thus, one of the most critical decisions facing the marketing manager is how much to spend on the promotional effort.

Unfortunately, many managers, failing to realize the value of advertising and promotion, treat the communications budget as an expense rather than an investment. Instead of viewing the dollars spent as contributing to additional sales and market share, they focus their attention on the impact of budget expenses against profits. As a result, when times get tough, such as in a recession, the advertising and promotional budget is the first to be cut. Moreover, the decision is not a one-time responsibility, as a new budget is formulated every year, each time a new product is introduced, or when either internal or external factors necessitate a change to maintain competitiveness.

While one of the most critical decisions to be made, budgeting has perhaps been the most resistant to change, with new insights and/or methods occurring infrequently. A comparison of advertising and promotional texts over the past 10 years would reveal the same methods for establishing budgets are discussed, and the theoretical basis for this process remains rooted in economic theory and marginal analysis. (Advertisers also use an approach based on **contribution margin**—the difference between the total revenue generated by a brand and its total variable costs—but, as noted by Robert Steiner, *marginal analysis* and *contribution margin* are essentially synonymous terms.)[1] We begin our discussion of budgeting with an examination of these theoretical approaches.

Theoretical Issues in Budget Setting

Most of the models used to establish advertising budgets can be categorized as taking an economic or a sales response perspective. A discussion of each of these approaches follows.

Marginal analysis

Exhibit 9–1 graphically represents the concept of **marginal analysis.** As advertising/promotional expenditures increase, sales and gross margins also increase to a point and level off. Profits are shown to be a result of the gross margin minus advertising expenditures. Using this theory to establish its budget, a firm would continue to spend advertising/promotional dollars so long as the marginal revenues created by these expenditures exceed the incremental advertising/promotional costs. As shown on the graph, the optimal expenditure level would be established at that point where marginal costs were equal to the marginal revenues that they generate (Point *A*). If the sum of the advertising/promotional expenditures exceeded the revenues these efforts generated, one would conclude the appropriations were too high, and scale down the budget. If revenues were higher, a higher budget might be in order. (We see later in this chapter that this approach might also be applied to the allocation decision.)

While marginal analysis seems logical intuitively, certain weaknesses with this approach limit its usefulness. These weaknesses include the assumptions (1) that sales are a direct result of advertising and promotional expenditures and this effect can be measured and (2) that advertising and promotion are solely responsible for sales. Let us examine each of these assumptions in more detail.

1. Assumption that sales are a direct measure of advertising and promotions efforts. In Chapter 8, we discussed the fact that the advertiser needs to set

➤ *Exhibit 9–1*
Marginal analysis

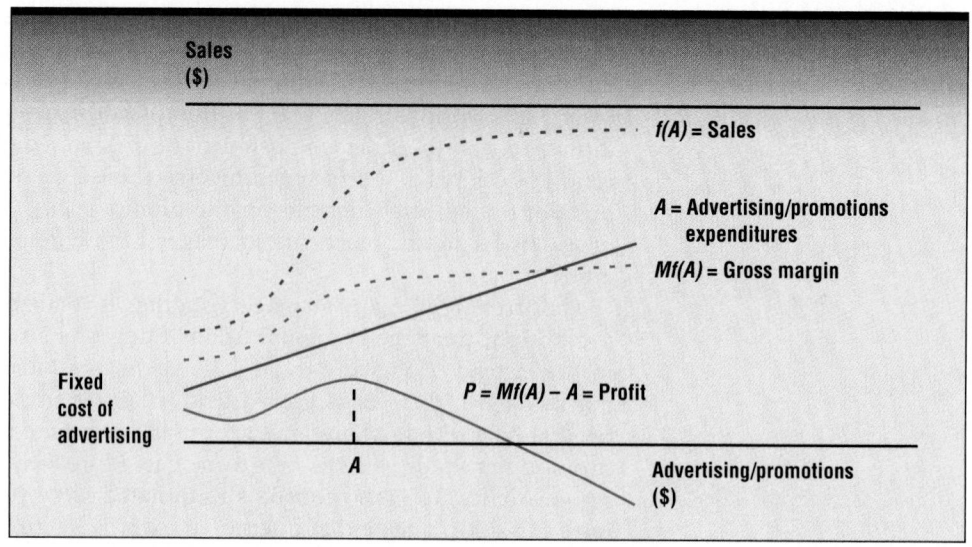

communications objectives that contribute to accomplishing overall marketing objectives but at the same time are separate. One reason cited for this strategy is that it is often difficult, if not impossible, to demonstrate the effects of advertising and promotions on sales. In studies using sales as a direct measure, it has been almost impossible to establish the contribution of advertising and promotion. As noted by Frank Bass, "There is no more difficult, complex, or controversial problem in marketing than measuring the influence of advertising on sales."[2] Or, in the words of David Aaker and James Carman, "Looking for the relationship between advertising and sales is somewhat worse than looking for a needle in a haystack."[3] Thus, to try to show that the size of the budget will lead to an impact directly on the sales of the product is misleading. A more logical approach would be to examine the impact of various budgets on the attainment of communications objectives.

As we saw in the discussion of communications objectives, sales are not the only goal to be attained through the promotional effort. Awareness, interest, attitude change, and other communications objectives are often sought, and while the bottom line may often be to sell the product, these objectives may serve as the basis on which the promotional program is developed.

2. Assumption that sales are determined solely by advertising and promotion. Under this assumption, the remaining elements of the marketing mix (price, product, and distribution) are ignored. The promotional function is considered to be the one and only factor impacting sales. As has been noted in previous chapters, the effects of product quality, pricing, and/or distribution also contribute to a company's success. In addition, environmental factors may impact the effectiveness of the promotional program—leading the marketing manager to assume the advertising was or was not effective when some other factor may have helped or hindered the accomplishment of the desired objectives (see Exhibit 9–2).

Overall, you can see that while the economic approach is a logical one that applies one perspective to the budgeting process, the difficulties associated with determining the effects of the promotional effort on sales and revenues limit its applicability. Marginal analysis as a basis for budgeting is, as a result, seldom used (with the exception of direct-response advertising).

Sales response models

While examining Exhibit 9–1, you may have wondered why the sales curve was drawn to show sales leveling off even though advertising and promotions efforts continued to increase. The fact is, the relationship between advertising and sales has

➤ *Exhibit 9–2*
Leadership and responsiveness to a growing market contributes to Lockheed's corporate growth

This new business lineup includes an F-28, Boeing 757, DC-10, and Boeing 747.

Look who's coming to Lockheed.

Leveraging skills proven on more than 200,000 aircraft, Lockheed is now the most experienced and fastest-growing aircraft maintenance and modification company in the world. New airline customers come to Lockheed centers every day.

Forecasts say the world's commercial fleet will grow by as much as 50%, and existing commercial and military fleets will be used longer. That means a bigger market, and the opportunity for Lockheed to grow stronger in this thriving service industry. One example: a new partnership agreement with Japan Airlines will help fill the bays with 747s at our newest center in San Bernardino, California.

Establishing leadership positions on existing capabilities is a cornerstone of Lockheed's plan to build shareholder value and create the premier aerospace company in the world.

Lockheed leads.

Watch NOVA on PBS, Tuesdays at 8 p.m.

been the topic of much research and discussion designed to determine the shape of the response curve.

Almost all advertisers subscribe to one of two models of the advertising/sales response function. These two response curves, the **concave-downward function** and the **S-shaped response curve,** are described below.

The concave-downward function   After reviewing over 100 studies of the effects of advertising on sales, Julian Simon and Johan Arndt concluded the effects of advertising budgets follow the microeconomic law of diminishing returns.[4] That is, as the amount of advertising increases, its incremental value decreases. The logic is that those with the greatest potential to buy will likely act on the first (or earliest) exposures, whereas those less likely to buy are not likely to change as a result of the advertising. Of those who may be potential buyers, each additional advertisement will supply little or no new information that will affect their decision. Thus, according to this model, the effects of advertising would quickly begin to diminish, as shown in Exhibit 9–3a. Budgeting under this model would indicate that less advertising dollars may be necessary to create the optimal influence on sales.

The S-shaped response function   A second model assumed by many advertising managers is the sales response model shown in Exhibit 9–3b. As can be seen, this model projects an S-shaped response function to the budget outlay, with the response again being measured in sales.

According to the S-shaped response model, initial outlays of the advertising budget have little impact—as indicated by the essentially flat sales curve in range A. After a certain budget level has been reached (the beginning of range B), advertising and promotional efforts begin to have an effect, as additional increments of expenditures result in an increased sales level. This incremental gain continues only to a point, however, because at the beginning of range C the impact of additional expenditures

➤ *Exhibit 9–3*   **Advertising sales/response functions**

A. The concave-downward response curve

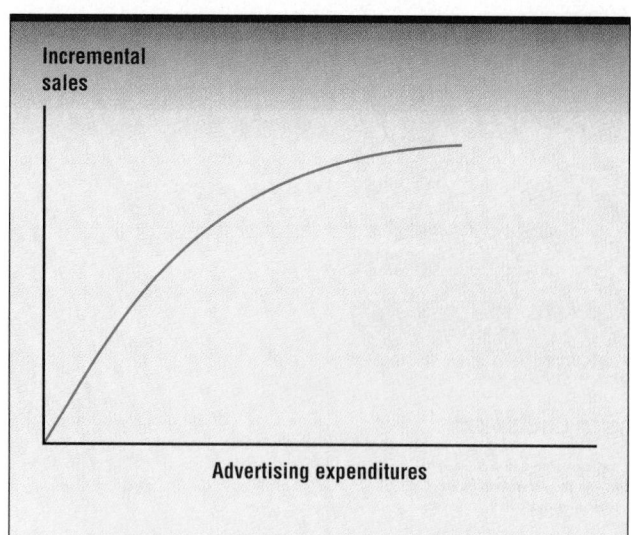

B. The S-shaped response function

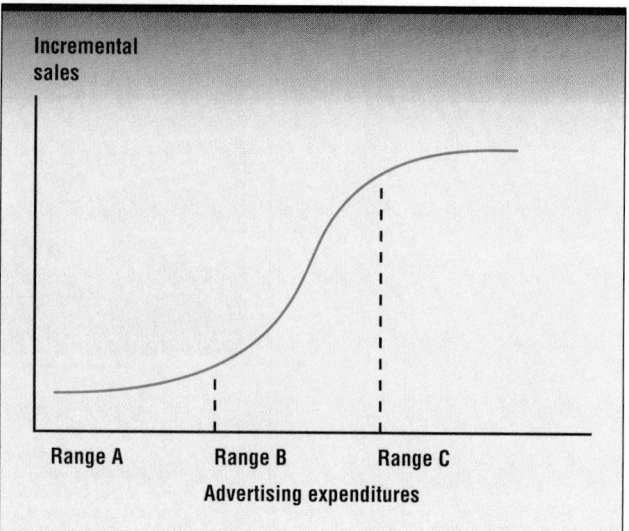

begins to return little or nothing at all in the way of sales. This model suggests a small advertising budget is likely to have no impact beyond the sales that may have been generated through other means (word of mouth, etc.). At the other extreme, more does not necessarily mean better, as additional dollars spent beyond range B have no additional impact on sales and for the most part can be considered wasted. As with marginal analysis, one would attempt to operate at that point on the curve in area B where the maximum return for the money is attained.

As with marginal analysis, weaknesses in these sales response models render the models academic—that is, of limited use to practitioners for direct applications. Many of the same problems seen earlier—the use of sales as a dependent variable, measurement problems, and so on—limit the usefulness of these models. At the same time, you should keep in mind the purpose of discussing such models. Even though marginal analysis and the sales response curves may not be directly applicable, their value lies in providing the manager with some insight into a theoretical basis of how the budgeting process should work. Some empirical evidence indicates the models may have validity. For example, one study, based on industry experience, has provided support for the S-shaped response curve; the results indicated that a minimum amount of advertising dollars must be spent before a noticeable effect on sales will occur.[5] The studies discussed in earlier chapters on learning and the hierarchy of effects also demonstrate the importance of repetition on gaining awareness and on subsequent higher-order objectives such as adoption. Thus, while we may not be able to say these models provide a tool for setting the advertising and promotional budget directly, we can use them to guide our appropriations strategy from a theoretical basis. As you will see later in this chapter, having a theoretical basis offers an advantage over many of the methods currently being utilized for budget setting and allocation.

Additional Factors Considered in Budget Setting

While the theoretical bases just discussed should be considered in establishing the budget appropriation, a number of other issues have also been shown to be necessary for consideration. Some of these are discussed here.

Situational factors influencing the budget

As we stated earlier, a weakness in attempting to use sales as a *direct* measure of response to advertising is that various situational factors may be having an effect. In one very comprehensive study, 24 variables were shown to affect the advertising-sales ratio.

➤ *Exhibit 9–4* **Factors influencing advertising budgets**

Factor	Relationship of Advertising/Sales	Factor	Relationship of Advertising/Sales
Product factors		**Customer factors**	
Basis for differentiation	+	Industrial products users	−
Hidden product qualities	+	Concentration of users	+
Emotional buying motives	+	**Strategy factors**	
Durability	−	Regional markets	−
Large dollar purchase	−	Early stage of brand life cycle	+
Purchase frequency	Curvilinear	High margins in channels	−
Market factors		Long channels of distribution	+
Stage of product life cycle		High prices	+
Introductory	+	High quality	+
Growth	+	**Cost factors**	
Maturity	−	High profit margins	+
Decline	−		
Inelastic demand	+		
Market share	−		
Competition			
Active	+		
Concentrated	+		
"Pioneer" in market	−		

Note: + relationship means the factor leads to a positive effect of advertising on sales; − relationship indicates little or no effect of advertising on sales.

Exhibit 9–4 lists these factors, and their relationships.[6] For example, a product characterized by emotional buying motives, hidden product qualities, and/or a strong basis for differentiation would see a noticeable impact of advertising on sales (see Exhibit 9–5). Products characterized as large dollar purchases would be less likely to benefit. Likewise, products in the maturity or decline stages of the product life cycle would be less likely to notice an impact on sales. Other factors involving the market, customer, costs, and strategies employed were also shown to have different effects.

The results of this study are interesting although limited. The factors presented here relate primarily to the percentage of sales dollars allocated to advertising and the factors influencing these ratios. As we will see later in this chapter, the percentage of sales method of budgeting has inherent weaknesses in that the advertising and sales effects may be reversed. Thus, in the case of these factors, we cannot be sure whether the situation actually led to the advertising sales relationship or vice versa. Thus, while these factors should be considered in the budget appropriation decision, they should not be used as the sole determination as to where and when to increase or decrease expenditures.

Keys to budget setting

A survey of the *Advertising Age* Editorial Sounding Board (92 executives of the top 200 advertising companies in the United States—representing the client side—and 130 executives of the 200 largest advertising agencies and 11 advertising consultants—representing the agency side) yielded the results shown in Exhibit 9–6, page 301, regarding factors gaining and losing in importance in budget setting. As can be seen in this exhibit, there is some lack of consensus as to what is becoming more or less important in determining the size of the budget. While clients—referring to their own companies—most commonly cite intended changes in advertising strategy and/ or creative approaches as important in setting the ad budget, those on the agency side are more likely to cite *profit contribution goals* or other financial targets of the client as growing in importance. Some disagreement is seen in respect to which factors are decreasing in importance also, as only the level of the previous year's spending appears as a key factor to both groups.

Overall, the responses of these two groups reflect, in part, their perceptions as to how budgets are set. To understand fully why differences in the relative importance

➤ *Exhibit 9–5*
A strong basis for differentiation could show a noticeable effect of advertising on sales

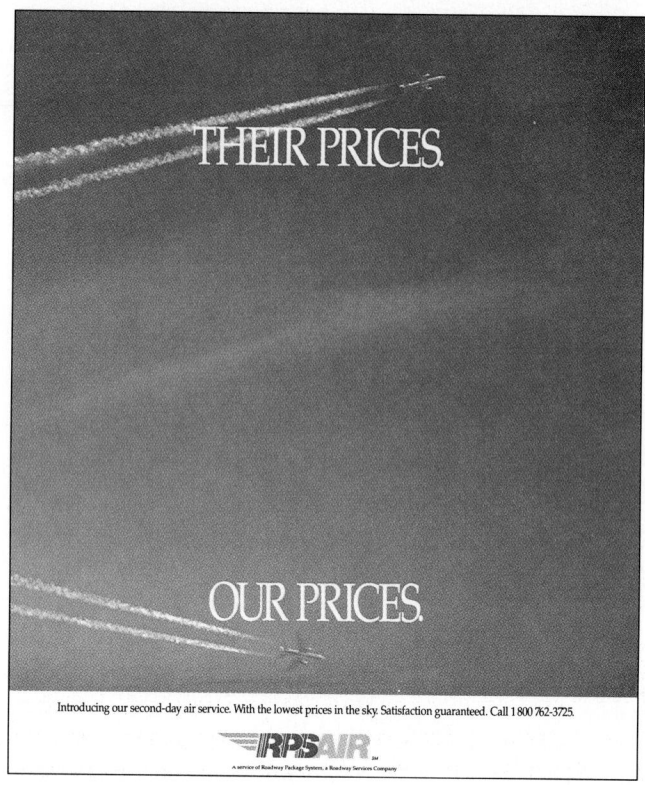

of these factors might be indicated, it is important to understand the approaches currently employed in budget setting. The next section of this chapter examines these.

Budgeting Approaches

As just discussed, the theoretical approaches to establishing the promotional budget are seldom employed. In smaller firms, they may never be used. Rather, a number of different methods developed through practice and experience are implemented. This section reviews some of the more traditional methods employed for setting budgets and the relative advantages and disadvantages of each. However, before discussing each of these methods, it is important for you to understand two things: First, it is common for a firm to employ more than one method; and second, the budgeting approaches utilized by firms vary according to the size and sophistication of the organization. Let us proceed with a discussion of each of the more commonly employed methods and then return to a discussion of these two points.

Top-Down Approaches

The approaches discussed in this section may be referred to as **top-down approaches** because a budgetary amount is established (usually at an executive level), and then the monies are passed down to the various departments (as shown in Exhibit 9–7, page 302). As you will see, these budgets are essentially predetermined and have no true theoretical basis. Top-down methods include the affordable method, arbitrary allocation, percentage of sales, competitive parity, and return on investment (ROI).

The affordable method

In the **affordable method** (often referred to as the all-you-can-afford method), the firm determines the amount of monies to be spent in various areas such as production and operations and, having done so, allocates remaining dollars to advertising and promotion, considering this to be the amount it can afford. The task to be performed by the advertising/promotions function is not considered, and the likelihood of under- or overspending is high, as no guidelines for measuring the effects of various budgets are established.

> *Exhibit 9-6*
Importance of factors in budget setting

Advertisers—Referring to Own Companies	
Increasing in Importance	
Intended changes in advertising strategy and/or creative approach	51%
Competitive activity and/or spending levels	47
Profit contribution goal or other financial target	43
Decreasing in Importance	
Level of previous year's spending, with adjustment	17
Senior management dollar allocation or set limit	11
Volume share projections	8

Agencies—Referring to Client Companies	
Increasing in Importance	
Profit contribution goal or other financial target	56%
Competitive activity and/or spending levels	43
Intended changes in advertising strategy and/or creative approach	37
Decreasing in Importance	
Projections/assumptions on media cost increases	25
Level of previous year's spending, with adjustment	24
Modifications in media strategy and/or buying techniques	17

In the Pacific Printing example discussed in Promotional Perspective 9–1, the owner of the company allocated his money to various sources such as equipment and remodeling, leaving little for advertising and promotion. When asked how he arrived at the budget, the owner said, "This is all that I could afford after my expenses." As noted, this approach is not uncommon among small firms. Unfortunately, it is also not uncommon in large firms either—particularly those that are not marketing driven and either do not understand or do not believe in the role and function of advertising and promotion. For example, many high-tech firms will focus on new product development and engineering, assuming the product, if good enough, will sell itself. In many of these companies, little monies are left for performing the advertising and promotions tasks.

The logic for using this approach stems from a "We can't be hurt with this method" thinking. That is, if we know what we can afford, and we do not exceed it, we will not get into financial problems. While this may be true in a strictly accounting sense, this method does not reflect sound managerial decision making from a marketing perspective. Often, using this method does not result in enough money being allocated to get the product off the ground and into the market. In terms of the S-shaped sales response model discussed earlier, the firm is operating in range A. Or the firm could be spending more than is necessary, operating in range C on the curve. In other instances, once the market gets tough and sales and/or profits begin to fall, this method would likely lead to budget cuts at a time when they very well might need to be increased.

Arbitrary allocation

Perhaps an even weaker method than the affordable method for establishing a budget is that of **arbitrary allocation.** While the previous method at least gave some thought to economic considerations, in this approach virtually no theoretical basis is considered, and often the budgetary amount is set by fiat; that is, the budget is determined by management solely on the basis of what is felt to be necessary and/or effective. In a discussion of how managers set advertising budgets, Melvin Salveson reported that often these decisions may reflect "as much upon the managers' psychological profile as they do economic criteria."[7] While Salveson was referring to larger corporations, the approach is no less common in small firms and nonprofit organizations.

➤ *Exhibit 9–7*
Top-down versus bottom-up approaches to budget setting

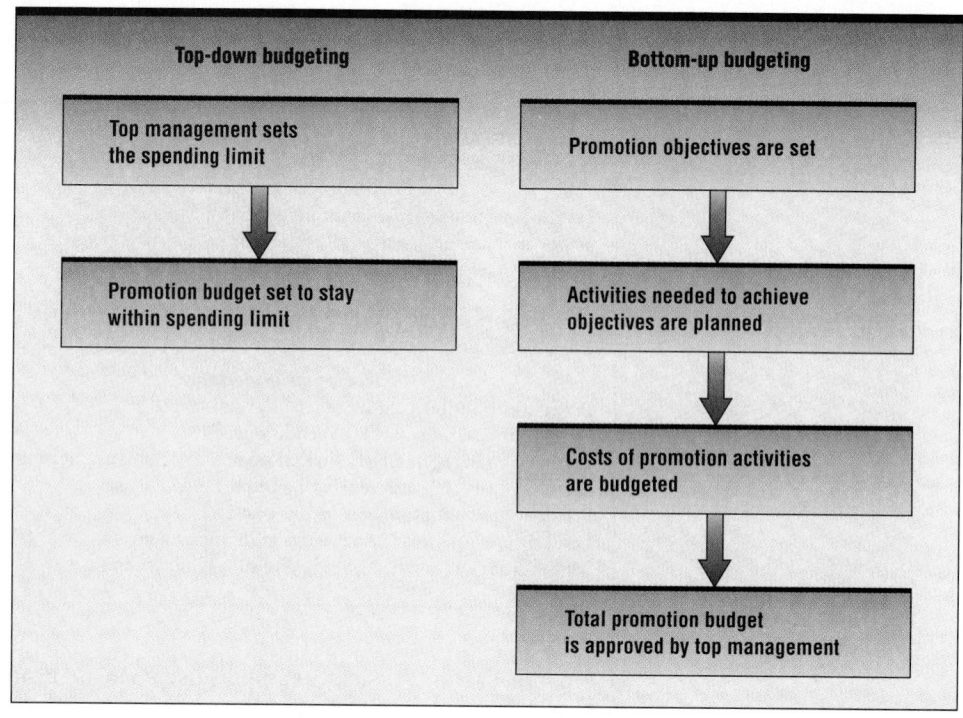

The arbitrary allocation approach has no obvious advantages. No systematic thinking has occurred, no objectives have been budgeted for, and the concept and purpose of advertising and promotion have been largely ignored. Other than the fact that the manager believes some monies must be spent on advertising and promotion and then picks a number, there is no good explanation as to why this approach continues to be used. At the same time, budgets continue to be set this way, and our purpose in discussing it is to point out that this method is employed—not recommended.

➤ *Exhibit 9–8*
Alternative methods for computing percentage of sales for Entree Cologne

Method 1: Straight % of sales	
1993 Total dollar sales	$1,000,000
Straight % of sales at 10%	$100,000
1994 Advertising budget	$100,000
Method 2: % of unit cost	
1993 Cost per bottle to mfr.	$4.00
Per unit cost allocated to adv.	1.00
1994 Forecasted sales, 100,000 units	
1994 Advertising budget (100,000 × $1.00)	$100,000

Percentage of sales

Perhaps the most commonly used method for budget setting (particularly in large firms) is the **percentage of sales method.** In this method, the advertising and promotions budget is based on the sales of the product, with the amount to be determined in either of two ways: (1) taking a percentage of the sales dollars or (2) assigning a fixed amount of the unit product cost to promotion and multiplying this amount by the number of units sold. These two methods are shown in Exhibit 9–8.

A second variation of the percentage of sales method is offered by using a **percentage of projected future sales** as a base. (This is reflected in method 2 provided in Exhibit 9–8.) Again, this method may use either a straight percentage of projected sales method or a unit cost projection, as shown above. In the straight percentage method, sales are projected for the coming year based on the marketing manager's estimates. The budget is established by taking a percentage of these sales. Often an industry standard percentage much like those presented in Exhibit 9–9 will be used to make this determination.

One advantage offered by using future sales as a base is that the budget is not based on last year's sales. As the market changes, these changes and the effect they will have on sales must be factored into the next year's forecast rather than relying on past data. As a result, the budget is more likely to reflect current conditions and, as such, be more appropriate.

Examination of the budgets of the different industries shown in Exhibit 9–9 reveals the percentage allocated varies from one industry to the next, with some

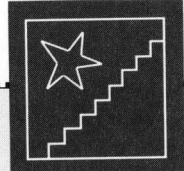

Promotional Perspective 9–1

Poor Budgeting Dooms a Printer

Pacific Printing, which had been in the printing business for over 20 years, decided it wanted to enter the photocopying business. The company's interest in entering this market was motivated by a proliferation of copy services that had sprung up in the city, giving the owner of the printing company the impression there was money to be made in this business. After clearing out a back room in the print shop, the owner's next move was to purchase the top-of-the-line Xerox copy machine—for cash. On taking delivery of the copier, this same owner called in an advertising consultant to help him embark on an advertising and promotional strategy that would position him among the leaders. He explained his goals to the consultant and asked for a proposal for a promotional plan, including the figure the consultant thought was necessary to make the program work.

When the consultant returned a week later and presented the advertising and promotional budget he was proposing, the print shop owner was shocked. He explained to the consultant he had never dreamed of spending anywhere near that amount and, in fact, only had about a tenth of the proposed budget available. The consultant—himself now a bit shocked—asked the owner how he had arrived at the figure he had established. His answer was, "After I purchased the copy machine, and cleared out the back room, this was all that I felt that I could afford." The consultant left without the contract, and Pacific Printing never got off the ground in the photocopying business.

firms budgeting a very small percentage (for example, 4.4 in construction and mining), whereas others spend a much higher proportional amount (for example, 8.6 percent in the beverage industry). (The actual dollar amounts spent may vary quite markedly according to the company's total sales figure. Thus, a smaller percentage of sales in the food industry may actually result in significantly more advertising dollars being spent!)

Proponents of the percentage of sales method cite a number of advantages to this approach. First, they argue it is financially safe and keeps ad spending within reasonable limits, as it bases spending on the past year's sales or what the firm expects to sell in the upcoming year. Thus, there will be sufficient monies to cover this budget, with increases in sales leading to budget increases, and decreases resulting in decreases accordingly. Second, the percentage of sales method is simple, straightforward, and easy to implement. Regardless of which basis—past or future sales—is employed, the calculations necessary to arrive at a budget are not difficult. Finally, this budgeting approach is generally stable. While the budget may vary with increases and decreases in sales, for the most part, as long as these changes are not drastic, the manager will have a fairly reasonable idea of the parameters of the budget.

At the same time, the percentage of sales method has some serious disadvantages that render it less than an optimal budgeting strategy. Perhaps the most serious is the basic premise on which the budget is established: *sales.* Using sales as the basis for setting the advertising appropriation is analogous to putting the cart before the horse. Rather than considering advertising as the cause of sales, the roles are reversed, with the level of sales determining the amount of advertising and promotions dollars to be spent. The result is a reversal of the cause-and-effect relationship between advertising and sales.

A second problem with this approach is actually one of the characteristics cited as an advantage earlier: stability. The position of proponents is that if all firms use a similar percentage, then stability will be brought to the marketplace. What happens if someone varies from this standard percentage? The problem here is that this method does not allow for changes in strategy either internally or from competitors. A firm wishing to be aggressive may wish to allocate more monies to the advertising

➤ *Exhibit 9–9* **Advertising-to-sales ratios (by industry), 1991**

Industry	Ad Dollars as Percent of Sales	Ad Dollars as Percent of Margin	Industry	Ad Dollars as Percent of Sales	Ad Dollars as Percent of Margin
Abrasive, asbestos, misc minerals	1.1	3.9	Computer communication equipment	1.9	4.0
Adhesives & sealants	2.7	5.9	Computer peripheral equip, NEC	1.9	4.1
Agriculture chemicals	0.7	3.1	Computer storage devices	1.4	4.8
Agriculture production-crops	2.2	7.1	Computers & software-wholesale	0.6	5.2
Air cond, heating, refrig equip	1.7	6.5	Construction, mining, matl handle equip	4.4	12.9
Air courier services	1.2	9.9	Convert paper, paprbd, ex boxes	2.3	5.2
Air transport, scheduled	1.9	65.5	Dairy products	4.1	11.2
Aircraft & parts	0.6	3.1	Drug & proprietary stores	1.6	5.6
Aircraft parts, aux equip, NEC	0.8	3.1	Durable goods-wholesale, NEC	3.6	7.6
Auto & home supply stores	2.2	8.9	Educational services	6.9	15.7
Auto rent & lease, no drivers	2.4	3.6	Electrical indl apparatus	2.0	6.2
Automatic regulating controls	3.3	11.5	Electrical measure & test instruments	2.6	5.4
Bakery products	8.0	47.6	Electr, other elec equip, ex computrs	2.2	5.6
Beverages	8.6	14.6	Electric lighting, wiring equip	2.5	8.5
Books: publng & printing	2.9	6.0	Electromedical apparatus	1.3	2.2
Broadwoven fabric mill, cotton	4.3	21.7	Electronic comp, accessories	0.7	2.3
Business services, NEC	2.7	6.5	Electronic components, NEC	1.0	3.4
Cable & other pay TV services	2.9	6.0	Electronic computers	3.6	7.2
Calculate, acct mach, ex comp	1.7	4.4	Electronic connectors	1.0	4.2
Catalog, mail-order houses	6.9	17.7	Electronic parts, equip-whsl, NEC	2.0	7.5
Chemicals & allied prods-whsl	4.2	18.0	Engineering services	0.4	1.9
Chemicals & allied products	2.3	6.1	Engines & turbines	1.3	6.6
Cmp programming, data process	0.2	0.6	Engr, acc, resrch, mgnt, rel svcs	1.4	6.7
Computer & comp software stores	0.6	3.1	Equip rental & leasing, NEC	0.7	2.4
Computer integrated system design	1.5	4.1	Fabricated plate work	1.0	3.7
Computer processing, data prep svc	1.5	2.9	Fabricated rubber products, NEC	0.7	3.9
Computer programming service	1.7	8.9	Facilities support mgmt svcs	1.9	11.6
Commercial printing	2.7	10.4	Farm machinery & equipment	1.1	4.5
Communications equipment, NEC	2.1	4.9	Finance-services	0.8	6.9
Communications services, NEC	1.3	3.2	Food & kindred products	6.3	14.9
Computer & office equipment	1.6	3.3			

and promotions budget—a strategy that would not be possible with a percentage of sales method, unless the manager was willing to deviate from industry standards.

Unfortunately, this method of budgeting may result in severe misappropriation of funds. If one believes advertising and promotion have a role to perform in marketing a product, then one should believe allocating more monies to advertising will, as shown in the S-shaped curve, generate incremental sales (to a point). Products with low sales will have smaller promotion budgets, which in turn will hinder sales progress. At the other extreme, very successful products may have an excess budget—some of which may be better appropriated elsewhere.

The percentage of sales method is also difficult to employ for new product introductions (see Exhibit 9–10). If no past sales histories are available, there may exist no basis for establishing the budget. Projections of future sales may be difficult, particularly if the product is highly innovative and/or may have fluctuating sales patterns.

Finally, if the budget is contingent on sales, decreases in sales will lead to decreases in budgets when they may need to be increased. To continue to cut the advertising and promotion budgets may add impetus to the downward sales trend. On the other hand, some of the more successful companies have been those that have allocated additional funds during hard times or downturns in the cycle of sales. As was indicated in the ad shown in the chapter lead-in, companies that have maintained or increased their ad expenditures during recessions achieved increased visibility and

had higher growth in both sales and market share (as compared to those that reduced advertising outlays). For example, Sunkist Growers can attribute at least some of its success in establishing and maintaining its strong image to the fact that it has maintained consistent levels of advertising expenditures over 80 years—despite recessions.[8]

While the percentage of future sales method has been proposed as a remedy for some of the problems discussed here, the reality is that problems with forecasting, cyclical growth, and uncontrollable factors have limited the effectiveness of this approach as well.

Competitive parity

If you asked marketing managers if they ever set their advertising and promotions budgets based on what their competitors allocated, they probably would deny it. Yet if you examined the advertising expenditures of these companies, both as a percentage of sales and in respect to the media in which they are being allocated, you would see little variation in the percentage of sales figures for firms within a given industry. Such results are not likely to have happened by chance alone, as the expenditures of competitors are available from a variety of sources, including companies that provide competitive advertising information, trade associations, and other advertising industry periodicals.

In the **competitive parity method,** budget amounts are established by matching the percentage sales expenditures of the competition. The argument here is that to set budgets in this fashion takes advantage of the collective wisdom of the industry— that is, uses the knowledge of others as well as oneself. A second advantage offered is that this method takes the competition into consideration, which leads to stability in the marketplace by minimizing marketing warfare. If the competition knows others are thought to be less likely to match their increases in promotional spending, they are less likely to take an aggressive posture to attempt to gain market share. Thus, the likelihood of unusual or unrealistic ad expenditures is minimized.

The competitive parity method has a number of disadvantages, however. For one, the method ignores the fact that advertising and promotions are designed to accomplish specific objectives by addressing certain problems and opportunities. Second, it assumes that because firms have equal, or nearly equal, expenditures, their programs will be equally effective. Such an assumption ignores the contributions of creative executions and/or media allocations as well as the success or lack thereof of various promotions. Further, it ignores possible advantages of the firm itself; for example, some firms simply make better products than others.

In addition to the disadvantages cited above, there is no guarantee the competition will continue to pursue their existing strategies. Given that competitive parity figures must be determined by examination of competitors' previous years' promotional expenditures (short of corporate espionage), changes in market emphasis and/or spending may not be recognized until the competition has already established an advantage. Further, there is no guarantee the competition will not increase or decrease its own expenditures, regardless of what other companies do. Finally, promotional wars may not be avoided. Companies like Coke and Pepsi and Anheuser-Busch and Miller have been notorious for their spending wars, with each responding to the others' increased outlays.

In summary, it is unlikely that a firm will employ the competitive parity method as a sole means of establishing the promotional budget. This method is typically used in conjunction with the percentage of sales or other methods. It is not a wise strategy to ignore the competition. Managers must always be aware of what competitors are doing; they should not just emulate them in setting their own goals and developing their own strategies (see Exhibit 9–11).

Return on investment (ROI)

As previously noted, in employing the percentage of sales method, sales dictate the level of advertising appropriations. At that time we stated this relationship is backward and advertising should be seen as a contributor to sales. In the marginal analysis and S-shaped curve approaches, it is expected that incremental investments in advertising and promotions dollars should lead to increases in sales. The key word here is *investment*.

In the **ROI budgeting method,** advertising and promotions are considered as investments, just as plant and equipment and the like are in other areas of the firm. Thus, the budgetary appropriation (investment) should then lead to certain returns. As with other aspects of the firm's efforts, advertising and promotion are expected to meet a certain level of return.

While the ROI method appears to be good on paper, the reality is that it is almost never possible to assess the returns provided by the promotional effort—at least so long as sales continue to be the basis for evaluation. Thus, while managers are certain to pose the question as to how much return they are getting for such expenditures, the bottom line is that it still remains a question, and ROI remains a virtually unused method of budgeting.

Summary of Top-Down Budgeting Methods

Having just read this section, you are probably asking yourself why we even discussed this material. The budgeting methods examined are either not recommended for use or, when they are used, have severe disadvantages that limit their effectiveness.

➤ *Exhibit 9–11* **Managers must always be aware of what competitors are doing and how they are advertising their products**

IF IT HAD A 20-VALVE HIGH-PERFORMANCE ENGINE, IT WOULD BE OUR COMPETITION.

Acura Vigor GS

Imagine settling back in a comfortable leather seat, escaping the pressures of the outside world. You adjust the volume on your one-of-a-kind sound system and take in the unobstructed view. But instead of turning the page of your book, you downshift and turn the corner.

As luxuriously furnished as the Acura Vigor GS is, aesthetics never take a backseat to performance. So, the real beauty of its leather- and wood-trimmed interior is the fact that it was designed to enhance the driving experience. From the way the seats hold your body in place to the way the controls respond to your touch. And knowing you have standard anti-lock brakes and a driver's side air bag will surely help you relax.

Add all that to a 2.5-liter, 176-horsepower engine and you realize that the Acura Vigor is one car that not only offers you the comforts of home, but the power to leave it very quickly. For more information or your nearest dealer, call 1-800-TO-ACURA.

ⒶACURA PRECISION CRAFTED PERFORMANCE

Nevertheless, it is necessary to understand the various methods considered and used so that you might recognize their limitations. This is particularly true since, in reality, these are the methods most commonly employed by marketers, as demonstrated by the research studies cited in Exhibit 9–12. While these studies did not report on why top-down methods are so commonly employed, it would seem likely that tradition and top management's desire for control may be two of the major contributing factors.

As shown in Exhibit 9–12, the use of percentage of sales methods remains high, particularly that based on anticipated sales. Fortunately, both the affordable and arbitrary methods appear to be on the decrease, as is the use of quantitative methods. On the increase is the use of a method not yet discussed—the objective and task method. Let us now turn our discussion to this method, reserving our discussion of quantitative models until later.

Build-up Approaches

The major flaw associated with the top-down methods is that they are judgmental approaches that lead to predetermined budget appropriations often not linked to objectives and the strategies designed to accomplish them. A more effective budgeting strategy would be to consider the communications objectives established and budget according to what is deemed necessary to attain these goals. The promotional planning model established in Chapter 1 indicates the budget decision is an interactive process with the communications objectives, on the one hand, and the promotional mix alternatives, on the other. The idea is to budget so these promotional mix strategies can be implemented to achieve the stated objectives. Methods for budget setting under this approach are now considered.

➤ *Exhibit 9–12*
Comparison of general methods used by consumer advertisers to set advertising budgets

Method	Percentage of Respondents Using Each Method		
	San Augustine and Foley (1975)	Patti and Blasko (1981)	Lancaster and Stern (1983)
Quantitative methods	4	51	20
Objective and task	12	63	80
Percentage anticipated sales	52	53	53
Unit anticipated sales	12	22	28
Percentage past sales	16	20	20
Unit past sales	12	n.a.	15
Affordable	28	20	13
Arbitrary	16	4	n.a.
Match competitors	n.a.	24	25
Outspend competitors	n.a.	n.a.	8
Share of voice/market	n.a.	n.a.	5
Previous budget	n.a.	n.a.	3
Others	20	n.a.	12

n.a. = not applicable
Note: Totals exceed 100% due to multiple responses and rounding.

Objective and task method

As previously noted, it is important that objectives setting and budgeting go hand in hand rather than in a sequential step fashion. It is difficult to establish a budget with no specific objectives in mind, and setting objectives without regard to the budget available makes no sense. For example, the objective of Pacific Printing may have been to create awareness of the availability of its copy services throughout the southern California market. With the minimal budget the owner had established, it is obvious that attainment of this goal was impossible.

The **objective and task method of budget setting** utilizes a **build-up approach**, employing a three-step process: (1) defining the communications objectives to be accomplished, (2) determining the specific strategies and tasks that will be required to attain these objectives, and (3) estimating the costs associated with the performance of these strategies and tasks. The total budget is based on the accumulation of these costs.

Implementing the objective and task approach is somewhat more involved. In using this method, the manager is required to monitor and evaluate this process throughout and change existing strategies according to the attainment and/or nonattainment of objectives. As shown in Exhibit 9–13, this process involves several steps. Let us examine these in more detail.

1. **Isolation of objectives.** On presentation of the promotional planning model, a company will have two sets of objectives to be accomplished—the marketing objectives for the product and the communications objectives. On establishing the former, the task now involves determining the specific communications objectives that will be designed to accomplish these goals. As in any objective setting process, communications objectives must be specific, attainable, and measurable as well as time constrained.

2. **Determination of tasks required.** Again referring to the promotional planning process, a number of elements are involved in the strategic plan designed to attain the objectives established (these strategies will constitute the remaining chapters in this text and may involve all the elements of the promotional mix). These tasks may include advertising in various media, sales promotions, and/or other elements of the promotional mix, each with its own role to perform.

3. **Estimation of required expenditures.** Build-up analysis requires determining the estimated costs associated with the tasks developed in the previous step. For

➤ *Exhibit 9–13*
The objective and task method

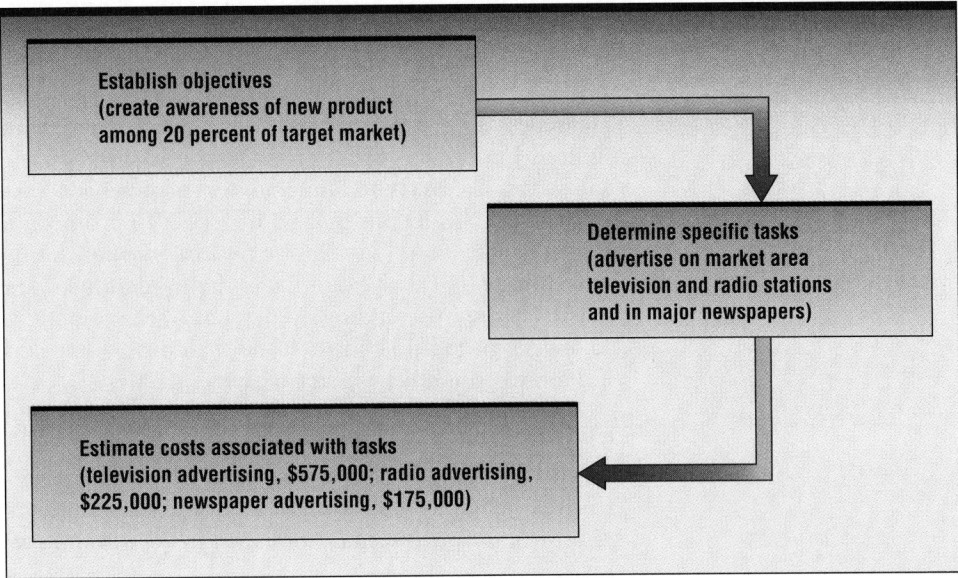

example, this would involve costs for developing awareness through advertising, trial through sampling, and so forth.

4. Monitoring. As will be seen in Chapter 20 on measuring effectiveness, methods can be applied to determine how well one is doing with respect to attaining established objectives. Performance in this regard should be monitored and evaluated in light of the budget appropriated.

5. Reevaluation of objectives. Once specific objectives have been obtained, monies might be better spent on new goals. Thus, if one has achieved the level of awareness sought, the budget should be altered to stress a higher-order objective such as evaluation or trial.

The major advantage of the objective and task method is that the budget is driven by the objectives to be attained. Thus, rather than being established at the top and passed down, the managers closest to the marketing effort will have input and specific strategies that will be considered in the budget setting process.

The major disadvantage of this method is determining which tasks will be required as well as the costs associated with each. In many cases, these determinations are not easily made. For example, specifically what tasks would be necessary to attain awareness among 50 percent of the target market? How much will it cost to perform these tasks? While these decisions may be easier to determine for certain objectives—for example, estimating the costs of sampling required to stimulate trial in a defined market area—it is not always possible to know exactly what is required and/or how much it will cost to complete the job. While this process becomes easier if one has had past experience to use as a guide—either with the existing product or a similar one in the same product category—it is especially difficult for new product introductions. As a result, the budget setting process using this method is not as easy to perform or as stable as some of the methods discussed earlier. Given this disadvantage, many marketing managers have not adopted the objective and task method for allocating the budget. Rather, they have stayed with some of the top-down approaches discussed earlier for setting the total expenditure amount.

The objective and task method—while offering advantages over other methods previously discussed—is more difficult to implement when there is no track record for the product. Thus, budgeting for new product introductions tends to be a special case. The following section addresses this problem.

Payout planning

The first months of a new product's introduction typically require heavier-than-normal advertising and promotion appropriations to stimulate higher levels of awareness and subsequently trial. After studying more than 40 years of Nielsen figures, James O. Peckham has estimated the average share of advertising to share of sales ratio necessary to launch a new product successfully is approximately 1.5:2.0.[9] Translated, this means that with respect to promotion, a new entry should be spending at approximately twice the desired market share, as shown in the two examples in Exhibit 9–14. For example, in the food industry, brand 101 gained a 12.6 percent market share by spending 34 percent of the total advertising dollars in this category. Likewise, brand 401 in the toiletry industry had a 30 percent share of advertising dollars to gain a 19.5 percent share of sales.

To determine how much to spend, marketers will often develop a **payout plan.** This plan determines the investment value of the advertising and promotion appropriation. The basic idea is to project the revenues the product will generate over two to three years, as well as the costs that will be incurred. Based on an expected rate of return, the payout plan will assist in determining what advertising and promotions

> *Exhibit 9–14*
Share of advertising/sales relationship (two-year summary)

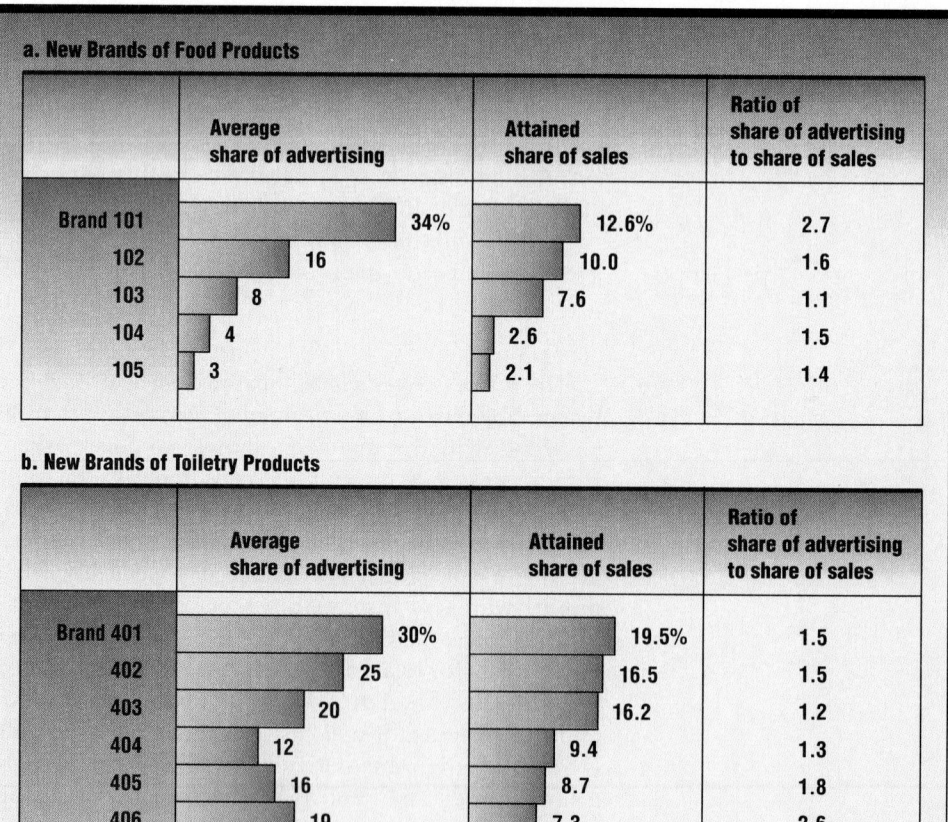

a. New Brands of Food Products

	Average share of advertising	Attained share of sales	Ratio of share of advertising to share of sales
Brand 101	34%	12.6%	2.7
102	16	10.0	1.6
103	8	7.6	1.1
104	4	2.6	1.5
105	3	2.1	1.4

b. New Brands of Toiletry Products

	Average share of advertising	Attained share of sales	Ratio of share of advertising to share of sales
Brand 401	30%	19.5%	1.5
402	25	16.5	1.5
403	20	16.2	1.2
404	12	9.4	1.3
405	16	8.7	1.8
406	19	7.3	2.6
407	14	7.2	1.9
408	10	6.0	1.7
409	7	6.0	1.2
410	6	5.9	1.0
411	10	5.9	1.7
412	6	5.2	1.2

expenditures will be necessary and at what time this return might be expected. An example of a three-year payout plan is shown in Exhibit 9–15. The product would lose money in year 1, almost break even in year 2, and finally begin to show substantial profits by the end of year 3.

The advertising and promotion figures are higher in year 1, declining in years 2 and 3. This appropriation is consistent with that suggested earlier by Peckham and reflects the additional outlays necessary to make as rapid an impact as possible. (Keep in mind that shelf space is limited, and a store owner is not likely to wait around for a product to become successful!) In addition, it must reflect the companies' guidelines for new product expenditures, as companies generally have established time periods in which the product must begin to show a profit. Finally, it should be kept in mind that building market share may be more difficult than maintaining it—thus, the substantial drop-off in expenditures in the later years.

In summary, while the payout plan is in itself not always perfect, it does guide the manager in establishing the budget. When used in conjunction with the objective and task method, it provides a much more logical approach to budget setting than the top-down approaches previously discussed.

Quantitative models

Attempts to apply *quantitative models* to budgeting have met with limited success. For the most part, these methods have employed **computer simulation models** involving statistical techniques such as multiple regression analysis to determine the relative contribution that the size of the budget has on the sales response to advertising. Because of problems associated with these methods, their acceptance and use have been limited—as is demonstrated in the figures reported earlier in Exhibit 9–12. At the same time, as is evident in this same exhibit, some advertisers have found the quantitative approach to be satisfactory and continue to employ this method. Unfortunately, the value of quantitative models has yet to reach the promised potential. Perhaps as computers continue to find their way into the advertising domain, better models may be forthcoming. The specific discussion of these models is beyond the scope of this text, however, and we will limit our discussion to noting that such methods do have merit but may need more refinement before achieving widespread success.

Summary of Budgeting Methods

The preceding discussion of budgeting approaches indicates there is no universally accepted method of setting a budget figure. Weaknesses in each method may make them unfeasible or inappropriate. At the same time, as is indicated in Exhibit 9–12, the use of the objective and task method continues to increase, whereas less sophisticated methods are declining in favor. In addition to the increased use of the objective and task method, more advertisers are employing the payout planning approach. By using these approaches in combination with the percentage of sales methods, these advertisers are more likely to arrive at a useful and more sophisticated method of budget setting. For example, many firms now start the budgeting process by establishing the objectives they need to accomplish and budget for them.

➢ *Exhibit 9–15*
Example of three-year payout plan ($ millions)

	Year 1	Year 2	Year 3
Product sales	15	35.5	60.75
Profit contribution (@ $0.50/case)	7.5	17.75	30.38
Advertising/promotions	15	10.5	8.5
Profit (loss)	(7.5)	7.25	21.88
Cumulative profit (loss)	(7.5)	(0.25)	21.63

However, the budget may be constrained by the application of a percentage of sales, or other method, when considering whether or not it is affordable. In addition, competitors' budgets may also influence this decision.

Allocating the Budget

Once the budget has been appropriated, the next step is to allocate it. The allocation decision involves determining which markets, products, and/or promotional elements will receive the funds appropriated. In this section, we discuss the factors influencing this decision.

Allocating to Advertising and Promotion Elements

As noted earlier in this chapter, advertisers have begun to shift some of their budget dollars away from traditional advertising media and into sales promotions targeted at both the consumer and the trade. In addition, direct marketing and other promotional tools are also receiving increased attention and competing for more of the promotional budget (see Exhibit 9–16). The advantage of more target selectivity has led to an increased emphasis on direct marketing while a variety of new media (which will be discussed in Chapter 15) have provided marketers with previously unavailable ways to reach prospective customers.

Marketers have also noted that rapidly rising media costs, the ability of sales promotions to motivate trial, maturing of the product and/or brand, and the need for more aggressive promotional tools have also led to shifts in strategy.[10] (We discuss consumer and trade promotions and the reasons for some of these changes in Chapter 17).

Some marketers have also effectively used the allocation decision as a strategy for stretching the advertising dollar—that is, to get more impact from the same amount of monies—as is demonstrated in the General Motors example discussed in Promotional Perspective 9–2.

Client/Agency Policies

Another factor that may influence budget allocation is the individual policy of the company or the advertising agency. The agency may discourage the allocation of

➢ *Exhibit 9–16*
Companies like Edible Advertising offer a novel way to promote a product or a company

monies to sales promotion, preferring to spend them on the advertising area. While the agency position is that promotional monies are harder to track in terms of effectiveness, and they may be used improperly if not under its control, it has also been noted that in many cases commissions are not made on this area and this fact might contribute to the agency's reluctance.[11]

The orientation of the agency or firm may also directly influence where monies are spent. Many ad agencies are managed by top officers who have ascended through the creative ranks and as a result are more willing and inclined to emphasize the creative budget. Others may have preferences for specific media. For example, in 1985, BBDO Worldwide, one of the largest advertising agencies in the United States, began to position itself as an expert in cable television programming and as a result began to spend more of the clients' monies in this medium. Other agencies have also acquired reputations as being more inclined to prefer one advertising medium over others. All in all, both the agency and the client may have specific preferences and favor certain aspects of the promotional program, perhaps based on past successes, that will influence to a large degree where dollars are spent.

Market Size

While the budget should be allocated according to the specific promotional tools necessary to accomplish the stated objectives, the *size* of the market will affect the decision. In smaller markets, it is often easier and less expensive to reach the target market. Too much of an expenditure in these markets will lead to saturation and a lack of effective spending. In larger markets, the target group may be more dispersed and thus more expensive to reach. Think, for example, about the cost of purchasing media in Chicago or New York City versus a smaller market like Columbus, Ohio, or Birmingham, Alabama. The former would be much more costly and as such would necessitate a higher budget appropriation.

Market Potential

For a variety of reasons, some markets hold more potential than do others. Marketers of snow skis would find greater returns on their expenditures in Denver, Colorado, than they would in Ft. Lauderdale, Florida. Imported Mexican beers sell better in the border states (Texas, Arizona, California) than they do in the Midwest. A disproportionate number of imported cars are sold in California and New England, relative to the rest of the United States. In those instances that particular markets hold higher potential, the marketing manager might decide to allocate additional monies to them. (Keep in mind, however, that just because a market does not have high sales does not mean it is to be ignored. The key here is *potential*—and a market with low sales but high potential may be a candidate for additional appropriations.)

A variety of methods for estimating marketing potential are employed. Many marketers conduct research studies to forecast demand and/or use secondary sources of information such as those provided by government agencies or syndicated services such as Dun & Bradstreet, A. C. Nielsen, and Audits and Surveys. One source for consumer goods information is the *Survey of Buying Power,* published annually by *Sales & Marketing Management* magazine. The *Survey of Buying Power* contains population, income, and retail sales data on states, counties, metropolitan statistical areas, and cities in the United States and Canada with populations of 40,000 or more.

Market Share Goals

Two recent studies appearing in *Harvard Business Review* discussed advertising spending with the goal of maintaining market share and increasing market share.[12] In the first of these, John Jones compared the brand's share of market with its share of advertising voice (the brand's share of the total value of the main media exposure in the product category). Jones classified the brands as "profit taking brands, or

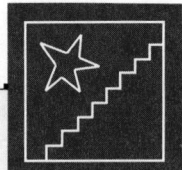

Promotional Perspective 9–2

How Much Needs to Be Spent to Market a Car?

When General Motors announced in 1991 it intended to cut over 70,000 jobs during the next five years, those in the advertising and promotion industry obviously took note. Surely such major cutbacks would also have to be felt in the communications budget as well. Not everyone agrees with this forecast, however. Some believe that if the entire GM organization was run as well as the advertising and marketing division, no cutbacks of any sort would be necessary. They point out that GM is already being outspent on a dollars-per-vehicle basis by 8 of the top 10 auto companies (see chart). In addition, since the company cannot afford to lose any more sales and market share, they predict that few, if any, cuts would be forthcoming.

Some analysts think that while the overall budget—over $2.3 billion was spent in the first nine months of 1991—may remain the same, the allocation of these monies may shift dramatically. As one executive noted, "The GM ad/marketing budget is best described as a living organism that takes many different forms but will stay the same size." Should this be true, someone in the GM organization will gain, while someone else will lose.

One area that might take a hit is the corporate campaign created by McCann-Erickson titled "Putting quality back on the road." Most of the divisions don't want the overall campaign, preferring a "hard-sell" approach conducted for each car on its own. Also likely to experience cuts is the ad/marketing staff.

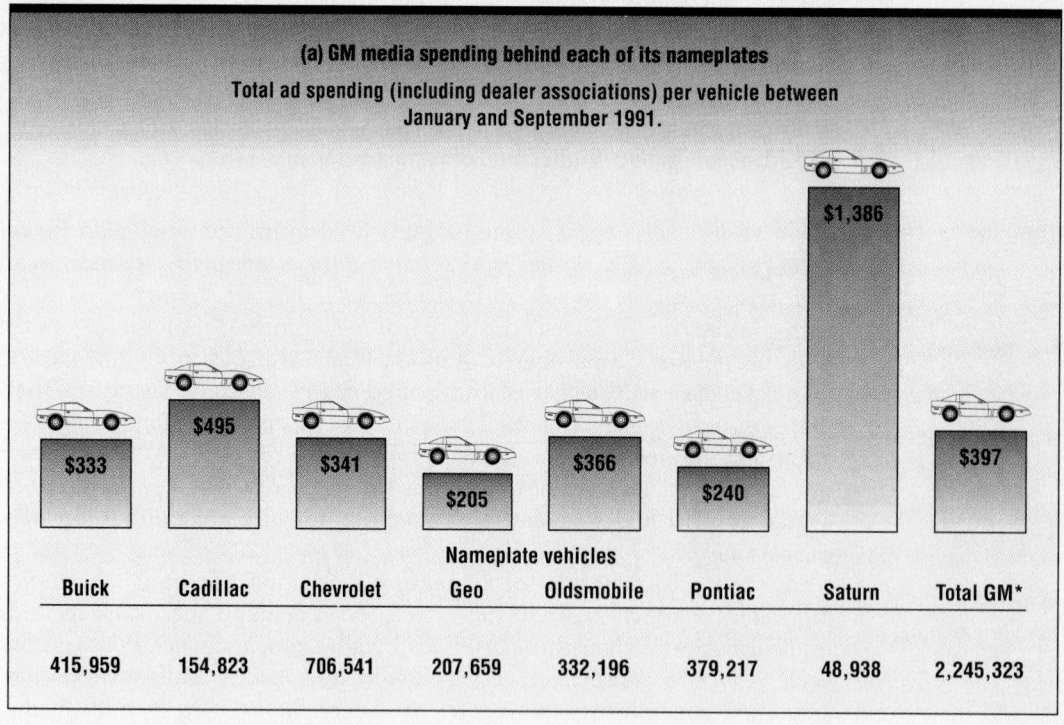

(a) GM media spending behind each of its nameplates

Total ad spending (including dealer associations) per vehicle between
January and September 1991.

	Buick	Cadillac	Chevrolet	Geo	Oldsmobile	Pontiac	Saturn	Total GM*
Per vehicle	$333	$495	$341	$205	$366	$240	$1,386	$397
	415,959	154,823	706,541	207,659	332,196	379,217	48,938	2,245,323

Nameplate vehicles

*Includes $111 million in corporate advertising.

Some of the work the ad agencies used to perform, such as research on the market and on various aspects of the advertising program, has been absorbed by GM in recent years, and while it continues to be conducted, fewer persons may be working more to do it.

Dealers may also feel the pinch. Dealer incentives could be reduced from $750 to $600 per year freeing $300 million ($150 × 2 million vehicles) for other forms of advertising.

The winners are the individual divisions. The recent successes of Cadillac and Saturn support the notion that the individual brands should promote themselves. Oldsmobile's lack of an image will likely get an infusion through more ad dollars (see the accompanying chart). Also likely to gain are the direct-marketing

agencies. Cadillac's successful mailing to 170,000 potential customers did not go unnoticed by the other divisions. (Chrysler also mailed out 400,000 videotapes to potential minivan buyers in 1991, and auto manufacturers do keep an eye on the competition!)

GM appears to be one of those companies that will not slash its advertising budget during a recession. As this perspective indicates, cuts do not necessarily have to occur if creative allocation is employed!

Source: Larry Collins and Eric Schmuckler, "Which Way GM?" *Mediaweek*, January 13, 1992, pp. 16–22; and, "What Happened to Advertising," *Business Week*, September 23, 1991, pp. 66–72.

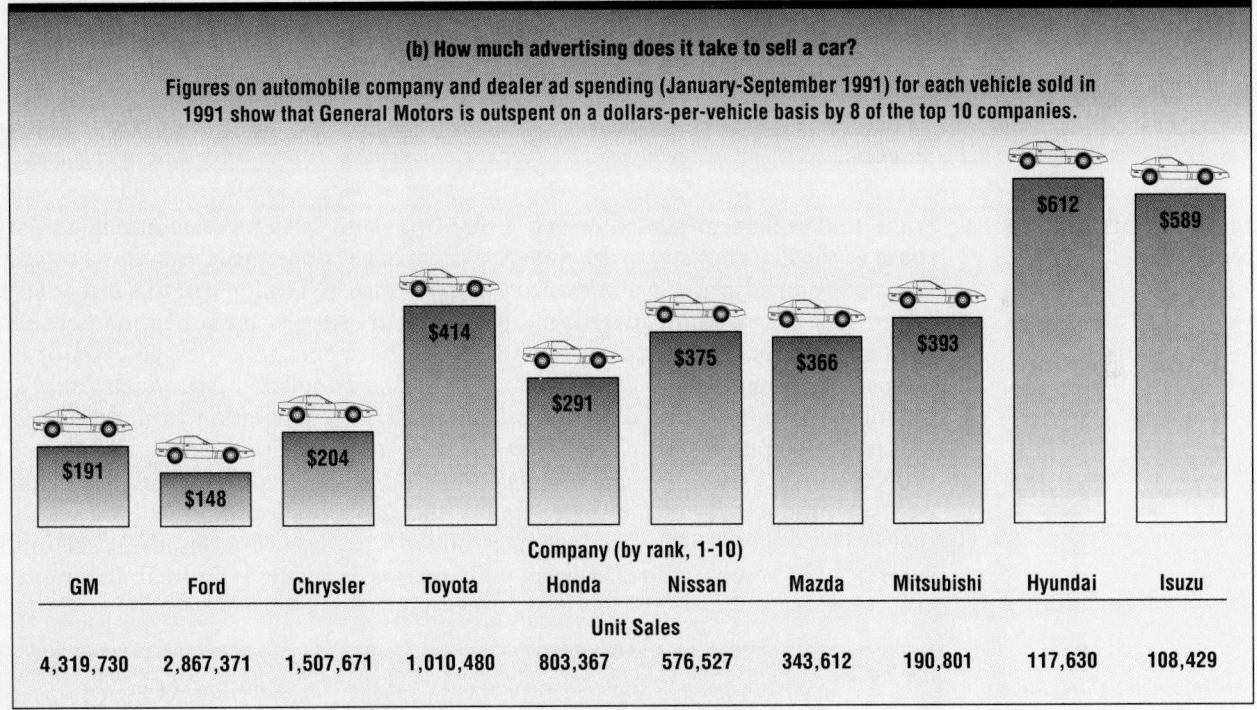

(b) How much advertising does it take to sell a car?

Figures on automobile company and dealer ad spending (January–September 1991) for each vehicle sold in 1991 show that General Motors is outspent on a dollars-per-vehicle basis by 8 of the top 10 companies.

Company (by rank, 1-10)

GM	Ford	Chrysler	Toyota	Honda	Nissan	Mazda	Mitsubishi	Hyundai	Isuzu
$191	$148	$204	$414	$291	$375	$366	$393	$612	$589

Unit Sales

GM	Ford	Chrysler	Toyota	Honda	Nissan	Mazda	Mitsubishi	Hyundai	Isuzu
4,319,730	2,867,371	1,507,671	1,010,480	803,367	576,527	343,612	190,801	117,630	108,429

underspenders" and "investment brands, those whose share of voice is clearly above their share of market." The results of his study indicated that for those brands with small market shares, profit takers are in the minority; however, as the brands get more powerful, or increase their market share, nearly three out of five have a proportionately smaller share of voice.

Jones notes that three factors can be cited to explain this change. First, new brands generally receive higher than average advertising support. Second, older, more mature brands are often "milked"—that is, when they reach the maturity stage, advertising support is reduced. And third, an advertising economy of scale whereby advertising works harder for well-established brands, a lower expenditure is required. Jones concludes that for larger brands, it may be possible to reduce advertising expenditures and still maintain market share. Smaller brands, on the other hand, have to continue to maintain a large share of voice to maintain and gain share.

James Schroer addressed the advertising budget in a situation in which the marketer wishes to increase market share. His analysis suggests that to have a growing market share, marketers should:

- Segment markets rather than focus on a national advertising effort, focusing on those markets where competition is weak and/or underspending.
- Determine their competitors' cost positions—in other words, determine how long the competition can continue to spend at the current or increased rate.
- Resist the lure of short-term profits that result from ad budget cuts.
- Consider niching strategies as opposed to long-term wars.

Exhibit 9–17 reflects Schroer's suggestions for spending priorities in various markets.

Economies of Scale in Advertising

Some studies have presented evidence that firms and/or brands maintaining a large share of the market have an advantage over smaller competitors and thus can spend less money on advertising and realize a better return.[13] The logic of this is that larger advertisers can maintain advertising shares that are smaller than their market shares because they may get better advertising rates, have declining average costs of production, and may accrue the advantages of advertising several products jointly. In addition, more favorable time and space positions, cooperation of middle people, and favorable publicity are seen as more likely to accrue. Reviewing the studies in support of this position, and then conducting research over a variety of small-package products, Kent Lancaster found that this situation did not hold true and that in fact larger brand share products might actually be at a disadvantage in this regard.[14] His results indicated firms with leading brands are not maintaining their

> *Exhibit 9–17*

The share of voice (SOV) effect and ad spending: priorities in individual markets

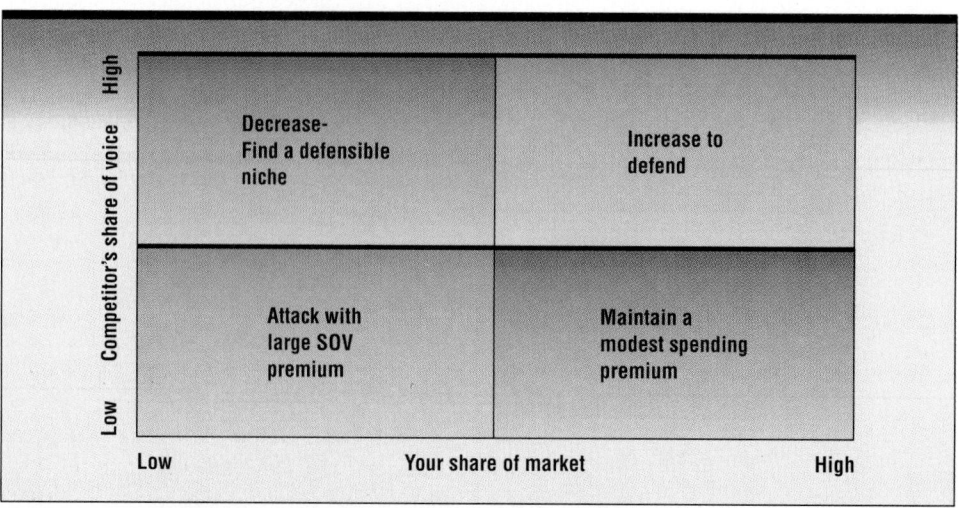

brand shares with lower advertising shares; the leading brands spend an average of 2.5 percentage points more than their brand share on advertising. More specifically, this study concluded the following:

1. There is no evidence to support the position that larger firms can support their brands with lower relative advertising costs than smaller firms.
2. There is no evidence that the leading brand in a product group enjoys lower advertising costs per sales dollar than do other brands.
3. There is no evidence of a static relationship between advertising costs per dollar of sales and the size of the advertiser.

The results of this study, and others that have shown similar results, would indicate there are really no **economies of scale** to be accrued as a result of the size of the firm or the market share of the brand.[15]

Organizational Characteristics

In a review of the literature on how allocation decisions are made between advertising and sales promotion, George Low and Jakki Mohr concluded organizational factors also played an important role in determining how communications dollars are spent.[16] The authors note that the following factors all influence the allocation decision:

- The organization's structure—that is centralized versus decentralized, formalization, and complexity.
- Power and politics in the organizational hierarchy.
- The use of expert opinions (for example, consultants).
- Characteristics of the decision maker (i.e., preferences and experience).
- Approval and negotiation channels.
- Pressure on senior managers to arrive at the "optimal" budget.

Low and Mohr note that each of the above factors influences the relative amounts assigned to advertising and promotion, and these factors vary from one organization to another.

One example of how these factors might influence allocations relates to organizational structure and the level of interaction between marketing and other functional departments such as accounting and operations. The authors note the relative importance of advertising versus sales promotion might vary from department to department, as accountants—being dollars-and-cents minded—would argue for the sales impact of promotions, while operations would argue against sales promotions because of sudden surges in demand that might result, thereby throwing off production schedules and so on. The net effect on the budget allocation would be that the marketing department might be influenced by the thinking of either of these groups in making its decision.

The use of outside consultants to provide expert opinions might also affect the allocation decision, based on the preferences of these people. Likewise, trade journals, academic journals, and even books might also be considered as valuable inputs into the decision maker's thinking. In sum, it seems obvious that a number of factors must be taken into account in the budget allocation decision. Factors such as market size and potential, specific objectives sought, as well as previous company and/or agency policies and preferences may all influence this decision.

SUMMARY

As you have probably concluded on reading this chapter, the budget decision is not typically based on supporting experiences or strong theoretical foundations. Nor is it one of the more soundly established elements of the promotional program.

The major problem associated with the budgeting methods now employed is that they are not based on the sound theoretical approach—economic models are limited; they often try to demonstrate the effects on sales directly; and they ignore other elements of the marketing mix. Some of the methods discussed have no theoretical basis and ignore the actual role advertising and promotion are meant to perform.

One possible suggestion for improving the budget appropriation is to tie the measures of effectiveness to communications objectives rather than to the broader-based marketing objectives. As noted in this chapter, one method for doing this would be to employ the objective and task approach, with communications objectives. While this approach may not be the ultimate solution to the budgeting problem, it would be an improvement over those methods currently being employed.

In other instances, marketers have found it advantageous to employ a combination of methods. For example, some companies establish the dollar amount of the budget by using a percentage of sales method, then allocate these monies by employing an objective and task approach. Others may consider combining payout planning and objective and task approaches.

As in the budget determination decision, a number of factors must be considered when allocating advertising and promotions dollars. Market size and potential, agency policies and preferences, and those of management itself may influence the allocation decision.

KEY TERMS

contribution margin
marginal analysis
concave-downward function
S-shaped response curve
top-down approaches
affordable method
arbitrary allocation

percentage of sales method
percentage of projected future sales
competitive parity method
ROI budgeting method

objective and task method of budget setting
build-up approach
payout plan
computer simulation models
economies of scale

DISCUSSION QUESTIONS

1. Discuss the marginal analysis approach to budget setting. What are some weaknesses that limit its application?
2. Compare the S-shaped response curve and the concave-downward sales response models. What types of products and/or services would be most likely to be characterized by each?
3. Discuss how you would explain to a small-business owner the reasons it would be necessary to budget a larger amount to advertising and promotion, basing your argument on the S-shaped response function.
4. What are some factors that have been increasing in importance in the budget-setting process? What are some factors that seem to be decreasing in importance?
5. Discuss the three factors cited by John Jones as reasons why brands can be categorized as profit takers or underspenders. Give an example of each.

6. In the percentage of sales approach to budget setting, a large difference may exist between percentages set by different companies. Give examples of companies setting a low figure. A high figure. Why are these figures so different?
7. Discuss the strategies recommended by Schroer that are essential for brands pursuing a growing market share.
8. What factors may influence the budget allocation decision? Give an example of each of these.
9. Some advertisers believe economies of scale are accrued in the advertising process. Discuss their reasons for taking this position. Does research evidence support this position?
10. What are some of the possible reasons that the use of quantitative models in the budgeting process is declining?

part V

Developing the Integrated Marketing Communications Program

chapter 10

Creative Strategy: Planning and Development

chapter objectives

➤ To discuss what is meant by advertising creativity and examine the role of creative strategy in advertising.

➤ To examine creative strategy development and the roles of various client and agency personnel involved in this process.

➤ To examine the process that guides the creation of advertising messages and the various research inputs into the stages of the creative process.

➤ To examine various approaches used for determining major selling ideas that form the basis of an advertising campaign.

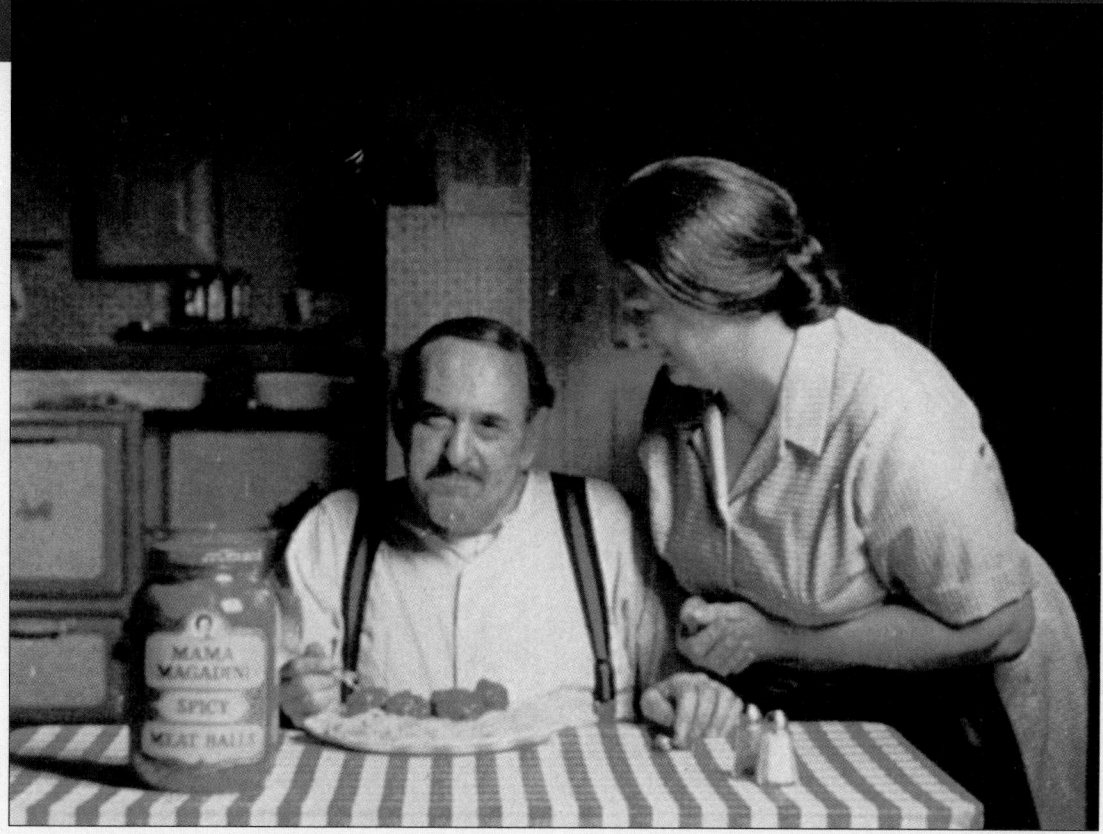

Agency Creatives Are Forced to Go Bland

A number of years ago, the advertising agency for Alka-Seltzer created a commercial showing a blueberry-pie eating contest that winds up with one rotund competitor telling a young kid on the circuit the secret to eating mountains of pies. The ads ends with the line, "Next time you overeat, take what the guys who overeat *for a living* take." Another Alka-Seltzer commercial showed a beefy Italian-American couple and featured the husband delivering one of the all-time classic advertising lines—"Mama Mia! That's a spicy meatball!"—as his wife looks on adoringly. Both of these humorous spots won numerous awards and were seen as creative ways to sell the product. However, in today's advertising environment, probably neither would have made it to the air. Nutrition activists or overweight people would likely have negative reactions to the pie-eating spot, while the "Mama mia" spot would be considered anti-Italian and violate today's code of ethnic sameness or it might offend women.

Creative personnel in advertising agencies are feeling more restricted than ever. "Political correctness" has infiltrated the advertising world, making the lives of ad agency creatives more difficult and limiting the images and messages that major advertisers can send to the American consumers. Many creative people have seen their ideas squelched out of concern that they might offend someone or be misinterpreted. For example, a

radio spot for the brokerage firm of PaineWebber was pulled after the company received letters from a handful of angry piano teachers who took offense at a line in the spot where one mother comments on the excellent recital of a second mother's daughter, saying, "She plays like she studied in Europe." The second mother's response "She did, thank you PaineWebber," was seen as implying that you have to go to Europe to study the piano.

Subaru had to change an ad for its SVX sports car that promised, "You can drive it so fast, you'll get so many tickets you'll lose your license." While the agency saw the ad as a tongue-in-cheek reference to speed, consumer activists didn't get the joke, and several networks refused to run the ad.

Many other restrictions face advertisers. Funeral scenes are considered taboo because they are too depressing. Bacon and eggs cannot be shown together in the same commercial, and visits to the dentist can make no reference to pain. Larry Postaer, creative director of Rubin, Postaer & Associates in Los Angeles, has noted that limitations on advertising creativity and concern that an ad may offend someone are probably at an all-time high. One of his agency's clients, American Honda, has made it a strategy to not show people in its advertising, if possible, to reduce the chance that they might represent segments of the population that could object to stereotyping.

(continued)

Ad agency executives argue the restrictions on creative people result in bland ads. The head of one large New York agency notes, "The walls have closed in. . . . Advertising has gotten timid." The result, he says, is a mass of ads that are "not quite totally homogeneous." Others believe bland advertising is costing marketers money and hurting the advertising industry. They argue that because bland ads have less impact on the consumer, advertisers must spend much more money running the ads to achieve some impact. Moreover, the sameness of commercials is leading consumers to turn them off or ignore them.

So how did advertising get in such a quandary? Many say it is the result of a more conservative society and special-interest groups who call for consumer boycotts or find other ways to make life difficult for companies whose actions they find to be inappropriate, offensive, or in poor taste. Others note references to race, sex, religion, and economic class have become taboo as women, minorities, ethnic, and other large groups battle against discrimination and stereotyping. Some believe the recession has led middle managers to become increasingly worried about job security, so they are unwilling to risk their jobs by approving a controversial or potentially offensive ad.

Not all advertisers have gone bland. Some continue to take risks and are reaping the benefits. For example, Levy's rye bread won legions of fans in the 1960s with ads showing various ethnic groups such as Native Americans, a plump Italian woman, and a round-cheeked Irish cop as part of its "You don't have to be Jewish to love Levy's" campaign. Levy's has used these ads several times in recent years with little complaint, and the most recent flight resulted in a 10 percent sales increase. Bugle Boy received over 17,900 reader response cards from an ad campaign in *Rolling Stone* that used an overtly sexual theme to advertise its casual wear for young men.

Some advertising people defend ads that are risqué or even offensive by noting their ads are not supposed to appeal to everybody. For example, Deutsch Inc. has built a reputation for taking creative risks and having a flip attitude with ads like "Your mother wears Nikes," for British Knights sneakers. Creative director Donnie Deutsch says, "The business of advertising is segmentation. . . . If I'm doing an advertisement for 16-year-old street kids that a 50-year-old rich woman in Florida feels good about, I'm probably not doing my job. You can't have it both ways." Many creative people are concerned their clients would rather have it the bland way.

Source: Jon Berry, "Think Bland," Adweek's Marketing Week, November 11, 1991, pp. 22–24.

O ne of the most important components of an integrated marketing communications program is the advertising message. While the fundamental role of an advertising message is to communicate information, it does much more. The commercials we watch on television or hear on radio and the print ads we see in magazines and newspapers or on billboards are a source of entertainment, motivation, fascination, fantasy, and sometimes irritation as well as information. Ads and commercials appeal to, and often create or shape, the consumers' problems, desires, and goals. From the marketer's perspective, the advertising message provides a way of telling or demonstrating to consumers how the product or service can solve a problem or help satisfy desires or achieve goals. Advertising can also be used to create images or associations and position a brand in the consumer's mind as well as transform the experience of buying and/or using a product or service. Many consumers have never driven or even ridden in one, yet they perceive BMW automobiles as "The Ultimate Driving Machine." Many people feel good about sending Hallmark

> *Exhibit 10–1*
Excellent advertising helps make consumers feel good about sending Hallmark cards

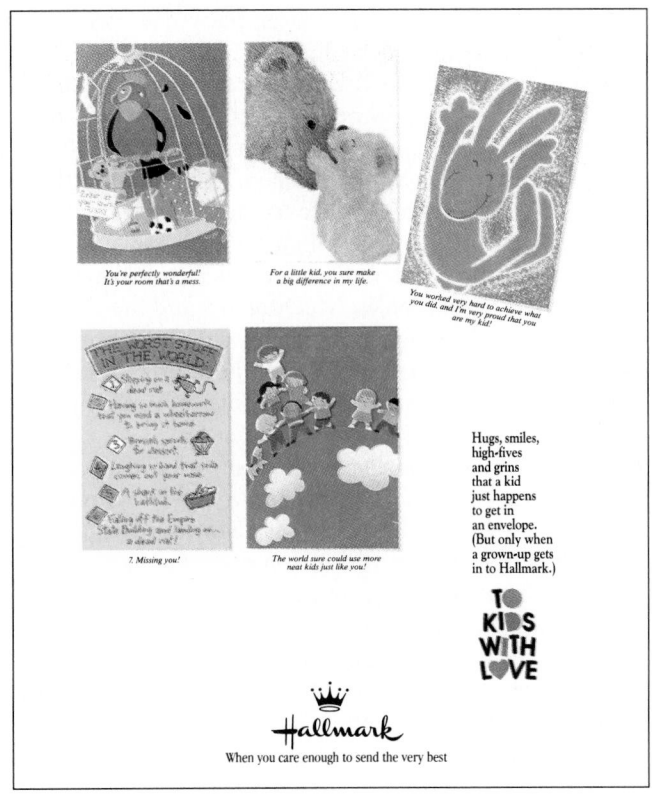

greeting cards because they have internalized the company's advertising theme, "When you care enough to send the very best" (Exhibit 10–1).

One only has to watch an evening of commercials or peruse a few magazines to realize there are myriad ways to convey an advertising message. Underlying all of these messages, however, is a <u>creative strategy</u> that involves determining what the advertising message will say or communicate and <u>creative tactics</u> dealing with how the message strategy will be implemented or executed. In this chapter, we focus on advertising creative strategy. We consider what is meant by creativity, particularly as it relates to advertising, and examine a well-known approach to creativity in advertising.

Attention is also given to the creative strategy development process and various approaches to determining the *big idea* that will be used as the central theme of the advertising campaign and translated into attention-getting, distinctive, and memorable messages. As was discussed in the opening vignette, creative specialists are finding it more and more difficult to come up with big ideas that will break through the clutter yet satisfy the concerns of their risk-averse clients. At the same time, however, their clients are continually challenging them to find the creative idea or message that will strike a responsive chord with their target audience.

Some of you may not be directly involved in the design and creation of advertisements, as you may choose to work in another agency department or on the client side of the business. However, because creative strategy is often so crucial to the success of the firm's promotional effort, everyone involved in the promotional process should have some understanding of the creative strategy and tactics that underlie the development of advertising campaigns and messages, as well as the creative options available to the advertiser. Also, individuals on the client side as well as agency people outside of the creative department must interact and work with the creative specialists in developing the advertising campaign, implementing it, and evaluating its effectiveness. Thus, marketing and product managers, account representatives, researchers, and media personnel must appreciate the creative process and develop a productive relationship with creative personnel.

The Importance of Creativity in Advertising

For many students—as well as many advertising and marketing practitioners—the most interesting aspect of advertising is the creative side. We have all at one time or another been intrigued by an ad and admired the creative insight that went into it. A great ad is a joy to behold and often an epic to create, for the cost of producing many television commercials can reach $500,000 or more. Many companies, however, see this as money well spent. They realize the manner in which the advertising message is developed and executed is often critical to the success or failure of the promotional program, which in turn can influence the effectiveness of the entire marketing program. Companies such as Procter & Gamble, Anheuser-Busch, Coca-Cola, Pepsi-Cola, Nike, McDonald's and many others spend millions of dollars each year to produce advertising messages and hundreds of millions more to purchase media time and space to run these ads. While these companies make excellent products, they also realize creative advertising is a very important part of their marketing success.

Good creative strategy and execution can often be the primary factor in determining the success of a product or service or reversing the fortunes of a troubled or struggling brand. For example, Marlboro cigarettes became the top-selling brand and has held that position for over two decades on the strength of its "Marlboro Country" advertising campaign.

Creative advertising can also help create interest and excitement in a mundane and otherwise ordinary product. For example, carpeting has been traditionally viewed as a very dull product to advertise. However, when Du Pont introduced its revolutionary new Stainmaster carpet fibers in 1987, its agency used a humorous

➤ *Exhibit 10–2a*   **The creative use of humor has been effective in getting consumers to request Stainmaster carpeting**

CONTROL TOWER: Flight 124 fly runway
    heading to
3,000. Right turn to two-seven-zero. You
    are cleared for take-off.
AVO: Presenting Du Pont
certified Stainmaster carpet.

Stainmaster gives you
a revolutionary level of protection
against stains and spills
that's unsurpassed by any other carpet
    you can buy today.

Because you never know . . .
STARTER: Gentlemen, start your engines.
AVO: Stainmaster.
AVO: From Du Pont Carpet Fibers.

appeal featuring a cute little boy launching his dinner onto the floor to demonstrate the product's stain resistance (Exhibit 10–2a). The Stainmaster commercial quickly became one of the most popular on television and, more importantly, was very effective in getting consumers to request specifically the Stainmaster brand when purchasing carpeting.[1] Du Pont has continued to use humorous appeals featuring toddlers terrorizing their mothers' rugs, and the commercials are among the most popular on television (Exhibit 10–2b).

Creative advertising can be a tremendous asset to a promotional program. But the reverse is also true. An advertising campaign that is poorly conceived or executed can be a liability. Many companies have solid marketing and promotional plans and spend substantial amounts of money on advertising, yet have difficulty coming up with a creative advertising campaign that will differentiate them from their competitors. For example, Burger King changed its advertising campaign theme eight times in the past 10 years and changed agencies four times in search of an advertising approach that would give the chain a strong position and identity in the fast-food market. However, as discussed in Promotional Perspective 10–1, Burger King is still hungry for the right campaign.

Just because an ad or commercial is creative or popular does not mean it will increase sales or revive a declining brand. Many ads have won awards for creativity but have failed to increase sales. In some instances, the failure to generate sales has

➤ *Exhibit 10–2b*

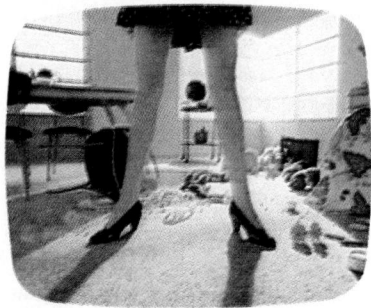 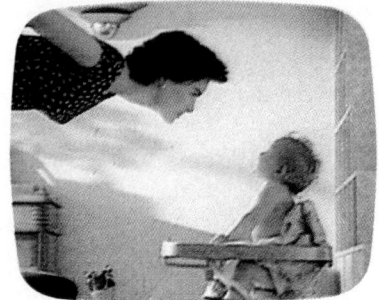 

MOTHER: That's mommy's little
    sweetheart.
SFX: VROOM,VROOM.
(MUSIC)
(MUSIC)
(MUSIC)
(MUSIC)

(MUSIC)
(MUSIC)
(MUSIC)
ANNCR: (VO) Now there's
a new Stainmaster carpet
that handles foot traffic
like never before.

(MUSIC)
(MUSIC)
(MUSIC)
(MUSIC)
New Stainmaster Xtra Life. It
    stays beautiful longer.
(MUSIC)
Only from Du Pont.

Promotional Perspective 10–1

Still Hungry for the Right Campaign

In the late 1970s and early 1980s, Burger King used successful advertising such as the popular "Have it your way" theme and a hard-hitting "Battle of the burgers" campaign touting the superiority of its flame broiling to McDonald's frying process to become the second largest fast-food chain in the country. However, by 1986, Burger King's 13 percent increase in sales came primarily from new restaurants; sales in existing stores were up less than 1 percent. Burger King's problems have continued into the 1990s as its market share slipped from 19.9 percent in 1987 to 19.2 percent in 1990 and U.S. sales remained flat in 1991.

Burger King's problems are due in part to the fact that the fast-food market is growing only 2 to 3 percent per year and has become very competitive. In addition to archrival McDonald's, which outspends Burger King more than 2 to 1 on advertising, the chain faces severe competition from Taco Bell, with its successful "value menu" discount strategy, and the growing number of pizza, chicken, and Mexican fast-food outlets. However, many analysts believe one of the company's biggest problems over the past decade has been its inability to come up with a consistent, effective, and memorable advertising campaign that gives Burger King a strong image and position in the fast-food market.

In the past 4 years, Burger King has gone through four advertising agencies, and over the past 10 years the chain has created and scrapped eight campaign themes (see exhibit). After abandoning the battle of the burgers campaign in 1986, Burger King introduced the notorious "Herb the Nerd" campaign. The $40 million campaign featured a nerdy man in horn-rim glasses, white socks, and gaudy plaid clothes who was supposedly the only person in America never to have tasted a Whopper. The campaign generated publicity; however, much of it was negative, as the ads were criticized as being stupid, silly, and gimmicky. Sales dropped 2 percent during the campaign, and Herb was pulled off the air after three months.

After putting Herb to rest, the company tried two more themes in 1986 and 1987, including "This is a Burger King town" and "Fast food for fast times." A few months into the latter campaign, Burger King fired J. Walter Thompson, its agency of 11 years, and awarded its advertising business to N. W. Ayer, Inc. The new ad campaign developed by Ayer used the theme "We do it like you'd do it" and emphasized the personal contact customers get at Burger King as well as flame broiling, having it your way, and quality food.

It was hoped the new theme would satisfy Burger King's appetite for a successful campaign and a strong identity in the market. However, after a few months, the campaign was falling flat, along with sales, and top executives at Pillsbury, Burger King's parent company, were critical of the advertising. In early 1989, Pillsbury sold Burger King to Grand Metropolitan PLC, a British company, and a new marketing team was hired. One of the first moves made by the new marketing vice president, Gary Langstaff, was to fire N. W. Ayer and hire a new agency.

Grand Met actually hired two agencies for its new acquisition. D'Arcy Masius Benton & Bowles (DMB&B) was given responsibility for Burger King's image advertising, while Saatchi & Saatchi Advertising Inc. handled promotional oriented ads. In early 1989, the new agencies developed a very successful promotion for the elusive children's market—BK Kids Club. Later that year, yet another new advertising theme was introduced using the slogan "Sometimes you've gotta break the rules." The new theme, which was the brainchild of Langstaff, was seen as a reprisal of "Have

cost the agency the account. For example, many advertising people believe some of the best ads of all time were those done for Alka-Seltzer a number of years ago, including the classic "Mama Mia! That's a spicy meatball!" and "I can't believe I ate the whole thing" commercials. While the ads won numerous creative awards, Alka-Seltzer sales reportedly declined and the agency lost the account. Many advertising and marketing people have become very ambivalent toward, and in some cases, even critical of, advertising awards.[2] They argue that agency creative people are often too concerned with creating ads that win awards rather than sell their clients' products.

As we saw in Chapter 8, the success of an ad campaign cannot always be judged in terms of sales. However, many advertising and marketing personnel, particularly those on the client side, believe advertising must ultimately lead the consumer to purchase the product or service or the creativity means little. Finding a balance between creative advertising and effective advertising is difficult. To better understand this dilemma, we turn our attention to the issue of creativity and its role in advertising.

it your way" and an appeal to the consumer's desire to be treated as an individual. Langstaff argued that the campaign would position Burger King as an alternative to cookie-cutter McDonald's.

Soon after the campaign was unveiled, however, it began to receive sharp criticism from Burger King's powerful franchisees. Many of them thought consumers simply didn't understand what the slogan was supposed to mean, while some believed the rule-breaking theme sent the wrong message to kids. Langstaff vowed to stay with the theme and stated he would not be "coerced" by franchisees or the media into scrapping it after a few months. However, after 18 months, the angry franchisees finally were having it their way as Burger King dropped the campaign in April 1991 and Langstaff resigned.

The latest in the long line of unsuccessful campaigns is "Your Way, Right Away," yet another variation of the "Have it your way" theme. The new theme calls for a return to elements used successfully in the 1970s: flame-broil cooking of its hamburgers, custom preparation, and taste. Burger King hopes to stay with the new theme for a while as the chain realizes its lack of consistency has been even more damaging than many of its misguided campaigns. However, given Burger King's track record, many people would probably be reluctant to bet their Whopper on the campaign theme lasting too long. Perhaps by the time you read this, Burger King will have found yet another campaign theme—or another agency.

Source: "Burger King is Hungry—For the Right Ad Campaign," *Business Week,* March 16, 1987, pp. 82–84; "Tempers Are Sizzling over Burger King's New Ads," *Business Week,* February 12, 1990; Scott Hume, "BK brakes the 'rules,'" *Advertising Age,* February 25, 1991, pp. 1, 50; and Matthew Grimm, "The Biggest Battle at Burger King," *Adweek's Marketing Week,* April 8, 1991, pp. 20–21.

Burger King's many advertising campaigns

HAVE IT YOUR WAY
1974–76—BBDO Worldwide

AREN'T YOU HUNGRY?
1981–83—J. Walter Thompson

BATTLE OF THE BURGERS
1983–86—J. Walter Thompson

HERB THE NERD
1986—J. Walter Thompson

THIS IS A BURGER KING TOWN
1987—J. Walter Thompson

FAST FOOD FOR FAST TIMES
1987—J. Walter Thompson

WE DO IT LIKE YOU'D DO IT
1988–90—N. W. Ayer

SOMETIMES YOU'VE GOTTA BREAK THE RULES
1989–91—DMB&B/Saatchi & Saatchi

YOUR WAY. RIGHT AWAY
1991—DMB&B/Saatchi & Saatchi

Advertising Creativity

What Is Creativity?

Creativity is probably one of the most commonly used terms in advertising. Advertisements are often described as being creative. The people who develop ads and commercials are known as "creative types" or "creatives." And advertising agencies develop reputations for their creativity. Perhaps the reason so much attention is focused on the concept of creativity is because many people view the specific challenge given to those who develop an advertising message as being *creative.* It is their job to turn all of the input, such as information regarding product features and benefits, marketing plans, consumer research, and communication objectives, into a creative concept that will bring the advertising message to life. This begs the question, What is meant by *creativity?*

The Creative Education Foundation defines **creativity** as "a quality possessed by persons that enables them to generate novel approaches in situations, generally reflected in new and improved solutions to problems."[3] Some scientists have described creativity as a "feat of mental gymnastics engaging the conscious and subconscious parts of the brain. It draws on everything from knowledge, logic, imagination, and intuition to the ability to see connections and distinctions between ideas and things."[4]

Different Perspectives of Advertising Creativity

Perspectives of what constitutes creativity in advertising vary. At one extreme are those who argue that advertising is creative only if it sells the product. Advocates of this position are more concerned with the impact an advertising message or campaign has on sales than with whether it is novel, innovative, or wins awards. At the other end of the continuum are those who judge the creativity of an ad in terms of its artistic or aesthetic value and argue that creative advertising must be novel, unique, and original. They contend creative ads are different and can break through the competitive clutter, grab the consumer's attention, and have some impact.

As you might expect, perspectives of advertising creativity often depend on the role or position of those involved in the creative process. A study by Elizabeth Hirschman examined the perceptions of various individuals involved in the creation and production of TV commercials including management types (product managers and account executives) and creatives (art director, copy writer, commercial director, and producer).[5] She found that product managers and account executives viewed an ad as a promotional tool whose primary purpose is to communicate favorable impressions to the marketplace. They believed the utility of a commercial should be evaluated in terms of its fulfillment of the client's marketing and communication objectives.

In contrast to this client orientation, the perspective of those on the creative side were much more self-serving as:

> In direct contrast to this client orientation, the art director, copywriter, and commercial director viewed the advertisement as a communication vehicle for promoting their own aesthetic viewpoints and personal career objectives. Both the copywriter and art director made this point explicitly, noting that a desirable commercial from their standpoint was one which communicated their unique creative talents and thereby permitted them to obtain "better" jobs at an increased salary.[6]

In her interviews, Hirschman also found that the product manager was much more risk averse and wanted a more conservative commercial than the creative people, who wanted to maximize the impact of the message.

The answer as to what constitutes creativity in advertising is probably somewhere between the two extreme positions noted above. To break through the clutter and make an impression on the target audience, an ad often must be unique and entertaining. As noted in Chapter 6, research has shown that a major determinant of whether a commercial will be successful in changing brand preferences is its "likability" or the viewer's overall reaction to the spot.[7] Television commercials and print ads that are well designed and executed and generate emotional responses can create positive feelings that are transferred to the product or service being advertised. Many creative people believe this type of advertising will come about only if they are given considerable latitude in developing advertising messages. But ads that are creative only for the sake of being creative often fail to communicate a relevant or meaningful message to consumers that will lead to the purchase of a product or service.

All of those involved in the planning and development of an advertising campaign must understand the importance of balancing the "It's not creative unless it sells!" perspective with the novelty/uniqueness and impact position. Marketing and product managers or account executives must recognize that imposing too many sales- and marketing-oriented communication objectives on the creative team can result in mediocre advertising, which is often ineffective in today's highly competitive and cluttered media environment. At the same time, the creative specialists must recognize that the goal of advertising is to assist in selling the product or service and good advertising must be able to communicate in a manner that helps the client achieve this goal.

Advertising creativity should be viewed as "the ability to generate fresh, unique, and appropriate ideas that can be used as solutions to communication problems. This perspective recognizes that creative advertising ideas are those that are novel, original, *and* appropriate. To be appropriate and effective, a creative idea must be relevant or have some importance to the target audience. Many ad agencies recognize the importance of developing advertising that is creative and different yet communicates relevant information to the target audience. Exhibit 10–3 shows the D'Arcy Masius Benton & Bowles agency's "Universal Advertising Standards." These nine principles were developed by the agency to guide its creative efforts and help achieve superior creativity consistently. An examination of these standards shows the agency views a creative advertising message as one built around a core creative or "power idea" and uses excellent design and execution to communicate information that interests and is relevant to the target audience.

Advertising creativity is not the exclusive domain of those who work on the creative side of advertising. The nature of the advertising and promotion business requires creative thinking from everyone involved in the promotional planning process. Individuals in the agency, such as account executives, media planners, researchers, and attorneys, as well as those on the client side, such as marketing and brand managers, must all be creative in seeking solutions to problems encountered in

➤ *Exhibit 10–3* **D'Arcy Masius Benton & Bowles' Universal Advertising Standards**

1. Does this advertising position the product simply and with unmistakable clarity?

The target audience for the advertised product or service must be able to see and sense in a flash *what* the product is for, *whom* it is for, and *why* they should be interested in it.

Creating this clear vision of how the product or service fits into their lives is the first job of advertising. Without a simple, clear, focused positioning, no creative work can begin.

2. Does this advertising bolt the brand to a clinching benefit?

Our advertising should be built on *the most compelling and persuasive* consumer benefit—not some unique-but-insignificant peripheral feature.

Before you worry about how to say it, you must be sure you are saying *the right thing*. If you don't know what the most compelling benefit is, you've got to find out before you do anything else.

3. Does this advertising contain a Power Idea?

The Power Idea is the vehicle that transforms the strategy into a dynamic, creative communications concept. It is the core creative idea that sets the stage for brilliant executions to come.

The ideal Power Idea should:

—Be describable in a simple word, phrase, or sentence without reference to any final execution.

—Be likely to attract the prospect's attention.

—Revolve around the clinching benefit.

—Allow you to brand the advertising.

—Make it easy for the prospect to vividly experience our client's product or service.

4. Does this advertising design in Brand Personality?

The great brands tend to have something in common: the extra edge of having a Brand Personality. This is something beyond merely identifying what the brand *does* for the consumer; all brands *do* something, but the great brands also *are* something.

A brand can be whatever its designers want it to be—and it can be so from day one.

5. Is this advertising unexpected?

Why should our clients pay good money to wind up with advertising that looks and sounds like everybody else's in the category? They shouldn't.

We must dare to be different, because sameness is suicide. We can't be outstanding unless we first stand out.

The thing is not to *emulate* the competition but to *annihilate* them.

6. Is this advertising single-minded?

If you have determined the right thing to say and have created a way to say it uncommonly well, why waste time saying anything else?

If we want people to remember one big thing from a given piece of advertising, let's not make it more difficult than it already is in an overcommunicated world.

The advertising should be all about that *one big thing*.

7. Does this advertising reward the prospect?

Let's give our audience something that makes it easy—even pleasurable—for our message to penetrate: a tear, a smile, a laugh. An emotional stimulus is that special something that makes them want to see the advertising again and again.

8. Is this advertising visually arresting?

Great advertising you remember—and can play back in your mind—is unusual to look at: compelling, riveting, a nourishing feast for the eyes. If you need a reason to strive for *arresting* work, go no further than Webster: "Catching or holding the attention, thought or feelings. Gripping. Striking. Interesting."

9. Does this advertising exhibit painstaking craftsmanship?

You want writing that is really *written*. Visuals that are *designed*. Music that is *composed*.

Lighting, casting, wardrobe, direction—all the components of the *art* of advertising are every bit as important as the *science* of it. It is a sin to nickel-and-dime a great advertising idea to death.

Why settle for good, when there's great? We should go for the absolute best in concept, design and execution.

This is our craft—the work should sparkle.

"Our creative standards are not a gimmick," Steve emphasizes. "They're not even revolutionary. Instead, they are an explicit articulation of a fundamental re-focusing on our company's only reason for being.

"DMB&B's Universal Advertising Standards are the operating link between our vision today—and its coming reality."

Promotional Perspective 10–2

Absolut Results

In 1980, Absolut was a relatively unknown brand of Swedish vodka imported to the United States by Carillon Importers. The brand had a small advertising budget of less than $1 million and sales of about 12,000 cases a year. About this time, Geoff Hayes, an executive art director at TBWA, the agency for Absolut, came up with a creative concept for an advertising campaign playing off the distinctive shape of the bottle. The initial ad, "Absolut Perfection," featured a picture of the Absolut bottle with a halo and the first of the two-word headlines that would become the campaign's signature. Subsequent ads in the campaign have continued making the bottle the hero of the advertisements by depicting it with visual puns and accompanying witty headlines.

The objective of the ad campaign has been to build awareness of the brand and to make Absolut a "fashionable symbol of smartness and sophistication that consumers would want to be associated with." This goal has been accomplished through outstanding creative execution that makes the Absolut ads break through the clutter and stand out. Underlying this creativity, however, is a spirit of cooperation between the media and creative departments of TBWA and a unique creative alliance between the agency and Carillon Importers.

Michael Roux, chairman of Carillon Importers, recognized early that the advertising campaign could be carried further by playing on the name Absolut and the distinctive shape of the bottle and tailoring the print ads for the magazines or regions where they appear. For example, for New York City area media, the agency created "Absolut Manhattan" showing Central Park in the shape of a vodka bottle. Ads in the Los Angeles area used the tag line "Absolut L.A." and featured a swimming pool shaped like an Absolut bottle. Ads appearing in publications such as *Skiing* or *Ski* show ski slopes curving around pine trees formed in the shape of the bottle and the tag line "Absolut Peak."

Absolut's annual media schedule consists of up to 100 magazines, including various consumer and business publications.

The creative and media departments work together selecting magazines and deciding on ads that will appeal to the readers of each publication. In many cases, the creative department is asked to create media-specific ads to run in a particular publication. For example, the media department suggested ads be

---

planning, developing, and executing an advertising campaign. Promotional Perspective 10–2 discusses how creative synergy between the media and creative departments of the TBWA agency and the creative thinking of its client has resulted in soaring sales for Absolut vodka.

Planning Creative Strategy

The Participants

As we saw in Chapter 3, marketers usually hire advertising agencies to develop and implement their ad campaigns because they are specialists in the creative function of advertising. However, the development of creative strategy also involves representatives from the client side and other people from within the agency as well as the creative staff. Consider, for example, developing an advertising campaign for a consumer package-goods company. Representatives from the client side may include one or more product or brand managers responsible for developing the marketing plan and sales and profitability objectives for the brand. A product group and/or marketing manager may also be involved in the development of, and ultimately will

designed for playbills (theater programs) and the creative response was "Absolut Bravo," which featured roses adorning the clear bottle. Although it was not on the media list, the creatives developed an "Absolut Centerfold" ad for *Playboy,* which featured its playmate bottle ("11-inch bust, 11-inch waist, and 11-inch hips) and an "Absolut Data Sheet" listing ambitions ("To always be cool, with or without ice"), turn-ons (Swedish massages, ice, olives), turn-offs (drinking and driving).

TBWA executives acknowledge the important role their client plays in the success of the Absolut campaign. For example, the chairman of TBWA noted, "Very early on, our creative people saw that here was a client who didn't just talk about wanting break-through creative work—most clients did that. He demanded it, he bought it, and he actually ran it." In describing the unique creative-media collaboration, TBWA's president recognizes the role of the client: "What Carillon has done for us is give us a more open mind and put more demand on all departments to be creative in their ideas than might be the case otherwise."

While Carillon has demanded creativity and excellence from the creative and media departments of TBWA, it has also been willing to pay for it. The production budget for Absolut's ads exceed the media budgets of some of its competitors. Michael Roux paid the late artist Andy Warhol $65,000 for a painting of an Absolut bottle and five years' reproduction rights. Roux has also commissioned painting from other contemporary artists such as Keith Haring, Kenny Scharf, and Armond Arman. Carillon's annual media budget for Absolut has grown to more than $25 million.

Carillon's willingness to take risks and its demands for creativity from itself and its agency have resulted in phenomenal sales success for Absolut. Despite a declining U.S. liquor market, Absolut sales have grown more than 33 percent per year for the past five years. In 1990, Carillon Importers sold 2.7 million cases of Absolut, and it has become the number one imported vodka and number two super-premium spirit of any kind sold in America. The advertising campaign has produced *Absolut Results.*

Source: Valerie H. Free, "Absolut Original," *Marketing Insights,* Summer 1991, pp. 64–72; Steve Blount and Lisa Walker, *The Best of Ad Campaigns!* (Rockport, Mass: Rockport Publishers, 1988), pp. 20–32; and Gary Levin, " 'Meddling' in Creative More Welcome," *Advertising Age,* April 9, 1990, pp. S-4, S-8.

have to approve, the marketing plan and objectives. From this plan comes the overall advertising and promotional strategy that will guide development of the creative and media strategies as well as other aspects of the promotional mix.

The product and marketing managers from the client side work closely with the account executives from the agency whose responsibility is to communicate the client's objectives to creative and media personnel in the agency. Account executives, along with other agency personnel such as researchers, often work closely with the client in analyzing the market and customers and helping formulate marketing and promotional strategies. Account executives must also work closely with the agency personnel because they are responsible for "selling" the agency's creative and media plan to the client.

Generating creative concepts and the design and production of the actual advertising message are usually the responsibility of a creative team consisting of a copywriter and an art director. Copywriters generally contribute the written or verbal elements of the message, while art directors concern themselves with the visual presentation of the ad or commercial. It is important for copywriters and art directors to visualize how their verbal and visual presentations will interact with one another. Thus, it is not uncommon for each to think in terms of both words and pictures.

The copywriter–art director team works together to generate creative ideas and concepts that can be the basis of the advertising message. The actual production and implementation of the ad or commercial usually involves other individuals such as artists, typographers, photographers, commercial directors and producers, and film editors.

The Creative Challenge

Despite all the input and background information provided to them, those who work on the creative side of advertising often face a real challenge. They must take all the research, creative briefs, strategy statements, communication objectives, and other input and transform this information into an advertising message. Their job is to write copy, design layouts and illustrations, or produce commercials that effectively communicate and execute the central idea or theme on which the campaign is based. Rather than simply stating the attribute or benefits of a product or service, they must put the advertising message into some embellished form that will engage the attention and interest of the audience and make the advertisement memorable.[8]

The job of the creative team is challenging because every marketing situation is different, and each campaign or advertisement may require a different creative approach. One can find numerous lists of rules or guidelines that successful advertising copywriters have developed for creating effective advertising.[9] Most advertising people, however, would probably argue there is no magic formula, pattern, or recipe to follow for developing effective advertising. As advertising copywriter Hank Sneiden notes in his book *Advertising Pure and Simple:*

> Rules lead to dull stereotyped advertising, and they stifle creativity, inspiration, initiative, and progress. The only hard and fast rule that I know of in advertising is that there are no rules. No formulas. No right way. Given the same problem, a dozen creative talents would solve it a dozen different ways. If there were a sure-fire formula for successful advertising, everyone would use it. Then there'd be no need for creative people. We would simply program robots to create our ads and commercials and they'd sell loads of product—to other robots.[10]

Sneiden's perspective on rules and formulas suggests that every advertising situation is different and requires a unique creative approach. However, creative teams do sometimes follow approaches that have been shown to be effective or are popular among consumers. They may even imitate a creative idea or execution. For example, the popular parody ads for the Eveready Battery Company's Energizer batteries have been imitated by numerous national and local advertisers.

Many advertising people take a negative view of copycat ads, arguing they violate the cardinal rule of good advertising. For example, Laurel Clutter, vice chairman of the FCB/Leber Katz Partners agency, notes: "You're not differentiating your product if you use the same executional gimmick as someone else. It's extremely lazy and you might wind up reinforcing the other company's advertising and brand name instead of your own."[11]

Taking a Creative Risk

Many creative people argue they sometimes follow proven approaches or formulas when creating ads because they are safe and less likely to fail. They note that clients are often very *risk averse* and feel uncomfortable with advertising that is too different. For example, according to Bill Tragos, chairman of TBWA, the advertising agency noted for its excellent creative work for Absolut vodka, Evian, and many other clients, "Very few clients realize that the reason that their work is so bad is that they are the ones who commandeered it and directed it to be that way. I think that at least 50 percent of an agency's successful work resides in the client."[12]

Many creative people agree with this position and note it is important for clients to be willing to take some risk if they want breakthrough advertising that gets noticed and has an impact. For example, one of the fastest-growing and most successful agencies is Weiden & Kennedy, best known for its excellent creative work for Nike and Subaru (Exhibit 10–4). The agency's founders believe a key element to Weiden & Kennedy's success has been a steadfast belief in taking risks when most agencies and their clients have been retrenching and becoming more conservative.[13] They note the agency's ability to develop great advertising is much easier because clients such as Nike are willing to take risks and go along with the agency's priority system, which places the creative work first and the client/agency relationship second. The agency has even terminated relationships with large clients such as Gallo and Miller Brewing when they interfered too much with the creative process.

Not all companies or agencies agree that advertising has to be risky to be effective, however. Many marketing managers are more comfortable with advertising that communicates product or service features and benefits and gives the consumer a reason to buy. They argue their advertising campaigns are multimillion-dollar investments whose goal is to sell the product rather than finance the whims or interests of their agency's creative staff. They argue that some creative people seem to have lost sight of advertising's bottom line: Does it sell?

The issue of how much latitude creative people should be given and the amount of risk the client should be willing to take is ongoing and open to considerable debate. However, one point that is generally agreed on by clients and agency personnel is that the ability to develop novel, yet appropriate approaches to communicating with the customer makes the creative specialist valuable—and often hard to find.

> *Exhibit 10–4*
Weiden & Kennedy's belief in taking risks has resulted in creative advertising for clients such as Subaru

The Subaru Legacy

Weld a peace sign to the hood and make believe you're driving a Mercedes that gets really great gas mileage.

THE BRAZEN audacity. To compare a Subaru* Legacy* to one of Germany's finest and most-revered automobiles.

Hey, why not. They both are designed to do the same thing. Transport people and their stuff from point A to point B. And they both perform that basic automotive function effectively and comfortably.

For example, the Legacy LSi Sedan, which costs many thousands less than the cheapest Mercedes, offers most of the amenities you'd only expect from a fine, absurdly priced luxury car:

Soft grain leather seats. All-Wheel Drive. Compact disc player. Moonroof. Driver's-side air bag. The 4-Channel Anti-Lock Braking System which monitors each wheel to help prevent the car from locking up during emergency stops. And the Legacy is also blessed

with numerous other engineering features which translate into the type of durability Subaru is famous for.

(Important selling point—93% of all Subaru cars registered in the last 10 years are still on the road and running today.¹)

Now, if you've read this far, you'd probably like a second opinion about the Legacy. Alright, here's one from *Car and Driver*: "The Subaru Legacy is the nicest driving, least expensive, and best equipped 4-wheel drive sedan on the market."²

We repeat—nicest driving, least expensive, best equipped.

So if you're into haughty status symbols, go into the closet and grab that medallion off that ancient Nehru jacket and affix it to the hood. Or, then again, with all the money you'll be saving on your new Legacy you could just imagine you're driving the world's peppiest, most elegantly styled Brink's truck.

Subaru Legacy LSi

Subaru. What to drive.™

¹ Based on R.L. Polk & Co., registration statistics. ² May, 1990. For additional information, 1-800-284-8684. © Subaru of America, 1991.

Creative Personnel

The image of the creative advertising person, which is frequently perpetuated in novels, movies, and TV shows, is often one of a freewheeling, free-thinking, and eccentric personality. Many advertising and marketing people think individuals who work on the creative side of advertising tend to be somewhat different from those on the managerial side. The educational background of creative personnel is often in nonbusiness areas such as art, literature, music, humanities, or journalism, so their interests and perspectives tend to differ from those with a business education or background. Creative personnel tend to be more abstract and less structured, organized, and conventional in their approach to, and solution of, a problem, more often relying on intuition than logic. One study examined the personality types of highly creative writers and architects, two types of professionals similar to creative people working in advertising. Highly creative people were found to be significantly more open to experience, more flexible, more unconventional, more playful, more aggressive, more independent, and more inner-directed. They were also found to be more intuitive and perceptual in their orientation.[14]

Advertising creatives are sometimes stereotyped as strange or odd. This may stem from the fact that creative personnel are often viewed as being independent and withdrawn nonconformists who dress differently and do not always work the conventional 9-to-5 schedule. Of course, from the perspective of the creatives, it is the marketing or brand managers, account executives, and other management personnel who are strange or different. (Many creatives refer to account executives or product managers as "suits" in reference to the fact that they often wear coats and ties all day.) In many agencies, it is unlikely that you could tell the creative personnel from the account representatives or other executives by their dress or demeanor. Yet the differences in the creative and managerial personalities and perspectives must be recognized and tolerated for creative people to do their best work and to ensure successful interaction and cooperation among all those involved in the advertising process.

Most agencies thrive on creativity, for it is the major component in the product they produce. Thus, they must create an environment that fosters, and is conducive to, the development of creative thinking and creative advertising. The client must also learn to recognize and understand the differences in the perspectives of the creative personnel versus those of marketing and product managers. While the client has the ultimate responsibility for approving the advertising, the opinions and work of the creative specialist must be considered and respected when evaluating advertising ideas and content. The evaluation of the creative's ideas and work is discussed in more detail in Chapter 11.

* The Creative Process

Some advertising people have argued that creativity in advertising is best viewed as a process and that creative success is most likely when some organized approach is followed. This does not mean there is an infallible blueprint or formula to follow to create effective advertising. As we saw earlier, many advertising people reject and resist attempts to standardize creativity or develop rules or guidelines to follow. However, most advertising creative professionals do follow a process when approaching the task of developing an advertisement.

One of the most popular and well-known approaches to creativity in advertising was developed by James Webb Young, a former creative vice president at the J. Walter Thompson agency. Young stated that

> the production of ideas is just as definite a process as the production of Fords; that the
> production of ideas, too, runs an assembly line; that in this production the mind
> follows an operative technique which can be learned and controlled; and that its
> effective use is just as much a matter of practice in the technique as in the effective use
> of any tool.[15]

Young's model of the creative process contained five steps or stages:

1. **Immersion** Gathering raw material and information through background research and immersing yourself in the problem.
2. **Digestion** Taking the information, working it over, and wrestling with it in the mind.
3. **Incubation** Putting the problems out of your conscious mind and turning the information over to the subconscious and letting it do the work.
4. **Illumination** The appearance or birth of an idea—the "Eureka! I have it!" phenomenon.
5. **Reality or verification** Looking back at the idea to see if it still looks good or solves the problem, then shaping and developing the idea to practical usefulness.

Young's process of creativity is very similar to an approach outlined much earlier by English sociologist Graham Wallas, who suggested that creative thought involved four stages:

1. **Preparation** Gathering background information needed to solve the problem through research and study.
2. **Incubation** Getting away and letting ideas develop.
3. **Illumination** Seeing the light or solution.
4. **Verification** Refining and polishing the idea and seeing if it is an appropriate solution.

These models of the creative process are valuable to those working in the creative area of advertising, as they offer an organized way of approaching an advertising problem. These approaches stress the need for preparation or gathering of background information that is relevant to the problem as the first step in the creative process. As we have seen in earlier chapters, the advertiser and agency start by developing a thorough understanding of the product or service, the target market of interest, and the competition. Attention is also focused on the role of advertising in the marketing and promotional program.

These models do not say much about how this information will be synthesized and used by the creative specialist. This part of the process is unique to the individual and, in many ways, is what sets apart the great creative minds and strategists in advertising. In the following section we examine how various types of research and information can provide input to the creative process of advertising.

Inputs to the Creative Process: Preparation/Incubation/Illumination

Background research

Only the most foolish creative person or team would approach an assignment without first learning as much as possible about the client's product or service, the target market, the competition, and any other relevant background information. The creative specialist should also be knowledgeable of and open to information about the general trends, conditions, and developments in the marketplace as well as research on specific advertising approaches or techniques that might be effective. The creative specialist can acquire background information in numerous ways. Some of these informal fact-finding techniques have been noted by Sandra Moriarty and include:

- Reading anything related to the product or market such as books, trade publications, or general interest articles, research reports, and the like.
- Asking everyone involved with the product for information such as designers, engineers, sales personnel, and consumers.
- Listening to what people are saying or talking about among themselves. Visits to stores, malls, restaurants, or even the agency cafeteria can be

informative. Listening to the client can be particularly valuable since he or she often knows the product and market the best.

- Using the product or service and becoming familiar with it. This is imperative if the creative person is going to develop ads for it. The more you use a product, the more you know and can say about it.
- Working in and learning about the client's business. This is another way of gathering relevant background information. A creative person may want to work in a client's business to understand better the person trying to be reached.[17]

To assist in the preparation, incubation, and illumination stages, many agencies provide creative people with both general and product-specific preplanning input. **General preplanning input** can include books, periodicals, trade publications, scholarly journals, pictures, and clipping services, which gather and organize magazine and newspaper articles on the product, the market, and the competition, including the latter's advertisements. This input can also come from research studies conducted by the client, agency, media, or other sources.

Another important type of general preplanning input is information concerning trends, developments, and happenings in the marketplace. Information is available from a variety of sources including local, state, and federal government organizations, secondary research suppliers, and research reports available from various industry trade associations as well as advertising and media organizations. For example, advertising industry groups such as the American Association of Advertising Agencies and media organizations such as the National Association of Broadcasters (NAB) and Magazine Publishers of America (MPA) publish reports and newsletters that provide information on market trends and developments and how they might affect consumers (Exhibit 10–5).

➤ *Exhibit 10–5*
The *MPA Research Newsletter* is a valuable source of information on market trends

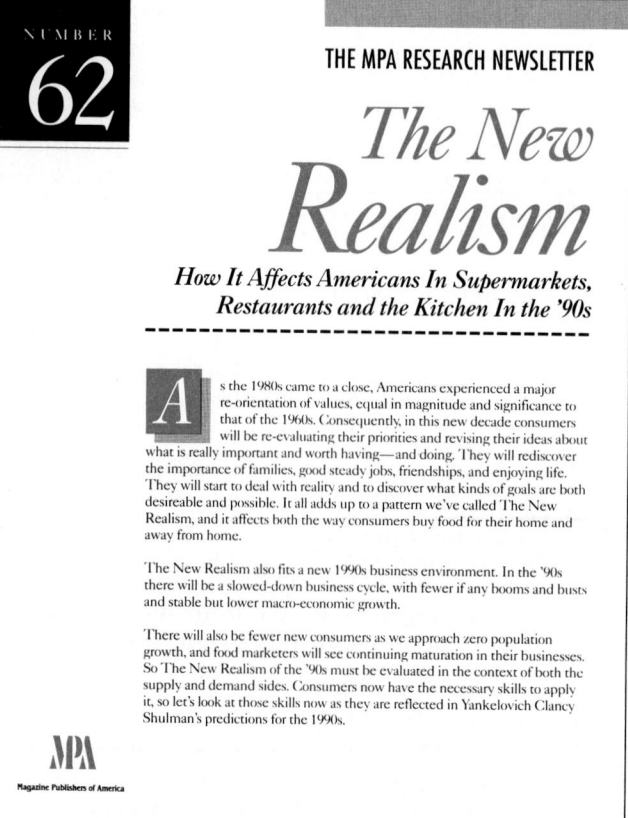

NUMBER

62

THE MPA RESEARCH NEWSLETTER

The New
Realism

How It Affects Americans In Supermarkets,
Restaurants and the Kitchen In the '90s

- -

A s the 1980s came to a close, Americans experienced a major re-orientation of values, equal in magnitude and significance to that of the 1960s. Consequently, in this new decade consumers will be re-evaluating their priorities and revising their ideas about what is really important and worth having—and doing. They will rediscover the importance of families, good steady jobs, friendships, and enjoying life. They will start to deal with reality and to discover what kinds of goals are both desireable and possible. It all adds up to a pattern we've called The New Realism, and it affects both the way consumers buy food for their home and away from home.

The New Realism also fits a new 1990s business environment. In the '90s there will be a slowed-down business cycle, with fewer if any booms and busts and stable but lower macro-economic growth.

There will also be fewer new consumers as we approach zero population growth, and food marketers will see continuing maturation in their businesses. So The New Realism of the '90s must be evaluated in the context of both the supply and demand sides. Consumers now have the necessary skills to apply it, so let's look at those skills now as they are reflected in Yankelovich Clancy Shulman's predictions for the 1990s.

MPA
Magazine Publishers of America

Individuals involved in developing creative strategy can also gather relevant and timely information by reading various industry and business publications. For example, during the Persian Gulf War, publications such as *Advertising Age* and *The Wall Street Journal* carried numerous articles that discussed the public's reactions to the war and reported the results of studies concerning how consumers might change their spending plans or respond to commercials shown during television coverage of the war.[18]

Product/service-specific research

In addition to general background research and preplanning input, creative people are also provided with **product-** (or service-) **specific preplanning input.** This information generally comes in the form of specific studies conducted on the product or service, the target audience, or a combination of the two. Quantitative and qualitative consumer research such as attitude studies; market structure and positioning studies such as perceptual mapping, lifestyle research; focus group interviews; and studies providing demographic and psychographic profiles of users of a particular product, service, or brand are examples of the types of product-specific preplanning input that can be provided to creative personnel.

A very valuable source of product-specific preplanning input for profiling the target audience is available from large-scale studies done by syndicated research firms such as Simmons Market Research Bureau (SMRB) or by Mediamark Research, Inc. (MRI). These firms do annual surveys of nearly 30,000 adults covering areas such as their possession and consumption of a wide range of products and services and individual brands, usage of all major advertising media, and their demographic and lifestyle characteristics. These studies also break users into three usage rate categories—heavy, medium, and light. This information can be used to develop a profile of consumers who use a particular product or service as well as various user groups, such as the heavy or light users of a product and/or brand. Simmons and MRI data are designed to primarily be used in media planning (as is discussed in Chapter 12). However, this information is also very helpful to the creative team members as it provides them with a better understanding of demographic and psychographic characteristics of the audience for which an advertising message must be created.

Many of the product- or service-specific studies that are helpful to the creative team are conducted by the client or the agency. For example, a number of years ago, the BBDO ad agency developed an interesting approach for finding ideas around which creative strategies could be based called **problem detection.**[19] This research technique involves asking consumers familiar with a product (or service) to generate an exhaustive list of things that bother them or problems they encounter when using it. These problems are then rated by consumers for their importance, and various brands can be evaluated in terms of their association with each problem. The outcome of a problem detection study can provide valuable input for product improvements, reformulations, or new products. This process can also provide ideas for the advertising creative strategy regarding attributes or features to emphasize as well as guidelines for positioning new or existing brands.

Some agencies conduct psychographic studies annually and use this information to construct detailed psychographic or lifestyle profiles of product or service users. One such agency is DDB Needham Worldwide, which conducts a large-scale psychographic study each year using a sample of 4,000 U.S. adults. The agency uses the Life Style Study to provide its creative teams with a better understanding of the target audience for which they are developing ads.

For example, information from the agency's Life Style Study was used by the creative team in developing a speculative presentation outlining an ad campaign for Southwestern Bell Mobile Systems. Psychographic research revealed the potential

cellular phone user was self-confident, ambitious, outgoing, physically active, and liked to exert influence over his business associates. He also considered himself a trendsetter and valued his time. This psychographic profile, along with demographic information showing the typical mobile phone user to be a 25-to-54-year-old male, earning more than $35,000 a year, and spending one to seven hours a week in his car on business or commuting, led the agency to conclude the target customer was a yuppie. However, the yuppie image was becoming negative by the end of the 1980s, so the agency wanted to avoid developing an ad showing a yuppie-type talking on his car phone. The creative team decided on a humorous campaign in which a variety of animals were portrayed as cellular phone users. However, the headlines and copy of each ad appealed to the psychographic characteristics of the mobile phone user identified in the Life Style Study (Exhibit 10–6). The agency won the account, and Southwestern Bell has been very pleased with the award winning campaign.[20]

Qualitative research input

Many agencies, particularly larger ones with strong research departments, have their own research programs and specific techniques they use to assist in the development of creative strategy and provide input to the creative process. In addition to the various quantitative research studies, qualitative research techniques such as in-depth interviews or focus groups can also provide the creative team with valuable insight at the early stages of the creative process. **Focus groups** are a research method whereby consumers (usually 10 to 12) from the target market are led through a discussion regarding a particular topic. Focus groups are used in marketing research to gain insight and understanding as to why and how consumers use a product or service, what is important to them in choosing a particular brand, what they like and don't like about various products or services, and any special needs they might have that aren't being satisfied. A focus group session might also include a discussion of advertising-related issues such as types of appeals to use or evaluations of the advertising of various companies.

In the creative process, focus group interviews are valuable because they bring the creative people and others involved in creative strategy development into contact with the consumer. By watching and listening to a focus group, copywriters, art directors, and other creative specialists can get a better sense of who the target audience is, what they are like, and who they need to write, design, or direct to in the creation of an advertising message.

Generally, creative personnel are open to any research or information that will help them understand the client's target market better and assist in generating creative ideas. Some marketers and advertising agencies use an anthropological approach to better understand consumers and the cultural meaning brands have to them. Promotional Perspective 10–3 on page 338 discusses how this research is being used to develop creative advertising strategies and ad campaigns.

➤ *Exhibit 10–7*
Viewer reaction profiles can be used to measure consumer evaluations of proposed ads

Commercial _____   Respondent I.D. _____

TELEVISION COMMERCIAL REACTION PROFILE

How well do you think each of the words below describes the ad you have just seen?

Extremely well	5
Very well	4
Fairly well	3
Not very well	2
Not well at all	1

ridiculous	imaginative	meaningful to me	humorous
unique	jolly	tender	amusing
serene	enthusiastic	exhilarated	soothing
playful	stupid	worth remembering	original
merry	gentle	vigorous	lovely
energetic	exciting	irritating	terrible
ingenious	for me	novel	important to me
phony	valuable		

Inputs to the Creative Process: Verification/Revision

The verification/revision stage of the creative process evaluates the resultant ideas from the illumination stage, rejects any that may be inappropriate, and refines and polishes those that remain and gives them final expression. Some of the techniques used at this stage include directed focus groups to evaluate creative concepts, ideas, or themes; message communication studies; portfolio tests; and evaluation measures such as the viewer reaction profile shown in Exhibit 10–7.[21]

At this stage of the creative process, members of the target audience may be asked to evaluate rough creative layouts and to indicate what message or meaning they get from the ad, what they think of the execution style, or their reactions to a slogan or theme. The creative team can get some insight into how a TV commercial might communicate its message by having members of the target market evaluate the ad in storyboard form. A storyboard is a series of drawings used to present the visual plan or layout of a proposed commercial. It contains a series of sketches of key frames or scenes along with a description of the copy or audio portion that will accompany each scene (Exhibit 10–8, page 340).

Testing a commercial in storyboard form is often difficult because storyboards are often too abstract for most consumers to understand. Thus, to make the creative layout more realistic and easier to evaluate, an aniamatic may be produced whereby a videotape of the storyboard is produced along with an audio soundtrack. Storyboards and aniamatics are useful for research purposes as well as for presenting the creative idea to other agency personnel or to the client for discussion and approval before proceeding further in the creative production process.

At this stage of the process, the creative team is attempting to find the best creative approach or execution style before moving ahead with the campaign themes and going into actual production of the ad. The verification/revision process may include more formal and extensive pretesting of the ad before a final decision is made to use this creative approach. Pretesting and other related procedures are examined in detail in Chapter 20.

Creative Strategy Development

Just like any other area of the marketing and promotional process, the creative aspect of advertising is guided by specific goals and objectives and requires development of a creative strategy. As noted at the beginning of the chapter, creative strategy focuses on what the advertising message will say or communicate and guides the development of all messages used in the ad campaign.

Promotional Perspective 10–3

People Watching Helps Advertisers Better Understand Consumers

Suppose you work for an ad agency and have been assigned to work on an ice cream account the agency just acquired. Your assignment is to determine what ice cream really means to the typical consumer. Think for a moment about how you might approach this problem. You might propose a quantitative survey to ask consumers what attributes are important to them in choosing a brand of ice cream, what flavors they prefer, when they like to eat it, and the like. Or you could propose doing qualitative research such as focus group interviews to let consumers tell you in their own words what ice cream means to them, whey they eat it, and how they buy it. Quantitative studies such as surveys and qualitative research such as focus groups are very commonly used to answer this type of question. However, some marketers and ad agencies are going beyond surveys and focus groups and are studying consumers by observing them and becoming involved in their everyday lives.

Researchers at Young & Rubicam, one of the country's largest agencies, call their research approach "ethnography," an anthropological term that refers to the study of cultures by living with a family and observing how they go about their lives. Young & Rubicam researchers used this approach to address the question posed above—what does ice cream mean to American consumers?—for its Breyer's ice cream account. The agency's researchers visited six families at home to observe their ice cream indulgence. They photographed people eating ice cream and taking that first lick. They looked in freezers, inspected bowls and utensils, and watched people put various toppings on America's favorite dessert. The director of marketing research at Kraft Inc., which owns the brand, noted, "We learned about people's response to ice cream and found that it is a very sensual, inner-directed experience." He noted it was hoped the research would guide the agency in developing more effective advertising.

Young & Rubicam also used ethnographic research in developing a new advertising campaign for the U.S. Postal Service. The agency sent an anthropologist out with a mail carrier to learn how people interact with their letter carriers and found that in rural areas, letter carriers "are seen as a contact with society, an antidote to loneliness." Television commercials in the new campaign profiled individual letter carriers, emphasizing the human dimension of postal service with the theme "We Deliver for You."

Young & Rubicam conducts ethnographic research for a number of other clients such as General Foods, Johnson & Johnson, and Colgate. The director of research at the agency says, "Ethnography eliminates some of the distance between us and consumers and brings them alive for our creative staff. . . . The biggest mistake ad agencies make is to presume they know people just because they have a lot of quantitative data."

Other agencies, marketers, and consultants use observational research to get a more realistic picture of consumers and their behavior than can be obtained from interviews. Some researchers believe techniques such as focus groups result in consumers portraying themselves as they would like to be rather than as they really are. For example, DDB Needham Worldwide used a more basic form of anthropological research—hanging around in supermarkets—to observe the purchase decision for a General Mills children's fruit snack product. Mothers interviewed in focus group sessions said they bought the product because of its "wholesomeness." However, the observational research revealed the purchase decision process was very different: a child would beg the mother to put the product in the cart, and the brand was almost irrelevant. An associate director of strategic planning and research at the agency noted the wholesomeness response coming out of focus group interviews was a category motivator that encouraged consumers to buy the product but not a specific brand. Many researchers think more traditional research methods elicit less-than-sincere responses, particularly with low-interest or low-involvement product categories.

Some people believe anthropological research may intrude too far into consumers' lives. For example, in 1989, a California

---

As we stressed in previous chapters and in the discussion of the creative process, creative strategy should be based on a number of factors. These include a thorough analysis of the target audience; the basic problem, issue, or opportunity the advertising must address; the major selling idea or key benefit the message needs to communicate; and any required or mandatory supportive information that needs to be included in the advertisement. Once these factors are determined, a creative strategy statement that describes the message appeal and execution style that will be used in the ad should be developed. Many advertising agencies have these various elements stated or outlined in a document known as the copy or creative platform.

Copy Platform

We will refer to the written document that specifies the basic elements of the creative strategy as a **copy platform.** This document is referred to in various agencies by

couple sued Nissan Motors, claiming a company researcher from Japan who rented a room from them during a temporary assignment invaded their privacy. The researcher had been studying U.S living and car-buying patterns, in part by observing and taking notes while living with the couple. While the couple charged he misrepresented and concealed the real reason for his stay, Nissan called the suit absurd, and seven months later it was dropped.

Source: Gary Levin, "Anthropologists in Adland," *Advertising Age,* February 24, 1992, pp. 3, 49; and Ron Alsop, "People Watchers Seek Clues to Consumers' True Behavior," *The Wall Street Journal,* September 4, 1986, p. 29.

Ethnographic research was used in developing the "We Deliver for You" campaign for the U. S. Postal Service

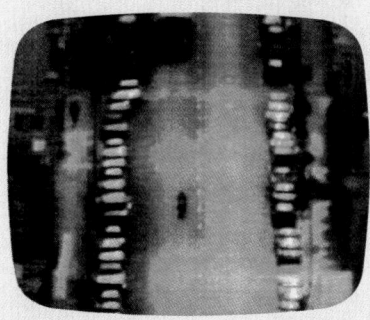

AN: The spirit of the Olympic Games, it's about being the best you can be. They call him "Iron Legs" and he wants to be the best at what he does. Richard Lo isn't an Olympic athlete, he's a letter carrier. His route includes some of the cruelest hills in San Francisco. He climbs them everyday, delivering up to 300 pounds of mail.

different names, such as a creative platform or work plan, creative blueprint, or a creative contract. The account representatives or manager assigned to the account usually prepare the copy platform. In larger agencies, an individual from research or the strategic planning department may prepare the copy platform. Individuals from the agency team or group assigned to the account, including creative personnel as well as representatives from media and research, have input into preparing this document. The advertising manager and/or the marketing and product managers from the client side are also involved in the process and must ultimately approve the copy platform. Exhibit 10–9 (page 341) provides an example of a copy platform outline that can be used to guide the creative process. Just as there are different names for the copy platform, there are variations in the outline and format used, and agencies are likely to vary in the information and level of detail they include in the copy platform.

➤ *Exhibit 10–8* **Some insight into consumers' response to a commercial can be gained by showing them a storyboard layout**

SFX: CAR AND FOOT TRAFFIC AMBIENCE
VO: Why did the chicken cross the road?
To open a 7/24 Savings Plan at San Diego Trust.
Because with $500 in savings...

...he can avoid getting henpecked by monthly charges on a checking account.
What's more, he can access his nest egg through our huge ATM network...
SFX: BANK AMBIENCE
...and round-the-clock phone service.

VO: And of course, the interest he'll earn on savings isn't just chicken feed.
So open a 7/24 Savings Plan at San Diego Trust.
And give yourself a good reason to...
SFX: COCKA DOODLE DOO

➤ *Exhibit 10–9*
Copy platform outline

1. Basic problem or issue the advertising must address
2. Advertising and communication objectives
3. Target audience
4. Major selling idea or key benefits to communicate
5. Creative strategy statement (campaign theme, appeal, and execution technique to be used)
6. Supportive information and requirements

➤ *Exhibit 10–10*
Hathaway has run its "Man in the Hathaway shirt" campaign for more than 40 years

Several components of the copy platform have already been discussed in previous chapters. For example, in Chapter 8, we examined the DAGMAR model and saw how the setting of advertising objectives requires specifying a well-defined target audience as well as developing a communications task statement regarding what message needs to communicated to this audience. Determining what problem the product or service will solve or what issue must be addressed in the ad helps in establishing communication objectives for the message to accomplish. Many copy platforms also include supportive information and requirements (elements that must appear in the ads such as brand identifications, disclaimers, and the like). The final two components of the copy platform, the development of the major selling idea and creative strategy development, are often the responsibility of the creative team or specialist and are the crux of the creative strategy since they form the basis of the advertising campaign.

Advertising Campaigns

Most advertisements are part of a series of messages that make up an advertising campaign. The **advertising campaign** often consists of multiple messages in a variety of media that center on a single theme or idea. Determining the central theme, idea, position, or image is a critical part of the creative process, as it sets the tone or direction for the development of the individual ads that make up the campaign. Some campaigns last only a short time, usually because they are ineffective or market conditions change, as was discussed in the Burger King example in Promotional Perspective 10–1. However, a successful campaign theme and creative strategy may last for several years or even longer. Philip Morris has been using the "Marlboro Country" campaign for over 25 years, while the "Man in the Hathaway shirt" campaign featuring the model with the distinctive eyepatch first appeared in 1951. The latter campaign has been modified by using celebrities in the ads such as Ted Turner and sports broadcaster Bob Costas (Exhibit 10–10). Exhibit 10–11 lists some of the more successful and enduring advertising campaign themes.

➤ *Exhibit 10–11*
**Examples of successful and
long-running advertising
campaigns**

Company or Brand	Campaign Theme
Marlboro cigarettes	"Marlboro Country"
Hathaway shirts	"The man in the Hathaway shirt"
Allstate Insurance	"You're in good hands with Allstate"
Hallmark cards	"When you care enough to send the very best"
Budweiser beer	"This Bud's for you"
United Airlines	"Fly the friendly skies"
BMW automobiles	"The ultimate driving machine"
State Farm Insurance	"Like a good neighbor, State Farm is there"
AT&T	"Reach out and touch someone"
Timex watches	"It takes a licking and keeps on ticking"
Dial soap	"Aren't you glad you use Dial?"
U.S. Army	"Be all that you can be!"

Once the creative theme or idea is established and approved, attention can then turn to the type of appeal and creative execution style or approach that will be used. However, before considering these parts of creative strategy, we examine how major selling ideas are determined.

The Search for the Major Selling Idea

As noted above, an important part of creative strategy is determining the central theme that will become the **major selling idea** of the ad campaign. As A. Jerome Jeweler states in his book *Creative Strategy in Advertising:*

> The major selling idea should emerge as the strongest singular thing you can say about your product or service. This should be the claim with the broadest and most meaningful appeal to your target audience. Once you determine this message, be certain you can live with it; be sure it stands strong enough to remain the central issue in every ad and commercial in the campaign.[22]

Some advertising experts argue that for an ad campaign to be effective it must contain a "big idea" that attracts the consumer's attention, gets a reaction, and sets the advertiser's product or service apart from the competitions'. Well-known ad man John O'Toole describes the **big idea** as

> that flash of insight that synthesizes the purpose of the strategy, joins the product benefit with consumer desire in a fresh, involving way, brings the subject to life and makes the reader or audience stop, look, and listen.[23]

Of course, the real challenge to the copywriter is coming up with the big idea to use in the ad, as many products and services offer virtually nothing unique, and it can be difficult to find something interesting to say about them. David Ogilvy, generally considered one of the most creative advertising copywriters ever to work in the business, has stated:

> I doubt if more than one campaign in a hundred contains a big idea. I am supposed to be one of the more fertile inventors of big ideas, but in my long career as a copywriter I have not had more than 20, if that.[24]

While really great ideas in advertising are difficult to come by, there are many examples of big ideas that became the basis of very creative and successful advertising campaigns. Some classic examples include the "We try harder" campaign, which positioned Avis as the underdog rental car company that provided better service than Hertz; the "Tastes great, less filling" argument theme used for over 20 years for Miller Lite beer; the "Pepsi Generation" theme and subsequent variations for Pepsi-Cola such as "The taste of a new generation"; and AT&T's "Reach out and touch someone" emotional ads for its long-distance service. More recent or current examples of big ideas that have resulted in memorable and effective advertising include the "Perception/Reality" campaign for *Rolling Stone* magazine and Nike's "Just do it" campaign (Exhibit 10–12).

> *Exhibit 10–12*
Nike's "Just do it" campaign is an example of a "big idea" in advertising

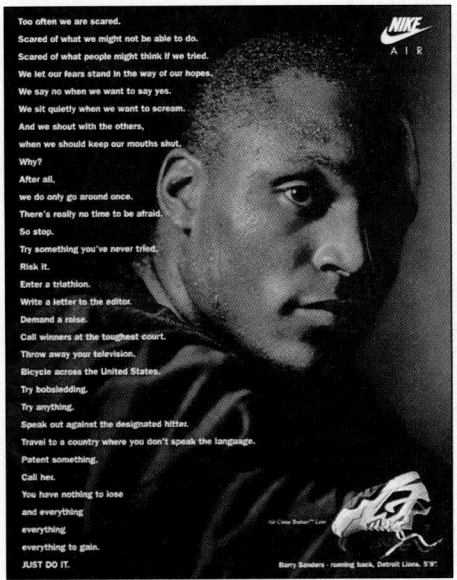

It is often difficult to pinpoint the exact source or inspiration for a big idea or to teach advertising people how to find them. However, several approaches can guide the creative team's search for a major selling idea and offer alternative solutions or options for developing effective advertising. Some of the best known and most discussed approaches include the following:

- The unique selling proposition.
- Creation of a brand image.
- Looking for the inherent drama.
- Positioning.

Unique selling proposition

The concept of the **unique selling proposition** (USP) was developed by Rosser Reeves, former chairman of the Ted Bates agency, and is described in his influential book *Reality in Advertising*. Reeves noted there are three characteristics of unique selling propositions:

1. Each advertisement must make a proposition to the consumer. Not just words, not just product puffery, not just show window advertising. Each advertisement must say to each reader: 'Buy this product and you will get this benefit.'
2. The proposition must be one that the competition either cannot or does not offer. It must be unique either in the brand or in the claim.
3. The proposition must be strong enough to move the mass millions, that is, to pull over new customers to your brand.[25]

Reeves said the attribute claim or benefit that formed the basis of the USP should dominate the ad and should be emphasized through repetitive advertising. The ad shown in Exhibit 10–13 for Mobil 1 synthetic motor oil is an example of a message that uses a unique selling proposition.

An important consideration in the use of Reeves's approach to developing the major selling idea is finding a truly unique product or service attribute, benefit, or inherent advantage that can be used in the claim. This may require considerable research on the product and consumers not only to determine the USP but also to document or substantiate the claim. As we shall see in Chapter 23, the Federal Trade Commission has become concerned with advertisers making claims of superiority or uniqueness without supporting data. Also, some companies have sued their competitors for making unsubstantiated uniqueness claims.[26]

➤ *Exhibit 10–13*
This ad for Mobil 1 uses a unique selling proposition

Advertisers must also consider whether the unique selling proposition affords them a *sustainable competitive advantage* that cannot be easily copied or imitated by competitors. In the package-goods field in particular, companies very quickly match a brand feature for feature, which means advertising based on USPs quickly obsolesces. For example, a few years ago, Procter & Gamble invented a combination shampoo and conditioner and used it to rejuvenate its struggling Pert brand. The reformulated brand was called Pert Plus and its market share rose from 2 percent to 12 percent, making it the leading shampoo. However, competing brands such as Revlon, Suave, and others quickly launched their own two-in-one formula products[27] (Exhibit 10–14).

➤ *Exhibit 10–14*
Procter & Gamble's combination shampoo and conditioner USP was quickly imitated by competitors

Creating a brand image

In many product and service categories, competing brands are often so similar it is very difficult to find or create a unique attribute or benefit to use as the major selling idea. Many of the package-goods products that account for much of the advertising dollars spent in the United States are difficult to differentiate on a functional or performance basis. Thus, the creative strategy used to sell these products is based on the development of a strong, memorable identity or meaning for the brand through image advertising.

The advertising person most associated with image advertising is David Ogilvy, who popularized the idea of brand image in his famous book *Confessions of an Advertising Man*. Ogilvy noted that with image advertising "every advertisement should be thought of as a contribution to the complex symbol which is the brand image." He argued that the image or personality of the brand is particularly important when brands are similar:

> The greater the similarity between brands, the less part reason plays in brand selection. There isn't any significant difference between the various brands of whiskey, or cigarettes, or beer. They are all about the same. And so are the cake mixes and the

➤ *Exhibit 10–15*

A. Designer jeans often use image advertising

B. Colognes and fragrances rely heavily on image advertising

detergents and the margarines. The manufacturer who dedicates his advertising to building the most sharply defined personality for his brand will get the largest share of the market at the highest profit. By the same token, the manufacturers who will find themselves up the creek are those shortsighted opportunists who siphon off their advertising funds for promotions.[28]

Image advertising has been used as the main selling idea for a variety of products and services including soft drinks, liquor, cigarettes, automobiles, airlines, financial services, perfumes/colognes, and clothing. Many consumers wear designer jeans, Ralph Lauren polo shirts, and Swatch watches or drink certain brands of beer or soft drinks because of the image of these brands. The key to successful image advertising is determining and developing an image that will appeal to product users. The ads for Lawman denim and The Baron cologne show examples of ads that have been successful in developing brand images (Exhibit 10–15).

Inherent drama

A somewhat different approach to determining the major selling idea is by finding the **inherent drama** or characteristic of the product that makes the consumer purchase it. The inherent drama approach expresses the advertising philosophy of Leo Burnett, founder of the Leo Burnett agency in Chicago. Burnett argued that the inherent drama "is often hard to find but it is always there, and once found it is the most interesting and believable of all advertising appeals."[29] He believed advertising should be based on a foundation of consumer benefits with an emphasis on the dramatic element in expressing these benefits.

Burnett was an advocate of a down-home type of advertising that presents the idea or message in a warm and realistic way. Some of the more famous advertisements

➤ *Exhibit 10–16*   **This commercial uses an inherent drama approach**

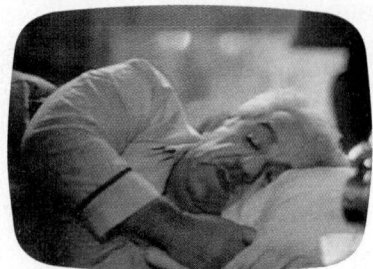

(SFX: RING)
SAM: Patrino.
(AVO): The news spread throughout the raisin business.
SAM: (ON PHONE) More raisins?
(AVO): Now Kellogg's puts two bigger scoops in Kellogg's Raisin Bran for even more raisins.

SAM: (GIVING ORDERS TO LOADERS) More raisins!
(AVO): Raisin brokers, raisin shippers and raisin raisers worked furiously to meet the Kellogg's demand.
SAM: (TO PICKERS) More raisins, more raisins!

(AVO): It's been tough on some of us...
SAM: (IN BED) More raisins.
(AVO): ...but it's been worth it. 'Cause now two scoops in Kellogg's Raisin Bran...
means even more raisins than ever before.
SAM: Mmmm - more raisins.

developed by the Leo Burnett agency using the inherent drama approach include those for Maytag appliances and Kellogg's cereals. Notice how the commercial shown in Exhibit 10–16 uses this approach to dramatize the fact that Kellogg's Raisin Bran cereal contains more raisins than ever before.

Positioning

The concept of **positioning** as a basis for advertising strategy was introduced by Jack Trout and Al Ries in the early 1970s and has become a popular basis of creative development.[30] From an advertising perspective, the basic idea of positioning is that advertising is used to establish or "position" the product or service in a particular place in the mind of the consumer.

Trout and Ries originally described positioning as the image consumers had of the brand in relationship to competing brands in the product or service category. However, the concept of positioning has been expanded beyond direct competitive positioning and, as was discussed in Chapter 5, can be done on the basis of product attributes, price/quality, usage or application, product users, or product class. Any of these can be used as the basis of a major selling idea that becomes the basis of the creative strategy and results in the brand occupying a particular place or position in the minds of the target audience. Actually, positioning can be done on the basis of a unique or distinctive attribute, which shows that the positioning and unique selling proposition approaches can overlap. Positioning approaches have been used as the foundation of a number of successful creative strategies (as was shown in numerous examples in Chapter 5) and continues to be important as a basis for creative strategy.

Ethical Perspective 10-1

Do Advertisers Go Too Far to Get Attention?

Advertisers are always searching for a creative or avant-garde idea that will break through the clutter and grab consumers' attention. We began this chapter, however, by discussing how many creative people think they are being stifled by restrictions that limit the images and messages they can deliver to the American public. Many creative people believe advertising has become too bland and boring as a result of advertisers being overly concerned with offending someone and making ads that are "politically correct." However, not all advertisers are concerned about whether their ads offend someone or are perceived as being in poor taste. Many advertisers are abandoning conventional advertising techniques and deliberately creating ads that are controversial and of questionable taste. Some experts call this new rage "shock advertising" and argue that its intent is not necessarily to sell a product but to elicit attention for a brand name by jolting consumers into staring at the ad.

The most controversial of the shock ad campaigns is a series of print ads being run around the world by Benetton, the Italian-based clothing manufacturer that has 6,500 stores in more than 100 countries. Probably the most criticized ad in the campaign is the one showing a family agonizing at the bedside of a dying AIDS patient. Some have called the picture, which was originally published not as an ad but in *Life* magazine, the most shocking photo ever used in an advertisement. The series also features an automobile fully ablaze after a car bomb went off and an agonizing photo of a boatload of refugees who appear to be swarming into the water.

Benetton readily admits its goal is to shock some people with its ads. Peter Fressola, a Benetton North America spokesman, has stated, "Yes, we mean to shock some people with our ads.

But people who are shocked by this have been living in a cocoon. They need to be shocked into seeing what's really going on in the world." He explains Benetton's position on the ads by noting: "We believe that when that many people see an image this powerful, it can raise their collective consciousness. And that can result in action."

Benetton, which creates its own advertising, has been regarded as the renegade of the advertising world since 1989 when it ran a print ad featuring a black woman nursing a white baby. While Benetton executives don't deny their ultimate goal is to sell clothing, they argue that their shock ads have a loftier objective of making social statements concerning issues that appeal particularly to young consumers such as racial prejudice or the spread of AIDS. However, not everyone agrees with this. Well-known advertising executive Jerry Della Femina suspects the real aim of the Benetton AIDS ad is free publicity and questions how far the company will go to shock people. Others have accused Benetton of exploiting human suffering to sell its products. The Benetton ads have been a subject of controversy in many other countries. Advertising self-regulatory organizations in Britain, France, and Spain have condemned the ads and urged magazines in these countries to reject many of them.

Benetton is not alone in the use of shock ads. Calvin Klein has been criticized for using advertising for its clothing and toiletries that often resembles soft pornography. The company created a controversy in 1991 when it ran a magazine-size supplement in an issue of *Vanity Fair* featuring explicit photos of semi-nude models that many considered in poor taste. Many advertising people believe shock ads can be used more readily by companies such as Calvin Klein and Benetton because their images as leading

(continued)

Positioning also is often the basis of a firm's creative strategy when it has multiple brands competing in the same market. For example, Procter & Gamble markets three lines of dishwashing detergents—Ivory Liquid, Joy, and Dawn—and positions each one differently. Ivory is positioned on the basis of its mildness, and Joy for its ability to deliver "shiny dishes," whereas Dawn is positioned as being the most effective at cutting through grease.

The approaches to determining the major selling ideas discussed above are very popular and are often used as the basis of the creative strategy for ad campaigns. These approaches represent specific "creative styles" that have become associated with some of the most famous and successful advertising creative minds and their agencies.[31] However, many other creative approaches and styles are available and are often used in advertising.

Also, agencies are by no means limited to any one creative approach. For example, the famous Marlboro Country campaign, which is a classic example of image advertising, was developed by the Leo Burnett agency, which is known more for the inherent drama approach, whereas many different agencies have followed the unique selling proposition approach advocated by Rosser Reeves and the former Ted Bates agency. The challenge to the creative specialist or team is to find a major selling idea,

(concluded)

edge and avant-garde fashion designers rely heavily on the images they create.

Advertising experts also note that the shock ad approach is popular among firms that have small advertising budgets and rely on publicity to increase their name awareness. For example, Bamboo Inc., a tiny lingerie maker, spent $2,000 to have a team of "street kids" rove around Manhattan spray-painting ads (using an environmentally safe paint that washes off) that stated, "From here it looks like you could use some new underwear." Next to the slogan is the Bamboo name. The agency that developed the campaign noted, "If you're Procter & Gamble, you don't do this type of advertising, but if you're an underdog, it pays to advertise in an underdog fashion."

Shock advertising is not confined, however, to fashion designers and small companies. Volvo has run a series of print ads featuring small, but graphic, photos of mangled Volvos and accident victims' accounts of how they survived terrible crashes because of the way the car is built. The director of communications at Volvo noted, "This is an attempt to make the issue of safety more engaging and compelling."

Many advertising critics are concerned about how far advertisers will go with the shock ad approach. While they see the eye-opening ads as a way of breaking through the clutter, some are concerned that shock advertising may change the way many companies advertise their products. However, many marketers counter by noting their ads are designed to appeal to narrowly defined market segments and they will let them decide whether the ads are too shocking.

Source: Bruce Horowitz: " 'Shock Ads': New Rage That Spawns Rage," *Los Angeles Times,* March 22, 1992, pp. D1, 7; and Adrienna Ward, " 'Socially Aware' or 'Wasted Money'?" *Advertising Age,* February 24, 1992, p. 4.

whether it be based on a unique selling proposition, brand image, inherent drama, position in the market, or some other approach, and use it as a guide to the development of an effective creative strategy.

In their search for a big idea, advertisers consider many different creative options that might grab the consumer's attention. However, as discussed in Ethical Perspective 10–1, many people believe some advertisers are going too far in their efforts to break through the advertising clutter and have an impact on consumers.

SUMMARY

The creative development and execution of the advertising message constitute an integral part of a firm's promotional program and are often the key to the success or failure of a marketing campaign. Marketers generally turn to advertising agencies to develop, prepare, and implement their creative strategy since they are specialists in the creative function of advertising. The specialist or team working on the creative side of advertising is responsible for developing an effective way of communicating the marketer's message to the customer. However, other individuals on both the client and agency sides must work with the creative specialists in developing the creative strategy, implementing it, and evaluating its effectiveness.

Much attention is focused on the concept of creativity in advertising, as the challenge facing the writers, artists, and others who develop the ads is to be creative and come up with fresh, unique, and appropriate ideas that can be used as solutions to communications problems. Creativity in advertising is best viewed as a process that contains several steps or stages, including preparation, incubation, illumination, and verification. Various sources of information and assistance are available to provide input and assistance and help the creative specialists determine the best campaign theme, appeal, or execution style.

Creative strategy development is guided by specific goals and objectives and is based on a number of factors including the target audience, the basic problem or issue the advertising must address, the objectives the message seeks to accomplish, and the major selling idea or key benefit the advertiser wants to communicate. These factors are generally stated in a copy platform, which is a work plan used to guide the development of the advertising campaign. An important part of creative strategy is determining the major selling idea that will become the central theme of the campaign. There are several approaches to doing this, including using a unique selling proposition, creating a brand image, looking for inherent drama in the brand, and using positioning.

KEY TERMS

creative strategy
creative tactics
creativity
advertising creativity
general preplanning input
product-specific
   preplanning input

problem detection
focus groups
storyboard
aniamatic
copy platform
advertising campaign
major selling idea

big idea
unique selling proposition
  (USP)
image advertising
inherent drama
positioning

DISCUSSION QUESTIONS

1. Discuss the meaning of advertising creativity. Choose a print ad and a TV or radio commercial you like and analyze them in terms of creativity.
2. How should advertising creativity be judged and who should be responsible for judging it—clients or agency creative specialists?
3. What is your opinion of advertising awards such as the Clios that are based solely on creativity? Should agencies pride themselves on their creative awards? Why or why not?
4. What are the various stages of the creative process? Do you agree with the notion that advertising creativity can or should follow a definitive process?
5. Assume you have been assigned to work on the development of an advertising campaign for a new brand of cereal. Discuss the various types of general and product-specific preplanning input you might provide for the creative team.
6. What is meant by a major selling or big idea? What are some of the approaches to developing major selling ideas? Provide examples of each approach.
7. What is meant by a unique selling proposition (USP)? Find an example of an ad that you feel uses a unique selling proposition as its major selling idea. Evaluate this ad against the three characteristics of USPs discussed in the chapter.
8. Discuss the role brand image plays in the advertising of a particular product/service category such as soft drinks, cologne, or airlines. Discuss the image used by various companies competing in this market.
9. Discuss the role positioning plays as a basis for advertising strategy. Find examples of two ads that use positioning as the basis for their creative approach.
10. Do you feel that companies such as Benetton are using "shock advertising" to make social statements or merely to get publicity that will ultimately help sell their products? Defend your position.

chapter **11**

Creative Strategy: Implementation and Evaluation

chapter objectives

➤ To analyze various types of appeals that can be used in the development and implementation of an advertising message.

➤ To analyze the various creative execution styles that can be used by advertisers and the types of advertising situations where they are most appropriate.

➤ To analyze various tactical issues involved in the creation of print advertising and television commercials.

➤ To consider how clients evaluate the creative work of their agencies and discuss guidelines for the evaluation and approval process.

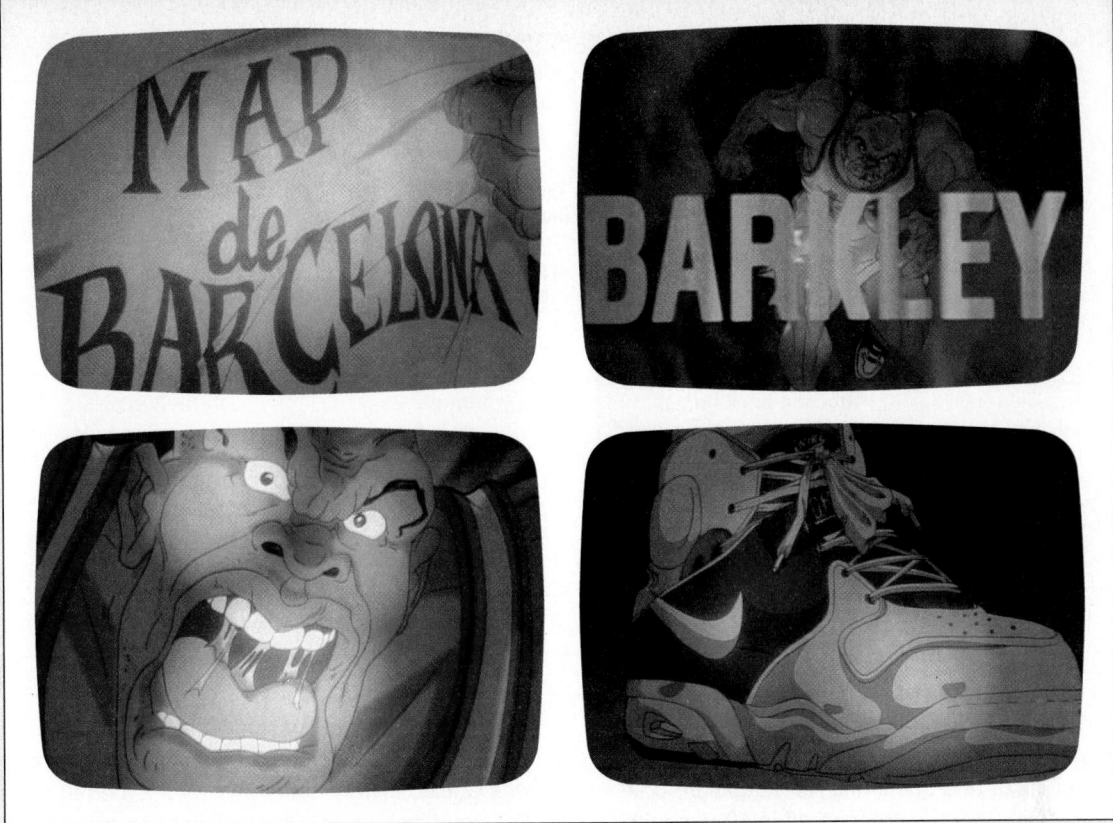

Consumers' Favorite Commercials

Before reading further, stop for a moment and think about the ads you have seen recently. Which ones caught your attention and really made an impression? Which TV commercial would you rate as the "most outstanding" one you have seen? How do you think your list of top commercials compares against that of other consumers? Every year, Video Storyboard Tests Inc., a New York City-based ad testing company, surveys more than 25,000 consumers across the country and asks them to name the most outstanding TV commercials they have seen recently. The accompanying exhibit lists the 25 most popular TV campaigns of 1991 along with their 1990 ranking and the name of the agency that handles the advertising.

In 1991, for the second straight year, the most popular commercials were those for Pepsi/Diet Pepsi. The popular Pepsi commercials included a humorous spot featuring supermodel Cindy Crawford drinking a Pepsi as two preteen boys watch in awe and gawk in admiration—of Pepsi's new can. Commercials for Diet Pepsi feature Ray Charles singing the familiar "You've got the right one baby, uh huh!" refrain accompanied by a trio of female singers. The innovative Energizer bunny parody commercials also continued to be very popular, while the campaign making the biggest leap on the popularity charts was for Du Pont's Stainmaster carpeting. The latest humorous spot in this campaign featured a toddler

terrorizing the carpeting as his mother chases him around the house in his walker. Nike's free-spirited "Just do it" commercials, many of which featured superstar athletes Bo Jackson and Michael Jordan, also continued to be very popular among consumers.

The top 10 also includes perennially popular campaigns for highly advertised companies and brands such as McDonald's, Coca-Cola, and Budweiser. However, Miller Lite beer did not finish in the top 10 for the first time in more than a decade after dropping the long-running "Tastes great–less filling" campaign featuring ex-jocks for the widely criticized "It's it and that's that" theme. Commercials for Bud Light also declined in popularity since Anheuser-Busch stopped using Spuds MacKenzie, the original party animal, in ads for the brand.

In the opening to Chapter 4, we discussed the new emphasis recession-weary consumers are putting on price and value. More evidence of just how important price and value have become to consumers is shown by the fact that a third of the top 25 commercials focused on low prices, special deals, and/or value. For example, Taco Bell cracked the top 10 with "59! 79! 99!" blaring as its sole jingle, slogan, and message. Pizza Hut jumped from the 25 spot to 10 on the strength of ads talking about price deals, while Burger King and Little Caesar also emphasized price and deals in many of their commercials.

Most Popular Television Commercials of 1991

1991 Rank	Brands	Ad Agencies	1991 Rank	Brands	Ad Agencies
1	Pepsi/Diet Pepsi	BBDO	15	Huggies	Oglivy & Mather
2	Energizer	Chiat/Day/Mojo	16	Taster's Choice	McCann-Erickson
3	DuPont Stainmaster	BBDO	17	Diet Coke	Lintas
4	Nike	Wieden & Kennedy	18	Johnson & Johnson baby shampoo	Lintas
5	McDonald's	Leo Burnett			
6	Coca-Cola	McCann-Erickson	19	Burger King	DMB&B/Saatchi & Saatchi
7	Little Ceasar	Cliff Freeman & Partners	20	AT&T	Ayer/Oglivy & Mather/Young & Rubicam/McCann-Erickson
8	Budweiser	DMB&B			
9	Taco Bell	Foote, Cone & Belding	21	Bud Light	DDB Needham
10	Pizza Hut	BBDO	22	Duracell	Ogilvy & Mather
11	Coors Light	Foote, Cone & Belding	23	Honda	Rubin Postaer & Associates
12	California Raisins	Foote, Cone & Belding	24	Wendy's	Backer Spielvogel Bates
13	Miller Lite	Leo Burnett	25	Jell-O	Young & Rubicam
14	Toyota	Saatchi & Saatchi			

(continued)

Creative ads for Infiniti (the nature campaign discussed in Chapter 8) and Isuzu (the Joe Isuzu liar campaign) both made the top 25 in 1990 but dropped off in 1991 as the companies changed campaigns. The car ads that did make the top 25, Toyota and Honda, both emphasized value in their commercials.

The popularity of commercials focusing on price is particularly interesting since most TV spots avoid reference to price and focus more on brand image. However, the creative director for the agency that created Taco Bell's screaming price commercials argues: "You can do it in a way that is entertaining, and people will like it. . . . I think our image is healthier than ever."

Many of the top campaigns that did not talk about price or value used an emotional-based appeal or execution, particularly cute kids. In addition to the Stainmaster spots, commercials for McDonald's, Coca-Cola, Huggies, Johnson & Johnson's baby shampoo, and Jell-O all used children to appeal to consumers' emotions. One of the most creative of the new campaigns on the list is the one for Taster's Choice instant coffee, which debuted at number 16. The campaign uses a continuing soap opera type of format featuring the ongoing saga of two flirtatious neighbors.

Some advertising and marketing executives are skeptical of the Video Storyboard popularity contest and question whether popular advertising really translates into sales. They note that many of these popular ads are for heavily advertised brands or companies and are cited as most outstanding since they are seen so often and thus have a greater chance of being remembered in a recall test. However, one executive perhaps best summarized many advertising and marketing people's opinions when he noted, "It's good to know people are at least paying attention to your message."

In Chapter 10, we discussed the importance of advertising creativity and examined the various steps in the creative process. We focused on determining *what* the advertising message will say or communicate. This chapter focuses on *how* the message will be implemented or executed. We examine various appeals and execution styles that can be used in developing the advertisement and tactical issues involved in the design and production of effective advertising messages. We conclude by presenting some guidelines or criteria that clients can use to evaluate the creative work of their agencies.

Appeals and Execution Styles

The **advertising appeal** refers to the basis or approach used in the advertisement to attract the attention or interest of consumers and/or to influence their feelings toward the product, service, or cause. An advertising appeal can also be viewed as "something that moves people, speaks to their wants or needs, and excites their interest."[1] The **creative execution style** refers to the manner or way in which a particular appeal is turned into an advertising message that is presented to the consumer. According to William Weilbacher:

> *Exhibit 11−1*
Goodyear uses a rational appeal to introduce a new product

> *Exhibit 11−1*
Goodyear uses a rational appeal to introduce a new product

The appeal can be said to form the underlying content of the advertisement, and the execution the way in which that content is presented. Advertising appeals and executions are usually independent of each other; that is, a particular appeal can be executed in a variety of ways and a particular means of execution can be applied to a variety of advertising appeals. Advertising appeals tend to adapt themselves to all media, whereas some kinds of executional devices are more adaptable to some media than others.[2]

Advertising Appeals

Hundreds of different appeals can be used as the basis for an advertising message. At the broadest level, these approaches are generally broken into two categories or classes—informational/rational appeals and emotional appeals. The use of rational versus emotional appeals was introduced in Chapter 7 in discussing message aspects of communication. Attention was given to the rational appeal of comparative advertising and the emotional appeals of fear and humor. In this section, we focus on additional ways of using rational and emotional appeals as part of creative strategy. We also consider how rational and emotional appeals can be combined in developing the advertising message.

Informational/rational appeals

Informational/rational appeals focus on the consumer's practical, functional, or utilitarian need for the product or service and emphasize features of a product or service and/or the benefits or reasons for owning or using a particular brand. The content of these types of messages emphasize facts, learning, and the logic of persuasion.[3] Rational-based appeals tend to be informative, and advertisers using this approach generally attempt to convince consumers that their product or service has a particular attribute or provides a specific benefit that is important to them or shows how the brand satisfies their needs. Their objective is to persuade the target audience to buy the brand because it is the best available or does a better job of meeting the consumers' needs. For example, Goodyear uses a rational appeal to explain why its new Aquatred tire represents a technological breakthrough and is a superior product (Exhibit 11−1).

Many rational motives can be used as the basis for advertising appeals, including comfort, convenience, economy, and health and sensory benefits such as touch, taste, and smell. In addition to these factors, a number of other rational motives or

➤ *Exhibit 11–2*
Jaguar uses a feature appeal ad to emphasize its quality and safety

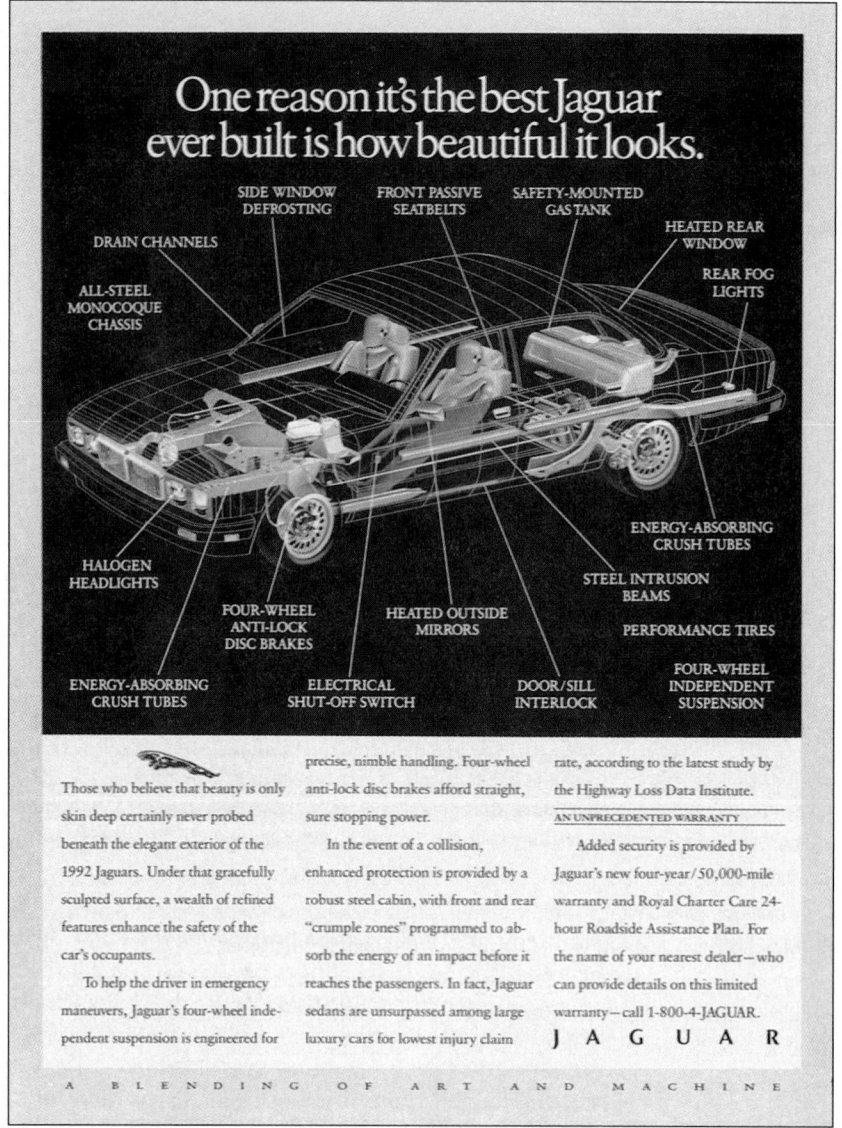

purchase criteria are commonly used in advertising such as quality, performance, dependability, durability, efficiency, efficacy, and performance. The particular features, benefits, or evaluative criteria that are important to consumers and can serve as the basis of an informational/rational appeal message vary from one product or service category to another as well as among various market segments.

William Weilbacher identified a number of different types of advertising appeals that fall under the category of rational approaches as they tend to be informative and focus primarily on product or service attributes and features. We briefly discuss each of these appeals and cite some examples of their use.

Ads that use a *feature appeal* focus on the dominant attributes or characteristics of the product or service. These types of ads tend to be highly informative and attempt to present the customer with a number of important product attributes or features that will lead to favorable attitudes and can be used as the basis for a rational purchase decision. Technical and high-involvement products often use this type of advertising approach. For example, the Jaguar ad shown in Exhibit 11–2 focuses on various product features to show how well built the car is and how these features enhance the safety of passengers.

➤ *Exhibit 11–3*
UPS promotes the low price of its Next Day Air Letter

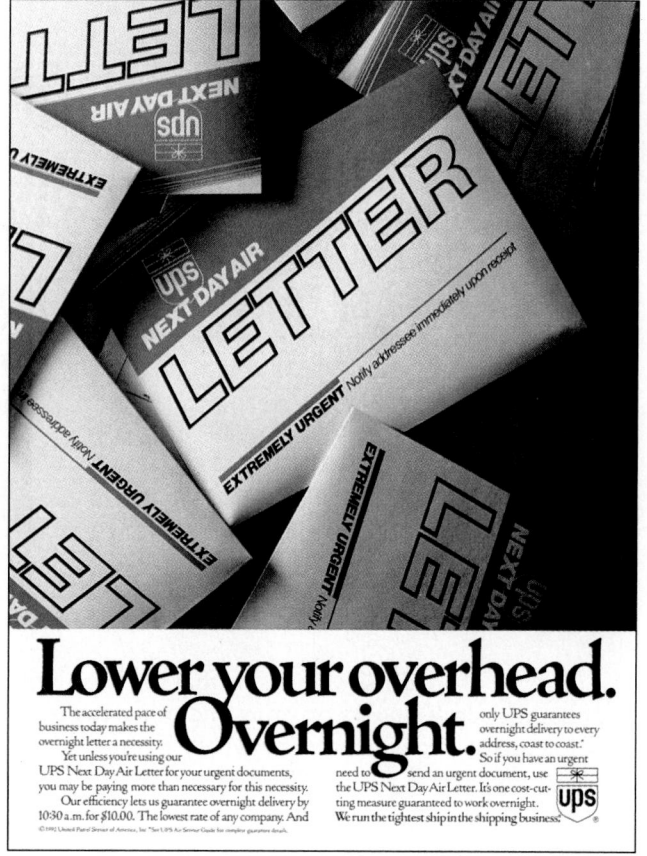

When a *competitive advantage appeal* is used, the advertiser makes either a direct or indirect comparison to another brand (or brands) and usually makes a claim of superiority on one or more attributes. This type of appeal was discussed in Chapter 7 under comparative advertising.

A *favorable price appeal* is one that makes the price offer the dominant point of the message. Price appeal advertising is used most often by retailers for announcing sales, special offers, or low everyday prices. However, as was discussed in the opening vignette, price appeal ads are also being used by national advertisers and have become very popular among consumers, particularly during the recent recession. Many companies, such as fast-food chains, have made price an important part of their marketing strategy through programs such as promotional deals and "value menus" or lower overall prices, and their advertising strategy is designed to communicate this. Many other types of advertisers use price appeals as well. For example, in Exhibit 11–3, United Parcel Service of America, Inc., uses a price appeal to promote the cost savings for the UPS Next Day Air Letter.

News appeals are those where some type of news or announcement about the product, service, or company dominates the advertisement. This type of appeal can be used for a new product or service or to inform consumers of some significant changes in the product/service such as a modification or improvement. This appeal works best when a company has important news or information it wants to communicate to its target market. The ad for American Airlines shown in Exhibit 11–4, which was used to announce major changes in its airfares, is a good example of a news appeal ad.

Product/service popularity appeals stress the wide use or popularity of a product or service by pointing out factors such as the number of consumers who use the brand or have switched to it or its leadership position in the market. The main point

> *Exhibit 11–4*
American Airlines announces its new fare structure in this news appeal type of ad

of this type of advertising appeal is that the popularity of the brand is evidence of the product/service's quality or value and other customers should consider using it. The ad for Sharp fax machines shown in Exhibit 11–5 is an example of this type of advertising appeal.

Emotional appeals

Emotional appeals relate to the consumers' social and/or psychological needs for purchasing a product or service. Many of the motives consumers have for their purchase decisions are emotional, and the "feelings" or overall affect one has for a brand are often just as important as, if not more than, knowledge of its features or attributes. Rational, informative-based appeals are viewed by advertisers for many products and services as dull and uninteresting. Moreover, many advertisers believe appeals to consumers' emotions work better at selling certain types of products, since many brands do not differ markedly from competing brands, making rational-based differentiation very difficult.

Many feelings or needs can serve as the basis for an advertising appeal designed to reach and influence consumers on an emotional level, as shown in Exhibit 11–6. These appeals are based on the psychological states or feelings that are directed to the self (such as pleasure or excitement) as well as those that have a more social orientation (such as status or recognition).

Advertisers can use emotional appeals in many ways in their creative strategy. Advertising using humor, sex appeals, or other types of appeals that are very entertaining, arousing, upbeat, and/or exciting can be used to affect the emotions of consumers and/or put them in a favorable frame of mind. Many TV advertisers use sentimental ads that are very poignant and create a "lump in the throat" of viewers. Companies such as Hallmark, AT&T, Kodak, and McDonald's often create commercials that evoke feelings of warmth, nostalgia, and/or sentiment. Marketers use emotional appeals hoping the positive feelings they evoke will transfer to the brand. It has been shown that positive mood states created by advertising can have a favorable effect on consumers' evaluation of a product.[4] Research has also shown that emotional advertising is better remembered than nonemotional messages.[5]

Another reason for using emotional appeals is to influence consumers' interpretations of their product usage experience. One way of doing this is through the

➤ *Exhibit 11–5*
This ad for Sharp fax machines uses a product popularity appeal

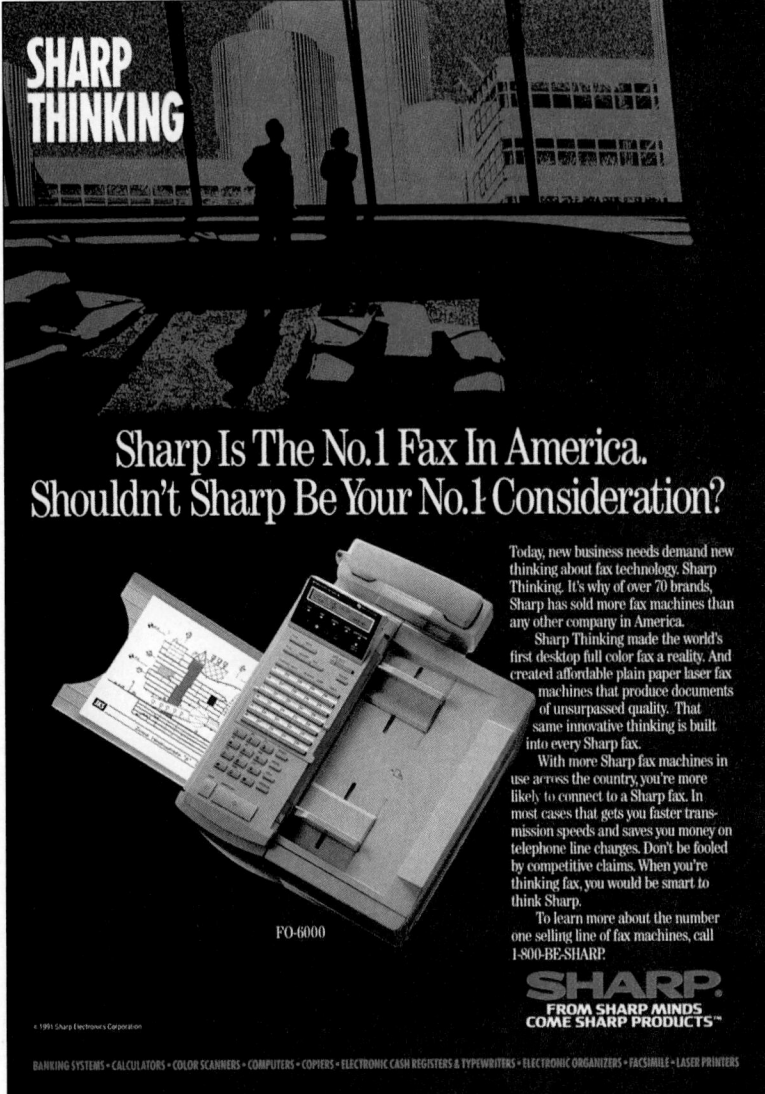

SHARP THINKING

**Sharp Is The No.1 Fax In America.
Shouldn't Sharp Be Your No.1 Consideration?**

Today, new business needs demand new thinking about fax technology. Sharp Thinking. It's why of over 70 brands, Sharp has sold more fax machines than any other company in America.

Sharp Thinking made the world's first desktop full color fax a reality. And created affordable plain paper laser fax machines that produce documents of unsurpassed quality. That same innovative thinking is built into every Sharp fax.

With more Sharp fax machines in use across the country, you're more likely to connect to a Sharp fax. In most cases that gets you faster transmission speeds and saves you money on telephone line charges. Don't be fooled by competitive claims. When you're thinking fax, you would be smart to think Sharp.

To learn more about the number one selling line of fax machines, call 1-800-BE-SHARP.

FO-6000

SHARP.
**FROM SHARP MINDS
COME SHARP PRODUCTS™**

© 1991 Sharp Electronics Corporation

BANKING SYSTEMS • CALCULATORS • COLOR SCANNERS • COMPUTERS • COPIERS • ELECTRONIC CASH REGISTERS & TYPEWRITERS • ELECTRONIC ORGANIZERS • FACSIMILE • LASER PRINTERS

➤ *Exhibit 11–6*
Bases for emotional appeals

Personal States or Feelings	Social-Based Feelings
Safety	Recognition
Security	Status
Love	Respect
Affection	Involvement
Happiness	Embarrassment
Joy	Affiliation/belonging
Nostalgia	Rejection
Sentiment	Acceptance
Excitement	Approval
Arousal/stimulation	
Sorrow/grief	
Pride	
Achievement/ accomplishment	
Self-esteem	
Actualization	
Pleasure	
Ambition	
Comfort	

use of what is known as transformational advertising. A **transformational ad** is defined as:

> one which associates the experience of using (consuming) the advertised brand with a unique set of psychological characteristics which would not typically be associated with the brand experience to the same degree without exposure to the advertisement.[6]

Transformational ads create feelings, images, meanings, and beliefs about the product or service that may be activated when consumers use it and thus "transforms" their interpretation of the usage experience. Christopher Puto and William Wells note that a transformational ad has two characteristics:

1. It must make the experience of using the product richer, warmer, more exciting, and/or more enjoyable than that obtained solely from an objective description of the advertised brand.
2. It must connect the experience of the advertisement so tightly with the experience of using the brand that consumers cannot remember the brand without recalling the experience generated by the advertisement.[7]

➤ *Exhibit 11–7*   Saab combines both rational and emotional appeals in this ad

21 LOGICAL REASONS TO BUY A SAAB.

In each of us, there is a tough, cold, logical side that wants to have hard facts, data and empirical evidence before it will assent to anything.

So when your impulsive, emotional side saw the exciting photograph on the facing page and yelled "Hey, look at this!," your logical side immediately asked to see some solid and relevant information about the Saab.

Here, then, are some of the more significant hard facts about Saabs, facts that make a strong logical argument in favor of owning a Saab:

1) Front-wheel drive. Once, Saab was one of the few cars in the U.S. that offered this. Since then, most other carmakers have discovered the superior handling and safety of front-wheel drive and have followed Saab's lead.

2) Turbocharging. More power without more engine displacement. Saab's third generation of turbocharging, incorporating an intercooler and Saab's Automatic Performance Control system, is still a generation or two ahead of any competition.

3) Four-valve technology. Doubling the number of valves per cylinder improves engine efficiency enormously. Yet another group of manufacturers is beginning to line up behind Saab.

4) Advanced ergonomics. That's just a way of saying that all instruments, controls and functional elements are designed so that they will be easy and natural to use. A legacy of Saab's aerospace heritage. Saab is the only car manufacturer which

also builds supersonic military jets.

5) Special steel underpanel. The Saab's smooth underside improves its aerodynamics and helps shed water to prevent rust.

6) Balance. 60% of the car's weight is borne by the front wheels, to maintain a consistent slight understeer and superior traction.

7) Rustproofing. A 16-step process that's designed to protect the car from the wetness and saltiness of Sweden's long winters.

8) Climate control. Your Saab is going to be comfortable inside, whatever is happening outside. Air conditioning is standard on all models, and effective insulation helps to control the temperature as well as the noise level inside.

9) High capacity electrical system. For reliable starts in subarctic cold.

10) Advanced Sound System. When you're in the Saab, the AM/FM cassette system sounds wonderful. When you get out, it can come with you, to provide the most theft deterrent possible.

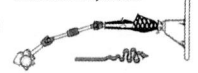

11) One of the world's safest steering wheels. Heavily padded and designed to collapse in a controlled manner in case of heavy impact.

12) Safety cage construction. Last year, the U.S. Highway Loss Data Institute ranked the safety of cars based on actual damage and injury claims. Saab 900's were safer than any other midsize sedans.

13) Fold-down rear seats. This

makes Saab the only performance sedan in the world that can provide up to 56 cubic feet of cargo space.

14) Large, 15-inch wheels. They permit good high-speed control with a very comfortable ride. They also permit larger disc brakes all around.

15) Price. It's modest, particularly when you see it against comparable Audi, BMW, Mercedes or Volvo models.

16) Side-cornering lights. These show you what you're getting into when you signal for a turn at night.

17) Front seats. Firmly supportive, orthopedically shaped and adjustable in practically every dimension you can imagine. They're even heated.

18) Saab dealers. They're all over the country, waiting to help you with specially trained mechanics and comprehensive stocks of Saab parts, and . . .

19) Saab accessories. These may be a bit too much fun for your logical side. They let you customize your Saab with factory-approved performance wheels, floor mats, fog lights and so on. And on. And on.

20) Saab's aircraft heritage. The first Saab automobile was designed by aircraft engineers who established a company tradition of carefully rethinking problems rather than just adopting the conventional solution.

21) The Saab driving experience. Best expressed on the facing page.

SAAB
The most intelligent cars ever built.

ONE EMOTIONAL REASON

➤ *Exhibit 11–8*

This ad serves as a reminder for HERSHEY'S KISSES chocolates

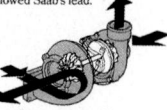

Three cheers for the holidays.

— HERSHEY'S KISSES —

The "Reach out and touch someone" campaign used by AT&T over the past decade to encourage consumers to keep in touch with family and friends via the telephone is an example of the successful use of transformational advertising. The success of this campaign has been cited as one reason for the growth of emotional and sentimental advertising in recent years.[8] McDonald's has also used transformational advertising very effectively to position itself as the fast-food chain where parents (or grandparents) can enjoy a warm and happy experience with their children.

Advertising researchers and agencies have been giving considerable attention to the role emotions play in consumer decision making and how advertising influences feelings. For example, Promotional Perspective 11–1 (page 360) discusses a technique known as emotional bonding that was developed by the McCann-Erickson agency in conjunction with advertising professors Rajeev Batra and Michael Ray and provides an example of how it was used in developing an emotional appeal ad campaign for a bank.

Combining rational and emotional appeals

In many advertising situations, the decision facing the creative specialist is not one of choosing between an emotional versus a rational appeal but rather determining how to combine the two approaches. Consumer purchase decisions are often made on the basis of both emotional and rational motives, and copywriters must give attention to both elements in developing effective advertising. As noted copywriters David Ogilvy and Joel Raphaelson have stated:

Few purchases of any kind are made for entirely rational reasons. Even a purely functional product such as laundry detergent may offer what is now called an emotional benefit—say the satisfaction of seeing one's children in bright clean clothes. In some product categories the rational element is small. These include soft drinks, beer,

cosmetics, certain personal care products and most old fashion products. And who hasn't experienced the surge of joy that accompanies the purchase of a new car?[9]

Well-known advertising copywriter Hal Riney suggested the balance of emotion and rationality in advertising depends on several factors, including

- The importance of what you have to say—more importance leads to more rationality.
- How familiar your message is—more familiarity leads to more emotion.
- The number of times the consumer will be exposed to your message—more repetition allows for more emotion.[10]

The need to appeal to both rational and emotional purchase motives has been recognized by many advertisers and agencies. The ad shown in Exhibit 11–7 for Saab automobiles is an example of how the company has attempted to address directly both the rational and emotional considerations involved in the purchase of an automobile.

The majority of advertising for products and services could probably be placed in one of the categories of rational or emotional appeals discussed above. But not every ad will fit neatly into these categories. For example, some ads such as the one for HERSHEY'S KISSES shown in Exhibit 11–8 can simply be classified as **reminder advertising.** This type of ad does not rely on any specific type of appeal, and its only objective is to keep the brand name in the mind of the consumer. Well-known brands and market leaders often use reminder advertising.

Advertisers introducing a new product often use **teaser advertising,** which is designed to create curiosity and build excitement and interest in a product or brand by talking about it but not showing it. Teaser ads are often used for new movies and are particularly popular among automotive advertisers when they introduce a new model or make significant changes in a car. The nature campaign used to introduce the Infiniti, discussed in Chapter 8, is an example of teaser advertising. A teaser campaign was also used by General Motors' Saturn division, which talked about the cars for months before showing them, and by Mazda, which used the technique to peak interest in its redesigned RX-7 sports car. Chrysler also recently used a teaser campaign before the introduction of its new Jeep model, the Grand Cherokee (Exhibit 11–9). Teaser campaigns can effectively generate interest and curiosity for a new product. However, advertisers must be careful not to extend them too long or they will lose their effectiveness.[11]

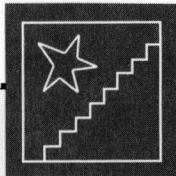

Promotional Perspective 11–1

Creating Emotional Bonds with the Customer

Advertisers have known for quite a while that emotions often play an important role in the consumer decision-making process and the use of emotional advertising can affect how consumers feel about brands. The McCann-Erickson advertising agency developed a proprietary research technique called *emotional bonding* that evaluates how consumers "feel" about brands and the nature of any emotional rapport they have with these brands compared to the ideal emotional state they associate with the overall product category. The basic concept of emotional bonding is that consumers develop three levels of relationships with brands, as shown below:

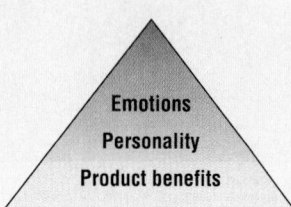

The most basic relationship indicates how consumers "think" about brands in respect to product benefits. This occurs, for the most part, through a rational learning process and can be measured by assessing how well advertising communicates product information. Consumers at this stage are often not very brand loyal, and brand switching is common. At the next stage, the consumer assigns a "personality" to a brand. For example, a brand may be thought of as self-assured, aggressive, and adventurous as opposed to compliant and timid or be regarded as responsible and orderly rather than frivolous and disorganized. In such instances, consumers' judgments of brands have moved well beyond their attributes or delivery of product/service benefits. Moreover, in most instances, consumers judge the personality of brands based on a rational assessment of overt or covert cues found in their advertising.

According to McCann-Erickson researchers, the strongest relationship that develops between a brand and the consumer is based on their feelings or emotional attachments to a brand. Consumers develop "emotional bonds" with certain brands, which results in positive psychological movement toward them.

Marketers' goal is to achieve this highest level of emotional linkage between their brand and the consumer. McCann-Erickson believes advertising can help develop and enrich emotional bonding between consumers and brands. McCann-Erickson and its subsidiary agencies use emotional bonding research to provide strategic input into the creative process and to determine how well advertising is communicating with the consumer.

Emotional bonding research was used by the Phillips Ramsey subsidiary of McCann-Erickson to develop advertising creative strategy in a campaign developed for San Diego Trust & Savings Bank. In the strategic phase, 300 consumers including customers and noncustomers of the bank were surveyed to determine (1) attributes customers use to select a financial institution; (2) the importance of various personality characteristics of financial institutions; and (3) the emotional states or feelings sought in a banking relationship. These measures were also acquired for San Diego Trust & Savings, its closest competitor, and the *ideal* financial institution.

The research revealed that the most important attributes used in selecting a financial institution were financial security, convenience, ability to control one's own money, and competitive products. The personality characteristics of the ideal financial institution included security, honesty, dependability, and responsibility. The ideal emotional states sought from a financial institution were feeling confident, secure, in control, and self-assured. The research also showed how San Diego Trust & Savings was perceived with regard to these factors. Based on this information, the agency's creative team developed an advertising campaign that incorporated each of these factors with the goal of bringing San Diego Trust closer to the ideal institution.

An important part of the new campaign is an emotional commercial that helps position San Diego Trust & Savings as a safe and secure financial institution where the customers are in control of their money. This positioning message is communicated in all of the bank's advertising and promotional messages. Both agency and bank marketing personnel believe the new campaign is helping to establish stronger emotional bonds between San Diego Trust & Savings and its customers.

Source: *Topline*, No. 4 (September 1989), McCann-Erickson, New York.

San Diego Trust & Savings used emotional bonding research in developing this commercial

(VO): Since most of us are too busy living to think about banks, isn't it

comforting to know that your money will always be safe, easy to get to and there

when you need it. San Diego Trust & Savings Bank.

Many ads are not designed to sell a product or service but rather to enhance the image of the company or meet other corporate goals such as soliciting investment or employee recruitment. This type of advertising is generally referred to as corporate image advertising and is discussed in more detail in Chapter 18.

Advertising Execution Once the specific advertising appeal that will be used as the basis for the advertising message has been determined, the creative specialist or team must then turn its attention to its execution. *Creative execution* refers to the way in which an advertising appeal is carried out or presented. While it is obviously important for an ad to have a meaningful appeal or message to communicate to the consumer, the manner in which the ad is executed is also important.

One of the best known advocates of the importance of creative execution in advertising was William Bernbach, founder of the Doyle Dane Bernbach agency. Bernbach's philosophy stressed that how you say something in advertising is very important. In his famous book on the advertising industry, *Madison Avenue,* Martin Mayer notes Bernbach's reply to David Ogilvy's Rule 2 for copywriter's that "what you say in advertising is more important than how you say it." Bernbach replied

> execution can become content, it can be just as important as what you say. . . . A sick guy can utter some words and nothing happens; a healthy vital guy says them and they rock the world.[12]

An advertising message or appeal can be presented in numerous ways:

- Straight-sell or factual message.
- Scientific/technical evidence.
- Demonstration.
- Comparison.
- Slice of life.
- Testimonial.
- Animation.
- Personality symbol.
- Fantasy.
- Dramatization.
- Humor.
- Combinations.

We now turn our attention to a closer examination of some of these formats and considerations involved in their use.

Straight-sell or factual message

One of the most basic types of creative executions is the *straight-sell* or *factual message.* This type of ad relies on a straightforward presentation of information concerning the product or service. This type of execution is often used with informational/rational appeals where the focus of the message is the product or service and its specific attributes and/or benefits. This type of appeal may list only one product claim such as the Puritan vegetable oil ad shown in Exhibit 11–10 or can provide a great deal of product information such as done in many automotive ads.

This type of appeal is often used in print ads, with a picture of the product or service occupying part of the ad, and the straightforward factual copy takes up the remainder of the ad space. Straight-sell or factual executions are also used in TV advertising, with an announcer generally delivering the sales message while the product/service is shown on the screen. Ads for high-involvement consumer products as well as industrial and other business-to-business products generally use this type of execution format.

Scientific/technical evidence

A variation of the straight-sell or announcement execution is where scientific or technical evidence or information is presented in the ad. Advertisers will often cite technical information in their ads, results of scientific or laboratory studies, or endorsements by scientific bodies or agencies as supportive evidence for their advertising claims. For example, Procter & Gamble used the endorsement it received from

➤ *Exhibit 11–10*
Puritan vegetable oil uses a straightforward factual claim

➤ *Exhibit 11–11*
Castrol GTX Motor Oil cites a scientific study in this ad

the American Council on Dental Therapeutics concerning the value of fluoride in helping prevent cavities as the basis of the advertising campaign that made Crest the leading brand on the market. The ad for Castrol GTX motor oil (Exhibit 11–11) uses this type of appeal in proclaiming it was the only brand to meet and exceed industry performance standards.

Demonstration

Demonstration advertising is designed to illustrate the key advantages or benefits of the product/service by showing it in actual use or in some contrived or staged situation. Demonstration executions can be very effective for convincing consumers of a product's utility or quality and for convincing them of the value or advantages of owning or using the brand. TV is particularly well suited for demonstrating executions since the benefits or advantages of the product can be shown or performed right on the screen. Although perhaps a little less dramatic than TV, demonstration ads can also be used as the basis for a print ad execution, as shown in the ad for IVAC's Controlled Release Infusion System (CRIS) in Exhibit 11–12.

Comparison

While comparative advertising was discussed in Chapter 7 as a type of advertising appeal, brand comparisons can also be the basis for the advertising execution. The comparison execution approach has become increasingly popular in recent years among advertisers since it offers a direct way of communicating a particular advantage

➤ *Exhibit 11–12* **This ad demonstrates the ease of use of a drug delivery system**

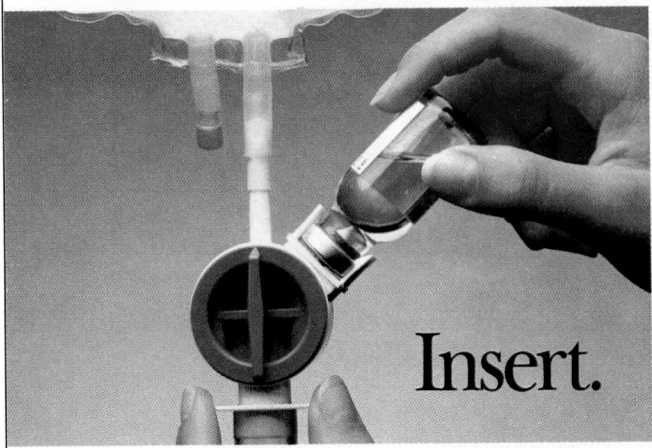

CRIS® The simple solution to drug delivery.

Insert.

Click.

CRIS, the Controlled Release Infusion System from IVAC, simplifies drug delivery. The CRIS system adapts to your existing IV administration sets and uses the primary IV solution to deliver secondary medications.

And the CRIS system delivers directly from previously reconstituted single-dose drug vials. So minibags and secondary sets are eliminated.

Designed for ease of use.
With the CRIS dial in the upright 12 o'clock position, the primary solution alone is infusing.

Administering a secondary drug is an easy two-step process. Simply insert a reconstituted single-dose vial onto the CRIS spike. Then click the dial clockwise into the 2 o'clock position.

The primary solution now flows through the vial and delivers the drug.

CRIS saves you time.
When administering medications, the CRIS system can save time.* Because you do not hang a minibag, prime a secondary set, or connect and disconnect additional tubing. And, with fewer connects and disconnects, the potential for needle sticks is greatly reduced.

For hospitals where nurses are responsible for administering medications, the CRIS system can also significantly reduce preparation time.

After the drug has been delivered using 60 ml of primary IV solution, the vial remains in place until the next dose is required. This ensures the sterility of the spike. And the primary IV solution continues to flow uninterrupted through the vial, eliminating the need to flush the line and reducing the potential for clotted lines and unscheduled restarts.

With the CRIS dial in the 2 o'clock position, the primary IV solution flows uninterrupted through the reconstituted vial and delivers the secondary medication to the patient.

CRIS delivers clinical benefits to your patients.
By using the primary IV solution for delivery, the CRIS system minimizes the total fluid volume to the patient. Plus, the CRIS device administers 100% of the labeled dose while some "piggyback" systems may leave from 7% to 16% undelivered in the secondary set and container.**

CRIS fits into your system.
The CRIS system works with the IV solution containers, administration sets and instruments you're now using.

The CRIS device remains as a part of the primary set, so you replace it only as frequently as you change the set.

And, because the primary solution continuously flushes the line, different medications can be administered

sequentially through the same CRIS device, without fear of incompatibility.

What's more, the CRIS system can be used with a roller clamp or electronic rate control, and heparin locks.

CRIS is easy to implement.
For years, IVAC's District Managers and Clinical Consultants have helped implement systems in hospitals throughout the country. Their experience will help to ensure a smooth and easy implementation of the CRIS system in your hospital.

IVAC also provides in-service instructional videos, educational literature, or on-site training.

To find out more about the CRIS system, call your IVAC District Manager. Or call us direct at 1-800-482-IVAC.

*Mangino P., ASHP Annual Meeting, Washington, D.C. 1987.
Smith C., Amen R: ASHP Annual Meeting, Washington, D.C. 1987.
Smith T., Kitrenos J: American Journal of Hospital Pharmacy 1986; 43: 1930-35.
**Documentation available upon request.*

IVAC
CORPORATION

Touching Lives Through Technology™
10300 Campus Point Drive, San Diego, CA 92121-1579

a brand may have over its competitors or positioning a new or lesser known brand with industry leaders. For example, in Exhibit 11–13, the Houston Acura Dealer Association uses a comparative execution to compare its lease program (and Legend model) to those of Mercedes and BMW.

Testimonials

Many advertisers prefer to have their messages presented by way of a *testimonial* whereby a person speaks on the behalf of the product or service based on his or her personal use of and/or experiences with it (Exhibit 11–14). Testimonial executions can use ordinary people such as satisfied customers discussing their own experiences with the brand and the benefits of using it. This approach can be very effective when the spokesperson delivering the testimonial is someone with whom the target audience can identify or the person has a particularly interesting experience or story to tell. The testimonial must be based on actual use of the product or service to avoid any legal problems, and the spokesperson must be credible.

Testimonials can be particularly effective when they come from a recognizable or popular source. For example, Ultra Slim-Fast used a variety of celebrities including Los Angeles Dodgers' manager Tommy Lasorda; talk show host Kathy Lee Gifford and her husband, sportscaster Frank Gifford; and former fashion model Christina Ferrare to deliver testimonials for the effectiveness of its product for losing weight.

A somewhat related but different execution technique from the testimonial is that of the *endorsement* whereby a well-known or respected individual such as a celebrity or expert in the product or service area speaks on the behalf of the company or the brand. When endorsers promote a company or its products or services, the message is not necessarily based on their personal use and/or experiences.

➤ *Exhibit 11–13*
This Acura ad uses a comparative execution

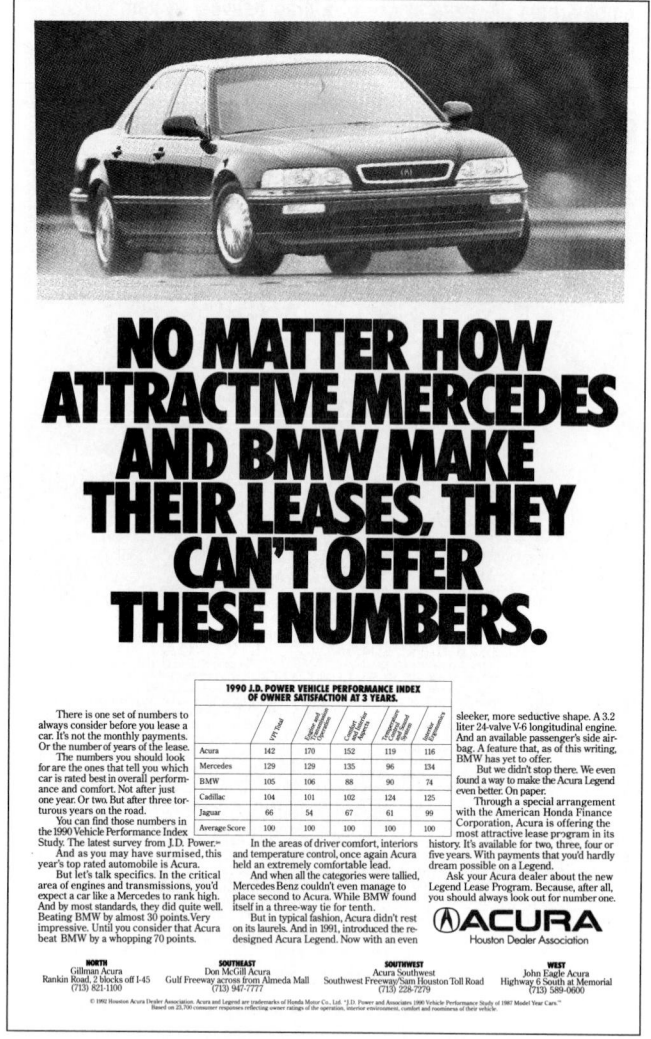

Slice of life

A widely used advertising format, particularly for package-goods products, is what is known as the *slice-of-life execution,* which is generally based on a problem/solution–type approach. This type of ad attempts to portray a real-life situation involving a problem or conflict that consumers might face in their daily lives. The ad then focuses on showing how the advertiser's product or service can resolve the problem.

Slice-of-life executions are often criticized for being unrealistic and irritating to watch. This stems from the fact that this technique is often used to remind consumers of problems of a more personal nature such as dandruff, bad breath, body odor, and laundry problems. Often these ads come across as contrived, silly, phony, or even offensive to consumers. However, many advertisers still prefer this execution style because they believe it is effective at presenting a situation or problem to which most consumers can relate and at registering the product feature or benefit that helps sell the brand.

For many years, Procter & Gamble was known for its reliance on slice-of-life advertising executions. In 1980, two thirds of the company's commercials used either the slice-of-life or testimonial execution format. However, P&G has begun breaking away from slice-of-life commercials and using other techniques such as humor, animation, and other less traditional execution styles. By 1990, only one in four of the company's ads relied on slice-of-life or testimonials.[13]

➤ *Exhibit 11–14*
This ad uses a testimonial execution

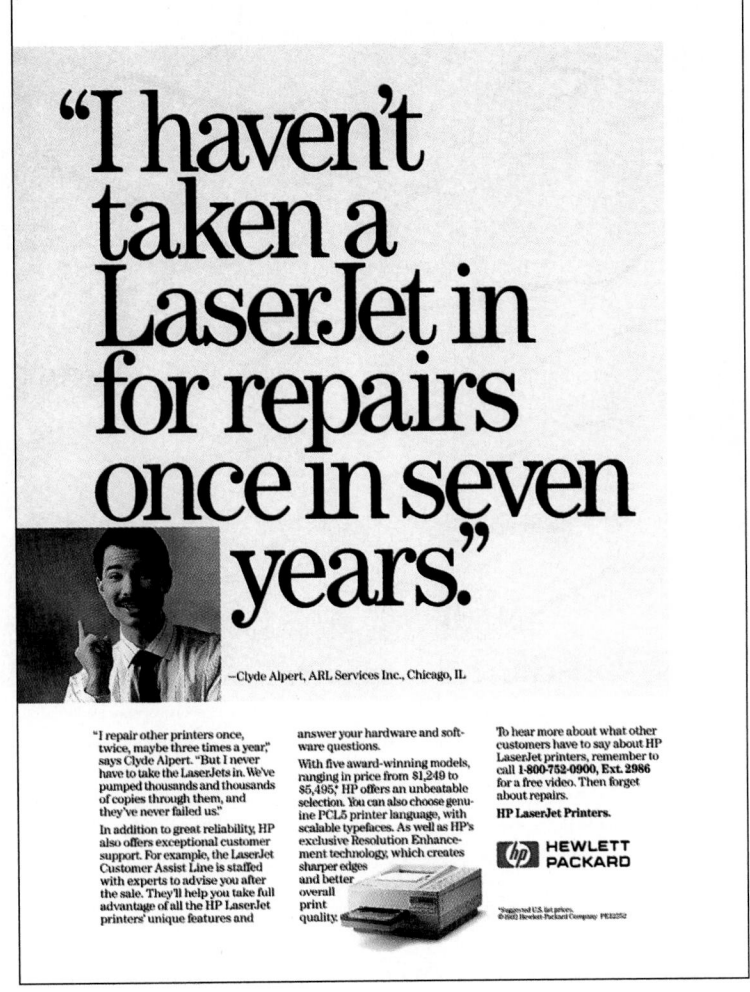

Slice-of-life or problem/solution execution approaches are not limited to consumer product advertising. A number of business-to-business marketers have begun using a variation of this execution style to demonstrate how their products and services can be used as solutions to business problems. In the late 1980s, a new advertising genre that some advertising people refer to as *slice of death* became popular. One well-known example of this type of advertising was the "Business realities" campaign used by AT&T Business Systems. The campaign was targeted toward businesspeople purchasing a phone system for their company (Exhibit 11–15). In describing the use of the slice-of-death ads, the director of advertising at AT&T noted, "Businesspeople are not always nice and polite to one another. They operate under a great deal of confusion and decisions are critical to their careers. What we're saying is don't make a mistake."[14] Slice-of-death ads have also been used by other business-to-business advertisers such as Apple and Wang.

Animation

An advertising execution approach that has increased in popularity in recent years is that of using animation. With this technique, animated scenes are drawn by artists or created on the computer, and cartoon, puppet, or some other type of fictional character may be used in the ad. Cartoon animation is a particularly popular execution technique for creating commercials targeted at children.

Animated cartoon characters and commercials have also been used very successfully by the Leo Burnett agency in campaigns for Green Giant vegetables (valley of

➤ *Exhibit 11–15*   **Slice-of-death ads remind executives of the consequences of making bad decisions**

Planned obsolescence is an unfortunate reality with many of today's business phone systems. Some manufacturers won't let you upgrade to a better system without first replacing most of your equipment.

And they make new technology available only in their latest systems.

AT&T is different. We respect your investment. Our systems are designed to be flexible. To adapt. To grow as you grow.

For example, AT&T Systems 85 & 75 allow you to add messaging, networking and other features as needed.

And we can incorporate new technology

as it becomes available. We're the first vendor to support the ISDN Primary Rate Interface, a standard that will allow today's customers an easy transition to the integrated networks of the future.

And our upgrade policies mean there are no unexpected costs or capability surprises.

AT&T protects your investment. Because we

believe the products and services you use today shouldn't be useless tomorrow.

From equipment to networking, from computers to communications, AT&T is the right choice. Call 1 800 247-1212.

 **AT&T**
The right choice.

the Jolly Green Giant) and Keebler cookies (the Keebler elves). Another example of a very successful use of animation execution is the ad campaign developed for the California Raisin Advisory Board, which—as noted at the beginning of the chapter—has been among the most popular campaigns on TV. A technique called "claymation" was used to create the dancing raisin characters used in these ads.

The use of animation as an execution style may increase as creative specialists discover the advanced animation techniques available using computer-generated graphics and other technological innovations. Some advertisers have begun using "Roger Rabbit"-style ads that mix animation with real people. For example, Nike used this technique to develop a very creative and entertaining commercial featuring basketball star Michael Jordan and cartoon character Bugs Bunny trouncing a foursome of bullies on the basketball court. Animation was also used by Nike for the "Barcelona Basketball" spot shown at the beginning of the chapter.

Personality symbol

Another type of advertising execution is that of developing a central character or personality symbol to deliver the advertising message and with which the product or service can be identified. This character can take the form of a person who is used as a spokesperson, such as Mr. Whipple for Charmin toilet tissue who would ask shoppers to "Please don't squeeze the Charmin," or invented characters such as Frank and Ed who helped make Bartles & Jaymes one of the leading brands of wine coolers.

Personality symbols can also be based on fantasy characters or animals. As was discussed in Chapter 7, the use of VIPs, or visual image personalities, is a popular

➤ *Exhibit 11–16*
Spuds MacKenzie was a very popular personality symbol for Bud Light

way of creating interest for low-involvement products. For example, Morris, the finicky feline, has been promoting 9-Lives cat food since 1969, while Charlie the Tuna first started tricking fishermen into catching him in Starfish tuna commercials in 1961, and Tony the Tiger has been touting Kellogg's Frosted Flakes are GRRReat for over two decades.

One of the most popular advertising personality symbols in recent years was Spuds MacKenzie, who was used to promote Bud Light beer (Exhibit 11–16). Spuds became a marketing phenomenon, appearing on talk shows and in movies and generating a multimillion-dollar industry of T-shirts and other Spuds paraphernalia. However, Anheuser-Busch also had to deal with complaints from various groups that it was using Spuds to appeal to minors. MADD (Mothers Against Drunk Drivers) and other groups complained about Spuds dolls being sold in toy stores and teenagers wearing Spuds T-shirts. Anheuser-Busch attributed the blame for this on merchandising pirates and noted that licensed Spuds products were not intended to be marketed to people under the legal drinking age. The company also noted it did not show Spuds commercials in prime time to avoid exposing him to those under 21. Anheuser-Busch stopped using Spuds at the end of 1989, a move the company said was based on a decision to change advertising directions rather than complaints over his use. Actually, the controversy over Spuds MacKenzie was mild compared to the furor over the use of another advertising personality symbol—"Old Joe," the cartoon character who appears in ads for Camel cigarettes. Ethical Perspective 11–1 discusses the controversy surrounding the "Smooth Character" campaign for Camels.

Fantasy

An execution technique that is very popular for emotional types of appeals such as image advertising is that of *fantasy*. Fantasy executions are particularly well suited for television, as the commercial can become a 30-second escape for the viewer into another realm or lifestyle. When fantasy executions are used, the product or service becomes a central part of the situation created by the advertiser. Cosmetics ads often use fantasy appeals to create images and symbolism that become associated with the brand.

Ethical Perspective 11–1

Old Joe Must Go

In late 1987, RJR Nabisco launched the "smooth character" advertising campaign featuring "Old Joe," a cartoon camel character. The campaign was soon criticized, however, as an effort by RJR to reposition Camels to appeal to young people. Critics argued that ads showing Old Joe accompanied by beautiful women, race cars, jet airplanes, and other appealing images are particularly intriguing and appealing to children. They also suggested the campaign was another example of the tobacco industry's efforts to sustain sales by attracting teenagers, as 90 percent of people who smoke start before they reach the age of 21.

The controversy surrounding the campaign heated up in 1991 when three studies published in the *Journal of the American Medical Association* concluded the smooth character ads were more successful at marketing Camels to children than to adults. One of the studies concluded the ad campaign boosted RJR's share of the children's cigarette market from less than 1 percent to 32.8 percent. Another of the studies found that 91.6 percent of six-year-olds associated Old Joe with cigarettes, a level nearly equal to the association of Mickey Mouse with the Disney Channel.

These findings led a powerful coalition of health groups—formed by the American Medical Association, the American Cancer Society, and the American Lung Association—to petition the Federal Trade Commission to take immediate action against RJR's use of the smooth character ads. In March 1992, the U.S. surgeon general, Antoine Novella, urged RJR to voluntarily stop using the Old Joe ads because of their appeal to children. She also asked billboard companies and magazine and newspaper publishers to stop running the ads.

Despite all the criticism and the requests to drop Old Joe, RJR says it has no intentions of stopping the campaign. RJR officials have been very critical of the conclusions of the studies published in *JAMA*, characterizing some of them as absurd. The company stated the campaign is targeted at adults and any appeal to children is unintentional. They note the company adheres to guidelines of the Tobacco Institute, the industry trade association, that are designed to shield children from advertising and promotion. Under the self-imposed measures, cigarette companies cannot advertise in publications read primarily by young people. They also cannot use models in ads who are, or appear to be, under the age of 25 nor can they offer free samples to people under 21.

RJR officials argue that young people's decision to smoke is primarily a result of peer group pressure and lifestyle rather than tobacco advertising. The company also points to the outdoor and print advertising campaign it began running in the fall of 1991 urging young people not to smoke.

Critics still contend the Old Joe ads are an example of the subtle ways tobacco companies appeal to children and that young people are the real target audience for the campaign. Moreover, they argue the only way the problem can be resolved is by banning all forms of tobacco advertising and promotion. It will be interesting to see how long Old Joe keeps smoking those Camels.

Source: Michael J. McCarthy, "Tobacco Critics See a Subtle Sell to Kids," *The Wall Street Journal*, May 3, 1990, pp. B1, 6; Judann Dagnoli, " 'Jama' Lights New Fire under Camel's Ads," *Advertising Age*, December 16, 1991, pp., 3, 32; Bruce Horowitz, "Furor over Smoking Camel," *Los Angeles Times*, December 11, 1991, pp. D1, 3; and Bruce Horowitz, "Cigarette Ads under Fire," *Los Angeles Times*, March 10, 1992, pp. D1, 6.

Dramatization

Another execution technique particularly well suited to television is that of dramatization where the focus is on telling a short story with the product or service as the star or hero. Dramatization is somewhat akin to slice-of-life execution in that it often relies on the problem/solution approach. However, rather than just using a typical situation or vignette as the setting for the ad, the drama technique uses more excitement or suspense in telling the story. According to Sandra Moriarty, there are five basic steps to a dramatic commercial:

> First is exposition, where the stage is set for the upcoming action. Next comes conflict, which is a technique for identifying the problem. The middle of the dramatic form is a period of rising action where the story builds, the conflict intensifies, the suspense thickens. The fourth step is the climax, where the problem is solved. The last part of a drama is the resolution, where the wrapup is presented. In advertising that includes product identification and call to action.[15]

The real challenge facing the creative team is how to encompass all these elements into a 30-second commercial. A good example of the dramatization execution technique is the ad for American Express Travelers Cheques shown in Exhibit 11–17.

> *Exhibit 11–17* **This American Express ad uses a dramatization approach**

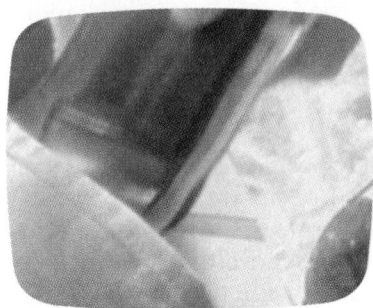

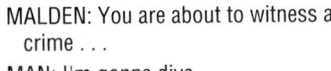

MALDEN: You are about to witness a
   crime . . .
MAN: I'm gonna dive.
I'm going to do the double reverse
   half-gainer with a pike.
WOMAN: O.K.
MAN: No, I'm all right.
WOMAN: Go ahead then.

MAN: O.K. Take a picture of this.
   This may be the last one.
MAN: Ready. Get a good one.
MALDEN: They're on vacation . . .
WOMAN: I'm watching.
MALDEN: They've saved all year . . .
WOMAN: I'm watching.

MALDEN: just for this.
WOMAN: Oooooh!
MALDEN: If cash is stolen, it's gone
   for good.
So carry these–American Express
   Travelers Cheques. If lost or stolen
   you can get these back.
Don't leave home without them.

Humor

Like comparisons, humor has been discussed as a type of advertising appeal, but this technique can also be used as a way of presenting other advertising appeals. Humorous executions are particularly well suited to television or radio, although some print ads attempt to use this style. The pros and cons of using humor as an executional technique are similar to those associated with its use as an advertising appeal and were discussed in Chapter 7.

Combinations

Many of the execution techniques discussed above can be combined to present the advertising message. For example, animation is often used to create personality symbols or to present a fantasy execution. Slice-of-life ads often are used to make a demonstration of a product or service, whereas comparisons are sometimes made using a humorous approach. It is the responsibility of the creative specialist(s) to determine whether more than one execution style can or should be used in creating the advertisement.

Creative Tactics

Our discussion thus far has focused on the development of creative strategy and various appeals and execution styles that can be used for the advertising message. However, once the creative approach, type of appeal, and execution style have been determined, attention turns to creating the actual advertisement. The design and production of advertising messages involves a number of activities such as writing copy, developing illustrations and other visual elements of the ad, and bringing all of the pieces together to create an effective message. In this section, we examine the verbal and visual elements of an ad and discuss tactical considerations in creating print ads and TV commercials.

Creative Tactics for Print Advertising

The three basic components of a print ad are the headline, the body copy, and the visual or illustrations. The headline and body copy portions of the ad are the responsibility of the copywriters, while artists, often working under the direction of an art director, are responsible for the visual presentation of the ad. Art directors also work with the copywriters to develop a layout or arrangement of the various components of the ad such as headlines, subheads, body copy, illustrations, captions, logos, and the like. We briefly examine some of the important considerations regarding the three components of a print ad and how they are coordinated.

Headlines

The term **headline** refers to the words in the leading position of the advertisement—the words that will be read first or are positioned to draw the most attention.[16] Headlines are usually set in larger type and are often set apart from the body copy or text portion of the ad to give them prominence. Most advertising people consider the headline the most important part of a print ad because of its key role and the various functions it must serve.

The most important function of a headline is attracting the readers' attention and making them interested in the rest of the message. While the visual portion of an ad is obviously important, the headline often shoulders most of the responsibility of attracting the readers' attention. Research has shown the headline is generally the first thing people look at in a print ad followed by the illustration. It has also been shown, however, that only 20 percent of readers go beyond the headline and read the body copy.[17] Thus, in addition to attracting attention, the headline must provide the reader with sufficient reason to read the copy portion of the ad, which contains more detailed and persuasive information about the product or service. To do this, the headline must, in a few words, put forth the main theme, appeal, or proposition of the advertisement. In some cases, a print ad may contain little, if any, body copy, so the headline must work with the illustration to communicate the entire advertising message.

Headlines also perform a segmentation function by engaging the attention and interest of consumers who may be most likely to buy a particular product or service. Advertisers begin the segmentation process by choosing to advertise in certain types of publications (e.g., a travel, general-interest, or fashion magazine). However, an effective headline goes even further in selecting good prospects for the product by addressing their specific needs, wants, or interests. For example, the headline used in the Audemars Piguet ad shown in Exhibit 11–18 suggests this unique watch is for a very elite target market.

Types of headlines   Numerous types of headlines can be used. The type used depends on several factors, including the creative strategy, the particular advertising situation (e.g., product type, media vehicle(s) being used, timeliness), and its relationship to other components of the ad such as the illustration or body copy. Headlines can be categorized as direct and indirect. **Direct headlines** are very straightforward and informative in terms of the message they are presenting and the target audience it is directed toward. Commonly used types of direct headlines include those offering a specific benefit, promise, or reason the reader should be interested in the product or service.

Other types of direct headlines are those that make an announcement or provide news or information to the reader. These types of headlines are particularly effective

➤ *Exhibit 11–18*

The headline of this ad is likely to engage the attention of a very elite target audience

➤ *Exhibit 11–19*

This ad uses a command headline

when the advertiser has something important or "new" to tell the target audience. For example, the American Airlines ad presented in Exhibit 11–4 uses a news-type headline to announce major revisions in its fare structure.

Another type of direct headline is one that uses a command format. Command headlines range from gentle or polite suggestions to strong statements regarding appropriate behaviors or actions. For example, many ads designed to promote prosocial behavior (making charitable donations or doing volunteer work) or deter certain types of behavior (drinking and driving, littering, smoking) often use a command headline. The ad for the Children's Defense Fund shown in Exhibit 11–19 uses a command headline.

Indirect headlines are not straightforward with respect to identifying the product or service or providing information regarding the point of the advertising message. However, indirect headlines are often more effective at attracting readers' attention and/or interest because they provoke curiosity or lure the reader into the body copy portion of the ad to learn an answer or get an explanation. Techniques for writing indirect headlines include the use of questions, provocations, how-to statements, or challenges.

Indirect headlines rely on their ability to generate curiosity or intrigue so as to motivate the reader to become involved with the ad and read the body copy to find out the point of the message. This can be risky if the headline is not provocative or interesting enough to get the readers' interest. Advertisers deal with this problem by using an interesting visual appeal that helps attract attention and offers an additional reason for reading more of the message. For example, in the ad shown in Exhibit 11–20, the question headline is accompanied by an amusing illustration to entice travelers to read the message to learn more about Delta's new Los Angeles to San Francisco shuttle and Person To Person service. Do you think this ad would have been as effective with a more traditional illustration such as a tired or harried business traveler?

➤ *Exhibit 11–20*
This ad combines a question headline with an amusing illustration to attract readers' interest

Subheads

While many ads have only one headline, it is also common to see print ads containing the main headline and one or more secondary headlines or **subheads.** Subheads usually appear in a smaller type size than the main headline and are generally larger than the type size used for the body copy. Subheads are usually found above or below the main headline, although they may also appear within the body copy. For example, the Delta ad shown in Exhibit 11–20 uses subheads in both of these positions.

Subheads are often used to enhance the readability of the message by breaking up or sectioning off large amounts of body copy and highlighting key sales points. Subheads are generally written to reinforce the headline and advertising slogan or theme.

Body copy

The main text portion of a print ad is referred to as the **body copy** (or sometimes as copy). While the body copy is usually the heart of the advertising message, getting the target audience to read it is often difficult. The copywriter generally faces a dilemma in writing the body copy; it must be long enough to communicate the advertiser's message yet short enough to hold the readers' attention and interest.

Body copy content often flows from the theme or points made in the headline or various subheads. However, the specific content of the copy depends on the type of advertising appeal and/or execution style being used. For example, straight-sell copy that presents relevant information, product features and benefits, or competitive advantages is often used with the various types of rational appeals discussed earlier in the chapter.

Emotional appeals often use narrative copy whereby the ad tells some type of story or provides an interesting account of a problem or situation involving the product. For example, the ad for General Foods International Coffees in Exhibit 11–21 uses a first-person narrative style in the body copy.

Sometimes a special form of narrative copy involving the use of dialogue/monologue copy is used. A dialogue presents a conversation between two people, while in

➤ *Exhibit 11–21*

This emotional appeal uses a narrative style in the body copy

➤ *Exhibit 11–22*

This Sanka ad uses a strong visual appeal to help communicate its message

the monologue, the person presents the message in his or her own words. Testimonial executions generally use the monologue style.

Advertising body copy can be written to go along with various types of creative appeals and executions such as comparisons, price appeals, demonstrations, humor, dramatizations, and the like. Copywriters choose a copy style that is appropriate for the type of appeal being used and is most effective for executing the creative strategy and communicating the advertiser's message to the target audience.

Visual elements

The third major component of a print ad is the visual element or illustration. The illustration is often a dominant part of a print ad and plays a very important role in determining its effectiveness. For example, in Chapter 10, we discussed how outstanding illustrations played a critical role in a successful ad campaign for Absolut vodka. The visual portion of an ad must attract attention, communicate an idea or image, and work in a synergistic fashion with the headline and body copy to produce an effective message.

A number of decisions have to be made regarding the visual portion of the ad—what "identification marks" should be included in the ad (brand name, company or trade name, trademarks, logos); whether to use photographs or hand-drawn or painted illustrations; what colors to use (or even perhaps to do the ad in black and white or with just a "splash of color"); and what the focus of the visual should be. While all of these factors are important, the latter is a very major decision in the design of a print ad.

A number of options are possible for the visual form used. For example, the illustration can focus on the product only, the product ready for use or in use, various product features, the benefits or outcomes from using the product or service, comparisons of products, symbolism or imagery, or a combination of these factors. For example, the Sanka ad shown in Exhibit 11–22 focuses on the product set against a background of fresh water to reinforce the message of natural decaffein-ation and fresh taste.

Layout

While each of the individual components of a print ad are important, the key factor is how these elements are blended into a finished advertisement. A **layout** refers to the physical arrangement of the various parts of the ad including the headline, subheads, illustrations, body copy, and any identifying marks. The layout shows where the various parts of the ad will be placed and provides those working on the ad with some ideas and guidelines. For example, the layout helps the copywriter determine how much space he or she has to work with and how much copy can or should be written. The layout can also guide the art director in determining the size and type of photographs to be used. Layouts are often done in rough form and presented to the client so the advertiser can visualize what the ad will look like before giving preliminary approval. This is very important as the agency should have client approval of the layout before moving to the more costly stages of print production.

Creative Tactics for Television

As consumers, we see so many TV commercials that it becomes easy to take for granted the amount of time, effort, and money that goes into making them. Creating and producing commercials that break through the high level of clutter on TV and communicate effectively is a very detailed and expensive process. On a cost-per-minute basis, commercials are the most expensive productions seen on television.[18]

TV is a unique and powerful advertising medium because it contains the elements of sight, sound, and motion, which can be combined to create a variety of advertising appeals and executions. However, television is also a very different advertising medium in that, unlike a print message, the viewer does not control the rate at which the message is presented, so there is no opportunity to review points of interest or reread things that are not communicated clearly. As with any form of advertising, one of the first goals in creating TV commercials is to get the viewers' attention and then maintain it. This can be particularly challenging because of the clutter, and television commercials are often viewed while doing other things (reading a book or magazine, talking).

As with print ads, TV commercials have several components. Two of the major elements of a commercial are the video and audio, which must work together to create the right impact and communicate the advertiser's message.

Video

The video or visual elements of a commercial are what is seen on the television screen. The visual portion generally dominates what is presented in a commercial and must attract the viewers' attention and communicate an idea, message, and/or image. In many commercials, a number of visual elements have to be coordinated to produce a successful ad. Decisions have to be made regarding the main focus of the visual such as the product, the presenter, action sequences, demonstrations, and the like, as well as the setting(s), the talent or characters who will appear in the commercial, and various other factors such as lighting, graphics, color, and identifying symbols.

Audio

The audio portion of a commercial also includes several elements such as voices, music, and sound effects. Voices are used in different ways in commercials. They may be heard through the direct presentation of a spokesperson or as a dialogue or conversation among various people appearing in the commercial. A common method for presenting the audio portion of a commercial is through a **voice-over** whereby the message is delivered or action on the screen is narrated or described by the voice of an announcer who is not visible. A recent trend among major advertisers is to use distinctive celebrities to do voice-overs for their commercials. For example, actor Gene Hackman does many of the voice-overs for United Airline spots, while Michael Douglas does the voice-overs for Infiniti automobile commercials.

Music is also a very important part of many TV commercials and can play a variety of roles and functions.[19] In many commercials, the role of music is primarily to provide a pleasant background or help create the appropriate mood or setting. For example, advertisers often use "needledrop," which Linda Scott describes as follows:

> Needledrop is an occupational term common to advertising agencies and the music industry. It refers to music that is prefabricated, multipurpose, and highly conventional. It is, in that sense, the musical equivalent of stock photos, clip art or canned copy. Needledrop is an inexpensive substitute for original music; paid for on a one-time basis, it is dropped into a commercial or film when a particular normative effect is desired.[20]

In many commercials, the role of music is much more central to the advertising message. It can be used to help get attention, break through the advertising clutter, communicate a key selling point, help establish an image or position, or add emotion and feeling. For example, music can work through a classical conditioning process whereby it creates positive feelings or affect that become associated with the adver-tised product or service.[21] Music can also create a positive mood state that may make the consumer more receptive toward the advertising message.[22]

Music often plays a very important role in the creative strategy for TV commer-cials. For example, a few years ago, Anheuser-Busch developed its "The Night Belongs to Michelob" advertising campaign designed to associate Michelob with nighttime excitement. A number of popular musicians, including Phil Collins and Genesis, Roger Daltrey, Wang Chung, and Frank Sinatra, appeared in the ads singing songs related to the nighttime theme. In 1992, Nike developed a very popular commercial set around the classic Beatles song "Instant Karma." The company paid a large sum of money for the rights to use the music.

Another important musical element in both TV and radio commercials is **jingles,** which are catchy songs about a product or service that usually carry the advertising theme and a simple message. For example, Doublemint gum has used the well-known "Double your pleasure, double your fun with Doublemint, Doublemint gum" jingle for years. The jingle is very memorable and serves as a good reminder of the mint flavor taste of the product. Jingles can be used by themselves as the basis for a musical commercial. For example, commercials for Diet Pepsi are built around Ray Charles singing the jingle for the brand, which incorporates the "You've got the right one, baby! Uh huh!" slogan. In some commercials, jingles are used more as a form of product identification and often appear at the end of the message. Jingles are often done by companies that specialize in writing commercial music for advertising. These "jingle-houses" work with the creative team to determine the role music will play in the commercial and the message that needs to be communicated through the music and/or the jingle.

Planning and production of television commercials

One of the first decisions that has to be made in planning a TV commercial is the type of appeal and execution style that will be used. Television is well suited to both rational and emotional advertising appeals or combinations of both. Various exe-cution styles that are often used with rational appeals, such as a straight-sell or announcement, demonstration, testimonial, or comparison, work well on TV. While these execution styles are often used in TV commercials, advertisers recognize that they often need to do more than talk about, demonstrate, or compare their products or services. They realize their commercials must break through the clutter and grab the attention and interest of viewers. For example, when Honda redesigned its popular

➤ *Exhibit 11–23*
The creative "Art Gallery" commercial was used to introduce the redesigned Accord

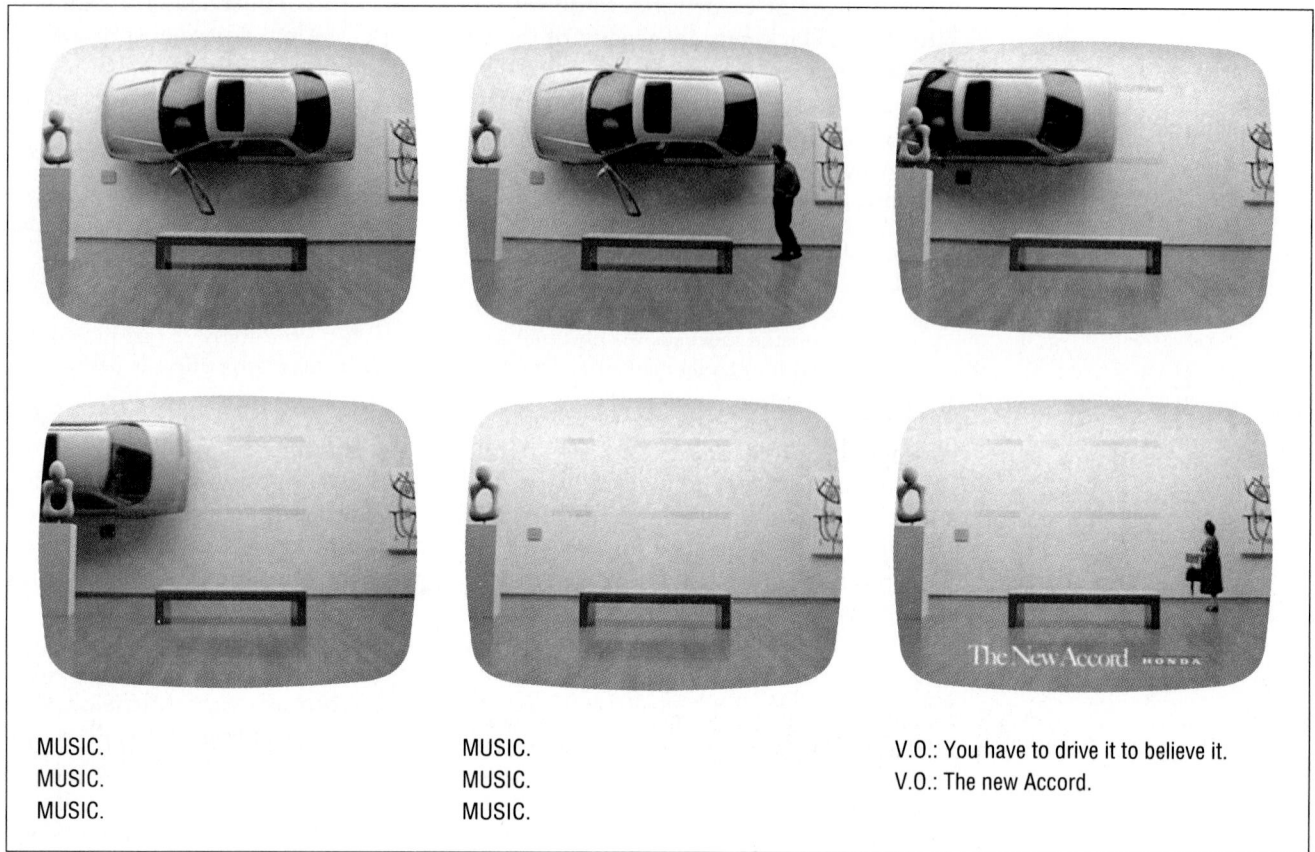

MUSIC.
MUSIC.
MUSIC.

MUSIC.
MUSIC.

V.O.: You have to drive it to believe it.
V.O.: The new Accord.

Accord model in 1990, the agency developed a very creative commercial to introduce it. The spot, shown in Exhibit 11–23, showed a man strolling through an art gallery where he comes to an Accord mounted on a wall like a painting. Through elaborate special effects, he climbs into the car and drives off, leaving faint tire tracks on the wall, to the amazement of the little old lady in the last frame of the commercial. The commercial caught the attention and fascination of many consumers, who wondered how it was done. It also received media attention and was featured on TV and news programs in segments on how it was filmed. (To produce the ad, the agency built a room inside a large drum that could be rotated to place the three walls in various positions.)

In addition to engaging the consumers' attention and interest, advertisers must often appeal to emotional, as well as rational, buying motives. Television is essentially an entertainment medium, and many advertisers recognize that their commercials are successful because they entertain as well as inform. For example, a close examination of the 25 most popular TV campaigns discussed at the beginning of this chapter would show that many of them are characterized by commercials with strong entertainment value. Television is particularly well suited to drama and emotion. No other advertising medium can touch the emotions and feelings of consumers as well as TV. Various types of emotional-oriented appeals such as humor, fear, or fantasy work very well on television. Television also works well for dramatizations and story-telling types of executions. For example, Global Perspective 11–1 discusses how Nestlé has had great success in the United States with a soap opera/continuing story type of advertising genre it originally used in a campaign in the United Kingdom.

➢ *Exhibit 11–24* **Three phases of production for electronic media**

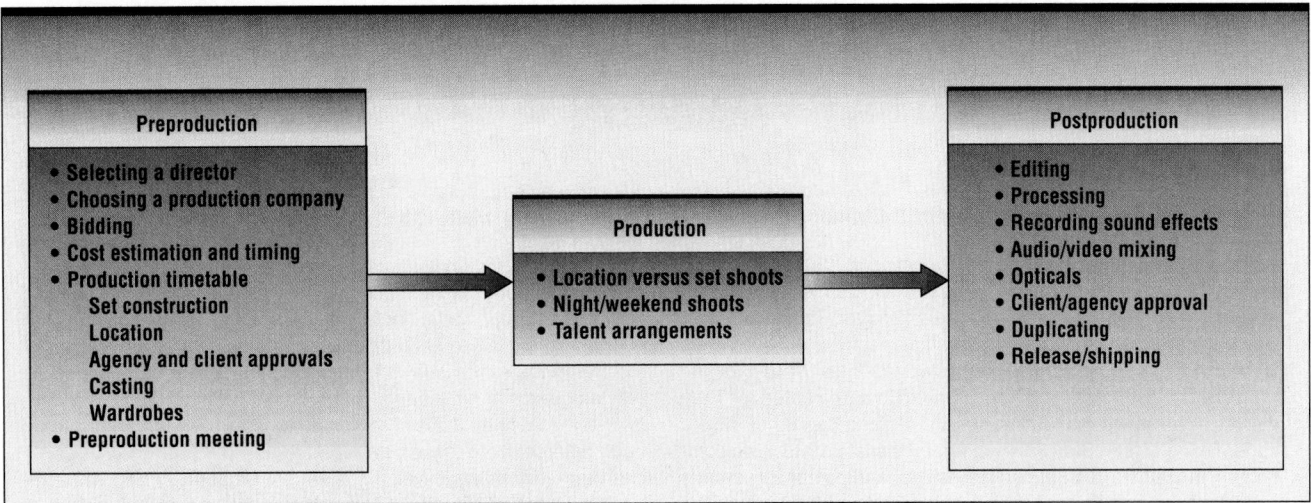

Planning the commercial The various elements of a TV commercial are brought together in a document known as a script. A **script** is a written version of a commercial that provides a detailed description of its video and audio content. The script indicates the various audio components of the commercial such as the copy to be spoken by voices, music, and sound effects. The video portion of the script provides the visual plan of the commercial such as camera actions and angles, scenes, transitions, and other important descriptions. Scripts also show how the video corresponds to the audio portion of the commercial and thus provide an idea of how these two important parts of a commercial fit together.

Once the basic script of the commercial has been conceived, the writer and art director get together to produce a storyboard, a series of drawings used to present the visual plan or layout of a proposed commercial. The storyboard contains still drawings of the video scenes along with the audio that accompanies each scene. Storyboards are very helpful because, like a layout for a print ad, they provide those involved in the production and approval of the commercial with a good approximation of what the final commercial will look like. In some cases, an aniamatic, a videotape of the storyboard along with the accompanying audio soundtrack, may be produced if a more finished form of the commercial is needed for client presentations or pretesting.

Production Once the storyboard or aniamatic of the commercial is approved, it is ready to move to the production phase. The production process for a commercial actually involves three stages:

1. **Preproduction**—all the work and activities that occur before the actual shooting/recording of the commercial.
2. **Production**—the period during which the commercial is filmed or videotaped and recorded.
3. **Postproduction**—activities and work that occurs after the commercial has been filmed and recorded.

The various activities that occur in each phase are shown in Exhibit 11–24. Before the final production process begins, however, the client must usually review and approve the creative strategy and the various tactics that will be used in creating the advertising message.

Global Perspective 11–1

Taster's Choice Borrows a Cup of Creativity from the U.K.

For more than 20 years after its introduction in 1967, advertising for Nestlé Beverage Company's Taster's Choice ® freeze-dried instant coffee focused primarily on the product. Taster's Choice was positioned as the instant coffee that "tastes closest to fresh brewed," and the advertising emphasized how freeze drying locked in the coffee's flavor. The premium image created for Taster's Choice helped make it one of the leading brands of instant coffee in the United States. However, by the late 1980s, the competition in the U.S. market had intensified, and competing brands were outspending Taster's Choice on advertising and promotion by four to one. Moreover, Nestlé was concerned that U.S. consumers were beginning to perceive coffee as a commodity and becoming highly responsive to price and sales promotion.

In 1990, Nestlé and its advertising agency, McCann-Erickson New York, decided to abandon the product/oriented advertising and develop a more emotionally driven campaign. McCann-Erickson conducted emotional bonding research (see Promotional Perspective 11–1) among instant-coffee drinkers and found that typical users of Taster's Choice were discriminating, self-assured, and sophisticated. These personality traits were also seen as matching well with the premium image of Taster's Choice.

Nestlé and McCann-Erickson decided to develop a campaign that would involve consumers emotionally in the advertising and in the brand. Some competitors were using emotional appeals, such as General Foods International Coffees (shown in Exhibit 11–21). However, one emotional dimension that was absent in coffee advertising was romance. Thus, the client and agency decided the new campaign for Taster's Choice would add a touch of romance to the brand's sophisticated image.

Generally, at this point, an ad agency would have to begin thinking about how the creative strategy would be executed. However, McCann-Erickson's London office had created a campaign for Nestlé U.K.'s Gold Blend instant coffee brand that fit very well with the creative strategy chosen for Taster's Choice in the United States. The campaign was based on soap opera-style commercials featuring two flirtatious neighbors, whose relationship develops in each episode. In the ads, the coffee plays a background role to the evolving romantic tension between the couple. The campaign was introduced in 1987, and Gold Blend sales increased 20 percent in the United Kingdom within 18 months.

Nestlé and McCann-Erickson decided to use the first two commercials from the British campaign in the United States,

which started off with the female neighbor borrowing some Taster's Choice from her next door neighbor. Some minor modifications had to be made, including changes in voice-overs and shortening the ad to U.S. broadcast standards. The third commercial in the series shows the couple meeting again unexpectedly as guests at his sister's dinner party. The spot ends with an invitation to dinner. Subsequent spots in the U.S. campaign have been different from those developed for the U.K. campaign, but it has been just as effective.

The "brewing romance" campaign developed an avid following in Britain as tabloids chronicled the series, viewers wrote in for autographs of the actors who played the couple and even sent in script suggestions. Nestlé has the whole country anticipating the couple's wedding. The romance isn't so far along in the United States, but consumer reactions appear to be just as feverish. Prior to execution No. 3, Taster's Choice received hundreds of letters from consumers voicing their enthusiasm for the campaign. The debut of each new "episode" became a major media event. The fourth installment had its premiere on ABC's "Good Morning America" in February 1992. The segment included live interviews with the "charming neighbors," actors Sharon Maughan and Tony Head. In addition, Taster's Choice took out ads in *TV Guide* to promote both the third and fourth executions. This marked the first time that print ads were used to promote a television commercial. For example, one *TV Guide* ad advertised a sneak peek at execution No. 4, during the ABC movie of the week, *When Harry Met Sally*. The first two episodes generated more positive mail and phone calls than any other campaign in Nestlé's history.

In addition, Taster's Choice was involved in a special sponsorship deal with MGM-UA Home Video: because of its classy modern-day romantic image, Taster's Choice became the official sponsor of the 50th anniversary edition of the classic movie *Casablanca*.

The actors and the campaign have received tremendous publicity, including write-ups in *People*, *USA Today*, and *The New York Times*. As noted at the beginning of the chapter, the Taster's Choice campaign has also become a favorite among consumers polled in the Video Storyboard survey.

The Taster's Choice serial advertising campaign is an example of how successful the serial format can be when executed properly. By combining romance with a touch of mystery and witty dialogue, viewers have come to know and love the two charming neighbors who keep meeting over coffee. Their slow-brewing re-

---

Client Evaluation and Approval of Creative Work

While the creative specialists have much of the responsibility of determining the advertising appeal and execution style to be used in a campaign, the client must evaluate and approve the creative approach before any ads are produced. A number of people on the client side may be involved in evaluating and approving the creative work of the agency, including the advertising or communications manager, product or brand managers, marketing director or vice president, representatives from the legal department, and sometimes even the president or chief executive officer (CEO) of the company or the board of directors.

lationship has the press and viewers across the country begging for more.

Nestlé will likely have the relationship between the neighbors develop at the same pace as the U.K. campaign, which means it will be a long, drawn-out affair. In the U.K. campaign, it took four years for the couple to kiss. Nestlé will want to keep the relationship moving slowly, as the campaign is not only capturing consumer interest and anticipation, but is selling coffee as well. In the fourth quarter of 1991, Taster's Choice share of the $935 million instant coffee market was 27.3 percent, compared to 23.7 percent in the first quarter of 1990. Given these results, Nestlé is likely to keep the romance "brewing" for quite a long time.

Source: Judann Dagnoli and Elena Bowes, "A Brewing Romance," *Advertising Age,* April 8, 1991, p. 22; Bradley Johnson, "Romance Warms," *Advertising Age,* February 24, 1992, p. 4; Bradley Johnson and Joe Mandese, "Nestle, ABC Strike Taster's Choice Deal," *Advertising Age,* Februray 3, 1992, p. 3; and Bradley Johnson and Alison Fahey, "Taster's Choice Says Play it Again," *Advertising Age,* April 13, 1992, p. 4.

TONY: Hey, I'll walk you home.
SHARON: Thank you for a lovely dinner.
TONY: Aren't you going to invite me in?
(SILENCE)
For coffee.
SHARON: Well, I do have Taster's Choice.

TONY: Then how can I refuse?
ANNCR: Savor the sophisticated taste of Taster's Choice.
SHARON: Well. . .
TONY: Just one more cup?
SHARON: You, uh, said that two cups ago.

TONY: You know how much I love your coffee.
SHARON: Then by all means, take it with you.
(SILENCE)
(SILENCE)

The amount of input each of these individuals has in the creative evaluation and approval process varies depending on the company's policies, the importance of the product to the company, the role of advertising in the marketing program, and the advertising approach being recommended. For example, you may recall the discussion in Chapter 1 of how the Chiat/Day agency had to sell the "1984" commercial used to introduce the Macintosh personal computer to Apple's board of directors, who expressed concern over the way viewers might interpret and react to the commercial. Earlier in the chapter, we noted that Procter & Gamble has been moving away from the use of testimonials and slice-of-life advertising executions to somewhat riskier and more lively forms of advertising. However, the company remains very conservative and has been slow to adopt the more avant-garde ads used by many of its competitors. Many agencies that do the advertising for various P&G brands recognize that quirky executions that challenge the company's subdued style and corporate culture are not likely to be approved.[23]

In many cases, top management is involved in selecting an ad agency and must approve the theme and creative strategy for the campaign. Evaluation and approval of the individual ads proposed by the agency often rest with the advertising and product managers with primary responsibility for the brand. The account executive and a member of the creative team present the creative concept to the client's advertising and product and/or marketing managers for their approval before beginning actual production of the ad. Evaluation of the advertising by the company's and the agency's legal department is also very important, so it can be determined whether the ad might be interpreted as being deceptive or breaking any laws or regulatory codes (the legal and regulatory aspects of advertising are discussed in Chapter 23).

Once the creative approach has been determined and approved, the attention then turns to the production process, which involves a variety of activities and tasks required to produce the ad or commercial and put it into a finished form suitable for use by the media. The client reviews and approves the final version of the ad after the production stage. However, a careful evaluation should be made before the ad actually enters production, since this stage requires considerable time and money, as suppliers are hired to perform the various functions required to produce the actual ad. The client's evaluation of the print layout or commercial storyboard can be difficult since the advertising or product manager is generally not a creative expert and must be careful not to reject viable creative approaches or to accept ideas that will result in inferior advertising. Personnel on the client side can use certain guidelines to judge the efficacy of creative approaches suggested by the agency.

Guidelines for Evaluating Creative Output

Advertisers might use numerous criteria to evaluate the creative approach suggested by the agency. In some instances, the client may want to have the rough layout or storyboard pretested to get quantitative information to assist in the evaluation. However, in most instances, the evaluation process is done on a more subjective basis whereby the advertising or product manager relies on qualitative considerations to make a judgment. Some of the most important and basic criteria or guidelines that might be used in evaluating creative approaches are discussed below.

- **Is the creative approach consistent with the brand's marketing and advertising objectives?** One of the most important factors the client must consider is whether the creative appeal and execution style being recommended by the agency are consistent with the marketing strategy for the brand and the role advertising and promotion has been assigned in the overall marketing program. This means the creative approach must be compatible with the image of the brand and the way it is positioned in the marketplace and should contribute to the marketing and advertising objectives.

- **Is the creative approach consistent with the creative strategy and objectives and does it communicate what it is supposed to?** The advertising appeal and execution must meet the communications objectives laid out in the copy platform, and the ad must say what the advertising strategy calls for it to say. Often, creative specialists lose sight of what the advertising message is supposed to be communicating and come up with an approach that fails to execute the advertising strategy. Individuals responsible for reviewing and approving the approach under consideration should ask the creative specialists to explain how the appeal or execution meets the advertising strategy and contributes to the meeting of objectives.

- **Is the creative approach appropriate for the target audience?** Generally, much time has been spent defining, locating, and attempting to understand the target audience for the advertiser's product or service. Careful consideration should be given to whether the ad appeal or execution being recommended will appeal to, be understood by, and communicate effectively with the target audience. This involves a careful consideration of all elements of the ad and how the audience will respond to them. The advertiser does not want to approve advertising that he or she believes will receive a negative reaction from the target audience. For example, it has been suggested that advertising targeted to older consumers should use models that are 10 years younger than the average age of the target audience since most people feel that they are younger than their actual chronological age.[24] Thus, the client may not want to approve an ad that contains a model that appears too old to the target audience.

  Advertisers also face a considerable challenge developing ads for the teenage market because of the rapidly changing styles, fashions, language, and values of this age group. Advertisers may find they are using an advertising approach, spokesperson, or even an expression that is no longer popular among teens or has been overused. An example is the expression "Not!" that became popular among young people after being used in "Saturday Night Live" comedy skits, on MTV, and repeated in the hit movie Wayne's World. The expression was used in a number of commercials as even advertisers such as Disneyland began using it. However, some critics think the expression was overused and may have been picked up a bit late by advertisers.

- **Does the creative approach communicate a clear and convincing message to the customer?** Most ads are supposed to communicate a sales message to the customer. This means the ad must be designed to tell the audience about the attributes, features, benefits, and so forth, of the product or service and provide them with a reason (or reasons) to buy the brand. Advertising for some products, such as automobiles, often is quite detailed and attempts to provide a great deal of information to the consumer for use in making a decision. However, advertisers must be careful not to put too much information and detail into an ad, as it is unlikely that most consumers will have the capacity or interest to attend to it all. The key factor is that the main selling points and supportive information be in the ad and come through to the audience and that extraneous ideas, words, and information be eliminated.

- **Does the creative execution overwhelm the message?** A very common criticism of advertising, and TV commercials in particular, is that so much attention and emphasis are put on creative execution that the advertiser's message gets overshadowed. Many commercials have been very creative and entertaining for viewers but have failed to register the brand name and/or selling points effectively.

  For example, a few years ago, the agency for North American Philips Lighting Corp. developed an award-winning campaign that focused on the humorous results when light bulbs fail at just the wrong time. The humorous spots included an older woman who appears to accidentally vacuum up her screeching cat after a light bulb blows, and another showed two men trying to defuse a time bomb when the lights go out. Another commercial in the campaign showed an elderly couple using Philips Pastel bulbs to create a romantic mood (Exhibit 11–25). While the purpose of the campaign was to help Philips make inroads into General Electric's dominance in the light bulb market, many consumers did not notice the Philips brand name. When the campaign first aired, a Video Storyboard survey showed that many thought the ads were for GE light bulbs rather than for Philips. The agency that created the campaign argued its own surveys taken a year later showed that brand awareness and sales increased considerably. However, some advertising

➤ *Exhibit 11–25* **Some advertising people felt that the Philips Lighting commercials may have been too creative and overwhelmed the message**

(Partial overhead of living room. Man reads paper. Wife walks in with Pastel bulbs, goes straight to lamp).
ANNCR: For a change of mood,
(Wife turns off lamp, as husband ignores her).
ANNCR: Change to Philips Softone Pastel™ light bulbs.
(Woman switches on lamp. It now gives a warm peach hue to the whole room).
MUSIC. (Piano riff)
(Shot over piano as man sings).
MAN: I'm in the mood for love. Simply because. . .

(Woman slides into frame with bottle of champagne).
MAN: (Singing). . .you're near me.
(Suddenly, the cork pops out and flies at the man).
MAN: Funny but when you're. . .
SFX: Cork pop.
(Cork hits man on forehead leaving a little impression).
SFX: Bop!
(He's stunned into silence for a brief moment. He launches back into the song with great enthusiasm).
MAN: near me.

(Woman puts bottle in bucket at left of piano and slides next to him).
MAN: I'm in the mood for love.
ANNCR: Make everything seem more beautiful. . .
(All the colors are represented. Each bulb lights up in sequence from left to right. "Philips" clicks on). . .
ANNCR: with new Softone Pastels. It's time to change your bulb to Philips.

people still think the ad may have been too creative and entertaining and overwhelmed the message.[25]

With the increasing amount of clutter in most advertising media, it may be necessary to use a unique or novel creative approach to gain the viewer's or reader's attention. However, care must be taken to ensure that too much emphasis is not put on the execution of the message and that the consumer can remember who the advertiser is and what it is attempting to sell. The primary function of an ad is to communicate information that can influence the sale of a product or service. While clients want to make sure the sales message is not lost at the expense of creative execution, they must also be careful not to stifle the efforts of the creative specialists and force them into producing dull and boring advertising.

• **Is the creative approach appropriate for the media environment in which it is likely to be seen?** As was discussed in earlier chapters, each media vehicle has its own particular climate or environment that results from the nature of its editorial content, the type of reader or viewer it attracts, and the nature of the advertisements it contains. Consideration should be given to how well the ad fits into the media environment in which it will be shown. For example, the Super Bowl not only has become the most popular sporting event in the country in terms of viewership but also has become a showcase for commercials. People who know or care very little about advertising know how much a 30-second commercial costs an advertiser, and many pay as much attention to the ads as the game itself. Thus, many advertisers feel compelled to develop new ads for the Super Bowl or to save new commercials for the game so as to be noticed by the scrutinizing eye of the consumer.

• **Is the advertisement truthful and tasteful?** The ultimate responsibility for determining whether an ad deceives or offends the target audience really lies with the client. Most companies have standards regarding factors such as deceptive and/or offensive advertising, and it is the job of the advertising or product manager to evaluate the approach suggested by the creative specialists against these standards. If necessary, the firms's legal department may be asked to review the ad to determine whether the creative appeal, message content, or execution could cause any problems for the company. It is much better to catch and correct any potential legal problems before the ad is prepared and shown to the public than after the fact.

The factors discussed above are basic criteria the advertising manager, product manager, or other personnel on the client side can use in reviewing, evaluating, and approving the ideas offered by the creative specialists. There may be other factors specific to the firm's advertising and marketing situation that must be considered in evaluating the work of the creative team. Also, there may be situations where it is acceptable to deviate from the standards the firm usually uses in judging creative output. As we shall see in Chapter 20, the client may want to move beyond these subjective criteria and use more sophisticated pretesting methods to determine the value of a particular approach suggested by the creative specialist or team.

SUMMARY

In this chapter, we examined how the advertising message will be implemented and executed. Once the creative strategy that will guide the advertising campaign has been determined, attention turns to the specific type of advertising appeal and execution format to be used to carry out the creative plan. The appeal refers to the central message used in the ad to elicit some response from consumers or influence their feelings. Appeals can be broken into two broad categories of rational and emotional. Rational appeals focus on consumers' practical, functional, or utilitarian need for the product or service, whereas emotional appeals relate to social and/or psychological reasons for purchasing a product or service. Numerous types of appeals are available to advertisers under each category.

The creative execution style refers to the way the advertising appeal is presented or carried out in the message. A number of commonly used execution techniques were examined in the chapter, along with considerations for their use. Attention was also given to various tactical issues involved in creating print and TV advertising. The various components of a print ad include headlines, body copy, illustrations, and layout. We also examined the visual or video and audio components of TV commercials and various considerations involved in the planning and production of commercials.

Creative specialists are responsible for determining the advertising appeal and execution style as well as the tactical aspects of creating advertisements. However, the client must review, evaluate, and approve the creative approach before any ads are produced or run. A number of criteria can be used by advertising, product or brand managers, and others involved with the promotional process to evaluate the approach being taken in the advertising messages before approving final production.

KEY TERMS

advertising appeal
creative execution style
informational/rational
   appeals
emotional appeals
transformational ad

reminder advertising
teaser advertising
headline
direct headlines
indirect headlines
subheads

body copy
layout
voice-over
jingles
script

DISCUSSION QUESTIONS

1. Discuss the difference between an advertising appeal versus a creative execution style. Choose several ads and analyze the particular appeal and execution style used in each.

2. For what type of marketing situation would an advertiser be likely to use a news appeal or announcement type of ad? Find an example of this type of advertising appeal and describe why it is appropriate.

3. Discuss what is meant by transformational advertising? For what types of products or services would a transformational ad be most suitable?

4. Some advertising people argue that the distinction between rational and emotional advertising appeals is irrelevant as all advertising includes aspects of both. Do you agree or disagree with this statement?

5. Discuss the logic of developing advertising that combines rational and emotional appeals? Find an example of an advertisement that does this and analyze it.

6. Choose an example of an advertisement you believe uses an inappropriate appeal and/or execution style. What type of appeal or creative execution format do you think would be more appropriate?

7. Discuss the ethical implications of using personality symbols who might be appealing to young people for advertising alcohol or tobacco? Do you agree with the position of the advertisers who argue they do not intentionally try to reach young people with ads using these personality symbols?

8. What are the various roles of the headline in a print advertisement? Find examples of print ads that use direct and indirect headlines.

9. Discuss the role music plays in TV commercials. How would you explain the decision of companies such as Nike to pay large sums of money for the right to use songs such as "*Instant Karma*" in their commercials?

10. Choose a current advertising campaign and analyze it with respect to the creative guidelines discussed in the last section of the chapter. Do you think the advertising meets all of the guidelines discussed?

chapter 12

Media Planning and Strategy

chapter objectives

➢ To introduce the key terminology necessary to understand media planning.

➢ To provide an understanding of the development of a media plan.

➢ To provide an understanding of the process of developing and implementing media strategies.

➢ To introduce sources of media information and characteristics of media.

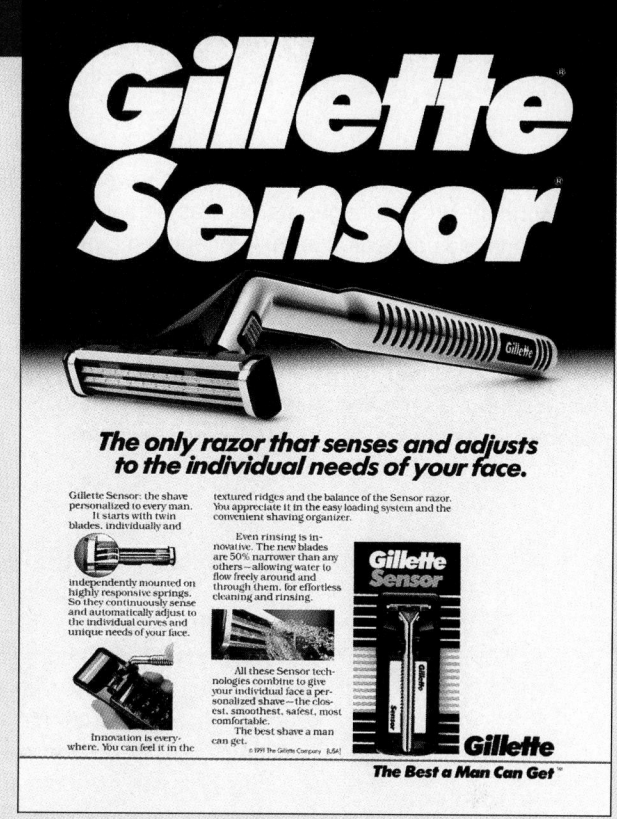

Media Strategies Determine the Success of New Brands

The failure rate of new brand and/or product introductions in the U.S. marketplace is almost frightening. Some managers estimate as many as 86 percent never make it. The reasons behind successful and nonsuccessful introductions are varied, but many managers are now focusing on the marriage between marketing strategy, creative execution, and media planning and buying as the key ingredients to success.

Three recent success stories demonstrate this quite well: AT&T's Universal Card, the first national bank card to simplify credit card use by combining charge card purchases and long-distance calling in one bill; Gillette Sensor, the first shaving system with movable blades; and Lever 2000, the first bar soap to consolidate synthetic products with coconut brands. Each of these products was innovative and well positioned, and each had a very successful media strategy behind it. The media strategies they employed differed in each case.

For the Universal Card and Sensor, the winning media combinations began with high-profile TV events—the 1990 Academy Awards for the former and the 1990 Super Bowl for Sensor. For the Universal Card, three consecutive pages of print ads appeared beginning the very next day in national newspapers such as *The Wall Street Journal* and *USA Today.* This media blitz resulted in over 250,000 people calling AT&T within 24 hours of the Oscar show. Since then, 12.5 million cards have been issued, with charges exceeding $13.2 billion in 1991 alone.

Like the Universal Card, Gillette's Sensor used a high-profile TV event followed by a print blitz the next day. The campaign also included a heavy emphasis on advertising to the trade and a teaser campaign that started three weeks before the Super Bowl. In the teaser campaign, 30-second TV spots shown on national sporting events proclaimed, "On January 28, 1990, Gillette will change the way you shave forever." More TV spots followed the day after the game, along with ads in *Time, Newsweek,* and *USA Today.* Sales were so high, Gillette ran out of Sensors in some parts of the country and had to pull back on the media buy. By the time the second phase of the Sensor launch occurred on NCAA basketball's Final Four, NBA games, prime-time TV, and national print, the shaver was well on its way to an 11.5 percent market share of the $356 million market. The Sensor is now sold in 17 countries in Europe, the Far East, and North America.

Lever 2000 employed a markedly different media strategy, but achieved no less spectacular results. The product was first test marketed in Atlanta using spot TV and print magazines such as *American Health, Reader's Digest, People,* and *Time.* After four regional tests, Lever

(continued)
went to a national audience. Network TV spots were aired on sports shows (the target market was primarily males), and print ads appeared in male-oriented magazines such as *Time* and *Rolling Stone.* Fitness boards were used in gyms throughout the country—the first time any Lever Brothers product had employed this medium. By 1991, Lever 2000 had 7.5 percent of the $970 million soap market and the annual advertising budget reached $25 million—the most ever spent on a Lever soap intro-

duction. Buoyed by the successful use of these media, Lever continues to search for innovative new media and has tested spots on Turner Broadcasting's new Checkout Channel, among other leading-edge media options.

Based on these results, it would seem obvious that the media did contribute to the product introductions' successes.

Source: Richard Brunelli, "The New Math of New Brands," Mediaweek, *March 9, 1992, pp. 12–15.*

The success of the Universal Card, Sensor, and Lever 2000 introductions demonstrates the importance that media can play in the marketing of products and services. In each case, effective media plans and strategies were a critical ingredient to a successful marketing campaign. The primary objective of the media plan is to develop a framework that will allow for delivery of the message to the target audience in the most effective and cost-effective manner possible—that is, to communicate what the product and/or brand can do.

This chapter presents the various methods of message delivery available to the marketer, examines some key considerations used in making media decisions, and discusses the process of developing media strategy and plans. In succeeding chapters, we explore the relative advantages and disadvantages of the various media and examine each in more detail.

An Overview of Media Planning

The media planning process is not an easy one, as a number of options are available to the planner. These options include mass media such as television, newspapers, radio, and magazines (and the choices available within each of these categories) as well as out-of-the-home media such as outdoor advertising, transit advertising, and electronic billboards. In addition, a variety of support media such as direct marketing, specialty advertising, and in-store point-of-purchase options must also be considered.

While at first glance the choice between these alternatives might seem relatively straightforward, this is often not the case. Part of the reason media selection becomes so involved is due to the nature of the media themselves. For example, TV provides the opportunity to combine both sight and sound—an advantage not offered by other media. Magazines may be able to convey more information and may keep the message available to the potential buyer for a much longer time. Newspapers also offer their own specific advantages, as do outdoor, direct media, and each of the others. Thus, the characteristics of each alternative must be considered, along with many other factors. This process becomes even more complicated when the manager has to choose between alternatives within the same medium—for example, choosing between *Time* and *Newsweek* or between "Roseanne" and "Murphy Brown."

In addition to the nature of the media, the potential for achieving effective communications through a well-designed media strategy warrants the added attention. An example of the power of an effective media strategy was demonstrated by an innovative and somewhat controversial media program employed by Pioneer Electronics in the late 1970s. This strategy involved placing ads in male-oriented magazines such as *Playboy, Penthouse,* and *Rolling Stone.* Stereo manufacturers had previously advertised only in magazines targeted to audiophiles such as *Stereo Review* and *Hi Fidelity.* This broadening of media use to general-interest consumer magazines contributed to their doubling of sales every year for six years and changed the nature of stereo advertising for an entire industry.

> *Exhibit 12–1*
Expenditures of top advertisers in various media

AD $ SUMMARY COMPANY RANKINGS

LNA/ARBITRON MULTI-MEDIA SERVICE
January - December 1991

RANK	COMPANY	10-MEDIA TOTAL	MAGAZINES	SUNDAY MAGAZINES	NEWSPAPERS	OUTDOOR	NETWORK TELEVISION	SPOT TELEVISION	SYNDICATED TELEVISION	CABLE TV NETWORKS	NETWORK RADIO	NATIONAL SPOT RADIO
1	PROCTER & GAMBLE CO	1,166,454.5	142,900.1	4,309.9	3,699.4	516.6	515,697.1	283,650.3	131,782.6	67,824.3	10,809.7	5,264.5
2	PHILIP MORRIS COMPANIES INC	1,110,355.7	215,073.3	12,397.0	17,792.7	69,679.3	389,466.5	206,161.9	135,686.7	24,075.7	6,569.7	33,452.9
3	GENERAL MOTORS CORP	1,056,501.2	250,443.7	15,804.0	35,682.0	6,389.8	527,831.6	109,901.5	38,425.9	32,354.4	17,185.3	22,473.0
4	PEPSICO INC	542,040.4	7,832.8	136.7	2,315.4	2,892.6	204,571.9	78,384.0	17,393.4	15,116.4	3,556.9	15,201.1
5	FORD MOTOR CO	517,700.2	149,633.7	3,417.4	27,154.8	1,706.2	217,456.4	78,384.0	17,393.4	14,035.7	6,021.7	2,496.9
6	SEARS ROEBUCK & CO	462,340.0	21,583.4	1,704.8	88,674.9	416.0	187,874.5	37,430.3	26,044.4	20,321.5	66,474.5	11,815.7
7	TOYOTA MOTOR CORP	442,511.9	105,354.5	1,852.2	11,131.1	1,773.7	173,664.9	123,869.9	16,513.8	8,098.5	- -	253.3
8	GENERAL MILLS INC	419,077.2	17,450.2	447.0	275.9	640.1	151,432.0	201,032.3	13,809.0	31,835.3	1,668.6	486.8
9	CHRYSLER CORP	414,781.1	106,682.0	12,137.2	7,404.0	1,019.7	176,181.8	68,104.0	5,582.7	12,904.0	14,639.6	10,126.1
10	AMERICAN TELEPHONE & TELEGRAPH CO	391,693.5	48,838.2	5,251.3	28,290.8	552.4	171,955.0	61,733.1	18,824.2	19,305.5	30,108.9	6,834.1
	TOP 10 TOTAL	6,523,455.7	1,065,791.9	57,457.5	222,421.0	85,586.4	2,716,131.7	1,431,670.8	433,085.8	245,871.3	157,034.9	108,404.4
11	MCDONALDS CORP	387,386.0	6,247.6	3.5	307.7	6,947.3	171,833.8	149,055.1	32,979.4	16,224.4	- -	3,787.2
12	KELLOGG CO	381,291.2	4,951.4	32.3	150.5	16.6	236,569.2	71,440.2	58,389.6	9,535.2	- -	206.2
13	UNILEVER NV	371,396.5	81,027.1	337.7	597.3	486.2	154,615.5	84,300.9	36,900.9	8,063.0	1,137.2	3,930.7
14	JOHNSON & JOHNSON	371,079.1	56,330.9	2,663.0	368.5	- -	239,823.3	23,690.5	38,272.6	9,521.2	- -	409.1
15	NEWS CORP LTD	358,564.2	17,016.7	1,441.2	240,491.8	558.7	40,832.1	25,415.6	13,061.9	4,243.1	1,879.0	13,624.1
16	ANHEUSER-BUSCH COS INC	327,880.1	20,002.6	1,120.1	5,754.4	11,616.3	122,922.1	92,447.6	23,390.6	31,407.6	- -	19,218.8
17	GRAND METROPOLITAN PLC	326,679.5	83,087.4	4,091.9	2,110.5	7,656.1	103,272.5	64,389.8	42,502.1	11,389.8	- -	8,179.4
18	TIME WARNER INC	311,308.4	66,816.8	6,568.2	32,736.2	528.3	63,606.9	68,782.4	40,289.2	29,300.7	1,386.1	1,293.6
19	NESTLE SA	307,647.2	77,066.9	5,387.8	3,200.4	376.2	108,991.4	63,914.4	33,057.8	10,365.2	774.0	4,513.1
20	AMERICAN HOME PRODUCTS CORP	290,588.3	15,802.6	40.5	- -	- -	173,277.5	66,403.5	7,785.7	19,087.8	6,194.7	1,996.0
21	RJR NABISCO INC	285,513.3	61,810.3	6,251.6	3,169.5	51,713.7	112,669.8	8,775.9	22,136.9	17,794.8	808.8	382.0
22	SONY CORP	262,847.9	55,450.6	38,411.6	29,723.5	378.0	65,629.8	39,965.1	21,534.0	8,429.7	1,042.2	2,283.4
23	WALT DISNEY CO	257,311.4	27,967.2	3,853.1	23,712.6	356.9	93,799.6	71,852.4	26,456.4	5,972.0	721.7	2,619.5
24	HONDA MOTOR CO LTD	242,462.7	58,112.6	1,971.1	10,628.3	1,251.4	116,973.9	35,170.4	5,103.7	4,751.1	- -	8,500.2
25	VALASSIS INSERTS	239,587.8	- -	2.5	239,585.3							
	TOP 25 TOTAL	11,244,999.3	1,697,482.6	129,633.6	814,957.5	167,472.1	4,520,949.1	2,297,274.6	834,946.6	431,956.9	170,978.6	179,347.7

Likewise, the AT&T Universal Card strategy has changed the way credit cards are marketed. In the past, direct mail constituted the primary media emphasis. Perhaps based in part on AT&T's success, Mastercard's targeting of 18-to-24-year-olds relied heavily on radio time and special promotions.[1]

The product and/or service being advertised affects the media planning process. As demonstrated in Exhibit 12–1, firms have found that some media are more useful to them in conveying their messages to specific target audiences than are others. For example, Procter & Gamble tends to rely more heavily on television advertising, whereas General Motors prefers print media. The result is placement of advertising dollars in these preferred media—and significantly different media strategies.

Some Basic Terms and Concepts

Before beginning our discussion of media planning, we review some basic terms and concepts used in the media planning and strategy process.

Media planning consists of the series of decisions involved in the delivery of the promotional message to the prospective purchasers and/or users of the product or brand. Media planning is a process, meaning a number of decisions are made, and each of these may be altered or abandoned as the plan develops.

The **media plan** requires development of specific **media objectives** and specific **media strategies**—or plans of action—designed to attain these objectives. Once the decisions have been made, and the objectives and strategies formulated, this information is organized into the media plan—the guide for media selection.

The **medium** is the general category of available delivery systems, which includes broadcast media such as TV and radio, print media such as newspapers and magazines, direct mail, outdoor advertising, and other support media. The **media vehicle** is the specific carrier within a medium category. For example, *Time* and *Newsweek* are print vehicles, whereas specific television programs such as "Beverly Hills 90210" and "60 Minutes" are broadcast vehicles. As you will see in succeeding chapters, each vehicle has its own characteristics as well as its own relative advantages and disadvantages. Specific decisions must be made as to the value of each in delivering the message.

Reach is a measure of the number of different audience members exposed at least once to a media vehicle (or vehicles) in a given period of time. **Coverage** refers to the potential audience that might receive the message through a vehicle. (It is important to distinguish between *coverage* and *reach,* as the former relates to potential audience, whereas the latter refers to the actual audience delivered. The importance of this distinction will become more obvious to you later in this chapter.) Finally, **frequency** refers to the number of times the receiver is exposed to the media vehicle in a specified period.

The Media Plan

The media plan determines the best way to get the advertiser's message to the market. In a very basic sense, the goal of the media plan is to find that combination of media that enables the marketer to communicate the message in the most effective manner to the largest number of potential customers at the minimum cost.

The activities involved in the development of this plan and the purposes of each are presented in Exhibit 12–2. As you can see, a number of decisions must be made throughout this process. These decisions are not set in stone, however. As the plan evolves, events may occur that necessitate that changes be made. As a result, many advertisers find it necessary to frequently alter and update their objectives and strategies.

In addition to the difficulties associated with frequently making revisions, the media planning process is further complicated by a number of other problems. Let us review some of these.

Problems in Media Planning

Unfortunately, the media strategy decision has not become a standardized task. A number of problems exist, each of which contributes to the difficulty involved in establishing the plan and at the same time reduces its effectiveness. Some of these problems are described next.

Insufficient information

While a great deal of information about markets and the media exists, media planners often require more than is available. Some information may not be available for a variety of reasons, whereas other information may be of limited value because of measurement problems. Some data are just not measured, either because they cannot be or because to do so would be too expensive. For example, continuous measures of radio listenership exist, but only periodic listenership studies are reported due to sample size and cost constraints. Second, there are problems with some of the measures of audience size in television and print as well as the examples shown in Promotional Perspective 12–1 show.

A third measurement problem may occur as a result of the timeliness of the measurements, as some audience measures are taken only at specific times of the year (for example, **sweeps periods**—February, May, July, and November—that are used for measuring television audiences and setting advertising rates). This information is then generalized to succeeding months, so future planning decisions must be made on past data that may not reflect current behaviors. Think about planning for TV advertising for the fall season. There are no data on the audiences of new shows, and audience information, if taken on existing programs during the summer, may not be an accurate indicator of how these programs will do in the fall because summer viewership is generally much lower. While the advertisers are able to review these programs before they are aired, they do not have actual audience figures.

The lack of available information is an even more pronounced problem with small advertisers. Because of their limited budgets, many of these advertisers may not be able to afford to purchase the information they require. As a result, their decisions are made on limited or out-of-date data or no data at all.

Inconsistent terminologies

Problems arise because the cost bases used by different media often vary. In addition, the standards of measurement used to establish these costs are not always consistent. For example, print media may present cost data in terms of the cost to reach a

➤ *Exhibit 12–2* **Activities involved in developing the media plan**

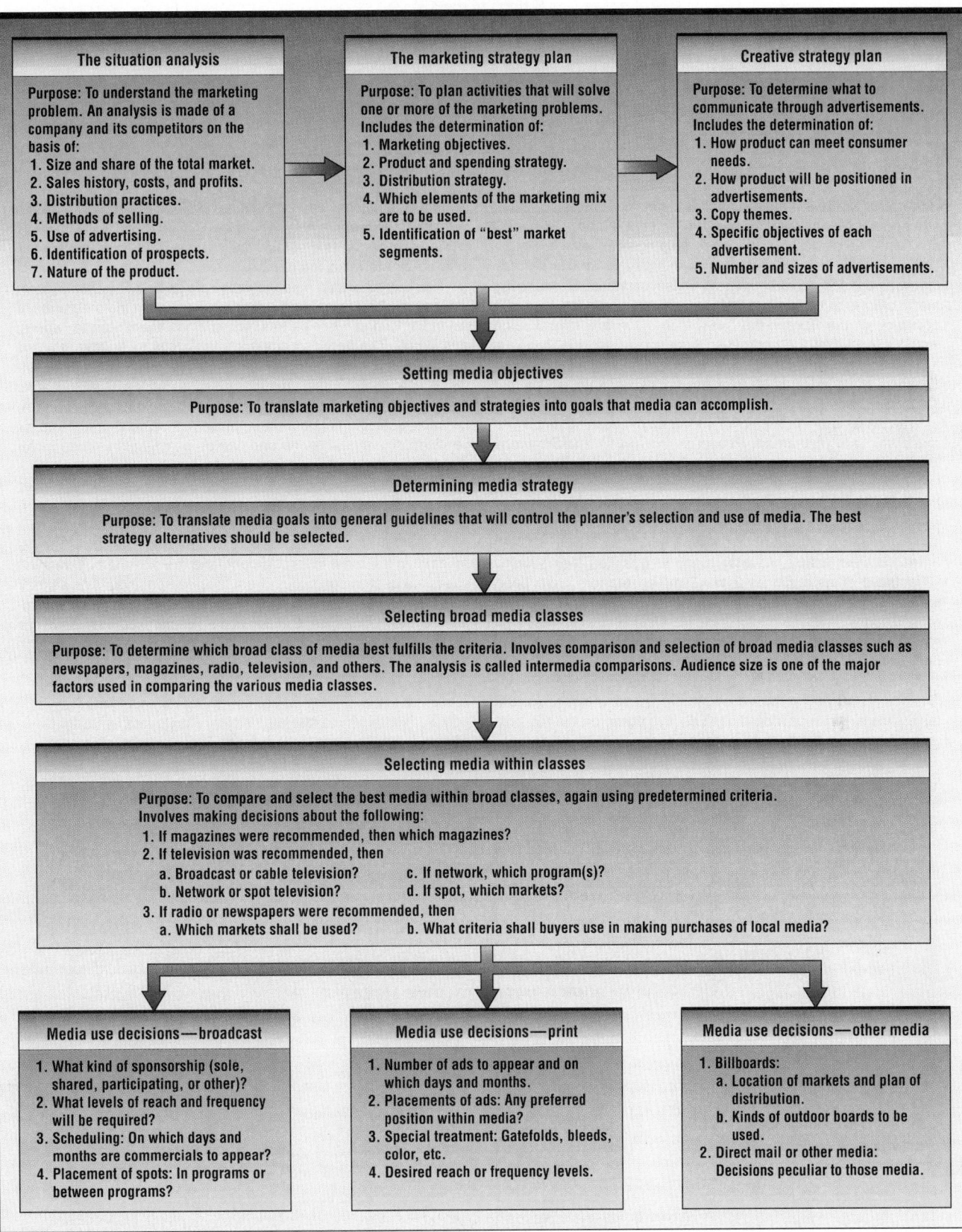

The situation analysis

Purpose: To understand the marketing problem. An analysis is made of a company and its competitors on the basis of:
1. Size and share of the total market.
2. Sales history, costs, and profits.
3. Distribution practices.
4. Methods of selling.
5. Use of advertising.
6. Identification of prospects.
7. Nature of the product.

The marketing strategy plan

Purpose: To plan activities that will solve one or more of the marketing problems. Includes the determination of:
1. Marketing objectives.
2. Product and spending strategy.
3. Distribution strategy.
4. Which elements of the marketing mix are to be used.
5. Identification of "best" market segments.

Creative strategy plan

Purpose: To determine what to communicate through advertisements. Includes the determination of:
1. How product can meet consumer needs.
2. How product will be positioned in advertisements.
3. Copy themes.
4. Specific objectives of each advertisement.
5. Number and sizes of advertisements.

Setting media objectives

Purpose: To translate marketing objectives and strategies into goals that media can accomplish.

Determining media strategy

Purpose: To translate media goals into general guidelines that will control the planner's selection and use of media. The best strategy alternatives should be selected.

Selecting broad media classes

Purpose: To determine which broad class of media best fulfills the criteria. Involves comparison and selection of broad media classes such as newspapers, magazines, radio, television, and others. The analysis is called intermedia comparisons. Audience size is one of the major factors used in comparing the various media classes.

Selecting media within classes

Purpose: To compare and select the best media within broad classes, again using predetermined criteria. Involves making decisions about the following:
1. If magazines were recommended, then which magazines?
2. If television was recommended, then
   a. Broadcast or cable television?   c. If network, which program(s)?
   b. Network or spot television?   d. If spot, which markets?
3. If radio or newspapers were recommended, then
   a. Which markets shall be used?   b. What criteria shall buyers use in making purchases of local media?

Media use decisions—broadcast

1. What kind of sponsorship (sole, shared, participating, or other)?
2. What levels of reach and frequency will be required?
3. Scheduling: On which days and months are commercials to appear?
4. Placement of spots: In programs or between programs?

Media use decisions—print

1. Number of ads to appear and on which days and months.
2. Placements of ads: Any preferred position within media?
3. Special treatment: Gatefolds, bleeds, color, etc.
4. Desired reach or frequency levels.

Media use decisions—other media

1. Billboards:
   a. Location of markets and plan of distribution.
   b. Kinds of outdoor boards to be used.
2. Direct mail or other media: Decisions peculiar to those media.

Promotional Perspective 12–1

Research Methods Cause Controversy

Advertising costs are determined by the number of persons that can be reached through the medium. In print media, such costs are based on circulation and readership figures; while in broadcast, the basis is ratings. As in any industry, firms compete directly to provide advertisers with these services. Because so many billions of dollars are spent on advertising each year, the accuracy of the figures the services provide are critical. One would expect that the competing firms would provide accurate information, and this information would be consistent if properly obtained. Many advertisers think this is the way it should be, but it is not the way it is!

The two primary providers of information regarding magazine readership are Mediamark Research Inc. (MRI) and Simmons Market Research Bureau (SMRB). Because of the importance media buyers place on these figures, they have become crucial to the individual publications. As the vice president of one top ad agency noted, "If the readership numbers shift just a hair, there is a big shift in the number of ad pages." Yet MRI and SMRB rarely agree on their results, causing many to question their validity. Differences of as much as 3 to 13 million readers have been shown for the top five magazines listed by each service, yet both organizations stand by their results. Differences in research methodologies are cited as the cause of the discrepancies, and both believe their methods are correct.

In the TV industry, the two competing organizations are ScanAmerica (a service provided by Arbitron) and Nielsen. As the table shows, these providers don't always agree on the top programs or the size of their audiences either.

Interestingly, Nielsen and Arbitron use identical methodologies and sample sizes and still get different results. Once again, both

agency and network researchers have raised questions about the validity of the results. As a result, the Big 3 networks (ABC, CBS, NBC) have begun to pressure these organizations to change the way they determine the ratings.

Radio listenership figures hardly fare better. The primary provider of market information—Arbitron—relies on the memories of listeners 12 and older as to which stations they listen to, where, and when. The service compares its results to another service called Radar, which measures network listening audiences, offering validation for their results based on how well they match. Unfortunately, the differences continue to grow further apart, increasing suspicions about their validity. Since no formal basis for verification is available, no one can be exactly sure which is the most accurate.

As can be seen, none of the media services seems to offer verifiable figures. So how do advertisers use this information? A variety of approaches are taken, including using the service that provides the most consistent results, the one that presents the medium in the most favorable light, and the one the buyers think offers the best methodology (from their perspective). And as they continue to use these results, they continue to clamor for improved methodologies and verifiable results—as they have for years.

Source: Joe Mandese, "Rival Ratings Don't Match Up," *Advertising Age,* February 24, 1992, p. 50; Joe Mandese, "Arbitron Tries to Tune up Ratings," *Advertising Age,* September 9, 1991, p. S11; Betsy Spethmann, "Agencies Hope for Research Standard," *Advertising Age,* September 9, 1991, p. S10; Joanne Lipman, "Readership Figures for Periodicals Stir Debate in Publishing Industry," *The Wall Street Journal,* September 2, 1987.

ScanAmerica vs. Nielsen

According to Nielsen, the number one show in November 1991 was "60 Minutes," but ScanAmerica says it was "Roseanne."

ScanAmerica				Nielsen			
Top 10 Programs	Nielsen Rank	Network	ScanAm. Rating	Top 10 Programs	ScanAm. Rank	Network	Nielsen Rating
1. "Roseanne"	2	ABC	21.1	1. "60 Minutes"	2	CBS	22.6
2. "60 Minutes"	1	CBS	18.8	2. "Roseanne"	1	ABC	21.3
3. "Full House"	4	ABC	18.8	3. "Cheers"	8	NBC	19.5
4. "Home Improvement"	9	ABC	18.7	4. "Full House"	3	ABC	19.4
5. "Family Matters"	—	ABC	18.6	5. "Murphy Brown"	15	CBS	19.1
6. "A Different World"	12	NBC	18.4	6. "Coach"	11	ABC	18.0
7. "Monday Night Football"	11	ABC	18.3	7. "Designing Women"	24	CBS	17.2
8. "Cheers"	3	NBC	17.9	8. "Major Dad"	29	CBS	17.2
9. "The Cosby Show"	16	NBC	17.8	9. "Home Improvement"	4	ABC	17.2
10. "Step by Step"	—	ABC	17.6	10. "Murder, She Wrote"	14	CBS	17.2

thousand people (cost per thousand—CPM), whereas broadcast media may refer to cost per ratings point (CPRP), and outdoor refers to the number of "showings." Audience information that is used as a basis for these costs has also been collected by different methods. Finally, terms that actually mean something different (such as *reach* and *coverage*) may be used synonymously, adding to the confusion.

Time pressures

It seems that advertisers are always in a hurry—sometimes because they need to be, other times because they *think* they need to be. In the former case, actions by a competitor may require rapid response. For example, the cutting of airfares by one carrier requires immediate response by others. In the latter case, a false sense of urgency may be dictating time pressures. In either situation, media selection decisions may be made without proper planning and analyses of the markets and/or media. In other instances, there may just not be enough time to analyze all the information available.

Measures of effectiveness

Because it is so hard to measure the effectiveness of advertising and promotions in general, it is also difficult to determine the relative effectiveness of various media or media vehicles. While progress is being made in this regard (particularly in the area of direct-response advertising), in many situations, the media planner is forced to assume the impact of these alternatives.

Because of these problems, not all media decisions are quantitatively determined. Sometimes managers may have to assume the image of a medium in a market in which they are not familiar, anticipate the impact that recent events may cause, or make judgments without full knowledge of all the available alternatives.

While the problems just discussed may complicate the media decision process, they by no means render it an entirely subjective exercise. In the remainder of this chapter, we explore in more detail how media strategies are developed and ways of increasing their effectiveness.

Developing the Media Plan

In the promotional planning model presented in Chapter 1, we discussed the process of identifying target markets, establishing objectives, and formulating strategies for attaining these objectives. The development of the media plan and strategies follows a similar path—the primary difference being that the focus is more specifically keyed to determining the *best* way to deliver the message. Otherwise, the process—shown in Exhibit 12–3—is very similar, involving a series of stages: (1) market analysis, (2) establishment of media objectives, (3) media strategy development and implementation, and (4) evaluation and follow-up. Each of these is discussed in turn, with specific examples provided. In addition, an example of an actual media plan is included in Appendix B to Chapter 12, and we refer to this plan throughout the remainder of this chapter to exemplify each phase further.

➤ *Exhibit 12–3* **Developing the media plan**

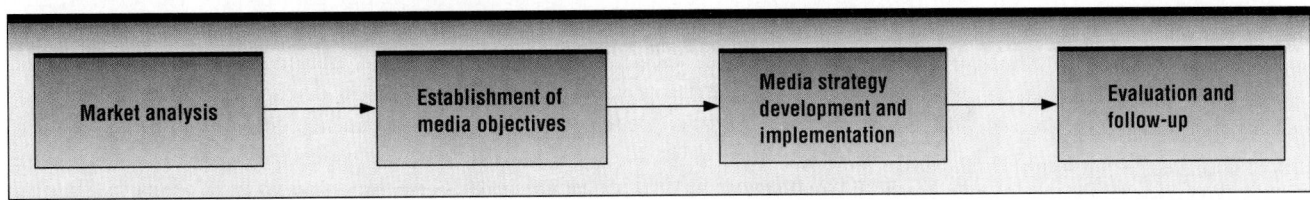

Market Analysis and Target Market Identification

While an extensive examination of the market has already been performed in the situation analysis stage of the overall promotional planning process, this initial analysis is broader in that it involves a complete review of internal and external factors, competitive strategies, and the like. In the development of media strategy, a market analysis is again performed, although this time the specific focus is on the media and delivering the message. The key questions to be asked at this stage are:

- To whom shall we advertise (who is the target market)?
- What internal and external factors may influence the media plan?
- Where (geographically) and when should we focus our efforts?

To Whom Shall We Advertise?

While a number of target markets might be derived as a result of the situation analysis, the decision as to which specific groups to go after may involve the media planner working as a team with the client, account representative, marketing department, and creative directors. A variety of factors may be used to assist the media planners in this decision—some of which will require primary research, whereas others will be available from published sources (secondary sources) of information.

One example of secondary information is that provided by the *Simmons Market Research Bureau (SMRB)*. SMRB provides syndicated data on audience size and composition for approximately 100 publications, as well as broadcast exposure and data on usage of over 800 consumer products and services. This information is provided in the form of raw numbers, percentages, and indexes. As can be seen in Exhibit 12–4, information is given on (1) the number of adults in the United States by each category under consideration; (2) the number of users; (3) the percentage of users falling into each category (for example, the percentage of users that are female); (4) the percentage of each category that uses the product (for example, the percentage of all females using); (5) an index number; and (6) the same information (as 2 through 5) classified by heavy, medium, and light users. (While not shown here, both Simmons and its major competitor, *Mediamark Research, Inc. [MRI]*, also provide lifestyle information as well as media usage characteristics of the population.)

In many instances, media planners are more concerned with the percentage figures and the index numbers than they are with the raw numbers. The reasons for this vary, but it is primarily due to the fact that they may have their own data from other sources—both primary and secondary—with which they feel more comfortable; the numbers provided may not be specific enough for their needs; or because of the methods by which the data were collected, they believe the numbers provided may be questionable. The total (raw) numbers provided by Simmons and MRI are then used in combination with, or as a supplement to, their own figures.

On the other hand, the **index number** is often relied on as a good indicator of the potential of the market. This index number is derived from the formula:

$$\text{Index number} = \frac{\text{Percentage of users in a demographic segment}}{\text{Percentage of population in the same segment}} \times 100$$

This number serves as a guide as to the use of a product by a particular segment. An index number over 100 means use of the product is proportionately greater in that segment than one that is average (100) or less than 100. For example, in the MRI data shown in Exhibit 12–5, it can be seen that the age groups 35–44, 45–54, and 55–64 are more likely to be heavy users of lipstick and lip gloss than are those in the other age segments, as are those with a household income of $35,000+. Most occupation groups are heavy users, with the exception of those in precision crafts, and those in the category "other employed." Thus, marketers—depending on their overall strategy—may wish to use this information to determine which groups are now using the product and to target this group, or they may wish to identify a group that is currently using the product less in an attempt to develop that segment.

➤ *Exhibit 12–4* **Market research profile of cola users**

	TOTAL U.S. '000	ALL USERS A '000	B % DOWN	C % ACROSS	D INDX	HEAVY USERS EIGHT OR MORE A '000	B % DOWN	C % ACROSS	D INDX	BOTTLED A '000	B % DOWN	C % ACROSS	D INDX	CANNED A '000	B % DOWN	C % ACROSS	D INDX
TOTAL ADULTS	182456	107986	100.0	59.2	100	34162	100.0	18.7	100	64427	100.0	35.3	100	77735	100.0	42.6	100
MALES	87118	57364	53.1	65.8	111	19037	55.7	21.9	117	33966	52.7	39.0	110	41533	53.4	47.7	112
FEMALES	95338	50622	46.9	53.1	90	15125	44.3	15.9	85	30461	47.3	32.0	90	36202	46.6	38.0	89
18–24	25530	17961	16.6	70.4	119	7633	22.3	29.9	160	11523	17.9	45.1	128	13715	17.6	53.7	126
25–34	44118	29093	26.9	65.9	111	10646	31.2	24.1	129	17994	27.9	40.8	116	22039	28.4	50.0	117
35–44	37521	23183	21.5	61.8	104	6716	19.7	17.9	96	13883	21.5	37.0	105	17172	22.1	45.8	107
45–54	25346	14302	13.2	56.4	95	4240	12.4	16.7	89	8281	12.9	32.7	93	9798	12.6	38.7	91
55–64	21009	11029	10.2	52.5	89	2655	7.8	12.6	67	5946	9.2	28.3	80	7563	9.7	36.0	84
65 OR OLDER	28934	12419	11.5	42.9	73	2271	6.6	7.8	42	6801	10.6	23.5	67	7449	9.6	25.7	60
18–34	69647	47054	43.6	67.6	114	18279	53.5	26.2	140	29517	45.8	42.4	120	35754	46.0	51.3	120
18–49	120585	78177	72.4	64.8	110	27394	80.2	22.7	121	48074	74.6	39.9	113	58377	75.1	48.4	114
25–54	106984	66577	61.7	62.2	105	21603	63.2	20.2	108	40158	62.3	37.5	106	49009	63.0	45.8	108
35–49	50938	31123	28.8	61.1	103	9115	26.7	17.9	96	18557	28.8	36.4	103	22623	29.1	44.4	104
50 OR OLDER	61871	29810	27.6	48.2	81	6768	19.8	10.9	58	16353	25.4	26.4	75	19358	24.9	31.3	73
GRADUATED COLLEGE	35347	18823	17.4	53.3	90	4256	12.5	12.0	64	10728	16.7	30.4	86	13919	17.9	39.4	92
ATTENDED COLLEGE	35167	20303	18.8	57.7	98	6323	18.5	18.0	96	11597	18.0	33.0	93	15374	19.8	43.7	103
GRADUATED HIGH SCHOOL	70823	43928	40.7	62.0	105	15062	44.1	21.3	114	26676	41.4	37.7	107	31808	40.9	44.9	105
DID NOT GRADUATE HIGH SCHOOL	41119	24932	23.1	60.6	102	8521	24.9	20.7	111	15426	23.9	37.5	106	16634	21.4	40.5	95
EMPLOYED MALES	67846	46006	42.6	67.8	115	15993	46.8	23.6	126	27566	42.8	40.6	115	33752	43.4	49.7	117
EMPLOYED FEMALES	57394	30497	28.2	53.1	90	9317	27.3	16.2	87	18245	28.3	31.8	90	22414	28.8	39.1	92
EMPLOYED FULL–TIME	112285	69201	64.1	61.6	104	22930	67.1	20.4	109	41409	64.3	36.9	104	50475	64.9	45.0	106
EMPLOYED PART–TIME	12955	7302	6.8	56.4	95	2380	7.0	18.4	98	4402	6.8	34.0	96	5692	7.3	43.9	103
NOT EMPLOYED	57216	31483	29.2	55.0	93	8852	25.9	15.5	83	18616	28.9	32.5	92	21569	27.7	37.7	88
PROFESSIONAL/MANAGER	31819	17101	15.8	53.7	91	4515	13.2	14.2	76	10036	15.6	31.5	89	12604	16.2	39.6	93
TECHNICAL/CLERICAL/SALES	39581	22672	21.0	57.3	97	7008	20.5	17.7	95	13089	20.3	33.1	94	16905	21.7	42.7	100
PRECISION/CRAFT	14839	10235	9.5	69.0	117	4012	11.7	27.0	144	6535	10.1	44.0	125	7470	9.6	50.3	118
OTHER EMPLOYED	39001	26494	24.5	67.9	115	9775	28.6	25.1	134	16151	25.1	41.4	117	19187	24.7	49.2	115
SINGLE	40179	26098	24.2	65.0	110	10217	29.9	25.4	136	16252	25.2	40.4	115	19644	25.3	48.9	115
MARRIED	108808	64055	59.3	58.9	99	18481	54.1	17.0	91	37570	58.3	34.5	98	45904	59.1	42.2	99
DIVORCED/SEPARATED/WIDOWED	33469	17834	16.5	53.3	90	5464	16.0	16.3	87	10606	16.5	31.7	90	12188	15.7	36.4	85
PARENTS	60855	40631	37.6	66.8	113	13482	39.5	22.2	118	25180	39.1	41.4	117	30061	38.7	49.4	116
WHITE	156458	90780	84.1	58.0	98	28116	82.3	18.0	96	53093	82.4	33.9	96	65803	84.7	42.1	99
BLACK	20509	13774	12.8	67.2	113	5160	15.1	25.2	134	9041	14.0	44.1	125	9432	12.1	46.0	108
OTHER	5489	3432	3.2	62.5	106	885	2.6	16.1	86	2293	3.6	41.8	118	2500	3.2	45.5	107
NORTHEAST–CENSUS	38593	22160	20.5	57.4	97	5368	15.7	13.9	74	16028	24.9	41.5	118	14293	18.4	37.0	87
MIDWEST	44281	24898	23.1	56.2	95	7327	21.4	16.5	88	12677	19.7	28.6	81	19201	24.7	43.4	102
SOUTH	62591	39118	36.2	62.5	106	14519	42.5	23.2	124	24320	37.7	38.9	110	26905	34.6	43.0	101
WEST	36991	21811	20.2	59.0	100	6947	20.3	18.8	100	11402	17.7	30.8	87	17337	22.3	46.9	110
COUNTY SIZE A	75891	43359	40.2	57.1	97	12309	36.0	16.2	87	26324	40.9	34.7	98	30712	39.5	40.5	95
COUNTY SIZE B	54708	33119	30.7	60.5	102	10665	31.2	19.5	104	19543	30.3	35.7	101	24116	31.0	44.1	103
COUNTY SIZE C	27729	16793	15.6	60.6	102	5938	17.4	21.4	114	9674	15.0	34.9	99	12452	16.0	44.9	105
COUNTY SIZE D	24127	14715	13.6	61.0	103	5250	15.4	21.8	116	8886	13.8	36.8	104	10456	13.5	43.3	102
METRO CENTRAL CITY	57518	35162	32.6	61.1	103	11223	32.9	19.5	104	19989	31.0	34.8	98	26734	34.4	46.5	109
METRO SUBURBAN	85780	49004	45.4	57.1	97	14390	42.1	16.8	90	29956	46.5	34.9	99	34168	44.0	39.8	93
NON METRO	39158	23820	22.1	60.8	103	8549	25.0	21.8	117	14482	22.5	37.0	105	16834	21.7	43.0	101
TOP 5 ADI'S	40412	23079	21.4	57.1	96	6233	18.2	15.4	82	15097	23.4	37.4	106	15727	20.2	38.9	91
TOP 10 ADI'S	57709	32644	30.2	56.6	95	9067	26.5	15.7	84	21381	33.2	37.0	105	22081	28.4	38.3	90
TOP 20 ADI'S	83116	47625	44.1	57.3	97	13722	40.2	16.5	88	29571	45.9	35.6	101	33506	43.1	40.3	95
HSHLD. INC. $75,000 OR MORE	21409	11472	10.6	53.6	91	3137	9.2	14.7	78	6677	10.4	31.2	88	8465	10.9	39.5	93
$60,000 OR MORE	36836	20296	18.8	55.1	93	5450	16.0	14.8	79	11854	18.4	32.2	91	14883	19.1	40.4	95
$50,000 OR MORE	53155	29435	27.3	55.4	94	8401	24.6	15.8	84	17518	27.2	33.0	93	21230	27.3	39.9	94
$40,000 OR MORE	75291	42438	39.3	56.4	95	12102	35.4	16.1	86	24710	38.4	32.8	93	31064	40.0	41.3	97
$30,000 OR MORE	102396	59510	55.1	58.1	98	17769	52.0	17.4	93	35324	54.8	34.5	98	43174	55.5	42.2	99
$30,000 – $39,999	27105	17072	15.8	63.0	106	5667	16.6	20.9	112	10614	16.5	39.2	111	12111	15.6	44.7	105
$20,000 – $29,999	30317	18768	17.4	61.9	105	6373	18.7	21.0	112	10822	16.8	35.7	101	13883	17.9	45.8	107
$10,000 – $19,999	29855	18353	17.0	61.5	104	6479	19.0	21.7	116	11297	17.5	37.8	107	13108	16.9	43.9	103
UNDER $10,000	19888	11355	10.5	57.1	96	3541	10.4	17.8	95	6985	10.8	35.1	99	7571	9.7	38.1	89
HOUSEHOLD OF 1 PERSON	23383	11336	10.5	48.5	82	2915	8.5	12.5	67	6621	10.3	28.3	80	7727	9.9	33.0	78
2 PEOPLE	59547	31809	29.5	53.4	90	9263	27.1	15.6	83	17730	27.5	29.8	84	22690	29.2	38.1	89
3 OR 4 PEOPLE	72643	46028	42.6	63.4	107	15192	44.5	20.9	112	28128	43.7	38.7	110	33353	42.9	45.9	108
5 OR MORE PEOPLE	26884	18813	17.4	70.0	118	6793	19.9	25.3	135	11948	18.5	44.4	126	13965	18.0	51.9	122
NO CHILD IN HSHLD.	109702	59165	54.8	53.9	91	17626	51.6	16.1	86	33808	52.5	30.8	87	41560	53.5	37.9	89
CHILD(REN) UNDER 2 YEARS	15048	10548	9.8	70.1	118	4030	11.8	26.8	143	6875	10.7	45.7	129	7752	10.0	51.5	121
2 – 5 YEARS	25473	17985	16.7	70.6	119	6250	18.3	24.5	131	11774	18.3	46.2	131	13493	17.4	53.0	124
6 – 11 YEARS	34011	23085	21.4	67.9	115	7433	21.8	21.9	117	14221	22.1	41.8	118	17375	22.4	51.1	120
12 – 17 YEARS	33774	22170	20.5	65.6	111	7394	21.6	21.9	117	13733	21.3	40.7	115	16230	20.9	48.1	113
RESIDENCE OWNED	124747	69384	64.3	55.6	94	19886	58.2	15.9	85	40350	62.6	32.3	92	49466	63.6	39.7	93
VALUE: $70,000 OR MORE	69554	36947	34.2	53.1	90	9297	27.2	13.4	71	21652	33.6	31.1	88	26509	34.1	38.1	89
VALUE: UNDER $70,000	55193	32437	30.0	58.8	99	10588	31.0	19.2	102	18699	29.0	33.9	96	22957	29.5	41.6	98

While the index is a useful aid, it should not be used alone. Rather, percentages and product usage figures must also be considered to get an accurate picture of the market. While the index for a particular segment of the population may be very high, leading one to believe this is an attractive segment to target, this may be a result of a low denominator—that is, a very small proportion of the population in this segment. An example of how this might occur is provided in Exhibit 12–6. While the 18-to-24-year-old age segment has the highest index, it also has both the lowest product usage and the lowest population percentage of any segment. If the marketer

➤ *Exhibit 12–5*

Lipstick and lip gloss usage—women*

	Heavy Users Index	Medium Users Index	Light Users Index
Used lipstick and/or lip gloss in last 7 days 78.87%			
Number of times used in last 7 days			
Heavy—more than 10 times 25.37%			
Medium—7 to 10 times 28.02%			
Light—less than 7 times 25.48%			
Base: Women			
Age			
18–34	96	83	89
35–44	112	101	83
45–54	139	110	78
55–64	112	110	92
65 or over	84	107	104
Employment			
Professional	124	109	76
Executive, administrative, managerial	137	96	91
Clerical, sales, technical	130	103	84
Precision, crafts	77	84	78
Other employed	89	101	98
Household income			
$50,000 or more	134	112	77
$40,000–$49.9	115	110	92
$35,000–$39.9	113	97	97
$25,000–$34.9	93	97	111
$15,000–$24.9	94	99	103
Less than $15,000	58	85	123

*Mediamark Research, Spring 1992.

➤ *Exhibit 12–6*

How high indexes can be misleading

Age Segment	Population in Segment (percent)	Product Use in Segment (percent)	Index
18–24	15.1	18.0	119
25–34	25.1	25.0	100
35–44	20.6	21.0	102
45+	39.3	36.0	91

relies solely on the index, while ignoring product use, he or she would be ignoring a full 82 percent of product users.

Further, keep in mind that while Simmons and MRI provide demographic, geographic, and psychographic information, other factors may also be important—and in fact may be more useful in defining specific markets.

What Internal and External Factors May Be Operating?

Media strategies will be influenced by both *internal* and *external* factors operating at any given time. Internal factors may involve the size of the media budget, managerial and administrative capabilities, or the organization of the agency, as demonstrated in Exhibit 12–7. External factors may include the economy (the rising costs of media), changes in technology (the availability of new media), competitive factors, and the like. While some of this information may require primary research to determine, a substantial volume of information is also available through secondary sources including magazines, syndicated services, or even the daily newspaper.

Exhibit 12–8 presents one such example of a service that provides competitive information. As shown, the BAR/LNA Multi-Media Service provides media spending figures for various brands competing in the same market. Competitive information is also available from a variety of other sources, as shown in Appendix A to Chapter 12.

Where to Promote?

The question of where to promote relates to geographical considerations. As noted in Chapter 9, companies often find that sales are stronger in one area of the country than another and may allocate advertising expenditures according to the market potential of an area. For example, for years, Maxwell House coffee has had a much

➤ *Exhibit 12–7* **Organizing the media buying department**

While various firms and advertising agencies may have different ways of organizing the media buying department, three seem to be the most common. The first form employs a product/media focus, whereas the second places more emphasis on the market itself. The third organizes around media classes alone.

Form 1 In this organizational arrangement, the media buyers and assistant media buyers are responsible for a product or group of products and/or brands. Their media planner both plans and buys for these products/brands in whichever geographic areas they are marketed. For example, if the agency were responsible for the advertising of Hart skis, the media planners would determine the appropriate media in each area for placing the advertisements for these skis. The logic underlying this approach is that the planner knows the product and will identify the best media and vehicles for promoting the same.

Form 2 In this approach, the market is the focal point of attention. Media planners become "experts" in a particular market area and are responsible for planning and buying for all products/brands the firm and/or agency markets in those areas. For example, a planner may have responsibility for the Memphis, Tennessee, market. If the agency has more than one client who wishes to market in this area, the media selection for all of the brands/products is the responsibility of the same person—in this case, the logic being that his or her knowledge of the media and vehicles in the area allows for a more informed media choice. The nonquantitative characteristics of the media would get more attention under this approach.

Form 3 Organizing around a specific class of media—for example, print or broadcast—is a third alternative. In this case, the purchasing and development unit will handle all the agency print or broadcast business. Members of the media department become specialists who are brought in very early in the promotional planning process. Planners perform only planning functions, while buyers are responsible for all purchases. The buying function itself may be specialized with specific responsibilities for specialty advertising, national buys, local buys, etc. Their knowledge of the media and the audience each serves is considered a major benefit. In addition, by handling all the media buys, their ability to negotiate better deals is stronger.

As to which strategy works best, who is to say? Each has been in use for some time, and proponents have reasons for their organization. Discussions with media personnel in ad agencies tend to indicate the second approach requires that the agency be of substantial size and have enough clients to support the geographical assignment, whereas the third alternative seems to be the most common design.

greater brand share in the East than it has had in the West. The question that needs to be asked is, Where will the advertising be more wisely spent? Should General Foods allocate additional promotional dollars to those markets where the brand is already the leader so as to maintain market share, or does more potential exist in those markets in which the firm is not doing as well—that is, in areas in which there is more room to grow? Perhaps the best answer to this question is that the firm should spend advertising and promotion dollars where they will be the most effective, that is, in those markets where they will be most likely to achieve the desired objectives. Unfortunately, as we have seen so often, it is not always possible to measure directly the impact of promotional efforts. At the same time, certain tactics can be employed to assist the planner in making this determination.

Using indexes to determine where to promote

As was stated previously, media planners often use indexes to guide their efforts. In addition to those provided by Simmons and MRI, three additional indexes may also be found to be useful:

1. *The Survey of Buying Power Index* One common source of information is the **Survey of Buying Power Index,** published annually by *Sales and Marketing Management* magazine. The Survey of Buying Power is conducted for every major metropolitan market in the United States and is based on a number of factors, including population, effective buying income, and total retail sales in the area. Each of these factors is individually weighted and a "buying power index" is derived that charts the potential of a particular metro area, county, or city relative to the United States as a whole. The resulting index provides the media planner with insight into the relative value of that market, as shown in Exhibit 12–9. When used in combination with other market information, the Survey of Buying Power is useful to the marketer in determining which geographic areas should be targeted.

➤ *Exhibit 12–8*

LNA/ARBITRON MULTI-MEDIA SERVICE
January - December 1991

CLASS/COMPANY/BRAND	CLASS CODE	QUARTERLY AND YEAR-TO-DATE ADVERTISING DOLLARS (000)										
		10-MEDIA TOTAL	MAGAZINES	SUNDAY MAGAZINES	NEWSPAPERS	OUTDOOR	NETWORK TELEVISION	SPOT TELEVISION	SYNDICATED TELEVISION	CABLE TV NETWORKS	NETWORK RADIO	NATIONAL SPOT RADIO
G330 RESTAURANTS, HOTEL DINING & NIGHT CLUBS							CONTINUED					
CARLSON COS INC (CONTINUED)	G330											
TGI FRIDAYS RESTAURANTS												
04		3,607.4	- -	- -	77.8	27.5	- -	442.8	- -	- -	2,826.8	232.5
91 YTD		11,389.5	- -	- -	106.6	101.3	- -	480.2	- -	- -	9,847.1	854.3
90 YTD		8,126.1	- -	- -	61.5	220.4	- -	135.0	- -	- -	6,416.2	1,293.0
COMPANY TOTAL												
Q1		3,147.5	- -	- -	13.9	28.2	- -	46.9	- -	- -	2,841.9	216.6
Q2		3,101.4	- -	- -	5.7	38.1	- -	34.5	- -	- -	2,697.8	325.8
Q3		1,736.4	- -	- -	9.7	108.6	- -	0.8	- -	- -	1,480.6	136.7
Q4		3,813.6	- -	- -	77.8	123.6	- -	552.9	- -	- -	2,826.8	232.5
91 YTD		11,798.9	- -	- -	106.6	298.5	- -	635.1	- -	- -	9,847.1	911.6
90 YTD		8,429.6	- -	- -	61.5	277.5	- -	381.4	- -	- -	6,416.2	1,293.0
CASSANO ENTRS	G330											
CASSANO PIZZA&SUBS REST												
Q1		29.1	- -	- -	- -	- -	- -	29.1	- -	- -	- -	- -
Q2		73.2	- -	- -	- -	- -	- -	73.2	- -	- -	- -	- -
Q3		98.3	- -	- -	- -	- -	- -	98.3	- -	- -	- -	- -
Q4		5.8	- -	- -	- -	- -	- -	5.8	- -	- -	- -	- -
91 YTD		206.4	- -	- -	- -	- -	- -	206.4	- -	- -	- -	- -
90 YTD		203.4	- -	- -	- -	- -	- -	203.4	- -	- -	- -	- -
CATCH A RISING STAR	G330											
CATCH A RISING STAR NIGHTCLUB												
Q1		12.2	- -	- -	12.2	- -	- -	- -	- -	- -	- -	- -
Q2		5.2	- -	- -	5.2	- -	- -	- -	- -	- -	- -	- -
Q3		12.3	- -	- -	12.3	- -	- -	- -	- -	- -	- -	- -
Q4		15.5	- -	- -	4.2	- -	- -	- -	- -	- -	- -	- -
91 YTD		45.2	5.7	5.6	33.9	- -	- -	- -	- -	- -	- -	- -
90 YTD		73.4	5.7	5.6	73.4	- -	- -	- -	- -	- -	- -	- -
CHESAPEAKE BAY SEAFOOD HOUSE	G330											
CHESAPEAKE BAY SEAFOOD HOUSE RESTAURANT												
Q2		201.4	- -	- -	- -	- -	- -	201.4	- -	- -	- -	- -
Q3		329.0	- -	- -	- -	- -	- -	329.0	- -	- -	- -	- -
Q4		54.0	- -	- -	- -	- -	- -	54.0	- -	- -	- -	- -
91 YTD		584.4	- -	- -	- -	- -	- -	584.4	- -	- -	- -	- -
90 YTD		246.8	- -	- -	97.8	- -	- -	149.0	- -	- -	- -	- -
CHESAPEAKE FINANCIAL CORP	G330											
ARBYS RESTAURANTS												
Q1		5,193.8	- -	- -	82.8	74.2	- -	4,881.9	- -	- -	- -	154.9
Q2		5,259.2	- -	- -	69.7	90.6	- -	4,920.0	- -	- -	- -	178.9
Q3		5,764.9	- -	- -	74.3	119.7	- -	5,326.0	- -	- -	- -	244.9
Q4		5,661.6	- -	- -	64.9	104.0	- -	5,353.9	- -	- -	- -	138.8
91 YTD		21,879.5	- -	- -	291.7	388.5	- -	20,481.8	- -	- -	- -	717.5
90 YTD		27,565.9	- -	0.4	482.6	386.3	- -	26,217.5	- -	- -	- -	479.1
COMPANY TOTAL												
Q1		5,193.8	- -	- -	82.8	74.2	- -	4,881.9	- -	- -	- -	154.9
Q2		5,259.2	- -	- -	69.7	90.6	- -	4,920.0	- -	- -	- -	178.9
Q3		5,764.9	- -	- -	74.3	119.7	- -	5,326.0	- -	- -	- -	244.9
Q4		5,661.6	- -	- -	64.9	104.0	- -	5,353.9	- -	- -	- -	138.8
91 YTD		21,879.5	- -	- -	291.7	388.5	- -	20,481.8	- -	- -	- -	717.5
90 YTD		27,676.8	- -	0.4	482.6	386.3	- -	26,328.4	- -	- -	- -	479.1

2. *The Brand Development Index* The rate of product usage by geographical area is an additional factor that could be integrated into the decision process through the use of the **Brand Development Index (BDI).** This index is represented as follows:

$$\text{BDI} = \frac{\text{Percentage brand total U.S. sales in the market}}{\text{Percentage of total U.S. population in the market}} \times 100$$

The BDI considers the percentage of the brand's total U.S. sales that occur in a given market area as compared with the percentage of the total population in the market. The resulting BDI is an indication of the sales potential that exists for that brand in that market area. An example of this calculation is shown in Exhibit 12–10. As with the index previously discussed, the higher the index number, the more market potential that exists. In this case the index number of 312 indicates this market has high potential for brand development.

3. *The Category Development Index* The **Category Development Index (CDI)** is computed in the same manner as the BDI, the only difference being the CDI uses information regarding the product category (as opposed to the brand) in the numerator, as is represented in the following formula:

$$\text{CDI} = \frac{\text{Percentage of product category total sales in market}}{\text{Percentage of total U.S. population in market}} \times 100$$

The CDI then provides information with respect to potential for development of the total product category, rather than specific brands. When this information is combined with the BDI, a much more insightful promotional strategy may be developed. For example, consider the market potential for coffee in the United States. One might first look at how well the product category does in a specific market area, finding that in some areas such a Utah and Idaho the category potential is lower (see Exhibit 12–11). In analyzing the BDI, the company may find that relative to other brands in this area it may be doing very well or very poorly. This information can then be used in determining how well a particular product category and a particular brand are performing and in determining what media weight (or quantity of advertising) would be required to gain additional market share, as shown in Exhibit 12–12, page 401.

> *Exhibit 12–9*
Survey of Buying Power Index

Rhode Island

POPULATION

S&MM ESTIMATES: 12/31/90

METRO AREA County City	Total Population (Thousands)	% Of U.S.	Median Age Of Pop.	18-24 Years	25-34 Years	35-49 Years	50 & Over	Households (Thousands)	Total Retail Sales ($000)	Food ($000)	Eating & Drinking Places ($000)	General Mdse. ($000)	Furniture/ Furnish. Appliance ($000)	Automotive ($000)	Drug ($000)
PROVIDENCE–PAWTUCKET–WOONSOCKET	921.4	.3674	34.1	11.8	17.0	20.1	28.4	347.2	6,621,140	1,390,972	740,007	750,465	291,612	1,175,964	301,155
Bristol	49.0	.0196	35.9	10.9	15.5	20.9	30.5	17.6	239,949	66,787	27,747	2,630	6,814	53,545	13,682
Kent	162.1	.0646	35.9	8.9	16.9	22.3	29.2	62.4	1,687,207	275,155	168,616	307,478	55,278	301,666	58,221
Warwick	85.9	.0342	36.9	8.7	16.7	21.4	31.5	33.6	1,241,231	159,242	114,017	300,202	47,168	189,376	34,648
Providence	598.9	.2388	33.8	12.2	17.3	19.2	28.7	227.4	3,832,852	814,370	442,223	400,598	197,994	690,435	198,710
Cranston	76.4	.0305	37.3	9.5	17.5	20.7	32.8	29.5	513,493	116,552	55,772	21,447	43,116	94,507	34,699
East Providence	50.6	.0202	36.9	9.1	16.9	19.4	33.3	20.0	405,889	72,226	38,188	22,368	20,077	130,818	20,625
• Pawtucket	73.0	.0291	33.7	10.2	19.1	17.8	29.7	29.9	514,684	105,502	42,451	110,785	21,226	73,536	34,132
• Providence	161.4	.0644	29.6	18.0	17.6	16.5	24.0	59.1	931,996	174,406	59,502	63,388	169,702	39,520
• Woonsocket	44.1	.0176	33.3	10.9	17.9	17.9	28.9	17.7	292,009	70,461	20,413	36,712	12,715	72,514	14,174
Washington	111.4	.0444	32.6	14.2	16.2	21.9	24.3	39.8	861,132	234,660	101,421	39,759	31,526	130,318	30,542
SUBURBAN TOTAL	642.9	.2563	35.5	10.5	16.6	21.4	29.3	240.5	4,882,451	1,040,603	550,237	543,466	194,283	860,212	213,329
OTHER COUNTIES															
Newport	87.5	.0349	33.8	11.8	17.6	22.3	25.5	32.8	703,842	121,062	118,031	34,174	29,726	176,816	18,994
TOTAL METRO COUNTIES	921.4	.3674	34.1	11.8	17.0	20.1	28.4	347.2	6,621,140	1,390,972	740,007	750,465	291,612	1,175,964	301,155
TOTAL STATE	1,008.9	.4023	34.1	11.8	17.0	20.3	28.1	380.0	7,324,982	1,512,034	858,038	784,639	321,338	1,352,780	320,149

RETAIL SALES BY STORE GROUP

EFFECTIVE BUYING INCOME

S&MM ESTIMATES: 12/31/90

METRO AREA County City	Total EBI ($000)	Median Hsld. EBI	A $10,000-$19,999	B $20,000-$34,999	C $35,000-$49,999	D $50,000 & Over	Buying Power Index
PROVIDENCE–PAWTUCKET–WOONSOCKET	13,161,017	28,441	19.4	25.5	18.6	20.9	.3714
Bristol	727,359	30,275	19.2	26.8	17.6	23.9	.0182
Kent	2,422,662	30,869	17.0	27.8	21.2	21.1	.0756
Warwick	1,322,227	31,519	16.5	27.6	21.5	21.8	.0463
Providence	8,427,416	27,115	20.2	24.4	17.8	20.3	.2319
Cranston	1,237,230	31,764	17.7	24.6	19.9	25.2	.0323
East Providence	777,080	30,763	18.3	25.3	21.5	22.1	.0219
• Pawtucket	997,942	25,377	21.5	26.0	17.8	16.3	.0286
• Providence	1,924,178	20,802	24.2	23.5	13.4	14.8	.0558
• Woonsocket	566,843	23,811	22.3	24.4	16.8	15.5	.0165
Washington	1,583,580	30,461	18.6	28.1	19.4	22.3	.0457
SUBURBAN TOTAL	9,672,054	31,087	17.8	26.1	20.0	23.3	.2705
OTHER COUNTIES							
Newport	1,414,978	31,746	17.5	24.8	19.4	25.8	.0388
TOTAL METRO COUNTIES	13,161,017	28,441	19.4	25.5	18.6	20.9	.3714
TOTAL STATE	14,575,995	28,696	19.2	25.5	18.6	21.3	.4102

While the indexes just discussed provide important insights into the market potential for the firm's products and/or brands, this information is supplemental to the overall strategy determined earlier in the promotional decision-making process. In fact, much of this information may have already been provided to the media planner. At the same time, it may be used more specifically by the media department in determining the media weights to assign to each area. This decision ultimately affects the budget allocated to each area as well as other factors such as reach, frequency, and scheduling.

Establishing Media Objectives

Just as the situation analysis leads to establishment of marketing and communications objectives, the media situation analysis should lead to determination of specific media objectives. The media objectives are not ends in themselves. Rather, they are designed to lead to the attainment of communications and marketing objectives. As such, media objectives are the goals to be attained by the media program and should be limited to those that can be accomplished through media strategies. Examples of media objectives may include: Create awareness in the target market through the following:

• Use broadcast media to provide coverage of 80 percent of the target market over a six-month period.

• Reach 60 percent of the target audience at least three times over the same six-month period.

• Concentrate heaviest advertising in winter and spring, with lighter emphasis in summer and fall.

Calculating BDI

$$BDI = \frac{\text{Percentage of brand sales in South Atlantic region}}{\text{Percentage of U.S. population in South Atlantic region}} \times 100$$

$$= \frac{50}{16} \times 100$$

$$= 312$$

Using CDI and BDI to determine market potential

$$CDI = \frac{\text{Percentage of product category sales in Utah/Idaho}}{\text{Percentage of total U.S. population in Utah/Idaho}} \times 100$$

$$= \frac{1\%}{1\%} \times 100$$

$$= 100$$

$$BDI = \frac{\text{Percentage of total brand sales in Utah/Idaho}}{\text{Percentage of total U.S. population in Utah/Idaho}} \times 100$$

$$= \frac{2\%}{1\%} \times 100$$

$$= 200$$

Developing and Implementing Media Strategy

Having determined what is to be accomplished, efforts turn to consideration of *how* to achieve these objectives—that is, the development and implementation of media strategies. As noted, media strategies evolve directly from the actions required to meet objectives and involve the criteria presented in Exhibit 12–13.

Developing a Media Mix

A wide variety of media and media vehicles are available to the advertiser. While it is possible that only one medium and/or vehicle might be employed, it is much more likely that a number of alternatives will be used. The objectives sought, the characteristics of the product or service, the size of the budget, and individual preferences are just some of the factors that might be considered in determining what combination of media will be used.

As an example, consider a promotional situation in which a product requires a visual demonstration to be communicated effectively. In this case, TV might be the most effective medium. If the promotional strategy calls for the use of coupons to stimulate trial, print media will be necessary.

By employing a media mix, advertisers are usually able to add more versatility to their media strategies, as each of the various media contributes its own distinct advantages (as is demonstrated in succeeding chapters of this text). By combining media, it may be possible to increase coverage, reach, and frequency levels while also improving the likelihood of achieving overall communications and marketing goals.

Determining Target Market Coverage

The media planner assumes the responsibility for determining which target markets should receive the most media emphasis. (In the Denny's plan, this was determined to be adults ages 25 to 54 in 28 core markets—see "General Overview," Appendix B.) Developing media strategies involves a matching of the most appropriate media to this market by asking the question, "Through which media and media vehicles can I best get my message to prospective buyers?" The issue here is to get coverage of the market, as represented in Exhibit 12–14. As can be seen in this exhibit, the optimal goal would be to achieve coverage *b*—that is, to attain full market coverage.

But this is a very unlikely and overly optimistic scenario. In more realistic situations, conditions *c* or *d* are most likely to occur. In the former (*c*) the coverage of the media does not allow for coverage of the entire market, leaving some potential customers without exposure to the message. In the latter, the marketer is faced with a problem of overexposure—defined as **waste coverage**—in which the coverage of the media exceeds the targeted audience. Waste coverage refers to the shaded area extending beyond the target audience. If this coverage reaches persons who are not sought as buyers, and who are not potential users, then this coverage is "wasted."

➤ *Exhibit 12–12*
Using BDI and CDI indexes

	High BDI	**Low BDI**
High CDI	High market share Good market potential	Low market share Good market potential
Low CDI	High market share Monitor for sales decline	Low market share Poor market potential

High BDI and high CDI	This market usually represents good sales potential for both the product category and the brand.
High BDI and low CDI	The category is not selling well, but the brand is; probably a good market to advertise in, but should be monitored for declining sales.
Low BDI and high CDI	The product category shows high potential but the brand is not doing well; a determination as to reasons is necessary.
Low BDI and low CDI	Both the product category and the brand are not doing well; not likely to be a good place for advertising.

(This term is used to explain the coverage that reaches nonpotential buyers and/or users. One may not be part of the intended target market but for various other reasons may still be considered as potential—for example, those who may be buying the product as a gift for someone else.)

The goal of the media planner is to attempt to extend the coverage of the media to as many of the members of the target audience as possible while at the same time minimizing the amount of waste coverage. The typical situation usually involves trade-offs. Sometimes one has to live with less coverage than desired, whereas at other times coverage has to include members not specifically targeted, as the media most likely to be effective may also expose others not sought. In this latter instance, waste coverage is justified based on the fact that the media employed are likely to be the most effective means of delivery available and the cost of the waste coverage is exceeded by the value gained from the use of these media.

When watching a professional football game on TV, you may have noticed a number of commercials for stock brokerage firms such as Dean Witter Reynolds and Shearson Lehman Hutton. Not all viewers are candidates for stock market services and might constitute waste coverage. At the same time, a very high percentage of potential customers can be reached with this strategy, and the program is considered a good media buy because the ability to generate market coverage outweighs the disadvantages of high waste coverage.

Exhibit 12–15 represents an example of how information provided by Simmons can be used to match media to target markets. A profile of magazines read and television shows watched by those who engage in aerobics is shown. (You can practice the use of index numbers here!) From Exhibit 12–15 you can see that *Shape, Self,* and *Vanity Fair* magazines would likely be wise selections, whereas *Road and Track, Sports Afield,* or *True Story* would be less likely to lead to the desired exposures.

➤ *Exhibit 12–13*
Criteria considered in the development of media plans

- Developing a media mix
- Determining target market coverage
- Determining geographic coverage
- Scheduling
- Determining reach versus frequency
- Creative aspects and mood
- Flexibility
- Budget considerations

Determining Geographic Coverage

Snow skiing is much more popular in some areas of the country than in others. Thus, it would not be the wisest of strategies to promote skis in those areas where interest is not as high—unless it would be possible to generate an increase in interest. It may be possible to promote an interest in skiing in the Southeast. However, the likelihood that we would experience a notable increase in sales of ski equipment is not very high, given the market's distance from snow. As a result the objective of weighting certain geographic areas—known as **geographical weighting**—more than others makes sense, and the strategy of exerting more promotional efforts and dollars in these areas naturally follows. (See Denny's "Overall Parameters," Appendix B.)

➤ *Exhibit 12–14*
Marketing coverage possibilities

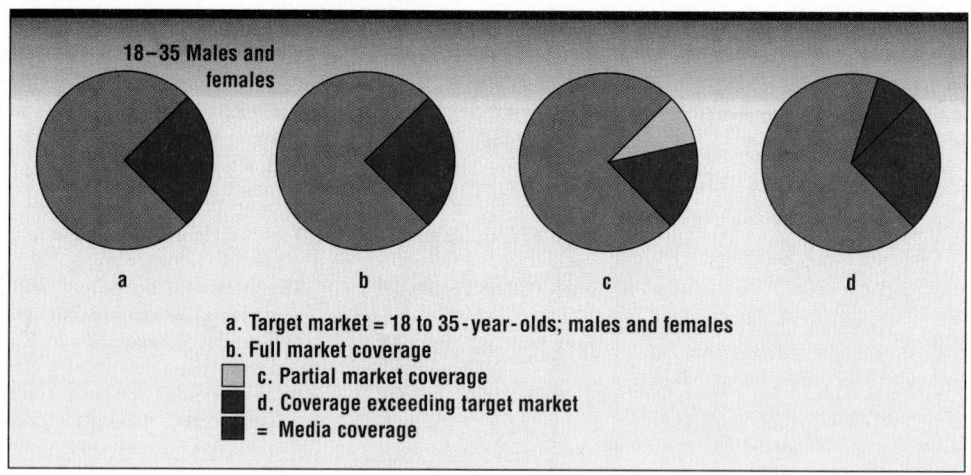

18–35 Males and females

a   b   c   d

a. Target market = 18 to 35-year-olds; males and females
b. Full market coverage
☐ c. Partial market coverage
■ d. Coverage exceeding target market
■ = Media coverage

➤ *Exhibit 12–15*
Magazines purchased by people who engage in aerobics

	TOTAL U.S. '000	AEROBICS A '000	B % DOWN	C ACROSS %	D INDX	20 OR MORE DAYS A '000	B % DOWN	C ACROSS %	D INDX
REDBOOK	10533	1074	9.1	10.2	157	760	10.1	7.2	174
ROAD & TRACK	3838	*133	1.1	3.5	53	**55	0.7	1.4	35
ROLLING STONE	6154	496	4.2	8.1	124	317	4.2	5.2	124
SCIENTIFIC AMERICAN	1835	*137	1.2	7.5	115	**57	0.8	3.1	75
SELF	2957	594	5.0	20.1	310	466	6.2	15.8	381
SESAME STREET MAGAZINE	3606	444	3.8	12.3	190	292	3.9	8.1	196
SEVENTEEN	3532	259	2.2	7.3	113	*165	2.2	4.7	113
SHAPE	1664	252	2.1	15.1	234	*185	2.4	11.1	269
SKI	1764	*176	1.5	10.0	154	**102	1.4	5.8	140
SKIING	1535	*161	1.4	10.5	162	**86	1.1	5.6	135
SMITHSONIAN	6299	464	3.9	7.4	114	219	2.9	3.5	84
SOAP OPERA DIGEST	6437	756	6.4	11.7	181	433	5.7	6.7	162
SOUTHERN LIVING	7213	675	5.7	9.4	144	506	6.7	7.0	169
SPORT	3012	**153	1.3	5.1	78	**67	0.9	2.2	54
THE SPORTING NEWS	3348	*179	1.5	5.3	82	**128	1.7	3.8	92
SPORTS AFIELD	3370	**91	0.8	2.7	42	**37	0.5	1.1	27
SPORTS ILLUSTRATED	21035	1002	8.5	4.8	73	611	8.1	2.9	70
STAR	10704	814	6.9	7.6	117	470	6.2	4.4	106
SUNDAY MAGAZINE NETWORK	34831	2761	23.3	7.9	122	1828	24.2	5.2	127
SUNSET	3255	269	2.3	8.3	127	185	2.4	5.7	137
TV GUIDE	39127	2620	22.1	6.7	103	1565	20.7	4.0	97
TENNIS	1548	**102	0.9	6.6	102	**82	1.1	5.3	128
TIME	24413	1734	14.7	7.1	110	1165	15.4	4.8	115
TRAVEL & LEISURE	2520	189	1.6	7.5	116	*144	1.9	5.7	138
TRUE STORY	3060	*312	2.6	10.2	157	**234	3.1	7.6	185
USA TODAY	6199	459	3.9	7.4	114	328	4.3	5.3	128
USA WEEKEND	34618	2192	18.5	6.3	98	1369	18.1	4.0	96
U.S. NEWS & WORLD REPORT	13465	830	7.0	6.2	95	596	7.9	4.4	107
US	4059	453	3.8	11.2	172	311	4.1	7.7	185
VANITY FAIR	1974	292	2.5	14.8	228	*173	2.3	8.8	212

*Projection relatively unstable because of sample base—use with caution
†Number of cases too small for reliability—shown for consistency only

Scheduling

Obviously, companies would like to keep their advertising in front of the consumer at all times as a constant reminder of the product and/or brand name. In reality, this is not possible for a variety of reasons (not the least of which is the budget!), nor may it always be necessary. The primary objective of *scheduling* is to time the promotional efforts so they will coincide with the highest potential buying times. While for some products these times may not be easily identifiable, for others they are very obvious. Three scheduling methods available to the media planner are represented in Exhibit 12–16.

Continuity refers to a continuous pattern of advertising. Continuous may mean advertising every day, every week, or every month—the *key* is that a regular (continuous) pattern is developed with no gaps or no-advertising periods. Examples of such strategies might include advertising for food products, laundry detergents, or other products consumed on an ongoing basis without regard for seasonality.

> *Exhibit 12–16*
Three methods of promotional scheduling

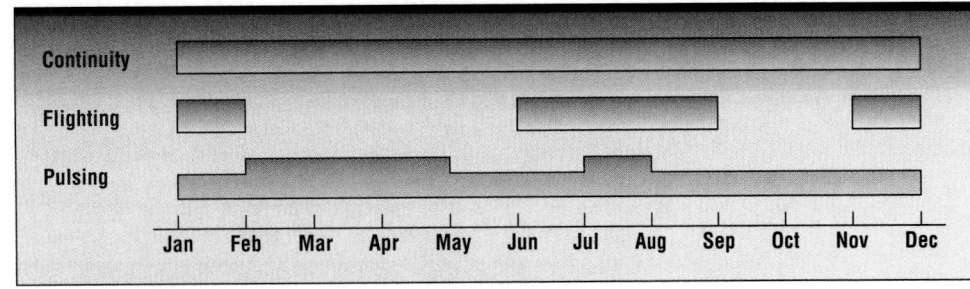

A second method, **flighting,** employs a less regular schedule, with intermittent periods of advertising and nonadvertising. At some time periods, there may be heavier promotional expenditures, and at others there may be no advertising. Many banks, for example, spend no monies on advertising in the summer, while maintaining advertising throughout the rest of the year. Snow skis are another example of a seasonal product that might be advertised very heavily between October and April; less in May, August, and September; and not at all in June or July.

The final method, **pulsing,** is actually a combination of the first two. In a pulsing strategy, continuity is maintained, but at certain times a heavier emphasis on promotional efforts is required. An example of a pulsing strategy is that used in the automobile industry, where advertising continues throughout the year but may increase at certain times like April (income tax refund check time), September (new models being brought out), and the end of the model year. Again, the scheduling strategy depends on the objectives, buying cycles, and the budget, among other factors. It should also be understood there are certain advantages and disadvantages to each scheduling method, as shown in Exhibit 12–17. (Notice that in the Denny's media plan, flighting is recommended as the best television advertising strategy while a continuous radio schedule is employed; again, see Appendix B.)

Determining Reach versus Frequency

You probably noticed that the topic heading for this section included the word *versus.* There is a reason for this: Given that advertisers face a variety of objectives, and given that they have budget constraints, the decision is usually one of having to trade off reach and frequency. The issue becomes one of determining whether to advertise to have the message be seen or heard by more persons or by a smaller number of persons more often. The information necessary to make this decision becomes one of how much reach and frequency are needed, respectively. Let us explore these issues.

How much reach is necessary?

Thinking back to the hierarchies discussed in Chapter 6, you will recall that the first stage of each of the models requires awareness of the product and/or brand. As a hierarchy, the more persons aware, the more persons likely to be at each of the subsequent stages. Achieving awareness requires reach—that is, exposing potential buyers to the message. For new brands or products, a very high level of reach is to be sought, as the objective is to have as many persons as are potential buyers aware of the new entry. At the same time, high reach is also desired at later stages of the hierarchy. For example, at the trial stage of the adoption hierarchy, a promotions strategy employing cents-off coupons or free samples might be employed. An objective of the marketer is to reach a larger number of people with these samples, in an attempt to make consumers aware of the product, get them to try it and develop favorable attitudes toward it. (In turn, these attitudes might lead to purchase.)

The problem arises because there is no known way of determining how much reach is required to achieve levels of awareness, attitude change, or buying intentions, nor can we be sure an ad placed in a vehicle will actually reach the intended

➤ *Exhibit 12–17*
Characteristics of scheduling methods

Continuity	
Advantages	Serves as a constant reminder to the consumer
	Covers the entire buying cycle
	Allows for media priorities (quantity discounts, preferred locations, etc.)
Disadvantages	Higher costs
	Potential for overexposure
	Limited media allocation possible
Flighting	
Advantages	Cost efficiency of advertising only during purchase cycles
	May allow for inclusion of more than one medium or vehicle with limited budgets
	Weighting may offer more exposure and advantage over competitors
Disadvantages	Increased likelihood of wearout
	Lack of awareness, interest, retention of promotional message during nonscheduled times
	Vulnerability to competitive efforts during nonscheduled periods
Pulsing	
Advantages	All of the same as the previous two methods
Disadvantages	Not required for seasonal products (or other cyclical products)

audience. (There has been some research with respect to the former of these problems, and we allude to this research soon when we discuss effective reach.)

For example, if you were to buy advertising time on the TV program "60 Minutes," does this mean everyone who is tuned to this program will see the ad? The answer is no; many will leave the room, be distracted during the commercial, and so on, as shown in Exhibit 12–18. (The exhibit also provides a good example of the difference between reach and coverage.) Likewise, if I expose everyone in my target group to the message one time, will this be sufficient to create a 100 percent level of awareness? The answer again is no, as research indicates one exposure is not likely to be enough. This then leads us to the next question: What *frequency* of exposure is necessary for the ad to be seen and to have an impact?

What frequency level is needed?

With respect to its use in media planning, *frequency* carries a slightly different meaning. (Remember when we said one of the problems in media planning was that terms often take on different meanings?) In the latter instance, *frequency* refers to the number of times one is exposed to the media vehicle and not necessarily the ad itself. While one study has estimated the actual audience to the commercial may be as much as 30 percent lower than that exposed to the program, all researchers do not agree on this figure.[2] For example, Exhibit 12–18 demonstrates that depending on the program, this number may range from a low of 12 percent to as high as 40 percent. At the same time, most advertisers do agree that a 1:1 exposure ratio does not exist. So, for example, while your ad may be placed in a certain vehicle, the fact that someone has been exposed to that vehicle does not ensure your ad has been seen. As a result, the frequency level expressed in the media plan is not the same as that of actual ad exposure and is an overstatement of the actual level of exposure to the ad that might be expected. This overstatement has led some media buyers to refer to the reach of the media vehicle as "opportunities to see" an ad rather than actual exposure to the ad itself.

Because the advertiser has no sure way of knowing whether exposure to a vehicle results in exposure to the ad, the media and advertisers have adopted a compromise position and agree that one exposure to the vehicle constitutes reach, given that this

> *Exhibit 12–18*   **Who's still there to watch the ads?**

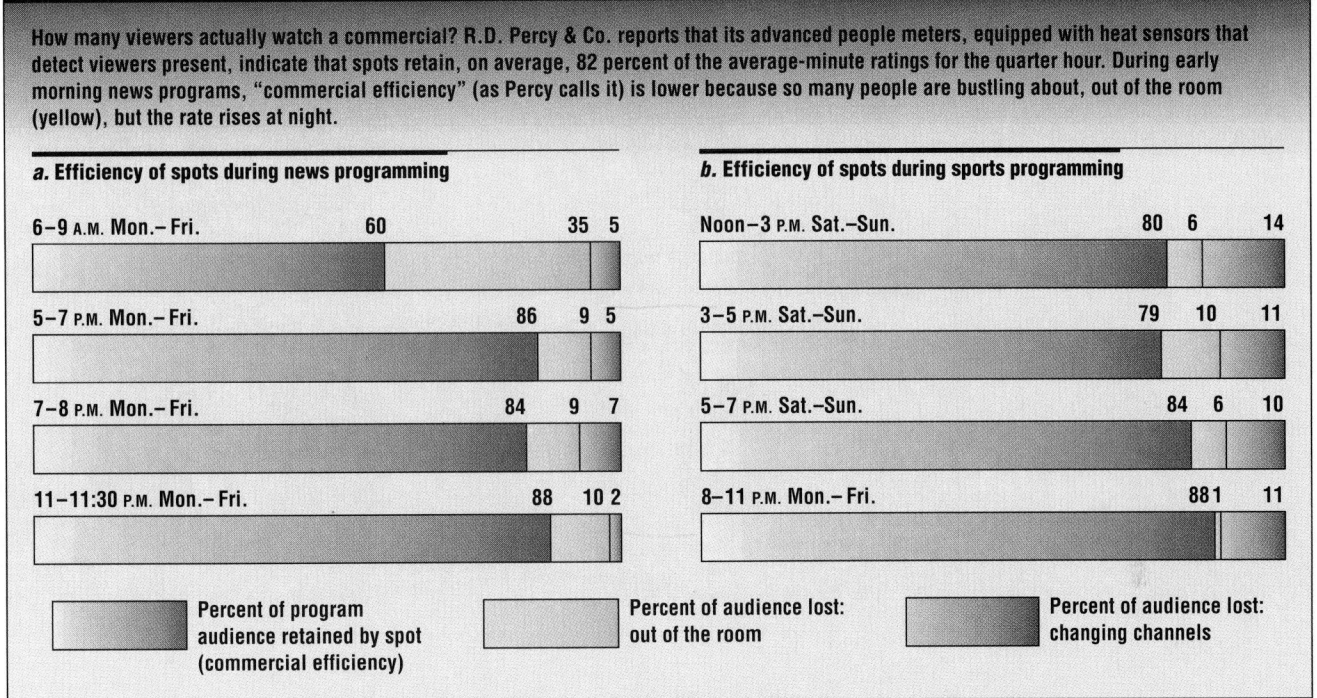

How many viewers actually watch a commercial? R.D. Percy & Co. reports that its advanced people meters, equipped with heat sensors that detect viewers present, indicate that spots retain, on average, 82 percent of the average-minute ratings for the quarter hour. During early morning news programs, "commercial efficiency" (as Percy calls it) is lower because so many people are bustling about, out of the room (yellow), but the rate rises at night.

a. Efficiency of spots during news programming

6–9 A.M. Mon.–Fri.   60   35   5
5–7 P.M. Mon.–Fri.   86   9   5
7–8 P.M. Mon.–Fri.   84   9   7
11–11:30 P.M. Mon.–Fri.   88   10   2

b. Efficiency of spots during sports programming

Noon–3 P.M. Sat.–Sun.   80   6   14
3–5 P.M. Sat.–Sun.   79   10   11
5–7 P.M. Sat.–Sun.   84   6   10
8–11 P.M. Mon.–Fri.   88   1   11

Percent of program audience retained by spot (commercial efficiency)   Percent of audience lost: out of the room   Percent of audience lost: changing channels

exposure must occur for the viewer even to have an "opportunity to see" the ad. Thus, this figure is used in the calculation of reach and frequency levels. This compromise does not, however, help determine the level of frequency required to make an impact. And, as has been stated, the exact number is not known. The creativity of the ad, the involvement of the receiver, noise, and a variety of other intervening factors confound any attempts to make this precise a determination.

At this point, we are fairly certain the question in your mind must be: "If nobody knows this stuff, how do they make these decisions?" It is a very good question, and the truth is that the decisions are not always made on hard data—remember, we said there is some creativity to media planning. Or, as noted by Joseph Ostrow, executive vice president–director, Communications Services with Young and Rubicam, "Establishing frequency goals for an advertising campaign is a mix of art and science but with a definite bias toward art."[3] Let us first examine the process involved in setting reach and frequency objectives and then discuss the logic of each.

The process of establishing reach and frequency objectives

It is possible to be exposed to more than one media vehicle with an ad, resulting in repetition (frequency). For example, if one ad is placed on one TV show one time, the number of persons exposed would be the reach. Assume the ad was placed on two shows. The total number exposed once is **unduplicated reach.** At the same time, some people would see the ad twice. Thus, the reach of the two shows, as depicted in Exhibit 12–19, would include a number of persons who were reached by each show (C). This overlap in reach is referred to as **duplicated reach.**

Both unduplicated and duplicated reach figures are important. In respect to the former, an indication of potential new exposures is provided, whereas duplicated reach provides an estimate of frequency. Most media buys are likely to include both forms of reach. Let us consider an example.

A measure of potential reach in the broadcast industry is the television (or radio) **program rating.** While this number is expressed as a percentage figure, an estimate of the total number of homes reached could easily be calculated by taking this

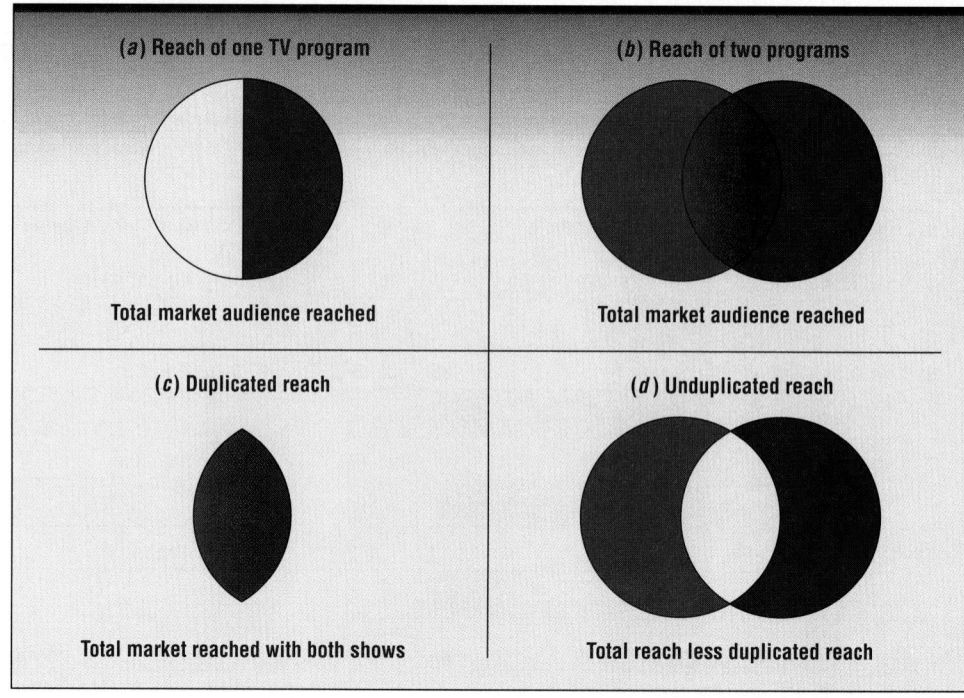

(*a*) Reach of one TV program

Total market audience reached

(*b*) Reach of two programs

Total market audience reached

(*c*) Duplicated reach

Total market reached with both shows

(*d*) Unduplicated reach

Total reach less duplicated reach

percentage number times the number of homes with television sets. For example, if there are 93.1 million homes with TV sets in the United States and the program has a rating of 30, then the calculation would be 0.30 × 93.1, or 27.93 million homes. (We go into much more detail on ratings and other broadcast terms in Chapter 13.)

To estimate the reach obtained through a media buy, the media buyer typically uses a numerical indicator determined by gross ratings points (GRPs). A discussion of the concept of gross ratings points and an example of its use follows.

Using gross ratings points (GRPs)

When the marketer wants to know how many potential audience members might be exposed to a series of commercials, he or she uses the program rating described earlier. The average number of times the home is reached during this period is the frequency of exposure. A summary measure can be used that combines these two figures and provides the media buyer with an indication of the weight the schedule will deliver. This number is a commonly used reference point known as **gross ratings points,** or **GRPs**. The formula used in calculating GRPs is

$$\text{GRP} = \text{Reach} \times \text{frequency}$$

GRPs are based on the total audience that might be reached by an advertising buy and uses a duplicated reach estimate.*

Given that GRPs are not a direct measure of actual reach, the advertiser must ask, How many GRPs are needed to attain a certain reach? and How do these GRPs translate into effective reach? For example, how many GRPs must one purchase to attain an unduplicated reach of 50 percent, and what is the frequency of exposure this schedule will deliver? The following example may help you to understand how this process works.

---

*A figure found to be more useful by advertisers is that of **target ratings points** (**TRPs**). TRPs refer to the number of persons in the primary target audience that the media buy will reach—and the number of times. This figure is more useful in determining the efficiency of the advertising in that it does not include waste coverage. However, it is calculated in the same manner as GRPs and is still subject to the same limitations. In the remainder of this chapter, we use only the term *GRPs,* except in specific instances where the distinction is necessary.

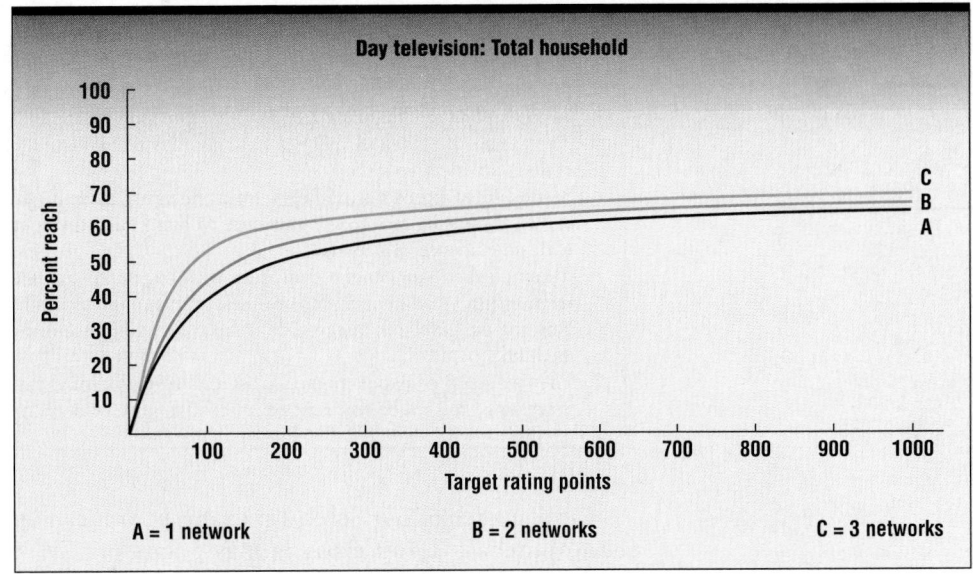

First, it is necessary to understand what these ratings points represent. A purchase of 100 GRPs might mean 100 percent of the market is exposed once or 50 percent of the market is exposed twice or 25 percent of the market is exposed four times, and so on. As you can see, this information must be more specific for the marketer to use effectively. In respect to the first question (How many GRPs are necessary?), the manager needs to know how many members of the intended audience the schedule actually reaches. The chart shown in Exhibit 12–20 helps make this determination.

In referring to Exhibit 12–20, you can see that a purchase of 100 TRPs on one network would yield an estimated reach of 32 percent of the total households in the target market. This figure would climb to 37.2 percent if two networks were used, and 44.5 percent on three. Working backward through the formula for GRPs (TRPs), the estimate of frequency of exposure—3.125, 2.688, and 2.247, respectively—demonstrates the trade-off between reach and frequency levels that would be attained.

In February 1987, Seven-Up purchased 1,400 GRPs in a four-week period to introduce a new ad campaign. This purchase employed 189 separate TV spots and was estimated to reach 96 percent of the target audience an average of 14 times. To determine if this was a wise media buy, we need to know the answer to the second question—was this an effective reach figure? Certainly, reaching 96 percent of the target market is attractive. But what about the frequency level? Why was this number so high? And was it likely to be effective? In other words, does this level of GRPs affect awareness, attitudes, and purchase intentions?

A number of researchers have explored this issue. David Berger, vice president and director of research at the Foote, Cone & Belding advertising agency, has determined that 2,500 GRPs are likely to lead to approximately a 70 percent probability of high awareness, whereas 1,000 to 2,500 would be approximately 33 percent likely, and less than 1,000 would result in almost no likelihood.[4] David Olson obtained similar results and further showed that as awareness increased, trial of the product would also increase, although at a significantly slower rate.[5] In both cases, it was evident that a high number of GRPs would be required to make an impact.

Exhibit 12–21 presents a summary of the effects that can be expected at different levels of exposure, based on a review of research in this area. As this exhibit shows, a number of factors may be operating, and direct relationships may be difficult to establish.[6]

In addition to those results shown in Exhibit 12–21, Ostrow has shown that while the number of repetitions increases awareness rapidly, much less of an impact is likely for attitudinal and behavioral responses.[7]

1. One exposure of an advertisement to a target group within a purchase cycle has little or no effect in all but a minority of circumstances.
2. Since one exposure is usually ineffective, the central goal of productive media planning should be to emphasize enhancing frequency rather than reach.
3. The weight of evidence suggests strongly that an exposure frequency of two within a purchase cycle is an effective level.
4. Beyond three exposures within a brand purchase cycle or over a period of four or even eight weeks, increasing frequency continues to build advertising effectiveness at a decreasing rate but with no evidence of decline.
5. Although there are general principles with respect to frequency of exposure and its relationship to advertising effectiveness, differential effects by brand are equally important.
6. Nothing we have seen suggests that frequency response principles or generalizations vary by medium.
7. The frequency of exposure data from this review strongly suggest that wearout is not a function of too much frequency per se; it is more of a creative or copy problem.

Getting back to our Seven-Up example, you can imagine how expensive it had to be to purchase 1,400 gross ratings points on TV. Now that you have additional information, we will ask again, "Was this a good buy?"

Determining effective reach

Given that the marketer is faced with a budget constraint, he or she must decide whether it is in the best interest to increase reach at the expense of frequency or vice versa; that is, increase the frequency of exposure but to a smaller audience. As shown, a number of factors will influence this decision. For example, a new product or brand introduction would attempt to maximize reach—particularly unduplicated reach—to create awareness in as many persons as possible as quickly as possible. At the same time, if the product were a high-involvement product, or one whose benefits may not be very obvious, a certain level of frequency will be necessary to achieve effective reach.

Effective reach represents the percent of a vehicle's audience reached at each effective frequency increment. This concept is based on the assumption that one exposure to an ad may not be sufficient to convey the desired message. As we saw earlier, the exact number of exposures necessary for the ad to make an impact is not known with certainty, although advertisers have settled on a minimum of three as the required number. Thus, effective reach (exposure) is shown in the shaded area in Exhibit 12–22 in the range of 3 to 10 exposures. Below 3 exposures is considered insufficient reach, while beyond 10 is considered excessive exposure and thus ineffective reach. The 3 to 10 exposure level is no guarantee of having effective communication. As stated, different messages may require more or less exposures. In the advertising industry, the 3 to 10 exposure rate is often used as a rule of thumb as to what constitutes effective reach.

Since they do not know precisely the number of times the viewer will actually be exposed, advertisers typically purchase GRPs that lead to a frequency of exposure greater than three in an attempt to ensure the likelihood of effective reach.

Determining effective reach is further compounded by the fact that when calculating GRPs, advertisers use a figure that they refer to as **average frequency.** *Average frequency* refers to the average number of times the target audience reached by a media schedule is exposed to the vehicle over a specified period. The problem with using this figure can easily be seen by examining the scenario below.

Consider the following media buy in which:

50 percent of audience is reached 1 time.

30 percent of audience is reached 5 times.

20 percent of audience is reached 10 times.

Average frequency = 4.0

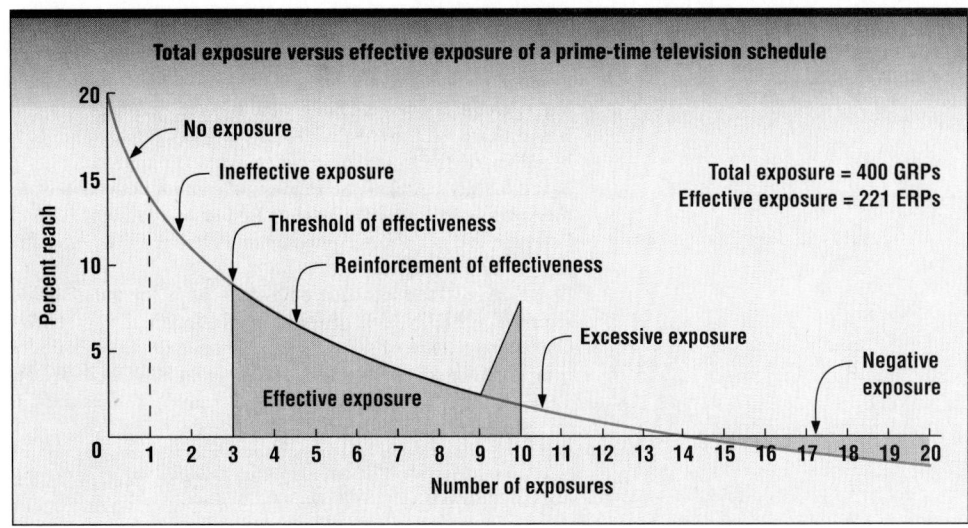

Total exposure versus effective exposure of a prime-time television schedule

Total exposure = 400 GRPs
Effective exposure = 221 ERPs

- No exposure
- Ineffective exposure
- Threshold of effectiveness
- Reinforcement of effectiveness
- Excessive exposure
- Negative exposure
- Effective exposure

Percent reach

Number of exposures

In this media buy, the average frequency is 4.0, which is slightly over the number established as effective. Yet at the same time, a full 50 percent of the audience had only a one-time exposure. Thus, the average frequency number can be misleading, and including this number in calculations of GRPs might result in underexposing the audience.

Even though the use of GRPs has its problems, this does not mean it cannot provide useful information to the marketer. It has been established that a certain level of GRPs is necessary to achieve awareness and increases in GRPs are likely to lead to more exposures and/or to more repetitions—both of which are necessary to have an effect on higher-order objectives. Perhaps the best advice for purchasing GRPs is offered by Ostrow. He recommends the following strategies:[8]

1. Instead of using average frequency, the marketer should decide what minimum frequency goal is needed to reach the advertising objectives effectively and then maximize reach at that frequency level.
2. To determine effective frequency one must consider three elements including marketing factors, message factors, and media factors.

A summary of the factors cited in the second recommendation are shown in Exhibit 12–23.

In summary, the reach versus frequency decision—while extremely critical—is a very difficult one to make. A number of factors must be considered, and concrete rules do not always apply. The result is a decision that many times is "more of an art than a science."

Considering Creative Aspects and Mood

The context of the medium in which the ad is to be placed may also affect viewers' perceptions. Given a specific creative strategy, certain media may be required to operationalize that creativity. For example, television—because it provides both sight and sound—may be more effective in generating emotions than other media, and magazines may create different perceptions than will newspapers. In developing a media strategy, both creativity and mood factors must be considered. Let us examine each in more detail.

Creative aspects

A number of cases exist that demonstrate it is possible to significantly increase the success of a product through a strong creative campaign. At the same time, to implement this creativity, it is necessary to employ a medium that will support such a strategy. For example, the Absolut vodka campaign discussed in Chapter 10 and the campaign of Obsession cologne, an ad for which was shown in Chapter 4, used

➤ *Exhibit 12–23*
Factors important in determining frequency levels

Marketing factors
• **Brand history**   Is the brand a new brand or an established one? New brands generally require higher frequency levels than do established brands.
• **Brand share**   An inverse relationship exists between brand share and frequency. The higher the brand share, the lower the frequency levels required.
• **Brand loyalty**   An inverse relationship exists between loyalty and frequency levels, as the higher the loyalty, the lower the level of frequency required.
• **Purchase cycles**   Shorter purchasing cycles require higher frequency levels to maintain top-of-mind awareness.
• **Usage cycle**   Products used on a daily basis (or more) will quickly be used and need to be replaced. A higher level of frequency is desired.
• **Competitive share of voice**   Higher frequency levels are required when a high level of competitive noise exists and when the goal is to meet or beat competitors.
• **Target group**   The ability of the target group to learn and to retain messages has a direct effect on frequency.

Message or creative factors
• **Message complexity**   The more simple the message, the less frequency required.
• **Message uniqueness**   The more unique the message, the lower the frequency level required.
• **New versus continuing campaigns**   New campaigns require higher levels of frequency to register the message.
• **Image versus product sell**   Creating image requires higher levels of frequency than does a specific product sell.
• **Message variation**   Single messages require less frequency; a variety of messages requires more.
• **Wearout**   Higher frequency may lead to wearout. This effect must be tracked and used to evaluate frequency levels.
• **Advertising units**   Larger units of advertising require less frequency than smaller ones to get the message across.

Media factors
• **Clutter**   The more advertising that appears in the media used, the more the need for frequency to break through the clutter.
• **Editorial environment**   An ad that is consistent with the editorial environment will require lower levels of frequency to communicate.
• **Attentiveness**   The higher the level of attention achieved by the media vehicle, the less frequency is required. Low attention-getting media will require more repetitions.
• **Scheduling**   Continuous scheduling requires less frequency than does flighting or pulsing.
• **Number of media used**   The lower the number of media used, the lower the level of frequency required.
• **Repeat exposures**   Media that allow for more repeat exposures—for example, monthly magazines—require less frequency.

print media to communicate their messages effectively. Kodak and McDonald's, among others, have effectively used TV to create emotional appeals. In some situations, the media strategy to be pursued may be the driving force behind the creative strategy. Promotional Perspective 12–2 describes how media departments and creative departments are working more closely together, and how sometimes the media persons may dictate creative strategy.

Mood

Certain media are more or less effective in enhancing the creativity of a message because these media create a mood that carries over to the communication itself. For example, think about the mood created by the following magazines: *Gourmet, Skiing, Travel,* and *House Beautiful.* Each of these special-interest vehicles brings the reader into a particular mood. The promotion of fine wines, ski boots, luggage, and home products are enhanced by this mood. As a further example, think about the

Promotional Perspective 12–2

Media and Creative Team Up to Become More Effective

In many advertising agencies, the creative department is often credited with the relative successes and failures of advertising campaigns. After all, it is the "creatives" who are responsible for putting together such appeals as Nike's "Just do it," or Pepsi's "Uh-huh" campaigns. For years, members of the media department have taken a backseat to the creatives, seemingly just doing their jobs while their colleagues got all the credit. The typical scenario is that the creative staff dreams up the concept and the media planners determine the appropriate media. Well, in some agencies, this is no longer the case.

More and more, the creative department is turning to the media department to work together in developing more effective ads. At DDB Needham, the media department claims to be in the driver's seat, with creative following its guidelines. DDB Needham's "Personal Media Mapping" program, according to the agency, reverses the system by having media tell creative what it should develop based on the optimal media strategy it has derived.

The Personal Media Mapping program works something like this. A task force consisting of creatives and media planners meets early in the strategy phase to "map" out the media the client is most likely to employ. With a clear-cut vision of the media plan, creative comes up with a theme. Much discussion occurs. For example, planners on the Mobil Oil account determined their target audience rose at 6:15 A.M., read the newspapers, and then turned to their favorite radio station to listen to traffic reports for morning drive time. This knowledge led to radio spots as well as consecutive "Drive Your Engine Clean" ads in morning newspapers throughout the country. The Absolut vodka ads discussed earlier in Chapter 10 are another excellent example of the media-driven approach, as are ads run by Amtrak and Colgate-Palmolive.

This new team effort between media and creative is implemented in a variety of forms. In some agencies, task forces such as that described above are used. In others, the media and creative departments are located next to each other to stimulate interaction. In others, media persons are asked to sit in on creative strategy sessions and/or to comment on creative campaigns being proposed.

Regardless of the form such team work takes, the bottom line is that advertisers have learned that to reach the consumer, it is important to know their lifestyles, attitudes, and their media habits. They have also learned that the proliferation of new media have changed the way consumers make choices. And they know that to communicate effectively, they will have to use these media and develop specific creative appeals around them. As noted by Page Thompson, executive vice president and media director at DDB, "The consumer is in ultimate control."

In the advertising agencies, it would appear the media departments are gaining some control as well!

Source: David Kalish, "Media First," *Marketing and Media Decisions,* September 1990, pp. 24–25; Gary Levin, "Meddling in Creative More Welcome," *Advertising Age,* April 9, 1990, p. S-4.

---

different image that might be created for your product if you advertised it in these media:

New York Times versus *National Enquirer*

Architectural Digest versus *Reader's Digest*

A highly rated prime-time TV show versus an old rerun

As noted, the message may require a specific medium and a certain media vehicle to achieve its objectives. Likewise, certain media and vehicles have images that in turn may carry over to the perceptions of messages placed within them.

Flexibility   To have an effective media strategy, a degree of *flexibility* must be included. Because of the rapidly changing marketing environment, strategies may need to be modified. If the plan has not built in some flexibility, opportunities may be lost and/or the company may not be able to address adequately threats that develop. This need for flexibility may result from

1. ***Market opportunities*** Sometimes a market opportunity may arise that the advertiser wishes to take advantage of. For example, the development of a new advertising medium may offer an opportunity that was not previously available.

2. *Market threats* Occasions may arise in which internal or external factors may pose a threat to the firm, and a change in media strategy is dictated. For example, a competitor may alter its media strategy to gain an edge. Failure to respond to this challenge may create problems for the firm.

3. *Availability of media* Sometimes a desired medium (or vehicle) is not available to the marketer. This may occur because the medium does not reach a particular target segment or because there is no longer any time or space available in that medium. In the former instance, there are still some areas of this country where certain media do not reach. In the latter, while the media may be available, limited advertising time or space may have already been sold or cutoff dates for entry may have passed. Alternative vehicles or media may then have to be considered.

4. *Changes in media or media vehicles* A change in the medium or in a particular vehicle may necessitate change in the media strategy employed. For example, the advent of cable television opened a new opportunity for message delivery. Likewise, a drop in ratings or a change in editorial format may lead the advertiser to use different programs or print alternatives.

Each of these factors requires that the media strategy be developed with a degree of flexibility that allows the manager to adapt to specific market situations.

Budget Considerations

One of the more important decisions in the development of media strategy is that of cost estimating. The value of any strategy can be determined by how well it delivers the message to the audience with the lowest cost and the least amount of waste. We have already explored a number of other factors, such as reach, frequency, and availability, that affect this decision. Given these factors, it is the goal of the marketer to arrive at the optimal delivery by balancing cost with each of these. (Once again, The Denny's Plan demonstrates how this issue is addressed; see Appendix B, General Overview.) As the following discussion shows, understanding and using cost figures may not be as easy as it first seems.

Cost bases

Advertising and promotional costs can be categorized in two ways. The **absolute cost** of the medium or vehicle is the actual total cost required to place the message. For example, a full-page color ad in *Newsweek* magazine would cost approximately $115,000. **Relative cost** refers to the relationship between the price paid for advertising time or space and the size of the audience delivered and is used to compare media vehicles. Relative costs are important because the manager must try to optimize audience delivery within the constraints of the budget. Thus, given that a number of alternatives are available for delivering the message, an evaluation of the relative costs associated with these choices must be made. The way media costs are provided and problems in comparing these costs across media often make such evaluations difficult. Let us examine these in more detail.

Determining relative costs of media To evaluate alternatives, advertisers must compare the relative costs of media as well as vehicles within these media. Unfortunately, the broadcast, print, and out-of-home media do not always provide the same cost breakdowns, nor necessarily do vehicles within the print media. Following are the cost bases used.

1. *Cost per thousand* For years the magazine industry has provided cost breakdowns on the basis of **cost per thousand (CPM)** people reached. The formula used for making this computation is

$$\text{Cost per thousand (CPM)} = \frac{\text{Cost of ad space (absolute cost)} \times 1,000}{\text{Circulation}}$$

➤ *Exhibit 12–24*
Cost per thousand computations—*Time* versus *Newsweek*

	Time	*Newsweek*
Per page cost	$135,000	$115,000
Circulation	4.5 million	3.5 million
Calculation of CPM	$\dfrac{135,000 \times 1,000}{4,500,000}$	$\dfrac{115,000 \times 1,000}{3,500,000}$
CPM	$30.00	$32.85

➤ *Exhibit 12–25*
Comparison of cost per ratings point—"Married with Children" versus "Murder, She Wrote"

	"Married with Children"	"Murder, She Wrote"
Cost per spot ad	$5,100.00	$4,300.00
Rating	32	30
Reach (total persons)	560,000	525,000
Calculation	$5,100/32	$4,300/30
CPRP	$159	$143

Exhibit 12–24 provides an example of this computation for two alternative vehicles within the same medium—*Time* and *Newsweek*—and shows that (all other things being equal) *Time* is a more cost-effective buy, even though the absolute cost is higher. (We come back to "all other things being equal" in a moment.)

2. *Cost per ratings point* The broadcast media provide a different comparative cost figure, referred to as **cost per ratings point (CPRP)** (or cost per point, CPP), based on the following formula:

$$\text{Cost per ratings point (CPRP)} = \frac{\text{Cost of commercial time}}{\text{Program rating}}$$

An example of this calculation for a local market buy such as San Diego is shown in Exhibit 12–25, which indicates "Murder, She Wrote" would be more cost-effective.

3. *Milline rate* For newspapers, the cost-efficiency formula is based on the **milline rate,** which is the cost per line of space per million circulation. As shown in Exhibit 12–26, the cost of advertising in the *Pittsburgh Post Gazette* is significantly higher than that of the *Philadelphia Inquirer* (again, all things being equal).

As you can see, it is difficult to make the comparisons across various media. For example, what is the broadcast equivalent of cost per thousand, or the milline rate? In an attempt to provide some standardization of relative costing procedures, the broadcast and newspaper media have begun to provide their cost-efficiency measures in terms of cost/000 utilizing the following formulas:

$$\text{Television:} \quad \frac{\text{Cost of 1 unit of time} \times 1,000}{\text{Program rating}}$$

$$\text{Newspapers:} \quad \frac{\text{Cost of ad space} \times 1,000}{\text{Circulation}}$$

While the comparison of media on a cost per thousand basis is important, intermedia comparisons can be misleading if the numbers used are taken at face value. The ability of TV to provide both sight and sound, the longevity of magazines, and other characteristics of each medium make it difficult to make direct comparisons based on cost/000 alone. Thus, the media planner should use these numbers but must also consider the specific characteristics of each of the media and media vehicles in the decision.

➤ *Exhibit 12-26*
Milline rate comparisons—
Pittsburgh Post Gazette **versus**
Philadelphia Inquirer

	Pittsburgh Post Gazette	Philadelphia Inquirer
Cost per page	$13,000.00	$9,150.00
Cost per line	$7.20/line	$9.25/line
Circulation	168,500	984,000
Calculation	$\text{Milline rate} = \dfrac{\text{Line rate} \times 1,000,000}{\text{Circulation}}$	
Milline rate	$\dfrac{\$7.20 \times 1,000,000}{168,500}$ $\$42.73$	$\dfrac{\$9.25 \times 1,000,000}{984,000}$ $\$9.40$

Other factors must also be considered when evaluating the cost efficiency utilizing cost/000. The cost/000 figure may be either an *overestimation* or an *underestimation* of the actual cost efficiency. Consider, for example, a situation when a certain degree of waste coverage is inevitable. In this case, the circulation figure (using the *Time* magazine figures to demonstrate our point) exceeds the target market. As noted earlier, if these persons reached by this message are not potential buyers of the product, then having to pay to reach them results in a cost/000 figure that reflects a lower cost than is true, as shown in scenario A of Exhibit 12–27.

Given the figures in scenario A, it is necessary to use the potential reach to the target market—the destination sought—rather than the overall circulation figure, as those not in the target market are not of interest. In using the target market audience, you may find that a medium with a much higher cost/000 figure is a wiser buy if it is reaching more potential receivers.

CPM may also be an underestimate of cost efficiency. Magazine advertising space sellers have argued for years that because more than one person may read an issue, the actual reach is underestimated. They have argued for making comparisons using a **readers per copy** figure in calculating cost/000. This new cost-efficiency determination would include a **pass-along rate,** estimating the number of persons to whom the magazine has been "passed along to" as the true circulation figure. Referring to scenario B in Exhibit 12–27, you can see how this might lower the cost-efficiency estimates. Consider, as an example, a family in which the father, mother, and two teenage children all read each issue of *Time* magazine. Assume such families constituted 33 percent of *Time*'s circulation base. While the circulation figure includes only one magazine, in reality there are four potential exposures in these households, increasing the total reach to 9 million. As a result, the companies argue that magazines are being judged unfairly if cost/000 figures are used alone.

While the readers per copy figure seems to make sense intuitively, in reality it has the potential to be extremely inaccurate. The actual number of times the magazine changes hands is extremely difficult to determine. While the scenario of the family reading *Time* is easy enough to understand and estimate the readership, consider these occasions: How many persons in a fraternity read each issue of *Sports Illustrated* or *Playboy* that is delivered? How many members of a sorority or on a dorm floor read each issue of *Cosmopolitan* or *Self?* How many of either group read each issue of *Business Week?* While research is conducted to make these determinations, obtaining the estimates of pass along is very subjective, and using these figures to estimate reach is highly speculative. Thus, while these figures are regularly provided by the media, managers are very careful in using them directly. At the same time—and once again—the art (versus science) of media buying enters, for many magazines' managers may have a good idea that the reach is greater than the circulation figure provided. In these cases, the circulation figure is treated as a conservative estimate of reach.

In addition to the potential for over- and/or underestimation of cost efficiencies, CPMs are limited in that they describe only *quantitative* estimates of the value of media. Thus, while they may be good for comparing very similar vehicles (such as *Time* and *Newsweek*), they are less valuable in making intermedia comparisons. We have already noted some differences between the various media that prohibit making

> *Exhibit 12–27*
Cost per thousand estimates

Scenario A: Overestimation of Efficiency

Target market: 18–49
Magazine circulation: 4,500,000
Circulation to target market: 65% (2,925,000)
Cost per page: $135,000

$$CPM = \frac{\$135,000 \times 1,000}{4,500,000} = \$30.00$$

$$CPM \text{ (actual target audience)} = \frac{\$135,000 \times 1,000}{2,925,000} = \$46.15$$

Scenario B: Underestimation of Efficiency

Target market: all age groups, male and female
Magazine circulation: 4,500,000
Cost per page: $135,000
Pass-along rate: 3* (33% of households)

$$CPM \text{ (based on readers per copy):} = \frac{\text{Page cost} \times 1,000}{\text{Circulation} + 3(1,500,000)}$$

$$= \frac{\$135,000 \times 1,000}{9,000,000} = \$15.00$$

*Assuming pass along was valid.

direct comparisons, and in the next section, we discuss other characteristics of media that must be considered.

In looking back at what you have just read, you can see that the development of media strategy involves a number of factors that must be considered. As you can now see, Ostrow may not be that far off when he calls this process an art rather than a science, as so much of this process requires going beyond the numbers.

Evaluation and Follow-Up

All plans require some evaluation to assess their performance. The media plan is no exception.

In outlining the planning process, we stated that objectives are established and strategies are developed for the purpose of attaining them. Having implemented these strategies, marketers need to know whether or not they were successful. Measures of effectiveness must consider two factors: (1) How well did these strategies perform the media objectives established? and (2) How well did this media plan contribute to attaining the overall marketing and communications objectives? If the strategies employed were successful, they should be used in the future plans; if not, then some analysis as to why they were not should be undertaken.

The problem with measuring the effectiveness of the media strategies is probably obvious to you at this point. At the very outset of this chapter, we suggested the planning process was limited by problems with measurements and lack of consistent terminology (among others). While these problems limit the degree to which we can assess the relative effectiveness of various strategies, that does not mean it is impossible to make such determinations. Sometimes it is possible to show that a plan has worked. Even if the evaluation procedure is not 100 percent foolproof, it is better than no attempt.

The Use of Computers in Media Planning

Attempts to improve on the media buying process through the use of computers have received a great deal of attention. While advanced planning models have been around since at least 1963, for the most part, these models have met with limited success. Programs based on linear programming, simulation, and iteration have been adopted by only a relatively small number of agencies.

> *Exhibit 12–28*
BAR/LNA information is also available on the PC

COMPANY/BRAND $

LNA/ARBITRON MULTI-MEDIA SERVICE
January - December 1991

PARENT COMPANY/BRAND	CLASS CODE	YEAR-TO-DATE ADVERTISING DOLLARS (000)										
		10-MEDIA TOTAL	MAGAZINES	SUNDAY MAGAZINES	NEWSPAPERS	OUTDOOR	NETWORK TELEVISION	SPOT TELEVISION	SYNDICATED TELEVISION	CABLE TV NETWORKS	NETWORK RADIO	NATIONAL SPOT RADIO
FORCE E												
FORCE E SPORTING GOODS	G717	44.5	44.5	- -	- -	- -	- -	- -	- -	- -	- -	- -
FORCE FIN												
FORCE FIN DIVING EQUIPMENT	G419	47.5	47.5	- -	- -	- -	- -	- -	- -	- -	- -	- -
FORD AUTO DEALERS ASSOCIATION												
FORD DEALERS ASSN LEASING	T119-9	1,948.1	- -	- -	- -	- -	- -	1,884.3	- -	- -	- -	63.8
FORD DEALERS ASSN VARIOUS AUTOS	T119-9	84.4	- -	- -	84.4	- -	- -	- -	- -	- -	- -	- -
FORD DEALERS ASSOCIATION	T119-9	93,105.3	- -	- -	7,220.9	488.6	- -	82,089.3	- -	- -	- -	3,386.5
FORD DLRS ASSN PARTS & SERVICE	T119	499.1	- -	- -	- -	- -	- -	499.1	- -	- -	- -	- -
FORD MOTOR CO DEALERS ASSN	T119-9	321.4	- -	- -	- -	- -	- -	305.7	- -	- -	- -	15.7
FORD-LINCOLN-MERCURY DEALERS ASSN	T119-9	19.2	- -	- -	19.2	- -	- -	- -	- -	- -	- -	- -
LINCOLN DEALERS ASSOCIATION	T119-9	10.9	- -	- -	- -	- -	- -	- -	- -	- -	- -	10.9
LINCOLN-MERCURY DEALERS ASSN CAPRI	T119-9	13.5	- -	- -	- -	13.5	- -	- -	- -	- -	- -	- -
LINCOLN-MERCURY DEALERS ASSN LEASING	T119-9	1,150.6	- -	- -	38.3	- -	- -	904.6	- -	- -	- -	207.7
LINCOLN-MERCURY DEALERS ASSN TOWN CAR	T119-9	0.9	- -	- -	- -	0.9	- -	- -	- -	- -	- -	- -
LINCOLN-MERCURY DEALERS ASSN TRACER	T119-9	1.8	- -	- -	- -	1.8	- -	- -	- -	- -	- -	- -
LINCOLN-MERCURY DEALERS ASSOCIATION	T119-9	28,820.0	- -	- -	4,752.5	302.0	- -	22,595.5	- -	- -	- -	1,170.0
COMPANY TOTAL	T119-9	126,055.2	- -	- -	12,115.3	806.8	- -	108,278.5	- -	- -	- -	4,854.6

Computers have been employed, however, in the automation of each of the four steps involved in planning and strategy development. While the art of media strategy has not been mechanized, advances in the quantitative side have significantly improved the managers' decision-making capabilities while also saving substantial time and effort. Let us briefly examine some of these methods.

The Use of Computers in Market Analysis

Earlier in this chapter, we discussed the use of Simmons and MRI data and provided examples of each. In Chapter 5, we reviewed the information provided in PRIZM, VALS, VISION, and other such systems. All these data have been computerized and are available for access either through an interactive system or on the agency's own PC. For example, MRI offers its clients interactive capabilities with its mainframe or its MEMRI software data base that can be used on a personal computer for cross tabulation of media and demographic data, reach and frequency estimates, and cost rankings, in addition to numerous other applications. The interactive capabilities also allow for an interface with PRIZM, VALS, and VISION data. Simmons also allows access to PRIZM, ACORN, VALS, and others.

Other market analysis programs are also available. Programs such as ClusterPlus and Market America include demographic, geographic, psychographic, and product and media use information that can be used for media planning. In addition, census tract information and socioeconomic data are accessible. These systems are linked to Arbitron and Nielsen local market data for use in scheduling and targeting to specific groups.

In addition to customer analyses, other information used in the analysis stage is available. Exhibit 12–28 is an example of the BAR/LNA data reviewed earlier that are also available through computer access.

The analyses of these data would assist in determining which markets and which groups should be targeted for advertising and promotions. By using this information, along with other data, the marketer can also readily define media objectives.

The Use of Computers in Media Strategy Development

In the strategy development phase, we discussed the need to make decisions regarding coverage, scheduling, costs, and the trade-off between reach and frequency, among others. Perhaps one of the primary benefits to media planners to accrue from computers is the development of programs to assist in the development of these strategies. While there are far too many of these programs to review in this text, we would like to provide you with a very small sampling just to demonstrate our point.

Reach and frequency analyses on the computer

Exhibit 12–29 demonstrates one example of how software programs are being used to determine reach and frequency levels and are also assisting in the decision as to which alternative is best. As shown in Exhibit 12–29, various media mixes for television and radio at different TRPs are computed, with reach and frequency estimates, the number of persons reached three or more times, and the costs provided. The program also has determined—based on the combination of reach, fre-

➤ *Exhibit 12–29*
San Diego Trust & Savings Bank
reach and frequency analyses

	Product Message		
Media Mix (A 25–54)	**Reach Frequency (% / X)**	**3+ Level (%)**	**1st Quarter Weekly Cost**
TV (125)	84 / 4.5	51	$21,480
TV (125) R (125)	91 / 8.2	71	29,450
TV (125) R (150)*	92 / 9.0	73	31,045
TV (150)	86 / 5.2	57	25,660
TV (150) R (125)	92 / 9.0	73	33,625
TV (150) R (150)	92 / 9.8	74	35,220
TV (175)	89 / 5.9	61	29,930
TV (175) R (125)	93 / 9.7	75	37,900
TV (175) R (150)	93 / 10.5	76	39,490
TV (200)	90 / 6.7	65	34,255
TV (200) R (125)	93 / 10.5	76	42,225
TV (200) R (150)	93 / 11.3	78	43,820

(Based on a three-week flight.)
*Recommended.

quency levels, frequency of exposures three or more times, and cost/000 — that a mix of 125 TRPs on television and 150 TRPs on radio would result in the best buy. Keep in mind that this recommendation considers only the most efficient combination of these factors and does not allow for the "art" of media buying.

The preceding is just one of the many examples of how computer programs — in this case, the Telmar system — are being used in the media strategy development phase.

Other computer-based media planning programs are available, including:

- **Manas** — calculates cost and audience estimates for various media plans, accessing ratings data.
- **IMS** — planning system linked to MRI, SMRB, and SRDS helps planners rank different media options according to rates and audience delivery.
- **Telmar** — allows planners to analyze media data, devise media plans, and create flowcharts, and is linked to major syndicated data services.
- **Media Management Plus** — ranks stations in each market according to delivery potential and costs, and calculates projected ratings.
- **AdWare** — provides Arbitron and Nielsen information, calculates media costs, projects GRPs, etc.
- **Tapscan** — uses syndicated data useful in media planning.
- **TV Conquest** — combines Nielsen, Donnelley, and Simmons data to provide demographic, product usage, and ratings information.

The above are just a sampling of some of the many computer-based media planning programs available. Unfortunately, space does not allow for a complete list or a more in-depth description.

The one area in which computers have not yet provided a direct benefit is in the evaluation stage of the media plan. While these programs do generate what they consider to be optimal solutions to the use of TRPs, GRPs, and media mixes and allow for pre- and postbuy analyses, the true test is what happens when the plan is implemented. We reserve our discussion of the evaluation process until the chapter on measuring effectiveness.

Characteristics of Media

To this point, we have discussed the elements involved in the development of media strategy. One of the most basic elements in this process was said to be the matching of media to markets. In the following chapters, you will see that each medium has its own characteristics that make it more or less advantageous for the attainment of

Media	Advantages	Disadvantages
Television	Mass coverage High reach Impact of sight, sound, and motion High prestige Low cost per exposure Attention getting Favorable image	Low selectivity Short message life High absolute cost High production costs Clutter
Radio	Local coverage Low cost High frequency Flexible Low production costs Well-segmented audiences	Audio only Clutter Low attention getting Fleeting message
Magazines	Segmentation potential Quality reproduction High information content Longevity Multiple readers	Long lead time for ad placement Visual only Lack of flexibility
Newspapers	High coverage Low cost Short lead time for placing ads Ads can be placed in interest sections Timely (current ads) Reader controls exposure Can be used for coupons	Short life Clutter Low attention-getting capabilities Poor reproduction quality Selective reader exposure
Outdoor	Location specific High repetition Easily noticed	Short exposure time requires short ad Poor image Local restrictions
Direct mail	High selectivity Reader controls exposure High information content Opportunities for repeat exposures	High cost/contact Poor image (junk mail) Clutter

specific objectives. Before examining these media specifically, it is helpful to establish an overall framework in which some of these characteristics are defined and compared.

Exhibit 12–30 represents an overall comparison of media and some of the characteristics by which they are evaluated. This is a very general comparison, and an analysis of the various media options must be undertaken for each situation. However, it provides you with a good starting point from which to make comparisons. The following chapters in this text discuss in more depth the characteristics of various media and their relative advantages and disadvantages with respect to accomplishing advertising and promotions objectives.

SUMMARY

This chapter has presented an overview of the determination of media objectives, development of the media strategy, and the formalization of these in the form of a media plan. In addition, sources of media information, characteristics of media, and an actual plan were provided.

The media strategy must be designed to supplement and support the overall marketing and communications objectives. As such, the objectives of this plan are designed to provide delivery of the message the program has developed.

The basic task involved in the development of media strategy is to determine the best matching of media to the target market, given the constraints of the budget. The media planner attempts to balance reach and frequency and to deliver the message to the intended audience with a minimum of waste circulation. At the same time, a number of additional factors must be considered, all of which affect the media decision.

Media strategy development has been referred to by one well-known practitioner as an art rather than a science. The reason for this assessment was based on the fact that while much quantitative data are available to the planner, there is also a reliance on creativity and/or nonquantifiable factors.

This chapter was designed to provide you with an overview of the media planning and strategy development process. A number of factors were considered, including the development of a proper media mix, determining target market and geographic coverage, scheduling, balancing reach and frequency, and creative aspects. In addition, budget considerations and the need for flexibility in the schedule were discussed. Finally, the use of computers in the media planning process was considered.

KEY TERMS

media planning
media plan
media objectives
media strategies
medium
media vehicle
reach
coverage
frequency
sweeps periods
index number
Survey of Buying Power
   Index

Brand Development
   Index (BDI)
Category Development
   Index (CDI)
waste coverage
geographical weighting
continuity
flighting
pulsing
unduplicated reach
duplicated reach
program rating
gross ratings points
   (GRPs)

target ratings points
   (TRPs)
effective reach
average frequency
absolute cost
relative cost
cost per thousand (CPM)
cost per ratings point
   (CPRP)
milline rate
readers per copy
pass-along rate

DISCUSSION QUESTIONS

1. Explain how advertisers use index numbers provided by SMRB and MRI. How is this number derived?
2. What is a brand development index? A category development index? How can marketers use these indices?
3. What is meant by waste coverage? Is there ever a time when high waste coverage may be justified? Cite examples.
4. What is a gross ratings point? Explain why GRPs may be misleading.
5. Describe the difference between absolute cost and relative cost. Which is most relevant to the media buyer?
6. What is meant by readers per copy? How is this figure derived? What are some of the problems associated with this number?
7. Discuss the market situation being described by: high BDI and high CDI; high BDI and low CDI; low BDI and high CDI; and low BDI and low CDI.
8. Describe some of the bases used for determining relative media costs. Discuss some of the problems inherent in using these to make cross-media comparisons.
9. Obtain cost, circulation, and ratings information for some of your local media. Using the relative cost formulas provided in the text, compare the efficiencies of each.
10. Explain the difference between GRPs and TRPs. Many marketers argue that only TRPs are relevant. Explain why they might make this argument.

Appendixes
to Chapter 12

Appendix A   Sources of Media Information

Cross-reference guide to advertising media sources

	General Information	Competitive Activities	Market Information (geographic)	Audience Information (target groups)	Advertising Rates
Nonmedia information (general marketing)	1, 11, 18, 19, 26, 28, 29	1, 23	11, 12, 18, 19, 21, 24, 26, 30	18, 19, 26	
Multimedia or intermedia	1, 18, 19, 26	1, 15	21	2, 14, 31	2
Daily newspapers		17		5, 18, 19, 25, 26	2, 30
Weekly newspapers					30
Consumer magazines	16	15		18, 19, 26	2, 30
Farm publications				5, 32	2, 30
Business publications			7, 9	7, 32	2, 30
Network television		8, 15		4, 18, 19, 20, 26	2
Spot television		8, 15		4, 18, 19, 20, 26	2, 30
Network radio		8, 22		13, 18, 19, 20, 26, 27	2
Spot radio		22		4, 6, 13, 20, 26	2, 30
Direct mail					2, 30
Outdoor		15			2, 10
Transit					2

1. *Advertising Age*
2. Advertising agency media estimating guides
3. American Business Press, Inc. (ABP)
4. Arbitron Ratings Company
5. Audit Bureau of Circulations (ABC)
6. Birch Radio, Inc.
7. Business/Professional Advertising Association (B/PAA) Media Data
8. Broadcast Advertisers Reports (BAR)
9. Business Publications Audit of Circulation (BPA)
10. *Buyer's Guide to Outdoor Advertising*
11. *State and Metropolitan Area Data Book*
12. *Editor & Publisher Market Guide*
13. C. E. Hooper, Inc., "Hooperatings"
14. Interactive Market Systems (IMS)
15. Leading National Advertisers (LNA), Inc.
16. Magazine Publishers Association, Inc. (MPA)
17. Media Records, Inc.
18. Mediamark Research, Inc. (MRI)
19. Mendelsohn Media Research, Inc. (MMR)
20. Nielsen Media Research Company
21. PRIZM
22. Radio Expenditure Reports
23. SAMI Burke, Inc.
24. *Sales and Marketing Management Survey of Buying Power*
25. Scarborough's Newspaper Ratings Company, Ltd.
26. Simmons Market Research Bureau: *Study of Media and Markets*
27. Sindlinger Report
28. *Standard Directory of Advertisers*
29. *Standard Directory of Advertising Agencies*
30. Standard Rate and Data Service
31. Telmar
32. Verified Audit Circulation Corporation (VAC)

Source: Arnold M. Bantam, Donald W. Jugenheimer, and Peter B. Turk, *Advertising Media Sourcebook,* 3rd ed. (Lincolnwood, Ill.: NTC Business Books, 1989), pp. 8–9.

Appendix B Denny's Restaurants 1991 Media Plan*

General Overview

Denny's media plan reflects a promotion-driven marketing strategy and business development that is very geographically skewed. By focusing the available budget behind promotions in our most important geography, we believe advertising awareness levels that are well ahead of our share of voice in this heavily advertised category are achieved.

In light of the numerous promotions to be supported over the 1991 calendar year, it has been decided to focus on 28 core markets, representing 40 percent of total U.S. households and 75 percent of total sales, through the use of spot television primarily. Although national media will be considered as a base to provide some form of national presence, budget limitations prohibit any extensive use of these media vehicles; therefore, the top 28 sales markets ranked on sales volume and BDI will receive the majority of support.

The advertising programs scheduled for 1991 fall into two categories:

• Long-term equity building programs.
• Short-term price/product programs.

Both types of programs will run in all Denny's Restaurants nationally so the media will include some form of national presence with heavier emphasis in key sales markets.

Overall Parameters

• Advertising period: calendar year 1991.
• Budget: $21.2 million.
• Geography: primary—28 core markets (40 percent of United States/75 percent of Sales); secondary—National.
• Target audience: Adults 25–54 (system promotions) and kids 2–10 (Flintstones).

Long-Term Equity Programs

• Birthday.
• Grand Slam (menu introduction).
• Late Night.
• Flintstones.

General objective: Increase guest counts/customer base over a longer term period.

Birthday

In order to motivate people to come to Denny's, this program offers them a free meal on their birthday, which they can choose from the special "Birthday Menu" between breakfast, lunch, or dinner. The purpose of the promotion is not only to motivate people by giving them the "free meal," but it is also directed at increasing repeat business by them plus any potential customers they may bring.

Objective

Promote trial and repeat business via the offer of a free birthday meal.

Strategies/tactics

Use network radio over a 12-month period, recognizing:

• Cost efficiency versus television, thereby providing awareness and continuity throughout the entire year.

*Courtesy of Denny's Inc.

- Schedule flights around the beginning and end of each month to increase awareness around the new "Birthday Month."
- Ability to provide national support.

Target

Adults 25–54.

Grand Slam (Menu Introduction)

The Denny's "Grand Slam" breakfast has met considerable success since its launch and has always been one of the most popular entrees on the Denny's menu. For 1992, the "Grand Slam" concept will be expanded beyond the breakfast daypart to offer nine great new Grand Slam entrees for breakfast, lunch, and dinner.

Objective

Increase trial and repeat business via the introduction of new "Grand Slam" menu items. In addition, increase lunch and dinner business along with breakfast.

Strategies

- Use spot TV in the core 28 markets to introduce the new Grand Slam menu over three different phases/support periods:
  Phase I (introduction): 500 TRPs/4 weeks.
  Phase II: 400 TRPs/3 weeks.
  Phase III: 400 TRPs/3 weeks.
- Spot TV will provide support throughout baseball season to take advantage of the "Grand Slam" theme/tie-in with Major League Baseball.
- Use network radio (general/MLB-CBS package) for continuity throughout promotion period (baseball season):
  Cost efficient.
  Extends reach of overall campaign.
  Excellent advertising environment (CBS/MLB package).

Target

Adults 25–54.

Late Night

The Late Night promotion is Denny's marketing effort to give customers something really different from other restaurants. Since Denny's is open 24 hours a day, through advertising, promotions, in-store merchandising, and a special menu with various kinds of dishes, they offer "night owls" a better way to stay awake in a warm, comfortable, and friendly place.

Objective

To increase guest counts during the graveyard daypart. Being a 24-hour operation, Denny's has the advantage and opportunity of increasing business during this daypart.

Strategies

Use spot radio in all top sales markets to reach "night owls" owing to its:

- Ability to deliver the target without waste.
- Low out-of-pocket cost (versus television).
- Merchandising/promotional opportunities.

Executional considerations:

- Station selection: Schedules to be placed on top ranking overnight stations (Monday–Sunday; 11 P.M.–5 A.M.).
- It is recommended to purchase schedules on at least 3 stations and approximately 17 TRPs per market per week. Actual total number of spots per market per week are in the range of 40–90 but may vary depending on available ratings.
- Available research has indicated the overnight audience (11 P.M. to 5 A.M.) is approximately 10 percent that of the 6 A.M. to 7 P.M. audience. Consequently, ratings are roughly 10 percent of daytime. 17 TRPs per week in overnight should deliver the equivalent level of commercial units as the 6 A.M. to 7 P.M. time period, which typically averages roughly 150 TRPs per week.
- Commercial unit: 100 percent 60-second spots.

Target

Adults 25–54 (primary): adults 18–34 (secondary).

Flintstones

Directed to families with kids between 2 and 10 years old, this promotion attracts young families with kids by offering special Flintstones premiums. Every two months, the special premiums will be available in the restaurants (e.g., Dino Racers, Flintstone's vehicles, etc.). In addition, a special Flintstones Kid Menu has been created offering more "personable" service and ultimately increasing interest in repeat visits.

Objectives

Increase guest counts in the segment of families with kids 10 years old and under through the use of Flintstone's premiums/merchandise available to kids 2–10.

Strategies/tactics

- Use spot TV over three flights (two weeks per flight) promoting three different kids premiums in 25 markets, recognizing:
    Broad reach against target.
    High impact of television/showcase opportunity.
- Use a daypart mix of: 50 percent kids weekend/50 percent kids other (either early morning or kids afternoon, depending on market-by-market availabilities and efficiencies).
- Use national cable over three flights (two weeks per flight) to supplement the spot TV buy, recognizing:
    Opportunity for alternative programs/dayparts targeted to kids.
    Ability to provide "national" support efficiently (covers all Denny's markets).
    Low out-of-pocket cost for national support.
    Ability to extend reach against kids (basic cable share increasing versus network affiliate shares declining).
- Use top cable kids' programming on:
    TBS/TNT.
    USA.
    Nickelodeon.
    Family Channel.

Target

Kids 2–10.

Short-Term Price/ Product Promotions

Grand Slam (Baseball Cards)

General objective is to increase guest counts/sales in a more immediate, shorter-term period.

This six-week promotion is scheduled to enhance the Grand Slam menu introduction, which will be promoted during the baseball season. It consists of collectible holographic baseball cards that people can get when they order one of the special meal items on the "Grand Slam" menu. There are 26 different cards featuring a "grand slam" slugger from each Major League team.

Objective

To stimulate trial and repeat business for the Grand Slam meal concept, via the distribution of a collectible series of hologrammed baseball cards (6 million for 26 teams) distributed within the restaurants over a six-week period.

Strategies

- Target the "baseball fan" defined primarily as men 18–49.
- Utilize baseball broadcasts as the primary vehicle to reach the defined target recognizing that:
    The one behavior that separates the "core fan" from the casual fan or the general population is the need to tune in live broadcasts of the seasonal games.
    "In game" ratings invariably exceed support programming (e.g., Pre/post game, talk, anthology shows).
    Aggressive reach/frequency goals can be attained in this manner.
- Focus on local/regional versus national efforts, recognizing that baseball interest has always been "home team" oriented. Local broadcasts:
    Are higher rated than national broadcasts.
    Benefit from "the flavor" of the home team announcers (with the attendant possibilities of high awareness "value-added" opportunities).
    Can be structured to go beyond flagship stations, thereby achieving virtual national coverage.
- Utilize special "opportunistic" vehicles as available, as a means:
    To stimulate immediate broad reach relatively "early" in the promotion period.
    To "showcase" and enhance impact of the promotion.
- Utilize sports print media that collectively can provide:
    Alternative cost effective means to reach and impact the fan.
    An opportunity to explain the promotion in greater detail.
    An opportunity to reach the baseball card collector, an important subsegment within the target, and estimated to number between 7 and 10 million people (including children and teens not addressed in the adult target definitions).
    In conjunction with broadcast, an opportunity to generate a sense of "preemptive presence" that can enhance impact and sense of importance of the promotion to the baseball fan.

Target

Men 18–49/the "baseball fan."

Holiday Mug

To stimulate business during the holiday season, special "Holiday" coffee mugs will be available in all restaurants during December. They can be used for personal use and also as gifts or stocking stuffers during the holidays.

Objective

Increase sales/guest counts via the availability of a special "holiday" coffee mug.

Strategy

- Use spot television in select key sales markets, recognizing
  Visual impact, showcase opportunity.
  Budget limitations prohibit any sort of national effort.

Target

Adults 25–54.

Denny's Restaurants 1991 media flowchart

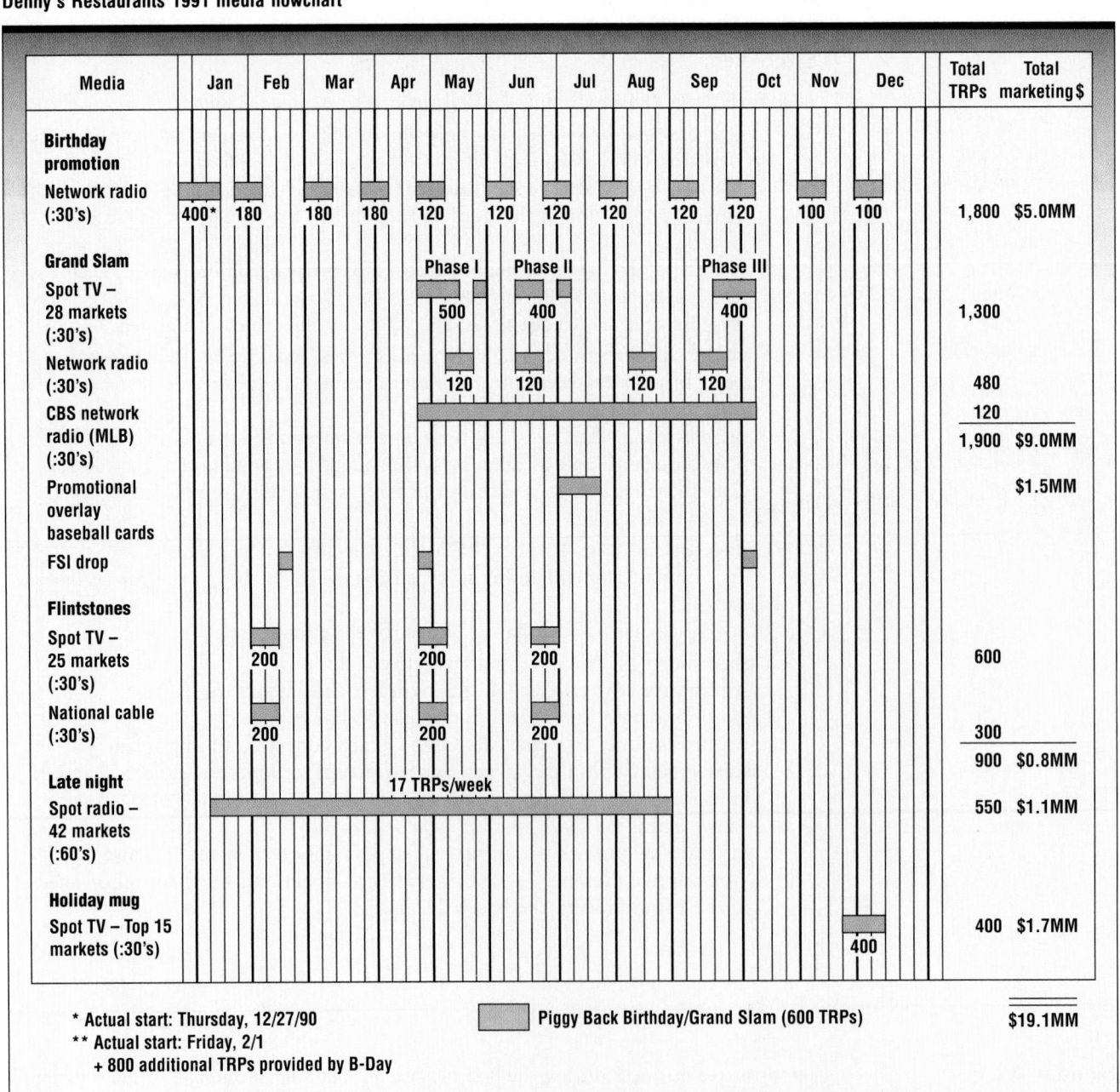

Media	Jan	Feb	Mar	Apr	May	Jun	Jul	Aug	Sep	Oct	Nov	Dec	Total TRPs	Total marketing$
Birthday promotion Network radio (:30's)	400*	180	180	180	120	120	120	120	120	120	100	100	1,800	$5.0MM
Grand Slam Spot TV – 28 markets (:30's)					Phase I 500	Phase II 400			Phase III 400				1,300	
Network radio (:30's)					120	120		120	120				480	
CBS network radio (MLB) (:30's)													120	
													1,900	$9.0MM
Promotional overlay baseball cards														$1.5MM
FSI drop														
Flintstones Spot TV – 25 markets (:30's)		200			200	200							600	
National cable (:30's)		200			200	200							300	
													900	$0.8MM
Late night Spot radio – 42 markets (:60's)				17 TRPs/week									550	$1.1MM
Holiday mug Spot TV – Top 15 markets (:30's)												400	400	$1.7MM

* Actual start: Thursday, 12/27/90
** Actual start: Friday, 2/1
  + 800 additional TRPs provided by B-Day

▨ Piggy Back Birthday/Grand Slam (600 TRPs)

$19.1MM

Denny's Restaurants 1991 Grand Slam promotion

Media	April	May	June	July	August	September	October	Total TRPs	Total cost $
Grand Slam									
- menu introduction		Phase I	Phase II			Phase III			
Spot TV (:30's)		500	400			400		1,300	
Network radio (:30's)		120	120 120 120		120 120	120 120 120		1,080	
CBS network radio (MLB) (:30's)								120	
								2,500	$9.0MM
- Baseball cards								Total units	
Synd. TV (MLB)								9	
CBS network TV All Star Game								1	
Regional cable fill								TBD	
ESPN MLB (Sun)								6	
Regional local/radio								14	
Print								–	

▦ Denotes split copy (Birthday/Grand Slam) $1.5MM

▦ Baseball promotion copy - 16 units total   Combined total: $10.5MM

chapter 13

Evaluation of Broadcast Media

chapter objectives

➤ To examine the structure of the television and radio industries and the role of each medium in the advertising program.

➤ To examine the advantages and limitations of television and radio as advertising media.

➤ To examine the various issues, concepts, and considerations of relevance in using television and radio in the media program.

➤ To explain how advertising time is purchased for the broadcast media, how audiences are measured, and how rates are determined.

➤ To consider future trends and developments regarding television and radio and how they will influence the use of these media in advertising.

Advertising's Biggest Showcase

Americans love their football, and Super Bowl Sunday has become an unofficial national holiday. The game usually draws the largest TV audience of the year. Its appeal spans various age groups, sexes, and regions of the country. The Super Bowl is even developing a global appeal as it is now seen in more than 50 countries. While most consumers think about the Super Bowl as the biggest football game of the year, many marketers view it as the premier marketing event as well. During the past decade, the Super Bowl has become the biggest and most important advertising showcase, particularly for companies with deep pockets and a willingness to spend more than $800,000 for a 30-second spot.

The Super Bowl began to become a showcase for new commercials in 1984 when Apple ran its highly publicized "1984" spot to introduce the Macintosh personal computer (discussed in Promotional Perspective 1–1). Since then, many advertisers have used the game to introduce new campaigns or show off their agency's creative talents. For example, Coca-Cola used the 1989 game to sponsor a segment of the halftime show and run ads for diet Coke in 3-D. This marked the first time 3-D commercials had been run on television. For each of the past four years, Anheuser-Busch has spent over $1 million to produce special "Bud Bowl" commercials featuring teams of helmeted Budweiser bottles battling Bud Light

bottles in an animated football game. Pepsi and Nike have also used the Super Bowl to unveil new commercials including the latter's popular "Hare Jordan" spot featuring Michael Jordan and Bugs Bunny.

Despite the high cost of advertising on the Super Bowl, many advertisers think it is well worth the money. They point out the Super Bowl is usually the best-watched program of the year as more than 110 million viewers watch the game. Many advertisers also believe the Super Bowl is one occasion where as much attention is paid to the commercials as to the program. Many consumers actually wait to see the new ads that often debut during the telecast, and the spots often receive a considerable amount of hype and publicity. Studies have also shown that recall of the average Super Bowl spot is nearly two and a half to three times higher than the recall of the average prime-time commercial. Moreover, some advertisers think that advertising on the Super Bowl is an indication the company has made it to the "big leagues," which will command respect from customers and competitors. Some companies are also turning their Super Bowl advertising into events that transcend the game. For example, for the 1992 Super Bowl, Anheuser-Busch developed an integrated promotional program around its Bud Bowl ads that included point-of-purchase displays and game cards that gave

(continued)
consumers the opportunity to play along and win a $1 million grand prize.

Not all advertisers believe, however, the Super Bowl is a super media buy. Many think the costs of advertising time has gotten too expensive, and competition among advertisers to outdo one another has made the clutter level during the game too high. Moreover, many media people believe advertising on the game can be a risky proposition since many people attend Super Bowl parties to watch the game. During the commercial breaks, they may be socializing, discussing the game, or getting something to eat or drink. There is also always the possibility the game will be a blowout, which means much of the audience may be tuned out by the third or fourth quarter.

Some advertisers think the large amount of money required to advertise on the Super Bowl can go a lot further and buy many more spots during other programs or time periods. One such advertiser is Frito-Lay, which advertised during the big game for several years. However, rather than advertising on the 1992 Super Bowl, the company sponsored counterprogramming during halftime of the game on a special live episode of Fox Broadcasting's "In Living Color" show. A Frito-Lay spokesman noted the company was able to sponsor the entire 30-minute show for about the same amount of money it would have cost to air two Super Bowl spots. A special minute-by-minute analysis of Nielsen ratings showed the counterprogramming move was effective as ratings of the Super Bowl halftime show declined while those for the "Doritos Zaptime/In Living Color Super Halftime Party" increased.

As the cost of advertising time on the Super Bowl continues to escalate, advertisers may take a hard look at whether it is really an efficient media buy. However, the American consumers' passion for football and the Super Bowl is likely to continue and advertisers who can afford it will continue to be a part of advertising's biggest showcase.

Source: "Super Bowl XXVII Fact Book," Adweek's Marketing Week, January 13,1992, pp. 19–25; Bruce Horowitz, "Many Advertiser's Shelve Super Bowl Game Plans," Los Angeles Times, January 14, 1992, pp. D1, 3; "Fox Halftime Ploy Works," Advertising Age, March 3, 1992, p. 20; and Joanne Lipman, "Super Bowl Is Advertisers' Biggest Turf," The Wall Street Journal, January 8, 1990, p. B1.

A major reason the Super Bowl is advertising's biggest showcase is because it appears on America's primary form of entertainment—the television set. TV has virtually saturated households throughout the United States, and many other countries as well, and has become a mainstay in the lives of most people. The average American household watches nearly seven hours of TV a day, and the "tube" has become the predominant source of news and entertainment for many people. Seventy-five percent of the TV households in the United States have a videocassette recorder (VCR), and many people have turned portions of their homes into entertainment centers with large-screen TV sets, VCRs, and stereos. On any given evening between the prime-time hours of 8 and 11 P.M., more than 90 million people are watching TV. Popular shows such as "Roseanne" or "Cheers" may have more than 40 million viewers. The large numbers of people who watch television during the evening, as well as other times of the day, are important to the TV networks and stations because they can sell time on these programs to marketers interested in reaching the viewing audience with their advertising messages. Moreover, the characteristics of TV that make it a great medium for news and entertainment also provide advertisers with an opportunity for making creative ads that can have a strong impact on consumers.

Radio is also an integral part of our lives. Many of us wake up to clock radios in the morning and rely on radio programs to inform and/or entertain us while we drive to work or school. For many people, radio is a constant companion in their cars, at home, or even at work. The average American listens to the radio more than three hours each day.[1] Like TV viewers, radio listeners are an important audience for marketers.

In this chapter, we examine the broadcast media of TV and radio, including the general characteristics of each as well as their specific advantages and disadvantages. We examine how advertisers use television and radio as part of their advertising and media strategies, how they buy TV and radio time, and how audiences are measured and evaluated for each medium. We also examine the various factors that have changed the role of television and radio as advertising media and consider future developments that will continue to do so.

An Overview of Radio and Television

Radio and television are the most pervasive media in the lives of most American consumers. Think for a moment about the number of TV sets and radios in your home. Over 98 percent of the 93.1 million U.S. households own a TV set, and 65 percent own two or more sets. Ninety-nine percent of all television homes have color TV sets (Exhibit 13–1). The typical person spends an average of three and a half hours a day watching television.[2] Radio is clearly the most ubiquitous of all the media as the number of radio sets in the United States is estimated to total 558 million, or over five per household.[3] This number includes the 180 million radios in cars, trucks, and vans. Obviously, advertisers recognize the value of the broadcast media for reaching the consumer, as more than $27 billion was spent on TV advertising and over $8.4 billion on radio in 1991.[4]

➤ *Exhibit 13–1* **The growth of television ownership in the United States**

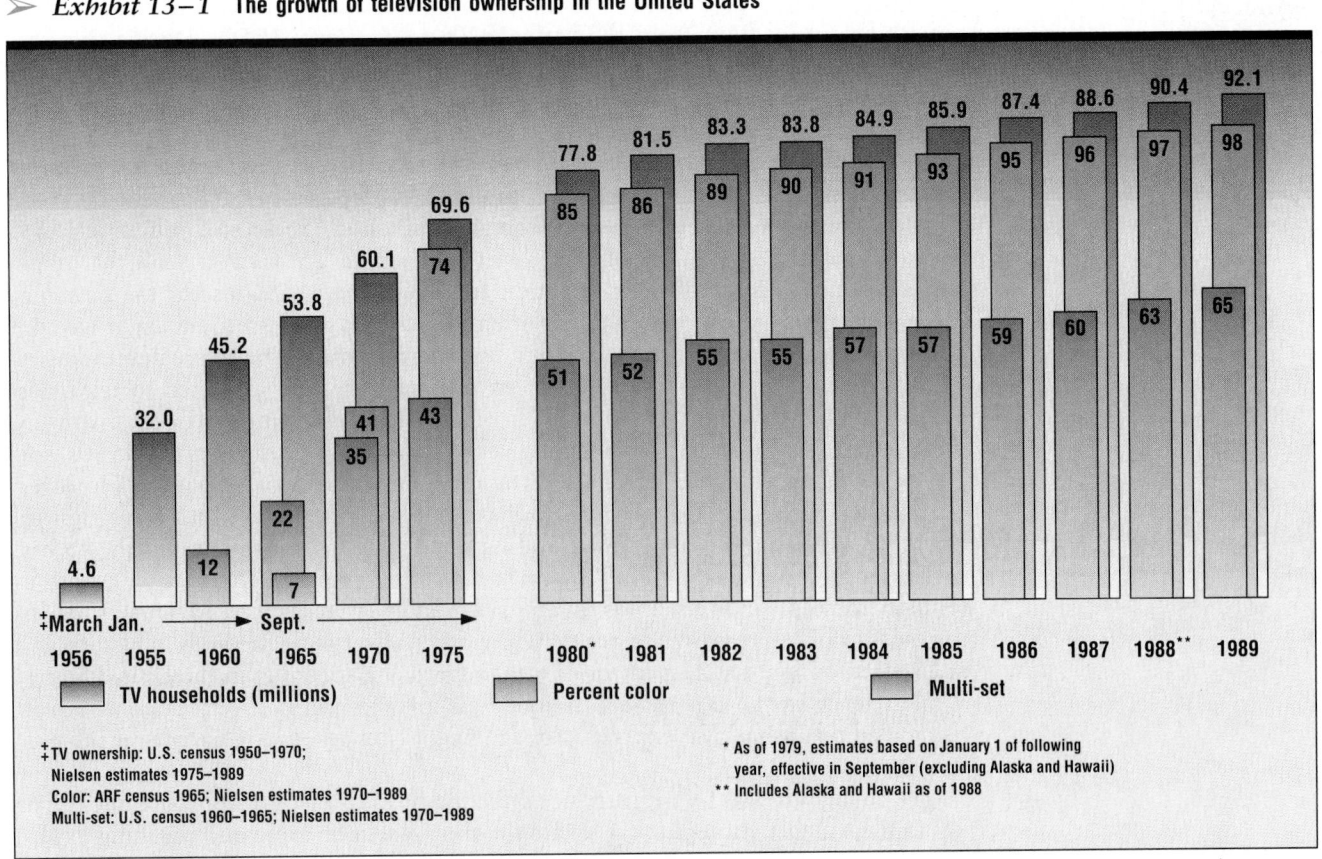

Radio and television have certain similarities as broadcast media. Unlike the print media, radio and television are time- rather than space-oriented and are sold in segments ranging from a few seconds to as much as an hour. Both radio and TV programming are organized similarly. Some stations belong to a network or nation-wide system of programming, and others are independent producers and buyers of programming. Time on both media is sold on a network or nationwide basis as well as on a local market basis. Radio and TV both rely on the public airways to broadcast their programs, must be licensed to operate, and are regulated by the Federal Communications Commission (FCC). Both media use similar methods for gathering information on the size and composition of their audiences. Finally, both are often referred to as low- or passive-involvement media since consumers can pick up messages and be influenced by either radio or TV commercials without actively attending to them. Think about how often you turn on the radio or even the television for "background" entertainment while doing something else (such as reading this book).

While radio and television do share these characteristics, as advertising media vehicles they differ in many ways. Because radio offers only an audio message, it is more limited in its ability to communicate and present the advertiser's appeal. Radio is also a relatively low-cost medium and more adaptable to changing conditions and situations but lacks the impact and prestige of television. However, radio and TV often compete with one another for advertisers' media dollars. And the competition between the two is becoming greater with the availability of low-cost local cable channels in many areas.

The Changing Role of the Broadcast Media

For nearly 70 years, the **broadcast media** of radio and television have been a dominant part of the lives of most Americans. Radio was a major news, information, and entertainment medium from the early 1920s to the early 1950s. During this era, advertisers embraced radio by developing and placing advertising messages for the new medium and also by creating and producing programs that would attract audiences and serve as a vehicle for their commercials. The golden era of radio came to an abrupt halt, however, beginning in 1950 with the introduction of television as a national medium. As can be seen in Exhibit 13–1, the number of households in the United States with TV sets increased from 4.6 million in 1950 to 32 million in 1955.

Radio stations saw many of their listeners become TV viewers, and the major networks turned most of their attention to developing programs for the new medium. Advertisers began turning their attention to TV as well, recognizing it was the best medium for reaching the increasing number of families that were developing as the baby boom moved into full gear. Advertisers were also attracted to television because of the creative opportunities it offered for presenting and demonstrating their products. Radio went through a very difficult period during the 1960s and 1970s, as many advertisers neglected the medium in favor of television. However, during the 1980s, many advertisers rediscovered the advantages and opportunities available through radio advertising and its popularity is continuing into the 1990s.

Television experienced unprecedented growth over the past four decades, both in terms of increases in households owning a set and with respect to advertisers' use of the medium. TV has grown faster than any other advertising medium in history and in 1991 accounted for 22 percent of total advertising spending in the United States. While television has experienced tremendous growth and is a very popular advertising medium, it has also experienced significant changes, particularly over the past decade or so.

The changes in the TV industry are affecting how advertisers approach the use of TV in their media strategies. For example, the growth of cable and resulting explosion in channels and fragmentation of the viewing audience means advertisers have to rethink how they will use television. More attention is being paid to using TV to reach specific segments of customers rather than mass markets. The trend toward shorter spots and zapping of commercials means advertisers face significant challenges in developing commercials that attract and hold the viewer's attention. Despite these changes, however, television is still a very powerful advertising medium that plays an important role in the media strategy of many marketers.

Television

It has often been said that television represents the ideal advertising medium. The ability of TV to combine visual images, sound, motion, and color presents the advertiser with the opportunity to develop creative and imaginative appeals unlike any other medium. However, television does have certain problems or limitations that limit or even prevent its use by many advertisers. Let us examine some of the specific advantages and limitations of television as an advertising medium.

Advantages of Television

Creativity and impact

Perhaps the greatest advantage of television is the opportunity it provides for presenting the advertising message. The interaction of sight and sound offers tremendous creative opportunity and flexibility in developing the message and makes it possible to create dramatic and life-like representations of products and services. TV commercials can be used to convey a mood or image for a brand as well as to develop emotional or entertaining appeals that may help make an otherwise dull product appear exciting or interesting.

Television is also an excellent medium for demonstrating a product or service. For example, print ads are effective for showing a car and communicating information regarding its features, but only a TV commercial can put you in the driver's seat and give you the sense of actually driving, as shown by the Acura commercial in Exhibit 13–2.

➤ *Exhibit 13–2* **This television commercial helps demonstrate the sensation of driving a car**

(MUSIC THROUGHOUT)
COBURN: Acura would like to pose the following question:

Could your heart benefit from the use of another 24 valves?

The Acura Legend Coupe.

Coverage and cost effectiveness

Television advertising also makes it possible to reach large audiences. Nearly everyone, regardless of age, sex, income, or education level, watches at least some television and most people do so on a regular basis. The average number of hours of household television usage per day has risen from five and a half hours in 1965 to level off at about seven hours in 1991. According to Nielsen estimates, over 235 million people are in the television households, 77 percent of whom are adults 18 years and older.

Marketers selling products and services that appeal to broad target audiences find that television gives them an opportunity to reach mass markets and often at very good cost efficiencies. For example, the average prime-time TV show reaches 11 million homes, while a top-rated show such as "Cheers" may reach nearly 22 million homes. In 1991, the average cost per thousand (CPM) was $9 for network evening shows and $2.39 for daytime weekday shows.[5]

Because of its ability to reach large audiences and the cost efficiencies it offers, TV is a particularly popular medium among companies selling mass consumption products. Companies with widespread distribution and availability of their products and services use TV to reach the mass market and deliver their advertising messages at a very low cost per thousand. Television has become a highly dominant and indispensable medium to large consumer package-goods companies, automobile manufacturers, and major retailers. In 1990, the top 100 national advertisers accounted for 77 percent of all monies spent on network TV advertising and 42 percent of the dollars spent on spot television.[6] Companies such as Procter & Gamble spend more than 80 percent of their media advertising budget on various forms of TV—network, spot, cable, and syndicated programs. Exhibit 13—3 shows the top 25 network TV advertisers in 1991 and their expenditures.

Captivity and attention

Television is basically intrusive in that commercials impose themselves on viewers as they watch their favorite programs. Unless a special effort is made to avoid commercials, most of us end up being exposed to thousands of them each year. The increase in viewing options and the penetration of VCRs, remote controls, and other automatic devices have made it easier for TV viewers to avoid commercial messages. For example, a recent study of consumers' viewing habits found the audience for commercials declines an average of 17 percent from that of the program (an issue discussed later in this chapter).[7] However, the remaining viewers are likely to be exposed and devote some attention to many advertising messages. As discussed in

➤ *Exhibit 13—3*
Top 25 network TV advertisers (1991)

Rank	Advertiser	1991	Rank	Advertiser	1991
1	General Motors Corp.	$527.8	13	McDonald's Corp.	171.8
2	Procter & Gamble Co.	515.7	14	Unilever NV	154.6
3	Philip Morris Cos.	389.5	15	General Mills	151.4
4	Johnson & Johnson	239.8	16	Anheuser-Busch Cos.	122.9
5	Kellogg Co.	236.6	17	Honda Motor Co.	117.0
6	Ford Motor Co.	217.5	18	RJR Nabisco	112.7
7	PepsiCo	204.6	19	Nestle SA	109.0
8	Sears, Roebuck & Co.	187.9	20	Eastman Kodak Co.	105.6
9	Chrysler Corp.	176.2	21	Grand Metropolitan	103.3
10	Toyota Motor Corp.	173.7	22	Bristol-Myers Squibb Co.	95.4
11	American Home Products Corp.	173.3	23	Coca-Cola Co.	95.2
			24	Walt Disney Co.	93.8
12	AT&T Co.	172.0	25	Warner-Lambert Co.	84.1

Note: Dollars are in millions.

Chapter 6, the low-involvement nature of consumer learning and response processes may mean television advertising has the potential to have an effect on consumers simply through heavy repetition and exposure to catchy slogans, jingles, and the like.

Selectivity and flexibility

Television has often been criticized for being a nonselective medium since it is difficult to reach a precisely defined and small market segment through the use of TV advertising. While this is true to some extent, selectivity is possible since there are variations in the composition of television audiences as a result of program content, broadcast time, and geographic coverage. Audiences may vary by time of the day or night when they watch television, the programs watched, and even the day of the week. For example, Saturday morning TV caters to children; Saturday and Sunday afternoon programs are geared to the sports-oriented male; and weekday, daytime shows appeal heavily to homemakers. With the growth of cable television, advertisers are able to refine their television coverage further by appealing to groups with specific interests such as sports, news, or music. The ad for MTV shown in Exhibit 13–4 promotes the value of the network for reaching teens and young adults.

➤ *Exhibit 13–4*
MTV promotes its ability to reach the youth market

Flexibility is also possible through television advertising, as advertisers can adjust their media strategies to take advantage of potential that may exist in different geographic markets through local or spot advertisements in specific market areas. Ads can also be scheduled to be seen repeatedly or to take advantage of special occasions. For example, Gillette has traditionally been a major sponsor during the baseball World Series Classic every fall, which allows it to advertise heavily to men who constitute the primary market for many of the company's products.

Limitations of Television

Although television has many advantages and is unsurpassed from a creative perspective, the medium has several disadvantages that limit or preclude its use by many advertisers. These problems include high costs, the lack of selectivity, the fleeting nature of a television message, commercial clutter, and distrust of TV ads.

Costs

Despite the efficiency of TV in reaching large audiences, it is an expensive medium in which to advertise. The high cost of using television stems not only from the expense of buying airtime but also from the costs of producing a quality commercial. In a survey of 1987 commercial production costs, the American Association of Advertising Agencies found that the average national brand 30-second spot cost $156,000 to produce.[8] Even local ads can be very expensive to produce and often are not of high quality. The high costs of producing and airing commercials may be less of a problem for major advertisers with large budgets. However, high costs often price small- and medium-sized advertisers out of the market, as they cannot afford to develop and run a TV advertising program.

Lack of selectivity

As discussed in the previous section, some selectivity is available in television through variations in programs and with the growth of cable TV. Many advertisers, however, are seeking a very specific, and often small, target audience and find the coverage of TV often extends beyond their market, thus reducing its cost effectiveness, as was discussed in Chapter 12. Geographic selectivity can be a problem to local advertisers such as a retailer since a station bases its rates on the total market area it reaches. For example, stations in Pittsburgh, Pennsylvania, reach viewers in western Pennsylvania, eastern Ohio, northern West Virginia, and even parts of Maryland. The small company or retailer whose market is limited to the immediate Pittsburgh area may find TV to be an inefficient media buy since the stations cover a geographic area that is larger than the merchant's trade area.

The audience selectivity of television is improving as advertisers are able to target certain groups of consumers through the type of program or day and/or time when they choose to advertise. However, TV still does not offer the advertiser the same audience selectivity as other media such as radio, magazines, newspapers, or direct mail for reaching precise segments of the market.

Fleeting message

TV commercials usually last only 30 seconds or less and leave nothing tangible for the viewer to examine or consider. As was noted earlier, television commercials became shorter and shorter as the demand for a limited amount of broadcast time intensified and advertisers sought to get more impressions from their media budgets. As can be seen in Exhibit 13–5, 30-second commercials became the norm in the mid-1970s. However, in September 1986, the three networks began accepting 15-second spots across their full schedules (except during children's viewing time), and since 1988 these shorter spots have been accounting for more than a third of all network commercials.

➤ *Exhibit 13–5* **Changes in percentage of network commercials by length**

Commercial Length	1965	1975	1980	1985	1987	1988	1989	1990	1991
15	—	—	—	10	31	36	38	35	34
30	23	93	96	84	65	61	57	60	62
60	77	6	2	2	2	2	2	2	2
All others	—	1	2	4	2	1	3	3	2

An important factor in the decline in commercial length has been the spiraling inflation in media costs that occurred over the past decade. With the average cost of a prime-time spot reaching over $100,000, many advertisers saw shorter commercials as the only way to keep their media costs in line. Fifteen-second spots typically sell for half the price of a 30-second spot. Thus, by using 15- or even 10-second commercials, advertisers think they can run additional spots and reinforce the message or reach a larger audience.

The trend toward shorter commercials means advertisers must be able to get consumers' attention and communicate an idea, message, or selling proposition in a very short period. However, many advertisers believe shorter commercials can deliver a message just as effectively as longer spots and, of course, for much less money. A large-scale study compared the performance of 15- and 30-second spots and found that, where the average 30-second spot scored a 100 for communication performance on the index, the typical 15-second spot scored a 76. The 15-second spots also scored well on the average number of ideas played back per viewer—2.6 for the 15s versus 2.9 for the 30s. Finally, the 30- and 15-second spots were rated about equally with regard to viewers' sense of the importance of the main idea created by the commercial.[9]

Several years ago, many advertising people predicted 15-second spots would become the dominant commercial unit by the early 1990s. However, the growth in the use of 15-second commercials peaked at 38 percent in 1989 and declined to 35 percent in 1990 and 34 percent in 1991. The decline in the use of 15-second spots may be due to several factors, including creative considerations, lower prices for network time, and a desire by the network to restrict their use to deal with clutter.[10]

Clutter

The problems of fleeting messages and shorter commercials are compounded by the fact that the advertiser's message is only one of many spots and other nonprogramming material seen during a commercial break, so it may have trouble being noticed amid all of the clutter. One of the greatest concerns advertisers have expressed recently with regard to TV advertising is the potential decline in effectiveness because of *clutter*. The next time you watch television, count the number of commercials, promotions for the news or upcoming programs, or public service announcements that appear during a station break and you will appreciate why clutter is a major concern. With all of these messages competing for our attention, it is easy to understand why the viewer often comes away confused or even annoyed and often unable to remember or properly identify the product or service advertised.

A major cause of clutter has been the shift among advertisers to the use of shorter commercials. Compounding this has been the use by some advertisers of **split-30s**, 30-second spots in which the advertiser promotes two different products with separate messages. Clutter has also resulted from the networks and individual stations making more time available for commercials or redistributing time to popular programs. For many years, the amount of time available for commercials was restricted by the Code Authority of the National Association of Broadcasters and was limited to

9.5 minutes per hour during prime time and 12 minutes during nonprime time. However, the code was suspended in 1982 by the Justice Department on the grounds it violated antitrust law. Initially, the networks did not alter their time standards. However, over the past several years, they have increased the number of commercial minutes in their schedules to compensate for lower rates that resulted from declines in the size of their viewing audiences and softening demand for advertising.

As we saw in Chapter 7, advertisers and agencies have become very concerned about clutter and have been pressuring the networks to cut back on the commercials and other sources of clutter. The networks may be ready to act on the problem. For example, ABC slightly reduced its prime-time commercial load for the 1992-93 season and was considering reducing the clutter level of certain shows to determine if advertisers would pay a premium for programs with lower clutter levels.[11]

Limited viewer attention

When advertisers buy time on a TV program, they are not purchasing guaranteed exposure but rather the opportunity to communicate a message to the viewing audience. However, while advertisers often pay large sums for the opportunity to reach large numbers of consumers, there is increasing evidence and concern that the size of the viewing audience during a commercial break is reduced. Reductions in the size of the audience for a commercial may occur because people leave the room to go the bathroom or to get something to eat or drink, or they are distracted in some other way during a commercial break.

Research psychologist Peter Collett spent five months examining the viewing behavior of 20 families using a hidden video camera. The results of his study showed there is a weak relationship between presence in front of the TV and whether someone actually watches the programs and commercials. The subjects in his study watched only about 65 percent of each program and only 50 percent of commercials. However, Collett did find an interesting pattern; a large segment of viewers watched less than 10 percent of a commercial, while another segment watched more than 90 percent of a spot. Collett concluded viewers' attention to a commercial is a function of a number of factors including the nature of the spot, the positioning of the ad in the commercial break, the presence of other people in the room, and the programming environment.[12]

Getting consumers to pay attention to commercials has become an even greater challenge in recent years. The increased penetration of VCRs into most households and the prevalence of remote control devices have led to the problems of zipping and zapping. **Zipping** occurs when consumers fast forward through commercials during the playback of a program previously recorded on a VCR. A study by Nielsen Media Research found that while 80 percent of recorded shows are actually played back, viewers zip past more than half of the commercials.[13]

Zapping refers to the use of a remote control device to change channels and switch away from commercials. The Nielsen study found that most commercial zapping occurs at the beginning and, to a somewhat lesser extent, at the end of a program. Zapping at these points is likely to occur because commercial breaks are so long and predictable. Zapping has also been fueled by the emergence of 24-hour continuous format programming on cable channels such as CNN, MTV, and ESPN. Viewers can switch over for a few news headlines, sports scores, or a music video and then back to the program. Research profiling zappers has shown that young adults zap more than older adults, and men are more likely to zap than women.[14]

The obvious issue facing advertisers is how to inhibit zapping. The networks use certain tactics to hold viewers' attention such as previews of the next week's show or short closing scenes at the end of a program. Some programs start with action sequences before opening credits and commercials to hold the viewers' attention. A few years ago, Anheuser-Busch began using the "Bud Frame" during sports programming in

➤ *Exhibit 13–6* **Developing creative commercials may be one answer to the zapping problem**

(SFX:) DOOR OPENS.
(DOOR CLOSES)
(SFX:) HAT TOSSED, CATCHES HOOK.
(SFX:) RADIO CLICKED ON.
NEWSMAN: . . .Special Bulletin. Early this morning, people all over town have reported unusual sightings in their Easter Baskets

NEWSMAN: Peanut Butter Easter Eggs.
ANNCR: Anyone who knows . . .Reese's Peanut Butter Eggs . . .are Easter's best.
Two great tastes that taste great together. . . all dressed up for the holiday.
NEWSMAN: Reaction in Washington is highly optimistic.

RABBIT: Ahhhhhh. . .
(SFX:) RADIO RECEPTION GOES HAYWIRE.
RECEPTION CLEARS.
NEWSMAN: The Easter Bunny. . .has done it again.
ANNCR: Reese's Peanut Butter Easter Eggs.
ANNCR: They're getting quite a reception.

which the ad frames the live coverage of a sporting event. The ultimate answer to zap-proofing commercials is to produce creative and meaningful advertising messages that will attract and hold the viewers' attention (Exhibit 13–6). However, this is easier said than done, and as more viewers gain access to remote controls, the zapping problem is likely to continue.

Distrust and negative evaluation

To many critics of advertising, the TV commercial personifies everything that is wrong with the industry. Critics of advertising often single out television commercials because of their pervasiveness as well as the intrusive nature of the medium. Consumers are seen as defenseless against the barrage of TV ads since they are unable to control the transmission of the message and what appears on their screen. Studies have shown that of the various forms of advertising, distrust is generally the highest for TV commercials.[15] Also, concern has been raised over the effects of television advertising on specific groups such as children or the elderly.

When to Use Television Advertising

The various advantages of television, particularly its powerful impact and ability to reach large audiences, make it a very important medium for many advertisers. For these companies, the decision is not *whether* to use this form of advertising but rather *how* they can use it most effectively. However, as we have discussed in the preceding pages, TV has its limitations as an advertising medium. Thus, companies considering whether to use television must consider several factors, including the following.[16]

- Do we have a large enough budget to finance the production of quality commercials? This is particularly important for large companies competing on a national or regional level since they want to protect the image of their brands as well as that of their company. Many local companies produce commercials for a fraction of the cost of national ads (and it is often evident), but they are not attempting to compete on a national level against firms with high-quality commercials.
- Do we have a large enough media budget to sustain a continuous schedule and generate the exposures needed to have an impact on the target audience? Television advertising may be a very efficient media buy for many companies, but the absolute costs of buying commercial time and sustaining a TV schedule can be very expensive, particularly on a national level.
- Is there a large market for our product or service, and can this market be reached efficiently through a specific network, station, or program? Because of the costs of TV advertising, a firm selling to a specialized market must consider whether there is a way to target this audience through television effectively. Many companies are taking advantage of the specialized audiences reached through cable and independent stations and are making TV part of their media mix.
- Is it necessary to make a strong impact on the market through the use of a creative advertising campaign? Television is a very powerful medium, and many companies have used it to create messages that focus attention on their products or services and effectively differentiate them from competitors'. Television is the best medium for making a strong impact on consumers and adding prestige to a company and/or its brands.

Buying Television Time

A number of options are available to advertisers that choose to use TV as part of their media mix. Advertisers can purchase time in a variety of program formats that appeal to various types and sizes of audiences. Commercial time can be purchased on a national, regional, or local basis. An advertiser can sponsor an entire program, participate in the sponsorship, or use spot announcements during or between programs.

The purchase of TV advertising time is a highly specialized phase of the advertising business, particularly for large companies spending huge sums of money. The large advertiser that makes extensive use of television advertising generally utilizes agency media specialists or specialized media buying services to arrange the media schedule and purchase television time. Decisions have to be made regarding national or network versus local or spot purchases, selection of specific stations, sponsorship versus participation, different classes of time, and appropriate programs. Local advertisers may not have to deal with the first decision but do face all the others. In this section, we examine some of the considerations involved in the purchase of television time.

Network versus Spot

A basic decision that faces all advertisers is the allocation of their TV media budget among network versus local or spot announcements. Most national advertisers that are heavy users of TV use network schedules to provide national coverage and supplement this with regional or local spot purchases to reach markets where additional coverage is desired or needed. Each of these types of television advertising purchases is examined in more detail below.

Network advertising

A common way by which advertisers disseminate their messages is the purchase of airtime from a **television network.** A network assembles a series of affiliated local television stations, or **affiliates,** to which it supplies programming and services. These affiliates, most of which are independently owned, contractually agree to preempt time during specified hours for programming provided by the networks and to carry the national advertising within the program. The networks share the advertising revenue they receive during these time periods with the affiliates. The affiliates are also free to sell commercial time in nonnetwork periods and during station breaks in the preempted periods to both national and local advertisers.

The three major networks—NBC, ABC, CBS—each have affiliates throughout the nation such that they have almost complete national coverage. Thus, when an advertiser purchases airtime from one of these three national networks, the commercial is transmitted across the nation through the affiliate station network. Network advertising truly represents a mass medium, as the advertiser can broadcast its message simultaneously throughout the country with a network commercial.

A major advantage of network advertising is the simplification of the purchase process, as the advertiser has to deal with only one party or media representative to air a commercial nationwide. The networks also offer the most popular programs and generally control prime-time programming. Thus, advertisers interested in reaching the huge nationwide audiences will generally buy network time during the prime viewing hours of 8 to 11 P.M. eastern time.

Problems associated with network advertising limit its attractiveness to some companies. The major drawback is the high cost of network time. Exhibit 13–7 shows estimates of costs for a 30-second spot on the three networks' prime-time shows during the 1992–93 television season. As can be seen in this exhibit, many of the popular prime-time shows charge $200,000 or more for a 30-second spot. Thus, only advertisers with large budgets can afford to use network advertising on a regular basis.

Availability of time can also be a problem as more advertisers turn to network advertising to reach mass markets. Over the past several years, a large portion of the prime-time commercial spots, particularly on the popular shows, has been sold during the up-front market. The **up-front market** is a buying period that occurs before the upcoming television season when the networks sell a large part of their commercial time. Thus, advertisers hoping to use prime-time network advertising must plan their media schedules and often purchase TV time as much as a year in advance. In recent years, some problems have developed in the up-front market concerning guarantees that shows will deliver a certain number of viewers. Changes in the up-front market are discussed in Promotional Perspective 13–1.

A final problem with network advertising is that companies often have variations in the market potential for their products and may not want to pay for nationwide advertising. For example, Coors beer did not have a distribution network in a number of states including New York, New Jersey, and Pennsylvania until 1987. Thus, the company did not want to make heavy use of network advertising and reach consumers who could not purchase the product in their areas. Consequently, much of Coors' TV media budget was spent on spot advertising rather than network until distribution was established in most of the states.

While the majority of network advertising dollars go to the three major networks, several other types of networks have evolved in recent years, including the Fox Broadcasting Company, which broadcasts its programs over a group of affiliated independent stations. Cable TV networks also have developed to provide programming to local cable systems in cities throughout the country (cable television is discussed later in the chapter). Network television can also be purchased on a

> *Exhibit 13–7*
What the fall TV shows cost: estimated price of a 30-second spot on the big 3 networks

Monday

	7 p.m.	7:30 p.m.	8 p.m.	8:30 p.m.	9 p.m.	9:30 p.m.
ABC	Young Indiana Jones $95,000		NFL Monday Night Football $265,000			
CBS	Evening Shade $200,000	Hearts Afire $175,000	Murphy Brown $310,000	Love & War $190,000	Northern Exposure $225,000	
NBC	Fresh Prince $150,000	Blossom $140,000	NBC Monday Night Movies $140,000			

Tuesday

ABC	Full House $175,000	Hangin' With Mr. Cooper $180,000	Roseanne $290,000	Coach $280,000	Going to Extremes $130,000	
CBS	Rescue: 911 $115,000		CBS Tuesday Movie $125,000			
NBC	Quantum Leap $115,000		Reasonable Doubts $115,000		Dateline NBC $105,000	

Wednesday

ABC	The Wonder Years $125,000	Doogie Howser, M.D. $135,000	Home Improvement $225,000	Laurie Hill $120,000	Civil Wars $135,000	
CBS	The Hat Squad $80,000		In the Heat of the Night $90,000		48 Hours $135,000	
NBC	Unsolved Mysteries $150,000		Seinfeld $200,000	Mad About You $140,000	Law & Order $125,000	

Thursday

ABC	Delta $70,000	Room for Two $80,000	Homefront $95,000		PrimeTime Live $95,000	
CBS	Top Cops $80,000		Street Stories $85,000		Knots Landing $175,000	
NBC	A Different World $150,000	Rhythm & Blues $160,000	Cheers $300,000	Wings $225,000	L.A. Law $200,000	

Friday

ABC	Family Matters $125,000	Step by Step $120,000	Dinosaurs $110,000	Camp Wilder $90,000	20/20 $120,000	
CBS	Golden Palace $120,000	Major Dad $125,000	Designing Women $125,000	Bob $130,000	Picket Fences $130,000	
NBC	Final Appeal $70,000	What Happened? $70,000	The Round Table $80,000		I'll Fly Away $110,000	

Saturday

ABC	Covington Cross $55,000		Crossroads $75,000		The Commish $85,000	
CBS	Frannie's Turn $60,000	Brooklyn Bridge $75,000	Raven $60,000		Angel Street $55,000	
NBC	Here & Now $85,000	Out All Night $85,000	Empty Nest $135,000	Nurses $125,000	Sisters $125,000	

Sunday

	6 p.m.	6:30 p.m.				
ABC	Life Goes On $90,000	Funniest Videos $150,000	Funniest People $145,000	ABC Sunday Night Movie $125,000		
CBS	60 Minutes $220,000	Murder, She Wrote $150,000		CBS Sunday Night Movie $160,000		
NBC	Secret Service $50,000	I Witness Video $70,000		NBC Sunday Night Movie $180,000		

Source: Agency and network estimates   All times Central Time.

regional basis, making it possible for an advertiser's message to be aired in certain sections of the country with one media purchase.

Regional networks were created by the major TV networks in the early 1970s in response to complaints by smaller companies that access to network TV gave national companies an unfair competitive advantage. Facing legal action if they did not offer regional advertising packages, the networks agreed to do so. However, the networks agreed to make regional buys available only under the conditions that they could find advertisers interested in reaching remaining parts of the country during the time slot such that the network ultimately ended up with a national sale. An advertiser that makes a regional network purchase generally pays in proportion to the percentage of the country receiving the message plus a nominal fee for splitting the feed. The amount of money spent for regional network advertising represents less than 5 percent of network advertising revenue.[17] However, the increasing use of regional marketing by national advertisers is likely to result in increased regional network advertising.[18]

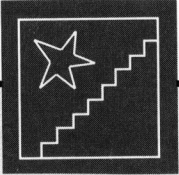

Promotional Perspective 13–1

The Up-Front Market Gets a Little Less Friendly

Every spring, representatives of advertising agencies, media buying services, and the major TV networks get together to kick off what has become known as the "up-front market" for network television advertising time. The networks sell a large part of their commercial time as much as 52 weeks in advance during this period. The process begins in April or May when advertisers release their network TV budget guidelines to their agencies. Media planners set rough buying goals in terms of audience targets and gross rating points and decide how much money will go to each network daypart. Once the networks announce their new prime-time schedules, the negotiating process begins.

During the buying process, network account executives and agency media buyers negotiate a package of programs. While the advertisers may prefer to buy a package consisting of all top-rated shows, the networks rarely sell these shows without including a few new or struggling series in the deal. Once the package is set, price negotiations begin, with actual rates depending on rating guarantees, cancellation options, and other points. After a deal is set, the networks put it on hold and allow the agency or media buying service some time to go over the buy with its client before making a commitment.

National advertisers buy anywhere from a third to three quarters of their network TV time for the upcoming year in the up-front market to secure guarantees or assurances that purchased rating levels will be met and to get lower prices than they could obtain in the "scatter market" after the season begins. Actual rates paid for commercial time in the up-front market depend on a number of factors, including the demand for network advertising time and a program's ratings from the previous season as well as ratings predicted for the upcoming season.

Billions of dollars in network time are purchased during the up-front season. Traditionally this has occurred with a handshake and a smile, as signed contracts are almost unheard of in the business. However, the cordial manner in which up-front market business occurs changed radically in 1990 as the networks sought to do away with guarantees, which is the practice of promising advertisers that shows will reach a specific number of viewers. The problem began during the 1989–90 season when audience measures by A.C. Nielsen indicated the total audience of the three networks fell 7 to 8 percent below guarantee levels. The drop was very costly as the networks had to provide several hundred millions of dollars in makegoods in the form of free advertising time to compensate for the lower audiences. The networks complained long and hard to Nielsen, which could offer no explanation for the vanishing viewers but stood by its numbers. However, the networks believed there were problems with the way Nielsen measured the television viewing and took it upon themselves to come up with alternatives to the traditional guarantees.

During up-front negotiations for the 1990–91 season, the three major networks banded together and decided to scrap the prevailing system and offer different, less-stringent guarantees. The new guarantees are based on a range of ratings rather than a specific rating or make guarantees for only a small portion of the prime-time schedule. The new policy also calls for the use of eight-year viewing trends for network television as well as for cable, syndication, and independent stations to project usage levels for TV. If usage levels reported by Nielsen Media Research drop below the projections, the network will adjust its guaranteed audience delivery numbers to ease its responsibility for make goods. If the usage levels reported by Nielsen were the same as the projections and the number of viewers delivered was below the guaranteed level, the networks would provide makegoods.

As might be expected, the new policy has drawn considerable criticism from the advertising community, which dislikes the idea of giving up guaranteed numbers and paying for viewers who are not being delivered. The networks have made several attempts in the past to change the guarantee system, and it is questionable as to whether they will be successful this time, as advertisers can turn to other alternatives such as cable TV, the Fox network, or syndicated shows. The purchase of network advertising time is always the result of considerable negotiation, and many media buyers believe guarantees will also be negotiated.

The factor that will probably determine the outcome of the battle over guarantees is supply and demand for network advertising time. Up-front sales reached a record $4.3 billion during the 1990–91 season but declined 19 percent to $3.5 billion for the 1991–92 and 1992–93 seasons. The networks are more likely to enforce the new system during strong demand for prime-time, but may have to relax their position when demand softens. One thing is certain: The way advertisers buy network time is clearly changing, and it is becoming harder to do it with a handshake and a smile.

Source: Joe Mandese, "Let the Season Begin," *Marketing & Media Decisions,* May 1988, pp. 36–34; Joanne Lipman, "Networks Try to Scrap Guarantees," *The Wall Street Journal,* May 10, 1990; and Joe Mandese, "Upfront Sales Fall 19%," *Advertising Age,* July 8, 1991, pp. 3, 38. Joanne Lipman, " 'Upfront' Gains Said to Be Sign of Rebound," *The Wall Street Journal,* July 10, 1992, B12.

Spot and local advertising

Spot advertising refers to commercials shown on local television stations, with the negotiation and purchase of time being made directly from the individual stations. All nonnetwork advertising done by a national advertiser is known as **national spot** advertising, whereas airtime sold to local firms such as retailers, restaurants, banks, and auto dealers is known as **local advertising.** Local advertisers desire media whose coverage is limited to the geographic markets in which they do business. As discussed earlier, this may be difficult to accomplish with TV because the broadcast area covered by a local station may extend beyond the retailer's trade area. However, many local businesses are large enough to make efficient use of TV advertising.

Spot advertising offers the national advertiser greater flexibility in adjusting to local market conditions. The advertiser can concentrate commercials in areas where market potential is the greatest or where additional support is needed. This appeals to advertisers with uneven distribution or limited advertising budgets, as well as those interested in test-marketing or introducing a product in limited market areas. National advertisers also often use spot television advertising through local retailers or dealers as a part of their cooperative advertising programs and as a way of providing local dealer support.

A major problem to the national advertiser in using spot advertising is that it can be more difficult to acquire since the time must be purchased from a number of local stations. Moreover, there are more variations in the pricing policies and discount structure of the individual stations than with the networks. However, this problem has been reduced somewhat by the use of **station reps** or individuals who act as sales representatives for a number of local stations and represent them in dealings with national advertisers.

Spot advertisements also are subject to more commercial clutter since local stations can sell time on network-originated shows only during station breaks between programs, except when network advertisers have not purchased all the available time. As discussed earlier, the abundance of ads and other nonprogram material during these station breaks or adjacencies means more clutter and can result in lower recall of the advertising. Viewership also generally declines during station breaks, as people may leave the room, zap to another channel, attend to other tasks, or cease watching television.

While spot advertising is mostly confined to station breaks between programs on network-originated shows, local stations sell time on their own programs, which consist of news, movies, syndicated shows, or locally originated programs. Also, independent stations are in most cities and can be used by spot advertisers. Local advertisers find the independent stations particularly attractive because they generally have lower rates than the major network affiliates. Exhibit 13–8 shows an ad for a local TV station promoting its programming.

➢ *Exhibit 13–8*
An independent station promotes itself

The decision facing most national advertisers is not whether to use either network or spot advertising but rather how to combine the two to make effective use of their television advertising budget. Another factor making spot advertising attractive to national advertisers is the growth in syndication.

Syndication

Advertisers may also reach TV viewers by advertising on **syndicated programs,** which are shows that are sold or distributed to local stations. There are several types of syndicated programming. **Off-network syndication** refers to reruns of network shows that are bought by individual stations. Shows that have become very popular in off-network syndication include "M*A*S*H," "The Cosby Show," and "The Golden Girls." The FCC prime-time access rule forbids large-market network affiliates from carrying these shows from 7 to 8 P.M. They are very popular among independent stations, which are not affected by this restriction. Other syndication restrictions include the number of episodes that must be produced before a show is eligible for syndication and limitations on network involvement in the financing or production of syndicated shows. The FCC may ease some of the rules involving the networks' role in producing and syndicating programs.[19]

Off-network syndication shows are very important to local stations as they provide them with quality programming that often has an established audience. The syndication market is also very important to the studios that produce programs and sell them to the networks. Most prime-time network shows initially lose money for the studios since the licensing fee paid by the networks does not cover production costs. Over four years—the times it takes to produce the 88 episodes regarded as the minimum needed to break into syndication—half-hour situation comedies often run up a deficit of nearly $12 million, and losses on a one-hour drama show can reach $30 million. However, the producers recoup their money when a show is sold to syndication. For example, "The Cosby Show" set a record a few years ago when it was sold into syndication for $800 million. In 1990, "Golden Girls" grossed nearly $300 million in syndication, and "Who's the Boss?" pulled in even more.[20]

First-run syndication refers to shows produced specifically for the syndication market. The first-run syndication market is made up of a variety of shows including some that did not make it as network shows and are moved into syndication while new episodes are being produced.

Under **barter syndication,** both off-network and first-run syndicated programs are offered free or for a reduced rate to local stations but with some advertising time presold to national advertisers. Usually, more than half of the advertising time is presold, and the remainder is available for sale by the local advertiser. Barter syndication allows national advertisers to participate in the syndication market with the convenience of a network-type media buy, while local stations get free programming and can sell the remainder of the time to local or spot advertisers. Recently, the straight barter deal has begun being replaced by more barter/cash arrangements, where the station pays for a program at a reduced rate and accepts a number of preplaced, bartered ads. Some of the top-rated barter syndicated programs include "Wheel of Fortune," "Jeopardy," "The Oprah Winfrey Show," and "Night Court." Exhibit 13–9 shows the program rating and share of audience of the top 20 syndicated programs for February 1991.

Syndication has become a very big business. The $3.4 billion in revenue generated in 1991–92 is comparable in size to any of the big three networks. Syndicated shows have become more popular than network shows in certain dayparts such as daytime and late fringe. In some markets, syndicated shows such as "Wheel of Fortune" draw a larger audience than the network news. Shows hosted by syndication personalities such as Phil Donahue, Oprah Winfrey, and Arsenio Hall have also become very popular.

Many national advertisers use syndicated shows because it is less expensive than network prime-time advertising and allows them to target certain audiences. For

➤ *Exhibit 13–9*
The top 20 syndicated programs (1991)

Program (Number of Markets)	Rating/Share of Audience February 1991 Nielsen Rating
"Wheel of Fortune" (194)	16.4/30
"Jeopardy" (184)	13.6/26
"Oprah Winfrey" (195)	11.5/32
"Entertainment Tonight" (155)	8.8/15
"Golden Girls" (95)	8.1/18
"Cosby Show" (184)	7.9/19
"Current Affair" (58)	7.4/16
"Cheers" (161)	7.3/18
"Inside Edition" (119)	7.3/15
"Donahue" (197)	6.8/25
"Night Court" (144)	6.1/14
"Who's the Boss" (140)	6.7/15
"Family Feud" (109)	5.9/15
"Hard Copy" (140)	5.6/14
"Sally Jessy Raphael" (164)	5.4/22
"Growing Pains" (120)	5.5/13
"M.A.S.H" (116)	5.1/15
"Perfect Strangers" (46)	4.6/8
"Regis & Kathie Lee" (162)	4.4/18
"People's Court" (152)	4.4/14

example, "Star Trek" is considered one of the hottest shows in syndication because it reaches the highly sought after, and often difficult to reach, young male audience. As can be seen in Exhibit 13–10, syndication is much more effective than the networks in reaching the children's and teenage market.

Syndication has certain disadvantages, such as more commercial time and thus more clutter. The audience for syndicated shows is often older and more rural, and syndicators do not supply as much research information as the networks do. Syndication also creates more problems for media buyers since a syndicated show might not be seen in a particular market or may be aired during an undesirable time period. Thus, media buyers have to look at each market and check airtimes and other factors in putting together a syndication schedule.[21]

Methods of Buying Time

In addition to deciding whether to use network versus spot advertising, advertisers must decide whether to sponsor an entire program, participate in a program, or use spot announcements between programs. Sponsorship of a program and participations are available on either a network or a local market basis, whereas spot announcements are available only from local stations.

Sponsorship

Under a **sponsorship** arrangement, an advertiser assumes responsibility for the production and usually the content of the program as well as the advertising that appears within it. In the early days of TV, most programs were produced and sponsored by corporations and were identified by their name such as the "Texaco Theater," the "Bell Telephone Hour," and the "Armstrong Circle Theater." Today most shows are produced either by the networks or through independent production companies that sell the program to the network.

Several major companies have been sponsoring special programs for many years such as the "Hallmark Hall of Fame" dramatic series and the "Kraft Masterpiece Theater." However, sole sponsorship of programs, which is usually limited to specials, has been declining steadily since the mid-1970s. Sole sponsorships may be making a comeback, however, as several companies including AT&T, General Electric, IBM, Clorox, and Chrysler have begun program sponsorships.

➤ *Exhibit 13–10*
Syndicated programs reach more children than the networks

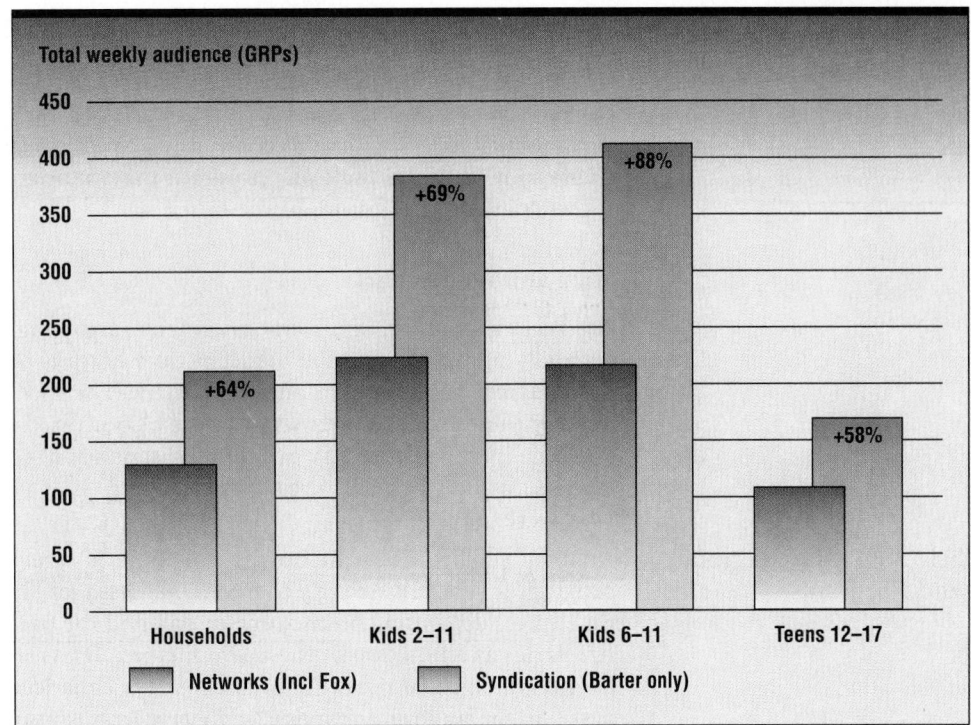

A company might choose to sponsor a program for several reasons. Sponsorship allows the firm to capitalize on the prestige of a high-quality program (such as those noted above) and thus enhance the image of the company and its products. A second reason for sponsorship is that the sponsor has control over the placement and content of its commercials. The commercials can be placed wherever the advertiser wants them in the program and can be of any length as long as the total amount of commercial time does not exceed network or station regulations. Advertisers introducing a new product line often will sponsor a program and run commercials that are several minutes long to introduce and explain the product. For example, IBM used this strategy to introduce its new generation of personal computers. While these factors make sponsorship attractive to some companies, the high costs of sole sponsorship limit this option to only large firms. Most commercial time is purchased through other methods such as participations.

Participations

Most advertisers either cannot afford the costs of sponsorship or want greater flexibility than that which results from sponsoring a program. Thus, nearly 90 percent of network advertising time is sold as **participations,** with several advertisers buying commercial time or spots on a particular program. An advertiser can participate in a particular program once or several times on a regular or irregular basis. Participating advertisers have no involvement or financial responsibility for the production of the program, as this is assumed by the network or individual station that sells and controls the commercial time.

There are several advantages to participation. First, the advertiser has no long-term commitment to a program, and expenditures can be adjusted to buy any number of participation spots that fit within the budget. This is particularly important to small advertisers with a limited budget. The second advantage is that the television budget can be spread over a number of programs, which provides for greater reach in the media schedule. This can be particularly important when introducing a new product or advertising campaign.

The disadvantage of participations is that the advertiser has little control over the placements of ads, and there may also be problems with availability. Preference is given to advertisers willing to commit to numerous spots, and the firm trying to buy single spots in more than one program may find that time is unavailable in certain shows, particularly during prime time.

Spot announcements

As discussed earlier, spot announcements are bought from the local stations and generally appear during the adjacent time periods of network programs (hence the term **adjacencies**), rather than within them. The spot announcements are most often used by purely local advertisers but are also utilized by companies with no network schedule (because of spotty or limited distribution) or by large advertisers that make dual use of network and spot advertising.

Selecting Time Periods and Programs

Another consideration in buying TV time is selecting the particular period and program for the advertiser's commercial messages. The cost of television advertising time varies depending on the time of day and the particular program, since audience size varies as a function of these two factors. Television time periods are divided into **dayparts,** which are specific segments of a broadcast day. The time segments that make up the programming day often vary from station to station. However, a typical classification of dayparts for a weekday is shown in Exhibit 13–11.

The various daypart segments attract different audiences both in size and nature, and thus advertising rates vary accordingly. Prime-time draws the largest audiences, with 8:30 to 9 P.M. being the most watched half-hour time period and Sunday being the most popular night for television. As noted earlier, firms wanting to advertise during prime time must pay premium rates. Thus, the prime-time daypart is dominated by the large national advertisers.

The various dayparts are important to advertisers since they attract different demographic groups. For example, daytime TV generally attracts women, whereas early morning attracts women and children. In recent years, daytime ratings have been declining as more and more of the traditional female viewers join the work force. With nearly 65 percent of women in the work force, many advertisers are turning to other dayparts such as early morning to reach them. The top early morning advertisers have increased their spending in this daypart in recent years to reach working women. The late-fringe (sometimes called late-night) daypart segment has become particularly popular among advertisers trying to reach young adults who tune into shows such as "The Tonight Show," "Late Night with David Letterman," and ABC's "Nightline."

Audience size and demographic composition also vary depending on the type of program. In recent years, situation comedies attracted the largest prime-time audiences, with women 18 to 34 comprising the greatest segment of the audience. Feature films ranked second, followed by general drama shows. Women 55 + were the largest audience segment for these programs.[22]

> *Exhibit 13–11*
Common television dayparts

Morning	7:00 A.M.–9:00 A.M., Monday through Friday
Daytime	9:00 A.M.–4:30 P.M., Monday through Friday
Early fringe	4:30 A.M.–7:30 P.M., Monday through Friday
Prime-time access	7:30 P.M.–8:00 P.M., Sunday through Saturday
Prime time	8:00 P.M.–11:00 P.M., Monday through Saturday and 7:00 P.M.–11:00 P.M., on Sunday
Late news	11:00 P.M.–11:30 P.M., Monday through Friday
Late fringe	11:30 P.M.–1:00 A.M., Monday through Friday

Cable Television

The growth of cable

Perhaps the most significant development in the broadcast media has been the growth and expansion of **cable television.** Cable, or CATV (community antenna television), which delivers TV signals through wire rather than the airways, was initially developed to provide reception to remote areas unable to receive broadcast signals. Cable then expanded to metropolitan areas and grew rapidly owing to the improved reception it offered and because it provided subscribers with a wider selection of stations. Cable has experienced extreme growth during the past two decades. In 1975, only 13 percent of TV households had cable. However, by early 1992, cable penetration reached 61 percent, or 57 million households, and by 1994, it is expected to exceed 65 percent.

Cable subscribers pay a monthly fee for which they receive an average of more than 30 channels, including the local network affiliates and independent stations, various cable networks, superstations, and local cable system channels. Cable networks and channels have a dual revenue stream as they are supported by both subscriber fees and advertising revenue. Cable operators also offer programming that is not supported by commercial sponsorship and is available only to households willing to pay a separate fee beyond the monthly subscription charge. These pay channels include HBO, Showtime, and the Movie Channel. Currently, these stations do not show advertising and are not of interest to marketers, except as competitors for the viewing audience of commercial TV. However, some speculate that pay channels may begin to accept advertising on a limited basis.

Cable television broadens the program options available to the viewer as well as the advertiser by offering specialty channels including all-news, popular music, country music, sports, weather, educational, and cultural channels as well as children's programming. Exhibit 13–12 shows the most popular cable channels along with the type of programming they carry and number of subscribers. Many cable systems also carry **superstations,** which are independent local stations that send their signals via satellite to cable operators to make available to subscribers. The five superstations in the United States are WWOR and WPIX in New York, WGN in

➤ *Exhibit 13–12*
Major cable networks

Network	Estimated Home Coverage (Millions)	Program Type
ESPN	59.1	Sports
CNN	58.4	News/information
USA	58.1	Entertainment/movies/sports
Nickelodeon	57.5	Youth interest
TBS	57.1	Entertainment/movies/sports
The Discovery Channel	56.0	Family/health/news/technology/science
MTV	55.2	Music (video)
TNT	54.9	Movies/sports
The Family Channel	54.6	Family/general/original
TNN	54.0	Country
Lifetime	53.0	News/information/women's interest
The Weather Channel	50.0	National/regional/local weather
Arts & Entertainment	50.0	Family/variety
Headline News	47.6	News/information
CNBC	44.0	News/information
VH-1	43.9	Music (video)
Black Entertainment TV	31.9	Ethnic
Prime Network	25.0	Sport
Entertainment Channel	21.0	Entertainment/news/gossip
The Travel Channel	17.0	World travel
CMT Country Music	16.0	Music (video)
The Learning Channel	15.6	Information

Chicago, WSBK in Boston, and WTBS in Atlanta (which like CNN is part of the Turner Broadcasting System, Inc.). Programming on superstations generally consists of sports, movies, and reruns of network shows. The superstations do carry national advertising and are a relatively inexpensive option for cable households across the country.

Cable has had a considerable influence on the nature of television as an advertising medium. First, the expanded viewing options available through cable have led to considerable audience fragmentation. Much of the growth in cable audiences has come at the expense of the three major networks. Cable channels now have about 20 percent of the prime-time viewing audience, while the share of the three networks has declined to 63 percent. Many cable stations have become very popular among consumers and have led advertisers to reevaluate their media plans and the prices they are willing to pay for network and spot commercials on network affiliate stations. The networks recognize the growing popularity of cable and are becoming involved with the cable industry. ABC purchased an 80 percent interest in ESPN, while NBC recently launched two cable channels—the Consumer News and Business Channel (CNBC) and Sports Channel America.

Advertising on cable

As can be seen in Exhibit 13–13, cable advertising revenues have increased steadily since the early 1980s and exceeded $3 billion in 1991. Much of this growth has come from advertising on the national cable networks such as CNN, ESPN, and MTV. However, many national advertisers have been shifting some of their advertising budgets to spot cable and purchasing through local operators as well as the national cable networks. Over the past four years, spot cable revenues have averaged 20 percent annual growth, reaching more than $100 million in 1991.[23]

As with broadcast TV, cable can be purchased on a national, regional, and local or spot level. Many large advertisers advertise on cable networks to reach larger numbers of viewers across the country with a single media buy. Regional cable advertising is also available on cable, primarily through sports and news channels that cover a certain geographic area.

As noted above, many advertisers are turning to spot advertising on local cable systems to reach specific geographic markets. Many national advertisers prefer spot cable because it affords them more precision in reaching specific markets, and they can save money by using a number of small, targeted media purchases rather than making one network buy. The growth in spot cable advertising is also being facilitated by the use of **interconnects** whereby a group of cable systems in a geographic area are joined for advertising purposes. These interconnects increase the size of the audience an advertiser can reach with a spot cable buy. For example, New York Interconnect reaches more than 3.3 million subscribers in the greater New York metropolitan area. More sophisticated interconnect systems are developing that will pool larger numbers of cable systems and allow spot advertisers to reach more viewers. These new systems will also allow local advertisers to make more selective cable buys as they can purchase the entire interconnect or one of several zones within the system.[24]

While spot cable is becoming very popular among national advertisers, it has some of the same problems as spot advertising on broadcast television. The purchasing process is very complicated and time consuming as media buyers must contact hundreds of cable systems in putting together a media schedule consisting of spot cable buys. Local cable systems also do not provide advertisers with strong support or have much information available on demographics, lifestyle, or viewership patterns.

Advantages of cable

Cable television has experienced tremendous growth as an advertising medium because it has some important advantages. One of the primary advantages of cable is

➤ *Exhibit 13–13*
Cable advertising revenue growth

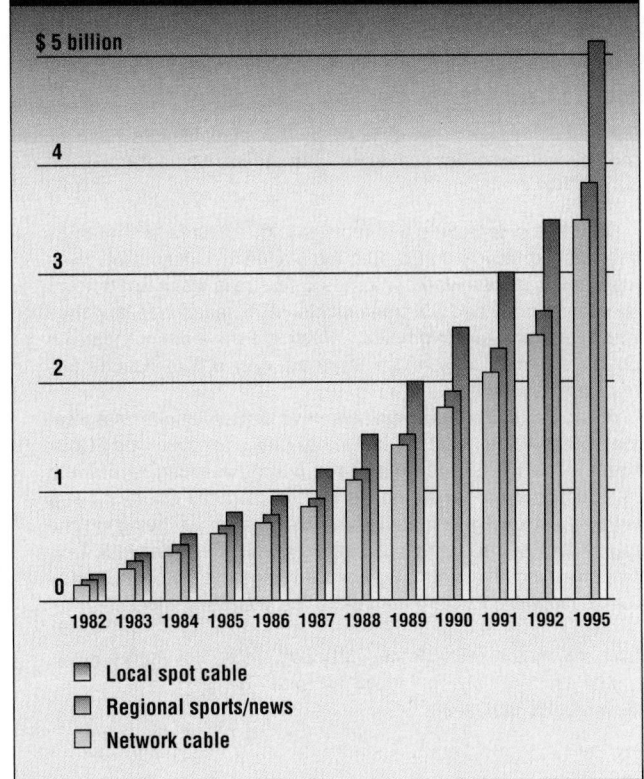

➤ *Exhibit 13–14*
Nickelodeon is very effective for advertising targeted at children

its selectivity. Cable subscribers tend to be younger, more affluent, and better educated than nonsubscribers and have greater purchasing power. Moreover, the specialized programming on the various cable networks reaches a very specific target market.

Many advertisers have turned to cable because of the opportunities it offers for **narrowcasting,** or reaching very specialized markets. For example, ESPN is very popular among advertisers whose primary target audience is the male sports enthusiast. Global Perspective 13–1 discusses how MTV is used by advertisers in the United States and many other countries that are interested in reaching teenagers and young adults. Nickelodeon claims to have more viewers of kids programs than the three networks combined and has become very popular among advertisers targeting this market (Exhibit 13–14). In recent years, a number of companies have been using cable to reach specific target markets. Gillette has been purchasing more time on cable stations such as TBS, CNN, USA Network, and MTV to reach 18-to-34-year-olds. RJR Nabisco advertises over 30 products on cable to reach children, teenagers, and women with greater efficiency.

Advertisers are also interested in cable because of its low cost and flexibility. Many advertisers have found that the cost of producing a program for cable TV is substantially lower than for a network show. A two-hour network program may cost about $2.5 million, whereas a half-hour cable show can be produced for anywhere from $3,000 to $15,000. Even if the advertiser does not produce the program, spot announcements on cable are considerably lower on most cable stations. This makes television a much more viable media option to smaller advertisers with limited budgets or those firms interested in targeting their commercials to a very well-defined target audience. Also, with cable, advertisers generally do not have to make large

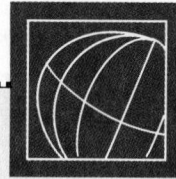

Global Perspective 13–1

MTV Goes International

MTV (Music Television) Network was launched in the United States in 1981 as a pioneering 24-hour rock video channel on cable television. The New York-based company, which is a unit of Viacom International, Inc., is seen in 49 percent of American homes, or approximately 45 million, and its growth parallels that of cable TV at 7 to 8 percent a year. However, MTV is seeking an audience far beyond the U.S. shores. It has expanded into 24 countries including Australia, Japan, and many European and South American nations.

The president of MTV argues that the station has an edge in attracting its target audience of 12-to-34-year-olds around the world and delivering them to advertisers. He notes this is the first international generation and that despite cultural differences, teenagers from various countries are much more similar to each other than they are to their parents as "they wear Levi's, shop at Benetton, wear Swatch watches, and drink Coca-Cola." Rock 'n' roll music is the greatest common denominator of young people around the world, and music is a global language that crosses borders very easily.

MTV has entered into a number of joint ventures to finance its overseas expansion. In Europe, the station broadcasts 24 hours a day, seven days a week, whereas in Australia it airs just 6 hours a week on Friday and Saturday nights. MTV Japan was launched in July 1988 and airs five hours a week in early morning hours on Tuesdays and Fridays, since there are only a few stations and time slots available.

A number of major advertisers have signed long-term agreements with MTV Europe including Levi, Toyota, Coca-Cola, Pepsi-Cola, JVC Stereo, and all the major American record and movie companies. While the network is currently operating at a loss in most foreign markets, MTV sees itself as being on the ground floor of the coming global communications network. One company executive stated the company's goal is "to be the global rock 'n' roll village where we talk to the youth worldwide."

Source: William K. Knoedelseder, Jr., "MTV Goes Global," *Los Angeles Times,* December 18, 1988 pt. IV, pp. 1,4; and Bob Meck, "Fountain of Youth," *Adweek,* April 8, 1991, p. 20.

MTV has expanded into many foreign countries

up-front commitments, which may be as much as a year in advance, required by the networks.

In addition to the lower costs, cable affords the advertiser much greater flexibility in the type of commercials that can be used. As noted earlier in the chapter, the typical network commercial has been reduced to 30 seconds or less in length. However, cable stations are willing to accept much longer ads, and many advertisers will use two- and three-minute commercials on cable programs. Some cable advertisers have used **infomercials,** which are commercials that range from three to thirty minutes in length. This longer format is used to communicate detailed information about a product or service, to demonstrate how to use it, or to discuss special features or advantages. For example, Procter & Gamble has used infomercials on Nickelodeon to teach children how to care for their teeth and to advertise Crest toothpaste. Direct-response advertisers often use these longer ads to describe their products to consumers and to encourage them to call in their order during the commercial. The use of infomercials by direct-response advertisers is discussed in Chapter 16.

The low costs of cable are also making it a very popular advertising medium among local advertisers. Retailers and merchants such as car dealers, furniture stores, restaurants, and many others are taking advantage of the low rates on local cable channels and are switching advertising spending from traditional media such as radio, newspapers, and even magazines. Local cable advertising is one of the fastest-growing segments of the advertising market, and cable systems expect to increase the percentage of revenue they earn from local advertising from 5 percent to 20 percent over the next several years.[25]

Limitations of cable

While cable has become increasingly popular among national, regional, and local advertisers, it still has a number of drawbacks to its appeal as an advertising medium. One of the major problems facing cable is that it is still overshadowed by the major networks, as households with basic cable service still watch considerably more network programming than cable shows. This stems from the fact that cable generally has less desirable programming and poorer production quality than broadcast TV.

Another drawback of cable is audience fragmentation. Although cable's share of the TV viewing audience has increased significantly, these viewers are spread out among the large number of channels available to cable subscribers. The number of viewers who watch any one cable channel is generally quite low. Even the more popular cable channels such as MTV, ESPN, or CNN have prime-time ratings of only about 1 or 2. The large number of cable stations has resulted in audience fragmentation and has made buying procedures more difficult, since numerous stations must be contacted to reach the majority of the cable audience in a market. There are also problems with the quality and availability of local ratings for cable stations as well as research on audience characteristics.

Another problem with cable is its lack of penetration, particularly in the major markets. As of February 1992, cable penetration was 60 percent in the New York City designated market area, 57 percent in the Los Angeles DMA, and 53 percent in Chicago. While cable penetration is now 61 percent of all U.S. television households, this still means nearly 40 percent of the market cannot be reached by advertising on cable.

The future of cable

Cable should continue to experience strong growth throughout the 90s as its audience share increases and advertisers spend more money to reach cable viewers. However, the cable industry also faces a number of challenges over the next decade such as competition from new channels, continued fragmentation of the existing audience, and increased government regulation. Advances in technology, such as video compression and fiber optics, will make it possible for cable systems to offer more channels and thus subject existing cable channels to greater competition. One study estimates that 90 percent of all cable subscribers will have an average of 75 channels by 1997.[26] This will lead to even further fragmentation of the cable audience and make it more difficult for cable networks and channels to charge the advertising rates needed to finance original programming.

Some of the growth in cable channels will come from **multiplexing,** or multiple channels transmitted from one network. Several of the major cable networks such as the Nashville Network and The Discovery Channel already own several channels, and MTV and ESPN have announced plans to launch multiple cable channels.[27] The cable networks will attract a more specialized audience with their separately programmed channels but will sell the combined, as well as individual channel, audiences to advertisers.

Recent years have seen a revolt against the cable industry, and various versions of a "re-regulation" bill have been submitted to Congress.[28] The bill would roll back the provisions of the Cable Television Act of 1984 and would allow local governments to regulate basic cable rates and force cable operators to pay licensing fees for local broadcast programming they now "retransmit" for free. The cable industry has been lobbying against the bill and also has been working to improve the image of cable. For example, the National Cable Television Association has developed an advertising campaign promoting the value of cable and the significant contributions cable networks make to the quality of television programming (Exhibit 13–15).

The future of cable as an advertising medium will ultimately depend on the size and characteristics of the audience the cable stations can reach with their programs. This in turn will depend on the ability of cable to offer programs that attract viewers and subscribers. Although cable has long been a stepchild in terms of program development and acquisition, this has begun to change. For example, CNN has become widely recognized for the quality of its programming and has become the authoritative source for news throughout the world. The position of CNN as the preeminent source of news and information was particularly evident during the

➤ _Exhibit 13–15_
This ad was part of a campaign promoting the value and contributions of cable

Where the African elephant was headed two years ago.

Where he is today because of cable.

This is the true story of a television program that changed the world. It's called _Ivory Wars._

This cable documentary, created by The Discovery Channel and the World Wildlife Fund, portrayed the mindless slaughter of African elephants.

When it was shown to delegates to the Convention on International Trade in Endangered Species, all 103 member nations enacted a ban on the sale of elephant ivory. As a result, the price of ivory has plummeted and demand has virtually disappeared.

Cable companies like yours spend over $3.2 billion a year to help fund programming that can make a difference. Not just in your living room. But in your world.

Cable contributes to life.

National Cable Television Association

Persian Gulf War in 1991 when the network scored record ratings. Even many of the stations affiliated with the three major networks preempted their networks in favor of CNN's coverage of the war.[29]

Cable stations have also begun competing against broadcast stations in the syndication market for reruns of popular shows. Some cable channels have also begun to produce more original programming such as movies, documentaries, and concerts that are attracting more viewers. Better programming will lead to higher ratings, which in turn will lead to more advertising dollars and the revenue needed to continue to develop better programs for cable.

Cable has become, and will continue to be, a particularly popular source of sports programming and is very important to advertisers interested in reaching the male market. There are already 17 regional cable sports networks, and companies such as Group W Sports Marketing make it possible for advertisers to buy multiple regions with one media buy (Exhibit 13–16). It is predicted that every sizable city in the country will have its own regional sports network within a few years.[30]

Cable networks are also paying large sums of money for the rights to sports programming. The deals by ESPN and the Turner Broadcasting System (TBS) for exclusive Sunday night coverage of National Football League games proved that cable networks could compete with the major networks in a sports bidding war. In 1990, ESPN negotiated a four-year, $400 million contract as Major League Baseball's exclusive national cable channel.[31]

As cable penetration increases, its programming improves, and more advertisers discover its efficiency and ability to reach very targeted market segments, cable's popularity as an advertising medium should continue to grow. Many advertising agencies have developed specialists to examine and plan for the use of cable in their clients' media schedules. However, as discussed above, the cable industry will also have to deal with a number of problems if it is to continue to grow and be profitable.

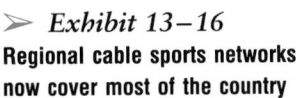

➤ *Exhibit 13–16*
Regional cable sports networks now cover most of the country

Measuring the Television Audience

One of the most important considerations in using television advertising concerns the size and composition of the viewing audience. Audience measurement is very critical to the advertiser as well as the networks and stations. From the advertisers' perspective, the viewing audience is very important. They want to know the size and characteristics of the audience they are reaching when they purchase time on a particular program. Also, the rates they pay are a function of audience size; so the advertiser wants to be sure audience measurements are accurate.

Audience size and composition are also important to the network or station, as these are what determine the amount they can charge for their commercial time. Shows are frequently canceled because they fail to attract enough viewers to make their commercial time attractive to potential advertisers. Determining audience size is not an exact science and has been the subject of considerable controversy through the years. In this section, we examine how audiences are measured and how advertisers use this information in planning their media schedules.

Audience Measures

Measurement of the size and composition of television audiences is performed by rating services. The standard source of national or network television audience information is the A. C. Nielsen Company, whereas local audience information is available from Nielsen and the Arbitron Company. For information on the demographic composition of television audiences, advertisers also use the Simmons reports and Mediamark Research (MRI), as discussed in Chapter 12.

Both Nielsen and Arbitron gather viewership information from a sample of television homes and then project this information to the total viewing area. The various techniques used to gather audience measurement information include diaries, electronic meters or recorders, and personal interviews. The rating services provide various types of information used in measurement and evaluation of a station's viewing audience. These are important to the media planner in making decisions regarding the value of buying commercial time on a program and are discussed before examining the rating services.

Television households

This figure refers to the number of households in the market that own a television set. The A. C. Nielsen Company estimates 91.7 million U.S. households owned at least one television set as of January 1992. Since over 98 percent of U.S. households own a TV set, television households generally correspond to the number of households in a given market.

Program rating

Probably the best known of all the audience measurement figures is the **program rating.** This number represents the percentage of TV households in an area that are tuned to a specific program during a specific time period. The program rating is calculated by dividing the number of households tuned to a particular show by the total number of households in the area. For example, if 12 million households (HH) watched a program such as the "CBS Evening News," the national rating would be 13.1, which is calculated as follows:

$$\text{Rating} = \frac{\text{HH tuned to show}}{\text{Total U.S. HH}} = \frac{12,000,000}{91,700,000} = 13.1$$

A **ratings point** represents 1 percent of all the television households in a particular area tuned to a specific program. On a national level, one ratings point represents 917,000 households. Thus, a top-rated program such as "Roseanne," which has an average rating of 21, would reach 19.3 million households each week (21 × 917,000).

The program rating is the key number to the stations since the amount of money they can charge for commercial time is based on this figure. Ratings points are very important to the networks, as well as individual stations, as a 1 percent change in a program's ratings over the course of a viewing season can mean millions of dollars in gains or losses in advertising revenue.

Households using television

The percentage of homes in a given area that are watching television during a specific time period is referred to as **households using television (HUT).** This figure is sometimes referred to as sets in use and is always expressed as a percentage. For example, if 50 million of the U.S. TV households have their television sets turned on at 10 P.M. on a Wednesday night, the HUT figure would be 54.5 percent (50 million ÷ 91.7 million). As Exhibit 13–17 shows, television usage varies widely depending on the time of day and season of the year.

Share of audience

Another important audience measurement figure is the **share of audience,** which refers to the percentage of households using television in a specified time period that are tuned to a specific program. This figure considers variation in the number of sets in use and the total size of the potential audience, since it is based only on those households that have their sets turned on. Share of audience is calculated by dividing the number of households (HH) tuned to a show by the number of households using television (HUT). Thus, for the "CBS Evening News" example, if 54.5 percent (or 50 million) of U.S. households had their sets turned on, the share of audience would be 24, which is calculated as follows:

$$\text{Share} = \frac{\text{HH tuned to show}}{\text{U.S. households using TV}} = \frac{12 \text{ million}}{50 \text{ million}} = 24$$

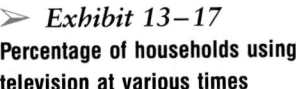

➣ *Exhibit 13–17*
Percentage of households using television at various times

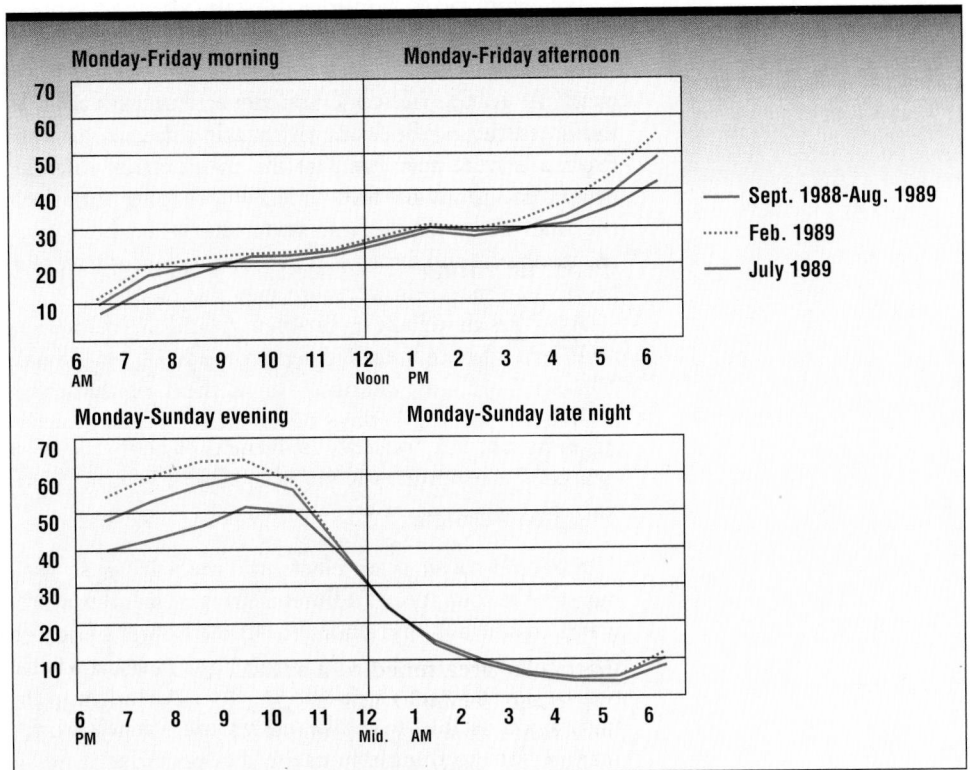

The share of audience figure will always be higher than the program rating unless all the households had their sets turned on (in which case, they would be equal). Share figures are important since they reveal how well a program does with the available viewing audience. For example, during late-night television, the size of the viewing audience drops substantially, so the best way of assessing the popularity of a program is to examine the share of the available audience it attracts relative to competing programs.

In addition to these figures, rating services will also provide an audience statistic known as **total audience**. This figure represents the total number of homes viewing any five-minute part of a telecast. This number can also be broken down to provide audience composition figures that are based on the distribution of the audience into demographic categories.

Network Audience Information

Nielsen television index

The primary source of national and network television audience information is the A.C. Nielsen Company's Nielsen Television Index (NTI), which provides daily and weekly estimates of television viewing and national sponsored network and major cable program audiences. For more than 20 years, Nielsen provided this information using a two-pronged system consisting of a national sample of metered households along with a separate sample of diary households. In the metered households, an electronic measurement device known as the **audimeter** (audience meter) was hooked up to the TV set to conduct a continuous measurement of the channels to which the set is tuned. Network viewing for the country—or the famous "Nielsen ratings"—was based on the results provided by audimeters placed in a national sample of homes carefully selected to be representative of the population of U.S. households. The metered households were also supported by a separate panel of households that recorded viewing information in diaries. Since the audimeter could measure only the channel to which the set was tuned, the diary panel was used to gather demographic data on the viewing audience.

For many years, considerable concern was expressed in the television and advertising industries over the audimeter/diary system. In particular, several problems were noted with the diary method. First, the information from diaries was not available to the network and advertising analysts for several weeks. Then studies indicated the method was overstating the size of some key demographic audiences. Problems were noted in that the cooperation rates among diary keepers were going down, and many of the women who kept a household's diary were not noting what the man in the home was watching when he was alone. The complex new video environment and explosion in viewing options were also making it difficult for diary keepers to maintain accurate viewing records.

As a result of these problems, and in response to competitive pressure from another audience measurement company from England, AGB, in fall 1987, the A. C. Nielsen Company changed its method of audience measurement by making the people meter the sole basis of its national rating system and eliminating the use of the diary panel.

The people meter

The **people meter** is an electronic measuring device that incorporates the technology of the old-style audimeter in a system that records not only what is being watched but also by whom in 4,000 homes. The actual device is a small box with eight buttons—six for the family and two for visitors—that can be placed on the top of the TV set (Exhibit 13–18). An accompanying remote control unit also makes it possible to make electronic entries from anywhere in the room. Each member of the sample household is provided a personal button on the system that is used to indicate his or her presence as viewer. The device is also equipped with a

➤ *Exhibit 13–18*
The people meter is now used by Nielsen for measuring national TV audiences

sonar sensor to alert the viewers entering or leaving the room to punch in or log out on the meter.

The viewership information the people meter collects from the household is stored in the home system until it is retrieved by Nielsen's computers. The data collected by the system include when the set is turned on, which channel is viewed, when the channel is changed, and when the set is off, in addition to the information on who is viewing. The demographic characteristics of the viewers are also in the system, and viewership can be matched to these characteristics. The Nielsen's operation center processes all this information each week for release to the television and advertising industries. Nielsen uses a sample of metered households in the nation's largest markets (New York, Los Angeles, and Chicago) to provide overnight viewing results.

Nielsen's switch to people meters has generally been viewed as an improvement over the diary panel system. However, initial reaction to the system was not all positive, particularly by some of the networks that saw estimates of their audience sizes by the new system coming out lower than under the old system. Promotional Perspective 13–2 discusses some of the background and continuing battle over the measurement of television audiences.

Arbitron

In fall 1991, the Arbitron Ratings Company launched a new national network ratings service called ScanAmerica. ScanAmerica began operations with a sample of only 1,000 households dispersed among five major markets—New York, Chicago, Los Angeles, Dallas, and Atlanta. However, Arbitron hoped to expand ScanAmerica to a nationally projectable sample of 2,000 households by 1993. A major feature of the ScanAmerica rating service, which uses a people meter system, is that it also gathers data on product usage patterns of audiences of specific network shows. CBS was the only network to subscribe to ScanAmerica along with a few major consumer package-goods companies and advertising agencies. Because of this lack of support Arbitron suspended operations of the national ratings service in September 1992.

Local Audience Information

Information on local audiences is important to both local advertisers and those firms making national spot buys. The two major sources of local audience information are again Nielsen and Arbitron. To measure television viewership in local markets, Nielsen provides the Nielsen Station Index (NSI). The NSI measures television station audiences in over 200 local markets known as **designated market areas (DMAs)**. DMAs are nonoverlapping areas used for planning, buying, and evaluating television audiences and are generally a group of counties in which stations located in a metropolitan or central area achieve the largest audience share. Nielsen uses audimeters for several of the larger markets such as New York, Chicago, and Los Angeles, whereas other markets are measured by diaries only. NSI reports information

Promotional Perspective 13–2

The Ongoing Battle over Television Audience Measurement

Since 1942, the TV and advertising industries have relied on the A.C. Nielsen Company to provide information on the size of nationwide television viewing audiences. The audience measurement numbers Nielsen provides have a tremendous influence on the content and business of television. They are the foundation on which program decisions and deals are made and advertising dollars are spent. For over 40 years, Nielsen relied on a two-pronged system that included a sample of households wired to audimeters, which recorded whether a TV set was turned on and the channel to which it was tuned, and another set of homes that maintained viewing diaries that could be used to determine audience composition characteristics such as demographics.

Concern over the accuracy of viewing diaries led the networks, as well as many advertisers and agencies, to challenge Nielsen's measurement system. In 1985, a number of the largest advertising agencies signed a contract with a new Nielsen competitor, AGB Television Research, the U.S. affiliate of an English company that had been providing ratings in Europe and Asia for years. Much of the interest in AGB centered around its new technology for measuring viewing audiences known as the people meter. The networks were also very interested in a challenge to Nielsen's monopoly and potential improvements in measurement technology and helped fund an initial test of AGB's system in Boston. In 1987, CBS canceled its contract with Nielsen for audience ratings and signed a one-year deal with AGB.

In response to the competitive threat from AGB, Nielsen began installing its own people meters and in 1987 announced the system would replace the National Audience Composition diary system used to record viewer demographics. Both Nielsen and AGB began producing people meter-based ratings in September 1987, and the two new systems produced radically different results. For example, during the first week, Nielsen's people meter rated ABC's "Monday Night Football" game at 15.3, while AGB gave it a rating of 11.9, a discrepancy of roughly 3 million households! After a year of confusion and debate, the industry decided to stay with Nielsen since it was a known entity. In August 1988, AGB announced it was suspending its U.S.-based ratings operation after losing $80 million.

Unfortunately, the controversy over the people meter and Nielsen's audience measures did not end when AGB left the market. The new measurement system showed considerable declines in the size of some audience segments for many prime-time shows. This meant advertisers expected to pay less money for commercial time on these shows. The controversy over the people meter came to a head in 1990 over what the networks

called an inexplicably steep decline in usage levels during the first quarter of the year. As discussed in Promotional Perspective 13–1, the ratings shortfall forced the networks to give away $150 million to $200 million worth of makegoods since their rating guarantees were not met. The networks responded by denouncing the accuracy of the people meter system, the sample composition, and its ability to produce statistically reliable results. Moreover, they all refused to renew their contracts for rating services with Nielsen. Nielsen responded by stating the people meter represents the state of the art in electronic measurement equipment and there were no major problems with the system.

The result of this latest controversy over Nielsen's audience measurement system was establishment of the Committee on Nationwide Television Audience Measurement (CONTAM), which includes representatives from the three major networks and the National Association of Broadcasters. CONTAM hired a media research firm to investigate the people meter system and recommend changes. While the report documented problems with the quality of Nielsen's measurement system, it also acknowledged the complexity and problems associated with measuring viewing audiences. Certain guidelines were developed for improving the cooperation rate of households in the Nielsen samples, obtaining better representation by monitoring all TV sets in a home, and developing a way of dealing with the problem of "button fatigue," whereby people fail to log in or out on the people meter.

Concern over the problems associated with audience measurement continue, and several new technologies are being tested. For example, Nielsen is working on a passive people meter based on an image recognition system. Arbitron, Nielsen's major rival in the United States, is testing a passive people meter system developed by a French company. There is also speculation that AGB may return to the United States with its own passive people meter system. Nielsen's new passive people meter system may even be able to track the viewing audience's attention to the tube on a second-by-second basis. This would yield accurate ratings of not just shows, but commercials as well. Many believe this would provide an answer to an issue that has challenged the television industry since the first ad appeared on TV in 1941 — How many people actually watch the commercial?

Source: Erik Larson, "Watching Americans Watch TV," *Atlantic Monthly*, March 1992, pp. 66–78; Wayne Walley, "Big 3 Nets Put Heat on Nielsen," *Advertising Age*, June 25, 1990, p. 60; Wayne Walley, "Nets Force Nielsen Showdown," *Advertising Age*, September 24, 1990, pp. 3, 60; and "Who's Gyping Whom in TV Ads?" *Fortune*, July 6, 1987, p. 78.

on viewing by time periods and programs and includes audience size and estimates of viewing over a range of demographic categories.

Arbitron provides audience measurement information for the 214 or so largest TV markets. Like Nielsen, Arbitron uses electronic meters and diaries for measuring audiences in the 13 largest markets, whereas only diaries are used in the other markets. Arbitron also defines its markets in terms of nonoverlapping geographic areas, each area known as an **area of dominant influence** (**ADI**). Each county in the

➤ *Exhibit 13–19* **Sample page of Arbitron ADI**

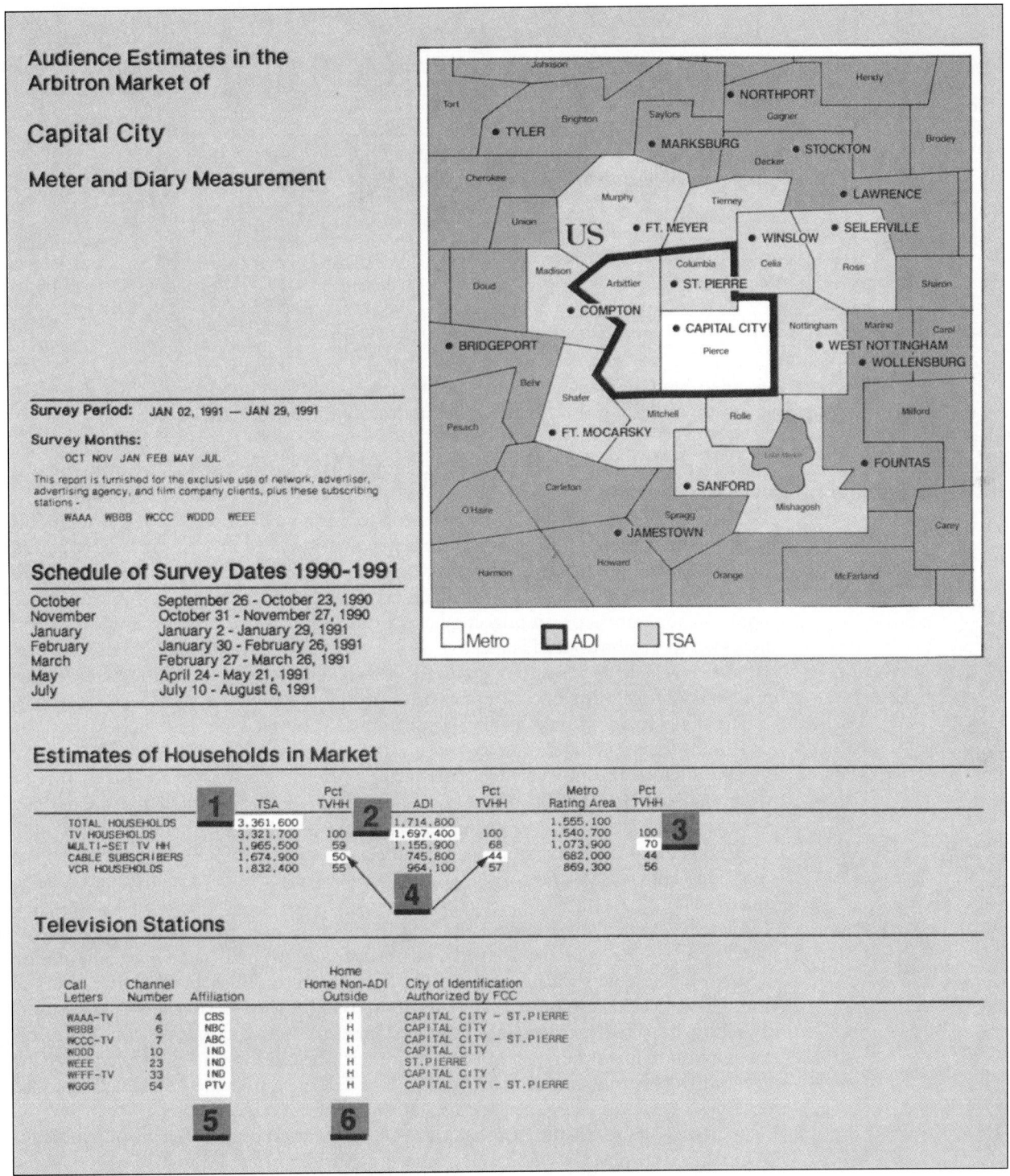

Audience Estimates in the Arbitron Market of

Capital City

Meter and Diary Measurement

Survey Period: JAN 02, 1991 — JAN 29, 1991

Survey Months:

OCT NOV JAN FEB MAY JUL

This report is furnished for the exclusive use of network, advertiser, advertising agency, and film company clients, plus these subscribing stations –

WAAA WBBB WCCC WDDD WEEE

Schedule of Survey Dates 1990-1991

October	September 26 - October 23, 1990
November	October 31 - November 27, 1990
January	January 2 - January 29, 1991
February	January 30 - February 26, 1991
March	February 27 - March 26, 1991
May	April 24 - May 21, 1991
July	July 10 - August 6, 1991

☐ Metro   ☐ ADI   ☐ TSA

Estimates of Households in Market

	1 TSA	Pct TVHH	**2** ADI	Pct TVHH	Metro Rating Area	Pct TVHH **3**
TOTAL HOUSEHOLDS	3,361,600		1,714,800		1,555,100	
TV HOUSEHOLDS	3,321,700	100	1,697,400	100	1,540,700	100
MULTI-SET TV HH	1,965,500	59	1,155,900	68	1,073,900	70
CABLE SUBSCRIBERS	1,674,900	50	745,800	44	682,000	44
VCR HOUSEHOLDS	1,832,400	55	964,100	57	869,300	56

4

Television Stations

Call Letters	Channel Number	Affiliation	Home Home Non-ADI Outside	City of Identification Authorized by FCC
WAAA-TV	4	CBS	H	CAPITAL CITY - ST.PIERRE
WBBB	6	NBC	H	CAPITAL CITY
WCCC-TV	7	ABC	H	CAPITAL CITY - ST.PIERRE
WDDD	10	IND	H	CAPITAL CITY
WEEE	23	IND	H	ST.PIERRE
WFFF-TV	33	IND	H	CAPITAL CITY
WGGG	54	PTV	H	CAPITAL CITY - ST.PIERRE

5   **6**

nation is assigned to an ADI, which is an exclusive geographic area consisting of all counties in which the home market stations receive a preponderance of viewing. Each ADI is also part of a greater unit called the total survey area, which includes counties outside the ADI where there is an audience for stations broadcasting from within the ADI. Arbitron also reports information for a metro rating area (MRA), which is an area within the ADI that generally corresponds to the U.S. government's metropolitan statistical areas. Exhibit 13–19 provides a sample page from Arbitron

➤ *Exhibit 13–20* **Top 20 television markets ranked by size and percentage of U.S. population***

Rank	TV households		Rank	TV households	
1. New York	6,479,500	7.35%	11. Houston	1,452,000	1.58%
2. Los Angeles	4,883,200	5.32%	12. Cleveland	1,421,800	1.55%
3. Chicago	2,999,700	3.27%	13. Minneapolis-St. Paul	1,380,100	1.50%
4. Philadelphia	2,637,400	2.87%	14. Seattle-Tacoma	1,379,400	1.50%
5. San Francisco-Oakland-San Jose	2,208,000	2.41%	15. Miami-Ft. Lauderdale	1,286,300	1.40%
6. Boston	2,126,300	2.32%	16. Tampa-St. Petersburg	1,243,100	1.35%
7. Washington, D.C.	1,718,100	1.94%	17. Pittsburgh	1,139,600	1.24%
8. Dallas-Ft. Worth	1,763,400	1.92%	18. St. Louis	1,110,900	1.21%
9. Detroit	1,718,100	1.87%	19. Sacramento-Stockton	1,045,700	1.14%
10. Atlanta	1,456,800	1.59%	20. Phoenix	1,021,500	1.11%
			Total, markets 1–20:	40,804,800	44.44%

*All data is from the Arbitron Company and represents the Arbitron Television household and population estimates for the 1991–92 season.

showing how a television market is measured, and Exhibit 13–20 shows the television household and population estimates for the top 20 ADIs.

Developments in Audience Measurement

The advertising industry is likely to see changes over the next several years in the way viewing audiences are measured. Technological developments and a very competitive research marketplace will continue to drive companies toward the never-ending quest for the ideal TV rating and measurement system. Many people believe people meters are only the first step in improving the way audiences are measured. While the people meter is seen as an improvement over the diary method, this system still requires cooperation on an ongoing basis from people in the metered homes. As was discussed in Promotional Perspective 13–2, work is continuing on developing passive measurement systems that require less involvement by people in metered homes and can produce more accurate measures of the viewing audience.

The main focus of new technology for measuring viewing audiences will be on developing commercial rating systems rather than just program ratings. Current systems such as the people meter or diary method measure the audiences for the programs surrounding the commercials rather than the commercials themselves. However, problems such as zipping and zapping as well as people leaving the room or turning attention away from the TV during commercial breaks have focused more attention on the need to develop accurate ratings of more than just program audience viewing.[32]

The development of a system that can provide second-by-second or minute-by-minute ratings could have a profound impact on the television and advertising industries. These new ratings would alter the content of TV programs as executives would have insight into how viewers respond to various parts of a show. Advertisers obviously have the greatest interest in commercial ratings as they could use this information to force the networks to lower their prices if the results showed a decline in viewership during commercial breaks. It would also provide greater insight into the types of commercials that attract and hold viewers' attention.[33]

Another important development is the tying together of television audience viewership information with the purchase behavior of the household through the use of **single-source data.** A number of companies including Information Resources, Nielsen, and Arbitron have developed single-source systems that are being tested in various markets.[34] These systems monitor the shows a household watches as well as the brands it purchases, coupon usage, magazine and newspaper readership, and demographics. We discuss the use of single-source data in more detail in Chapter 20.

It appears that the 1990s will see a considerable amount of change and developments in terms of viewing options, video technology, and audience measurement. These trends and developments must be carefully monitored by advertisers and

➤ *Exhibit 13–21*
Radio revenue growth ($ millions)

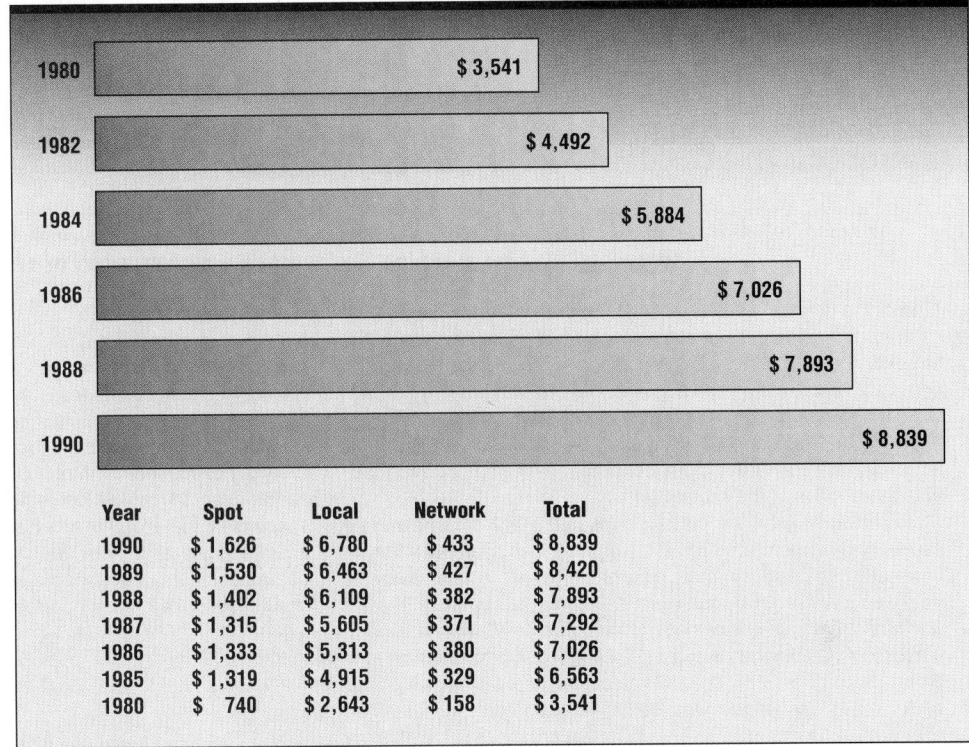

Year	Spot	Local	Network	Total
1990	$ 1,626	$ 6,780	$ 433	$ 8,839
1989	$ 1,530	$ 6,463	$ 427	$ 8,420
1988	$ 1,402	$ 6,109	$ 382	$ 7,893
1987	$ 1,315	$ 5,605	$ 371	$ 7,292
1986	$ 1,333	$ 5,313	$ 380	$ 7,026
1985	$ 1,319	$ 4,915	$ 329	$ 6,563
1980	$ 740	$ 2,643	$ 158	$ 3,541

media planners as well as by people in the television industry, as they can have a profound impact on audience size, composition, and the way advertisers use, and pay for the use of, television as an advertising medium.

Radio

Television has often been referred to as the ideal advertising medium, and to many people it personifies the glamour and excitement of the industry. Radio, on the other hand, has been called the "Rodney Dangerfield of media" in reference to the lack of respect many advertisers have for the medium and that it is often taken for granted by many advertisers.[35] As noted at the beginning of this chapter, the role of radio as both an advertising medium and an entertainment medium changed dramatically with television's rapid growth in popularity during the 1950s, 1960s, and 1970s. However, radio survived and has become a very healthy, although somewhat different, medium. Radio has evolved into a primarily local advertising medium, whereas it was dominated by network programming and national advertisers before the growth of television. In 1990, network advertising accounted for less than 5 percent of radio's revenue.[36] Radio has also become a medium characterized by highly specialized programming appealing to very narrow segments of the population.

The survival of radio is perhaps best demonstrated by the numbers. The number of radio stations in this country has grown to more than 9,000, including 4,987 commercial AM stations and 4,392 commercial FM stations. In 1987, over 557 million radios were in use, or an average of 5.7 per household. Radio reaches 77 percent of all Americans over the age of 12 each day and has grown into a ubiquitous medium that is background to many activities such as reading, driving, running, walking, working, and interacting. The pervasiveness of this medium has not gone unnoticed by advertisers, as radio advertising revenue has grown from $3.5 billion in 1980 to more than $8.8 billion in 1990 (Exhibit 13–21).

Radio has survived and flourished as an advertising medium because it offers advertisers certain advantages for communicating messages to their potential customers. However, radio has inherent limitations and thus plays a somewhat different role as an advertising medium. In this section, we examine the characteristics of radio and the role it plays in the advertiser's media strategy.

Promotional Perspective 13–3

A Successful Radio Campaign Has Motel 6 Leaving a Lot of Lights On

One of the largest portions of the 2.8 million room lodging industry is the economy or budget segment, which is dominated by the Motel 6 chain (the "6" originally stood for $6 a night when the company was founded in 1962). Although Motel 6 is the nation's largest chain of budget motels, before 1986 it had no marketing department, never had an advertising campaign, charged guests $1.49 to have their televisions connected, and did not even provide telephones in the motel rooms.

In 1986, Motel 6 hit bottom as it lost $18.7 million and its occupancy rate dropped to 66.7 percent. This prompted the investment company that had bought the chain to take steps to help turn it around. Phones were installed in every room; the TV hookup charge was dropped; rooms were refurbished; and a number of new motels were built, bringing the total number of Motel 6s to over 500. By 1988, Motel 6 had earnings of $5.3 million, and occupancy was up to 73.8 percent. While these changes were important in Motel 6's turnaround, the company's top executives agree that such a rapid reversal would not have been possible without its pervasive radio campaign featuring Tom Bodett, a 33-year-old-contractor-turned-writer, as spokesperson for the company.

Motel 6 originally went with radio in 1986 because it had a limited ad budget of just over $1 million and because it believed radio was the best way to reach travelers, most of whom arrived by car or truck and without a reservation. In the radio spots developed by the chain's ad agency, Bodett delivers a down-home, humorous message that tells travelers it is OK to be cheap and ends with the campaign slogan: "We'll leave the light on for you." Much of the success of the campaign comes from Bodett's country-style voice and delivery. It has also been suggested that Bodett is so effective because on radio his "real-folk" voice takes on a variety of faces. Older people envision him as a road-weary traveler, younger people see him as one of them, and businesspeople hear a harried salesperson.

While the exact reason is difficult to determine, there is little doubt that Bodett has been effective and has become very popular in the process. He has his own national radio show and even has his own fan club. Although he receives mountains of mail addressing him as the head of the chain, Motel 6's real president does not mind, noting, "He can be chairman of the board if he wants! ... He's contributed that much to the turnaround of this company." Bodett is heard in more than 70 different executions of Motel 6 spots, and in 1989 the company spent over $8 million on network and radio advertising. The success of the Motel 6 ads has led other motel chains such as Econ Lodges and Red Roof Inns to develop radio campaigns using celebrity spokespeople. However, none has been as successful as Bodett's folksy appeal.

Source: "King of the Road," *Marketing and Media Decisions,* March 1989, pp. 80–86.

Example of Motel 6 Radio Spot
"Hi. Tom Bodett for Motel 6 with a plan for anyone whose kids are on their own now. Take a drive, see some of the country and visit a few relatives. Like your sister Helen and her husband Bob. They're wonderful folks and always happy to pull the hide-a-bed out for you, but somehow the smell of mothballs just isn't conducive to gettin' a good night's sleep. And since Bob gets up at 5:30, well that means you do too. So here's the plan. Check into Motel 6. 'Cause for around 22 bucks, the lowest prices of any national chain, you'll get a clean, comfortable room, and Helen and Bob'll think you're mighty considerate. Well you are, but maybe more important, you can sleep late and not have to wonder if the towels in their bathroom are just for decoration. My rule of thumb is, if they match the tank and seat cover, you better leave 'em alone. Just call 505-891-6161 for reservations. I'm Tom Bodett for Motel 6. Give my best to Helen and Bob and we'll leave the light on for you."

One of the 70-plus radio spots for Motel 6 created by The Richards Group.

Advantages of Radio

Cost and efficiency

One of the main strengths of radio as an advertising medium is its low cost. Radio commercials are very inexpensive to produce. They require only a script of the commercial to be read by the radio announcer or a copy of a prerecorded message that can be broadcast by the station. The cost for radio time is also low. A minute on network radio can cost only $5,000, which translates into a cost per thousand figure of only $3 to $4. The low relative cost of radio makes it one of the most efficient of all advertising media, whereas the low absolute or actual cost means the budget needed for an effective radio campaign is often lower than for other media.

The low cost of radio also means advertisers can build more reach and frequency into their media schedules, given a certain budget. Advertisers can use different

➤ *Exhibit 13–22*
Breakdown of radio stations by type of program format

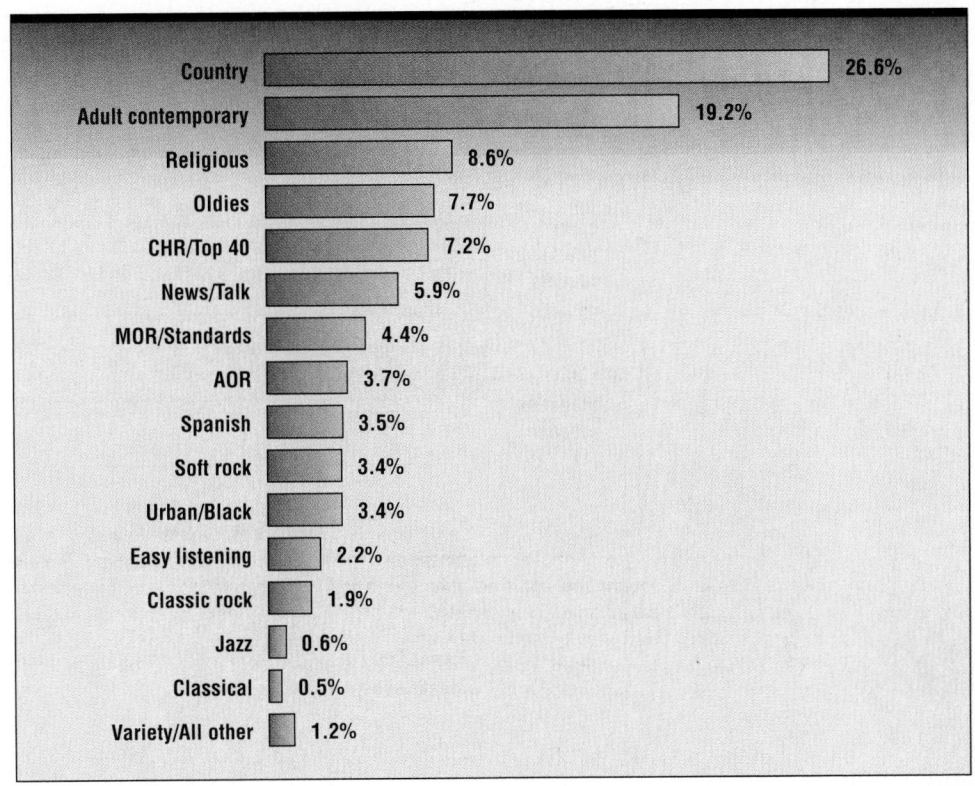

stations to broaden the reach of their messages and multiple spots to ensure an adequate frequency level. Many national advertisers have begun to recognize the cost efficiency of radio. A few years ago, Miles Laboratories spent its entire advertising budget of $600,000 for Bactine first-aid spray in this medium. While the media budget was too small to allow for much impact with TV ads, radio proved very effective in reaching its target audience of young mothers, which included working women as well as mothers staying at home. The effect of the radio campaign on Bactine sales was so favorable that Miles decided to allot 15 percent of its total ad budget to radio for other brands such as Alka-Seltzer and Flintstones vitamins.[37] Promotional Perspective 13–3 discusses how Motel 6 used radio advertising to help turn around the company.

Selectivity

Another major advantage of radio is the high degree of audience selectivity available through the various program formats and geographic coverage of the numerous stations. Radio enables companies to focus their advertising on specialized audiences such as certain demographic and lifestyle groups. Most areas have radio stations with formats such as rock 'n' roll, easy listening, classical music, country western, talk shows, and all news, to name a few. Exhibit 13–22 shows the breakdown of radio stations by type of programming format. Hard-to-reach consumers such as teenagers, college students, or working adults can be reached more easily through radio than most other media. Light television viewers spend considerably more time with radio than with television and are generally an upscale market in terms of income and education level.[38] As can be seen in Exhibit 13–23, light readers of magazines and newspapers also spent more time listening to radio. Radio has also become a popular way to reach specific non-English-speaking ethnic markets. For example, Los Angeles, New York City, and Miami have several radio stations that

➤ *Exhibit 13–23*
Time spent with radio by light users of various other media

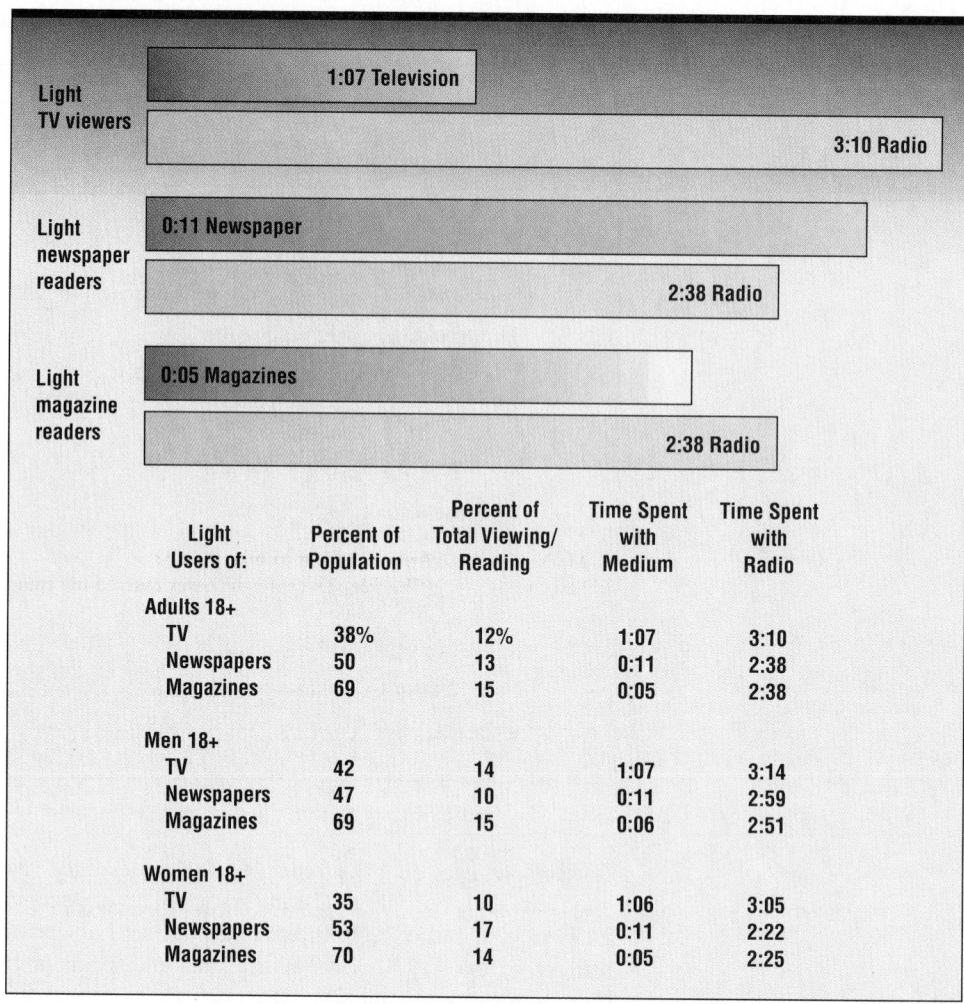

Light Users of:	Percent of Population	Percent of Total Viewing/ Reading	Time Spent with Medium	Time Spent with Radio
Adults 18+				
TV	38%	12%	1:07	3:10
Newspapers	50	13	0:11	2:38
Magazines	69	15	0:05	2:38
Men 18+				
TV	42	14	1:07	3:14
Newspapers	47	10	0:11	2:59
Magazines	69	15	0:06	2:51
Women 18+				
TV	35	10	1:06	3:05
Newspapers	53	17	0:11	2:22
Magazines	70	14	0:05	2:25

broadcast in Spanish and reach these areas' large Hispanic markets. As mass marketing declines and gives way to market segmentation and regional marketing, radio will continue to grow in importance.

Flexibility

Radio is probably the most flexible of all the advertising media, as it has a very short closing period, which means advertisers can change their message almost up to the time it goes on the air. Radio commercials can usually be produced and scheduled on very short notice. Advertisers can also adjust their messages to local market conditions and marketing situations very easily through radio.

Mental imagery

Another potential advantage of radio that is often overlooked is that it allows listeners to use their imagination when processing a commercial message. While the creative options of radio are limited, many advertisers have taken advantage of the absence of a visual element to let consumers create their own picture or image of what is happening in a radio message.

For example, a radio campaign for Molson Golden beer used a series of man-meets-woman vignettes as part of its advertising program for the brand in the United States. These spots took advantage of listeners' opportunity to fantasize and develop

➤ *Exhibit 13–24*
Molson beer made effective use of radio by letting listeners use their imaginations

FEMALE:	Excuse me, is this stool taken?
MALE:	Uh, no.
FEMALE:	Mind if I sit here?
MALE:	Help yourself.
FEMALE:	Thanks.
MALE:	Would you, uh, pass me the peanuts?
FEMALE:	Sure—(sound of a glass being knocked over)—oh, oh, I'm terribly sorry. Oh, I've ruined that tie, and it's so beautiful too. Let me wipe it up.
MALE:	(softly) That's OK.
FEMALE:	Um, that's a very interesting cologne you're wearing.
MALE:	Huh? It's beer!
FEMALE:	(Chuckle) Oh, no, I'm sorry. Let me buy you another one, please.
MALE:	No, that's all right—I'll just suck my tie.
FEMALE:	(Chuckle) Let me make it up to you. How about a Molson Golden?
MALE:	Molson Golden?
FEMALE:	Yah, imported from Canada. It's excellent. Crisp, clear, smooth—you'll really love it.
MALE:	Uh, yah, yah . . .
FEMALE:	You will?
MALE:	Are you trying to pick me up?
FEMALE:	(Chuckle) The thought never entered my mind.
MALE:	Well, think.
FEMALE:	(Chuckle)
ANNOUNCER:	Molson Golden beer, from North America's oldest brewery. Since 1786, Molson makes it golden. Imported by Martlet, Great Neck, New York.
MALE:	Well, you're not doing a very good job of this.
FEMALE:	I know, let me start over: Is this stool taken?
MALE:	(Shouts) Hold the peanuts!

their own images of the characters in the scenes developed in the commercials. An example of one of the Molson radio spots is shown in Exhibit 13–24.

It has also been suggested that radio can be used to reinforce television messages through a technique called **image transfer** whereby the images of a TV commercial are implanted into a radio spot.[39] This involves establishing the video image of a TV commercial, then using the audio portion (spoken words and/or jingle) as the basis for the radio campaign. The idea is that when consumers hear the radio message, they will make the connection to the TV commercial, which reinforces its video images. Image transfer offers advertisers a way of combining radio and TV ads and making them work together by reinforcing one another.

Merchandising value and support

Radio stations often become an integral part of many communities, and the radio personalities may become popular figures. Advertisers often use radio stations and personalities to enhance their involvement with a local market and to gain influence with local middlemen such as retailers.

Limitations of Radio

Several factors limit the effectiveness of radio as an advertising medium and must be considered by the media planner in determining the role the medium will play in the advertising program.

Creative limitations

A major drawback of radio as an advertising medium is the absence of a visual image. The radio advertiser cannot show the product, demonstrate it, or use any type of visual appeal or information. A radio commercial is, like a television ad, a short-lived and fleeting message that is externally paced, which does not allow the receiver to control the rate at which the message is processed. Because of the creative limitations of radio, many companies tend to ignore it, and agencies often assign junior people to the development of radio commercial messages.

Fragmentation

Another problem with radio is the high level of audience fragmentation that occurs because of the large number of stations. Radio listeners can choose from a large number of stations, and the percentage of the market tuned to any particular station is usually very small. For example, the top-rated radio station in many major metropolitan areas with a number of AM and FM stations may attract less than 10 percent of the total listening audience. Thus, advertisers that want to have broad reach in their radio advertising media schedule have to buy time on a number of stations to cover even a local market.

Chaotic buying procedures

It should be readily apparent how chaotic the media planning and purchasing process can become for the advertiser that wants to use radio on a nationwide spot basis. Acquiring information and evaluating and contracting for time with even a fraction of the 9,000 commercial stations that operate across the country can be very difficult and time consuming. This problem has been diminished somewhat in recent years as the number of radio networks increases and the growth in syndicated programs offering a package of several hundred stations expands.

Limited research data

Audience research data on radio are often limited, particularly as compared with television, magazines, or newspapers. Most radio stations are not large operations and lack the revenue to support detailed studies of their audiences. Also, most users of radio are local companies that are not able to support research on radio listenership in their markets. Thus, media planners do not have a great deal of audience information available to guide them in their purchase of radio time.

Buying Radio Time

The purchase of radio time is similar to that of television, as advertisers can make either network, spot, or local buys. Since these options were reviewed in examining ways of buying television time, they are discussed here only briefly.

Network versus Spot Radio

Network radio

Advertising time on radio can be purchased on a network basis using one of the national networks. In 1987, the Westwood One Network purchased Mutual Broadcasting Network and NBC Radio Network, leaving four major networks: ABC, CBS, Westwood, and United Stations. There are also more than 100 regional radio networks across the country. The advantage of using networks is that the advertiser can minimize the amount of negotiation and administrative work needed to get national or regional coverage, and the costs will be lower than if individual stations were used. However, the number of affiliated stations on the network roster and the type of audience they reach can vary considerably. Thus, the use of network radio results in less flexibility in selecting stations.

Spot radio

National advertisers can also use spot radio to purchase airtime on individual stations in various markets. The purchase of spot radio provides advertisers greater flexibility in selecting markets, individual stations, and airtime and making any

➤ *Exhibit 13–25*
Dayparts for radio

Morning drive time	6:00 A.M.–10:00 A.M.
Daytime	10:00 A.M.–3:00 P.M.
Afternoon/evening drive time	3:00 P.M.–7:00 P.M.
Nighttime	7:00 P.M.–12:00 A.M.
All night	12:00 A.M.–6:00 A.M.

➤ *Exhibit 13–26*
Sample radio rate card

GRID	I	II	III	IV	DAY/DAYPART
AAA	175	150	125	110	M-F 3P-8P SAT 10A-3P
AA	160	140	115	100	M-F 5:30A-10A SUN 10A-3P
A	150	130	110	95	M-F 10A-3P M-SUN 8P-1A
B	125	110	95	80	SA/SU 5:30A-10A R. O. S.
C	150	130	110	95	T. A. P.

* ALL RATES APPLY TO :30 OR :60 SECOND COMMERCIAL ANNOUNCEMENTS

adjustments in the message for local market conditions. Spot radio accounts for approximately 20 percent of radio time sold.

Local radio

By far the heaviest user of radio is the local advertiser, as nearly 78 percent of radio advertising time is purchased from individual stations by local companies. Auto dealers, retailing operations, restaurants, and financial institutions are among the heaviest users of local radio advertising.

Time Classifications

As with television, the broadcast day for radio is divided into various time periods or dayparts, as shown in Exhibit 13–25. The size of the radio listening audience varies widely across the various dayparts, and advertising rates follow accordingly. The largest radio audiences (and thus the highest rates) occur during the early morning and late afternoon drive times. Radio rates also vary according to the number of spots or type of audience plan purchased. Variation in radio rates is common depending on the supply and demand of time available in the local market and the ratings of the individual station. Rate information is available directly from the stations on their rate cards (see Exhibit 13–26) and is summarized in Standard Rate and Data Service's (SRDS) Spot Radio Rates and Data for both local stations and radio networks. However, many stations do not adhere strictly to rate cards and the rates published in SRDS. Radio rates vary according to market demand and time availability.

Audience Information

As noted earlier, one problem with radio is the lack of audience information. Because there are so many radio stations and thus many small, fragmented audiences, the stations cannot support the expense of detailed audience measurement. Also, owing to the nature of radio as incidental or background entertainment, it becomes very difficult to develop precise measures of radio listenership in terms of who listens at various time periods and for how long. There are now two major radio ratings services, with Arbitron being the primary supplier of audience information for local stations and the RADAR (radio's all-dimension audience research) studies, which supply information on network audiences.

Arbitron

Arbitron covers 260 local radio markets with one to four ratings reports per year. Arbitron uses a sample of representative listeners in each market and has them

> *Exhibit 13–27* **Partial page from Arbitron Radio Ratings Report**

Target Audience
PERSONS 18-49

	MONDAY-FRIDAY 6AM-10AM				MONDAY-FRIDAY 10AM-3PM				MONDAY-FRIDAY 3PM-7PM				MONDAY-FRIDAY 7PM-MID				WEEKEND 10AM-7PM			
	AQH (00)	CUME (00)	AQH RTG	AQH SHR	AQH (00)	CUME (00)	AQH RTG	AQH SHR	AQH (00)	CUME (00)	AQH RTG	AQH SHR	AQH (00)	CUME (00)	AQH RTG	AQH SHR	AQH (00)	CUME (00)	AQH RTG	AQH SHR
KCBQ																				
METRO	25	263	.2	.8	40	365	.3	1.3	36	340	.3	1.4	6	138		.5	51	356	.4	2.4
TSA	25	263			40	365			36	340			6	138			51	356		
KCBQ–FM																				
METRO	101	684	.7	3.1	117	768	.9	3.7	83	736	.6	3.2	23	354	.2	2.1	67	616	.5	3.2
TSA	101	684			117	768			83	736			23	354			67	616		
KCEO																				
METRO	11	110	.1	.3	8	81	.1	.3	10	95	.1	.4		8			1	8		
TSA	11	110			8	81			10	95				8			1	8		
KFMB																				
METRO	171	790	1.3	5.3	106	678	.8	3.3	141	1092	1.0	5.4	87	827	.6	7.9	92	567	.7	4.4
TSA	171	790			106	678			141	1092			87	827			92	567		
KFMB–FM																				
METRO	352	1714	2.6	10.9	197	1354	1.5	6.2	155	1344	1.1	6.0	51	785	.4	4.6	96	946	.7	4.6
TSA	352	1714			197	1354			155	1344			51	785			96	946		
KFSD																				
METRO	41	291	.3	1.3	67	295	.5	2.1	39	281	.3	1.5	16	237	.1	1.5	20	234	.1	1.0
TSA	41	291			67	295			39	281			16	237			20	234		
KGB																				
METRO	268	1800	2.0	8.3	275	1686	2.0	8.7	230	1693	1.7	8.8	92	928	.7	8.4	200	1326	1.5	9.6
TSA	268	1800			275	1686			230	1693			92	928			200	1326		
KGMG																				
METRO		8							2	16		.1		16				8		
TSA		8							2	16				16				8		

maintain a diary of their radio listening for a seven-day period. Audience estimates for the market are based on these diary records and reported by time period and selected demographics in the *Arbitron Ratings/Radio* book to which clients subscribe. Exhibit 13–27 provides a sample page from the Arbitron Ratings Report for persons in the 18-to-49 age target audience across the various dayparts. The three basic estimates in the Arbitron report include:

- Person estimates—the number of persons listening.
- Rating—the percentage of listeners in the survey area population.
- Share—the percentage of the total estimated listening audience.

These three estimates are further defined by using quarter-hour and cume figures.

The **average quarter-hour** (**AQH**) **figure** identifies the average number of persons estimated to have listened to a station during any 15-minute period of any given daypart. For example, station KCBQ has an average quarter-hour listenership of 2,500 during the weekday 6 A.M. to 10 A.M. daypart. This means that any weekday, for any 15-minute period during this time period, an average of 2,500 people between the ages of 18 and 49 are tuned to this station. This figure helps to determine the audience and cost of a spot schedule within a particular time period.

Cume is a term used for cumulative audience, which is the estimated total number of different people who listened to a station for a minimum of five minutes in a quarter-hour period within a reported daypart. In Exhibit 13–27, the cumulative audience of persons 18 to 49 for station KCBQ during the weekday morning daypart is 26,300. Cume provides an estimate of the reach potential of a radio station.

The **average quarter-hour rating** (**AQH RTG**) expresses the estimated number of listeners as a percentage of the survey area population. The **average quarter-hour share** (**AQH SHR**) is the percentage of the total listening audience tuned to each station and shows the share of listeners each station captures out of the total listening audience in the survey area. The average quarter-hour rating of station KCBQ during the weekday 6 A.M. to 10 A.M. daypart is 0.2 while the average quarter-hour share is 0.8.

Radar

In the RADAR studies, which are sponsored by the major radio networks, audience estimates are collected twice a year and are based on daily telephone interviews covering seven days of radio listening behavior. Each listener is called daily for a week and asked about radio usage from the day before until that moment. Network audience measures are provided by RADAR along with estimates of audience size for all stations and various segments. The audience estimates are time-period measurements for the various dayparts. RADAR also supplies reports that provide estimates of network audiences to all commercials and to commercials within various programs. The research is conducted year round and is published annually in *Radio Usage and Network Radio Audiences.*

As is the case with TV, media planners must use the audience measurement information to evaluate the value of various radio stations in reaching the advertiser's target audience and their relative cost. The media buyer responsible for the purchase of radio time works with information on target audience coverage, rates, time schedules, and availability to try to optimize the advertiser's radio media budget.

Developments in Radio

Radio survived the threat it encountered from television by becoming a more localized medium that could focus on specialized market segments. As the number of commercial radio stations increases, the specialization and fragmentation of the radio audience will continue. Particularly noteworthy is the growth of FM stations, which have a more limited range but have the advantage of broadcasting in stereo. Most radio sets sold today have both AM and FM capability, and 75 percent of radio listening and 60 percent of advertising spending is on FM stations.[40] This figure is even higher for young adults (18-34), where nearly 80 percent of listening occurs on FM because of the more youth-oriented format of FM stations and the superior fidelity of stereo.[41] AM stations have begun to respond to the challenge of FM by changing the format of their programs and getting permission from the FCC to broadcast in stereo. The aging of the population may be a benefit to AM stations, as older consumers are less likely to listen to music and tune into more talk shows, local information programs, news, and sports.

Another important trend in radio is the increasing number of radio networks and syndicated programs that offer advertisers a package of several hundred stations. This reduces the fragmentation and purchasing problems associated with radio and increases the appeal of the medium to national advertisers. In the 1990s, radio stations are expected to have more of their programs satellite-delivered from radio networks, which will reduce their programming costs. The U.S. government is also supporting development of a global radio network using satellites. The plan would require a new generation of radio sets capable of receiving satellite broadcasts and would offer broadcasters and advertisers a way of reaching a national and international market.[42]

Advertisers are continuing to discover ways to make effective use of radio in their media plans. However, radio, like all other advertising media, has been hurt by the cutback in advertising spending. Total radio advertising revenue was down 3 percent in 1991, the first decline in over a decade.[43] Local radio stations are beginning to experience more competition from cable advertising. A number of radio advertisers are switching to local cable because the rates are comparable with those of radio and there is the added advantage of TV's visual impact.[44] Concern has also been expressed over the continuing growth in the number of radio stations competing for a stagnant listener market with similar programming. Thus, a number of challenges face radio in its quest to continue to gain audiences and attract advertising revenue. While radio is no longer taken for granted by advertisers, the medium must deal with these problems if it is to sustain its growth.

SUMMARY

Television and radio, or the broadcast media, are the most pervasive media in most consumers' daily lives and offer advertisers the opportunity to reach vast audiences. Both broadcast media are time-, rather than space-, oriented and are organized similarly in that they utilize a system of affiliated stations belonging to a network, as well as individual stations, to broadcast their programs and commercial messages. Advertising on radio or TV can be done on national or regional network programs or may be purchased on a spot basis from local stations.

Television has grown faster than any other advertising medium in history and has become the leading medium for national advertisers. No other medium offers the creative capabilities of television, as the combination of sight, sound, and movement present the advertiser with a vast number of options for presenting a commercial message with high impact. Television also offers advertisers mass coverage at a low relative cost. Variations in programming and audience composition, along with the growth of cable television, are helping TV offer more audience selectivity to advertisers. While television is often viewed as the ultimate advertising medium, it has several limitations, including the high cost of producing and airing commercials, a lack of selectivity relative to other media, the fleeting nature of the message, and the problem of commercial clutter. The latter two problems have been compounded in recent years by the trend toward shorter commercials.

Information regarding the size and composition of TV audiences is provided on a national level by the A. C. Nielsen Company, whereas local audience information is provided by Nielsen along with the Arbitron Ratings Company. The amount of money networks or stations can charge for commercial time on their programs is based on these audience measurement figures. This information is also important to media planners, as it is used to determine the combination of shows needed to attain specific levels of reach and frequency with the advertiser's target market.

Future trends in television include the continued growth of cable and the resulting increase in available channels to cable households. The continued penetration of videocassette recorders poses a potential threat to traditional viewing patterns as consumers record shows to watch at their own leisure and fast forward through the commercials and as they watch more prerecorded programs such as movies. Developments and changes are likely to occur in the measurement of viewing audiences, with greater emphasis placed on measuring the number of people watching the commercial as well as the program.

The role of radio as an entertainment and advertising medium has changed with the rapid growth of television. Radio has evolved into a primarily local advertising medium that offers highly specialized programming appealing to very narrow segments of the market. Radio offers advertisers the opportunity to build high reach and frequency into their media schedules and the ability to reach selective audiences at a very efficient cost.

The major drawback of radio is its creative limitations owing to the absence of a visual image. The short and fleeting nature of the radio commercial along with the highly fragmented nature of the radio audience are also problems. As with television, the rate structure for radio advertising time varies with the size of the audience delivered. Information regarding radio audiences is provided by Arbitron for local markets and by the RADAR studies for network audiences.

A major trend in radio is the continued specialization and fragmentation of radio audiences. FM radio has begun to dominate the listening audience, although AM stations are responding to this challenge with changes in program formats and the addition of stereo broadcasting capabilities. Radio may face challenges in the future from cable television.

KEY TERMS

broadcast media	up-front market	syndicated programs
split-30s	regional networks	off-network syndication
zipping	spot advertising	first-run syndication
zapping	national spot	barter syndication
television network	local advertising	sponsorship
affiliates	station reps	participations

adjacencies
dayparts
cable television
superstations
interconnects
narrowcasting
infomercials
multiplexing
program rating
ratings point

households using
  television (HUT)
share of audience
total audience
audimeter
people meter
designated market areas
  (DMAs)
area of dominant
  influence (ADI)

single-source data
image transfer
average quarter-hour
  (AQH) figure
cume
average quarter-hour
  rating (AQH RTG)
average quarter-hour
  share (AQH SHR)

DISCUSSION QUESTIONS

1. Discuss the advantages and disadvantages of advertising on the Super Bowl. Do you think this event will continue to attract advertisers as the cost of a 30-second spot approaches $1 million? Why or why not?
2. Discuss how the changes that have occurred in the television industry over the past two decades have affected the use of TV as an advertising medium.
3. Discuss the specific advantages and disadvantages of television as an advertising medium.
4. Explain what is meant by zipping and zapping and how they affect television advertising. Discuss some ways advertisers can deal with the zapping problem.
5. Choose a particular television daypart other than prime time and analyze the products and services being advertised during this period. Why do you think these firms have chosen to advertise during this daypart?
6. What are the advantages and disadvantages of advertising on cable television networks or stations or a syndicated program? Choose a cable and a syndicated program and evaluate the types of products and services advertised during these shows.
7. Discuss the methods used to measure network television viewing audiences and local audiences. Do you believe the measurement methods being used for each are producing valid estimates of program audiences? Why or why not?
8. What are the advantages and limitations of advertising on radio? What types of advertisers are most likely to use radio?
9. Discuss how the concept of image transfer can be used in radio advertising. Provide an example of a radio campaign that is using this concept and evaluate it.
10. Discuss the future of television and radio as advertising media. What are some of the developments that may affect their use?

chapter **14**

Evaluation of Print Media: Magazines and Newspapers

➤ To examine the structure of the magazine and newspaper industries and the role of each medium in the advertising program.

➤ To examine the advantages and limitations of magazines and newspapers as advertising media.

➤ To examine the various types of magazines and newspapers and the value of each as an advertising medium.

➤ To examine how advertising space is purchased in magazines and newspapers, how readership is measured, and how rates are determined.

➤ To consider future trends and developments regarding magazines and newspapers and how they will influence their use as advertising media.

Is There Life after College?—This Magazine May Tell You

The transition from college to the cold, cruel "real world" is often difficult for many students. However, the publishers of *Cosmopolitan* have come out with a new spinoff magazine designed to help make the transition a little easier for coeds. In February 1992, the first issue of *Cosmopolitan's Life After College* was published, and about 500,000 copies were distributed to campus bookstores, drugstores, supermarkets, and other outlets in hundreds of major college communities. More than 25,000 editions were also given to career planning and placement offices at many schools.

The focus of the new magazine is on helping young women achieve their career goals and adjusting to life off campus. It includes articles with tips about landing that first job, dressing for the corporate world, managing finances, and social life in the real world. Articles in the premier issue included "Write the Perfect Resume," "Killer Interview Questions," "Meeting Men in the Real World," and "The Office Romance: Can It Ever Work?" Seth Hoyt, publisher of *Life After College,* believes the new magazine can be helpful to women during a critical stage in their lives. The first issue included a questionnaire to find out more about readers' demographics, career plans, and other information that will be helpful in planning future issues.

Life After College is positioned differently from its older sister publication *Cosmopolitan,* which has a wide appeal among college-age women. The covers feature professional, yet chic younger women rather than the sexy and glamorous models with the plunging necklines who appear on the cover of *Cosmo.* Hoyt thinks the magazine appeals to recent graduates or ambitious undergraduates who will use it as an information source. He also expects the magazine to have a considerable "back-end audience" of 22-to-26-year-old women who have postponed working or have been working for a few years and might want to switch jobs.

Although the decision to publish a separate magazine for this market was largely intuitive, it was also based on knowledge that *Cosmo* has a large college following and there are a lot of women who are out of school, out of work, and need the type of information *Life After College* will provide. The publishers do not expect the new magazine to be the type of publication young women would subscribe to; rather, it will be similar to bridal magazines whose readers purchase one or two issues to help in planning and preparation for the big event. Plans call for the new magazine to be a seasonal publication that comes out a few times a year.

While there is concern the new magazine might cannibalize some sales away from *Cosmo,* the publishers

(continued)
believe the new publication is unique from an editorial standpoint and will end up adding more readers to the *Cosmopolitan* franchise. A number of national magazines have tried in the past to appeal to the after-college market but have found the segment very transient and difficult to pin down. However, *Life After College* has an advantage since it is spinning off of an established maga-zine that has wide appeal with young women. It will be interesting to see if women rely on the new publication to help them answer the question of whether there is indeed "life after college."

Source: Reprinted with permission from Marketing News, *published by the American Marketing Association, Carrie Goerne, May 11, 1992.*

Magazines and newspapers have been in existence as advertising media for more than two centuries and for many years were the only major media available to advertisers. However, with the growth of the broadcast media, particularly television, reading habits declined as more consumers turned to TV viewing not only as their primary source of entertainment but also as a source of news and information. Despite the competition from the broadcast media, newspapers and magazines have remained important media vehicles, both to consumers and to advertisers.

Thousands of different magazines are published in this country appealing to nearly every specific consumer interest and lifestyle, as well as to the thousands of different businesses and occupations. By becoming a highly specialized medium that reaches a specific target audience, the magazine industry has grown and prospered. Newspapers are still the primary advertising medium in terms of both ad revenue and number of advertisers. Newspapers are particularly important as a local advertising medium for the hundreds of thousands of retail businesses and are often used by large, national advertisers as well.

Magazines and newspapers are an important part of our lives. For many consumers, newspapers are their primary source of product information, as they would not even think of going shopping without checking to see who is having a sale or clipping coupons from the weekly food section or Sunday inserts. Many people subscribe to and/or read a number of different magazines each week or month to become better informed or simply to be entertained. Individuals employed in various occupations rely on business magazines to keep them informed and updated on current trends and developments in their industries as well as in business in general.

While most of us are very involved with the print media, it is important to keep in mind that very few, if any, newspapers or magazines can survive without the support of advertising revenue. For example, consumer magazines generate an average of 48 percent of their revenues from advertising, whereas business publications receive nearly 73 percent.[1] Newspapers generate 70 percent of their total revenue from advertising. In many cities, the number of daily newspapers has declined because they could not attract enough advertising revenue to support their operations. The print media must be able to attract large numbers of readers or a very specialized audience to be of interest to advertisers.

The Role of Magazines and Newspapers

The role of magazines and newspapers in the advertiser's media plan differs from the broadcast media in that they allow the presentation of detailed information that can be leisurely processed at the reader's own pace. The print media are not intrusive like radio and television and generally require some attention and effort on the part of the reader for the advertising message to have an impact. For this reason, newspapers and magazines are often referred to as being **high-involvement media.**[2] Newspapers are a mass medium in that they are received in nearly 70 percent of American households on a daily basis. Magazines, however, reach a very selective audience and, like radio, can be valuable in reaching specific types of consumers and market segments. While both magazines and newspapers are print media, the advantages and disadvantages of the two are quite different, as are the types of advertising each attracts. In this chapter, we focus on these two major forms of print media. The specific advantages and limitations of each medium are examined along with factors that are important to the media planner in determining when and how to use newspapers and magazines in the media plan.

Magazines

Over the past several decades, magazines have been a rapidly growing medium that serves the educational, informational, and entertainment needs and interests of a wide range of readers in both the consumer and business markets. The number of consumer magazines has more than doubled since 1970 as hundreds of new magazines were introduced each year during the 1980s. In 1988 alone, 491 new consumer magazines were launched. More than half of these are published less than six times a year and nearly a third are published only once a year.[3] The American public's interest and involvement in magazines has led many advertisers to invest their media dollars in magazine advertising. The amount of money spent on advertising in consumer magazines has grown from slightly over $1 billion in 1970 to $6.5 billion in 1991.[4] Magazines rank second only to television as a medium for national advertisers. There has also been a tremendous growth in business publications, which serve the interests of various industries, businesses, and professions. The number of business publications has grown to more than 5,000, and advertising revenue in these magazines has increased from $836 million in 1970 to $4.1 billion in 1991.[5]

Magazines are the most specialized of all advertising media. While some magazines such as *Reader's Digest, Time,* or *TV Guide* are general mass-appeal publications, most are targeted to a very specific type of audience. There is a magazine designed to appeal to nearly every type of consumer in terms of demographics, lifestyle, activities, interests, or fascination. Numerous magazines are targeted toward specific businesses and industries as well as toward individuals engaged in various professions (Exhibit 14–1).

The wide variety of magazines makes this an appealing medium to a vast number of advertisers. Although television accounts for the largest amount of advertising expenditures among national advertisers, more companies advertise in magazines than any other medium. Users of magazines range from large consumer products

➤ *Exhibit 14–1*
Magazines targeted to a specific industry or profession

companies such as the Philip Morris Companies and General Motors Corporation that spend well over $200 million a year on magazine advertising to a small company advertising scuba equipment in *Skin Diver* magazine.

Classifications of Magazines

To gain some perspective on the various types of magazines available, and the advertisers that use them, it is useful to consider the way magazines are generally classified. Standard Rate and Data Service (SRDS), which is the primary reference source on magazines for media planners, divides magazines into three broad categories or classes based on the audience to which they are directed—consumer, farm, and business publications. Each of these broad categories is then further classified according to the editorial content and audience appeal of the magazine.

Consumer magazines

Consumer magazines are those that are bought by the general public for information and/or entertainment. SRDS divides consumer magazines into 51 classification groupings such as general interest, sports, travel, and women's. Another way of classifying consumer magazines is on the basis of distribution, as they can be sold through subscription or circulation, store distribution, or both. For example, *Time* and *Newsweek* are sold both through subscription and in stores, whereas *Woman's World* is sold only through stores. *People* magazine was originally sold only through stores but then added subscription sales as the magazine gained in popularity. Exhibit 14–2 shows the top 10 magazines in terms of subscriptions and single-copy sales, respectively. Magazines can also be classified by issue frequency, with weekly, monthly, and bimonthly being the most common.

Consumer magazines represent the major portion of the magazine industry, accounting for nearly two thirds of all advertising dollars spent in magazines. Moreover, the distribution of advertising revenue in consumer magazines is highly concentrated, as the top 25 magazines account for more than 70 percent of total consumer magazine advertising.

Consumer magazines are obviously best suited for marketers interested in reaching general consumers of products and services as well as for companies trying to reach a specific target market. The most frequently advertised product categories in consumer magazines are toiletries and cosmetics, tobacco products, alcoholic beverages, automobiles, food, and household products. Marketers of tobacco products and hard liquor spend a large amount of their media budgets in magazines since they are prohibited from advertising in the broadcast media.

While large national advertisers tend to dominate consumer magazine advertising in terms of expenditures, it should be noted that the more than 2,000 consumer magazines are also very important to smaller companies selling products that appeal to specialized markets. Special-interest magazines are very effective at assembling consumers with similar lifestyles or interests and offer marketers an efficient way to

> *Exhibit 14–2*
Top magazines

A. By Subscriptions		B. In Single Copy Sales	
1. *Modern Maturity*	22,450,003	1. *TV Guide*	6,458,237
2. *Reader's Digest*	16,269,637	2. *Woman's Day*	3,375,125
3. *TV Guide*	15,053,018	3. *National Enquirer*	3,390,837
4. *National Geographic*	9,763,406	4. *Family Circle*	2,808,713
5. *Better Homes & Gardens*	8,002,794	5. *Star*	2,792,823
6. *Good Housekeeping*	5,188,919	6. *Cosmopolitan*	2,103,870
7. *McCall's*	5,066,849	7. *People Weekly*	1,767,304
8. *Ladies' Home Journal*	5,065,131	8. *First For Women*	1,764,430
9. *Family Circle*	5,065,131	9. *Good Housekeeping*	1,401,546
10. *Woman's Day*	4,619,505	10. *Woman's World*	1,279,280

Excludes comics, publishers' packages, and bulletins

reach these people with a minimal amount of wasted coverage or circulation. For example, a manufacturer of high-quality, expensive running shoes such as New Balance or Saucony might find *Runner's World* to be the best vehicle for advertising to the serious runner (Exhibit 14–3).

Not only are these specialty magazines of value to firms interested in reaching a specific market segment, but the editorial content of many of these magazines also creates a very favorable advertising environment in which to advertise relevant products and services. For example, the avid skier often cannot wait for the first snowfall after reading the season's first editions of *Skiing* and *Ski* magazine and may be particularly receptive to ads for skiing products while reading these publications.

Farm publications

The second major SRDS category consists of all the magazines directed to farmers and their families. About 270 publications are tailored to nearly every possible type of farming or agricultural interest. Standard Rate and Data Service breaks farm publications into 11 classifications ranging from general-interest magazines aimed at all types of farmers (e.g., *Farm Journal, Successful Farmer, Progressive Farmer*) to those in specialized agricultural areas such as poultry (*Gobbles*), hog farming (*National Hog Farmer*), or cattle raising (*Beef*—see Exhibit 14–4). Also, a number of farm publications are directed at farmers in specific states or regions such as *Nebraska Farmer* or *Montana Farmer Stockman*. Farm publications are not classified under business publications because historically farms were not perceived as businesses.

➤ *Exhibit 14–3*
Runner's World is an excellent medium for reaching the serious runner

➤ *Exhibit 14–4*
Beef magazine is read by many cattlemen

Business publications

Business publications are those magazines or trade journals published for specific businesses, industries, or occupations. Standard Rate and Data Service has a separate edition for business publications in which approximately 5,200 magazines and trade journals are listed and broken into 159 categories. The major categories include:

1. Magazines directed at specific professional groups such as *National Law Review* for lawyers or *Architectural Forum* for architects.
2. Industrial magazines directed to businesspeople in various manufacturing and production industries such as *Iron Age, Chemical Week,* or *Industrial Engineering.*
3. Trade magazines targeted to wholesalers, dealers, distributors, and retailers such as *Progressive Grocer, Drug Store News, Women's Wear Daily,* or *Restaurant Business.*
4. General-business magazines aimed at executives in all areas of business such as *Forbes, Fortune,* or *Business Week* (general-business publications are also included in SRDS's consumer publications edition).

The numerous business publications reach specific types of professional people with particular interests and needs and provide them with important information relevant to their industry, occupation, and/or careers. Business publications are important to advertisers because they provide an efficient way of reaching the specific types of individuals who constitute their target market. Much marketing occurs at the trade and business-to-business level where one company sells its products or services directly to another. We examine the role of advertising in business-to-business marketing in greater detail in Chapter 21.

Advantages of Magazines

Magazines have a number of characteristics and qualities that make them particularly attractive as an advertising medium. The specific strengths of magazines include their selectivity, excellent reproduction quality, flexibility, permanence, prestige, readers' high receptivity to magazine advertising and involvement with the publication, and services they offer to advertisers.

Selectivity

One of the main advantages of using magazines as an advertising medium is their **selectivity** or ability to reach a specific target audience. Magazines are the most selective of all media with the exception of direct mail. The high degree of selectivity of magazines is because most magazines are published for special-interest groups. The thousands of magazines published in the United States reach all types of consumers and businesses and allow advertisers to target their advertising to segments of the population of the most interest to them. For example, *Modern Photography* is targeted toward photography buffs, *Stereo Review* reaches those with an avid interest in music, *American Baby* reaches new mothers, and *Ebony* focuses in on the upscale black market.

In addition to selectivity based on interests, magazines also can provide the advertiser with high demographic and geographic selectivity. *Demographic selectivity,* or the ability of a medium to reach specific demographic groups, is available through magazines in two ways. First, most magazines are, as a result of editorial content, aimed at fairly well defined demographic segments. For example, *Ladies Home Journal, MS, Self,* and *Cosmopolitan* are read predominantly by women; *Esquire, Playboy,* and *Sports Illustrated* are read mostly by men; and teenage girls can be reached through *Seventeen* or *Sassy.*

A second way magazines offer demographic selectivity is through special editions. Even magazines that appeal to broader audiences such as *Reader's Digest, Time,* or

Newsweek can provide a high degree of demographic selectivity through their special demographic editions. Most of the top consumer magazines offer different editions targeted at different demographic markets. Exhibit 14–5 describes *Newsweek 50 Plus,* a specific demographic edition offered by *Newsweek* magazine.

Geographic selectivity, whereby an advertiser can focus ads in certain cities or regions, is also possible through magazines. One way of achieving geographic selectivity is by using a magazine that is edited for, and targeted toward, particular areas. Numerous magazines are devoted to regional interests such as *Yankee* (New England), *Southern Living* (South), *Sunset* (West), and *Texas Monthly* (guess where?). One of the more successful media developments of recent years has been the growth of "city magazines" in most major American cities. Publications such as *Los Angeles Magazine, Philadelphia, Pittsburgh, Denver,* and *San Diego Magazine,* to name a few, provide residents of these areas with articles concerning lifestyle, happenings, events, and the like, in these cities and their surrounding metropolitan areas.[6] These magazines offer very high geographic selectivity and also tend to be read by a very upscale audience, as shown by the profile in Exhibit 14–6 of the *San Diego Magazine* reader.

Another way of achieving geographic selectivity in magazines is through the purchase of specific geographic editions of national or regional magazines. A number of publications divide their circulation into specific geographic groupings based on regions or major metropolitan areas and offer advertisers the option of concentrating their ads in these editions. For example, *Newsweek* breaks the United States

> *Exhibit 14–5*
Newsweek special edition description

Newsweek 50PLUS

Newsweek 50 Plus: On Target in a Changing World

Today, adults age 50+ comprise 26% of the U.S. population...and their consumer muscle has become even more spectacular!

■ Discretionary income: over $130 *billion*, more than half the U.S. total...

■ Total assets: $7 *trillion*, or 70% of the net worth of U.S. households.

Source: "The Shifting American Marketplace," Age Wave Inc., 1989

Today's most savvy marketers are targeting the 50+ market for all kinds of products and services. And now you can target them in Newsweek 50 Plus.

Just consider Newsweek 50 Plus's editorial environment. It reflects our long-standing enterprise in reporting on America's changing demographic profile and the entire issue of aging (including the newsweekly field's only editorial department on Aging). Enterprise that has earned Newsweek a National Magazine Award and special recognition by the AARP.

Newsweek: An Editorial Difference that Works for You

Your message in Newsweek 50 Plus appears in Newsweek's timely, lively editorial setting. Editorial that millions of active men and women over 50 rely on...week after week. Men and women in America's mainstream that you should be reaching.

Newsweek 50 Plus: Circulation and Audience Highlights

1992 Circulation: 500,000 individual subscribers age 50 or older

Subscriber Identification: Database match with Equifax Marketing Decision Systems and Donnelley Marketing Information Services.

Audience Profile: A valuable core market of affluent achievers

■ Total Adults: 3,276,000 (58% male/42% female)   ■ Professional/Managerial: 931,000

■ Total Adults, Age 50+: 2,497,000   ■ Median Age: 56.3 years

■ Attended/Graduated College: 1,926,000   ■ Median Household Income: $45,469

Source: 1991 Simmons (Newsweek estimates)

➤ *Exhibit 14–6*
The *San Diego Magazine* reader is very upscale

into 11 geographic areas and offers regional editions for each, as shown in Exhibit 14–7. In addition to these geographic regions, *Newsweek* offers advertisers their choice of editions directed to the top 40, 20, or 10 metropolitan areas. Many magazines allow advertisers to combine regional or metropolitan editions to best match the geographic market of interest to them.

In 1992, Standard Rate and Data Service listed 259 consumer magazines offering geographic and/or demographic editions. These editions are particularly attractive to regional and national advertisers. Regional advertisers can purchase space in editions that reach only areas where they have distribution, yet still enjoy the prestige of advertising in a major, national magazine. National advertisers can use the geographic editions to focus their advertising on areas with the greatest potential or those needing more promotional support. They also can use regional editions to test-market products or alternative promotional campaigns in various regions of the country.

Ads in regional editions can also list the names of retailers or distributors in various markets, thus encouraging greater local support from the trade. As noted in previous chapters, the trend toward regional marketing is increasing the importance of having regional media available to marketers. The availability of regional and demographic editions can also enhance the cost efficiency of magazines, as they result in a lower cost per thousand for reaching desired audiences.

Reproduction quality

One of the most valued attributes of magazine advertising is the reproduction quality that is possible for the ads. Magazines are generally printed on a high-quality paper stock and use printing processes that provide excellent reproduction in black and white or color. Since magazines are a very visual medium where illustrations are

➤ *Exhibit 14–7* **Geographic editions of *Newsweek* magazine**

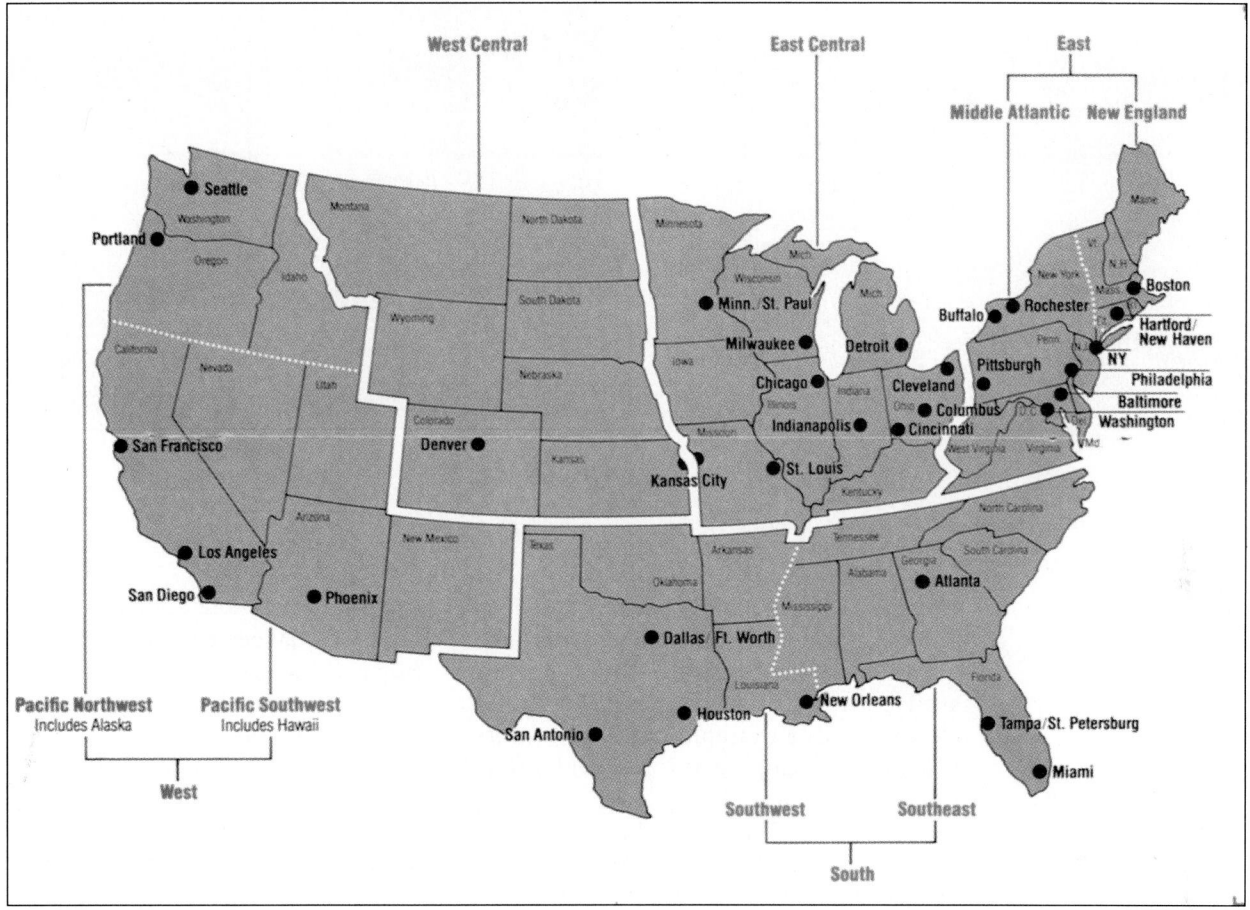

often a dominant and critical part of an advertisement, this is a very important property. The reproduction quality of most magazines is far superior to that offered by the other major print medium of newspapers, particularly when color is needed. The use of color has become a virtual necessity in most product categories, and more than two thirds of all magazine ads now use color.

Creative flexibility

In addition to their excellent reproduction capabilities, magazines also offer advertisers a great deal of flexibility in terms of the type, size, and placement of the advertising material. Some magazines offer (often at an extra charge) a variety of special options that can be used to enhance the creative appeal of the ad and usually increase attention and readership of the ad. Examples of such options include gatefolds, bleed pages, inserts, and creative space buys.

<u>Gatefolds</u> enable an advertiser to make a striking presentation by using a third page that folds out and gives the ad an extra large spread. Gatefolds are often found at the inside cover of most large consumer magazines or on some inside pages. Advertisers utilize gatefolds to make a very strong impression, and they are often used on special occasions such as the introduction of a new product or brand. For example, automobile advertisers often use gatefolds to introduce new versions of their cars each model year. Not all magazines offer gatefolds, however, and they usually must be reserved well in advance and are always sold at a premium.

<u>Bleed pages</u> are those where the advertisement extends all the way to the end of the page, rather than leaving a margin around the ad. Bleed pages are used to give

➢ *Exhibit 14–8* **Honeywell and Transamerica each spent nearly $1 million to produce and run pop-up ads**

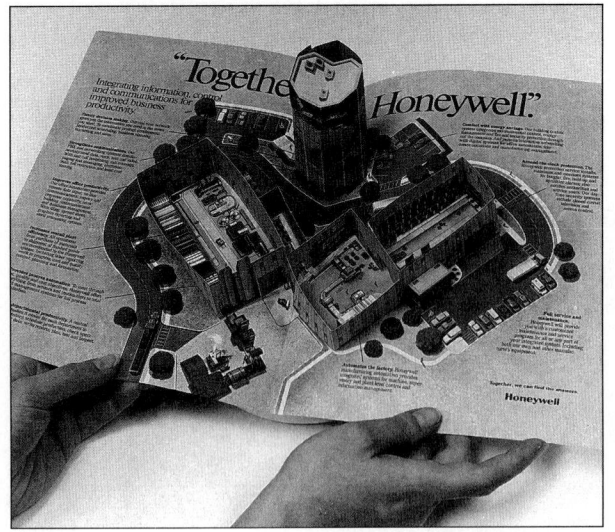

the advertisement an impression of being larger and to make a more dramatic impact in presenting the ad. Many magazines charge an extra 10 to 20 percent for bleed pages.

In addition to gatefolds and bleed pages, other types of creative options are available through magazines including unusual page sizes and shapes and other techniques. For example, some advertisers have grabbed the attention of magazine readers by developing ads that jump off of the page through the use of three dimensional pop-up ads. Honeywell ran a *pop-up ad* in *Business Week* to catch the eye of potential clients that showed a state-of-the-art corporate park in which all the buildings are equipped with the company's 24-hour fire and burglar alarms and other automated systems (Exhibit 14–8).

Transamerica Corporation also used pop-up construction to develop a corporate ad depicting the city of San Francisco and the company's corporate symbol—the Transamerica pyramid tower (Exhibit 14–8). The ad, which ran in *Time* magazine, promoted the Transamerica Insurance Companies as leaders in providing innovative insurance coverage. The cost of producing and running these pop-up ads one time was nearly $1 million, which begs the question of whether they are effective enough to justify the high costs. Research studies by Starch INRA Hooper indicate pop-up inserts outperform ordinary four-color ads nearly 2 to 1 in attention value. Both the Honeywell and Transamerica ads attained record-setting Starch "Noted" scores (the percentage of readers who remembered seeing the ad). Similarly, the "Seen/Associated" scores (the percentage of readers who could associate the ads with the company) for both inserts more than doubled those of ordinary four-color ads.

In addition to pop-up ads, inserts of various other forms can also be used in many magazines. These include return cards, recipe booklets, coupons, records, and even product samples. Cosmetic companies use "scratch and sniff" inserts to introduce new cologne or perfume fragrances, and some companies use them to promote deodorants, laundry detergents, or other products where the scent is important. Inserts are also used in conjunction with direct-response ads and as part of sales promotion strategies. For example, Gatorade developed a unique print insert known as the "Scorecard" as part of its event sponsorship association with the NCAA basketball tournament (Exhibit 14–9). The scorecard was part of a four-page ad insert in *Sports Illustrated* and was very effective in attracting reader interest and involvement. Follow-up market research showed that 85 percent of the 500 randomly selected male subscribers had noticed the Gatorade scorecard and 57 percent actively used it during the NCAA tournament.

The use of special inserts such as scented ads, pop-ups, singing ads, and other techniques are a way of breaking through the clutter in magazines and capturing the

➤ *Exhibit 14-9*
Gatorade's scorecard insert was an effective way of attracting reader interest and involvement

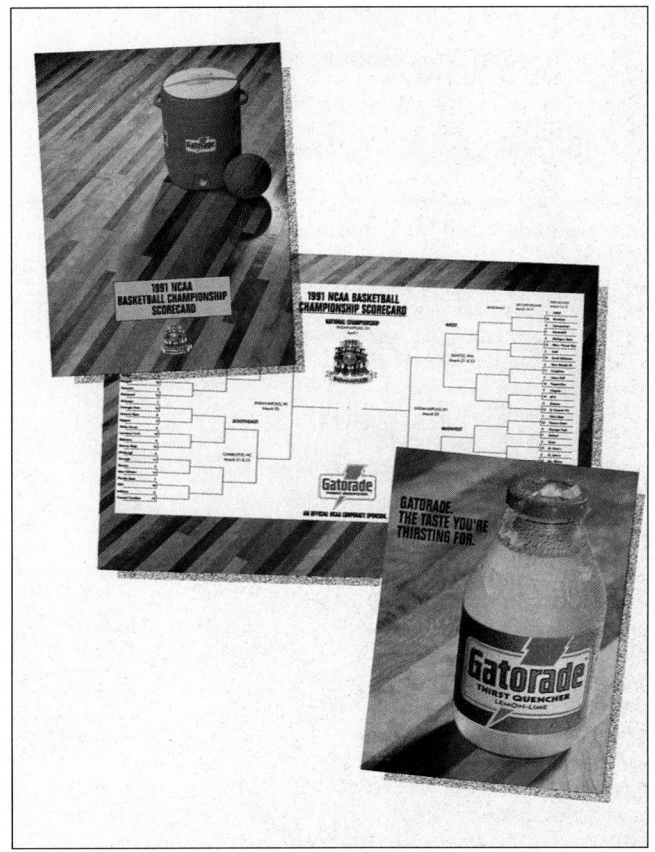

consumer's attention and interest. However, there recently has been some backlash against various types of *printaculars,* as is discussed in Ethical Perspective 14–1.

Creative space buys are another option made available by magazines. Some magazines allow advertisers to purchase space units in certain combinations so as to increase the impact of their media budget. For example, WD-40, an all-purpose lubrication product, used quarter-page ads on four consecutive pages of several magazines with a different use for the product mentioned on each page (refer back to Exhibit 5–20). This strategy allowed the company to get greater impact for its media dollars and was helpful in promoting the variety of uses for the product.

Permanence

Another distinctive advantage offered by magazines is their permanence or long life span. As mentioned in the previous chapter, television and radio are characterized by fleeting messages that have a very short life span, whereas newspapers are generally discarded soon after being read. Magazines, however, are generally read over several days and are often kept for reference. Thus, they are retained in the home longer than any other medium and are generally read or referred to on several occasions. A study of magazine audience readership found that readers devote an hour or more over a period of two to three days reading an average magazine.[7] Studies have also found that nearly 75 percent of consumers retain magazines for future reference.[8] One benefit of the longer life of magazines is that readership occurs at a less hurried pace, and there is more opportunity to examine and appraise ads in considerable detail. This means ads can use longer and more detailed copy, which can be very important for high-involvement and complex products or services. The permanence of magazines also means readers can be exposed to ads on multiple occasions, which can enhance readership, and the opportunity to pass magazines along to other readers is increased.

Ethical Perspective 14–1

Are Magazine Ads Becoming Too "Printacular"?

Getting the magazine reader's attention has become increasingly difficult in recent years as the number of ads appearing in most publications increases. To break through the clutter and get their ads noticed, magazine advertisers have been using a variety of techniques including scent strips, heavy-stock multipage inserts, and other types of *printaculars* or spectacular print ads. Some of the most elaborate printaculars have been the pop-up ads for Transamerica Corporation and Honeywell, as we saw in Exhibit 14–8.

A few years ago, Toyota took the concept of 3-D advertising a step further by inserting nearly 14 million pairs of three-dimensional glasses, made of cardboard and plastic, in issues of *Time, People,* and *Cosmopolitan.* Liquor advertisers have been big users of print spectaculars, particularly during the Christmas holiday season. In recent years, advertisers such as Seagram's and Brown-Foreman have used gimmicks such as musical ads that use tiny silicon chips to play Christmas songs when they are opened. In 1991, Absolut vodka wrapped designer scarves inside ads appearing in 200,000 issues of *Interview* magazine.

While printaculars may be effective in getting the magazine reader's attention, some marketers believe they do so at the expense of the other ads that appear in a publication. A backlash has developed against them as many advertisers do not want to run regular ads that have to compete with heavy inserts, pop-ups, computerized songs, or other distractions. Some advertisers and agencies are even asking publishers to notify them when they plan to run any spectacular inserts so they can decide whether to keep their regular page ads in the issue.

Many print advertisers and agencies argue that printaculars alter the appearance and feel of a magazine and the reader's relationship to it. One agency executive argues that readers will always flip immediately to the insert, which cuts down on the likelihood of other ads being seen. There is also concern that many of these gimmicks may be turning off the magazine reader. For example, Porsche ran a 20-page, heavy-stock insert that angered many of the other advertisers as well as readers who argued that it made it more difficult to go through the magazine.

Many magazine readers also complain about scent strips. For example, *TV Guide* decided it would no longer carry scented inserts after receiving hundreds of letters of protest about a scent-strip ad it carried for a new cologne. Complaints over scent strips often come from consumers who are allergic to the perfumed ads. To deal with this problem, some magazines are requiring that advertisers must use leak- and odor-proof sealants to protect readers.

While the printaculars may get a lot of attention, not all advertisers think they make sense from a financial perspective. In some cases, the ad inserts cost advertisers more than $1 each, and over $1 million may be spent to run the ad one time in one or a few publications. A few years ago, the Brown-Foreman Beverage Co. found that printaculars do not always work well. It ran an ad for Canadian Mist liquor that used a microchip to play "Deck the Halls" inside limited editions of *People* magazine. The campaign cost more than $1 million and the brand manager noted it did not lead to a significant increase in sales. Rather than using the costly inserts, Brown-Foreman decided to use the monies to develop splashier point-of-purchase displays.

This Cutty Sark ad was a parody of gimmicky Christmas messages

During the 1991 holiday season, many advertisers pulled away from printaculars. The most talked about print ad of the Christmas season was a Cutty Sark parody of ad gimmicks from Christmases past that looked like a printacular but actually did very little. The headline of the ad read, "A lot of people judge a product by how elaborate the gimmick in its Christmas ad is." However, when consumers pulled a cardboard tab that said, "Pull Here," nothing flipped open or popped-up and no songs were sung. Instead, the tab read, "A lot of people are wrong. Merry Christmas from everyone at Cutty Sark." An executive from the Della Femina, McNamee agency, which created the ad, noted its objective was to be "anti-trendy."

Many advertising people believe the novelty of many of the printaculars has simply worn off and they have become blasé to consumers. While it is unlikely that marketers will abandon printaculars, both publishers and advertisers will have to give more consideration to their use as magazine readers and other advertisers will be scrutinizing them.

Source: Scott Donaton and Pat Sloan, "Ad 'printaculars' under Scrutiny," *Advertising Age,* February 12, 1990; Bruce Horowitz, "No Room This Season for Splashy Print Ads," *Los Angeles Times,* December 12, 1991; and Bruce Horowitz, "Toyota Sets Sights on New Dimension in Ads to Bolster Sales of Corolla," *Los Angeles Times,* October 6, 1987, pt. IV, p. 8.

Prestige

Another positive feature of magazine advertising is the prestige the product or service may gain from advertising in publications with a favorable image. Companies whose products rely very heavily on perceived quality, reputation, and/or image often buy space in prestigious publications with high quality and involving editorial content and for which consumers have a high level of interest in the advertising pages. For example, *Esquire* and *Gentlemen's Quarterly* provide a very favorable environment for advertising men's fashions, and a clothing manufacturer may advertise its products in these magazines to enhance the prestige or image of its lines. *Architectural Digest* provides a very impressive editorial environment that includes high-quality photography and artwork. The upscale readers of the magazine are likely to have a very favorable image of the publication that may transcend to the products advertised on its pages. *Good Housekeeping* provides a unique consumer's refund or replacement policy for products that bear the limited warranty seal or that advertise in the magazine. This can increase the level of confidence a consumer has in a particular brand and reduce the amount of perceived risk associated with a purchase.

While most media planners recognize that the environment created by a publication is important, it can be difficult to determine the degree of prestige a magazine provides. Subjective estimates based on media planners' knowledge or experience may be used to assess a magazine's prestige as can objective measures such as reader opinion surveys.[9]

Consumer receptivity and involvement

With the exception of newspapers, consumers are more receptive to advertising in magazines than in any other medium. Magazines are generally purchased because the information they contain is relevant and interesting to the reader, and ads represent additional information that may be of value in making a purchase decision. For example, consumers often rely on magazines for information on travel as they may purchase publications such as *Travel & Leisure* or *Conde Naste Travel* to read articles about various resorts or parts of the world. The ads contained in these publications are also likely to be of interest to readers, particularly those who may be planning a trip.

A study conducted for the Magazine Publishers of America examined the various media as a source of knowledge and usable ideas for various products. It found that magazines are consumers' primary source of information for a variety of products and services including automobiles, food products, money matters, clothing and fashions, beauty and grooming, and personal and business travel (Exhibit 14–10).[10]

In addition to their interest or relevance, magazine ads are likely to be received favorably by consumers because, unlike broadcast ad, they are nonintrusive and can easily be ignored. Studies of magazine readers have shown that the majority of them welcome ads in magazines, whereas only a small percentage have negative attitudes toward magazine advertising.[11] Some magazines, such as bridal or fashion publications, are purchased as much for their advertising as editorial content.

In addition to being more receptive to advertising in magazines, consumers are also generally more involved with magazines than any other media. Consumers generally pay for magazines, and the amount they must lay out has nearly doubled over the past decade.[12] Some publications, such as *Unique Homes,* have single-copy prices as high as $7. Readers' high level of involvement with a magazine may make them more attentive and likely to recall the ads. Magazine Publishers of America–sponsored studies have shown that magazine readers are more likely to attend to and recall advertisements than are TV viewers.

Services

A final advantage of magazines is the special services some publications offer advertisers. Some magazines have merchandising staffs that call on trade intermediaries

➤ *Exhibit 14–10*
Magazines are an important source of information for many products and services

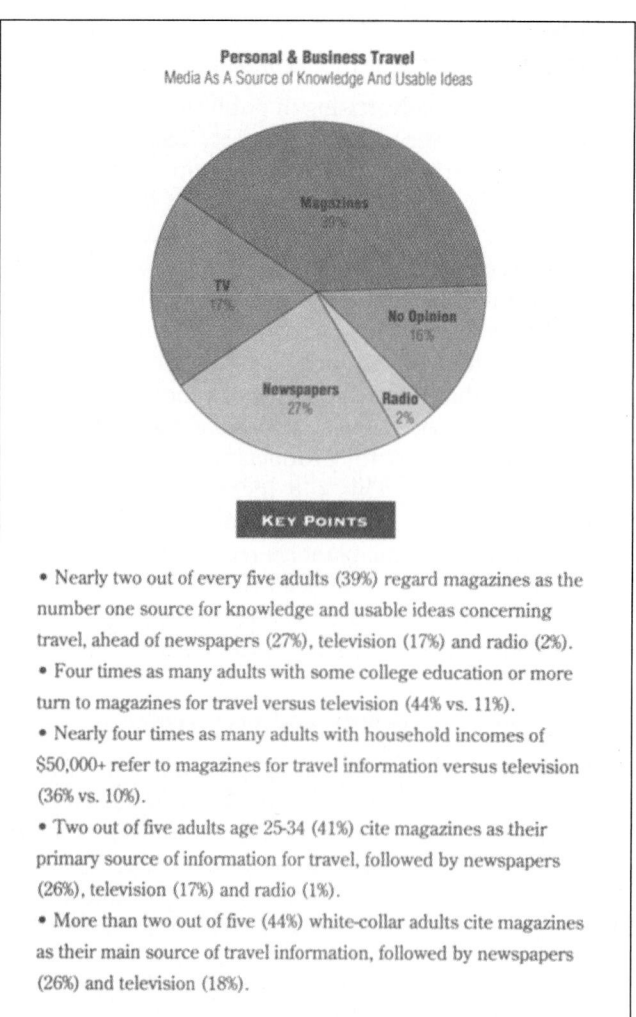

Personal & Business Travel
Media As A Source of Knowledge And Usable Ideas

Magazines 39%
TV 17%
No Opinion 16%
Radio 2%
Newspapers 27%

KEY POINTS

• Nearly two out of every five adults (39%) regard magazines as the number one source for knowledge and usable ideas concerning travel, ahead of newspapers (27%), television (17%) and radio (2%).

• Four times as many adults with some college education or more turn to magazines for travel versus television (44% vs. 11%).

• Nearly four times as many adults with household incomes of $50,000+ refer to magazines for travel information versus television (36% vs. 10%).

• Two out of five adults age 25-34 (41%) cite magazines as their primary source of information for travel, followed by newspapers (26%), television (17%) and radio (1%).

• More than two out of five (44%) white-collar adults cite magazines as their main source of travel information, followed by newspapers (26%) and television (18%).

such as retailers to let them know a product is being advertised in their publication and to encourage them to display or promote the item. Another service offered by magazines (usually the larger ones) is the availability of research studies that they conduct on consumers and make available to advertisers. These studies may deal with general consumer trends, changing purchase patterns, and media usage or may be relevant to a specific product or industry.

An important service offered by some magazines is the availability of **split runs** whereby two or more versions of an ad are printed in alternate copies of a particular issue of a magazine. This service is used to conduct a "split-run test," where some offer or inquiry inducing a way of prompting responses is included in each ad. This allows the advertiser to determine which ad generates the most responses or inquiries and thus provides some evidence as to their effectiveness.

Disadvantages of Magazines

Although the advantages offered by magazines are considerable, they have certain drawbacks. These include the costs of advertising, their limited reach and frequency, the long lead time required in placing an ad, and the problem of clutter and heavy advertising competition.

Costs

The costs of advertising in magazines obviously vary according to the size of the audience they reach and their selectivity. Advertising in large, mass circulation magazines such as *TV Guide, Reader's Digest,* or *Time* can be very expensive. For example, a full-page, four-color ad in *Time* magazine's national edition cost $134,400 in 1992. Popular positions such as back cover cost even more. The costs of ad space in more specialized publications with smaller circulation is less. A full-page, four-color ad in *Tennis* magazine (circulation of 755,000) cost $39,450 in 1992.

Like any medium, the expense of using magazines must be considered not only from an absolute cost perspective but also in terms of relative costs. Most magazines tend to emphasize their effectiveness in reaching specific target audiences and their ability to do so on a low cost per thousand basis. Also, as discussed above, an increasing number of magazines are offering demographic and geographic editions, which helps lower their costs. Media planners generally focus on the relative costs of a publication in reaching the advertiser's target audience. However, they may recommend a magazine with a high cost per thousand because of its ability to reach a small, specialized market segment. Of course, advertisers with limited budgets will be interested in the absolute costs of space in a magazine and the costs of producing quality ads for these publications.

Limited reach and frequency

Magazines are generally not as effective as other media in offering reach and frequency. Studies of magazine audiences have revealed that nearly 90 percent of adults in the United States read one or more consumer magazines each month. However, the percentage of adults reading any individual publication tends to be much smaller, and magazines are thus often described as having thin penetration of households. For example, the circulation of *TV Guide,* which is the third highest of any magazine, is just over 15 million. This represents only 20 percent of the 93 million households in the United States.

As can be seen in Exhibit 14–11, only 30 magazines had a paid circulation of greater than 2 million at the end of 1991. Thus, advertisers seeking broad reach must make media buys in a number of magazines, which means more negotiations, transactions, and the like. Magazines are generally not used as the sole basis of a broad reach strategy but rather are used in conjunction with other media.

The frequency level available through magazines can also be a problem since most are monthly—or at best, weekly—publications. Thus, the opportunity for building frequency through the use of the same publication is limited. Using multiple ads in the same issue of a publication is generally viewed as an inefficient way of building frequency. Most advertisers attempt to achieve frequency by adding additional magazines with a similar audience to the media schedule.

Long lead time

Another drawback of magazines is the long lead time needed to place an ad. Most major publications have anywhere from a 30- to a 90-day lead time, which means space must be purchased and the ad must be prepared well in advance of the actual publication date. Once the closing date for advertising is reached, no changes in the art or copy of the ad can be made. The long lead time required by magazines means magazine ads cannot be as timely as other media, such as radio or newspapers, in responding to current events or changing market conditions.

Clutter and competition

While the problem of advertising clutter is generally discussed in reference to the broadcast media, magazines also have this drawback. The clutter problem for magazines is really somewhat of a paradox, as the more successful a magazine becomes, the more advertising pages it attracts, which leads to greater clutter. In fact, magazines generally gauge their success in terms of the number of advertising pages they attract.

➤ *Exhibit 14–11*
Top 50 magazines in circulation

Rank	Magazine	Circulation	Rank	Magazine	Circulation
1	Modern Maturity	22,450,003	26	Smithsonian	2,140,349
2	Reader's Digest	16,269,637	27	Glamour	2,081,212
3	TV Guide	15,053,018	28	V.F.W. Magazine	2,063,354
4	National Geographic	9,763,406	29	NEA Today	2,034,846
5	Better Homes & Gardens	8,002,794	30	Field & Stream	2,002,732
6	Good Housekeeping	5,188,919	31	Money	1,933,864
7	McCall's	5,066,849	32	Home & Away	1,881,346
8	Ladies' Home Journal	5,065,135	33	Seventeen	1,851,665
9	Family Circle	5,065,131	34	Ebony	1,844,973
10	Woman's Day	4,619,505	35	Country Living	1,839,065
11	Time	4,073,530	36	Popular Science	1,837,026
12	Redbook	3,860,294	37	Life	1,815,916
13	National Enquirer	3,758,964	38	First for Woman	1,764,430
14	Playboy	3,547,165	39	Parents Magazine	1,752,474
15	People	3,380,832	40	Discovery	1,677,022
16	Sports Illustrated	3,297,493	41	Popular Mechanics	1,639,033
17	Newsweek	3,224,770	42	Adventure Road	1,523,853
18	Prevention	3,204,583	43	Outdoor Life	1,502,818
19	Star	3,102,026	44	Sunset	1,491,509
20	American Legion Magazine	2,935,379	45	Soap Opera Digest	1,447,483
21	AAA World	2,800,733	46	The Elks Magazine	1,442,326
22	Cosmopolitan	2,741,802	47	Golf Digest	1,421,797
23	Southern Living	2,361,076	48	Penthouse	1,390,919
24	Scholastic Teen Network	2,333,967	49	New Woman	1,350,392
25	U.S. News & World Report	2,237,009	50	Boy's Life	1,299,061

Figures are averages for six months ended December 31, 1991.

Magazine publishers do attempt to control the clutter problem by maintaining a reasonable balance of editorial pages to advertising. According to the Magazine Publishers of America, the average consumer magazine contains 48 percent advertising and 52 percent editorial.[13] However, many magazines contain ads on more than half of their pages, and in some publications, the amount of advertising is even higher. This clutter makes it difficult for the advertiser to gain the attention of the readers and draw them into the ad. Thus, many print ads use strong visual images, catchy headlines, or some of the creative techniques discussed earlier to grab the attention and interest of magazine readers.

While clutter is a problem for magazines, it is not viewed as serious an issue with the print media as for radio or television since, as noted earlier, consumers tend to be more receptive and tolerant of print advertising. Also, while they can control their exposure to a magazine ad simply by turning the page, broadcast ads are much more intrusive and difficult to ignore.

Magazine Circulation and Readership

Two of the most important considerations in deciding whether to utilize a magazine in the advertising media plan are the size and characteristics of the audience reached by the publication. Media buyers evaluate magazines on the basis of the vehicle's ability to deliver the advertiser's message to as many people as possible in the target audience. To do this, they must consider the circulation of the publication as well as its total readership and match these figures against the audience they are attempting to reach.

Circulation

Circulation figures represent the number of individuals that receive a publication, either through subscription or store purchase. The number of copies distributed to these original subscribers or purchasers is known as **primary circulation** and is used as the basis for the magazine's rate structure. The circulation for any particular issue of a magazine tends to fluctuate, particularly if it relies heavily on retail or newsstand sales. Thus, many publications base their rates on *guaranteed circulation* and provide advertisers with a rebate if the number of delivered magazines falls below the guarantee. To minimize the likelihood of rebating, most guaranteed circulation figures are conservative; that is, they are set safely below the average actual delivered circulation, and advertisers are not charged for any excess circulation.

Many publishers have become discontented with the guaranteed circulation concept since it requires them to provide refunds if guarantees are not met, but excesses in circulation result in a bonus for the advertiser. Thus, many publications have gone to a circulation rate base system whereby rates are based on a set average circulation. This figure is nearly always below the actual circulation delivered by a given issue, but there is no guarantee of circulation. However, it is unlikely circulations will fall below the rate base since this would reflect negatively on the publication and make it difficult to attract advertisers at prevailing rates.

Circulation verification   Given that circulation figures are the basis for a magazine's advertising rates and one of the primary considerations in selecting a publication, the credibility of circulation figures is very important. To ensure that the circulation figures for a magazine are accurate, most major publications are audited by one of the circulation verification services. Consumer magazine and farm publication circulations are audited by the Audit Bureau of Circulations (ABC). This organization, which was organized in 1914 and is sponsored by advertisers, agencies, and publishers, collects and evaluates information regarding the subscriptions and sales of magazines and newspapers to verify their circulation figures. Only publications with 70 percent or more paid circulation (which means the magazine was purchased at not less than half the magazine's established base price) are eligible for verification audits by ABC. Certain business publications are audited by the Business Publications Audit (BPA) of Circulation. Many of these are published on a **controlled-circulation basis,** meaning copies are sent (usually free) to individuals the publisher believes are important and able to influence sales to a company.

Circulation verification services play an important role in providing the media planner with reliable figures regarding the size and distribution of a magazine's circulation and helping evaluate its worth as a media vehicle. In addition to the circulation figures, the ABC statement provides other important information.[14] It shows how a magazine is distributed by state and county size as well as the percentage of the circulation sold at less than full value and the percentage arrears, which indicates how many subscriptions are being given away. This information is important since many advertisers believe that subscribers who pay for a magazine are more likely to read it than are those who get it at a discount or receive free copies.

Media buyers are generally skeptical about publications with circulation figures not audited by one of the verification services, and some companies will not advertise in unaudited publications. Circulation data, along with the auditing source, are available in Standard Rate and Data Service or from the publication itself. Exhibit 14–12 shows an example of an Audit Bureau of Circulations publisher's statement.

Readership and total audience

In addition to considering the primary circulation figures for a magazine, advertisers may also be interested in the number of people a publication reaches as a result of secondary or pass-along readership. **Pass-along readership** can occur when the primary subscriber or purchaser gives a magazine to another person to read or when the publication is read in places such as waiting rooms of doctor's offices or beauty salons, on airplanes, and so forth.

Advertisers generally attach greater value to the primary in-home reader versus the pass-along reader and the out-of-home reader, as the former generally spends more time with the publication, picks it up more often, and receives greater satisfaction

➤ *Exhibit 14–12*   **Example of an Audit Bureau of Circulations publisher's statement**

from it than the out-of-home reader. Thus, this reader is more likely to be attentive and responsive to ads. However, pass-along circulation can be very important to a publication, and the value of these readers should not be discounted. Pass-along readers are an important part of the audience of many publications and can greatly expand the magazine's readership. *People* magazine, which has a high number of pass-on and out-of-home readers, commissioned a media research study to determine that its out-of-home audience spends as much time reading the publication as do its primary in-home readers because of the nature and layout of the publication.[15]

The **total audience,** or **readership,** of a magazine can be determined by taking the readers per copy, which is the total number of primary and pass-along readers, and multiplying this figure by the circulation of an average issue. For example, a magazine that has a circulation of 1 million and 3.5 readers per copy has a total audience of 3.5 million. However, rate structures are generally based on the more verifiable circulation figures of a publication, and many media planners devalue a pass-along reader by as much as 50 percent. While total readership estimates are reported by major syndicated magazine research services, which are discussed below, these numbers are often viewed with suspicion by media buyers. As was discussed in Chapter 12, a controversy has developed over the estimates of magazine readership used by the two major research firms.

Audience Research for Magazines

While the circulation and total audience size of a magazine are important in selecting a media vehicle, the media planner is also interested in the match between the magazine's readers and the advertiser's target audience. The obvious question here is whether the magazine reaches the type of reader to whom the company is trying to sell its product or service. Information relevant to this question is available from several sources including the publication's own research and syndicated research studies.

➤ *Exhibit 14–13*
This reader profile comes from research done by the magazine

SAN DIEGO MAGAZINE

1989–1990 DEMOGRAPHICS

READER PROFILE

Sex	
Women	54.1%
Men	45.9%

Age	
18-24	5.3%
25-49	51.1%
50-59	16.0%
60 +	27.6%
Median Age	46.3

Marital status	
Married	74.0%
Single	13.4%
Divorced/Widowed	12.6%

Education	
Attended College	81.3%
Graduated College	53.2%
Post-Graduate Degree	22.2%

Home ownership	
Own Home	80.8%
Median Value	$245,455
Average Value	$332,710

Number people in home	
One	18.6%
Two	49.3%
Three	15.2%
Four Or More	16.9%
Average	2.4

Household income	
$30,000 +	88.6%
$50,000 +	70.4%
$75,000 +	49.3%
$100,000 +	32.2%
Median HHI	$74,202
Average HHI	$113,600

Net worth	
$100,000 +	82.8%
$250,000 +	62.0%
$500,000 +	40.0%
$1 Million +	21.8%
$5 Million +	2.6%
Median	$386,029
Average	$836,150

Head of household occupation	
Chairman/Pres./CEO/VP	13.6%
Top Management	29.4%
Middle Management	12.2%
Total Management	41.6%
Professional/Technical	16.2%
Business/Industry	50.1%
Total Prof./Business	66.3%

Professional activities	
(Purchase Or Approve Purchase)	
Computers & Services	59.2%
Communications Systems	50.3%
Advertising	32.1%
Office Furniture	28.5%
Insurance	24.3%
Business Gifts/Premiums	24.6%
Company Cars	20.4%
Plant or Office Space	16.8%

Most magazines provide media planners with reports and information detailing readers' demographics, financial profile, lifestyle, and product usage characteristics. The larger the publication, the more detailed and comprehensive the information it usually can supply about its readers. For example, the profile of the *San Diego Magazine* reader shown in Exhibit 14–13 comes from a study commissioned by the publication.

In addition to studies conducted by the magazines themselves, syndicated research studies are also available. For consumer magazines, primary sources of information concerning magazine audiences are Simmons Market Research Bureau's Study of

Media and Markets and the studies of Mediamark Research, Inc. (MRI). These studies provide the media planner with a broad range of information on the audiences of major national and regional magazines, including demographics, lifestyle characteristics, and product purchase and usage data. Most large advertising agencies and media buying services also conduct ongoing research that either focuses on or includes the media habits of consumers. This information can be used along with the above-mentioned sources in determining the value of various magazines in reaching particular types of product users.

Audience information for business publications is generally more limited than for consumer magazines. The widely dispersed readership and nature of business publication readers make audience research more difficult for these magazines. The media planner generally relies on information provided by the publication or by sources such as Standard Rate and Data Service. SRDS contains a business analysis of circulation for various publications that provides information on the title of the individual who receives the publication and the type of industry in which he or she works. This information can be of value in understanding the audience reached by various business magazines.

Purchasing Magazine Advertising Space

Cost elements

As noted earlier, magazine rates are primarily a function of the circulation of the publication. However, a magazine's advertising rates vary in response to a number of other variables including the size of the ad, its position in the publication, the particular editions (geographic, demographic) chosen, any special mechanical or production requirements, and the number and frequency of insertions.

Advertising space is generally sold on the basis of space units such as full page, half page, and quarter page, although some publications quote rates on the basis of column inches. The larger the ad, the greater the cost. However, many advertisers use full-page ads since they result in more attention and readership. Several studies have found that full-page ads generated 36 percent more readership than half-page ads.[16]

Advertisements can be produced or run using black and white, black and white plus one color, or four colors. The more color used in the ad, the greater the expense because of the increased printing costs. As can be seen in Exhibit 14–14, a full-page black and white ad in *Newsweek* cost $73,620 in 1992, whereas a four-color ad was $114,535. On average, a four-color ad will cost 30 percent more than a black-and-white ad. Advertisers generally prefer using color because of the greater visual impact it makes, plus the fact that color ads have been found to be superior for attracting and holding attention.[17] For example, Starch INRA Hooper, Inc., analyzed the effect of various factors such as ad position and color on the readership of magazine ads. The research shows that the noted scores (the percentage of readers who remember having previously seen the ad in a publication they read) are 45 percent higher for a four-color page ad than a black-and-white ad, and a four-color

> *Exhibit 14–14*
Newsweek national edition space rates

	B&W	B&1C	4C
Full page	$73,620	$96,605	$114,535
2 columns	57,655	75,690	95,430
Half page	46,020	60,370	74,435
1 column or square third	29,450	38,625	49,630
Half column	15,315	20,150	—
4th cover	—	—	146,815
2nd & 3rd cover	73,620	96,605	114,535
Line rate*	235	—	—

*14 Line Minimum

spread outperforms a black-and-white spread by 53 percent.[18] Ads requiring special mechanical production such as bleed pages or special inserts may also result in extra charges.

The rates for magazine advertising space can also vary according to the number of insertions and amount of money spent during a specific period. The more often an advertiser contracts to run an ad, the less the space charges. Volume discounts are based on the total space purchased within a contract year, as measured in dollars. Advertisers can also save money by purchasing advertising in magazine combinations or networks.

Magazine networks offer the advertiser the opportunity to buy space in a group of publications as a package deal. These networks may be offered by publishers who have a variety of magazines that reach audiences with similar characteristics. The ad for the Petersen Magazine Network shown in Exhibit 14–15 promotes the coverage its leisure-time–enthusiasts publications provide of the adult male market. Networks are also offered by publishers of a group of magazines with diversified audiences as well as independent networks that sell space in groups of magazines published by a variety of companies. For example, the News Network sells space in a group of news-oriented publications such as *Time, Newsweek,* and *U.S. News & World Report.*

➤ *Exhibit 14–15*
This publisher offers a network to reach adult males

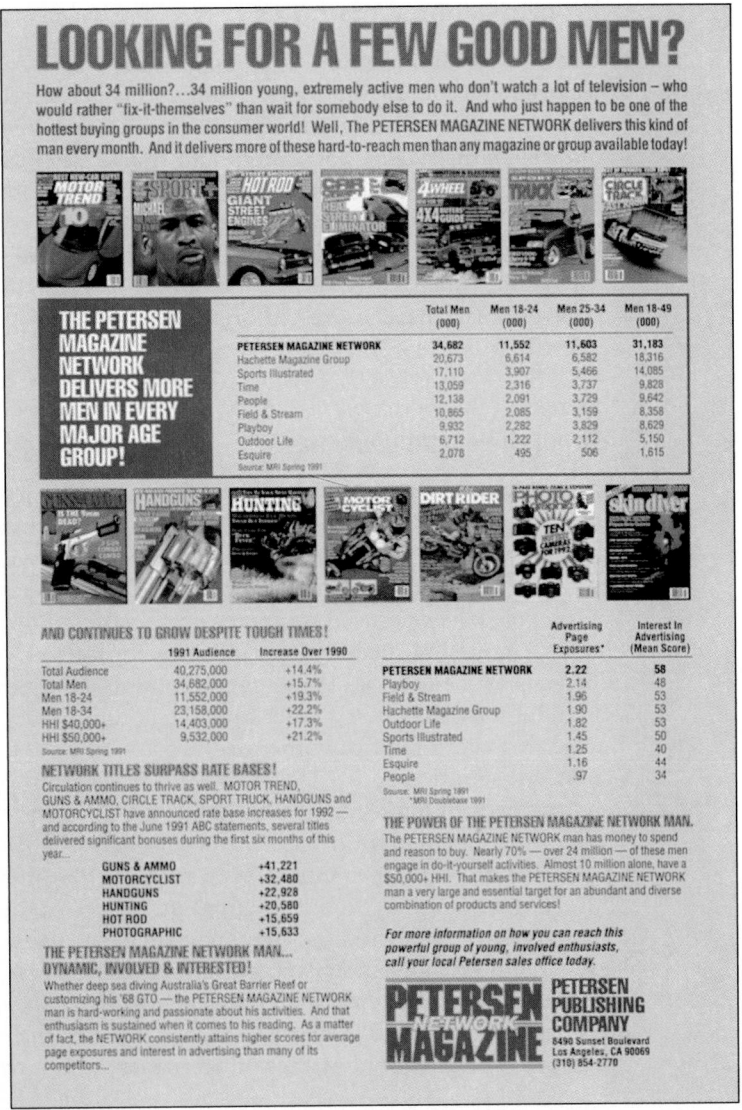

The Future of Magazines

Magazines have gone through a very difficult period over the past several years. The number of ad pages in magazines fell 3.7 percent in 1990 and 8.7 percent in 1991 as the industry suffered through its worst advertising drought since the mid-1970s. Advertising revenue declined by as much as 20 to 30 percent for some publications as marketers reduced their advertising budgets during the recession and discounting of advertising space became more pervasive. While ad revenue has been declining, publishers have also seen their costs increase. The cost of paper continues to rise, and the industry was hit hard in 1991 by a 22.6 percent increase in second-class postage rates. A number of well-known publications failed to survive the tough times including *Egg, Savvy, Fame,* and *Connoisseur.* Many magazines have been reducing personnel, trimming circulation, and using computers to increase productivity of their editorial staffs.

One of the major problems facing many magazines is that they will not be able to increase their advertising rates to cover increasing costs and declines in ad pages. Magazines are looking at a number of ways to improve their position, including strengthening their editorial platform, better circulation management, becoming involved in cross magazine and media deals, and using technological advances to make advertising in magazines more appealing to marketers.[19]

Stronger editorial platforms

It is likely that the number of magazines will shrink over the next several years because the economy and advertising industry cannot continue to support them all. Magazines with strong editorial platforms that appeal to the interests, lifestyles, and demographics of consumers and market trends of the 90s will have the best chance of attracting readers *and* advertisers. For example, magazines such as *Connoisseur,* which appealed to the conspicuous consumption lifestyle of the late 80s, have folded as recession-battered consumers return to more basic values. Publications such as *Parenting* and *Sports Illustrated for Kids* are doing very well as baby boomers have more children and they (the "mini-baby boomers") become older (Exhibit 14–16).[20]

Circulation management

Magazine publishers will also have to work to improve the quality of their circulation bases to remain profitable. During the 90s, circulation will become the major source of revenue for many publications, and they will have to carefully consider the costs of attracting and maintaining additional readers or subscribers. For many years, magazines focused on increasing their circulation under the assumption that higher circulation meant higher advertising rates. However, publishers are now realizing that the cost of attracting and maintaining the last 10 to 15 percent of their circulation base is often greater than the additional revenue generated as it represents subscribers who require numerous direct-mail solicitations, premium offers, or discount subscriptions.

A number of magazines including *Time, TV Guide, Redbook,* and *McCall's* have reduced their circulation base in recent years.[21] Many publishers believe they can pass on price increases more easily to their core readers or subscribers and offer advertisers a more loyal and focused audience. Many advertisers actually welcome the improvement in circulation management by magazines. They would rather reach a few hundred thousand fewer subscribers than pay for inefficient circulation and be hit with advertising rate increases each year. Many magazines are also using the monies saved on the circulation side to improve the editorial content of their publications, which should attract more readers and advertisers.

Cross-magazine and media deals

Another important development involves the way advertising space is sold; there will be a greater number of *cross- or multimagazine* and *cross-media* ad packages. **Cross- or multimagazine deals** involve two or more publishers offering their magazines to an advertiser as one package. *Newsweek* and Times Mirror Magazines (which includes specialty publications such as *Field & Stream* and *Ski*) recently entered into a cross-magazine arrangement with several advertisers including Kmart, Brown & Williamson, and American Isuzu.[22]

Many magazines are also becoming involved in **cross-media advertising** deals that include several different media opportunities from a single company or a partnership of various media providers. For example, General Motors negotiated an $80 million cross-media deal with Time Warner that includes advertising in the magazines owned by the media conglomerate such as *Time, Sports Illustrated,* and *Fortune,* on its cable television stations, and in home videos. Cross-media deals could account for as much as 20 percent of all media buys over the next several years.[23]

Advances in technology

Many advertisers are increasingly turning to magazines as a cost-efficient way of reaching specialized audiences. As marketers continue to move toward greater market segmentation, market niche strategies, and regional marketing, they are making greater use of magazines because of their high selectivity and ability to avoid wasted coverage or circulation. Magazines are using advances in technology to divide their audiences on the basis of demographics, psychographics, or regions and to deliver more personalized advertising messages. Two important developments in this area are the availability of selective binding technology and ink-jet imaging.

If Life Is A Journey, Here Are Two Things To Help You On Your Way.

The New Mazda 929.   *The Meaning of Life* free.

```
          GEORGE BELCH
        TEST DRIVE A MAZDA
    AND GET THE MEANING OF LIFE FREE
DAVE SMITH MAZDA          CUSH POWAY MAZDA
6435 MIRAMAR ROAD         13750 POWAY RD.

SAN DIEGO, CA 92121       POWAY, CA 92064
```

Take this certificate to your Mazda Dealer and test-drive any new Mazda before February 29, 1992. Then fill out this postage-paid card, have your dealer validate it and drop it in the mail. You will receive your free copy of *The Meaning of Life* (retail value $24.95) by mail.

Name _____ Address _____ City _____

State _____ Zip _____ Telephone _____ Date of test drive _____

Model Tested _____ Current Vehicle Owned _____

Do you plan to purchase a new car ____ yes ____ no. If yes, within ____ 3 months ____ 6 months ____ 9 months ____ 1 year

Authorized Dealership Signature _____ Dealer Code _____ Date _____

Limit one book per card. NOT TRANSFERABLE/NOT NEGOTIABLE. Mechanical reproduction or other facsimiles are not valid. Offer available from Mazda while supplies last, but you must redeem certificate by March 31, 1992. Please allow 6-8 weeks after mailing for shipment. Limit one book per family. Valid driver's license required. Void where prohibited. For a free brochure, call 1-800-639-1000.

© 1991 Mazda Motor of America, Inc.   DTMLAU

Many publications are now offering **selective binding**—a computerized production process that allows the creation of hundreds of copies of a magazine in one continuous sequence. Selective binding enables magazines to send different editorial or advertising messages to various groups of subscribers within the same issue of a publication. **Ink-jet imaging** makes it possible to personalize an advertising message such as the Mazda ad insert shown in Exhibit 14–17. A number of publications such as *American Baby, Farm Journal,* and *Modern Maturity* have been using these processes to insert ads into issues going to specific subscriber segments. Many publishers believe selective binding and ink-jet imaging will allow advertisers the opportunity to target their messages more finely and make magazines compete more effectively with direct mail and other direct-marketing vehicles.[24]

Publishers are also developing new technologies that will enhance the creative opportunities available to magazine advertisers. As was noted earlier, advertisers have been using a variety of techniques to capture readers' attention in print ads including sound, scents, moving images, and pop-up ads. Current technologies are being refined and made more cost effective, and a number of new technologies will be incorporated into print ads soon. These include the use of anaglyphic images, or three-dimensional materials that are viewed with colored glasses; lenticular or color images printed on finely corrugated plastic that seem to move when tilted; and pressure- or heat-sensitive inks that change color on contact. These new technologies will provide advertisers with ways of breaking through the advertising clutter. However, as shown in Exhibit 14–18, these new print technologies can be very costly.

➤ *Exhibit 14–18*
High costs for high-tech wizardry (per-piece costs of print technologies based on order of 1 million pieces)

Talking ads (6-second play)	$2.25*
Reflective light technology	$2.00+
Lenticular image 7″x10″	$1.00-$1.50*
Liquid-filled ads	$0.85
Singing ads	$0.81*
Heat-sensitive ink	$0.62
Stereo viewers	$0.55*
3D images	$0.23

Notes: Costs do not include binding into magazines.
*Cost of printing ad not included.

Moreover, as was discussed in Ethical Perspective 14–1, many advertisers and agencies are concerned that magazine ads that use these new technologies may do so at the expense of other ads in the publication and thus may bring pressure to publishers to control their use. Some creative people have also expressed concern that these new technologies are gimmicks that are being substituted for creative advertising ideas.[25]

Newspapers

Newspapers are the second major form of print media and represent the largest of all advertising media in terms of total advertising dollar volume. In 1991, more than $30 billion was spent on newspaper advertising, which represents about 24 percent of the total advertising expenditures in the United States.[26] Newspapers are an especially important advertising medium to local advertisers and particularly to retailers, which account for a large amount of newspaper advertising. However, newspapers also have characteristics that make them valuable to national advertisers. Many of the advertising dollars spent by local retailers are actually provided by national advertisers through cooperative advertising programs (which are discussed in Chapter 17). Like magazines, there are different classifications or types of newspapers; they vary in terms of their characteristics and their role as an advertising medium. We begin by examining the various ways by which newspapers can be classified.

Types of Newspapers

The traditional role of newspapers as a communication medium has been to deliver prompt and detailed coverage of news as well as supplying other information and features that appeal to readers. The vast majority of newspapers are daily publications serving a local community. However, other types of newspapers have special characteristics that can be valuable to advertisers including weekly, national, and special-audience newspapers.

Daily newspapers

Daily newspapers, which are published each weekday, are found in cities and larger towns across the country, with many areas having more than one daily paper. Daily newspapers are read by nearly 113 million adults each weekday.[27] They provide detailed coverage of news, events, and issues concerning the local area as well as business, sports, and other relevant information and entertainment. Daily newspapers can further be classified as morning, evening, or Sunday publications. In 1991, there were 1,586 daily newspapers in the United States, of which 67 percent were evening papers and 33 percent morning. There were also 875 Sunday newspapers, most of which were published by daily newspapers. Since 1965, the total circulation of daily newspapers has been between 60 and 63 million. However, the total number of dailies has been declining over the past 10 years, although the number of Sunday editions has been increasing.

Promotional Perspective 14–1

The National Strikes Out

The dream of many publishers is the successful introduction of a daily national newspaper. in 1982, the Gannett Company, one of the nation's leading newspaper publishers, caught the attention of the media world with the introduction of *USA Today,* which it developed along the lines of a general-interest magazine with particularly good coverage of sports, entertainment, and business news. The paper was launched amid considerable skepticism by the advertising industry and media community. *USA Today* was criticized for its lack of in-depth coverage of stories and heavy use of graphics. Some critics called it the fast food of journalism and nicknamed it "McPaper." It took more than five years and several hundred million dollars for *USA Today* to turn a profit. However, by 1987, it had become the leading national newspaper in terms of total readership and had turned a profit. Today the paper continues to be profitable and has a circulation of over 1.6 million.

While *USA Today* has been successful, the most recent attempt to introduce a national newspaper did not fare so well. In 1990, National American Sports Communications, a partnership controlled by Mexican media mogul Emilio Azcarraga Milmo, launched *The National,* the nation's first all-sports daily. The new paper was developed with the idea of providing total and in-depth coverage of sporting events and stories and hired well-known sports writer Frank Deford as its editor.

The paper was launched January 31, 1990, in the three major markets of New York, Chicago, and Los Angeles, with an advertising rate base of 250,000 readers. The plan called for the addition of a market a month until it was distributed nationally with a circulation of more than 1 million. The partnership that owned *The National* indicated it would be willing to spend $100 million over the five years it would take the paper to turn a profit.

Unfortunately, the new paper was surrounded by problems from the beginning; and it had a difficult time finding a day-to-day audience and maintaining advertisers once their charter discounts expired. A major problem the paper encountered was the trouble it had providing all of its editions with late scores, particularly from West Coast games. The paper also had trouble differentiating itself from the competition—most notably *USA Today,* which had a statistics-filled sports section and provided late scores and thus was beating *The National* at its own game. Media buyers also noted the paper was hurt by the saturation in the sports media marketplace, as many daily newspapers had upgraded their sports sections. The fact it was launched just as the recession was getting worse and many advertisers were cutting back on their advertising spending did not help.

While all of these problems contributed to the failure of *The National,* editor Frank Deford noted the paper's biggest problem was distribution. Unlike *USA Today,* which spent nearly $100 million right from the beginning to develop an internal distribution system, *The National* chose a less expensive route of hiring Dow Jones & Co. as its distributor. Thus, the paper was often published without late scores or wasn't delivered on time because issues were printed too late to go out on the Dow Jones trucks.

The National failed in its attempt to become a national daily newspaper

> ## "This is the last challenge in daily journalism for the 20th Century!"
>
> —Frank Deford, Editor,
> THE NATIONAL® Sports Daily

SPORTS DAILY
COMING IN JANUARY 1990

CALL PETE SPINA, ADVERTISING DIRECTOR AT 212 767-1177
IN NEW YORK, MARK FURLONG AT 212 767-1177
IN CHICAGO, TIM SCHLAX AT 312 984-0418
IN LOS ANGELES, BOB BLOCHER AT 213 479-1000
IN DETROIT, RON ENGLEHART AT 313 948-1880

However, the publishing partnership was not willing to invest tens of millions of dollars to establish an independent distribution network.

The National published its last issue June 13, 1991, 16 months after it was launched. The paper never obtained the circulation base it needed to attract the big national advertisers. The editor of the *Sporting News,* a weekly sports newspaper, summarized the problems of *The National* pretty well when he noted: "If you can't get your product to the people, no matter how good it is, you can't survive. Sports fans love features and in-depth reporting, but they want late scores." Unfortunately, *The National's* failure to deliver the scores to the readers meant it could not deliver the readers to the advertisers. In the newspaper business, that means you don't survive.

Source: Scott Donaton, "Distribution Strikes Out," *Advertising Age,* June 17, 1991, pp. 1, 49; and Patrick M. Reilly, "The National Tries to Counter Slow Start," *The Wall Street Journal,* July 16, 1990, p. B1.

Weekly newspapers

Most weekly newspapers originate in small towns or suburbs where the volume of news and advertising is not adequate to support a daily newspaper. These papers focus primarily on news, sports, and events relevant to the local area and usually ignore national and world news, sports, and financial and business news. Weeklies are the fastest-growing class of newspapers, and in 1992, there were 7,476 such papers in the United States. Weeklies appeal primarily to local advertisers because of their geographic focus and lower absolute cost. Most national advertisers avoid weekly newspapers because of their duplicate circulation with daily or Sunday papers in the large metropolitan areas and problems in contracting for and placing ads in these publications. However, the contracting and scheduling problems associated with using these papers have been reduced by the emergence of syndicates that publish the papers in a number of areas and sell ad space in all of their publications through one office.

National newspapers

While national newspapers are very common in Europe as well as many other foreign countries, only a handful exist in the United States. Newspapers in this country with national circulation include *The Wall Street Journal, The Christian Science Monitor,* and *USA Today.* All three are daily publications and have editorial content that has a nationwide appeal. *The Wall Street Journal* has the largest circulation of any newspaper in the country, selling over 2 million copies a day. *USA Today* represents the most recent successful national newspaper and has positioned itself as "the nation's newspaper" (Exhibit 14–19). Promotional Perspective 14–1 discusses the failed attempt to launch a national sports newspaper— *The National.*

National newspapers appeal primarily to large national advertisers and to regional advertisers that use specific geographic editions of these publications, if available. For example, *The Wall Street Journal* has six geographic editions in which ads can be placed.

Special-audience newspapers

A variety of papers offer specialized editorial content and are published for particular groups including labor unions, various professional organizations, industries, and hobbyists. For example, many individuals working in advertising and marketing read *Advertising Age,* which is the leading trade publication for these industries. Specialized newspapers are also published in areas with large foreign language–speaking ethnic groups such as Hispanics, Vietnamese, and Filipinos. Exhibit 14–20 shows an ad promoting a network of newspapers targeting the Hispanic market.

Newspapers targeted at various religious groups compose another large class of special-interest papers. For example, more than 140 Catholic newspapers are published across the United States. Another type of special-audience newspaper is one most of you probably read regularly during the school year—the college newspaper. Over 1,300 colleges and universities publish a newspaper and offer advertisers an excellent medium for reaching college students (Exhibit 14–21, page 503).

Newspaper supplements

Although not a category of newspapers per se, many papers include magazine-type supplements, primarily in their Sunday editions. Sunday supplements, as they are often called, have been a part of most newspapers for many years and come in

➤ *Exhibit 14–19*
USA Today is a national newspaper

➤ *Exhibit 14–20*
Ad promoting a paper targeted to Hispanics

various forms. One type is the syndicated Sunday magazine such as *Parade* or *USA Weekend* that is distributed in hundreds of papers throughout the country. *Parade* has a circulation of over 32 million, whereas *USA Weekend* is carried by more than 350 newspapers with a combined circulation of more than 13 million. These publications are very similar to national magazines and carry both national and regional advertising.

Some large papers publish local Sunday supplements distributed by the parent paper. These supplements contain stories that are of more local interest, and ad space may be used by either local or national advertisers. While the *New York Times Sunday Magazine* is the best known of the local supplements, several other papers such as the *Washington Post, San Francisco Examiner,* and *Los Angeles Times* have their own Sunday magazines (Exhibit 14–22, page 504). In some areas, papers have begun carrying regional supplements as well as specialized weekday supplements that cover specific topics or interests such as food, sports, and entertainment. Supplements are valuable to advertisers that want to use the newspaper yet get four-color reproduction quality in their ads.

Types of Newspaper Advertising

In addition to there being several different types of newspapers, the ads appearing in these papers can also be divided into different categories. The major classifications of newspaper advertising are display and classified. In addition to these two dominant categories, other special types of ad and preprinted inserts also appear in newspapers.

Display advertising

Display advertising is found throughout the newspaper and generally uses illustrations, headlines, white space, and other visual devices in addition to the copy text. Display ads account for approximately 70 percent of the advertising revenue of the average newspaper. Two types of display advertising appear in newspapers—local and national (general).

Local advertising refers to ads placed by local organizations, businesses, and individuals who want to communicate with consumers in the market area served by

➤ *Exhibit 14–21*
College newspapers are an excellent way of reaching students

the newspaper. Local advertising comes primarily from retailers. Supermarkets and department stores are among the leading local display advertisers along with the numerous other retailers and service operations such as banks and travel agents. Local advertising is sometimes referred to as *retail advertising* because retailers account for so much of the local ads found in a newspaper. However, it should be noted that local advertising includes other forms of advertising. Local advertisers account for approximately 85 percent of newspaper display advertising.

National or *general newspaper advertising* refers to display advertising done by marketers of branded products or services that are sold on a national or regional level. These ads are designed to create and maintain demand for a company's particular product or service and to complement the efforts of local retailers that stock and promote the advertiser's products. Major retail chains, automobile companies, and airlines are heavy users of newspaper advertising.

Classified advertising

Classified advertising also provides newspapers with a substantial amount of revenue. These ads are arranged under subheads according to the product, service, or offering being advertised. Employment, real estate, and automotive are the three major categories of classified advertising. While most classified ads include only text set in uniform type, some newspapers also accept classified display advertising. These ads are run in the classified section of the paper but use illustrations, larger type sizes, white space, borders, and even color to enhance their appearance.

Special ads and inserts

Special advertisements in newspapers include a variety of governmental and financial reports and notices and public notices of changes in business and personal relationships. Other types of advertising also appear in newspapers such as political or special-interest ads promoting a particular candidate, issue, or cause. **Preprinted inserts** are another type of advertising distributed through newspapers. These ads do not appear in the paper itself but rather are printed by the advertiser and then taken to the newspaper to be inserted before delivery. Many retailers use inserts such as

➤ *Exhibit 14–22*
The *Los Angeles Times* promotes
its Sunday magazine

circulars, catalogs, or brochures in specific circulation zones of the newspaper to reach shoppers in their particular trade area.

Advantages of Newspapers

Newspapers have a number of characteristics that make them popular among both local and national advertisers. These include their extensive penetration of local markets, flexibility, geographic selectivity, reader involvement, and the special services newspapers offer.

Extensive penetration

One of the primary advantages of newspapers is the high degree of market coverage, or penetration, they offer an advertiser. In most areas, 70 percent or more of households read a daily newspaper, and the reach figure may exceed 90 percent among some groups such as higher-income and -education-level households. Most areas are served by one or two daily newspapers, and often the same company owns both, publishing both a morning and an evening edition. Thus, by making one space buy, the advertiser can achieve a high level of overall reach in a particular market.

The extensive penetration of newspapers makes them a truly mass medium and provides advertisers with an excellent opportunity for reaching all segments of the population with their advertising message. Also, since many newspapers are published and read daily, the advertiser can build a high level of frequency into a media schedule with newspapers.

Flexibility

Another advantage of newspapers is the flexibility they offer the advertiser. Newspapers provide flexibility in several ways. First, they are flexible in terms of requirements for producing and running the advertisements. Newspaper ads can be written, laid out, and prepared in a matter of hours, and for most dailies the closing time by which the ad must be received is usually no more than 24 hours (although closing

Promotional Perspective 14–2

Using Newspaper Advertising to Respond to "Black Monday"

On October 19, 1987, individuals investing in the stock market experienced a very traumatic event when, after five years of unprecedented growth, the Dow Jones industrial average dropped 508 points. The crash was the worst in the history of the market in terms of point and percentage decline as well as dollar losses. Nearly all investors were affected by the event, which became known in the financial world as "Black Monday."

In the aftermath of Black Monday, the financial community was faced with an extraordinarily difficult marketing and communications problem. While there was uncertainty over what to tell investors, they knew they must react quickly or face a further erosion in investor confidence. The situation called for not only an immediate response but also detailed and thoughtful information and advice to reassure worried investors. To deal with this crisis, many financial services companies turned to newspapers to reach their clients and offer them reassuring words.

Merrill Lynch, one of the largest financial services companies, reacted to Black Monday by creating an ad headlined "After October 19: A perspective" on Tuesday morning and placing it in newspapers on Wednesday. The full-page ad ran in 10 local newspapers in addition to two national newspapers, *The Wall Street Journal* and *USA Today*. Merrill Lynch followed the first ad with a second one on Friday, October 23, headlined "Now, What about Next Week?" which updated the company's clients and the country as well as informing them about extended weekend hours when brokers would be available. Subsequent ads ran in 150 local newspapers as well as in international publications. A number of key people were involved in the creation of the ads including not only the advertising agency but also the chairman, the director of global services, and the director of financial market research at Merrill Lynch.

Merrill Lynch's director of advertising indicated newspapers were a natural choice for the reassurance campaign, as the medium gave the company the ability to turn information around quickly and to go into detail to deliver as much information as possible. He noted, "Getting the message out in a timely manner was as important as the message itself." Thus, the newspaper's ability to produce detailed and timely information made it the appropriate medium for this situation.

Source: Tamara Goldman, "Big Spenders Develop Newspaper Strategies," *Marketing Communications*, June 1988, pp. 24–29.

Merrill Lynch reacted quickly to Black Monday with newspaper ads

After October 19: A perspective.

On October 19, investor uncertainty abruptly turned into an unprecedented market decline. In one day the Dow Jones Industrial Average fell 22½ percent.

But the selling was not caused by any particular bad news, and there is no evidence that it was justified by the fundamental values of the stocks being sold.

Buy, sell, hold?

The worst thing to do right now would be to sell at distressed prices.

It's crucial at this point to get your bearings in this totally new environment, and decide upon a rational and prudent course of action.

Without minimizing the seriousness of a market decline of some 40 percent since its high last August, it is also correct to say that for investors who remain steady under fire this new market is studded with values. But before seeking them out, it makes sense to take a good, careful look around.

What will happen next?

Some historical perspective: One of the reasons for our optimism is the magnitude of the decline we've just been through. Some of the worst declines in history have not exceeded 50 percent in the initial selloff. Even those that were followed by poor economic fundamentals recovered as much as 50 percent of the losses in subsequent months.

One of the concerns in the bond market, and the barrier to long-term economic growth, was the fear of resurging inflation. The dangers on the inflation front seem very limited at this juncture.

A better environment ahead.

The fundamentals of the economy may be called into question, but we believe the markets are overreacting to events, and that the economic outlook is sound.

It cannot be said too strongly or too often: however severe this shock has been, this is no time to sell.

In fact, it is a time to take advantage of opportunities in financial assets.

Reducing risks with bonds.

The bond market has been at best unkind to investors for the past few months, but our fixed-income analysts point out that this week's big equity selloff was accompanied by some strengthening in the bond market.

We feel that long-term Treasury bonds currently yielding in the neighborhood of 10 percent offer a very satisfying return with relatively little risk.

Partly because of the stock market decline, the Federal Reserve Board is no longer so likely to pursue a tighter monetary course, which would tend to push interest rates upward.

The Industrial Renaissance.

In the stock market, the quest for value should focus on the major long-term resurgence of the industrial sector of the economy. For investors who want to make a move now, and who have the patience to hold on through short-term volatility, we are recommending a small group of companies in the heavy industrial and closely-related sectors that we believe have the potential to lead the recovery in the stock market.

We also see opportunities in utilities and certain insurance companies.

It's no time to go it alone.

At times like these, it's more important than ever to have continuing access to the kind of information and insight that can help you exploit the opportunities that uncertainty creates.

For our part, we continue offering our clients the reassurance of our financial strength, our proud tradition of trustworthiness and our leadership in providing professional guidance and service.

At Merrill Lynch, we remain confident in the financial markets, and in the underlying value of financial assets in this climate.

We recognize that emotions run high during times like these; however, it is critical that reason and objectivity prevail now more than ever.

We urge all investors to take no action out of fear, and to make careful and thoughtful decisions before taking any action at all.

Whatever volatility we face in the days ahead, we are committed to demonstrate to you the highest degree of professionalism and service. We urge you to take a long-term view and prepare yourself to participate in the opportunities we see ahead in a fundamentally sound economy.

© 1987 Merrill Lynch & Co., Inc.

---

dates for special ads such as those using color and Sunday supplements will be longer). The short production time and closing dates make newspapers an excellent medium for responding to current events or presenting timely information to consumers. For example, both national and local advertisers run ads each year congratulating the winning team in the Super Bowl, NBA Championships, World Series, and other popular contests. Promotional Perspective 14–2 discusses how Merrill Lynch, the financial services firm, took advantage of the timeliness of newspapers to respond to the "Black Monday" stock market crash a few years ago.

A second dimension of newspapers' flexibility stems from the creative options they make available to advertisers. Newspaper ads can be produced and run in various sizes, shapes, and formats or make use of color or special inserts to gain the attention and interest of the readers. Ads can be run in Sunday magazines or other supplements, and a variety of scheduling options are possible, depending on the advertiser's purpose.

Geographic selectivity

Newspapers generally offer advertisers more geographic or territorial selectivity than any other medium except direct mail. Advertisers can vary their coverage for various areas by choosing a paper—or combination of papers—that reaches the areas with the greatest sales potential. National advertisers take advantage of the geographic selectivity of newspapers to concentrate their advertising in specific areas they have problems reaching with other media or to take advantage of strong sales potential in a particular area. For example, automobile advertisers such as BMW, Mercedes, and Volvo use heavy newspaper media schedules in California and the New York/New Jersey areas to capitalize on the high sales potential for luxury import cars in these markets.

A number of companies such as General Motors, AT&T, and Campbell are using newspapers as part of their regional marketing strategies. Newspaper advertising provides them with more flexibility to feature products on a market-by-market basis, to respond and adapt campaigns to local market conditions, and to tie into more retailer promotions and thus foster more support from the trade.[28]

Local advertisers such as retailers are interested in geographic selectivity or flexibility within a specific market or trade area. Their media goal is to concentrate their advertising on the area from which they draw most of their customers. Many newspapers now publish several geographic or zone editions that provide local advertisers with the opportunity to do this. For example, the *Los Angeles Times* publishes 11 geographic or zone editions. Exhibit 14–23 shows a map of the 11 areas for which a specific edition is published.

Reader involvement and acceptance

Another important feature of newspapers is the level of involvement and acceptance consumers have with newspapers and the ads they contain. The typical daily newspaper reader spends an average of 45 minutes a day reading the weekday newspaper and 62 minutes reading the Sunday paper.[29] Most consumers rely heavily on newspapers not only for news, information, and entertainment but also for information for making consumption decisions.

Many consumers actually purchase a newspaper *because* of the advertising it contains rather than despite it. Consumers use retail ads to determine product prices and availability and to see who is having a sale. One aspect of newspapers that is helpful to advertisers is the readers' knowledge and involvement with particular sections of the paper. Most of us know that ads for automotive products and sporting goods are generally found in the sports section of most papers, whereas ads for financial services are found in the business section. The weekly food section found in many newspapers is popular for recipe and menu ideas as well as for the grocery store ads and coupons offered therein by many stores and companies. Exhibit 14–24 (page 508) shows readership figures for various sections of newspapers for adults.

The value of newspaper advertising as a source of information has been shown in several studies. One study found that consumers look forward to newspaper ads more than for other media, whereas another showed that 80 percent of consumers indicated newspaper ads were most helpful to them in doing their weekly shopping. Newspaper advertising has also been rated the most believable of all forms of advertising in numerous studies.

➤ *Exhibit 14–23* **The *Los Angeles Times* publishes 11 zone editions**

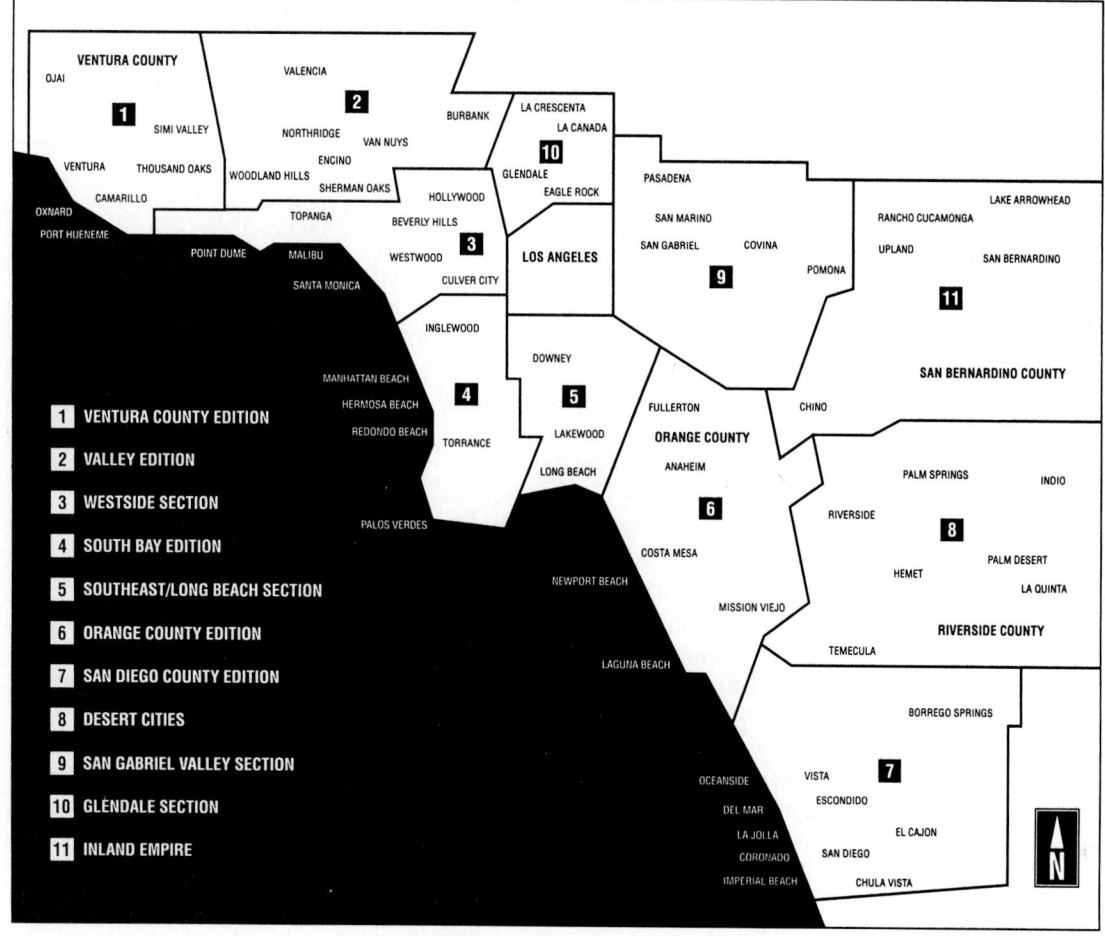

Services offered

While newspapers have numerous advantages as an advertising medium for reaching and communicating with consumers, they also can be valuable to the advertiser in terms of the special services they offer. For example, many newspapers offer merchandising services and programs to manufacturers that help convince local retailers they should stock, display, and promote the company's product and make the trade aware of newspaper ads being run for the item.

Many newspapers are also an excellent source of local market information through their knowledge of market conditions and research they conduct such as readership studies and consumer surveys. Exhibit 14–25 (page 509) shows a list of studies available from the Union-Tribune Publishing Company, publisher of the major daily newspaper in San Diego.

Newspapers can also be of assistance to small companies through the free copywriting and art services they provide. Small advertisers without an agency or advertising department often rely on the newspaper to assist them in the writing and production of their ads.

Limitations of Newspapers

While newspapers have a considerable number of advantages, like all media they also have disadvantages and limitations that must be considered in evaluating and using them as media vehicles. The limitations of newspapers include their reproduction problems, short life span, lack of selectivity, and clutter.

➤ *Exhibit 14–24*
Daily newspaper pages or sections usually read (total adult readers, by sex)

	Percent of Weekday Audience:		
	Adults	Men	Women
Read every page	58%	59%	56%
Read certain pages/sections	42	41	44
General news	93	92	94
Editorial page	78	77	79
Entertainment (movies, theaters)	78	75	82
Sports	77	87	67
Comics	74	74	74
Food, cooking	74	67	81
TV, radio listings	74	72	76
Business, finance	73	77	70
Classified	73	74	71
Home furnishings, improvement	73	68	78

Poor reproduction

One of the greatest limitations of newspapers as an advertising medium is their poor reproduction quality. The coarse paper stock used for newspapers, the absence of color, and the lack of time papers have available for high-quality reproduction limits the quality of most newspaper ads. Newspapers have improved their reproduction quality in recent years, and color reproduction has become more readily available. Also, advertisers desiring high-quality color in newspaper ads can turn to several alternatives such as using free-standing inserts or Sunday supplements. However, these are more costly and may not be desirable to many advertisers. As a general rule, if the visual appearance of the product is important, the advertiser will not rely on newspaper ads. For example, ads for food products or fashions generally use magazines so as to capitalize on their superior reproduction quality and color.

Short life span

Unlike magazines, which may be retained around the house for several weeks, the life span of a daily newspaper is generally less than a day. In most homes, the daily paper is read and discarded within 24 hours. Thus, an ad is unlikely to have any impact beyond the day of publication, and repeat exposure to an ad is very unlikely. Further compounding this problem is the short amount of time many consumers may spend with the newspaper and the possibility they may not even open certain sections of the paper. These problems can be offset somewhat by using high frequency in the newspaper schedule and by advertising in a section of the paper where consumers are likely to look for ads if they are in the market for a particular product or service.

Lack of selectivity

While newspapers do have the advantage of offering advertisers geographic selectivity, they are not a selective medium in terms of demographics or lifestyle characteristics. As noted earlier, most newspapers have extensive penetration and reach broad and very diverse groups of consumers. This makes it difficult for marketers to focus specifically on narrowly defined market segments through the newspaper. For example, a manufacturer of fishing rods and reels will find newspapers to be very inefficient because of the wasted circulation that results from reaching all the non-fishermen who purchase a newspaper. Thus, they are more likely to use special-interest magazines such as *Field & Stream* or *Fishing World* to advertise their equipment. Any newspaper ads for their products will be done through cooperative plans whereby retailers share the costs or spread them over a number of sporting goods featured in the newspaper ad.

➤ *Exhibit 14–25*

Newspaper publishers such as the Union-Tribune conduct numerous studies on local markets

➤ *Exhibit 14–26*

Island ads are a way of attracting attention

SAN DIEGO COUNTY MARKET

San Diego Market - Buy The Numbers '92 - '93
Gives you a look at the San Diego market, ranking it nationally, as well as within the Southern California market. Provides information on the economy, demographics (by county and zip code) and media coverage. It also includes a section on advertising opportunities available in the Union-Tribune.
$50 (75 pages, 9/91)

Continuing Analysis Of Shopping Habits In San Diego (CASH)
This semi-annual study presents share of shopper traffic and consumer profiles for local retail stores. Based on San Diego County households, this study covers 83 categories including apparel, appliances, materials/tools, and household furnishings.
$75 (172 pages, 10/91)

Quick Market Stats
A four-page review of the San Diego market, media and Union-Tribune circulation and readership.
FREE (4 pages, 12/91)

San Diego County Consumer Expenditures
FACTS report shows total annual consumer expenditures in San Diego County for selected store categories. Separate zone figures are included.
FREE (#247, 1 page 12/91)

San Diego Regional Shopping Center Study
This annual study provides shopper traffic, shopping frequency, travel time, cross-shopping , readership studies and other demographic characteristics of San Diegans who shop at one or more of the fifteen largest shopping centers in the county.
FREE (45 pages, 7/91)

Southern California Business Activity Centered in Three Key Counties: SD, Orange, & LA
FACTS report matching San Diego County's population, buying income and retail sales against three primary Southern California counties and seven secondary counties.
FREE (#240, 1 page, 10/90)

1990's Promise Continued Population Boom for San Diego
FACTS report ranking San Diego County with 14 major metropolitan areas in the nation, based on current population and projected population growth through 1994 .
FREE (#246, 1 page, 3/91)

San Diego, An Important Hispanic Market
FACTS report offering total and percentage ranking of Hispanic market population for San Diego County based on the ten highest ranked cities in the nation. It also offers readership information as well as demographic characteristics.
FREE (#246, 3 pages, 3/91)

The San Diego Hispanic Market
A presentation with the demographics of the Hispanic market in San Diego County, including a full-color map detailing the percent penetration of the San Diego County Hispanic market by zip code.
FREE (10 pages, 8/91)

The San Diego Asian Market
A report on the demographics of the San Diego County Asian market, including a full-color map that details the percent penetration of the Asian market in San Diego County by zip code.
FREE (10 pages, 7/91)

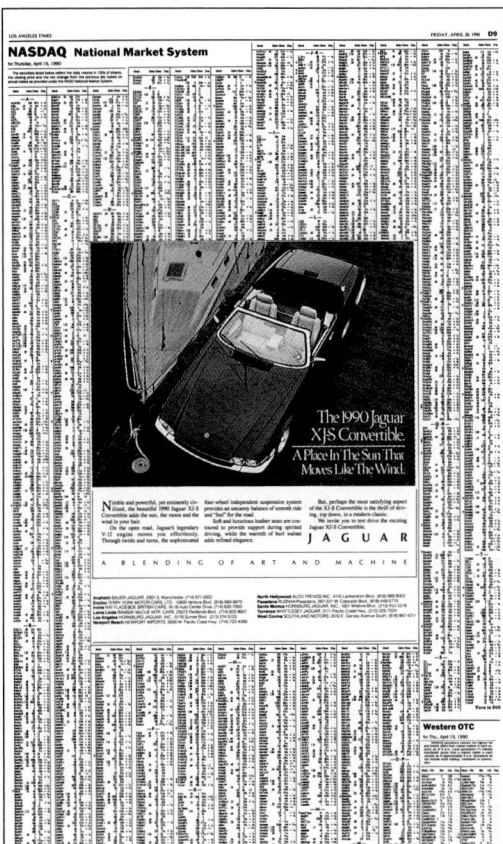

Clutter

Newspapers, like most other advertising media, suffer from clutter since there are so many advertisements competing for the reader's attention. Sixty-four percent of the average daily paper in the United States is devoted to advertising. Thus, the advertiser's message must compete with numerous other ads for consumers' attention and interest. Moreover, the creative options in newspapers are somewhat limited by the fact that nearly every ad is in black and white. Thus, it can be very difficult for the newspaper advertiser to break through the clutter unless more costly measures such as large space buys or color are used. Some advertisers use creative techniques such as "island ads," whereby the ad is surrounded by editorial material. Island ads are often found in the middle of the stock market quotes on the financial pages of many newspapers (Exhibit 14–26).

The Newspaper Audience

As with any medium, the media planner must understand the nature and size of the audience reached by a newspaper in considering its value in the media plan. As was noted above, newspapers as a general class of media do an excellent job of penetrating most households. Thus, the typical daily newspaper provides advertisers the opportunity to reach most of the households in a market. However, while local advertisers are interested in the ability of a newspaper to cover a particular market or trade area, national advertisers are concerned with reaching broad regions or even the entire country. Thus, they must purchase space in a number of papers to achieve the desired level of coverage.

The basic sources of information concerning the audience size of newspapers come from the circulation figures available through rate cards, on publisher's statements, or through Standard Rate and Data Service's *Newspaper Rates and Data.* Circulation figures for many newspapers are verified by one of the auditing services such as Audit Bureau of Circulations (discussed previously). While the rate cards or publisher's statements are used by local advertisers to get information concerning circulation figures and advertising rates, advertisers using a number of papers in their media plan generally find SRDS a convenient source.

Newspaper circulation figures are generally reported for three categories in addition to total circulation. These categories include city zone, the retail trading zone, and all other areas. The **city zone** is a market area composed of the city where the paper is published and contiguous areas similar in character to the city. The **retail trading zone** is the market outside the city zone whose residents regularly trade with merchants within the city zone. The "all other" category refers to all circulation not included in the city or retail trade zone.

In some instances, circulation figures are provided only for the primary market, which is the city and retail trade zones, and the other area. The circulation patterns across the various categories are considered by both local and national advertisers in evaluating and selecting newspapers.

National advertisers that use newspapers often buy them based on the size of the market area they cover. For example, a large advertiser such as General Motors may decide to purchase advertising in the "first 10 markets," "first 50 markets," "first 100 markets," and so on. The national advertiser gets different levels of market coverage depending on the number of market areas purchased.

Audience information

Circulation figures provide the media planner with the basic data for assessing the value of newspapers and their ability to cover various market areas. However, the media planner is also interested in the characteristics of a newspaper's readers so as to match them against those of the advertiser's target audience. Data on newspaper audience size and characteristics are available from commercial research services and from studies conducted by the papers.

Commercial studies providing readership information for the top 100 or so major markets are supplied by the Simmons-Scarbough Syndicated Research Associates. These studies cover more than 150 daily newspapers and provide reach and frequency estimates for various demographic groups. The audience information available from these studies is valuable to the media planner for comparing newspapers with other media vehicles that generally have similar data available. Many advertising executives and media planners believe the newspaper industry must expand the amount of audience research data available or risk losing more advertising dollars to magazines and television.

Many newspapers commission and publish their own audience studies so as to provide current and potential advertisers with information on readership and characteristics of readers such as demographics, shopping habits, and lifestyles. These studies are often designed to provide information to advertisers as well as to help promote the effectiveness of the newspaper in reaching various types of consumers. Since they are sponsored by the paper itself, many advertisers are somewhat skeptical over the results of these studies. Careful attention must be given to the research methods and conclusions drawn by these studies when using them to make media decisions.

Purchasing Newspaper Space

Advertisers are faced with a number of options and pricing structures when purchasing newspaper space. The cost of advertising space depends not only on the newspaper's circulation but also on factors such as premium charges for color or special sections as well as discounts available. Also, the purchase process and the rates paid for newspaper space differ for national versus local advertisers. We first consider the rate differential for national versus local advertisers.

National versus local rates

According to the American Association of Advertising Agencies, national advertising rates are, on average, 66 percent higher than those paid by local advertisers. Newspapers attribute the higher national rates to the added costs they incur in serving national advertisers, along with several other factors.

National and local advertisers differ in the method by which they purchase newspaper space. National advertisers are represented by an advertising agency and purchase space through a sales agent or "rep" representing the newspaper. The sales agents work for organizations representing a number of independent newspapers and/or newspaper chains. Their job is to supply the media buyer with information regarding the newspaper they represent and to promote the advantages of the newspaper in reaching specific markets and other services they offer to advertisers and their agencies. The representatives are paid commissions by the individual newspapers on the space they sell. The advertising agency also receives a 15 percent commission on any space purchased for clients.

Local advertisers usually deal directly with the newspaper's advertising department through the local representatives or reps working in the advertising sales department of the newspaper. These reps work with the local advertisers by making them aware of information and services provided by the newspapers and sometimes (for small advertisers) helping them plan and prepare their ads. While local sales reps receive a commission on the space they sell, the 15 percent agency commission or discount is not granted to local advertisers. However, the space rate for local advertisers is generally much lower than the rate charged national advertisers.

The differential rate structure for national versus local advertisers has been the source of considerable controversy. Newspaper publishers claim the rate differential is justified for several reasons. First, they argue it costs more to handle national advertising since a 15 percent commission must be granted to advertising agencies and commissions must also be paid to the independent sales reps who solicit non-local advertising. National advertising is also less dependable than local advertising since the national advertiser usually does not advertise in newspapers on a continual basis like a local advertiser. Thus, they argue that the costs of handling their business will be higher than for a local advertiser.

They also argue that national advertisers often request considerable merchandising assistance from newspapers to assist in implementing special promotions. Finally, newspaper publishers contend demand for national advertising is inelastic and thus will not increase if rates are lowered or decrease if rates are higher. Thus, there is no incentive to lower the rates charged the national advertiser.

National advertisers do not view these arguments as valid justification for the rate differential charged by newspapers. They argue that the costs of handling national advertising are not greater than for local business. They point out that many national advertisers use newspapers on a regular basis, and since they use an agency to prepare their ads, they are less likely to request special services. National advertisers also note that the large and costly staff maintained by many newspapers to assist in the design and preparation of advertising is used mostly by local advertisers.

Some newspapers are making efforts to narrow the rate differential for national and local advertisers to a more reasonable level (Exhibit 14–27).[30] National advertisers will still pay higher rates to cover the agency commission paid by the newspapers, but the rates they pay will be more in line with those paid by local advertisers. However, the rate differential still remains for many papers. A survey by

➤ *Exhibit 14–27*
Some newspapers have narrowed the rate differential for national and local advertisers

We treat National Advertisers like one of the family!

We want national advertisers who buy *The Columbus Dispatch* to feel welcome. So now we give you the same range of volume discounts that our local advertisers enjoy. And there are no annoying restrictions!

Plus, *The Dispatch* lets you dominate the $16 billion effective buying power of the Columbus MSA, delivering 73% of the MSA's nearly one million adults on Sunday and 55% daily.*

For more information and our latest rate book, call National Advertising Manager Leonard Zane at 614-461-5183. In Ohio call toll-free 800-282-0263.

The Columbus Dispatch
Morning & Sunday

* Source: Scarborough's 1987 Newspaper Audience Ratings Study

➤ *Exhibit 14–28*
Standard advertising units

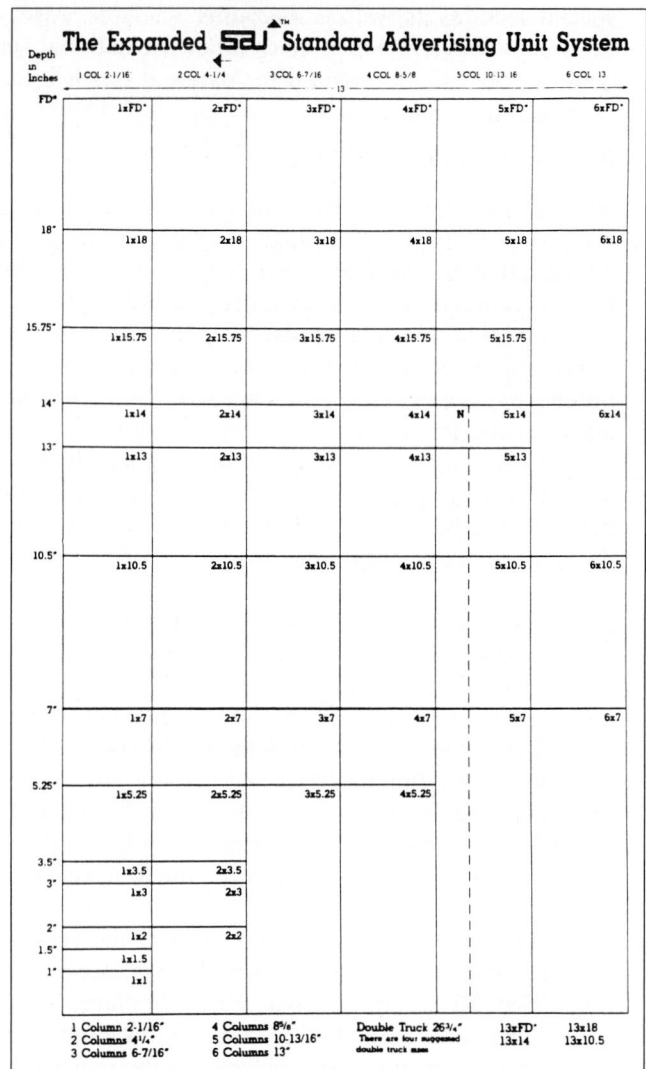

News-Inc. of national and local rates for 22 newspapers in large and small markets found that the premiums paid by national advertisers ranged from 9 to 109 percent.[31] Many marketers sidestep the national advertiser label and the higher rates by channeling their newspaper ads through special category plans, cooperative advertising deals with retailers, and local dealers and distributors that pay local rates. However, the rate differential does limit many national advertisers from making newspapers a larger part of their media mix.[32]

Newspaper Rates

Traditionally newspaper space for national advertisers has been sold by the agate line system. An **agate line** measures 1/14 inch in depth and one column wide; thus, there are 14 lines per inch. The size of an ad would generally be specified in terms of total agate lines, or "lineage," which is determined by the number of lines and columns the ad covered. For example, an ad that is 10 inches deep by 2 columns wide would contain 280 agate lines ($2 \times 10 \times 14$). Thus, the total cost for the ad would depend on the newspaper per-line rate. If the paper charged $3 per agate line, the ad would cost $840.

The problem with this system is that newspapers use page formats of varying width. Some have six columns per page, whereas others have eight or nine. Thus, the size, shape, and costs of an ad vary depending on the column format used by the paper. This results in a complicated production and buying process for national advertisers purchasing space in a number of newspapers.

To address this problem and make newspapers more comparable to other media that sell space and time in standard units, the newspaper industry developed **standard advertising units (SAUs)** and switched to this system in 1984. Under this system, all newspapers will use column widths 2 1/16 inches wide, with tabloid-size papers having five columns per page and standard or broadcast papers being six columns in width. The *column inch* is used as the unit of measurement to create the 57 standard-size units or format sizes, as shown in Exhibit 14–28.

The national advertiser can prepare one ad in a particular SAU, and it would fit every newspaper in the country that accepts SAUs and rates would be quoted on that basis. Since over 1,400 or about 90 percent of the daily newspapers use the SAU system, the purchase and production process has been simplified tremendously for national advertisers.

Newspaper rates for local advertisers continue to be based on the column inch, which is one inch deep by one column wide. Advertising rates for the local advertiser are quoted per column inch, and total space costs are calculated by multiplying the number of column inches by the cost per inch.

Rate structures

While the column inch and standard advertising unit are used for determining basic newspaper advertising rates, the media planner must consider other options and factors. Many newspapers charge **flat rates,** which means they offer no discount for large quantity or repeated space buys. Others may have an **open-rate structure,** which means various discounts are available. These discounts are generally based on frequency or bulk purchases of space and are dependent on the number of column inches purchased in a year.

Newspaper space rates also depend on any special requests the advertiser has such as preferred position or the use of color. The basic rates quoted by a newspaper are **run of paper,** or **ROP,** which means the paper can place the ad on any page or in any position it desires. While most newspapers try to place an ad in a position requested, the advertiser can ensure a specific section and/or position on a page by paying a higher **preferred position rate.** Color advertising is also available in many newspapers on a ROP basis or can be utilized through the use of preprinted inserts or Sunday supplements.

Advertisers can also buy newspaper space based on **combination rates** whereby a discount is offered for using several newspapers as a group. The most frequently used combination rate occurs when a publisher owns both a morning and an evening newspaper in a market and offers a reduced single rate for using the same ad in both newspapers, generally within a 24-hour period.

Combination discounts are also available when the advertiser buys space in several newspapers owned by the publisher in a number of markets or in multiple newspapers affiliated in a syndicate or newspaper group. Exhibit 14–29 shows an ad for the Network of City Business Journals. Advertisers can place their messages in business journals in 50 cities with one media buy through this group.

Comparing newspaper rates

As with other media, advertisers are interested in comparing the rates of newspapers with different rates and circulation on some common basis. The traditional standard for comparing newspapers has been to compute their **milline rate,** which is the cost per line of space per million circulation. The formula for this calculation is

$$\text{Milline} = \frac{1,000,000 \times \text{Rate per line}}{\text{Circulation}}$$

➤ *Exhibit 14–29* **The Network of City Business Journals is an example of a newspaper group**

Thus, a newspaper with a circulation of 500,000 and a rate of $1.50 per line would have a milline rate of

$$\frac{1,000,000 \times 1.50}{500,000} = \$3.00$$

Since most newspapers have switched away from the agate line- to the column inch-based rate method, the cost per thousand method (CPM) is now used to make cost comparisons among newspapers. The CPM comparison uses the space unit the advertiser is buying (i.e., the particular SAU) in the numerator of the formula to compare newspapers with different circulation bases. For example, a full-page or 6 × FD SAU ad (6 columns wide by full depth [FD]) in Newspaper A may cost $5,400 and $3,300 in Newspaper B. If the circulations of the two papers are 165,000 and 116,000, respectively, the CPM for this particular SAU in each paper would be calculated as follows:

$$\text{Newspaper A} = \frac{\$5,400 \times 1,000}{165,000} = \$32.73$$

$$\text{Newspaper B} = \frac{\$3,300 \times 1,000}{116,000} = \$28.45$$

The use of the CPM criterion as a comparison basis is more convenient than using the agate line method. It also allows the media planner to make intermedia comparisons between newspapers and other media that could not be done with the milline rate. Thus, the milline rate comparison method is rarely used by media planners in comparing the relative costs of newspapers.

The Future of Newspapers

Newspapers remain the largest advertising medium in terms of total advertising volume, despite the tremendous growth of the broadcast media and cable advertising in particular. However, newspapers have fallen behind TV and magazines as a medium for national advertisers. Newspapers accounted for only 5 percent of the $73 billion spent by national advertisers in 1991.[33] Newspapers' major strength lies in their role as a medium that can be used effectively by local advertisers on a continual basis. While it is unlikely that newspapers' importance as a local advertising medium will change in the near future, they will face greater competition from other advertising media and direct marketers. Newspapers must address a number of problems and issues.

Competition from other media

The newspaper industry's battle to increase its share of national advertising volume has proven to be very difficult. Not only is there the problem of reproduction quality and rate differentials, but newspapers are also facing competition from other media competing for both national and local advertisers' budgets. The newspaper industry is particularly concerned about the "bypass," or loss of advertisers to direct marketing and telemarketing.[34]

Many firms are developing large data bases that identify their best prospects and targeting telephone and direct-mail promotions directly to them. Much of the money spent on these programs is coming at the expense of newspaper advertising budgets. For example, it has been estimated that in markets of 250,000 households, newspapers are losing nearly $1 million a year in revenue to direct marketers. In markets of 1 million or more households, the annual losses are estimated to be more than $4 million.[35]

To deal with this problem, many newspapers will have to gear up to compete as direct marketers. Many papers are already building data bases by collecting information from readers that can be used by potential advertisers to target specific groups or for direct marketing. In addition to their data bases, newspapers have a distribution system that can reach nearly every household in a market every day. In the future, it is likely that many newspapers will find ways to make their extensive data bases and distribution systems available to marketers that want to target consumers with direct-marketing efforts.[36]

The intermedia battle that newspapers find themselves involved in is no longer limited to national advertising. Local radio and TV stations (particularly cable stations), as well as the expanded number of Yellow Pages publishers, are aggressively pursuing local advertisers. Thus, newspapers will have to fight harder to retain many of their local advertisers.

Circulation

Like magazines, many newspapers are taking a closer look at their circulation and analyzing whether the cost of getting additional circulation is justified by the advertising revenue it generates. For many papers, circulation revenue is accounting for more of their total revenue and they are raising newsstand and home-delivery rates. Several major metropolitan newspapers have found that advertisers use newspapers to reach consumers within specific geographic areas and do not want to pay for readers in outlying areas. Thus, some papers are eliminating what has been called "ego circulation" and focusing more on regional editions in their immediate trade area.[37]

Cross-media buys

Another area where newspapers may be following the lead of magazines is in the area of cross-newspaper and media buys. Newspapers within, as well as across, various regions are banding together to offer national advertisers a package of newspapers rather than requiring them to purchase space in individual papers. For example, General Motors used a $20 million, 100-plus newspaper buy for the regionalized rollout of its new Saturn automobile. A number of newspaper networks are being formed to help newspapers compete for more of the media expenditures of national advertisers.[38]

Cross-media buys involving newspapers and other media vehicles are also likely to become more prevalent. For example, the *Washington Post* has been involved in a cross-media deal with *Newsweek,* while large media companies that own newspapers, magazines, and broadcast media are also offering cross-media packages to advertisers.

Attracting and maintaining readers

The growth of newspapers as an advertising medium may also be limited by a decline in the popularity of the medium itself. Newspaper readership has been on a steady decline for the past two decades. In 1970, nearly 70 percent of the adult population read a newspaper on the average weekday. By 1990, this percentage had fallen to 62 percent. Additionally, the percentage of U.S. households receiving a daily newspaper declined from 77 percent in 1980 to 67 percent in 1990. The decline in newspaper readership can be attributed to several factors, including the fast-paced, time-poor lifestyle of the modern, dual-income household along with the continued growth, popularity, and viewing options offered by TV.

A number of newspapers have made changes to make their papers more interesting and easier and faster to read. These changes include the increased use of color and graphics as well as expanded coverage of sports and entertainment. Some papers have begun providing short summaries of articles in each section of the paper so readers can peruse them and decide what they want to read. Exhibit 14–30 shows an example of an ad used in a campaign by the *Los Angeles Times* to announce format changes and encourage people to read the new, faster-format *Times.*

Of particular concern to publishers is the decline in newspaper readership among important market segments such as women and young adults. A 1991 survey by Simmons Market Research Bureau found that 60 percent of women read a newspaper on a typical day, compared with 67 percent in 1981. Newspapers and advertisers are concerned over the decline in readership among women since they are far more likely than men to be making buying decisions. To attract more women readers, many newspapers are introducing new women's sections and revising old ones to make them more interesting and appealing to the modern woman. This means

➤ *Exhibit 14–30*
The *Los Angeles Times* used testimonial ads to tell readers about the new easier-to-read format

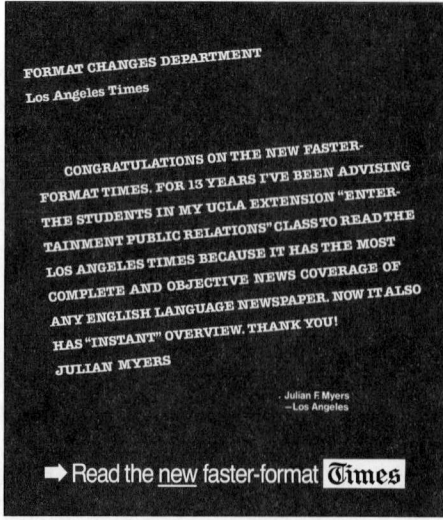

including articles on issues such as health, parenting, and careers such as how working women with children manage their time.[39]

Newspapers are also concerned over where their future readers will come from as the current generation of young people in this country are very dependent on the broadcast media. Fifty-three percent of adults between the ages of 18 and 24 read a newspaper every day and only 45 percent of those in the 30-to-44-year-old age group. Many newspapers are making special efforts to attract teenage readers in hope that they will become and remain regular newspaper readers. Some publishers are creating special sections to attract younger readers. These sections rely heavy on color and graphics and focus on topics of relevance to young people by including articles on local issues, fashion, music, and entertainment.[40]

The newspaper industry faces a serious challenge if it is to increase circulation and readership and continue to attract advertising revenue. This means making newspapers more interesting and appealing to readers by targeting specific groups as well as expanding services and efforts to advertisers to encourage them to continue using the newspaper as an advertising medium.

SUMMARY

Magazines and newspapers, the two major forms of print media, play an important role in the media plans and strategy of many advertisers. Magazines are a very selective medium and are very valuable to the advertiser for reaching specific types of customers and market segments. The three broad categories or classes of magazines are consumer, farm, and business publications. Each of these three categories can be further classified according to the editorial content and audience appeal of the publication.

In addition to their high selectivity, the advantages of magazines include their excellent reproduction quality, long life, prestige, flexibility, and readers' high receptivity to magazine advertising. Disadvantages of magazines include their high cost, limited reach and frequency, the long lead time they require, and the advertising clutter in most publications.

Two of the most important considerations of the media planner in deciding whether to use a magazine are size and characteristics of the audience reached by the publication. Media buyers consider the circulation of a publication as well as its total readership and compare these figures against the audience the advertiser is attempting to reach. Circulation figures are used as the basis for a magazine's advertising space rate structure. For most major publications, these figures are audited by a circulation verification service such as the Audit Bureau of Circulations.

Advertising space rates in magazines vary according to a number of factors such as the size of the ad, position in the publication, particular editions purchased, the use of color, and the number and frequency of insertions. Rate comparisons for magazines are made on the basis of the cost per thousand criterion, although other factors such as the editorial content of the publication and its ability to reach specific target audiences must also be considered.

Newspapers represent the largest advertising medium in terms of total volume, with over a fourth of all advertising dollars going to them. Newspapers are an especially important medium to local advertisers, particularly retailers. Newspapers are also used by national advertisers, with automobile, tobacco, and airline companies being among the heaviest users.

Newspapers are a broad-based medium and reach a large cross section of households in a particular area. In addition to their broad reach or penetration, newspapers have other advantages including flexibility, geographic selectivity, reader involvement, and special services they provide. Drawbacks of newspapers include their lack of high-quality ad reproduction, short life span, clutter, and lack of class selectivity.

The rates newspapers charge national advertisers are, on the average, 66 percent higher than those paid by a local advertiser. This differential rate structure for national versus local advertisers has been the source of considerable controversy, and some papers are beginning to reduce the rates paid by national advertisers. The buying and selling of newspaper ad space have changed significantly in recent years to simplify the use of the medium by national advertisers.

Trends toward market segmentation and regional marketing are prompting many advertisers to make more use of newspapers and magazines. However, both magazines and newspapers are facing increasing competition from other media such as radio, cable television, and direct marketing. Both magazines and newspapers are giving closer attention to improving the quality of their circulation bases and cross-media deals. Rising costs are presenting problems for magazines, whereas declining readership is a problem for newspapers.

KEY TERMS

high-involvement media
selectivity
gatefolds
bleed pages
split runs
primary circulation
controlled-circulation
 basis
pass-along readership
total audience/readership

magazine networks
cross- or multimagazine
 deals
cross-media advertising
selective binding
ink-jet imaging
display advertising
classified advertising
preprinted inserts
city zone

retail trading zone
agate line
standard advertising units
 (SAUs)
flat rates
open-rate structure
run of paper (ROP)
preferred position rate
combination rates
milline rate

DISCUSSION QUESTIONS

1. Discuss how the role of magazines and newspapers as advertising media differs from that of television and radio.
2. More than 2,000 consumer and over 5,000 business magazines are published in the United States. How can the market support such a large number of magazines?
3. How can advertisers increase the selectivity of their magazine and newspaper advertising?
4. Explain why advertisers of a product such as cosmetics or women's clothing would choose to advertise in a publication such as *Vogue,* which devotes most of its pages to ads rather than editorial.
5. What are the differences between magazine circulation and total audience or readership? If you were a media buyer, which of the two would you use in making your magazine buys?
6. If you were purchasing magazine advertising space for a golf club manufacturer, what factors would

you consider? Would your magazine selections be limited to golfing publications? Why or why not?
7. Do you believe advertisers and agencies have a right to be notified when a magazine in which they have an ad scheduled plans to run a printacular such as a multipage insert or pop-up ad? Defend your position.
8. Do you agree with the policy of most newspapers whereby national advertisers are charged a higher rate than local advertisers? How might newspapers attract more business from national advertisers, aside from reducing the rate differential?
9. What are the specific advantages and limitations of newspapers and magazines as advertising media?
10. Discuss the future of both newspapers and magazines as advertising media. How might newspapers deal with declining readership?

chapter **15**

Support Media

chapter objectives

➢ To introduce the various support media available to the marketer in developing a promotional program.

➢ To provide an understanding of the advantages and disadvantages of support media.

➢ To explain how audience measurement for support media is provided.

Advertisers Tie In to Movies

The brands that appear in movies do not just happen to be there. Almost every time you watch a movie these days you also watch a slew of advertisements. Besides the obvious ads that appear before the movie begins, more products are making their way into the actual movie. Some sources estimate that some movies, such as *Robin Hood: Prince of Thieves* and *Terminator 2: Judgment Day,* could get approximately $10 to $15 million each in marketing support through tie-ins with marketers. (Tie-ins may include product placements in movies as well as promotional events such as games, toys, and so on.)

Product placements are very common. For example, Wrigley's gum appeared in *Jungle Fever;* Miller beer was very prominently displayed in the bar scene in *Thelma and Louise;* Pizza Hut had a showing in *The Rocketeer;* and Pepsi and Subway received exposure on *Terminator II.* In the 1992 showing of *Wayne's World,* Pizza Hut, Pepsi, Dorito's, Reebok, and Nuprin were all prominently promoted, while some movies such as *Point Break* have dozens of product placements in them.

Promotional tie-ins are also used frequently. In these tie-ins, the advertiser may get a product placement as well as the opportunity to promote products associated with the movie. For example, Pepsi offered "Thirst Terminator" cups (*Terminator II*), and McDonald's promoted a Dick Tracy Crimestopper Game (*Dick Tracy*) as movie spin-offs. Advertising expenditures on tie-ins were estimated to be about $30 to $40 million in 1991 (see accompanying chart).

While many advertisers consider product placements and tie-ins to be an excellent way to promote their brands—Dairy Queen is a veteran of the tie-in game—others are not so pleased. Both McDonald's and Hardee's, both of which tied in to *Days of Thunder,* thought they were shortchanged. Also dissatisfied was Black & Decker, which settled a lawsuit against 20th Century Fox. The movie company promised to show a Black & Decker power tool in the movie *Die Hard II* in exchange for in-store movie promotions. When the scene featuring the tool ended up on the cutting room floor, Black & Decker sued for more than $150,000 in damages to offset the costs of the promotion.

Consumers and the media are also showing their dissatisfaction. Ad critic Michael Jacobson estimates more than 100 brand-name products appeared in the top five grossing films of 1990, and he has asked the Federal Trade Commission (FTC) to require movie companies to inform consumers of product placements through on-screen disclosures. Other consumer groups have asked for notices to be made before the movies begin. The FTC notes it has no control over the content of movies.

Summer marketing partnerships

- **"Robin Hood: Prince of Thieves"**
  Distributor: Warner Bros.
  Release date: June 14
  Tie-in partners: Kenner Toys, Ralston Purina

- **"The Rocketeer"**
  Distributor: Walt Disney Pictures
  Release date: July 3
  Tie-in partners: M&M/Mars, Pizza Hut

- **"Terminator 2 : Judgement Day"**
  Distributor: Tri-Star Pictures
  Release date: July 12
  Tie-in partners: Subway, Diet Pepsi, Hero cologne

- **"101Dalmations" (re-lease)**
  Distributor: Walt Disney Pictures
  Release date: June 12
  Tie-in partners: Cheerios, Mattel

- **"Radio Flyer"**
  Distributor: Columbia Pictures
  Release date: July 19
  Tie-in partners: Dairy Queen, Scott Paper, Kraft marshmallows

- **"Bill & Ted's Excellent Adentures II"**
  Distributor: Orion Pictures
  Release date: June 19 or 26
  Tie-in partners: Ralston Purina, Kenner Toys Butterfinger

- **"Bingo!"**
  Distributor: Tri-Star Pictures
  Release date: Aug.16
  Tie-in partners: Skippy dog food

Source: *Advertising Age*

(continued)

Hollywood argues that product placements add realism to the movies, many of the placements are not paid for, and the director typically requests a particular brand to convey certain attributes or a specific setting. They argue that brands must be shown if the movie is to appear realistic. They also contend that merely placing a product in a movie does not mean the consumer will be harmed.

Meanwhile, the likelihood of a brand X beer or soda being consumed in a movie is not very high—it just wouldn't seem real!

Source: Steven W. Colford and Marcy Magiera, "Products in Movies: How Big a Deal," Advertising Age, *June 10, 1991, pp. 12; Marcy Magiera, "Hollywood Cools off Summer Film Tie-Ins,"* Advertising Age, *April 15, 1991, p. 3; and Cara Appelbaum, "Summer's Blockbuster Brand Tie-Ins,"* Adweek's Marketing Week, *July 8, 1991, p. 4.*

The increased use of product placements and movie tie-ins described here is just one example of the increasing number of alternative media available to the marketer. Advertisements seem to be popping up everywhere—in places you never expect them to be and in situations in which you may not even realize you are seeing one.

In this chapter, we review a number of support media—some of which are new to the marketplace, others that have been around a while—discussing the relative advantages and disadvantages, cost information, and audience measurement of each. We refer to these media as **support media** because for large advertisers, particularly national advertisers, the media reviewed in the previous chapters dominate their media strategies. Support media are used to reach those persons in the target market that these media may not have reached and to reinforce, or support, the message communicated therein.

You may be surprised at how many different ways there are to deliver the message and how often you are exposed to them. Let's begin by examining the scope of the support media industry and then some of the many alternatives available to the marketer.

The Scope of the Support Media Industry

Some of the less commonly used support media are often referred to by a variety of titles. **Alternative media, nonmeasured media,** and **nontraditional media** are just some of the more commonly used terms. Essentially, these terms describe a vast variety of channels used to deliver communications and to promote products and services. Consider these:

- A California company offers advertising space on an arm band that is used to protect drivers' left arms from sunburn.

> *Exhibit 15–1*
Estimated gross billings by media category show that outdoor ads are still the most popular

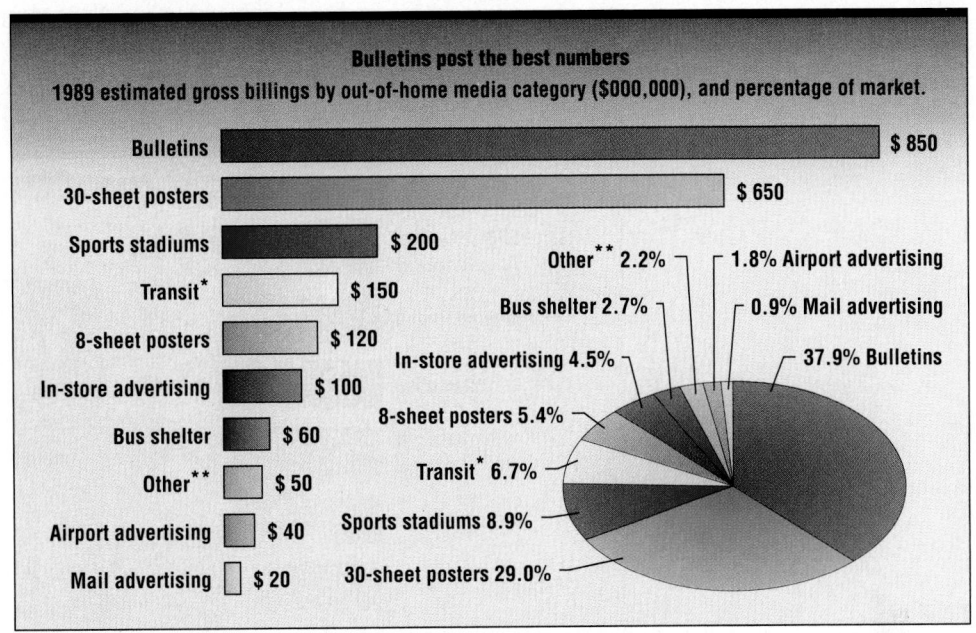

Bulletins post the best numbers
1989 estimated gross billings by out-of-home media category ($000,000), and percentage of market.

Bulletins	$ 850
30-sheet posters	$ 650
Sports stadiums	$ 200
Transit*	$ 150
8-sheet posters	$ 120
In-store advertising	$ 100
Bus shelter	$ 60
Other**	$ 50
Airport advertising	$ 40
Mail advertising	$ 20

Other** 2.2%
1.8% Airport advertising
Bus shelter 2.7%
0.9% Mail advertising
In-store advertising 4.5%
37.9% Bulletins
8-sheet posters 5.4%
Transit* 6.7%
Sports stadiums 8.9%
30-sheet posters 29.0%

* Includes bus, train and cab.
** Includes painted walls, trucks, air banners, movie theaters, golf course signage, etc.

- Another will put your ad at the bottom of a golf cup.
- Still another will place your ad at the bottom of a drinking cup so it will be seen everytime one takes a drink.

You can see why these media may be considered nontraditional.

At the same time, these media are not necessarily nontraditional in respect to their use by large and small companies. Many advertisers, as well as the top 100 advertising agencies, have increased their use of these media, and as new alternatives are developed, this use is likely to continue to grow. Figures relating to "nontraditional" media do not include some of the more commonly used support media, such as outdoor advertising, specialty advertising, transit advertising, and advertising in the Yellow Pages. Let us examine some of these in more detail.

Out-of-Home Media

Out-of-home advertising here refers to a variety of advertising forms including outdoor (billboards and signs), transit (both inside and outside the vehicle), skywriting, and a variety of other media. While outdoor advertising is one of the more commonly employed media—as shown in Exhibit 15–1—the others have also been increasing in use.

Outdoor Advertising

It is believed that outdoor advertising has been in existence since the days of cave dwellers, and it is known that both the Egyptians and Greeks employed this form of communication as early as 5,000 years ago. Outdoor certainly is one of the more pervasive communication forms—particularly if you live in an urban or suburban area.

Even though outdoor accounts for only about 1 percent of all advertising expenditures, and the number of billboards has decreased, it has been a steadily growing medium in terms of dollars billed. In 1982, approximately $888 million was spent in this area, whereas in 1990 this figure had risen to an estimated $1.6 billion.[1] Much of this continued growth can be attributed to the longtime users such as tobacco and spirits advertisers, but a number of new product categories have also increased expenditures in outdoor. For example, the increase in the number of females in the work force has led to more advertising of products targeted to this

➤ *Exhibit 15–2*
1990 outdoor spending by category

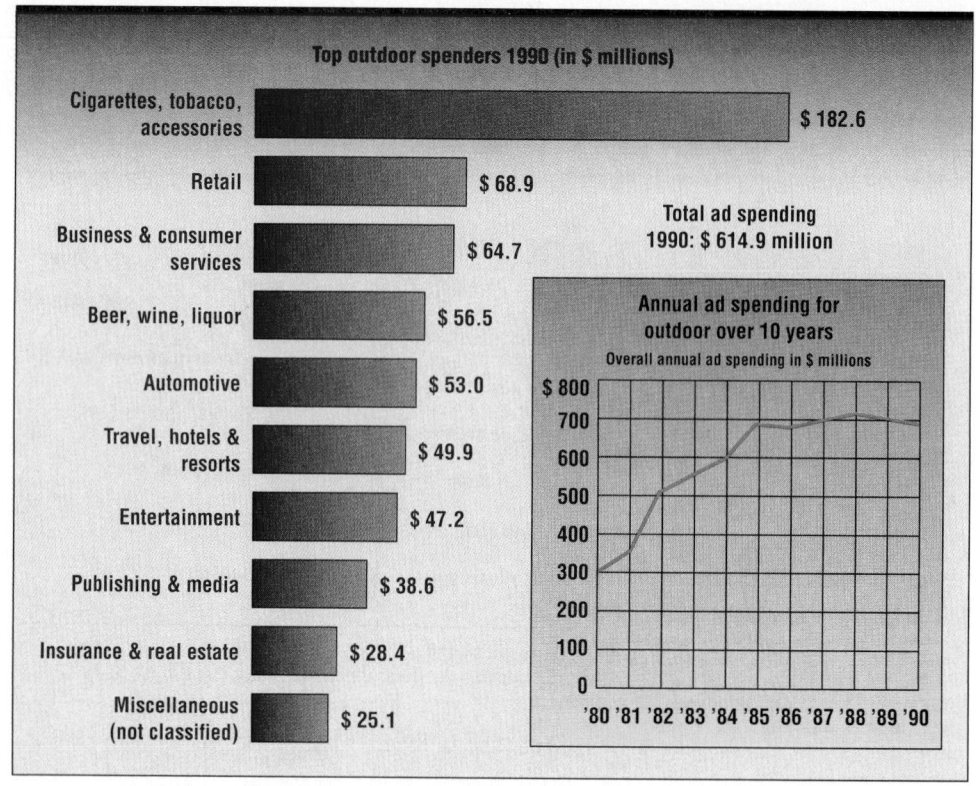

segment, whereas travel companies, entertainment and amusement attractions, insurance companies, and automotive companies have also seemingly "discovered" this medium, as demonstrated in Exhibit 15–2.

A major reason for the continued success of outdoor is the ability of this medium to remain innovative through technology. As can be seen in Exhibit 15–3, billboards no longer are limited to standard two-dimensional boards, as three-dimensional forms and extensions are now used to attract attention. In addition, electronic billboards and inflatables, like the one shown in Exhibit 15–4 that was used to promote Tropicana Orange Juice, have also opened new markets. You probably have been exposed to either sign boards or electronic billboards at sports stadiums, in supermarkets, in the campus bookstore and dining halls, in shopping malls, on the freeways, or on the sides of buildings from skyscrapers in New York City to Mailpouch Tobacco signs on the sides of barns in the Midwest. This is truly a pervasive medium.

At the same time, outdoor has its critics. Ever since former President Lyndon Johnson's wife, Lady Bird, instigated a campaign to rid the interstate highways of billboard advertising—the Highway Beautification Act of 1965—there has been a controversy regarding its use. A number of cities and states have passed, or currently have pending, legislation limiting the use of this advertising form, considering it unsightly and obtrusive. In addition, a study conducted by the University of Michigan Survey Research Center showed that as many as 19 percent of those polled

➤ *Exhibit 15–3*   **Outdoor advertising goes beyond two dimensions**

 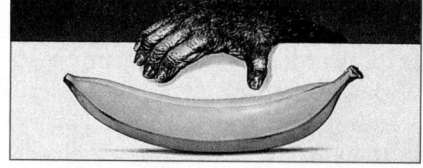 

➤ *Exhibit 15–4*
Inflatables bring new meaning to outdoor advertising

favored doing away with outdoor advertising, and 64.5 percent favored "reasonable" regulation.[2] Ethical Perspective 15–1 (page 526) discusses some of the current problems advertisers are facing.

In addition, media buyers have not completely adopted the medium, partially because of image problems and because of the belief that outdoor is difficult to buy. (Approximately 80 percent of outdoor advertising is purchased by local merchants and companies.) Let us examine some of the advantages and disadvantages of the medium in more detail.

Advantages and disadvantages of outdoor

Outdoor offers the advertiser a number of advantages, including:

1. **Wide coverage of local markets**   With proper placement, a broad base of exposure is possible in local markets, with both day and night presence. A 100 GRP **showing** (the percentage of duplicated audience exposed to an outdoor poster daily) could yield possible exposure to an equivalent of 100 percent of the marketplace on a daily basis, or the equivalent of 3,000 GRPs over a month. This level of coverage is likely to yield high levels of reach.

2. **Frequency**   Because purchase cycles are typically for 30-day periods, those persons reached are usually exposed a number of times, resulting in high levels of frequency.

3. **Geographic flexibility**   Outdoor can provide a great deal of flexibility, given possibilities of placement along highways, near store locations, or via mobile billboards—almost anywhere that laws permit. Local, regional, or even national markets may be covered.

Ethical Perspective 15–1

Billboards—Effective Medium or Environmental Eyesore?

Mention the word *billboard* and you will raise the ire of environmentalists in a hurry. But the word *billboard* is synonymous with effective advertising to many of those in business as well as other fields.

While the war on outdoor advertising began many years ago, perhaps the most significant battle occurred in the mid-1960s when President Johnson's wife, Lady Bird, initiated the anti-outdoor advertising campaign that resulted in passage of the Highway Beautification Act of 1965, which banned billboards on federally funded highways. Since then, a series of other battles have been fought, with both sides claiming victories.

Opponents of outdoor billboards argue the industry is its own worse enemy. They claim they are not against billboards in general—they say they would never suggest the Strip in Las Vegas take down its signs—but rather are against the seemingly endless intrusion into their personal lives and the environment. Their argument is that the proliferation of signs has become obnoxious and an eyesore. As evidence to support their claim, they note that even signs that supposedly are designed to show concern for the environment are being used as a new way to get a billboard where they are not supposed to be. They also argue that harmful products are being promoted, and minorities and the poor are often the targets of the medium.

Billboard "enemies" have taken actions ranging from defacing the boards to government legislation, and they have enlisted a substantial army. Their results have been effective. Four states now ban billboard advertising (Vermont, Hawaii, Maine, and Alaska), while a fifth (Rhode Island) has put a stop to the erecting of new ones. In addition, a number of cities have their own restrictions and/or bans. San Diego, New York, Denver, Jacksonville, St Louis, and Maricopa County, Arizona, restrict the number and location of billboards, and Albuquerque, Houston, and Tacoma are considering such actions.

Battles are also being fought at the federal level. While the Visual Pollution Control Act of 1991, designed to hasten the demise of outdoor ads, was defeated in the Senate, the Intermodal Surface Transportation Efficiency Act (ISTEA), which bans construction of new billboards on scenic highways, was signed into law by President Bush. Under this law, federal officials, armed with a $428 million compensation fund, are putting an end to thousands of billboards not in compliance with the Highway Beautification Act of 1965. The program may result in the demolition of over 114,000 billboards nationwide.

Those on the advertisers' side have established their own position and their own battle tactics. Their actions range from information dissemination—informing minority leaders of the damage done to minority-owned businesses when billboards are defaced—to "billboard police," who watch for those who might destroy or deface a billboard. They are also armed with what many consider to be the most powerful Washington lobby, the victors in the battle against the Visual Pollution Control Act. Proponents of outdoor note it is an extremely effective medium, as evidenced by its faster growth rate than both print and broadcast. They cite technological innovations such as electronic billboards as a major contributor to their success.

Not everyone has joined the fray. While the defacing of billboards appears to be on the increase, and consumers are generally in favor of increased regulation, most of those surveyed are against defacing or other nonlegislated tactics designed to bring down the boards. They seem to be torn between not wanting the boards and yet not wanting too much legislation and/or destruction. When the battle will end, if ever, is hard to tell.

Source: Adam Snyder, "Outdoor Forecast: Sunny, Some Clouds," *Adweek's Marketing Week*, July 8, 1991, pp. 18–19; Scott Hume, "Regulate Outdoor Ads: Poll," *Advertising Age*, August 13, 1990, p. 20; Alison Fahey, "Outdoor Ads Coming Down," *Advertising Age*, August 27, 1990, p. 3; and Susan C. Schena, "Next Exit: Gas, Lodging and Food from the Folks Who Cleaned the Highway," *San Diego Business Journal*, June 3, 1991, p. 17.

4. Creativity   As shown in Exhibit 15–3, outdoor ads can be very creative and, as a result, attract attention. The use of large print, colors, and other elements allows for a high degree of creativity.

5. Ability to create awareness   Because of its impact (and the requirement of a simple message), outdoor can lead to a high level of awareness.

At the same time, however, there are some limitations to outdoor, many of which are related to the advantages cited earlier:

1. **Waste coverage** While it is possible to reach very specific audiences, in many cases, the purchase of outdoor results in a high degree of waste coverage. It is not likely that all persons driving by a billboard or all persons within an area are likely to be part of the target market.

2. **Limited message capabilities** Because of the speed with which most persons pass by outdoor ads, exposure time is limited. As a result, messages are limited to a few words and/or an illustration. Lengthy appeals are not possible.

3. **Wearout** Because of the high level of frequency of exposures mentioned earlier, outdoor may also lead to a quick wearout. Because daily routines do not vary much, people are likely to see the same ad numerous times and get tired of seeing it.

4. **Cost** Because of the decreasing signage available, and the higher cost associated with inflatables, the cost of outdoor advertising is high in both an absolute and a relative sense.

5. **Measurement problems** One of the more difficult problems regarding outdoor advertising lies in the accuracy of measuring reach, frequency, and other effects. (As will be seen in the measurement discussion, this problem is currently being addressed, though it has not been resolved.)

6. **Image problems** As noted, outdoor advertising has suffered some image problems as well as some disregard among consumers.

In sum, outdoor advertising has both advantages and disadvantages for the marketer. At the same time, some of these problems may not be inherent in some of the other forms of out-of-home advertising. As such, they may offer alternatives for consideration. A brief discussion of some of these alternatives follows.

Additional out-of-home media

A variety of other forms of outdoor advertising are also available. As you read about these, keep in mind the advantages and disadvantages of outdoor in general mentioned earlier and consider whether these alternatives have the same advantages and/or provide a possible solution to the disadvantages.

Aerial advertising Airplanes pulling banners, skywriting (in letters as high as 1,200 feet), and blimps all constitute another form of outdoor advertising, **aerial advertising,** available to the marketer. Generally these media are not expensive in absolute terms and can be useful for reaching specific target markets. For example, Coppertone has often used skywriting over beach areas to promote its tanning lotions, Gallo used skywriting to promote its wine coolers (Bartles & Jaymes), whereas local advertisers have promoted special events, sales, and the like. Exhibit 15–5 shows a few of the many products, services, and/or events that have used this medium.

Mobile billboards Another outdoor medium is that of **mobile billboards** (see Exhibit 15–6, page 528). Companies have painted Volkswagen Beetles with advertisements called Beetleboards, and others have painted trucks and vans. Still others have advertised on small billboards, mounted them on trailers, and driven around and/or parked in the geographic areas being targeted. Costs depend on the area and the mobile boards company's fees, though both small and large organizations have found the medium affordable. Valvoline, Citicorp, and Knott's Berry Farm are a few advertisers that have used this medium.[3]

In-store media Advertisers are spending billions of dollars to promote their products in supermarkets and other types of stores with media beyond those typically used, such as displays, banners, and shelf signs. These point-of-purchase materials

➤ *Exhibit 15–5*
Aerial advertising is used by a variety of advertisers

➤ *Exhibit 15–6*
An example of a mobile billboard

now include a variety of different types of media including video displays on shopping carts, kiosks that provide recipes and coupons at the ends of counters and at cash registers, LED (light-emitting diode) boards, and ads that broadcast over in-house screens, to mention a few. Exhibit 15–7 lists a few of the many in-store options.

Much of the attraction of the point-of-purchase media is based on figures provided by the Point of Purchase Advertising Institute (POPAI) that state approximately two thirds of consumers' purchase decisions are made in the store, with some impulse categories demonstrating an 80 percent rate.[4] As a result, many advertisers are spending more of their dollars closer to the place where decisions are made, as is reflected in the examples provided in Promotional Perspective 15–1 (page 530).

➤ *Exhibit 15–7* **In-store media options**

Company/Program	Medium	Store Coverage	How Sold
ActMedia			
Act Now	Co-op couponing/ sampling	8,000	Event basis-2 weekends per event
Aisle Vision	Ad posters inserted in stores' directory signs.	8,000	4-week cycles
Carts	Ad placed on frame inside/outside shopping cart	8,000	4-week cycles
Impact	Customized in-store promotion events	Up to 20,000	Event basis-Runs in 2–3 week periods
Instant Coupon Machine	Coupon dispensers mounted into shelf channels	8,000	4-week cycles
POP Radio	Live format in-store radio network	6,500 Grocery 8,500 Drug	4-week cycles
Shelf Take-One	Two-sided take-one offers in plastic see-thru cartridges placed at shelf	12,000 Grocery 5,400 Drug	4-week cycles
Shelf Talk	Plastic frames on shelf near product	10,000 Grocery 5,400 Drug	4-week cycles
Advanced Promotion Technologies			
Vision System	Scanner-driven, card-based promotion system using audio/video at checkout	30	4-week cycles
Catalina Marketing			
Checkout Coupon	Scanner-driven coupon program that generates coupons at checkout	4,100	Event basis
Donnelly Marketing			
Convert	Solo/customized promotion events	Up to 10,000	4-week cycles
In-Store Advertising	Two-sided LED display units that hang above 5 high-traffic areas	5,200	Event basis
Marketing Force	In-store demos & customized events	Up to 20,000	4-week cycles
Media One, Inc.			
SuperAd	Back-lit ads placed in checkout lanes	6,000	4-week cycles
Stratmar Systems			
Field Services	In-store demos & customized events	8,000	Event basis
StratMedia	Shopping cart ad program	2,000 Mass merchandisers; 1,500 Drug	6-week cycles
Supermarket Communications Systems			
Good Neighbor Direct	Bulletin Board distribution center	8,100	4-week cycles
Turner Broadcasting			
The Checkout Channel	Television vehicle that directly targets consumers at the checkout line	150 + stores	4-week cycles
VideOcart, Inc.	Electronic video terminals mounted to shopping carts	50	4, 8 or 12-week increments of a 26-week cycle

Miscellaneous outdoor media   Advertisements on parking meters, automatic teller machines, trash cans, ski lift poles, and even restroom walls have all added to the pervasiveness of this medium. Exhibit 15–8 (page 531) shows how Campbell Soup uses ads on chairlift poles at ski resorts to reach potential customers. The next time you are out, take a few moments to observe how many different forms of outdoor advertising you are exposed to.

Audience measurement in out-of-home advertising

A number of sources of audience measurement are available to someone considering the use of outdoor advertising:

• Simmons Market Research Bureau conducts research annually for the Institute of Outdoor Advertising, providing demographic data, exposures, and the like.
• Audience Measurement by Market for Outdoor (AMMO) are audience estimates provided by Marketmath, Inc., for outdoor showings in over 500 markets. Published annually, the reports are based on a series of local market travel studies and circulation audits and provide demographic characteristics of audiences.

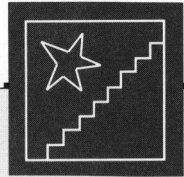

Promotional Perspective 15–1

In-store Becomes One of Advertisers' Favorite Choices

Many advertisers believe the best way to promote their products and services is to "be where the action is"—that is, shorten the time between the consumers' exposure to the message and when they shop. One way of doing this is through in-store-media, one of the fastest-growing advertising media in the United States.

In-store media include point-of-purchase radio, shopping cart ads, bulletin boards, end-of-aisle videos, and coupon dispensers to mention a few. In addition, special events designed especially for the store are gaining in popularity. While in-store media are not a new discovery to marketers, their rapid growth has caught some agencies by surprise, and they are scrambling to become part of the action. Because in-store media are not typically purchased through ad agencies, the agencies realize they are losing potentially millions of dollars in commissions.

Consider some of these examples:

- Videocart, Inc., a normal shopping cart with a small computer screen bolted to its front rail, has signed Procter & Gamble, Pepsi, Nabisco, and Ralston Purina. These companies pay approximately $4 to reach 1,000 users compared to about $7 for a newspaper ad and $10 to $12 for a nighttime TV commercial.

- In-Store Advertising, which places electronic signage in supermarkets, topped $30 million in sales in 1990, with ads in over 3,600 stores. Clorox Co. and Kraft General Foods are just a few of the companies using this service.

- Adgraphics expanded its Shoppers Video network to over 400 stores. The company places about 20 monitors in a store, displaying 15-second computer-animated graphics.

- ADDvantage Media Group is going national with its interactive "Shoppers Calculator," an interactive device hooked onto shopping cart handles that features print ads alongside solar-powered calculators so shoppers can tally their purchases.

The most successful of these ventures to date is the Videocart. While it costs Videocart between $95,000 and $125,000 to equip each store, the fees charged advertisers more than cover the cost. Videocart believes the business the carts generate easily covers the advertisers' costs for placing the ads, and most store owners agree. As a result, the company expects to be in over 5,000 stores by the end of 1994.

How do the stores know the Videocarts work? In test markets, the stores participating in Videocart tests averaged a 33 percent sales increase on those products featured on the carts (according to the company). The least effective carts generated 29 percent, and the most effective, 38.7 percent. For products that offered specials, the average sales increase was 167 percent. Getting to the consumer at the point of purchase obviously pays!

Source: Scott Hume, "Improved VideOcart Starts Test," *Advertising Age,* November 12, 1990, p. 66; Joshua Levine, "The Ultimate Sell," *Forbes,* May 13, 1991, pp. 108–9; Alison Fahey, "Actmedia Is Ready to Fight Back," *Advertising Age,* March 19, 1990, p. 18; and Alison Fahey, "Advertising Media Crowd into Aisles," *Advertising Age,* June 18, 1990, p. 18.

An opportunity too small to miss.

Micromarketing works. And we can prove it.

The medium is VideOcart— an interactive computer screen on a supermarket cart, manufactured in alliance with IBM. Shoppers find it helpful, friendly and fun.

The strategy is radical localization — a message custom-tailored to the shoppers in a particular store, on a particular week, delivered precisely at the moment of maximum leverage. In the supermarket aisle, as the customer approaches your product. It's a burst of national marketing energy at the personal point-of-sale. In about a hundred major market stores by the end of '91. In over 2000 stores by the end of '93.

The result is unprecedented behavior change. Measured by actual scanner data—a 33% *average* sales increase. That's without price promotion. All for less than half the cost-per-viewer of a TV spot delivered to a mass market sometime during the week before they shop.

The brands on board are some of the biggest names in marketing. P & G, Pepsico, Wal-Mart, Kraft/General Foods, Kroger, Nabisco, Hershey and more. They know micromarketing is the future. They know VideOcart is the most powerful micromarketing medium available today. Do they know something you don't know?

POWER AT THE POINT OF SALE.

- The Institute of Outdoor Advertising is a trade organization of the outdoor advertising industry. This organization gathers cost data and statistical information for outdoor advertising space purchases.
- Harris Media Systems employs a mathematical model using data supplied by the Traffic Audit Bureau (TAB) and segmented by time period and billboard

➤ *Exhibit 15—8*
Campbell Soup employs a variety of advertising media

size. The data provide audience figures in the top 50 metropolitan areas and are available to subscribers on any IBM-compatible computer.

- The Point of Purchase Advertising Institute is a trade organization of point-of-purchase advertisers collecting statistical and other market information on point-of-purchasing advertising.
- The Outdoor Advertising Association of America (OAAA) is the primary trade association of the industry, providing members assistance in respect to research, creative ideas, and more effective use of the medium.
- The Media Market Guide (MMG) provides physical dimensions, population characteristics, and media opportunities for the top 100 media markets.
- The Traffic Audit Bureau (TAB) is the auditing arm of the industry. TAB conducts traffic counts on which the published rates are based.
- The Traffic Audit Bureau for Media Measurement provides outdoor advertisers with data regarding exposures to a variety of outdoor media including bus shelters, aerial banners, in-store media, billboards, and the like. This organization was formed in response to complaints that the current methodologies employed might be outdated and overstating the reach provided by these media.

One of the weaknesses associated with outdoor advertising was stated as that of audience measurement. Space rates have typically been published on the basis of the number of desired showings, as shown in Exhibit 15–9. For example, a 100 showing would theoretically provide coverage to the entire market. In San Diego, California, this would mean coverage of approximately 1,950,000 persons for a monthly rate of $30,600 to $37,200. Along with the rate information provided, the companies offering outdoor billboards also provide reach and frequency estimates associated with the showings. Unfortunately, there is no valid way to determine whether the showings promised are performing as they are said to be. As such, the buyer is somewhat at the mercy of the selling agent when making a purchase.

Because of criticism evolving about this problem, the industry has implemented a gross ratings point system similar to that employed in the television industry. While the system has helped, problems associated with the use of GRP's discussed earlier in this text are also present here and as such limit the usefulness of this information. In addition, the new service provided by Harris Media Systems is believed by many to be a significant improvement over the AMMO system, resulting in more credible information.[5]

➤ *Exhibit 15–9*
Posting space rates, San Diego market (per-month basis)

Showing Size	1 Month	3 Months	6 Months	12 Months
#25 (15 posters)	$10,650	$10,350	$10,050	$ 9,750
#50 (30 posters)	21,300	20,700	20,100	19,500
#75 (45 posters)	31,950	31,050	30,150	29,250
#100 (60 posters)	37,200	35,700	33,000	30,600

Transit Advertising

A second form of out-of-home advertising is **transit advertising.** While similar to outdoor in the sense that billboards and electronic messages may be employed, transit is targeted to the millions of people who are exposed to commercial transportation facilities, including buses, taxis, commuter trains, elevators, trolleys, airplanes, and subways.

While transit advertising has been around for a long time, recent years have seen a renewed interest in this medium. In part due to the increased number of women in the work force (they can be reached on their way to work more easily than at home), audience segmentation, and the rising cost of TV advertising, transit ad spending has increased from $43 million in 1972 to over $225 million in 1989.[6] Much of this spending has come from package-goods companies such as Colgate, H. J. Heinz, Kraft-General Foods and Weight Watchers, which have cited lower costs and improved frequency of exposures as motivations to buy transit.

Types of transit advertising

There are actually three types, or forms, of transit advertising: (1) **inside cards,** (2) **outside posters,** and (3) station, platform, or **terminal posters.** A brief description of each of these follows.

Inside cards   If you have ever ridden a commuter bus, you have probably noticed the cards placed above the seats and luggage area advertising restaurants, television or radio stations, or a myriad of other products and services. A more recent innovation is the use of electronic message boards that carry current advertising information. While these message boards fulfill the same functions as inside cards, the ability to change the message and the visibility provide the advertiser with a more attention-getting medium.

At the same time, transit cards can be controversial. For example, in the New York subway system, many of the ads for chewing gum, soup, and Smokey the Bear have given way to public service announcements for AIDS prevention, unwanted pregnancies, rape, cures for callouses and corns, and infant mortality. While subway riders may agree that such issues are important and should be brought to the public's attention, they have voiced their complaints over the pervasiveness of these ads. The ads have been called depressing, intrusive, and a lot more unprintable names.

A variation on inside transit advertising is shown in Exhibit 15–10. The airline ticket holder has been shown to be a very effective form of advertising communication. This form of advertising takes advantage of a captive audience as well as being a medium that keeps the message in front of the passenger during the time he or she is holding the ticket.

Outside posters   Various forms of outdoor transit posters are used by advertisers to promote products and services. These posters may appear on the sides, back, and/or roofs of buses, taxis, trains, and subway and trolley cars. Some examples are shown in the ad for Transportation Displays, Inc., a leading outdoor and transit advertising company (Exhibit 15–11, page 534).

The increased sophistication of this medium was demonstrated in a test market in Barcelona, Spain, during the 1992 Summer Olympics. Viatex—a joint venture between Atlanta-based Bevilaqua International (a sports marketing company), Saatchi & Saatchi Lifestyle Group, and Warrec Company, a Connecticut-based international

➤ *Exhibit 15–10*
Airline ticket holders are used to promote a variety of products

business firm—mounted electronic billboards on the side of buses. These monitors flashed Olympic news and ads that could change by the time of day. In addition, electronic beacons located throughout the city were activated as the bus drove by—changing the message for the various locations.

Station, platform, and terminal posters Floor displays, island showcases, electronic signs, and other forms of advertisements that appear in train or subway stations, airline terminals, and the like, are all forms of transit advertising. As can be seen in Exhibit 15–12, these advertisements can be very attractive and attention getting. Gannett Transit has recently introduced electronic signs on platforms in subway stations in New York.

Advantages and disadvantages of transit advertising

Some of the advantages of using transit advertising include:

1. Exposure Long length of exposure to an ad is one advantage that is particularly true with indoor forms. The average ride on mass transit is approximately 30 to 44 minutes, allowing for plenty of exposure time.[7] Likewise, as was noted in the airline ticket example discussed earlier, the audience is essentially a captive one, with nowhere else to go and nothing much to do. As a result, they may be more likely to read the ads—and read them more than once.

A second form of exposure provided is that regarding the absolute number of persons exposed. It was estimated that in 1989, approximately 9 million people rode mass bus transportation, providing a very substantial number of potential viewers.[8]

2. Frequency Because our daily routines are very standard, those who ride buses, subways, and the like, will be exposed to the ads a repeated number of times. If you rode the same subway to work and back every day, in one month, you would have the opportunity to see the ad approximately 20 to 40 times.

3. Timeliness Many shoppers use mass transit to reach their destinations. An advertisement promoting a product or service at a particular shopping area could result in a very timely communication.

➤ *Exhibit 15–11*

Outside transit posters are used on a variety of vehicles

➤ *Exhibit 15–12*

Terminal posters can be used to attract attention

4. Geographic selectivity   For local advertisers in particular, transit advertising provides an opportunity to reach a very select segment of the population. A purchase of a location in a particular neighborhood or area of the city would lead to exposure to those persons of specific ethnic backgrounds, demographic characteristics, and so on.

5. Cost   Transit advertising tends to be one of the least expensive media in terms of both absolute and relative costs. An ad on the side of a bus can be purchased for a very reasonable CPM.

Some disadvantages are also associated with transit. These include the following.

1. Image factors   To many advertisers, transit advertising does not carry the image they would like to use to represent their products or services. Some advertisers may think having their firm's name on the side of a bus or on a bus stop bench may not reflect well on the image of the firm.

2. Reach   While it was earlier stated that an advantage of transit advertising was the ability to provide exposure to a large number of persons, these persons may have certain lifestyles and/or behavioral characteristics that may not be true of the target market as a whole. For example, in rural or suburban areas, mass transit is very limited or nonexistent. As a result, the media would not be as effective for reaching these persons as it might be in inner-city and metropolitan areas.

3. Waste coverage   While we discussed geographic selectivity as a possible advantage, not everyone who rides a transportation vehicle or is exposed to transit advertising is a potential customer. For many products that may not have specific geographic segments, this form of advertising incurs a good deal of waste coverage.

Another problem with respect to an inability to target a specific group is related to the routes assigned to buses. For example, the same bus may not run the same route every day. To save wear and tear on the bus, some companies alternate city routes—with much stop and go—with longer suburban routes to attempt to reduce strain on the vehicle. Thus, a bus that goes downtown one day—and reaches the desired target group—may be in the suburbs the next, where there may be little market potential.

4. Copy and creative limitations Because of the nature of transit advertising, the marketer is limited in both the creativity and copy used. With respect to the former, it may be very difficult to place colorful and attractive advertisements on cards or benches. With respect to the latter, while much copy might be provided on inside cards, on the outside of vehicles like buses and taxis the message will be much more fleeting, and short-copy points will be necessary.

5. Mood of the audience If you have ever ridden mass transportation at rush hour, little needs to be said about the effects of mood. Sitting or standing on a crowded subway may not be conducive to reading advertising, let alone creating the mood the advertiser would like for you to be in. As noted previously, certain ad messages may contribute to this less than positive feeling. Likewise, hurrying through an airport may create anxieties that limit the effectiveness of the ads placed there.

In summary, transit advertising has its obvious advantages as well as disadvantages, and an advantage for one product or service advertiser may be a disadvantage to another. Transit advertising can be an effective medium; however, one must understand the strengths and weaknesses associated with this form of advertising to use it properly.

Audience measurement in transit advertising

As with outdoor advertising, the cost basis for transit is the number of showings. In transit advertising, a 100 showing means one ad would appear on or in *each vehicle* in the system, whereas a showing of 50 would mean half of the vehicles would carry the ad. If you are placing such ads on taxicabs, it may be extremely difficult—if not impossible—to determine who is being exposed to them.

Rate information is available from the sellers of transit advertising, and audience information is very limited. As a result, much of the information that can be used in the purchase of transit ads may not be coming from purely objective sources.

Specialty Advertising

According to the Specialty Advertising Association International, **specialty advertising** is

an advertising, sales promotion, and motivational communications medium which employs useful articles of merchandise imprinted with an advertiser's name, message, or logo. Unlike premiums, with which they are sometimes confused, these articles (called advertising specialties) are always distributed free—recipients don't have to earn the specialty by making a purchase or contribution.[9]

As can be seen by this description, specialty advertising is often considered both an advertising medium as well as a sales promotion medium. In our discussion, we treat it as a supportive advertising medium.

There are over 20,000 different **advertising specialties** items including ballpoint pens, coffee mugs, keytags, calendars, T-shirts, and matchbooks. In addition, non-conventional specialties such as plant holders, wall plaques, and gloves with the advertiser's name printed on them have also been used to promote a company or its product, as have glassware, trophies, awards, and vinyl products, as shown in Exhibit 15–13. In fact, advertisers spend over $5 billion per year in specialty advertising items. The growth of this medium (342 percent) during the 1970s makes this the fastest-growing of all advertising or sales promotions media.[10]

➤ *Exhibit 15–13*
Examples of specialty advertising items

If you stop reading for a moment and look around your desk (or bed or beach blanket), you probably have some specialty advertising item around you. It may be the pen you are using, a matchbook, or even a book cover with the campus book-store name on it. Specialty items are used for a variety of promotional purposes. They may be used to thank a customer for patronage, to keep the name of the company in front of the person, to introduce new products, or to reinforce the name of an existing company, product, or service. Advertising specialties are also very often used to support other forms of product promotions.

Advantages and Disadvantages of Specialty Advertising

Like any other advertising medium, specialty advertising has both advantages and disadvantages that it offers to the marketer. Some of the advantages include the following.

1. Selectivity   Because specialty advertising items are generally distributed directly to target customers, the medium offers a high degree of *selectivity*. Selectivity reduces waste coverage, and the communication is distributed to the desired recipient.

2. Flexibility   As the variety of specialty items included in Exhibit 15–13 demonstrates, this medium provides for a high degree of *flexibility*. A message as simple as a logo or as long as is necessary can be distributed through a variety of means. In addition, both small and large companies may employ this medium and are limited seemingly only by their own creativity.

3. Frequency   Most forms of specialty advertising are designed for *retention*. As a result, items such as key chains, calendars, and pens remain with the potential customer for a long time, providing the opportunity for repeat exposures to the advertising message at no additional cost.

4. Cost   While the cost of some specialty items may be rather expensive (leather items, etc.) most of them are very inexpensively priced, making them affordable to almost any size organization or firm. With the high number of repeat exposures, on a cost per exposure basis, the relative cost of this advertising medium is even less.

5. Supplementing other media   One of the major advantages of specialty advertising is its ability to supplement other media. Because of its low cost and repeat exposures, the simplest message can reinforce the appeal or information provided through other forms. For example, Saab-Scandia of North America presented new car buyers with a series of advertising specialties to support its "dedicated delivery" program promoted through print media. Document organizers, tire gauges, and tape deck cleaning kits were just some of the items used to reinforce the point that Saab wanted its customers to be satisfied.

Disadvantages of specialty advertising include the following.

1. Image While most forms of specialty advertising are received as friendly reminders of the store or company name, the firm must be careful in the specialty item chosen. The potential for "cheapening" the company image exists if a very inexpensive or improperly designed advertising form is utilized.

2. Saturation With so many firms and organizations now using this advertising medium, the potential exists for saturation of the marketplace. While one might argue that we can always use another ballpoint pen or book of matches, the value to the receiver declines if replacement is too easy, and the likelihood of retention of the item and even notice of the message is reduced. The more unique the specialty, the more value it is likely to have to the receiver.

Audience Measurement in Specialty Advertising

Owing to the nature of the industry, specialty advertising has no established ongoing audience measurement system similar to those discussed with other media. Research has been conducted in an attempt to determine the impact of this medium, however, including the following reports.

A study by Schreiber and Associates indicated 39 percent of people receiving advertising specialties could recall the name of the company as long as 6 months after receiving the message, whereas a second study conducted by A. C. Nielsen found that 31 percent of respondents were still using at least one specialty they had received at least 12 months earlier.[11]

A study by Gould/Pace University indicated the inclusion of a specialty item in a direct-mail piece generated a greater response rate and dollar purchases per sale were 321 percent greater than mail pieces without such items.[12] Finally, a report by Richard Manville Research, Inc., reported the average household had almost four calendars and if they had not been given such items free, two thirds stated they would purchase one—an indication of the desirability of this particular specialty item.[13]

The trade organization of this field is the Specialty Advertising Association (SAA) International. The SAA assists users in the development and utilization of specialty advertising forms. The organization also provides promotional and public relations support for specialty advertising and disseminates statistical and educational information.

Yellow Pages Advertising

When we think of advertising media, many of us overlook one of the most commonly used forms in existence—the Yellow Pages. While almost all of us use the Yellow Pages frequently, we often tend to forget it is advertising. In 1990, some 200 publishers produced more than 6,500 Yellow Pages throughout the United States and generated $8.9 billion in advertising expenditures.[14]

Most of the industry's advertising revenues are accounted for by nine big operators. The seven regional Bell companies, the Donnelley Directory, and GTE Directories account for more than 90 percent of the advertising revenues.[15] Local advertisers constitute the bulk of the ads in these directories (approximately 90 percent), through national advertisers such as Motorola and others use the directories as well.[16]

Interestingly, there are a variety of forms of Yellow Pages (because AT&T never copyrighted the term, any publisher can use it) including:

- **Specialized directories**—directories targeted at select markets such as Hispanics, blacks, Asian, and women. Also included in this category are 800 directories, Christian directories, and many others.
- **Audiotex**—the "talking Yellow Pages" offers oral information on advertisers.

- **Other services**—some Yellow Pages directories offer coupons and free-standing inserts. In Orange County, telephone subscribers received samples of Golden Graham and Cinnamon Toast Crunch cereals when their Yellow Pages were delivered.

The Yellow Pages are often referred to as a **directional medium** in that ads do not create awareness or demand for products or services, but rather point consumers in the direction where their purchases can be made once they have decided to buy.[17] The Yellow Pages are thus considered to be the final link in the buying cycle—as shown in Exhibit 15–14.

Advantages and disadvantages of Yellow Pages

The Yellow Pages offer the following advantages to advertisers:

1. **Wide availability** As noted, a variety of directories are published. According to the Yellow Pages Publishers Association, there are more than 17.6 billion references to the Yellow Pages yearly.[18]

2. **Action oriented** The Yellow Pages are referred to when consumers are considering, or have decided to take, action. As such, it is the final link in the buying process.

3. **Costs** Ad space and production costs are relatively low compared to other media.

4. **Frequency** Because of its longevity (Yellow Pages are published yearly), consumers will return to the directories time and time again. The average adult refers to the Yellow Pages an estimated 1.87 times per week.[19]

5. **Nonintrusiveness** Because consumers choose to use the Yellow Pages, it is not considered to be an intrusion. Studies have shown that most consumers rate the Yellow Pages very favorably.[20]

Disadvantages of the Yellow Pages include:

1. **Market fragmentation** Since Yellow Pages are essentially local media, they tend to be very localized. Add to this the increasing number of specialized directories, and the net result is a very specific offering.

2. **Timeliness** Because Yellow Pages are printed only once a year, they may often be outdated. Companies may have relocated, gone out of business, or changed phone numbers in the period between new books.

3. **Lack of creativity** While the Yellow Pages are somewhat flexible, they are limited in respect to their creative aspects.

➤ *Exhibit 15–14*
The Yellow Pages are often the final link in the buying cycle

4. **Lead times**   Printing schedules require that ads be placed a long time before the publications appear. As a result, it is impossible to get an ad in after the deadline, and advertisers need to wait a long time before the next edition.

Other Media

In addition to some of the more commonly thought of media, there are numerous other ways to promote products. Some of these are reviewed here.

Advertising in Movie Theaters and on Videotapes

Two methods of delivering the message that are quickly increasing—to the dismay of many—is the use of movie theaters and videotape rentals to promote products and/or services. Commercials shown before the film and previews have seemingly replaced cartoons, with both local and national sponsorships. On videotapes, companies have placed ads before the movies as well as on the cartons containing the rentals. For example, Nestlé has run ads on videotapes of the movies *Dirty Dancing, Mr. Mom,* and *To Live and Die in L.A.,* among others. Pepsi has run ads on *Top Gun, Innerspace,* and *Stand And Deliver,* among others. Dozens of other advertisers have also employed this medium. Consumer reaction to ads in movie theaters and on videotapes seems to be mixed. As shown in Exhibit 15–15, most people think ads on videotapes are annoying or very annoying (67.5 percent). At the same time, this survey showed that as many as 57 percent watch these commercials. The same seems to hold true for advertising in movie theaters. In an *Advertising Age*/Gallup survey, a national sample of moviegoers indicated that 35 percent were against a ban on ads in movie theaters, with another 21 percent unsure of whether such a ban should be enacted.[21] The survey was taken after Walt Disney Co. announced it would stop showing its movies in any theater that runs on-screen advertising along with the films. While advertisers were infuriated, Disney claimed its surveys showed customers were extremely irritated by such ads and as a result might quit coming to the theaters.[22]

Advantages of movie theater and videotape advertising

Both of these media provide a number of advantages to the advertiser, including the following.

1. **Exposure**   The number of persons attending movies is substantial as ticket sales approach $5 billion per year.[23] At the same time, the number of households using VCRs is also increasing. The result of these growth figures is that more people

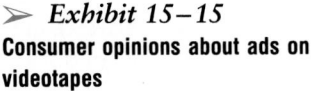
➤ *Exhibit 15–15*
Consumer opinions about ads on videotapes

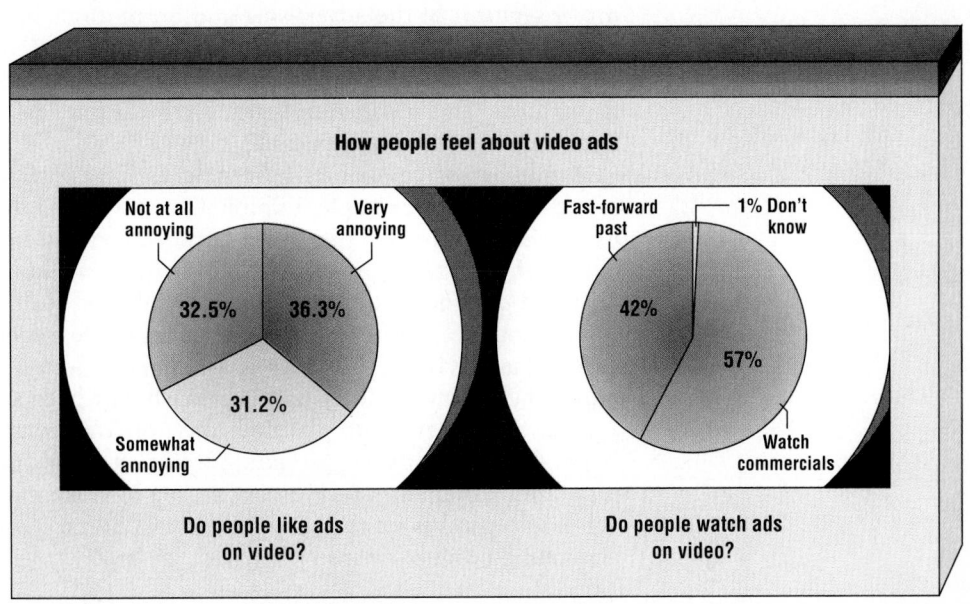

are likely to be exposed to the ads. In addition, these viewers constitute a "captured audience," who also are known to watch less television than the average.[24]

2. **Mood**   Assuming the movie is well liked, the mood can carry over to the product advertised. For example, in the *Top Gun* ad mentioned, the setting was identical to that in the movie, and a carryover of the mood was very likely.

3. **Cost**   The cost of advertising in a theater varies from one setting to the next. However, both in terms of absolute and relative costs per exposure the costs are low.

4. **Recall**   Research indicates approximately 87 percent of viewers can recall the ads they saw in a movie theater the next day. This compares with an approximately 20 percent recall rate for television.[25]

5. **Clutter**   The *lack* of clutter is another advantage offered by advertising in movie theaters. Most theaters limit the number of ads to only a few, and as long as this remains the rule, less clutter will occur than does in other media.

Disadvantages of movie and videotape advertising

Some of the disadvantages associated with these advertising media are given below.

1. **Irritation**   Perhaps the major disadvantage of this form of advertising is that many people do not wish to see advertising in these media. A number of studies have indicated a high degree of *irritability* may be created by these ads.[26] This dissatisfaction could also carry over to the product itself, to the movies, or to the theaters.

2. **Cost**   While the cost of advertising in local theaters has been cited as an advantage because of the low rates charged, ads exposed on a national basis cost as much as $425,000 per minute to reach 25 million viewers. This cost reflects a rate 20 percent higher than an equal exposure on television.

While only two disadvantages of theater advertising have been mentioned, the first of these is a strong one. Many persons believe that because they have paid to see a movie (or rent a videotape), advertising is an intrusion. In the Michael Belch and Don Sciglimpaglia study, many moviegoers stated that not only would they not buy the product advertised, but they would also consider boycotting it. Given that this is the case, advertisers should be very cautious in their use of this medium. Should the use of movies be desired, a different alternative—placing products in the movies—might be considered as an alternative. Let us discuss this approach.

Product Placements in Movies and Television

At the outset of this chapter, you read a brief report on the effectiveness of promoting a product through the movies. While this form of advertising does not constitute a major segment of the advertising and promotions business, it is a mode of delivery that has proved to be effective for some companies. (Note: Like specialty advertising, some persons consider **product placement** as a promotion rather than as an advertising form. This distinction is not a critical one, and we have therefore decided to treat it as a form of advertising.)

A number of companies have paid to have their products used in movies and music videos. For example, Exhibit 15–16 shows how Justin Boots was able to get its product featured in the movie *City Slickers*. Essentially, this form of advertising is sort of advertising without an advertising medium in the sense that the realism provided does not lead the audience member to realize that the product promotion is going on, yet the impact is real. For example, when Reese's Pieces candies were used in the movie *ET*, sales rose 70 percent and were added to the concessions of 800 movie theaters where they had previously not been sold.[27]

Likewise, the move to place products on TV programs is also on the increase. In 1988, CBS broke its long-standing tradition of not mentioning brand names in its programs. Companies such as Coca-Cola (a Coke machine on "TV 101") and Pine Sol (a sweepstakes on the soap "All My Children") are just a few of the companies employing product tie-ins.

➤ *Exhibit 15–16*
Many companies use movies to promote their products

Advantages of product placements

A number of advantages of product tie-ins have been suggested.

1. Exposure A large number of people see movies each year (approximately 1 billion admissions in 1991). [28] The average film is estimated to have a life span of three and one-half years (with 75 million exposures), and most, if not all, of these moviegoers are very attentive audience members. Coupling this with the increasing home video rental market and network and cable television (for example, HBO, Showtime, Movie Channel), the potential for exposure for a product placed in a movie is enormous. In addition, this form of exposure is not subject to zapping—at least not in the theater.

High exposure numbers are also offered for television tie-ins, based on the ratings and (at least in the case of soaps) the possibility to direct the ad to a defined target market.

2. Frequency Depending on how the product is used in the movie (or program), there may be ample opportunity for *repeated exposures* (or even more if you are among the many people who like to watch a program or movie more than once). For example, in promoting Honda scooters, the advertising agency Dailey and Associates had the product used in movies as well as in the television program "Knight Rider." In the latter, the scooter was in front of the viewer in a series of different scenes, with total airtime of over five minutes!

3. Support for other media In the Honda advertising example just cited, the other media advertising the product included an appeal consistent with that in the television show. Coors has used the character E.T.—from the film of the same name in which Coors had placed its product—to support its public relations efforts by asking people not to drive when drinking. Kimberly-Clark Corporation created a sweepstakes, coupon offer, and TV-based ad around their Huggies diapers featured in the movie *Baby Boom*.

4. Source association In an earlier chapter in this book, we discussed the advantages of source identification. When many potential consumers see their favorite movie star riding a Honda, wearing Adidas, or eating Reese's Pieces, this association may lead to a favorable product image. For example, when the star of the movie *Risky Business* (Tom Cruise) appeared in a pair of Ray-Ban sunglasses, the sales of Ray-Bans immediately increased from 18,000 to over 360,000 units.[29]

5. Cost While the cost of placing a product may range from as little as providing free samples to as much as a million dollars, these are extremes. As shown in Exhibit 15–17, the CPM for this form of advertising can be very low, owing to the high volume of exposures this medium generates.

> *Exhibit 15–17*
CPM for motion picture advertising

Title of Film	Theater Boxoffice	Audience[1]	Weeks in Release	Cost per Thousand[2]
Batman Returns	145,480,492	29,750,600	4	.16
Beauty and the Beast	141,838,563	29,000,500	35	.17
Lethal Weapon 3	135,799,341	27,770,820	9	.18
Wayne's World	121,115,040	24,767,900	22	.20
Hook	118,965,084	24,328,240	24	.21
The Addams Family	113,379,166	23,185,920	22	.22
Basic Instinct	110,987,913	22,696,910	17	.22

1. Audience figure is based on an average ticket price of $4.89 from Motion Picture Association of America, Inc., data and statistics, published in June 1992.
2. CPM is the cost for reaching 1,000 consumers with an advertisement multiplied by 1,000, divided by the total audience (the average cost of a product placement is $5,000).

6. Recall   A number of firms have measured the impact of product placements on next-day recall. Results ranged from Johnson's Baby Shampoo registering 20 percent to Kellogg's Corn Flakes registering 67 percent (on the movie *Raising Arizona*). Average recall is approximately 38 percent. Again, you can see that these scores are better than those reported for television viewing.

Disadvantages of product placements

Some disadvantages are also associated with product placements.

1. High absolute cost   While we have just stated the CPM may be very low for product placement in movies, the absolute cost of placing the product may be very high, precluding some advertisers from its use. For example, the cost of placing a product in the movies averages approximately $7,500, with many placements being substantially higher.[30]

2. Time of exposure   While the method by which Ray-Bans and Reese's candy were exposed to the audience led to an obvious impact, the viewer's noticing the product is not a guarantee. Some product placements are more conspicuous than others and thus have a greater chance of being seen by viewers. However, other placements may not result in a prominent featuring of the product. In such a case, the advertiser runs the risk of not being seen—although it must be remembered the same risk is present through other forms of media advertising.

3. Limited appeal   The advertisement of the product in this media form is limited in respect to the appeal that can be made. There is no potential for discussing product benefits or providing detailed information. Rather, appeals are limited to source association, use, and enjoyment. The endorsement of the product is an indirect one, and the flexibility for product demonstration is subject to its use in the film.

4. Lack of control   In many movies, the advertiser has no say over how often and when the product will be shown. Miller beer, for example, found its placement on the movie *Dragnet* did not work as well as expected, whereas Fabergé developed an entire Christmas campaign around its Brut cologne and its movie placement, only to find the movie was delayed until February.

5. Public reaction   Many TV viewers and moviegoers are incensed at the idea of placing ads in the programs (movies). These viewers maintain the barrier between program content and commercials should remain and have vowed to fight future efforts.

Audience measurement for product placements

To date, no form of audience measurement other than that available from the providers is available. As a result, the potential advertiser may often have to make a decision based on his or her own creative insights as to potential effectiveness and/or rely on the credibility of the source. At the same time, however, at least one study has demonstrated the potential effectiveness beyond those examples just cited. As noted in a study by Eva Steortz, product placements have an average recall of 38 percent.[31]

In-Flight TV Commercials

Another rapidly growing medium is that of **in-flight television commercials.** While in-flight videos have been a common occurrence on international flights for some time, the use of the same on domestic flights was not as common. Even less common was including commercials in these videos. In 1990, about $18 million in commercials were booked on flights ($12 million on international flights), and advertisers expect a 25 percent growth rate throughout the 1990s.[32] Much of the attraction of this medium is the captive audience, and this audience offers desirable characteristics to many advertisers (for example, business travelers). While not all airlines now offer in-flight commercials—only about 15 percent of all travelers could be reached in 1990—companies such as Japan Air Lines, Delta, TWA, and British Airways are participating.

Advantages and disadvantages of in-flight advertising

Advantages of in-flight advertising include:

1. A desirable audience The average traveler is 45 years old with a household income of $83,700. Both business and tourist travelers tend to be upscale and an attractive audience to companies targeting these groups.

2. A captured audience As noted earlier in the discussion about ticket covers, the audience in the airplane cannot leave the room. In many cases, particularly on long flights, passengers are willing (and even happy) to have commercials to watch.

3. Cost The cost of in-flight commercials is lower than the costs of business print media. For example, in 1990, the CPM to reach adults with at least a $75,000 household income on United and Northwest Airlines with a 30-second commercial was $82.60. A four-color spread in *Forbes* and *Fortune* would have cost $156.20 and $181.60, respectively.[33]

4. Segmentation capabilities In-flight allows the advertiser to reach specific demographic groups, as well as travelers to a specific destination. For example, Martell cognac targeted first-class passengers only on JAL's New York to Tokyo route.[34]

Disadvantages of in-flight advertising include:

1. Irritation As noted, many consumers are not pleased with the idea of advertisements in general, believing they are already too intrusive. In-flight ads are just one more place, they think, in which advertisers are intruding.

2. Limited availability Many airlines now limit the amount of time they will allow for in-flight commercials. Japan Air Lines, for example, allows a mere 220 seconds per flight, regardless of its length.

3. Lack of attention While cited earlier as an advantage, many passengers may decide to tune out the ads, not purchase the headsets required to get the volume, or simply ignore the commercials.

4. Wearout Given projections for significant increases in the number of in-flight ads being shown, airline passengers may soon be inundated by these commercials. In this case, the possibility of wearout increases.

SUMMARY

This chapter introduced you to the vast number of support media available to the marketer. These media, often referred to as nontraditional or alternative media, are just a few of the many ways advertisers attempt to reach their target markets. We have barely scratched the surface in our presentation here.

Support media offer a variety of advantages. Cost, ability to reach the target market, and flexibility are just a few of those cited in this chapter. In addition, many of the media discussed here have effectively demonstrated the power of their specific medium to get results.

But each of these support media has disadvantages. Perhaps the major weakness with most of these is the lack of audience measurement and verification. Unlike many of the media discussed earlier in this text that provide audience measurement figures, many nontraditional media do not offer this service. As a result, the advertiser is forced to make decisions without hard data or must rely on the information provided by the media.

As the number and variety of support media continues to grow, it is likely the major weaknesses will be overcome. When that occurs, these media may no longer be considered nontraditional or alternative.

KEY TERMS

support media
alternative media
nonmeasured media
nontraditional media
out-of-home advertising
showing
aerial advertising

mobile billboards
in-store media
transit advertising
inside cards
outside posters
terminal posters
specialty advertising

advertising specialties
Yellow Pages advertising
directional medium
product placement
in-flight television
    commercials

DISCUSSION QUESTIONS

1. Discuss some of the advantages and disadvantages of outdoor advertising.
2. The text notes that users of transit advertising must rely on audience information provided by companies selling transit advertising space. Discuss some of the problems that might occur from this situation.
3. What is meant by a 100 GRP showing? Give examples of how GRPs are used in outdoor advertising. In transit.
4. Give examples of some of the new out-of-home media. Why have these become so popular?
5. Describe some of the various sources available for audience measurement for out-of-home media.

6. Discuss the advantages and disadvantages associated with transit advertising.
7. What are some of the reasons in-store media may be effective in increasing sales.
8. Discuss some advantages and disadvantages associated with Yellow Pages advertising.
9. Many consumers have expressed their dissatisfaction with advertisements on videotapes and in movie theaters. Discuss some reasons for this dissatisfaction.
10. Discuss some of the various types of products that might be successfully advertised on in-flight commercials. Explain your reasoning.

chapter 16

Direct Marketing

chapter objectives

➤ To introduce the area of direct marketing as a communications tool.

➤ To present the strategies and tactics involved in direct marketing.

➤ To demonstrate the use of direct-marketing media.

➤ To illustrate the scope and effectiveness of direct marketing.

The High-Tech Presidential Election

The 1992 presidential election was different from all previous ones in at least one respect—the communications tools used by the candidates to reach the voting public. The traditional use of mass media and door-to-door visits was supplemented by a very sophisticated direct-marketing campaign. Some of the strategies employed, such as saturation data base mailing and factual ads, were borrowed directly from consumer products marketers. Others, such as the direct mailing of videocassettes to party members, were specifically designed for the campaign. Some observers believe this campaign may change the way political candidates market themselves forever.

The basic thrust of the new strategy was to get away from mass media messages, replacing them with highly targeted ones that were tuned through survey research. The use of mass media television buys, for the first time since the Kennedy-Nixon race, constituted only a small percentage of the media budget, as the overall direct-marketing effort received the bulk of the emphasis.

The Republicans employed Michael Dawidziak, a number cruncher specializing in manipulating voter lists and census data. Dawidziak combined a variety of lists including voter registration lists, telephone books (to weed out deceased voters), demographic data, and credit

card lists, and he developed different telemarketing scripts to target specific voters.

Another Republican-employed strategist, Eddie Mahe, used a specifically targeted message and high-speed phone bank to effectively employ telemarketing. The phone banks automatically dialed and screened out busy signals and answering machines. Once the call got through, the "negative phone ads" told the potential voter when the opposition did something he or she was not likely to condone (like voting for a tax increase!).

The Democrats made extensive use of direct mail, sending videos to potential voters. In at least one market, no TV time and no other direct-mail or telemarketing techniques were employed. The cost of the videotape, including a four-color mailer and pitch letter, was about $1.25—one fourth of the cost four years earlier.

In his bid for the Democratic nomination, Jerry Brown used 30-minute infomercials. The program consisted of three seven-minute "soft" segments punctuated by two-minute money pitches. Besides offering the advantage of specific targeting, the direct-marketing campaign offered the candidates a very effective method for tracking ad placements. The tracking technology—named Polaris after the computer system designed to track

WHO GETS A CAMPAIGN VIDEO PITCH?

1. RAW DATA...
Voter data on CD ROM
Census data
Mailing-list data

2. IS REFINED...
Phone banks and polling

3. THEN MANIPULATED...
Number-crunching, which results in a prediction test

4. INTO VOTING PITCHES
Voter likely won't vote for candidate — No video
Voter likely will vote for candidate — Video with fund-raising pitch
Voter likely is undecided — Video with brand image pitch
(Cost of tape: $1.09–$1.35)

(continued)

nuclear submarines—produced an electronic signature to help the system detect when and where the ads ran. As a result, candidates knew exactly when and where their ads—and those of their competitors—aired. Polaris enabled the candidates to be sure their ads were aired when they were supposed to and also provided them with complete knowledge of the competitors' schedule.

Were American voters ready for 30-minute political infomercials, 800 phone numbers, and videocassettes? At the time of this writing it was too early to tell, but one thing is certain—mass marketing of presidential candidates is a lot less likely in the future.

Source: Dan Koeppel, "The High-Tech Election," Adweek's Marketing Week, March 2, 1992, pp. 18–21.

As you can see by the opening discussion, direct-marketing tools are not limited to use by product and service marketers. You can also see that the importance of direct marketing in the communications program continues to increase as marketers focus more on specific target markets.

While most companies continue to rely primarily on the other promotional mix elements to move their products and services through intermediaries, an increasing number are going directly to the consumer. These companies believe that while the traditional use of promotional mix tools such as advertising, sales promotion, personal selling, and so on are effective in creating brand image, conveying information, and/or creating awareness, by going direct, these same tools can be used to generate an immediate behavioral response. As such, direct marketing constitutes a valuable tool in the integrated communications program, though at the same time seeks somewhat different objectives.

In this chapter, we discuss direct marketing and its role as a communications tool. Direct marketing is one of the fastest-growing forms of promotion in terms of dollar expenditures—and for many marketers it is rapidly becoming the medium of choice for reaching consumers. Stan Rapp and Thomas Collins in their book *Maximarketing* propose that direct marketing be the driving force behind the overall marketing program.[1] They present a nine-step model that involves creating a data base, reaching prospects, developing the sale, and developing the relationship. We begin our discussion by defining direct marketing and then examine direct-marketing media and their use in the overall communications strategy. The chapter concludes with a basis for evaluating the direct-marketing program and a discussion of the advantages and disadvantages associated with this marketing tool.

Defining Direct Marketing

As noted in Chapter 1, **direct marketing** refers to a system of marketing by which organizations communicate directly with target customers to generate a response or transaction. This response or transaction may take the form of an inquiry, a purchase, or even a vote. In his *Dictionary of Marketing Terms*, Peter Bennett defines direct marketing as:

> The total of activities by which the seller, in effecting the exchange of goods and services with the buyer, directs efforts to a target audience using one or more media (direct selling, direct mail, telemarketing, direct-action advertising, catalogue selling, cable TV selling, etc.) for the purpose of soliciting a response by phone, mail or personal visit, from a prospect or customer.[2]

Before proceeding further, it is necessary to distinguish between direct marketing and **direct-marketing media.** As you can see in Exhibit 16–1, direct marketing refers to an aspect of total marketing—that is, it involves marketing research, segmentation, evaluation, and the like, just as our planning model presented in Chapter 1 did. Likewise, direct marketing uses a set of direct-response media, including direct mail, telemarketing, interactive television, print, and other media. These media are essentially the tools by which direct marketers implement the communications process.

It has been estimated that the purchases of products and services through direct-response advertising exceeded $200 billion in 1991.[3] The types of firms that use this marketing method range from major retailers such as Wards and Sears to publishing companies to computer retailers to financial services. In addition, business-to-business and industrial marketers have significantly increased their direct-marketing efforts.

The Growth of Direct Marketing

Direct marketing has been in existence since the invention of the printing press in the 15th century. Ben Franklin was a very successful direct marketer in the early 1700s, and Warren Sears and Montgomery Ward (you may have heard of these guys!) were employing this medium in the 1880s.

The major impetus behind the growth of direct marketing may have been the development and expansion of the U.S. Postal Service, as the catalog was now available to both urban and rural dwellers. The impact of the catalog, as is described in Promotional Perspective 16–1, revolutionized America's buying habits.

The catalog alone does not account for the rapid growth of direct marketing. Much of this growth has been attributed to a number of factors in American society, each of which has led to the increased attractiveness of this medium—both to the buyer and to the seller.

- **The use of consumer credit cards** The adoption of credit cards (there are now an estimated 350 million MasterCard and Visa cards in circulation worldwide) made it feasible to purchase both low- and high-ticket items through direct-response channels and also assured the seller that he or she would be paid. Since the 1950s, credit card sales have increased to the point where $220.9 billion was purchased via MasterCards alone in 1991.[4] Of course, not all of this was through direct marketing; but a high percentage of direct purchases do use this method of payment, and companies such as American Express, Diners Club, MasterCard, and Visa are among some of the heaviest direct advertisers.

- **Direct-marketing syndicates** Companies specializing in list development, statement inserts, catalogs, and sweepstakes opened many new opportunities to companies that previously had not explored this method of marketing. The number of these companies continues to expand, creating even more new users.

- **The changing structure of American society and the market** Perhaps one of the major factors contributing to the success of direct marketing is that America is now a land of "money-rich and time-poor" people.[5] The rapid

➤ *Exhibit 16–1* Direct marketing—an aspect of total marketing

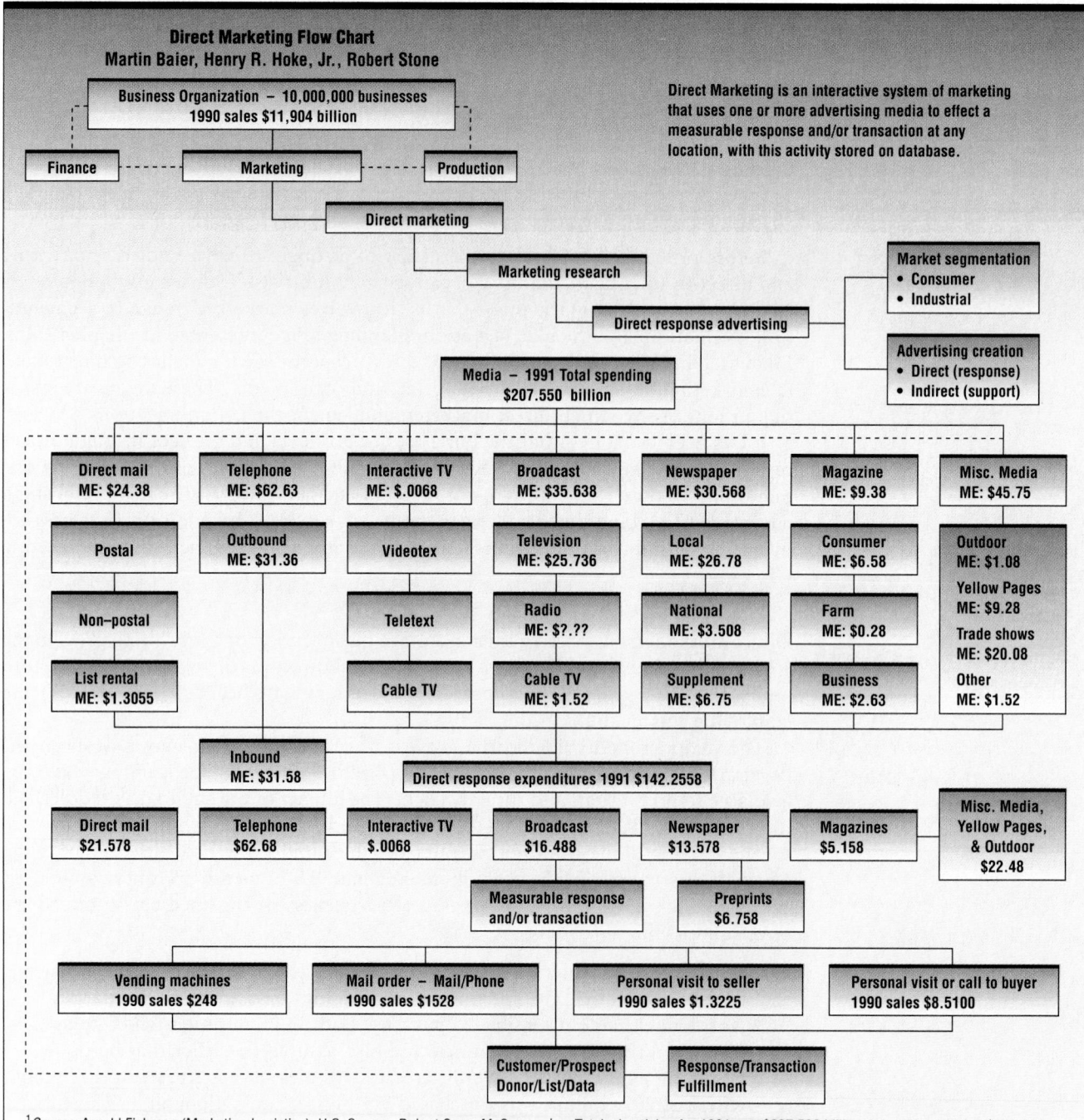

Direct Marketing Flow Chart
Martin Baier, Henry R. Hoke, Jr., Robert Stone

Direct Marketing is an interactive system of marketing that uses one or more advertising media to effect a measurable response and/or transaction at any location, with this activity stored on database.

[1] *Source:* Arnold Fishman (Marketing Logistics), U.S. Census, Robert Coen, McCann Erickson (Media Figures).

[2] Personal visit to seller includes $1.580 billion of Consumer Product Sales at retail plus 90% of Consumer Services Sales. 10% of Consumer Service Sales are conducted by salespeople visiting the buyer.

[3] *Source:* Sandra Perrick, past president of the American Telemarketing Association. Approximately half of Telemarketing Expenditures are for Outbound Calls; 50% for inbound.

[4] The Mail Order Sales Figure excludes roughly $49 billion of charitable mail order contributions which are not included in the $11.904 billion of U.S. Aggregate Sales.

*Dollars in billions; ME: Media Expenditures, + Subsegments not included in totals.

Total advertising for 1991 was $207.596 billion. It is estimated that $142.256 billion of the $207.596 or 68% of this volume is direct response advertising. New section of the flow chart reports direct response components of overall media advertising expenditures. A growing percentage of Broadcast, Newspaper, and Magazine advertising dollars can be categorized as direct response advertising. The percentage is growing rapidly as marketers learn the efficiency of measuring advertising performance.

Promotional Perspective 16–1

The Sociocultural Impact of Catalogs

No one has expressed more vividly the sociocultural impact of catalogs than Daniel Boorstin, the Pulitzer Prize winning historian and chief librarian of Congress. It was not merely facetious to say that many farmers came to live more intimately with the good Big Book of Ward's or Sears, Roebuck than with the Good Book. The farmer kept his Bible in the frigid parlor, but, as Edna Ferber remarked in *Fanny Herself* (1917), her novel of the mail-order business, the mail-order catalogue was kept in the cozy kitchen. That was where the farm family ate, and where they really lived. For many such families, the catalogue probably expressed their most vivid hopes for salvation. It was no accident that pious rural customers without embarrassment called the catalogue "the Farmer's Bible." There was a familiar story of the little boy who was asked by his Sunday School teacher where the Ten Commandments came from, and who unhesitatingly replied that they came from Sears, Roebuck. . . .

Farm children now learned from the new Bible of their consumption community. In rural schoolhouses, children were drilled in reading and spelling from the catalogue. They practiced arithmetic by filling out orders and adding up items. They tried their hand at drawing by copying the catalogue models, and acquired geography by studying the postal-zone maps. In schoolrooms that had no other encyclopedia, a Ward's or Sears catalogue handily served the purpose; it was illustrated, it told you what something was made of and what it was good for, how long it would last, and even what it cost. Many a mother in a household with few children's books pacified her child with the pictures in the catalogue. When the new book arrived, the pictures in the old catalogue were indelibly fixed in the memory of girls who cut them up for paper dolls. . . . The children of rural America thought of the big books from Sears and Ward's as exhaustive catalogues of the material world.

Source: Nat Ross, "A History of Direct Marketing," in *Direct Marketing Fact Book* (Direct Marketing Association, New York, 1985), p. 5. Reprinted with permission of the Direct Marketing Association, Inc.

increase of dual-income families (in 1991 an estimated 57.5 percent of women were in the work force)[6] has meant more income. At the same time, trends toward physical fitness, do-it-yourself, and home entertainment have reduced the time available for shopping and have increased the attractiveness of direct purchases.

- **Technological advances** The rapid technological advancement of the electronic media (to be discussed later in this chapter) and of computers has made it easier for the consumer to shop and for the marketer to be successful in reaching the desired target markets. By 1992, 79 million television homes received home shopping programs, and home channel purchases totaled over $2.55 billion per year.[7]

- **Miscellaneous factors** A number of other factors have contributed to the increased effectiveness of direct marketing including changing values, more sophisticated marketing techniques, improved image of the industry, and so on. Those factors that have contributed to the growth of this direct marketing will also assure its success in the future. The variety of companies employing direct marketing (see Exhibit 16–2) demonstrates the potential offered by this approach.

Direct-Marketing Decisions

To successfully implement direct-marketing programs, companies must make a number of decisions. As in other marketing programs, decisions involve determining (1) what the programs objectives will be; (2) which markets to target—determined through the use of a list or marketing data base; (3) what direct marketing strategies will be employed; and (4) how to evaluate the effectiveness of the program.

➤ *Exhibit 16−2* **A variety of companies employ direct marketing**

Magnavox CATV	American Express
A division of North American Philips Corp., the company markets cable television equipment worldwide. Eastern Europe, China, and Argentina have become some of its most valued clients.	The company targeted the top 1% of American Express Cardmembers offering them a "By Invitation Only" Platinum Card membership. The membership offered private gallery tours, private access to the Bob Hope Celebrity Pro-Am Golf Tournament, and private forums with editors of *The New Republic* magazine, among other activities.
Quaker and CBS	**Philip-Morris, Inc.**
Quaker Oats Co. and CBS have combined in the first network TV/consumer products direct-marketing campaign. Ten full-page coupons from Quaker were sent to over 18 million households during the fall TV premiere period. Included in the customized package were promotions for new and returning CBS shows, with highlights on family-oriented shows such as "Major Dad."	Philip-Morris sent buyers of competing Winston and Camel brand cigarettes a fancy package containing a fold-out colored ad and $3 worth of coupons good for a carton of its newly introduced Marlboro Mediums. The outside of the box contained the new Marlboro Medium logo and 5 packs of cigarettes.
General Motors	**Lexus**
Cadillac, Pontiac, and Oldsmobile have all used direct mail. The GM divisions sent both letters and product demonstrations on videotape. Oldsmobile offered a free videotape to anyone who called an 800 number, while Pontiac mailed a video to over 250,000 Chrysler minivan owners.	Lexus tied a direct-mail campaign with a promotional offer. The mailer included a brochure of the Lexus (see Exhibit 16–3), a personal invitation to test drive the new model ES 250, and a promotional incentive. For all those who accepted the invitation to test drive the car, a certificate good for 2 years' free regularly scheduled maintenance would be validated.

Direct-Marketing Objectives

As previously noted, the direct marketer seeks a direct response. Thus, the objectives of the program normally seek a behavior—for example, test drives, votes, contributions, and/or sales. A typical objective for these programs would be defined through a set response—for example, a 2 to 3 percent response rate.

Not all direct marketing seeks a behavioral response, however. Many organizations and companies use direct marketing for building an image, maintaining customer satisfaction, and informing and/or educating customers in an attempt to potentially lead to future actions.

Developing a Marketing Data Base

As we have discussed throughout this text, market segmentation and targeting are critical components of any promotional program. This fact is no less true for direct marketers. To segment and target their markets, direct marketers make use of a data base. Essentially, a data base is a listing of customers and/or potential customers. At the very least, this list may contain names, addresses, and ZIP codes, while many data bases are much more sophisticated including information on demographics and psychographics, purchase transactions and payments, personal facts, neighborhood data, and even credit histories. This data base serves as the foundation on which the direct-marketing programs evolve. For example, data bases are used to perform the following functions:[8]

- **Improving the selection of market segments** Some consumers are more likely to be potential purchasers, users, voters, and so on than are others. By analyzing the characteristics of the data base, a higher potential audience can be targeted. For example, catalog companies have become very specialized, targeting only potential customers who are most likely to want, need, and/or purchase their products. Companies such as Lands' End, Lillie's Kids, and Talbots have successfully culled their lists and become much more efficient.
- **Stimulating repeat purchases** Once a purchase has been made, the customer's name and other information is entered into the data base. As present customers, these people are proven to be direct-marketing users and

➤ *Exhibit 16–3*
Lexus is just one of the many car companies now using direct marketing

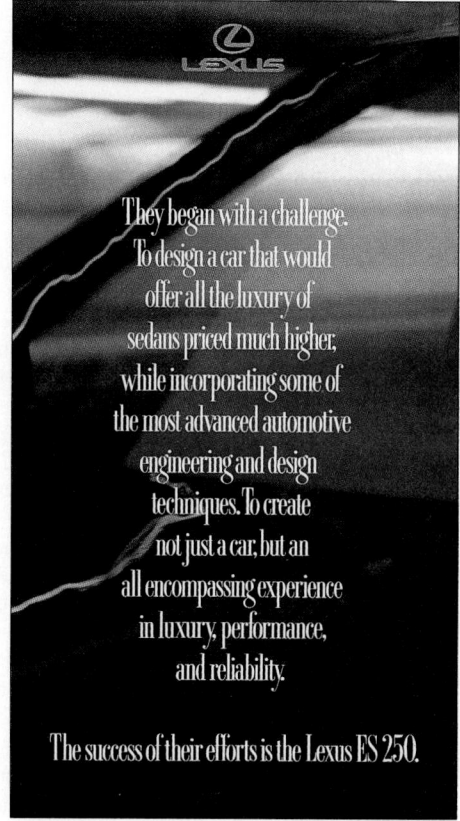

They began with a challenge. To design a car that would offer all the luxury of sedans priced much higher, while incorporating some of the most advanced automotive engineering and design techniques. To create not just a car, but an all encompassing experience in luxury, performance, and reliability.

The success of their efforts is the Lexus ES 250.

often offer high potential for repurchase. Magazine companies, for example, routinely send out renewal letters and/or phone subscribers before the expiration date. Other companies, ranging from window cleaners to carpet cleaners to automobile companies, build a base of customers and contact them when they are "due" to repurchase.

- **Cross-selling** Customers who demonstrate a specific interest also constitute strong potential for other products of the same nature. For example, the National Geographic Society has successfully sold globes, maps, videotapes, travel magazines, and an assortment of other products to subscribers, who obviously have an interest in geography and/or travel. Likewise, companies like Victoria's Secret have expanded their clothing lines primarily through sales to existing customers.

In addition to the above examples, numerous other companies have established comprehensive data bases on existing and potential customers (some of these are shown in Exhibit 16–4). Seemingly everyone from cigarette companies to banks has used data bases, to the point where some groups are concerned about invasion of privacy, as demonstrated in Ethical Perspective 16–1.

Direct marketers are concerned as well. The Direct Marketing Association (DMA), the trade association for direct marketers, has asked its members to adhere to ethical rules of conduct in their marketing efforts, noting that if the industry does not police itself, the government will do so.

Sources of data base information

There are many sources of information for these data bases. These sources include:

- **The U.S. Census Bureau** The 1990 census data provide information on almost every household in the United States. Data include household size, demographics, income, and other information.

> *Exhibit 16–4*
Data collection activity by major marketers

Marketers are using advertising, direct mail, and interactive telephone programs to collect data on their current and potential customers, who they can then recontact about new products, consumer research, or promotions. Here's a sample of recent activity.

Marketer	Brand(s)	Program
Procter & Gamble Company	Cheer Free, Cascade LiquiGel, NyQuil LiquiCaps	Collects data through reply cards in FSIs offering free product samples by mail. P&G can recontact them about future line extensions or related new products.
MCI Communications Corporation	Long-distance service	Friends & Family program offers 20% discount to customers who identify people called regularly. MCI then targets those names with mail and phone solicitations.
AT&T/Walt Disney World		Callers enter joint sweepstakes using interactive phone program and are asked about Disney product and resort usage for future contacts by company.
Kimberly–Clark Corporation	Huggies diapers	Buys lists of new mothers and sends coupons, brochures, and new-product information during babies' diaper-wearing stage.
Pepsi–Cola Company	Pepsi	"Summer Chill Out" promotion developed mailing list with discount card offered to kids.
Hallmark Cards	Greeting cards	Envelope glued in magazine ad, when filled out with information on demographics and where card buyers shop, it's redeemable for free greeting card.
Coca–Cola Company	Coca–Cola Classic	"Pop Music" promotion provides CD buyers' names to partner Sony Corporation.
Philip Morris Cos.	Merit cigarettes	"Blind" FSI mail-in coupon offered unidentified product sample as part of contest promotion.

- **The U.S. Postal Service**   Postal ZIP code and the extended four-digit code provides information on both household and business locations.
- **List services**   A variety of providers of lists are available (an example of one such provider is shown in Exhibit 16–5). These providers vary in quality depending on the accuracy of the list and its currency.
- **Standard Rates and Data Service**   The SRDS provides information regarding two types of lists—consumer lists and business lists. These lists are provided in two volumes of information entitled *Direct Mail List Rates and Data* and provide over 50,000 list selections in hundreds of classifications.
- **Simmons Market Research Bureau**   SMRB conducts an annual study of customers who buy at home through the mail or via telephone (see Exhibit 16–6). Information is provided in respect to total orders placed, type of products purchased, demographics, and purchase satisfaction, among others.
- **Direct Marketing Association, Inc.**   The trade organization of the Direct Marketing Association is responsible for promoting direct marketing and providing statistical information on direct-marketing use. The organization publishes a *Fact Book of Direct Marketing* containing information regarding use, attitudes toward direct marketing, rules and regulations, and so forth.

Ethical Perspective 16–1

Data Base Marketing—Marketing Advantage or Invasion of Privacy?

Data base marketing has become so sophisticated and effective that hardly a major corporation fails to use this marketing tool. Through the use of advanced computer technologies, companies have compiled an extensive array of information about customers and potential customers. Consider these examples:

- Philip Morris Inc., R. J. Reynolds, Brown & Williamson, and other tobacco companies have spent hundreds of millions of dollars to collect the names, addresses, and brand preferences of close to 70 percent of the nation's million smokers. These smokers are sent samples, coupons, catalogs, posters, and even marketing surveys in an attempt to get them to purchase the company's brands.

- Private researchers using topologically integrated geographic encoding and referencing systems (TIGER maps) provide businesses with information on every street and almost every household in America. The information details the average age, education, and income of neighborhoods, the growth and affluence of the community, and in some cases, even the occupants' brand usage and preferences.

- Financial institutions routinely examine customers' product and service usage (checking accounts, savings programs, etc.) to determine potential adopters of new offerings.

As noted, some believe the amount of data now available on American citizens is excessive and has become an invasion of privacy. In a Gallup study conducted in 1991, 78 percent of the adults polled said they were concerned about privacy issues, with 45 percent of respondents noting they were "very concerned." These people think that since access to this data is so easy, unscrupulous businesspeople may take advantage of the personal information. Some marketers note that banks could theoretically deny loans based on neighborhood profiles; cigarette companies could target teenagers or minority groups; and endless other companies could provide a deluge of junk mail and unwanted product samples.

Data base marketing has become so sophisticated that as census and postal information are combined, it has become possible to target a particular side of the street or selected floors within a high-rise office building or even an individual. With the knowledge of the demographics, lifestyles, spending habits, and so on of these people, companies may know more about them than they know about themselves.

Because these lists are readily sold to a variety of clients, including government agencies, the privacy of the individual is becoming less and less guarded. To many, "Big Brother," the fictional character in the George Orwell book *1984,* is here!

Source: Sam Fulwood III, "Data Crunchers: Marketing Boon or Invasion of Privacy?" *Los Angeles Times,* May 19, 1991, pp. D1; "Smoking Out the Elusive Smoker," *Business Week,* March 16, 1992, pp. 62–63; Scott Hume, "Consumers Target Ire at Data Bases," *Advertising Age,* May 6, 1991, p. 3.

In addition to these sources of information, consumer goods manufacturers, banks, credit bureaus, retailers, charitable organizations, and other business operations provide lists and selected other information available for purchase. Companies also build their own data bases through completed warranty cards, surveys, and so on.

Direct Marketing Strategies and Media

As with all other communications programs discussed throughout this text, decisions must be made as to the message to be conveyed, the size of the budget, and so on. Perhaps the major difference between direct-marketing programs and other promotional mix programs is in respect to the use of media. We next examine media employed in direct-marketing programs.

As shown in Exhibit 16–1, direct marketing employs a number of media including direct mail, telemarketing, direct-response broadcasting, and print. Each of these media is used to perform specific functions, although they generally follow what direct marketers refer to as a one- or two-step approach.

In the **one-step approach,** the medium is used directly to obtain an order. For example, you probably have seen TV commercials for products like wrench sets, workout equipment, or magazine subscriptions in which the viewer is urged to phone in using an 800 number to place an order immediately. Usually these ads allow for the use of a credit card or C.O.D., as well as a mail-in address. Their goal is to generate an immediate sale when the ad is shown.

➤ *Exhibit 16–5*   **An example of the variety of lists available**

MAIL RESPONSE LISTS

QUANTITY		PRICE
AUTOMOTIVE		
15,000,000	American Car Buyers/Foreign/or USA Models	Inquire
208,000	AutoWeek Subscribers	$60/M
146,000	Babcox Business Leaders	$65/M
160,000	Beverly Hills Motoring Accessories Buyers	$95/M
165,000	4 Wheel & Off Road Subs	$60/M
48,000	Hearst Motor Bookbuyers	$50/M
49,500	Hot Rod Magazine	$60/M
328,000	Classic Motor Books	$55/M
218,000	Auto/Truck Do-It-Yourselfers	$60/M
74,000	Cars & Parts Magazine	$70/M
BEAUTY/HEALTH/DIET		
800,000	American Health Magazine	$65/M
1,000,000	Bio-Energetics Research Buyers	$70/M
339,000	Comfortably Yours	$85/M
1,700,000	Cosmetique Beauty Buyers	$55/M
32,000	Cardiac Alert Subs	$85/M
33,000	Executive Fitness Letter	$75/M
912,000	Health Magazine	$60/M
480,000	Health Conscious Americans	$50/M
224,000	Tufts University Newsletter	$65/M
550,000	University of California—Berkeley Wellness Letter	$70/M
135,000	Vegetarian Times	$65/M
200,000	Weider Health and Fitness	$65/M
2,400,000	Prevention Magazine	$60/M
821,000	Weight Watchers Magazine	$65/M
BOOKBUYERS		
2,200,000	Better Homes & Gardens	$60/M
642,000	Barnes & Noble	$70/M
840,000	Boardroom Bookbuyers	$85/M
330,000	Warren, Gorham & Lamont	$90/M
	Bantam Bookbuyers	Inquire
	Book of the Month Club	Inquire
	CMG (College Bookbuyers)	Inquire
	Doubleday Bookbuyers	Inquire
	Literary Guild	Inquire
	MacMillan Bookbuyers	Inquire
	Prentice Hall, Inc.	Inquire
	Time-Life—INQUIRE BY SUBJECT	Inquire
BUSINESS MAGAZINES		
25,000	American Banker	$110/M
36,000	Apartment Management	$60/M
1,161,000	Boardroom Reports	$85/M
236,000	Business Week Subs at Business	$98/M
377,000	Business Month	$70/M
36,000	Cash Flow	$95/M
115,000	The Economist	$125/M
731,000	Forbes	$95/M
67,000	Government Executive	$85/M
74,060	High Technology	$80/M
560,000	Inc. Magazine	$90/M
57,000	Industrial Safety Hygiene News	$70/M
389,000	Kiplinger Washington Letter	$85/M
129,000	Plant Engineering	$65/M
	Cahners Magazines	Inquire
	Chilton Magazines	Inquire
	Gralla Publications	Inquire
	Hayden Publications	Inquire
	Hitchcock Magazines	Inquire
	Hunter Publications	Inquire
	McGraw Hill Publications	Inquire
	Penton/IPC Magazines	Inquire
	Technical Publishing	Inquire

Many types of **privately owned** specialty lists of people are also available, such as:

- **MAIL ORDER BUYERS** of various direct mail, TV or magazine products.
- **SUBSCRIBERS** to magazines, newsletters
- **CONTRIBUTORS** to fund-raising campaigns
- **CREDIT CARD HOLDERS,** charge customers

These lists can be related to your specific product or purpose. If your offer is not in competitive conflict with such lists, the owner will authorize use of his names for your mailing. **A SAMPLE MAILING PIECE MUST BE SUBMITTED WITH YOUR ORDER FOR APPROVAL.** These **RESPONSE LISTS** are an additional tool to target specific segments of your direct mail market.

PRICES, QUANTITIES, AND MINIMUMS (usually 5,000 – Inquire) for such lists are completely at the discretion of the list owner, and are subject to change. *Please inquire for details and current prices before placing your order.* Orders for RESPONSE LISTS are not commissionable and cannot be charged on credit cards.

These two pages are a *representative* group of such private response lists. Many, many more are available.

QUANTITY		PRICE
BUSINESS PRODUCT BUYERS		
110,000	Amsterdam Business	$80/M
64,060	Atlas Pen & Pencil	$75/M
112,000	Baldwin Cooke Co	$80/M
2,000,000	Day Timers	$85/M
240,000	Drawing Board	$70/M
75,000	Grayarc	$55/M
244,000	Delmart	$50/M
CHILDREN		
203,000	American Baby	$60/M
52,000	Baby Talk	$60/M
55,000	Bear Necessities	$80/M
500,000	Child Color Portraits	$50/M
715,000	Children's Reading Institute	$55/M
611,000	Childcraft	$75/M
280,000	Electric Company	$60/M
818,000	Encyclopedia Britannica Buyers	$55/M
43,000	Gifted Children Monthly	$75/M
630,000	Grolier Enterprises	$65/M
280,000	Humpty Dumpty Magazine	$60/M
308,000	Jack & Jill Magazine	$60/M
63,000	Muppet Magazine	$60/M
1,600,000	Field Publications	$60/M
86,000	Teen Beat	$50/M
645,000	Young Miss Magazine	$50/M
CONTRIBUTORS		

QUANTITY		PRICE
435,000	American Museum Natural History	$75/M
400,000	Animal Welfare Donors	$65/M
437,000	Greenpeace	$65/M
4,000,000	Health	$65/M
1,313,000	Humanitarian	$65/M
226,000	National Foundation Cancer Research	$60/M
148,000	National Glaucoma Research	$75/M
1,497,000	Political	$65/M
248,000	Political/Conservative	$65/M
162,000	Political/Liberal	$65/M
4,000,000	Religious	$65/M
586,000	Hands Across America Donors	$55/M
COMPUTERS/DATA/PROCESSING		
2,800,000	Personal Computer Owners/ Type of Brand	Inquire
700,000	Business Computer Owners/ Type of Brand	Inquire
260,000	Professionals Using Computers	Inquire
665,000	Brandon Computer Professionals	$75/M
255,000	Byte Magazine	$100/M
113,000	Computerworld Magazine	$125/M
70,000	Computer Systems News	$87/M
137,580	Compute! Magazine	$80/M
160,000	Datamation	$80/M
400,000	Family and Home Office Computing	$80/M
135,000	MIS Week	$110/M
453,000	PC Magazine	$100/M
CONSUMER MAGAZINES		
250,000	Americana Magazine	$65/M
93,000	Art & Antiques Magazine	$80/M
380,000	Atlantic Monthly	$80/M
148,000	American History Illustrated	$70/M
73,000	Birdwatchers Digest	$60/M
110,000	Collectors Mart	$60/M
1,160,000	Contest Newsletter	$70/M
1,100,000	Davis Publications	$55/M
295,000	Early American Life	$70/M
110,000	Fate Magazine	$65/M
919,000	Insight Magazine	$55/M
1,000,000	Life Magazine	$70/M
112,000	New Age Journal	$75/M
346,000	National Audubon Society	$70/M
2,700,000	Newsweek	$60/M
1,613,000	Popular Science	$55/M
59,000	Spy Magazine	$75/M
335,000	Success Magazine	$75/M
12,000,000	TV Guide Subscribers	$55/M
852,000	TV Guide Cable Subscribers	$65/M
2,100,000	U.S. News & World Report	$70/M
	Regional Magazines (By City)	Inquire
CREDIT CARD HOLDERS		
10,200,000	American Express Co	$95/M
113,000	Carte Blanche	$80/M
670,000	Diners Club	$80/M
388,000	Diners—Mail Order Buyers	$85/M
382,000	Diners—Airline Ticket Buyers	$90/M
200,000	Syndicated Bank Cardholders (Purchased in monthly VISA and MASTERCARD statements)	$65/M
4,480,000	Credit Card Service Bureau	$65/M
1,395,000	Bloomingdales	$65/M
175,000	Chargit—Credit Card Holders	$65/M
390,000	First Travel Club Cardholders	$70/M
	INQUIRE-MISCELLANEOUS PRODUCT BUYERS W/CARDS	
CULTURAL		

The **two-step approach** may actually involve the use of more than one medium. In this strategy, the first effort is designed to screen or qualify potential buyers. The second effort has the responsibility of generating the response. For example, many companies use telemarketing to screen on the basis of interest, then follow up to interested parties with more information designed to achieve an order or use personal selling to close the sale.

> *Exhibit 16–6*
SMRB provides information on
consumers who ordered
merchandise by mail or phone in
last 12 months (adults)

	Total U.S. (000)	Ordered by Mail or Phone			
		A (000)	B % Down	C Across %	D Indx
Total adults	182456	95992	100.0	52.6	100
Males	87118	40255	41.9	46.2	88
Females	95338	55737	58.1	58.5	111
18–24	25530	11357	11.8	44.5	85
25–34	44118	22980	23.9	52.1	99
34–44	37521	22190	23.1	59.1	112
45–54	25346	14426	15.0	56.9	108
55–64	21009	12310	12.8	58.6	111
65 OR OLDER	28934	12730	13.3	44.0	84
18–34	69647	34338	35.8	49.3	94
18–49	120585	64032	66.7	53.1	101
25–54	106984	59596	62.1	55.7	106
35–49	50938	29694	30.9	58.3	111
50 OR OLDER	61871	31960	33.3	51.7	98
Graduated college	35347	21821	22.7	61.7	117
Attended college	35167	20563	21.4	58.5	111
Graduated high school	70823	37744	39.3	53.3	101
Did not graduate high school	41119	15865	16.5	38.6	73
Employed males	67846	32877	34.2	48.5	92
Employed females	57394	36598	38.1	63.8	121
Employed full-time	112285	61317	63.9	54.6	104
Employed part-time	12955	8158	8.5	63.0	120
Not employed	57216	26517	27.6	46.3	88
Professional/manager	31819	20165	21.0	63.4	120
Technical/clerical/sales	39581	23409	24.4	59.1	112
Precision/craft	14839	6942	7.2	46.8	89
Other employed	39001	18960	19.8	48.6	92
Single	40179	17392	18.1	43.3	82
Married	108808	62881	65.5	57.8	110
Divorced/separated/widowed	33469	15719	16.4	47.0	89
Parents	60855	34648	36.1	56.9	108
White	156458	85309	88.9	54.5	104
Black	20509	8270	8.6	40.3	77
Other	5489	2413	2.5	44.0	84
Hshld income $75,000 or more	21409	13601	14.2	63.5	121
$60,000 or more	36836	23133	24.1	62.8	119
$50,000 or more	53155	32827	34.2	61.8	117
$40,000 or more	75291	46006	47.9	61.1	116
$30,000 or more	102396	61323	63.9	59.9	114
$30,000–$39,999	27105	15318	16.0	56.5	107
$20,000–$29,999	30317	15656	16.3	51.6	98
$10,000–$19,999	29855	12608	13.1	42.2	80
Under $10,000	19888	6405	6.7	32.2	61

Direct mail

This direct-marketing medium constitutes what has been commonly referred to as "junk mail"—the unsolicited mail you find in your mailbox. The amount of advertising dollars spent in direct mail continues to be one of the highest of all advertising media, with an estimated $24.38 billion spent in this area in 1991.[9] Direct mail is not restricted to small companies seeking our business in an unsolicited manner. Well-known and -respected companies such as General Electric, American Express, and Citicorp have increased their expenditures in this area, as has Audi.

While many advertisers shied away from direct mail in the past, fearful of the image that might be created or harboring the belief that direct mail was useful only for low-cost products, this is no longer the case. For example, Porsche Cars North America, Inc., uses direct mail to target high-income, upscale consumers who

➤ *Exhibit 16–7*
Porsche used direct mail to target high income physicians

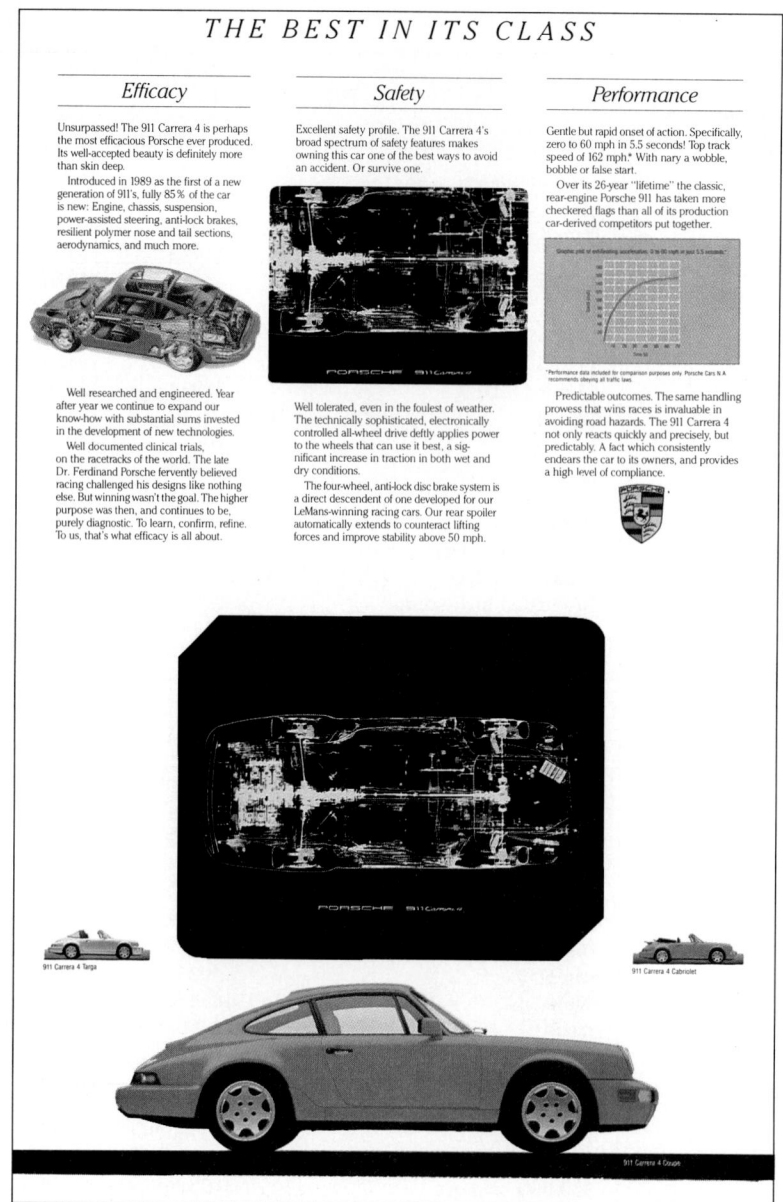

constitute the market segment with the highest potential for purchasing its expensive sports cars. Exhibit 16–7 shows a direct mail piece that was sent to a very precisely defined target market—physicians in specialties with the highest income levels. The list of these physicians was also screened to match the demographics of Porsche buyers and narrowed further to specific geographic areas. As can be seen in this exhibit, the direct mail piece sent to the physicians was an x-ray of a Porsche 911 Carrera 4 that was written in the language of the medical audience. This creative direct-mail campaign generated one of the highest response rates of any mailing Porsche had done in recent years.[10]

Keys to the success of direct mail are the **mailing list** that constitutes the data base from which names are generated and the ability to segment markets. Lists have now become more current and more selective, eliminating waste coverage. Segmentation on the basis of geography (usually through ZIP codes), demographics, and lifestyles has led to increased effectiveness. The most commonly employed lists are those individuals who are past purchasers of direct-mail products!

➤ *Exhibit 16–8*   **Catalog shopping increases**

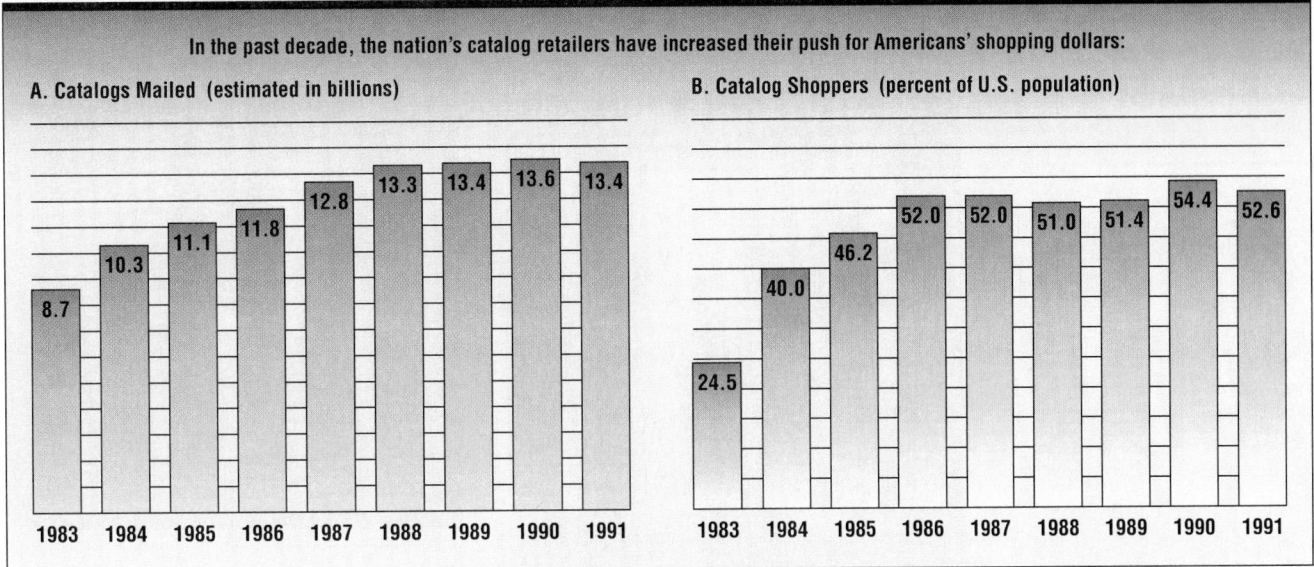

In the past decade, the nation's catalog retailers have increased their push for Americans' shopping dollars:

A. Catalogs Mailed (estimated in billions)

1983	1984	1985	1986	1987	1988	1989	1990	1991
8.7	10.3	11.1	11.8	12.8	13.3	13.4	13.6	13.4

B. Catalog Shoppers (percent of U.S. population)

1983	1984	1985	1986	1987	1988	1989	1990	1991
24.5	40.0	46.2	52.0	52.0	51.0	51.4	54.4	52.6

The importance of the list has led to a business of its own. In 1990 there were an estimated 38 billion names on lists, and many companies have found it profitable to sell the names of purchasers of their products and/or services to list firms. Companies such as A. B. Zeller and Metromail provide such lists on a national level, whereas in almost any metropolitan area there are firms providing the same service on a local basis. In 1990, the list business accounted for $1.3 billion in sales of names.

Catalogs

A major participant in the direct-marketing business is the catalog company. As shown in Exhibit 16–8, the number of catalogs mailed and the number of catalog shoppers have increased significantly since 1984. (The slight decline shown in 1991 is a result of more effectively targeted lists, according to the DMA.) Catalog sales in 1991 reached an estimated $30 billion.

Many companies use catalogs in conjunction with their more traditional sales and promotional strategies. For example, companies like Sears, Nordstrom, and J. C. Penney sell directly through catalogs but also use this medium to inform consumers of product offerings available in the stores. Others rely solely on catalog sales—for example, L. L. Bean—while others have started out exclusively as catalog companies and have now branched into retail outlets, such as Sharper Image, Lands' End, and Banana Republic. Exhibit 16–9 shows just a few of the many companies that market through catalogs.

Broadcast media

The success of direct marketing in the broadcast industry is truly remarkable. Direct-response TV is estimated to have generated over $500 million in sales in 1991.[11] Some believe this figure may even be higher. For example, one company in California sold almost $50,000 a day in a diet program at $19.95 per order, whereas others have sold products costing into the hundreds of dollars successfully. Perhaps the most amazing thing about these sales figures is that the advertising time purchased to sell these products was among the least expensive available in the medium. (Direct

➤ *Exhibit 16–9*
A few of the many companies that market through catalogs

advertisers often purchase advertising time at the last moment to obtain a discount from the published rates. They also often purchase time on programs with low ratings or reruns, as the consumer is less likely to leave an interesting show or event to place the phone order!)

Two broadcast media are available to the direct marketer—television and radio. While radio was used quite extensively in the 1950s, its use and effectiveness have dwindled substantially in recent years. Thus, the majority of direct-marketing broadcast advertising now occurs on TV and receives the bulk of our attention here.

Direct marketing in the broadcast industry involves two forms of advertising—**direct-response advertising** and **support advertising.** In direct-response advertising,

➤ *Exhibit 16–10*   **One of the many products that use infomercials to inform consumers**

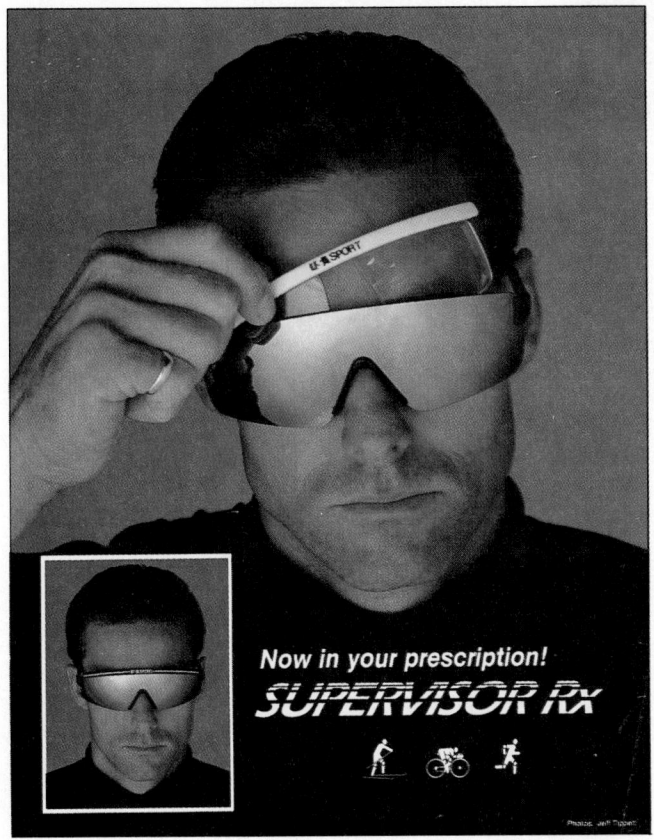

US-A SPORT®
Convertible Sportglass

What makes a great sport sunglass? For some, contemporary styling comes immediately to mind. Adequate U.V. protection is a must. It should also act as a barrier to wind, dust, and snow. For the active individual who may encounter any number of conditions in the course of a day, a sport sunglass must serve many functions.

Unquestionably, the greatest protection is provided by the wrap-around design of quality shield glasses. The panoramic view offered by this style is appealing, as is the added benefit of its ability to block side light and foreign particles. The aerodynamics are perfect for sports like skiing and bicycling. A number of things can make one shield glass superior to all others.

OPTICS Despite the popularity of cylinder shield glasses on the market, the serious optical professional would question recommending them due to their obvious distortion. A six-base spherical lens (the same curvature as the human eye) provides optimum optics, therefore doing what a sunglass should do—help the eyes, not hurt them.

ADJUSTABILITY Active people come in a variety of sizes, but unfortunately, not all sport glasses are designed to allow for that. During demanding sports, a person may run, jump, ride, spin, twist, fall, or flip. It's essential that a sportglass fit right, stay put, and not fall off.

PRESCRIPTIONABILITY Sixty percent of all people could benefit from corrective lenses. This includes many sport enthusiasts whose abilities might be hampered by their poor vision. Until now, these individuals have had limited choices in sunwear.
They could:
 • wear conventional sunglasses with contacts
 • wear prescription sunglasses
 • wear clip-ons or over glasses

None of these options offers the advantage of full wrap-around protection. Whether individuals wear eyeglasses or contact lenses, they still experience the discomfort that sweat in the eyes and cold weather conditions cause.

A NATURAL CHOICE FLASHSPORT
There is a new product on the market: Flashsport Rx. It's the world's first patented shield glass that converts from nonprescription to prescription and back again instantly. Flashsport has a six-base curve spherical polycarbonate lens which is available in two sizes—narrow (135 mm x 45mm) and deep (140mm x 50mm) - and five colors - gold mirror, blue/green mirror, smoke, clear, and high contrast amber. These distortion-free lenses block 100% U.V. to 400 nm. Patented multi-adjustable temples not only adjust for length, but also curvability, by bending from paddle tip to cable. This provides a custom fit and also allows instant pantoscopic angle adjustment. Cyclists will appreciate the ability to make these adjustments without removing

their helmet. Prescriptionability is the most dramatic feature: Rx lenses are bonded to an interchangeable bumper/sweat bar, which is available in six colors bearing the USA Sport or Campagnolo logos. These are easily inserted into removed from the Flashsport at will. The Flashsport Rx is a boon to contact lens wearers: it's a sport-glass designed to meet all their needs. For driving or everyday use, they can wear the Flashsport as a sunglass; for active sports such as bicycling, skiing, or windsurfing, the Rx insert is snapped into place and the shield instantly becomes a prescription sunglass. This means that one excellent sportglass can serve the needs of everyone whether or not they wear prescription or contact lenses. The Flashsport Rx... from Sport Optics International, Inc.

Sport Optics International • 6191 Cornerstone Court East #101 • San Diego • CA 92121 • FAX (619) 546-8921 • (619) 546-1221 • **1-800-456-7842**

the product or service is offered and a sales response is solicited, either through the one- or two-step approach previously discussed. Examples include ads for Soloflex, Nordic Track, and record albums, discs, and/or tapes and/or tips on football or basketball betting. Support advertising is designed to do exactly that—support other forms of advertising. Ads for Publishers Clearing House or Reader's Digest or other companies informing you to look in your mailbox for a coming sweepstakes entry are examples of this use of broadcast medium.

Infomercials

The lower cost of commercials on cable and satellite channels has led advertisers to a new form of advertising—the infomercial. An **infomercial** is essentially a longer than average advertisement, ranging from as few as 3 to as long as 60 minutes. Most are 30 minutes long. Many infomercials are produced by the advertisers and are designed to be viewed as regular TV shows, with the purpose of gaining sales by having consumers dial an 800 or 900 number to place an order. Programs such as "Amazing Discoveries" and Richard Simmons' "Deal-A-Meal" promote products and services and diet programs, respectively, while other infomercials promote spray cleaners made from "100 percent natural oranges" (Citrus Miracle) or self-improvement tapes that promise to raise one's IQ and/or bring "meaningful and lasting love relationships" (Brain Supercharger)—see Promotional Perspective 16–2.

At the same time, not all infomercials are of this nature. For example, Sport Optics International, marketer of the USA/sport sunglasses shown in Exhibit 16–10,

Promotional Perspective 16–2

Infomercials—Tact or Tacky?

Perhaps the most controversial form of advertising message now airing is that of the infomercial. Supporters argue that infomercials are an excellent source of direct, nonhyped product information, while their opponents call the same ads everything from tacky, to sleazy, to deceptive.

There is evidence to support both contentions. For example, Time Life Music, the third largest U.S. mail-order company, was the first Fortune 500 company to successfully air an infomercial. The half-hour commercial starring Rick Dees and titled "The Rock 'N Roll Era" has received national acclaim and has been called by some the best half-hour commercial ever produced. The ad is laden with both information and entertainment in its countdown of the top 40 songs of the "Rock 'N Roll Era." General Motors also has used this format to tout its new Saturn line of cars, offering the prospective consumer a great deal of truthful information about the car.

On the other side, opponents of infomercials consider the ads to be tacky at best and potentially harmful. They argue that the majority of infomercials are produced and marketed by "hucksters" and claim the advertisers are trying to disguise the commercials as TV programs. They refer to the list of "hottest shows" as evidence of their position in that they are not really shows at all, but advertiser-produced 30-minute commercials. They note that products such as Euro-Trym Diet Patch (an adhesive disk that attached to the skin and was supposed to curb the appetite — but didn't), Y-Bron (an impotence remedy), and Foliplexx (a baldness treatment), all of which have been declared deceptive by the Federal Trade Commission, are representative of what is wrong with the infomercial industry. They are especially concerned because they think viewers tend to believe things they see on TV more so than they do those seen in print.

Certainly there is some truth in both sides' claims. Infomercial producers admit there have been abuses in the industry but claim such abuses are on the decline. They note that the formation of a trade organization and establishment of content guidelines suggested by government regulators will go far in gaining them respectability.

In the meantime, the growth figures for infomercials also reflect their growing popularity—or at least acceptability. Consider the following:

- The number of infomercial telecasts increased from 2,500 a month in 1985 to over 21,000 a month in 1991.
- Almost every affiliate of the major networks accepts infomercials.
- An estimated $800 million in sales were expected through infomercials in 1992 alone.

While proponents argue that these figures demonstrate the favorable reactions to infomercials, at least one opponent notes, "Most people are holding their nose but taking the money . . . . It's a lure and a curse." Only time—and consumers' spending—will tell.

Source: Richard Zoglin, "It's Amazing! Call Now!" *Time,* June 17, 1991, p. 71,; Steven W. Colford and Alison Fahey, "Infomercials Find New Venues," *Advertising Age,* May 27, 1991, p. 37; "Fortune 500-Time Life Music Tests Infomercial Concept," *Direct Response TV Infomercials Newsletter,* Fall 1990, pp. 1–3.

The Ten Hottest Shows

The hottest infomercials, as of the latest ratings, as measured by the number of telecasts for each show in May 1990.

Rank	Show	Telecasts
1.	Liquid Luster	1605
2.	Amazing Discoveries	1328
3.	Snackmaster	1198
4.	Stainerator	977
5.	Mega Memory	777
6.	Second Paycheck	720
7.	Daily Mixer	583
8.	Beauty Breakthrough	574
9.	Soloflex	388
10.	Kitchen Mate	287

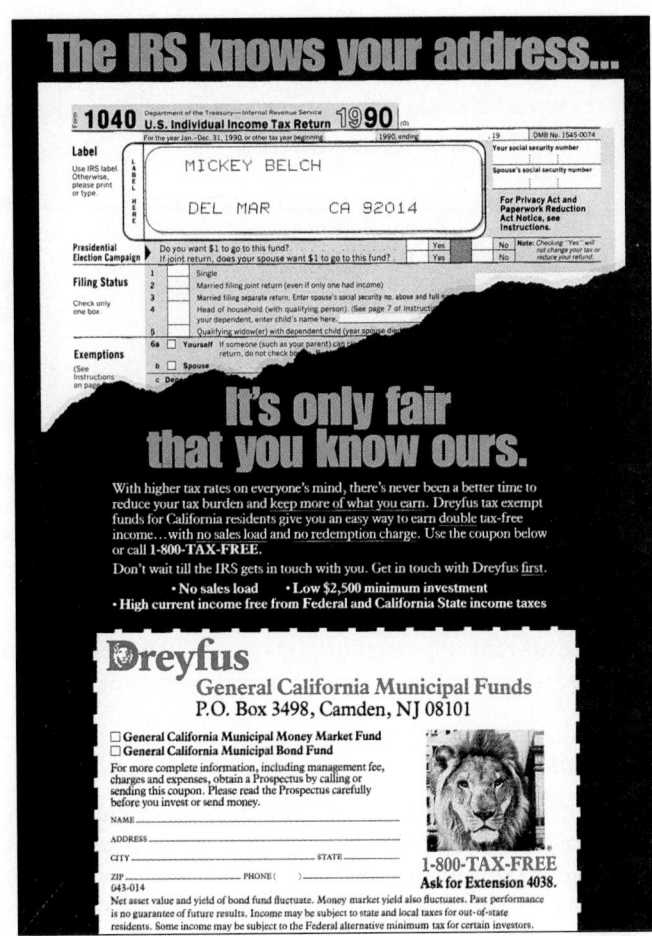

have used infomercials to tell their product story. Companies such as Volvo, General Motors, AT&T, and Time-Life are also experimenting with the format. In 1990, approximately $500 million of sales were generated by infomericals, and 1992 figures were expected to exceed $800 million.[12]

As to their effectiveness, at least one study indicates the infomercials get watched. Bruskin Goldring market research found that 25- to 49-year-olds watch the most infomercials, people in the $30,000 to $40,000 income range watch at an above average rate, and of those who have purchased goods through infomercials, 21 percent make more than $40,000 a year.[13]

At the same time, some are not sold on the idea of what they consider advertisements disguised as programs. Four consumer groups (the Consumer Federation of America, Center for the Study of Commercialism, Center for Media Education, and Telecommunications Research and Action Center) have asked the FCC to require all infomercials to display a symbol that indicates a "paid ad" or "sponsored by" so they won't be confused with regular television programming.[14]

Print media

Difficult media to employ for direct marketing are magazines and newspapers. Because these ads have to compete with the clutter of other ads, and because the cost of the space is relatively expensive, response rates may be lower and the profits not as high as in other media. This does not mean these media are not used (as is evidenced by the fact that expenditures totaled over $40 billion in 1991),[15] only that the returns may not have been as great. Exhibit 16–11 provides an example of a

➤ *Exhibit 16–12*
The telemarketing boom

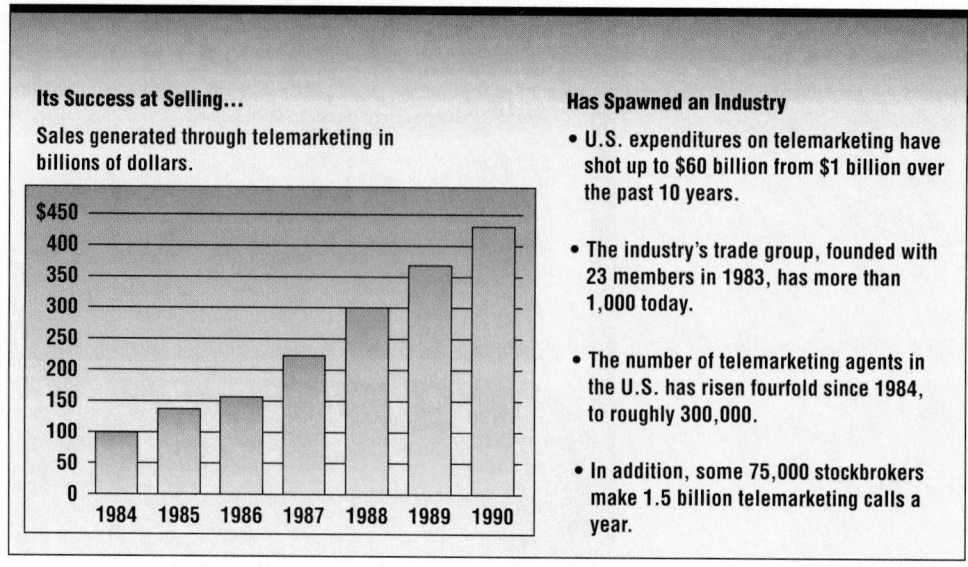

Its Success at Selling...

Sales generated through telemarketing in billions of dollars.

Has Spawned an Industry

• U.S. expenditures on telemarketing have shot up to $60 billion from $1 billion over the past 10 years.

• The industry's trade group, founded with 23 members in 1983, has more than 1,000 today.

• The number of telemarketing agents in the U.S. has risen fourfold since 1984, to roughly 300,000.

• In addition, some 75,000 stockbrokers make 1.5 billion telemarketing calls a year.

direct ad that appeared in a magazine. You can find many more in specific interest areas, whether it be financial newspapers, sports, sex, or hobby magazines.

Telemarketing

If you have a telephone, you probably do not have to be told about the rapid increase in the use of **telemarketing.** Again, both profit and charitable organizations have employed this medium effectively in both one- and two-step approaches. It has been estimated that over 118 million Americans receive nearly 3 billion telemarketing phone calls each year, with approximately 6 percent of these resulting in a completed transaction.[16] While 6 percent may seem to be a very low figure, as can be seen in Exhibit 16–12, the fact is that telemarketing is a very big industry and it continues to grow.

As telemarketing continues to grow and expand in scope, a new dimension referred to as **audiotex** or **tele-media** has evolved. Tom Eisenhart refers to tele-media as the "use of telephone and voice information services (900, 800, and 976 numbers) to market, advertise, promote, entertain, and inform."[17] Many tele-media programs are interactive. While many people still think of 900 and 976 numbers as "ripoffs" or "sex, lies, and phone lines," over 7,000 programs are carried on 900 networks alone, with companies such as Tele-Lawyer, a legal information services organization; Bally's Health & Tennis Corp., the nation's largest health-club chain, and NutraSweet constituting over 75 percent of these. Exhibit 16–13 shows more specifically where such calls are going.

Telemarketing and tele-media programs have responded to public complaints and criticisms. "Dial-a-Porn" and other such programs constitute a diminishing share of the 800, 900, and 976 offerings. As more and more large companies increase their usage of these services, the tarnished image now shared by many consumers will likely subside.

The new electronic media

Over the past few years technological advances have opened up a number of new media for marketers. While these alternatives vary in many respects, a summary classification that might best describe these new media is that of electronic media. A review of some of these follows.

➤ *Exhibit 16–13*
**I'd pay to find out! (percentage of
total 900 calls made to specific
applications)**

	1991	1992*
Information	35.6%	32.5%
Entertainment	20.1	18.4
Messaging	11.6	8.4
Ordering	7.1	8.6
Sweepstakes	5.9	6.0
Fund raising	5.4	6.4
Polling/surveying	3.5	4.6
Lead generation	2.9	3.4
Couponing	2.1	3.2
Dealer **locators**	1.6	1.8
Customer services	0.9	1.1
Other	3.3	5.6

*Estimate

Teleshopping The development of the toll-free 800 telephone number, combined with the widespread use of credit cards, has led to a dramatic increase in the number of persons who shop via their television sets. Jewelry, kitchenware, insurance, and a variety of other companies have now employed this medium to promote (and sell!) their products. In 1992, there were five home shopping channels in the United States accounting for over $2.55 billion worth of sales.

Videotext (electronic teleshopping) Unlike infomercials and home shopping channels, which rely on broadcast or cable video channels, **videotext** is an information retrieval service that occurs through one's personal computer. Videotext uses a telephone, television, and hand-held keyboard and allows subscribers to request electronic pages of text stored miles away in a computer, as shown in Exhibit 16–14.

With only a minimal knowledge of computers, home shoppers can select the information they want as though they were using an index of a book. Shoppers can purchase products, services such as airline tickets, play games, get stock market reports, view the latest headlines, and pay bills. Advertisers may provide their messages in the forms of logos or names or in longer segments, depending on the costs they wish to assume and the message they wish to convey.

The country's leading information retrieval services companies—CompuServe, Dow Jones, Prodigy (a joint venture between Sears and IBM), and the Source—have increased their information offerings over the years, making this medium more attractive to marketers. As of 1991, Prodigy had over a million subscribers, and advertisers such as Sharp Electronics, KLM Royal Dutch Airlines, Oldsmobile, Holiday Inn, Panasonic, and others promoted their products through this service.[18] In addition, Prodigy announced a joint venture with *USA Today* to offer the opportunity for consumers to buy classified advertising.

Some of the companies that have used videotext services, the marketing objectives they sought to achieve, and their reasons for participating are shown in Exhibit 16–15.

While videotext in theory offers a great new method of shopping and a new avenue for advertisers, at this time the system has met with only limited success. While the number of subscribers and advertisers have both been on the increase, some of the major providers such as Times Mirror's Gateway system have abandoned their efforts. Until personal computers have made a much greater penetration of the home market—as forecasts had predicted—the value of this medium will likewise not reach its potential in the consumer market.

Advantages and disadvantages of the new electronic media Given the lack of time experienced by so many dual working families, the ability of the new electronic

➤ *Exhibit 16–14* **How videotex works**

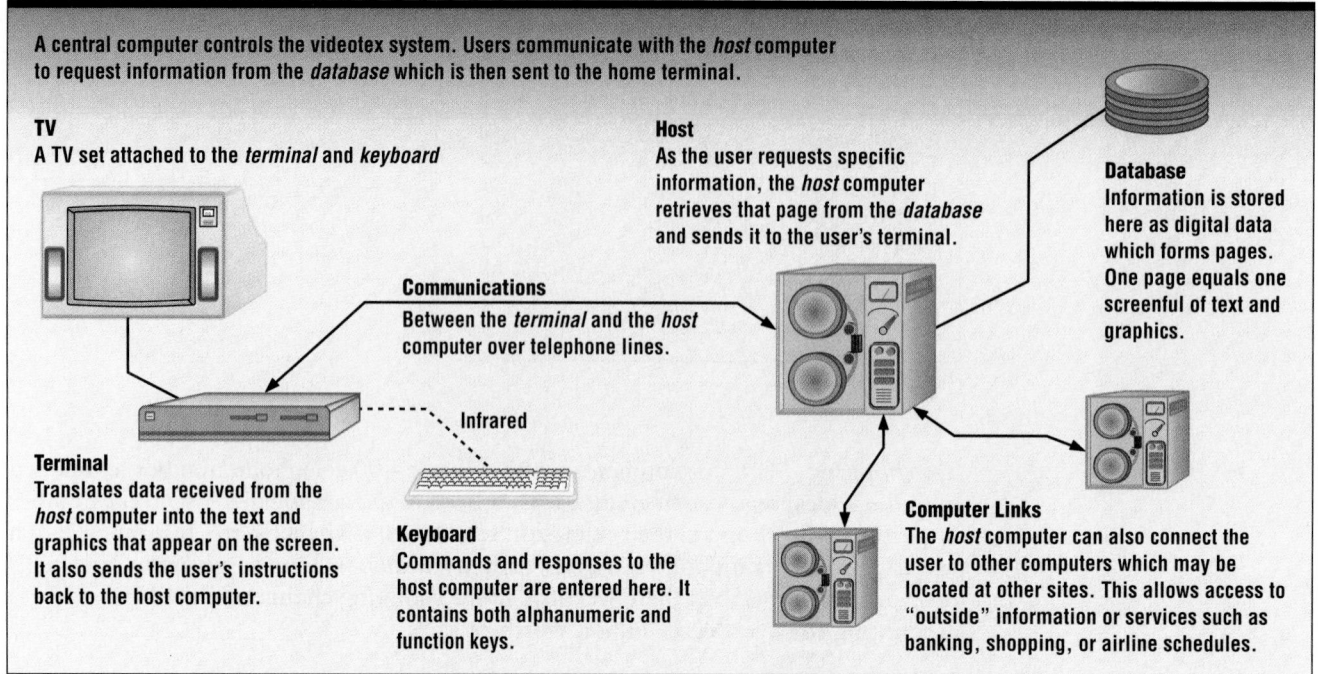

A central computer controls the videotex system. Users communicate with the *host* computer to request information from the *database* which is then sent to the home terminal.

TV
A TV set attached to the *terminal* and *keyboard*

Communications
Between the *terminal* and the *host* computer over telephone lines.

Infrared

Terminal
Translates data received from the *host* computer into the text and graphics that appear on the screen. It also sends the user's instructions back to the host computer.

Keyboard
Commands and responses to the host computer are entered here. It contains both alphanumeric and function keys.

Host
As the user requests specific information, the *host* computer retrieves that page from the *database* and sends it to the user's terminal.

Database
Information is stored here as digital data which forms pages. One page equals one screenful of text and graphics.

Computer Links
The *host* computer can also connect the user to other computers which may be located at other sites. This allows access to "outside" information or services such as banking, shopping, or airline schedules.

Note: This Times Mirror system uses the term *videotex*. However, we use the term *videotext* in the text to refer to the generic electronic teleshopping media.

media to offer an alternative shopping medium holds great potential. The visual aspects of television allow for demonstrations and product representations not available through catalogs and provide the potential consumer with much more information for decision making. The information retrieval systems offer an almost unlimited opportunity for marketers.

At the same time, as noted, the success that was expected for these media has not been achieved. A number of reasons have been hypothesized, including:

• Computers have not been adopted at the rate expected for home use.
• Many people are still not comfortable with shopping without being able to handle the merchandise; that is, they prefer to feel the material, see the colors, try on the product, and so on, and not just buy it.
• Shopping may be a form of relaxation. To many people, a day in the shopping mall or downtown is a form of entertainment. It gets them out of the house, takes their mind off work, and provides them with an opportunity to interact socially. Some people feel that since they work hard to enjoy their money, at least they can take the time to enjoy spending it!
• Consumers have preferred to get their news in the traditional manner—e.g., TV, radio, and newspapers.
• Pricing was based on the minute rather than monthly contracts, thus being less attractive to advertisers.
• Information offerings were limited.

Michael J. Major notes that many of these problems have been corrected, and projections for videotext are much more optimistic. He notes that in France, over 5.5 million videotext screens were in use (60 percent of phone subscribers), and, as a result, the future for this service appears to be more rosy.[19]

One area in which the use of videotext has been adopted, and continues to increase in use, is the *industrial sector*. In those situations where companies are bidding on government or private industry contracts that require meeting specifications, the

➤ *Exhibit 16–15*
Why marketers chose videotext

Service Providers	Marketing Objective	Reason for Participating
Sears	Reach affluent homeowners	Subscriber demographics; interactive advertising
Buffums The Broadway Robinson's	Reach affluent department store customers	Targeted advertising; new distribution channel; electronic catalog
Williams-Sonoma Crabtree & Evelyn	Reach an affluent segment accustomed to mail-order shopping	Targeted advertising, with ordering capability
Ticketron Waldenbooks	Market a product with a limited shelf life, where inspection isn't necessary for purchase	Complex ad message, with frequent updating
Hallmark	Develop an electronic version of current product	New distribution channel, offered with electronic mail
Bache	Market time-sensitive information (The Wachtel Report)	"Instant" distribution
The Grocer	Build repeat business	Ease of reordering through videotex
Computerland	Reach electronics consumers	Receptivity of videotex subscribers to electronic products

electronic media offer a distinct advantage over existing methods. For example, where specifications previously had to be mailed to prospective bidders, these specs are now available immediately through the video screen. When changes in specifications are required, which is common, they are noted almost immediately, saving valuable time and effort to all parties involved.

In sum, while the electronic media may not be the answer for all marketers, or for all shoppers, they do satisfy the needs of a particular segment of society. The commitment made by the companies offering such services, as well as the success experienced by many of those who have advertised in these media, suggests there is a bright future for advertisers in this area.

Direct Selling

One final element of the direct-marketing program involves direct selling. **Direct selling** involves the direct, personal presentation, demonstration, and sales of products and services to consumers in their homes. Avon, Amway, Mary Kay Cosmetics, and Tupperware are some of the more well-known U.S. direct-selling companies (Exhibit 16–16). Close to 5 million people engage in direct selling throughout the world; 98 percent of these are independent contractors not employees of the firm they represent). These 5 million generate approximately $12 billion in sales.[20]

The three forms of direct selling are:

1. **Repetitive person-to-person selling** The salesperson visits the buyer's home, job site, or other location to sell frequently purchased products or services (for example, Amway).
2. **Nonrepetitive person-to-person selling** The salesperson visits the buyer's home, job site, or other location to sell infrequently purchased products or services (for example, encyclopedia companies such as World Book and Encyclopedia Britannica).
3. **Party plans** The salesperson offers products or services to groups of people through home or office parties and demonstrations (for example, Tupperware and PartyLite Gifts, Inc.).

➤ *Exhibit 16–16*
Tupperware is one of the many companies using direct selling to market its products

Evaluating the Effectiveness of the Direct-Marketing Program

Because of ability to generate a direct response, measuring the effectiveness of direct-marketing programs is not difficult. Using an effectiveness measure known as **cost per order** (CPO), advertisers can evaluate the relative effectiveness of an ad in as little as eight minutes based on the number of calls generated. If the advertiser targets a $5 return per order and a broadcast commercial costs $250, the ad is considered effective if at least 50 orders are generated. Similar measures can be developed for print and direct-mail ads.

For direct-marketing programs that may not have an objective of generating a behavioral response, traditional measures of effectiveness can be applied. (We discuss these measures in Chapter 20.)

Advantages and Disadvantages of Direct Marketing

Many of the advantages of direct marketing have already been presented. A review of these and some additions follow.

1. Selective reach   Direct marketing provides the advertiser the opportunity to reach a large number of persons as well as a more effective reach through the elimination or reduction of waste coverage. With respect to the former, intensive coverage may be obtained through broadcast advertising or through the mail. While everyone may not drive on highways where there are billboards, or pay attention to TV commercials, virtually everyone receives mail. In the latter case, a good list allows for a minimal amount of waste, as only those offering the highest potential are targeted. For example, a political candidate can direct a message at a very select group of people (those living in a certain ZIP code or members of the Sierra Club), whereas compact disc companies might target recent purchasers of compact disc players.

2. Segmentation capabilities   As just mentioned, it is possible to purchase lists of recent product purchasers, bank card holders, recent automobile buyers, or a variety of others. These lists may allow segmentation on the basis of geographic area, occupation, demographics, and job titles, to mention a few. When combining this information with that of the geo-coding capabilities of PRIZM or VISION (discussed in Chapter 5), effective segmentation strategies can be developed.

3. Frequency   Depending on the medium utilized, it may be possible to build *frequency* levels. As noted, the program vehicles used for television advertising are usually some of the more inexpensive available; thus, the cost of purchasing repeat times is not prohibitive. At the same time, this may not be so easily accomplished

➤ *Figure 16–17*
An example of a high-quality direct-mail piece that attracts consumers' attention

through the mail, as an irritation factor may be associated with receiving the same mail repeatedly.

4. Flexibility   Direct marketing can take on a variety of creative forms. The direct mail piece for the Cadillac Eldorado shown in Exhibit 16–17 is an example of a very attractive and high-quality message that attracts the consumer's attention. Direct-mail pieces also allow for the possibility of detailed copy and the ability to provide a great deal of information.

5. Timing   While many media may require long-range planning and long closing dates, direct-response advertising can be much more *timely*. Direct mail, for example, can be put together very quickly and distributed to the target population. As noted earlier, the television programs typically used for direct-response advertising are older, less sought programs and, as a result, are much more likely to appear on the station's "list of available spots." In addition, a common strategy is to purchase available time at the last possible moment to get the best price.

6. Personalization   No other advertising medium can provide the ability to personalize the message as well as direct marketing—specifically direct mail. Parents with children at different age levels can be approached with their child's name included in the appeal. Automobile owners will be mailed letters directly congratulating them on their new auto purchase and offering them accessories. Recent computer purchasers will be sent software solicitations. Graduating college students receive very personalized information, some of which recognizes their specific needs and offers solutions (such as credit cards!).

7. Costs   While the CPM for direct mail may be very high on an absolute and a relative basis, one must keep in mind a previous discussion we have presented. Given the ability of direct mail to specifically target the audience and eliminate waste coverage, the actual CPMs are reduced. The cost of the ads used on television are often among the lowest available.

A second factor contributing to the cost effectiveness of direct-response advertising is the **cost per customer purchasing.** Because of the low cost of media, it is possible—in fact, necessary—to have a very low cost associated with each sale generated.

8. Measures of effectiveness   No other medium can measure the effectiveness of its advertising efforts as well as can direct-response advertisers.

Disadvantages of direct marketing include the following.

1. Image factors   As we noted at the outset of our discussion of direct marketing, the mail segment of this industry is often referred to as "junk mail." The reason for this terminology is very simple: Many people believe the unsolicited mail they receive is promoting junk, whereas others dislike the idea they are being solicited. Some companies, including Motorola, GM, and Air Products & Chemicals—senders of direct mail—say they throw out the majority of junk mail received. This problem is particularly relevant given the increased volume of mail that is being sent. (One study estimates the typical American receives 14 pieces of junk mail per week.)[21] Likewise, the advertisements on television are often low-budget ads and are often for lower-priced products. The combination of these two elements contributes to the image that something less than the best products are marketed in this way. (Note: Some of this image is being overcome by the home shopper channels, in which very expensive products are being promoted.)

2. Accuracy   One of the advantages cited earlier was that of being able to target potential customers specifically. This ability is most characteristic of direct mail and telephone marketing. The effectiveness of both of these methods is, however, directly related to the accuracy of the lists utilized. Lists must be kept current, as many people move, change occupations, and so on, and if the lists do not keep pace with these moves, the result may be a decrease in selectivity. The rapid advancement of the computerized list has greatly improved the capabilities to keep current and has reduced the incidence of bad names being included.

3. Content support   In our discussion of the objectives to be accomplished in developing a media strategy in Chapter 12, we discussed mood and content of the medium. Magazines were cited as mood creating, and it was argued that this would contribute to the overall effectiveness of the ad placed therein. In direct-response advertising, the ability to create mood is limited to broadcast and print methods (those surrounded by program and/or editorial content), with direct mail being unlikely to do so.

SUMMARY

This chapter has introduced you to the rapidly growing field of direct marketing. As you have learned (we hope!), direct marketing involves a variety of methods and media. While once thought of primarily as direct mail and telemarketing, the number of ways that direct marketing can be employed offers many different types of companies and organizations a powerful promotional and selling tool.

The growth of direct marketing continues to outpace other advertising and promotional areas, with many of the Fortune 500 companies now employing sophisticated direct marketing strategies. Data base marketing has become a critical component of many marketing programs.

Advantages of direct marketing include the ability to specifically target and reach one's market, flexibility, frequency, and timing. The ability to measure program effectiveness, costs, and personalized and custom messages are also cited as advantages of direct-marketing programs.

At the same time, a number of disadvantages are associated with the use of direct marketing. Image problems, the intrusive nature of the medium, and the proliferating sale and use of data bases have caused some marketers to be hesitant to use direct-marketing tools. However, self-policing of the industry and the increased utilization by large, sophisticated companies and organizations have led to significant changes and improvements. As a result, the use of direct marketing has increased and will continue to do so.

KEY TERMS

direct marketing
direct-marketing media
data base
one-step approach
two-step approach
mailing list

direct-response
  advertising
support advertising
infomercial
telemarketing
audiotex

tele-media
videotext
direct selling
cost per order (CPO)
cost per customer
  purchasing

DISCUSSION QUESTIONS

1. Discuss some of the factors that have contributed to the growth of direct marketing. Explain why.
2. Describe what is meant by a data base. What functions do data bases perform?
3. Bring to class some examples of direct mail you have received. Try to determine if you can tell the data base from which your name was derived.
4. Discuss the advantages and disadvantages of infomercials.
5. Discuss some of the reasons direct marketing has been receiving more attention from marketers.
6. What is the difference between the one-step and two-step approaches used in direct marketing?
7. What are some of the problems associated with direct marketing?
8. Discuss some of the reasons videotext was not adopted as rapidly as expected.
9. Name some companies that currently employ direct-selling methods. What form of direct selling do they employ?

chapter 17

Sales Promotion

chapter objectives

➢ To understand the role of sales promotion in a company's marketing and promotional program and to examine reasons for the increasing importance of sales promotion.

➢ To examine the various objectives of sales promotion programs.

➢ To examine the various types of consumer- and trade-oriented sales promotion tools and factors to consider in using them.

➢ To understand how sales promotion is coordinated with advertising.

➢ To consider potential problems and abuse by companies in their use of sales promotion.

The Times Are A-Changing

For many years, advertising was the major component in the promotional mix of most consumer product firms. Two decades ago, nearly 70 percent of marketers' promotional dollars were spent on advertising campaigns designed to create or reinforce brand awareness and image and build long-term loyalty to products. However, during the inflationary period of the late 1970s and early 1980s, a surge of interest in sales promotion began as manufacturers would raise prices to stay ahead of inflation, then offer various incentives to both consumers and retailers to keep sales perking.

To encourage consumers to keep buying their brands, marketers began using more coupons, refunds, rebates, price-off deals, and other incentives. At the same time, marketers discovered a very powerful promotional tool known as the trade allowance whereby they provided retailers with discounts, often in return for extra shelf space, an end-aisle display, or a spot on the store's roster of weekly advertised specials. The idea behind the trade allowances was that retailers would pass on the discounts to their shoppers in the form of lower prices or special deals. However, not only did retailers often fail to pass on the discounts, but many also became addicted to the trade deals and began demanding that manufacturers provide them.

Many marketers were pleased to accommodate the retailers since the trade deals seemed to move the most product through their stores. As the market for many consumer products matured and growth disappeared, brand managers came to rely on trade promotions for short-term volume gains. They would try to buy growth with promotional dollars rather than building the brand franchise and consumer loyalty. However, many companies were also beginning to discover they had little choice in the matter. The big supermarket chains would cut back on a brand's shelf space, give more facings to a competitor, or even drop a product if they did not get the kind of trade allowances they wanted.

By the mid- to late 1980s, a fundamental change had occurred in the way most consumer products companies were marketing their products. The proportion of total marketing expenditures that companies allocated to sales promotion rose sharply, while the proportion spent on media advertising declined at nearly the same rate. By 1987, nearly two thirds of consumer products companies' promotional budget was being spent on consumer and trade promotion and only one third on media advertising. By 1991, advertising's share of the promotional budget had dropped to just 25 percent while nearly half of the budget went to trade promotions and the remaining 25 percent to consumer promotions.

Over the past few years, many marketers have become concerned that they are too reliant on sales

573

(continued)

promotion. At the same time, however, market forces keep pressure on them to continue with the promotions and allocate less money to advertising. These forces include the recession, a decline in consumer brand loyalty, and consumers' weariness of the constant barrage of media advertising.

The recession has made consumers more price and deal sensitive while making it more difficult for marketers to meet financial goals. Many product managers are scrambling to increase quarterly sales rather than investing in image advertising and building brand equity. They believe advertising takes too long to show any results and its effect is too difficult to measure. Thus, they continue to shift their marketing dollars from media advertising into consumer promotions such as coupons, contests, or sweepstakes. Even when they do advertise, marketers often build some type of promotional component into their ads such as a contest or sweepstakes.

Many marketing people would like to see a return to the good old days where media advertising was king and

consumers developed strong loyalties to heavily and cleverly advertised products and services. A number of companies are growing tired of being "held hostage" by retailers and are showing more interest in moving their money back toward the consumer. For example, Edwin Artzt, chairman of Procter & Gamble, noted, "Advertising is a longer-term investment, and it shouldn't be intruded upon by short-term needs." P&G, the leading advertiser in the world, is steering more of its marketing budgets into advertising.

It will be interesting to see if marketers try to shift the marketing pendulum in the direction of advertising or continue to pursue the short-term sales jumps that sales promotions can deliver and retailers have been demanding. For now, most marketing people realize sales promotion is here to stay and they had better learn to play by the new rules if they want to compete.

Source: Daniel M. Gold, "A Shift in Direction," Adweek's Marketing Week, *April 13, 1992; and Jennifer Lawrence, "P&G's Artzt on Ads: Crucial Investment,"* Advertising Age, *October 28, 1991, pp. 1, 53.*

arketers have come to recognize that advertising alone is often not enough to move their products off store shelves and into the hands of consumers. Companies are increasingly turning to sales promotion methods targeted at both consumers and the wholesalers and retailers that distribute their products as a way of stimulating demand for them. More and more companies are developing fully integrated marketing communication programs that include consumer and trade promotions that are coordinated with advertising, direct marketing, and publicity/public relations campaigns as well as sales force efforts.

This chapter focuses on sales promotion and its role in a firm's integrated marketing communications program. We examine how marketers use both consumer- and trade-oriented promotions to influence the purchase behavior of consumers as well as wholesalers and retailers. We explore the objectives of sales promotion programs as well as the various types of sales promotion tools that can be used at both the consumer and trade level. We also consider how sales promotion can be integrated with other elements of the promotional mix as well as problems that have arisen from marketers becoming overly dependent on the use of consumer and trade promotions, particularly the latter.

The Scope and Role of Sales Promotion

Sales promotion has been defined as "a direct inducement that offers an extra value or incentive for the product to the sales force, distributors or the ultimate consumer with the primary objective of creating an immediate sale."[1] Several important aspects of sales promotion should be kept in mind as you read this chapter.

First, sales promotion involves some type of inducement that provides an *extra incentive* to buy. This incentive is usually the key element in a promotional program and can include a coupon or price reduction, the opportunity to enter a contest or sweepstakes, a money-back refund or rebate, or an extra amount of a product. The incentive may also be a free sample of the product, which is given in hopes of generating a future purchase, or a premium, which also serves as a reminder of the brand name and reinforces its image, such as the Kix T-shirt offer (Exhibit 17–1). Most sales promotion offers attempt to add some value to the product or service. While advertising appeals to the consumer's mind and emotions in hopes of giving

➢ *Exhibit 17–1*

Kix uses a T-shirt offer as a premium incentive

➢ *Exhibit 17–2*

Coupons with expiration dates attempt to accelerate the purchase process

the individual a reason to buy, sales promotion appeals more to the pocketbook and provides an extra incentive for purchasing a brand.

Sales promotion can also be used to provide an inducement to marketing intermediaries such as wholesalers and retailers. A trade allowance or discount provides retailers with a financial incentive to stock and promote a manufacturer's products. A trade contest may be directed toward wholesalers or retail personnel to give them extra incentive to perform certain tasks or meet sales goals.

A second point regarding sales promotion is that it is essentially an *acceleration tool* that is designed to speed up the selling process and is often used to maximize sales volume.[2] By providing an extra incentive, sales promotion techniques can motivate consumers to purchase a larger quantity of a brand or shorten the purchase cycle of the trade or consumers by encouraging them to take more immediate action.

Companies may also use limited time offers such as price-off deals to retailers or a coupon with an expiration date (Exhibit 17–2) to accelerate the purchase process. Offering coupons with expiration dates can also help manufacturers control the financial liability better than offering coupons without expiration dates. Sales promotion attempts to maximize sales volume be motivating customers who have not been responsive to advertising or other efforts to purchase a brand. The ideal sales promotion program is one that generates sales that would not otherwise be achieved by other means such as advertising. However, as we shall see later, many sales promotion programs end up being used more by current users of a brand rather than attracting new users.

A final point regarding sales promotion activities is that they can be targeted to different parties in the marketing channel. As shown in Exhibit 17–3, sales promotion can be broken into two major categories: consumer-oriented promotions and trade-oriented promotions. The various activities involved in **consumer-oriented sales promotion** includes couponing, sampling, premiums, bonus packs, price-offs, rebates, contests, sweepstakes, and event sponsorship. These promotions are directed at the consumers who purchase goods and services and are designed to provide them with an inducement to purchase the marketer's brand.

As was discussed in Chapter 2, consumer-oriented promotions are part of a promotional "pull strategy" and work along with advertising to encourage consumers to purchase a particular brand and thus create demand for it. Consumer-oriented promotions can also be used by retailers to encourage consumers to shop in their particular stores. For example, many grocery stores use their own coupons or sponsor contests and other promotions to increase store patronage.

Trade-oriented sales promotion includes activities such as promotional allowances, dealer contests and incentives, point-of-purchase displays, cooperative advertising, trade shows, and other programs designed to motivate distributors and retailers to carry a product and make an extra effort to promote or "push" it to their customers. Nearly 70 percent of all sales promotional dollars are spent on trade promotions, with the remaining 30 percent going to consumer-oriented promotions. Many marketing programs include both trade- and consumer-oriented sales promotion programs, as it is important to stimulate both groups to maximize the effectiveness of the marketing and promotional program.

> *Exhibit 17–3*
Types of sales promotion activities

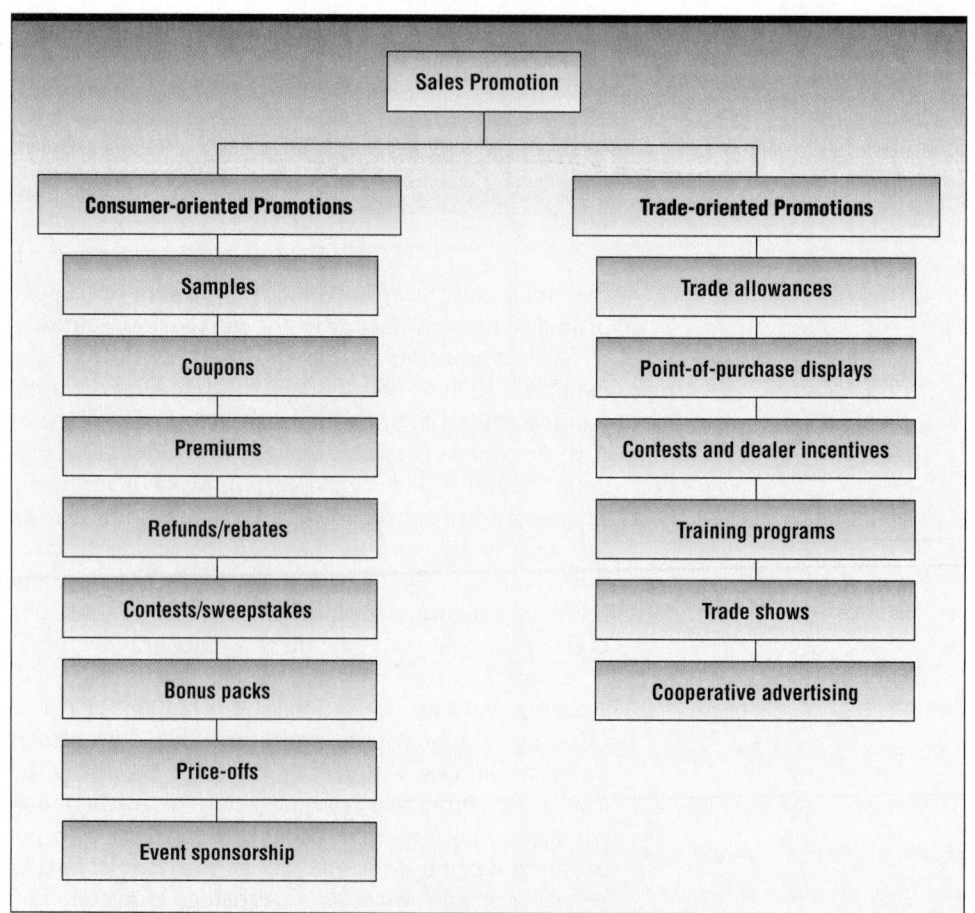

The Growth of Sales Promotion

While sales promotion has been around for a long time, its role and importance in manufacturers' marketing programs have increased dramatically. Total estimated expenditures on sales promotion increased at an average rate of 13 percent during the 1980s, increasing from $49 billion in 1980 to more than $140 billion in 1991. During this same period, spending on national advertising increased at a slower rate, particularly during the past three years.[3]

Not only has the total amount of money spent on sales promotion increased, but the percentage of marketers' budgets allocated to promotion has also risen dramatically. Annual studies by Donnelley Marketing track the marketing spending of major package-goods companies in three categories: trade promotion, consumer promotion, and media advertising. Exhibit 17–4 shows the long-term trend of allocations to each of these three categories. As can be seen in this exhibit, the percentage of the marketing budget spent on consumer promotions has held steady over the past decade while the allocation to trade promotions has increased dramatically.

Particularly noteworthy is the shift in marketing dollars from media advertising to trade promotion. In 1991, the marketers surveyed by Donnelley spent nearly half of their marketing budgets on promotional programs targeted to the trade. This increase in trade promotion has come almost totally at the expense of media advertising. In the most recent Donnelley survey, marketers indicated they expected trade spending to decline somewhat in the future with corresponding increases in consumer promotions and media advertising.[4] However, many marketing people believe it will be difficult to reverse the flow of marketing dollars to the trade for some of the reasons discussed below.

Reasons for the Shift in Marketing Dollars to Sales Promotion

In the opening to this chapter, we examined some developments that have led to the increased emphasis on sales promotion and the decline in media advertising. Given the magnitude of the shift in the way marketers allocate their marketing budgets, it is important to understand the factors that underlie these changes.

➤ *Exhibit 17–4*
Long-term allocations to trade promotion, advertising, and consumer promotion

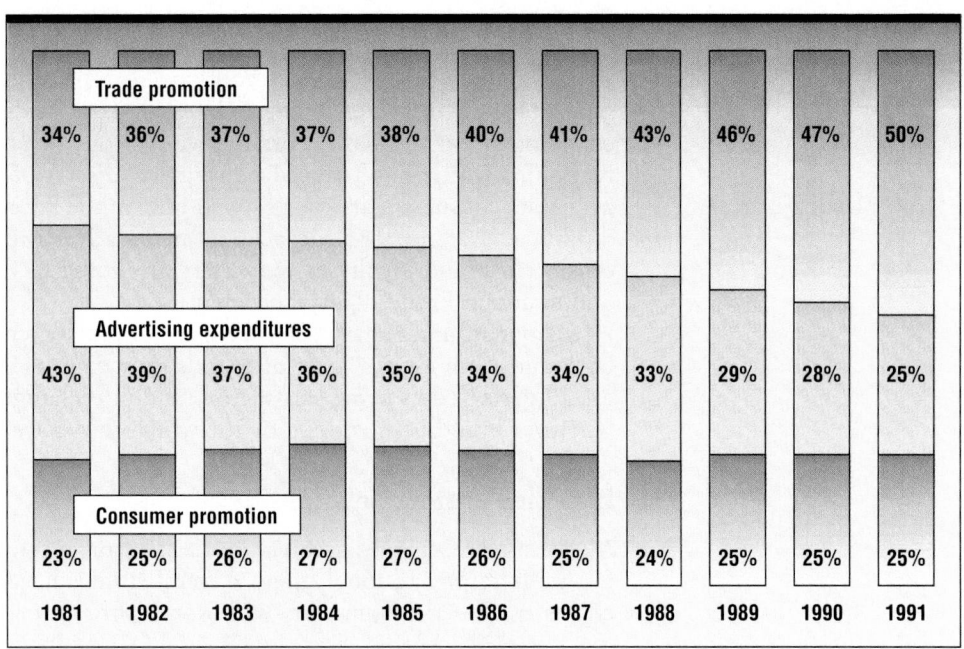

	1981	1982	1983	1984	1985	1986	1987	1988	1989	1990	1991
Trade promotion	34%	36%	37%	37%	38%	40%	41%	43%	46%	47%	50%
Advertising expenditures	43%	39%	37%	36%	35%	34%	34%	33%	29%	28%	25%
Consumer promotion	23%	25%	26%	27%	27%	26%	25%	24%	25%	25%	25%

The growing power of retailers

One reason for the increase in sales promotion is the power shift in the marketplace from manufacturers to retailers. For many years, manufacturers of national brands had the power and influence, and retailers were just passive distributors of their products. Consumer products manufacturers created consumer demand for their brands by using heavy advertising and some consumer-oriented promotions, such as samples, coupons, and premiums, and they could exert pressure on retailers to carry the products. Moreover, retailers did very little research and sales analysis; they relied on manufacturers to provide them with information regarding the sales performance of individual brands.

In recent years, however, several developments have resulted in power transferring from the manufacturers to the retailers. With the advent of optical checkout scanners and computers, retailers gained access to data concerning how quickly products turn over, which sales promotions are working, and which products make money. Retailers use this information to analyze sales of manufacturers' products and have been demanding discounts and other types of promotional support from manufacturers of lagging brands. Companies that fail to comply with retailers' demands for more trade support often face reductions in shelf space or even having their product dropped.

Another factor that has contributed to the increased power of retailers is the consolidation of the grocery store industry, which has resulted in larger chains with greater buying power and clout. As was noted in the chapter opening, these large chains have become accustomed to trade promotions and can use their power to pressure manufacturers to provide deals, discounts, and allowances.

The more powerful and sophisticated retailers are demanding greater sales and profit performance from manufacturers' brands and now have the ability to determine if they are getting it. This has led many companies to turn to trade promotions to generate sales for their brands and/or offer more attractive deals to retailers. However, since companies have only so much money available for marketing communications, the increases in trade promotion have come at the expense of advertising.

Declining brand loyalty

Another major reason for the increase in sales promotion is that consumers have become less brand loyal in recent years and are purchasing more on the basis of price, value, and convenience. You may recall from Chapter 4 (Exhibit 4–21), the percentage of consumers who are brand loyal is under 50 percent for most product categories.[5] The decrease in brand loyalty is due to a number of factors including the recession, which has reduced consumers' discretionary income. With less money available, consumers are more apt to buy on the basis of price rather than loyalty to a particular brand. The cutbacks in media advertising have also contributed to the erosion in brand loyalty as marketers are doing less to differentiate their products and maintain brand equity and image.

Many consumers have also become "brand switchers" and are willing to switch back and forth among a set of brands they view as essentially equal. These brands are all perceived as being satisfactory and interchangeable, and consumers purchase whatever brand is on special or for which they have a coupon.

Increased promotional sensitivity

Marketers are making greater use of sales promotion because consumers respond favorably to promotional offers. Several studies have shown the percentage of purchases made in conjunction with some sort of promotional offer has increased sharply over the past decade.[6] One recent study found consumers indicating 54 percent of their purchases were made under some promotional inducement, with price promotions, coupons, and point-of-purchase displays being the most important.[7] A recent national survey of 7,500 households found that over 90 percent of consumers had taken advantage of some form of promotion in the past month. Coupons were particularly popular among consumers and seen as a way of getting greater value.[8]

An obvious reason for consumers' increased sensitivity to sales promotion offers is that they are a way to save money. Another reason is that many purchase decisions are made in the store by consumers who are price sensitive, increasingly time poor, and facing "hyperchoice," or too many choices.[9] Annual studies conducted by the Roper Organization have shown that the percentage of consumers who know what brand they want to buy and plan on purchasing when they enter a store declined from 56 percent in 1988 to 46 percent by mid-1991.[10] When consumers make purchase decisions in the store, they are very likely to be attentive and responsive to promotional deals. Buying a brand that is on special or being displayed can also simplify the decision-making process and deal with the problem of overchoice. Professor Leigh McAlister has described this process quite well:

> As consumers go down the supermarket aisle they spend 3 to 10 seconds in each product category. They often don't know the regular price of the chosen product. However, they do have a sense of whether or not that product is on promotion. As they go down the aisle, they are trying to pensively fill their baskets with good products without tiresome calculations. They see a "good deal" and it goes in the cart.[11]

The net effect of declining loyalty and increasing promotional sensitivity is that marketers are finding it increasingly necessary to use sales promotion techniques to attract and maintain customers. In many product categories, promotions are becoming very common, which encourages increasingly sophisticated and price-sensitive consumers to use them.

Brand proliferation

A major aspect of many firms' marketing strategies over the past decade has been the development of new products. Over 10,000 new products were introduced to the marketplace in 1991, as compared with only 2,689 in 1980. The market has become saturated with new brands that often lack any significant advantages that can be used as the basis of an advertising campaign. Thus, companies have become increasingly dependent on sales promotion to encourage consumers to try these brands. In Chapter 4, we saw how sales promotion techniques can be used as part of the "shaping process" to lead the consumer from initial trial to repeat purchase at full price. Marketers are relying more on promotional tools such as samples, coupons, rebates, premiums, and other innovative promotions to achieve trial usage of their new brands and to encourage repeat purchase.

Promotions are also important in getting retailers to allocate some of their precious shelf space to new brands. The competition for shelf space allocation for new products in supermarkets and other stores is enormous. Retailers are more open to new brands with strong sales promotion support that will bring in more customers and thus help boost their sales and profits.[12] Many retailers require manufacturers to provide them with special discounts or allowances just to get them to handle a new product. These *slotting fees or allowances,* which are discussed later in the chapter, can make it expensive for a manufacturer to introduce a new product. Global Perspective 17–1 discusses how slotting fees and other factors are leading some companies to launch new products in foreign countries before bringing them to the United States.

Global Perspective 17–1

Testing Products in Foreign Markets

The introduction of new products is a very important part of the marketing strategy of most consumer products companies. New products are the primary source of growth for many companies and often account for a substantial amount of their profits. However, a number of factors are making it very difficult to launch new products in the U.S. market. One major problem is that too many products are already clogging retailers' shelves. Over the past seven years, shelf space in supermarkets has grown 2.5 percent a year while the number of new products stocked has grown 7.4 percent. More than 10,000 new products hit the supermarket shelves in 1991 alone.

The increasing demand for a limited amount of shelf space has also made it very expensive for manufacturers to launch new products. Most supermarkets now require manufacturers to pay "slotting fees" to stock their products, and it can cost a company as much as $9 million just to get a product on the shelves nationally. Once a new product hits the store shelves, it can soak up millions more in advertising and promotional support to compete against entrenched brands or other new products.

The high costs of entering the U.S. market may not be a problem for large companies such as Procter & Gamble, Colgate, or Kraft General Foods. However, they can be prohibitive to smaller companies that lack the money to pay the exorbitant slotting fees and promotional expenses required to launch a new product. To get around this problem, some companies are launching their new products in foreign countries to test consumer reaction and to generate cash that can be used to enter the U.S. market.

Several smaller companies have used foreign countries as their test markets. For example, Carewell Industries recognized it could not afford the slotting fees required by U.S. supermarket chains and decided to launch its new flexible Dentax toothbrush in several Asian and European countries. Stores in Malta, Greece, and Malaysia-Singapore were happy to take the product because American brands have a very strong appeal in Asian and underdeveloped European markets. The company recorded approximately $4 million in sales in 1991, which it is using to invest in U.S. distribution.

Nice-Pak Products launched its Pudgies baby wipes in the United Kingdom two years ago to refine its marketing plans in a controlled market. The firm's vice president of marketing noted it was easier to launch a new product in the United Kingdom than doing even a regional launch in the United States as securing distribution in three supermarket chains provides access to

Pudgies were test marketed in the United Kingdom before entering the U.S. market

nearly 70 percent of the market. To launch Pudgies in the United Kingdom, Nice-Pak relied primarily on sampling to induce product trial. Pudgies samples were wrapped in maternity magazines offered in doctors' offices.

Nice-Pak learned several other things in the U.K. test launch regarding packaging that is helping it enter the United States. Consumers reacted very favorably to the bright yellow container featuring a bouncing baby bear on the label. Also, consumers in the United Kingdom are sensitive to environmental issues, which led Nice-Pak to develop a refill package that allows consumers to keep refilling the same container. The refill packaging was a major factor in Wal-Mart's decision to stock the new brand.

The global marketplace is becoming a very familiar venue even for small companies. Some marketing experts expect that more small and medium-sized companies will launch their product overseas before trying to enter the United States, which still has the most lucrative consumer market in the world. Foreign countries could become the out-of-town test market of the future as marketers may want to see "if it will play in Greece or Singapore" as well as in Peoria.

Source: David Kiley, "America's New Test Market? Singapore," *Adweek's Marketing Week*, February 4, 1991, p. 22; and "Why New Is Old Hat," *Forbes*, July 22, 1991, pp. 302–3.

Fragmentation of the consumer market

Many companies are finding that the consumer market has become increasingly fragmented and difficult to market to. A myriad of media options are available to consumers, with the growth of cable television, radio, and special-interest magazines making it difficult to find efficiencies in mass media. As traditional mass media-based strategies such as advertising become less effective, marketers are turning to more

➢ *Exhibit 17–5*
Many promotions are targeted to a local market

segmented, highly targeted approaches. For example, with the increasing focus on regional marketing, more major companies are tailoring their promotional efforts to specific geographic markets and even to certain retail chains.[13] Sales promotion tools have become one of the primary vehicles for doing this through programs tied into local flavor, themes, or events. For example, Burger King spends nearly half of its advertising budget on local tie-ins and promotions designed to build traffic in its restaurants. Pizza Hut also runs a number of local promotions (Exhibit 17–5).

Marketers are also shifting more of their promotional efforts to direct marketing, which often includes some form of sales promotion incentive such as a coupon or premium offer. Many marketers use information they get from sources such as premium offers and sweepstakes to build data bases that can be used for future direct-marketing efforts. The Donnelley Survey of Promotional Practices found that nearly two thirds of package-goods companies are building consumer data bases or have plans to do so.[14] Exhibit 17–6 shows the percentage of companies using various sales promotion tools to help build a consumer data base. As marketers continue to shift from media advertising to direct marketing, it is likely that promotional offers will be used.

Short-term focus

Many businesspeople believe the increase in sales promotion is motivated by marketing plans and reward systems geared to short-term performance and focus on the immediate generation of sales volume.[15] Some think the package-goods brand management system has contributed to marketers' increased dependence on sales promotion. Brand managers use sales promotions routinely, not only as a way of introducing new products or defending against the competition, but also to meet quarterly or yearly sales and market share goals. Brand managers are not the only individuals who champion the use of sales promotion. The sales force may have short-term quotas or goals to meet and also may receive requests from retailers and wholesalers for promotions. Thus, they may pressure marketing or brand managers to use promotions to help them move the products into the retailers' stores.

Consumer and trade promotions are viewed by many managers as the most dependable way of generating short-term sales, particularly when they are price related. The reliance on sales promotion is particularly high in mature and slow-growth markets where it is even more difficult to stimulate consumer demand

> *Exhibit 17–6*
Consumer data base sources

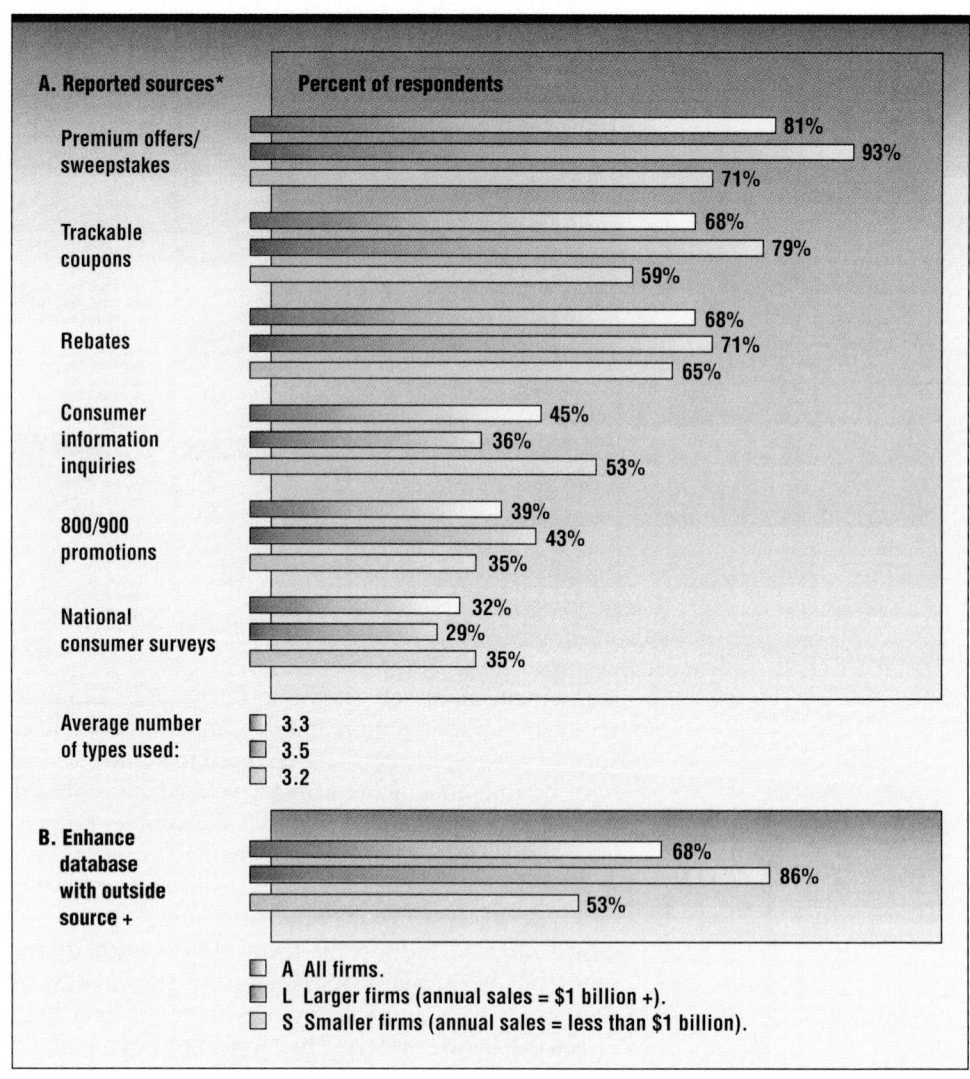

* Of those respondents who are building or plan to build a consumer database within the next 12 months.

through advertising. This has led to considerable concern that managers have become too dependent on the "quick sales fix" that can result from a promotion and the brand franchise may be eroded by too many deals.

Increased accountability

In addition to pressuring their marketing or brand managers and sales force to produce short-term results, many companies are demanding to know what they are getting from their promotional expenditures. Many companies have shifted their promotional dollars from advertising to sales promotion because of an increasing emphasis on economic accountability. In companies struggling to meet their sales and financial goals, top management is demanding more measurable and accountable methods of relating promotional expenditures to sales and profitability. For example, Philip Morris's Kraft General Foods unit and other companies have begun using computerized sales information from checkout scanners in determining compensation for marketing personnel. Part of the pay managers receive depends on the sales a promotion generates relative to its costs.[16]

Managers who are being held accountable to produce results often prefer to use price discounts or coupons since they are more likely to produce a quick and easily measured jump in sales. They often prefer some type of promotion over advertising since it takes longer for an ad campaign to show some impact and the effects are more difficult to measure. Also, as was noted earlier, marketers are also feeling pressure from the trade as powerful retailers are demanding performance from manufacturers' brands and are using their scanner technology to determine which products are moving off of their shelves.

Competition

Another factor that led to the increase in sales promotion is the manufacturers' reliance on trade and consumer promotions to gain or maintain competitive advantage. The markets for many products are mature and have become stagnant. Marketers have found it increasingly difficult to affect sales through advertising. Exciting, breakthrough creative ideas are difficult to come by, and consumers' attention to mass media advertising continues to decline. Rather than allocating large amounts of money to media budgets to run dull ads, many marketers have turned to sales promotion.

Many companies are tailoring their trade promotions to key retail accounts and developing strategic alliances with retailers that include both trade and consumer promotional programs. However, retailers may use a promotional deal made with one company as leverage to seek an equal or better deal with its competitors. Consumer and trade promotions are easily matched by competitors, and many marketers find themselves in a "promotional trap" whereby they have little choice but to continue using them or be at a competitive disadvantage. We discuss this problem in more detail later in the chapter.

Clutter

The increasing problem of advertising clutter has led many advertisers to turn to consumer promotions to attract consumers' attention and interest to their ads. The use of a promotional offer in an ad often attracts the interest of consumers and thus may be a useful way of breaking through the clutter that is prevalent in most media today. A premium offer may help attract attention to an ad as will a contest or sweepstakes (Exhibit 17–7). Some studies have shown that ad readership scores are higher for print advertisements with coupons than for ads without them.[17] However, more recent studies by Starch INRA Hooper, Inc., have found that magazine ads with coupons do not generate higher readership than those without coupons.[18]

Concerns over the Increased Role of Sales Promotion

A number of factors have contributed to the increased use of sales promotion by consumer product manufacturers. However, many marketing and advertising executives are very concerned over this shift in the allocation of the promotional budget and how it affects *brand equity*. As was noted in Chapter 1, brand equity can be thought of as a type of intangible asset of added value or "goodwill" that results from the favorable image, impressions of differentiation, and/or strength of attachment a consumer has to a brand. Another term often used synonymously with brand equity is *consumer franchise*.

Some critics argue that the sales promotion increases are coming at the expense of brand equity as every dollar that goes into promotion rather than advertising devalues the brand.[19] They point out that trade promotions in particular are contributing to the destruction of brand franchises and equity as they encourage consumers to purchase primarily on the basis of price. Studies conducted by advertising agency DDB Needham Worldwide show that the percentage of consumers who say they purchase well-known brands has declined from 77 percent in 1975 to 62 percent in 1990.[20]

Proponents of advertising argue that marketers must maintain strong brand franchises if they want to be able to differentiate and charge a premium price for them.

➤ *Exhibit 17–7*
Promotional offers can help attract attention to an ad

They argue that advertising is still the most effective way of building the long-term franchise of a brand as it informs consumers of a brand's features and benefits, creates images, and helps build and maintain brand loyalty. However, many marketers are not investing in their brands as they take monies away from media advertising to fund short-term promotions. If this trend continues, there is concern that brands will lose the equity that advertising helped create and be forced to compete primarily on the basis of price.

Many of the concerns raised over the increase in sales promotion are justified. However, not all sales promotion activities detract from the value or equity of a brand. It is important to distinguish between consumer-franchise-building and nonfranchise-building sales promotions.

Consumer-Franchise-Building and Nonfranchise-Building Promotions

Sales promotion activities that are effective in communicating distinctive brand attributes and that contribute to the development and reinforcement of brand identity are often referred to as **consumer-franchise-building (CFB) promotions.**[21] Consumer sales promotion efforts cannot make consumers loyal to a brand that is of little value or that does not provide them with a specific benefit. However, some promotional activities can help make consumers aware of a brand and, by communicating its specific features and benefits, contribute to the development of a favorable brand image. Consumer-franchise-building promotions are designed to build long-term brand preference and help the company achieve the ultimate goal of full-price purchases that are not dependent on a promotional offer.

For many years, franchise or image building was viewed as the exclusive realm of advertising, whereas the role of sales promotion was viewed as generating short-term sales increases. However, many marketers have recognized the image building potential of sales promotion and are paying attention to the CFB value of their

promotional programs. One sales promotion expert describes the acceptance of the image-building potential of sales promotion as follows:

> Today's marketers who appreciate the potential of sales promotion as an ongoing strategy that works to build a brand's franchise recognize that promotion's potential goes well beyond mere quick-fix, price-off tactics. The promotion professional is familiar with a variety of approaches to generating consumer involvement—i.e., sweepstakes, special events, premiums, or rebates—and understands that the given campaign must work in harmony with long-term goals and brand positioning.[22]

Companies can use sales promotion techniques in a number of ways to contribute to their franchise-building efforts. Rather than using a "one-time offer," many companies are developing promotional programs that encourage repeat purchases and long-term patronage. For example, many credit cards have developed promotional programs where consumers earn bonus points every time they use their card to charge a purchase. These points can then be redeemed for various items. Most airlines, as well as many hotel chains, have developed frequent flyer or guest programs to encourage loyalty and repeat patronage.

An example of a successful consumer-franchise-building promotion is the "Bone China Sweepstakes" for Palmolive dishwashing liquid and liquid dishwasher detergent shown in Exhibit 17–8. For many consumers, an important factor in choosing a dishwashing product is that it does not harm or damage dishes. The "Trust Your Best with Our Best" association with expensive Royal Doulton bone china helps to position the Palmolive products as being gentle enough to use on even the most expensive dishes. Colgate-Palmolive has run this successful promotion for several years.

Nonfranchise-building promotions are designed to accelerate the purchase decision process and generate an immediate increase in sales. These activities do little or nothing to communicate information about a brand's unique features or the benefits of using it and thus contribute very little to the building of brand identity and image. Price-off deals, bonus packs, and rebates or refunds are examples of non-FB sales promotion techniques. Trade promotions receive the most criticism for being non-franchise building and for good reason. First, many of the promotional discounts and allowances given to the trade are never passed on to consumers, thus they do nothing to contribute to the brand franchise. Moreover, most trade promotions that are forwarded through the channels reach the consumers in the form of lower prices or special deals and lead consumers to buy on the basis of price rather than brand equity.

Many specialists in the promotional area have stressed the need for marketers to use sales promotion tools as a franchise builder and to create long-term continuity in their promotional programs.[23] Whereas non-FB promotions merely borrow customers from other brands, well-planned CFB activities can convert consumers to loyal customers. Short-term non-FB promotions have their place in a firm's promotional mix, particularly when competitive developments warrant such activities. However, the limitations of non-FB activities must be recognized in the development of a long-term marketing strategy for a brand.

Consumer-Oriented Sales Promotion

In this section, we examine the various sales promotion tools and techniques a marketer can use to influence consumers. We study the various consumer-oriented promotions shown in Exhibit 17–3 and discuss their advantages and limitations as well as issues that must be considered in using them. However, before examining the different types of consumer-oriented promotions, we consider some objectives marketers have for sales promotion programs targeted to the consumer market.

Objectives for Consumer-Oriented Sales Promotion

As the use of sales promotion techniques continues to increase, companies must consider what they hope to accomplish through their consumer promotions and how they interact with other promotional activities such as advertising, direct marketing, or personal selling. As noted earlier, marketers often implement sales promotion programs to gain short-term sales increases with little attention given to the long-term cumulative effect promotions may have on the brand's image and position in the marketplace. This often leads to ill-conceived promotions that do little more than create short-term spikes in the sales curve.

Not all sales promotion activities are designed to achieve the same objectives. As with any promotional mix element, marketers must plan the use of consumer promotions by conducting a situation analysis and determining the specific role sales promotion will have in the integrated marketing communications program. Attention must be given to what the promotion is designed to accomplish and to whom it should be targeted. By having clearly defined objectives and measurable goals for their sales promotion programs, managers are forced to think beyond the short-term sales fix (although this can be and often is a goal).

While the basic goal of most consumer-oriented sales promotion programs is to induce purchase of a brand, the marketer might have a number of different objectives for both new and established brands. Some of the specific objectives for consumer-oriented sales promotion programs are examined below.

Obtaining trial and repurchase

One of the most important uses of sales promotion techniques is to encourage consumers to try a new product or service. While thousands of new products are introduced to the market every year, as many as 90 percent of them fail within the first year. Many of these failures are due to the fact that the new product or brand lacks the promotional support needed either to encourage initial trial by a sufficient number of consumers or to induce enough of those trying the brand to repurchase it.

Many new brands are merely new versions of an existing product and usually do not offer benefits that are so unique that advertising alone can induce trial. Sales promotion tools have become an important part of new brand introduction strategies, as the level of initial trial can be increased through the use of techniques such as sampling, couponing, and refund offers.

The success of a new brand depends not only on getting initial trial but also on inducing a reasonable percentage of those who try the brand to repurchase it and establish ongoing purchase patterns. Promotional incentives such as coupons or refund offers are often included with a sample to encourage repeat purchase after trial. For example, when Lever Brothers introduced its new Lever 2000 brand of bar soap, millions of free samples were distributed along with a 75-cent coupon. The samples allowed consumers to try the new soap, while the coupon provided an incentive to purchase it.

Increasing consumption of an established brand

While sales promotion is very important in the introduction of a new product or brand, many marketing managers are responsible for established brands competing in mature markets, against established competitors, and where consumer purchase patterns are often well set. Awareness of an established brand is generally high as a result of cumulative advertising effects, and many consumers may have tried the brand at one time. These factors can create a very challenging situation for the brand manager who hopes to increase sales of the product or defend its market share against a competitor. Sales promotion can be an effective way to generate some new interest in or excitement for an established brand or to help increase sales or to defend market share against competitive threats.

Marketers can attempt to increase sales for an established brand in several ways, and sales promotion can play an important role in each. One way of increasing product consumption is by identifying new or additional uses for the brand. Sales promotion techniques such as providing recipe books or calendars that show various ways of using the product are often used to accomplish this. One of the best examples of a brand that has found new or extended uses is Arm & Hammer baking soda. Exhibit 17–9a shows a clever promotion for the brand that was timed to coincide with the change to daylight-saving time.

Another strategy for increasing sales of an established brand is to use promotions that attract nonusers of the product category or users of a competitive brand. Attracting nonusers of the product category can be very difficult, as consumers may not see a need for the product or have an interest in using it. However, sales promotions can be designed to appeal to nonusers. For example, the Toro Company developed a very successful promotion called "Snow Insurance" to attract consumers who questioned whether they might have a need for a snow thrower because of the mild winters experienced by many areas of the country a few years ago.

Toro's sales promotion agency developed a "S'no Risk®" program whereby Toro offered a refund of from 50 percent to 100 percent of the purchase price if snowfalls were 20 percent to 50 percent less than the average for a given community (Exhibit 17–9b). Toro underwrote the program through an insurance policy with premiums based on the number of sales. The promotion ran from June until December, and by December 10, sales exceeded season projections by 20 percent and promotion projections by 30 percent.[24]

A more common strategy for increasing sales of an established brand is to attract consumers who use a competitive brand. This can be done by providing users of a competitive brand with an incentive to switch such as a coupon, premium offer, bonus pack, or price deal. Promotions can also be used to get users of a competitive brand to try another brand through sampling or other types of promotional programs.

One of the most successful promotions ever used for attracting users of a competitive brand was the "Pepsi Challenge." In this campaign, Pepsi took on its archrival, industry leader Coca-Cola, in a hard-hitting comparative promotion that

> *Exhibit 17—9*

A. Arm & Hammer used this promotion to show another use for the product

B. Toro's S'no Risk ® promotion helped attract new users

challenged consumers to taste the two brands in blind taste tests (Exhibit 17—10). The Pepsi Challenge promotion included national and local advertising, couponing, and trade support as part of a fully integrated promotional program. The campaign was used for several years and was considered instrumental in helping Pepsi move ahead of Coke and become the market share leader in supermarket sales. As a result of the campaign, Coke launched a variety of counterattacks including the controversial decision to change its formula and launch New Coke in 1986.

Defending current customers

With more new brands entering the market every day and competitors attempting to take away their customers through aggressive advertising and sales promotion efforts, many companies are turning to sales promotion programs to hold present customers and defend their market share. A company can use sales promotion techniques in several ways to retain its current customer base. One way is to "load" them with the product and thus take them out of the market for a certain time. Special price promotions, coupons, or bonus packs can be used to encourage the consumer to stock up on the brand. This not only keeps consumers using the company's brand but also reduces the likelihood they would switch brands in response to a competitor's promotion.

Enhancing advertising and marketing efforts

A final objective for consumer trade promotions is to enhance or support the advertising and marketing effort for the brand. Sales promotion techniques such as

➤ *Exhibit 17–10* **The Pepsi Challenge was a very successful promotion**

ANNCR: All across America people are taking the Pepsi Challenge. In California here's what they are saying.

TRACY KUERBIS: Pepsi really is the better drink.

DAVE JOHNSON: I've proven to myself now that I like Pepsi better.

ANNCR: Nationwide

more people prefer the taste of Pepsi over Coca-Cola.

CHERIE BOOTH: I think today's test was very honest.

DAVE: Pepsi has a better product and that's probably why they are running a test like this because it's obvious how many people over here have picked Pepsi.

SUZANNE MACK: Being able to compare the two, I'd pick Pepsi.

CHERIE: If somone offered me either or, I choose the Pepsi.

ANNCR: What will you say? Take the Pepsi Challenge and find out.

contests or sweepstakes are often used to help draw attention to an ad and increase the consumer's level of interest or involvement with the message and the product. Sales promotion programs also can help encourage retailers to stock, display, and promote a brand during the promotional period. Cooperation from the trade is important to the success of a promotional program.

Consumer-Oriented Sales Promotion Techniques

In this section, we examine the various sales promotional techniques used by marketers and the role they play in meeting the various objectives discussed above. Exhibit 17–11 shows the extent to which these various consumer promotions are used by the largest as well as by the smaller package-goods companies. The Donnelley Marketing Survey of Promotional Practices found that on average the largest package-goods firms use 8.1 of the 10 types of promotions, whereas the smaller firms use 6.3.[25]

Sampling

Sampling involves a variety of procedures whereby consumers are given some quantity of a product for no charge to induce trial. Sampling is generally considered to be the most effective way of generating trial, although it is also the most expensive. As a sales promotion technique, sampling is often used to introduce a new product or brand to the market. However, as can be seen in Exhibit 17–11, sampling is also used for established products—particularly by large companies. Some companies do not use sampling for established products since samples may be ineffective in inducing a satisfied user of a competitive brand to switch and may result in giving the product away to the firm's current customers—who would buy it anyway. There may be an exception to this when significant changes or modifications (new and improved) are made in a brand.

Manufacturers of package-goods products such as food, health, cosmetics, and toiletries are heavy users of sampling since their products meet the three criteria that are important for an effective sampling program:

1. The products are of relatively low unit value, so samples do not cost too much.
2. The products are divisible, which means they can be broken into small sample sizes that are adequate for demonstrating the brand's features and benefits to the user.

➤ *Exhibit 17–11*
Types of consumer promotions used by large and small firms

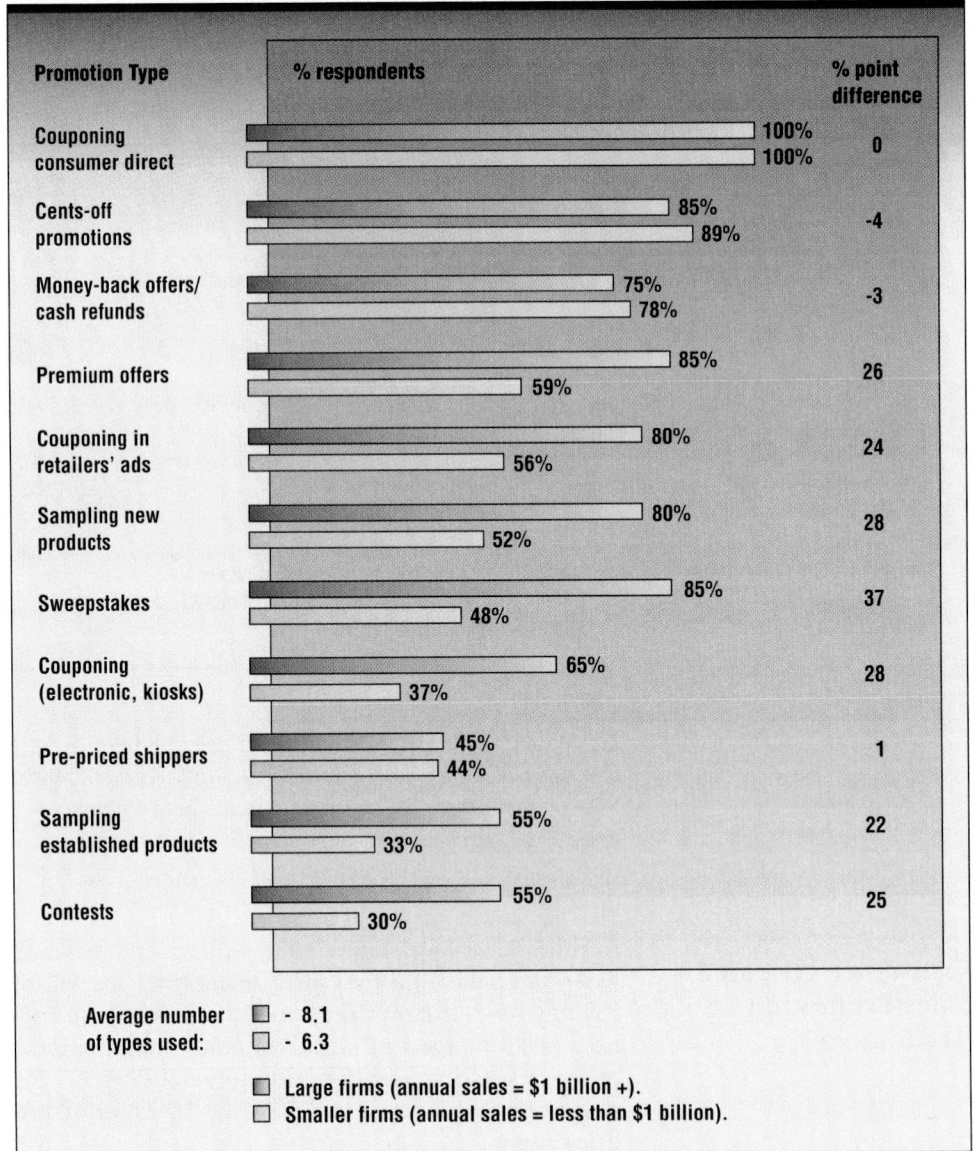

➤ *Exhibit 17–11*
Types of consumer promotions used by large and small firms

Promotion Type	% respondents	% point difference
Couponing consumer direct	100% / 100%	0
Cents-off promotions	85% / 89%	-4
Money-back offers/cash refunds	75% / 78%	-3
Premium offers	85% / 59%	26
Couponing in retailers' ads	80% / 56%	24
Sampling new products	80% / 52%	28
Sweepstakes	85% / 48%	37
Couponing (electronic, kiosks)	65% / 37%	28
Pre-priced shippers	45% / 44%	1
Sampling established products	55% / 33%	22
Contests	55% / 30%	25

Average number of types used: ■ - 8.1   □ - 6.3

■ Large firms (annual sales = $1 billion +).
□ Smaller firms (annual sales = less than $1 billion).

3. The purchase cycle for these products is relatively short, so the consumer will consider making an immediate purchase or will not forget about the brand when the next purchase occasion for the product does occur.

Benefits and limitations of sampling

There are several important benefits of using a sampling program. First, samples are an excellent way of inducing a prospective buyer to try a product or service. One expert estimates approximately 75 percent of the households receiving a sample will try it.[26] The trial rates generated by a sampling program are much higher than those produced by advertising or other sales promotion techniques.

Getting the consumer to try a product leads to a second benefit of sampling—a sample allows the consumer to experience the brand directly and thus gain a greater appreciation for its benefits. This can be particularly important when a product's features and benefits are difficult to describe through other means such as advertising. Many products such as foods, beverages, and cosmetics are examples of products where subtle features are most appreciated when experienced directly.

Obviously the marketer must believe the brand has some unique or superior benefits for a sampling program to be worthwhile. If this is not the case, the sampled

➤ *Exhibit 17–12* **Summary of sampling methods**

Eight Basic Sampling Media	Uses	Limitations
1. Door-to-door	Virtually any product can be delivered in this way	Most expensive means of sampling Problem with leaving perishables if occupant absent Illegal in some areas
2. Direct mail	Best for small, light products that are nonperishable	Rising postal costs
3. Central location	Best for perishables such as food or when personal demonstration is required	If in-store, same offer must be made to all retailers (Robinson-Patman Act) Usually involves cost of sales training If in public place, may be illegal in some areas
4. Sample pack in stores	Best method for attracting retail support, because retailers sell the packs at a premium unit price	Requires retail acceptance like any other new product May necessitate special production for trial sizes
5. Cross-product sampling in or on pack	Good for low-cost sampling of a manufacturer's other products	Trial limited to users of "carrier" product Restricted for large products
6. Co-op package distribution	Good for narrow audiences such as college students, military personnel, brides	Little appeal to trade
7. Newspaper or magazine distribution	Relatively low-cost method of sample distribution for flat or pouchable products	Seem to be regarded by media vehicle recipients as "cheap" and are often disregarded, resulting in less trial than with other sampling methods Limited to certain product types
8. Any of above with coupon	Increases postsample trial rate by using purchase incentive	Additional cost of coupon handling

consumers revert back to other brands and do not become repeat purchasers. The costs of a sampling program can be recovered only by getting a sufficient number of consumers to become regular users of the brand at full retail price.

Another possible limitation to sampling is that the benefits of some products are difficult to gauge immediately, and the learning period required to appreciate the brand may require supplying the consumer with larger amounts of the brand than is affordable. For example, a product such as an expensive skin cream that is promoted as being effective at preventing or reducing wrinkles would have to be used over an extended period before any effects might be noticed.

Sampling methods

One basic decision the sales promotion or brand manager must make concerns the method by which the sample will be distributed. The sampling method chosen is important not only in terms of costs but also in terms of influencing the type of consumer who receives the sample. The goal in choosing a sampling method is to find an effective, cost-efficient method that gets the product to the best prospects for trial and subsequent repurchase. Some of the more widely used sampling methods, along with the pros and cons of each, are shown in Exhibit 17–12. Some of the basic distribution methods include door-to-door, direct-mail, in-store, and on-package approaches.

Door-to-door sampling, whereby the sample is delivered directly to the prospect's residence, is sometimes used, particularly if it is important to control where the samples are delivered. While virtually any type of product samples can be delivered this way, this method is on the decline because of the expenses involved. Some companies may have their samples delivered directly as part of a cooperative effort where several product samples are sent at once to a household or through services such as Welcome Wagon, which calls on new residents in an area.

Sampling through the mail is common for small, lightweight products that are nonperishable such as the sample of Fab 1 Shot detergent shown in Exhibit 17–13a. A major advantage of this method is that the marketer has more control over where and when the product will be distributed and can target the sample to specific market areas. Many marketers are making increased use of information from companies such as Claritas' PRIZM-target marketing programs or National Decision Systems VISION to better target their sample mailings. The main drawbacks to through-the-mail sampling are postal restrictions and increasing postal rates.

In-store sampling has become an increasingly popular method of distributing samples, particularly for food products. This method is usually carried out by hiring temporary workers or "demonstrators" who set up a table or booth, prepare small samples of the product, and pass them out to shoppers. The in-store sampling approach can be very effective for food products, since consumers have an opportunity to taste the item and the demonstrator can give the consumer additional information about the product while it is being sampled. Demonstrators also will often give consumers a cents-off coupon for the sampled item to encourage immediate trial purchase. While this sampling method can be very effective, it can also be expensive and requires a great deal of planning, as well as the cooperation of retailers.

On-package sampling, whereby a sample of a product is attached to another item, is another common sampling method (See Exhibit 17–13b). This procedure can be very cost-effective, particularly for multiproduct firms that can attach a sample of a new product to an existing brand. However, the sample is distributed only to consumers who purchase the item to which the sample is attached. Thus, the sample will not reach nonusers of the "carrier" brand. This sampling method can be expanded by attaching the sample to multiple carrier brands and by including samples with products not made by the company.

Other methods

The four sampling methods discussed above are the most common ways of distributing product samples. However, a number of other methods are used to distribute samples such as inserting packets in magazines or newspapers (particularly Sunday

➤ *Exhibit 17–13*

A. Product sample sent through the mail

B. Armor All uses on-package samples for related products

supplements). Some firms such as tobacco and cereal companies make samples available to consumers who call free numbers to request them or mail in sample request forms. As was discussed in Chapter 16, these types of sampling methods are becoming very popular because they can help marketers build a data base that can be used for direct marketing.

Many companies also make use of specialized sample distribution services such as Gift Pax, Inc., Ruben H. Donnelley Corporation, and D. L. Blair. These companies help the company identify consumers who are nonusers of a product or users of a competitive brand and develop appropriate procedures for distributing a sample to them. As college students, many of you probably receive sample packs at the beginning of the semester that contain trial sizes of a variety of products such as mouthwash, toothpaste, headache remedies, and deodorant.

Couponing

The oldest, yet most widely used and effective sales promotion tool is the *cents-off coupon*. Coupons have been around since 1895 when the C. W. Post Company started using the penny-off coupon to sell its new Grape-Nuts cereal. In recent years, coupons have become increasingly popular with consumers, which may explain their explosive growth among manufacturers and retailers who use them as sales promotion incentives. As can be seen in Exhibit 17–11, coupons are the most popular sales promotion technique and are used by all the package-goods firms in the Donnelley Survey.

Over the past two decades, the number of coupons distributed by marketers has increased from 16 billion in 1968 to 292 billion in 1991.[27] Coupon distribution rose dramatically during the 1980s, increasing at an average annual growth rate of 11 percent (Exhibit 17–14). Coupon redemption, which had plateaued at the end of the 1980s and had even shown a slight decline in 1990, increased more than 5 percent in 1991 to 7.46 billion. This increase was the highest since 1986 and was attributed to the recession as consumers turned to coupons to save money.[28] According to studies by NCH Promotional Services, nearly 80 percent of U.S. households use coupons and 39 percent use five or more coupons per week. The average face value of coupons has increased from 21 cents in 1981 to 54 cents in 1991.

Adding additional fuel to the coupon explosion is the vast number of coupons distributed through retailers that are not even included in the aforementioned figures. In most markets, a number of grocery stores make manufacturers' coupons even more attractive to consumers by doubling their face value (Exhibit 17–15).

➤ *Exhibit 17–14*
Trend in coupon distribution (billions of coupons)

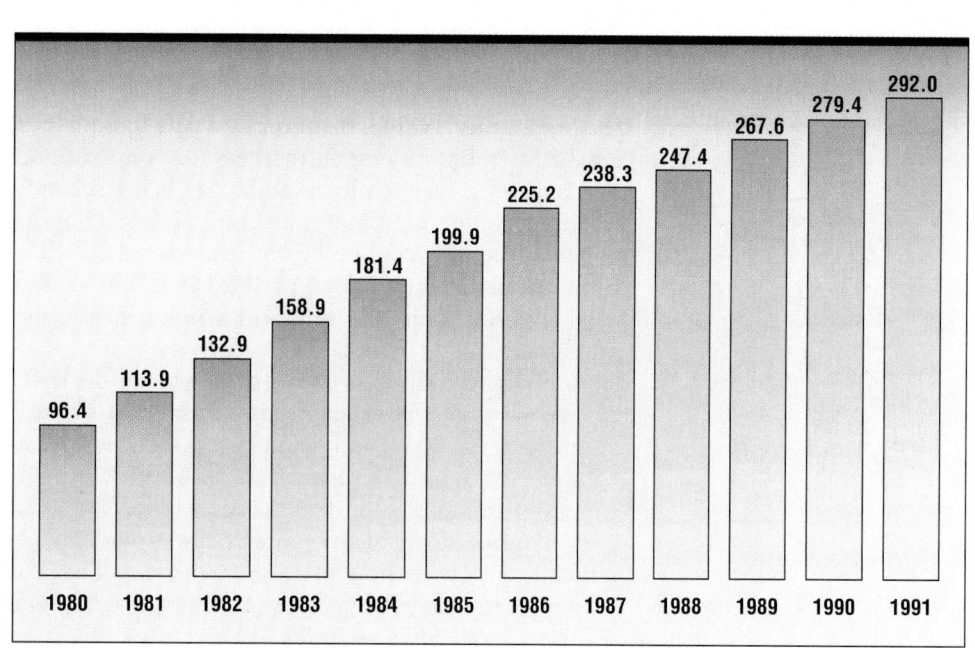

96.4	113.9	132.9	158.9	181.4	199.9	225.2	238.3	247.4	267.6	279.4	292.0
1980	1981	1982	1983	1984	1985	1986	1987	1988	1989	1990	1991

Advantages and limitations of coupons

Coupons have a number of advantages that make them popular sales promotional tools for both new and established products. First, coupons make it possible to offer a price reduction to those consumers who are price sensitive without having to reduce the price for everyone. Price-sensitive consumers generally seek out or purchase *because* of coupons, whereas those who are not as concerned about price buy the brand at full value. Coupons also make it possible to reduce the retail price of a product without relying on retailers for cooperation, which can often be a problem.

Coupons are generally regarded as being second only to sampling as a promotional technique for generating trial. Since a coupon lowers the price of a product, the consumer's level of perceived risk associated with trial of a new brand is reduced. Coupons can encourage repurchase after initial trial. As was shown earlier, many new products include a cents-off coupon inside the package to encourage repeat purchase.

Coupons can also be useful promotional devices for established products. They can be used to encourage nonusers to try a brand, to encourage repeat purchase among current users, and to get users to try a new and improved version of a brand. Coupons may also be helpful in getting users of a product to trade up to more expensive brands.

A number of problems are associated with the use of coupons. First, it can be difficult to estimate how many consumers will use a coupon and when. Response to a coupon is rarely immediate, as the average amount of time taken to redeem a

➤ *Exhibit 17–16* **Factors affecting coupon redemptions**

1. Method of distribution	12. Area of country
2. Product class size	13. Competitive activity
3. Audience reached by coupon	14. Size of coupon drop
4. Consumer's "need" for product	15. Size of purchase required for redemption
5. Brand's consumer franchise/market share	16. Level of general support for advertising and promotion
6. Degree of brand loyalty	17. Consumer attitude and product usage/number of potential users
7. Brand's retail availability/distribution	18. Period of time since the coupons were distributed
8. Face (monetary) value of coupon	19. Growth trend
9. Whether new or old (established) brand	20. Timing, if brand is subject to seasonal influences
10. Design and appeal of coupon ad	21. Demographics, such as age, family size, annual income, and expenditures
11. Discount offered by coupon	22. General level of misredemption in the couponed area

coupon is anywhere from two to six months. While redemption may be expedited through the use of an expiration date, coupons are generally not as effective as sampling for inducing initial product trial in a short period. A number of factors can influence the redemption of a coupon, as shown in Exhibit 17–16.

A problem associated with using coupons to attract new users to an established brand is that it is very difficult to prevent the coupons from being received and used by consumers who already use the brand. For example, General Foods decided to reduce its use of coupons for Maxwell House coffee when research revealed the coupons were being redeemed primarily by current users.[29] Thus, rather than attracting new users, the coupons end up reducing the company's profit margins among consumers who would probably purchase the product anyway.

Another problem associated with the use of coupons is the cost. Couponing program expenses include the face value of the coupon redeemed plus costs for production, distribution, and handling of the coupons. Exhibit 17–17 shows the calculations used to determine the costs of a couponing program. The costs of a couponing program should be tracked very closely by the marketer to ensure the promotion is economically feasible.

Yet another concern in the use of coupon promotions is misredemption or the cashing of a coupon without the purchase of the brand. Coupon misredemption or fraud occurs in a number of ways, including:

- Redemption of coupons by consumers for brands not actually purchased.
- Redemption of coupons by sales clerks in exchange for cash.
- The gathering and redemption of coupons by store managers or owners without the accompanying sale of the product.
- The gathering or printing of coupons by criminals who sell them to unethical merchants, who in turn redeem them.

A 1989 study by the Grocery Manufacturers of America and the Food Marketing Institute estimated coupon misredemption at 7.1 percent and reported it is costing marketers nearly $273 million a year.[30] More recent estimates of coupon misredemption are as high as $500 million. While efforts are being made to solve this problem, marketers must still allow a certain percentage for misredemption when estimating the costs of a couponing program. Ways of dealing with the coupon misredemption, such as improved coding, are being developed, but it still remains a problem.

Coupon distribution

Coupons can be disseminated to consumers in a number of ways, including distribution in newspapers and magazines, through direct mail, and in or on packages. Distribution of coupons through newspaper free-standing inserts (FSIs) is by far the

Cost per Coupon Redeemed: An Illustration	
1. Distribution cost	$ 80,000
10,000,000 circulation × $8/M	
2. Redemptions at 3.1%	310,000
3. Redemption cost	$ 77,500
310,000 redemptions × $.25 face value	
4. Handling cost	$ 24,800
310,000 redemptions × $.08	
5. Total program cost	$182,300
Items 1 + 3 + 4	
6. Cost per coupon redeemed	58.8¢
Cost divided by redemptions	
7. Actual product sold on redemption	$248,000
(misredemption estimated at 20%)	
310,000 × 80%	
8. Cost-per-product moved	73.5¢
Program cost divided by product sold	

most popular method for delivering coupons to consumers. FSIs accounted for nearly 80 percent of all coupons distributed in 1990, which represents a 20 percent increase in their share of total distribution over 1985. The growth in coupon distribution through FSIs has come at the expense of vehicles such as manufacturers' ads in newspapers (newspaper ROP), newspaper co-op ads, and magazines.

A major advantage of media-delivered coupons is the brand exposure that results, particularly from newspapers. Also, many consumers actively search the newspaper for coupons, especially on Sundays or "food days" (when grocery stores advertise their specials). Thus, the likelihood of the consumer at least noticing the coupon is enhanced. Distribution of coupons through magazines can take advantage of the high selectivity of the publication for reaching specific target audiences. Finally, distribution of coupons through the media can be done at reasonable costs, particularly through the free-standing inserts.

While the distribution of coupons through FSIs has been increasing, this growth has resulted in a clutter problem. Consumers are being bombarded with too many coupons, and although each FSI publisher offers product exclusivity in its insert, this advantage may be negated when there are three inserts in a Sunday paper. Redemption rates of FSI coupons have declined from the 7 percent range to only 2.5 percent and are even lower for some products (Exhibit 17–18). In addition to the clutter problem and low redemption rates, the costs of using FSIs have increased substantially over the past few years, as the cost per thousand circulation has gone from an average of $3 to nearly $8.

These problems with FSIs are leading many marketers to look at alternative ways of delivering coupons that will result in less clutter and higher redemption rates, such as direct mail. Over the long term, it is expected that many marketers will switch out of FSIs and into other coupon delivery methods.[31]

The direct-mail method of distributing coupons increased for several years, although it declined somewhat in 1990, and now accounts for 4 percent of all coupons distributed. The bulk of coupons disseminated via direct mail are sent by local retailers or through co-op mailings whereby a packet of coupons for a number of different products is sent to a household. These include couponing programs such as Donnelley Marketing's Carol Wright, Metromail's Red Letter Day, Advo Systems' Mailbox Values, and Val-Pak Direct Marketing Systems

Direct-mail couponing has several advantages. First, the mailing can be sent to a broad audience or targeted to specific geographic or demographic segments. Some co-op coupon programs such as Donnelley's Carol Wright have several special-market mailings to groups such as teenagers, senior citizens, Hispanics, and other

> *Exhibit 17–18*
Coupon redemption rates by
media 1990 (grocery products)

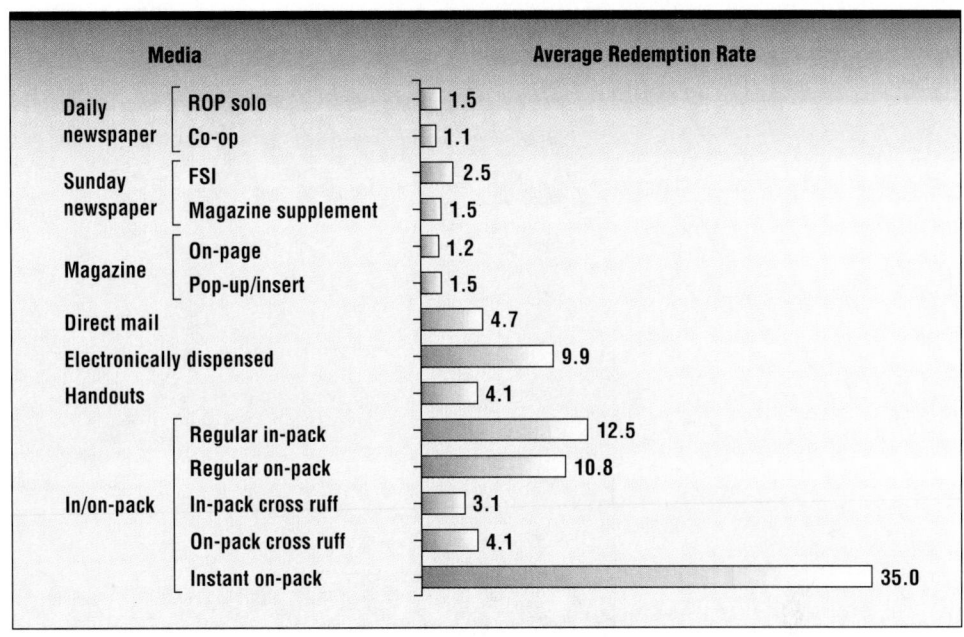

Media		Average Redemption Rate
Daily newspaper	ROP solo	1.5
	Co-op	1.1
Sunday newspaper	FSI	2.5
	Magazine supplement	1.5
Magazine	On-page	1.2
	Pop-up/insert	1.5
Direct mail		4.7
Electronically dispensed		9.9
Handouts		4.1
In/on-pack	Regular in-pack	12.5
	Regular on-pack	10.8
	In-pack cross ruff	3.1
	On-pack cross ruff	4.1
	Instant on-pack	35.0

segments. The firm that mails its own coupons can be particularly selective in its selection of recipients. Another important advantage of direct-mail couponing is their higher redemption rate. Direct-mail couponing is a more effective way of gaining the attention of consumers and results in redemption rates of nearly 5 percent, which is much higher than that of FSIs.

The major disadvantage of the direct-mail method of coupon delivery is the expense relative to other distribution methods. The cost per thousand figure for distributing coupons through co-op mailings ranges from $10 to $15, and a solo mailing can have a CPM as high as $100. Also, the higher redemption rate of mail-delivered coupons may result from the fact that many of the coupon recipients are already users of the brand who take advantage of the coupons sent directly to them.

Placing coupons either inside or on the outside of the package is another method for distributing them. The in/on package coupon has virtually no distribution costs and a much higher redemption rate than other couponing methods. There are several types of in/on package coupons. An in/on pack coupon that is redeemable for the next purchase of the same brand is known as a **bounce-back coupon.** The logic of using this type of coupon is to provide consumers with an inducement to repurchase the brand.

Bounce-back coupons are often used with product samples to encourage the consumer to purchase the product after trying a sample. They may also be included in or on the package during the early phases of a brand's life cycle to encourage repeat purchase or to act as a defensive maneuver for a mature brand that is facing competitive pressure and wants to retain its current users. The main limitation of bounce-back coupons is that they go only to purchasers of the brand and thus are not effective for attracting nonusers. Exhibit 17–19 shows a bounce-back coupon placed on the package for Kellogg's Eggo brand waffles.

Another type of in/on pack coupon is the **cross-ruff coupon,** which is redeemable on the purchase of a different product, usually one made by the same company but occasionally through a tie-in with another manufacturer. Cross-ruff coupons have a redemption rate of 3.1 to 4.1 percent and can be effective in encouraging consumers to try other products or brands. Companies with wide product lines such as cereal manufacturers are common users of these coupons.

➤ *Exhibit 17–19*
An example of a bounce-back coupon

Yet another type of package coupon that some companies use is the **instant coupon.** This coupon is attached to the outside of the package, and the consumer rips it off and redeems it at the checkout stand. Instant coupons have redemption levels of 35 percent and provide the consumer with an immediate point-of-purchase incentive. Some companies prefer to use instant coupons rather than price-off deals since the latter require more cooperation from retailers and can be more expensive since every package must be reduced in price.

Couponing trends

Marketers are continually searching for new and more effective couponing techniques. The enormous increase in the number of coupons distributed by manufacturers has led to what might be called "coupon clutter." Households are receiving more coupons than they can possibly notice, clip, save, and remember to use. Some companies are introducing in-store coupon distribution techniques through vending machines, electronic dispensers, or personal distributors whereby consumers can request and receive coupons right in the store. These distribution methods are preferred by some companies that believe coupons are most effective if they are given to consumers when they are ready to make a purchase. These techniques allow consumers to choose coupons they are interested in, removing the need to clip coupons from print ads and then remembering to bring them to the store.

Companies are also seeking ways of using coupons to attract the customers of their competitors. Estimates are that 65 percent to 85 percent of a manufacturer's coupons are used by current customers. Thus, marketers are attempting to target their coupons to users of competitive brands through marketing research and telemarketing. Even though precise targeting of coupons is expensive in terms of distribution costs, it can be more cost-effective than newspaper couponing for attracting new users. Promotional Perspective 17–1 discusses how technological advances are leading to more effective ways of using coupons and assessing their impact.

Promotional Perspective 17–1

Getting More Out of Coupons

While the use of coupons is increasing, companies are still facing enormous inefficiencies in their couponing programs. Problems such as misredemption and fraud, high processing costs, and difficulty in targeting coupons and tracking their effectiveness have made it hard for companies to get their money's worth out of their couponing promotions. Moreover, it is estimated that as many as 80 percent of coupons are used by loyal customers who would buy the company's products at full price.

Many of these problems are being addressed through technological advances made possible through the use of bar-coded coupons. While bar codes have been used for several years on products, many companies realize they can be useful on coupons as well. More than 70 percent of U.S. supermarkets are equipped with scanning devices to read the bar codes, and a number of companies have evolved to use the bar coding and provide services to firms using coupons.

The use of bar codes on coupons has a number of advantages to both manufacturers and retailers. First, the costs of handling coupons are reduced, as processing that used to be done by hand is now handled automatically by the scanner. The scannable coupons make for faster checkouts and help reduce fraud and misredemption since scanning prevents an item from being substituted for the product on the coupon or the use of a coupon for a large-package size when a smaller size is actually purchased.

Another major benefit of the bar-coded coupons is the potential they offer companies for improving the distribution of their coupons to specific market segments rather than using relatively untargeted distribution methods. For example, Catalina Marketing Corporation developed a method for distributing coupons at supermarkets by identifying a customer's purchases through bar codes and printing coupons for a competitor's product for use on a future shopping trip. This system makes it possible for marketers to reach users of competitive brands with their coupons rather than people who already use their brand.

Companies are also using this system to link purchases of products that are in some sense related. For example, a consumer who purchases a caffeine-free cola would be issued a coupon for decaffeinated coffee.

Another benefit of the new technologies is that they provide companies with information on the effectiveness of their couponing programs as well as those of their competitors. Companies such as Burke Marketing Research Services track coupon redemption at the brand level and offer subscribers the opportunity to monitor their own, as well as competitors' promotional efforts, analyze what type of household is making a purchase, and determine what brand lost sales owing to a coupon-induced switch. Also, by tracking the timing of coupon redemptions, a company can gauge the effectiveness of its media plan.

Another company trying to make couponing more effective is Actmedia, which has developed the Instant Coupon Machine that

Catalina Marketing promotes its checkout coupons

You're Looking At The Reason The FSI Is An Obsolete Medium.

FSI's have no idea what's in a consumer's head. Or on it. Lacking the capacity to identify your target customer, they just throw themselves at everyone. Talking to people who'd never want to buy your product.

This kind of mass waste was completely unavoidable in the old days. But now, with Checkout Coupon,® you can pick out the customers you want, and deliver coupons only to them. On a national basis reaching 65 million shoppers each week.

© 1992 Catalina Marketing Corporation.

Far too many FSI's go to waste. Checkout Coupon eliminates waste by issuing coupons based solely on purchase behavior.

Using scanner data right at the checkstand, we issue coupons only when a shopper buys a product you've specified in advance. Such as a competitive brand.

So instead of promoting where there's no growth potential, call us about Checkout Coupon. Catalina Marketing, 721 East Ball Road, Anaheim, CA 92805. (800) 955-9770.

CHECKOUT COUPON

can be affixed to store shelves. The company claims its Instant Coupon Machine has generated an average coupon redemption rate of 24 percent, which is significantly higher than the 2 or 3 percent redemption rate for free-standing inserts.

With more and more coupons being dispensed by companies every year, marketers must find ways to improve the efficiency and effectiveness of their couponing programs. These new technologies offer companies greater opportunities to get their money's worth from their couponing dollars.

Source: Merri Rosenberg, "Using High Tech to Make Coupons Pay," *Adweek,* November 11, 1985, p. 6; "Stealing the Right Shoppers," *Forbes,* July 10, 1989, pp. 104–5; and Michael Burgi, "Coupon Machine Off at Fast Clip," *Advertising Age,* May 6, 1991, p. 31.

Premiums

Premiums are another type of sales promotion device used by many marketers. A **premium** is an offer of an item of merchandise or service either free or at a low price that is used as an extra incentive for purchasers. More than $4 billion was spent on consumer premiums in 1992, including direct premiums and mail-in offers. Marketers' use of premium offers is changing, as many are eliminating toys and gimmicks in favor of "value-added" premiums that reflect the quality of the product and are consistent with its image and positioning in the market. The two basic types of premium offers are those that are offered free and the self-liquidating premium.

Free premiums

Free premiums are usually inexpensive gifts or merchandise included in the product package or sent to consumers who make mail-in requests along with a proof of purchase. In/on package premiums are examples of commonly used free premium offers. These include towels or glasses packed in detergent boxes; toys, balls, trading cards, or other items included in cereal packages; or samples of one product included with another (Exhibit 17–20). A recent survey found that in/on package premiums are consumers' most preferred type of promotion.[32]

Package-carried premiums are used because they have high impulse value and can provide an extra incentive to the consumer to use the product. However, several problems are associated with the use of in/on pack premiums. First, there is the cost factor, which results from the premium itself as well as from extra packaging efforts

➢ *Exhibit 17–20*
Colgate toothpaste is used as an in-package premium for Life cereal

that are sometimes needed. Finding desirable premiums at reasonable costs can be difficult, particularly for adult markets. Using a poor premium may hurt sales.

Another problem with these premiums is the possible restrictions the firm may face from regulatory agencies such as the Federal Trade Commission, and the Food and Drug Administration or from industry codes regarding the type of premium used. Strict guidelines have been developed by the National Association of Broadcasters regarding the advertising of premium offers to children. Concern has been expressed over the potential for premium offers to entice children to request a brand to get the promoted item and then never consume the product.

Mail-in premium offers usually require the consumer to send in one or more proof-of-purchase symbols to receive premium items. Since most free mail-in premium offers require more than one proof of purchase, they can encourage repeat purchase and reward brand loyalty. However, a major drawback of mail-in premiums is that they do not offer immediate reinforcement or reward to the purchaser and thus may not be effective in providing extra incentive to purchase the brand. Few consumers take advantage of mail-in premium offers; the average redemption rate is estimated to be between 2 and 4 percent.[33]

Self-liquidating premiums

Self-liquidating premiums are those that require the consumer to pay some or all of the cost of the premium plus handling and mailing costs. The items used as self-liquidating premiums are usually purchased in large quantities by the company and offered to consumers at prices that are lower than would be paid at retail. The marketer usually does not attempt to make a profit on the premium item but only wants to cover costs and offer a value to the consumer.

In addition to the cost savings, self-liquidating premiums offer several advantages to marketers. By offering values to consumers through the premium products, the advertiser can create interest in the brand and goodwill that may enhance the brand's image. These premiums can also encourage trade support and gain in-store displays for the brand and the premium offer. Also, self-liquidating premiums are often tied in directly to the advertising campaign and may be an effective way of extending an advertising message and contributing to the consumer-franchise-building effort for a brand. For example, the Michelob Night Hits tape offer helped reinforce the "Night belongs to Michelob" campaign theme used for the brand (Exhibit 17–21).

In some instances, marketers have used product containers and packages to develop self-liquidating premiums. Fast-food restaurants often sell beverages in containers with logos of local sports teams or movie, television, or cartoon characters on them. Some companies offer attractive packages for their products that can be saved and reused such as decorative canisters for the kitchen, wine decanters, or jars for nuts and candy. Package premium offers can also have a functional relationship to the product such as the squeeze-bottle used in many beverage premium offers.

Self-liquidating premium offers have the same basic limitations as mail-in premiums in that they have a very low redemption rate. It is estimated that fewer than 10 percent of U.S. households have ever sent for a premium, and less than 1 percent of self-liquidating offers are actually redeemed.[34] Low redemption rates can leave the marketer with a large supply of items with a logo or some other brand identification that may make them very hard to dispose of. Thus, it is important to test consumers' reaction to a premium incentive and to determine whether they perceive the offer as a value. Another option is to use premiums with no brand identification. However, this can detract from the consumer-franchise-building value of a premium.

Contests and Sweepstakes

Contests and sweepstakes have become an increasingly popular consumer-oriented promotion. The number of nationally advertised contests and sweepstakes has increased from about 300 in 1975 to more than 1,000 in 1991 as companies look for

➢ *Exhibit 17–21*
An example of a premium offer that is supportive of brand image and position

ways to generate interest and excitement among consumers for their products and services. Many marketers view these types of promotions as having an appeal and glamour that tools such as cents-off coupons lack. Contests and sweepstakes are exciting to consumers because, as one expert has noted, consumers have a "pot-of-gold at the end of the rainbow mentality" and think they can win the big prizes being offered.[35]

There are differences between contests and sweepstakes. A **contest** is a promotion whereby consumers compete for prizes or money on the basis of skills or ability, and winners are determined by judging the entries or ascertaining which entry comes closest to some predetermined criteria (e.g., picking the winning teams and number of total points in the Super Bowl or NCAA Basketball Tournament). Contests usually provide a purchase incentive by requiring a proof of purchase to enter or an entry form that is available from a dealer or advertisement.

A **sweepstakes** is a promotion whereby winners are determined purely by chance and cannot require a proof of purchase as a condition for entry. Sweepstakes require only that the entrant submit his or her name for consideration in the drawing or selection of the prize or prizes. While this is often done on an official entry form, handwritten facsimile entries must also be permitted. Another form of a sweepstakes is a **game,** which also has a chance element or odds of winning associated. The use of scratch-off cards with instant winners is a popular promotional tool. Some games occur over a longer period and require more involvement by consumers. Games such as bingo are popular among retailers and fast-food chains as a way of building store traffic and repeat purchase.

Because they are easier to enter, sweepstakes attract more entries than contests and have become a more widely used sales promotion technique. Also, they are easier and less expensive to administer since every entry does not have to be checked or judged. Choosing the winning entry in a sweepstakes requires only the random selection of a winner from the pool of entries or generation of a number to match against those held by sweepstakes entrants.

Contests and sweepstakes can get the consumer involved with a brand by making the promotion product relevant. For example, contests that ask consumers to suggest a name for a product or to submit recipes that use the brand can increase involvement levels. Some contests require consumers to read an advertisement or package or visit a store display to gather information needed to enter. Marketers must be careful not to make their contests too difficult to enter, as this may discourage participation among key prospects in the target audience and the contest may attract only habitual or professional contest entrants.

Sweepstakes can also be used to generate interest in or excitement over a brand. In an increasingly cluttered media environment, sweepstakes can provide consumers with an extra incentive for attending to an ad. As the president of one of the leading sweepstakes consulting firms has noted:

> Sweepstakes are the insurance policy for an ad campaign. It's a way to get attention in a world where everyone else is trying to get attention too. They also generate a sense of immediacy since there's always a deadline for entries.[36]

Contest and sweepstakes promotions can sometimes be an effective way of dealing with specific problems. For example, British Airways was faced with the problem of attracting American tourists to Europe in the middle of the wave of terrorist violence in summer 1986. The company used a six-month promotion whereby passengers were eligible to participate in an in-flight skill game as well as an instant-win sweepstakes with free roundtrip tickets on the Concorde, a shopping spree at Harrods, the famous London department store, and a Rolls-Royce Silver Spirit among the prizes. The promotion drew 1 million entries in one week, and within 60 days of the start of the promotion, the airline was back to the load factor of the previous year.[37] A similar promotion was repeated in 1991 when the Persian Gulf War caused a significant decline in international travel (Exhibit 17–22).

As with other sales promotion techniques, sweepstakes can be particularly effective at franchise building when they are directly tied to the creative theme being used in the advertising campaign. For example, the Quaker Oats Microwave Sweepstakes was an effective way to promote the new microwave preparation feature of the product (Exhibit 17–23, page 605).

Problems with contests and sweepstakes

While the use of contests and sweepstakes continues to increase, a number of disadvantages and problems are associated with these types of promotions. Many sweepstakes and/or contest promotions often do little to contribute to the consumer-franchise-building effort for a product or service and may even detract from it. The sweepstakes or contest often becomes the dominant focus and overshadows the brand. Thus, little has been accomplished other than to give out substantial amounts of money and/or prizes. Many promotional experts question the effectiveness of contests and sweepstakes, and some companies have even stopped using them. Companies cut back on their use of sweepstakes because of concern over their effectiveness and fears that consumers might become overdependent on them.[38]

Also, numerous legal problems and considerations affect the design and administration of contests and sweepstakes. These promotions are regulated by a number of different federal agencies, and each of the 50 states has its own rules to follow. The regulation of contests and sweepstakes has helped clean up the abuses that plagued the industry in the late 1960s and has resulted in more favorable perceptions of these promotions among consumers. Companies still must be careful, however, in designing a contest or sweepstakes and awarding prizes. Most firms use consultants or firms specializing in the design and administration of contests and sweepstakes to avoid any legal problems. However, as discussed in

> *Exhibit 17–22* **British Airways used a sweepstakes to overcome a difficult situation**

Promotional Perspective 17–2 on page 606, companies can still run into problems with contests and other types of promotions.

A final problem that continues to detract from the effectiveness of contests and sweepstakes is the presence of professionals or hobbyists who submit large numbers of entries but have no interest in or intention to purchase the product or service. Because most states make it illegal to require a purchase as a qualification for a sweepstakes entry, consumers can enter as many times as they wish. Professional players enter as many as several hundred entries per sweepstakes, depending on the nature of the prizes and the number of entries the promotion attracts. Newsletters are even available that inform them of all the contests and sweepstakes being held, the entry dates, estimated probabilities of winning for various numbers of entries, information on how to enter, and solutions to any puzzles or other information that might be needed to enter a contest. The presence of these professional entrants not only defeats the purpose of the promotion but may also deter entries from consumers who think their chance of winning is limited.

Refunds and Rebates

Refunds or rebates are offers to return some portion of the product purchase price, usually after supplying some sort of proof of purchase. Consumers are generally very responsive to refund or rebate offers, particularly as the size of the savings increases. Thus, refunds and rebates are used by all types of companies ranging from package-goods companies to manufacturers of major appliances and automobiles. The use of money-back offers/cash refunds ranks second to coupons among package-goods companies.

Refund offers are often used by package-goods marketers to induce trial of a new product or to encourage users of another brand to switch. The savings offered through a cash refund offer may be perceived by the consumer as an immediate value that lowers the cost of the item. The savings are realized only if the refund or rebate

➤ *Exhibit 17–23*
**This sweepstakes helped promote
a new product feature**

➤ *Exhibit 17–23*
**This sweepstakes helped promote
a new product feature**

offer is redeemed by the consumer. Redemption rates for refund offers typically range from 1 to 3 percent for print and point-of-purchase offers to 5 percent for in/on package offers.[39]

Refund offers can also encourage repeat purchase. Many offers require consumers to send in multiple proofs of purchase as a condition for receiving the refund. In some cases, the size of the refund offer may even increase as the number of purchases gets larger. Many package-goods companies are switching away from cash refund offers only to the use of coupons or cash/coupon combinations (see Exhibit 17–24, page 607). By using coupons in the refund offer, the marketer enhances the likelihood of repeat purchase of the brand.

The use of refunds—or as they are more commonly referred to, rebates—has become a widely used form of promotion for consumer durables. Products such as cameras, sporting goods, appliances, televisions, audio and video equipment, computers, and automobiles frequently use rebate offers to appeal to price-conscious consumers. The use of rebates for expensive items such as automobiles was begun by Chrysler Corporation in 1981 to boost sales and generate cash for the struggling company. Rebates have since become a very common promotional technique not only in the auto industry and other durable products but for package-goods products as well.

Evaluating refunds and rebates

As noted earlier, refunds and rebates can be effective sales promotional tools for creating new users and for encouraging brand switching or repeat purchase behavior or as a way of offering a temporary price reduction. In many instances, the refund or rebate offer may be perceived as an immediate savings or value even though the money is not received until the offer is redeemed, and many consumers will never follow through on the refund or rebate offer. Thus, a perception of a price reduction is operating and can influence purchase even though the consumer may fail to realize the savings. This means the marketer can reduce price for much less than if a direct price-off deal were used.

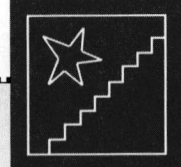

Promotional Perspective 17–2

Promotions Don't Always Go as Planned

As the U.S. economy struggled through a prolonged recession, many marketers turned to sales promotions to pry dollars from reluctant consumers. Contests, sweepstakes, premiums, and other types of offers are often used by marketers to give consumers an extra incentive to buy their products. However, these promotions don't always go as planned and can be flops that can embarrass a company or even create legal problems. Several major companies known for their marketing excellence have experienced major promotional blunders in recent years.

In the summer of 1991, Coca-Cola spent millions of dollars gearing up for and advertising its "Magi-can" promotion. The promotional concept was simple—when consumers opened certain cans of Coke, a prize such as a $5 bill would pop out. However, Murphy's Law (whatever can go wrong will) quickly took over. First, there were problems with the device designed to propel the prizes out of the Magi-can and many malfunctioned. Then several supermarkets reported problems with vandals opening the entire stock of Coke cans in search of the prize. There were also reports of children drinking the nonpotable water used to fill the prize cans. Coke ran full-page ads in national newspapers explaining the problems it was encountering. However, by then it was too late, and the ill-fated promotion was canceled after a few weeks.

Pepsi also encountered problems with a promotion planned for the 1991 Super Bowl. Pepsi planned to broadcast a special toll-free telephone number during its Super Bowl commercials that consumers could call at halftime to see if they were one of three $1 million prize winners. The promotion was designed as a countermove against the "Crack the Code" promotion Coke was airing during its halftime commercials. Coke planned to show viewers how to decode the special game pieces—by holding them to their TV screens—to see if they had won one of the big prizes.

Both promotions were canceled before the Super Bowl telecast. Pepsi dropped its promotion when the Federal Communications Commission expressed concern that the millions of calls the promotion was expected to generate could disrupt the nation's communications system. Coke decided it was not appropriate to run a lighthearted promotion with the Persian Gulf War underway and ran an ad explaining its position instead.

Some companies have found their promotional snafus can cause them major legal problems. A few years ago, the Beatrice Company initiated a promotion tied to ABC's "Monday Night Football." Contestants could win prizes if the numbers on their scratch-off cards matched the number of touchdowns and field goals in weekly Monday night games. A major problem arose, however, when a salesman for Procter & Gamble, who was also a computer buff, cracked the contest code. With the help of his friends, he collected thousands of cards, mostly from Beatrice

salespeople, and identified 4,000 winners worth $21 million in prize money.

Beatrice contended "The Scratch Gang" violated the rules of the game in obtaining some tickets and the contest's defect nullified all prize claims and canceled the contest. Millions of dollars in lawsuits were filed, and although the case was eventually settled out of court, Beatrice suffered considerable embarrassment and loss of goodwill.

Kraft also found out how expensive it can be when a promotion is not executed properly. The company ran a "Ready to Roll" sweepstakes in Chicago and Houston in June 1980 whereby consumers in these cities had a chance to match game pieces from newspaper free-standing inserts with pieces found in Kraft Singles American cheese. However, the FSI was printed incorrectly and every piece turned out to match, making everyone a winner! Hundreds of consumers had matching pieces indicating they had won a Dodge minivan and thousands more had won cash prizes.

Kraft declared the contest null and void but still had to develop some way to compensate the winners. Minivan winners were awarded $250 and lesser amounts were given to those who had winning pieces for other prizes. Consumers with winning tickets were also eligible to enter a drawing for four minivans and various other prizes. Kraft estimated the cost of pulling unpurchased packages off the shelf and paying consolation prizes at nearly $3.8 million. The original plans for the sweepstakes budgeted $36,000 for prizes. There is no way of estimating how much goodwill was lost among the thousands of consumers who thought they won big prizes.

One of the greatest concerns a company has is that a product or promotional offer can end up being a health hazard. Taco Bell had to halt a promotion where plastic sports bottles were being sold for 99 cents when it was discovered they had tops that could easily be swallowed by small children. The company quickly recalled 300,000 bottles that had been sold and halted plans to sell another 2 million.

Most consumer promotions don't encounter problems of the magnitude discussed in these examples. However, many marketers are becoming more innovative and trying to do more creative things in their promotions. A lot of embarrassment and money can be saved by carefully evaluating a promotion and recognizing that Murphy's Law often applies.

Bruce Horowitz, "The Pratfalls in Promotions," *Los Angeles Times*, April 28, 1991, pp. D1, 8; "Kraft Snafu Could Cost $4 Million," *Advertising Age*, July 10, 1989, p. 53; and Laurie Baum, "How Beatrice Lost at Its Own Game," *Business Week*, March 2, 1987, p. 66.

Some problems are associated with refunds and rebates. Many consumers are not motivated by a refund offer because of the delay in receiving the reward and the effort required to obtain the savings. Many consumers view the refund or rebate process of saving cash register receipts and proofs of purchase, filling out forms, and mailing in the offer as a hassle and do not want to be bothered by it.[40] A study of

➤ *Exhibit 17–24*
A cash/coupon combination refund offer

➤ *Exhibit 17–24*
A cash/coupon combination refund offer

consumers' perceptions of rebates found a negative relationship between the use of rebates and the perceived efforts and difficulties associated with the redemption process.[41] It was also found that consumers perceive manufacturers as offering rebates to sell products that are not faring well. Nonusers of rebates were particularly likely to perceive the rebate redemption process as too complicated and to have negative perceptions of manufacturers' motives for offering rebates. Thus, companies using rebates must simplify the redemption process and use other promotional elements such as advertising to retain consumer confidence in the brand.

When small refunds are being offered, marketers might find other promotional incentives such as coupons or bonus packs more appropriate and effective. Marketers must be careful not to overuse refund or rebate offers and thus confuse consumers over the real price and value of a product or service. Also, consumers can become dependent on rebates and delay their purchases or only purchase brands for which a rebate is available. Many retailers have become disenchanted with rebates and the burden and expense of administering these programs and have eliminated rebating programs.[42]

Bonus Packs

Bonus packs offer the consumer an extra amount of a product at the regular price by providing larger containers or extra units (Exhibit 17–25). Bonus packs result in a lower cost per unit for the consumer and thus provide extra value, as well as more of the product, for the money. There are several advantages to using bonus pack promotions. First, the bonus pack gives marketers a direct way of providing extra value to the consumer without having to get involved with things such as coupons or refund offers. The additional value of a bonus pack is generally obvious to the consumer and can have a strong impact on the purchase decision right at the time of purchase.

Bonus packs can also be an effective defensive maneuver against a competitor's promotion or introduction of a new brand. By loading current users with large amounts of their product, a marketer can often remove these consumers from the market and make them less susceptible to a competitor's promotional efforts. Bonus packs often receive favorable response from retailers and may result in larger purchase orders and favorable display space in the store as well.

Bonus pack promotions can be particularly effective when cooperation and relationships with retailers are favorable. It should be noted, however, that bonus packs often require additional shelf space and generally do not provide any extra profit margins for the retailer. Thus, the marketer can encounter problems with these promotions if trade relationships are not favorable. Another problem with bonus packs is that they may appeal primarily to current users who probably would have purchased the brand anyway or to promotion-sensitive consumers who may not become loyal to the brand.

Price-Off Deals

Another type of consumer-oriented promotion technique is the direct **price-off deal,** which provides the consumer with a reduction in the regular price of the brand. Price-off reductions are typically offered right on the package itself through specially marked price packs, as shown in Exhibit 17–26. Typically price-offs range from 10 to 25 percent off the regular price, with the reduction coming out of the manufacturer's profit margin, not the retailer's. It is very important to maintain the retailer's margin during a price-off promotion to maintain its support and cooperation.

Marketers use price-off promotions for several reasons. First, price-offs are controlled by the manufacturer, which enables them to ensure the promotional discount reaches the consumer rather than being kept by the trade. As with a bonus pack, price-off deals usually present a readily apparent value to the shopper, particularly when he or she has a "reference price point" for the brand and thus recognizes the value of the discount.[43] Thus, price-offs can provide a strong influence at the point of purchase when price comparisons are being made. Price-off promotions can also encourage consumers to purchase larger quantities and thus preempt competitors' promotions and assist in obtaining trade support.

Price-off promotions may not be favorably received by retailers since they can create pricing and inventory problems. Most retailers will not accept packages with a specific price shown on the package. Thus, the familiar X amount off the regular price must be used. Also, as with bonus packs, price-off deals often appeal primarily to regular users rather than attracting nonusers. Finally, it should be noted that the

> *Exhibit 17–27*
Event sponsorships soar

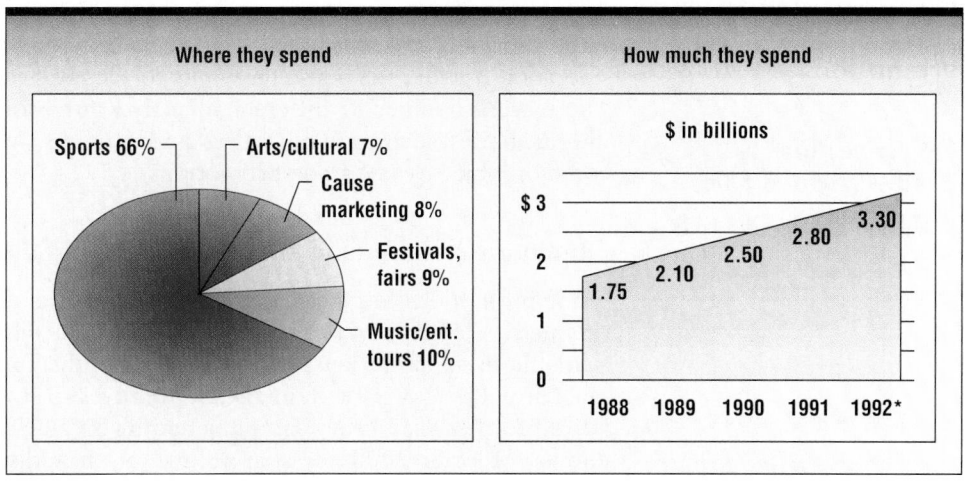

Where they spend

Sports 66% — Arts/cultural 7%
Cause marketing 8%
Festivals, fairs 9%
Music/ent. tours 10%

How much they spend

$ in billions

$3 — 2 — 1 — 0

1.75 2.10 2.50 2.80 3.30

1988 1989 1990 1991 1992*

*Projected.

Federal Trade Commission has a set of specific regulations regarding the conditions that price-off labels must meet and the frequency and timing of their use.

Event Sponsorship

Another type of consumer-oriented promotion that has become increasingly popular in recent years is **event sponsorship** whereby a company develops sponsorship relations with a particular event. An estimated 4,500 companies spent $3.3 billion on event sponsorships in 1992, nearly double the amount spent in 1988 (Exhibit 17–27). Sports receive two thirds of the event sponsorship monies. Among the more popular sporting events for sponsorship are golf and tennis tournaments, auto racing, and running events.[44] Bicycle racing, beach volleyball, skiing, and various water sports are also attracting corporate sponsorship. Traditionally, cigarette-, beer-, and automobile-related companies have been among the largest sports event sponsors. However, a number of other companies have become involved in event sponsorship such as Procter & Gamble, which spends over $30 million a year in this area and has begun using the services of events-marketing agencies.[45]

Many marketers are attracted to event sponsorship because it offers them a way of getting their company and/or product names in front of consumers. Moreover, by choosing the right events for sponsorship, companies can get visibility among consumers who constitute their target market. For example, RJR Nabisco is heavily involved in sponsorship of automobile racing under its Winston and Camel cigarette brands. The company's market research indicated racing fans fit the demographic profile of users of these brands very well and consumers would purchase a product that was instrumental in sponsoring their favorite sport.[46] For tobacco companies, which are prohibited from advertising on radio and television, event sponsorship also provides them with a way to have their brand names seen on TV.

Marketers also are attracted to event sponsorship because of the opportunities it offers for promotional tie-ins to regional markets. Events such as stock car races are very popular in southern states and are an effective way of reaching consumers in this region. Hanes Hosiery puts its Underalls panty hose logos on race cars and sponsors races to reach women in the South where its sales are weak.[47] As traditional media advertising becomes more crowded and expensive and regional marketing trends increase, it is likely that more companies will turn to event sponsorship.

A number of challenges face the event sponsorship industry, including charges that it is weak on research. As marketers become interested in targeted audiences, they will want more evidence of an event's effectiveness. The sponsorship industry also faces a potential problem as the Internal Revenue Service is considering changing its guidelines on taxing corporate sponsorships of nonprofit organizations. This change in the tax code could result in major cutbacks in sponsorships by corporations.[48]

Trade-Oriented Sales Promotion

Objectives for Trade-Oriented Sales Promotion

As with consumer-oriented promotions, sales promotion programs targeted to the trade should be based on well-defined objectives and measurable goals and a consideration of what the marketer wants to accomplish by using the trade promotion. There are a number of different objectives for promotions targeted to marketing intermediaries such as wholesalers and retailers. We examine some of the more common objectives of trade promotions.

Obtain distribution and support for new products

Trade promotions are often used to encourage retailers to give shelf space to new products. Manufacturers recognize that only a limited amount of shelf space is available in supermarkets, drugstores, and other major retail outlets. Thus, they must provide retailers with financial incentives to stock new products. For example, Lever Brothers used heavy sampling and high value coupons in the successful introduction of Lever 2000 bar soap. However, in addition to these consumer promotions, the company used discounts to the trade to encourage retailers to stock and promote the new brand.

While trade discounts or other types of special price deals may be used to encourage retailers and wholesalers to stock a new brand, marketers may use other types of promotions to get them to "push" the brand. Merchandising allowances may be used to get retailers to display a new product in high-traffic areas of a store, while incentive programs or contests may be used to encourage wholesaler or retail store personnel to push a new brand.

Maintain trade support for established brands

Trade promotions are often designed to maintain distribution and trade support for established brands. Brands that are in the mature phase of their product life cycle are vulnerable to losing wholesale and/or retail distribution, particularly if they are not differentiated or face competition from new products. Trade deals are often used to induce wholesalers and retailers to continue to carry weaker products because the discounts increase their profit margins. Brands with a smaller market share often rely heavily on trade promotions since they lack the funds required to differentiate themselves from competitors through media advertising.

Even if a brand has a strong market position, trade promotions may be used as part of an overall marketing strategy. For example, H. J. Heinz Co. increased its marketing spending by $100 million in 1992 and allocated virtually all of the money to trade promotions while cutting back substantially on advertising. A Heinz executive said the move was made in response to the weak economy, noting, "Price elasticity is what it's all about, and no amount of advertising will sell as well as price in this environment."[49] He also noted the increased trade promotion had resulted in substantial sales volume and market share increases for its brands.

Encourage retailers to display and promote established brands

Another objective of trade-oriented promotions is to encourage retailers to display and promote an established brand. A particularly important goal of trade promotion is to obtain retail store displays of a product away from its regular shelf location. A typical supermarket has approximately 50 display areas at the end of aisles, near checkout counters, and elsewhere. Marketers want to have their products displayed in these areas because it increases the probability shoppers will come into contact with them. Even a single display can often increase a brand's sales significantly during a promotion.

Manufacturers often use multifaceted promotional programs to encourage retailers to promote their products at the retail level. For example, Exhibit 17–28 shows a brochure for a promotion the Van Camp Seafood Company used for its Chicken of the Sea tuna brand. The promotion included a variety of promotional tools

> *Exhibit 17–28* **This multifaceted promotion is designed to encourage retailer participation and support**

designed to increase retailer participation such as manufacturer-sponsored advertising in local newspapers, display cards, and even free shoes for purchasing a specified number of cases. The program also encouraged retailers to participate by showing various promotional offers targeted toward consumers such as coupons and rebate offers.

Build retail inventories

Manufacturers often use trade promotions to build the inventory levels of retailers or other channel members. There are several reasons manufacturers use trade promotions to "load" a retailer with their products. First, wholesalers and retailers are more likely to push a product when they have high inventory levels rather than storing it in their warehouses or back rooms. Building channel members' inventories also ensures they will not run out of stock and thus miss sales opportunities.

Finally, some manufacturers sell seasonal products and believe it is important to offer large promotional discounts so retailers will stock up on their products before the peak selling season begins. This enables the manufacturer to smooth out seasonal fluctuations in its production schedule and passes on some of the inventory carrying costs to retailers or wholesalers. Moreover, when retailers stock up on a product before the peak selling season, they often will run special promotions and offer discounts to consumers to reduce excess inventories.

Types of Trade-Oriented Promotions

Manufacturers can use a variety of trade promotion tools as inducements for wholesalers and retailers. We examine some of the most frequently used types of trade promotions and some of the factors that must be considered in using them.

Contests and incentives

Manufacturers may develop contests or special incentive programs to stimulate greater selling effort and support from reseller management or sales personnel. Contests or

➤ *Exhibit 17–29*
This contest was targeted toward food-service distributors

incentive programs can be directed at managers who work for a wholesaler or distributor as well as toward store or department managers at the retail level. Manufacturers often sponsor contests for resellers and use prizes such as trips or valuable merchandise as rewards for meeting sales quotas or other types of goals they establish. Exhibit 17–29 shows an example of a contest the Van Camp Seafood Company sponsored for food-service distributors who call on restaurants.

An important target of contests or special incentives are the sales personnel of the wholesalers, distributors/dealers, or retailer. These salespeople are an important link in the distribution chain as they are likely to be very familiar with the market, more frequently in touch with the customer (whether it be another reseller or the ultimate consumer), and larger in number than the manufacturer's own sales organization.

Manufacturers often devise incentives or contests for these sales personnel. These programs may involve cash payments made directly to the retailer's or wholesaler's sales staff to encourage them to promote and sell a manufacturer's product. These payments are known as pm's, **push money,** or spiffs. For example, an appliance manufacturer may pay a $25 spiff to retail sales personnel for selling a certain model or size. In addition to cash payments, sales contests may be used whereby sales personnel can win valuable prizes such as trips or valuable merchandise for meeting certain goals established by the manufacturer. As can be seen in Exhibit 17–30, these incentives may be tied to product sales, new account placements, or merchandising efforts.

While contests and incentive programs can be very effective at generating reseller support, they also can be a source of conflict. These programs can cause problems between retail sales personnel and management. Some retailers want to maintain control over the selling activities of their sales staff. Their concern is that their salespeople may devote an undue amount of effort trying to win a contest or receive incentives offered by the manufacturer. These programs can also result in retail sales personnel becoming overly aggressive in pushing consumers to buy certain products.

➢ *Exhibit 17–30*
**Three forms of promotion
targeted to reseller salespersons**

- **Product or program sales**
  Awards are tied to the selling of a product; for example:
  - Selling a specified number of cases
  - Selling a specified number of units
  - Selling a specified number of promotional programs
- **New account placements**
  Awards are tied to:
  - The number of new accounts opened
  - The number of new accounts ordering a minimum number of cases or units
  - Promotional programs placed in new accounts
- **Merchandising efforts**
  Awards are tied to:
  - Establishing promotional programs (such as theme programs, etc.)
  - Placement of display racks, counter displays, and the like

Rather than selling the product or model that is best for the customer, salespeople push products that serve their own interests.

Many retailers refuse to allow their employees to participate in manufacturer-sponsored contests or to accept incentive payments. Retailers that do allow them often have strict guidelines and policies that must be followed, and management approval of the program is required.

Trade allowances

Probably the most commonly used trade promotion is some form of trade allowance, a discount or deal offered to the retailer or wholesaler to encourage them to stock, promote, or display the manufacturer's products. Several types of allowances generally are offered to retailers including buying allowances, promotional or display allowances, and slotting allowances.

Buying allowances   A buying allowance is a deal or discount offered to resellers in the form of a price reduction on merchandise ordered during a fixed period. These discounts are often offered in the form of an *off-invoice allowance,* which means a certain per case amount or percentage is deducted from the invoice. A buying allowance can also take the form of *free goods* whereby the reseller gets extra cases with the purchase of specific amounts (for example 1 free case with every purchase of 10 cases).

Buying allowances are used for several reasons. They are easy to implement and are well accepted, and sometimes expected, by the trade. They are also viewed as an effective way of encouraging resellers to buy the manufacturer's product since they will want to take advantage of the discounts being offered during the allowance period. Manufacturers offer trade discounts expecting wholesalers and retailers to pass the price reduction through to consumers, which will result in greater sales. However, as we see later, this is often not the case.

Promotional allowances   Manufacturers often offer allowances or discounts to retailers for performing certain promotional or merchandising activities in support of their brands. They are also sometimes referred to as a merchandising allowance. Promotional allowances can be given for providing special displays away from the product's regular shelf position, running in-store promotional programs, or including the product in an ad. The manufacturer generally has guidelines or a contract specifying the activity to be performed to qualify for the promotional allowance. The allowance is usually given as a fixed amount per case or a percentage deduction from the list price for merchandise ordered during the promotional period.

Slotting allowances   In recent years, manufacturers have been demanding and getting a special type of allowance for agreeing to handle a new product. Also called stocking allowances, introductory allowances, or street money, slotting allowances are fees that must be paid to retailers to provide a "slot" or position to accommodate the new product. Retailers argue that these fees are justified because there are costs associated with taking on a new product such as redesigning store shelves, entering the product into their computers, finding warehouse space, and informing store employees of the new product.[50] They also note they are assuming some risk in taking on a new product since a high percentage of new product introductions fail.

Slotting fees can range from a few hundred dollars per store to as much as $50,000 or more for an entire retail chain. Manufacturers that want to get their products on the shelves nationally can face several million dollars in slotting fees. Many marketers believe slotting allowances are a form of blackmail or bribery and argue that some 70 percent of these fees go directly to retailers' bottom lines.

Retailers can continue charging slotting fees because of their power and the limited availability of shelf space in supermarkets relative to the large numbers of products introduced each year. Some retailers have even been demanding **failure fees.** If a new product does not hit a minimum sales level within a certain time, a fee is charged to cover the costs associated with stocking, maintaining inventories, and then pulling the product.[51]

Large manufacturers with popular brands are less likely to pay slotting fees than smaller companies that lack leverage in negotiating with retailers. Many companies are concerned over the whole issue of trade promotions. Promotional Perspective 17–3 discusses how Procter & Gamble, one of the country's most powerful consumer products companies, is taking a stand against trade promotions.

Displays and Point-of-Purchase Materials

The next time you are in a store, take a moment to examine the various promotional materials used to display and sell products. Point-of-purchase displays are an important promotional tool because they can help a manufacturer obtain more effective in-store merchandising of products. Marketers use a variety of point-of-purchase materials including end-of-aisle displays, banners, posters, shelf cards, motion pieces, stand-up racks, and a number of other materials. In Exhibit 17–31, the WD-40 company reminds retailers of the importance of displays.

> *Exhibit 17–31*
WD-40 uses point-of-purchase displays to generate in-store sales

Displays can increase sales over 500 percent*

Displays not only draw attention, but recommend additional uses to help increase your inventory turns. To order displays, just contact your WD-40 representative.
*1989 Mueller Study

Promotional Perspective 17–3

P&G Changes the Rules on Trade Promotions

Consumer product manufacturers and retailers have been battling one another for years over issues such as shelf space and the allocation of promotional dollars. For the marketers, the name of the game is shelf space for both their existing brands and any new ones they might introduce, while the retailers' goal is to get more money from the manufacturers in the form of trade promotions. Over the past decade, retailers have been winning the battle as they have been demanding and getting a wealth of promotional subsidies from manufacturers.

Marketers have been anteing up promotional dollars in a variety of ways, including slotting fees for shelf space, price discounts, subsidies for retailer's store-sponsored advertising, and payments for in-store displays and special promotions. In 1970, manufacturers offered retailers trade promotion discounts averaging about 4 percent. Today, promotional discounts average anywhere from 10 to 15 percent. In 1991, nearly 50 percent of every dollar marketers spent on advertising and promotion went to retailers in the form of trade promotions versus only 35 percent in 1987.

While marketers provide retailers with promotional dollars to hold on to or acquire coveted shelf space, they also do so in anticipation that the savings will be passed through to consumers in the form of lower prices. However, Procter & Gamble claims only 30 percent of trade promotion discounts actually reach consumers in the form of lower prices as 35 percent is lost in inefficiencies and another 35 percent is pocketed by the retailers. Moreover, many marketers believe retailers are taking advantage of their promotional deals and misusing promotional funds.

For example, many supermarkets engage in a practice known as *forward buying* whereby they stock up on the product at the lower deal or off-invoice price and resell it to consumers at higher prices once the marketer's promotional period has ended. In some cases, retailers may take advantage of the promotional deals and then divert some of the product purchased at the low price to a store outside of their area or to a middleman who will resell it to other stores. One management consulting firm estimates these buying practices now account for more than half of supermarket profits.

In addition to not passing the discounts on to consumers, forward buying and diversion create other problems for manufacturers. The huge swings in demand that result from these practices cause production scheduling problems and mean that both manufacturers and retailers are always building toward or drawing down from a surge. Marketers are also concerned that the system leads to frequent price specials and leads consumers to make purchases on the basis of what's on sale rather than developing any loyalty to a brand.

The problems and concerns created by retailers' abuse of trade promotions have led one of the country's most powerful consumer products marketers to take action. In late 1991, Procter & Gamble adopted a policy of everyday low pricing (EDLP) whereby it has lowered the wholesale list price on nearly 40 percent of its product line by anywhere from 10 to 25 percent, while cutting promotional allowances to the trade. The price cuts leave the total cost of the product to retailers at about the same level it would have been with the trade promotion discounts. However, P&G hopes the EDLP program will help eliminate manufacturing and handling inefficiencies created by deal buying, lead to lower regular prices at the retail level, and help build brand loyalty among consumers.

As might be expected, many supermarket chains are angered by P&G's new policy. They prefer to operate on a "high-low" strategy of frequent price specials and argue the EDLP program puts them at a disadvantage against the warehouse, price club stores, and mass merchandisers that already use everyday low pricing. Some retailers have retaliated against the company by discontinuing or cutting back on the number of P&G items they sell, refusing to stock new products, or promoting rival brands. Procter & Gamble acknowledges that the EDLP program is meeting resistance, and it is receiving pressure from retailers to change it. However, the company remains committed to the program and believes the resistance will subside once retailers adjust their operations.

This is not the first time a major marketer has attempted to hold the line on promotions. Coca-Cola tried a similar move with its Hi-C brand in the early 1980s but abandoned the idea when competitors increased their deals and took away market share. There may be a difference this time, however, as P&G's size and strength and the popularity of its various brands put it in a better position than most marketers to weather retailers' wrath. Moreover, the lack of competitive moves by other companies to ambush P&G suggests many marketers are applauding the company for taking a stand on trade promotion abuses.

Many other major consumer products marketers are also re-examining their trade promotional expenditures and policies and may soon join P&G. While these programs may have different names and different tactics, their goal will be the same—to hold the line on trade promotion and reallocate this money back toward consumers. Several companies are also taking steps to track down and stop the practice of diverting. For example, Tropicana products suspended shipments to a company it suspected of diverting its products and won a $500,000 court settlement against the retailer. It will be interesting to see if the marketers can win the latest round in this ongoing battle with the trade.

Source: "Not Everyone Loves a Supermarket Special," *Business Week,* February 17, 1992, pp. 64–68; "P&G Plays Pied Piper on Pricing," *Advertising Age,* March 9, 1992, p. 6; Eric Hollreiser, "Laying It Out on the Table," *Adweek's Marketing Week,* April 27, 1992, pp. 18–20; and "Diverting," *Adweek's Marketing Week,* May 18, 1992, pp. 20–22.

In addition to point-of-purchase displays, many manufacturers help retailers by providing more efficient shelf space planning through the use of more effective **planograms,** which are configurations of products that occupy a shelf section in a store. Some manufacturers are developing computer-based programs that allow retailers to input information from their scanner data and determine the best shelf layouts by experimenting with factors such as product movement, space utilization, profit yields, and other factors.[52]

Sales Training Programs

Another form of manufacturer-sponsored promotional assistance is sales training programs for reseller sales personnel. Many products sold at the retail level require knowledgeable salespeople who can provide consumers with information about various brands and models including their features, benefits, advantages, and the like. Cosmetics, appliances, computers, consumer electronics, and sporting equipment are examples of products for which consumers often rely on knowledgeable retail sale personnel for assistance.

Manufacturers provide sales training assistance to retail salespeople in a number of ways. They may provide classes or training sessions that retail personnel can attend to increase their knowledge of a product or a product line. These training sessions present information and ideas on how to sell the manufacturer's product and may also include motivational components. Sales training classes for retail personnel are often sponsored by companies selling high-ticket items or more complex products such as personal computers, automobiles, or ski equipment.

Another way manufacturers provide sales training assistance to retail employees is through their own sales force. Sales representatives work with retail personnel to educate them about their product line and provide selling tips and other relevant information. The sales force can provide ongoing sales training for retail sales staff as they come into contact with them on a regular basis and can update them on changes in the product line, market developments, competitive information, and the like.

Manufacturers also provide training and sales assistance to reseller personnel in other ways. They provide them with detailed sales manuals, product brochures, reference manuals, and other material. Many companies now provide videocassettes for retail sales personnel that include product information, product-use demonstrations, and ideas on how to sell their product. Many of these selling aids can be used as sales tools to provide information to customers as well as sources of information for the sales staff.

Trade Shows

Another important promotional activity targeted to resellers is the **trade show,** a type of exhibition or forum where manufacturers can display their products to current as well as prospective buyers. In many industries, trade shows provide a major opportunity to display their product lines and interact with customers. They are often attended by important management personnel from large retail chains as well as by distributors and other reseller representatives.

A number of promotional functions can be performed at trade shows including demonstrating products, identifying new prospects, gathering customer and competitive information, and even writing orders for a product. Trade shows are particularly valuable for introducing new products as resellers are often looking for new merchandise to stock and may be receptive to information and presentations. They can also provide a manufacturer with valuable leads that can be followed up on through sales calls or direct marketing.

It is also important to recognize the social aspect of trade shows. Many companies use trade shows to interact with and entertain key customers and can be an important way of developing and maintaining relationships with the trade.

Cooperative Advertising

The final form of trade-oriented promotion we examine is **cooperative advertising** whereby the cost of advertising is shared by more than one party. There are three types of cooperative advertising. Although the first two are not part of trade-oriented promotional activity, we should recognize their objectives and purpose.

Horizontal cooperative advertising refers to advertising sponsored in common by a group of retailers or other organizations providing products or services to the market. Exhibit 17–32 shows an example of an ad representing cooperative effort among ski resorts in Summit County, Colorado.

Ingredient-sponsored cooperative advertising is that supported by raw materials manufacturers; the objective is to help establish end products that include materials and/or ingredients. Exhibit 17–33 shows an example of a cooperative ad run by Metal-Cladding, Inc., promoting the application of Du Pont's Teflon finishes to the coating of food-processing equipment.

The most common form of cooperative advertising, which is used as part of a trade-oriented promotional program, is **vertical cooperative advertising.** Co-op advertising, as it is commonly called, is a cooperative arrangement under which a manufacturer pays for a portion of the advertising a retailer runs to promote the manufacturer's product and its availability in the retailer's place of business. Manufacturers generally share the cost of advertising run by the retailer on a percentage basis (usually 50-50) up to a certain limit.

The limit or amount of the cooperative advertising funds the manufacturer provides to the retailer is usually based on a percentage of dollar purchases made from the manufacturer. Thus, if a retailer purchases $100,000 of product from a manufacturer, it will receive 3 percent or $3,000 of cooperative advertising money. Large retail chains often combine their co-op budgets across all of their stores, which gives them a larger sum of money to work with and more media options.

Cooperative advertising can take on several forms. Retailers may advertise a manufacturer's product as part of an ad featuring a number of different products (such as in a newspaper food ad or roto). In this case, the individual manufacturers reimburse the retailer for their portion of the ad. Another common arrangement is for the ad format to be prepared by the manufacturer and placed in the local media by the retailer. For example, Exhibit 17–34 shows a cooperative ad format that can be used by retailers in various market areas by just inserting their store name and location.

Once a cooperative ad is run, the retailer requests reimbursements from the manufacturer for its percentage of the media costs. Manufacturers usually have

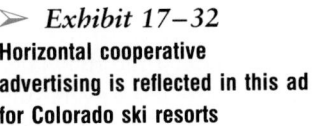

➤ *Exhibit 17–32*
Horizontal cooperative advertising is reflected in this ad for Colorado ski resorts

➤ *Exhibit 17–33 (left)*
This ad by Metal-Cladding, Inc.,is an example of ingredient-sponsored cooperative advertising

➤ *Exhibit 17–34 (right)*
An example of vertical cooperative advertising

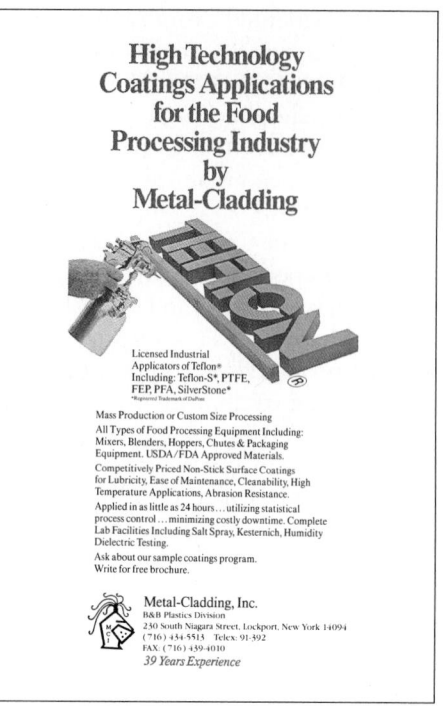

specific requirements that must be met for the ad to qualify for co-op reimbursements such as size, use of trademarks, content, and format. Verification that the ad was run is also required in the form of a tear sheet (print) or an affidavit from the radio or TV station (broadcast) along with an invoice.

As with other types of trade promotions, manufacturers have been increasing their cooperative advertising expenditures in recent years.[53] Some companies have been moving money out of national advertising and into cooperative advertising because they believe they can have greater impact with ad campaigns in local markets. There has also been a trend toward more cooperative advertising programs initiated by retailers rather than manufacturers. Many retailers approach manufacturers with catalogs, promotional events they are planning, or advertising programs they have developed in conjunction with local media and ask them to pay for a percentage cost of the program. Manufacturers often think they must go along with these requests, particularly when the retailer is large and powerful.[54]

Coordinating Sales Promotion and Advertising

Those involved in the promotional process must recognize and understand that sales promotion techniques usually work best when used in conjunction with advertising and the effectiveness of an ad campaign can be enhanced by consumer-oriented sales promotion efforts. Rather than viewing advertising and sales promotion as separate activities competing for a firm's promotional budget, they should be viewed as complementary tools. When properly planned and executed to work together, advertising and sales promotion can provide a *synergistic effect* much greater than the response that would be generated from either promotional mix element being used alone.

Evidence of this synergistic effect comes from a study conducted over 18 months for a package-goods company. The results of this study, shown in Exhibit 17–35, showed that while advertising increased sales a certain amount and sales promotion another amount, the combination of the two forms of promotion generated an additional level of sales.[55]

Proper coordination of the advertising and sales promotion efforts is essential if the firm wants to take advantage of the opportunities offered by each tool and get

> *Exhibit 17–35*
Interaction effect of advertising and sales promotion

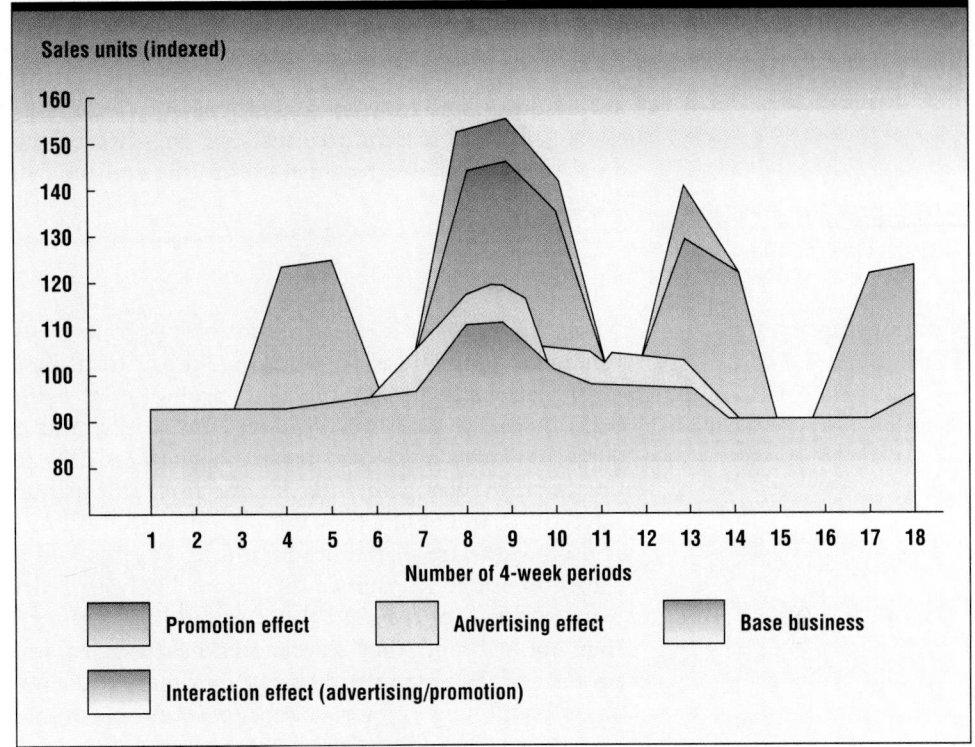

the most out of its promotional budget. Successful integration of advertising and sales promotion requires decisions concerning not only the allocation of the budget to each area but also the coordination of the ad and sales promotional themes, the target audience reached, and the timing of the various promotional activities.

Budget Coordination

As was noted at the beginning of this chapter, many companies are spending more money on sales promotion than on media advertising. It is difficult to say just what percentage of a firm's overall promotional budget should be allocated to advertising- versus consumer- and trade-oriented promotions. This allocation depends on a number of factors including the specific promotional objectives of the campaign, the market and competitive situation, and the stage of the brand in its life cycle.

Consider, for example, the way allocation of the promotional budget may vary according to the stage of a brand in the product life cycle. In the introductory stage, a large amount of the budget may be allocated to sales promotion techniques such as sampling and couponing to induce trial. In the growth stage, however, promotional dollars may be used primarily for advertising to stress brand differences and keep the brand name in the minds of consumers.

When a brand moves to the maturity stage, advertising plays primarily a reminder role to keep consumers aware of the brand. Consumer-oriented sales promotions such as coupons, price-offs, premiums, and bonus packs may be needed periodically to maintain consumer loyalty, attract new users, and protect against competition. Trade-oriented promotions are needed to maintain shelf space and accommodate retailer demands for better margins as well as encourage them to promote the brand. The study cited above on the synergistic effects of advertising and promotion examined a brand in the mature phase of its life cycle and found that 80 percent of its sales at this stage were due to sales promotions. When a brand enters the decline stage of the product life cycle, it is likely that most of the promotional support will be removed and expenditures on sales promotion are very unlikely.

Coordinating Ad and Promotional Themes

To integrate the advertising and sales promotional programs successfully, the theme of consumer promotions should be tied in with the advertising and positioning theme wherever possible. As was noted in evaluating the various sales promotion techniques, these tools should attempt to communicate a brand's unique attributes or benefits and to reinforce the sales message or campaign theme. In this way, the sales promotion effort contributes to the consumer-franchise-building effort for the brand.

Media Support and Timing

Media support for a sales promotion program is also critical and should be coordinated with the media program for the advertising campaign. Media advertising is often needed to deliver the sales promotional materials such as coupons, sweepstakes, contest entry forms, premium offers, and even samples. However, media support is also needed to inform consumers of a promotional offer as well as to create prior awareness, interest, and favorable attitudes toward the brand. By using advertising in conjunction with a sales promotion program, marketers can make consumers aware of the brand and its benefits and increase their responsiveness to the promotion. Consumers are more likely to redeem a coupon or respond to a price-off deal for a brand they are familiar with or have favorable feelings toward than for a brand they have never heard of or know nothing about. Moreover, product trial created through sales promotion techniques such as sampling or high-value couponing is more likely to result in long-term usage of the brand when accompanied by advertising.[56]

Using a promotion without prior or concurrent advertising can limit its effectiveness as well as risk damaging the image of the brand. Consumers may perceive the brand as being "promotion dependent" or of lesser quality. This can result in a lower likelihood of consumers developing favorable attitudes and long-term loyalty. Conversely, the effectiveness of an ad can be enhanced by a consumer promotion as consumers may be more likely to attend to an ad that contains a coupon, a premium offer, or an opportunity to enter a sweepstakes or contest.

An example of the effective coordination of advertising and sales promotion is the introductory campaign Lever Brothers Co. developed for its new Lever 2000 bar soap. As noted earlier in the chapter, Lever Brothers used high-value coupons, sent samples of the new bar to half of the U.S. households, and offered discounts to retailers as part of its introductory marketing blitz. However, the sales promotion efforts were accompanied by heavy advertising in print and TV. The advertising campaign used the theme "Presenting some of the 2000 body parts you can clean with new Lever 2000" (Exhibit 17–36).

Sales promotion was very important in inducing trial for Lever 2000 and continued after introduction in the form of couponing. However, the strong positioning created through effective advertising has been instrumental in converting consumers to regular users. A marketing manager noted that repeat sales of the brand have been about 40 percent, even after heavy discounting ended. Just six months after its introduction, Lever 2000 became the number two deodorant soap in dollar volume with an estimated 8.4 percent of the $1.5 billion bar soap market.[57]

To coordinate their advertising and sales promotion programs more effectively, many companies are having their sales promotion agencies become more involved in the advertising and promotional planning process. Rather than hiring agencies to develop individual, nonfranchise-building types of promotions with short-term goals and tactics, many firms are having their sales promotion and advertising agencies work together to develop more fully integrated promotional strategies and programs. Exhibit 17–37 shows how the role of sales promotional agencies is changing.

➤ *Exhibit 17–36*
A creative advertising campaign contributed to the sales success of Lever 2000

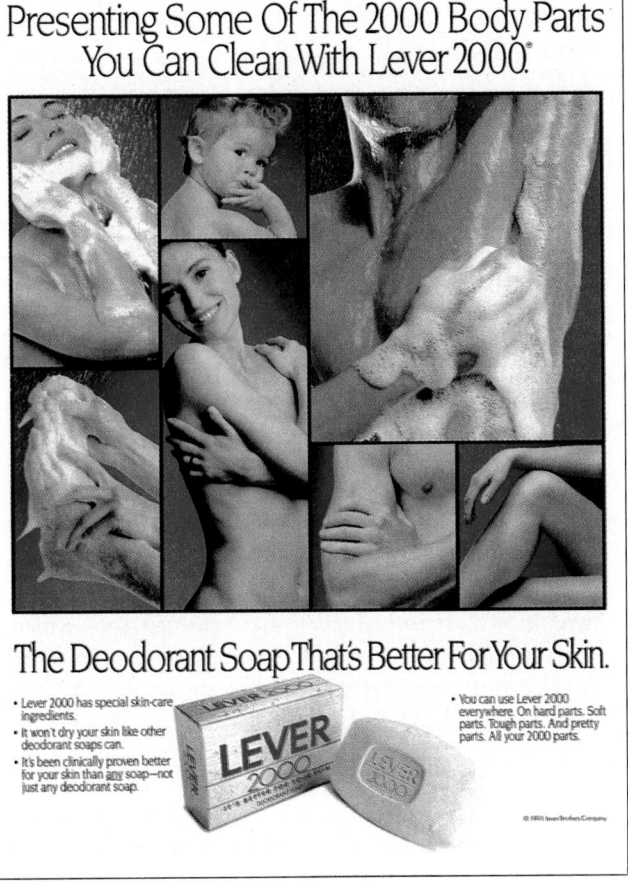

Sales Promotion Abuse

The increasing use of sales promotion in the marketing program is more than a passing fad and has been characterized as a change in the fundamental, strategic decisions regarding how companies market their products and services. However, the value of this increased emphasis on sales promotion has been questioned by several writers, particularly with regard to the lack of adequate planning and management of sales promotional programs.[58]

As the use of sales promotion techniques increases, an important factor to consider is whether marketers are becoming too dependent on and possibly even abusing this element of the marketing program. Consumer and trade promotions can be a very effective tool for generating short-term increases in sales. As was discussed at the beginning of this chapter, many brand managers would rather use some type of promotion to produce immediate sales than invest in advertising and build the brand's image over an extended time. As the director of sales promotion services at one large advertising agency noted:

> There's a great temptation for quick sales fixes through promotions. It's a lot easier to offer the consumer an immediate price savings than to differentiate your product from a competitor's.[59]

Overuse of sales promotion can be detrimental to a brand in several ways. A brand that is constantly promoted may lose perceived value from the perspective of the consumer. Consumers often end up purchasing a brand because it is on sale, they get a premium, or they have a coupon, rather than basing their decision on a favorable attitude they have developed. However, when the extra promotional incentive is not available, they may switch to another brand.

> *Exhibit 17–37*
Shifting role of the promotion agency

Traditional	New Improved
1. Primarily used to develop short-term tactics or concepts.	1. Used to develop long- and short-term promotional strategies, as well as tactics.
2. Hired/compensated on a project-by-project basis.	2. Contracted on annual retainer, following formal agency reviews.
3. Many promotion agencies used a mix—each one hired for best task and/or specialty.	3. One or two exclusive promotion agencies for each division or brand group.
4. One or two contact people from agency.	4. Full team or "core group" on the account.
5. Promotion agency never equal to ad agency– doesn't work up front in annual planning process.	5. Promotion agency works on equal basis with ad agency– sits at planning table up front.
6. Not directly accountable for results.	6. Very much accountable– goes through a rigorous evaluation process.

Alan Sawyer and Peter Dickson have used the concept of *attribution theory* to examine how the use of sales promotion may affect consumer attitude formation.[60] According to this theory, people acquire attitudes by observing their own behavior and considering why they acted in a certain manner. Consumers who consistently purchase a brand using a promotional tool such as a coupon or because of a price-off deal may "attribute" their behavior to the external promotional incentive rather than to a favorable attitude toward the brand. However, when no external incentive is available, consumers should be more likely to attribute their purchase behavior to favorable underlying feelings about the brand.

Another potential problem with consumer-oriented promotions is that a **sales promotion trap** or spiral can result when a number of competitors extensively use promotions.[61] Often a firm begins using sales promotions to differentiate its product or service from the competition. If the promotion is successful and leads to a differential advantage (or even appears to be doing so), competitors may quickly copy the promotional program. When all the competitors are using sales promotions extensively, it not only lowers profit margins for each firm but also may make it difficult for any one firm to hop off the promotional bandwagon.[62] This promotional dilemma is shown in Exhibit 17–38.

A number of industries such as cosmetics and airlines have fallen into this promotional trap. In the cosmetics industry, gift-with-purchase and purchase-with-purchase promotional offers, which were originally developed as a tactic for getting buyers to sample new products, have become a common, and costly, way of doing business.[63] In the airline industry, frequent flyer programs were begun several years ago to encourage loyalty to a particular carrier. However, nearly all the competitors quickly developed mileage-award programs out of fear of losing customers to airlines that offered them.

These programs have become very costly to administer and are costing the airlines millions of dollars every year. Moreover, since all of the major carriers have relatively comparable programs, they cannot be used as a source of differential advantage. Many airline executives long for the day when they can eliminate these programs.[64]

The effective use of sales promotions requires that marketers carefully consider both the short-term impact of a promotion as well as the long-term effect it may have on the brand. The ease with which competitors can develop a retaliatory promotion and the likelihood of their doing so should also be considered. Marketers must be careful not to damage the brand franchise with sales promotions or to get the firm involved in a promotional war that erodes the brand's profit margins and often threatens its long-term existence. Marketers are often tempted to resort to sales promotions to deal with declining sales and other problems rather than examining other aspects of the marketing program such as channel relations, price, packaging, product quality, or advertising.

> *Exhibit 17–38*
Sales promotion dilemma

All other firms	Our firm	
	Cut back promotions	**Maintain promotions**
Cut back promotions	Higher profits for all	Market share goes to our firm
Maintain promotions	Market share goes to all other firms	Market share stays constant; profits stay low

SUMMARY

For many years, advertising was the major promotional mix element of most consumer product companies. Over the past decade, however, marketers have been allocating more of their promotional dollars to sales promotion. Sales promotion programs can be classified as either being trade or consumer oriented.

This chapter focused on the role sales promotions play in a firm's marketing and promotional program. There has been a steady increase in the use of sales promotion techniques to influence and motivate consumers' purchase behavior. The growing power of retailers, erosion of brand loyalty, increase in new product introductions, fragmentation of the consumer market, short-term focus of marketing and product managers, and increase in advertising clutter are some of the reasons for this increase.

Sales promotions can be characterized as being either franchise-building or nonfranchise-building promotions. The former contribute to the development and reinforcement of brand identity and image, whereas the latter are designed to accelerate the purchase process and generate immediate increases in sales.

A number of consumer-oriented sales promotion techniques were examined in this chapter, including sampling, couponing, premiums, contests and sweepstakes, rebates and refunds, bonus packs, price-off deals, and event sponsorship. The characteristics of these promotional tools were examined, along with their specific advantages and limitations. Various types of trade-oriented promotions were also examined, including trade contests and incentives, trade allowances, displays and point-of-purchase materials, training programs, trade shows, and cooperative advertising.

Advertising and sales promotion should not be viewed as separate activities but rather as complementary tools. When planned and executed properly, advertising and sales promotion can produce a synergistic effect that is greater than the response generated from either promotional mix element alone. To accomplish this, there must be coordination of advertising and promotional themes, target audiences, and media scheduling and timing.

Consideration must also be given to the potential for sales promotional abuse. This can result when marketers become too dependent on the use of sales promotion techniques and sacrifice long-term brand position and image for short-term sales increases. In many industries, sales promotion traps or spirals develop when a number of competitors extensively use promotions and it becomes difficult for any single firm to cut back on promotion without risking a potential loss in sales. Overuse of sales promotion tools can not only result in lower profit margins but can also threaten the image and viability of a brand.

KEY TERMS

sales promotion
consumer-oriented sales
 promotion
trade-oriented sales
 promotion
consumer-franchise-
 building (CFB)
 promotions
nonfranchise-building
 promotions
sampling
bounce-back coupon

cross-ruff coupon
instant coupon
premium
self-liquidating premiums
contest
sweepstakes
game
bonus packs
price-off deal
event sponsorship
push money

failure fees
planograms
trade show
cooperative advertising
horizontal cooperative
 advertising
ingredient-sponsored
 cooperative advertising
vertical cooperative
 advertising
sales promotion trap

DISCUSSION QUESTIONS

1. What are the differences between consumer-oriented and trade-oriented sales promotions? Discuss the importance and role of each in a firm's integrated marketing communications program.
2. In 1991, marketers of consumer package goods spent 75 percent of their marketing dollars on sales promotion and only 25 percent on media advertising. Discuss some of the reasons sales promotion has become so important and is receiving an increasing portion of marketers' promotional budgets.
3. Discuss some of the long-term problems marketers might be creating as they continue to shift their marketing dollars to trade promotion and away from consumer advertising.
4. What are the differences between consumer-franchise-building and nonfranchise-building promotions? Find an example of a promotion you believe contributes to the franchise of the brand.

5. Discuss the advantages and limitation of coupons. What are some factors that influence consumers' use of coupons?
6. How might marketers measure the effectiveness of an event sponsorship promotion such as a golf or tennis tournament or an automobile race?
7. What is a slotting allowance? Do you think retailers are justified in charging manufacturers slotting fees? Why or why not?
8. Discuss the advantages of cooperative advertising from the perspective of the manufacturer and the retailer.
9. Why is it important that marketers use advertising in conjunction with sales promotion in the introduction of a new product?
10. What is meant by a sales promotion trap or spiral? What are the options for a company involved in such a situation?

chapter **18**

Public Relations, Publicity, and Corporate Advertising

chapter objectives

➤ To demonstrate the roles of public relations, publicity, and corporate advertising in the promotional mix.

➤ To differentiate between public relations and publicity and to demonstrate the advantages and disadvantages of each.

➤ To examine the reasons for corporate advertising and the advantages and disadvantages associated with this form of communication.

➤ To examine methods for measuring the effects of public relations, publicity, and corporate advertising.

Cause-Related Marketing Benefits Everyone—Or Does It?

Cause-related marketing—in which companies link with a charity or nonprofit organization as a contributing sponsor—has grown from relative obscurity to one of the hottest trends in business and industry. Most cause-related events are set up on a contract basis, where the charity or benefactor is guaranteed a fixed amount of money for use of its name during a promotion, regardless of the sales generated. A less common arrangement has the company donating a fee or a percentage of the sales of the product promoted—with a cap on the maximum amount to be received.

Companies like American Express (involved in the Statue of Liberty Restoration in 1983); Visa (contributing money to support the U.S. Olympic team based on Visa charges); Johnson & Johnson (contributing monies to curb domestic violence); and the Phoenix Phone Network of San Francisco (donating 10 percent of callers' long-distance phone bills to the church of their choice) are just a few of the many participating in cause-related marketing programs.

It would seem at first glance that everyone would win in cause-related arrangements. The charities would receive badly needed funds, and the sponsoring organization would be rewarded with favorable publicity and a positive image in the eyes of the public. In some instances, this has been the case. Kimberly-Clark, for example, has been involved with the Make a Wish Foundation and RIF (Reading Is Fundamental), donating a percentage of the value of the coupons redeemed and/or products sold during a set period. Kimberly-Clark found that during such periods, coupon redemption and sales were higher than usual, and the benefactors were rewarded handsomely.

Others are not so fortunate, however. According to Warner Canto of American Express Travel Related Services, "If your primary goal is to make money for a worthy cause, stay away from it. . . . It is not meant to be philanthropy. Its objective is to make money for your business." Canto would know; American Express has launched some of the most successful cause-related campaigns. The problem arises when the public thinks the sponsoring organization has other than philanthropic motives. Even well-meaning causes can be controversial. For example, supporting AIDS programs is not considered a good strategy because it is related to sickness and/or tragedy, and people might believe it is an attempt to benefit from others' misfortunes.

In many cases, the primary goal of the company is not the philanthropy, but rather the increased sales and profits. As noted by Mava Heffler of Johnson & Johnson, the Shelter-Aid Program, while having good intentions, was designed from the start to sell more product. "We

(continued)

weren't trying to come up with a good cause. . . . We were trying to come up with a good promotion that would move product, and this was it." The promotion, like other J&J promotions, received strong marketing support, including coupons, P-O-P displays, and local and national advertising. Ads were run on "Cagney & Lacey" and "Designing Women" TV programs in which the content revolved around domestic violence. In addition, the program received a big boost from the publicity it received in articles in *USA Today* and *McCall's,* and in a segment on "The Today Show."

Still other companies are unsure of the merits of cause-related programs. They note there may be sales gains, but there may be long-term image-related negative effects as well. Because it is so difficult to measure the direct impact of these promotions, the uncertainty keeps many companies from participating. Others do participate, but only in the safest of causes. Help for controversial causes will just have to wait.

Source: Bill Kelley, "Cause-Related Marketing: Doing Well While Doing Good," Sales & Marketing Management, *March 1991, pp. 60–66; Jim Berry, "The Official Phone Company of God,"* Adweek's Marketing Week, *July 22, 1991, p. 14.*

Cause marketing is just one of the many ways organizations integrate public relations programs with other elements of the promotional mix to more effectively market their products. Many companies believe they are directly benefiting from such programs. Besides the increased sales these programs generate, the positive publicity also provides long-term benefits.

Publicity, like public relations and corporate advertising, consists of promotional program elements that may be of great benefit to the marketer. As such, publicity constitutes an integral part of the overall promotional effort that must be managed and coordinated with the other elements of the promotions mix. However, these three tools do not always have the specific goals of product and service promotion as objectives, nor do they always involve the same methods you have become accustomed to as you have read this text. Typically, these activities are more involved in changing attitudes toward an organization or issue rather than in promoting specific products or affecting behaviors directly (though you will see that this role is changing in some firms). In this chapter, we explore the roles of public relations, publicity, and corporate advertising, the advantages and disadvantages of each, and the process by which these elements are employed. Some very interesting examples of such efforts—both successful and unsuccessful—are also included.

Public Relations

What is public relations? How does it differ from other elements discussed thus far? Perhaps a good starting point would be to define what the term **public relations** has traditionally meant and then to introduce its "new" role.

The Traditional Definition of Public Relations

While a variety of books define *public relations,* perhaps the most comprehensive is that offered by the *Public Relations News* (the weekly newsletter of the industry):

the management function which evaluates public attitudes, identifies the policies and procedures of an organization with the public interest, and executes a program of action (and communication) to earn public understanding and acceptance.[1]

As this definition indicates, public relations is a management function. The term *management* should be used in its broadest sense, in that it is not limited only to business managements but includes other types of organizations as well and extends to profit as well as nonprofit institutions and organizations.

Also, this definition of public relations defines a process that requires a series of stages including:

1. The determination and evaluation of public attitudes.
2. The identification of policies and procedures of an organization with a public interest.
3. The development and execution of a communications program designed to bring about public understanding and acceptance.

This process does not occur at just one time. To have an effective public relations program, an *ongoing* effort must be established and continued over months or even years.

Finally, this definition indicates public relations involves much more than activities designed to sell a product or service. The public relations program may involve some of the promotional program elements previously discussed but may use them in a different way and for a different purpose. For example, press releases may be mailed to announce new products or changes in the organization. Special events may be organized to create goodwill in the community, and advertising may be used to demonstrate the firm's position on a controversial issue.

The New Role of Public Relations

While the traditional definition of public relations described its role in the organization for many years, in an increasing number of marketing-oriented companies, a new set of responsibilities has been established for this function. Under its new role, public relations takes on a much broader—and more marketing-oriented—perspective, designed to promote the organization as well as its products and/or services.

Exhibit 18–1 demonstrates four different relationships that marketing and public relations have assumed in an organization. As can be seen, these relationships are defined by the degree of use of each function.

Class 1 relationships are those characterized by a minimal use of either function. Organizations with this design typically have very small marketing and/or public relations budgets and devote little time and effort in this regard. As noted, small social service agencies and nonprofit organizations are typically characterized by this classification.

Those organizations characterized by a *class 2* relationship have a well-established public relations function, but do very little in the way of formalized marketing activities. As indicated in Exhibit 18–1, colleges and hospitals typically have such a design, although in both cases the marketing activities are increasing. Both of these groups have moved in the direction of class 4 organizations in recent years, though public relations activities still dominate.

Many small companies are typified by a *class 3* organization in which marketing tends to dominate, whereas the public relations function is minimal. Private companies (without stockholders) and small manufacturers with little or no publics to appease tend to employ this design.

Class 4 enterprises have both a strong marketing and a strong public relations department. In many of these organizations, these two departments operate independently. For example, public relations may be responsible for the more traditional responsibilities described earlier, whereas marketing is responsible for promoting

> *Exhibit 18–1*

Four classes of marketing and public relations use

		Public Relations	
		Weak	Strong
Marketing	**Weak**	1 Example: Small social service agencies	2 Example: Hospitals and colleges
	Strong	3 Example: Small manufacturing companies	4 Example: Fortune 500 companies

specific products and/or services. At times, both groups may work together, and both report to top management. Many Fortune 500 companies employ multiple advertising agencies and public relations firms to promote them.

The new role of public relations might best be characterized by the class 4 categorization noted above, although with a slightly different relationship. Rather than each department operating independently, the two now work much more closely together, blending their talents to provide the best overall image of the firm and its product or service offerings. Public relations departments increasingly position themselves as a tool both to supplant and to support the traditional advertising and marketing efforts. The American Express and J&J examples discussed at the beginning of this chapter exemplify this new relationship.

William N. Curry notes that organizations must use caution in developing class 4 relationships.[2] Curry says public relations and marketing are not one and the same, and when one becomes dominant, the balance required to operate at maximum efficiency is lost. He notes that an organization that loses sight of the objectives and functions of public relations in an attempt to achieve marketing goals may in the long run be operating to its own detriment.

Integrating Public Relations into the Promotional Mix

Given the broader responsibilities of public relations, the issue now becomes one of integrating this element into the promotional mix. Philip Kotler and William Mindak suggest that a number of alternative organizational designs are possible, with either marketing or public relations being the dominant function, both being equal but separate functions, or the two performing the same roles.[3] While each of these designs has its merits, in this text we consider public relations as a promotional program element. This means that while a broader role will be defined, traditional responsibilities must still be assumed.

Whether a traditional role or a more marketing-oriented one is assumed, public relations activities are still tied to specific communications objectives. The need to assess public attitudes and to create a favorable corporate image is of no less importance than strategies designed to promote products or services directly.

The Process of Conducting Public Relations

The actual process of conducting public relations and integrating it into the promotional mix involves a series of tasks. These tasks involve both traditional and marketing-oriented activities.

The Determination and Evaluation of Public Attitudes

Given that public relations is concerned with attitudes toward the firm or specific issues beyond those directed at a product or service, the very first question you may ask is, Why? Why is the firm so concerned with the public's attitudes?

One reason is that these attitudes may impact sales of the firm's products. For example, sales of Coors beer have been very directly influenced by the boycotts against the company initiated by union members and minorities—both of whom have developed negative attitudes toward the brewer. The oil spill that occurred in Prince William Sound, Alaska, in 1989 when the tanker *Exxon Valdez* hit a submerged reef resulted in very unfavorable attitudes toward Exxon (the owner of the ship), which led to a number of protests, a boycott of Exxon products, and the return of thousands of the company's credit cards. Exhibit 18–2 shows an ad run by Exxon apologizing for the catastrophe and responding to the public relations problem it created. Promotional Perspective 18–1 (page 632) shows a few other companies that have faced similar nightmares.

Second, no one wants to be perceived as a "bad citizen." Corporations exist in communities, and their employees may both live and work there. Negative attitudes carry over to employee morale and may result in a less-than-optimal working environment internally and/or in the community.

As a result of this concern with the perceptions of the public, many firms conduct research designed to keep the firm abreast of the public's attitudes. Surveys of public

➤ *Exhibit 18–2*
Exxon apologizes for the Alaskan oil spill

AN OPEN LETTER TO THE PUBLIC

On March 24, in the early morning hours, a disastrous accident happened in the waters of Prince William Sound, Alaska. By now you all know that our tanker, the Exxon Valdez, hit a submerged reef and lost 240,000 barrels of oil into the waters of the Sound.

We believe that Exxon has moved swiftly and competently to minimize the effect this oil will have on the environment, fish and other wildlife. Further, I hope that you know we have already committed several hundred people to work on the cleanup. We also will meet our obligations to all those who have suffered damage from the spill.

Finally, and most importantly, I want to tell you how sorry I am that this accident took place. We at Exxon are especially sympathetic to the residents of Valdez and the people of the State of Alaska. We cannot, of course, undo what has been done. But I can assure you that since March 24, the accident has been receiving our full attention and will continue to do so.

L. G. Rawl
Chairman

EXXON

➤ *Exhibit 18–3*
Times Mirror ad designed to gain readers' views

attitudes are common among privately held corporations, utilities, and/or publicly held companies. The advertisement shown in Exhibit 18–3 is one way of collecting such information, whereas other, more standard research techniques are also used. The reasons for conducting this research are many, including the following.

1. **It provides input into the planning process.** Once the firm has determined the attitudes of the public, these attitudes serve as the starting point in the development of programs designed to maintain favorable positions or change unfavorable ones.
2. **It serves as an "early warning system."** Once a problem exists, it may require substantial efforts in time and money to correct it. By conducting research, the firm may be able to identify potential problems and handle them effectively before they become an issue.
3. **It secures support internally.** Should research indicate that a problem or potential problem exists, then it will be much easier for the public relations arm to gain the support it needs to address this problem.
4. **It increases the effectiveness of the communication.** By better understanding the problems and/or potential problems, the firm is better able to design communications that will effectively deal with them in the proper manner.[4]

Establishing a Public Relations Plan

In a survey of 100 top and middle managers in the communications field regarding their public relations programs, over 60 percent indicated their "programs" involved little more than the use of press releases, press kits for trade shows, and new product announcements.[5] Further, these tools were not formulated into a formal public relations effort but rather were used only as they felt they were needed. In

Promotional Perspective 18–1

Boycotts—The Public Relations Nightmare

To most consumers, Procter & Gamble (P&G) is a well-respected manufacturer and marketer of consumer products. To others, it is a company that engages in devil worship and contributes at least some of its profits to the Church of Satan. For decades, P&G has had to contend with and respond to rumors that link the company with the devil. At the center of the controversy is the P&G logo that featured a man in whose beard could be seen the numbers 666—the numbers linked with the devil in the Book of Revelations. Despite P&G's adamant denials, the rumors persist and have led to consumer boycotts of the company's products. P&G estimates that over the past decade it has had to respond to over 150,000 calls related to the satanism rumor and has initiated numerous lawsuits against boycotters. In some of these cases, P&G won the lawsuits and the rumors were stopped. In too many others, the source could not be identified even after thousands of dollars and hours were involved in the attempt.

Executives at Bumble Bee Seafoods, the third largest marketer of tuna in the United States, awoke one morning to full-page ads urging consumers to boycott the company for using tuna-catching methods that resulted in the inadvertent capturing and killing of dolphins. The sponsor of the ads, San Francisco-based Earth Island Institute, an environmental watchdog group, also held a press conference charging Bumble Bee with "the slaughter of dolphins" and "stinging the American consumer with a PR campaign founded on deceit."

Over the next weeks, Bumble Bee and its advertising agency spent thousands of hours planning and implementing a counterattack. This counterattack included the use of refutational ads, the company's own press conference, and lengthy negotiations with Earth Island. While no dollar amount of lost sales resulting from the boycott has been released, the company estimates it has spent in the hundreds of thousands of dollars fighting the negative publicity and boycott.

Besides the two boycotts cited here, a variety of other companies have been hit with boycotts as well: Coors Brewing Co. (minority discrimination); McDonald's (environmental irresponsibility); H. G. Heilman (targeting harmful products to blacks). Even countries are not safe. A boycott was called against all Japanese products, when a Japanese official called American workers lazy.

To the public relations department, the threat of or actual enactment of a boycott is nothing less than a nightmare. Besides the potential for lost sales, boycotts create additional forms of havoc. Time normally spent to promote the product or brand is now devoted to countering the boycott. Employees of the target of the boycott and their public relations agencies are taken away from their normal activities and required to devote extra time and energy to fight the battle. Dollars that might normally be spent in image-building public relations activities are now spent to counter negative communications.

Besides public relations costs, there are costs for court battles, employees' overtime, travel, and so on that would not necessarily be incurred. But perhaps the biggest cost of all is the long-term effect on image. Some people probably still believe McDonald's uses worms in its hamburgers—the basis for one of the boycotts against McDonald's; that Bumble Bee slaughters dolphins; and that Coors discriminates against blacks and Latinos, even though each of these companies spent thousands and thousands of dollars fighting these claims. To at least one company—P&G—it may just be easier to give in. After fighting the satanism rumors for decades, the company announced in 1991 that the P&G logo, in place since the founding of the company in the late 1800s, would be changed. It just took too much time and effort to fight.

Source: Laurie Freeman, "Devil Rumors Nick P&G Again," *Advertising Age*, May 7, 1990, p. 60; "Corridor Talk," *Adweek's Marketing Week*, March 25, 1991, p. 38; "Corridor Talk," *Adweek's Marketing Week*, July 25, 1991, p. 30; "Boycott of Bumble Bee Tuna Urged," *San Diego Union*, December 5, 1990, p. A-3.

other words, no structured program was evident in well over half of the companies surveyed! As we noted earlier, the public relations process is an ongoing one, requiring formalized policies and procedures for dealing with problems and opportunities. Just as you would not develop an advertising and/or promotions program without policies and procedures and a plan, you should not institute public relations efforts this way. Moreover, this plan needs to be integrated into the overall marketing communications program. Exhibit 18–4 provides some of the questions marketers need to ask to determine whether the public relations plan is an appropriate one.

Cutlip, Center, and Broom suggest a four-step process for developing a public relations plan: (1) define public relations problems; (2) plan and program; (3) take action and communicate; and (4) evaluate the program.[6] As you can see, these questions and the four-step planning process tie in very well with the promotional planning process stressed throughout this text.

➤ *Exhibit 18–4*
10 questions to evaluate marketing public relations plans

> 1. Does the plan reflect a thorough understanding of the company's business situation?
> 2. Has the PR (public relations) program made good use of research and background sources?
> 3. Does the plan include analysis of recent editorial coverage?
> 4. Do the PR people fully understand the product—its strengths and weaknesses?
> 5. Does the PR program describe several cogent, relevant conclusions from the research?
> 6. Are the program objectives specific and measurable?
> 7. Does the program clearly describe what the PR activity will be and its benefits to the company?
> 8. Does the program describe how its results will be measured?
> 9. Do the research, objectives, activities, and evaluations tie together?
> 10. Has the PR department communicated to marketing throughout the development of the program?

Developing and Executing the Public Relations Program

Because of the broad role that public relations may be asked to perform, the public relations (PR) program may need to extend beyond that of the promotional program. A broader definition of the target market, additional communications objectives, and different messages and delivery systems may be employed. Let us examine this process.

Determining relevant target audiences

The targets of public relations efforts may be varied, with different objectives established for each. Some may be directly involved in the product purchase, whereas others may affect the firm in a different way (for example, stockholders, legislators, etc.). In addition, these audiences may include persons both internal or external to the firm.

Internal audiences may include the employees of the firm, investors and stockholders, suppliers, members of the local community, and current customers. You may be wondering why members of the local community or customers of the firm are considered internal rather than external. According to John Marston, these groups should be considered internal because they are already connected with the organization in some way and constitute the group the firm would normally communicate with in the ordinary routine of work.[7] **External audiences** are those people who are not necessarily closely connected with the organization, for example, the public at large.

It may be necessary to communicate with these groups on an ongoing basis for a variety of reasons ranging from ensuring goodwill to introducing new policies, procedures, or even products. A few examples might help.

Employees of the firm The goals of maintaining morale and providing employees with an indication of the results of their efforts are often prime objectives of the public relations program. Organizational newsletters, notices on bulletin boards, paycheck envelope stuffers, direct mail, and annual reports are some of the methods used to communicate with these groups. Exhibit 18–5 shows an example of one such internal organization communication used by Hershey Foods.

Personal methods of communicating may be as formal as an established grievance committee or as informal as an office Christmas party. Other social events such as corporate softball and/or bowling teams are also used to create goodwill.

Stockholders and investors You may typically think of an annual report such as that shown in Exhibit 18–6 as providing stockholders and investors with financial information regarding the firm. While this is one purpose, annual reports also provide a communications channel in which this audience may be informed as to why the firm is or is not doing well, future plans, or other information that goes beyond just that of numbers.

For example, McDonald's has successfully used annual reports to fend off potential public relations problems. In 1989, the company ran a report on McDonald's

➤ *Exhibit 18–5*

An example of a newsletter used for internal corporate communication

➤ *Exhibit 18–6*

Annual reports serve a variety of purposes

recycling efforts to alleviate consumers' concerns about waste. In 1990, the report included a 12-page spread on food and nutrition. Other companies have employed similar strategies. In addition to the annual report, shareholders meetings, video presentations, or other forms of direct mail may be employed for this purpose. Companies have used these approaches to generate additional investments, to bring more of their stocks "back home" (that is, become more locally controlled and managed), and to produce funding to solve specific problems, as well as to promote goodwill.

Community members Those persons who live and work in the community in which a firm is located or doing business are often the target of public relations efforts. Such efforts may involve advertisements informing the community of activities that the organization is engaged in, for example, reducing air pollution, cleaning up water supplies, or as shown in Exhibit 18–7, protecting wildlife. (As you can also tell from Exhibit 18–7, the community can be defined very broadly!) Demonstrating to the public that the organization is a good citizen, and has their welfare in mind, may also be a reason for communicating to these groups.

Suppliers and customers An organization wishes to maintain a level of *goodwill* with its suppliers as well as its consuming public. It is obvious that consumers are less likely to wish to buy from a company that they do not think is socially conscious and might take their loyalties elsewhere. Likewise, suppliers may be inclined to exhibit the same behaviors.

Sometimes sponsoring a public relations effort results in direct evidence of success. For example, the "Say no to drugs" campaign resulted in a boon to companies manufacturing drug testing kits, hospitals offering drug rehabilitation programs,

➤ *Exhibit 18–7*
Chevron demonstrates public concern

➤ *Exhibit 18–8*
SDGE's Consumer Outreach Program is one of many targeting the San Diego community

The sheep that came home for winter.

Winds here can scream up to 70 miles per hour. Temperatures plummet to 20 below. This is Stillwater Valley, Montana. The winter home of a small, fledgling herd of Bighorn Sheep. A herd that for years has been struggling to survive. But people who work nearby are providing medication and food to nurture, protect and save these majestic animals. Hopefully helping each generation become healthier. Each generation larger.

Do people look after their neighbors so nature can grow strong?

People Do.

Chevron

To our customers:

SDG&E management believes it's important to have the benefit of public participation in our company's customer policies and practices. Decisions about gas and electric service affect everyone. Therefore, we want to involve a broad-based representation of customers in examining SDG&E's operations.

That's what our Consumer Outreach Program is all about—community involvement. The success of the program so far is due in large measure to the interest of those community representatives who have given their time and effort.

What has emerged is a growing consensus of customer attitudes, concerns and expectations relating to our company and its operations. I am much encouraged by the positive and constructive recommendations produced thus far.

Clearly, the Consumer Outreach Program is an important two-way means of communication on energy, a subject that touches the lives of every one of us. Please read the report that follows, and I believe you will share my optimism about the value of this program.

Jack E. Thomas

Jack E. Thomas,
Executive Vice President,
Utility Operations
San Diego Gas & Electric

and television news programs' ratings.[8] At the same time, indirect indications of the success of these efforts may include more customer loyalty, less antagonism, or greater cooperation between the firm and its suppliers or consumers.

Sometimes a public relations effort may be targeted to more than one of the groups cited above. For example, San Diego Gas & Electric (SDGE), the public utility company for the San Diego area, has suffered from extreme negative attitudes among its customers, brought about by high utility rates. This problem was aggravated when a series of management blunders resulted in even higher rates, and plans were announced to build a nuclear plant in one of the lagoons near the ocean, resulting in protests from consumers and environmentalists. Stockholders and potential investors lacked trust, and employee morale was at a low. (Company cars with the SDGE logo on the doors were vandalized and drivers were threatened to the point where the identifying logos had to be removed.)

The public relations plan developed to deal with these problems targeted a variety of publics and employed a number of channels. Television spots were used to show consumers how to save energy. Print ads explained the reasons for the energy purchases made by management, and public relations programs such as the Consumer Outreach Program shown in Exhibit 18–8 were developed. The outcome of these programs has been shown to have led to much more favorable attitudes among all the publics targeted (at least employees can put the SDGE logo back on their cars!).

Relevant audiences may also include those persons not directly involved with the firm. External audiences may include the press, educators, civic and business groups, governments, potential customers, and the financial community.

➤ *Exhibit 18–9*
The media employs public relations to enhance their image to the community

10 STANDS FOR SAN DIEGO

San Diego's 10 has always been committed to making San Diego a better place to live. And we make that commitment a reality with community projects that net real results — projects we're proud to sponsor:

▶ **CHILDREN'S LINE 10**

San Diego's 60,000 latchkey kids now have somewhere to turn — Children's Line 10, a special after-school phone line for kids home alone. There's always a trained volunteer on the line, ready to lend an ear when kids are scared, lonely or bored. In under 3 years, more than 20,000 kids dialed our 800 number.

▶ **TEAM 10**

San Diego's 10 is putting a little elbow grease into this community project. Four times a year, we ask volunteers to join us as we roll up our sleeves and improve our environment. Projects like neighborhood clean-ups, tree-planting, and school renovations. With our volunteer corps of hundreds, we're proving that a little muscle goes a long way.

▶ **VOLUNTEER 10**

Want to volunteer but don't know where? Volunteer 10 can help. One call puts you in touch with over 550 programs countywide that need volunteers. Volunteer 10 received 12,000 calls during its first two years.

▶ **10 LEADERSHIP AWARD**

Every Friday on 10News at 6:30, we salute a leader of San Diego — with the 10Leadership Award, presented by 10News reporter Leonard Villarreal. It's our way of honoring those who take action and get results. And a way of paying tribute to the unsung heroes of San Diego. These leaders are nominated by their peers and colleagues. And every year, we bring them together for a luncheon to once again say "thanks."

▶ **10 FRIENDS**

We're also giving kids a chance to form friendships with people of another generation — San Diego's older adults. 10Friends brings together schools and senior centers so participants can share experiences, learn from one another, and become friends. From Vista to Chula Vista, students and seniors are enjoying activities that are fun and rewarding.

▶ **CHANNEL 10 TOY DRIVE**

Thousands of kids have a Christmas they'll remember, thanks to the annual Toy Drive at San Diego's 10. In December 1990, we collected more than 25,000 toys for the Salvation Army to distribute to families in need. For the past 16 years, 10News Weathercaster "Captain" Mike Ambrose has generously given his talent and time to this project.

The media Perhaps one of the most critical of the external publics is that of the media. The media determines what you will read in your newspapers or see on television, what is news, and how this news will be presented. Because of the media's extreme power, the media should be informed of the actions of the firm. Thus, companies issue press releases and communicate through conferences, interviews, and special events as a means of disseminating information. The media are generally receptive to such information, as news people are interested in good stories so long as the communications are handled professionally.

One person who has mastered this task quite well is Steven Jobs, founder of Apple Computer. Jobs achieved extensive media coverage of his introduction of the Macintosh, and later the NeXT computers, by establishing a well-staged event in which the media were the first to see the new innovations. These events were very well attended and got both products off to an excellent start. Apple has continued to follow the model set by Jobs.

In turn, the media are also concerned about how the community perceives them. Exhibit 18–9 reflects an example of one of the public relations pieces distributed by a San Diego television station, demonstrating the variety of programs the station employs to benefit the community.

Educators A number of organizations provide educators with information regarding their activities. Organizations such as the Direct Marketing Association, the Specialty Advertising Association, and the American Association of Yellow Pages Publishers (as shown in Exhibit 18–10), among others, keep educators informed in an attempt to generate goodwill as well as exposure for their causes. These groups, as well as major corporations, provide information regarding new innovations, state-of-the-art research, or other items of interest.

Much of the reason underlying the release of this information is that educators are, to a degree, like the media—that is, they control the flow of information to certain parties—in this case, people like you.

> *Exhibit 18–10*
The Yellow Pages distribute information to college professors, in part through *Link* magazine

Civic and business organizations   The local Jaycees, Kiwanis, and other nonprofit civic organizations also serve as gatekeepers of information to those in their sphere of influence. Speeches made at organization functions, financial contributions, or sponsorships are all designed to create goodwill. Likewise, memberships of corporate executives on the board of directors of nonprofit organizations also generate positive public relations.

Governments   Direct efforts to influence government bodies at both a local and a national level are often employed as a public relations effort. Successful *lobbying* may mean immediate success for a product, whereas laws or regulations passed that may be detrimental to the firm may cost it millions. Imagine for a moment what the approval of NutraSweet meant to Searle or what could happen to the beer and wine industries should television advertising be banned.

Financial groups   In addition to current shareholders, potential shareholders and investors may be relevant target markets. Financial advisers, lending institutions, and others must be kept abreast of new developments as well as the financial information typically provided, as they offer the potential for new sources of funding. Press releases and corporate reports have played an important role in providing information to these publics.

Implementing the public relations program

Once the research has been conducted and the target audiences have been identified, the public relations program must be developed and delivered to the receivers. A number of public relations tools are available for this purpose.

The press release   As previously noted, one of the most important publics is that of the press. To have information used by the press, it must be factual, true, and/or of interest to the medium as well as its audience. As shown in Exhibit 18–11, the source of the **press release** can do certain things to improve the likelihood that the "news" will be disseminated.

In addition to those methods shown in Exhibit 18–11, the information needs to be of interest to the readers of that medium. For example, financial institutions may issue press releases to business trade media and/or to the editor of the business

➤ *Exhibit 18–11*
Getting the public relations story told

Jonathan Schenker of Ketchum Public Relations, New York, suggests four new technological methods to make life easier for the press and to increase the likelihood of getting one's story told:

1. *Telephone press conferences*   Since reporters cannot always get to a press conference, use the telephone to call them for coverage.
2. *In-studio media tours*   Satellite communications providing a story, and a chance to interview, from a central location such as a television studio save broadcast journalists time and money by eliminating their need to travel.
3. *Multicomponent video news releases (VNR)*   A five-component package consisting of a complete script in print and on tape, a video release with a live reporter, a local contact source at which to target the video, and a silent video news release that allows the station to fill in with its own news reporter lend an advantage owing to their budget-savings capabilities.
4. *Targeted newswire stories*   By targeting the public relations message, reporters are spared the need to read through volumes of news stories, selecting only those of interest to them and their target audiences.

section of a common-interest medium such as the newspaper. Information on the release of a new rock album is of more interest to radio disk jockeys than to television newscasters, whereas sports news also has its interested audiences.

Press conferences   We are all familiar with press conferences held by political figures. While used less often by organizations and corporations, this form of delivery can be very effective. The topic must be of major interest to a specific group before it is likely to gain coverage. Usually major accomplishments such as the awarding of the next Super Bowl or Olympics location or major breakthroughs, such as medical cures, emergencies, or catastrophies, are topics warranting a national press conference, whereas on a local level, community events, local developments, and the like may receive coverage. Press conferences are often used by companies when they have significant news to announce, such as the introduction of a new product or advertising campaign. For example, Coca-Cola held a press conference to announce that the cast from "Beverly Hills 90210" had signed on to represent Coke throughout the United States and international markets.

Exclusives   Although most public relations efforts may seek a variety of channels for distribution, an alternative strategy may be to offer one particular medium exclusive rights to the story. Should this medium or group reach a substantial number of persons interested in that area, offering an **exclusive** may enhance the likelihood of acceptance. As you watch television over the next few weeks, watch for the various networks' and local stations' offerings of exclusives. Notice the attention they pay to these exclusives and how the media actually use them to promote themselves.

Interviews   While you are watching television, or when you are reading magazines, pay close attention to the personal interviews being conducted. Usually, someone will have some specific questions or issues to be raised, and a spokesperson is provided by the firm for answering them. For example, when the *Challenger* space shuttle accident occurred, a spokesperson for Morton Thiokol, the company responsible for manufacturing the O-rings that contributed to the explosion, was interviewed to provide the company's perspective. When Chrysler was accused of selling cars used by employees as new, Lee Iacocca, the president of Chrysler, served as the interviewee to give the company's response to the charges.

Other methods of distributing information include photo kits, bylined articles (articles written by the firm, signed, and offered for publication), speeches, and trade shows. Of course, the specific mode of distribution to be used is determined by the nature of the story and the interest of the media and its publics.

Advantages and Disadvantages of Public Relations

Like the other program elements, there are both advantages and disadvantages to be accrued through the use of public relations.

Some of the advantages are:

- **Credibility**   Because public relations communications are not perceived in the same light as advertising—that is, the public does not realize the organization either directly or indirectly paid for the communications—they tend to have more credibility among the receivers. The fact that the medium is not being compensated for providing the information may lead the receiver to consider the news as more truthful and credible. For example, an article that appears in newspapers or magazines discussing the virtues of aspirin may be perceived as much more credible than an ad for the same product.

  Automotive awards presented in magazines such as *Motor Trend* have long been known to carry clout among potential car buyers. Now marketers have found that even lesser media mean a lot as well. General Motors' Pontiac division played up an award given to Pontiac as "the best domestic sedan" by *MotorWeek* in a 30-minute program carried by about 300 Public Broadcasting Service stations. Likewise, Chrysler trumpeted the awards given to its Jeep Cherokee by *4-Wheel & Off Road Magazine*.[9]

  Sometimes, news about a product may in itself serve as the subject of an ad. Exhibit 18–12 demonstrates how GM used favorable publicity from a variety of sources to promote its products. A number of auto manufacturers have also taken advantage of the high customer satisfaction ratings reported on by J. D. Powers & Associates, an independent research firm specializing in automotive research, in their ads.

- **Cost**   Both in absolute and relative terms, the cost of public relations is very low—particularly when considering the possible effects. While many firms employ public relations agencies and spend millions of dollars in this area, for smaller companies, this form of communication may be the most affordable of the alternatives available. Many public relations programs require little more than the time and expenses associated with putting the program together and getting it distributed and yet are still able to accomplish their objectives.

- **Avoidance of clutter**   Because of the nature of the communication—that it may be typically perceived as a *news item*—public relations messages are not subject to the clutter of advertisements. A story regarding a new product introduction or breakthrough is perceived as a news item and is likely to receive more attention. Referring back to Steven Job's introduction of the NeXT computer, all the major networks covered the story, as did major newspapers and magazines. Some (like CNN) devoted two- to three-minute segments to the introduction.

- **Lead generation**   Information provided about a technological innovation, a medical breakthrough, and the like, almost immediately results in a multitude of inquiries. These inquiries may provide the firm with the potential of some quality sales leads. For example, Vend-a-Video, a manufacturer of a videocassette vending machine, received dozens of inquiries regarding its product from one article that appeared in a trade magazine discussing the product's development. Leads from as far away as Germany and Brazil offered the company a potential source of sales.

- **Ability to reach specific groups**   Because some products may have appeal to only a small segment, it is not feasible to engage in advertising and/or promotions to reach this group. In addition, the firm or organization may not have the financial capabilities to engage in promotional expenditures. One of the best—and only—ways to communicate to these groups is that of public relations, through any of the delivery channels discussed.

➤ *Exhibit 18–12*   **These GM ads capitalized on favorable publicity**

- **Image building**   Effective public relations leads to development of a positive image for the organization or firm. A strong image is, in turn, insurance against later misfortunes. For example, in 1982, seven people in the Chicago area died after taking Extra Strength Tylenol capsules that had been laced with cyanide (by an as-yet-unidentified person). Within one week of the news of the poisonings, Tylenol's market share fell from 35 to only 6.5 percent. Strong public relations efforts combined with an already strong product and corporate image made it possible for the product to rebound (despite the opinions of many experts that the product had no chance of recovering!). A brand or firm with a lesser image would never have been able to come back. The ad shown in Exhibit 18–13 demonstrates the power of a strong image.

Perhaps the major disadvantage of using public relations is the potential for not completing the communications process. While it was mentioned earlier that public relations sometimes breaks through the clutter of commercials, it is also possible that while the message may be noted by the receiver, the connection to the source is not achieved. For example, many firms' public relations efforts are never associated with their sponsors.

One of the potential ways that public relations may misfire is through mismanagement and a lack of coordination with the marketing department. As was stated earlier in this chapter, some organizations have separate marketing and public relations departments. When these departments operate independently, the potential exists for inconsistent communications, redundancies in efforts, and so on.

WHY A STRONG BRAND IMAGE GIVES YOU AN ALMOST UNFAIR ADVANTAGE.

[In a world of parity products and services, nothing can tilt things more dramatically in your favor than powerful brand and corporate advertising.]

A brand or corporate image is not something that can be seen, touched, tasted, defined, or measured. Intangible and abstract, it exists solely as an idea in the mind. Yet it is often a company's most precious asset.

When in the 1980s, corporations laid out billions for the companies that owned brands like Kraft, Jell-O, Del Monte, Maxwell House and Nabisco, it wasn't the products themselves they were after, but the enduring power of warm images, feelings, and impressions associated with the brand names. In fact, when the dust finally settles, it will become clear that the megamergers, takeovers, and leveraged buyouts of that decade were primarily about the acquisition of brands.

Yet despite their enormous value, brands are not immune to neglect, and in the face of a tough economy and strong competition, companies are often tempted to sacrifice brand and corporate advertising for short-term promotion. While such strategies can yield immediate results, over time they can weaken and tarnish the brand.

Studies conducted on the PIMS (Profit Impact on Market Strategy) data base prove that companies that put more money behind (their) image advertising are more likely to be market dominators, ranking first in a category and having sales volume one-and-a-half times greater than the nearest competitor. Moreover, the larger the ratio of brand advertising to promotion, the greater the return on investment (ROI). When only a quarter of a company's advertising/promotion budget is spent on brand advertising, the ROI is 18%. When the ratio is increased to 50/50, the return can be over 70% higher.

Backing your brand in good times and bad–keeping that image in front of people–can mean higher profits as well as leadership.

PROTECTING AND NURTURING A brand is one of advertising's most important jobs. And that means choosing the media for your message with care. For more and more companies, the best environment is The Wall Street Journal. The Journal has always operated on the principle that there is a direct link between the quality of our editorial and the quality of the advertising we attract. Witness the impressive list of corporations appearing in any Journal issue.

In The Myers Marketing & Research survey of The Worldwide Marketing Leadership Panel, The Journal was awarded top honors in five separate categories, including editorial quality and reader involvement–more evidence of The Journal's unmatched stature and prestige.

If you're looking for a publication that can add value to your brand, there's no better brand than ours: The Wall Street Journal.

THE WALL STREET JOURNAL.
THE WORLD'S BUSINESS DAILY. IT WORKS.

© 1991 Dow Jones & Company, Inc. All Rights Reserved. Source: Myers Marketing & Research. 6A292

While other disadvantages may be associated with public relations, the two discussed here are the most common. The key to effective public relations is to establish a good program, worthy of public interest, and manage it properly. To determine if this program is working, it is necessary to measure the effectiveness of the public relations effort.

Measuring the Effectiveness of Public Relations

As with the other promotional program elements, it is important to evaluate the effectiveness of the public relations efforts. In addition to determining the contribution of this program element on the attainment of communications objectives, the evaluation offers additional advantages:

1. It tells management what has been achieved through public relations activities and actions.

2. It provides management with a quantitative means of measuring public relations achievements.

3. It provides management with a means of judging the quality of public relations achievements and activities.[10]

As shown in Exhibit 18–14, a number of criteria may be used to measure the effects of such programs. In addition to the methods provided in Exhibit 18–14, Raymond Simon suggests additional means for accomplishing this evaluation process, including:

- **Personal observation and reaction**   One method suggested is that of personal observation by one's superiors. This observation and evaluation should occur at all levels of the organization.

- **Matching objectives and results**   Specific objectives designed to attain the overall communications objectives may be established. Relating these objectives to actions, activities, or media coverage is suggested. For example, placing a feature story in a specific number of media may serve as an objective, quantitative, and measurable goal.

- **The team approach**   Harold Mendelsohn suggests that one way to achieve attitude and behavior modification through public information campaigns is to use the **team approach** whereby evaluators are actually involved in the campaign. [11] By using research principles and working together, actual rather than assumed intents and efforts will be developed—and potentially accomplished.

- **Management by objectives**   In this method, the executives and their managers act together to identify goals to be attained and the responsibilities of the managers in this endeavor. These goals are then used as a standard to measure accomplishments.

- **Public opinions and surveys**   Research in the form of public opinion surveys may be used to gather data to evaluate program goal attainment.

- **Audits**   Both internal and external audits might be used. **Internal audits** involve evaluations by one's superiors or peers within the firm to determine how well one (or one's programs) has (have) been performing. **External audits** are conducted by outside parties, including consultants, the client (in the case of a public relations agency), or others not within the organization itself.

In summary, the role that public relations is assuming in the promotional mix is changing. As public relations become more marketing oriented, the criteria by which they are evaluated will also need to change. At the same time, other—nonspecifically marketing-oriented—activities will continue to be the responsibility of the public relations department and will also serve as a basis for evaluation.

➤ *Exhibit 18–14*
Criteria for measuring the effectiveness of public relations

A system for measuring the effectiveness of the public relations program has been developed by Lotus HAL. The criteria used in the evaluation process include:

- The total number of impressions over time
- The total number of impressions on the target audience
- The total number of impressions on specific target audiences
- Percentage of positive articles over time
- Percentage of negative articles over time
- Ratio of positive to negative articles
- Percentage of positive/negative articles by subject
- Percentage of positive/negative articles by publication or reporter
- Percentage of positive/negative articles by target audience

Publicity

To many marketers, publicity and public relations are synonymous. In fact, publicity is really a subset of the public relations effort. Publicity refers to the generation of news about a person, product, or service that appears in broadcast or print media. As you can see by this definition, there is no clear distinction between publicity and what we have just been discussing under the heading of public relations.

There are, however, several major differences between publicity and public relations. First, the former is typically a *short-term* strategy, whereas public relations is a concerted program extending over a period of time. Second, public relations is designed to provide positive information about the firm and usually is controlled by the firm or an agent of the same. Publicity, on the other hand, is not always positive and is not always under the control of, or paid for by, the organization. In many cases, publicity—both positive and negative—originates from sources other than the firm.

In most organizations, control and dissemination of publicity constitute one of the functions to be performed by the public relations department. While part of the public relations effort, publicity requires special attention and effort. In this section, we discuss the role publicity plays in the promotional program and some of the ways marketers both use and react to these communications.

The Power of Publicity

Perhaps one of the factors that most sets off publicity from the other program elements is the sheer *power* this form of communication can generate. Unfortunately for the marketer, this power is not always realized in the way he or she would like it to be. Publicity can make or break a product or even a company, as is evidenced by the following examples:

- After receiving very favorable customer satisfaction ratings in the Power Initial Quality Survey, Buick LeSabre sales jumped 81.5 percent in the next month (compared to the same month the previous year).[12]
- San Francisco's Fog City Diner saw its orders for mussels triple to over 200 pounds a week after the diner and the mussel stew were featured in a Visa commercial.[13]
- When professional golfer John Daly, a well-known long driver, used a Cobra golf club in the televised Skins game, an order for 25,000 of the clubs was received from Japan the next day.
- The Suzuki Samurai is no longer aggressively marketed and the Audi 5000 is no longer marketed at all in the United States as a result of sales losses incurred after negative publicity in *Consumer Reports* and on "60 Minutes," respectively.

Earlier we discussed the substantial drop in Tylenol sales resulting from extensive media coverage of the tampering of its products while on store shelves. The Johnson & Johnson marketing efforts (including a strong public relations emphasis) designed to aid recovery were a model in proficiency that will be studied by students of marketing (both in the classroom and in the boardroom) for many years. By January 1983, almost 100 percent of the original brand share had been regained.

Further, as is demonstrated in Ethical Perspective 18–1, the ability to capitalize on positive publicity is not always under the marketers' control.

These examples demonstrate the impact of publicity and the potential for success and/or failure that it carries. But why? Why is publicity so potentially more powerful than advertising or sales promotions—or even other forms of public relations? A number of reasons are offered. The first is that publicity is highly *credible.*

Unlike advertising and sales promotions, publicity is not usually perceived as being sponsored by the company (and, of course, in the negative instances never is!). As a result, the consumer perceives this information as more objective and places more confidence in it. In fact, *Consumer Reports*—the medium responsible for at least one of the examples previously cited—recently ran an advertising campaign

Ethical Perspective 18–1

"60 Minutes" Provides Heartening News to Wine Industry

The wine industry received a much needed boost in 1992 from a very unexpected source—CBS's weekly "60 Minutes" program. The investigative reporters of "60 Minutes," a group feared by many of the companies they have reported on, aired a segment describing the health benefits of drinking red wine in moderation. The report indicated daily moderate consumption of red wine can reduce the risks of heart disease.

The good news couldn't have come at a better time. Over the past decade, wineries have been in the doldrums due to a continuing decline in wine consumption. Changing consumer attitudes and lifestyles, coupled with the anti-alcohol activists and the negative publicity surrounding alcohol abuse, had led to serious sales losses. The future appeared bleak.

The impact of the positive publicity generated by the "60 Minutes" segment was immediately felt. In the weeks following the report, supermarket sales increased as much as 54 percent over the previous year. After the initial flurry, sales have remained 25 percent higher than the same period a year before.

The wine industry seized the opportunity. The Wine Institute bought 2,000 video copies of the program and distributed them to members, wholesalers, and others involved in the industry. The California Association of Winegrape Growers made bumper stickers proclaiming "A gift for your heart . . . Enjoy a glass of red wine." One winery, Leeward Winery of Ventura, California, announced the news in the newlsetter it sends to its customers. The industry had its first market opportunity in years.

Then things changed. The Bureau of Alcohol, Tobacco and Firearms (BATF), the Treasury Department agency that enforces regulations governing the alcohol industry, told the industry to stop promoting the health benefits of wine. Federal regulations prohibit ads claiming wine has either curative or therapeutic effects if they are misleading or false. While the BATF never argued that the claims were false, it believed they were misleading since they never mentioned the negative effects of alcohol consumption.

Leeward fought back, arguing it should not be illegal to advertise health claims given that they have been proved to be accurate. Leeward thought it was not even an ethical issue, in that the reports and the claims were initially from outside, objective sources, and Leeward has the right to present scientific results. It believes it may be time to change the rules regarding advertising health claims for alcoholic products. Further, it claims a newsletter is not advertising anyway.

While the debate—and the legal action—continues, the larger wineries have decided not to get involved. The larger wineries are worried the BATC could revoke their licenses, and making such claims would open them up to potential product liability lawsuits. Leeward, a company selling only about 12,000 cases annually, would be less likely to be sued. So for now, the big guys are sitting back watching what at least one observer considers the David (Leeward) and Goliath (BATF) battle.

Source: Donna K. H. Walters, "To Your Health," *Los Angeles Times*, April 18, 1992, pp. D1–D2.

---

designed to promote its credibility by noting it does not accept advertising and therefore can be more objective in its evaluations.

In other instances, the information may be perceived as akin to an endorsement by the medium in which it appears. For example, publicity regarding a breakthrough in the durability of golf balls and reported by *Golf* magazine will go far in the promotion of this product. *Car & Driver's* "Car of the Year" reflects the magazine's perception of the quality of the auto selected, as previously noted.

Still another reason is the *news value* of publicity and the frequency of exposure it generates. When basketball stars Larry Bird and Kareem Abdul-Jabbar appeared together on a commercial for Lay's potato chips, the ad appeared on every major television network as well as a variety of cable sports programs both as paid commercials and free as the media publicized the campaign.

A similar effect was achieved by Big Boy Restaurants when the chain ran a national campaign asking consumers whether it should do away with the "Big Boy" holding a burger outside the front of each of its stores. All the major networks reported the results in the form of news, and thousands of letters were sent to the company asking them not to do away with the "kid."

The bottom line is that publicity is *news,* and as research has shown, people like to pass on information that has news value. Publicity thus results in a significant amount of word-of-mouth communication—free and credible information regarding the firm and its products.

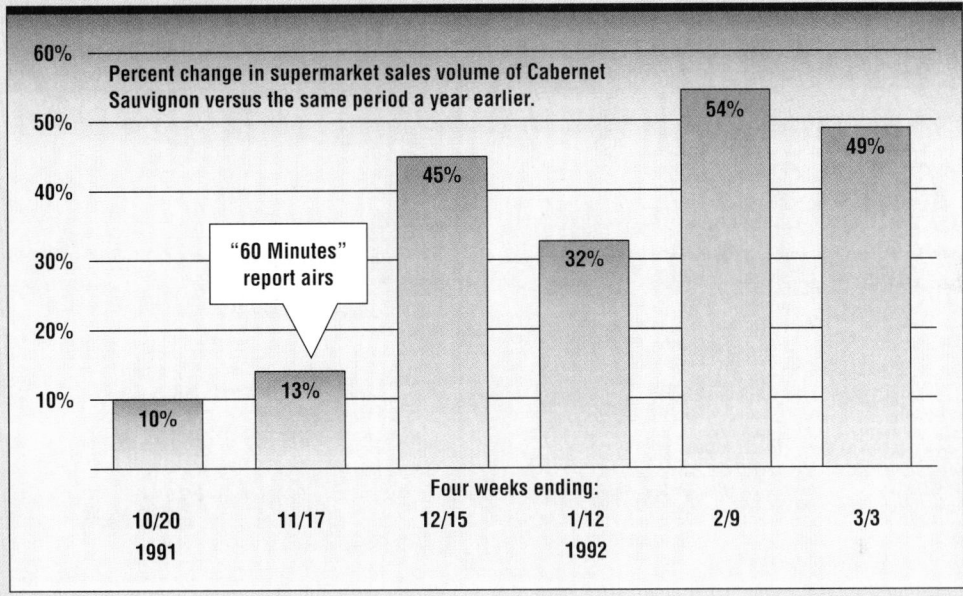

Heartening Report Sales of red wines such as Cabernet Sauvignon surged following a Nov. 17, 1991, report on CBS' "60 Minutes" that highlighted studies saying that daily moderate consumption of red wine can reduce the risks of heart disease.

The Control and Dissemination of Publicity

In some of the examples cited earlier, the control of publicity was not always in the hands of the company. While in some instances it is the firm's own blunder in allowing the information to leak out, in the case of Suzuki and Audi the firms could do little or nothing to stop the media from releasing the information. When publicity becomes news, it is reported on and carried by the media, sometimes despite the efforts of the firm. In these instances, the organization needs to react to the potential threat created by the news.

A good example of one company's efforts to respond to adverse publicity is shown in Exhibit 18–15. Tree Top's problems began when all the major news media carried stories relating that the chemical Alar, used by some growers to regulate the growth of apples, was a potential cause of cancer in children. Despite published denials by reliable scientific and medical authorities, including the Surgeon General, that Alar does not cause cancer, a few special-interest groups were able to generate an extraordinary amount of adverse publicity, causing concern among consumers and purchasing agents. A few school districts took apples off their menus, and even applesauce and juice were implicated. To state its position, Tree Top ran the ad shown in Exhibit 18–15 to help alleviate consumers' fears. In addition, a direct mailing was sent to nutritionists and day-care operators to further clarify Tree Top's position. The campaign was successful both in assuring consumers of the product's safety and in rebuilding consumers' confidence.

In other instances, however, publicity can be controlled and must be managed like any other promotional tool. For example, when the Food and Drug Administration

(FDA) instructed P&G to stop using "fresh" claims in its Citrus Hill orange juice, the company refused to do so. After a lengthy confrontation, the FDA eventually impounded thousands of gallons of the product, and the resulting publicity reflected negatively both on the brand and the organization.

Likewise, publicity can also work for the marketer. For example, New Retail Concepts, Inc., the marketer of No Excuses jeans, took advantage of the publicity surrounding the Donna Rice-Gary Hart scandal in 1987 by using Rice in its advertisements (Exhibit 18–16). The company scheduled a press conference with Rice to announce the affiliation the night after Gary Hart went on "Nightline" to say he would not reenter the presidential race.

When Hart later decided to return to the race, the commercial aired on a number of national news programs, as the ads were the only existing footage anyone had of Rice. Thus, the ads were shown in prime time at virtually no cost to the company—the company introduced its product with a very small advertising budget ($500,000), while gaining millions of dollars in free publicity.[14]

No Excuses did it again when Marla Maples, the girlfriend of Donald Trump, was to be used in a 15-second commercial touting the jeans. When two TV networks refused to air the spot, a variety of other media reported on their refusal, showing and discussing the ads. Again, valuable publicity was generated.[15]

To the degree that they are able, marketers like to have control over the time and place in which information is released. Courses are offered, and books have been written regarding the role of publicity in the public relations process and how to manage this function. These books involve such issues as how to make a presentation, whom to contact, how to issue a press release, and specific information for each medium addressed—including television, radio, newspapers, magazines, and direct-response advertising. In addition, they offer alternative media that may be used such as news conferences, seminars, events, and personal letters, as well as insights as to how to deal with government and other legislative bodies. Because this information is too extensive to include as a single chapter in this text, we suggest you pursue one of the many texts available on this subject for additional insights.

Advantages and Disadvantages of Publicity

As noted previously, publicity offers the advantages of credibility, news value, significant word-of-mouth communications, and a perception of being endorsed by the media. Beyond the potential impact of negative publicity, two major problems arise from the use of publicity.

Timing

Timing of the publicity is not always completely under the control of the marketer, however. Unless the information to be conveyed is perceived as having very high news value by the press, the timing of the communication release is entirely up to the media—if it gets released at all. Thus, the information may be released earlier than desired or too late to make much of an impact.

Accuracy

One of the major methods for getting publicity is the press release. Unfortunately, the information sometimes "gets lost in the translation"—that is, it is not always reported the way the provider wishes it to be. As a result, inaccurate information, omissions, or other errors may result. Sometimes when you see a publicity piece that has been written based on a press release, you wonder if they are even talking about the same topic!

Measuring the Effectiveness of Publicity

The methods employed for measuring the effects of publicity are essentially the same as those discussed earlier under the broader topic of public relations. Rather than to reiterate these methods here, we thought it might be more interesting to show you an actual example. Exhibit 18–17 provides a model developed by Ketchum Public Relations for tracking the effects of publicity. (I guess we just provided Ketchum with some free publicity!)

Corporate Advertising

One of the more controversial forms of advertising is that of **corporate advertising**. Actually an extension of the public relations function, corporate advertising does not promote any one specific product or service. Rather, it is designed to promote the firm overall—either by enhancing its image, assuming a position on a social issue or cause, or seeking direct involvement in something. Why is corporate advertising considered controversial? A number of reasons are offered:

1. **Consumers are not interested in this form of advertising** A Gallup and Robinson study reported in *Ad Age* indicated consumers were as much as 35 percent less interested in corporate ads than they were in product-oriented advertising.[16] Much of this disinterest may be because the consumer may not understand the reasons behind such ads. Of course, much of this confusion results from ads that may not be very good from a communications standpoint.

2. **A costly form of self-indulgence** Firms have been accused of engaging in corporate image advertising only to satisfy the egos of top management. While this may or may not be true, the impetus for this argument stems from the fact that corporate ads are not easy to write. That is, the message to be communicated is not as precise and specific as one designed to position a product, for example. As a result the top managers often dictate the content of the ad, with the copy then reflecting their ideas and images of the corporation.

> *Exhibit 18–17* **The Ketchum publicity tracking model**

Paul H. Alvarez, chairman and chief executive officer of Ketchum Public Relations, describes his firm's publicity tracking model as follows:

We have done a pretty good job in educating clients on what publicity programs can and cannot do, and what can be realistically expected. But true accountability requires *measured* results. Is publicity *measurable*?

Up to now, perhaps not. But Ketchum Public Relations has been working for three years on "The Ketchum Publicity Tracking Model," the first computer-based measurement system designed specifically to evaluate publicity programs. It goes beyond traditional accounting methods such as reporting to the client the number of column inches or the amount of broadcast time obtained, and total audiences reached. . . . It evaluates, via a publicity exposure index and a publicity value index, the amount of target audience exposure received and the degree to which planned messages were delivered to the target audience.

In planning a campaign to be evaluated by the model, the client and the firm agree upon standards of performance in two areas: the number of gross impressions to be achieved within the target audience, and the key messages to be delivered to that audience. The firm's computer is programmed with audience statistics from media in 120 top national markets. Performance standards for a given program are also programmed into the computer along with campaign results.

Results are printed out by media category, target audience reached and the quality (based on numerical values assigned to various 'selling' points in the copy) of the message delivered to the audience. It then produces two evaluative numbers: an overall exposure index and an overall value index. Taking 1.00 as a standard index for the campaign, the degree to which the index is above or below this figure shows to what extent performance was above or below the norm.

In the accompanying "Sample Tracking Report," based on a campaign in Orlando, Florida, the exposure index (1.08) and the value index (1.48) indicate that the program overall met expectations and exceeded the established norms.

The first column of figures in the report shows media exposure among designated market area (DMA) audiences. The second column records average size/length of exposure for each medium, which is translated into average media units (based on a norm of 1.00) and publicity exposure units.

The columns for average impact factor and publicity value units indicate the degree to which key "selling" points in the copy were mentioned in the exposures. Note that the average impact factor for network television is low (0.81). The reason is that although the subject of the campaign (a special event) was mentioned fairly often (1.93 average media units), mention of specific dates and other key copy points did not meet expectations.

The tracking model also demonstrates in advance what a publicity program will do. Thus it is a tool for deciding whether or not a program is worth carrying out. If the decision is "go," it then reports how well objectives were met. Instead of guesswork, we now have a method for placing accountability to the client on a factual basis.

Sample Tracking Report

Placement Type	DMA Target Audience (thousands)	Average Size/ Length	Average Media Units	Publicity Exposure Units (thousands)	Average Impact Factor	Publicity Value Units (thousands)
Newspapers	4,552	⅑ page	0.93	4,233	1.26	5,334
Magazines	268	½ page	1.66	455	1.47	656
Television (network)	95	5:10 min	1.93	183	0.81	149
Television (local)	504	6:05 min	2.13	1,073	1.81	1,946
Radio (local)	200	10:00	2.60	520	1.40	728
Totals	5,619		1.15	6,454	1.37	8,813

Publicity exposure norm = 5,960,000
Publicity exposure index (6,454/5,960) = 1.08
Publicity value index (8,813/5,960) = 1.48

Notes:
The publicity exposure norm is established by estimating the target audiences (adults 18–49, weighted 60 percent male, 40 percent female) and exposure of a "good" hypothetical placement schedule.

The publicity exposure index suggests the campaign's exposure was 1.08, as good as expected on a normal (= 1.00) basis.

The publicity value index suggests the impact value of the campaign was 1.48 times as good as expected on a normal (= 1.00) basis.

3. A belief that the firm must be in trouble Some critics believe the only reason firms engage in this form of advertising is because the company is in trouble—either in a financial sense or in the public's eye—and is advertising to attempt to remedy the problem.

There are a number of forms of corporate advertising, each with its own objectives in mind. The argument of these critics is that these objectives have become important only because the firm is not, or has not been, managing itself properly.

4. Corporate advertising is a waste of money Given that the ads do not directly appeal to anyone, are not understood, and do not promote anything specific, critics argue the monies could be better spent in other areas. Again, much of this argument has its foundation in the fact that the corporate image ads are often intangible. They typically do not ask directly for a purchase; they do not ask for investors; rather, they present a position or try to create an image. Because they are not specific, many critics believe their purpose is lost on the audience, and therefore these ads are not a wise investment of the firm's resources.

Despite these criticisms, and others, corporate advertising has become increasingly more prevalent since the 1970s. It has been estimated that more than 7 percent of all advertising dollars spent are for corporate advertising, meaning billions of dollars are spent on this form of communication.[17]

While corporate advertising has generally been regarded as the domain of companies such as USX, Kaiser Aluminum, and Boise Cascade—that is, companies with no products to sell directly to the consumer market—this is no longer the case. Procter & Gamble ran its first corporate spot in 1987, and other consumer products companies such as IBM and AT&T have also increased expenditures in this area.

As noted above, one of the criticisms leveled at the users of corporate advertising stems from the fact that so many people are not sure exactly what corporate advertising is or what its purpose is. This form of advertising has been used as a catchall for any type of advertising run for the direct benefit of the corporation rather than its products or services—a lot of advertising falls into this categorization.[18] For purposes of this text (and to attempt to bring some perspective to the term), we use the broader-based term of *corporate advertising* to describe various types of advertising designed to promote the organization itself rather than its products or services.

Objectives of Corporate Advertising

Corporate advertising may attempt to accomplish a number of objectives. This form of advertising may be designed with two goals in mind: (1) creating a positive image for the firm and (2) communicating the organization's views on social, business, and environmental issues. More specific applications include:

- Boosting employee morale and smoothing labor relations.
- Helping newly deregulated industries ease consumer uncertainty and answer investor questions.
- Helping diversified companies establish an identity for the parent firm, rather than relying solely on brand names.[19]

As these objectives indicate, corporate advertising is targeted at both internal and external audiences and involves the promotion of the organization as well as its ideas.

Types of Corporate Advertising

Attainment of the objectives is sought through implementing the various forms of corporate advertising. Each form is designed to achieve specific goals.

Image advertising

One form of corporate advertising is that devoted to the promotion of the organization's overall *image*. Such advertising may accomplish a number of objectives including that of creating *goodwill* both internally and externally, creating a position for the company, and generating resources—both human and financial. A number of methods are used.

1. General image or positioning ads As shown in Exhibit 18–18, ads are often designed to create an image of the firm in the mind of the public. As can be seen in the exhibit, Allstate is attempting to create the image of itself as a company that cares for its customers and places them in the security of "the good hands people."

➢ *Exhibit 18–18*
Allstate positions itself as "the good hands people"

➢ *Exhibit 18–19*
NBC ran ads to demonstrate the advantages of sponsoring the broadcast of the Olympic Games in Barcelona

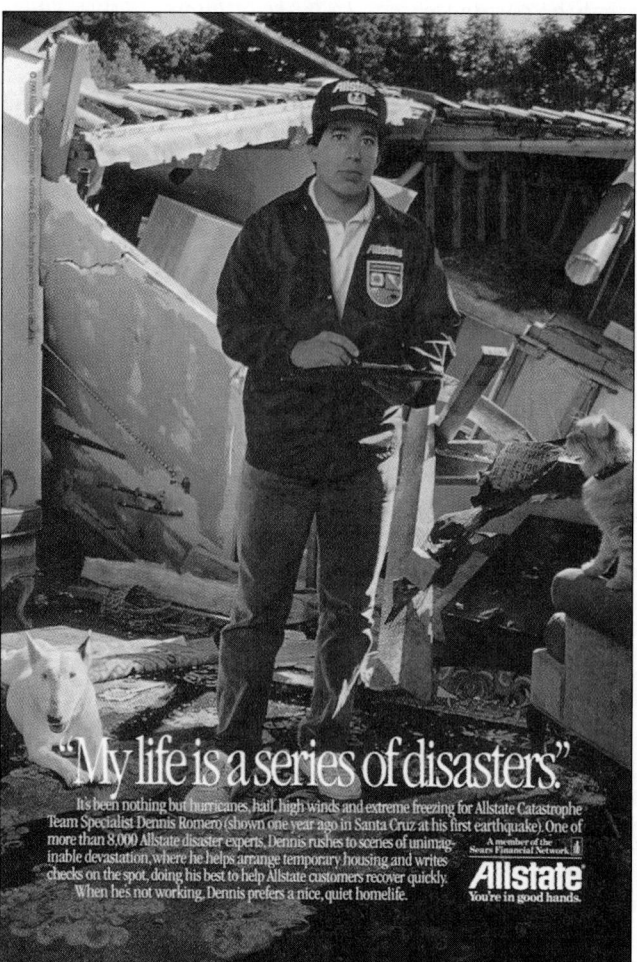

Other companies have used image advertising to attempt to change an existing image. The American Medical Association (AMA), responding to its less than positive image among many Americans who perceived doctors as inattentive and money-grubbers, ran a series of advertisements portraying doctors in a "more sensitive light." The AMA spent over $1.75 million highlighting the caring, sharing, and sensitive side of AMA members.[20] *Penthouse* magazine attempted to change its image with advertisers by running ads in trade magazines that showed *Penthouse* was not just a magazine with pictures of nude females.

2. Sponsorships   Often a firm runs corporate image advertising on programs or television "specials." For example, the Hallmark or IBM specials and documentaries on network television and Mobil and Gulf Oil program sponsorships on public television are designed to promote the corporation as a good citizen. By associating itself with high-quality and/or educational programming, the firm hopes for a carryover effect that benefits its own image.

Other examples of sponsorships include those run by American Express and Chrysler to support the refurbishing of the Statue of Liberty. In both of these instances, the sponsoring organizations benefited from the association, as did the charity that received the funds. American Express card usage during the campaign increased by 25 percent, and $1.7 million was raised for refurbishing the statue.[21] Certainly, a favorable corporate image was created!

➤ *Exhibit 18–21*
Deloitte & Touche creates an image for recruitment

➤ *Exhibit 18–20*
Some sponsors of the 1992 U.S. Olympic team

- Anheuser-Busch
- AT&T
- Bausch & Lomb
- Blue Cross and Blue Shield
- Bridgestone/Firestone
- Bristol-Myers Squibb
- Brother Industries
- The Coca-Cola Co.
- Eastman Kodak
- Hilton Hotels Corp.
- Kraft General Foods
- Mars Inc.
- Matsushita
- Maverick Ranch Lite Beef
- McDonald's
- J. C. Penney
- Pittsburgh Paint & Glass
- Ricoh
- 3M
- Time Inc. Magazines
- U.S. Postal Service
- Visa
- Xerox
- York International

Exhibit 18–19 touts the value of sponsoring the 1992 Summer Olympics broadcast on NBC from Barcelona, Spain, noting the opportunity to reach an "enormous and influential group of upscale decision makers." In addition to broadcast sponsorship, team sponsorships were sold for approximately $3 million to $5 million, while sponsorships that covered the teams and events were sold at between $10 million and $15 million.[22] Exhibit 18–20 shows some of the companies that decided a sponsorship would be good for them.

3. Recruiting The promotional piece for Deloitte & Touche presented in Exhibit 18–21 is a good example of corporate image advertising designed to attract college graduates. The ad is designed to promote a corporate image for the company. Thus, if you are a graduating senior considering a career in accounting, this ad would be of interest to you.

The Sunday employment section of most major metropolitan newspapers is an excellent place to see this form of corporate image advertising at work. Notice the ads contained in these papers and consider the image the firms are presenting.

4. Generating financial support Some corporate advertising is designed to generate investments in the corporation. By creating a more favorable image, the firm looks attractive to potential stock purchasers and investors. More investments mean more working capital, more monies for research and development, and so on. Thus, in this instance, corporate image advertising is almost attempting to make a sale—the product is the firm.

While there is no concrete evidence that corporate image advertising leads directly to increased investment, at least one study shows a correlation exists between the price of stock and the amount of corporate advertising done.[23] That is, those firms with higher dollars spent in corporate advertising also tend to have higher-priced

➤ *Exhibit 18–22* **The eight key attributes of reputation**

Quality of Management	
Most Admired	**Score**
Wal-Mart Stores	9.27
Rubbermaid	9.22
Merck	9.19
Least Admired	**Score**
CrossLand Savings	2.88
HomeFed	3.23
Continental Airlines/ Salomon	3.25

Financial Soundness	
Most Admired	**Score**
Merck	9.43
Wal-Mart Stores	9.00
Coca-Cola	8.91
Least Admired	**Score**
Continental Airlines Hold.	1.22
CrossLand Savings	1.50
HomeFed	1.74

Quality of Products or Services	
Most Admired	**Score**
Merck	9.26
Rubbermaid	8.97
Procter & Gamble	8.81
Least Admired	**Score**
Wang Laboratories	3.99
CrossLand Savings	4.07
Continental Airlines Hold.	4.16

Use of Corporate Assets	
Most Admired	**Score**
Merck	8.81
Wal-Mart Stores	8.81
Rubbermaid	8.53
Least Admired	**Score**
CrossLand Savings	2.19
HomeFed	2.21
Continental Airlines Hold.	2.83

Value as Long-Term Investment	
Most Admired	**Score**
Merck	9.09
Coca-Cola	8.64
Wal-Mart Stores	8.60
Least Admired	**Score**
CrossLand Savings	1.40
Continental Airlines Hold.	1.59
HomeFed	1.82

Innovativeness	
Most Admired	**Score**
Merck	9.03
Wal-Mart Stores	8.80
Rubbermaid	8.75
Least Admired	**Score**
Crossland Savings	3.32
Sears Roebuck	3.34
Wang Laboratories	3.45

Ability to Attract, Develop, and Keep Talented People	
Most Admired	**Score**
Merck	9.00
Wal-Mart Stores	8.60
Liz Claiborne	8.34
Least Admired	**Score**
CrossLand Savings	2.22
Continental Airlines Hold.	2.50
Wang Laboratories	2.72

Community and Environmental Responsibility	
Most Admired	**Score**
Merck	8.32
Johnson & Johnson	8.29
Rubbermaid	8.19
Least Admired	**Score**
Salomon	2.95
Continental Airlines Hold.	3.59
CrossLand Savings	3.62

stocks (though you must keep in mind that showing a direct relationship is very difficult to substantiate).

Many factors have been shown to affect corporate image. Exhibit 18–22 reveals the results of a survey conducted by *Fortune* magazine. As you can see, this thing called image is not unidimensional! The most admired firms represented in *Fortune's* survey did not gain their positions merely by publicity and word of mouth.

Creating a positive corporate image is also not likely to be accomplished just by running a few advertisements. Quality of products and services, innovativeness, sound financial practices, being a good corporate citizen, and engaging in sound marketing practices are just a few of the many factors that contribute to overall image.

Social, business, and environmental issue advertising

A second major form of corporate advertising is that of issue-oriented advertising, or as it is often called, **advocacy advertising.** Advocacy advertising has been defined as

concerned with the propagation of ideas and elucidation of controversial social issues of public importance in a manner that supports the position and interest of the sponsor.[24]

➤ *Exhibit 18–23* **Advocacy ads may take a position on an issue**

Heroes

A coffin draped in the American flag...surviving officers in dress uniforms, mourning their fallen comrade...families in black, quietly sobbing, trying to understand what cannot be understood.

We have seen it too many times, the final rites for our defenders—fallen not in foreign wars, but today, right here at home in hundreds of American cities and towns. Another kind of war—against crime—is killing one American law-enforcement officer in the line of duty every 57 hours.

Like those fallen in other wars, these men and women wear the many faces of America. They are black and they are white; they trace their roots back to Asia and Africa and Europe and the Americas. They are young and old, they are commanders, detectives, and foot soldiers in the battle against lawlessness.

Consider these numbers:
● 30,000 law-enforcement officers have been killed on duty in the history of the U.S.
● In 1987 (the most recent data available), 155 officers were killed, 21,273 were wounded and 63,842 were assaulted with a weapon.
● In the past 10 years, 1,525 police officers have been killed, 204,584 have been injured and 590,822 have been assaulted.

● Every day, 500,000 American law-enforcement officers subject themselves to these risks, on our behalf.

How do we honor them? And how do we keep their sacrifices vivid in the public consciousness? One way is through the construction of the National Law Enforcement Officers Memorial. Congress has declared that the memorial will be built on three acres of open space at Washington, D.C.'s Judiciary Square. Groundbreaking is planned for Spring 1989, and the memorial should be ready for dedication by Peace Officers' Memorial Day, May 15, 1990.

Apart from donating the land, Congress purposely allocated no money for the construction. That is to come from corporations, organizations and individual donors. The fund-raising goal for the memorial is $7.5 million; more than $1.2 million has been raised to date.

Join us in contributing to the National Law Enforcement Officers Memorial Fund, 1360 Beverly Road, Suite 305, McLean, VA 22101. Contributions are tax deductible. Your contribution also is a symbol of support for our hometown heroes, for their service and sacrifice. They deserve it. They've earned it.

Mobil

©1988 Mobil Corporation

How nuclear energy benefits a typical family of four.

Every year, the ospreys return to their wildlife preserve around the nuclear electric plant near Waterford, Connecticut, where nesting platforms have been built for them by the local utility.

It's one more example of how peacefully nuclear energy coexists with the environment. Because America's 111 operating nuclear plants don't burn anything to generate electricity, they don't pollute the air. They don't produce any greenhouse gases, either.

To help satisfy the nation's growing need for electricity without sacrificing the quality of our environment, we need more nuclear plants. For your family, and others as well.

If you'd like more information, write to the U.S. Council for Energy Awareness, P.O. Box 66080, Dept. OS26, Washington, D.C. 20035.

Nuclear energy means cleaner air.

© 1991 USCEA

While still seeking the objective of portraying an image for the company or organization, advocacy advertising does so in a much more indirect manner—that is, by adopting a position on a particular issue rather than promoting the organization itself.

Advocacy advertising—examples of which are shown in Exhibit 18–23—has increased in use over the past few years and has also met with increased criticism. The ads may be sponsored by a firm or by an industry association and are designed to provide the readers with insight as to how the firm operates or management's position on a particular issue.

Sometimes the advertising results as a response to negative publicity or because the firm was unable to place the message through public relations channels and thought its position warranted the expenditures. In other situations, the firm may just wish to have certain ideas accepted or have society understand its concerns.

While advocacy advertising has recently fallen under criticism from a number of sources—including consumer advocate Ralph Nader—as you can see in Exhibit 18–24, this form of communication has been around for some time. AT&T engaged in issues-oriented advertising as early as 1908 and continued to employ this form of communication throughout the 20th century. While critics contend that those with large advertising dollars may be able to purchase more ad space and time, and that the advocacy ads may be misleading, the checks and balances inherent in the system that control for regular product advertising also are operating in this area. For example, an ad run by the seven regional Bell operating companies that addressed

➤ *Exhibit 18–24*   **Advocacy ads have been used for years**

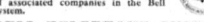

the threat of rapidly developing Japanese technologies in the telecommunications industry was perceived by some congressmen (the group the ads were designed to influence) as "Japan-bashing" and offensive. When the ad backfired, the campaign was immediately halted, and the agency responsible for developing it was fired.[25] The ultimate judge, of course, is always the reader.

Advantages and Disadvantages of Corporate Advertising

A number of reasons for the increased popularity of corporate advertising become evident when you examine the advantages of this form of communication. Some of these advantages are provided below.

1. It is an excellent vehicle for positioning the firm. Firms—like products—need to establish an image or position in the marketplace. Corporate image ads are one vehicle for accomplishing this objective. As we noted much earlier in this text, a well-positioned product is much more likely to achieve success than is one without an image or a vague one. The same holds true of the firm. Stop and think for a moment about the image that comes to mind when you hear of IBM, Apple, Johnson & Johnson, or Procter & Gamble. Now what comes to mind when you hear the words Unisys, USX, or Navistar? How many of the consumer brands can you name that fall under Beatrice Foods' corporate umbrella? (Swiss Miss, Tropicana, Cutty Sark, and others.) While we are not saying that these latter companies are not successful—because they certainly are—we are suggesting their corporate identity (or position) is not as well entrenched as those first cited. What is important is that those companies with strong positive corporate images may have an advantage over competitors that may be enhanced by promoting the company overall.

2. Corporate image advertising takes advantage of the benefits to be derived from engaging in public relations. As the public relations efforts of firms have increased, the attention paid to these events by the media has lessened. (Not because they are of any less value, but rather because there are more events to cover.) The net result is that when a company engages in a public relations effort, there is no guarantee it will receive press coverage and publicity. Corporate image advertising gets the message out, and though it may not be exactly the same as reading it from an objective source, the fact remains that what has been done can be communicated.

3. Corporate image advertising reaches a very different target market. Corporate image advertising is not—and should not always be—targeted to the general public. It is a special form of communication that may be targeted to a select group or target market. Often, corporate image advertising is targeted to investors and managers of other firms rather than to the general public. As such, it is not critical if everyone does not like or appreciate this form of communication, so long as the target market does. In this respect, this form of advertising may be accomplishing its objectives.

Some of the disadvantages of corporate advertising were alluded to earlier in this chapter. To these criticisms, we can add the following.

1. Questionable effectiveness There is no strong evidence to support the fact that corporate advertising works. Despite the data cited earlier that demonstrated a correlation between stock prices and corporate image advertising, many believe this correlation may have little meaning. For example, a study by Bozell & Jacobs Advertising of 16,000 ads concluded that corporate advertising contributed to only 4 percent of the variability in the company's stock price, compared with a 55 percent effect attributable to financial factors.[26] A second study also casts doubts on earlier studies that concluded that corporate advertising worked.[27]

2. The constitutionality and/or ethics Some critics contend that since larger firms have more monies, they can control public opinion and this is unfair and unethical. This point was briefly mentioned earlier and was resolved in the courts in favor of the advertisers. Nevertheless, many still see such advertising as unfair and immediately take a negative view of the sponsor.

As you can see, a number of valid points have been offered in support of arguments for and against corporate advertising. Two things are certain: (1) There is no definite conclusion as to who is right in this instance, and (2) the use of this communications form continues to increase.

Measuring the Effectiveness of Corporate Advertising

As you no doubt can tell from our discussion on the controversy and conflicting opinions surrounding corporate advertising, there needs to be some method for determining whether or not such advertising is effective. In this section, we focus on how such evaluations might be made.

- **Attitude surveys** One method of determining the effectiveness of corporate advertising is conducting attitude surveys to gain insights into both the public's and investors' reactions to ads. The "Phase II" study conducted by Yankelovich, Skelly & White (a market research firm in Connecticut) is perhaps one of the best-known applications of this measurement method.[28] In this study, the firm measured recall and attitudes toward corporate advertisers and reported that corporate advertising is more efficient in building recall for a company name than is product advertising alone. In addition, frequent corporate advertisers rated better than those with low corporate ad budgets on virtually all attitude measures.

- **Studies relating corporate advertising and stock prices** The Bozell & Jacobs study reported on earlier is one of a number of studies that have examined the effect of various elements of corporate advertising (for example, position in the magazine, source effects, etc.) on stock prices. As we reported earlier, conflicting conclusions have resulted from the studies, indicating that while the model for such measures seems logical, methodological problems may be accounting for at least some of the discrepancies.

- **Focus group research** Focus groups have been used both before and after the development of corporate advertisements to gain insights into what investors want to see in ads and their reactions after such ads have been developed. As with product-oriented advertising, this method also has its limitations, although it does allow for some effective measurements.

In sum, measuring the effectiveness of corporate advertising has employed some of the methods used to measure product-specific advertising. At the same time, research in this area has not kept pace with that of the consumer market (one study reported that only 35 of the Fortune 500 companies ever attempted to measure performance of their annual reports).[29] While a number of reasons have been cited for this lack of effort, the most commonly offered is that corporate ads are often the responsibility of those in the highest management positions in the firm, and these parties do not wish to be held accountable. Interestingly, those who should be most concerned with accountability are the ones most likely to shun this responsibility!

SUMMARY

We examined the role of the promotional elements of public relations, publicity, and corporate image advertising. In each case, we noted that these areas are all of significant importance to the marketing and communications effort and they are usually considered in a different way than the other promotional elements. The reasons for this special treatment stem from the fact that, first, they are typically not designed to promote a specific product or service and, second, because in many instances it may be harder for the consumer to make the association between the communication and its intent.

Public relations was shown to be useful in respect to traditional responsibilities, as well as in a more marketing-oriented role. In many firms, public relations is a separate department operating independently of marketing, whereas in others it is considered a support system. Many large firms may have an external public relations agency, just as they have an outside advertising agency.

In the case of publicity, another factor enters the equation—the lack of control as to the communication the public will receive. In the areas of public relations and corporate image advertising, the source remains the organization, and much more control is afforded. Dealing with publicity is often more of a reactive than a proactive approach. The effects of publicity may be more instrumental or detrimental to the success of a product or organization than all other forms of promotion combined.

While all publicity cannot be managed, the marketer must nevertheless recognize its potential impact. Publicity releases and the management of information are just two of the factors under the control of management. At the same time, proper reaction and strategy relating to uncontrollable events are also responsibilities.

Corporate advertising was described as being controversial. Much of this stems from the fact that because the source of the message in this form of communication is top management, the rules that are applied to other advertising and promotion forms are often not used. This element of communication definitely has its place in the promotional mix. However, to be effective, it must be used with each of the other elements, with specific communications objectives in mind.

Finally, it was noted that measures of evaluation and control are required for each of these program elements as they are for all others in the promotional mix. We have presented some methods for taking such measurements and some evidence as to why it is important to use them. As long as the elements of public relations, publicity, and corporate image advertising are considered an integral component of the overall communications strategy, they must respect the same rules as the other promotional mix elements to ensure success.

KEY TERMS

public relations
internal audiences
external audiences
press release

exclusive
team approach
internal audits
external audits

publicity
corporate advertising
advocacy advertising

DISCUSSION QUESTIONS

1. Explain what is meant by the term *cause marketing*. Cite examples of organizations that have used this strategy.
2. Discuss the difference between the "traditional" role of public relations and the "new" role.
3. Explain the difference between public relations and publicity. In what ways are they the same?
4. Why is publicity so powerful? Give examples of how publicity has worked for and against companies.
5. Some believe the new role of public relations should not be adopted by firms, noting that the responsibilities of public relations differ. Argue in support and defense of this position.
6. Give examples of organizations that might fit into each of the classes proposed by Kotler and Mindak. Cite examples of organizations that may have changed classes over the past few years.
7. What are the various forms that corporate advertising might assume? Give examples of each.
8. Describe some of the problems that might result from boycotts. Discuss some of the strategies for combatting boycotts.
9. What is meant by advocacy advertising? Bring examples of advocacy ads to class.
10. In the chapter, we mentioned Exxon's reaction to the Alaskan oil spill. Using the concepts presented in this chapter, discuss some of the things Exxon might have done to remedy the negative publicity generated.

chapter 19

Personal Selling

chapter objectives

➤ To examine the role of personal selling in the promotional mix.

➤ To examine the advantages and disadvantages of personal selling as a promotional program element.

➤ To demonstrate how personal selling is combined with other program elements in the design of a promotional program.

➤ To consider some of the ways to determine the effectiveness of the personal selling effort.

The Entire Staff Becomes Salespersons

Traditionally, there have been sales departments, marketing departments, advertising departments, and/or combinations of these. Advertising people worked on advertising, salespersons sold, and so on. Tradition, at least in some firms, has gone by the way, as more and more employees are being asked to perform different functions, with almost everyone being asked to at least help the selling effort.

Because of the sluggish economy, limited budgets, and an increased emphasis on selling, many corporations have enlisted everyone from top executives to the lowest-paid hourly employee as "on-the-street" sales representatives. Consider the following examples.

ITT-Sheraton launched a two-week international sales blitz to highlight its $1 billion investment in upgrading its properties throughout the world. The campaign included 44,000 face-to-face sales calls on prospective customers by people in every level of the organization, including 25,000 in North and South America; 17,000 in Europe, Africa, and the Middle East; and 2,000 in the United Kingdom. In addition, 175 customer appreciation events were held throughout North America.

All of the nonsales professionals were accompanied by ITT sales professionals. Beverage operators, chefs, and housekeepers each talked about how they contributed to make Sheraton a better place to stay, and how much they valued the customer.

IBM Corporation—the company that once taught its employees to sing company songs at sales meetings—now is teaching everyone in the organization to sing its praises. Each of the 344,000 employees is being encouraged to help promote and sell the latest version of its OS/2 2.0 operating system.

Both sales and nonsales employees have been armed with a sales kit that features an OS/2 2.0 brochure, reprints of an article about the developers of the program that ran in *Datamation* magazine, and a personal letter about the product from the vice president and general manager of IBM's personal systems. In addition, pocket cards explaining the advantages were provided to all employees to pass out to prospective buyers such as their dentists, doctors, friends, neighbors, and so on.

Employees are rewarded for their efforts. The more effort expended, the greater the reward. IBM expects at least 50,000 of the 344,000 employees to participate.

How are customers and potential customers reacting to the "new" sales forces? Most of them seem to like it. They like the added attention, and they like to get a feel for what goes on behind the scenes, and throughout

(continued)

all levels of the companies. In addition, the salespeople and the employees like it as well. As noted by Vice President Keefer D. Welch, director of sales at ITT-Sheraton, several employees have already made the switch into sales, and some latent talent is being discovered. The employees also say they are having fun, and (in the IBM model) being rewarded as well. It seems everyone is better off!

Source: Sandra Pesmen, "Feet on the Street," Business Marketing, *May 1992, pp. 20–21.*

Personal Selling

The ITT-Sheraton and IBM examples demonstrate a novel way organizations are integrating the personal selling function into the overall marketing communications program. In Chapter 1, we stated that while we recognized the importance of personal selling, and the role it plays in the overall marketing and promotions effort, this topic would not constitute a major emphasis in this text. While we do not wish to downplay the importance of this promotional mix element, we noted that personal selling is not typically under the control of the advertising and promotions department—usually being the responsibility of the sales manager. At the same time, the personal selling effort provides a valuable contribution to the promotional program. To develop a promotional plan effectively, the roles and responsibilities of the company's sales force must be considered and integrated into the communications program. Moreover, a strong cooperative effort between the departments is necessary.

This chapter focuses on the role personal selling assumes in the promotional mix, the advantages and disadvantages associated with this program element, and the basis for evaluating its contributions to attaining communications objectives. In addition, we explore the ways in which personal selling is combined with other program elements—both to lend support to them and to receive support from them.

The Scope of Personal Selling

Personal selling involves selling through a person-to-person communications process. The importance and/or emphasis placed on personal selling varies from firm to firm depending on a variety of factors including nature of the product and or service being marketed, size of the organization, and type of industry. In some organizations, personal selling may play the dominant role (in many industrial firms), while in others this role is minimized (low-priced consumer nondurable goods). However, personal selling should be used as a partner with, not a substitute for, the other promotional mix elements.

Exhibit 19–1 shows the results of a survey of marketing managers' perceptions of how the various elements of the promotional mix will change over the next few years. As this survey demonstrates, many managers believe sales management and personal selling are likely to increase in importance and are likely to increase the most among all of the elements of the promotional mix.

The Role of Personal Selling in the Promotional Mix

As noted, manufacturers may promote their products *directly* to consumers through advertising and promotions and/or direct-marketing efforts or *indirectly* through resellers and salespersons. (In many situations, the sales force may call on customers directly—for example, in the insurance industry or real estate business or in direct selling. However, in this chapter, we focus on the personal selling function as it exists in most large corporations—that is, as a link to resellers or dealing in business-to-business transactions.) Depending on the role defined by the organization, the responsibilities and specific tasks of salespersons may differ, but ultimately these tasks are designed to lead to the attainment of communications and marketing objectives.

➤ *Exhibit 19−1* **Change in relative importance of components of the promotional mix between now and 1995**

Strategy Statement	Change in Relative Importance					
	Greatly Decreased	Moderately Decreased	Same	Moderately Increased	Greatly Increased	Mean Rating*
Promotional strategy						
Special promotional activities such as promotional warranties, trade shows, dealer aids, and product displays.	0.0%	12.6%	48.5%	35.0%	3.9%	3.3
Public relations, public affairs, and community relations.	0.0	7.8	43.7	33.8	9.7	3.5
Product branding and promotional packaging.	0.0	8.7	47.6	35.0	8.7	3.4
Sales management and personal selling, including all sales management activities (e.g., training, supervision) and the sales efforts of your company management personnel.	1.0	2.9	28.4	52.9	14.7	3.8
Print media advertising in newspapers, magazines, and brochures.	0.0	17.6	52.0	24.5	5.9	3.2
Broadcast media advertising on radio/television.	0.0	15.8	51.5	25.7	6.9	3.2
Media advertising on cable TV, over-the-air pay TV, and videodiscs.	1.0	7.9	29.7	49.5	11.9	3.6

*1 = greatly decreased, 2 = moderately decreased, 3 = same, 4 = moderately increased, 5 = greatly increased.

Personal selling differs from the other forms of communication presented thus far in that messages flow from a sender (or group of senders) to a receiver (or group of receivers) directly (and usually face to face). Because of this *direct* and *interpersonal communication,* the sender is able to immediately receive and evaluate feedback from the receiver. This communications process—known as **dyadic communication** (between two persons or groups)—allows for more specific tailoring of the message and more personal communications than are available in many of the other media discussed. As a result, the message can be changed to address specific needs and wants of the receiver—a capability not available through nonpersonal media.

In some situations, this ability to focus on specific problems is mandatory, as a standard communication would not be sufficient. For example, consider an industrial buying situation in which the salesperson is an engineer. In promoting the company's products and/or services, the salesperson must be able to understand the specific needs of the client. This may mean understanding the tensile strength of materials or being able to read blueprints or plans to understand the requirements. Or consider a salesperson representing a computer graphics firm. Part of his or her responsibility for making a sale may involve the design of a software program to solve a problem unique only to this customer. Mass communications are not capable of accomplishing these tasks.

While the examples just given are both from industrial settings, personal selling is not restricted only to this market; it plays a critical role in the consumer market as well. As noted by the great entrepreneur Marshall Field: "The distance between the salesperson and the potential buyer is the most important three feet in business."[1] While Field was referring to the consumer as the buyer, we already have seen that resellers must be considered as well. Personal selling plays an important role in consumer products companies as they must secure distribution, motivate resellers to stock and promote the product, and so on.

Why is personal selling so important? Let's examine its role with respect to other promotional program elements.

Determining the Role of Personal Selling

One of the first questions the manager needs to ask when preparing the promotional program is, What will the specific responsibilities of personal selling be, and what role will it assume relative to the other promotional mix elements? To determine what this role should be, management should be guided by four specific questions:

1. What specific information must be exchanged between the firm and potential customers?
2. What are the alternative ways of carrying out these communications objectives?
3. How effective is each alternative in carrying out the needed exchange?
4. What is the cost-effectiveness of each alternative?[2]

Let's examine these in more detail.

- **Determining the information to be exchanged** In keeping with the objectives established by the communications models presented in Chapter 6, the salesperson may have a variety of messages to communicate, such as creating awareness of the product or service offering, demonstrating product benefits for evaluation, initiating trial, and/or closing the sale. In addition, answering questions, countering misconceptions, and discovering potentially unmet needs may also be necessary.

- **Examining promotional mix alternatives** In previous chapters, we discussed the roles of advertising and sales promotions, direct marketing, and public relations/publicity. Each of these program elements offers specific advantages and disadvantages, and each needs to be considered in developing the promotions mix. Likewise, personal selling is an alternative that must be considered, offering distinct advantages in some situations, while less appropriate in others—as evidenced in Exhibit 19–2.

- **Evaluating the relative effectiveness of alternatives** Depending on the target market and the objectives sought, each of the program elements must be evaluated in respect to its relative effectiveness. As noted, personal selling provides a number of characteristics that make it more effective in many situations. At the same time, advantages are provided by other program elements that may increase their attractiveness. For example, the ability to reach a large number of persons with one distinct and consistent message or the opportunity to repeat messages may be accomplished more effectively and more cost efficiently by advertising.

➤ *Exhibit 19–2* **When the sales force is a major part of the communications mix**

Product or Service	**Channels**
Complex products requiring customer application assistance (computers, pollution control systems, steam turbines) Major purchase decisions, such as food items purchased by supermarket chains Features and performance of the product requiring personal demonstration and trial by the customer (private aircraft)	Channel system relatively short and direct to end-users Product and service training and assistance needed by channel intermediaries Personal selling needed in "pushing" product through channel Channel intermediaries available to perform personal selling function for supplier with limited resources and experience (brokers or manufacturer's agents)
Price	**Advertising**
Final price negotiated between buyer and seller (appliances, automobiles, real estate) Selling price or quantity purchased enable an adequate margin to support selling expenses (traditional department store compared to discount house)	Advertising media do not provide effective link with market targets Information needed by buyer cannot be provided entirely through advertising and sales promotion (life insurance) Number and dispersion of customers will not enable acceptable advertising economies

- **Determining cost-effectiveness** One of the major disadvantages associated with personal selling is often considered to be the costs involved. (In 1991, Cahners Research estimated the average cost per sales call could be as high as $332.00.)[3] In evaluating program elements, their effectiveness must also be considered in terms of the costs associated with their use. While the cost of a personal sales call may not be prohibitive in industrial settings where a single purchase may be in the millions of dollars, the same cost may be unfeasible in a consumer market. Other media may be capable of communicating the required message at a much lower cost.

The Nature of Personal Selling

To integrate the personal selling effort into the overall promotional program properly, it is necessary to understand the nature of this tool. Let us look at how personal selling has evolved over the years and then examine some of the characteristics of personal selling.

The Evolution of Personal Selling

The personal selling task encompasses a variety of responsibilities (we discuss some of these in the next section). Like other aspects of the promotional mix, these responsibilities are constantly changing. As noted by Thomas Wotruba, the personal selling area is constantly evolving as the marketing environment itself evolves.[4] According to Wotruba, five distinct stages of personal selling evolution can be identified as shown in Exhibit 19–3:

1. **Provider stage** Selling activities are limited to accepting orders for the supplier's available offering and conveying it to the buyer.
2. **Persuader stage** Selling involves an attempt to persuade market members to buy the supplier's offerings.
3. **Prospector stage** Activities include seeking out selected buyers who are perceived to have a need for the offering as well as the resources to buy it.

➤ *Exhibit 19–3* **Characteristics of the stages in the evolution of selling**

Stages and Description	Characteristics of Stages			Examples
	Customer Needs	Type of Market	Nature and Intensity of Competition	
1. **Provider:** accepting orders and delivering to buyer.	Assumed to exist; not a concern	Sellers'	None	Route salespeople-drivers; some retail sales clerks
2. **Persuader:** attempting to convince anyone to buy available offerings.	Created, awakened	Buyers'	Undifferentiated; slight intensity	Telemarketer for photography studio; many new car dealer salespeople
3. **Prospector:** seeking out prospects with need for available offering as well as resources and authority to buy.	Considered but inferred	Segmented	Differentiated; growing	Car insurance salespeople calling on new car buyers; office supplies sellers calling on small businesses
4. **Problem-solver:** matching available offerings to solve customer-stated problems.	Diagnosed, with attention to customer input	Participative	Responsive and counteractive with increasing resources	Communication systems salespeople for a telephone company; architectural services seller calling on a building contractor
5. **Procreator:** creating a unique offering to match the buyer's needs as mutually specified, involving any or all aspects of the seller's total marketing mix.	Mutually defined; matched with tailored offering	Coactive	Focused; growing in breadth of market and service offerings	Materials handling equipment salesperson who designs and sells a system to fit a buyer's manufacturing facility

➤ *Exhibit 19–4* **Average cost per sales call by industry**

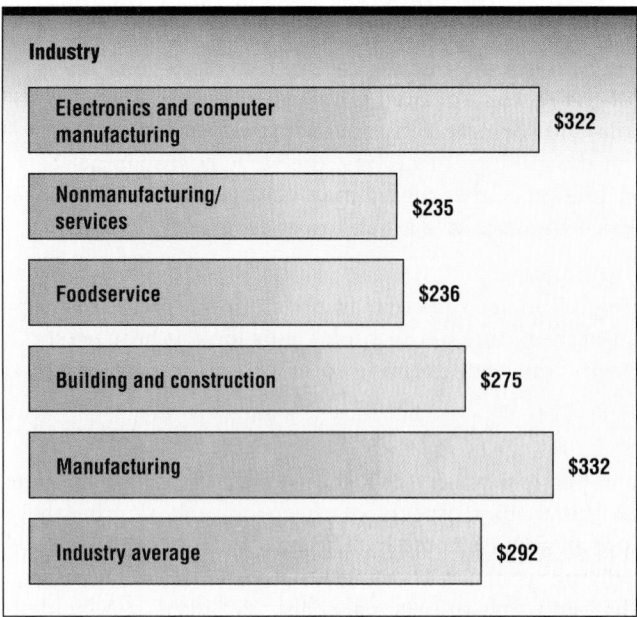

Industry	
Electronics and computer manufacturing	$322
Nonmanufacturing/ services	$235
Foodservice	$236
Building and construction	$275
Manufacturing	$332
Industry average	$292

➤ *Exhibit 19–5* **Number of research calls to close a sale**

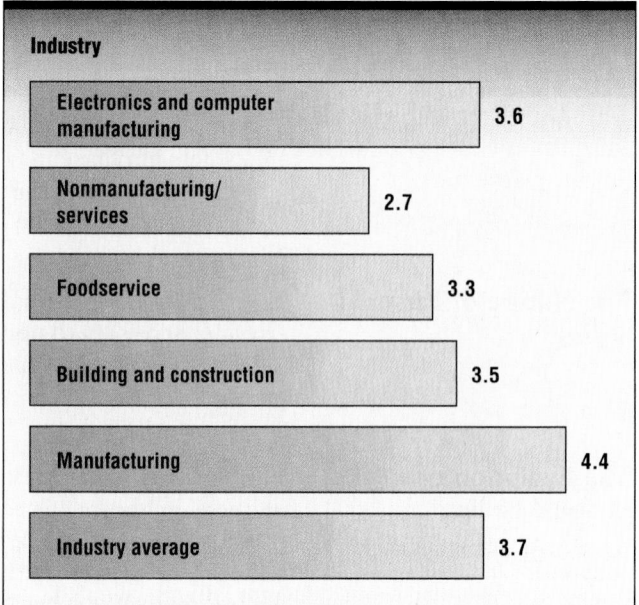

Industry	
Electronics and computer manufacturing	3.6
Nonmanufacturing/ services	2.7
Foodservice	3.3
Building and construction	3.5
Manufacturing	4.4
Industry average	3.7

4. **Problem-solver stage** Selling involves obtaining the participation of buyers in identifying their problems, which can be translated into needs, and then presenting a selection from the supplier's offerings that correspond with those needs and can solve those problems.

5. **Procreator stage** Selling defines the buyer's problems or needs and the solutions to those problems or needs through active buyer-seller collaboration and then creating a market offering uniquely tailored to the customer.

As noted by Wotruba, firms evolving through these five stages have to assume different market orientations, as well as different organizational designs, staffing, and compensation programs. In addition, the different stages require different promotional strategies, each being integrated with personal selling to achieve the maximum communications effect.

The costs of personal selling

In some industries, personal selling constitutes a substantial portion of the communications effort and may account for most of the promotional budget. The reasons for this are twofold: First, much attention is devoted to this function because of the advantages it offers over other communication methods; and second, it is an expensive form of communication. As demonstrated by Exhibit 19–4, the average cost per sales call varies by industry—ranging from a low of $235 to as high as $332 in the manufacturing sector. In both instances, the cost of a communication does not come cheap!

When the cost per sales call is compared with the cost per message delivered through other media (we saw in other chapters that these costs could be as low as 3 cents), this figure seems outrageous. But taking these numbers at face value may lead to an unfair comparison. In evaluating the costs of personal selling, it is necessary to consider the nature of the call, the objectives sought, and a determination as to whether other program elements could deliver the message as effectively. It may be that the higher costs cannot be avoided.

The costs associated with personal selling are even higher when you consider that one sales call is not likely to be enough to close a deal. This is particularly true in the industrial market, as shown in Exhibit 19–5, where multiple calls may be required.

➤ *Exhibit 19–6*
Types of sales jobs

Creative Selling
Creative selling jobs may require the most skill and preparation of any of the selling positions. In addition to prospecting, the salesperson must assess the situation, determine the needs to be met, present the capabilities for satisfying these needs, and get an order. In many instances the salesperson is the "point person" who has established the initial contact on behalf of the firm and who has the major responsibility for completing the exchange. He or she is, in fact, the "ordergetter."
Order Taking
Once the initial sale has taken place, the creative seller may be replaced (not physically!) by an order-taker. The role of the order-taker is much more casual. In many instances it may involve what is referred to as a *straight rebuy*– that is, the order does not change much (soft water or bottled water delivery persons are examples). In those instances where a slight change is considered, the order-taker may be involved in a modified rebuy, which may require some creative selling (for example, a salesperson calling on a wholesale food company may have a list of products to sell). Should a major purchase decision be required, however, the role of making the sale may again be turned to the creative seller.
Missionary Sales Reps
The missionary representative is essentially a support role. While performing many of the tasks assumed in creative selling, the missionary rep may not actually take the order. Rather the rep will introduce new products, new promotions, and/or new programs, with the actual order to be taken by the company's order-taker or by a distributor representing the company's goods. In addition, the missionary sales rep may have additional account service responsibilities. Missionary reps are most often employed in industries where a middleman is employed by the manufacturer for product distribution purposes (food products, pharmaceuticals, etc.).

The costs per closing a sale now appear even more intimidating (though in industrial markets the returns, as stated, may easily warrant the expense). A random survey of 4,000 businesses found in 1991 that it took an average of 3.7 personal calls to seal a deal. Manufacturing had the highest average number of calls at 4.4, while non-manufacturing services had the lowest at 2.7. The average cost to close a sale was $1,165.50 —a 14.3 percent increase over 1988 figures.[5]

Overall, personal selling is an expensive way of communicating. At the same time, however, personal selling usually involves more than just communicating and the returns (more direct sales) may be greater than those offered by the other program elements.

Personal selling responsibilities

Sales & Marketing Management uses three categories to classify salespersons including **order taking, creative selling,** and **missionary sales.**[6] (See Exhibit 19–6.) Of course, all firms do not treat each of these responsibilities the same, nor are their salespersons limited to only these tasks. As noted earlier, personal selling has evolved into additional responsibilities that both include and go beyond these. For example, with respect to the above tasks, job requirements may include: (1) locating prospective customers; (2) determining customers' needs and wants that are not being satisfied; (3) recommending a means of satisfying these needs and/or wants; (4) demonstrating the capabilities of the firm and/or the firm's products for providing this satisfaction; (5) closing the sale and taking the order; and (6) following up and servicing the account. Let's discuss these job classifications and some of the responsibilities assigned to each.

1. **Locating prospective customers** The process of locating prospective customers—often referred to as **prospecting**—involves the search for and qualification

➤ *Exhibit 19–7*
Giltspur offers salespersons expertise on how to qualify leads.

of prospective customers. Salespersons must follow up on **leads**—those persons who may be prospective customers—and **prospects**—those who need the product or service. In addition, they must determine whether these prospects are **qualified prospects**—that is, able to make the buying decision and afford it. Exhibit 19–7 shows an advertisement for a company that offers assistance to sales forces in determining who constitutes a qualified lead.

2. **Determining customer's needs and wants** At this stage, the salesperson is gathering more information on the prospect, and deciding on the best way to approach them. Determining what the customer needs or wants is required. In addition, the salesperson must make certain the person being approached is capable of making the purchase decison.

3. **Recommending a means of satisfying the customer's needs and wants** At this stage, the salesperson recommends a possible solution to the problem and/or needs of the potential customer. As noted earlier, this may entail providing information the prospect had not previously considered, or it may involve identifying alternative solutions that might work.

4. **Demonstrating the capabilities of the firm** Obviously, the salesperson would want his or her firm to be the choice for solving the prospect's needs. At this stage, the salesperson demonstrates the capabilities of the firm and shows the prospect why selecting that firm as the provider is the obvious choice. As you might expect, the importance of corporate image—created through advertising and other promotional tools—is an aid important to the salesperson.

5. **Closing the sale** The key ingredient to any sales presentation is the **close**—that is, getting the commitment of the prospect. For many salespersons, this is the most difficult of the selling tasks. Many salespersons are adept at prospecting, identifying customer needs, and making presentations, but they are reluctant to ask for the sale. Many managers, aware of this problem, work with their sales forces to assist them in closing the sale and helping reluctant and or uncertain buyers to make a decision.

6. **Following up and servicing the account**   Once the sale has been made, the responsibilities of the sales force are not ended. It has been said it is much easier to keep existing customers than it is to attract new ones. Follow-up activities require that the salesperson not terminate his or her efforts once the closing has been accomplished. Maintaining customer loyalty, repeat sales, and the opportunity to **cross sell**—that is, sell additional products and services to the same customer—are some of the advantages from maintaining customer satisfaction through follow-up activities.

It is important to remember that one of the advantages the salesperson offers is the opportunity to assess the situation firsthand and to adapt the sales message accordingly (hence, this is a *direct feedback* network). No other promotional element provides this opportunity. As a result, the successful salesperson is one who is constantly analyzing the situation, reading the feedback provided by the receiver, and presenting the message in a way that specifically meets the customer's needs.

While you might expect that this is an easy task, this may not always be the case. Sometimes buyers will not or cannot accurately express their needs. At other times, the salesperson may be required to become more of a problem solver for the client. More and more, successful salespeople are being asked to assist in the decision-making process of the buyers. The more salespeople can become entrenched in the planning and decision making, the more confidence and reliance the buyer places in them.

In other instances, the true motivation for purchasing may not be the one that is offered. While you might expect that buyers are basing their decisions on rational and objective factors, this may not always be the case. Even in industrial markets (where product specifications may be critical) or in reseller markets (where product movements and/or profits are important), many purchase decisions are made on what might be considered nonrational criteria (not irrational, but involving other than purely cost or other product benefits). Since it is generally believed these purchase situations involve less emotion and more rational thinking than many consumer purchases, this is an important insight.

Consider the dilemma that faces the marketer. If he or she provides advertising and promotions that speak only to the rational purchase motives—which is what one might expect one should do—he or she may be unable to make the sale. On the other hand, how could an advertiser possibly know all the emotional or nonrational criteria influencing the decision, let alone integrate this information into its messages? Once again, you can see the importance of the personal sales effort, as this may be the only way to uncover the many motivations for purchasing, and addressing them.

Global Perspective 19–1 compares personal selling techniques in the United States versus Japan. As you can see in this discussion, the Japanese seem to be more willing to respond to the variety of needs and wants of their customers and, as a result, may be more successful than their American competitors.

Based on the information just provided, the importance that personal selling plays in the promotional mix should now be more obvious. This program element provides for opportunities that are not offered by any other form of message delivery. While the variety of tasks performed by salespeople offers some distinct advantages to the marketing program, these same tasks may also constitute disadvantages, as you will now see.

Advantages and Disadvantages of Personal Selling

The nature of personal selling positions this promotional tool uniquely among those available to the marketer, offering some distinct advantages, including the following.

- **Allowing for two-way interaction**   The ability to interact with the receiver allows the sender to determine the impact of the message. As such, resolutions to problems in comprehension or objections or more in-depth discussions of certain selling points can be provided immediately. In other forms of mass communications, this direct feedback is not available, and such information cannot be immediately obtained—if it can be obtained at all.

Global Perspective 19–1

"Wet Selling"—Do The Japanese Do It Better?

A great deal of time and effort is expended in the United States to establish effective personal selling techniques. Colleges offer courses, training programs and seminars are conducted, and consultants are employed to improve our selling techniques. Even with all of this effort and expense, it appears that the Japanese may be doing the job better, both internationally and here in the United States.

One thing that makes the Japanese selling method so successful is what the Japanese refer to as a "wet" approach—wet meaning flexible, accommodating, caring, and humanistic. The foundation of this approach is respect, and the Japanese go out of their way to demonstrate to the potential buyer that they honor and value their business and the relationship. This respect is implemented through strong customer service and results in a high degree of customer satisfaction. It is also reflected in a partnership between the salesperson and the customer, with both working together to solve the customers' problems and meet their needs.

The American salesperson—at least in the eyes of George Leslie, president of Meitec America, Inc,—takes more of a "dry" approach. According to Leslie, American salespeople approach

an account armed with slick brochures, and not much else. He believes that they are not knowledgable about their products, offer only cursory customer service, and certainly do not treat their clients with respect. Customers are considered expendable (up until the time that they may be lost), they are treated with hard logic rather than empathy, and the partnerships are never formed. In essence, the American salesperson has very little commitment to the buyer.

Some American salespeople are learning from the "wet" approach. These salespeople have adopted the Japanese style, in part because they believe that it will work, and also because they feel that the American buyers now being approached by the Japanese will come to expect it. According to Leslie, the American salesperson is at a crossroads. He or she can either accept the more responsive "wet" approach, or take a defeatist attitude that it is not possible to compete that way here. It will be interesting to see which way they turn.

Source: George Leslie, "U.S. Reps Should Learn to Sell 'Japanese Style',' *Marketing News*, October 29, 1990, p. 6.

- **Tailoring of the message** Because of the direct interaction, messages can be tailored to the receiver. Because of this more precise message content, the sender is better able to address specific concerns, problems, and needs of the consumer. In addition, he or she is able to determine when to move on to the next selling point, ask for the sale, or close the deal.

- **Lack of distraction** In many personal selling situations, a one-to-one presentation is conducted. In these situations, the likelihood of distractions is minimized, and the buyer is generally paying more attention to the sales message. Even in those situations in which the presentation is made by a group of salespersons, or in which more than one decision maker is present, the setting may be less distracting than those in which nonpersonal mass media are employed.

- **Involvement in the decision process** Through consultative selling, the seller has become more of a partner in the buying decision process, acting in conjunction with the buyer to solve problems. The net result of this is more involvement and more reliance on the salesperson and his or her products and services.

As you can see, the advantages of personal selling focus primarily on the dyadic communications process, the ability to alter the message, and the opportunity for direct feedback. Sometimes, however, these potential advantages are not always realized. In fact, they may become disadvantages.

Some of the disadvantages associated with personal selling include the following.

- **Inconsistent messages** Earlier we stated that the ability to adapt the message to the receiver was a distinct advantage of personal selling. At the same time, the lack of a standardized message can become a disadvantage. The message to be communicated is generally well thought out, planned, and designed by the marketing staff with a particular communications objective in mind. Once this message has been determined, it is communicated to all receivers. The salesperson may alter this message—sometimes not in the way the marketer intended. Thus, the marketing staff may be at the mercy of the sales force with respect to what exactly is communicated. (Sales communications aids may offset this problem to some degree, as you will see later in this chapter.)

- **Sales force/management conflict** Unfortunately, there are situations in even the best of marketing companies in which one has to wonder if the sales staff and marketing staff know they work for the same company and for the same goals. Because of failures to communicate, corporate politics, and a myriad of other reasons, the sales force and marketing managers may not be working as a team. As a result, the marketing staff may not understand the problems faced by the sales staff, or the salespeople may not understand why marketing people do things the way they do. The result is that the sales force may not use materials provided from marketing, that marketing may not be responsive to the field's assessment of customer needs, and so forth. The bottom line is that the communications process is not as effective as it could be primarily because of a lack of internal communications and/or conflicts.

- **High cost** We discussed earlier the high cost involved in personal selling. As the cost per sales call continues to climb, the marketer may often find that mass communications may be a more cost-effective alternative.

- **Poor reach** This program element is not as effective for reaching as many members of the target audience as are other elements. Even if money were no object (not a very likely scenario!), the sales force has only so many hours and so many people they are able to reach in a given time. Further, the frequency with which these accounts are reached is also low.

- **Potential ethical problems** Because the manager does not have complete control over the messages the salespeople communicate and because of the emphasis on "making the sale"—income and advancements are often directly tied to sales—there is always an opportunity to "bend the rules." Salespeople may say and do things they know are not entirely ethical and may not be in the best interest of the firm in order to get a sale. The potential for this problem has led to a renewed emphasis on ethics in the marketplace and, as shown in Ethical Perspective 19–1, has forced managers to devote additional attention to this issue.

Combining Personal Selling with Other Promotional Tools

As with the other program elements, personal selling is usually used as one component of the promotional mix. Rarely—if ever—is personal selling used alone. Rather, this promotional tool both supports and is supported by other program elements.

Combining Personal Selling and Advertising

When considering specific market situations and communications objectives, the advantages of advertising make this program element more effective in the early stages of the response hierarchy (for example, in creating awareness and interest), whereas personal selling is more likely to be used in the later stages (for example, stimulating trial, getting the order, etc.). Thus, each may be more or less appropriate depending on the objectives sought. In developing a promotional mix, these elements can be combined so as to compensate for the weaknesses of the other, thus creating a situation where these elements complement each other.

For example, consider the situation involved in a new product introduction. Given an adequate budget, the initial objective might be to reach as many persons in the target market as quickly and as cost effectively as possible. Since the primary

Ethical Perspective 19–1

Analyzing Ethical Behavior in the Sales Force

There is a growing concern among businesses for ethics in the marketplace. Because of the emphasis on sales as the evaluative criterion for those involved in personal selling and the negotiation process inherent in all personal selling situations, many managers believe this area is of prime concern. They think something must be done to ensure that the sales force conducts its business "above board."

But why should businesses care about ethics? So long as the sales numbers keep coming in, are ethics relevant? There are a number of reasons to be ethical. First and foremost is the moral issue. Other issues can also be cited, many of which may not come directly to mind. For example:

1. **Mental health issues**   Many believe that to be an effective manager, one must have a clear conscience. Advancing to a management position through unethical means may cause the manager extreme discomfort and stress later.
2. **Corporate image**   Evidence indicates that in the long run, sales are not aided by unethical behaviors. On the other hand, the negative effects that might accrue to the firm accused of unethical behaviors can be detrimental. In addition, some firms report they are much more likely to conduct business with organizations of high moral and ethical fiber.
3. **Penalties**   For firms found guilty of unethical behaviors, fines and penalties may be assessed. Besides the loss of corporate image, more tangible factors such as financial penalties and/or "blacklisting" may result.

What can managers do to ensure the sales force conducts itself in an ethical and moral fashion? Thomas Wotruba suggests a framework for analyzing and promoting ethical behavior. His framework includes a four-stage process:

1. **Recognizing what actions are possible in a given situation, who would be affected, and what the outcomes would be.** Essentially, this initial step is an "ethical situation analysis," in which it is recognized who might be affected by unethical actions, alternatives are delineated, and potential outcomes determined.
2. **Determining the morally correct alternative.** In many situations, the salesperson is faced with alternative actions that might be taken. Each of these may lead to higher probabilities of completing the sale, but each might also have more serious moral implications. Considering the issues in the first stage, the various alternatives and their outcomes must be considered, with the best one selected.
3. **Assigning priority to moral values.** Managers have a variety of values they wish to satisfy. The goal at this stage is to prioritize moral values, so they will be chosen and the salesperson will act in a morally correct manner. The salesperson (and managers) must learn to think ethically and to have moral values at the top of the value list.
4. **Translating intentions into actions.** It is not enough to just have the right moral values and intentions. These intentions must be put into action. Planning for these actions, working around unexpected impediments and unexpected difficulties, overcoming fatigue and frustrations, and resisting distractions in pursuit of the final goal are the essential ingredients to effective implementation.

What will this ethical behavior mean to the firm? As noted by Wotruba, more ethical acts can result in two types of outcomes: (1) fewer negative consequences, and (2) more positive outcomes. He notes that these rewards can be both intrinsic and extrinsic, leading to more sales, greater profits, and increased customer satisfaction as well as improved working conditions, more happy and healthy salespersons, and perhaps an even better world to live in—at least in the workplace.

Source: Thomas R. Wotruba, "A Comprehensive Framework for the Analysis of Ethical Behavior, with a Focus on Sales Organizations," *Journal of Personal Selling and Sales Management* 10 (Spring 1990), pp. 29–42.

objective is awareness, and a simple message is all that is required, advertising would likely be the most appropriate medium.

Now suppose specific benefits needed to be communicated that were not very obvious or easy to comprehend, and a product demonstration would be useful. Or consider a situation in which the objective is to ask for the sale. In these situations, advertising is not likely to be sufficient, and personal selling would be a more appropriate tool. In common marketing situations such as these, you can see how well the combination of advertising and personal selling work together to attain the objectives sought.

A number of studies bear out this complementary relationship. A study by Theodore Levitt showed that sales reps from well-known companies are better received than those from companies that did not spend advertising dollars to create awareness.[7] (Once they were in the door, however, the buyer expected the salesperson to

perform better than those from lesser known companies.) Once a salesperson from a less well known company was able to get in to see the buyer—if he or she were able—the salesperson would have an approximately equal likelihood of making the sale. In risky situations, the well-advertised company representative would again have the advantage.

In other studies, John Morrill found that selling costs were as much as 2 percent to 28 percent lower if the buyer had received an advertising message before the salesperson's arrival.[8] McGraw-Hill Corporation, in a review of 54 studies, concluded the combination of advertising and personal selling was important given that "less than 10 percent of industrial decision makers had been called upon by a salesperson from a specific company about a specific product in the previous two months."[9]

These studies suggest that by combining advertising and personal selling, the company is likely to improve reach, reduce costs, and improve the probability of a sale (assuming the advertising is effective—a concern reflected in the ad shown in Exhibit 19–8). As you can see, this certainly leads to a complementary relationship.

Combining Personal Selling and Public Relations

The job descriptions presented earlier demonstrate that personal selling involves much more than just selling products and/or services. In many situations, the personal selling agent may be the best source of public relations available to the firm. In their day-to-day duties, salespersons are representing the firm and the products of that firm. Their personalities, servicing of the account, cooperation, and empathy not only influence the sales potential but also reflect on the organizations they represent.

The salesperson may also be used directly in a public relations role. For example, in many firms, the salesperson is encouraged to participate in community activities, such as the Jaycees, Little League, or other social organizations. In other instances,

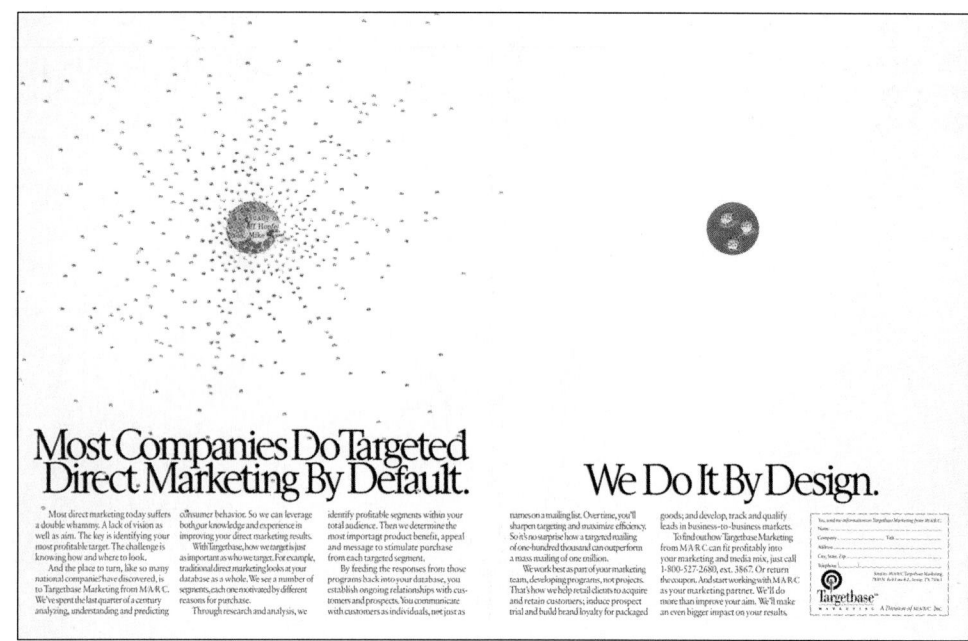

the sales force, in conjunction with the company, has sacrificed time from their daily duties to assist persons in time of need. For example, following a catastrophic flood, a beer company in the Northeast distributed water in its cans to flood victims, using the sales force to make the deliveries. After a Los Angeles earthquake, local companies donated food and their sales forces' time to aid quake victims, whereas Coors provided free water in its cans to residents of Pittsburgh when a barge break contaminated the drinking water. After the riots in Los Angeles in the spring of 1992, a number of organizations joined to help rebuild the ravaged community. As you might expect, these actions do not go unnoticed and result in goodwill toward both the company and its products while at the same time benefiting society.

Combining Personal Selling and Direct Marketing

Companies have found that by integrating direct marketing—specifically telemarketing—into their field sales operations, they are becoming more effective in their sales efforts. The cost of a sales call and the cost associated with closing the sale are already very high and on the increase. Many marketers have reduced these costs by combining the telemarketing and sales efforts. A number of companies now offer consulting services to help organizations in that endeavor, as shown in Exhibit 19–9. The telemarketing department is used to screen leads and—after qualifying potential buyers on the basis of interest credit ratings, and the like—pass on the leads to the sales force. The net result is a higher percentage of sales closings, less wasted time by the sales force, and a lower cost per sale average.

As shown in Exhibit 19–10, there has been a rapid growth in the use of the telemarketing-sales combination for many firms, as they have determined the phone can be used effectively for service and follow-up functions as well as for growth-related activities. Supplementing personal selling efforts with the phone calls in turn frees the sales force and allows them to spend more time selling.

The telemarketing staff, in addition to selling and supporting the sales efforts, has provided a public relations dimension. By being able to communicate more often with the buyer, goodwill is created, enhancing the likelihood of customer satisfaction and loyalty.

In addition to telemarketing, other forms of direct marketing have been employed successfully. For example, many companies send out lead cards to screen prospective customers on their level of interest. The salesperson then follows up on those expressing a genuine interest, saving valuable time and increasing the potential for a sale.

➤ *Exhibit 19–10*
The growth of telemarketing as a sales function: reasons for growth (in percent)

	Telephone Sales and Service	Field Sales
Total growth related	58.0	61.8
Overall business growth or expansion	44.7	43.1
Adding product lines	10.2	8.0
Adding territories	3.1	10.7
Total system related	20.8	7.5
Added centralized telemarketing dept.	11.5	1.8
Added/changed computer system	6.2	4.4
Centralized sales and marketing	3.1	1.3
Customer demand	10.5	10.2
Cost efficiencies	1.4	0
Other	2.0	2.2
Can't tell/no response	9.8	18.2

Note: Adds to more than 100 percent owing to multiple mentions.

Combining Personal Selling and Sales Promotions

The program elements of sales promotions and personal selling are also used to support each other. For example, many of the sales promotions targeted to resellers are presented and distributed by the sales force, who will ultimately be responsible for removing them or replacing them as well.

While trade sales promotions are designed to support the reseller, and are often targeted to the ultimate consumer, many other promotional tools are designed to assist the sales staff. Flip charts, leave-behinds, and specialty advertisements may be designed to assist salespeople in their presentations, to serve as reminders, or just to create goodwill. The number of materials available may range from just a few to hundreds, depending on the company. (If you ever get the chance, look into the trunk of a car of a consumer products salesperson. You will find everything from pens to calendars to flip charts to samples to lost baseball mitts—all but the last of which are provided to assist in the selling effort.)

Likewise, many sales promotions are targeted at the sales force itself. Sales incentives such as free trips, cash bonuses, or gifts are often used to stimulate sales efforts. And—as we saw with resellers—contests and sweepstakes may also be employed.

It is important that the elements of the promotional program work together, as each has its specific advantages and disadvantages. While personal selling is valuable in efforts to accomplish certain objectives, and in its support of other promotional tools, it must be supported by the other elements. Ads, sales promotions, and the like may be targeted to the ultimate user, resellers, or to the organization's sales force.

Evaluating the Personal Selling Effort

Like all other elements of the promotional mix, the personal selling function must be evaluated with respect to its contribution to the overall promotional effort. As we stated earlier, the costs of personal selling are often high, but the returns may be just as high.

Because the sales force is under the control and supervision of the sales manager, evaluations are typically based on sales criteria. Sales analyses may be performed with respect to total sales volume, by territories, by product line, by customer type, or by sales representative.[10] In addition, other sales-related criteria such as new account openings, customer contacts, and/or service records can be used. Customer relations and personal characteristics are also sometimes considered, as shown in Exhibit 19–11.

From a promotional perspective, sales performances are important, as are the contributions of individuals in generating these sales. On the other hand, the promotions manager is charged with evaluating the performance of the personal selling effort as one program element contributing to the overall promotional program. As such, he or she needs to use different criteria in determining its effectiveness.

➤ *Exhibit 19–11*
Criteria used to evaluate sales forces

Quantitative Measures	
Sales Results	**Sales Efforts**

Orders
    Number of orders obtained
    Average order size (units or dollars)
    Batting average (orders ÷ sales calls)
    Number of orders canceled by customers
Sales volume
    Dollar sales volume
    Unit sales volume
    By customer type
    By product category
    Translated into market share
    Percentage of sales quota achieved
Margins
    Gross margin
    Net profit
    By customer type
    By product category
Customer accounts
    Number of new accounts
    Number of lost accounts
    Percentage of accounts sold
    Number of overdue accounts
    Dollar amount of accounts receivable
    Collections made of accounts receivable
	Sales calls
	    Number made on current customers
	    Number made on potential new accounts
	    Average time spent per call
	    Number of sales presentations
	    Selling time versus nonselling time
	    Call frequency ratio per customer type
	Selling expenses
	    Average per sales call
	    As percentage of sales volume
	    As percentage of sales quota
	    By customer type
	    By product category
	    Direct selling expense ratios
	    Indirect selling expense ratios
	Customer service
	    Number of service calls
	    Displays set up
	    Delivery cost per unit sold
	    Months of inventory held by customer type
	    Number of customer complaints
	    Percentage of goods returned

Qualitative Measures	

Selling skills
    Knowing the company and its policies
    Knowing competitors' products and sales
        strategies
    Use of marketing and technical backup
        teams
    Understanding of selling techniques
    Customer feedback (positive and negative)
    Product knowledge
    Customer knowledge
    Execution of selling techniques
    Quality of sales presentations
    Communication skills
	Sales-related activities
	    Territory management: sales call
	        preparation, scheduling, routing, and
	        time utilization
	    Marketing intelligence: new-product
	        ideas, competitive activities, new
	        customer preferences
	    Follow-ups: use of promotional brochures
	        and correspondence with current and
	        potential accounts
	    Customer relations
	    Report preparation and timely submission
	Personal characteristics
	    Cooperation, human relations,
	        enthusiasm, motivation, judgment, care
	        of company property, appearance,
	        self-improvement efforts, patience,
	        punctuality, initiative, resourcefulness,
	        health, sales management potential,
	        ethical and moral behavior

Criteria for Evaluating Personal Selling Contributions to the Promotional Program

A number of criteria may be used to evaluate the contribution of the personal selling effort. These include:

- **Providing marketing intelligence**—the ability of the sales force to feed back information regarding competitive programs, customer reactions, market trends, and other factors that may be important in the development of the promotional program.
- **Follow-up activities**—the use and dissemination of promotional brochures and correspondences with new and existing customers; providing feedback as to the effectiveness of various promotional programs.

- **Program implementations**—the number of promotional programs implemented; the number of shelf and/or counter displays used and so forth; the implementation and assessment of cooperative advertising programs.
- **Attainment of communications objectives**—the number of accounts to whom presentations were made (awareness, evaluation), the number of trial offers accepted (trial), and the like.

When combining these criteria with those used by the sales department, the promotions manager should be able to gain an accurate assessment of the effectiveness of the personal selling program. On the other hand, the ability to make these evaluations requires a great deal of cooperation between the departments.

SUMMARY

This chapter discussed the nature of personal selling and the role this program element plays in the promotional mix. The role personal selling plays in the integrated marketing communications program varies depending on the nature of the industry, competition, and market conditions. In many industries (for example, industrial markets) the personal selling component may receive the most attention, while in others (for example, consumer nondurables) it plays a minor role. However, managers in both industries believe the importance of this program element will continue to increase over the next few years.

Personal selling offers the marketer the opportunity for a dyadic communications process—that is, a two-way exchange of information. As a result, the salesperson can instantaneously assess the situation and the effects of the communication and adapt the message if necessary.

While this exchange offers the opportunity to tailor the message to the needs and wants of the receiver specifically, it also offers the disadvantage of an unstandardized message, as the final message communicated is under the control of the salesperson. In an attempt to develop a standard communication, marketers provide their reps with flip charts, leave-behinds, and other promotional pieces to assist them in their presentations and to provide information to the prospective buyer.

Evaluation of the personal selling effort is usually under the control of the sales department, as sales is the most commonly used criterion. At the same time, the promotions manager must assess the contribution personal selling is providing by using nonsales-oriented criteria.

KEY TERMS

personal selling
dyadic communication
provider stage
persuader stage
prospector stage
problem solver stage

procreator stage
order taking
creative selling
missionary sales
prospecting

leads
prospects
qualified prospects
close
cross sell

DISCUSSION QUESTIONS

1. Discuss some of the advantages and disadvantages of using personal selling as part of the promotional program.
2. Describe some of the recent changes in technology that might affect how personal selling activities are conducted.
3. What are some criteria typically used by marketers to evaluate personal selling's contribution to the promotional program?
4. In what situations, and for what types of products, might personal selling be effective? Give examples.
5. Discuss some of the advantages and problems involved in the recruitment of other nonsales employees to join in the selling effort.

6. Describe the five stages involved in the evolution of selling. Explain the salesperson's role at each stage.
7. Explain the responsibilities of these various sales jobs: creative selling, order taking, missionary sales.
8. Describe the six job responsibilities of the sales force and the requirements of each.

9. Explain why the sales force might be one of the more vulnerable areas of the firm in respect to unethical behaviors. Discuss some of the problems that might occur from unethical behaviors.
10. Discuss Wotruba's framework for analyzing and promoting ethical behavior in the sales organization.

chapter **20**

Measuring the Effectiveness of the Promotional Program

chapter objectives

➢ To discuss reasons for measuring advertising effectiveness.

➢ To examine the various dependent measures used in assessing advertising effectiveness.

➢ To evaluate alternative methods for conducting measures of advertising effectiveness.

➢ To review the requirements of conducting proper effectiveness research.

Advertisers Are Getting Emotional over Effectiveness Measures

Given the billions of dollars spent on advertising and promotion in the United States each year, the need to measure the effectiveness of these communications programs is obvious. While some standard measures are available to let the advertiser know if ads are working or not, some advertisers are willing to try almost anything to measure effectiveness.

A variety of "wacky" methods have been employed. Advertising researchers have strapped gadgets around TV viewers to measure how fast their hearts beat and/or how much their palms sweat. Some have traced consumers' brain waves, while others have followed consumers around supermarkets to watch their reactions to promotional displays.

Some of the more recent undertakings have focused on consumers' emotional responses to ads. The thinking behind this approach is that while people may lie, their emotions don't. So if you want to get a true picture of advertising effectiveness, see how consumers "feel" about the ad rather than what they think about it.

Because consumers may underestimate their emotional responses to ads, or may feel uncomfortable about expressing their feelings, or may be unable to find the right words to describe their reactions, one of the country's top advertising agencies, BBDO Worldwide, has invented the "Emotional Measurement System," a propri-

etary device that uses photographs of actors' faces to help consumers choose their reactions to commercials. A variety of clients are using the system including Gillette's Atra Plus razors; Pepsi-Cola; Polaroid; and Wrigley's gum.

The BBDO system was developed after three years (and tens of thousands of dollars) of research that resulted in a special stack of 53 pictures that show people laughing, crying, and even cringing. The "Photodeck" was carefully selected from among 1,800 pictures of six actors and supposedly contains the full range of possible consumer emotions.

After watching commercials, focus group participants are asked to select pictures from the stack that best describe how they feel about the ad. The pictures tell the agency if the emotion it is seeking is being delivered by the ad. The researchers tabulate the responses, then plot them on a "perceptual map" to determine whether the response is positive or negative, active or passive. The methodology has received high praise from two of the clients—Wrigley and Gillette—as well as the creative department of the agency.

Not everyone shares the "emotional high" that BBDO does, however. While most advertising researchers agree it is important to attempt to measure emotions, some believe this system has too many flaws. Barbara Feigin, director of strategic services at Grey Advertising in

Some samples of "Photodeck," which BBDO believes represents the gamut of human emotions.

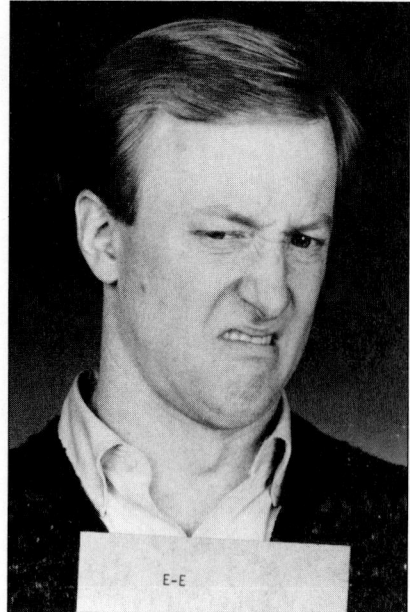

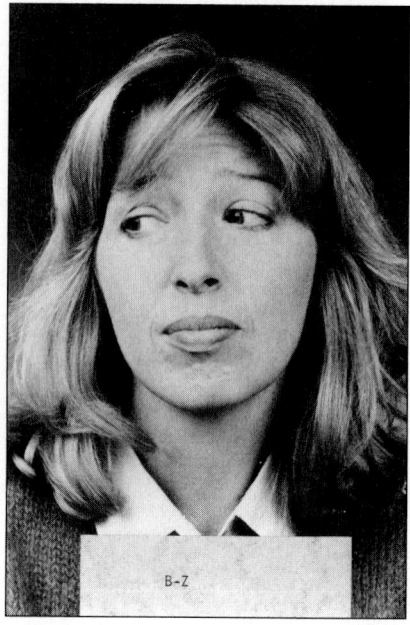

(continued)

New York, is not sold on the idea. She agrees that the idea of measuring emotions is good, but notes, "Do all people take away the same thing from the same picture? I don't think so." Others have said the system is a "large step forward" but think there is "a hell of a long distance" between measuring emotional response and manipulating it. Still others believe the system is little more than a marketing ploy to gain new clients.

Regardless of the arguments against the system, BBDO expects it may constitute the wave of the future in advertising research. Other faces will continue to express different emotions.

Source: Gary Levin, "Emotion Guides BBDO's Ad Tests," Advertising Age, January 29, 1990, p. 12; Bruce Horovitz, "Trying to Get a Better Picture of How People Feel About an Ad," Los Angeles Times, February 16, 1990, p. D6.

The search for ways to measure the effectiveness of advertising is constant. Both clients and agencies are continually striving to determine whether their communications are working and are employing a variety of methods for doing so. Unfortunately, there seems to be little agreement on the best method to use. This disagreement is not regarding the need for advertising research—almost everyone agrees that research is required—rather, it is on the ways the research is conducted and in how the results are used.

Measuring the effectiveness of the promotional program is a critical element in the promotional planning process. Research allows the marketing manager to evaluate the performance of specific program elements and provides input into the next period's situation analysis. It is a necessary ingredient to a continuing planning process and yet is a task that often is not carried out.

In this chapter, we discuss some reasons firms should measure the effectiveness of their advertising and promotional programs and why many decide not to. In addition, we examine how, when, and where such measurements can be conducted. Most of our attention is devoted to measuring the effects of advertising because much more time and effort has been expended developing evaluation measures in advertising than in the other promotional areas. This does not mean these areas are of any less importance, only that there is less to report on.

Before beginning this discussion, however, it is important to understand that in this chapter we are concerned with research that is conducted in an evaluative role—that is, to measure the effectiveness of advertising and promotion and/or to assess various strategies before implementing them. This is not to be confused with research discussed earlier in this text that served as input into the development of the promotional program. While evaluative research may occur at various times throughout the promotional process (including the development stage), it is conducted specifically to assess the effects of various strategies. We begin our discussion with the reasons research to measure effectiveness should be conducted as well as some of the reasons firms do not do so.

Arguments for and against Measuring Effectiveness

Almost any time one engages in a project or activity—whether for work or fun—some measure of performance occurs. For example, in sports you may compare your golf score against par, or when skiing, you may compare your time on a race course to others. In business, employees are generally given objectives to accomplish, and their job evaluations are based on their ability to achieve these objectives. Advertising and promotion should not be an exception. It is important to determine how well the communications program is working and to measure this performance against some standards. Some of the reasons for taking such measures follow.

Reasons for Measuring Effectiveness

Assessing the effectiveness of advertisements both before they are implemented and after the final versions have been completed and fielded offers a number of advantages:

1. **Avoiding costly mistakes** The top three advertisers in the United States spent over $6 billion in advertising and promotion in 1991. The top 100 spent a total of over $35 billion. This is a lot of money to be throwing around without some understanding as to how well it is being spent. If the program is not achieving its objectives, the marketing manager would want to know so as not to continue to spend (waste!) money on it.

Just as important as the out-of-pocket costs is the *opportunity* loss that accrues from poor communications. If the advertising and promotions program is not accomplishing its objectives, not only is the money spent lost but so too is the potential gain that could result from an effective program. Thus, the value of measuring the effects of advertising might not be considered so much a savings of money as it is an opportunity to make money, as is demonstrated by Promotional Perspective 20–1.

2. **Evaluating alternative strategies** Typically a firm may have a number of alternative strategies under consideration. For example, there may be some question as to which medium should be used or whether one message is more effective than another. In another instance, the decision may be between the use of two alternative promotional program elements. Research may be designed to assist the manager in determining which strategy is most likely to be effective and should be employed. For example, Coors often tests alternate versions of its advertising in different cities to determine which ad communicates most effectively.

3. **Increasing the efficiency of advertising in general** You may have heard the expression "Can't see the forest for the trees!" Sometimes advertisers get so close to the project they lose sight of what it is they are seeking, and because they know what they are trying to say, they expect their audience will also understand. They may use technical terms or jargon that they think everyone is familiar with, when they are not. At other times, the creative department may get too creative, or too sophisticated, losing the meaning that needs to be communicated. An added benefit of conducting research is the opportunity to develop more efficient and effective communications. As you can see, the reasons for evaluating communications are valid and somewhat obvious. But not everyone agrees with the need to evaluate. The next section examines some of the reasons.

Reasons Why Effectiveness Measures Are Not Used

A number of reasons for not measuring the effectiveness of advertising and promotions strategies are also offered.

1. **Cost** Perhaps the most commonly cited reason for not testing (particularly among smaller firms) is the expense associated with such efforts. To conduct good

Promotional Perspective 20–1

How Testing Saved a Bank Program

A San Diego-Based bank with assets of over $1 billion and a strong community image of conservatism decided to initiate an innovative and somewhat risky checking and savings program. Because it would be the first in the market with this program, the bank would stand to gain a sizable market share, as well as enhance its image as the most innovative financial institution in the market. At the same time, because the program had the potential to be confusing to customers, the bank also was threatened with the potential for failure, not only with the program itself but also as a reflection on the bank's image.

After much planning and discussion, the marketing manager and program director decided on a program they considered profitable to the bank and also attractive to the customer. The program was developed, and preliminary print ads and statement stuffers were developed.

In discussing the program with the institution's marketing consultants, some questions arose—both with the program and in the way it was to be communicated. After much deliberation, all parties involved agreed to a pretest of both the communications before implementation.

To make a long story short, the decision to test was the correct one. While it cost the bank approximately $14,000 and delayed initiation by one month, the results demonstrated two important facts:

1. The advertisements and statement stuffers designed to communicate the program were difficult to understand and would not have accomplished the objectives intended.
2. Not only was the advertising flawed, but also the program as it was designed was virtually unattractive to the target market and would have attracted few investors.

The initial month's newspaper advertising alone would have cost the bank approximately $62,000, and the program—had it failed initially—would not have been recoverable.

As a result of the research, both the ad and the program were changed. While the changes were easy to make, they were significant in respect to their impact on the proposed program. After making the changes and implementing the program and the advertising, the bank tracked the results. Both the program and the ad were extremely effective, leading to a very successful introduction.

As you can see, both out-of-pocket and opportunity costs warranted the investment in research (and may have saved a few jobs in the process!).

research can be expensive, both in terms of time and money. As a result, many managers decide time is critical and they must implement the program while the opportunity is available. Second, many managers explain that they believe the monies spent on research could be better spent on improved production of the ad, additional media buys, and the like, and they elect to allocate their budgets to these priorities rather than testing and evaluation.

While the former of these arguments may have some merit, there is very little in the second. Imagine what would happen if a poor campaign were developed, or if the incentive program did not motivate the targeted audience. Not only would you be spending money without the desired effects, but also the effort could possibly do more harm than good. Spending more money to buy media does not remedy a poor message nor substitute for an improper promotional mix. For example, one of the nation's leading brewers watched its test-market sales for a new brand of beer fall short of expectations and decided more media time was the answer. The solution, it thought, was to buy all the TV time available in the market for December and January so long as it matched its target audience. At the end of January, sales had not improved. On final analysis—the product was abandoned in the test market— it was determined the problem was not in the media but rather in the message, as no reason to buy was communicated. In this case, research would have identified the problem, and millions of dollars and a brand might have been saved. The moral of this story is that spending monies that might have been used for research to gain increased exposure to the wrong message is not a sound management decision.

2. Research problems A second reason cited for not measuring effectiveness is that it is very difficult to isolate the effects of advertising. Each of the marketing mix variables affects the success of a product or service. Because it is not always possible to measure the contribution of each marketing element directly, some managers become frustrated and decide not to test at all. Their argument is one of, "If I can't determine the specific effects, why spend the money?"

This argument also suffers from weak logic. While we agree that it may not always be possible to determine that the contribution made by promotions is an exact dollar or sales amount, proper use of research can provide useful results.

3. Disagreement as to what to test The objectives sought in the promotional program may differ by industry, by stage of the product life cycle, or even for different people within the firm. The sales manager may want to see the impact promotions has on sales, top management may wish to know the impact on corporate image, whereas those involved in the creative process may wish to assess recall and/or recognition of the ad. The lack of agreement as to what to test often results in no testing.

Again, there is little rationale for this position. With the proper design, many, if not all, of the above might be measured. Since every promotional element is designed to accomplish its own objectives, there is no reason research cannot be used to measure their effectiveness in doing so.

4. The objections of creative It has been argued by many—and denied by others—that the creative department does not want its work to be tested and many agencies are reluctant to have their work submitted for testing. This is both true and false. Members of advertising agencies' creative departments often agree that they do not wish to be evaluated on the creative aspects of ads. Their arguments are that the tests are not true measures of the creativity and effectiveness of the ads; that applying measures stifles their creativity; and that the more creative the ad, the more likely it is to be successful. They argue they should be allowed to be creative and not subject to the limiting guidelines that marketing may impose. The advertisement run by the Chiat Day Advertising Agency shown in Exhibit 20–1 reflects how many of those in the advertising business feel about this subject.

At the same time, the marketing manager is ultimately responsible for the success of the product or brand. Given the substantial dollar amounts being allocated to advertising and promotion, the burden for the proper use of these monies is part of the job requirements he or she is expected to perform. It is the manager's right, and responsibility, to know how well a specific program—or a specific ad—will perform in the market. As such, the manager is ultimately responsible to ensure that measures of effectiveness are employed.

5. Time A final reason often given for not testing is a lack of time. The lack of time takes on two dimensions: (1) managers believe they already have too much to do and just can't seem to get around to testing; and (2) managers think research takes time and they don't want to wait to get the message out, fearing they might miss the window of opportunity.

Planning might be the solution to the former of these arguments. While a variety of reports have appeared in the media about the overworked and time-poor managers, the value of research should require that it be conducted. Proper planning would ensure that this would happen.

The second argument can also be overcome with proper planning. While timeliness is critical, getting the wrong message out is of little or no value and may even be harmful, as noted earlier. There will be occasions where market opportunities may require quick market entry and may necessitate choosing between testing and immediate implementation. However, even in this case, some testing may help avoid mistakes or improve effectiveness. In most instances, proper planning and scheduling will allow for research to be undertaken.

➤ *Exhibit 20–1*
Chiat Day expresses its feelings toward testing

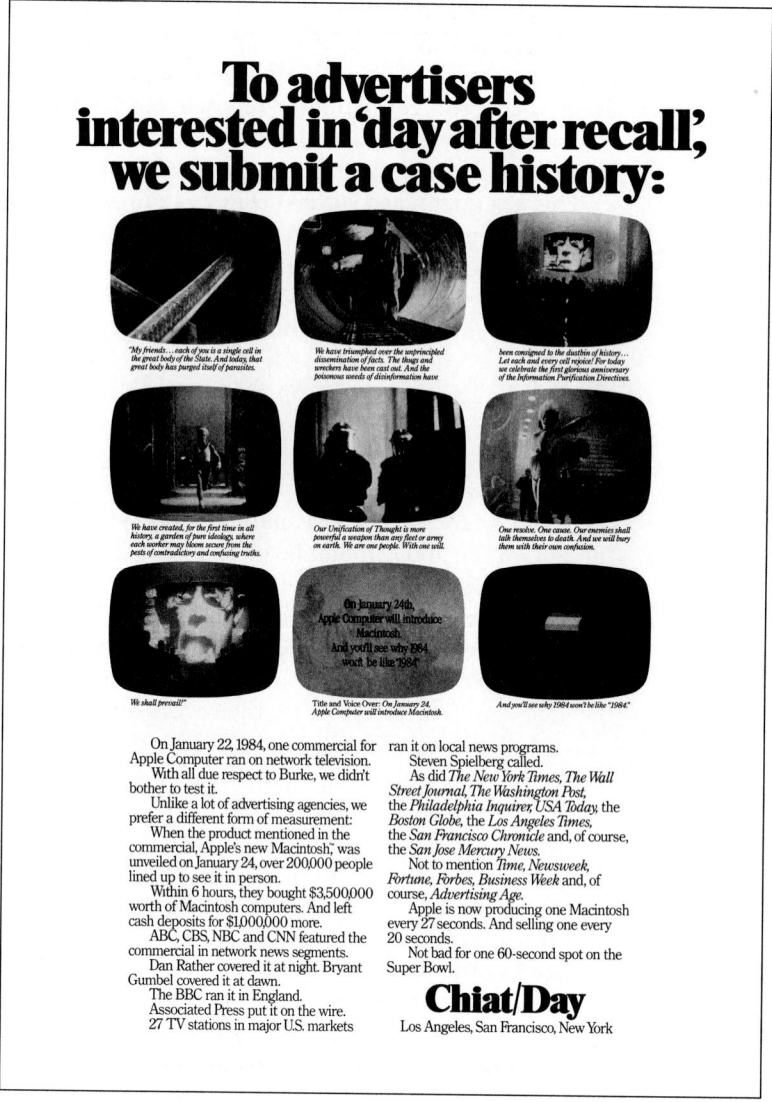

To advertisers interested in 'day after recall', we submit a case history:

On January 22, 1984, one commercial for Apple Computer ran on network television.

With all due respect to Burke, we didn't bother to test it.

Unlike a lot of advertising agencies, we prefer a different form of measurement:

When the product mentioned in the commercial, Apple's new Macintosh," was unveiled on January 24, over 200,000 people lined up to see it in person.

Within 6 hours, they bought $3,500,000 worth of Macintosh computers. And left cash deposits for $1,000,000 more.

ABC, CBS, NBC and CNN featured the commercial in network news segments.

Dan Rather covered it at night. Bryant Gumbel covered it at dawn.

The BBC ran it in England.

Associated Press put it on the wire.

27 TV stations in major U.S. markets ran it on local news programs.

Steven Spielberg called.

As did *The New York Times, The Wall Street Journal, The Washington Post,* the *Philadelphia Inquirer, USA Today,* the *Boston Globe,* the *Los Angeles Times,* the *San Francisco Chronicle* and, of course, the *San Jose Mercury News.*

Not to mention *Time, Newsweek, Fortune, Forbes, Business Week* and, of course, *Advertising Age.*

Apple is now producing one Macintosh every 27 seconds. And selling one every 20 seconds.

Not bad for one 60-second spot on the Super Bowl.

Chiat/Day

Los Angeles, San Francisco, New York

Conducting Research to Measure Advertising Effectiveness
What to Test

We now examine how to measure communications effects. More specifically, this section considers what elements to evaluate, as well as where and how such evaluations should occur.

In Chapter 6, we discussed the components of the communications model (source, message, media, receiver) and the importance of understanding the role of each in the promotional program. Given the importance placed on understanding these factors, it follows that it is necessary to determine how each is affecting the communications process. In addition, other decisions that must be made in the promotional planning process must also be evaluated.

Source factors

An important question to be asked is whether the spokesperson being used is effective and how the target market will respond to him or her. For example, John McEnroe, considered by many to be the obnoxious "bad boy" of tennis because of his sometimes abrasive on-court antics, proved to be an extremely successful spokesperson for Dunlop, Nike, and Bic. Or, as often happens, a product spokesperson may be an excellent source initially but, owing to a variety of reasons, may lose impact over time. For example, Bill Cosby is a spokesperson for Kodak. At one time or another, he has also been a representative for Ford, Jell-O, Texas Instruments, and E.F. Hutton, among others—which might bring his credibility into question (as discussed in Chapter 7). In other instances, characteristics of the source (changes in attractiveness or likability) or other external factors may lead to changes in source effectiveness.

Message variables

Both the message and the means by which this message is being communicated constitute bases for evaluation. For example, in the brewery's new product entry example discussed earlier, it was stated that the message never provided a reason for the consumer to try the new product. In other instances, the message may not be strong enough to "pull readers into the ad" by attracting their attention or clear enough to be used to make an evaluation. Sometimes the message may be memorable, but not achieve some of the other goals set by management. For example, the 1991 "Chill Out" campaign run by Pepsi achieved very strong results in respect to memorability and consumers expressed strong liking for the ads, but Pepsi's sales during the period grew at a rate significantly lower than did Coke's.[1] A number of factors regarding the message and its delivery may have an impact on its effectiveness, including the headline, illustrations, text, and layout.

Many ads are never seen by the public because of the message they convey. For example, a Susan Anton ad in which she was eating a piece of Pizza Hut pizza was considered too erotic for the company's small-town image. Likewise, an ad created for General Electric (GE) in which Uncle Sam gets slapped in the face (to demonstrate our growing trade imbalance) was killed by the company's chairman.[2]

Media strategies

Just as there are a number of media decisions to be made, there is also a need to evaluate these decisions. Research may need to be designed to determine which media class (for example, broadcast versus print), subclass (newspaper versus magazines), or specific vehicles (which newspapers or magazines) generate the most effective results. In addition, the location within a particular medium (front page versus back page) and size or length of time of the ad or commercial merit examination. For example, research has demonstrated that by choosing a larger ad, reader attention to that ad will increase.[3] Similarly, those involved in direct-response advertising on television have found that it is more effective to advertise on some programs than on others. As noted by one successful direct-marketing advertiser who found that old television shows yield more responses than first runs:

> The fifth rerun of "Leave It to Beaver" will generate much more response than will the first run of a prime-time television program. Who cares if you miss something you have seen four times before? But you do care when it's the first time you've seen it.[4]

Another factor that must be considered is that of the **vehicle option source effect.** The vehicle option source effect is "the differential impact that the advertising exposure will have on the same audience member if the exposure occurs in one media option rather than another."[5] There are differences in the way persons perceive ads that result from the context in which the ad appears.[6]

A final factor to be considered with respect to media decisions involves scheduling. The evaluation of flighting versus pulsing or continuous schedules is an important one to consider, particularly given the increasing costs of media time. Likewise, there may be opportunities associated with increasing advertising weights in periods of downward sales cycles or recessions. The manager experimenting with these alternative schedules and/or budget outlays should attempt to measure the differential impact that may result.[7]

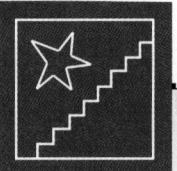

Promotional Perspective 20–2

Large Ad Budgets, Sales, and Effective Ads

Many marketers often lament that they cannot effectively compete against their competitors with larger, and thus more powerful, advertising budgets. To these managers, large automatically means effective. But a number of companies have found this is not necessarily the case—large advertising expenditures do not always result in more effective ads—at least when the criterion used to measure effectiveness is sales.

Take Pepsi as an example. During the first six months of 1991, Pepsi, perennially a large budget advertiser, ran its "Chill Out" campaign. In the second half of the year, the famous "You've got the right one baby, uh-huh" campaign featuring singer Ray Charles was used. While both of these campaigns ranked higher than Coke's in viewer recall, sales during the period grew at only 2 percent—much less than would be expected when a campaign scores as well as Pepsi's did.

Similar results have been found in regard to print advertising. Two of the world's best remembered automobile print ads in 1990 were created by two of the smallest budget advertisers—Porsche and Jaguar. While the domestic auto advertisers spent over $1 billion in magazine advertising, only three American carmakers cracked the top 10 most memorable ads list. Tiny ad budget companies like Alfa Romeo and Rolls-Royce ranked far above such big spenders as Ford, Chrysler, and GM.

A variety of factors have been cited for the foreign ads' successes. The novelty and "exoticness" of foreign cars, the product's ability to draw consumers into the ads, and the general inherent appeal of the brands have been mentioned. Still, experts cite the Porsche ads as "breakthrough" ads that are visually appealing and thus able to capture viewers' attention and memory.

Once again, however, when sales is used as the criterion, the ads would not test out as effective. Not very many Rolls-Royces were sold in the United States, and Porsche sold only 7,000 cars. (In fact, Porsche sales continue to decline.) Others in the top 10 such as Peugeot and Alfa Romeo are not showing significant sales increases either.

The seemingly conflicting results raise two points. First, having a substantial advertising budget is not necessary for creating memorable ads, and second, a lot more goes into creating sales than just advertising.

Excitement, novelty, and imagination lead to greater recall than does just large expenditures. But recall itself does not mean more sales. The prices of foreign cars would seem to be an obvious factor affecting sales of autos with memorable ads. Coke's special promotions, strong dealer relations, and discounting strategies have been suggested as reasons its sales continue despite Pepsi's better ads.

What does it all mean? It seems many factors go into creating memorable ads, and even more go into generating sales. Thus, attempting to show direct impact on sales as a measure of the advertising's success might lead to "throwing the baby out with the bathwater"—that is, getting rid of an effective ad because the wrong effectiveness measure was used.

Source: "Pepsi: Memorable Ads, Forgettable Sales," *Business Week*, October 21, 1991, p. 36; and Bruce Horovitz, "Car Firms that Spend the Most on Ads Aren't the Ones Whose Messages Sink in, Survey Says," *Los Angeles Times*, September 24, 1991, p. D1.

Budgeting decisions

A number of studies have been conducted that have examined the effects of budget size on advertising effectiveness and the effects of various ad expenditures on sales. A number of companies have also attempted to determine if increasing their ad budget will directly impact sales. The results of these studies have shown that this relationship is often hard to determine. Much of this difficulty may be because sales is often used as an indicator of effectiveness, which may confound the results as is demonstrated in Promotional Perspective 20–2. More definitive conclusions may be possible if other dependent variables—such as the communications objectives stated earlier—are used.

When to Test

Virtually all test measures can be classified according to the time in which they are conducted. **Pretests** are those measures taken before implementation of the campaign, whereas **posttests** occur after the ad or commercial has been in the field. A variety of pretests and posttests are available to the marketer, each with its own methodology designed to measure some aspect of the advertising program. Exhibit 20–2 provides a good classification scheme and categorization of these various testing methods.

	Advertising-related test (reception or response to the message itself and its contents)	**Product-related test** (impact of message on product awareness, liking, intention to buy, or use)

Laboratory measures (respondent aware of testing and measurement process)	**Cell I**
	
	Pretesting procedures
	1. Consumer jury
	2. Portfolio tests
	3. Readability tests
	4. Physiological measures
	    Eye camera
	    Tachistoscope
	    GSR/PDR
		Cell II
		
		Pretesting procedures
		1. Theater tests
		2. Trailer tests
		3. Laboratory stores

Real-world measures (respondent unaware of testing and measurement process)	**Cell III** Pretesting procedures 1. Dummy advertising vehicles 2. Inquiry tests 3. On-the-air tests Posttesting procedures 1. Recognition tests 2. Recall tests 3. Association measures 4. Combination measures	**Cell IV** Pretesting and posttesting procedures 1. Pre- and posttests 2. Sales tests 3. Minimarket tests

Pretesting

Pretests may occur at a number of points, from as early on as idea generation to rough execution to testing the final version before implementing it. In addition, more than one type of pretest may be used. For example, concept testing (which is discussed later in this chapter) may take place at the very earliest development of the ad or commercial. At this point, little more than an idea, basic concept, or positioning statement may be under consideration. In other instances, layouts of the ad campaign including headlines, some body copy, and rough illustrations may be used. For television commercials, storyboards and animatics may be tested.

The methodologies employed to conduct pretests may vary. Focus groups are often employed in which participants freely discuss the meanings they get from the ads, consider the relative advantages of alternatives, and even suggest improvements or additional themes. Sometimes in addition to the focus groups, or as an alternative, participants are asked to evaluate the ad on a series of rating scales. Different agencies may use their own set of measures, and in-home interviews, mall intercept, or laboratory methods may be used to gather the data.

The advantage of pretesting at this stage is to gain feedback relatively inexpensively. Any problems with the concept or the way it is to be delivered are identified before spending large amounts of money in development. Sometimes, more than one version of the ad is evaluated to determine which is most likely to be effective.

The disadvantage is that the final product may be much more effective in communicating than are the mock-ups, storyboards, or animatics. The mood-enhancing and/or emotional aspects of the message are very difficult to communicate in this format. Another disadvantage often cited is that of time delays. Many marketers believe being first in the market offers them a distinct advantage over competitors. Thus, they will forgo research to save time and ensure this position.

Posttesting

Posttesting is also common among both advertisers and ad agencies (with the exception of testing commercials for wearout). Exhibit 20–3 presents the results of a study that examined ad agency and advertisers' use of various advertising research methods. As can be seen, the percentage of organizations that evaluate finished commercials and TV campaigns is very high. Posttesting is designed to perform two roles: (1) to determine if the campaign is accomplishing the objectives sought; and (2) to serve as input into the next period's situation analysis. As with pretests, a variety of posttest measures are available, most of which involve survey research methods.

Where to Test

In addition to considering when to test, decisions must be made as to *where* these tests should occur. As was shown in Exhibit 20–2, these tests may take place in either laboratory or field settings.

Laboratory tests

Laboratory tests are those in which persons are brought to a particular location where they are shown ads and/or commercials and either asked questions about them or have their responses measured by other methods—for example, pupil dilation, eye tracking, or galvanic response measures.

The major advantage of the lab setting is the *control* it affords the researcher. Changes in copy, illustration, formats, colors, and the like, can easily be manipulated at a small cost, with the differential impact of each assessed. Thus, it becomes much easier for the researcher to isolate the contribution that each factor makes.

The major disadvantage is the lack of *realism*. Perhaps the greatest effect of this lack of realism is a **testing bias**. When people are brought into a lab—even if it has been designed to look like a living room—they know they are to be tested. As a result, they may think they have to be sensitive to the ads and scrutinize them to a much greater degree than they typically might, given a more natural setting. In this case, "everyone becomes an expert." A second problem with this lack of realism is the fact that the *natural viewing situation*—complete with distractions or comforts of the home—is not duplicated. Sitting in a lab setting may not be the same as viewing at home on the couch, with the wife/husband and kids, dog, cat, and parakeet chirping in the background. (A bit later you will see that some testing

➤ *Exhibit 20–3*
General findings about copy research

	Total		Agencies		Advertisers	
	No.	**%**	**No.**	**%**	**No.**	**%**
Total respondents	112	100.0	39	100.0	73	100.0
Undertake preliminary, background, or strategic research in preparation for advertising campaigns	104	92.9	39	100.0	65	89.0
Evaluate copy ideas, storyboards, other formats before rough commercial	85	75.9	34	87.2	51	69.9
Evaluate rough commercial execution of other formats before finished commercial	102	91.1	38	97.4	64	87.7
Evaluate finished commercials	105	93.8	35	89.7	70	95.9
Evaluation of television campaigns	98	87.5	37	94.9	61	83.6
Test competitive commercials	73	65.2	27	69.2	46	63.0
Test commercials for wearout	29	25.9	9	23.1	20	27.4

techniques have made progress in correcting this deficiency—no, they did not bring in the dogs and the parakeets!) Overall, however, the control offered by this method probably outweighs the disadvantages, which accounts for the frequent use of lab methods.

Field tests

Field tests are tests of the ad or commercial under natural viewing situations. In this testing format, the realism that is not present with lab methods is available, as are all the factors cited above (distractions, comforts, noise). In addition, the effects of repetition, program content, and even the presence of competitive messages are considered.

The major disadvantage of field tests is the lack of control, as it may be difficult or impossible to isolate causes of viewers' evaluations. Events that might not normally be operating may be present during the test, biasing the results. Competitors may learn of the research and attempt to sabotage it, and field tests usually take more time and money to conduct, so the results are not as quickly available to be acted on. Thus, while realism is gained, it is gained at the expense of other important factors. It is up to the researcher to determine which trade-offs will be required.

How to Test

Our discussion of the factors that should be tested, as well as where and when this testing would occur, was general and was designed to establish a basic understanding of the overall process as well as some key terms. In this section, we are more specific in discussing some of the more commonly used methods employed at each stage. Before this discussion, however, it is important to establish some criteria on which advertisements and commercials should be judged.

Conducting evaluative research is not easy. Nevertheless, some standards are considered necessary, and in 1982, 21 of the largest U.S. advertising agencies endorsed a set of principles aimed at "improving the research used in preparing and testing ads, providing a better creative product for clients, and controlling the cost of TV commercials."[8] This set of nine principles, called **PACT (Positioning Advertising Copy Testing)**, defines *copy testing* as research "which is undertaken when a decision is to be made about whether advertising should run in the marketplace. Whether this stage utilizes a single test or a combination of tests, its purpose is to aid in the judgment of specific advertising executions.[9] The nine principles determined to define a good copy testing procedure are shown in Exhibit 20–4.

As you can see by this list of principles, advertisers and their clients have expressed a concern for developing *appropriate* testing methods. Adherence to the principles included here might not make for perfect testing methods, but it would go a long way toward improving the state of the art and would help alleviate at least one of the arguments cited earlier for not testing. Having established the guidelines for good testing procedures, we now turn our attention to how such testing occurs.

➢ *Exhibit 20–4*
Positioning Advertising Copy Testing (PACT)

1. Provide measurements that are relevant to the objectives of the advertising
2. Require agreement about how the results will be used in advance of each specific test
3. Provide multiple measurements (because single measurements are not adequate to assess ad performance)
4. Be based on a model of human response to communications—the reception of a stimulus, the comprehension of the stimulus, and the response to the stimulus
5. Allow for consideration of whether the advertising stimulus should be exposed more than once
6. Recognize that the more finished a piece of copy is, the more soundly it can be evaluated and requires, as a minimum, that alternative executions be tested in the same degree of finish
7. Provide controls to avoid the biasing effects of the exposure context
8. Take into account basic considerations of sample definition
9. Demonstrate reliability and validity

The Testing Process

Testing may occur at various points throughout the development of the advertisement or advertising campaign. This research may be of the following types: (1) concept generation research, (2) rough, prefinished art, copy, and/or commercial testing, (3) finished art or commercial pretesting, and (4) market testing of ads or commercials (posttesting).

Concept Generation and Testing

Exhibit 20–5 describes the process involved in advertising **concept testing.** Concept testing is conducted very early in the campaign development process, with the primary objective of exploring the targeted consumer's response to a potential ad or campaign to having the consumer evaluate advertising alternatives. Positioning statements, copy, headlines, and/or illustrations may all be under scrutiny. The material to be evaluated may be as simple as a single headline or may involve a rough drawing or sketch of the ad. In addition, elements such as the colors used, print type, package designs, and even point-of-purchase materials may be evaluated.

The methods employed for concept testing may vary. One of the more commonly used is that of focus groups. These focus groups usually consist of 8 to 10 people considered to be in the target market for the product. For example, in testing new concepts for Jell-O gelatin, Young & Rubicam assessed reactions of mothers and children (the mothers being the buyers; the children, the ultimate consumers). The number of groups to be used varies, depending on group consensus, strength of response, and/or the degree to which participants like or dislike the concepts. It is not unusual for a number of groups to be employed (some companies report using as many as 50 or more to develop the campaign), although usually less than 10 are required to test a concept sufficiently.

While focus groups continue to be a favorite methodology used by marketers, they are often overused. A variety of reasons may contribute to this overuse. The methodology is attractive in that results are easily obtained, directly observable, and immediate. A variety of issues can be examined, and consumers are free to expand and/or go into depth in areas they might consider important. Also, focus groups don't require quantitative analysis. Unfortunately, many managers are uncertain about surveys or research methods that require numbers and statistics. Focus groups are qualitative in nature and require much less skill and effort for interpretation. Weaknesses with focus groups—as shown in Exhibit 20–6—demonstrate that there

➤ *Exhibit 20–5*
Concept testing

Objective:	A concept test is designed to explore consumers' responses to various ad concepts as expressed in words, pictures, or symbols.
Method:	Alternative concepts are exposed to consumers who match the characteristics of the target audience. Reactions and evaluations of each are sought through a variety of methods including focus groups, direct questioning, and survey completion. Sample sizes vary depending on the number of concepts to be presented and the consensus of responses.
Output:	Output consists of qualitative and/or quantitative data evaluating and comparing alternative concepts.

➤ *Exhibit 20–6*
Weaknesses associated with focus group research

- The results are not quantifiable.
- Sample sizes are too small to generalize to larger populations.
- Group influences may bias participants' responses.
- One or two members of the group may steer the conversation or dominate the discussion.
- Consumers become instant "experts."
- Members may not represent the target market (are focus group participants a certain type of person?).
- Results may be taken to be more representative and/or definitive than they really are.

are appropriate and inappropriate circumstances in which this methodology should be employed.

Another way of gathering consumers' opinions of concepts is the use of mall intercepts in which consumers in shopping malls are approached and asked to evaluate rough ads and/or copy. Rather than participating in a group discussion, individual assessments are gathered through the use of questionnaires, rating scales, and/or rankings.

Rough, Prefinished Art, Copy, and/or Commercial Testing

Because of the high cost associated with the production of an ad or commercial (many network commercials cost in the hundreds of thousands of dollars to produce), advertisers are increasingly spending more monies testing at early stages where only a rendering of the final ad is evaluated. Slide photographs of the artwork posted on a screen and animatic and photomatic roughs have all been used to test at this stage. (See Exhibit 20–7 for an explanation of terminology.) Because such tests can be conducted for about $3,000, research at this stage is becoming ever more popular.

The cost of the test is only one factor to be considered. The test is of little or no value if it does not provide relevant and accurate information. Thus, rough tests must provide an indication of how the finished commercial would perform. Some studies have demonstrated that the *reliability* of these testing methods is favorable and the results do typically correlate very well with the finished ad.[10]

Most of the tests conducted at the prefinished stage involve lab settings, although some on-air field tests are also available. Some of those more commonly employed include:

1. Comprehension and reaction tests One of the key concerns to the advertiser is whether the ad or commercial conveys the meaning intended. The second item of concern is the reaction the ad generates. Obviously, the advertiser does not want an ad that evokes a negative reaction or is offensive to someone. **Tests of comprehension and reaction** are designed to assess these responses. (Which makes you wonder why some ads are ever brought to the marketplace!)

Tests of comprehension and reaction employ no one standard procedure. Personal interviews, group interviews, and focus groups have all been used for this purpose, and sample sizes have varied according to the needs of the client, although it is very rare for less than 50 or more than 200 respondents to be tested.

2. Consumer juries Using consumers representative of the target market to evaluate the probable success of an ad is the basis of this method. Members of the group may be asked to rate or rank order a selection of layouts or copy versions presented in pasteups on separate sheets. (The verdict is the final outcome!) The objectives sought and methods employed in **consumer juries** are shown in Exhibit 20–8,[11] and an example of some questions asked of jurists is shown in Exhibit 20–9.

➤ *Exhibit 20–7*
Rough testing terminology

A rough commercial is an unfinished execution that may fall into three broad categories:

Animatic roughs	Live-action rough
Succession of drawings/cartoons	Live motion
Rendered artwork	Stand-in/nonunion talent
Still-frames	Nonunion crew
Simulated movement:	Limited props/minimal opticals
Panning/zooming of frame/rapid sequence	Location settings
Photomatic roughs	Finished
Succession of photographs	Live motion/animation
Real people/scenery	Highly paid union talent
Still-frames	Full union crew
Simulated movements:	Exotic props/studio sets/special effects
Panning/zooming of frame/rapid sequence	

➤ *Exhibit 20–8*
Consumer juries

Objective:	Potential viewers (consumers) are asked to evaluate ads and to give their reactions to and evaluation of them. When two or more ads are tested, viewers will usually be asked to rate or rank order the ads according to their preferences.
Method:	Respondents are asked to view ads and rate or rank them according to two methods: (1) the order of merit method or (2) the paired comparisons method. In the former, the respondent is asked to view the ads, then rank them from one to *n* according to their perceived merit. In the latter, ads are compared only two at a time, with each ad being compared to every other ad in the group, and the winner listed. The best ad is that which wins the most times. Consumer juries typically employ 50 to 100 participants.
Output:	An overall reaction to each ad under consideration as well as a rank ordering of the ads based on the viewers' perceptions.

➤ *Exhibit 20–9*
Questions asked in a consumer jury test

1. Which of these advertisements would you most likely read if you saw it in a magazine?
2. Which of these headlines would interest you the most in reading the ad further?
3. Which advertisement convinces you most of the quality or superiority of the product?
4. Which layout do you think would be most effective in causing you to buy?
5. Which advertisement did you like best?
6. Which advertisement did you find most interesting?

While the jury method offers the advantages of *control* and *cost-effectiveness*, serious flaws in the methodology limit its usefulness. For example:

- **The consumer may become a self-appointed expert.** One of the benefits sought from the jury method is the *objectivity* and *involvement* in the product or service that the targeted consumer can bring to the evaluation process. It is possible, however, that knowing that they are being asked to critique advertisements, the participants try to become more *expert* in their evaluations—paying more attention and being more critical than they might typically be. The result may be a less-than-objective evaluation and/or a potential for evaluation on other elements than those sought.
- **The number of ads that can be evaluated is limited.** Whether *order of merit* or *paired comparison methods* are used, the ranking procedure becomes very involved and tedious as the number of alternatives under consideration increases. For example, consider the ranking of 10 ads. While the top two and the bottom two ranked may very well reveal differences, those ranked in the middle may not really yield much discriminating information. In the paired comparison method, the number of evaluations required can easily be calculated by the formula

$$\frac{n(n-1)}{2}$$

So in a situation where six alternatives were to be considered, 15 evaluations would have to be made. As the number of ads increases, the task would become even more unmanageable.

- **A halo effect is possible.** Sometimes participants may rate an ad good on all characteristics because they like a few and overlook specific weaknesses or bad attributes. This tendency, called the **halo effect,** distorts the rankings or ratings and defeats one of the values offered—the ability to control for specific components. (Of course, the reverse may also occur, that is, rating an ad bad overall due to only a few bad attributes.)
- **Preferences for specific types of advertising may overshadow objectivity.** Ads that involve emotions or pictures may receive higher ratings or rankings than those employing copy, facts, and/or rational criteria. Thus, even though the

latter form may prove to be more effective in the marketplace, they may be judged less favorably by the jurists if these persons prefer the former types.

Some of the problems noted here can be remedied by the use of *ratings scales* versus rankings. However, ratings are also not always valid, suffering from many of the problems noted above. Thus, while consumer juries have been used for a number of years and are still frequently employed, questions of bias have led researchers to question the validity of this method. As a result, a variety of other (methods discussed later in this chapter) are more commonly employed.

Pretesting Finished Ads   As shown in Exhibit 20–3, this stage of testing has received the most attention and participation among marketing researchers and their agencies. At this stage, a finished advertisement or commercial is used; however, it has not been presented to the market. As a result, it is still possible to make changes before fielding.

Many researchers prefer to test at this stage since the ad is in final form, which they believe provides a better test, and yet still has not been seen by the target market. A variety of test procedures are available for both print and broadcast ads, including both laboratory and field methodologies.

Print methods include the use of portfolio tests, analyses of readability, and the use of dummy advertising vehicles. Broadcast tests include theater tests and on-air tests, whereas both print and broadcast may use physiological measures. A discussion of each and identification of some of the firms providing such services follow.

Pretesting finished print messages

A number of methods for pretesting finished print ads are available, one of which is **Burke's Reflections test** described in Exhibit 20–10. While a number of different measures may be used, only the most commonly employed of these methods are discussed here.

Portfolio tests   This laboratory methodology is designed to expose a group of respondents to a portfolio consisting of both control and test ads. Having viewed the portfolio, respondents are asked to indicate what information they recall from the ads. The assumption is that the ads that yield the *highest recall* will be the most effective.

While **portfolio tests** offer the opportunity to compare the alternative ads under consideration directly, a number of weaknesses with this method may limit its applicability. These include the following.

1. Factors other than advertising creativity and/or presentation may be affecting recall. Interest in the product or product category, the fact that respondents know they are participating in a test, or interviewer instructions (among others) may account for more differences than the ad itself.
2. Recall may not be the best test. Some researchers argue that for certain types of products—those of low involvement—recognition (ability to recognize the ad when shown) may be a better measure than recall. Thus, by using recall, erroneous results might occur.

One way of determining the validity of this method is to correlate results obtained by the portfolio method with readership scores obtained once the product has been placed in the field. Whether such validity tests are being conducted or not is not readily known, although the use of portfolio methods continues to remain popular in the industry.

Readability tests   A test of the communications efficiency of the copy in a print ad is possible without ever conducting an interview with a potential reader. This test uses a formula known as the **Flesch formula**, named after its developer, Rudolph Flesch. In the formula, readability of the copy is assessed by determining the average

Objective:	A test designed to measure recall and readers' impressions of print advertisements.
Method:	Mall intercepts in two or more cities are used to screen respondents and have them take home "test magazines" for reading. Participants are phoned the next day to determine opinions of the ads, recall of ad contents, and other questions of interest to the sponsor. Approximately 225 persons constitute the sample.
Output:	Scores reported include related recall of copy and visual elements, sales messages, and other nonspecific elements. Both quantitative (table) scores and verbatim responses are reported.

number of syllables per 100 words. Human interest appeal in the material, length of sentences, and familiarity with certain words are also considered and correlated with the educational background of targeted audiences. Previously established norms for various target audiences have been established and serve as a basis for comparison. The test suggests that copy is most comprehended when sentences are short, words are concrete and familiar, and personal references are drawn.

This method eliminates many of the interviewee biases associated with other tests. Also, gross errors in understanding can be avoided. Finally, the fact that norms have been established offer an attractive standard for comparison.

Disadvantages are also inherent, however. The copy may become too mechanical, and the direct input of the receiver is not available. Without this input, other contributing elements, such as creativity, cannot be addressed. To be effective, therefore, this test should be used only in conjunction with other pretesting methods.

Dummy advertising vehicles　An improvement on the portfolio test is a methodology in which ads are placed in "dummy" magazines developed by an agency or research firm. The magazines contain regular editorial features of interest to the reader, as well as the test ads, and are distributed to a *random sample* of homes in predetermined geographic areas. Readers are instructed that the magazine publisher is interested in evaluations of editorial contents and they are to read the magazines as they normally would. Having completed this task, readers are interviewed on both the editorial contents and their reactions to the ads. Recall, readership, and interest-generating capabilities of the ad are assessed.

The advantage of this method is that it provides a more natural setting than does the portfolio test. Readership occurs in the participant's own home, the test more closely approximates a natural reading situation, and the reader may go back to the magazine—as they might typically do.

At the same time, the same disadvantages associated with portfolio tests are inherent here. The testing effect is not eliminated, and product interest may still bias the results. Thus, while this test methodology offers some advantages over the portfolio method, it is not a guaranteed measure of determining the advertising's impact.

Pretesting finished broadcast ads

While a variety of methods for pretesting broadcast ads are available, we again focus on the most popular of these.

Theater tests　One of the most popular laboratory methods for pretesting finished commercials has been that of **theater testing.** A number of variations in the methodologies employed exist, but before discussing these, it will be helpful to understand the basic theater testing concept.

Participants in theater tests are recruited by telephone, mall intercepts, and/or the mailing of tickets. Those sought are invited to view pilot films of proposed new television programs. In some instances, the show is actually being tested, but more commonly a standard program is used so audience responses can be compared with normative responses established by previous viewers. Sample sizes range from 250 to 600 participants.

➤ *Exhibit 20–11*
Alternative theater methodologies

Advertising Research Services (ARS) runs theater tests in four cities, on a total sample of 400 to 600 persons. Precommercial brand preferences are taken, and in this test, respondents are asked to choose from pictures of packages of brands—thus resulting in a recognition test rather than recall.

Viewers then watch a 30-minute television program with three sets of two commercials embedded in the program. Questions are then asked about the program. A second program of 30 minutes is then shown, with six additional commercials included. Any of the 12 commercials might be the test commercial. The measure of brand preference change is taken after the second program.

After approximately 72 hours, half of the sample is phoned to obtain a measure of recall. These results are compared against norms established from previous tests.

Advertising Control for Television (ACT), a lab procedure of the McCollum/Spielman Co., uses approximately 400 respondents representing four cities. The initial brand preference measure is taken by asking participants which brands they most recently purchased. Respondents are then divided into groups of 25 to view a 30-minute program with seven commercials inserted in the middle. Four are test commercials; the other three are control commercials with established viewing norms. After viewing the program, respondents are given a recall test of the commercials.

After completing the recall test, a second 30-minute program is shown, with each test commercial shown again. The second measure of brand preference is taken at this time, with persuasion measured by the percentage of persons who switched preferences from their most recently purchased brand to one shown in the test commercials.

When first entering the theater, viewers are informed that a drawing will be held for gifts and are asked to complete a product preference questionnaire asking which products they would prefer, should they win. This form also requests demographic data from the respondent. Participants may be seated in specific locations in the theater to allow observation by age, sex, and so on. The program and commercials are viewed, and a form asking for the viewer's evaluations is distributed. Participants are then asked to complete a second form for a drawing, so that changes in product preference can be noted. In addition to product/brand preference information, additional information regarding responses to the commercials may be obtained, including:

1. Interest in, and reaction to, the commercial.
2. Overall reaction to the commercial as measured by an adjective checklist.
3. Recall of various aspects of the commercial.
4. Interest in the brand under consideration.
5. Continuous (frame-by-frame) reactions throughout the commercial.

As noted, the methods of the theater testing operations vary. While all measure brand preference changes, each has its own way of conducting the tests. Some may not take all the measures listed above. Others may ask the consumers to turn dials or push buttons on a keypad to provide the continual responses, and so on. An example of some of these methodologies is shown in Exhibit 20–11.

Theater tests have both proponents and opponents. Those opposed to this methodology cite a number of disadvantages associated with this form of pretesting. First, they argue that the environment is too *artificial*—the lab setting is bad enough, but to ask respondents to turn dials or, as one service does, to wire people for physiological responses takes one too far from a natural viewing setting. Second, the contrived measure of brand preference change seems too simple and too phony to believe. Critics contend that participants will see through it and make changes because they think they are supposed to since they are being tested. Finally, the *group effects* of having others present and overtly exhibiting their reactions may affect viewers, who may not have had any reactions themselves.

Proponents, on the other hand, argue that such tests offer distinct advantages. In addition to the control offered, they cite the value of established norms (averages of commercials' performances) as an indication of how one's commercial will fare against others in the same product class that have been tested previously. Further, they argue the brand preference measure has been supported by actual sales results.

Despite the limitations of theater testing, most major consumer product companies use, or have used, it to evaluate their commercials. They argue that despite its shortcomings, this method allows for the identification of strong or weak commercials and a comparison to norms of other ads.

On-air tests   Some of the firms conducting theater tests also provide a second form of commercial testing in which the commercials are inserted into actual TV programs in certain test markets. Typically, the commercials are in finished form, although the testing of ads earlier in the developmental process is becoming more common. This form of testing is referred to as an **on-air test** and often includes single-source ad research (discussed later in this chapter). In addition to Information Resources, Burke Marketing Research, ASI Market Research, Inc., and Nielsen are well-known providers of on-air tests. Exhibit 20–12 describes one of these services—that of ASI's Recall Plus Test.

On-air testing techniques offer all the advantages of field methodologies, as well as all the disadvantages. In addition, negative aspects of the specific measures taken through the on-air systems have been cited. One concern that has been expressed is a problem associated with the use of **day-after recall scores**—the primary measure used in these tests. Lyman Ostlund notes that measurement errors created by the "natural environment" may result from the position of the ad in the series of commercials shown, the adjacent program content, and/or the number of commercials being shown.[12] While the testing services believe their methods overcome many of these criticisms, each still uses recall as a primary measure of effectiveness. Since recall tests may best reflect the degree of attention, and interest in an ad, attempts to claim that the tests may indicate the ad's impact on sales may be going too far. (In 28 studies reviewed by Jack Haskins, only 2 demonstrated that factual recall could be related to sales.)[13] This fact was also demonstrated in Promotional Perspective 20–2.

On the plus side, most of the testing services have offered evidence of both validity and reliability of the on-air pretesting of commercials. Both ASI and Burke claim their pretest and posttest results yield the same recall scores 9 out of 10 times—a strong indication of reliability and a good predictor of the effect the ad is likely to have when shown to the population as a whole.

In summary, on-air pretesting of finished or rough commercials offers some distinct advantages over lab methods and some indications as to the likelihood of success of the ad. Whether the measures used provide as much of an indication as the providers say they will still remains in question.

Physiological measures   A less commonly used method of pretesting finished commercials involves a laboratory setting in which physiological response variables are measured. These measures indicate the receiver's *involuntary* response to the ad and, as such, theoretically alleviate biases associated with voluntary measures reviewed to

> *Exhibit 20–12*
ASI Market Research—recall plus test

Objective:	Allows for the testing of finished or rough commercials to allow day-after recall and verbatim reactions.
Method:	One control and four test commercials are inserted into new 30-minute family television programs. The commercials and program are sent to two geographically dispersed cities and aired on CATV during prime-time viewing hours. Approximately 200 female viewers between the ages of 18 and 65 are randomly selected from all homes on the CATV system in the area. Commercials are then reexposed to viewers who recalled the ad, with more diagnostic questions then administered.
Output:	Day-after recall scores, verbatim responses to the commercials, and test-retest reliability scores are provided. Scores on competitive commercials (if used) are also provided.

this point. (Involuntary responses are those over which the individual has no control, such as heartbeat, reflexes, etc.) A variety of physiological measures have been used to test both print and broadcast ads.

1. Pupil dilation Research in **pupillometrics** is designed to measure dilation and constriction of the pupils of the eye in response to stimuli. *Dilation* is an activity most closely associated with action, whereas *constriction* involves the body's conservation of energy.

Advertisers have used pupillometrics to evaluate product and package design as well as to test ads, believing the interest value of the ad or preference for two ads could be determined. A stronger interest in (or preference for) an ad would be indicated by pupil dilation, as would arousal or attention-getting capabilities. Other attempts to determine the affective (liking or disliking) responses created by ads have met with less success.

Because of the high costs associated with this testing method, and some methodological problems, the use of pupillometrics has waned over the past decade. However, these methods can be useful in evaluating certain aspects of advertising.

2. GSR/EDR Galvanic skin response—also known as **electrodermal response**—measures the *resistance* or *conductance* the skin offers to a small amount of current passed between two electrodes. Response to a stimulus activates sweat glands, which in turn increases the conductance of the electrical current. Thus, reaction to advertising might be reflected in GSR/EDR activity. In their review of the research in this area, Paul Watson and Robert Gatchel have concluded that GSR/EDR (1) is sensitive to affective stimuli, (2) may present a picture of attention, (3) may be useful as measures of long-term advertising recall, and (4) is useful in measuring ad effectiveness.[14]

While a number of companies have (and many still do) offered skin response measures, this research methodology is not commonly used now.

3. Eye tracking A methodology that is more commonly employed is that of **eye tracking** (Exhibit 20–13). In eye tracking tests, viewers are asked to view an ad while a sensor aims a beam of infrared light at the eye. The beam follows the movement of the eye as it views the ad or commercial and provides information as to the exact spot on which the viewer is focusing. A *continuous* reading of responses is obtained, demonstrating what elements may be attracting attention, how long the viewer is focusing on specific elements of the ad, and the sequence in which these elements are being viewed.

By using eye tracking, researchers can identify strengths and weaknesses in an ad. For example, certain elements of an ad, such as attractive models or background occurrences, may distract the viewer's attention away from the brand or product being advertised. In such a case, steps may be taken to remedy this distraction before fielding the ad. In other instances, colors or illustrations may attract attention and create viewer interest in the ad.

4. Brain waves **Electroencephalographic (EEG) measures** can be taken from the skull to determine electrical frequencies in the brain. These electrical impulses are used in two areas of research:

- **Hemispheric lateralization** involves the determination of alpha activity in the left and right sides of the brain. It has been hypothesized that the left and

➤ *Exhibit 20–13*
Eye movement research

Objective:	To track viewers' eye movements to determine what viewers read or view in print ads and what attention is focused on in television commercials or billboards.
Method:	Fiber optics, digital data processing, and advanced electronics are used to follow eye movements of viewers and/or readers as they view an ad.
Output:	Relationship between what readers see, recall, and comprehend. Scan paths on print ads, billboards, commercials, and print materials. (Can also be used to evaluate package designs.)

right sides of the brain perform separate functions, with the right side processing visual stimuli, whereas the left processes verbal stimuli. The right hemisphere is thought to respond more to *emotional* stimuli, whereas the left responds to logical reason; and the left is responsible for recall, whereas the right determines recognition.[15] If these hypotheses are correct, the implications would be that advertisers could design the ads to increase learning and memory by creating stimuli to appeal to each hemisphere. However, some researchers believe lateralization is not a valid explanation of how the brain functions and that to design an ad to appeal to one side or the other would be highly implausible.

- **Alpha activity** refers to the degree of brain activation, with people being referred to as in an alpha state when they are inactive, resting, and/or sleeping. The theory is that a person in an alpha state is less likely to be processing information (recall correlates negatively with alpha levels) and that attention and processing requires moving one from this state. By measuring one's alpha level while viewing a commercial, it would be possible to assess the degree to which attention and processing are likely to occur.

While EEG research has attracted the attention of academic researchers, it has been much less successful in attracting the interest of practitioners.

Market Testing of Advertisements

Because the advertisement and/or campaign has been implemented does not mean there is no longer a need for testing. The fact that pretests have been conducted on smaller samples and may in some instances have questionable merit necessitates an examination of how the ad is doing in the field. In this section, we discuss some measures for posttesting an ad. Some of the tests are similar to those discussed in the previous section and many of the same companies provide these services.

Posttests of print ads

A variety of print posttests are available, including inquiry tests, recognition tests, and recall tests.

Inquiry tests   Used both in consumer- and business-to-business market testing, **inquiry tests** are designed to measure advertising effectiveness on the basis of *inquiries* generated from ads appearing in various print media. The inquiry may take the form of the number of coupons returned, the number of times a phone call is generated by the ad, or direct inquiries through reader cards. For example, you may have recently called in response to an ad in a local medium and were asked where you found out about the company or product or where you saw the ad. This is a very simple and easily employed measure of the advertisement or media effectiveness. More complex methodologies of measuring effectiveness through inquiries are also used. These methods may involve (1) running the ad in successive issues of the same medium, (2) running **split-run tests** in which variations of the ad are run in alternate copies of the same newspaper or magazine, and/or (3) running the same ad in different media. The measures taken by each of these methods will yield information on different aspects of the strategy. For example, in the first instance, one would be measuring the *cumulative* effects of the campaign, whereas in the second, specific elements of an ad or different versions of the ad would be examined. In the final method, the medium rather than the ad itself is the focus of the effectiveness measure.

While inquiry tests may yield some useful information, weaknesses in this methodology limit its effectiveness. For example, inquiries may not necessarily be a true measure of the attention-getting or information-providing aspects of the ad. The reader may be attracted to an ad, read it, and even store the memory provided but not be motivated to inquire at that particular time. Other factors such as time constraints, lack of a need for the product or service at the time the ad is run, or other factors may limit the number of inquiries. To conclude that the ad was not effective—or was less effective—may be erroneous, as attention-getting qualities, attitude change, awareness, and recall of copy points may all have been affected, although this might not be reflected. At the other extreme, a person with a particular need for the product may respond to the ad, regardless of specific elements of the ad. This person would then be considered as having responded to the ad for reasons associated with the ad, when in actuality he or she would have responded to any version.

The major advantages of inquiry tests may be that they are very inexpensive to implement and some feedback with respect to the general effectiveness of the ad or media used is possible. However, comparisons of alternative versions of an ad or specific creative aspects are usually not very effective.

Recognition tests   Perhaps the most commonly employed form of posttesting of print ads is the **recognition method**—most closely associated with Starch INRA Hooper. The *Starch Readership Report* allows the advertiser to assess the impact of an ad in a single issue of a magazine, over time, and/or across alternative magazines (see Exhibit 20–14). Starch measurements are taken for over 75,000 advertisements in more than 1,000 issues representing over 100 consumer, farm, and business magazines and newspapers per year. As can be seen in Exhibit 20–14, a number of measures of the ad's effectiveness are provided. An example of a Starch-scored ad is shown in Exhibit 20–15.

In addition to the *Starch Readership Report* described in Exhibit 20–14, Starch also offers the *Starch Impression Study* and the *Starch Ballot Readership Study.* The Starch Impression Study provides consumers' qualitative impressions of ads—for example, company image, important features, and so on—whereas the latter measures readership in business magazines.

The advantages claimed by the Starch methods are (1) the pulling power of various aspects of the ad can be assessed through the control offered, (2) a comparison to the effectiveness of competitors' ads can be determined through the use of the norms provided, (3) alternative ad executions can be tested, and (4) readership scores are a useful indication of the consumers' *involvement* in the ad or campaign. (With respect to this last statement, it is argued that the reader must read and become involved in the ad before the ad has an opportunity to communicate. To the degree that this readership can be shown, a direct indication of effectiveness is possible.)

Of the advantages cited above, perhaps the most valid is that of the ability to judge specific aspects of the ad. Many researchers have criticized other aspects of the Starch recognition method (as well as other recognition measures) based on the following:

1. The problem of false claiming   Research has indicated that in recognition tests, respondents may claim to have seen an ad when they have not. False claims may be a result of having seen similar ads elsewhere, expectations that such an ad would

➤ *Exhibit 20–14*
The Starch Readership Report

Objective:	To determine recognition of print advertisements as well as a comparison to other ads of the same variety or in the same magazine.
Method:	Samples are drawn from 20 to 30 urban areas reflecting the geographical circulation of the magazine. Personal interviewers are used to screen readers for qualifications and to determine exposure and readership. Samples include a minimum of 200 males and females, as well as specific audiences where required. Participants are asked to go through the magazines, looking at the ads, and provide specific responses.
Output:	Starch Readership Reports generate three recognition scores: • A Noted Score—the percentage of readers who remember seeing the ad • A Seen-Associated Score—the percentage of readers who recall seeing or reading any part of the ad identifying the product or brand • A Read-Most Score—the percentage of readers who reported reading at least one half of the copy portion of the ad

➤ *Exhibit 20–15*
Example of a Starch-scored advertisement

appear in the medium, or the personality of the respondent. In addition, interest in the product category has been shown to increase reporting of ad readership. Whether this false claiming is deliberate or not, such claims lead to an overreporting of effectiveness. On the flip side, factors such as interview fatigue may lead to an underreporting bias—that is, not reporting an ad that may have been seen.

2. Interviewer sensitivities Anytime research involves interviewers, there is a potential for bias. Respondents may believe they need to impress the interviewer or they might appear unknowledgeable if they continuously claim not to recognize an ad. In addition, there also exists the possibility of variance associated with interviewer instructions, recordings, and so on, regardless of the amount of training and sophistication involved.

3. Reliability of recognition scores By its own admission, Starch notes that the reliability and validity of its readership scores increase with the number of insertions tested. Essentially it is saying that to test just one ad on a single exposure may not produce valid or reliable results.

In sum, despite its critics, the Starch Readership studies continue to dominate the posttesting of print ads. The value provided by norms and the fact that reliability and validity can be improved with multiple exposures may underlie the decisions to employ this methodology.

Recall tests A number of tests to measure recall of print ads are available. Perhaps the most well known of these are the *SAMI-Burke Standard Print Test* and the *Gallup & Robinson Impact Test*—the latter of which is described in Exhibit 20–16. These **recall tests** are similar to those described earlier under the section on pretesting of broadcast ads in that they attempt to measure recall of specific ads.

In addition to the interviewer problems discussed in the section on recognition tests, other factors have been cited as disadvantages associated with recall tests. The

➤ *Exhibit 20–16*
Gallup & Robinson magazine impact research service

Objective:	To track recall of advertising (and client's advertisements) appearing in magazines to assess performance and effectiveness.
Method:	Test magazines are placed in participants' homes and respondents are asked to read the magazine that day. A telephone interview is conducted the second day to assess recall of ads, recall of copy points, and consumers' impressions of the ads. Sample size is 150 persons.
Output:	Three measurement scores are provided: • Proven Name Registration—the percentage of respondents who can accurately recall the ad • Idea Communication—the number of sales points the respondents can recall • Favorable Buying Attitude—the extent of favorable purchase reaction to the brand or corporation

reader's degree of involvement with the product and/or the distinctiveness of the appeals and visuals may lead to higher recall scores, although in general the method may actually lead to lower levels of recall than actually exist (though the advertiser would be happy with an error in this direction). Since critics contend the test is not strong enough to reflect recall accurately, many ads may be considered less effective than they really are and will be abandoned or modified without cause.

On the plus side, it is thought that recall can assess the impression on memory created by the ad. Proponents of recall tests contend the major concern may not be the score results themselves but rather how these scores are interpreted.

Posttests of broadcast commercials

A number of methods exist for the posttesting of broadcast commercials. Again, the most commonly used will be discussed here.

Day-after recall tests   As noted earlier in this chapter, the most popular method of posttesting employed in the broadcast industry is that of the **Burke Test** (Exhibit 20–17). While the Burke Test actually refers to a specific test provided by SAMI-Burke, Inc.—the *day-after recall (DAR)* test (Burke also offers a "selector" test, which adds additional measures to DAR)—the name *Burke Test* has almost become generic for all recall tests. It is important to recognize, however, that the methodology employed is the recall test and that firms such as Gallup & Robinson and ASI Market Research, Inc., provide the same services. In addition, variations and extensions on the basic DAR test are available.

While different organizations offer their own methodologies, the effectiveness measure is still the number of persons able to *recall* the ad. For example, in comparing the Burke and Gallup & Robinson tests, differences in the markets used, the number of respondents, and the selection of respondents (Burke calls the day after the ad until 200 persons are found who have seen a program, whereas Gallup & Robinson prerecruits viewers) are evident. At the same time, both tests provide scores reporting two basic factors:

1. **Unaided recall**   No aids are provided to the respondent. Rather, they are asked a simple question such as, "While watching [program] last night, did you see a commercial for [product category]?" Thus, the unaided recall score would reflect the percentage of respondents who recalled a particular commercial—a strong measure of memory.
2. **Aided recall**   In the aided test, "aids" are given, such as, "While watching [program] last night, did you see a commercial for [brand name]?" The percentage of respondents who can then recall the commercial is then reported as an "aided" score.

Because of advertisers' strong reliance on the measure, the Burke score may make or break an ad—sometimes erroneously.

➤ *Exhibit 20–17*
Burke DAR Test

Objective:	To determine the ability of the commercial to gain viewer attention, communicate an intended message, associate the brand name with the message, and affect purchase behavior.
Method:	Interviews take place the day after the commercial airs in numerous cities throughout the United States. A sample of 200 persons who confirmed that they watched the program in which the ad was placed are used. All individuals are asked if they remember a commercial, then all that they can remember about it.
Output:	Scores reflecting unaided and aided recall, indicating they remember the commercial and whether they can relate details about it.

As with the other methodologies discussed, recall tests are not without their critics. In addition to those problems cited earlier, the following disadvantages have been suggested:

1. DAR tests may favor *nonemotional* appeals. Because the respondent is asked to verbalize the message, thinking messages may be easier to recall than are emotional communications. Thus, the recall scores for emotional ads may be lower.[16]

2. Program content may influence recall. The surrounding program content in which the ad appears may lead to different recall scores for the same brand. The net result is a potential inaccuracy in the recall score and in the norms used to establish comparisons.[17]

3. The use of a prerecruited sample (Gallup & Robinson) may increase attention to the program and the ads contained therein because the respondents know they will be "tested" the next day. This effect would lead to a *higher* level of recall than really exists.

The major advantage of the day-after recall tests is that they are field tests. Thus, the natural setting is supposed to provide a more realistic response profile. A major reason for the high use of these tests is that norms are provided that give the advertisers a standard for comparison for how well their ads are performing.

Test marketing of broadcast ads   Many companies conduct tests designed to measure their advertising effects in specific test markets before releasing them nationally. In test marketing, the markets are chosen on the basis of their representativeness of the target market. For example, a company may test its ads in Portland, Oregon; San Antonio, Texas; or Buffalo, New York; if the demographic and socioeconomic profiles of these cities match the product's market. A variety of factors might be tested, including reactions to the ads (for example, alternative copy points), the effects of various budget sizes, or special offers. The ads are in finished form and are placed in the media in which they might normally appear, with measures of effectiveness taken after the ads have been run.

The advantage of test marketing of ads is the realism provided. Regular viewing environments are used and the testing effects are minimized. In addition, it has also been shown that a high degree of control can be attained if the test is designed successfully. For example, an extensive test market study was designed and conducted by Seagram and Time, Inc., over three years to measure the effects of advertising frequency on consumers' buying habits. This study demonstrated just how much could be learned from research conducted in a field setting but with some experimental controls. It also demonstrates quite effectively that with proper research, it may be possible to gain strong insights into the impact of advertising campaigns. (Many advertising researchers consider this study to be one of the most conclusive studies ever conducted in the attempt to demonstrate the effects of advertising on sales.)

The Seagram's study also reveals some of the disadvantages associated with test market measures—not the least of which are the cost and time factors. Few firms have the luxury to spend three years and hundreds of thousands of dollars to conduct

➢ *Exhibit 20–18*
Single-source ad tracking systems

BehaviorScan
1. 10 geographically dispersed test communities. Four examples: Pittsfield, MA; Rome, GA; Eau Claire, WI; and Visalia, CA
2. About 30,000 panel households
3. Requires cable television system

AdTel
1. Five geographically dispersed test communities. Three examples: Portland, ME; the Quad Cities (Davenport, IA; Moline, IL; etc.); and Boise, ID
2. About 12,000 panel households
3. Requires cable television system

ERIM
1. Two test communities: Sioux Falls, SD; and Springfield, MO
2. About 6,000 panel households
3. No requirement for cable television

Roper CollegeTrack
1. College students' product usage, purchases, and media habits
2. Combines Roper and CollegeTrack surveys on national samples

MarketSource
1. College and high school campuses
2. 1,600 locations throughout 500 college campuses
3. 500 high schools

such a test. In addition, as noted earlier, there is always the fear that competitors may discover and intervene in the research process.

Given both the advantages and disadvantages of test marketing, however, this testing methodology offers the possibility to provide substantial insight into the effectiveness of advertising. If care is taken to minimize the negative aspects of such tests, the results can be quite useful.

Single-source tracking studies **Single-source methods** track the behaviors of consumers from the television set to the supermarket checkout counter. Participants with cable TV in a designated area who agree to participate in the studies are provided with a card (similar to a credit card) that identifies their household and provides the research company with their demographics. The households are split into matched groups, with one group receiving an ad, whereas the other does not, and/or alternate ads are sent to each. Their purchases are then recorded from the bar codes of the products bought. Commercial exposures are then correlated with purchase behaviors.

Earlier in this chapter, we briefly mentioned the use of single-source ad research in pretesting broadcast commercials. A recent study demonstrates that the single-source methodology can also be used effectively to posttest ads, allowing for a variety of dependent measures and tracking the effects of increased ad budgets, alternative versions of ad copy, and even ad effects on *sales*.[18]

A 10-year study conducted by Information Resources, Inc.'s BehaviorScan service demonstrated long-term effects of advertising on sales. The study examined copy, media schedules, ad budgets, and the impact of trade promotions on sales in 10 markets throughout the United States, concluding that advertising can produce sales growth as long as two years after a campaign ends.[19]

(The study also concluded that results of copy recall and persuasion tests were unlikely to reliably predict sales.) As shown in Exhibit 20–18, a number of single-source methods have been used for this purpose—BehaviorScan (Information Resources, Inc.), AdTel (SAMI-Burke), and ERIM (A. C. Nielsen) among others.

Many advertisers believe these single-source measures will change the way research is conducted, as the advantages of control and the ability to measure the effects of the ads on sales directly are possible. A number of major corporations and

➤ *Exhibit 20–19*
Factors making or breaking tracking studies

1. Properly defined objectives
2. Alignment with sales objectives
3. Properly designed measures (e.g., adequate sample size, maximum control over interviewing process, adequate time between tracking periods)
4. Consistency through replication of the sampling plan
5. Random samples
6. Continuous interviewing (that is, not seasonal)
7. Evaluative measures must be related to behavior (attitudes have met this criterion; recall of ads does not)
8. Asking critical evaluative questions early to eliminate bias
9. Measure competitors' performance
10. Questions that ask where the advertising was seen or heard often provide misleading results (television always wins)
11. Building news value into the study
12. Using "moving averages" to spot long-term trends and avoid seasonality
13. Reporting data in terms of relationships rather than as isolated facts
14. Integrating key marketplace events with tracking results (for example, advertising expenditures of self and competitors, promotional activities associated with price changes in ad campaigns, introductions of new brands, government announcements, changes in economic conditions)

advertising agencies are now employing this method, including Campbell Soup Co., Colgate-Palmolive Co., Nestlé Foods Corp., General Foods, P&G, Pepsi-Cola Co.; Leo Burnett Advertising, USA, and J. Walter Thompson.

While single-source testing is a valuable tool, it still has some problems. As one researcher working with these data notes, "Scanner data focuses on short-term sales effects, and as a result captures only 10–30% of what advertising does."[20] Others have complained that the data are too complicated to deal with, as an overabundance of information is available. Still another disadvantage is the high cost of collecting single-source data.

Tracking print/broadcast ads   One of the more useful and adaptable forms of posttesting involves tracking the effects of the advertising campaign by taking measurements at regular intervals. **Tracking studies** have been used to measure the effects of advertising on awareness, recall, interest, and attitudes toward the ad and/or brand as well as purchase intentions. (Ad tracking may be applied to both print and broadcast ads but is much more commonly employed with the latter.) Personal interviews, telephone surveys, mall intercepts, and even mail surveys have been used. Sample sizes typically range from 250 to 500 cases per period, with quarterly or semiannual surveys being most common. The results of tracking studies yield perhaps the most valuable information available to the marketing manager for assessment of the current programs and planning for the future.

The major advantage of tracking studies is that the study can be tailored to each specific campaign and/or situation. By maintaining a standard set of questions, effects of the campaign can be tracked over time. In addition, the effects of various media can also be determined—although with a much lesser degree of effectiveness. Tracking studies have also been used to measure the differential impact of alternative budget sizes, the effects of flighting, brand or corporate image, and recall of specific copy points. Finally, when designed properly, as shown in Exhibit 20–19, tracking studies also offer the advantages of a high degree of reliability and validity.[21]

Some of the problems cited with the recall and recognition measures are inherent with tracking studies, as many other factors may be affecting both brand and advertising recall. Despite these limitations, however, tracking studies have been shown to be a very effective method for assessing the effects of advertising campaigns.

In summary, you can see that each of the testing methods considered in this chapter has its strengths and its limitations. The questions that may come to mind then are: Can we actually conduct testing of advertising effectiveness? or What can

Promotional Perspective 20–3

How AT&T Tested the "Slice of Death" Ads

When AT&T startled the advertising community with its "slice of death" ads (which were discussed in Chapter 11), it was not just the result of good luck or an effective creative director. The ads—which portray angry, frightened businesspeople coping with major telephone and computer problems—were developed using strong research methods.

From the start, research played a critical role. Participation in focus groups with small-businesspersons played a key role in establishing the original concept, as AT&T managers and ad agency personnel generated ideas from listening to years of problems being expressed. The promise that AT&T would offer these businesses would be "peace of mind."

To determine how to deliver the message, three alternative approaches were created in animatic form. Each was shown to a new set of focus groups, primarily to gain additional insights. Based on these results, the most serious "deadly confessions" version was selected.

Once the creative direction was established, the company used its in-house test/control persuasion and recall methodology to test it further. This test consisted of three components—a measure of day-after recall, attitude change, and extensive diagnostics. Target audience executives were chosen as respondents. The results of this testing indicated above-average levels of persuadability, criticism, and annoyance.

Focus groups were used in the next phase, primarily to determine if the quantitative results could be supported. They were. The company had to weigh the trade-offs between the criticisms and annoyances against the high attention-getting and persuadability factors. They decided to go with the campaign.

When the campaign broke nationally in March 1987, tracking results demonstrated that consumers responded almost immediately—and in a generally positive manner. Criteria such as "leadership in telephone systems" and "the company to call for telephone systems" and "dependable products" were the common evaluations.

But AT&T was not done yet. In an unusual move for advertisers, the company conducted research among its salespeople, asking them to provide their impressions of how the campaign affected them and their customers. Again, an enthusiastic "thumbs up" evaluation was shown.

The rest is history. The award-winning campaign was continued and even expanded. Three agencies were used to develop a cooperative effort that looked like only one shop was used. The results were—and continue to be—impressive.

Source: Adapted from Thornton C. Lockwood, "Behind the Emotion in 'Slice of Death' Advertising," *Business Marketing*, September 1988, pp. 87–93.

---

be done to ensure that we have a valid and reliable test? Promotional Perspective 20–3 provides an affirmative answer to the first of these questions, whereas the next section of this chapter suggests some answers to the latter.

Establishing a Program for Measuring Advertising Effects

There is no sure-fire method of testing advertising effectiveness. However, pressures to determine the contribution these ads are making to the overall marketing effort are increasing. While there is no simple solution to this problem, certain things can be done to help improve this measurement task. Let us first begin by reviewing the major problems with some existing methods and then examine some possible improvements.

Problems with Current Research Methods

In evaluating current testing methods against the criteria established by PACT (refer to Exhibit 20–4), it becomes obvious that some of the principles important to good copy testing can be accomplished rather readily, whereas others will require substantially more effort. For example, principle 6—providing equivalent test ads—should require a minimum of effort. The researcher can easily control the state of completion of the test communications. Also of relative ease are principles 1 and 2—providing measurements relative to the objectives sought and determining a priori how the results will be used.

We have seen throughout this text that each promotional medium, the message, and the formulation of the budget are all established with consideration of the marketing and communications objectives sought. By following the integrated marketing communications planning model, the roles of each of these elements will have been established. Thus, by the time one gets to the measurement phase, the criteria by which these programs will be evaluated should simply fall into place.

Of slightly more difficulty are principles 3, 5, and 8, although, once again, these factors are largely in the control of the researcher. For example, providing multiple measurements (principle 3) may require little more than budgeting accordingly to ensure that more than one test is conducted. At the most, it may require considering two alternative, but similar, measures to ensure reliability. Likewise, principle 5—exposing the test ad more than once—can be accomplished with a proper research design. Finally, sample definition (principle 8) requires little more than sound research methodology, as any test should use those consumers in the market targeted to assess its effectiveness. You would not use a sample of nondrinkers to evaluate potential new liquor commercials!

The more difficult factors to control—and the principles that perhaps may best differentiate between good and bad testing procedures—are those contained in the PACT requirements 4, 7, and 9. Fortunately, however, addressing each of these contributes to the attainment of the others.

The best starting point is principle 4, which states the research should be guided by and based on a model of human response to communications and this model must consider a number of responses including reception, comprehension, and behavioral response. The reason it is the best, in our opinion, is that it is the one least addressed by practicing researchers. If you recall, the material covered in Chapter 6 proposed a number of such models that might be used for fulfilling this principle's requirements. Yet even though these models have existed for quite some time, very few—if any—of the research methods commonly employed attempt to integrate this information into their methodologies. Most of these methods discussed here do little more than provide recall scores—despite the fact many researchers have shown that recall is a poor measure of effectiveness. Those that do claim to measure such factors as attitude change or brand preference change are often fraught with problems that severely limit their reliability. To have an effective measure, some relationship to the communications process must be included.

It might seem at first glance that principle 7—provide a nonbiasing exposure—might fall into one of the categories of being easier to accomplish. A review of both lab and field measures would indicate this is not that easy to do. Lab measures, while offering control, are artificial and lend themselves to testing effects. Field measures, while more realistic, often lose control. The Seagram and Time, Inc. study—while perhaps having the best of both worlds—is perhaps too large a task for most firms to undertake. While not perfect, some of the improvements associated with the single-source systems help to solve this problem. In addition, properly designed ad tracking studies provide truer measures of the impact of the communication. As technology develops, and more attention is paid to this principle, we should expect to see improvements in methodologies in the near future.

Last, but in no way least, is principle 9, the concern for reliability and validity. Most of those measures discussed have been shown to be lacking in one of these criteria, if not both, yet these are two of the most critical factors discriminating between good and bad research. The most basic of research classes always insists that research designs provide evidence of reliability and validity. If the study is properly designed, and by that we mean it addresses principles 1 through 8, it should meet these requirements.

Essentials of Effective Testing

Most simply put, good tests of advertising effectiveness must address the nine principles established by PACT. One of the easiest ways to accomplish this is by following the decision sequence model in formulating promotional plans. For example:

- **Establish communications objectives**   We have stated that except for a few instances—most specifically, direct-response advertising—it is extremely difficult if not impossible to show the direct impact of advertising on sales. Given this fact, the marketing objectives established for the promotional program do not typically serve as good measures of communication effectiveness. For example, it is very difficult (or too expensive) to demonstrate the effect of an ad on brand share or on sales. On the other hand, attaining communications objectives helps lead to the accomplishment of these marketing objectives and can be measured. As such they serve as viable dependent measures.

- **Employ a consumer response model** Early in this text we reviewed hierarchy of effects models and cognitive response models. Either or both of these lend themselves to providing an understanding of the effects of communications and as such lend themselves to serving as the communications goals we said are required.

- **Employ both pretests and posttests** From a cost standpoint—both actual cost outlays and opportunity costs—pretesting makes sense. As seen throughout this chapter, it may mean the difference between success and/or failure of the campaign or the product. At the same time, the use of posttesting drops off dramatically. Given some of the limitations of pretests, the much larger samples, and more natural setting of posttesting, this information may be required to determine the true effectiveness of the ad or campaign.

- **Understand and implement proper research** It is critical to understand research methodology. What constitutes a good design? Does it have validity and reliability? Does it measure what we want it to and what we need it to? There is no shortcut to this criterion, and there is no way to avoid it if you truly want to measure the effects of advertising.

A major study sponsored by the Advertising Research Foundation (ARF), involving interviews with between 12,000 and 15,000 people, addressed some of these issues.[22] While we do not have the space to go into depth regarding this study here, it should be noted that the research was designed to evaluate measures of copy tests, compare copy testing procedures, and examine some of the principles set forth by PACT. Information on this study has been published in a number of academic and trade journals and by the ARF.

Measuring the Effectiveness of Other Program Elements

Throughout this text, we have discussed promotional program elements in respect to how and when they should be used, the advantages and disadvantages of each, and so on. In some instances, we have discussed measures of effectiveness used to evaluate these programs. In this final section, we add a few additional measures that may not have been discussed earlier in an attempt to provide insights into how these program elements might be evaluated.

Evaluating the Effectiveness of Sales Promotions

Sales promotions are not limited to retailers and resellers of products. Sports marketers have found this tool to be a very effective means of attracting crowds and have been able to measure their relative effectiveness by the number of fans attending games. In such cases, a direct measure of effectiveness is possible.

Other measures of sales promotions are also available. Advertisers have used awareness tracking studies and have counted the number of inquiries, coupon redemptions, and sweepstakes entries as measures of the effectiveness of the promotion. They have also tracked sales during promotional and nonpromotional periods, while holding other factors constant.

One of the more recent and interesting technological developments designed to track the effectiveness of sales promotions at the point of sales is offered by Datatec Industries. This automated system, called Shopper Trak, places sensors in the store that track whether a person is coming or going, calculate the shopper's height (to differentiate between adults and children), and gauge traffic patterns. The system is designed to help retailers evaluate the effectiveness of various promotions or displays located throughout the store.[23]

Measuring the Effectiveness of Nontraditional Media

In Chapter 15, we noted that one of the disadvantages of employing nontraditional media is that they usually do not offer the capabilities to measure the effectiveness of the programs. While this is still true, some progress has been made. Consider these examples:

- **Measuring the effects of shopping cart signage**   Earlier we discussed some of the sales increases that have been shown when shopping cart signage was used. We have also noted throughout this chapter that while sales is a critical goal, many other factors may also contribute to, or detract from, this measure. (It should also be noted that these results have been provided by the companies offering these promotional media.) At least one study has examined the effectiveness of shopping cart signage on other than sales data.[24] This study used a personal interview technique in grocery stores to measure awareness of, attention to, and influence of this medium. Interestingly, the results of this study indicate a much lower level of effectiveness of this medium.

- **Effectiveness of ski-resort based media**   In Chapter 15, we discussed how some advertisers have used advertising on ski chair lifts and in other areas to attempt to reach selective demographic groups. Now the Traffic Audit Bureau (TAB) is tracking the effectiveness of this form of advertising in an attempt to provide advertisers with more reliable criteria on which to make a decision. The TAB data verify ad placements, while the media vendors have employed Simmons Market Research Bureau and Nielsen Media Research to collect ad impressions and advertising recall information.[25] These measures have been combined with sales tracking data to provide an indication of the medium's effectiveness.

Measuring the Effectiveness of Sponsorships

One of the more difficult promotional tools to evaluate is that of sponsorships. But as pressure continues to increase for the accountability of promotional expenditures, the billions of dollars spent annually to sponsor events will receive attention.

At least two companies have begun to offer services designed to measure the effectiveness of sports sponsorships. Events Marketing Research of New York specializes in custom research projects that perform sales audits in event areas, participant exit surveys, and economic impact studies. Joyce Julius & Associates of Ann Arbor, Michigan, provides sponsors with a measure that assigns a monetary value to the amount of exposure the sponsor receives during the event. The company reviews broadcasts and adds up the number of seconds a sponsor's product name or logo can be clearly seen (for example on signs or shirts). Thirty seconds of time is considered the equivalent of a 30-second commercial.[26] (Such a measure is of questionable validity.)

While the above measures, like the advertising effectiveness measures discussed earlier, have their inherent strengths and weaknesses, they offer the advertiser some information that may be useful in evaluating the effectiveness of promotional efforts. While not all promotional efforts can be effectively evaluated at this time, at least the first step has been taken in this regard.

SUMMARY

This chapter introduced you to issues involved in measuring the effects of advertising and promotions. These issues included reasons for testing, reasons companies do not test, and the review and evaluation of various research methodologies. Having done this, we arrived at a number of conclusions including: (1) advertising research to measure effectiveness is important to the promotional program, (2) not enough companies test their ads, and (3) problems exist with current research methodologies. In addition, we reviewed the criteria for sound research and suggested some things to do to accomplish effective studies.

All marketing managers want to know how well their promotional programs are working. This information is critical to planning for the next period, as program adjustments and/or maintenance are based on the results of the evaluation of the existing strategies. Problems often result when the measures taken to determine such effects are either inaccurate or improperly used.

This chapter demonstrated that testing must meet a number of criteria to be successful—as defined by PACT. In addition, these evaluations should occur both before and after the campaigns have been implemented.

A variety of research methods were discussed, many of which are provided by syndicated research firms such as SAMI-Burke, Arbitron, and A.C. Nielsen. In addition, companies have also developed their own testing systems.

Single-source research data such as BehaviorScan, ERIM, and AdTel were discussed and noted as a source of data for measuring the effects of advertising. These single-source systems offer strong potential for improving the effectiveness of ad measures in the future, as commercial exposures and reactions may be correlated to actual purchase behaviors.

KEY TERMS

vehicle option source effect
pretests
posttests
laboratory tests
testing bias
field tests
PACT (Positioning Advertising Copy Testing)
concept testing
tests of comprehension and reaction

consumer juries
halo effect
Burke's Reflections test
portfolio tests
Flesch formula
theater testing
on-air test
day-after recall scores
pupillometrics
electrodermal response
eye tracking
electroencephalographic (EEG) measures

hemispheric lateralization
alpha activity
inquiry tests
split-run tests
recognition method
recall tests
Burke Test
single-source tracking methods
tracking studies

DISCUSSION QUESTIONS

1. Discuss some of the reasons agencies and firms do not measure advertising effectiveness and why they should do so.
2. Discuss some of the components of the promotional plan that should be evaluated. Give examples.
3. The "bottom line" for advertisers is to evoke some behavior—for example, sales. However, sales may not be a true measure of advertising effects. Explain why it may be difficult to use sales as a measure of advertising effectiveness.
4. Describe some of the physiological measures of advertising that are used. Give examples of ads that might benefit from the use of these measures.
5. Describe some of the methods used to test other elements of the promotional mix.
6. What is a Burke score? How can it make or break an ad?
7. Discuss how tracking studies might be tied into the hierarchy of effects models.
8. Discuss the elements necessary to conduct good advertising testing research.
9. What is a Starch Test? What scores does this test provide?
10. Discuss the concept of single-source research. What advantages does it offer the marketer?

part VII

Special Topics and Perspectives

chapter 21

Business-to-Business Communications

chapter objectives

➢ To understand the differences between business-to-business and consumer product advertising and promotions.

➢ To understand the objectives of business-to-business communications.

➢ To recognize the role that various program elements play in the business-to-business promotional program.

➢ To examine the methods for evaluating promotional program effectiveness in business-to-business communications.

Business-to-Business Marketers Explore New Options

To many, marketing in the business-to-business market means personal selling and maybe an occasional ad in a trade magazine. They believe personal selling is the most important element of the promotional mix and is the lifeblood of the marketing program.

Others disagree. While they do not downplay the importance of personal selling, they do not rely exclusively, or in some cases, even extensively, on this promotional tool. Rather, they have adopted a variety of media that allow them to develop a truly integrated communications program. Consider these examples:

- Dell Computers and Polaroid Corporation use data bases containing segmentation information on existing and prospective customers. Dell keeps tabs on such factors as how recently customers bought, what they spent, how frequently they purchase Dell products, and what payment methods they used. Polaroid has established its data base over 10 years primarily through lead-generating direct-marketing campaigns. The company has increased its direct-marketing efforts to film and hardware products users in eight business-to-business segments.

- Minolta has developed a fax-on-demand (FOD) program, in which well-trained employees staff 800 and 900 call-in centers to answer customer and prospective customer inquiries. The employees answer the questions when they can and then immediately fax information to the caller. The customer has 24-hour access to the fax system and gets a response when needed, greatly increasing customer satisfaction and loyalty. Minolta, IBM, Canon, Xerox, and Du Pont have also developed FOD programs.

- Massachusetts Mutual Life Insurance Co. stoked the fires of its 100 general agents and 4,300 field associates with a baseball-oriented sales promotion program. A series of four-color illustrations was mailed to the company's agents during the spring "Get Your Hits" sales drive. Included with the illustrations was a wall-sized scorecard that agents used to tally their new accounts and a "rule book" that spelled out the contest rules.

- Intel employed a dazzling commercial for the Intel486 chip that took viewers on a magical mystery tour of the insides of a personal computer. The special effects were reminiscent of the 1982 film *Tron* in which a computer whiz was sucked into a computer and had to fight for his life in a giant video game competition.

- Other companies have also employed a variety of techniques, including DEC and Apple (electronic catalogs), Tyson Foods (audiotex promotions and sweepstakes), and Lotus (computer disks and local area network tie-ins).

713

(continued)

All of these companies have expressed pleasure and success with these new media. They indicate the new programs allow them to increase sales, improve customer satisfaction, and market much more efficiently, while saving money.

Their customers seem to like the ideas as well. Customer complaints are down, sales are up, and, in general, the customers are no longer bored by "stale" marketing techniques. To many, business-to-business marketing no longer is synonymous with personal selling.

Source: "New Options in Business: A User's Guide," Business Marketing, *May 1992.*

Often when we think of advertising and promotions, it is in regard to consumer products or resellers of these products. But about $100 billion a year is spent advertising products used in business and industrial markets.[1] The objectives sought in these communications and the strategies designed to achieve them are often different from those we have discussed in earlier chapters.

The lead-in to this chapter reflects the new thinking of the business-to-business marketer. While business-to-business marketers may have been considered unidimensional, plain, or even boring in the past, this certainly is no longer the case. Business-to-business advertising is becoming more creative, more innovative, more emotional, and more interesting. The "slice of death" ads discussed earlier are but one example of how communications to this industry are changing, and as you will see as this chapter progresses, business-to-business advertising is becoming more sophisticated and, in many ways, more similar to the consumer market.

Business-to-Business Communications

Before we discuss how business-to-business communications are used, it is important to establish an understanding of exactly what it is we are referring to when we use this term. Had you opened an advertising and/or promotions text just a few years ago, you probably would not have found a chapter titled "Business-to-Business Advertising." Rather, you would have noted titles such as "Industrial Marketing" or "Industrial Advertising." Much of the material would have dealt with topics such as advertising in the industrial sector and advertising to manufacturers.

As the United States has moved from an industrial to a service economy (approximately two thirds of the national economy is now accounted for by the latter), a new and different target market has evolved. This market still includes those involved in the industrial sector but has been broadened to include a "nation of office workers."

➤ *Exhibit 21–1*
Participants in a buying center

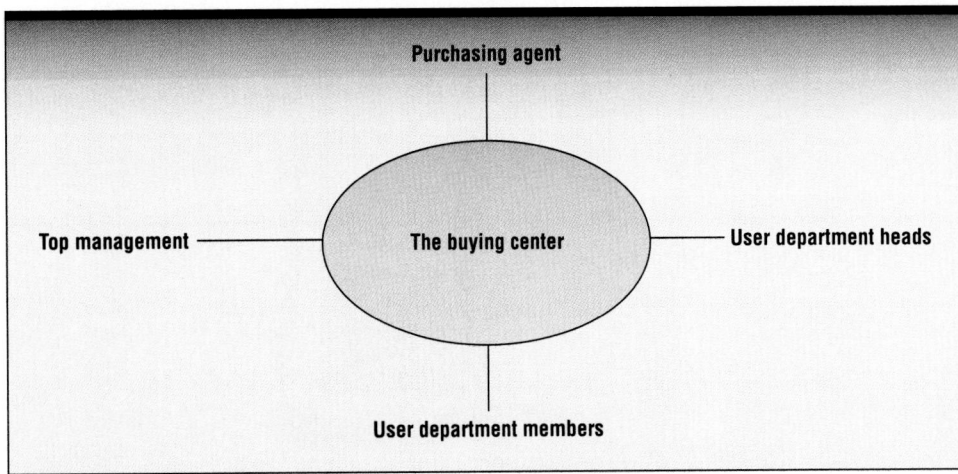

Along with this new market came the need to broaden the title given to advertising and promotions used to communicate with this new segment. Many of those involved in business communications thought the title of *industrial advertising* was somewhat misleading, it did not represent the true nature of the industry, and it was not current with the profession. A few years ago, the industry began to refer to itself as *business-to-business*. For this text, we use the term **business-to-business advertising**, although we want you to recognize that this term still includes communications targeted to the industrial sector. (When it is important to distinguish between industrial and service sectors, we will specifically cite the market we are referring to.)

Differences between Business-to-Business and Consumer Communications

The primary difference between business-to-business and consumer-oriented communications is that the latter is generally targeted at those consumers who will *actually use* the product or service in its final form, whereas business-to-business communications are directed to companies involved in the production of goods or services designed to facilitate the operation of the enterprise. These products are typically thought of as having a **derived demand**—that is, their demand is generated or driven by the need for other goods or services.

To understand the role of business-to-business communications, consider what is involved in the manufacturing of an automobile. While the auto is the final consumer product, the materials that are used to manufacture the car—steel, rubber, leather, plastic, and so on—must be purchased, as do the building, equipment, and the products used to market it. There is competition among suppliers to attempt to gain the auto manufacturer's business. Goodyear and Firestone may compete for the tire business, USX and Wheeling-Pittsburgh may want to sell the steel, and so on. All the elements of the promotional mix are employed in an attempt to sell these products.

While there are a number of differences between business-to-business and consumer communications, perhaps nine key characteristics best differentiate the areas.[2]

1. The decision maker While in consumer markets the consumer and decision maker may be the same person—or persons in those products/services characterized by joint decision making—this may not be the case in the business-to-business setting. In the latter market, one person may perform both roles, but more typically, the buying decision is made by a **buying center** or committee. The buying center is often formalized and includes individuals from throughout the organization, as shown in Exhibit 21–1.

In this case, all those involved must be reached and influenced, with different message and media strategies possibly required for each. Sometimes the decision maker is not readily apparent to the marketer.

2. Communications Communications are designed to support the sales effort. As elements of the promotional mix, advertising and promotions may take on a

➤ *Exhibit 21–2*
Brock Control Systems ads show consequences of the wrong decision

major role or a supportive one. In business-to-business marketing, the latter of these roles is typically assumed by advertising. Thus, communications tend to be much more information based, rational, and designed to generate leads or inquiries in support of the sales staff. As noted by one business-to-business agency:

> Each ad should make it desirable for the potential customer to contact the manufacturer, all inquiries should be responded to in the same day, and all information should help the customer sell the product or service to their management.[3]

3. Purchase decisions Whereas purchase decisions may be very quick in the consumer market, the more common case in the business-to-business setting is a *long-range* perspective. Immediate sales are rare, as committee decisions, budgetary considerations, and buying formulas may need to be addressed before the actual purchase is made. In some industrial situations, it is not uncommon to be operating on three- to five-year purchase cycles. Since many of the products have long life cycles, decisions are much less frequent and much more involved.

4. Buyer involvement The buyer generally is involved in the decision to purchase a consumer product. In business-to-business settings, this involvement may take on a different dimension. If a consumer product does not live up to expectations, the buyer is unhappy and suffers the consequences. If a poor decision is made in an industrial setting, the entire organization may suffer—and more than the

➤ *Exhibit 21–3*
The performance ratings top business-to-business marketers give advertising agencies

Planning			
Creative			
Account service			
Complete service			
Cost control			
Flexibility			
Client/agency size match			
Poor	**Fair**	**Good**	**Excellent**

Average ratings

➤ *Exhibit 21−4*
Top business marketers' most common complaints about agencies

Complaint	Percent Responding
Lack of industry experience	20%
High costs/lack of structure	15%
Inability to listen	8%
Tendency to overact	6%
Slow response	4%
Unqualified employees	2%
Undefined objectives	1%

buyer's personal satisfaction is at stake. The buyer may lose his or her job or the firm may experience other consequences, as is demonstrated in the ad for Brock Control Systems shown in Exhibit 21−2.

5. Integration of communications elements While business-to-business marketing efforts are rapidly improving, many marketers have considered this sector to be less sophisticated than those involved in consumer marketing. One of the prime reasons for this opinion is that the advertising and marketing programs had commonly not been integrated in the industrial firms, with each seemingly going its own direction.

In a survey conducted by *Business Marketing* magazine, 40 percent of the top marketers in industrial companies regarded their ad agency's planning expertise to be only fair to poor (see Exhibit 21−3) and complete service even worse. Some of this performance evaluation can be attributed to the lack of industry experience of the agency, whereas high costs and other factors were also cited, as shown in Exhibit 21−4.

Some of the factors cited in that survey are being overcome as business-to-business marketers become more sophisticated and begin to apply many of the same methods employed in the consumer market or, as shown in the chapter introduction, many innovative methods more applicable to the business-to-business sector. One example of this can be seen in the area of market segmentation. Just as the consumer market previously relied mainly on demographic segmentation, so too (until even more recently!) did business-to-business marketers. Now, as demonstrated by Promotional Perspective 21−1, the use of psychographics is becoming more common in segmenting business markets. Behavioral models such as the **Social Style Model**—a model suggesting businesspersons' "social styles" will influence how they react on the job—and the **CUBE Model** (Comprehensive Understanding of Business Environments)—in which values and lifestyles of corporate buying groups are detailed—are being used to assist in the segmentation process.[4]

6. Budget allocations The bulk of marketing monies in business-to-business sectors has traditionally been allocated to support of the sales organization. As a result, advertising and promotions expenditures often receive less of the marketing budget. Likewise, marketing research—used extensively by consumer products firms—receives much less support in the industrial sector (constituting only about 4 percent of the overall advertising budget).[5]

7. Evaluation measures In Chapter 20, we discussed the variety of measures of advertising effectiveness employed by consumer products firms. Later in this chapter, you will see that the industrial sector employs its own measures, some of which are similar to those of consumer products companies but most of which assume their own orientation. Usually, these measures are tied directly to sales rather than communications objectives.

8. Message content The content of the communications message of consumer products advertisers may be designed to create awareness, interest, or other communications objectives and may employ both rational and emotional approaches. While the use of emotional appeals has recently increased, business-to-business communications tend to focus on the use of information presented in a logical and rational format. Humor, sex, and other forms of emotional appeals have been used

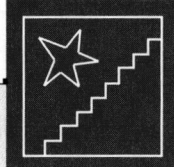

Promotional Perspective 21-1

Segmenting by Corporate Cultures

While consumer products companies have employed psychographics in their market segmentation analyses for years, the same has not been true of business-to-business marketers. Just as consumer companies have considered the effects of cultures on the purchase decision process, so now do business-to-business companies—only the focus is on the culture of the organization, or corporate culture. As noted by Philip Monchar of Total Research Corporation of Princeton, New Jersey, knowing the psychological profile of members of an organization is important because they will have adopted the corporate culture and will know what is and is not acceptable behavior. Monchar's research on corporate executives of 303 large and middle-size firms has led to the identification of three corporate culture segments: the "happy doers," "middle of the roads," and "satisfaction seekers."

Happy doers constitute approximately 36 percent of the sample, according to the study. These persons are more interested in maintaining a smooth operation than they are in their customers' satisfaction. They are least likely to change vendors, they are satisfied with their current suppliers, and purchase decisions are usually made by a single top-level manager relying on little input.

Middle of the road cultures (about 33 percent of the sample) are characterized by a willingness to work with multiple vendors.

However, all vendors must meet the company's model of the "personalized service caterer" that handles specific orders and unusual circumstances. Decisions are made after long studies of the issues, and formal evaluations are conducted frequently.

Satisfaction seekers (30 percent of the sample) are considered by Monchar as the most promising targets. They are the most customer oriented, are frequently dissatisfied with current vendors' prices and performances, and are most likely to conduct formal evaluations. As a result, they are most likely to switch suppliers. At the same time, however, they are the most cautious about making decisions, making them much slower than the other groups and involving more persons.

Advertising strategies can be developed to appeal to each segment, according to Monchar. For example, he notes that to reach "satisfaction seekers," ads should stress a company's ability to provide services quickly and accurately. To reach the "middle of the roaders," suggestions that the provider can offer tailored services in a given time frame are likely to work. He does not say how to reach the "happy doers"!

Source: Adapted from "Segmenting Markets by Corporate Culture," *Business Marketing*, July 1988, pp. 50–51.

in relatively few instances, as most ads tend to be very technical, information laden, and factual. The use of testimonials is also a very common business-to-business approach.

9. Media use   As you should expect, the media used by those involved in business-to-business advertising are often very different from the media employed in the consumer products sector. Since the media employed is the topic of a later section of this chapter, we will not go into this in depth here. The media tend to be more specifically targeted, whereas in the consumer products market, mass media such as television and radio are more commonly used.

In summary, there are obviously many differences between the communications strategies of industrial and consumer products companies. Much of this can be attributed to the nature of the industries, whereas some may be a result of marketing sophistication. Still others can be attributed to the fact that business-to-business marketers may define the objectives of advertising and promotions differently than their consumer market counterparts.

Establishing Business-to-Business Communications Objectives

The objectives that have been established earlier in this text are just as relevant for business-to-business marketers as they are for consumer products firms. Obviously, business-to-business advertisers have marketing objectives they wish to accomplish, and they should establish communications objectives as a means for attaining these goals. Likewise, establishing a *corporate image* is no less important for industrial firms than it is for their consumer counterparts.

However, as we have stated, business-to-business marketers have often concentrated their efforts directly on attaining sales. To this end, the emphasis in advertising

> *Exhibit 21–5*   **Business-to-business ads are becoming more interesting**

and promotions has been to support sales efforts, and sales have been used as the measure of their success. In this text, we take the position that communications and sales objectives need not be independent. That is, in business-to-business markets there is a need to achieve the same objectives as those sought in consumer markets to reach sales goals. These objectives include creating awareness; establishing a favorable image or position in the marketplace; and generating consumer interest, knowledge, and trial of the product, among others.

Developing and Implementing the Business-to-Business Program

Developing Business-to-Business Promotional Strategies

Just as the objectives of business-to-business programs have been different from those of consumer markets, so too have the strategies employed to achieve these objectives. These differences are becoming less distinct, however.

In the past, personal selling has been the primary promotional tool used by business-to-business marketers. As a result, much less emphasis has been focused on the development of advertising and promotional programs. Advertising was used almost exclusively to create awareness of products, and the messages were typically very rational, information laden, and somewhat unexciting. Recently, the role of advertising in the business-to-business promotional program has changed. For example, the use of color, illustrations, models, and emotional appeals has become more common, as the role ascribed to this promotional element has expanded. As demonstrated in the ad shown in Exhibit 21–5, attractive and interesting ads are no longer only the domain of consumer products marketers.

At the same time, this change in advertising strategy does not reflect a reduced emphasis on providing information and knowledge. Rather, it stems from the realization that to be seen and read, the advertisement must gain the attention of the receiver. These ads must be designed to cut through the clutter of other competing ads and to assist in the attainment of communications objectives such as knowledge, evaluation, and attitude formation. Thus, more attractive and creative advertising is designed to accomplish these objectives.

Likewise, advertising strategies designed to achieve trial have increased. As you can see in the Nomadic Display, Inc., ad shown in Exhibit 21–6, the ad goes beyond just providing product information and actually attempts to move the reader to action—in this case, asking for more information or a trial demonstration.

In addition to advertising and promotions programs, business-to-business marketers have realized the importance of other promotional program elements. While personal selling continues to play a significant role in the promotional mix, public relations and direct-marketing efforts have also increased. The use of direct mail and telemarketing have helped reduce selling costs by screening prospects, determining interest levels and qualifications, and serving as a more cost-effective means of disseminating information to prospective customers. Public relations programs designed to achieve better customer relations and the use and management of publicity have also increased. As noted earlier, a variety of support media have also been employed.

Sales promotions, like advertising, have become more creative and, along with the other promotional elements, have taken on a support role. An excellent example of

➤ *Exhibit 21–6*
This business-to-business ad is designed to stimulate trial

this is provided in the materials shown in Exhibit 21–7. In addition to the ad, a direct-mail brochure, a leave-behind promotional piece, and a demo disk are all used to promote the product. (These promotional materials generated the best response the Tektronix Division has had in years!)

Given the high costs of personal sales calls, support provided by advertising and promotional efforts is a direct benefit to be realized by industrial firms. Studies conducted by the American Business Press (ABP) and the Forsyth Group estimate that business publication advertising enhances personal selling efforts at only 31 cents per contact—far less than the $292 cost per sales call.[6] In addition, sales inquiries occurring through these activities may result in the generation of leads from sources the sales force previously had no knowledge of or time to explore on their own, increasing market coverage.

Implementing the Business-to-Business Program

As was noted earlier, an estimated $100 billion was spent by the largest business-to-business marketers in the advertising and promotion of their products, services, and corporate image in 1991. Exhibit 21–8 yields some interesting insights into the allocation of the business-to-business promotional budget. Those program elements that lead to the closest contact with the buyer and are most directly related to selling (for example, trade shows, catalogs, and direct mail) are most frequently used. The largest percentage of the budget is typically allocated to advertising in specialized business publications. Let us examine these allocations in more detail.

Advertising

Because of the broad reach of advertising, many of the media used to reach the consumer market receive less of the budget in the business-to-business sector.

➤ *Exhibit 21–7*
Tektronix uses a variety of promotional materials

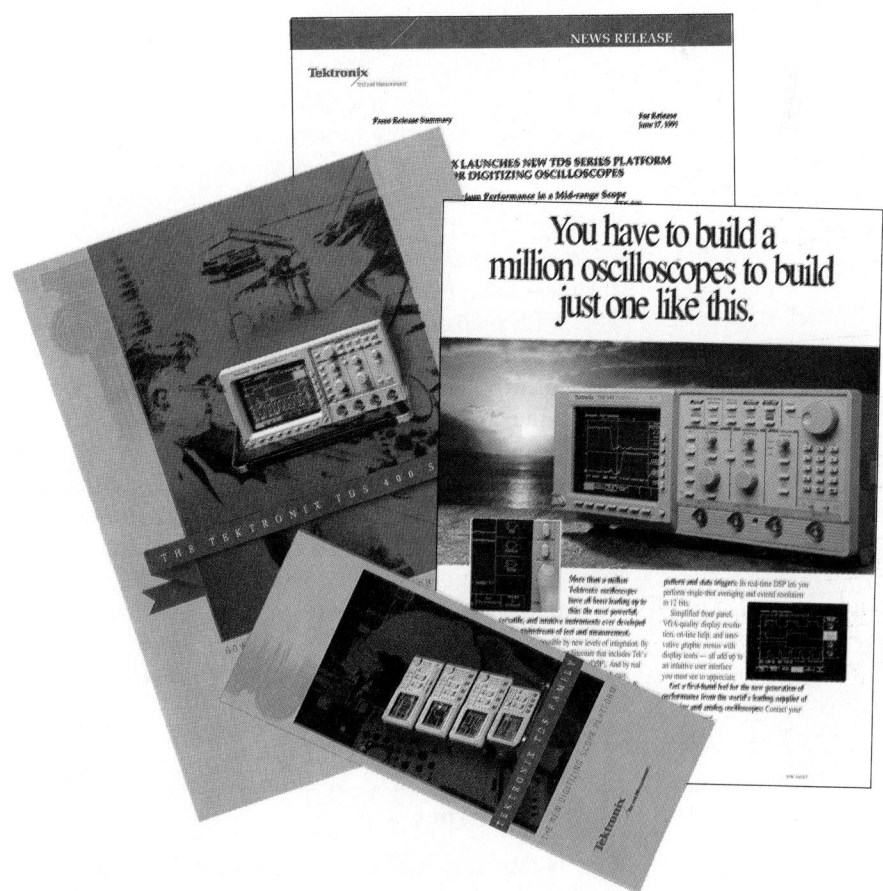

➤ *Exhibit 21–8*
Promotional allocations of business-to-business marketers

Promotional Area	Percent of Firms Using	Average Percent of Budget
Special business publications	80%	24.4%
General business publications	17%	3.5%
Farm publications	3%	.1%
Medical publications	7%	1.2%
Consumer publications	6%	.7%
Newspapers	8%	1.0%
Telemarketing	11%	1.0%
Direct mail	66%	6.8%
Network TV	1%	.1%
Spot TV	4%	.9%
Spot radio	5%	.7%
Directories	29%	1.7%
Company catalogs	61%	15.2%
Trade shows/exhibits	74%	13.2%
Dealer/distributor aids	25%	2.5%
Internal house organs	23%	1.4%
External house organs	23%	2.1%
AV (slide/movie/etc.)	36%	1.9%
Specialty advertising	27%	1.4%
Outdoor transit	3%	.2%
Publicity/PR	60%	4.7%
Research	18%	5%
Video tape	35%	2.3%
Other	22%	3.3%

Advertising tends to be concentrated in business publications that reach specific markets with much less being allocated to general business media. Exhibit 21–9 shows the hundred leading advertisers in specialized business publications. Exhibit 21–8 shows that 80 percent had advertised in one of the many trade publications available, while only 17 percent had used more general business publications. Much less of the advertising dollar is spent on broadcast, outdoor, or other media that do not allow for specific targeting.

While broadcast media have not been used extensively in the past, this trend is changing. As Exhibit 21–10, page 724 demonstrates, when used properly, even the broadest-reaching medium—television—may be used effectively.

In fact, many of the mass media are experiencing an increase in business-to-business advertisements, owing to an increase in the business-to-business mass market. With such a large number of persons employed in the service business, marketers have often found that their advertising may now employ the use of mass media, with significantly less waste coverage than previously expected. This is particularly true given the ability to "narrowcast" through cable television. Programs that reach specific audiences such as Moneyline, the Financial News Network, and so on, have allowed advertisers to reach specific target audiences through broadcast media. (Notice the increasing number of ads for copy machines, computers, or other office equipment now being shown on prime-time television, an example of which is shown in Exhibit 21–11, page 725.)

Radio also has seen an increase in business-to-business ads. Advertisers have found radio to be effective in reaching business audiences during drive time and news segments. In addition, a study conducted by the Radio Advertising Bureau indicated that as much as 53 percent of the work force listens to the radio while at work.[7] Certain radio formats also tend to have a higher business listening audience.

Direct marketing

Just as the consumer market has discovered the advantages of direct marketing, so too has the business-to-business marketer—particularly the benefits associated with

➤ *Exhibit 21-9* **Top 100 specialized business publication advertisers**

Company	Ad Spending	Company	Ad Spending
1. AT&T Co.	$39,946,298	51. AMP Inc.	$5,119,504
2. IBM Corp.	$34,457,114	52. Amoco Corp.	$5,052,446
3. Hewlett-Packard Co.	$30,078,614	53. Ashton-Tate Corp.	$4,991,876
4. Microsoft Corp.	$23,224,142	54. Dow Chemical Co.	$4,972,772
5. Northgate Computer Systems Inc.	$20,858,436	55. Okidata	$4,774,665
6. Digital Equipment Corp.	$19,783,696	56. Sun Microsystems Inc.	$4,677,870
7. NEC Technologies Inc.	$18,698,664	57. Hilton Hotels Corp.	$4,623,810
8. Canon USA Inc.	$17,034,612	58. American Express Co.	$4,605,323
9. Dell Computer Corp.	$15,983,945	59. Xerox Corp.	$4,543,437
10. Compaq Computer Corp.	$15,253,780	60. Adobe Systems Inc.	$4,420,424
11. General Motors Corp.	$14,904,654	61. Andersen Corp.	$4,403,465
12. Eastman Kodak Co.	$14,749,399	62. North American Philips Corp.	$4,383,571
13. Motorola Inc.	$14,603,014	63. Mobil Corp.	$4,366,132
14. Zeos International Ltd.	$13,248,200	64. Wyse Technology Inc.	$4,304,170
15. Texas Instruments Inc.	$13,233,967	65. AST Research Inc.	$4,303,498
16. Time Warner Inc.	$12,686,437	66. Data General Corp.	$4,255,980
17. Sony Corp.	$12,166,123	67. Bell Atlantic Corp.	$4,223,392
18. Toshiba America Inc.	$12,040,651	68. Samsung America Inc.	$4,197,654
19. Panasonic Co.	$11,968,356	69. Caterpillar Inc.	$4,186,545
20. Intel Corp.	$11,891,263	70. Eaton Corp.	$4,151,269
21. E.I. du Pont de Nemours & Co.	$11,386,238	71. Rockwell Intl. Corp.	$4,130,189
22. Oracle Systems Corp.	$11,214,148	72. Honeywell Inc.	$3,975,446
23. PC Connection Inc.	$10,951,520	73. Bull HN Information Systems Inc.	$3,914,849
24. General Electric Co.	$10,525,918	74. MCI Communications Corp.	$3,856,765
25. ITT Corp.	$10,234,589	75. The Hearst Corp.	$3,856,201
26. Apple Computer Inc.	$9,781,617	76. Borland Intl. Inc.	$3,759,207
27. Computer Associates Intl. Inc.	$9,334,536	77. Hoechst Celanese Corp.	$3,686,504
28. NCR Corp.	$9,275,111	78. American Airlines Inc.	$3,658,030
29. 3M Co.	$8,581,555	79. Seagate Technology Inc.	$3,649,264
30. Lotus Development Corp.	$8,376,537	80. Software Publishing Corp.	$3,389,365
31. NYNEX Corp.	$8,303,036	81. WordPerfect Corp.	$3,332,184
32. Siemens Corp.	$7,447,131	82. Georgia-Pacific Corp.	$3,303,417
33. Epson America Inc.	$7,336,313	83. 3 Com Corp.	$3,170,185
34. Ford Motor Co.	$7,005,531	84. The Hertz Corp.	$3,057,384
35. BellSouth Corp.	$6,754,399	85. MagneTek Inc.	$3,012,127
36. CompuAdd Inc.	$6,656,828	86. Tyson Foods Inc.	$2,993,683
37. Philip Morris Companies Inc.	$6,555,938	87. Dow Jones & Co. Inc.	$2,967,067
38. Unisys Corp.	$6,358,951	88. Pfizer Inc.	$2,882,256
39. Northern Telecom Ltd.	$6,219,168	89. National Semiconductor Corp.	$2,863,545
40. RJR Nabisco Holdings Corp.	$6,191,038	90. Dresser Industries Inc.	$2,832,109
41. Novell Inc.	$6,119,980	91. Trans World Airlines Inc.	$2,820,092
42. Fujitsu	$5,980,490	92. Walt Disney Co.	$2,814,904
43. Sharp Electronics Corp.	$5,898,979	93. Chrysler Corp.	$2,796,069
44. Intergraph Corp.	$5,748,430	94. Northwest Airlines Inc.	$2,780,171
45. Everex Systems Inc.	$5,739,507	95. Emerson Electric Co.	$2,589,538
46. Allied-Signal Inc.	$5,652,379	96. McDonnell Douglas Corp.	$2,367,472
47. Mitsubishi Intl. Corp.	$5,620,003	97. Chevron Corp.	$2,310,612
48. Tandon Corp.	$5,528,975	98. Boeing Co.	$2,035,674
49. GTE Corp.	$5,436,907	99. Tenneco Inc.	$1,475,672
50. Westinghouse Electric Corp.	$5,198,129	100. Schlumberger Ltd.	$1,472,897

Figures measured by ad spending in business trade publications. Ad expenditure totals were compiled by *Business Marketing* based on data provided by MMS-Rome Reports, a New York-based market research company.

telemarketing. As noted in Exhibit 21-8, 66 percent of the firms indicated they used direct mail in their promotional mix, and 11 percent had used telemarketing. While the telemarketing expenditure was estimated to account for only an average of 1 percent of the overall budget (another study estimated this figure could be as high as 6 percent), it must be remembered that the costs of telemarketing are very low. In addition, many of the firms surveyed may not have considered sales calls as a direct part of telemarketing, leading to a lower cost estimation. Nevertheless, studies have

➤ *Exhibit 21–10*
Using television in
business-to-business advertising

While most business-to-business advertisers use little or no television in their promotional plans, Jeffrey W. Kaumeyer, of Hammond Farrell, Inc., a New York advertising agency specializing in industrial marketing, notes that given three essential conditions, a number of possibilities for television exist:

The Essential Conditions

1. The prospects must be concentrated geographically.
2. The sales pitch must be boiled down to one simple, compelling human message.
3. Television must be complemented by the other, more basic components in a complete marketing communications plan.

The Possibilities
Ten other situations when television should be considered:

1. A first-class memorable spot can be produced for less than $197,000.
2. Purchase patterns are cyclical or heavily seasonal.
3. Buying influences are large in number and growing.
4. The most important buying influencers are hard to get in to see.
5. Speed of communication is essential.
6. The objective is to breathe life into a tired product and/or sales force.
7. Competitors' spending is "drowning out" your message.
8. You can continue to maintain at least a modest national presence.
9. Your marketing effort could use the support of indirect influences.
10. Your agency is making a good profit on your business (spot TV buying is not lucrative to the agency!).

shown that the use of telemarketing among business-to-business marketers is increasing. The reasons for the increasing attractiveness of this medium include:

1. **Coverage**   Telemarketing efforts can lead to significantly more contact with customers and potential customers. Thus, more persons can be exposed to the marketing communication and reached in much less time.
2. **Costs**   We have already discussed the high cost per sales call of field salespersons. Add in the benefits offered as a prescreening device, and as a follow-up strategy, and telemarketing becomes an even more attractive alternative.
3. **Sales**   Business-to-business sales account for approximately 80 percent of the sales generated through telemarketing. At an average sale of $1,500,[8] this effort is well spent.
4. **Market research**   The telephone allows the business-to-business marketer to engage in instant market research. The direct contact this medium provides between the marketer and customer allows the marketer to gain the customer's insights almost immediately while at the same time being able to gauge the response and follow up or probe.

As can be seen in Exhibit 21–12, page 726, the use of direct-marketing methods—particularly telemarketing—is being applied to a number of sales and marketing functions. All indications are that this trend is likely to continue and probably increase as personal selling and other media costs continue to climb.

Trade shows

As shown in Exhibit 21–8, after specialized business advertising, the business-to-business marketer is most likely to utilize trade shows as a means of communication. In 1991, 74 percent of the firms noted they had employed this medium, with an estimated 13.2 percent of the budget being allocated to this communications tool. (As can be seen in Exhibit 21–13, page 727, the trade show exhibit is an important part of this expenditure.)

➤ *Exhibit 21–11*   **Business-to-business ads are becoming more common on television**

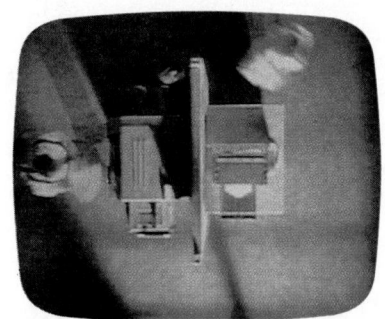
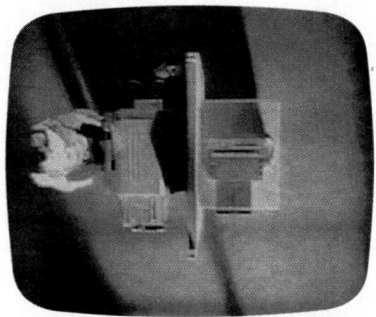

VO: Running around all day, (VIDEO: MAN RUNNING AROUND IN CIRCLES IN FAST MOTION) copying thermal faxes onto plain paper? STOP! (VIDEO: MAN FREEZE FRAMES)	Get a RICOH plain paper laser FAX 3200L (VIDEO: SHOT OF FAX 3200L). You'll get your faxes printed laser perfect on plain bond paper-FAST! (VIDEO: PEOPLE TAKING FAXES) And you can get one for less than any other fax of its kind.	So stop running around. Get a RICOH fax. (VIDEO: PEOPLE ENTERING MEETING) And get down to business. (VIDEO: PEOPLE SIT DOWN) (:04 DEALER TAG) (VIDEO: FOUR FAXES RECEIVING, RICOH LOGO APPEARS, AND OLYMPIC RINGS)

The reasons for the extensive use of this medium are many. First, the *cost per contact* is significantly lower when one uses trade shows than it would be through the field sales force. Equally important is the quality of the sales contact, as the majority of those attending trade shows have some influence in the purchase decision process, and most of those in attendance are there specifically to seek new ideas or suppliers. The net result of this cost/contact combination is that the estimate to close a sale at a trade show is approximately $142 versus the over $1,100 cost we cited earlier to do the same through the sales force.[9] Given these numbers, you can see why firms state they use this communications medium.

Sales promotions

In 1990, business-to-business marketers spent approximately 10 percent of their promotional budgets on sales promotions.[10] These promotions include video materials (other than films), point-of-sales materials, permanent display racks, and videotapes among others. As Exhibit 21–8 shows, 35 percent of the firms reported having used videotapes, constituting an average 2.3 percent of the promotional budget. Earlier in this text, we indicated that the use of videotapes in the consumer market was increasing particularly in the automotive industry. Business-to-business marketers have also found this to be an extremely beneficial medium, as the tapes allow for product introductions and demonstrations at a cost far less than making a personal sales call. In addition, the tapes can increase the reach to the target market

➤ *Exhibit 21–12*
Applications of telemarketing in business-to-business communications

Application/Integration	Percentage
Customer service	83.5
Customer discretion or whoever is available to the customer at the time.	31.5
Telephone representatives refer service requests to the field.	24.7
Field representatives refer service requests to telephone representatives.	23.2
Separate field and telephone accounts/territories.	4.1
Order taking	88.8
Field representatives refer orders to telephone representatives.	30.7
Customer discretion or whoever is available to the customer at the time.	28.3
Telephone representatives refer orders to the field.	26.7
Separate field and telephone accounts/territories.	3.1
Handling complaints	84.7
Field representatives refer complaints to telephone representatives.	31.1
Customer discretion or whoever is available to the customer at the time.	24.5
Telephone representatives refer complaints to the field.	21.1
Separate field and telephone accounts/territories.	7.8
Product prepurchase information	87.4
Field representatives refer inquiries to telephone representatives.	32.9
Customer discretion or whoever is available to the customer at the time.	26.6
Telephone representatives refer inquiries to the field.	24.1
Separate field and telephone accounts/territories.	3.8
Lead generation	99.9
Telephone representatives refer leads to the field for follow-up.	40.0
Marketing/advertising services assigns leads to both.	37.7
Field representatives refer leads to telephone reps for follow-up.	22.2
Lead qualification	75.0
Telephone representatives qualify leads then hand them off to the field for follow-up.	34.4
Field representatives qualify leads, then hand them off to telephone representatives for follow-up.	28.1
Marketing/advertising services assigns lead follow-up to both.	12.5
Prospecting	78.6
Telephone representatives refer prospects to the field for follow-up.	38.5
Field representatives refer orders to telephone reps for follow-up.	29.3
Marketing/advertising services assigns prospects to both.	10.8
Full account management	97.6
Shared accounts: Telephone and field representatives exchange information on sales/service activity by phone, fax, mail, and electronic mail.	92.4
Separate telephone and field accounts/territories.	5.2
Dealer locator	79.3
Customer discretion or whoever is available to the customer at the time.	29.2
Telephone representatives refer inquiries to the field.	25.0
Field representatives refer inquiries to telephone representatives.	20.9
Separate field and telephone accounts/territories.	4.2

Note: Only integration methods mentioned by a significant number of respondents are mentioned above.

in a lot less time. The role of many of these materials is to provide the sales force with aids to assist it in the selling effort and to be used as leave-behinds to reinforce the selling effort.

Incentives

The use of incentives is an important part of the business-to-business communications budget. The majority of that money is spent on merchandise incentives provided to the company's sales force, dealers, distributors, and customers. This merchandise includes the use of specialty advertising materials, whereas others may be televisions, VCRs, radios, computers, and even award trips (see Exhibit 21–14) that are given as motivational tools. Another category not specifically mentioned in this category is cash incentives—most of which are provided directly to one's own sales force.

> *Exhibit 21–13*
Trade show exhibits constitute an important part of the business-to-business marketer's communications efforts

Imagine this...

...as a rental exhibit.

Feeling the pinch of diminishing budgets and shrinking corporate staffs, yet still have the need to put your best foot forward? Impact Exhibits, with more than a decade of global marketing experience, can rent you a custom-designed tradeshow exhibit to showcase your company anywhere in the world.

And there's more! Impact's award-winning design team is backed by a quality-oriented, nonstop service and support staff that can help

you surround your one-of-a-kind exhibit with a wide range of value-added marketing services... from pre-show planning and training to lead management and fulfillment.

Discover why clients like Kodak and Commodore and Upjohn entrust their corporate images to us. For more information on Impact Exhibits and our worldwide custom-design rental program, call **1-800-321-1148** today.

IMPACT
EXHIBITS, INC.

> *Exhibit 21–14*
Norwegian Cruise Lines offers its services as an incentive to business-to-business employers

Public relations

While constituting only about 4 to 5 percent of the budget, 8 out of 10 industrial companies report they have a formalized public relations function.[11] Because the public relations media typically used include business paper articles, trade magazines, and journals, the use of public relations has been used in much more of a marketing role than for other reasons mentioned in Chapter 18 — as demonstrated in Exhibit 21–15. The use of articles and press releases to provide detail on new product innovations and/or developments is common in this market. Many customers have come to rely on these articles to keep abreast of new developments in the marketplace.

Videotext

Earlier in this book, we discussed the medium known as videotext and noted consumer use had not reached its expectations. This is not the case in the business-to-business market. Some well-known companies such as IBM, Digital Equipment Corp., AT&T, and Honeywell are already employing this means of communication and have found it to be very successful. Given the large volumes of specific information that are often required by industrial firms, the capabilities of videotext make this medium a viable tool.

One market in which videotext has been most useful is that of the government sector. Information regarding new laws, changes in product specifications, or contracts open for bid is very quickly and effectively communicated through this

➤ *Exhibit 21–15*
The major emphasis top marketers place on public relations programs

	Percent Responding*
Marketing/product support	85%
Corporate image building	19%
Employee communications	11%
Community relations	6%
Special events	6%
Financial/investor tours	5%

*Response adds to more than 100% due to multiple mentions.

method. Since government decisions are typically (at least in theory!) based on comparative bids for products or services provided, communication of information relevant to the structuring of the bid is important, and timing is critical.

In summary, the relative use of each of the program elements discussed here varies from one firm to the next. The use of each of these tools is dictated by the objectives to be accomplished as well as the budgets provided, just as was the case in consumer-oriented companies. Also, as was the case in consumer products companies, marketing research is needed as an input into the promotional program and to evaluate the effectiveness of these programs. The use of research constitutes the basis of our discussion in the next section.

The Role of Research in the Business-to-Business Promotional Program

Throughout this text, we have discussed the contribution of research to the promotional process—both as an *input* into decision making as well as a *measure of the effectiveness* of various programs. The business-to-business market is no exception to this rule. In this section, we examine the business-to-business marketers' use of research as an aid to identification and entry into various markets. In the final section, we examine the use of research as a measure for evaluating the effectiveness of the promotional effort.

Research Input into the Decision Process

One factor that makes business-to-business marketing different is that there often may be **multiple buying influences.** The roles of influencer, decision maker, purchaser, and user may not always be assumed by the same individuals. In this case, the marketing manager must identify all those involved in the purchase decision process. This may mean the manager may have to identify prospects by industry, by size of plant, and by title or job function. Otherwise, the advantages to be gained from specialized business media are lost, as the message will go unseen. To assist in this task, the manager has a number of secondary sources available.

Standard Industrial Classification (SIC) data

SIC data are provided by the U.S. Bureau of Management and Budget and provide a numerical description of a company based on the product it produces. Companies carry a four- to seven-digit code, with each additional identifying code number more specifically identifying the manufactured product or service. Most major libraries contain SIC classification data, or the same can be acquired from the U.S. Government Printing Office in Washington, D.C.

Dun & Bradstreet

Dun & Bradstreet publishes a plant list index based on SIC codes. While the government codes list the products made by plants, it does not carry the reverse information—that is, the names and number of plants manufacturing SIC code products. This information is provided by Dun & Bradstreet.

➢ *Exhibit 21–16*
A sampling of trade publications

Publication	Industry
Industry Specific	
Banking Industry	Banking
Beverage Industry	Bottling
American Cemetery	Cemetery and monuments
Interior Textiles	Drapery
Dairy Field	Dairy
Library Journal	Education
Product Marketing	Cosmetics
Executive Jeweler	Jewelry
Coal Age	Coal mining
General Industry	
Advertising Age	Advertising
Sales & Marketing Management	Sales/marketing
Forbes	Financial/business
Computer World	Computers

➢ *Exhibit 21–17*
Research studies used by business-to-business marketers

	Percent Responding
Market position studies	56%
Readership studies	46
Customer attitude studies	42
Focus groups	37
New product feasibility studies	37
Competitive environment analyses	35
Brand preference studies	33
Market potential studies	31
Company image studies	27
Prospect feedback studies	20

*Response adds to more than 100% due to multiple mentions.

MCC Media Data Form

The MCC Media Data Form provides information regarding an industry publication's circulation as well as its universe, or number of companies engaged in the business this medium is addressing.

Census of Manufactures

The Census of Manufactures provides reports on 452 SIC manufacturing industries in the United States, including number of establishments, employment, payrolls, hours worked, value added by manufacturing, quantity and value of products shipped, materials consumed, and capital expenditures.

U.S. Industrial Outlook

U.S. Industrial Outlook is a yearly report provided by the U.S. government detailing sales, shipments, and forecasts for selected industries. The report also identifies key trends, innovations, and foreign impacts on the market.

Trade publications

In addition to those sources cited above, business-to-business marketers also rely on an estimated 3,000 trade publications. Not all of these are relevant to each industry, as each provides specific information of interest and relevance to its own audience, as shown in Exhibit 21–16. Still other trade magazines have a more general appeal, creating a broader base of interest.

Of course, business-to-business marketers also engage in *primary* research. This research may serve as input to the planning process or as a measure of effectiveness. Promotional Perspective 21–2 reports on the increasing use of focus groups—a research method often used in consumer marketing—to provide business-to-business insights.

Evaluating Promotional Efforts

While 9 out of 10 business-to-business marketers consider marketing research to be important in their communications programs, Exhibit 21–17 seems to indicate this importance is attributed more to research input rather than to evaluation. As can be

Promotional Perspective 21–2

Business Marketers Turn to Focus Groups

The use of focus group research in the consumer market research community seems to have been adopted by almost everyone. Unlike their consumer counterparts, however, business-to-business marketers have been much slower to adopt this research technique. However, enthusiasm is growing for focus groups among many in the business-to-business industry.

Focus groups are especially suited to meet a number of the business marketing community's most pressing needs. Focus groups provide the opportunity to probe customers' needs and motivations, providing marketers with new insight into the buying process. In addition, as noted by Gary Willets, director of marketing research at NCR, focus groups allow for group dynamics not possible through personal interviews or surveys. Other advantages include the ability to observe the buyers through one-way mirrors.

One key advantage cited by Bonnie Keith, corporate marketing research manager at Digital Equipment Corp., is the opportunity to expose a broader range of employees to the customers' views. By bringing in employees from various aspects of the organization, these employees can acquire firsthand information about the customers' decision process. Keith notes that focus groups can be executed very quickly and are easier to understand than quantitative surveys.

As usual, not everyone believes focus groups are the panacea for all of the business-to-business marketers' research needs. Jean-Anne Matter, director of research at Ketchum Advertising, Pittsburgh, warns that focus groups are often used for the wrong purpose. She suggests that many marketers are deceived by what they consider "reality" when the opinions expressed are those of only a few, and only a "small slice" of what is really going on is provided. Matter adds that focus groups are becoming popular because they offer easy solutions and because researchers do not want to deal with complex quantitative information. Gary Willets also cautions researchers to be sure the groups are typical and not to be tempted to think they will provide all of the insights required.

Both Willets and Matter agree that focus groups should be used in combination with quantitative research methods. They note that both of these research techniques have their merits and should not be considered substitutable for each other.

The problems cited here are not specific to focus group research activities conducted in the business-to-business sector. Consumer researchers have seen the same advantages and disadvantages. Just as the use of focus groups has continued to increase in the consumer market, expectations are that the business-to-business marketer will likewise become more enchanted with the technique. According to Thomas L. Greenbaum, executive vice president of Clarion Marketing Communications, "The industrial sector is getting much more sophisticated and is catching up with the consumer products sector. They are beginning to use focus groups in much the same way the consumer side did in the early 1970s and 1980s." To at least some researchers, this increased usage may not necessarily mean increased sophistication.

Source: B. G. Yovovich, "Focusing on Customers' Needs and Motivations," *Business Marketing,* March 1991, pp. 41–43.

seen, of the top 10 research studies used, none of these is specifically oriented to measuring the effects of advertising and promotions. (While focus groups are also cited, these groups are primarily used to "provide in-depth views of sales prospect attitudes" rather than to evaluate ads.) Of the approximately 5 percent of the promotional budget spent specifically on advertising research, approximately 23 percent is used to pretest the effectiveness of ads or to follow up the effects once the ad campaign has been implemented.[12] The remaining 77 percent is again used as input into the advertising program.

Interestingly, even though the number of dollars spent on evaluative research appears low, a number of research services are available to the business-to-business advertiser, as shown in Exhibit 21–18. These services provide a variety of effectiveness measures.

Throughout this chapter, we have repeatedly mentioned that business-to-business marketers tend to emphasize the use of advertising and promotional tools to assist in the sales support effort. It should come as no surprise, then, that the measures most commonly employed to determine the relative effectiveness of these programs also employ the criterion of assessing contribution to the selling effort. Examination of the measures of advertising effectiveness that are employed by business-to-

➤ *Exhibit 21–18*
A sampling of effectiveness measures available to business-to-business advertisers

Ad-Sell Performance Study	McGraw-Hill telephone survey of 100 magazine readers. Scores: established contact; created awareness; aroused interest; built preference; kept customers sold
Ad-Chart	Chilton Marketing Research Co. survey of 100 readers. Scores: % noticed ad; % started to read; % read half or more; total readership index; informativeness index; cost-effectiveness index
Beta Research	Conducts studies in health-care field. Scores: likelihood of reading; changes in opinion of product as a result of ad; informativeness of ad; believability of ad
Fosdick Ad Evaluation	Surveys 100 respondents. Scores: buyers who read ad; buyers who did not read ad; nonbuyers who read ad; nonbuyers who did not read ad
Gallup & Robinson	Reports on 150 respondents. Scores: proved name registration; idea communication; favorable attitude
Starch Readership Reports	Readership of ads. Scores: noted; associated; read most
Advalue	Readership by 100 persons. Scores: recall seeing; readership; ad effect; action taken; future purchase; salesperson contact; ad comparisons
Ad Lab	Mail survey sent to 750 to 1,500 subscribers. Scores: total sample noting; total sample who started to read; total sample reading more than half; total finding ad informative/useful; buyers noting/specified; buyers/specifiers starting to read; buyers/specifiers reading more than half; buyers/specifiers finding ad or editorial informative/useful

➤ *Exhibit 21–19*

The *Copy Chasers* criteria for evaluating business-to-business advertisements

1. The successful ad has a high degree of visual magnetism.
2. The successful ad selects the right audience.
3. The successful ad promises a reward.
4. The successful ad backs up the promise.
5. The successful ad talks person to person.
6. The successful ad presents the selling proposition in logical sequence.
7. The successful ad invites the reader into the scene.
8. Successful advertising is easy to read.
9. Successful advertising has been purged of nonessentials.
10. Successful advertising emphasizes the service, not the source.

business advertisers reflects the emphasis placed on these efforts, as does Promotional Perspective 21–3.

In addition to some of the more commonly employed criteria used in the general-interest and/or consumer market (read most, awareness, attention, recall), more behavioral (and sales-oriented) items such as readership by purchase decision, built preference, kept customers sold, referred ad to someone else, and specified or purchased product, among others, are offered. In Exhibit 21–19, the criteria used by *Copy Chasers*—a panel of experts who evaluate business-to-business ads for *Business Marketing* magazine—provide insight into what is considered necessary to communicate effectively in this market.

As you can see, in the business-to-business market, the expectations of the role to be performed by advertising are somewhat different than what might be expected in the consumer market. The question to be asked here is, Should advertising be expected to generate such results? Or is this also a potential reason as to why so little is spent on measuring advertising effectiveness in the business-to-business market?

In sum, marketing and advertising research in business markets tends to be more oriented to that conducted for providing input into the marketing and promotional programs. As the role of advertising continues to change in this area, the amount and types of research used may follow.

Promotional Perspective 21–3

Business Publishers Promote Their Own Cause

For years, the business-to-business marketer viewed advertising's role as merely a support mechanism for personal selling. Selling advertising to these marketers was not easy, and the emphasis had to be on the use of advertising to aid the selling effort. It should come as no surprise then that when the American Business Press (ABP) ran an ad titled "It Pays to Advertise (Proof that Advertising Works)," this proof was related to sales. When the ABP's advertising insert appeared in business-to-business publications, the advertising effectiveness report was organized around the steps to a sale. Following the same format, here are the highlights of that report, demonstrating that business-to-business advertising has been shown to be effective in:

• **Making contact** A study showed that a large steel company's sales force called on 15 buying influencers in the client's company (steel products). The study also showed that over 150 additional people were influential in the decision. While the salespersons only reached the 15, their advertisements reached all 150.

• **Generating leads** Another study analyzed over 375,000 leads generated over 20 years from 1968 to 1989. The results showed that 82.4 percent of the inquirers never saw salespeople from the company they inquired about; 61 percent didn't even know the company made the product; 35.6 percent purchased the product; and 19.2 percent bought the advertised product.

• **Generating brand awareness** Studies have reported that advertising in business-to-business publications (1) increased name recognition by 2.5 times; (2) products advertised have as much as 250 percent higher name awareness than those not advertised; and (3) the higher the level of advertising investment, the higher the brand awareness achieved.

• **Building preference** Brand awareness in the chemical process industries have shown that advertised products had a 330 percent greater preference than those not being advertised.

• **Increasing sales** A medium level of advertising exposure to end-users increased sales by 80 percent in one study, while a high level of exposure increased them by 157 percent. Medium exposure to dealers led to an increase of 66 percent, while a high level led to 299 percent.

• **Lowering costs of sales/increasing market share** A number of studies have also shown that business-to-business advertising also lowers the cost of sales and increases market share as well as contributes to profits.

The report summarized over 30 years of case histories and research studies and was presented in a 12-page supplement appearing in a variety of business-to-business publications. Its purpose was to demonstrate the effectiveness associated with advertising in ABP media. The ad demonstrates its point quite well—business-to-business advertising obviously works. It also demonstrates another point—selling is still the main criterion for evaluating business-to-business advertising effectiveness.

Source: "It Pays to Advertise," American Business Press, 1991.

SUMMARY

This chapter has presented a slightly different perspective of the use of advertising and promotion. The business-to-business advertiser views the role of advertising and promotions somewhat differently than those in the consumer products industries. Whereas the latter may perceive the role of advertising and promotions to affect communications objectives, in the business-to-business sector, it is generally considered to be a sales support aid.

Because of the role advertising and promotions are asked to assume, the message and media strategies designed to accomplish the sales support objectives are again different from those that might be more commonly employed in the consumer products market. Messages tend to be more information laden, more straight to the point, and designed to elicit inquiries or answer questions. The use of illustrations, humor, and/or sex are much less commonly employed.

The media employed by industrial advertising are also different. It was noted that no less than 3,000 trade journals exist in the area, with the vast majority of firms reporting they use these. Trade shows and sales incentives were also commonly employed. Videotext—somewhat of a disappointment in the consumer products market—has found a great reception in the industrial sector.

Finally, the measures used to determine the effectiveness of business-to-business strategies were also shown to be sales support oriented. Criteria such as number of inquiries generated, referrals, and actual purchases are often employed to determine the relative effectiveness of alternative strategies.

KEY TERMS

business-to-business advertising
derived demand

buying center
Social Style Model

CUBE Model
multiple buying influences

DISCUSSION QUESTIONS

1. Explain why *business-to-business advertising* has replaced the use of the term *industrial advertising*.
2. What are some reasons business-to-business advertising has tended to be more rational and product specific in its appeals?
3. Explain some of the differences in media strategies employed by business-to-business and consumer products marketers.
4. Discuss some of the criteria used to evaluate business-to-business ads. How do they differ from those used in the consumer products market?
5. Find examples of business-to-business ads that reflect service sector and industrial sector products. Discuss the appeals used in each.
6. Why has the use of mass media such as television and consumer magazines for advertising business-to-business products and services been increasing?
7. Why are trade shows such an important medium for the business-to-business advertiser?
8. Business-to-business advertising has become more interesting, employing more color, more emotional appeals, and, in general, less information. Cite some reasons why this has occurred.
9. Discuss the nine differences between consumer and business-to-business communications.
10. Explain how public relations and publicity are being employed in the business-to-business market.

chapter 22

International Advertising and Promotion

chapter objectives

➤ To examine the importance of international marketing and the role of international advertising and promotion.

➤ To examine the various factors in the international environment and how they influence advertising and promotion decisions.

➤ To consider the issue of global versus localized marketing and advertising and the pros and cons of each.

➤ To examine the various decision areas of international advertising.

➤ To examine the role of other promotional mix elements in the international marketing program.

Marketers Go Global

In his 1983 book *The Marketing Imagination,* Harvard marketing professor Theodore Levitt argued the world was becoming a common marketplace where people have the same basic needs, wants, and tastes no matter where they live. Levitt called on marketers to develop global marketing strategies and true global brands that could be sold the same way in every country using worldwide product, market, and advertising standardization. Many multinational companies heeded the call for global marketing and began consolidating their advertising by hiring large superagencies with international marketing capabilities rather than using local agencies in various countries. These agencies were given the charge of helping companies turn their products and services into global brands that could be promoted with the same advertising theme and approach worldwide.

While a number of companies such as Gillette, Coca-Cola, Procter & Gamble, Philip Morris, and others were successful in turning many of their products into global brands, not everyone agreed with Levitt's call for globalization. Critics of global marketing and advertising argued that while consumers in various countries share some similarities, a number of differences make it difficult to reach them all with the same advertising appeal. They argued that advertisers needed to adapt their advertising campaigns to local markets to accommodate differences in culture, language, values, lifestyles, and other factors.

Many companies abandoned their attempts at global advertising, dismissing it as impractical, and returned to more localized approaches that would be responsive to the differences in various countries or regions. However, global advertising is still alive and well and boasts prestigious firms among its recent converts including Merrill Lynch, Joseph E. Seagram & Sons, Xerox, Chase Manhattan Bank, H. J. Heinz, Nike, Digital Equipment Corp., and Seiko.

Merrill Lynch began using a global advertising strategy for the first time by running spots on CNNs international feeds to Europe, Asia, and Latin America. Seagram's created a global brands division in 1991 and began its first worldwide campaign for Martell cognac. The company was impressed by the success of that effort and decided to launch a $40 million global campaign for Chivas Regal scotch.

Chase Manhattan Bank recently began a $75 million worldwide TV and print campaign using the theme "Profit from experience." Chase's corporate director of marketing explained the rationale for the global campaign by noting the bank's customers "span the globe and travel the globe. . . . They can only know one Chase in their minds, so why should we confuse them?"

(continued)

Seiko launched its first global image advertising campaign in the fall of 1991 by tying into its role as the official timekeeper of the 1992 Summer Olympics. The Olympics-themed messages used the slogan "The measure of greatness" in reference to its timekeeping role. Although Seiko had run similar ads in various countries before, they were always created locally and used different messages. The new campaign marked the first time Seiko used one message that was centrally created and shown all over the world.

Marketing and advertising experts attribute the increase in global advertising to several factors, including the fact that many global brands are now sold primarily on the basis of image. They also point to the deregulation of many foreign broadcast networks and the formation of pan-regional cable or satellite-delivered programming and the removal of many trade barriers in the European Community as factors encouraging the use of global advertising. Levitt has noted that several industries such as high-tech products and fashion are particularly ripe for global marketing because people around the world "speak the same language" when it comes to these areas.

Some companies are still skeptical about the merits of marketing their product the same way around the world. However, many companies recognize that the world is shrinking fast and global marketing is fast becoming a global reality.

Source: Gary Levin, "Ads Going Global," Advertising Age, *July 22, 1991, pp. 4, 42; Alison Fahey, "Seiko Times First Global Ad to Olympics,"* Advertising Age, *July 22, 1991, pp. 3, 37; and Theodore Levitt,* The Marketing Imagination *(New York: Free Press, 1983).*

The primary focus of the text to this point has been on the development of integrated marketing communications programs for products and services sold to the U.S. market. Many American companies have traditionally devoted most of their marketing efforts to the domestic market, since they often lack the resources, skills, or incentives to go abroad. This is changing very rapidly, however, as U.S. corporations recognize the opportunities that foreign markets offer for new sources of sales and profits as well as the necessity of marketing their products internationally. As we saw in the opening vignette, many companies are striving to develop *global brands* that can be advertised and promoted the same way the world over (Exhibit 22–1).

In this chapter, we look closely at international advertising and promotion and the various issues marketers must consider in communicating with consumers around the globe. We examine the environment of international marketing and how companies often must adapt their promotional programs to conditions in each country. Attention is given to the debate over whether a company should use a global marketing and advertising approach or whether it needs to tailor it specifically for various countries.

➤ *Exhibit 22–1*
Seiko uses global advertising to sell its product around the world

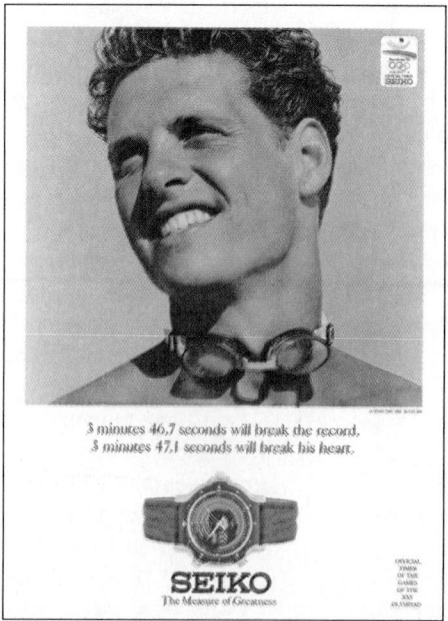

We also examine how firms organize for international advertising, select agencies, and consider various decision areas such as research, creative strategy, and media selection. While the primary focus of this chapter is on international advertising, we also consider issues involved in using other promotional mix elements in international marketing, including sales promotion, personal selling, and publicity/public relations. Let's begin by discussing some of the reasons international marketing has become so important to companies.

The Importance of International Marketing

U. S. companies are focusing on international markets for a number of reasons. Many firms are recognizing that the U.S. market offers them limited opportunity for expansion because of slow population growth, saturated markets, intense competition, and an unfavorable marketing environment. For example, U.S. tobacco companies face declining domestic consumption as a result of restrictions on their marketing and advertising efforts and the growing antismoking sentiment in this country. Companies such as R. J. Reynolds and Philip Morris are turning to foreign markets in Asia and South America where there are fewer restrictions and cigarette consumption is growing.[1] Many U.S.-based brewers such as Anheuser-Busch, Miller Brewing Co., Coors, and others are also looking to international markets to sustain growth as beer sales in this country continue to decline and regulatory pressures increase.[2]

Companies are also focusing attention on international markets because of the opportunities they offer for growth and profits. The dramatic economic, social, and political changes that have occurred around the world in recent years are opening markets in areas such as Eastern Europe and China. The growing markets of Western Europe, the Far East, Latin America, and other parts of the world present tremendous opportunities to marketers of consumer products and services as well as business-to-business marketers.

The importance, as well as the potential profitability, of international marketing has long been recognized by a number of U.S. companies such as IBM, Ford, General Motors, Exxon, Du Pont, and Colgate Palmolive, which generate much of their sales and profits from foreign markets. Gillette sells over 800 products in more than 200 countries, while Procter & Gamble markets 165 products overseas and had international sales of $12.4 billion in 1991. Kellogg's earns 35 percent of its profits outside of the United States and has nearly 50 percent of the European cereal market. Coke, Pepsi, Nike, McDonald's, and many other U.S. companies and brands are known all over the world (Exhibit 22–2).

➤ *Exhibit 22–2*
McDonald's is familiar to consumers around the world

Many U.S.-based companies have been entering joint ventures or forming strategic alliances with foreign companies to market their products internationally. For example, General Mills and Swiss-based Nestlé recently entered into a joint venture to create Cereal Partners Worldwide (CPW). The joint venture is designed to take advantage of General Mills' popular product line and Nestlé's powerful distribution channels in Europe, Asia, Latin America, and Africa.[3] Nestlé has also entered into joint ventures with Coca-Cola to have the beverage giant distribute its instant coffee and tea throughout the world. Häagen-Dazs entered into a joint venture in Japan with Suntory Ltd. and has seen its sales in Asia double since 1989.[4]

International markets are important to small and midsized companies as well as the large multinational corporations. Many of these firms find they often can compete more effectively in foreign markets where they may face less competition, can appeal to specific market segments, or where markets have not yet reached the maturity stage of their product life cycle. For example, the WD-40 Company has saturated the U.S. market with its lubricant product and now gets much of its sales growth from Europe, Canada, and Japan (Exhibit 22–3).

It has also become increasingly important for U.S. companies to adopt an international marketing orientation because imports are taking a larger and larger share of the domestic market for many products and are likely to continue to do so. Japanese companies, which have captured significant portions of the U.S. consumer electronics, motorcycle, and automobile markets, are moving into other product areas such as soft drinks, cosmetics, laundry detergents, and clothing.[5] The United States has been running a continuing **balance-of-trade deficit** whereby the monetary value of our imports exceeds that of our exports. American companies are realizing that we are shifting from being an isolated, self-sufficient, national economy to being part of an interdependent *global economy*. This means U.S. corporations must defend against foreign inroads into the domestic market as well as learn how to market their products and services to other countries.

While many U.S. companies are becoming more aggressive in their pursuit of international markets, some of the largest multinational corporations, and most formidable marketers, are European companies such as Unilever, Nestlé, Siemens, Phillips, and Renault as well as the various Japanese automobile and electronic manufacturers and package-goods companies such as Suntory, Shiseido, and Kao.

➤ *Exhibit 22–3*
The WD-40 Company gets much of its sales growth from foreign markets

Role of International Advertising and Promotion

Advertising and promotion are important parts of the international marketing program of firms competing in the global marketplace. While more than $130 billion is spent on advertising in the United States each year, advertising expenditures outside of the United States have increased dramatically over the past decade and are nearing $300 billion.[6] Exhibit 22–4 shows the top 25 advertisers in terms of advertising spending outside the United States. While U.S.-based Procter & Gamble is ranked number one in terms of worldwide spending, the Anglo-Dutch consumer products conglomerate Unilever NV emerged as the top advertising spender outside the United States in 1990. Of the top 25 spenders on advertising outside this country, only 6 are headquartered in the United States, 10 are based in Japan and 9 in Europe. These figures indicate the importance foreign-based multinational corporations place on the international marketplace. It is also important to note that many of these companies spend a considerable amount of money advertising their products in the United States.

More and more companies are recognizing that an effective promotional program is important for companies competing in foreign markets. As Vern Terpstra notes in his book *International Marketing:*

> Promotion is the most visible as well as the most culture bound of the firm's marketing functions. Marketing includes the whole collection of activities the firm performs in relating to its market, but in other functions the firm relates to the market in a quieter, more passive way. With the promotional function, however, the firm is standing up and speaking out, wanting to be seen and heard.[7]

However, in addition to its importance, many companies are realizing the challenge and difficulties they face in developing and implementing advertising and promotion programs for international markets. Companies planning on marketing and advertising their products or services abroad face an unfamiliar marketing environment and customers with a different set of values, customs, consumption patterns and habits, as well as differing purchase motives and abilities. Not only may the language vary from country to country, but also several may be spoken within a country, such as in India or Switzerland. Many U.S. companies also find that media options are much more limited in many foreign countries owing to lack of availability or limited effectiveness. As a result of all these factors, different creative and media strategies as well as changes in other elements of the advertising and promotional program are often required for foreign markets.

➤ *Exhibit 22–4*
25 leading advertisers in spending outside the United States

Rank	Advertiser	Headquarters	Primary business	Countries in which spending was reported for 1990	Non-U.S. spending 1990	'90-'89 % chg	U.S. spending 1990	W'wide spending 1990	Non-U.S. as % of w'wide
1	Unilever NV	Rotterdam/London	Food	Argentina, Australia, Austria, Brazil, Britain, Canada, Chile, Denmark, Finland, France, Germany, Greece, India, Italy, Japan, Malaysia, Mexico, Netherlands, Pan Arabia, Puerto Rico, South Africa, Spain, Switzerland, Taiwan, Turkey	$1,364.7	16.2	$568.9	$1,933.9	70.6
2	Procter & Gamble Co.	Cincinnati	Personal care	Austria, Britain, Canada, Chile, Denmark, France, Germany, Greece, India, Italy, Japan, Lebanon, Mexico, Netherlands, Pan Arabia, Philippines, Puerto Rico, Spain, Taiwan, Thailand	1,135.6	14.6	2,284.5	3,420.1	33.2
3	Nestle SA	Vevey, Switzerland	Food	Argentina, Austria, Brazil, Britain, Canada, Chile, France, Germany, Greece, India, Italy, Japan, Malaysia, Netherlands, Pan Arabia, Philippines, Puerto Rico, Spain, Switzerland, Taiwan, Thailand	603.5	7.3	635.9	1,239.4	48.7
4	PSA Peugeot-Citroen SA	Paris	Automotive	Argentina, Britain, France, Germany, Italy, Netherlands, Norway, Pan Arabia, Spain, Switzerland	597.1	20.2	9.1 *	606.3	98.5
5	Philip Morris Cos.	New York	Food	Argentina, Austria, Britain, Canada, Denmark, France, Germany, Hong Kong, Indonesia, Italy, Japan, Lebanon, Malaysia, Netherlands, Pan Arabia, Spain, Taiwan	511.2	5.9	2,210.2	2,721.4	18.8
6	Toyota Motor Corp.	Toyota City, Japan	Automotive	Australia, Britain, Canada, Germany, Indonesia, Japan, Norway, Pan Arabia, Switzerland, Thailand	458.5	28.6	580.7	1,039.2	44.1
7	Renault SA	Paris	Automotive	Austria, Britain, France, Germany, Italy, Netherlands, Pan Arabia, Spain, Turkey	442.0	4.8	0.0	442.0	100.0
8	Fiat SpA	Turin, Italy	Automotive	Britain, France, Germany, Italy, Netherlands, Spain, Switzerland	440.9	14.4	0.7 *	441.6	99.8
9	Canon Inc.	Tokyo	Electronics	Canada, France, Germany, Japan, Netherlands	411.0	55.2	119.5	530.5	77.5
10	General Motors Corp.	Detroit	Automotive	Austria, Britain, Canada, Finland, France, Germany, Italy, Netherlands, Norway, Pan Arabia, Spain, Switzerland	409.0	23.5	1,502.8	1,911.8	21.4
11	Matsushita Electric Industrial Co.	Osaka, Japan	Electronics	Britain, Canada, Germany, Hong Kong, Japan, Malaysia, Pan Arabia, Taiwan	398.8	3.2	330.2	729.0	54.7
12	Ford Motor Co.	Dearborn, Mich.	Automotive	Australia, Austria, Britain, Canada, Finland, France, Germany, Italy, Netherlands, Norway, Pan Arabia, Spain, Sweden, Switzerland, Taiwan	387.1	17.6	616.0	1,003.1	38.6
13	Henkel Group	Duesseldorf	Soaps	Austria, France, Germany, Italy, Netherlands, Spain	378.1	49.9	0.2 *	378.3	99.9
14	Hitachi Ltd.	Tokyo	Electronics	Japan, Pan Arabia	368.5	24.4	20.7 *	389.3	94.7
15	Mars Inc.	McLean, Va.	Food	Austria, Britain, Canada, France, Germany, Japan, Netherlands, Switzerland	332.5	17.4	272.4	604.9	55.0
16	Nissan Motor Co.	Tokyo	Automotive	Australia, Britain, Canada, Germany, Japan, Netherlands, Norway, Pan Arabia, Switzerland, Thailand	330.7	(7.6)	410.2	740.9	44.6
17	Kao Corp.	Tokyo	Soaps	Hong Kong, Japan, Taiwan	321.9	(0.5)	24.6 *	346.5	92.9
18	Volkswagen AG	Wolfsburg, Germany	Automotive	Canada, France, Germany, Norway, South Africa, Spain, Sweden	319.6	13.6	138.5	458.1	69.8
19	Philips NV	Eindhoven, The Netherlands	Electronics	Argentina, Austria, Brazil, Chile, Finland, France, Germany, Greece, Hong Kong, Italy, Japan, Netherlands, Pan Arabia, Spain, Sweden, Turkey	314.6	32.9	177.7	492.3	63.9
20	Ferrero SpA	Perugia, Italy	Food	Germany, Italy	291.6	30.6	6.8 *	298.4	97.7
21	Coca-Cola Co.	Atlanta	Food	Argentina, Austria, Britain, Canada, Chile, Germany, Israel, Italy, Japan, Lebanon, Mexico, Netherlands, Philippines, Puerto Rico, Spain, Thailand, Turkey	287.0	9.4	377.2	664.2	43.2
22	Suntory	Tokyo	Beer, spirits	Japan	283.3	(9.1)	5.8 *	289.0	98.0
23	Toshiba Corp.	Tokyo	Electronics	Germany, Hong Kong, Japan, Pan Arabia	274.0	(0.6)	18.7 *	292.7	93.6
24	NEC Corp.	Tokyo	Electronics	Germany, Japan, Malaysia, Netherlands	269.0	0.5	24.9 *	293.9	91.5
25	Mitsubishi Motor Corp.	Tokyo	Automotive	Australia, Japan, Norway, Pan Arabia	268.1	(3.2)	67.9 *	336.0	79.8

The International Environment

Just as with domestic marketing, companies engaging in international marketing must carefully analyze and consider the major environmental factors of each market in which they compete. The major environmental factors affecting international marketing include economic, demographic, cultural, and political/legal variables. Exhibit 22–5 shows some of the factors marketers must consider in each category when analyzing the environment of each country or market. Consideration of these factors is important not only in evaluating the viability and/or potential of each country as a market but also in designing and implementing a marketing and promotional program.

Economic Environment

A country's economic conditions indicate its present and future potential for consuming, as products and services can be sold only to countries where there is enough income to buy them. This is generally not a problem in developed countries such as the United States, Canada, Japan, and most of Western Europe, as consumers in these industrialized nations generally have higher income levels and standards of living. Thus, they have the capability and an interest in purchasing a variety of products and services. Developed countries have the **economic infrastructure** in terms of the communications, transportation, financial, and distribution networks needed to conduct business in these markets effectively. Not only do many developing countries lack purchasing power, but there are also limited communications networks available to firms that might want to promote their products or services to these markets.

For most companies, industrialized nations represent the greatest marketing and advertising opportunities for the reasons cited above. A 1990 report by Starch INRA Hooper and the International Advertising Association showed that the United States spent more money on advertising than nearly all other nations combined.[8] Per capita

➤ *Exhibit 22–5*
Forces in the international marketing environment

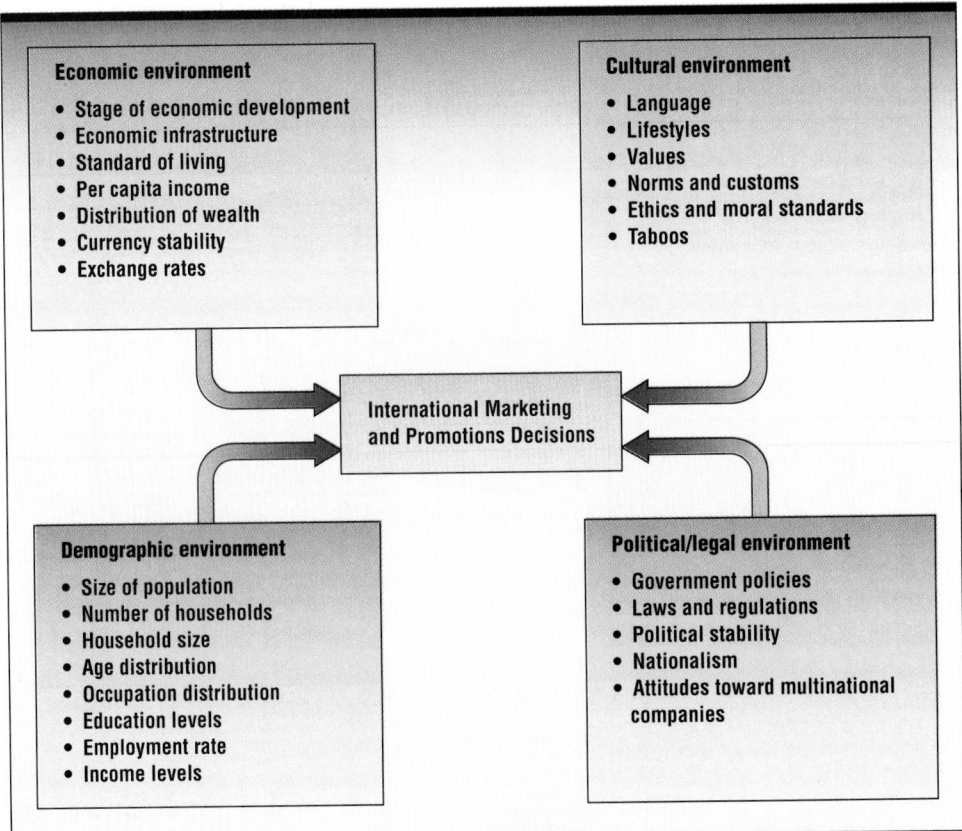

Economic environment
- Stage of economic development
- Economic infrastructure
- Standard of living
- Per capita income
- Distribution of wealth
- Currency stability
- Exchange rates

Cultural environment
- Language
- Lifestyles
- Values
- Norms and customs
- Ethics and moral standards
- Taboos

International Marketing and Promotions Decisions

Demographic environment
- Size of population
- Number of households
- Household size
- Age distribution
- Occupation distribution
- Education levels
- Employment rate
- Income levels

Political/legal environment
- Government policies
- Laws and regulations
- Political stability
- Nationalism
- Attitudes toward multinational companies

spending on advertising was also the highest in the United States at $513, compared with an average of $110 for the other 53 countries. Exhibit 22−6 lists the countries with more than $1 billion in advertising expenditures in 1990.

As can be seen in this exhibit, advertising expenditures are greatest in the more highly developed countries. However, most of these countries have stable population bases, and their markets for many products and services are already saturated. Many marketers are turning their attention to other parts of the world that have growing economies and rapidly developing consumer markets. For example, the "four tigers" of Asia—South Korea, Singapore, Hong Kong, and Taiwan—continue to be one of the fastest-growing markets in the world. It is predicted that these countries will account for nearly a quarter of the world's gross national product by the turn of the century and increases in per capita income are expected to follow. Many U.S. companies already have a strong presence in these countries including Colgate-Palmolive, Du Pont, Quaker Oats, and Coca-Cola.[9]

Marketers are also focusing on some of the developing countries that have expanding populations and present future growth opportunities. For example, Swiss-based Nestlé, which is the world's largest food company, estimates that 20 percent of the world's population in Europe and North America consumes 80 percent of its products. While Nestlé continues to target the European and American markets with ads such as the one shown in Exhibit 22−7, the company is also focusing attention on Third World nations as the "market of tomorrow."[10]

Demographic Environment

In addition to considering the economic environment of a country, international marketers must also examine its various demographic characteristics. Major demographic differences exist between various countries as well as within them. Marketers must consider a variety of demographic factors including income levels and distribution, age and occupation distributions of the population, household size, education, and employment rates. In some countries, factors such as literacy rates must be considered, as many people cannot read and thus they would not respond well to print ads. Demographic data can provide insight into the living standards and lifestyles in a particular country that can be helpful in planning an advertising campaign.

➤ *Exhibit 22−6*
Advertising expenditures by country, 1990

Country	Total Reported 1990 Advertising Expenditures (in millions of U.S. $)
United States	$128,640.00
Japan	38,433.60
United Kingdom	15,816.00
Germany	13,944.40
France	12,891.90
Spain	10,350.20
Italy	5,709.70
Netherlands	4,334.70
Switzerland	4,098.00
Australia	3,847.90
Brazil	3,186.50
Korea, South	2,826.10
Sweden	2,729.30
Mexico	2,199.30
Finland	1,800.20
Taiwan	1,569.30
Denmark	1,377.20
Belgium	1,283.30
Norway	1,233.30
Austria	1,012.00

➤ *Exhibit 22–7 (Left)*
Nestlé advertises its products to countries all over the world

➤ *Exhibit 22–8 (Right)*
This Heineken ad did not translate well into some languages

Demographic data provide marketers with insight into the market potential of various foreign markets. For example, China already has over 1 billion people, and by the year 2000, the population of India is expected to reach nearly 1 billion. Latin America remains one of the world's largest potential markets, although the meager per capita income of most consumers in the region is still a problem. Brazil, which has the largest consumer market in South America, is expected to have a population of 200 million by the year 2000 and will be a growth market for many products and services. Countries such as Thailand and Indonesia are also attracting the attention of many marketers. For example, Indonesia has more people under the age of 16 than the United States and they are very receptive to Western ways and products.[11]

Cultural Environment

Another extremely important aspect of the international marketing environment is the culture of each country. Among the most important cultural variables for marketers to consider are the language, the customs, the tastes, the attitudes, the lifestyle, the values, and the ethical/moral standards of each society. Nearly every country exhibits cultural differences that influence both the needs and wants of consumers and also how they go about satisfying them.

Marketers must be sensitive to foreign cultures not only in determining what products and services they can be sold but also in communicating with them. Advertising is often the most effective method of communicating with potential buyers and creating markets in other countries. However, advertising can also be one of the most difficult aspects of the international marketing program because of problems in attempting to develop messages that will be received and properly interpreted and understood in various countries.

International advertisers often have problems with language. The advertiser must know not only the native tongue of the country but also the nuances, idioms, and subtleties of the language. International marketers must be aware of the connotation of words and symbols used in their messages and understand how advertising copy and slogans are translated. In Chapter 6 (Global Perspective 6–1), we discussed some of the problems marketers often encounter in translating their advertising messages and brand names into various languages.

The Heineken ad shown in Exhibit 22–8 is another example of the problem international marketers sometimes encounter with language differences. Although

➤ *Exhibit 22–9*
1991 per capita package consumption of deodorant in various countries

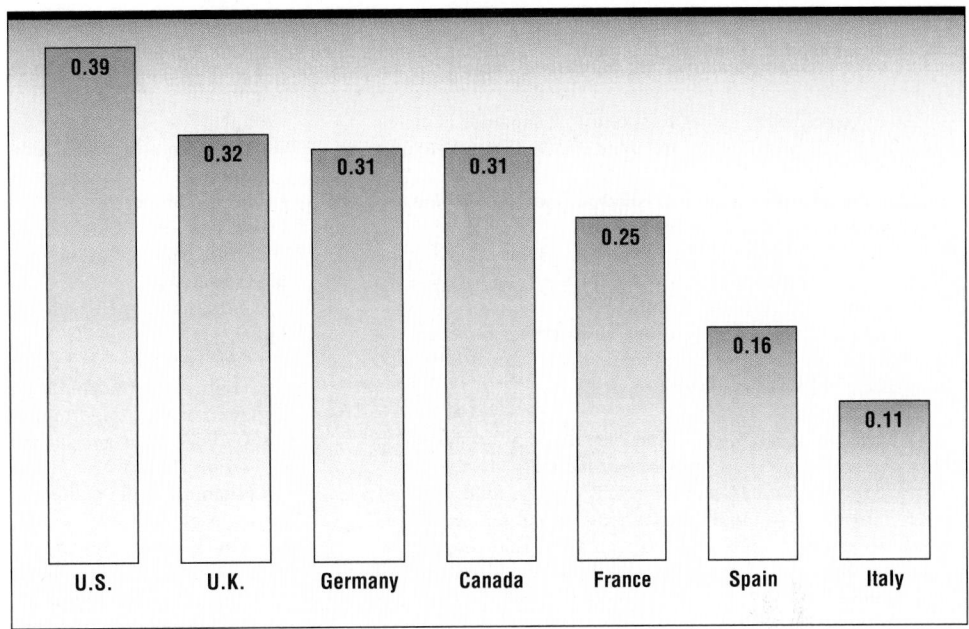

this ad worked well in the United States and other English-speaking countries, the line "you don't have to make a great fuss" could not be translated in a meaningful way into many other languages.

In addition to language, advertisers can encounter problems with the connotative meaning of signs and symbols used in their messages. For example, Pepsodent toothpaste was unsuccessful in Southeast Asia because it promised white teeth to a culture where black or yellow teeth are symbols of prestige. An American ad campaign using various shades of green in the ads was a disaster in Malaysia where the color symbolizes death and disease.

Problems arising from language diversity and differences in the signs and symbols can usually be best solved with the help of local expertise. Marketers should consult local employees or use an ad agency that is very knowledgeable in the local language and can help verify that the advertiser is saying what it wants to say. Many companies also turn to agencies specializing in the translation of advertising slogans and copy into foreign languages to assist in the development of their messages for different countries.

Tastes, traditions, and customs are also an important part of cultural considerations. The customs of a society affect what products and services are sold to a country as well as the way they must be marketed. In France, cosmetics are used heavily by men as well as women and advertising to the male market is common. There are also culturally acquired differences in grooming and hygiene habits of consumers in various countries. For example, U.S. consumers are very concerned with personal hygiene; many wash their hair every day and use products such as deodorant daily. However, consumers in many other Western countries are not as fanatical over personal hygiene. Exhibit 22–9 shows per capita deodorant consumption in the United States versus six European countries.

One of the more difficult markets for many American advertisers to understand is Japan because of its unique values and customs.[12] For example, the Japanese have a very strong commitment to the group, and social interdependence and collectivism are as important to the Japanese as individualism is to most Americans. Ads stressing individuality and nonconformity have traditionally not been prevalent in Japan, but Westernized values have become more prevalent in Japanese advertising in recent years.[13] However, the Japanese have a strong distaste for ads that confront or disparage the competition and tend to prefer soft- rather than hard-sell appeals.[14]

➤ *Exhibit 22–10* **Advertising appeals for the Japanese market**

The Appeals That Do Not Work In Japan	The Art of Selling—Japanese Style
A copywriter who wishes to appeal to a Japanese audience would be wise to forget the following fundamental American appeals: • *Be the first person in your neighborhood to own the Frammis washing machine . . .* (Japanese buyers would never want to be out of step with their neighbors. Nor would they wish to appear to be superior. This is considered to be very bad taste.) • *FREE . . . this $4.96 volume . . . no strings attached . . .* (The average Japanese buyer would simply not believe that something is given for nothing.) • *Less work for mother . . .* (The Japanese housewife wants her family to know that she has personally prepared every bite of food. TV dinners are virtually unknown in Japan. Several years ago, food processors were introduced in Japan. They were a dismal failure. Why? Because Japanese housewives want to do all that chopping and blending by hand. Anything less would be considered an insult to the family.) • *Act today—and save 10 percent off the price of this brand-new model hi-fi phonograph . . .* (Price is not considered a significant appeal to the Japanese buyer. They are more concerned with the dependability and reliability of the company.) • *Here's a great way to express your individuality and set yourself apart from the crowd . . .* (The Japanese consider individuality to be a bad thing. There is a saying that Japanese children learn—almost from the first day of school: The nail that stands the highest is the nail that gets hit by the hammer.) • *Now . . . for the very first time . . .* (In America, a phrase like this would be very appealing. In Japan, it is guaranteed to lose customers. The Japanese buyer simply does not want to be first to own something.)	So what appeals does a copywriter use when attempting to sell something to a Japanese audience? I discussed this matter with Bruce Guilfoile, who is a Japanese-American account executive at McCann Erickson Hakuhodo, Inc.—one of Tokyo's major advertising agencies. (They are also one of the major agencies specializing in Japanese direct response.) Guilfoile told me which appeals I must use—as a copywriter in Japan. • *Our company has been in business for over 35 years . . .* (Stability is considered a great virtue in Japan—and this appeal is viewed as very important to the people of Japan.) • *Our TV set is guaranteed to last longer than any other TV set on the market . . .* (Reliability is the major value that the Japanese look for when buying a product.) • *Our company has the strength of the Rock of Gibraltar . . .* (Image is very important to the Japanese.) • *This is an idea whose time has come . . .* (The Japanese are great believers in timing. Even if an idea seems incredibly "hot," they will wait—until the time is right. Once they are committed to a course of action, it would take wild horses to get them to change.) • *Buy this product . . . it will help bring greater harmony to your life . . . at home and at the office . . .* (Beyond a doubt, this is the most appealing thing you could be saying to a Japanese. They are intensely concerned about their human relations. Any product that claims to improve human relations is guaranteed to sell in Japan.)

Exhibit 22–10 lists advertising appeals one copywriter suggests would not work well in Japan, along with some appeals that would help sell a product.

Religion is another aspect of culture as it affect norms, values, and behavior patterns. Religious beliefs have a much stronger influence on people's lives in Middle Eastern and Far Eastern countries than in most Western societies. For example, in most Islamic countries, it is nearly impossible to conduct business deals during the holy season of Ramadan. The Islamic religion forbids the eating of pork, while cows are considered sacred in the Hindu religion, which stresses abstinence from beef.

Religious values can also have a strong influence on moral and ethical standards. For example, in many Arab countries such as Saudi Arabia, advertisers must be aware of various taboos resulting from conservative applications of the Islamic religion. Alcohol and pork are forbidden in the country and cannot be advertised. The ban is so strict that even images of pigs as stuffed toys cannot appear in ads. Human nudity is forbidden, as are pictures of anything sacred such as images in the shape of a cross or photographs of Mecca. The faces of women may not be shown in photographs, so for items such as cosmetics, drawings of women's faces are used in advertisements.[15]

Political/Legal Environment

The political and legal environment in a country is one of the most important factors influencing the advertising and promotional programs of international marketers. Regulations differ in every country owing to economic and national sovereignty considerations, nationalistic and cultural factors, and the goal of protecting consumers not only from false or misleading advertising but, in some cases, from advertising in general. It is difficult to make generalized statements regarding advertising regulation at the international level, as some countries are increasing government regulation and control of advertising, whereas others are decreasing them. Government regulations and restrictions can affect various aspects of a company's advertising program, including:

- The type of products that may be advertised.
- The content or creative approach that may be employed.
- The media that all advertisers (or different classes of advertisers) are permitted to employ.
- The amount of advertising a single advertiser may employ in total or in a specific medium.
- The use of foreign languages in advertisements.
- The use of advertising material prepared outside the country.
- The use of local versus international advertising agencies.
- The specific taxes that may be levied against advertising.[16]

A number of countries ban or restrict the advertising of various products. Cigarette advertising is banned in some or all media in numerous countries besides the United States including Argentina, Canada, England, France, Italy, Norway, Sweden, and Switzerland. The Australian government recently enacted legislation limiting tobacco advertising to point of purchase beginning in 1993. The ban also excludes tobacco companies from sponsoring sporting events.[17] Tobacco ads were banned from television in the United Kingdom in 1991 although they are still permitted on radio and other media. In China, tobacco and liquor advertising are banned except in hotels where only foreigners can stay and shop.

While international marketers are accustomed to restrictions on the advertising of products such as cigarettes, liquor, or pharmaceuticals, they often are surprised by restrictions on other products or services. For example, margarine cannot be advertised in France nor can restaurant chains. For many years, the French government restricted the advertising of tourism because it encourages the French to spend their francs outside of the country.[18] In some countries, such as China and Malaysia, jeans cannot be advertised since they are considered too Western and decadent.

Many countries restrict the media advertisers can use. Some of the most stringent advertising regulations in the world are found in Scandinavian countries. For example, Denmark began phasing in advertising on a limited basis in 1987, while commercial TV and advertising began in Sweden in 1992.[19] In both countries, the amount of time available for commercials is limited. Media availability in Saudia Arabia is very limited, as television and radio advertising is banned, and the limited number of magazines and newspapers are subject to government and religious restrictions.[20] While tobacco and alcohol are officially banned from Spanish television, advertisers of low-tar cigarettes and wine and beer may buy TV time after 9:30 P.M. if they pay a 100 percent surcharge.

In addition to restrictions on the type of products that can be advertised and the media that can be used, many governments have rules and regulations that affect the advertising message. France has just begun to permit comparative advertising, but has very strict guidelines governing its use. Germany frowns on comparative advertising and requires a rigorous fairness test before making comparative claims. Brazil's self-regulatory advertising codes are so strict that no advertiser has been able to create a comparative message that hasn't been challenged and stopped.[21]

Many countries restrict the types of claims advertisers can make, the words they can use, and the way products can be represented in ads. In Greece, specific claims

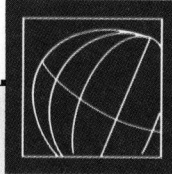

Global Perspective 22–1

Europe 1992 May Change Ad Regulations

At the end of 1992, the 12 members of the European Community (EC)—Belgium, France, Germany, Italy, Luxembourg, the Netherlands, Denmark, Ireland, the United Kingdom, Greece, Spain, and Portugal—were scheduled to begin implementing their plan to create a single European market and remove many of the barriers to trade among the EC nations. The "1992" plan as it was called for years is designed to create a single European market, which currently consists of 344 million consumers and rivals the United States and Japan in world trade power. The EC is expected to get larger; Sweden and Austria have already applied for membership, and Eastern European countries and former Soviet republics are also expected to join.

Many global marketers believe the changes that will be occurring with the implementation of the 92 plan will make it much easier to market and advertise their products in Europe. Part of the plan calls for uniform standards for TV commercials rather than requiring marketers to prepare several versions of their ads to comply with different regulations in various European countries. However, marketers hoping to create one campaign for the entire European market may still encounter problems if they are selling their products to children or using children in their commercials.

Rather than having the European Community draft legislation on children's advertising, the advertising industry is advocating self-regulation. The EC commissioner in charge of competition has challenged the advertising industry to come up with a self-regulation policy. The European Association of Advertising Agencies' (EAAA) advertising and children committee has drafted a self-regulation code that it hopes to have in place soon.

The EAAA committee is trying to reduce the more than 50 restrictions found in various EC nations to 12. The 12-point self-regulatory code proposed by the EAAA committee allows children to appear in ads but not verbally endorse a product or act as a presenter. Children cannot request products or make product comparisons in commercials but could handle or consume the product. The code also allows premiums or gifts to be featured in ads targeted to children.

The chairman of the EAAA committee has noted that a major objective of the new self-regulatory code is to do away with some of the more unusual local regulations. For example, under current laws in the Netherlands, confectionery ads must not be aimed at children, air before 8 P.M., or feature children younger than 14. A toothbrush must also appear on the screen either at the top or bottom during the entire spot or fill the whole screen for the last 1.5 seconds. In Spain and Germany, war toys cannot be advertised. Other rules commonly found in European countries restrict the use of children in commercials or allow them to appear only if they do not endorse a product. For example, in France, children cannot be presenters in commercials or appear without adults.

Marketers advertising their products in Europe may still find regulatory problems in other countries such as Greece and Sweden. Greece is trying to reinstate a 1987 law banning all toy advertising. The law was struck down by the EC in 1991 for restricting trade. International toy companies argue that the ban is being promoted by local toy companies in Greece to deter foreign competition.

The European country with some of the strictest advertising laws is Sweden, which is not currently part of the European Community and where commercial television just began in 1992. Swedish laws forbid targeting advertising to children under age 12, and no commercials of any kind can air before, during,

for a product, such as "20 percent less calories" are not permitted in an advertising message.[22] In addition, copyright and other legal restrictions make it difficult to maintain the same name from market to market. For example, diet Coke is known as Coca-Cola Light in Germany, France, and many other countries because of legal restrictions prohibiting the use of the word *diet* (Exhibit 22–11, page 748).

Government regulations and restrictions can also influence the use of foreign languages in advertising as well as the production of the ad. A study conducted for the International Advertising Association revealed that of the 46 countries surveyed, more than 90 percent permitted the use of foreign languages in print ads and direct mail.[23] However, only 72 percent allowed foreign-language commercials on television, on radio, or in cinema ads, and 25 percent of the countries restricted foreign-language ads to media targeted to foreigners in their country. The study also found that 22 percent of the countries prohibited the use of foreign-produced ads and foreign talent, whereas 38 percent had partial restrictions. For example, Revlon had

or after children's programs. However, Sweden has applied to join the EC and may have to change some of its strict advertising laws since they violate EC rules on the free movement of goods.

The acceptance of a self-regulatory code for children's advertising by the European Community would be welcome by marketers interested in developing pan-European advertising strategies and campaigns. However, it is unlikely that all of the European countries will agree on a self-regulatory code that challenges their long-standing concerns over advertising to children. Marketers may still have to deal with different rules and regulations when it comes to the sensitive area of children's advertising.

Children's advertising is not the only area that may be affected. The EC's European Parliament has already proposed a ban on all tobacco advertising and severe restrictions on pharmaceutical ads and food claims. There is also speculation that advertising for alcoholic beverages could also face restrictions. The EC rules are supposed to take precedence in member countries, although a nation may keep its own rules if they are more restrictive.

Source: Laurel Wentz, "Playing by the Same Rules," *Advertising Age*, December 2, 1991, p. S–2; Laurel Wentz, "Europe 92: How Smart Marketers Cash In," *Advertising Age*, December 2, 1991, pp. S–1, 9; and Laurel Wentz and Andrew Rosenbaum, "Ad Restrictions Loom in Europe," *Advertising Age*, April 23, 1990, p. 72.

What restrictions apply in which countries

Restrictions on TV advertising to children in Europe

	Belgium	Finland	France	Germany	Greece	Ireland	Italy	Nether.	Portugal	Spain	U.K.
Use of children restricted		X	X		X	X			X		
Limitations on confectionery spots	X	X						X			X
Limitations on toy spots					X	X			X		
Premiums, competitions banned	X								X		
Limitations on when spots can air					X			X	X		

Source: Laurel Wentz, "Playing by the Same Rules," *Advertising Age*, December 2, 1991, p. S–2. The accompanying chart shows what restrictions currently apply in various European countries.

to spend an extra $100,000 to film nearly identical versions of a Jontue perfume commercial in Australia and Colombia since both countries refused to accept the version of the ad produced in the United States.[24]

These restrictions are motivated primarily by economic considerations, as many countries require local production of at least a portion of television commercials to help build local film industries and create more jobs for local producers of print and audiovisual materials. However, nationalistic and cultural factors also contribute to these restrictions, along with a desire to prevent large foreign ad agencies from dominating the advertising business in a country and thus hampering its development.

In some countries, steps are being taken to ease some of the legal restrictions and other barriers facing international advertisers. Global Perspective 22–1 discusses how the European Community's "1992" movement is helping create a more standardized legal environment for advertisers in many European countries.

➤ *Exhibit 22–11*
**Diet Coke must use a different
name in some countries**

Global versus
Localized Advertising

The discussion of differences in the marketing environment of various countries suggests that each market is different and requires a distinct marketing and advertising program. However, in recent years, a great deal of attention has been focused on the concept of **global marketing** whereby a company utilizes a common marketing plan for all countries in which it operates, thus selling the product in essentially the same way everywhere in the world. **Global advertising** would fall under the umbrella of global marketing as a means of implementing this strategy by using the same basic advertising approach in all markets.

The concept of global marketing is not new, as debate over standardization versus localization of marketing and advertising programs was begun over a decade ago.[25] However, the idea of global marketing has become popularized in recent years by the theorizing of Theodore Levitt, who suggests the worldwide marketplace has become homogenized and the basic needs, wants, and expectations transcend geographic, national, and cultural boundaries.[26] One writer has described Levitt's position on global marketing as follows:

> Levitt's vision of total worldwide standardization is global marketing at the extreme. He argues that, thanks to cheap air travel and new telecommunications technology, consumers the world over are thinking—and shopping—increasingly alike. According to Levitt, "The New Republic of Technology homogenizes world tastes, wants and possibilities into global marketing proportions, which allows for world standardized products.[27]

Not everyone, however, agrees with Levitt's global marketing theory, particularly with respect to advertising, as they argue that products and advertising messages must be designed and/or adapted to meet the differing needs of consumers in various countries.[28] We will consider the advantages and problems of global marketing—and advertising in particular.

> *Exhibit 22–12*
Coke uses the "Can't Beat the Real Thing" theme in the United States

Advantages of Global Marketing and Advertising

The idea of a global marketing strategy and advertising program offers certain advantages to a company, including:

- Economies of scale in production and distribution.
- Lower marketing and advertising costs as a result of reductions in planning and control.
- Lower advertising production costs.
- Abilities to exploit good ideas on a worldwide basis and introduce products quickly into various world markets.
- A consistent international brand and/or company image.
- Simplification of coordination and control of marketing and promotional programs.

Advocates of global marketing and advertising contend that standardized products are possible in all countries if marketers emphasize quality, reliability, and low prices. They argue that people everywhere want to buy the same products and live the same way. The results of product standardization are lower design and production costs as well as greater marketing efficiency, which translates into lower prices for consumers. Additionally, product standardization and global marketing enable companies to roll out products faster into world markets, which is becoming increasingly important as product life cycles become shorter and competition increases.

At the beginning of the chapter, we discussed several examples of companies using global advertising. Many other companies have been very successful using a global advertising approach. For example, Coca-Cola uses the same basic advertising theme all over the world for many of its soft drinks to project a consistent image and position. For the past several years, advertising for its flagship brand Coca-Cola Classic has been using "Can't Beat the Real Thing" in the United States and a slight variation "Can't Beat the Feeling" in foreign markets (Exhibit 22–12).[29] (Coca-Cola is developing a new slogan for the brand that will have a stronger global appeal.[30] The new ad campaign may be running by the time you read this.) Global advertising not only allows Coca-Cola to communicate a consistent image to consumers around the world, but it also saves the company

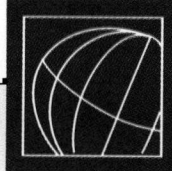

Global Perspective 22–2

Gillette Goes Global with Sensor

Probably few, if any, marketers understand as much as the Gillette Company about how men around the world go about the daily ritual of shaving. The company knows that German men shave more often than American men, take longer, and get better results because they follow directions meticulously. Frenchmen use more shaving cream and moisturizers and generally take better care of their skin than other Europeans. Men in southern European countries shave an average of only four times per week, lower than in most other European countries. While Gillette acknowledges there are some differences in shaving habits, it is convinced men around the world relate to shaving in basically the same ways. Few men look forward to their morning shave, and while they become emotionally attached to their shaving habits, the promise of a smoother, closer, and more comfortable shave appeals to men around the globe.

In 1990, Gillette introduced a new shaving system that appeals to the desire of men everywhere for a better shave. The new Sensor shaving system features twin blades individually mounted on springs that automatically adjust to the contours of a man's face. The Sensor was launched in the United States with $3 million worth of advertising during the Super Bowl. In addition, as part of its global strategy for the introduction of the Sensor, Gillette began running nearly identical commercials in 18 other countries almost simultaneously. The advertising theme used in the global campaign was "The best a man can get" and featured a montage of shots showing highly charged images of men in various roles (playing football and basketball, holding a child, kissing a woman) interspersed with explanations of the Sensor's new technology.

The only elements of the Sensor commercials that changed from country to country were the sports scenes and language. The football scenes shown in the American spots were replaced with shots of soccer for commercials shown in other countries.

The commercial was also translated into 26 languages to take into account language subtleties that might cause misinterpretation of the advertising theme. For example, in France, the theme was changed to *La perfection au masculine,* which translates into "perfection, male style" to overcome problems with the word *perfection,* which is a feminine word in French.

Gillette's decision to use a global advertising theme for the Sensor launch was based in part on previous experience the company had using a single campaign for its Contour Plus shaving system in Europe (which is the European version of the Atra plus sold in the United States). Gillette executives estimated the company saved millions of dollars in packaging, advertising, and production costs by using the single campaign, which boosted sales significantly.

Gillette is also using the global advertising strategy to market the Sensor in Japan, where it is also stressing the American image of the brand. The Japanese have a strong affinity for American products and respond very favorably to brand names and packaging in English. Gillette uses the same ad it uses in the United States, although the voice-over says the theme, "The best a man can get," in Japanese. The Sensor is sold in the same packaging used in the United States with the brand name shown in bold English letters and a Japanese version of it in tiny letters in a corner.

Sensor has turned out to be a global success for Gillette. It is one of the most successful new products in the company's 100-year history. More than 20 million Sensor razors were sold in the first three months after the product introduction and first-year sales exceeded forecasts by 30 percent. The Sensor campaign has also been very popular in Japan, where it has helped Gillette gain market share against Schick, the leading brand.

Gillette has made the Sensor a truly global brand with worldwide, mass market appeal. The company hopes to build on the

---

money. Coca-Cola estimates it saves more than $8 million a year because it does not have to develop new advertising appeals and imagery for the more than 155 countries where Coke is sold.

Another example of a marketer that has effectively used global marketing is the Gillette Company. Global Perspective 22–2 discusses how Gillette used global advertising to launch its new Sensor shaving system, which has become one of the most successful new products in the company's history.

Problems with Global Advertising

While the concepts of global marketing and advertising have received a great deal of attention recently, not everyone agrees with the strategy. Opponents of the standardized, global approach argue that differences in culture, market, and economic development; consumer needs and usage patterns; media availabilities; and legal

success it has had with the Sensor to develop an international line of men's grooming and skin-care products. Gillette has proven that men around the world share many similarities when it comes to shaving and they can be reached with a global advertising appeal.

Source: Yumiko Ono, "Gillette Tries to Nick Schick in Japan," *The Wall Street Journal*, February 4, 1991, pp. B1, 3; Joshua Levine, "Global Lather," *Forbes*, February 5, 1990, pp. 146–48; and Lawrence Ingrassia, "Gillette Hopes New Sensor Razor Will Give It a Competitive Edge," *The Wall Street Journal*, October 4, 1989, p. B6.

Gillette uses global advertising for the new Sensor shaving system

restrictions make it extremely difficult to develop an effective universal approach to marketing and advertising. They argue that advertising is particularly difficult to standardize because of cultural differences in circumstances, language, traditions, values, beliefs, lifestyle, music, and so on. Moreover, some experts argue that cultural change is occurring not necessarily in the direction of commonality of culture but rather in the direction of cultural diversity. Thus, advertising's job of informing and persuading consumers and moving them toward favoring and using a particular brand can only be done within a given culture.

Another problem marketers face when using a global campaign is that consumer usage patterns and perceptions of a product may vary from one country to another. Thus, advertisers must adjust their marketing and advertising approaches to different problems or situations they may be facing in various markets. For example, when

Nestlé Corporation introduced its Nescafe instant coffee brand, the company faced at least five different situations in various parts of the world, including:

1. In the United States, where the idea of instant coffee had great penetration but where Nescafe had the minor share.
2. In continental Europe, where Nescafe had the major share of the market, but the idea of instant coffee was in the early stages.
3. In the tea-drinking countries, such as the United Kingdom and Japan, where tea drinkers had to be converted not just to coffee but to instant coffee.
4. In Latin America, where the preferred coffee was a heavy one that could not be duplicated with an instant version.
5. In Scandinavia, where Nestlé had to deal with the ingrained custom of keeping a pot of coffee on the stove from early morning until late at night.

Nestlé had to use different advertising strategies for each market with varying executions, as a global campaign would not have been able to address the varying situations adequately.[31] Exhibit 22–13 shows examples of Nescafé ads used in Japan and Norway.

Many experts believe it is very difficult to standardize products and advertising messages. They argue not only that there is the problem of cultural differences but also that marketing a standardized product the same way all over the world can turn off consumers, alienate employees, and blind a company to diversities in customer needs. For example, when McDonald's expanded to Puerto Rico, it alienated consumers by using American TV ads dubbed in Spanish and then by using Hispanic ads that were brought in from New York, which subsequent research showed looked too Mexican.[32]

Parker Pen also encountered problems when it attempted to use global advertising in the mid-1980s. Parker encountered resistance from local managers in its foreign branches who resented the home office centralizing the advertising function with one worldwide agency and mandating the type of advertising appeal used in their markets.[33]

Concerns and problems over the use of global advertising have led some major companies to move away from a completely standardized approach. For example,

➤ *Exhibit 22–13*

A. Nescafe instant coffee ad used in Japan

B. Nescafé instant coffee ad used in Norway

the Colgate-Palmolive Company has used global advertising for many of its brands including the Colgate, Palmolive, Fab, and Ajax product lines, and the company continues to endorse the use of global appeals. Under its new marketing strategy, however, advertising is often modified for a specific country or region, particularly where local creativity can improve the advertising over the global standard.[34] An example of this new approach is the advertising used for Colgate toothpaste (see Exhibit 22–14). The globe/smile image is used as the visual in nearly every country where Colgate is marketed, although the copy is often varied. This ad for the Russian market appeared in the Moscow edition of *Reader's Digest*.

Some marketing experts argue that much of the attention being focused on the advantages of global advertising stems from large ad agencies trying to increase business by encouraging clients to use one agency to handle their marketing communications worldwide.[35] Indeed, some agencies such as London-based Saatchi & Saatchi, which is one of the world's largest agencies with offices in 58 countries, are

➤ *Exhibit 22–14*
Advertising for Colgate toothpaste uses a consistent visual image but the copy may vary for various markets

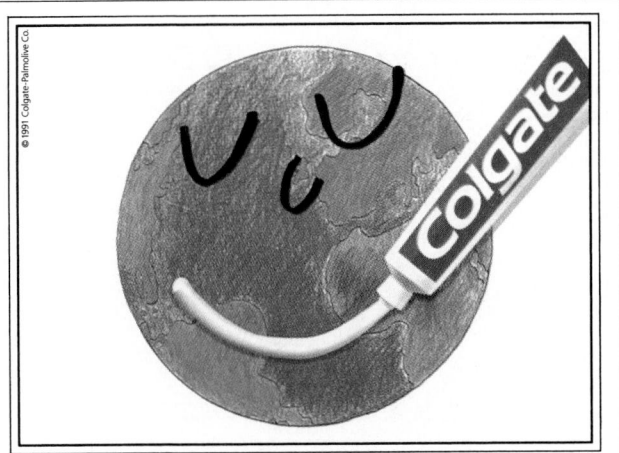

МИР ГОВОРИТ «КОЛГЕЙТ»–
ПОДРАЗУМЕВАЕТ ЗУБНАЯ ПАСТА.
МИР ГОВОРИТ ЗУБНАЯ ПАСТА–
ПОДРАЗУМЕВАЕТ «КОЛГЕЙТ».

Для людей в более чем 160 странах мира зубная паста «Колгейт» вот уже 100 лет является синонимом высочайшего качества. Люди больше доверяют пасте «Колгейт», чем другим пастам, потому что она содержит кальций и фтор, которые способствуют укреплению зубов и защищают их от кариеса.

С помощью пасты «Колгейт» вы и ваша семья смогут сохранить зубы здоровыми. Вашей семье также понравится освежающий вкус ментола.

Чистите зубы пастой «Колгейт» и вы убедитесь сами, что «Колгейт» означает качество.

ЗУБНАЯ ПАСТА НОМЕР ОДИН В МИРЕ.

Translation:

COLGATE. WHAT THE WORLD CALLS TOOTHPASTE.
THE WORLD SAYS COLGATE, THE WORLD MEANS TOOTHPASTE.
THE WORLD SAYS TOOTHPASTE, THE WORLD MEANS COLGATE.

In the past 100 years since it was first introduced, Colgate toothpaste has come to mean superior quality to people in over 160 countries. In fact, more families trust Colgate than any other toothpaste in the world because it contains calcium and fluoride for stronger teeth and unsurpassed cavity protection. Colgate will also help keep your family's teeth healthy. And it has a fresh, minty taste they'll love. Brush with Colgate. And see for yourself that, when the world says "Colgate," they mean quality.

THE NUMBER ONE TOOTHPASTE IN THE WORLD.

> *Exhibit 22–15*   **The Saatchi & Saatchi advertising agency is a proponent of global brands and advertising**

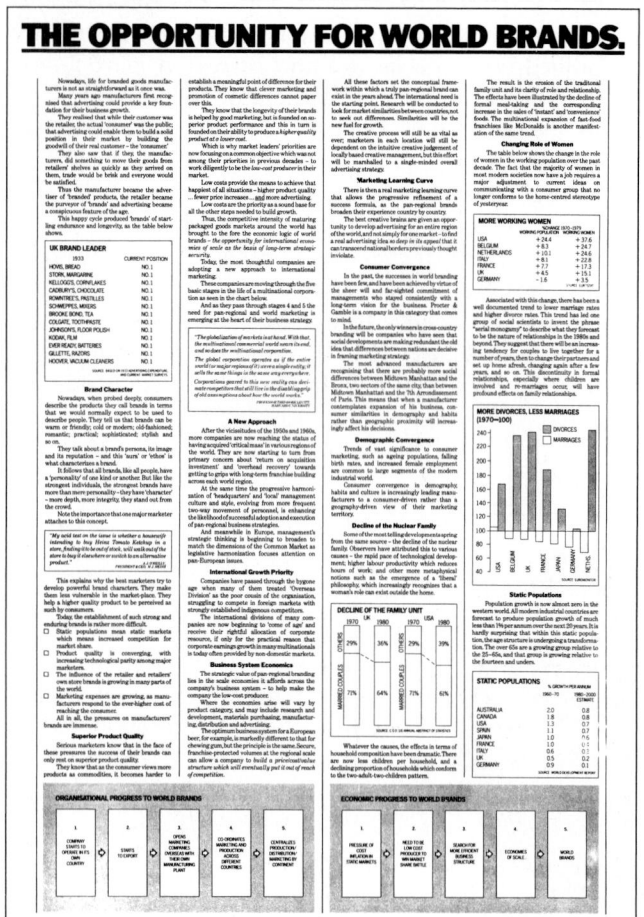

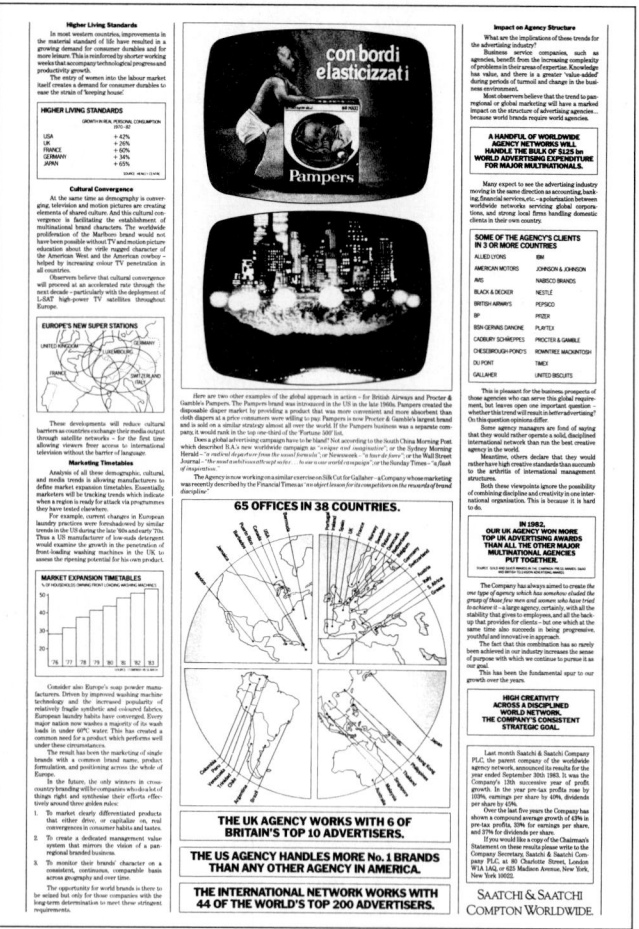

strong proponents of global marketing and have developed global campaigns for a number of clients including British Airways and Procter & Gamble. Saatchi & Saatchi views the opportunity for global brands and advertising as very plausible for a number of reasons including convergence in demographic and cultural trends and an increasing spillover of media across national borders, fueled by the growth and development of satellite television (Exhibit 22–15).

When Is Globalization Appropriate?

While globalization of advertising is viewed by many in the advertising industry as a difficult task, some progress has been made in learning what products and services are best suited to worldwide appeals. Products that can take advantage of global marketing and advertising opportunities include:

1. Brands that can be adapted for a visual appeal that avoids the problems of trying to translate words into dozens of languages.
2. Brands that are promoted with image campaigns that lend themselves to themes that play up to universal appeals such as sex or wealth.
3. High-tech products coming to the world for the first time; new technology products coming on the world at once and not steeped in the cultural heritage of the country.
4. Products with nationalistic flavor if the country has a reputation in the field.[36]

Many companies and brands rely heavily on visual appeals that are easily adapted for use in global advertising campaigns. For example, Nike used global advertising to launch the Air 180 running shoe, which was the company's first worldwide

➤ *Exhibit 22–16*
Visual appeals work well in global advertising

product launch. The commercials contained no spoken language, relying on visual imagery.[37] Reebok also has used global advertising that relies on visual imagery. For example, as part of its "Life is short. Play hard" campaign, Reebok used a global ad showing a man sky-surfing wearing a pair of Reebok Pump SXT cross trainers. International airlines such as British Airways and Singapore Airlines also use corporate image ads that rely heavily on visual appeals (Exhibit 22–16).

Products such as jewelry, liquor, and cigarettes are examples of items in the second category that can be promoted using image advertising. Marlboro uses its "Marlboro Country" theme featuring the cowboy around the world, whereas many cosmetic companies use similar image campaigns in many countries.

Levitt, as well as many advertisers, believes consumers are very similar with regard to emotional desires and motives and that emotions such as joy, sentiment, excitement, and many others are universal. Thus, it is common to find global advertising campaigns using emotional and image appeals. One advertising executive summarized this point very well:

> What it all boils down to is that we are all human. We share the gift of emotional response. We feel things. And we feel them in remarkably similar ways. We speak different languages, we observe different customs, but we are wired to each other and to an ultimate power source that transcends us in a way that makes us subject to a common emotional spectrum.[38]

High-tech products targeted to consumers such as personal computers, calculators, and electronic items such as VCRs, televisions, and audio equipment are examples of products in the third category. Also included in this category are various types of business-to-business products and services such as computer systems. Several business-to-business marketers have begun using global advertising campaigns, such as Digital Equipment Corp. and Xerox. For example, Xerox has been promoting itself as the "document company" in the United States as well as in foreign markets (Exhibit 22–17). Products in the fourth category include Swiss chocolates, French wine and champagnes, and German beer or automobiles.

Global Products, Local Messages

While the pros and cons of globalized marketing and advertising continue to be debated, many companies are taking what might be called an in-between approach by standardizing their products and basic marketing strategy but localizing their

➤ *Exhibit 22–17*
Business-to-business marketers such as Xerox have begun to use global advertising

advertising messages. This approach suggests similar desires, goals, needs, and uses for products and services exist, but advertising must be tailored to the local realities and conditions in each market. This approach has been described by agencies as "Think global, act local" and by Grey Advertising as "Global vision with a local touch."[39] Rather than using a global advertising message that will be seen by diverse markets, advertisers are tailoring their ad executions to local cultures and situations.

Although some marketers use global advertisements with little or no modification, most companies allow for some flexibility in their global execution and adapt their messages to respond to differences in language, market conditions, or other factors. For example, Coca-Cola and many other global marketers use a format called **pattern advertising** whereby their ads follow a basic approach but themes, copy, and sometimes even visual elements can be adjusted.

An excellent example of the use of pattern advertising is a campaign used by the Coca-Cola Company in various markets around the world. Coke's agency, McCann-Erickson Worldwide, created an award-winning commercial for the U.S. market showing American football star "Mean Joe" Greene giving his jersey to a young boy who had given him a bottle of Coke after a tough game. Reactions to the ad were so positive that Coke decided to use the same format and adapt it to other countries by creating ads featuring stars of the more popular international sport of soccer. Ads in South America used the popular Argentine star Maradonna while those in Asia used Thai star Niwat tossing their jerseys to an admiring young fan.

Another way global marketers adapt their campaigns to local markets is by producing a variety of ads that use a similar theme and format and allowing managers in various countries or regions to select those messages they believe will work best in their markets. This approach was used by Seagram's in the worldwide campaign the company developed for Chivas Regal scotch.[40] Seagram tested four campaigns in seven countries and decided to use a campaign with the theme "There will always be a Chivas Regal." A series of ads using universal images and a Chivas "crest" was created and translated into 15 languages. Marketing executives in the 34 countries where the campaign is running can choose specific ads in the series for their markets.

Although many marketers are striving to develop global brands, research suggests most are doing so by using a localized approach. A 1988 study by Robert Hite and Cynthia Fraser examined the international advertising strategies of successful U.S. multinational corporations and found that only 9 percent used totally standardized or global advertising for all foreign markets. Thirty-seven percent of the companies used all localized advertising, and the remaining 54 percent used a combination strategy of standardizing some portions of their advertising but adapted it for local markets.[41] A major risk of the global or standardized approach was believed to be a lack of communication owing to cultural differences. A more recent study by Ali Kanso surveyed international advertising managers of U.S. consumer durable goods manufacturers and found the majority of these companies used a localized advertising approach rather than standardization.[42] This study also found, however, that most of these companies used some standardized messages.

The "Think global, act local" approach appears to be the dominant strategy used by many international advertisers. Most managers believe it is important to adapt various components of their advertising messages such as the language, models, scenic backgrounds, message content, symbols, and other elements to blend with the culture and frame of reference of consumers in various countries. Many companies are making these tactical adjustments to their advertising messages to make them more appropriate for various countries and regions. However, at the same time, many are pursuing global strategies that will allow them to turn their products into global brands.

Decision Areas in International Advertising

As is the case with domestic marketing, certain organizational and functional decisions must be made by companies developing advertising and promotional programs for international markets. These decisions include organization, agency selection, advertising research, creative strategy and execution, and media strategy and selection.

Organizing for International Advertising

One of the first decisions a company must make when it decides to market its products to other countries is how to organize the international advertising and promotion function. This decision is likely to depend on how the company is organized overall for international marketing and business. Three basic options for organizing the international advertising and promotion function are centralization at the home office or headquarters, decentralization of decision making to local foreign markets, or a combination of the two alternatives.

Centralization

Many companies prefer centralization of the international advertising and promotion function whereby all decisions such as agency selection, research, creative strategy and campaign development, media strategy, and budgeting are done at the firm's home office. Complete centralization is likely when market and media conditions are similar from one country to another, when the company has only one or a few international agencies handling all of its advertising, when the company can use standardized advertising, or when it desires a consistent image worldwide. Centralization might also be used when a company's international business is small and it operates through foreign distributors or licensees who do not become involved in the marketing and promotional process.

Many companies also prefer the **centralized organizational structure** to protect their foreign investments and keep control of the marketing effort and corporate and/or brand image. For example, Delta Airlines has a highly centralized structure for international advertising, with all creative work and media placement controlled out of the company's headquarters in Atlanta. According to the company's advertising and sales promotion director, Delta is very concerned about how its name and image are presented in various markets, as "What Delta is in America, Delta is in Europe."[43]

The centralized approach can result in considerable cost savings, as it reduces the need for staff and administration at the local subsidiary level. As the trend toward globalized marketing and advertising strategies continues, companies are likely to move more toward centralization of the advertising function to maintain a unified world brand image rather than presenting a different image in each market. Some foreign managers may actually prefer centralized decision making, as it removes them from the burden and responsibility of advertising and promotional decisions and means they do not have to defend local decisions to the home office. However, many marketing and advertising managers in foreign markets oppose centralized control, as they argue that such a structure is too rigid and makes it difficult to adapt the advertising and promotional program to local needs and market conditions. As noted earlier, Parker Pen encountered such resistance when it attempted to implement a global advertising strategy.

Decentralization

Under a **decentralized organizational structure,** marketing and advertising managers in each market have the authority to make their own advertising and promotional decisions. Local managers can select advertising agencies, develop budgets, conduct research, approve creative themes and executions, and select advertising media. Companies using a decentralized approach put a great deal of trust and faith in the judgment and decision-making ability of personnel in local markets. This approach is often used when companies believe local managers know the marketing situation in foreign countries the best. It is also thought they are more effective and highly motivated when given control and responsibility for the advertising and promotional program in their markets. Decentralization also may be needed in small or highly unique markets where headquarters' involvement is not worthwhile or advertising tailored to the local market is needed.

Combination

While there is an increasing trend toward centralizing the international advertising function, many companies actually use a combination of the two approaches. With the combination approach, the home office, or headquarters, has the most control over advertising policy, guidelines, and operations in all markets. The international advertising manager works closely with the representatives from the international agency (or agencies) and sets advertising and promotional objectives, has budgetary authority, is responsible for approving all creative themes and executions, and approves media selection decisions, particularly when they are made on a regional basis or overlap with other markets.

Advertising managers in regional or local offices are responsible for submitting advertising plans and budgets for their markets, which are reviewed and considered by the international advertising manager. Local managers play a major role in working with the agency in adapting appeals to their particular markets and making media selection decisions.

The combination approach allows for consistency and uniformity in a company's international advertising, yet still permits local input and adaptation of the promotion program. Most consumer product companies find that local adaptation of advertising is necessary for foreign markets yet desire control of the overall worldwide image they project. One company that uses a combination approach is Eastman Kodak. Kodak provides central strategy and support to local offices and acts as consultants to them. Although each country is autonomous, the main office controls the quality of advertising and advertising policy. Media buying is done on a local level. However, the main office becomes involved in special media opportunities and overall strategy for events such as Olympic sponsorship and regionalized campaigns.

Agency Selection

One of the most important decisions a firm engaged in international marketing must make is the selection of an advertising agency. The company has three basic alternatives in selecting an agency to handle its international advertising. First, the company can choose a major agency with both domestic and overseas offices. Many U.S. agencies have offices all over the world and have become truly international agencies (Exhibit 22–18).

Many companies prefer to use a U.S.-based international agency, as this gives them greater control and convenience and also facilitates coordination of overseas advertising. In many cases, companies use the same agency to handle international as well as domestic advertising. For example, Texas Instruments had 28 agencies handling its advertising around the world before hiring one agency to handle both its foreign and domestic business. Eastman Kodak cut a 50-agency international roster down to 2 large international agencies.

As was discussed in Chapter 3, there has been a flurry of mergers and acquisitions in the advertising agency business in the United States in recent years. Many agencies have been merging or making acquisitions, both at home and in other countries, to be able to offer full-service global marketing and advertising operations to clients seeking more business in foreign markets.

Large agencies are subject to acquisition as well. Ogilvy & Mather was acquired in a hostile takeover by the London-based WPP Group in 1989.[44] The WPP Group also purchased another large New York agency, J. Walter Thompson, in 1987 on the same premise that large mega-agencies can offer clients greater global marketing strengths and service synergies.

A second alternative for the international marketer is to choose a domestic agency that—rather than having its own foreign offices or branches—is affiliated with agencies in other countries or belongs to a network of foreign agencies. An agency may acquire a small minority interest in several foreign agencies or become part of an organization of international agencies. This allows the agency to remain independent yet sell itself as an international agency offering multinational coverage and contacts.

➤ *Exhibit 22–18*
Lintas: Worldwide has offices all over the world. Its Australia office was chosen as the International Agency of the Year in 1991

Ad Age Turned The World Upside Down To Find The International Agency Of The Year.

Amazing agency from down under comes out on top. Lintas: Australia was chosen by *Ad Age* to be 1991 International Agency of the Year for its advertising that was judged to be "fresh, attention-grabbing and persuasive." Lintas was selected out of 72 agencies from 23 countries. All around the world people are discovering the surprising world of Lintas.

LINTAS:WORLDWIDE

➤ *Exhibit 22–19*
Criteria for selecting an agency to handle international advertising

- Ability of agency to cover relevant markets
- Quality of agency work
- Market research, public relations, and other services offered by agency
- Relative roles of company advertising department and agency
- Level of communication and control desired by company
- Ability of agency to coordinate international campaign
- Size of company's international business
- Company's desire for local versus international image
- Company organizational structure for international business and marketing (centralized versus decentralized)
- Level of involvement of company with international operations

The advantage of this arrangement is that the client can use a domestic-based agency yet still have access to foreign agencies that have a detailed knowledge and understanding of market conditions, media, and so on, in each local market. There may be several problems with this approach, however, as the local agency may have trouble coordinating and controlling the efforts of independent agencies and/or there may be variations in the quality of work of network members. Thus, companies considering this option must ask the local agency questions regarding its ability to coordinate and control the activities of its affiliates and the quality of their work in specific areas such as creative and media.

The third alternative the international marketer has is to select a local agency for each national market in which it sells its products or services. As noted earlier, local agencies often have the best knowledge and understanding of the marketing and advertising environment in a country or region and thus may be able to develop the most effective advertising.

Some companies like to choose local agencies because it gives them the flexibility to choose the best local talent in each market. In many countries, smaller, independent agencies may be doing the best creative work and, because of their independence, may be more willing to take risks and thus develop the most effective ads. Another reason for choosing local agencies is to increase the involvement and morale of foreign subsidiary managers by giving them responsibility for managing the promotion function in their markets. Some companies have their subsidiaries choose a local agency, as they are often in the best position to evaluate local agencies and will be the ones who must work closely with them.

Criteria for agency selection

The selection of an agency to handle a company's international advertising depends on how the firm is organized for international marketing and the type of assistance it needs to meet its goals and objectives in foreign markets. Exhibit 22–19 lists some of the criteria a company might use in deciding agency selection.

Some companies may choose a combination of the three alternatives discussed above because their involvement in each market differs, as does the advertising environment and situation in each country. Several experts in international marketing and advertising advocate the use of international agencies by international companies, particularly those firms moving toward global marketing and striving for a consistent corporate or brand image around the world.[45] The trend toward mergers and acquisitions and the formation of mega-agencies with global marketing and advertising capabilities suggests the international agency approach will become the preferred arrangement among large companies.

Advertising Research

Research plays the same important role in the development of international advertising and promotion programs that it does domestically, as its purpose is to help managers make more informed and better decisions. However, many companies do not conduct advertising research in international markets. Probably the main reason for this is the high cost of conducting research in foreign markets, coupled with the limited budgets many firms have for international advertising and promotion. For many companies, international markets have not represented a large percentage of their overall sales; thus, investments in research have been difficult to justify. Rather than making advertising decisions on the basis of quality marketing information, generalizations based on casual observations of foreign markets have guided the promotional process.

As companies increase their emphasis and investment in international marketing, they are recognizing the importance of conducting marketing and advertising research to better understand the characteristics and subtleties of consumers in foreign markets.[46] There are a number of areas where information from research on foreign markets can help firms make better advertising decisions, including:

- Information on demographic characteristics of markets.
- Information on cultural differences such as norms, lifestyles, and values.
- Information on consumers' product usage, brand attitudes, and media usage and preferences.
- Copy testing to determine reactions to different types of advertising appeals and executions.
- Research on the effectiveness of advertising and promotional programs in foreign markets.

A great deal of information is available to marketers through secondary sources. One of the most valuable sources of information for companies based in this country is the U.S. Department of Commerce. The Department of Commerce works closely with American companies to help them sell their products overseas through its International Trade Administration (ITA) division. The ITA publishes a regular series, called *Overseas Business Reports,* that provides valuable information on most major world markets including economic and marketing data as well as various laws and regulations. Information on various markets is also sometimes available from government agencies in other countries; such information is often made available through their embassies or consulates.

Other important sources of secondary information are various international organizations such as the United Nations. The *United Nations Statistical Yearbook,* which is published annually, provides demographic and economic data on more than 200 countries. Yearbooks and other reports are also available for other parts of the world such as Latin America, Europe, and Asia. Other international organizations that can provide valuable information on world markets include the International Monetary Fund and regional organizations such as the Japanese External Trade Organization or the European Community.

Information related to specific aspects of consumer needs and decision making in foreign markets such as product and brand attitudes, usage patterns, and media habits are generally more difficult to find, particularly in developing countries. However, more information is becoming available in these areas. For example, A. C. Nielsen has developed a large international data base that tracks purchase patterns of over 2,000 product classes in 25 countries, and Predicast has a foreign intelligence syndicated service. NCH Promotional Services now collects information on coupon distribution and redemption patterns in the United States as well as a number of European countries (Exhibit 22–20). Information on media usage in European countries has increased tremendously over the past decade also.[47]

Much of the information advertisers need to make informed decisions must be gathered from research generated by the company and/or advertising agency. Companies often find that consumer needs and wants, purchase motives, and usage patterns vary from one country to another, and research is needed to understand these differences. Some companies and their agencies conduct psychographic research in

➢ *Exhibit 22–20*
NCH Promotional Services is a source of information on coupon distribution and use in various countries

foreign markets to determine activities, interests, and opinions as well as product usage patterns. Research relevant to some of these issues may also be available from other sources. For example, a recent survey conducted by *Advertising Age International* and the research firm of Yankelovich, Clancy Shulman looked at purchase habits and brand loyalty of consumers in the United Kingdom, Germany, and France. As can be seen in Exhibit 22–21, consumers in all three countries indicated that value for their money was the most important factor in their purchase decisions and are very open to buying products from other countries. The survey also found that consumers in the United Kingdom are most loyal to a brand, while German customers are least loyal.[48]

It is also important for advertisers to conduct research on consumers' reactions to the advertising appeal and execution style they plan to use in foreign markets. One agency researcher recommends testing the basic premise and/or selling idea to be used in a global campaign first to be sure it has some relevance to the target audience in the various markets where it will appear:

> The logic behind this is that if the basic premise or selling idea has little relevance or appeal in a significant number of the markets, there is no value, at this time, of proceeding further by testing executions. If the premise or selling idea "works" either via testing, or you conclude from other upfront research and market analysis that it could work, you would then move to the second phase—executional testing. Here the primary focus should be on comprehension of the strategic message and its explicit or implicit support. . . . The test at this phase should also focus on the central cross-cultural emotional or symbolic issue through a custom-designed research methodology.[49]

Creative Decisions

Another decision facing the international advertiser is determining the appropriate advertising messages for each market. Creative strategy development for international advertising is basically similar in process and procedure to domestic advertising. Advertising and communications objectives should be formulated based on the marketing strategy and market conditions in foreign markets. Major selling ideas must be developed, and specific appeals and execution styles must be chosen.

An important factor that influences the development of creative strategy for international marketers is the issue of global versus localized advertising. As was noted earlier in the discussion of the two approaches, global advertising uses the same basic appeal and execution style, with perhaps minor variations, in all countries. If the

➤ *Exhibit 22–21* **Importance of purchase criteria in the United Kingdom, France, and Germany**

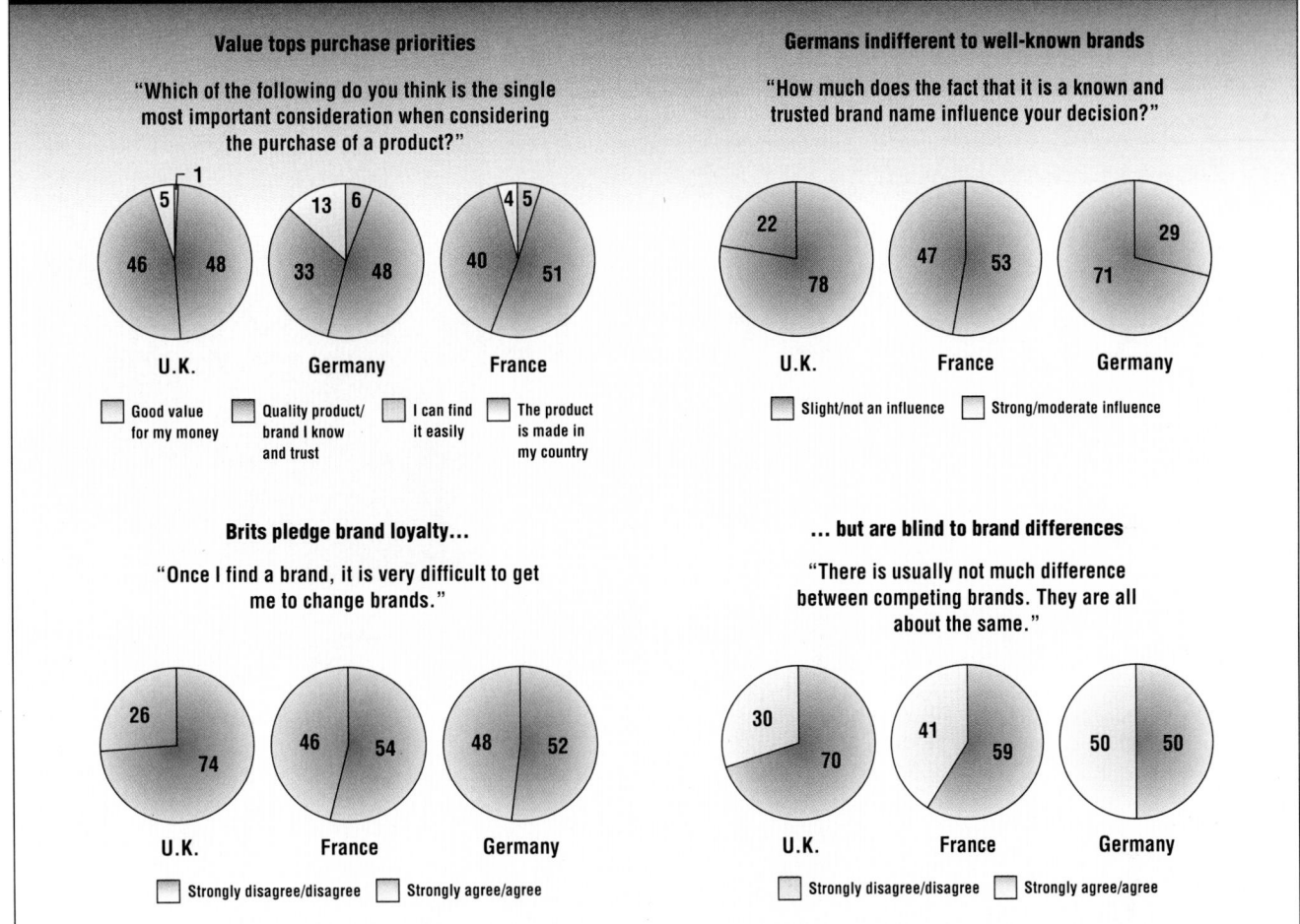

Value tops purchase priorities

"Which of the following do you think is the single most important consideration when considering the purchase of a product?"

U.K.   Germany   France

☐ Good value for my money   ☐ Quality product/ brand I know and trust   ☐ I can find it easily   ☐ The product is made in my country

Germans indifferent to well-known brands

"How much does the fact that it is a known and trusted brand name influence your decision?"

U.K.   France   Germany

☐ Slight/not an influence   ☐ Strong/moderate influence

Brits pledge brand loyalty...

"Once I find a brand, it is very difficult to get me to change brands."

U.K.   France   Germany

☐ Strongly disagree/disagree   ☐ Strongly agree/agree

... but are blind to brand differences

"There is usually not much difference between competing brands. They are all about the same."

U.K.   France   Germany

☐ Strongly disagree/disagree   ☐ Strongly agree/agree

standardized approach is taken, the challenge facing the creative team is to develop advertising that will transcend cultural differences and communicate effectively in every country.

When companies follow a **localized advertising strategy,** the creative team must determine what type of selling idea, ad appeal, and execution style will work in each market. A product may have to be positioned differently in each market depending on consumers' usage patterns and habits. For example, General Foods found that in France, people drink very little orange juice and almost none at breakfast. Thus, when the company decided to market its Tang instant breakfast drink in France, the agency developed ads positioning the brand as a refreshment for any time of day rather than as a substitute for orange juice, which was the approach used in the United States.[50]

Attention must also be given to what type of advertising appeal or execution style will be most effective in each market. Emotional appeals such as humor may work well in one country but not another because of differences in cultural backgrounds and consumer perceptions of what is or is not funny. While humorous appeals are common in the United States and Britain, they are not used often in Germany, where consumers tend to be more serious and do not respond favorably to humor in advertising.

Some countries such as France, Italy, and Brazil are more tolerant of and receptive to sexual appeal and nudity in advertising than are other societies. Grey Advertising found that an ad it developed for Camay soap in the United States, which featured

➤ *Exhibit 22–22*
Häagen-Dazs' sexy ads have worked well in Britain

It is the

intense

flavour of
the finest ingredients
combined with

fresh

cream that is
essentially Häagen-Dazs

Häagen-Dazs

FRESH CREAM ICE CREAM
Dedicated to Pleasure

a man touching a woman's skin while she bathed, would be a disaster in Japan. Even the idea of a man being in the bathroom with a female in Japan would be considered taboo.[51]

Marketers sometimes find they can change consumer purchasing patterns by taking a creative risk. For example, Häagen-Dazs broke through cultural barriers in Britain, where ice cream consumption is only a third of the level in the United States and consumers usually purchase low-grade and low-priced local brands. A sexy advertising campaign showing seminude couples feeding the ice cream to one another helped get British consumers to pay premium prices for Häagen-Dazs (Exhibit 22–22). The company also used an avant-garde billboard campaign in Japan showing a young couple kissing in public which is a near-taboo. The posters were so popular many were taken.[52]

Media Selection

One of the most difficult decision areas for the international advertiser is that of media strategy and selection. U.S. firms generally find major differences in the media outside the United States, and media conditions may vary considerably from one area to another, particularly in developing countries. Media planners face a number of problems in attempting to communicate advertising messages to consumers in foreign countries.

First, the types of media available in each country are different. Many homes in developing countries do not have television sets. And in some countries, television advertising is not accepted or the amount of commercial time is severely limited. For example, in Germany, TV restrictions include limiting advertising time to 20 minutes a day on each of the government-owned channels, restricting commercials to four five-minute breaks, and banning them on Sundays and holidays. Germany's two privately owned television stations, however, are permitted to devote up to 20 percent of airtime to commercials.

In the Netherlands, TV spots on the Dutch networks are limited to 5 percent of airtime and must be booked up to a year in advance. Programs also do not have fixed time slots for ads, making it impossible to plan commercial buys around desired programs. Some countries, such as Denmark, just began accepting television commercials in 1987 by allowing a daily five-minute block of advertising time on regional channels.[53]

The number of television sets in other parts of the world such as India and China is increasing tremendously. However, there is still controversy over television advertising in many countries. For example, in India, commercials are restricted to only 10 percent of programming time and must appear at the beginning or end of a program.[54]

The characteristics of media may differ from country to country in terms of their coverage, cost, quality of reproduction, restrictions, and the like. Another problem international advertisers face is obtaining reliable media information such as circulation figures, audience profiles, and costs. In some countries, media rates are negotiable and/or may fluctuate owing to unstable currencies and economic conditions. Thus, a number of factors and concerns face advertisers when putting together their international media plans and schedules.

The goal of international advertisers in choosing media is to select those vehicles that reach their target audience most effectively and efficiently. This means paying attention to the various media options regarding their ability to reach the appropriate people in each market and their costs. Media selection is often done on a localized basis, even when a centrally planned, globalized campaign is used. Many advertisers do this because they believe local agencies or media buyers have more knowledge of local media and better opportunities to negotiate rates, and it gives subsidiary operations more control and ability to adapt to media conditions and options in their market. Media planners have two options available—using national or local media or using international media.

Local media

Many advertisers choose local media of a country to reach its consumers. Print is the most used medium on a worldwide basis, since television commercial time is limited in many countries, as is the number of homes with TV sets. Many foreign countries not only have magazines that are circulated on a countrywide basis but also have national or regional newspapers as well. While newspapers are primarily a medium for local retail advertising in the United States, in many countries, they contain advertising directed to a national audience. Also, as in the United States, most countries have magazines appealing to special interests or activities and thus allow for targeting and selectivity in media selection.

As discussed earlier, restrictions and regulations have limited the development of TV as a dominant advertising medium in many countries. However, TV is a primary medium for obtaining nationwide coverage in most developed countries and is an important medium because of the tremendous creative opportunities it offers. Restrictions on television may be lessening in some countries, and time availability may increase. For example, in 1986, the French government awarded the first fully commercial TV channel license. The number of TV stations and television advertising in Italy exploded in the past decade since government restrictions against private broadcasting were lifted.[55] Advertising groups are using economic, legal, and political pressure to get more television commercial time from reluctant European governments. The increase in TV channels through direct broadcasting by satellite to many European households, which is discussed below, may hasten this process.[56]

In addition to print and television, many other local media are available to advertisers including radio, direct mail, billboards, cinema, and transit advertising. These media provide international advertisers with greater flexibility and the opportunity to reach specific market segments and local markets within a country. Most international advertisers rely heavily on national and local media in their media plans for foreign markets.

International media

The other way for the international advertiser to reach audiences in various countries is through the use of international media that have multimarket coverage. The primary focus of international media has traditionally been magazines and newspapers. A number of U.S.-based, consumer-oriented publications have international editions including *Time, Newsweek, Reader's Digest,* and *National Geographic* and the newspaper *USA Today.* Exhibit 22–23 shows the various countries where *Cosmopolitan* is published. U.S.-based business publications with foreign editions include *Business Week, Fortune, Harvard Business Review,* and *The Wall Street Journal.*

The international publications offer advertisers a way to reach large audiences on a regional or worldwide basis. Readers of these publications are usually upscale, high-income individuals who are desirable target markets for many products and services. There are, however, several problems with these international media that can limit their attractiveness to many advertisers. Their reach in any one foreign country may be low, particularly for specific segments of a market. Also, while the audiences of these publications are desirable to companies selling business or upscale consumer products and services, they do not cover the mass consumer markets or specialized market segments very well. Other U.S.-based publications in foreign markets offer advertisers ways of reaching specific market segments.

While print remains the dominant medium for international advertising, many companies are turning their attention to international commercial television. Package-goods companies in particular, such as Gillette, McDonald's, Pepsi, and Coca-Cola, view television advertising as the best way to reach mass markets and effectively communicate their advertising messages. Satellite technology has assisted and helped spread the development and growth of cable television in other countries as well as making global television networks a reality.

A number of satellite networks operating in Europe beam entertainment programming across several countries. For example, British Sky Broadcasting (BSkyB), which was formed by the merger of Sky Television and British Satellite Broadcasting, reaches 13 percent of all TV households in the United Kingdom and is expected to reach 36 percent by 1995.[57]

The main incentive to the growth of these satellite networks has been the severely limited program choices and advertising opportunities on government-controlled stations in most of Europe. However, many European countries are planning new channels as governments move to preserve cultural values and protect advertising revenues from going to foreign-based networks. The next major development in European broadcasting is **direct broadcast by satellite** (**DBS**) to homes and communities equipped with small, low-cost receiving dishes. The first DBS satellite was launched by West Germany in 1987, and Britain and Scandinavian countries are expected to have DBS satellites soon.

➤ *Exhibit 22–23*
Cosmopolitan is published in 28 countries

The World's Largest selling young woman's magazine

A Success in any Language

COSMOPOLITAN

Hearst Magazines International
959 8th Avenue, New York NY 10019 (212) 649 2631 FAX (212) 541 4212

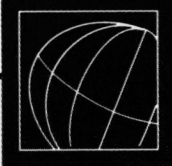

Global Perspective 22–3

Couponing around the World

Coupons have been a common part of the marketing scene in the United States for nearly a hundred years, but the last decade has seen a tremendous increase in couponing. The number of coupons distributed in the United States climbed from 96 billion in 1980 to 292 billion in 1991. Coupon redemption over this period has nearly doubled, going from 3.81 billion in 1980 to 7.46 billion in 1991. While the United States is the world's leading couponing market, several other countries are beginning to experience the same couponing growth that occurred in the United States during the 1980s.

NCH Promotional Services tracks coupon distribution and use in major world markets including the United States, Canada, and several European countries. In Canada, which is the second largest market in the world for couponing, distribution reached 25 billion in 1990, a 45 percent increase since 1989. Nearly 20 billion of these were store coupons distributed in retailer advertisements, while the remainder were manufacturer coupons. Coupon redemption in Canada is about 1 percent compared to 2.5 percent in the United States.

In the European Community, couponing is gaining in popularity as a marketing tool, although most European consumers trail those in the United States when it comes to coupon use. U.S. consumers redeemed 77 coupons per household in 1990 compared to 26 in Canada, 18 in Belgium, 17 in the United Kingdom, and 3 each in Italy and Spain. Europe's largest coupon market is in the United Kingdom, where more than 5 billion coupons were distributed in 1990 and redemption increased by 21 percent to 376 million. This was the largest percentage increase in coupon redemption of any country.

Couponing has not experienced as much growth in other parts of Europe, such as Spain or Italy. Coupon distribution has declined 36 percent in Spain over the past four years. The decline is due to the structure of the retail market, which depends on wholesalers as redemption middlemen. This leaves many openings for misredemption tactics. There have also been only modest increases in coupon distribution and redemption in Italy where the coupon market is dominated by a few multinational companies. Most coupons in Italy are distributed on or in packages or in stores.

France has only a small amount of couponing activity because the retailer market is highly concentrated and has a negative attitude toward coupons. Only 20 million coupons are redeemed each year in France, which has about the same popu-

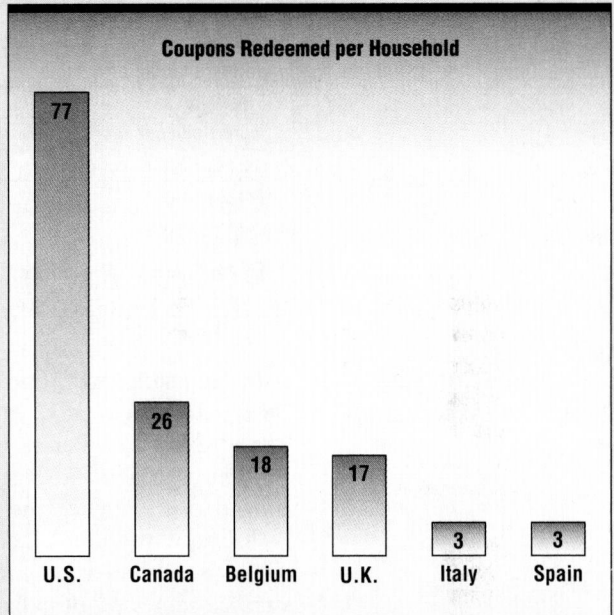

lation as the United Kingdom. In the Netherlands and Switzerland, major retailers refuse to accept coupons. Couponing has just become legal in Denmark, and manufacturers have not yet begun to use them. In Germany, couponing is not used much since the discount given on the coupon cannot be greater than 1 percent of the product's value.

Coupons first appeared in Japan in 1976, although many consumers have been reluctant to use them. In 1990, a ban on coupons in newspapers was lifted, and Japanese newspapers have started coupon advertising, with some running entire pages of ads with coupons. Free-standing inserts are also allowed although the number of FSIs that can be distributed is limited.

Source: *Coupon Distribution and Redemption Patterns 1991 International Edition* (Chicago: NCH Promotional Services, 1991). Betsy Spethman, ''Countries Crave Coupons,'' *Advertising Age*, July 15, 1991, p. 26; and David Kiburn, ''Japan's Coupon Move May Aid U.S. Marketers,'' *Advertising Age*, June 4, 1990, p. 30.

companies have found it difficult to do any promotions on a pan-European basis because sales promotion rules vary so much from one country to another. While the "1992" program may result in a more standardized legal environment in Europe, laws regarding sales promotion are still likely to vary. To deal with many of the problems and decision areas in the design of sales promotion programs for foreign markets, many companies use local agencies to develop them or turn to international sales promotion companies.

➤ *Exhibit 22–24*
Which European countries allow these promotions?

Promotion	U.K.	Spain	West Germany	France	Italy
In-pack premiums	●	●	●	▲	●
Multiple-purchase offers	●	●	▲	●	●
Extra product	●	●	▲	●	●
Free product	●	●	●	●	●
Mail-in offers	●	●	●	●	●
Purchase-with-purchase	●	●	●	●	●
Cross-promotions	●	●	●	●	●
Contests	●	●	▲	●	●
Self-liquidating premiums	●	●	●	●	●
Sweepstakes	▲	▲	●	▲	▲
Money-off coupons	●	●	●	●	▲
Next-purchase coupons	●	●	●	●	▲
Cash rebates	●	●	▲	●	●
In-store demos	●	●	●	●	●

● Permitted   ● Not permitted   ▲ May be permitted

Management of Sales Promotion in Foreign Markets

Although sales promotion programs of multinational companies have traditionally been managed locally, this is changing somewhat as marketers create global brands. Many global marketers recognize the importance of giving local managers the autonomy to design and execute their own sales promotion programs. However, how local promotions influence and contribute to global brand equity must also be considered.

Kashani and Quelch developed a framework for analyzing the role of centralized or headquarters versus local management in sales promotion decisions based on various stages of globalization (Exhibit 22–25). This model suggests headquarters' influence will be the greatest for global brands and at a minimum for local brands since they do not require international coordination. Global brands require a high degree of uniformity in marketing communications and thus the promotional program should be determined at the headquarters level. Decisions regarding overall promotional strategy including international communication objectives, positioning, allocation of the communications budget to sales promotion versus advertising, and weight of consumer versus trade promotions would be made at the headquarters level.[63]

Kashani and Quelch note that while the promotional strategy for global brands is determined by global product managers at headquarters, implementation of the programs should be left to local management. They also note it is important to make the promotional strategy broad enough to allow for differences that may be encountered during implementation in diverse local markets. Headquarters is also responsible for encouraging the cross-fertilization of ideas and practices among local managers and facilitating the transfer of information.

Regional brands often usually do not require the same level of standardization as global brands, and the promotional strategy can be developed by regional offices and carried out at the local level. However, regional promotions should be designed to avoid contradictory brand communications and promotional activities that might interfere or upset local activities in nearby markets. The role of national-level brand managers is defined as *adoption* and *adaptation*. They determine what promotional ideas will be adopted from the region and adapt them to local conditions.

For local brands, central coordination is needed, and decisions regarding promotional strategy, program design, and execution are left to local managers. Of course, local managers may benefit from information about the types of promotions used in other local markets and their effectiveness.

➤ *Exhibit 22–25*
Influence and roles in international sales promotion

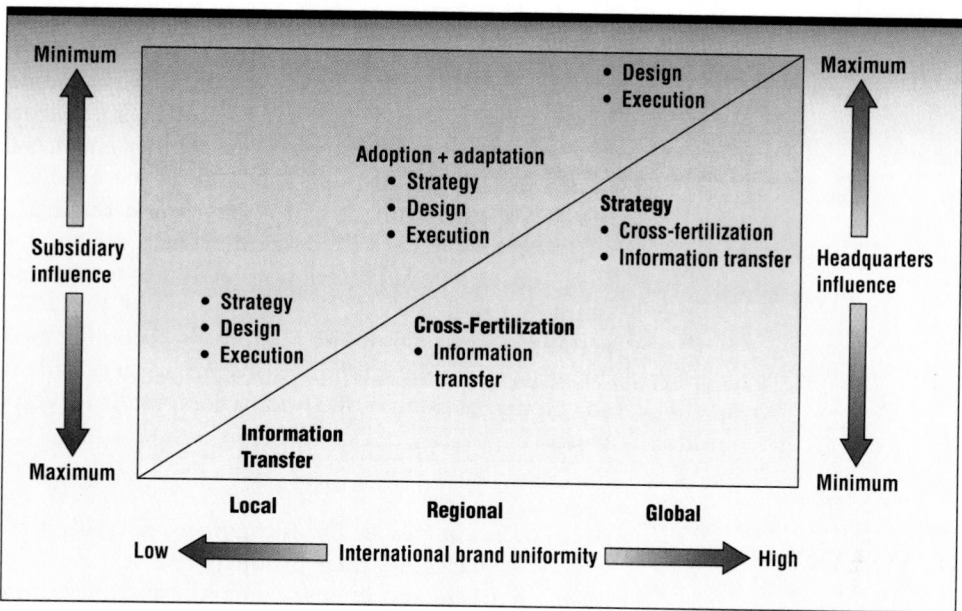

Personal Selling

Personal selling is an important promotional tool for many companies engaged in international marketing. Companies selling industrial and high-technology products generally rely heavily on personal selling as the primary method for communicating with their customers. The same emphasis on personal selling occurs when these companies market their products internationally. Consumer products firms may also use personal selling to call on distributors, wholesalers, or major retailing operations in foreign markets. Because of low wages in many developing countries, some companies hire large sales staffs to perform missionary activities and support selling and advertising efforts.

Because it involves personal contact and communication, personal selling is generally even more culture bound than advertising. Thus, most companies use sales representatives from the host country to staff their sales force, and personal selling activities and sales programs are adapted to each market. Management of the sales force is usually decentralized to the local subsidiaries; however, the international marketer sets the general sales policy and offers advice to foreign managers on the role personal selling should play in their market, the development of the sales program, and various aspects of sales management.

Public Relations

Many companies involved in international marketing are recognizing the importance of using public relations to support and enhance their marketing and advertising efforts.[64] Public relations activities are needed to deal with local governments, media, trade associations, and the general public, as all these groups may feel threatened by the presence of a foreign multinational. The job of public relations agencies in foreign markets is not only to help the company sell its products or services but also to present the firm as a "good corporate citizen" involved with and concerned about the future of the country.

Companies generally must have a favorable reputation and image if they are to be successful in foreign markets. Those with negative reputations or images may face pressure from the media and local governments or ultimately even boycotts by consumers. For example, Nestlé has been a target of consumer boycotts in several countries, including the United States, for its aggressive marketing of infant formula to mothers in Third World countries. To deal with this problem, the company stopped the advertising of the product and the distribution of free samples and set up a commission to monitor compliance.[65]

Often, public relations efforts are needed to deal with specific problems a company faces in international markets. For example, the G. D. Searle Company had problems getting its NutraSweet low-calorie sweetener into some markets because of strong sugar lobbies in Australia, Canada, and Europe fighting to retain sugar as the only sweetener in beverages. These lobbies encouraged the foreign press to pick up on some of the unfavorable news about the product that was published in the U.S. media. To deal with this problem, Searle retained Burson-Marsteller, the second largest PR company in the world, to help design factual ads about the product and to conduct other public relations activities to counter the problems and get the facts out about it.

Like advertising, public relations is becoming more of a global activity, and, like ad agencies, public relations firms are merging with and/or acquiring overseas offices so companies can use one firm to communicate with appropriate parties all over the world.

SUMMARY

Many U.S. companies are recognizing not only the opportunities but also the necessity of marketing their products and services internationally because of the saturated markets and intense competition from both domestic and foreign competitors. Advertising and promotion are important parts of the international marketing program of a multinational corporation. Advertising is generally the most cost-effective way of communicating with buyers and creating a market in other countries.

Companies engaging in international marketing must carefully analyze the major environmental forces in each market in which they compete, including economic, demographic, cultural, and political/legal factors. These factors are important not only in assessing the potential of each country as a market but also in designing and implementing advertising and promotional programs.

A company can take two basic approaches toward international marketing—a global marketing strategy or a localized approach. In recent years, much attention has been focused on global marketing whereby a standard marketing program is used in all markets. Global advertising falls under this strategy, as the same basic advertising approach is used in all markets. Opponents of the standardized or global approach argue that differences in culture, market, and economic conditions, and consumer needs and wants make it impractical to develop a universal approach to marketing and advertising. Many companies use an in-between approach by standardizing their basic marketing strategy but localizing advertising messages to fit each market.

There are a number of important decision areas in the development of advertising and promotional programs for international markets. These include organization, agency selection, advertising research, creative strategy and execution, and media strategy and selection. Companies can use either a centralized or a decentralized organizational structure for their international advertising operations or a combination of the two. Many American companies use a U.S.-based international agency to handle their international advertising or use a domestic agency that has affiliates in other countries. A third alternative is to select a local agency for each market.

In addition to advertising, sales promotion, personal selling, and public relations are also part of the promotional mix of international marketers. Sales promotion programs usually must be adapted to local markets and various factors have to be taken into consideration, including stage of market development, market maturity, consumer perceptions of promotional tools, trade structure, and legal restrictions and regulations. Personal selling may be the most important element of some companies' international marketing programs. However, personal selling is often more culture bound than advertising. Public relations programs are also important to international marketers, as they must develop and maintain favorable relationships with governments, media, and the citizens of foreign countries.

KEY TERMS

balance-of-trade-deficit
economic infrastructure
global marketing
global advertising
pattern advertising

centralized organizational
    structure
decentralized
    organizational structure

localized advertising
    strategy
direct broadcasting by
    satellite (DBS)

**DISCUSSION
QUESTIONS**

1. Why are international markets becoming so important to U.S. companies? Discuss the role of advertising in a firm's international marketing program.

2. Choose two foreign countries and discuss the problems a U.S. consumer packaged goods company might encounter in developing an advertising and promotion program in these markets.

3. What various environmental factors must be considered in developing an international marketing program? Discuss how these environmental forces would influence advertising and promotion.

4. Professor Theodore Levitt argues that the worldwide marketplace is becoming homogenized and the basic needs, wants, and expectations of consumers transcend geographic, national, and cultural boundaries. Do you agree with the position taken by Levitt? Why or why not?

5. Discuss the pros and cons of global advertising? What types of products and services lend themselves to global advertising?

6. What are the three ways a company can organize for international advertising and promotion?

7. What are the three basic alternatives a company has in selecting an agency to handle its international advertising? Under what conditions or type of situation might each alternative be used?

8. Discuss the various factors that must be taken into consideration in developing a sales promotion program in foreign markets.

9. How would the planning and implementation of a sales promotion program differ for global brands versus regional or local brands?

10. Discuss the role of personal selling and publicity/public relations in the marketing communication program of international marketers.

chapter 23

Regulation of Advertising and Promotion

chapter objectives

➤ To examine how advertising is regulated including the role and function of various regulatory agencies.

➤ To examine how self-regulation of advertising occurs and to evaluate this regulatory mechanism.

➤ To examine how advertising is regulated by various federal and state governmental agencies.

➤ To examine the operation, procedures, and programs of the Federal Trade Commission in regulating advertising.

➤ To examine rules and regulations that affect sales promotion and direct marketing.

Volvo's Monster Truck Ad Controversy

Over the past 25 years, Swedish automaker Volvo has spent millions of dollars advertising the safety and durability of its cars to U.S. consumers, often going to great lengths to demonstrate how well its cars are built. One of its ads showed a Volvo with six other Volvos stacked on top of it, while another showed a six-ton truck being lowered onto the roof of a Volvo. In both of these ads, the Volvo did not sag under the weight and pressure. The advertising theme used by Volvo for many years was "A car you can believe in." However, these ads, along with a recent commercial the company ran, have given some people reason to question whether Volvo has been running advertising they could believe in.

In the ads showing the Volvo holding up the other cars and the heavy-duty truck, the car was propped up with jacks placed between the car's tires. The jacks were hidden by shadows and thus invisible to viewers. Volvo defended the ads, stating they were intended to show the strength of Volvo's roofs and bodies, which were not reinforced, rather than to claim the tires and suspension of a Volvo could support the heavy load.

While the roofs of the Volvos used in these ads were not reinforced, this was not the case in another commercial. In October 1990, Volvo aired its infamous "Bearfoot monster truck ad" showing a pickup truck with huge, oversized tires driving over the top of a row of cars,

crushing the roofs of all of them except the Volvo. The commercial was produced in Texas where a local resident who had been invited to watch the filming noticed the cars used in the ad had been tampered with. He contacted the Texas Attorney General's Office, which investigated and found the ad was deceptive.

The roof of the Volvo used in the ad was reinforced with steel and plywood while the rival vehicles had their roof supports weakened. Also, the ad represented the monster truck car-crushing exhibition as a real event rather than acknowledging it was a staged dramatization.

The monster truck ad created a major controversy for both Volvo and its advertising agency, Scali, McCabe, Sloves, which had handled the automaker's advertising for 23 years. The incident received a tremendous amount of media coverage. Some journalists called it the worst product-demonstration rigging to hit the advertising industry in decades, and others noted it damaged the credibility of the entire advertising industry. In November 1990, the agency resigned the $40 million account, noting it had the ultimate responsibility for the rigged commercial. Volvo also ran full-page ads in national newspapers apologizing for the commercial.

In addition to Volvo losing credibility and the agency losing its largest account, the misleading commercial also

(continued)

cost the two parties money. In August 1991, Volvo and Scali, McCabe, Sloves each agreed to pay a $150,000 penalty as part of a settlement with the Federal Trade Commission. This marked the first time the FTC had required an advertising agency, not just an advertiser, to pay for a deceptive ad. Volvo was also required to run ads in Texas newspapers explaining the settlement and submit documentation of four older Volvo ads that made structural superiority claims, including the two stacking ads discussed above. The FTC reviewed these ads and concluded they were not deceptive since they made no claims about the strength of the tires or suspension of the cars.

Volvo did not admit to any guilt in its settlement with the FTC and has stated it was not aware of the changes made to the cars used in the monster truck commercial. Volvo has hired a new agency, and its advertising still stresses durability and safety. However, it is unlikely we will be seeing any monster trucks rolling over or stacked on top of Volvos in future commercials.

Source: Krystal Miller and Jacqueline Mitchell, "Car Makers Test Gray Areas of Truth in Advertising," The Wall Street Journal, November 19, 1990, pp. B1,5; Bruce Horowitz, "Volvo, Agency Fined $150,000 Each for TV Ad," Los Angeles Times, August 22, 1991, p. D2; Steven W. Colford and Raymond Serafin, "Scali Pays for Volvo Ad: FTC," Advertising Age, August 26, 1991, p. 4; and Raymond Serafin and Jennifer Lawrence, "Four More Volvo Ads Scrutinized," Advertising Age, November 26, 1990, p. 4.

Suppose you are the advertising manager for a consumer products company and have just reviewed a new commercial your advertising agency has created. You are very excited about the ad, as it presents some new claims regarding the superiority of your brand that should help differentiate it from the competition. However, before you can consider approving the commercial for use, you must have answers to a number of questions such as: Are the claims verifiable? If research was done, were proper procedures used in collecting the data and analyzing and presenting the findings? Do we have the proper research results to support our claims? Did we have the right people in the study and/or were there any conditions that might have biased the results? Are the claims made in the ad consistent with the research data?

Before approving the commercial, you decide to have it reviewed by the company's legal department and also ask your agency to have its attorneys examine it. Assuming the internal and agency reviews are acceptable, the ad will then be sent to the major networks, which will have their censors examine it. If they have any problems with the commercial, they may ask for more information or send it back for modification. None of the networks will run the commercial until it has received approval from its Standards and Practices Department.

Once the ad is approved and aired, it is subject to scrutiny from a number of state and federal regulatory agencies, such as the state attorney general's office and the Federal Trade Commission. Individual consumers or competitors who find the ad misleading or have some other concern may file a complaint with the National Advertising Division of the Council of Better Business Bureaus. You must also consider that disparaged competitors may sue you if they feel your ad has distorted the facts and misleads consumers. If you lose the litigation, your company may have to retract the claims and pay the competitor for damages, which may run into millions of dollars.

After considering all these regulatory issues, you must ask yourself if the new ad can meet all these challenges and whether it is worth the risk. Maybe you ought just to continue with the old approach that made no specific claims and simply said your brand was great.

As can be seen from the two scenarios presented above, regulatory concerns can play a major role in the advertising decision-making process. Advertisers operate in a complex environment of local, state, and federal rules and regulations. Additionally, a number of advertising and business-sponsored associations, consumer groups and organizations, and the media attempt to promote honest, truthful, and tasteful advertising through their own self-regulatory programs and guidelines. The legal and regulatory aspects of advertising are very complex. A number of parties are concerned over the nature and content of advertising and its potential to offend, exploit, mislead, and/or deceive consumers. Numerous guidelines, rules, regulations, and laws constrain and restrict advertising.

In most situations, these rules and regulations primarily influence individual advertisers and their messages, but there are situations where advertising for an entire industry can be affected. For example, cigarette advertising was banned from the broadcast media in 1970, and currently there is strong sentiment for a total ban on the advertising of tobacco products.[1] Legislation is also being considered that would further restrict the advertising of alcoholic beverages, including beer and wine.[2]

As was noted above, regulation and control over various aspects of advertising come from self-regulation by various groups within the advertising industry and from external state and federal regulatory agencies such as the Federal Trade Commission (FTC), the Federal Communications Commission (FCC), the Food and Drug Administration (FDA), and the U.S. Post Office. In recent years, attorneys general in a number of states have become more active in advertising regulation also. In the Volvo case discussed in the chapter opening, a state attorney general's office led the investigation of the deceptive advertising claim. While only the governmental agencies (federal, state, and local) have the force of law, most advertisers also abide by the guidelines and decisions of internal regulatory bodies. In fact, internal regulation from various groups such as the media or National Advertising Review Board probably has more influence on the day-to-day operations and decision making of advertisers and agencies than do governmental rules and regulations.

All involved in the advertising decision-making process, both on the client and agency side, must be aware of various bodies that regulate advertising and promotion including the general intent of their regulatory efforts, how they operate, and how they influence and affect advertising and other promotional mix elements. In this chapter, we examine the major sources of advertising regulation including efforts by the industry at voluntary, self-regulation and external regulation by governmental agencies. We also examine some regulations marketers must consider in other areas such as sales promotion and direct marketing.

Self-Regulation

For many years, the advertising industry has practiced and promoted the use of voluntary **self-regulation** to regulate and control advertising. Most advertisers and their respective agencies, as well as the media, recognize the importance of maintaining consumer trust and confidence and for advertising to be perceived as truthful and nonoffensive. Self-regulation has also been viewed by advertisers as a way to limit interference with and control over advertising by the government, as this may result in more stringent and troublesome regulations. Self-regulation and control of advertising emanate from all segments of the advertising industry including individual advertisers and their agencies, business and advertising associations, and the media.

Self-Regulation by Advertisers and Agencies

The self-regulatory process actually begins with the interaction of the client and the agency when creative ideas are generated and submitted for consideration. Most companies have specific guidelines, standards, and policies to which advertising for their products or service must adhere. Advertisers recognize that their ads are a reflection of the company, and thus they carefully scrutinize all messages to ensure they are consistent with the image the firm wishes to project. Companies also carefully review their ads to be sure any claims they make are reasonable and verifiable and do not mislead or deceive consumers. Ads are usually examined by corporate attorneys to avoid any potential legal problems, which not only could be time-consuming and expensive to the firm but also could result in negative publicity and embarrassment.

Internal control and regulation also come from the advertising agency, as most agencies have standards regarding the type of advertising they either want or are willing to produce. Most reputable agencies attempt to avoid ads that might offend consumers or that they believe may be misleading. Agencies are responsible for verifying all product claims made by the advertiser and ensuring adequate documentation or

substantiation is available. As such, they can be held legally responsible for fraudulent or deceptive claims and in some cases have been fined when their clients have been found guilty of engaging in deceptive advertising.

Many agencies have a creative review board or panel composed of experienced personnel who examine ads for content and execution as well as their potential to be perceived as offensive, misleading, and/or deceptive. Additionally, most agencies either employ or retain lawyers who also review the ads and determine whether they might pose any potential legal problems for the agency and the client. Exhibit 23–1 shows an ad for a legal firm specializing in advertising law.

Self-Regulation by Trade Associations

While many advertisers and their agencies have internal policies and standards they follow in developing their advertising, many industries have also developed self-regulatory programs. This is particularly true in industries where advertising is prone to controversy such as liquor and alcoholic beverages, drugs, and various products marketed to children. These trade and industry associations have developed their own advertising guidelines or codes that member companies are expected to abide by. For example, the Wine Institute (Exhibit 23–2), the U.S. Brewers Association, and the Distilled Spirits Council of the United States Inc. all have guidelines that member companies are supposed to follow in advertising alcoholic beverages. Other industry trade associations with advertising guidelines and programs include the Toy Manufacturers Association, Motion Picture Association of America, the Pharmaceutical Manufacturers Association, and the Proprietary Association (the trade association for nonprescription drug makers), among others.[3] Ethical Perspective 23–1, page 780, discusses how the Distilled Spirits Council recently revised its Code of Good Practice to help liquor manufacturers remain competitive in a declining market.

Many professions also maintain advertising guidelines through local, state, and national organizations. Professional associations such as the American Medical Association and the American Bar Association for years restricted advertising by their members on the basis that promotional activities such as advertising would lower the

➤ *Exhibit 23–2* **Wine Institute Code of Advertising Standards**

GUIDELINES. These guidelines shall apply only to voluntary subscribers of this Code of Advertising Standards.

1. Wine and wine cooler advertising should encourage the proper use of wine. Therefore subscribers to this code shall not depict or describe in their advertising:
   a. The consumption of wine or wine coolers for the effects their alcoholic content may produce.
   b. Direct or indirect reference to alcohol content or extra strength, except as otherwise required by law or regulation.
   c. Excessive drinking or persons who appear to have lost control or to be inappropriately uninhibited.
   d. Any suggestion that excessive drinking or loss of control is amusing or a proper subject for amusement.
   e. Any persons engaged in activities not normally associated with the moderate use of wine or wine coolers and a responsible life style. Association of wine use in conjunction with feats of daring or activities requiring unusual skill is specifically prohibited.
   f. Wine or wine coolers in quantities inappropriate to the situation or inappropriate for moderate and responsible use.
   g. The image of wine and wine coolers in advertising and promotion shall be adult-oriented and socially responsible. Comparative or competitor-derogatory advertising is inappropriate.
2. Advertising of wine has traditionally depicted wholesome persons enjoying their lives and illustrating the role of wine in a mature life style. Any attempt to suggest that wine directly contributes to success or achievement is unacceptable. Therefore, the following restrictions shall apply to subscribers of this code:
   a. Wine and wine coolers shall not be presented as being essential to personal performance, social attainment, achievement, success or wealth.
   b. The use of wine and wine coolers shall not be directly associated with social, physical or personal problem solving.
   c. Wine and wine coolers shall not be presented as vital to social acceptability and popularity.
   d. It shall not be suggested that wine or wine coolers are crucial for successful entertaining.
3. Any advertisement which has particular appeal to persons below the legal drinking age is unacceptable. Therefore, wine and wine cooler advertising by code subscribers shall not:
   a. Show models and personalities in advertisements who are under the legal drinking age. Models should appear to be 25 years of age or older.
   b. Use music, language, gestures or cartoon characters specifically associated with or directed toward those below the legal drinking age.
   c. Appear in children or juvenile magazines, newspapers, television programs, radio programs or other media specifically oriented to persons below the legal drinking age.
   d. Be presented as being related to the attainment of adulthood or associated with "rites of passage" to adulthood.
   e. Suggest that wine or a wine cooler product resembles or is similar to another type of beverage or product (milk, soda, candy) having particular appeal to persons below the legal drinking age.
   f. Use current or traditional heroes of the young such as those engaged in pastimes and occupations having a particular appeal to persons below the legal drinking age.
   g. Use amateur or professional sports celebrities, past or present.
4. Code subscribers shall not show motor vehicles in such a way as to suggest that they are to be operated in conjunction with wine or wine cooler use.
   Advertising should in no way suggest that wine or wine coolers be used in connection with driving motorized vehicles such as automobiles, motorcycles, boats, snowmobiles, or airplanes.
5. Wine and wine cooler advertising shall not appear in or directly adjacent to television or radio programs or print media which dramatize or glamorize over-consumption or inappropriate use of alcoholic beverages.
6. Wine and wine cooler advertising by code subscribers shall make no reference to wine's medicinal or caloric values.
7. Wine and wine cooler advertising by code subscribers shall not degrade the image or status of any ethnic, minority or other group.
8. Wine and wine cooler advertising shall not be directed to underage drinkers or pregnant women. Wine and wine cooler advertising shall not portray excessive drinking.
9. Wine and wine cooler advertising by code subscribers shall not exploit the human form, feature provocative or enticing poses, nor be demeaning to any individual.
10. A distinguishing and unique feature of wine is that it is traditionally served with meals or immediately before or following a meal.

Therefore, when subscribers to this code use wine advertising which visually depicts a scene or setting where wine is to be served, such advertising shall include foods and show that they are available and are being used or are intended to be used.

This guideline shall not apply to the depiction of a bottle of wine, vineyard, label, professional tasting etc. where emphasis is on the product.

All advertising—including, but not limited to direct mail, point-of-sale, outdoor, displays, radio, television and print media—should adhere to both the letter and the spirit of the above code.

status of the professional in the eyes of the public and would lead to unethical and fraudulent claims. However, professional codes that restrict advertising have been the target of attack from governmental regulatory agencies as well as various consumer groups that argue the public has a right to be informed about the services provided by the professional and his or her qualifications and background. They also argue that advertising by professionals will lead to improvements in professional services, as consumers become better informed and are better able to shop around for these services.[4]

In 1977, the Supreme Court held that state bar associations' restrictions on advertising are unconstitutional and that attorneys have First Amendment freedom

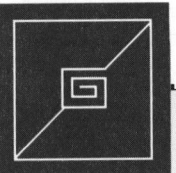

Ethical Perspective 23–1

A Change in Advertising Codes Creates a Controversy

Although no specific law prohibits advertising of hard liquor on radio or television, ads for spirit products are rarely seen or heard over the airways. Ads for liquor have been effectively banned for over five decades as a result of a code provision of the National Association of Broadcasters and by agreements of liquor manufacturers and their self-governing body, the Distilled Spirits Council, not to broadcast advertising for spirits of any kind. However, in November 1987, members of the Distilled Spirits Council revised their "Code of Good Practice," with one of the key changes being a decision by the industry to permit television advertising for "spirits coolers" that contain no more than 7 percent alcohol by volume. Spirit coolers have the same alcohol content as a wine cooler but are made from rum, a distilled spirit, rather than wine. The council also amended its code to allow spirits ads on closed-circuit TV in hotels and restaurants and on airline movie screens.

One of the reasons for the decision by the council was to help manufacturers of hard liquor remain competitive with other alcoholic beverages. Sales of distilled spirits have been declining over the past five years and television advertising is viewed as a way of reversing the sales slide. The council defended its decision by arguing that there is no difference between a malt-based cooler, a wine-based cooler, and a liquor-based cooler and this is an area where distilled spirits have a right to be competitive.

Much of the controversy over the advertising of spirit coolers has involved Bacardi Breezer, a rum-spiked cooler Bacardi Imports Inc. began marketing in 1988. The controversy stems in large part from a tag line in the commercial that says "Bacardi Light Rum Makes the Difference," leading critics to argue that these are as much rum ads as Breezer ads. Bacardi defends the ads and denies that they push rum, arguing that the references to rum are a simple case of line extension. Bacardi also argues that the Breezers have about the same alcohol content as beer and considerably less than most wines, both of which are advertised heavily on television. The company has supplied documentation of the product's alcohol content to the television networks as well as independent and local stations.

Bacardi's arguments regarding the alcohol content of its new drink have not convinced the policymakers at the three major networks as they continue to refuse to accept commercials for any drink containing distilled spirits. The director of broadcast standards for ABC noted, "If we're not responsible self-regulators, the government will step in," whereas another network executive noted that any erosion in current standards could lead to a backlash that would result in a ban of alcoholic beverage advertising on television. The vice president of program practices at NBC has argued that "our viewers make a distinction between spirit-based drinks on one hand, and brewed or fermented drinks, on the other."

Bacardi has skirted the problem of the networks' refusal to run its commercial by advertising Bacardi Breezers on independent stations and the local spot market where station owners make their own decisions concerning what ads to air. This media strategy has proven successful as the product became the number 3 liquor brand in its first year in national distribution with sales of more than 5 million cases.

Consumer health groups are very upset over the incursion of liquor marketers into television advertising in any form. The National Council on Alcoholism has expressed concern over the precedents being set by the Bacardi Breezer ads as well as the acceptance of spirit ads for hotels and airlines. The Center for Science in the Public Interest has called the acceptance of spirit ads "backdoor advertising" and argues that it could lead to the advertising of other forms of distilled spirits on television.

Other liquor companies such as Brown Forman Corp. are test marketing spirit coolers but have no plans to advertise them on TV. However, as distilled spirits sales continue to decline, other liquor marketers may be tempted to advertise these products on television to compete with beer and wine. Of course, it is likely that they will face considerable controversy if they do so.

Source: Bruce Horowitz, "Liquor Industry Plan for 'Spirits Coolers' Ads on TV Gets Icy Reception," *Los Angeles Times,* April 5, 1988, p. 10; Ron Alsop, "Despite Ban, Liquor Marketers Finding New Ways to Get Products on Television," *The Wall Street Journal,* March 14, 1988, p. 27; John B. Hinge and Kathleen Deveny, "Bacardi's TV Ads for Rum-Laced Cooler Are under Fire," *The Wall Street Journal,* July 22, 1991, pp. B1,3.

of speech rights to advertise.[5] Following this ruling, many restrictions on advertising were removed by a number of professional associations, and advertising by lawyers and other professionals has become common[6] (Exhibit 23–3). In 1982, the Supreme Court upheld an order by the FTC permitting advertising by dentists and physicians, which has resulted in ads by medical and dental organizations as well as by individual practitioners.[7]

Research has shown that consumers generally favor increased use of professional advertising. However, the professionals continue to have reservations about its use, as they are concerned advertising will have a negative impact on their image, credibility, and dignity and see benefits to consumers as unlikely.[8] Advertising by professionals is likely to gain in popularity, particularly by individuals entering the profession.

➤ *Exhibit 23–3*   **Advertising by lawyers has become common as a result of a 1977 Supreme Court ruling**

Man:
We were being strangled by our debts. We couldn't sleep, our work suffered. . . We'd heard about bankruptcy, but didn't know much about it.

Lawyer:
By the time the Brill's came to Jacoby & Meyers, they were being harrassed by their creditors, their wages were attached and their home was in foreclosure. We stopped all that.

Man:
We figured, our creditors were using lawyers to protect their rights. Why shouldn't we?

Lawyer: The Brill's just needed a chance to get a fresh start.

Jacoby & Meyers
   When it's time to call a lawyer about a bankruptcy.

Associations such as the American Bar Association and the American Medical Association have developed guidelines for advertising by their members to help maintain standards and guard against misleading, deceptive, or offensive ads.

While industry associations' guidelines are meant to show that member firms and individuals are concerned with the impact and consequences of their advertising, their effectiveness is limited to the ability of the association or profession to enforce the code or restrictions. Associations have no legal basis for enforcing these guidelines and must usually rely on peer pressure from members or other nonbinding sanctions to get advertisers to comply with these standards.

Self-Regulation by Businesses

A number of self-regulatory mechanisms have been established by the business community in an effort to control advertising practices. The largest and best known of these is through the **Better Business Bureau** (BBB). The BBB is not limited to one particular industry but rather promotes fair advertising and selling practices in all industries. Established in 1916 to handle consumer complaints about local business practices and particularly advertising, local BBBs are located in principal cities throughout the United States, supported entirely by dues of the more than 100,000 member firms.

The local BBBs receive and investigate complaints from consumers and other companies regarding the advertising and selling tactics of businesses in their area. Each local office has its own individual operating procedures for handling these complaints; however, the general procedure is to contact the violator and, if the complaint proves true, to request that the practice be stopped or changed. If the violator does not respond, negative publicity may be used against them or the case may be referred to appropriate governmental agencies for further action.

While the BBBs provide effective control over advertising practices at the local level, the parent organization of the local offices, the **Council of Better Business Bureaus,** plays a major role in monitoring and control of advertising at a national level. The council often assists new industries in the development of codes and standards for ethical and responsible advertising practices and also provides ongoing information concerning advertising regulations and legal rulings to advertisers, agencies, and the media. The council also plays an important self-regulatory role through its National Advertising Division (NAD) and Children's Advertising Unit. The NAD works closely with the **National Advertising Review Board** (NARB) to sustain truth, accuracy, and decency in national advertising. The NAD/NARB has become the advertising industry's primary self-regulatory mechanism and, as such, warrants additional discussion.

➤ *Exhibit 23–4*
Sources of NAD cases and decisions, 1991

Sources	Number	Percent	Decisions	Number	Percent
NAD monitoring	12	14	Substantiated	16	18
Competitors' challenges	63	71	Modified/discontinued	66	75
Local BBBs	2	2	Referred to NARB	4	5
Consumer complaints	5	6	Referred to government	2	2
Other	6	7		88	100%
	88	100%			

NAD/NARB

In 1971, four associations—the American Advertising Federation (AAF), the American Association of Advertising Agencies (AAAA), the Association of National Advertisers (ANA), and the Council of Better Business Bureaus—joined forces to establish the **National Advertising Review Council** (NARC). The NARC was established to sustain high standards of truth, accuracy, morality, and social responsibility in national advertising. The council has two operating arms: the National Advertising Division of the Council of Better Business Bureaus and the National Advertising Review Board. The NAD/NARB constitutes the advertising industry's most effective self-regulatory mechanism.

The NAD maintains an advertising monitoring program that is the source of many of the cases it reviews along with complaints received from consumers and consumer groups, local BBBs, and competitors' challenges (Exhibit 23–4). The NAD acts as the investigative arm of the NARC and, after initiating or receiving a complaint, determines the issue, collects and evaluates data, and makes the initial decision on whether the advertiser's claims are substantiated. The NAD may ask the advertiser to supply appropriate substantiation for the claim in question. If this is done, the case is dismissed. If the NAD does not find the substantiation to be satisfactory, it negotiates with the advertiser to secure modification or permanent discontinuance of the advertising. For example, Kellogg's agreed to modify advertising for its Special K cereal when the NAD questioned the claim that Special K's "200-calorie breakfast helps you keep the muscle while you lose the fat." Kellogg substantiated the claim on the basis that Special K contains the highest protein of all breakfast cereal. However, the NAD questioned whether it was appropriate for Kellogg to direct the claim to quick weight-loss dieters who might benefit more from supplementary protein. Kellogg agreed to change subsequent advertising to state that Special K contributes to a nutritionally balanced diet and exercise program.[9]

If the NAD and the advertiser fail to resolve the controversy, an appeal can be made by either party for a review by a five-person panel from the National Advertising Review Board. The NARB is composed of 50 executives including 30 national advertisers, 10 advertising agency representatives, and 10 representatives from the public sector. If the NARB panel agrees with the NAD and rules against the advertiser, the advertiser must discontinue the advertising in accordance with the panel decision. If the advertiser refuses to comply, the NARB refers the matter to the appropriate government agency and indicates the fact in its public record. Exhibit 23–5 shows a flowchart of the steps in the NAD/NARB review process.

Although the NARB has no power to order an advertiser to stop running an ad or no sanctions it can impose, advertisers who participate in the full process of an NAD investigation and NARB appeal rarely refuse to abide by the panel's decision.[10] Most cases do not even make it to the NARB panel. For example, in 1991, of the 88 NAD investigations, 16 ad claims were substantiated, 66 were modified or discontinued, 4 were referred to the NARB for resolution, and 2 to the government (Exhibit 23–4).

The NAD/NARB is a valuable and effective self-regulatory body. Cases brought to the NAD/NARB are handled at a fraction of the cost (and there is much less publicity) than if they were processed through a governmental agency such as the FTC. The system also works because judgments are made by the advertiser's peers,

➤ *Exhibit 23–5*   **National Advertising Division resolution process**

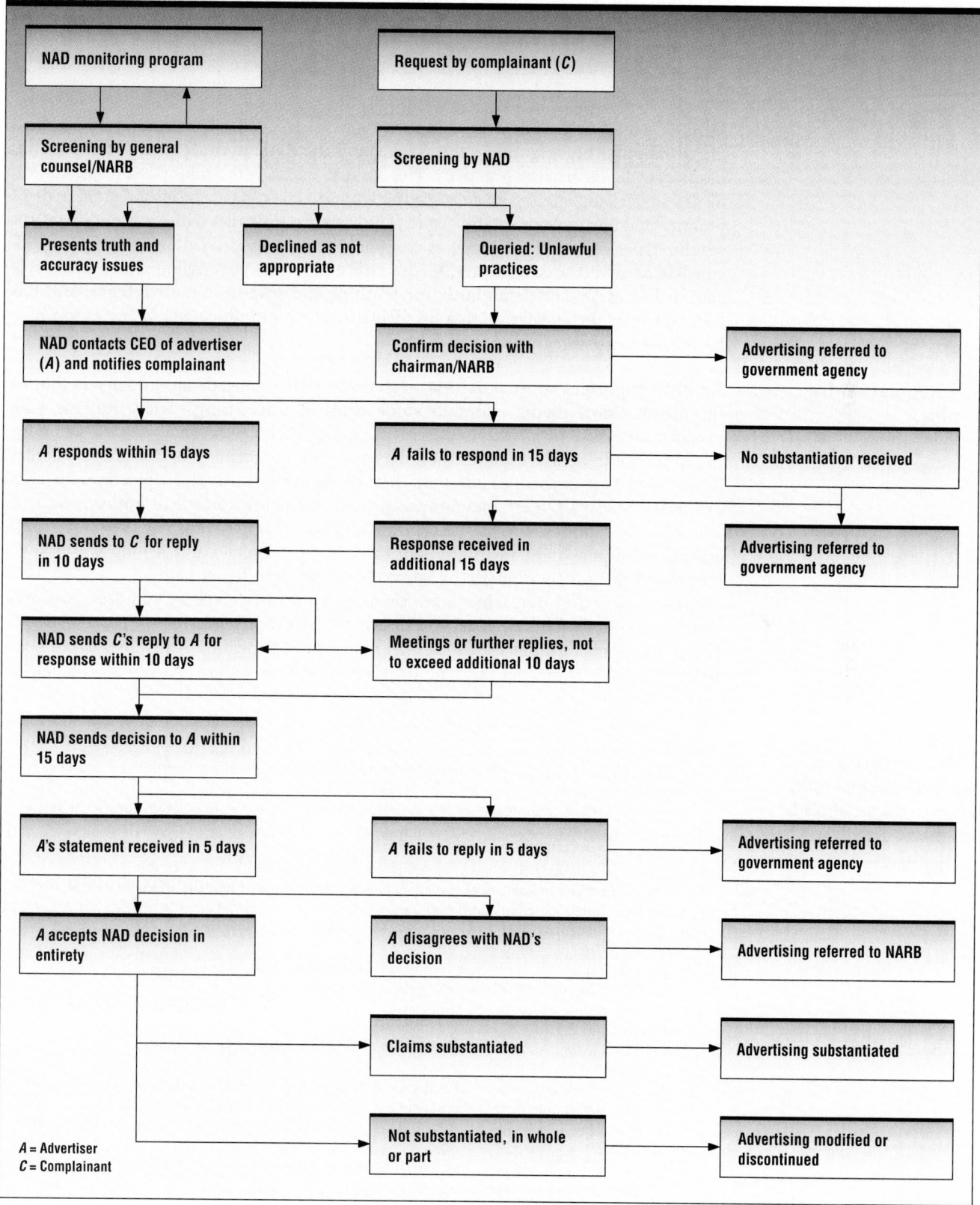

and most companies feel compelled to comply with their decision. Firms may prefer self-regulation rather than government intervention, as many companies will challenge competitor's unsubstantiated claims through self-regulatory groups such as the NARB.[11]

Advertising associations

Various groups in the advertising industry have also favored self-regulation. The two major national organizations, the AAAA and the AAF, actively monitor and police industrywide advertising practices. The AAAA, which is the major trade association of the advertising agency business in the United States, has established standards of practice and has its own creative code. The organization also will issue guidelines for specific types of advertising such as comparative messages (Exhibit 23–6). The AAF consists of advertisers, agencies, media, and numerous advertising clubs. The association has established standards for truthful and responsible advertising and has been active in the legislative area of advertising and in influencing agencies to abide by its code and principles.

Self-Regulation by Media

Another important self-regulatory mechanism in the advertising industry is that of the media. Most media maintain some form of advertising review process and, except in the case of political advertising, may reject any ads they regard as objectionable. Some media exclude the advertising of an entire product class, whereas others may ban individual ads that they think are offensive or objectionable. For example, *Reader's Digest* does not accept advertising for tobacco or liquor products, whereas for many years *Ms.* magazine refused to accept ads for Virginia Slims cigarettes because the editors thought the slogan "You've come a long way baby" overstated the advances made by women in their fight for equality.

Newspapers and magazines have their own set of advertising requirements and restrictions that often vary depending on the size and nature of the publication. Large, established publications such as major newspapers or magazines often have strict standards regarding the type of advertising they accept. As noted in Chapter

> *Exhibit 23–6*
> **American Association of Advertising Agencies policy statement and guidelines for comparative advertising**

The Board of Directors of the American Association of Advertising Agencies recognizes that when used truthfully and fairly, comparative advertising provides the consumer with needed and useful information.

However, extreme caution should be exercised. The use of comparative advertising, by its very nature, can distort facts and, by implication, convey to the consumer information that misrepresents the truth.

Therefore, the Board believes that comparative advertising should follow certain guidelines:

1. The intent and connotation of the ad should be to inform and never to discredit or unfairly attack competitors, competing products, or services.
2. When a competitive product is named, it should be one that exists in the marketplace as significant competition.
3. The competition should be fairly and properly identified but never in a manner or tone of voice that degrades the competitive product or service.
4. The advertising should compare related or similar properties or ingredients of the product, dimension to dimension, feature to feature.
5. The identification should be for honest comparison purposes and not simply to upgrade by association.
6. If a competitive test is conducted, it should be done by an objective testing source, preferably an independent one, so that there will be no doubt as to the veracity of the test.
7. In all cases the test should be supportive of all claims made in the advertising that are based on the test.
8. The advertising should never use partial results or stress insignificant differences to cause the consumer to draw an improper conclusion.
9. The property being compared should be significant in terms of value or usefulness of the product to the consumer.
10. Comparatives delivered through the use of testimonials should not imply that the testimonial is more than one individual's thought unless that individual represents a sample of the majority viewpoint.

14, some magazines such as *Parents* or *Good Housekeeping* regularly test products advertised therein and offer a "Seal of Approval" and refund offers for products that are later found to be defective. Such policies are designed to enhance the credibility of the publication and increase the reader's confidence in the products advertised in these magazines.

Advertising on television and radio has been regulated for years through codes developed by the industry trade association—the National Association of Broadcasters (NAB). Both the radio code (established in 1937) and the television code (1952) provided the standards for broadcast advertising for many years. Both codes prohibit the advertising of certain products such as hard liquor and also have standards regarding the manner in which products can be advertised. However, in 1982, the NAB suspended all of its code provisions after portions dealing with time standards and required length of commercials in the television code were found to be in restraint of trade by the courts. While the NAB codes are no longer in force, many individual broadcasters, such as the major television networks, have adopted major portions of the code provisions into their own standards.[12]

Probably the most stringent review process of any media is that of the three major television networks. All three networks maintain "Standards and Practices" divisions, which carefully review all commercials submitted to the network or individual affiliate stations. Advertisers are required to submit all commercials intended for airing on the network or an affiliate station for review.

Commercials at various stages of the production process are submitted for review by sending a script, storyboard, animatic, or finished commercial (when the advertiser believes there is little chance of objection). The network reviewers consider whether the proposed commercial meets acceptable standards and is appropriate for certain audiences. For example, different standards are used for ads designated for prime-time versus late night spots or for children's versus adults' programs. An example of the three networks' guidelines for children's advertising is shown in Exhibit 23–7. Most of these guidelines remain in effect, although ABC and NBC are

➤ *Exhibit 23–7*
A sampling of the TV networks' guidelines for children's advertising

Each of the major television networks has its own set of guidelines for children's advertising, although the basics are very similar. A few rules, such as the requirement of a static "island" shot at the end, are written in stone; others, however, occasionally can be negotiated.

Many of the rules below apply specifically to toys. The networks also have special guidelines for kids' food commercials and for kids' commercials that offer premiums.

	ABC	CBS	NBC
Must not overglamorize product	✓	✓	✓
No exhortative language, such as "Ask Mom to buy . . ."	✓	✓	✓
No realistic war settings	✓		✓
Generally no celebrity endorsements	✓	Case-by-case	✓
Can't use "only" or "just" in regard to price	✓	✓	✓
Show only two toys per child or maximum of six per commercial	✓		✓
Five-second "island" showing product against plain background at end of spot	✓	✓	✓ (4 to 5)
Animation restricted to one third of a commercial	✓		✓
Generally no comparative or superiority claims	Case-by-case	Handle w/care	✓
No costumes or props not available with the toy	✓		✓
No child or toy can appear in animated segments	✓		✓
Three-second establishing shot of toy in relation to child	✓	✓ (2.5 to 3)	
No shots under one second in length		✓	
Must show distance a toy can travel before stopping on its own		✓	

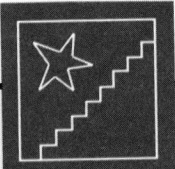

Promotional Perspective 23–1

Television Networks Change Standards for Commercials

Although you may sometimes find it hard to believe, every commercial shown on network television is reviewed by the networks' broadcast standards and practices division. The network reviewers, or censors as they are sometimes called, examine nearly 1,000 commercials a week to determine if they are in good taste, are potentially offensive to any particular groups, and are not deceptive. The networks often require companies to provide information that supports the claims made in their commercials to ensure they do not mislead consumers or provide advertisers with a competitive advantage based on claims they cannot substantiate.

The networks have long maintained their own standards and rules regarding the content of television advertising, and many of the ads they reject often end up being shown on cable and independent television stations. However, as the networks see their viewing audiences declining and continue to lose advertising revenue to cable, they are changing their standards and loosening some restrictions.

ABC is revising its guidelines and will loosen long-standing restrictions on endorsements and competitive advertising claims. The network plans to change a number of restrictions such as its ban against having doctors or actors portraying doctors appear as endorsers for health-care products. Under the new guidelines, doctors will be permitted to endorse products, although the network will require manufacturers to provide documentation that a significant number of health-care professionals of the sort represented in the commercial recommend the product. Commercials in which actors portray doctors would be considered on a case-by-case basis.

Another change being proposed by ABC would allow celebrities to endorse products outside of their profession in advertising targeted to children, although they still would not be permitted to endorse products related to their profession. The ABC vice president in charge of commercial standards has argued that children today are more sophisticated when it comes to sales pitches from celebrity endorsers. However, the president of the consumer group Action for Children's Television (ACT) has criticized the idea of having sports or rock heros endorse children's products, arguing, "Children cannot separate a sales pitch from a real-life situation. Seeing a hero using a product means to them that 'my friend wants me to have this product.' "

The changes being made by ABC will cover several other areas such as the advertising of weight-loss products and alcoholic beverages. Under the new guidelines, before and after diet photos will be allowed in ads for weight-loss products or plans if the advertiser can provide proof of its claims along with evidence the plan is safe and reasonable. The sound of off-camera drinking will be allowed in alcoholic beverage commercials, although drinking on camera will still not be permitted. While guidelines in these areas are being liberalized, ABC is adding new restrictions in other areas, including the formal prohibition of ads for coolers made from distilled spirits and 900-number telephone commercials targeted to children. Standards for product demonstrations are also being tightened and will require written documentation of claims.

Another important change ABC is considering would require advertisers to mediate their own false or misleading competitive advertising claims. Traditionally, advertisers have complained to the networks first if they had problems or concerns over claims made by a competitor in a television commercial. This proposal received a considerable amount of criticism from advertisers and agencies who argue there will be no incentive for a company making a questionable claim to respond quickly since its commercial would keep running while the challenge was being resolved. Many advertisers and agencies believe a challenge should be handled by the networks first since they can take a misleading ad off the air while the dispute is being settled. After hearing these complaints about the proposed changes in the ad challenge plan, ABC is reconsidering the proposal.

ABC has noted the changes being made are part of its periodic review process and will affect only a small percentage of the 50,000 commercials the network reviews every year. NBC and CBS have also revised and updated their commercial standards and operate under guidelines similar to those being adopted by ABC. Perhaps we have finally seen the last television commercial where an actor claims, "I'm not a doctor, but I play one on TV."

Source: Jane Hall, "ABC Considers Loosening Rules on Commercials," *Los Angeles Times,* September 11, 1991, pp. D1,4; and Joe Mandese, "ABC Loosens Rules," *Advertising Age,* September 9, 1991, pp. 2,8.

reconsidering their position on celebrity endorsements as will be discussed in Promotional Perspective 23–1.

It is estimated that each of the three major networks receives over 50,000 commercials a year for review, with nearly two thirds being accepted and only 3 percent rejected. The remaining 30 percent are revised and resubmitted for review, with most problems being resolved through negotiation.[13]

Network standards regarding acceptable advertising are constantly changing. In 1987, the networks began to allow advertisers of lingerie products to use live models rather than mannequins, and advertising for contraceptives has recently been appearing on some stations. It is likely that network standards will continue to change as society's values and attitudes toward certain issues and products change. Promotional Perspective 23–1 discusses recent changes the networks have made in their guidelines. Many advertising people believe these changes are being made in response to competition from independent and cable stations, which tend to be much less stringent in their requirements for commercials. However, television is probably the most carefully scrutinized and frequently criticized of all forms of advertising, and the networks must be careful not to offend their viewers and detract from the credibility of advertising.

Appraising Self-Regulation

As can be seen from the preceding discussion, there are a number of sources of internal regulation or self-regulation in advertising. The three major participants in the advertising process—the advertisers, the agencies, and the media—all work both individually and collectively to encourage truthful, ethical, and responsible advertising. The advertising industry views self-regulation as an effective mechanism for controlling abuses in advertising and avoiding the use of offensive, misleading, or deceptive practices and prefers this form of regulation to government intervention. Self-regulation of advertising has been effective and in many instances has probably led to the development of standards and practices higher than those imposed by law and beyond the proper scope of legislation.

However, there are limitations to self-regulation, and this process has been criticized in a number of areas. For example, concern has been expressed over the fact that it often takes the NAD six months to a year to resolve a complaint, during which time a company has often stopped using a commercial anyway. Concern has also been expressed over budgeting and staffing constraints, which limit the NAD/NARB system's ability to investigate more cases and complete them more rapidly.[14] Self-regulation has also been criticized for being self-serving to the advertisers and advertising industry and lacking the power or authority to be a viable alternative to federal or state regulation.

Many critics do not believe advertising can or should be controlled solely by self-regulation. They argue that regulation by governmental agencies is necessary in many instances to ensure that advertising provides consumers with accurate information and does not mislead or deceive them. Negative perceptions of self-regulation have prompted many parties to turn to the federal and state government for control and regulation of advertising. We now focus our discussion on governmental regulation of advertising.

Federal Regulation of Advertising

Governmental control and regulation of advertising stem from various federal, state, and local laws and regulations, with enforcement being the task of various government agencies. The most important source of external regulation comes from the federal government, particularly through the **Federal Trade Commission** (FTC). Thus, we focus most of our attention on federal regulation of advertising and the operation and policies of the FTC.

Background on Federal Regulation of Advertising

Federal regulation of advertising actually originated in 1914 with the passage of the **Federal Trade Commission Act** (FTC Act), which created the FTC, the agency that is today the most active in, and has the primary responsibility for, the control and regulation of advertising. The FTC Act was originally passed to help enforce antitrust laws, such as the Sherman and Clayton acts, by helping to restrain unfair methods of competition. The main focus of the five-member commission given the power to enforce the act was in protecting competitors from one another; the issue of false or misleading advertising was not even mentioned. In 1922, the Supreme Court upheld an FTC interpretation that false advertising was an unfair method of competition, but in the 1931 Raladam case (*FTC v. Raladam Co.*), the Court ruled the commission could not prohibit false advertising unless there was evidence of injury to a competitor by the ads.[15] This ruling limited the power of the FTC to protect consumers from false or deceptive advertising and led to a consumer movement that resulted in an important amendment to the FTC Act.

In 1938, the **Wheeler-Lea Amendment** was passed, which amended section 5 of the FTC Act to read:

> Unfair methods of competition in commerce and unfair or deceptive acts or practices in commerce are hereby declared to be unlawful.

The amendment empowered the FTC to act against advertising if there were evidence of injury to the public, and proof of injury to competition was not necessary. The Wheeler-Lea Amendment also gave the FTC the power to issue cease and desist orders and levy fines on violators and extended its jurisdiction over false advertising of foods, drugs, cosmetics, and therapeutic devices. This amendment also provided the FTC with access to the injunctive power of the federal courts. Initially this pertained only to the marketing of food and drug products but was expanded in 1972 to include all products where there is a threat to the public's health and safety.

In addition to the FTC, numerous other federal agencies are responsible for, or involved in, the regulation of advertising. The authority of these agencies is limited, however, to a particular product area or service, and these agencies often rely on the FTC to assist in the handling of false or deceptive advertising cases. Thus, we examine the FTC and its operations in more detail before discussing these other federal agencies.

The Federal Trade Commission

The FTC is charged with the responsibility of protecting both consumers and businesses from anticompetitive behavior and unfair and deceptive practices. The major divisions of the FTC include the Bureaus of Competition, Economics, and Consumer Protection (Exhibit 23–8). The Bureau of Competition is responsible for enforcing antitrust laws, whereas the Bureau of Economics aids and advises the commission on the economic aspects of its activities and prepares economic reports and surveys. The Bureau of Consumer Protection investigates and litigates cases involving acts or practices alleged to be deceptive or unfair to consumers. The National Advertising Division of the Bureau of Consumer Protection is responsible for enforcing those provisions of the FTC Act that forbid misrepresentation, unfairness, and deception in national advertising.

As noted, the FTC has had the power to regulate advertising since the passage of the Wheeler-Lea Amendment. However, it was not until the early 1970s—following criticism of the commission in a book by "Nader's Raiders" and a special report by the American Bar Association for its lack of action against deceptive promotional practices—that the FTC became active in the regulation of advertising.[16]

The authority of the FTC was increased considerably throughout the 1970s. A particularly important piece of legislation affecting the commission was the Magnuson-Moss Act of 1975, which resulted in dramatic broadening of the FTC's powers and a substantial increase in its budget. The first section of this act dealt with consumers' rights regarding product warranties and allowed the commission to require restitution for deceptively written warranties where the consumer lost more than $5. The second section, the FTC Improvements Act, gave the FTC the power to establish **trade regulation rules** (TRRs), industrywide rules that defined unfair practices before they occurred.

During the 1970s, the FTC made enforcement of laws regarding false and misleading advertising a top priority, as several new programs were instituted, budgets were increased, and the commission became a very powerful regulatory agency. However, many of these programs, as well as the expanded powers of the FTC to develop regulations on the basis of "unfairness," became the source of controversy. At the source of this controversy has been the fundamental issue of what constitutes unfair or deceptive advertising.

What is deceptive or unfair advertising?

Advertising has a responsibility in most economic systems of providing consumers with information they can use to make consumption decisions. However, if this

➤ *Exhibit 23–8* **The Federal Trade Commission organization**

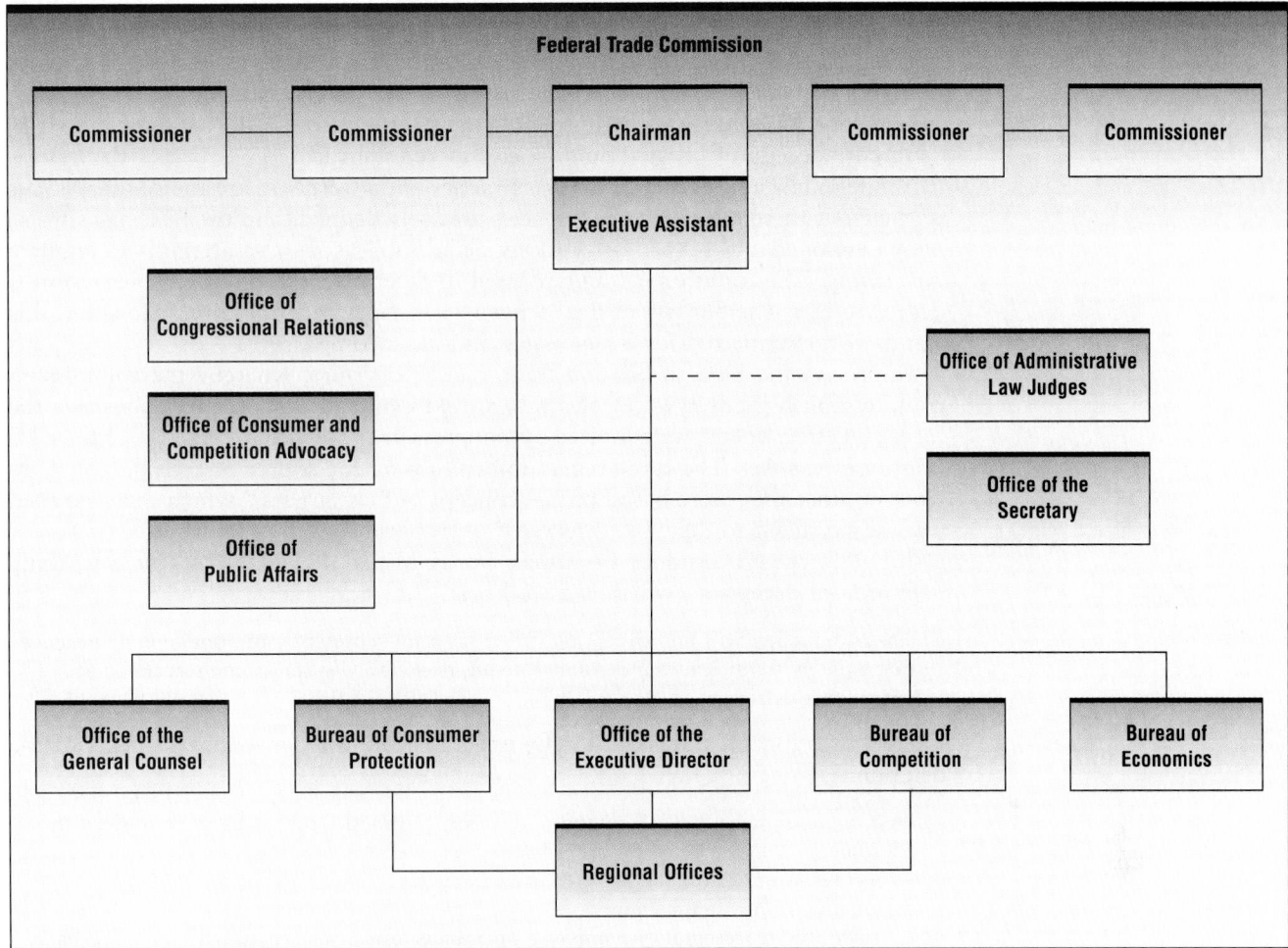

information is untrue or misleads the consumer, then the advertising is not fulfilling this basic function. The problem that arises, however, concerns just what constitutes an untruthful or deceptive ad. Deceptive advertising can take a number of forms, ranging from an intentional false or misleading claim by the advertiser to ads that may be true in a literal sense but may leave some consumers with a false or misleading impression.

The issue of deception, including its definition and measurement, has received considerable attention from the FTC and other regulatory agencies. One of the problems regulatory agencies must deal with in determining deception is distinguishing between false or misleading messages and those that, rather than relying on verifiable or substantiated objective information about a product, rely on subjective claims or statements about a product, a practice known as puffery.

Puffery has been legally defined as

advertising or other sales presentations which praise the item to be sold with subjective opinions, superlatives, or exaggerations, vaguely and generally, stating no specific facts.[17]

The use of puffery in advertising is common. For example, Bayer aspirin calls itself the "Wonder drug that works wonders," whereas Nestlé claims, "Nestlé makes the very best chocolate." Superlatives such as the "greatest," "best," and/or "finest" are puffs frequently used in advertising.

Puffery has generally been viewed as a form of "poetic license" or allowable exaggeration for the advertiser. The FTC has taken the position that consumers expect exaggeration or inflated claims in advertising and puffery is recognizable by consumers and will not lead to deception since it is not believed. However, some studies have shown consumers may believe puffery claims and may perceive them as literally true.[18] One study found that consumers could not distinguish between a verifiable fact-based claim and puffery and were just as likely to believe both types of claims.[19] Ivan Preston has argued that puffery has a detrimental effect on consumers' purchase decisions by burdening them with untrue beliefs and refers to it as "soft core deception" that should be considered illegal.[20]

While unfair and deceptive acts or practices in advertising are the primary focus of the FTC, these terms have never been precisely defined, and the FTC has continually developed and refined a "working definition" used in its attempts to regulate advertising. The traditional standard used in determining if an advertising claim is deceptive was whether it had the "tendency or capacity to deceive." However, this standard was criticized for being vague and all-encompassing.

Efforts by the FTC to develop trade regulation rules, whereby the commission could establish industrywide rules that would define unfair practices and have the force and effect of law, were limited by Congress in 1980 with the passage of the FTC Improvements Act. The trade regulation rules were the source of considerable controversy since they were based on the concept of "unfairness," which critics argued was very difficult to define and received overly broad use by the FTC.

In 1983, the FTC, under Chairman James Miller III, put forth a new working definition of **deception,** which is as follows:

> The commission will find deception if there is a misrepresentation, omission or practice that is likely to mislead the consumer acting reasonably in the circumstances to the consumer's detriment.[21]

The commissioners' statement briefly explained the three essential elements of the definition:

> First, there must be a representation, omission or practice that is likely to mislead the consumer.
>
> Second, we examine the practice from the perspective of a consumer acting reasonably in the circumstances.
>
> Third, the representation, omission or practice must be a "material" one. The basic question is whether the act is likely to affect the consumer's conduct or decision with regard to a product or service. If so, the practice is material, and consumer injury is likely because consumers are likely to have chosen differently but for the deception.[22]

The goal of then Chairman Miller, who drafted this definition, was to help the commission determine which cases were worth pursuing and to prevent the FTC from dealing with those considered trivial. Miller argued that for an advertisement to be considered worthy of challenge by the FTC, it should be seen by a substantial number of consumers, it should lead to significant injury, and the problem should be one that market forces are not likely to remedy. However, concern has been expressed that this revised definition will put a greater burden on the FTC to prove that deception has occurred and to prove that a deceptive act influenced the consumers' decision-making process in a detrimental way.

What constitutes unfairness remains a controversial issue. However, two of the factors the FTC considers in evaluating an ad for deception are (1) whether there are significant omissions of important information and (2) whether advertisers can substantiate the claims made for the product or service. The FTC has developed several programs that address these issues.

Affirmative disclosure

A problem in determining deception is that an ad can be literally true, yet leave the consumer with a false or misleading impression if the claim is true only under certain conditions or circumstances or if there are limitations to what the product can or cannot do. Thus, under its **affirmative disclosure** requirement, the FTC may require advertisers to include certain types of information in their ads so consumers will be aware of all the consequences, conditions, and limitations associated with the use of a product or service. The goal of affirmative disclosure is for consumers to have sufficient information to make an informed decision. An ad may be required to define the testing situation, conditions, or criteria used in making a claim. For example, fuel mileage claims in automobile ads are based on Environmental Protection Agency (EPA) ratings since they offer a uniform standard for making comparisons. The requirement that cigarette advertisements contain a warning concerning the health risks associated with smoking is also an example of an affirmative disclosure requirement.

A recent example of an affirmative disclosure ruling involves the case filed by the Federal Trade Commission against Campbell Soup in 1989 for making deceptive and unsubstantiated claims for its soups. Campbell's ads run as part of its "Soup is good food" campaign linked the low fat and cholesterol content of its soup with a reduced risk of heart disease. However, the advertising failed to disclose that the soups are high in sodium, which may increase the risk of heart disease. In a consent agreement accepted in 1991, Campbell agreed that, for any soup containing more than 500 milligrams of sodium in an eight-ounce serving, it will disclose the sodium content in any advertising that directly or by implication mentions heart disease in connection with the soup. Campbell also agreed it would not imply a connection between soup and a reduction in heart disease in future advertising.[23]

Advertising substantiation

A major area of concern to regulatory agencies in protecting consumers and promoting fair competition is whether advertisers can support or substantiate the claims made in their ads. For many years, there were no formal requirements concerning substantiation of advertising claims. Many companies would make specific claims in their ads without having any documentation or support such as laboratory tests and clinical studies available. In 1971, the FTC adopted an **advertising substantiation** program that required advertisers to have documentation to support the claims made in their ads and to prove they are truthful.[24] This program was broadened in 1972 to include the requirement that advertisers must substantiate their claims before the ad appears. The program requires substantiation of claims made with respect to safety, performance, efficacy, quality, or comparative price of a product.

The FTC's substantiation program has had a major effect on the advertising industry, as it has shifted the burden of proof from the commission to the advertiser. Before the substantiation program, the FTC was required to prove that an advertiser's claims were unfair or deceptive when challenging a case. In a number of cases, advertisers have been ordered by the FTC to cease making inadequately substantiated claims.

Ad substantiation seeks to provide consumers with a basis for believing advertising claims such that they can make rational and informed decisions and to deter companies from making claims they cannot adequately support. The FTC has taken the perspective that it is illegal and unfair to consumers for a firm to make a claim for a product without having a "reasonable basis" for making the claim. In their decision to require advertising substantiation, the commissioners made the following statement:

> Given the imbalance of knowledge and resources between a business enterprise and each of its customers, economically it is more rational and imposes far less cost on society, to require a manufacturer to confirm his affirmative product claims rather than impose a burden on each individual consumer to test, investigate, or experiment for himself. The manufacturer has the ability, the know-how, the equipment, the time and resources to undertake such information, by testing or otherwise, ... the consumer usually does not.[25]

Many advertisers have expressed considerable concern and responded negatively to the FTC's advertising substantiation program. They argue it is too expensive to document all their claims and most consumers either would not understand or would not be interested in the technical data and information used to substantiate the same. Some advertisers have argued they might choose to avoid the substantiation issue by using puffery claims, which do not require substantiation.

Generally, advertisers making claims covered by the substantiation program should have available prior substantiation of all claims. However, in 1984, the FTC issued a new policy statement that suggested after-the-fact substantiation might be acceptable in some cases and it would solicit documentation of claims only from advertisers that are under investigation for deceptive practices.

The FTC's Handling of Deceptive Advertising Cases

Consent and cease and desist orders

Allegations that a firm is engaging in unfair or deceptive advertising come to the attention of the FTC from a variety of sources including complaints from competitors, consumers, other governmental agencies, or the commission's own monitoring and investigations. Once the FTC decides a complaint is justified and warrants further action, it notifies the offender, who then has 30 days to respond to the complaint. The advertiser can agree to negotiate a settlement with the FTC by signing a **consent order**, which is an agreement to stop the practice or advertising in question. This agreement is for settlement purposes only and does not constitute an admission of guilt by the advertiser. Most FTC inquiries are settled by consent orders, as this saves the advertiser the cost and possible adverse publicity that might result if the case were to go further.

If the advertiser chooses not to sign the consent decree and contests the complaint, a hearing can be requested before an administrative law judge employed by the FTC but not under its influence. The judge's decision may be appealed to the full five-member commission by either side. The commission either affirms or modifies the order or dismisses the case. If the complaint has been upheld by the administrative law judge and the commission, the advertiser can appeal the case to the federal courts.

The appeal process described above may take some time, and the FTC may want to stop the advertiser from engaging in the deceptive practice. One instrument the FTC has at its disposal as a result of the Wheeler-Lea Amendment is the power to issue **cease and desist orders**. The cease and desist order requires that the advertiser stop the specified advertising claim within 30 days and prohibits the advertiser from engaging in the objectionable practice until after the hearing is held. Violation of a cease and desist order is punishable by a fine of up to $10,000 a day. A number of firms have violated the terms of a cease and desist order and have had to pay substantial fines, although most firms usually comply. The FTC complaint procedure is summarized in Exhibit 23–9.

Corrective advertising

By using consent and cease and desist orders, the FTC is usually able to stop a particular advertising practice it believes is unfair or deceptive. However, a problem may still exist even if an advertiser ceases using a deceptive ad, since consumers can still retain some or all of the deceptive claim in memory. To address this problem of residual effects of prior deceptive advertising, in the 1970s the FTC developed a program known as **corrective advertising**. Under this program, an advertiser found guilty of deceptive advertising can be required to run additional advertising designed to remedy the deception or misinformation contained in previous ads.

The impetus for corrective advertising was a case involving the Campbell Soup Company in which marbles were placed in the bottom of a bowl of vegetable soup

➤ *Exhibit 23–9* **FTC complaint procedure**

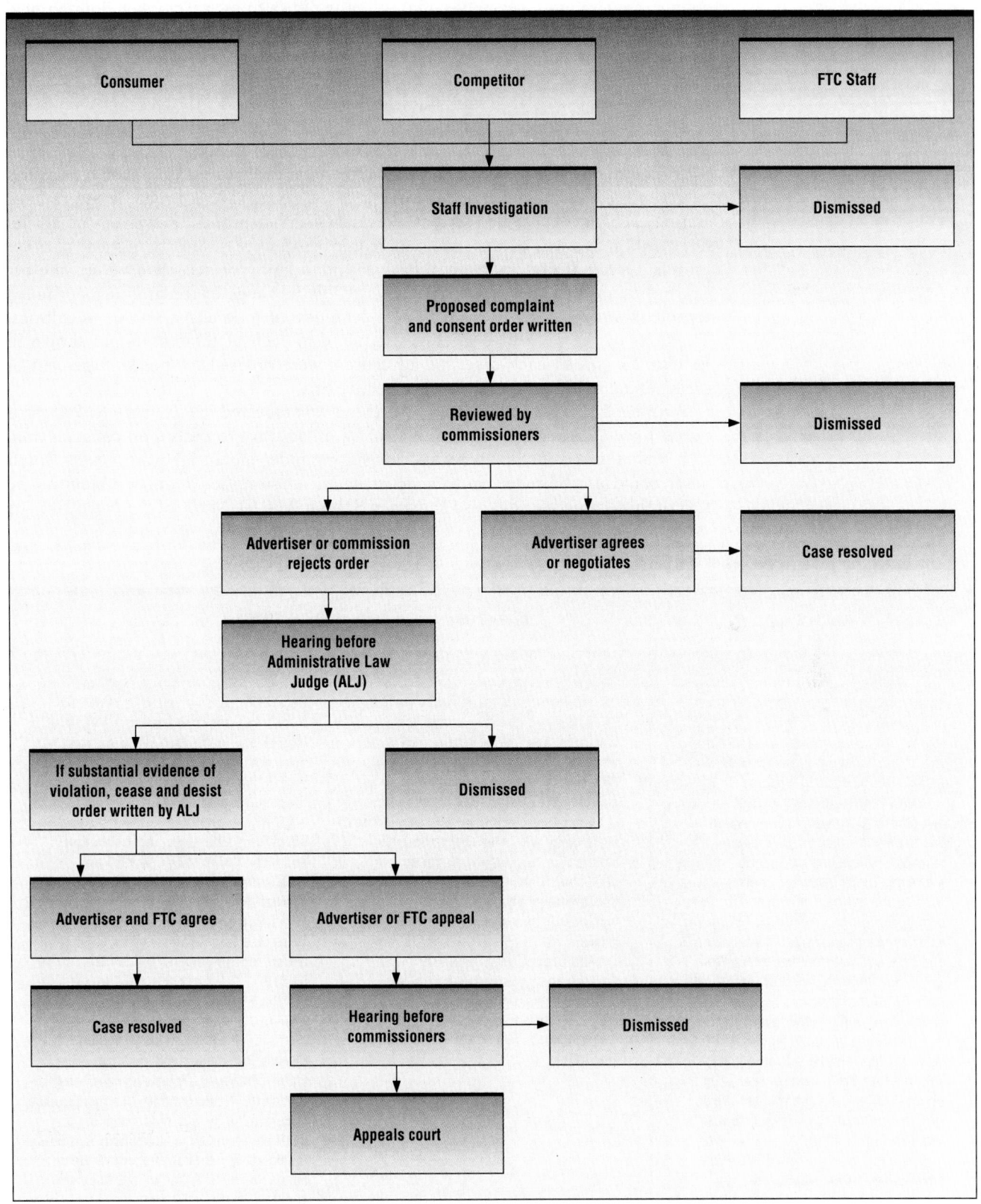

to force the solid ingredients to the surface. This created a false impression that the soup contained more vegetables than it really did (although Campbell Soup argued that if the marbles were not used, all the ingredients would settle to the bottom, leaving an impression of fewer ingredients than actually existed!). While Campbell Soup agreed to stop the practice, a group of law students calling themselves SOUP (Students Opposed to Unfair Practices) argued to the FTC that this would not remedy false impressions created by prior advertising and contended Campbell Soup should be required to run advertising to rectify the problem.

Although the FTC did not order corrective advertising in the Campbell case, it has been required in a number of subsequent cases. For example, Profile Bread ran ads stating each slice contained fewer calories than other brands. However, the ad did not mention this was because slices of Profile bread were thinner than those of other brands. Ocean Spray cranberry juice was found guilty of deceptive advertising because it claimed to have more "food energy" than orange or tomato juice but failed to note it was referring to the technical definition of food energy, which is calories. The texts of the corrective messages required in each of these cases are shown in Exhibit 23–10. In each case, the advertisers were ordered to spend 25 percent of their annual media budget to run corrective ads.

Another case where corrective advertising was required involved the STP Corporation for claims regarding the ability of its oil additive to reduce oil consumption. STP was required to run corrective ads stating independent laboratory tests it had made could not be relied on to support its oil consumption reduction claims. The text of this corrective ad is also shown in Exhibit 23–10. Many of the corrective ads

➤ *Exhibit 23–10*   **Examples of corrective advertising messages**

Profile Bread	Ocean Spray	STP
"Hi, (celebrity's name) for Profile Bread. Like all mothers, I'm concerned about nutrition and balanced meals. So, I'd like to clear up any misunderstanding you may have about Profile Bread from its advertising or even its name. "Does Profile have fewer calories than any other breads? No. Profile has about the same per ounce as other breads. To be exact, Profile has seven fewer calories per slice. That's because Profile is sliced thinner. But eating Profile will not cause you to lose weight. A reduction of seven calories is insignificant. It's total calories and balanced nutrition that count. And Profile can help you achieve a balanced meal because it provides protein and B vitamins as well as other nutrients. "How does my family feel about Profile? Well, my husband likes Profile toast, the children love Profile sandwiches, and I prefer Profile to any other bread. So you see, at our house, delicious taste makes Profile a family affair." (To be run in 25 percent of brand's advertising, for one year.)	"If you've wondered what some of our earlier advertising meant when we said Ocean Spray Cranberry Juice Cocktail has more food energy than orange juice or tomato juice, let us make it clear: we didn't mean vitamins and minerals. Food energy means calories. Nothing more. "Food energy is important at breakfast since many of us may not get enough calories, or food energy, to get off to a good start. Ocean Spray Cranberry Juice Cocktail helps because it contains more food energy than most other breakfast drinks. "And Ocean Spray Cranberry Juice Cocktail gives you and your family Vitamin C plus a great wake-up taste. It's... the other breakfast drink." (To be run in one of every four ads for one year.)	As a result of an investigation by the Federal Trade Commission into certain allegedly inaccurate past advertisements for STP's oil additive, STP Corporation has agreed to a $700,000 settlement. With regard to that settlement, STP is making the following statement: "It is the policy of STP to support its advertising with objective information and test data. In 1974 and 1975 an independent laboratory ran tests of the company's oil additive which led to claims of reduced oil consumption. However, these tests cannot be relied on to support the oil consumption reduction claim made by STP. "The FTC has taken the position that, in making the claim, the company violated the terms of a consent order. When STP learned that the test did not support the claim, it stopped advertising containing that claim. New tests have been undertaken to determine the extent to which the oil additive affects oil consumption. Agreement to this settlement does not constitute an admission by STP that the law has been violated. Rather, STP has agreed to resolve the dispute with the FTC to avoid protracted and prohibitively expensive litigation."

run in the STP case appeared in business publications to serve as a notice to other advertisers that the FTC was enforcing the corrective advertising program.

One of the most publicized corrective advertising cases involved Listerine mouthwash. In 1975, the FTC charged that since 1921 the Warner-Lambert Company had run ads promoting Listerine as being effective in the prevention of colds and sore throats. However, the FTC ruled the company had no valid support for this claim. In addition to ordering the company to stop using it, Warner-Lambert was required to run $10 million worth of corrective ads over a 16-month period stating, "Listerine would not help prevent colds or sore throats or lessen their severity." Listerine appealed the FTC decision all the way to the Supreme Court, which rejected the argument that corrective advertising violates advertisers' First Amendment rights. The order was upheld, forcing Warner-Lambert to run corrective messages.

Corrective advertising is probably the most controversial of all the FTC programs. Advertisers have argued that corrective advertising infringes on First Amendment rights of freedom of speech. The effectiveness of corrective advertising campaigns has also been questioned, as has the FTC's involvement in the business of creating advertisements through requiring particular content in corrective messages.[26] Proponents and opponents of corrective advertising continue to argue the benefits and pitfalls of this program. Exhibit 23–11 presents 10 summary conclusions on corrective advertising made by William Wilkie, Dennis McNeill, and Michael Mazis after studying over a decade of corrective advertising cases and research.

Current Status of Federal Regulation by the FTC

During the 1970s, the FTC became a very powerful and active regulator of advertising in the United States. However, by the 1980s Congress had become very concerned over the FTC's broad interpretation of unfairness, which led to the restrictive legislation of the 1980 FTC Improvements Act. Concern over the meaning of "unfair" advertising remains on the grounds that it is vague and subject to whatever meaning an individual wants to assign to it.[27]

During the 1980s, the FTC became less active and cut back its regulatory efforts. This change was in large part due to the laissez-faire attitude of the Reagan administration toward the regulation of business in general. The FTC's focus changed to handling only the most blatant cases of deception and to pursuing cases involving true eccentrics and charlatans, such as a company that sold "muscle building" pills

➤ *Exhibit 23–11*
Summary conclusions on corrective advertising

1. The FTC is empowered to order corrective advertising as a remedy against deceptive advertising campaigns.
2. There are important legal constraints as to when and in what manner the FTC can employ this remedy form.
3. Corrective advertising holds the potential to yield beneficial effects for consumers.
4. Corrective advertising appears to hold the potential to affect the sales and/or image of the advertised brand.
5. There is little evidence of a systematic FTC program for corrective advertising:
   * Bursts of case activity have been followed by long periods of inactivity.
   * Philosophical and personnel changes occurred throughout the 1970s and early 1980s at both the staff and commissioner levels.
   * Past orders have used a wide range of requirements for corrective advertising.
6. Consent negotiations between FTC staff members and company representatives have played a key role in the exact requirements in almost every case to date.
7. Consumer effectiveness of corrective advertising has not been the primary concern of the orders issued to date.
8. In communication terms, past corrective advertising orders against major advertisers appear to have been weak.
9. In terms of consumer impacts, the major corrective advertising orders appear *not* to have been successful in remedying consumer misimpressions across the marketplace.
10. If corrective advertising is to continue as an FTC remedy, some changes in the form of the orders will be required.

and frauds involving diamond investments scams and oil-land lotteries.[28] Concern was expressed that the FTC had become too narrow in its regulation of national advertising, forcing companies and consumer groups to seek relief from other sources such as state and federal courts or through self-regulatory groups such as the NAD/NARB.[29]

In 1988–89, an 18-member panel chosen by the American Bar Association undertook a study of the FTC as a 20-year follow-up to the 1969 report used by President Richard Nixon to overhaul the commission. The report filed by the commission expressed strong concern over the FTC's lack of sufficient resources and staff to regulate national advertising effectively and called for more funding to be provided to the commission. The committee suggested the FTC should retain its authority to use "unfairness" as the basis for issuing industrywide rules as well as complaints against individual advertisers.[30] The report called on the Bush administration to become more involved in the enforcement of advertising regulations. The Federal Trade Commission has taken more of an activist role under the Bush administration. Promotional Perspective 23–2 discusses the resurgence of the FTC under its new director and the active role it has taken in regulating advertising over the past several years.

While most advertisers have relied on self-regulatory mechanisms and the FTC to deal with deceptive or misleading advertising by their competitors, many companies are becoming more active by filing lawsuits against competitors they believe are making false claims. One piece of legislation that has become increasingly important in this regard is the Lanham Act.

The Lanham Act

This act was originally written in 1947 as the Lanham Trade-Mark Act to protect words, names, symbols, or other devices adopted to identify and distinguish a manufacturer's products. The **Lanham Act** was amended to encompass false advertising by prohibiting "any false description or representation including words or other symbols tending falsely to describe or represent the same." While the FTC Act did not provide individual advertisers with the opportunity to sue a competitor for deceptive advertising, civil suits are permitted under the Lanham Act.

More and more companies are using the Lanham Act to sue competitors for their advertising claims, particularly since comparative advertising has become so common. For example, the act was used against Bristol-Myers' Body on Tap Shampoo to stop the company from using TV ads showing tests indicating the product's superiority. It was argued the tests were not valid and the use of a slinky model in the ad distracted from the presentation of the results in the message.[31]

American Home Products (AHP) sued Johnson & Johnson for claims in Tylenol ads that ibuprofen-based analgesics, including AHP's Advil brand, cause stomach irritation. A U.S. district court fined Jartran Inc. a record $20 million in punitive damages on top of the $20 million awarded to U-Haul International to compensate for losses resulting from ads comparing the companies' prices and equipment that were ruled deceptive.

In several recent cases, companies have sued a competitor for damages resulting from false advertising claims. In 1990, Princeton Graphics Operating L.P., a subsidiary of Intelligence Systems, sued Japanese electronics giant NEC Corp. after a court ruled NEC ran false ads for its personal computer monitors. NEC was found guilty of falsely advertising that its Multisync monitor was compatible with IBM's PS/2 personal computer in order to capture market share. Princeton Graphics is seeking $25 million on the grounds that NEC's false advertising cost the company several million dollars of sales and a much greater amount from a lost opportunity to sell the company.[32]

In late 1991, a court ordered Ralston Purina Co. to pay Alpo Petfoods $12 million for damages caused by making false claims that its Purina Puppy Chow dog food could ameliorate and help prevent joint disease. The court ruled the claim was

Promotional Perspective 23–2

The Resurgence of the FTC

After nearly a decade of relative inactivity, the Federal Trade Commission (FTC) has once again become active in the regulation of advertising. Many attribute the renewed level of involvement to the leadership of Janet D. Steiger, who was appointed chairwoman in August 1989. Steiger promised to put teeth back into the FTC and aggressively develop a program that would provide strong national consumer protection. She has requested more funding by Congress to make up for the cutbacks that occurred during the Reagan administration and resulted in the agency's budget being reduced by a third and its staff by half.

Steiger has vowed to restore the FTC's image as a vigorous law-enforcement agency and is backing up her promises with action. In Steiger's first two years in office, the FTC filed as many consumer protection complaints as in the previous four years. In 1990, the commission opened 37 percent more preliminary investigations in consumer protection and 47 percent more full-phase investigations than in the year before. Steiger has shown particular interest in cracking down on misleading advertising in areas such as health, nutrition, weight loss, and environmental claims as well as telemarketing, 900 numbers, and advertising to children and the elderly.

The FTC sent a strong message to advertisers recently regarding its intention to become more aggressive and proactive in policing health claims when it ruled that Kraft Inc. ran deceptive advertising for its Kraft Singles cheese slices. Kraft had aired commercials for the product claiming its cheese slices are an important source of calcium because each contains 5 ounces of milk. The FTC complained the ads suggested each slice had as much calcium as five ounces of milk and they incorrectly implied Kraft Singles have more calcium than nondairy imitation cheese slices.

Even though the Kraft Singles ads did not expressly claim they had the equivalent amount of calcium as milk, the FTC ruled the ads could be interpreted this way. The commission's argument was based on the fact that the ads failed to mention that calcium is lost in the processing of cheese and visual elements in the ad reinforced the impression of equivalent amounts of calcium. For example, one ad showed the visual image of milk being poured into a glass up to a five-ounce mark that was then superimposed on a package of Kraft Singles while the milk ingredient and its calcium value were mentioned in the audio portion of the ad. The FTC order against Kraft forbids it from misrepresenting any nutrient in any of its cheese-related products. The commission noted that a pattern of deception had been established by the advertising for Kraft Singles and therefore it had to impose the order inhibiting misleading nutritional claims in any Kraft cheese or cheese-related products.

Many advertisers and agencies see the Kraft ruling as a sign the FTC plans on dealing vigorously with deceptive advertising. In December 1990, the FTC slapped sanctions on both Lewis Galoob Toys and its agency for misrepresenting the performance of several of the company's toys. The company and the agency promised to avoid making deceptive advertising claims and agreed to disclose that assembly may be required when a toy is shown fully assembled in a commercial. The commission has several other major cases pending including one against Fibre Trim, a weight-loss product. The FTC is taking issue with several Fibre Trim claims, including one that says it is a high-fiber supplement.

Many critics argued that advertisers had begun to get out of control during the 1980s as their claims went virtually unchecked by the federal government. However, with the resurgence of the Federal Trade Commission, it is very likely that advertisers, as well as their agencies, will be much more careful about the types of claims they make.

Source: Ray O. Werner, ed., "Legal Development in Marketing," *Journal of Marketing* 55, no. 4 (October 1991), pp. 99–100; S. J. Diamond, "New Director Putting Vigor Back into FTC," *Los Angeles Times*, March 29, 1991, pp. D1,4; and Joanne Lipman, "FTC Puts Advertisers on Notice of Crackdown on Misleading Ads," *The Wall Street Journal*, February 4, 1991, p. B6.

based on faulty data and the company continued the campaign after learning the research was in error. Alpo was awarded the money as compensation for lost revenue and the costs of advertising it ran in response to the Puppy Chow campaign.[33]

One legal expert noted, "The ability of one business to challenge another's advertising under section 43(a) of the Lanham Act is the most significant development in advertising regulation in the past ten years."[34] The ease of suing competitors for making false claims was facilitated even more with passage of the Trademark Law Revision Act of 1988. According to this law, anyone is vulnerable to civil action who "misrepresents the nature, characteristics, qualities or geographical origin of his or her or another person's goods, services or commercial activities." This wording closed a loophole in the Lanham Act, which did not mention another person's goods, as it had prohibited only false claims about one's own goods or services. While many disputes over comparative claims are never contested or are resolved through the NAD, it is likely that more companies will take rivals to court under the Lanham Act for several reasons, including the broad information discovery powers available under federal civil procedure rule, the speed with which a competitor can stop the offending ad through a preliminary injunction, and the possibility of collecting damages.[35]

Additional Federal Regulatory Agencies

The Federal Communications Commission

The FCC was founded in 1934 to regulate broadcast communication and has jurisdiction over the radio, television, telephone, and telegraph industries. The FCC has the authority to license broadcast stations as well as to remove a license or deny renewal to stations not operating in the public's interest. The FCC's authority over the airways gives it the power to control advertising content and to restrict what products and services can be advertised on radio and television. The FCC can eliminate obscene and profane programs and/or messages and those it finds in poor taste. While the FCC can eliminate ads that are deceptive or misleading, it generally works closely with the FTC in the regulation of advertising.

Many of the FCC's rules and regulations for television and radio stations have been eliminated or modified. The FCC no longer limits the amount of television time that can be devoted to commercials. However, on October 1, 1991, the Children's Television Act went into effect. The act limits advertising during children's programming to 10½ minutes an hour on weekends and 12 minutes an hour on weekdays. Under the Reagan administration, the controversial **Fairness Doctrine,** which required broadcasters to provide time for opposing viewpoints on important issues, was also repealed on the grounds that it was counterproductive. It was argued that the Fairness Doctrine resulted in a reduction in the amount of discussion of important issues because a broadcaster might be afraid to take on a paid controversial message on the grounds it might subsequently be required to provide equal free exposure for opposing viewpoints.

It was under this doctrine that the FCC required stations to run commercials about the harmful effects of smoking before passage of the Public Health Cigarette Smoking Act of 1970 (which banned broadcast advertising of cigarettes). Many stations still provide time for opposing viewpoints on controversial issues on the basis that this is consistent with the station's public service requirement and not necessarily directly related to fairness.

The Food and Drug Administration

Now under the jurisdiction of the Department of Health and Human Services, the FDA has authority over the labeling, packaging, branding, ingredient listing, and advertising of packaged foods and drug products. The FDA is authorized to require caution and warning labels on potentially hazardous products and also has limited authority over nutritional claims made in food advertising. This agency has the authority to set rules for promoting these products and also has the power to seize food and drugs on charges of false and misleading advertising. Like the FTC, the Food and Drug Administration has become a very aggressive regulatory agency in recent years. Promotional Perspective 23–3 discusses the changes that have occurred at the FDA since David A. Kessler took over as commissioner in early 1991.

The U.S. Postal Service

The U.S. mail is essentially a major advertising medium, as a large number of marketers use the mail to deliver advertising and promotional messages. The Post Office Department has control over advertising involving the use of the mail and ads involved with lotteries, fraud, and obscenity regulations. The postmaster general has

Promotional Perspective 23–3

The FDA Declares War on Misleading Food Claims

For years, the Food and Drug Administration was viewed as a toothless federal agency whose bark was worse than its bite. However, this perception changed quickly when David A. Kessler, a 40-year-old physician-lawyer, took over as commissioner of the FDA in early 1991. Kessler wasted little time showing companies that laissez-faire food labeling practices that had become common during the 1980s would no longer be acceptable and that the FDA meant business.

After only a few months in office, Kessler ordered the seizure of some 2,400 cases of Procter & Gamble's Citrus Hill Fresh Choice orange juice on the basis that the term *fresh* on the product label was false and misleading and confusing to consumers since Citrus Hill was produced from concentrate. Procter & Gamble had argued that FDA policy limiting the use of the word *fresh* did not apply because it was being used as a trademark, not as a descriptor. However, the FDA would not accept the trademark argument, and P&G finally agreed to remove all references to "fresh" from its packaging. Kessler's actions against P&G quickly caught the attention of other marketers using the word *fresh* on its labels. Ragu Foods removed the "fresh" claim from the label of its Ragu pasta sauce, while Nestlé and Kraft did the same with their sauces.

The FDA is going after a number of other commonly used descriptive labeling terms it believes are often abused such as *natural, light, no cholesterol,* and *fat free.* In May 1991, the FDA ordered the "no cholesterol" claim removed from products such as Mazola corn oil and HeartBeat canola oil. The FDA may do the same for a number of other products that use the no-cholesterol claim, for though it is technically correct, consumers tend to incorrectly assume these products are low in fat also.

The FDA is also cracking down on nutritional claims implied by brand names it thinks send a misleading message to consumers. For example, Great Foods of America was not permitted to continue to use the HeartBeat trademark under which it sells most of its foods. The FDA argued the trademark goes too far in implying the foods have special advantages for the heart and overall health. The company had spent more than $10 million on advertising over three years to build up the brand name and now must spend millions more to inform consumers of the name change. The company changed the name of its product to Smart Beat and is considering suing the FDA over the ruling.

Congress supplied Kessler and the FDA the ammunition it needed to embark on the labeling crusade when it passed the Nutritional Labeling and Education Act in 1990. The new law requires straightforward labels for all foods starting in 1993. While this act applies only to food labels, it may soon affect advertising of food products as well. A bill recently introduced in Congress would force the Federal Trade Commission, which has jurisdiction over advertising, to ensure food ads comply with the new FDA standards.

For years, many marketers made labeling decisions and nutritional claims based on what they thought they could get away with. However, it appears the 1990s will bring a new regulatory era in which marketers will have to be very careful over any health or nutritional claims they make for their products. Companies whose products have legitimate health advantages or benefits will be able to say so. However, those companies that stretch the truth may find themselves up against government agencies whose bite is even worse than their bark.

Source: Steven W. Colford and Julie Liesse, "FDA Label Plans under Attack," *Advertising Age,* February 24, 1992, pp. 1, 50; Steven W. Colford, "FDA, FTC May Team up to Tackle Label, Ad Claims," *Advertising Age,* May 27, 1991, pp. 3, 35; "The Cholesterol Is in the Fire Now," *Business Week,* June 10, 1991, pp. 34–35; and David Kiley, "FDA Seizes Citrus Hill," *Adweek's Marketing Week,* April 26, 1991, pp. 6, 7.

the power to impose legal sanctions for violations of these statutes as well as fraudulent use of the mail. The fraud order under U.S. Postal Service regulations has been used frequently to control deceptive advertising by numerous direct-response advertisers. These firms advertise on television or radio or in magazines and newspapers and use the U.S. mail to receive orders and payment. Many have been prosecuted by the Post Office Department for use of the mail in conjunction with the sale of a fraudulent or deceptive offer.

Bureau of Alcohol, Tobacco, and Firearms

The Bureau of Alcohol, Tobacco, and Firearms (BATF) is an agency within the Treasury Department that enforces laws, develops regulations, and is responsible for tax collection for the liquor industry. The BATF regulates and controls the advertising of alcoholic beverages. The agency determines what information will be provided in ads as well as what constitutes false and misleading advertising. It is also responsible for the inclusion of warning labels on alcohol advertising and the banning of the use of active athletes in beer commercials. The BATF can impose strong sanctions for violators.

State Regulation

In addition to the various federal rules and regulations, advertisers must also concern themselves with numerous state and local controls over advertising. An important development in state regulation of advertising was the adoption, in 44 states, of the Printers' Ink Model Statutes as a basis for advertising regulation. These statutes were drawn up in 1911 by *Printers Ink,* which for many years was the major trade publication of the advertising industry. Many states have since modified the original statutes and adopted laws similar to those of the Federal Trade Commission Act that serve as a basis for false and misleading advertising.

In addition to recognizing decisions by the federal courts regarding false or deceptive practices, many states have special controls and regulations governing the advertising of specific industries or practices. As the federal government became less involved in the regulation of national advertising during the 1980s, many state attorneys general began to enforce state laws regarding false or deceptive advertising. For example, the attorneys general in New York and Texas initiated investigations of advertising by Kraft, Inc. regarding claims in ads saying the pasteurized cheese used in Cheez Whiz was real cheese.[36] McDonald's was asked by attorneys general in three states to stop running ads claiming its food is high in nutrition on the basis that the ads were deceptive.[37]

The **National Association of Attorneys General** (NAAG) began making concerted moves against a number of national advertisers as a result of inactivity by the FTC during the Reagan administration. In 1987, the NAAG developed enforcement guidelines on airfare advertising that were adopted by more than 40 states. The NAAG also is involved in other regulatory areas including car rental price advertising, and in 1989, it began studying automobile manufacturer and dealer ads as well as advertising dealing with nutrition and health claims in food ads.[38] In 1991, a group of attorneys general from various states reached an agreement with Pfizer Corporation and its advertising agency to stop making deceptive claims regarding the ability of Pfizer's Plax mouthwash to reduce plaque.[39]

The NAAG's foray into regulating national advertising has raised the issue of whether the states working together can create and implement uniform national advertising standards that would, in effect, supersede federal authority. However, an American Bar Association panel concluded the Federal Trade Commission is the proper regulator of national advertising and recommended the state attorneys focus on practices that harm consumers within a single state.[40] This report also called for cooperation between the FTC and the state attorneys general.

Advertisers have become increasingly concerned over the trend toward increased regulation of advertising at the state and local levels, as this could have a severe impact on national advertising campaigns if they had to be modified for various states or municipalities. However, new FTC Chairwoman Janet Steiger has argued that businesses that advertise and sell nationwide need a national advertising policy. While she has called for greater cooperation between the states and the Federal Trade Commission, she argues that national advertising should be under the aegis of the FTC.[41] However, the advertising industry is still keeping a watchful eye on changes in advertising rules, regulations, and policies at the state and local level.

Regulation of Other Promotional Areas

Thus far, this chapter has focused primarily on the regulation of advertising. However, other elements of the promotional mix also come under the surveillance of various federal, state, and local laws and various self-regulatory bodies. In this final section, we examine some of the rules, regulations, and guidelines that affect sales promotion and direct marketing.

Sales Promotion

Both consumer- and trade-oriented promotions are subject to various regulations. The Federal Trade Commission regulates many areas of sales promotion through the Marketing Practices Division of the Bureau of Consumer Protection. Many promotional practices are also policed by state attorney general offices and local regulatory agencies. Various aspects of trade promotion such as allowances are regulated by the Robinson-Patman Act, which gives the FTC broad powers to control discriminatory pricing practices. We briefly examine some of the specific sales promotion tools and discuss the regulations that affect their use.

- **Contests and sweepstakes** As was noted in Chapter 17, numerous legal considerations affect the design and administration of contests and sweepstakes, and these promotions are regulated by a number of federal and state agencies. There are two important considerations in developing contests (including games) and sweepstakes. First, marketers must be careful to ensure their contest or sweepstakes is not classified as a *lottery,* which is considered a form of gambling and violates the Federal Trade Commission Act as an unfair method of competition and many state and local laws. A promotion is considered a lottery if a prize is offered, if winning a prize depends on chance and not skill, and the participant is required to give up something of value in order to participate. This latter requirement is referred to as *consideration* and is the basis on which most contests, games, and sweepstakes avoid being considered a lottery. Generally, as long as consumers are not required to make a purchase as a condition for entering a contest or sweepstakes, consideration is not considered to be present and the promotion is not considered a lottery.

    The second important requirement in the use of contests and sweepstakes is that the marketer provide full disclosure of the promotion. The FTC as well as many state and local governments have regulations that require marketers using contests, games, and sweepstakes to make certain all of the details are given clearly and they follow prescribed rules to ensure the fairness of the game.[42] Disclosure requirements include the exact number of prizes to be awarded and the odds of winning, the duration and dates of termination of the promotion, and making available lists of winners of various prizes (Exhibit 23–12). The FTC also has specific rules governing the way games and contests are conducted such as requirements that game pieces be randomly distributed, a game not be terminated before the distribution of all game pieces, and additional pieces cannot be added during the course of a game.

- **Premiums** Another sales promotion area subject to various regulations is the use of premiums. A common problem associated with premiums is a misrepresentation of their value. Marketers that make premium offers should list their value as the equivalent price at which the merchandise is usually sold when offered for sale on its own. Marketers must also be careful in the use of premium offers to special audiences such as children. While premium offers for children are legal, their use is controversial as many critics argue that they encourage children to request a product for the premium rather than its value. The National Advertising Division's Children's Advertising Review Unit (CARU) has voluntary guidelines concerning the use of premium offers. However, a recent study of children's advertising commissioned by CARU found the single most prevalent violation was devoting virtually an entire commercial message to information about a premium. CARU guidelines state advertising targeted to children must emphasize the product rather than the premium offer.[43]

- **Trade allowances** Marketers using various types of trade allowances must be careful not to violate any stipulations of the Robinson-Patman Act, which

prohibits price discrimination. Certain sections of the Robinson-Patman Act prohibit a manufacturer from granting wholesalers and retailers various types of promotional allowances and/or payments unless they are made available to all customers on proportionally equal terms.[44] Another form of trade promotion regulated by the Robinson-Patman Act is vertical cooperative advertising. The FTC monitors cooperative advertising programs to ensure that co-op funds are made available to retailers on a proportionally equal basis and these payments are not used as a disguised form of price discrimination.

Direct Marketing

As we saw in Chapter 16, direct marketing is growing rapidly. Many consumers are now purchasing products directly from companies in response to television and print advertising or direct selling. The Federal Trade Commission enforces laws in a number of areas that relate to direct marketing including mail-order offers, the use of 900 telephone numbers, and direct-response television advertising. In addition to the FTC, the United States Postal Service enforces laws dealing with the use of the mail to deliver advertising and promotional messages or receive payments and orders that may have been delivered by other means such as print or broadcast advertising.

A number of laws govern the use of mail-order selling. The FTC and Postal Service police direct-response advertising closely to ensure the ads are not deceptive or misleading or misrepresent the product or service being offered. Laws also forbid mailing unordered merchandise to consumers and rules govern the use of "negative option" plans whereby a company proposes to send merchandise to consumers and expects payment unless a notice of rejection or cancellation is sent by the consumer.[45] The FTC also has rules designed to encourage direct marketers to promptly ship merchandise that has been ordered. Companies that cannot ship merchandise within the time period stated in the solicitation (or 30 days if no time is stated) must provide buyers with an option to cancel the order and receive a full refund.[46]

The direct-marketing industry is also scrutinized by various self-regulatory groups, such as the Direct Marketing Association and the Direct Selling Association, that have specific guidelines and standards member firms are expected to adhere to and abide by. Exhibit 23-13 shows part of the Code of Ethics of the Direct Selling Association.

➤ *Exhibit 23–13* **The Direct Selling Association has a Code of Ethics for companies engaged in direct selling**

DIRECT SELLING ASSOCIATION

CODE OF ETHICS

PREAMBLE

The Direct Selling Association, recognizing that companies engaged in direct selling assume certain responsibilities toward consumers arising out of the personal-contact method of distribution of their products and services, hereby sets forth the basic fair and ethical principles and practices to which member companies of the association will continue to adhere in the conduct of their business.

INTRODUCTION

The Direct Selling Association is the national trade association of the leading firms that manufacture and distribute goods and services sold directly to consumers. The Association's mission is "to protect, serve and promote the effectiveness of member companies and the independent businesspeople marketing their products and to assure the highest level of business ethics and service to consumers." The cornerstone of the Association's commitment to ethical business practices and consumer service is its Code of Ethics. Every member company pledges to abide by the Code's standards and procedures as a condition of admission and continuing membership in the Association. Consumers can rely on the extra protection provided by the Code when they purchase products or services from a salesperson associated with a member company of the Direct Selling Association. For a current list of Association members, contact DSA, 1776 K St., N.W., Washington, DC 20006, (202) 293-5760.

A. CODE OF CONDUCT

1. Deceptive or Unlawful Consumer Practices

No member company of the Association shall engage in any deceptive or unlawful consumer practice.

2. Products or Services

The offer of products or services for sale by member companies of the Association shall be accurate and truthful as to price, grade, quality, make, value, performance, quantity, currency of model, and availability.

3. Terms of Sale

A written order or receipt shall be delivered to the customer at the time of sale, which sets forth in language that is clear and free of ambiguity:
A. All the terms and conditions of sale, with specification of the total amount the customer will be required to pay, including all interest, service charges and fees, and other costs and expenses as required by federal and state law;
B. The name and address of the salesperson or the member firm represented.

4. Warranties and Guarantees

The terms of any warranty or guarantee offered by the seller in connection with the sale shall be furnished to the buyer in a manner that fully conforms to federal and state warranty and guarantee laws and regulations. The manufacturer, distributor and/or seller shall fully and promptly perform in accordance with the terms of all warranties and guarantees offered to consumers.

5. Pyramid Schemes

For the purpose of this Code, pyramid or endless chain schemes shall be considered consumer transactions actionable under this Code. The Code Administrator shall determine whether such pyramid or endless chain schemes constitute a violation of this Code in accordance with applicable federal, state and/or local law or regulation.

SUMMARY

Regulation and control of advertising stem from internal or self-regulation as well as from external control from federal, state, and local regulatory agencies. For many years the advertising industry has promoted the use of voluntary self-regulation to regulate advertising and limit interference with, and control over, advertising by the government. Self-regulation of advertising emanates from all segments of the advertising industry, including advertisers and their agencies, business and advertising associations, and the media.

The NAD/NARB has become the primary self-regulatory mechanism for national advertising and has been very effective in achieving its goal of voluntary regulation of advertising. The various media also have their own advertising guidelines, with the major television networks maintaining the most stringent review process and restrictions.

Traditionally, the federal government has been the most important source of external regulation, with the Federal Trade Commission serving as the major watchdog of advertising in the United States. The FTC protects both consumers and businesses from unfair and deceptive practices and anticompetitive behavior. The FTC became very active in the regulation of advertising during the 1970s when several new programs and policies were initiated, including affirmative disclosure, advertising substantiation, and corrective advertising. In 1983, the FTC developed a new working definition of deceptive advertising.

During the 1980s, the commission became less active in the area of advertising regulation, focusing its attention on the pursuit of individual violators rather than emphasizing the regulation of entire industries. However, the FTC has recently become more active in the policing of false and deceptive advertising. Many companies have taken their own initiative in regard to deceptive advertising by filing lawsuits under the Lanham Act against competitors that make false claims. Many states, as well as the National Association of Attorneys General, have also become very active in exercising their jurisdiction over false and misleading advertising.

A number of laws also govern the use of other promotional mix elements such as sales promotion and direct marketing. The Federal Trade Commission regulates many areas of sales promotion as well as direct marketing. Various consumer-oriented sales promotion tools such as contests, games, sweepstakes, and premiums are subject to various regulations. Various trade promotion practices such as the use of promotional allowances and vertical cooperative advertising are regulated by the Federal Trade Commission under the Robinson-Patman Act. The FTC also enforces laws in a variety of areas that relate to direct marketing and mail-order selling.

KEY TERMS

self-regulation
Better Business Bureau
Council of Better
  Business Bureaus
National Advertising
  Review Board
National Advertising
  Review Council

Federal Trade
  Commission
Federal Trade
  Commission Act
Wheeler-Lea Amendment
trade regulation rules
puffery
deception
affirmative disclosure

advertising substantiation
consent order
cease and desist orders
corrective advertising
Lanham Act
Fairness Doctrine
National Association of
  Attorneys General

DISCUSSION QUESTIONS

1. The chapter opening discussed how Volvo used jacks to help support the weight from the other cars stacked on top of one of its cars in a demonstration commercial. Volvo defended the use of the jacks, arguing the ad was intended to demonstrate the strength of its roofs and bodies rather than the suspension. Do you agree with this argument? Do you think consumers' interpretation of the ad may have been different if they were aware of the use of the jacks?

2. Evaluate the role of self-regulation of advertising through organizations such as the NAD/NARB. What are the incentives of advertisers to cooperate with self-regulatory bodies?

3. Discuss the role of the Federal Trade Commission in regulating advertising. Do you believe the FTC should play a more active

role in the regulation of advertising? Why or why not?

4. What is meant by deceptive advertising? Evaluate the new definition of *deception* written by former FTC Chairman Miller.

5. Campbell Soup was accused of running deceptive ads recently, not because of any claims it made for the product but because its advertising did not warn consumers that Campbell soups are high in sodium. Do you believe advertisers should be found guilty of deceptive advertising for what they do not say, or should their responsibility be limited to the claims they do make?

6. What is meant by puffery? Find examples of several ads that use puffery. Do you think advertisers should be permitted to use puffery? Why or why not?

7. Do you believe advertisers should be required to substantiate their claims before running an ad, or is

it acceptable to provide documentation in response to a challenge of their advertising claims?

8. What is the purpose of corrective advertising? How should the FTC determine the extent of the corrective advertising effort required of an advertiser and the media in which it should appear? How would you determine whether corrective advertising has accomplished its purpose?

9. Over the past few years, the Federal Trade Commission and the Food and Drug Administration have become very proactive and aggressive in moving against marketers that make potentially deceptive or misleading health claims for their products. Discuss the factors that have led to the resurgence of these two regulatory agencies. What are the implications of the changes in the FTC and FDA for advertisers?

10. Discuss some rules and regulations that affect the use of nonadvertising elements of the promotional mix such as sales promotion and direct marketing. Do you believe these promotional areas require as much regulatory attention as advertising? Why or why not?

chapter 24

Evaluating the Social, Ethical, and Economic Aspects of Advertising

chapter objectives

➤ To consider various perspectives concerning the social, ethical, and economic aspects of advertising.

➤ To examine and evaluate the social criticisms of advertising.

➤ To examine the economic role of advertising and its effects on consumer choice, competition, and product costs and prices.

➤ To examine and evaluate perspectives regarding the economic effects of advertising.

The Debate over Tobacco and Alcohol Advertising

The advertising of tobacco and alcohol has been a source of controversy for many years. Cigarette advertising was banned from the broadcast media in 1970, and recently a number of groups have been calling for a total ban on the advertising of all tobacco products. There is also strong sentiment to severely restrict the advertising and promotion of alcoholic beverages including wine and beer. In 1989, the Surgeon General's Workshop on Drunk Driving made a number of recommendations concerning the advertising of alcoholic beverages including placing conspicuous warning labels in all alcohol ads, banning the use of celebrities with strong "youth appeal" in alcohol ads and promotions, prohibiting alcoholic beverage companies from sponsoring sporting events, prohibiting alcohol ads on college campuses, and requiring dissemination of health and safety messages to the public.

The pressure to restrict tobacco and alcoholic beverage advertising continues to grow. In March 1991, the Advertising Sensibility and Family Education Act was introduced in Congress and calls for health and safety warnings in alcoholic beverage ads. The National Commission on Drug Free Schools has begun including underage alcohol abuse in its reports and has called on the federal government to fund counter-usage advertising. Tobacco advertisers also face mounting pressure from various health groups that have called for a ban on ciga-

rette advertising. These groups have also expressed considerable concern over the sponsorship of sporting events such as NASCAR races and tennis tournaments by tobacco companies. They argue that sponsorship of these events along with advertising on stadium signage is a "backdoor" way of getting the brand names of tobacco products on television.

A major focus of the antismoking and drinking activists has turned to one of the most fundamental parts of the marketing strategies of tobacco and beer companies—their linkage with professional sports. Tobacco and beer companies are major supporters of sports in the United States. Beer companies recognize the demographic fit between sports audiences and their target markets, which is males between the ages of 21 and 35. Brewers are now the second-largest industry sponsor of network television sports, ranking only behind the automobile industry. The three major brewers, Anheuser-Busch, Miller Brewing, and Coors, spent more than $280 million in advertising on television sporting events and sports sponsorships in 1990. Budweiser signage appears in 80 percent of the professional sports stadiums around the country. Tobacco companies are also heavy users of stadium signage and sponsor a number of sporting events such as the Virginia Slims women's tennis tour.

(continued)

Critics of beer and cigarette company involvement with sports focus most of their arguments on teenagers and children. They argue that while the media buys of sports programming, sponsorships, and stadium signage may be directed at older audiences, they inevitably reach young people as well. For example, Arbitron, which measures television viewing audiences, estimates the World Series telecast draws more than 2 million viewers under the age of 17, and the Daytona 500 auto race draws more than a million young viewers. There is also concern that the association of beer and tobacco companies with sports sends the wrong message to young people, who often admire the athletes.

While the pressure mounts to restrict alcohol and tobacco advertising and its close relationship with professional sports, advertisers as well as the advertising industry are doing more than just arguing that these companies have a First Amendment right to advertise their legal products. The alcoholic beverage industry and individual companies are pouring millions of dollars into advertising that promotes responsible drinking. For example, Anheuser-Busch recently developed a "Family talks about drinking program" directed at the issue of underage drinking.

The advertising industry has also noted that a ban on advertising of these products would have a harmful economic impact. The Leadership Council on Advertising, which consists of media and advertising executives, recently released a study that claims an end to beer and wine advertising on television would result in a loss of more than 4,000 jobs and lead to enormous reductions in network TV sports programming. Without revenue from beer advertising, the networks would have less money to pay for sports programming, and some major sporting events would move to pay cable.

The study also suggests that a ban on tobacco advertising would result in a loss of nearly 8,000 jobs in the newspaper industry and 4,000 related to magazines. It is estimated that 165 magazines would fold as a result of the ad ban, including many targeted at blacks and Hispanics. The study also suggests consumers would have to pay higher prices for magazines, which would lead to circulation declines and even more problems for magazines.

Proponents of the advertising ban are quick to point out problems with the conclusions drawn by the Leadership Council study. They argue the loss of advertising revenue from tobacco and sports companies as well as sponsorship monies would be made up by other companies. They point to the banning of cigarette advertising from television and radio as an example, noting that none of the dire economic predictions occurred. However, the Leadership Council counters by noting the media business is much different now than 20 years ago with the advent of pay cable, pay-per-view, and the vast number of special-interest magazines.

Many people believe further restrictions on tobacco and alcohol advertising are inevitable as politicians respond to the public's concerns over tobacco-related illness and problems associated with drinking. However, this discussion points out there may be economic consequences associated with the way this social issue is addressed.

Source: Matthew Grim, "The Next Crusade? Tobacco, Beer & Sports," Adweek's Marketing Week, May 27, 1991, pp. 18–23; Jill Abramson, "Alcohol Industry Is at Forefront of Efforts to Curb Drunkenness," The Wall Street Journal, May 21, 1991, pp. A1,12; and Joanne Lipman, "Foes Claim Ad Bans Are Bad Business," The Wall Street Journal, February 27, 1990, pp. B1,6.

If I were to name the deadliest subversive force within capitalism, the single greatest source of its waning morality—I would without hesitation name advertising. How else should one identify a force that debases language, drains thought, and undoes dignity.[1]

The primary focus of this text has been on the role of advertising and other promotional variables as marketing activities used to convey information to, and influence the behavior of, consumers. We have been concerned with examining the advertising and promotion function in the context of a business and marketing environment and from a perspective that basically assumes these activities are appropriate. However, as can be seen in the above quote from noted economist Robert Heilbroner, not everyone shares this viewpoint. Advertising is the most visible of all business activities and is prone to scrutiny by those who are concerned over the methods and approaches used by advertisers to sell their products and services.

Because of its high visibility and pervasiveness, along with its persuasive character, advertising has been the subject of a great deal of controversy and criticism. Numerous books are critical of advertising, including not only its methods and techniques but also the social consequences that result from it. Various parties and

➤ *Exhibit 24–1*
Anheuser-Busch addresses the problem of underage drinking with the "Family Talk About Drinking" program

scholars including economists, politicians, sociologists, government agencies, social critics, special-interest groups, and consumers have attacked advertising for a variety of reasons including its excessiveness, the way it influences society, the methods used by advertisers, its supposed exploitation of consumers, and its effect on our economic system.

Advertising Ethics

In the previous chapter, we examined the regulatory environment in which advertising and promotion operates. While many laws and regulations determine what advertisers can and cannot do, not every issue is covered by a rule or guideline. In many situations, advertisers must make decisions regarding appropriate and responsible actions based on *ethical considerations* rather than on what is legal or within industry guidelines. **Ethics** are moral principles and values that govern the actions and decisions of an individual or group.[2]

While a particular action or practice may be within the law, this does not necessarily mean it is ethical. A good example of this is the issue of target marketing, which we discussed in Chapter 5 (Ethical Perspective 5–1). No laws restrict tobacco companies from targeting advertising and promotion for new brands to blacks. However, given the high level of lung cancer and smoking-related illnesses among the black population, many people would consider this an unethical business practice.

Throughout this text we have presented a number of Ethical Perspectives to show how various aspects of advertising and promotion often involve ethical considerations. Ethical issues often must be considered in making advertising and promotion

decisions. And advertising and promotion are areas where a lapse in ethical standards or judgment can result in actions that are highly visible and often very damaging to a company.

The role of advertising in society is controversial and at times has resulted in attempts at restricting or banning advertising to various groups or for certain products. The chapter opening discussed the current controversy raging over whether tobacco and alcohol advertising should be banned. These decisions involve very complex economic considerations as well as social issues. Companies such as Anheuser-Busch recognize the need to reduce alcohol abuse and drunken driving, particularly among young people. The company has instituted numerous programs to deal with this problem including the "Family Talk About Drinking" program (Exhibit 24–1).

Criticism of advertising often focuses on the actions of specific advertisers as well. Groups such as the National Organization for Women and Women Against Pornography have been critical of advertisers such as Guess? for depicting women as sex objects in their ads and of Calvin Klein for promoting sexual permissiveness and using erotic ads (Exhibit 24–2).

Advertising is a very powerful force, and this text would not be complete without considering the various criticisms regarding its social and economic effects as well as some of the defenses against these charges. We consider the various criticisms of advertising from a societal and ethical perspective and then appraise the economic effects of advertising.

The various perspectives presented in this chapter reflect judgments of people with different backgrounds, values, and interests. You may see nothing wrong with the advertising of beer on television or the sexually suggestive ads run by Calvin

Klein. Some of your fellow students, however, may view these issues quite differently and oppose these actions on moral and ethical grounds. Many people believe advertising is the subject of so much criticism today because it is being judged by a variety of groups with different norms, values, and ethical standards. While we attempt to present the arguments on both sides of these controversial issues, you may have to draw some of your own conclusions as to who is right or wrong.

Social and Ethical Criticisms of Advertising

Much of the controversy over advertising stems from the ways it is used by many companies as a selling tool and because of the impact advertising has on society's tastes, values, and lifestyles. Criticism of the specific techniques used by advertisers includes arguments that it is deceptive or untruthful, it is offensive or in bad taste, and it exploits certain groups such as children. Each of these criticisms is discussed along with responses of advertisers to these attacks. We then turn our attention to criticisms concerning the influence of advertising on values and lifestyles, as well as charges that it perpetuates stereotyping and advertisers can exert influence and control over the media.

Advertising as Untruthful or Deceptive

One of the major attacks against advertising is that many ads are misleading or untruthful and deceive the consumer. Deceptive advertising and attempts by industry and government to regulate and control it were discussed in the previous chapter. As was noted in that discussion, advertisers should have a reasonable basis for making a claim about product performance and, in many instances, may be required to provide substantiating evidence to support their claims. However, deception can occur in a more subtle way as a result of how the consumer perceives the ad and the resulting impact on beliefs.[3] The difficulty of determining just what constitutes deception, along with the fact that advertisers have the right to use puffery and thus make subjective claims about their products, tends to complicate the issue of whether an ad is untruthful or misleading. However, a concern of many critics is the extent to which advertisers are deliberately untruthful or misleading in their advertising.

While there are occasionally situations where advertisers have made overtly false or misleading claims, these cases usually have involved smaller companies and represent an extremely small portion of the $130 billion spent on advertising each year. Most advertisers do not design their messages with the intention of misleading or deceiving consumers. Not only would such practices be considered unethical by most firms, but they would also be risking their reputation and subjecting themselves to prosecution by various regulatory groups or government agencies. National advertisers in particular invest large sums of money to develop loyalty to, and enhance the image of, their brands. Thus, these companies are not likely to risk the consumer trust and confidence they enjoy by intentionally deceiving consumers.

The problem of untruthful or fraudulent advertising may exist more at the local level and in specific areas such as direct mail and other forms of direct-response advertising. However, a number of deceptive and misleading advertising cases have involved large national advertisers. National advertisers often test the limits of various industry and governmental rules and regulations to make claims that will give their brands an advantage in highly competitive markets. As was noted in the previous chapter, problems with unsubstantiated or misleading advertising claims increased during the 1980s. However, government agencies such as the FTC and FDA are putting more pressure on advertisers that deceive consumers.[4]

While many critics of advertising would probably accept the argument that most advertisers are not out to deceive or mislead consumers deliberately, they are still concerned over whether consumers are receiving proper information to make an informed choice. They argue that advertisers usually present only information that is favorable to their position and thus do not always tell consumers the "whole

➤ *Exhibit 24–3* **"Advertising Principles of American Business" of the American Advertising Federation (AAF)**

1. **Truth** Advertising shall reveal the truth, and shall reveal significant facts, the omission of which would mislead the public.
2. **Substantiation** Advertising claims shall be substantiated by evidence in possession of the advertiser and the advertising agency prior to making such claims.
3. **Comparisons** Advertising shall refrain from making false, misleading, or unsubstantiated statements or claims about a competitor or his products or service.
4. **Bait advertising** Advertising shall not offer products or services for sale unless such offer constitutes a bona fide effort to sell the advertised products or services and is not a device to switch consumers to other goods or services, usually higher priced.

5. **Guarantees and warranties** Advertising of guarantees and warranties shall be explicit, with sufficient information to apprise consumers of their principal terms and limitations or, when space or time restrictions preclude such disclosures, the advertisement shall clearly reveal where the full text of the guarantee or warranty can be examined before purchase.
6. **Price claims** Advertising shall avoid price claims that are false or misleading, or savings claims that do not offer provable savings.
7. **Testimonials** Advertising containing testimonials shall be limited to those of competent witnesses who are reflecting a real and honest opinion or experience.
8. **Taste and decency** Advertising shall be free of statements, illustrations, or implications that are offensive to good taste or public decency.

truth" about a product or service. The director of the FTC's Bureau of Consumer Protection has noted

> When you advertise a particular quality or characteristic of your product, you should disclose facts that tend to undermine or refute the specific claims you have made.[5]

Many believe advertising should be primarily informative in nature and should not be permitted to use puffery or embellished messages. Others argue that advertisers have the right to present the most favorable case for their products and services and should not be restricted to just the provision of objective, verifiable information.[6] They note that consumers can protect themselves from being persuaded against their will and that the various industry and governmental regulatory bodies and mechanisms are sufficient to keep advertisers from deceiving or misleading consumers. Exhibit 24–3 shows the Advertising Principles of the American Advertising Federation, which many advertisers use as a guideline in preparing and evaluating their ads.

Advertising as Offensive or in Bad Taste

Another common criticism of advertising, particularly by consumers, is that ads are offensive, tasteless, irritating, boring, obnoxious, and so on. A survey by the Ogilvy & Mather advertising agency found that only 59 percent of people like advertising. Half of the consumers surveyed considered most ads as being in poor taste versus 43 percent two years prior, and the percentage who believe advertising provides useful information slipped from 76 percent to 71 percent.[7]

Sources of distaste

Consumers can be offended or irritated by advertising in a number of ways. Some are offended if a product or service, such as contraceptives or personal hygiene products, is advertised at all. It is only in the last few years that publications began accepting ads for condoms, as the AIDS crisis forced them to reconsider their restrictions on advertising for the product (Exhibit 24–4). The major television networks gave their affiliates permission to accept condom advertising in 1987.[8] However, the first condom ad did not appear on network TV until November 1991, when the Fox Broadcasting Co. broadcast a spot. The three major networks are reviewing their policies regarding condom ads.[9]

A study of prime-time television commercials found there is a strong product class effect with respect to the type of ads consumers perceived as distasteful or irritating. The most irritating commercials were ads for feminine hygiene products, whereas commercials for women's undergarments and hemorrhoid products were close behind.[10] Another study found that consumers are more likely to dislike advertisements for products they do not use and for brands they would not buy.[11] Despite the

➤ *Exhibit 24–4 (left)*
Many magazines and television stations now accept ads for condoms

➤ *Exhibit 24–5 (right)*
Maidenform used celebrities to discuss women's lingerie

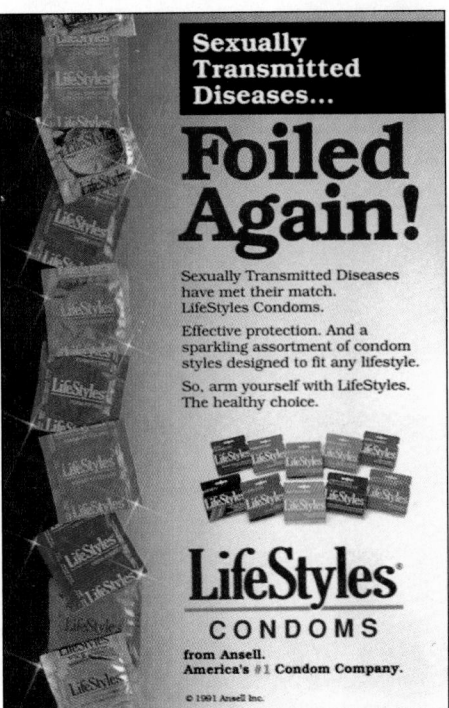

fact that people may find them offensive, ads for personal products such as herpes medication, douches, home pregnancy tests, and colon cancer detection kits have become more common on television and in print and the public more accepting of them.[12] However, advertisers still must be careful as to how these products are presented and the language and terminology used in the ads. There are still many rules, regulations, and taboos advertisers must deal with to have their TV commercials approved by the networks.[13]

Another way advertising can offend consumers is by the type of appeal or the manner of presentation. For example, many people take offense to the use of appeals that exploit consumer anxieties. Fear appeal ads, particularly for products such as deodorants, mouthwash, and dandruff shampoos, have often been criticized for attempting to create anxiety and using a fear of social rejection as a way of selling these products. Some ads for home computers were also criticized for attempting to create anxiety in parents over the need for their young children to be able to use a computer or fail in school.

Sexual appeals

The advertising appeals that have received the most criticism for being offensive or in poor taste are those using sexual appeals and/or nudity. These techniques are often used to gain consumers' attention and in some cases may not even be appropriate to the product being advertised. Even if the sexual appeal is appropriate for the product, many people may be offended by it. Concern has been expressed over both the use of nudity in advertising and also sexually provocative and suggestive ads. For example, in 1987, Playtex broke new ground in advertising when its television commercials for bras began using models instead of mannequins. Playtex's major competitor, Maidenform, did not take long to react and made the first commercial showing a woman removing her bra—albeit while remaining fully attired in a sweater.[14] Maidenform also developed what some thought was a rather risqué campaign featuring famous celebrities such as actors Michael York, Omar Sharif, Christopher Reeves, and Corbin Bernsen discussing their feelings about women and lingerie (Exhibit 24–5). Maidenform recently dropped the celebrity ads and began a new campaign critical of negative stereotyping of women (Exhibit 24–6).[15]

➤ *Exhibit 24–6*   **Maidenform's new ads lament the stereotyping of women**

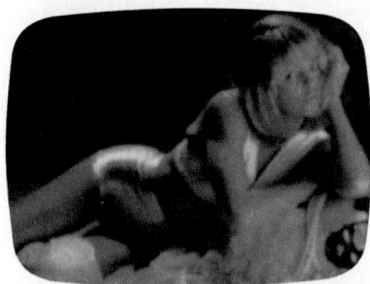

Somehow, women always seem to be portrayed like this. Or like this. Like this.	Or like this. Like this. Or like this. While there are many stereotypes of women. . .	there aren't many women who fit them. A simple truth known by all women. . . most men. . . and one lingerie company.

Many advertising critics are concerned that sexually suggestive ads are being increasingly used by companies with nonsexual products such as laundry detergents and athletic shoes. Borateem bleach ran a print ad showing the arms of six men reaching out to grab a woman dressed in skin-tight, zebra-striped shorts and wearing a bracelet that looked like handcuffs. The president of the agency that created the ad noted, "The company had to find a way to grab attention for a product in a pretty dull category."[16] Exhibit 24–7 shows a risqué sexual appeal used by Travel Fox, a small footwear company trying to compete against industry giants Nike and Reebok. The company president noted, "The shock appeal absolutely worked" but indicated the company would no longer use sex to sell its shoes because of the controversy created by the ad.[17]

Advertisers also complain about the double standard that exists for TV programs and commercials, noting that even the most suggestive commercials are bland compared with what is shown in many television programs. The networks argue, however, they have to scrutinize commercials more carefully because ads encourage people to imitate behaviors, whereas programs are merely meant to entertain. Network executives also note the complaints of parents who are concerned about their children seeing these ads, since they cannot always be there to change the channel or turn off the set when a suggestive or provocative ad comes on TV.

Because of the increasing clutter in the advertising environment, it is likely that advertisers will continue to use sexual appeals and other techniques that many people find offensive but catch the attention of consumers in their target audience. How far the advertisers can go with these appeals, however, will probably depend on the public's reactions to the ads. When the public thinks they have gone too far, they are likely to pressure the advertisers to change their ads and the media to no longer accept ads that are too explicit or offensive. It has been suggested that a return to sexual conservatism in this country, sparked by the fear of AIDS, has led many

> *Exhibit 24–7*
Travel Fox used a sexual appeal to sell shoes

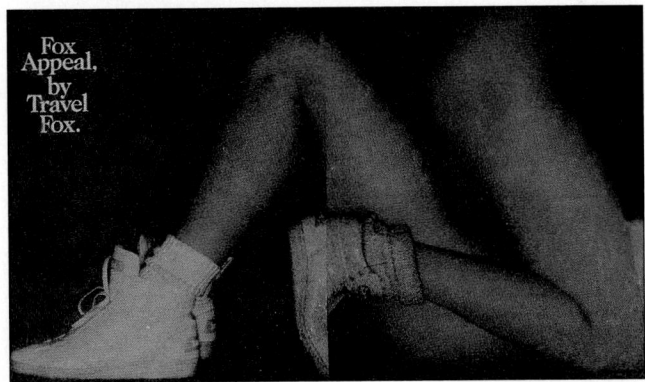

advertisers to tone down the use of explicit sexual appeals and imagery in their ads.[18] Ethical Perspective 24–1 discusses whether advertisers have gone too far with their sexual appeals.

Advertising and Children

One of the most controversial topics advertisers must deal with is the issue of advertising to children. The advent and growth of television have provided advertisers with a vehicle through which children can be readily and easily reached. Sources have estimated that children between the ages of 2 and 11 watch an average of 26 hours of television a week and may see between 22,000 and 25,000 commercials a year.[19] Studies have also shown that television is an important source of information for children about products.[20] Concern has also been expressed over marketers' use of other promotional vehicles and techniques such as radio ads, point-of-purchase displays, premiums in packages, and the use of commercial characters such as the Smurfs as the basis for television shows.

Critics argue that children, particularly young ones, are especially vulnerable to advertising because they lack the necessary experience and knowledge to understand and evaluate critically the purpose of persuasive advertising appeals. Research has shown that preschool children cannot differentiate between commercials and television programs, do not perceive the selling intent of commercials, and cannot distinguish between reality and fantasy.[21] Research has also shown that children need more than a skeptical or critical attitude toward advertising, as they must understand how advertising works in order to use their cognitive defenses against it effectively.[22] Because of children's limited ability to interpret the selling intent of a message or tell the difference between the program and a commercial, critics charge that advertising to children is inherently unfair and deceptive and thus should be banned or severely restricted.

At the other extreme are those who argue that advertising is a part of life and children must learn to deal with it as part of the **consumer socialization process** of acquiring the skills needed to function in the marketplace.[23] They argue that existing rules' restrictions are adequate for controlling children's advertising.

This issue received a great deal of attention in 1979 when the Federal Trade Commission held hearings to examine proposed changes in regulations regarding advertising to children. An FTC staff report recommended:

- Banning all television advertising for any product directed to or seen by audiences composed of a significant proportion of children who are under age 8 because they are too young to understand the selling intent of advertising.
- Banning advertising for sugary products that pose a dental health risk from TV shows seen by significant numbers of children between ages 8 and 11.
- Allowing continued TV advertising of less hazardous sugared foods to the 8-to-11-year-old group but only if individual food advertisers fund "balancing" nutritional and/or health disclosures.[24]

Ethical Perspective 24–1

Ads: Too Sexy for Their Own Good?

According to some advertisers, the "new vulgarity" is the key to advertising success. The "new vulgarity," which includes nasty language and images as well as graphic sex, has apparently caught on in advertising circles and with certain audiences. Steve Hayden, the chief creative director of BBDO Los Angeles, notes these forms of ads have a "whole group of people behind them saying 'Right on.'" Others state that receivers get a "vicarious thrill" when they see and hear such ads.

Who are these groups that like these type of ads? Hayden believes the Yuppie generation is one such segment, and a survey conducted by *Advertising Age* indicates college students are another. According to the *Ad Age* survey, "Nothing catches the eyes of college students better than the naked truth . . . and Calvin Klein knows it." Three of the top 10 favorite print ads with this group were Calvin Klein ads. Joe Venaglia, president of College Market Consultants, notes, "Sexy ads will always do well on the college level. . . . There is evolution of sex in advertising. . . . Students are in a questioning environment, so it's only natural they follow the trend."

Not everyone, however, is so enamored with sexy ads. A variety of groups believe that what may have been considered sexy and acceptable 10 years ago may no longer be. A coalition of consumer groups has recently come out against sexy ads, calling the Swedish bikini team beer ads run by Stroh's Brewery the winners of the Harlan Page Hubbard Lemon irresponsible advertising award. (The ad featured a bevy of blond beauties drinking the beer, and the models later made the front cover of *Playboy*.) In addition, a variety of other U.S. government groups have begun investigating this ad and others that may appeal to underage drinkers. Stroh's is facing sexual harassment charges that allege its advertising was a contributory factor.

Some industry experts also believe sexy ads may be outdated. They cite as an example the Calvin Klein insert that appeared in *Vanity Fair* at a reported cost of $1 million. While the 116-page insert featuring torrid sexual images generated much publicity, it apparently had no noticeable impact on sales. Others also think that in an age of AIDS and severe economic woes, "narrow sexual advertising" is not in tune. Anheuser-Busch is one company that agrees and has abandoned its "cheesecake" advertising, replacing it with women in more "equal roles." The maker of Budweiser and Michelob (among others) believes women no longer tolerate the old-time sexual portrayals.

Who is right is a question worthy of debate. According to Lillian-Maresch, president of Generation Insights, a Minneapolis consulting firm,

> Baby boomers are going through a midlife transition. They may appreciate these (sexy) ads artistically or aesthetically, but at a time when people are more reluctant than ever to purchase, image alone is no longer sufficient to drive the kind of sales boost that we used to see. People are looking for a more rational reason to buy.

Isn't this the same group that BBDO's Steve Hayden said really liked the ads? And what about all you college students? Didn't you vote the Calvin Klein Obsession ad as one of your top two favorites two years in a row? Just what is going on here? Maybe we just need to watch the sales of Calvin Klein, Stroh's, and Anheuser-Busch.

Source: Betsy Sharkey "Nasty Boys (and Girls): Beyond the Big Bland-Out," *Adweek*, June 18, 1990, p. 44; Ira Teinowitz, "This Bud's for Her," *Advertising Age*, October 28, 1991, p. 1; John P. Cortez and Ira Teinowitz, "More Trouble Brews for Stroh Bikini Team," *Advertising Age*, December 9, 1991, p. 45; Anita M. Busch, "Sexier the Better, Student Body Says," *Advertising Age*, February 5, 1990, p. S-1; and Teri Agins, "Klein Jeans' Sexy Insert Didn't Spur Sales," *The Wall Street Journal*, May 5, 1992, p. B1.

The FTC proposal was intensely debated, with the advertising industry and a number of companies arguing strongly against it. Their opposition was based on several factors including advertisers' right of free speech under the First Amendment to communicate with those consumers who make up their primary target audience.[25] They also argued that studies have shown children are more capable of perceiving persuasive intent than was originally believed, inability to perceive such intent does not necessarily lead to incorrect beliefs about products, and there was no evidence of a relationship between television advertising of sugared foods and inci-

➤ *Exhibit 24—8* **Children's Advertising Review Unit guidelines for children's advertising**

PRINCIPLES

Five basic principles underlie these guidelines for advertising directed to children:

1. Advertisers should always take into account the level of knowledge, sophistication, and maturity of the audience to which their message is primarily directed. Younger children have a limited capability for evaluating the credibility of what they watch. Advertisers, therefore, have a special responsibility to protect children from their own susceptibilities.
2. Realizing that children are imaginative and that make-believe play constitutes an important part of the growing up process, advertisers should exercise care not to exploit that imaginative quality of children. Unreasonable expectations of product quality or performance should not be stimulated either directly or indirectly by advertising.
3. Recognizing that advertising may play an important part in educating the child, information should be communicated in a truthful and accurate manner with full recognition by the advertiser that the child may learn practices from advertising that can affect his or her health and well-being.
4. Advertisers are urged to capitalize on the potential of advertising to influence social behavior by developing advertising that, wherever possible, addresses itself to social standards generally regarded as positive and beneficial, such as friendship, kindness, honesty, justice, generosity and respect for others.
5. Although many influences affect a child's personal and social development, it remains the prime responsibility of the parents to provide guidance for children. Advertisers should contribute to this parent-child relationship in a constructive manner.

dence of tooth decay.[26] Opponents of the ban also argued that parents should generally be involved in helping children interpret advertising and can refuse to purchase products they believe are undesirable for their children.

The FTC proposal was defeated, and changes in the political environment that resulted in less emphasis on government regulation of advertising have ended much of the debate over this issue. However, concern over advertising to children remains, and parent and consumer groups such as the Center for Science in the Public Interest and Action for Children's Television are still active in putting pressure on advertisers regarding what they feel are inappropriate or misleading ads for children. ACT was instrumental in getting Congress to approve the Children's Television Act in October 1990. The act limits the amount of commercial time in children's programming to 10½ minutes on weekends and 12 minutes for weekdays.

Children are also protected from the potential influences of television commercials by network censors and industry self-regulatory groups such as the Council of Better Business Bureau's Children's Advertising Review Unit (CARU). CARU has strict self-regulatory guidelines for children's advertising regarding the type of appeals, product presentation and claims, disclosures and disclaimers, the use of premiums, safety, and use of techniques such as special effects and animation. The five basic principles underlying the CARU guidelines for all advertising addressed to children under 12 years are presented in Exhibit 24—8.

As we saw in Chapter 23, the major networks also have strict guidelines for ads targeted to children. For example, in network TV ads, only 10 seconds can be devoted to animation and special effects, whereas the final 5 seconds are reserved for displaying all the toys shown earlier in the ad, disclosing whether they are sold separately and whether accessories such as batteries are included. Networks also require 3 seconds of every 30-second cereal ad to portray a balanced breakfast, usually by showing a picture of toast, orange juice, and milk.[27]

Advertising to children has been, and will remain, a controversial topic. A recent study found that marketers of products targeted to children believe advertising to them is beneficial because it provides useful information on new products and does not disrupt the parent-child relationship. However, the general public did not have such a favorable opinion, as older consumers and those from households with children had particularly negative attitudes toward children's advertising.[28]

It is important to many companies that they be able to communicate directly with children. However, only by being sensitive to the naiveté of children as consumers will they be able to do so freely and avoid potential conflict with those who believe children should be protected from advertising.

Social and Cultural Consequences

Concern is often expressed over the impact of advertising on society, particularly with respect to its influence on values and lifestyles. While a number of factors influence the cultural values, lifestyles, and behavior of a society, the overwhelming amount of advertising and its prevalence in the mass media lead many critics to argue that advertising plays a major role in influencing and transmitting social values. In his book *Advertising and Social Change,* Ronald Berman notes the major role advertising is playing relative to other institutions:

> The institutions of family, religion, and education have grown noticeably weaker over each of the past three generations. The world itself seems to have grown more complex. In the absence of traditional authority, advertising has become a kind of social guide. It depicts us in all the myriad situations possible to a life of free choice. It provides ideas about style, morality, behavior.[29]

While there is general agreement that advertising is an important social influence agent, opinions as to the value of its contribution are often negative. Advertising is criticized for a number of reasons including charges that it encourages materialism, it manipulates consumers to buy things they do not really need, it perpetuates stereotyping, and advertisers control the media. Each of these criticisms is discussed below.

Advertising encourages materialism

Many critics claim advertising has an adverse effect on consumer values by encouraging **materialism,** which is defined as a preoccupation with material things rather than intellectual or spiritual concerns. The United States is undoubtedly the most materialistic society in the world, which many critics attribute to advertising that

- Seeks to create needs rather than merely showing how a product or service fulfills them.
- Surrounds consumers with images of the good life and suggests the acquisition of material possessions leads to contentment and happiness and adds to the joy of living.
- Suggests material possessions are symbols of status, success, and accomplishment and/or will lead to greater social acceptance, popularity, sexual appeal, and so on.

The ad shown in Exhibit 24–9 for Rolls-Royce automobiles is an example of how advertising might promote materialistic values.

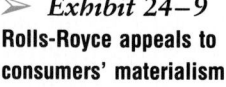

➤ *Exhibit 24–9*
Rolls-Royce appeals to consumers' materialism

The criticism of advertising on the grounds that it encourages materialistic values assumes several things. First, it assumes materialism is undesirable and is sought at the expense of nonmaterialistic goals. Many believe materialism is an acceptable part of the **Protestant ethic,** which stresses hard work and individual effort and initiative and views the accumulation of material possessions as evidence of success. Others argue that the acquisition of material possessions is not necessarily bad and, in fact, has an important economic impact by encouraging consumers to keep consuming even though their basic needs may be met. Most Americans believe economic growth is essential and materialism is both a necessity and an inevitable part of this progress.

Economist John Kenneth Galbraith, often a very vocal critic of advertising, has noted the role advertising plays in industrialized economies by encouraging consumption:

> Advertising and its related arts thus help develop the kind of man the goals of the industrial system require—one that reliably spends his income and works reliably because he is always in need of more. . . . In the absence of the massive and artful persuasion that accompanies the management of demand, increasing abundance might well have reduced the interest of people in acquiring more goods. . . . Being not pressed by the need for these things, they would have spent less reliably to get more. The consequence—a lower and less reliable propensity to consume—would have been awkward for the industrial system.[30]

It has also been argued that an emphasis on material possessions does not rule out consumers being interested in intellectual or spiritual cultural values. Defenders of advertising argue that interest in higher-order goals is more likely when basic needs have been met. Also, Raymond Bauer and Stephen Greyser have argued that consumers may purchase material things in the pursuit of nonmaterial goals.[31] For example, the purchase of an expensive stereo system may be made to enjoy music rather than simply to impress someone or acquire a material possession.

Even if one assumes materialism is undesirable, there is still the issue of whether advertising is responsible for creating and encouraging these values. While many critics argue that advertising is a major contributing force to materialistic values, others argue that advertising merely reflects or mirrors the values of society rather than molding or shaping them.[32] They argue that consumers' values are defined by the society in which they live. Moreover, they say these value systems are the results of extensive longtime socialization or acculturation.

The argument that advertising is responsible for creating a materialistic and hedonistic society has also been addressed by Stephen Fox in his book *The Mirror Makers: A History of American Advertising and Its Creators.* Fox concludes advertising has become a prime scapegoat for our times and advertising merely reflects society on itself. In discussing the effect of advertising on cultural values, he notes:

> To blame advertising now for those most basic tendencies in American history is to miss the point. It is too obvious, too easy, a matter of killing the messenger instead of dealing with the bad news. The people who have created modern advertising are not hidden persuaders pushing our buttons in the service of some malevolent purpose. They are just producing an especially visible manifestation, good and bad, of the American way of life.[33]

Exhibit 24–10 shows an ad developed by the American Association of Advertising Agencies (AAAA) that suggests advertising is a reflection of society's tastes and values and not vice versa. This ad was part of a campaign that addressed some of the common criticisms of advertising.

While it is probably unrealistic to hold advertising as solely accountable for our materialism, it does contribute by portraying products and services as symbols of status, success, and achievement and by encouraging consumption. As Richard Pollay has noted:

> While it may be true that advertising reflects cultural values, it does so on a very selective basis, echoing and reinforcing certain attitudes, behaviors, and values far more frequently than others.[34]

➤ *Exhibit 24–10*
The advertising industry argues that advertising is a reflection of society

The extent to which advertising is responsible for materialism, as well as the desirability of such values, are deep philosophical issues that will continue to be part of the debate over the societal value and consequences of advertising.

Advertising makes people buy things they do not need

A common criticism of advertising is that it has the power to manipulate consumers and make them buy things they do not need. Many critics argue that advertising should be limited to providing information that can be useful in making purchase decisions and not be persuasive. Information advertising, which reports factual, functional information such as price, performance, and other objective criteria, is viewed as acceptable and desirable. Persuasive advertising, however, which plays on consumers' emotions, anxieties, and psychological needs and desires such as status, self-esteem, and attractiveness, is viewed as undesirable and unacceptable. Persuasive advertising is criticized for fostering dissatisfaction and/or discontent among consumers and encouraging them to purchase products and services to solve these problems. It is charged that advertising exploits consumers and persuades them to go beyond basic needs or necessities, as was noted in discussing materialism.

Defenders of advertising offer a number of rebuttals to these criticisms. First, in response to the argument that only informational advertising is acceptable, they point out that a substantial amount of advertising is essentially informational in nature.[35] Also, it is difficult to separate desirable informational advertising from undesirable persuasive advertising. For example, Shelby Hunt, in examining the *information-persuasion dichotomy,* points out that even advertising that most observers would categorize as very informative is often very persuasive.[36] He argues that the basic purpose of advertising is to persuade and highly informative ads are often very effective in persuading consumers to purchase a product. Hunt notes

if advertising critics really believe that persuasive advertising should not be permitted, they are actually proposing that no advertising be allowed, since the purpose of all advertising is to persuade.[37]

➤ *Exhibit 24–11*
The AAAA responds to the claim that advertising makes consumers buy things they do not need

DESPITE WHAT SOME PEOPLE THINK, ADVERTISING CAN'T MAKE YOU BUY SOMETHING YOU DON'T NEED.

Some people would have you believe that you are putty in the hands of every advertiser in the country.

They think that when advertising is put under your nose, your mind turns to oatmeal.

It's mass hypnosis. Subliminal seduction. Brain washing. Mind control. It's advertising.

And you are a pushover for it.

It explains why your kitchen cupboard is full of food you never eat.

Why your garage is full of cars you never drive.

Why your house is full of books you don't read, T.V.'s you don't watch, beds you don't use, and clothes you don't wear.

You don't have a choice. You are forced to buy.

That's why this message is a cleverly disguised advertisement to get you to buy land in the tropics.

Got you again, didn't we? Send in your money.

ADVERTISING
ANOTHER WORD FOR FREEDOM OF CHOICE.
American Association of Advertising Agencies

Defenders of advertising also take issue with the argument that advertising should limit itself to dealing with basic functional needs. In our society, most lower-level needs recognized in Maslow's hierarchy such as the need for food, clothing, and shelter are satisfied, and it is natural for people to move from basic needs to higher-order ones such as self-esteem and status or self-actualization. Consumers are free to choose the degree to which they want to attempt to satisfy their desires, and advertisers should associate their products and services with the satisfaction of higher-order needs.

Proponents of advertising offer two other important defenses against the charge that advertising makes people buy things they do not really need. First, this criticism attributes too much power to the ability of advertising to make consumers do things against their will and assumes consumers have no ability to defend themselves against advertising. Second, it ignores the fact that consumers have the freedom to make their own choices when confronted with persuasive advertising. While they will readily admit the persuasive intent of their business, advertisers also are quick to note it is extremely difficult to make a consumer purchase a product he or she really does not want or need, as Coca-Cola discovered when it attempted to reformulate Coke in 1985. Ethical Perspective 24–2 discusses how the "green marketing" movement has failed to get consumers to forgo low price for products that make environmental claims.

If advertising were as effective and as powerful as the critics claims, we should not see products with multimillion-dollar advertising budgets failing in the marketplace. The reality is that consumers do have a choice, and they are not being forced to buy. Persuasion, it can be argued, is very much a part of our lives, and consumers have the ability to ignore ads for products and services they do not really need or that fail to interest them. Exhibit 24–11 shows an ad from the campaign by the American Association of Advertising Agencies that refutes the argument advertising makes consumers buy something they do not need.

Ethical Perspective 24–2

Is Green Marketing Turning Brown?

Over the past decade, many marketers have been developing new products, reformulating many of their existing brands, and changing their packaging to make their products more environmentally friendly. While some of these changes were made in response to stricter environmental laws and regulations, many were made to satisfy consumers' growing desire for "green" or "environmentally friendly" products. The "green marketing" movement trend was in full steam as we entered the 1990s. Marketing research and opinion polls showed environmental awareness was at an all-time high and consumers were willing to pay a premium for environmentally sensitive products. Many marketers saw green marketing as a way of gaining an edge over their competitors. Others worried about what would happen if they did not respond to the increased environmental sensitivity of consumers.

As green marketing became popular, environmental claims began popping up everywhere—on packages, in advertisements, on coupon inserts, and any other place consumers might see them. Marketers have been linking their products to numerous environmental issues such as recycling, energy conservation, saving the ozone, and preserving the rain forests. However, the avalanche of environmental ads has created considerable confusion and skepticism among consumers because there have been scores of bogus or misleading claims. Advertising claims that promoted trash bags, disposable diapers, and laminated juice cartons as biodegradable or easily recyclable were withdrawn following complaints from regulators. Part of the problem was that there have been no standards or guidelines for environmental labeling and advertising claims. (However in July of 1992 the Federal Trade Commission issued a set of voluntary guidelines for environmental marketing claims.)

Despite all these problems, most marketers expected the green marketing movement to continue into the 90s. However, recent evidence suggests it may be wilting. While marketing surveys continue to show that consumers are willing to pay anywhere from 7 to 20 percent more for environmentally sensitive products, these intentions are not being followed through at the cash register. Many retailers and manufacturers attribute the lack of consumer interest in green products to the recession as most people are more concerned over saving money than saving the Earth. They note most green products typically cost more than major brands, which often are discounted and for which consumers may have a coupon.

While many consumers consider themselves environmentalists, they often are not willing to pass up a bargain and pay more for products with environmental benefits. Also, in addition to the higher prices and confusion over environmental claims, many consumers do not like the quality of certain green products or find them less convenient to use. Research by the Roper Organization suggests green products have found a small niche market of consumers who are very involved in pro-environment practices

and are willing to spend an average of 7.4 percent more for green products. These "true-blue greens" account for 11 percent of the population and consist primarily of highly educated, affluent women.

While the green movement is slowing down in the United States, this is not the case in Europe and Japan where consumers tend to be much more environmentally conscious. For example, in Europe, Procter & Gamble sells many of its household products such as cleaners and detergents in refills that come in throw-away pouches. However, P&G says U.S. consumers would not take to the pouches.

Consumer apathy toward green marketing might be a temporary phenomenon that has been caused by the recession or it may be more enduring. It is likely that many marketers will continue to develop products and packaging that is environmentally friendly. However, it remains to be seen if they will continue to use environmental claims in their advertising that will get consumers to pay more for these products. It may be that most consumers are "basic brown" when its comes to green products.

Source: Valerie Reitman, " 'Green' Product Sales Seem to Be Wilting," *The Wall Street Journal,* May 18, 1992, p. B1; Scott Hume, "What Separates True Blues from Basic Browns," *Advertising Age,* October 26, 1991, p. GR-4; Bruce Horowitz, " 'Green' Honeymoon Is Over," *Los Angeles Times,* May 12, 1992, pp. D1,6; and Steven W. Colford, "FTC green guidelines may spark ad efforts," *Advertising Age,* August 3, 1992, pp. 1, 29.

Advertising and stereotyping

Advertising is often accused of creating and perpetuating stereotypes through its portrayal of certain groups including women and ethnic minorities such as blacks and Hispanics.

Women   One area where advertising has received much criticism is for its stereotyping of women. Critics have charged that advertising generally depicts women as homemakers or mothers and has failed to acknowledge the changing role of women in our society. Concern has also been expressed over women being shown as decorative objects or sexually provocative figures. A number of studies have examined advertising's portrayal of women and the problem of female stereotyping. A decade ago, Alice Courtney and Thomas Whipple reviewed the findings of nearly 70 studies in this area and concluded

> advertising portrays the typical woman in a limited and traditional role, that woman's place in advertising is seen to be in the home, and that her labor force roles are under-represented. Women are typically portrayed as housewives and mothers, as dependent upon men, and sometimes subservient. Women are often "used" as sexual or decorative objects in advertising but are seldom shown or heard in authoritative roles, such as announcers or voice overs. On the other hand, men are depicted as the voices of authority, the older and wiser advice-givers and demonstrators. They are shown in a wider range of occupations and roles in their working and leisure lives or as beneficiaries of women's work in the home.[38]

While sexism and stereotyping of women still exist, advertising's portrayal of women is improving in many areas.[39] Many advertisers have begun to recognize the changing role of women in our society and the importance of portraying them realistically. The increase in the number of working women has resulted not only in women having more influence in family decision making but also in more single-female households, which means more independent choice decisions. Thus, many advertisers are making special efforts to depict women in a favorable manner by showing them in a diversity of roles reflecting their changing place in society and avoiding stereotyping. For example, as was noted in Ethical Perspective 24–1, some companies have developed nonsexist advertising policies.[40] The ad shown in Exhibit 24–12 is an example of how advertisers are changing their portrayals of women.

Feminist groups such as the National Organization for Women (NOW) continually attack advertising that portrays women in traditional sexist roles. NOW has also been critical of advertising for portraying women as sex objects and has argued such advertising contributes to the problem of violence against women. NOW and other groups often protest to advertisers and their agencies against ads they believe are insulting to women and have even called for boycotts against offending advertisers.

Blacks/Hispanics   Blacks and Hispanics have also been the target of stereotyping in advertising. For many years, advertisers virtually ignored blacks and Hispanics as identifiable subcultures and viable markets. Thus, advertisements were often not targeted to these ethnic groups, and the use of blacks and Hispanics as spokespersons, communicators, models, or actors in advertisements was very limited. A 1983 study examining the portrayal of Hispanics in general-interest magazines found a very low incidence of use of Hispanic models—of 206 ads containing models, only 3 used Hispanics, despite the fact that Hispanics comprise nearly 10 percent of the readership of these publication.[41]

Several more recent studies have examined the incidence of minorities in advertising. One study reported an 11 percent incidence of blacks in television commercials.[42] A recent study by Robert Wilkes and Humberto Valencia examined the portrayal of blacks and Hispanics in commercials shown on network television and found that blacks appeared in 26 percent of all ads that used live models.[43] Hispanics, however, appeared in only 6 percent of the commercials with live models.

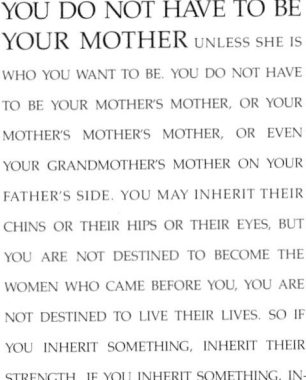

YOU DO NOT HAVE TO BE YOUR MOTHER UNLESS SHE IS WHO YOU WANT TO BE. YOU DO NOT HAVE TO BE YOUR MOTHER'S MOTHER, OR YOUR MOTHER'S MOTHER'S MOTHER, OR EVEN YOUR GRANDMOTHER'S MOTHER ON YOUR FATHER'S SIDE. YOU MAY INHERIT THEIR CHINS OR THEIR HIPS OR THEIR EYES, BUT YOU ARE NOT DESTINED TO BECOME THE WOMEN WHO CAME BEFORE YOU, YOU ARE NOT DESTINED TO LIVE THEIR LIVES. SO IF YOU INHERIT SOMETHING, INHERIT THEIR STRENGTH. IF YOU INHERIT SOMETHING, IN-HERIT THEIR RESILIENCE. BECAUSE THE ONLY PERSON YOU ARE DESTINED TO BECOME IS THE PERSON YOU DECIDE TO BE.

Another study analyzed the portrayal of blacks in business ads and found that the number of trade journal advertisements depicting blacks increased from 4.9 percent in 1966 to 10.6 percent in 1976 and stayed at the same level in 1986.[44] However, this study also found that the number of blacks in business ads as a percentage of the total people shown in these ads has not increased significantly over the past 20 years.

In recent years, not only has the use of blacks in advertising increased, but so has the depiction of their social and role status. The study of business ads concluded business-to-business advertisers are sensitive to changes in the status of blacks in business. The studies discussed here have also found that ads are increasingly likely to be racially integrated. While the use of Hispanics in television advertising is still rather low, the manner in which they are depicted is changing as marketers recognize they represent a very viable and expanding market.[45] Not only are advertisers being careful to avoid ethnic stereotyping, but they are also striving to develop advertising that has specific appeal to various ethnic groups (Exhibit 24–13).

Advertisers must be sensitive to the portrayal of specific groups of people in their ads. There is little question that advertising has been guilty of stereotyping women and ethnic groups in the past and, to a certain extent, still does so today. Advertisers might argue that in some cases this has been justified. For example, some women are content as homemakers and have no problem with ads depicting them as such. However, as the role of women changes, advertisers must change their portrayal of them and avoid demeaning stereotypes. Advertising must also consider the increasing importance of minority groups in our society and not only increase the incidence of their use in ads but also avoid stereotyping or negative role portrayals. Ethical Perspective 24–3 on page 826 discusses how some advertisers are addressing the problem of race relations in their advertising.

Advertising and the media

The fact that advertising plays such an important role in financing the media has led to concern on the part of many people that advertisers can influence or even control the media. We consider arguments on both sides of this controversial issue.

➤ *Exhibit 24–13*
Mattel appeals to black consumers in this ad

Arguments supporting advertiser control Some critics charge the media's dependence on advertisers' support makes them susceptible to various forms of influence, including exerting control over the editorial content of magazines and newspapers; biasing editorial opinions to favor the position of an advertiser; limiting coverage of a controversial topic, issue, or story that might reflect negatively on a company; and influencing the program content of television.

Newspapers and magazines receive nearly 70 percent of their total revenue from advertising, whereas commercial television and radio derive virtually all their income from advertisers. Small, financially insecure newspapers, magazines, or broadcast stations are the most prone to influence and pressure from advertisers, particularly companies that account for a large amount of the medium's advertising revenue. A local newspaper may be reluctant to print an unfavorable story about an automobile dealer or grocery store chain on whose advertising it depends.

While larger, more financially stable media should be less susceptible to an advertiser's influence, they may also be reluctant to carry stories detrimental to companies that purchase large amounts of advertising time or space. For example, since cigarette commercials were taken off radio and TV in 1970, tobacco companies have allocated most of their budgets to the print media. The tobacco industry outspends all other national advertisers in newspapers, and cigarettes constitute the second largest category of magazine advertising behind transportation. This has led to charges that magazines and newspapers avoid printing articles on the hazards of smoking to protect this important source of ad revenue.[46]

Individual television stations as well as the major networks also can be influenced by advertisers. Programming decisions are made largely on the basis of what shows will attract the largest number of viewers and thus be most desirable to the advertiser. Critics of television argue this often results in lower quality television, as educational, cultural, and informative programming is usually sacrificed for shows that get high ratings and appeal to the mass markets. Advertisers have also been accused of pressuring the networks to change their programming. Many advertisers have begun withdrawing commercials from programs that contain too much sex and violence, often in response to threatened boycotts of their products by consumers if they advertise on these shows.

The networks have had difficulty attracting sponsors for several controversial programs. In 1981, ABC had trouble attracting sponsors for its movie *The Day*

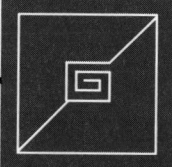

Ethical Perspective 24–3

Using Advertising to Address Social Problems

In recent years, some companies have been criticized for targeting their advertising to certain market segments. For example, as we saw in Chapter 5, tobacco marketer R.J. Reynolds received considerable criticism when it test-marketed Uptown, a high-tar menthol cigarette targeted at blacks, and its Dakota brand, which was to be targeted to low-income, young women with low education levels. The G. Heilman Brewing Company also created a controversy when it tried to market a high-alcohol malt liquor called PowerMaster to blacks. Many other alcoholic beverage and tobacco companies have been criticized for advertising their brands in inner-city areas where there are problems with teenage drinking, alcoholism, and high levels of smoking-related illnesses.

The criticism has not been limited to alcohol and cigarette advertising. Athletic shoe companies such as Reebok and Nike have also been attacked. Critics argue that these companies use athletes who are very popular among inner-city youth to endorse their products and thus create demand for products this group cannot afford. There have even been charges that Nike and Reebok are in some way responsible for incidents where young people have been killed for their Reebok "pumps" or Nike "Air Jordans."

Nike executives strongly reject the argument they are exploiting the young black market or contributing to inner-city problems. The company has recently begun to address the problems of race relations in its advertising. In June 1992, Nike began airing a commercial featuring black movie director Spike Lee, who has directed several other commercials for the company, serving as a peacemaker between two racially divided basketball teams. In the scene where he tries to mediate the bickering between the black and white teams, Lee says, "If we're gonna live together, we gotta play together." Lee decided to remove a scene in the commercial in which he holds up a Nike shoe because it did not fit in. He noted the spot "has nothing to do with selling sneakers."

While Nike and Lee may think the commercial does not have anything to do with selling sneakers, not everyone sees it this way. Officials at the Center for the Study of Commercialism criticized Nike for advertising itself as racially sensitive, arguing the basic goal of the message is to sell shoes. Nike's director of advertising defends the spot, noting the company tries to address racial problems and has posed the question, "Is it better not to do it at all? Are we supposed to turn our back on social issues?"

Nike is not the only company addressing the issue of race relations in its advertising. Italian clothing manufacturer Benetton has been linking itself with racial harmony in its worldwide advertising for nearly a decade. Even the company's trademark and advertising slogan, "United Colors of Benetton," symbolizes its commitment to racial and multicultural harmony. Benetton has used some powerful imagery to promote racial harmony including ads showing a black and white men handcuffed together, a white man kissing a black woman, and a black woman breast-feeding a white baby. Many magazines in the United States and other countries have refused to run some of the Benetton ads, arguing they might offend some people.

Apparel maker Esprit has also addressed racism in its ads. The company sponsored a promotion that asked young people to comment on things they would like to change in the world. Many said they wanted to see better relations between blacks and whites, and Esprit ran print ads that featured the written statements they received on the topic. Another clothing company trying to appeal to diverse ethnic groups is Cross Colours of Los Angeles, whose advertising slogan is "Clothing without prejudice."

Many sociologists believe the Los Angeles riots in May 1992 have brought the problem of racial relations to the forefront of social problems confronting this country. People such as Spike Lee are concerned advertisers will jump onto the racial harmony bandwagon as they did with the environmental movement in recent years. If this occurs, it may become even more difficult for advertisers that truly want to address social problems to make a statement in their advertising. On the other hand, if advertising is effective in influencing our purchase behavior, maybe it can also make us aware of the need to get along better with one another.

Source: Bruce Horowitz, "Can Ads Cure Social Ills?" *Los Angeles Times*, June 2, 1992, pp. D1,6; and Gary Levin, "Benetton Gets the Kiss-off," *Advertising Age*, July 22, 1991, pp. 1,40.

After, which depicted life in the United States following a nuclear war. Many advertisers did not want to be associated with the program because they believed sponsorship might result in their being perceived as antinuclear. In 1989, NBC had trouble getting advertisers for the movie *Roe vs. Wade,* which was the story of the woman whose case led to the 1973 Supreme Court ruling legalizing abortion. Several companies withdrew their sponsorship as a result of threats from antiabortion groups to boycott advertisers that bought time in the movie.[47]

Arguments against advertiser control   The commercial media's dependence on advertising means advertisers can exert influence on its character, content, and coverage of certain issues. However, media executives offer several reasons as to why it is incorrect to assume advertisers control or exert undue influence over the media.

➤ *Exhibit 24–14*
This ad points out how advertising lowers the cost of magazines for consumers

First, they point out it is in the best self-interest of the media that they not be influenced too much by advertisers. To retain public confidence, they must report the news fairly and accurately and not be perceived as biased or attempting to avoid controversial issues. Media executives point to the vast amount of topics they cover and the investigative reporting they often do as evidence of their objectivity. It is in their best interest to build a large audience for their publications or stations so they can make their medium more valuable to advertisers and charge more for advertising space and time.

Media executives also note that an advertiser needs the media more than they need any individual advertiser, particularly when the medium has a large audience or does a good job of reaching a specific market segment. Many publications and stations have a very broad base of advertising support and can afford to lose an advertiser that might attempt to exert too much influence or control. This is particularly true for the larger, more established, and financially secure media. For example, a consumer products company would find it difficult to reach its target audience effectively and efficiently without network television and could not afford to boycott a network because of disagreement over editorial policy or program content. Likewise, even the local advertiser in a small community may be dependent on the local media such as the newspaper, as it may be the most cost-effective media option available.

The media in the United States are basically supported by advertising, and this support means we can enjoy them for free or for a fraction of what it would cost without advertising. The alternative to an advertiser-supported media system is support by users through higher subscription costs for the print media and a fee or some type of pay-per-view system with television. Another alternative is government-supported media such as that used in many other countries for television and even newspapers. However, this raises the problem of government control and runs counter to most people's desire for freedom of the press. Although not perfect, a system of advertising-support media provides us with the best option for receiving information and entertainment. The ad in Exhibit 24–14, which was part of the AAAA campaign, notes how advertising lowers the cost of magazines for consumers.

Summarizing the Social Effects of Advertising

We have examined a number of advertising issues and criticisms and have attempted to analyze the arguments both for and against these concerns. Many people do not have a high opinion of advertising and have serious concerns over its impact on society. While advertisers are expected to comply with and follow numerous rules, regulations, policies, and guidelines, they do not cover every advertising situation. Moreover, what one individual views as distasteful or unethical may be acceptable to another.

Negative opinions regarding advertising have been around almost as long as the field itself, and it is unlikely they will ever disappear. However, the advertising industry must remain cognizant of, and address the various issues and concerns over, the effects of advertising on society. Advertising is a very powerful institution, but it will remain so only as long as consumers have faith and trust in the ads they see and hear every day. Many of the problems and controversies discussed here can be avoided if individual decision makers make ethical considerations an important element of the advertising planning process.[48] As the famous adman David Ogilvy once noted in discussing the social responsibility of advertisers: "The consumer is not a moron; she is your wife."

Economic Effects of Advertising

In addition to being scrutinized from a social perspective, considerable attention has been given to examining the economic impact of advertising. Advertising plays an important role in a free market system such as ours by making consumers aware of products and services and providing them with information that can be used for decision making. Advertising's economic role goes beyond this basic function of information provision, however, as it is viewed as a powerful force that can affect the functioning of our entire economic system.

Advertising is viewed by many as a positive force that encourages consumption and fosters economic growth. Proponents of advertising note it has very positive economic consequences, as it not only informs customers of available goods and services but also facilitates entry into markets for a firm or a new product or brand; leads to economies of scale in production, marketing, and distribution, which in turn leads to lower prices; and accelerates the acceptance of new products and hastens the rejection of inferior or unacceptable products.

Critics of advertising are much less favorable in their assessment of advertising's role and effect on our economic system. They view advertising as a detrimental force that not only fails to adequately perform its basic function of information provision but also adds to the cost of products and services and discourages competition and market entry, which leads to industrial concentration and results in higher prices for consumers.

In their analysis of advertising, economists generally take a macroeconomic perspective whereby they consider the general economic impact of advertising on an entire industry or on the economy as a whole rather than its effect on an individual company or brand. Our examination of the economic impact of advertising focuses on these broader macrolevel issues. We consider a number of the major issues regarding the role and impact of advertising on our economy including its effect on consumer choice, competition, and product costs and prices.

Effects on Consumer Choice

Some critics argue advertising hampers consumer choice, as large advertisers use their power to limit our options to a few well-advertised brands. Economists argue that advertising is used to achieve (1) **differentiation,** whereby the products or services of large advertisers are perceived as unique or better than competitors', and (2) brand loyalty, which enables large national advertisers to gain control of the market, usually at the expense of smaller brands.

Larger companies often end up charging a higher price and are able to achieve a more dominant position in the market than smaller firms that either cannot or do not compete against them and their large advertising budgets. When this occurs, advertising not only restricts the choice alternatives to a few well-known and heavily advertised brands but also becomes a substitute for competition based on price or product improvements.

Heavily advertised brands dominate the market in certain product categories such as soft drinks, beer, and cereals.[49] However, advertising generally does not create brand monopolies and reduce the opportunities for new products to be introduced to consumers. In most product categories, a number of different brands are on the store shelves and new products are being introduced all the time. As was noted in Chapter 17, over 10,000 new products were introduced in 1991, and the number of new products continues to increase every year.

The opportunity to advertise new brands gives companies the incentive to develop new brands and improve their existing ones. When a successful new product such as a personal computer or wine cooler is introduced, competitors quickly follow and use advertising to inform consumers about their brand and to attempt to convince them it is superior to that of the original manufacturer. Companies such as Apple Computer recognize that advertising has been an important part of their success (Exhibit 24–15).

Effects on Competition

One of the most common criticisms economists have with advertising concerns its effects on competition. They argue it is the power in the hands of the large firms with the huge advertising budgets that creates a **barrier to entry,** which is a condition that makes it difficult for other firms to enter the market. This results in less competition and higher prices. Economists note that smaller firms already in the market find it difficult to compete against the large advertising budgets of the industry leaders and are often driven out of business. For example, in the U.S. beer industry, the number

➤ *Exhibit 24–15*
Apple chairman John Scully acknowledges the importance of advertising

of brewers has declined from 170 in 1970 to less than 50 in 1989. In their battle for market share, industry giants Anheuser-Busch and Miller, which have over 60 percent of the market, have increased their ad budgets substantially. Anheuser-Busch alone spent $459 million on advertising in 1990. However, on a per barrel basis, these companies are spending much less than smaller firms, making it very difficult for the latter to compete.

Large advertisers clearly enjoy certain competitive advantages. First, there are certain **economies of scale** in advertising, particularly with respect to factors such as media costs. Firms such as Procter & Gamble and Philip Morris Companies, which spend over $2 billion a year on advertising and promotion, are able to make large media buys at a reduced rate, which can then be allocated to their various products at a lower cost.

Large advertisers usually sell more of a product or service, which means they may have lower costs and can afford to allocate more monies to advertising and thus use the costly but more efficient media such as network television. Their large advertising outlays also give them greater opportunity to differentiate their products and develop brand loyalty. To the extent that these factors occur, smaller competitors are at a disadvantage, and new competitors are deterred from entering the market.

While advertising may have an anticompetitive effect on a market, there is no clear evidence that advertising alone reduces competition, creates barriers to entry, and thus increases market concentration. Lester Telser noted that high levels of advertising are not always found in industries where firms have a large market share. He found an inverse relationship between product class advertising intensity and market share stability of the leading brands.[50] These findings run contrary to many economists' position that industries controlled by a small number of firms have high advertising expenditures and high advertising budgets result in stable brand shares for market leaders.

Defenders of advertising also note it is unrealistic to attribute a firm's market dominance and barriers to entry solely to advertising. There are a number of other factors to consider such as price, product quality, distribution effectiveness, production efficiencies, and competitive strategies. For many years, products such as Coors beer and Hershey chocolate bars were dominant brands even though these companies spent little on advertising. Hershey did not begin advertising until 1970, 66 years after the company was founded. The company relied on the quality of its products, its favorable reputation and image among consumers, and its extensive channels of distribution to market its brands. Industry leaders often tend to dominate markets because of their superior product quality and because they have the best management and competitive strategies, not simply because of the size of their advertising budgets.[51]

While market entry against large established competitors is difficult, companies with a quality product at a reasonable price often find a way to break into a market. Moreover, they usually find that rather than impeding their entry into the market, advertising actually facilitates their market entry by making it possible to communicate the benefits and features of their new product or brand to consumers. For example, Hyundai introduced its Korean-made cars to the U.S. market in 1986 and by 1988 was selling more than 200,000 vehicles a year. Hyundai has captured a significant portion of the U.S. automobile market by offering quality and reliable cars at a low price and telling consumers about them through advertisements such as the one shown in Exhibit 24–16.

Effects on Product Costs and Prices

A major area of debate among economists, advertisers, and consumer advocates and policymakers concerns the effects of advertising on product costs and prices. Critics argue that advertising results in increases in the prices consumers pay for products and services, citing a number of reasons for this. First, they note the large sums of money spent on advertising a brand constitute an expense that must be covered, and

➤ *Exhibit 24–16*
Advertising has helped Hyundai enter the automobile market in the United States

thus the consumer ends up paying for it through higher prices. This basic "somebody must pay for it" argument is a common criticism made by consumer advocates. Several studies have shown that firms with higher relative prices advertise their products more intensely than do those with lower relative prices.[52]

A second way advertising can result in higher prices is by increasing product differentiation and by adding to the perceived value of the product in the mind of the consumer. As noted by Paul Farris and Mark Albion, product differentiation occupies a central position in theories of advertising's economic effects.[53] The fundamental premise here is that advertising increases the perceived differentiation of physically homogeneous products and enables advertised brands to command a premium price. Albion and Farris offer some ways advertising can increase product differentiation, which are shown in Exhibit 24–17.

Critics of advertising generally point to the differences in prices between national brands and private label brands that are physically similar, such as aspirin or tea bags, as evidence of the added value created by advertising. The consumers' willingness to pay a higher price for heavily advertised national brands rather than purchasing the lower-priced, nonadvertised brand because of this added value is seen as wasteful and irrational. However, consumers do not always buy for rational, functional reasons, as the emotional, psychological, and social benefits derived from purchasing a national brand can be important to many people. Moreover, as noted by Albion and Farris,

> Unfortunately there seems to be no single way to measure product differentiation, let alone determine how much is excessive or attributable to the effects of advertising. . . . Both price insensitivity and brand loyalty could be created by a number of factors such as higher product quality, better packaging, favorable use experience and market position. They are probably related to each other but need not be the result of advertising.[54]

➤ *Exhibit 24–17*
Some views on how advertising increases product differentiation

Common Assumptions About Products and Consumers

A. Products can be described according to various product attributes or benefits provided to the consumer.

B. Different brands possess varying amounts of these attributes.

C. Consumers differ according to their desire for various attributes (preference functions).

D. Consumers do not perceive all brands as perfect substitutes for each other; therefore, "product differentiation" is said to exist. Price is not the sole criterion for selecting a brand to purchase.

Central Underlying Concepts

Market segmentation:

Certain groups of consumers with similar preference functions may perceive a subset of the total number of brands as being closer substitutes than the other brands.

Brand loyalty:

Brands perceived by a group of consumers to offer the "best" combination of attributes will be purchased more often by that group of consumers.

Price inelasticity:

Consumers will be willing to pay more for the brands that come closest to offering a combination of attributes that corresponds with their "ideal" brand.

Effects of Advertising

Advertising further differentiates products, increases brand loyalty, and increases price elasticity of demand.

A1. Introducing new attributes into the choice decision ("polyunsaturated fats are better for your health").

B1. Influencing consumers' assessment of the product's performance on a given attribute. (Although experience may play an important role, many qualities may be unmeasurable or impossible for consumers to judge from inspection and use—Crest has fluoride; Anacin dissolves faster.)

C1. Influencing the combination of attributes regarded as "ideal" (preference function)—for example, fewer preservatives are preferred.

Proponents of advertising offer several other counterarguments to the claim that advertising increases prices. They acknowledge that advertising costs are, at least in part, paid for by consumers. However, this does not mean consumers are paying more because of advertising, as it may actually help lower the overall cost of a product. For example, it has been argued that advertising helps firms achieve economies of scale in production and distribution by providing information to, and stimulating demand among, mass markets. These economies of scale help cut the cost of producing and marketing a product, which can in turn lead to lower prices—if the advertiser chooses to pass the cost savings on to the consumer. The ad shown in Exhibit 24–18, from the AAAA campaign, emphasizes this point. (The decline in calculator prices was also due to improvements in technology and lower costs resulting from the development of microchips.)

Advertising can also lower prices by making a market more competitive, which usually leads to greater price competition. A study by Lee Benham found that prices of eyeglasses were 25 to 30 percent higher in states banning eyeglass advertising versus those that permitted eyeglass advertising.[55] Robert Steiner analyzed the toy industry and concluded advertising resulted in lower consumer prices. He argued that a curtailment or removal of TV advertising would be very detrimental to the level of consumer prices for toys.[56] Finally, as was noted in discussing the effects of advertising on choice, advertising is a means to market entry rather than a deterrent and helps stimulate product innovation, which makes markets more competitive and helps keep prices down.

Overall, it is difficult to reach any firm conclusions regarding the relationship between advertising and prices. After conducting an extensive review of this area, Farris and Albion concluded

the evidence connecting manufacturer advertising to prices is neither complete nor definitive . . . consequently, we cannot say whether advertising is a tool of market efficiency or market power without further research.[57]

➤ *Exhibit 24–18*
This ad suggests advertising can lead to lower product costs

However, some economists disagree with this conclusion. For example, James Ferguson argues that economic theory indicates advertising cannot increase the cost per unit of quality to consumers because if it did, consumers would not continue to respond positively to advertising.[58] He notes that advertising lowers the costs of information about brand qualities, leads to increases in brand quality, and lowers the average price per unit of quality.

Summarizing Economic Effects

Albion and Farris suggest that economists' perspectives regarding the effects of advertising can be divided into two principal models or schools of thought, each of which makes different assumptions regarding the influence of advertising on the economy. Exhibit 24–19 summarizes the main points of the Advertising = Market Power and the Advertising = Information perspectives.

Advertising = Market power

This model reflects traditional economic thinking and views advertising as a way of changing consumers' tastes, lowering their sensitivity to price, and building brand loyalty among buyers of advertised brands. This results in higher profits and market power for the large advertiser, reduces competition in the market, and leads to higher prices and fewer choice alternatives for consumers. Proponents of this viewpoint are generally negative in their assumptions regarding the economic impact of advertising.

Advertising = Information

This model takes a more positive viewpoint of advertising's economic effects, as it views advertising as providing consumers with useful information, increasing their price sensitivity, which moves them toward lower-priced products, and increasing competition in the market. Advertising is viewed as a means of communicating with consumers and telling them about a product and its major features and attributes.

➤ *Exhibit 24–19* **Two schools of thought on advertising's role in the economy**

Advertising = Market Power		Advertising = Information
Advertising affects consumer preferences and tastes, changes product attributes, and differentiates the product from competitive offerings.	Advertising	Advertising informs consumers about product attributes and does not change the way they value those attributes.
Consumers become brand loyal and less price sensitive and perceive fewer substitutes for advertised brands.	Consumer buying behavior	Consumers become more price sensitive and buy best "value." Only the relationship between price and quality affects elasticity for a given product.
Potential entrants must overcome established brand loyalty and spend relatively more on advertising.	Barriers to entry	Advertising makes entry possible for new brands because it can communicate product attributes to consumers.
Firms are insulated from market competition and potential rivals; concentration increases, leaving firms with more discretionary power.	Industry structure and market power	Consumers can compare competitive offerings easily and competitive rivalry is increased. Efficient firms remain, and as the inefficient leave, new entrants appear; the effect on concentration is ambiguous.
Firms can charge higher prices and are not as likely to compete on quality or price dimensions. Innovation may be reduced.	Market conduct	More informed consumers pressure firms to lower prices and improve quality, innovation is facilitated via new entrants.
High prices and excessive profits accrue to advertisers and give them even more incentive to advertise their products. Output is restricted compared with conditions of perfect competition.	Market performance	Industry prices are decreased. The effect on profits due to increased competition and increased efficiency is ambiguous.

More informed and knowledgeable consumers result in pressure on companies to provide high-quality products at lower prices, and efficient firms remain in the market, whereas inefficient firms leave as new entrants appear. Proponents of this model assume the economic effects of advertising are favorable and view it as contributing to more efficient and competitive markets.

These two perspectives take very divergent views regarding the economic impact and value of advertising. We have considered arguments on both sides regarding the effect of advertising on consumer choice, competition, and product costs and prices. It is unlikely the debate over the economic effects and value of advertising will be resolved soon. Many economists will continue to take a negative view of advertising and the effects it has on the functioning of the economy, whereas advertisers will continue to view it as an efficient way for companies to communicate with their customers and as an essential component of our economic system.

Exhibit 24–20, which is an excerpt from a speech given by famous adman Leo Burnett, summarizes the perspective of most advertising people on the economic effects of advertising. Perhaps the only area of agreement is that advertising is a major economic force that has a significant effect on the functioning of our economy.

➢ *Exhibit 24–20*
This message summarizes the viewpoint of proponents of the advertising industry regarding its economic effects

> To me it means that if we believe to any degree whatsoever in the economic system under which we live, in a high standard of living and in high employment, advertising is the most efficient known way of moving goods in practically every product class.
> My proof is that millions of businessmen have chosen advertising over and over again in the operations of their business.
> Some of their decisions may have been wrong, but they must have thought they were right or they wouldn't go back to be stung twice by the same kind of bee.
> It's a pretty safe bet that in the next ten years many Americans will be using products and devices that no one in this room has even heard of. Judging purely by past performance, American advertising can be relied on to make them known and accepted overnight at the lowest possible prices.
> Advertising, of course, makes possible our unparalleled variety of magazines, newspapers, business publications, and radio and television stations.
> It must be said that without advertising we would have a far different nation, and one that would be much the poorer—not merely in material commodities, but in the life of the spirit.
> Leo Burnett

This excerpt is from a speech given by Leo Burnett on the occasion of the American Association of Advertising Agencies 50th Anniversary, April 20th, 1967.

SUMMARY

Advertising is a very powerful institution and has been the target of considerable criticism regarding its social and economic impact. Much of the criticism of advertising concerns the specific techniques and methods used by advertisers, as well as advertising's effect on societal values, tastes, lifestyles, and behavior. Critics argue that advertising is deceptive and untruthful; that it is often offensive, irritating, or in poor taste; and that it exploits certain groups such as children. Many people believe advertising should be informative only and advertisers should not use subjective claims, puffery, embellishment, or persuasive techniques.

Advertising often offends consumers by the type of appeal or manner of presentation used, with sexually suggestive ads and the use of nudity receiving the most criticism. Advertisers argue that their ads are consistent with contemporary values and lifestyles and are appropriate for the target audiences they are attempting to reach. Advertising to children is an area of particular concern, as critics argue that children lack the experience, knowledge, and ability to process and evaluate persuasive advertising messages rationally. Although an FTC proposal to severely restrict advertising to children was defeated, advertising to children remains an issue.

The pervasiveness of advertising and its prevalence in the mass media have led critics to argue that it plays a major role in influencing and transmitting social values. Opinions as to advertising's contribution to values are often very negative. Advertising has been charged with encouraging materialism, manipulating consumers to buy things they do not really want or need, perpetuating stereotyping through its portrayal of certain groups such as women and minorities, and controlling the media.

Advertising has also been scrutinized with regard to its economic effects. The basic economic role of advertising is to provide consumers with information to assist them in making consumption decisions. Advertising is viewed by some as a detrimental force that has a negative effect on competition, product costs, and consumer prices. Economists' perspectives regarding the economic effects of advertising follow two basic schools of thought: the Advertising = Market Power model and the Advertising = Information model. Arguments consistent with each perspective were considered in analyzing the economic effects of advertising.

KEY TERMS

ethics
consumer socialization
  process

materialism
Protestant ethic
differentiation

barrier to entry
economies of scale

DISCUSSION QUESTIONS

1. Evaluate the proposed restrictions on alcohol advertising discussed at the beginning of the chapter. Do you agree with the proposed limitations? Do you feel they will be effective in curbing alcohol comsumption?

2. Discuss the role of ethical considerations in advertising and promotion. How do ethical consideration differ from legal considerations?

3. Find examples of three ads that you find irritating, offensive, or in bad taste. Discuss the basis of your displeasure with these ads.

4. Many advertisers complain that a double standard exists for television programs versus commercials, as the networks scrutinize commercials more closely than the shows. Do you agree with the networks' position that commercials should be held to higher standards than programs? Why or why not?

5. Evaluate the arguments for and against advertising to children. Do you agree with the proposal the FTC put forth in 1979 to ban or limit severely children's advertising?

6. With which position do you agree?
   - "Advertising determines American consumers' tastes and values and is responsible for creating a materialistic society."
   - "Advertising is a reflection of society and mirrors its tastes and values."

7. Discuss the arguments for and against the claim that advertising exerts too much influence over or even controls the media.

8. Discuss the role of advertising as an economic force, giving attention to arguments for and against its effects on the economy.

9. Do you believe advertising increases or decreases the costs of products and services? Defend your position.

10. Compare the Advertising = Market Power and Advertising = Information perspectives regarding the economic effects of advertising.

Glossary of Advertising and Promotion Terms

80/20 rule (5)   The principle that 80 percent of sales volume for a product or service is generated by 20 percent of the customers.

5-Ws model of communication (6)   A model of the communications process that contains five basic elements: who? (source), says what? (message), in what way? (channel), to whom? (receiver), and with what effect? (feedback).

AIDA model (6)   A model that depicts the successive stages a buyer passes through in the personal selling process including: attention, interest, desire, and action.

absolute costs (12)   The actual total cost of placing an ad in a particular media vehicle.

adjacencies (13)   Commercial spots purchased from local television stations that generally appear during the time periods adjacent to network programs.

advertising (1)   Any paid form of nonpersonal communication about an organization, product, service, or idea by an identified sponsor.

advertising agency (3)   A firm that specializes in the creation, production, and placement of advertising messages and may provide other services that facilitate the marketing communications process.

advertising appeal (11)   The basis or approach used in an advertising message to attract the attention or interest of consumers and/or influence their feelings toward the product, service, or cause.

advertising campaign (10)   a comprehensive advertising plan that consists of a series of messages in a variety of media that center on a single theme or idea.

advertising creativity (10)   The ability to generate fresh, unique, and appropriate ideas that can be used as solutions to communication problems.

advertising manager (3)   The individual in an organization who is responsible for the planning, coordinating, budgeting, and implementing of the advertising program.

advertising specialties (15)   Items used as giveaways to serve as a reminder or stimulate remembrance of a company or brand such as calendars, T-shirts, pens, key tags, and the like. Specialties are usually imprinted with a company or brand name and other identifying marks such as an address and phone number.

advertising substantiation (23)   A Federal Trade Commission regulatory program that requires advertisers to have documentation to support the claims made in their advertisements.

advocacy advertising (18)   Advertising that is concerned with the propagation of ideas and elucidation of social issues of public importance in a manner that supports the position and interest of the sponsor.

aerial advertising (15)   A form of outdoor advertising where messages appear in the sky in the form of banners pulled by airplanes, skywriting, and on blimps.

affect referral decision rule (4)   A type of decision rule where selections are made on the basis of an overall impression or affective summary evaluation of the various alternatives under consideration.

affiliates (13)   Local television stations that are associated with a major network. Affiliates agree to preempt time during specified hours for programming provided by the network and carry the advertising contained in the program.

affirmative disclosure (23)   A Federal Trade Commission program whereby advertisers may be required to include certain types of information in their advertisements so consumers will be aware of all the consequences, conditions, and limitations associated with the use of the product or service.

affordable method (9)   A method of determining the budget for advertising and promotion where all other budget areas are covered and remaining monies are available for allocation.

agate line (14)   Unit of newspaper space measurement, 1 column wide by $\frac{1}{14}$ inch deep. (Thus, 14 agate lines = 1 column inch).

agency evaluation process (3)   The process by which a company evaluates the performance of its advertising agency. This process includes both financial and qualitative aspects.

alpha activity (20)   A measure of the degree of brain activity that can be used to assess an individual's reactions to an advertisement.

animatic (10)   A preliminary version of a commercial whereby a videotape of the frames of a storyboard is produced along with an audio soundtrack.

(Note: Numbers in parentheses after term indicate chapter(s) where term is discussed.)

arbitrary allocation (9)   A method for determining the budget for advertising and promotion based on arbitrary decisions of executives.

area of dominant influence (ADI) (13)   A geographic survey area created and defined by Arbitron. Each county in the nation is assigned to an ADI, which is an exclusive geographic area consisting of all counties in which the home market stations receive a preponderance of viewing.

attitude toward the ad (6)   A message recipient's affective feelings of favorability or unfavorability toward an advertisement.

attractiveness (7)   A source characteristic that makes him or her appealing to a message recipient. Source attractiveness can be based on similarity, familiarity, or likability.

audimeter (13)   An electric measurement device that is hooked to a television set to record when the set is turned on and the channel to which it is tuned.

audiotex (15)   The use of telephone and voice information services to market, advertise, promote, entertain, and inform consumers.

average frequency (11)   The number of times the average household reached by a media schedule is exposed to a media vehicle over a specified period.

average quarter-hour figure (AQH) (13)   The average number of persons listening to a particular station for at least five minutes during a 15-minute period. Used by Arbitron in measuring the size of radio audiences.

average quarter-hour rating (13)   The average quarter-hour figure estimate expressed as a percentage of the population being measured. Used by Arbitron in measuring the size of radio audiences.

average quarter-hour share (13)   The percentage of the total listening audience tuned to each station as a percentage of the total listening audience in the survey area. Used by Arbitron in measuring the size of radio audiences.

B

baby boomers (2)   The generation of Americans born between 1946 and 1964.

balance-of-trade deficit (22)   A situation where the monetary value of a country's imports exceeds its exports.

barrier to entry (24)   Conditions that make it difficult for a firm to enter the market in a particular industry, such as high advertising budgets.

barter syndication (13)   The offering of television programs to local stations free or at a reduced rate but with some of the advertising time presold to national advertisers. The remaining advertising time can be sold to local advertisers.

behavioristic segmentation (5)   A method of segmenting a market by dividing customers into groups based on their usage, loyalties, or buying responses to a product or service.

benchmark measures (8)   Measures of a target audience's status concerning response hierarchy variables such as awareness, knowledge, image, attitudes, preferences, intentions, or behavior. These measures are taken at the beginning of an advertising or promotional campaign to determine the degree to which a target audience must be changed or moved by a promotional campaign.

benefit segmentation (5)   A method of segmenting markets on the basis of the major benefits consumers seek in a product or service.

Better Business Bureau (BBB) (23)   An organization established and funded by businesses that operates primarily at the local level to monitor activities of companies and promote fair advertising and selling practices.

big idea (10)   A unique or creative idea for an advertisement or campaign that attracts consumers' attention, gets a reaction, and sets the advertiser's product or service apart from the competition.

billings (3)   The amount of client money agencies spend on media purchases and other equivalent activities. Billings are often used as a way of measuring the size of advertising agencies.

bleed pages (14)   Magazine advertisements where the printed area extends to the edge of the page, eliminating any white margin or border around the ad.

body copy (11)   The main text portion of a print ad. Also often referred to as copy.

bonus packs (17)   Special packaging that provides consumers with extra quantity of merchandise at no extra charge over the regular price.

bounce back coupon (17)   A coupon offer made to consumers as an inducement to repurchase the brand.

brand development index (BDI) (12)   An index that is calculated by taking the percentage of a brand's total sales that occur in a given market as compared to the percentage of the total population in the market.

brand extension strategy (2)   The strategy of applying an existing brand name to a new product.

brand loyalty (4)   Preference by a consumer for a particular brand that results in continual purchase of it.

brand manager (3)   The individual in an organization responsible for planning, implementing, and controlling the marketing program for a particular brand. Brand managers are sometimes referred to as product managers.

broadcast media (14)   Media that use the airwaves to transmit their signal and programming. Radio and television are examples of broadcast media.

build-up approach (9)   A method of determining the budget for advertising and promotion by determining the specific tasks that have to be performed and estimating the costs of performing them. See objective and task method.

Burke reflections test (20)   A method for pretesting finished print advertisements where consumers take home test magazines to read and are contacted the next day to determine opinions of the ads, recall of ad content, and other questions of interest to the advertiser.

Burke test (20)   A method of posttesting television commercials using a day-after recall test provided by SAMI-Burke, Inc.

business-to-business advertising (2, 21)   Advertising used by one business to promote the products and/or services it sells to another business.

buying center (6, 21)   A committee or group of individuals in an organization who are responsible for evaluating products and services and making purchase decisions.

C

cable television (13)   A form of television where signals are carried to households by wire rather than through the airways.

carryover effect (8)   A delayed or lagged effect whereby the impact of advertising on sales can occur during a subsequent time period.

category development index (CDI) (12)   An index that is calculated by taking the percentage of a product category's total sales that occur in a given market area as compared to the percentage of the total population in the market.

category extension (2)   The strategy of applying an existing brand name to a new product category.

category management (3)   An organizational system whereby managers have responsibility for the marketing programs for a particular category or line of products.

cease and desist order (23)   An action by the Federal Trade Commission that orders a company to stop engaging in a practice that is considered deceptive or misleading until a hearing is held.

central route to persuasion (6)   One of two routes to persuasion recognized by the elaboration likelihood model. The central route to persuasion views a message recipient as very active and involved in the communications process and as having the ability and motivation to attend to and process a message.

centralized organizational structure (22)   A method of organizing for international advertising and promotion whereby all decisions are made in a company's home office.

centralized system (3)   An organizational system whereby advertising along with other marketing activities such as sales, marketing research, and planning are divided along functional lines and are run from one central marketing department.

city zone (14)   A category used for newspaper circulation figures that refers to a market area composed of the city where paper is published and contiguous areas similar in character to the city.

classical conditioning (4)   A learning process whereby a conditioned stimulus that elicits a response is paired with a neutral stimulus that does not elicit any particular response. Through repeated exposure, the neutral stimulus comes to elicit the same response as the conditioned stimulus.

classified advertising (14)   Advertising that runs in newspapers and magazines that generally contains text only and is arranged under subheadings according to the product, service, or offering. Employment, real estate, and automotive ads are the major forms of classified advertising.

clients (3)   The organizations with the products, services, or causes to be marketed and for which advertising agencies and other marketing promotional firms provide services.

clutter (7, 13)   The nonprogram material that appears in a broadcast environment, including commercials, promotional messages for shows, public service announcements, and the like.

cognitive dissonance (4)   A state of psychological tension or postpurchase doubt that a consumer may experience after making a purchase decision. This tension often leads the consumer to try to reduce it by seeking supportive information.

cognitive processing (4)   The process by which an individual transforms external information into meanings or patterns of thought and how these meanings are used to form judgments or choices about behavior.

cognitive responses (6)   Thoughts that occur to a message recipient while reading, viewing, and/or hearing a communication.

collateral services (3)   Companies that provide companies with specialized promotional services such as package design, sales promotion, media buying, market research, and ad production.

combination rates (14)   A special space rate or discount offered for advertising in two or more periodicals. Combination rates are often offered by publishers who own both morning and evening editions of a newspaper in the same market.

commission system (3)   A method of compensating advertising agencies whereby the agency receives a specified commission (traditionally 15 percent) from the media on any advertising time or space it purchases.

communication (6)   The passing of information, exchange of ideas, or process of establishing shared meaning between a sender and a receiver.

communication objectives (1, 8)   Goals that an organization seeks to achieve through its promotional program in terms of communication effects such as creating awareness, knowledge, image, attitudes, preferences, or purchase intentions.

communication task (8)   Under the DAGMAR approach to setting advertising goals and objectives, something that can be performed by and attributed to advertising such as awareness, comprehension, conviction, and action.

comparative advertising (7, 11)   The practice of either directly or indirectly naming one or more competitors in an advertising message and usually making a comparison on one or more specific attributes or characteristics.

compensatory decision rule (4)   A type of decision rule for evaluating alternatives where consumers consider each brand with respect to how it performs on relevant or salient attributes and the importance of each attribute. This decision rule allows for a negative evaluation or performance on a particular attribute to be compensated for by a positive evaluation on another attribute.

competition-oriented pricing (2)   A strategy whereby prices are set based on what a firm's competitors are charging.

competitive advantage (2)   Something unique or special that a firm does or possesses that provides an advantage over its competitors.

competitive parity method (9)   A method of setting the advertising and promotion budget based on matching the absolute level of percentage of sales expenditures of the competition.

compliance (7)   A type of influence process where a receiver accepts the position advocated by a source to obtain favorable outcomes or to avoid punishment.

computer simulation models (9)   Quantitative based models that are used to determine the relative contribution of advertising expenditures on sales response.

concave downward function (9)   An advertising/sales response function that views the incremental effects of advertising on sales as decreasing.

concentrated marketing (5)   A type of marketing strategy whereby a firm chooses to focus its marketing efforts on one particular market segment.

concept testing (20)   A method of pretesting alternative ideas for an advertisement or campaign by having consumers provide their responses and/or reactions to the creative concept.

conditioned stimulus (4)   In classical conditioning, a stimulus that becomes associated with an unconditioned stimulus and capable of evoking the same response or reaction as the unconditioned stimulus.

conjunctive decision rule (4)   A type of decision rule for evaluating alternatives where consumers establish minimally acceptable levels of performance for each important product attribute and accept an alternative only if it meets the cutoff level for each attribute.

consent order (23)   A settlement between a company and the Federal Trade Commission whereby an advertiser agrees to stop the advertising or practice in question. A consent order is for settlement purposes only and does not constitute an admission of guilt.

consumer behavior (4)   The process and activities that people engage in when searching for, selecting, purchasing, using, evaluating, and disposing of products and services so as to satisfy their needs and desires.

consumer franchise-building promotions (17)   Sales promotion activities that communicate distinctive brand attributes and contribute to the development and reinforcement of brand identity.

consumer juries (20)   A method of pretesting advertisements by using a panel of consumers who are representative of the target audience and provide ratings, rankings, and/or evaluations of advertisements.

consumer-oriented sales promotion (17)   Sales promotion techniques that are targeted to the ultimate consumer such as coupons, samples, contests, rebates, sweepstakes, and premium offers.

consumer socialization process (24)   The process by which an individual acquires the skills needed to function in the marketplace as a consumer.

contest (17)   A promotion whereby consumers compete for prizes or money on the basis of skills or ability, and winners are determined by judging the entries or ascertaining which entry comes closest to some predetermined criteria.

continuity (12)   A media scheduling strategy where a continuous pattern of advertising is used over the time span of the advertising campaign.

contribution margin (9)   The difference between the total revenue generated by a product or brand and its total variable costs.

controlled circulation basis (14)   Distribution of a publication free to individuals a publisher believes are of importance and responsible for making purchase decisions or are prescreened for qualification on some other basis.

cooperative advertising (2, 17)   Advertising programs in which a manufacturer pays a certain percentage of the expenses a retailer or distributor incurs for advertising the manufacturer's product in a local market area.

copy platform (10)   A document that specifies the basic elements of the creative strategy such as the basic problem or issue the advertising must address, the advertising and communication objectives, target audience, major selling idea or key benefits to communicate, campaign theme or appeal, and supportive information or requirements.

copywriter (3, 10)   Individuals who help conceive the ideas for ads and commercials and write the words or copy for them.

corporate advertising (18)   Advertising designed to promote overall awareness of a company or enhance its image among a target audience.

cost per order (CPO) (15)   A measure used in direct marketing to determine the number of orders generated relative to the cost of running the advertisement.

cost per ratings point (12)   A computation used by media buyers to compare the cost efficiency of broadcast programs that divides the cost of commercial time on a program by the audience rating.

cost per thousand (12)   A computation used in evaluating the relative cost of various media vehicles that represents the cost of exposing 1,000 members of a target audience to an advertising message.

cost plus system (3)   A method of compensating advertising agencies whereby the agency receives a fee based on the cost of the work it performs plus an agreed on amount for profit.

counterargument (6)   A type of thought or cognitive response a receiver has that is counter or opposed to the position advocated in a message.

coverage (12)   A measure of the potential audience that might receive an advertising message through a media vehicle.

creative boutique (3)   An advertising agency that specializes in and provides only services related to the creative aspects of advertising.

creative execution style (11)   The manner or way in which a particular advertising appeal is transformed into a message.

creative selling (19)   A type of sales position where the primary emphasis is on generating new business.

creative strategy (10)   A determination of what an advertising message will say or communicate to a target audience.

creative tactics (10)   A determination of how an advertising message will be implemented so as to execute the creative strategy.

creativity (10)   A quality possessed by persons that enables them to generate novel approaches, generally reflected in new and improved solutions to problems.

credibility (7)   The extent to which a source is perceived as having knowledge, skill, or experience relevant to a communication topic and can be trusted to give an unbiased opinion or present objective information on the issue.

cross-media advertising (14)   An arrangement where opportunities to advertise in several different types of media are offered by a single company or a partnership of various media providers.

cross/multimagazine deals (14)   An arrangement where two or more publishers offer their magazines to an advertiser as one media package.

cross-ruff coupon (17)   A coupon offer delivered on one product that is redeemable for the purchase of another product. The other product is usually one made by the same company but may involve a tie-in with another manufacturer.

cross sell (19)   A term used in personal selling that refers to the sale of additional products and/or services to the same customer.

culture (4, 22)   The complexity of learned meanings, values, norms, and customs shared by members of a society.

cume (13)   A term used for cumulative audience, which is the estimated total number of different people who listened to a radio station for a minimum of five minutes during a particular daypart.

D

DAGMAR (8)   An acronym that stands for defining advertising goals for measured advertising results. An approach to setting advertising goals and objectives developed by Russell Colley.

data base   A listing of current and/or potential customers for a company's product or service that can be used for direct-marketing purposes.

day-after recall scores (20)   A measure used in on-air testing of television commercials by various marketing research companies. The day-after recall score represents the percentage of viewers surveyed who can remember seeing a particular commercial.

dayparts (12)   The time segments into which a day is divided by radio and television networks and stations for selling advertising time.

decentralized organizational structure (22)   A method of organizing for international advertising and promotion where managers in each market or country have decision-making authority.

decentralized system (3)   An organizational system whereby planning and decision-making responsibility for marketing, advertising, and promotion lies with a product/brand manager or management team rather than a centralized department.

deception (23)   According to the Federal Trade Commission, a misrepresentation, omission, or practice that is likely to mislead the consumer acting reasonably in the circumstances to the consumer's detriment.

decoding (6)   The process by which a message recipient transforms and interprets a message.

demographics (2)   Distribution of a population on selected characteristics such as age, sex, income, education, occupation, and geographic dispersion.

demographic segmentation (5)   A method of segmenting a market based on the demographic characteristics of consumers.

departmental system (3)   The organization of an advertising agency into departments based on functions such as account services, creative, media, marketing services, and administration.

derived demand (21)   A situation where demand for a particular product or service results from the need for other goods and/or services. For example, demand for aluminum cans is derived from consumption of soft drinks or beer.

designated market area (DMA) (13)   The geographic areas used by the Nielsen Station Index in measuring audience size. DMAs are nonoverlapping areas consisting of groups of counties from which stations attract their viewers.

differentiated marketing (5)   A type of marketing strategy whereby a firm offers products or services to a number of market segments and develops separate marketing strategies for each.

differentiation (24)   A situation where a particular company or brand is perceived as unique or better than its competitors.

direct-action advertising (2)   Advertising designed to produce an immediate effect such as the generation of store traffic or sales.

direct broadcast by satellite (DBS) (22)   A television signal delivery system whereby programming is beamed from satellites to special receiving dishes mounted in the home or yard.

direct channels (2)   A marketing channel where a producer and ultimate consumer interact directly with one another.

direct headline (11)   A headline that is very straightforward and informative in terms of the message it is presenting and the target audience it is directed toward. Direct headlines often include a specific benefit, promise, or reason for a consumer to be interested in a product or service.

direct marketing (1, 16)   A system of marketing by which an organization communicates directly with customers to generate a response and/or transaction.

direct-marketing media (16)   Media that are used for direct-marketing purposes including direct mail, telemarketing, print, and broadcast.

direct-response advertising (2)   A method of direct marketing whereby a product or service is promoted through an advertisement that offers the customer the opportunity to purchase directly from the manufacturer.

direct selling (1, 16)   The direct personal presentation, demonstration, and sale of products and services to consumers usually in their homes or at their jobs.

directional medium (15)   Advertising media that are not used to create awareness or demand for products or services but rather to inform customers as to where purchases can be made once they have decided to buy. The Yellow Pages are an example of a directional medium.

display advertising (14)   Advertising in newspapers and magazines that uses illustrations, photos, headlines, and other visual elements in addition to copy text.

dyadic communication (19)   A process of direct communication between two persons or groups such as a salesperson and a customer.

E

economic infrastructure (22)   A country's communications, transportation, financial, and distribution networks.

economies of scale (9, 24)   A decline in costs with accumulated sales or production. In advertising, economies of scale often occur in media purchases as the relative costs of advertising time and/or space may decline as the size of the media budget increases.

effective reach (12)   A measure of the percentage of a media vehicle's audience reached at each effect frequency increment.

electrodermal response (20)   A measure of the resistance the skin offers to a small amount of current passed between two electrodes. Used as a measure of consumers' reaction level to an advertisement.

electroencephalographic (EEG) measures (20)   Measures of the electrical impulses in the brain that are sometimes used as a measure of reactions to advertising.

emotional appeals (7, 11)   Advertising messages that appeal to consumers' feelings and emotions.

encoding (6)   The process of putting thoughts, ideas, or information into a symbolic form.

evaluative criteria (4)   The dimensions or attributes of a product or service that are used to compare different alternatives.

event sponsorship (17)   A type of promotion whereby a company develops sponsorship relations with a particular event such as a concert, sporting event, or other activity.

evoked set (4)   The various brands identified by a consumer as purchase options and that are actively considered during the alternative evaluation process.

exchange (1)   Trade of something of value between two parties such as a product or service for money. The core phenomenon or domain for study in marketing.

exclusive (18)   A public relations tactic whereby one particular medium is offered exclusive rights to a story.

expertise (7)   An aspect of source credibility where a communicator is perceived as being knowledgeable in a given area or for a particular topic.

external analysis (1)   The phase of the promotional planning process that focuses on factors such as the characteristics of an organization's customers, market segments, positioning strategies, competitors, and marketing environment.

external audiences (18)   In public relations, a term used in reference to individuals who are outside of or not closely connected to the organization such as the general public.

external audits (18)   Evaluations performed by outside agencies to determine the effectiveness of an organization's public relations program.

external search (4)   The search process whereby consumers seek and acquire information from external sources such as advertising, other people, or public sources.

eye tracking (20)   A method for following the movement of a person's eyes as he or she views an ad or commercial. Eye tracking is used for determining which portions or sections of an ad attract a viewer's attention and/or interest.

F

failure fee (17)   A trade promotion arrangement whereby a marketer agrees to pay a penalty fee if a product stocked by a retailer does not meet agreed-upon sales levels.

Fairness Doctrine (23)   A Federal Communications Commission program that required broadcasters to provide time for opposing viewpoints on important issues.

fear appeals (7)   An advertising message that creates anxiety in a receiver by showing negative consequences that can result from engaging in (or not engaging in) a particular behavior.

Federal Trade Commission (FTC) (23)   The federal agency that has the primary responsibility for protecting consumers and business from anticompetitive behavior and unfair and deceptive practices. The FTC regulates advertising and promotion at the federal level.

Federal Trade Commission Act (23)   Federal legislation passed in 1914 that created the Federal Trade Commission and gave it the responsibility to monitor deceptive or misleading advertising and unfair business practices.

feedback (6) Part of message recipient's response that is communicated back to the sender. Feedback can take a variety of forms and provides a sender with a way of monitoring how an intended message is decoded and received.

field of experience (6) The experiences, perceptions, attitudes, and values that senders and receivers of a message bring to a communication situation.

field tests (20) Tests of consumer reactions to an advertisement that are taken under natural viewing situations rather than in a laboratory.

financial audit (3) An aspect of the advertising agency evaluation process that focuses on how the agency conducts financial affairs related to serving a client.

first-run syndication (13) Programs produced specifically for the syndication market.

fixed-fee arrangement (3) A method of agency compensation whereby the agency and client agree on the work to be done and the amount of money the agency will be paid for its services.

flat rates (14) A standard newspaper advertising rate where no discounts are offered for large quantity or repeated space buys.

Flesch formula (20) A test used to assess the difficulty level of writing based on the number of syllables and sentences per 100 words.

flighting (12) A media scheduling pattern in which periods of advertising are alternated with periods of no advertising.

focus groups (10) A qualitative marketing research method whereby a group of 10–12 consumers from the target market are led through a discussion regarding a particular topic such as a product, service, or advertising campaign.

frequency (12) The number of times a target audience is exposed to a media vehicle(s) in a specified period.

full-service agency (3) An advertising agency that offers clients a full range of marketing and communications services including the planning, creating, producing, and placing of advertising messages and other forms of promotion.

functional consequences (4) Outcomes of product or service usage that are tangible and can be directly experienced by a consumer.

G

game (17) A promotion that is a form of sweepstakes because it has a chance element or odds of winning associated with it. Games usually involve game card devices that can be rubbed or opened to unveil a winning number or prize description.

gatefolds (14) An oversize magazine page or cover that is extended and folded over to fit into the publication. Gatefolds are used to extend the size of a magazine advertisement and are always sold at a premium.

general preplanning input (10) Information gathering and/or market research studies on trends, developments, and happenings in the marketplace that can be used to assist in the initial stages of the creative process of advertising.

geographical weighting (12) A media scheduling strategy where certain geographic areas or regions are allocated higher levels of advertising because they have greater sales potential.

geographic segmentation (5) A method of segmenting a market on the basis of different geographic units or areas.

global advertising (22) The use of the same basic advertising message in all international markets.

global marketing (22) A strategy of using a common marketing plan and program for all countries in which a company operates, thus selling the product or services the same way everywhere in the world.

green marketing (2, 24) The marketing and promotion of products on the basis of environmental sensitivity.

gross ratings points (GRPs) (12) A measure that represents the total delivery or weight of a media schedule during a specified time period. GRPs are calculated by multiplying the reach of the media schedule by the average frequency.

group system (3) The organization of an advertising agency by dividing it into groups consisting of specialists from various departments such as creative, media, marketing services, and other areas. These groups work together to service particular accounts.

H

halo effect (20) The tendency for evaluations of one attribute or aspect of a stimulus to distort reactions to its other attributes or properties.

headline (11) Words in the leading position of the advertisement; the words that will be read first or are positioned to draw the most attention.

hemisphere lateralization (20) The notion that the human brain has two relatively distinct halves or hemispheres with each being responsible for a specific type of function. The right side is responsible for visual processing while the left side conducts verbal processing.

heuristics (4) Simplified or basic decision rules that can be used by a consumer to make a purchase choice, such as buy the cheapest brand.

hierarchy of effects model (6) A model of the process by which advertising works that assumes a consumer must pass through a sequence of steps from initial awareness to eventual action. The stages include awareness, interest, evaluation, trial, and adoption.

hierarchy of needs (4) Abraham Maslow's theory that human needs are arranged in an order or hierarchy based on their importance. The need hierarchy includes physiological, safety, social/love and belonging, esteem, and self-actualization needs.

horizontal cooperative advertising (17)   A cooperative advertising arrangement where advertising is sponsored in common by a group of retailers or other organizations providing products or services to a market.

households using television (HUT) (13)   The percentage of homes in a given area that are watching television during a specific time period.

I

identification (7)   The process by which an attractive source influences a message recipient. Identification occurs when the receiver is motivated to seek some type of relationship with the source and adopt a similar position in terms of beliefs, attitudes, preferences, or behavior.

image advertising (10)   Advertising that creates an identity for a product or service by emphasizing psychological meaning or symbolic association with certain values, lifestyles, and the like.

image transfer (13)   A radio advertising technique whereby the images of a television commercial are implanted into a radio spot.

indirect channels (2)   A marketing channel where intermediaries such as wholesalers and retailers are utilized to make a product available to the customer.

indirect headlines (11)   Headlines that are not straightforward with respect to identifying a product or service or providing information regarding the point of an advertising message.

industrial advertising (2)   Advertising targeted at individuals who buy or influence the purchase of industrial goods or other services.

inflight television commercials (15)   Commercials that appear in videos shown to airline passengers during a flight.

infomercials (13, 16)   Television commercials that are very long, ranging from several minutes to an hour. Infomercials are designed to provide consumers with detailed information about a product or service.

information processing model (6)   A model of advertising effects developed by William McGuire that views the receiver of a message as an information processor and problem solver. The model views the receiver as passing through a response hierarchy that includes a series of stages including message presentation, attention, comprehension, acceptance or yielding, retention, and behavior.

informational/rational appeals (11)   Advertising appeals that focus on the practical, functional, or utilitarian need for a product or service and emphasize features, benefits, or reasons for owning or using the brand.

ingredient sponsored cooperative advertising (17)   Advertising supported by raw material manufacturers with the objective being to help establish end products that include materials and/or ingredients supplied by the company.

inherent drama (10)   An approach to advertising that focuses on the benefits or characteristics that lead a consumer to purchase a product or service and uses dramatic elements to emphasize them.

in-house agency (3)   An advertising agency set up, owned, and operated by an advertiser that is responsible for planning and executing the company's advertising program.

ink-jet imaging (14)   A printing process where a message is reproduced by projecting ink onto paper rather than mechanical plates. Ink-jet imaging is being offered by many magazines to allow advertisers to personalize their messages.

innovation-adoption model (6)   A model that represents the stages a consumer passes through in the adoption process for an innovation such as a new product. The series of steps include: awareness, interest, evaluation, trial, and adoption.

inquiry tests (20)   Tests designed to measure advertising effectiveness on the basis of inquiries or responses generated from the ad such as requests for information, number of phone calls, or number of coupons redeemed.

inside cards (15)   A form of transit advertising where messages appear on cards or boards inside of vehicles such as buses, subways, or trolleys.

instant coupon (17)   Coupons attached to a package that can be removed and redeemed at the time of purchase.

in-store media (15)   Advertising and promotional media that are used inside of a retail store such as point-of-purchase displays, ads on shopping carts, coupon dispensers, and display boards.

integrated marketing communication (1)   An approach to promotional strategy that involves the coordination and integration of the various marketing and promotional programs by which an organization communicates with its customers.

integration processes (4)   The way information such as product knowledge, meanings, and beliefs is combined to evaluate two or more alternatives.

interconnects (13)   Groups of cable systems joined together for advertising purposes.

internal audiences (18)   In public relations, a term used to refer to individuals or groups inside of the organization or with a close connection to it.

internal audits (18)   Evaluations by individuals within the organization to determine the effectiveness of a public relations program.

internalization (7)   The process by which a credible source influences a message recipient. Internalization occurs when the receiver is motivated to have an objectively correct position on an issue and the receiver will adopt the opinion or attitude of the credible communicator if he or she believes the information from this source represents an accurate position on the issue.

internal search (4)   The process by which a consumer acquires information by accessing past experiences or knowledge stored in memory.

international media (22)   Advertising media that have multicountry coverage and can be used to reach audiences in various countries.

jingles (11)   Songs about a product or service that usually carry the advertising theme and a simple message.

laboratory tests (20)   Tests of consumer reactions to advertising under controlled conditions.

Lanham Act (23)   A federal law that permits a company to register a trademark for its exclusive use. The Lanham Act was recently amended to encompass false advertising and prohibits any false description or representation including words or other symbols tending falsely to describe or represent the same.

layout (11)   The physical arrangement of the various parts of an advertisement including the headline, subheads, illustrations, body copy, and any identifying marks.

lexicographic decision rule (4)   A type of decision rule where choice criteria are ranked in order of importance and alternatives are evaluated on each attribute or criterion beginning with the most important one.

line extension (2)   The strategy of applying an existing brand name to another product in the same category.

local advertising (13)   Advertising done by companies within the limited geographic area where they do business.

localized advertising strategy (22)   Developing an advertising campaign specifically for a particular country or market rather than using a global approach.

macroeconomic conditions (2)   Factors that influence the state of the overall economy such as changes in gross national product, interest rates, inflation, recession, and employment levels.

macro environment (2)   Uncontrollable factors that constitute the external environment of marketing including demographic, economic, technological, natural, sociocultural, and regulatory forces.

magazine networks (14)   A group of magazines owned by one publisher or assembled by an independent network that offers advertisers the opportunity to buy space in a variety of publications through a package deal.

mailing list (16)   A type of data base containing names and addresses of present and or potential customers who can be reached through a direct-mail campaign.

major selling idea (10)   The basis for the central theme or message idea in an advertising campaign.

marginal analysis (9)   A principle of resource allocation that balances incremental revenues against incremental costs.

market opportunities (2)   Areas where a company believes there are favorable demand trends, needs, and/or wants that are not being satisfied, and where it can compete effectively.

marketing (1, 2)   The process of planning and executing the conception, pricing, promotion, and distribution of ideas, goods, and services to create exchanges that satisfy individual and organizational objectives.

marketing channels (2)   The set of interdependent organizations involved in the process of making a product or service available to customers.

marketing mix (1, 2)   The controllable elements of a marketing program including product, price, promotion, and place.

marketing objectives (1, 8)   Goals to be accomplished by an organization's overall marketing program such as sales, market share, or profitability.

marketing plan (1)   A written document that describes the overall marketing strategy and programs developed for an organization, a particular product line, or a brand.

market segmentation (5)   The process of dividing a market into distinct groups that have common needs and will respond similarly to a marketing action.

market segments (2, 5)   Identifiable groups of customers sharing similar needs, wants, or other characteristics that make them likely to respond in a similar fashion to a marketing program.

mass media (6)   Nonpersonal channels of communication that allow a message to be sent to many individuals at one time.

materialism (24)   A preoccupation with material things rather than intellectual or spiritual concerns.

media objectives (12)   The specific goals an advertiser has for the media portion of the advertising program.

media plan (12)   A document consisting of objectives, strategies, and tactics for reaching a target audience through various media vehicles.

media planning (12)   The series of decisions involved in the delivery of an advertising message to prospective purchasers and/or users of a product or service.

media strategies (12)   Plans of action for achieving stated media objectives such as which media will be used for reaching a target audience, how the media budget will be allocated, and how advertisements will be scheduled.

media vehicle (12)   The specific program, publication, or promotional piece used to carry an advertising message.

medium (12)   The general category of communication vehicles that are available for communicating with a target audience such as broadcast, print, direct mail, and outdoor.

microeconomic trends (2)   Patterns or developments in economic factors such as consumer income, savings, debt, and expenditure patterns.

milline rate (14)   A unit for measuring the cost of newspaper advertising space in relation to circulation. The milline rate represents the cost per line of space per million circulation.

missionary sales (19)   A type of sales position where the emphasis is on performing supportive activities and services rather than generating or taking orders.

mnemonics (4)   Basic cues such as symbols, rhymes, and associations that facilitate the learning and memory process.

motivation research (4)   Qualitative research designed to probe the consumer's subconscious and discover deeply rooted motives for purchasing a product.

motive (4)   Something that compels or drives a consumer to take a particular action.

multiattribute attitude model (4)   A model of attitudes that views an individual's evaluation of an object as being a function of the beliefs that he or she has toward the object on various attributes and the importance of these attributes.

multiple buying influences (21)   The idea that a number of different individuals may influence the purchase process for a product or service within an organization.

multiplexing (13)   An arrangement where multiple channels are transmitted by one cable network.

narrowcasting (13)   The reaching of a very specialized market through programming aimed at particular target audiences. Cable television networks offer excellent opportunities for narrowcasting.

national advertisers (2)   Companies that advertise their products or services on a nationwide basis or in most regions of the country.

national advertising (3)   Advertising done by a company on a nationwide basis or in most regions of the country and targeted to the ultimate consumer market.

National Advertising Review Board (NARB) (23)   A part of the National Advertising Division of the Council of Better Business Bureaus. The NARB is the advertising industry's primary self-regulatory body.

National Advertising Review Council (NARC) (23)   An organization founded by the Council of Better Business Bureaus and various advertising industry groups to promote high standards of truth, accuracy, morality, and social responsibility in national advertising.

National Association of Attorneys General (23)   An organization consisting of state attorneys general that is involved in the regulation of advertising and other business practices.

national spot (13)   All nonnetwork advertising done by a national advertiser in local markets.

negotiated commission (3)   A method of compensating advertising agencies whereby the client and agency negotiate the commission structure rather than relying on the traditional 15 percent media commission.

noise (6)   Extraneous factors that create unplanned distortion or interference in the communications process.

noncompensatory integration strategies (4)   Types of decision rules used to evaluate alternatives that do not allow negative evaluation or performance on a particular attribute to be compensated for by positive evaluation or performance on some other attribute.

nonfranchise-building promotions (17)   Sales promotion activities that are designed to accelerate the purchase decision process and generate an immediate increase in sales but do little or nothing to communicate information about a brand and contribute to its identity and image.

nonpersonal channels (6)   Channels of communication that carry a message without involving interpersonal contact between sender and receiver. Nonpersonal channels are often referred to as mass media.

nonprice competition (2)   A strategy of using factors other than price, such as advertising or product differentiation, as a basis for competition.

objective and task method (9)   A build-up approach to budget setting involving a three-step process: (1) determining objectives, (2) determining the strategies and tasks required to attain these objectives, and (3) estimating the costs associated with these strategies and tasks.

off-network syndication (13)   Reruns of network shows bought by individual stations.

on-air tests (20)   Testing the effectiveness of television commercials by inserting test ads into actual TV programs in certain test markets.

one-sided message (7)   Communications in which only positive attributes or benefits of a product or service are presented.

one-step approach (16)   A direct-marketing strategy in which the medium is used directly to obtain an order (for example, television direct-response ads).

open rate structure (14)   A rate charged by newspapers in which discounts are available based on frequency or bulk purchases of space.

operant conditioning (instrumental conditioning) (4)   A learning theory that views the probability of a behavior as being dependent on the outcomes or consequences associated with it.

order taking (19)   A personal selling responsibility in which the salesperson's primary responsibility is taking the order.

out-of-home advertising (15)   The variety of advertising forms including outdoor, transit, skywriting, and other media viewed outside the home.

outside posters (15)   Outdoor transit posters appearing on buses, taxis, trains, subways, and trolley cars.

PACT (Positioning Advertising Copy Testing) (20)   A set of principles endorsed by 21 of the largest U.S. ad agencies aimed at improving the research used in preparing and testing ads, providing a better creative product for clients, and controlling the cost of TV commercials.

participations (13) The situation when several advertisers buy commercial time or spots on network television.

pass-along readership (14) The audience that results when the primary subscriber or purchaser of a magazine gives the publication to another person to read, or when the magazine is read in places such as waiting rooms in doctors' offices, etc.

pattern advertising (22) Advertisements that follow a basic global approach although themes, copy, and sometimes even visual elements may be adjusted.

payout plan (9) A budgeting plan that determines the investment value of the advertising and promotion appropriation.

percentage charges (3) The markups charged by advertising agencies for services provided to clients.

percentage of projected future sales method (9) A variation of the percentage of sales method of budget allocation in which projected future sales are used as the base.

percentage of sales method (9) A budgeting method in which the advertising and/or promotions budget is set based on a percentage of sales of the product.

perception (4) The process by which an individual receives, selects, organizes, and interprets information to create a meaningful picture of the world.

perceptual map (5) A "map" of perceptions of the positions of brands or products as perceived by consumers.

peripheral route to persuasion (6) In the elaboration likelihood model, one of two routes to persuasion in which the receiver is viewed as lacking the ability or motivation to process information and is not likely to be engaging in detailed cognitive processing.

personal selling (1) Person-to-person communication in which the seller attempts to assist and/or persuade prospective buyers to purchase the company's product or service or to act on an idea.

persuasion matrix (7) A communications planning model in which the stages of the response process (dependent variables) and the communications components (independent variables) are combined to demonstrate the likely effect that the independent variables will have on the dependent variables.

phased processing strategy (4) An information processing strategy in which more than one decision rule is applied during the purchase decision process.

planograms (17) A planning configuration of products that occupy a shelf section in a store that is used to provide more efficient shelf space utilization.

portfolio tests (20) A laboratory methodology designed to expose a group of respondents to a portfolio consisting of both control and test print ads.

positioning (5) The art and science of fitting the product or service to one or more segments of the market in such a way as to set it meaningfully apart from competition.

positioning strategies (5) The strategies used in positioning a brand or product.

posttests (20) Ad effectiveness measures that are taken after the ad has appeared in the marketplace.

preferred position rate (14) A rate charged by newspapers that insures the advertiser the ad will appear in the position requested and/or in a specific section of the newspaper.

premium (17) An offer of an item of merchandise or service either free or at a low price that is used as an extra incentive for purchasers.

preprinted inserts (14) Advertising distributed through newspapers that is not part of the newspaper itself, but is printed by the advertiser and then taken to the newspaper to be inserted.

press release (18) Factual and interesting information released to the press.

pretests (20) Advertising effectiveness measures that are taken before the implementation of the advertising campaign.

price elasticity (2) The responsiveness of the market to changes in price.

price-off deal (17) A promotional strategy in which the consumer receives a reduction in the regular price of the brand.

primacy effect (7) A theory that the first information presented in the message will be the most likely to be remembered.

primary circulation (14) The number of copies of a magazine distributed to original subscribers.

primary demand advertising (2) Advertising designed to stimulate demand for the general product class or entire industry.

problem detection (10) A creative research approach in which consumers familiar with a product (or service) are asked to generate an exhaustive list of problems encountered in its use.

problem recognition (4) The first stage in the consumer's decision-making process in which the consumer perceives a need and becomes motivated to satisfy it.

problem-solver stage (19) A stage of personal selling in which the seller obtains the participation of buyers in identifying their problems, translates these problems into needs, and then presents a selection from the supplier's offerings that can solve those problems.

procreator stage (19) A stage of personal selling in which the seller defines the buyer's problems or needs and the solutions to those problems or needs through active buyer-seller collaboration, thus creating a market offering tailored to the customer.

product differentiation (5) The process employed in making products appear different from others.

product manager (3) The person responsible for the planning, implementation, and control of the marketing program for an individual brand.

product placement (15) A form of advertising and promotion in which products are placed in television shows and/or movies to gain exposure.

product specific preplanning input (10) Specific studies provided to the creative department on the product or service, the target audience, or a combination of the two.

product symbolism (2)   The meaning that a product or brand has to consumers.

professional advertising (2)   Advertising targeted to professional groups.

program rating (13)   The percentage of TV households in an area that are tuned to a program during a specific time period.

promotion (1)   The coordination of all seller-initiated efforts to set up channels of information and persuasion to sell goods and services or to promote an idea.

promotional management (1)   The process of coordinating the promotional mix elements.

promotional mix (1)   The tools used to accomplish an organization's communications objectives. The promotional mix includes advertising, direct marketing, sales promotion, publicity/public relations, and personal selling.

promotional plan (1)   The framework for developing, implementing, and controlling the organization's communications program.

promotional pull strategy (2)   A strategy in which advertising and promotion efforts are targeted at the ultimate consumer to encourage them to purchase the manufacturer's brand.

promotional push strategy (2)   A strategy in which advertising and promotional efforts are targeted to the trade to attempt to get them to promote and sell the product to the ultimate consumer.

prospector stage (19)   A selling stage in which activities include seeking out selected buyers who are perceived to have a need for the offering as well as the resources to buy it.

prospects (19)   Those persons who may be prospective customers based on a need for the product or service.

Protestant ethic (24)   A set of values that stress hard work and individual effort and initiative and view the accumulation of material possessions as evidence of success.

provider stage (19)   A selling stage in which activities are limited to accepting orders for the supplier's available offering and conveying it to the buyer.

psychoanalytic theory (4)   An approach to the study of human motivations and behaviors pioneered by Sigmund Freud.

psychographic segmentation (5)   Dividing the product on the basis of personality and/or lifestyles.

psychosocial consequences (4)   Purchase decision consequences that are intangible, subjective, and personal.

public relations (1)   The management function that evaluates public attitudes, identifies the policies and procedures of an individual or organization with the public interest, and executes a program to earn public understanding and acceptance.

publicity (1)   Communications regarding an organization, product, service, or idea that is not directly paid for or run under identified sponsorship.

puffery (23)   Advertising or other sales presentations that praise the item to be sold using subjective opinions, superlatives, or exaggerations, vaguely and generally, stating no specific facts.

pulsing (12)   A media scheduling method that combines flighting and continuous scheduling.

pupillometrics (20)   An advertising effectiveness methodology designed to measure dilation and constriction of the pupils of the eye in response to stimuli.

purchase intention (4)   The predisposition to buy a certain brand or product.

push money (17)   Cash payments made directly to the retailers' or wholesalers' sales force to encourage them to promote and sell a manufacturer's product.

qualified prospects (19)   Those prospects that are able to make the buying decision.

qualitative audit (3)   An audit of the advertising agency's efforts in planning, developing, and implementing the client's communications programs.

qualitative media effect (7)   The positive or negative influence the medium may contribute to the message.

ratings point (13)   A measurement used to determine television viewing audiences in which one ratings point is the equivalent of 1 percent of all of the television households in a particular area tuned to a specific program.

rational appeal (7)   Communications in which features and/or benefits are directly presented in a logical, rational method.

reach (12)   The number of different audience members exposed at least once to a media vehicle (or vehicles) in a given period.

recall tests (20)   Advertising effectiveness tests designed to measure advertising recall.

receiver (6)   The person or persons with whom the sender of a message shares thoughts or information.

recency effect (7)   The theory that arguments presented at the end of the message are considered to be stronger and therefore are more likely to be remembered.

recognition method (20)   An advertising effectiveness measure of print ads that allows the advertiser to assess the impact of an ad in a single issue of a magazine over time and/or across alternative magazines.

reference group (4)   A group whose perspectives, values, or behavior is used by an individual as the basis for his or her judgments, opinions, and actions.

refutational appeal (7)   A type of message in which both sides of the issue are presented in the communication, with arguments offered to refute the opposing viewpoint.

regional networks (13)   A network that covers only a specific portion of the country. Regional network purchases are based in proportion to the percentage of the country receiving the message.

reinforcement (4)   The rewards or favorable consequences associated with a particular response.

relative cost (12)   The relationship between the price paid for advertising time or space and the size of the audience delivered; it is used to compare the prices of various media vehicles.

reminder advertising (11)   Advertising designed to keep the name of the product or brand in the mind of the receiver.

repositioning (5)   The changing of a product or brand's positioning.

resellers (2)   Intermediaries in the marketing channel such as wholesalers, distributors, and retailers.

response (6)   The set of reactions the receiver has after seeing, hearing, or reading a message.

retail/local advertising (2)   Advertising carried out by retailers and/or local merchants.

retail trading zone (14)   The market outside the city zone whose residents regularly trade with merchants within the city zone.

ROI budgeting method (return on investment) (9)   A budgeting method in which advertising and promotions are considered investments, and thus measurements are made in an attempt to determine the returns achieved by these investments.

rolling boards (15)   Advertising painted or mounted on cars, trucks, vans, trailers, etc., so the exposure can be mobile enough to be taken to specific target market areas.

run of paper   (14)   A rate quoted by newspapers that allows the ad to appear on any page or in any position desired by the medium.

S

S-shaped response curve (9)   A sales response model that attempts to show sales responses to various levels of advertising and promotional expenditures.

sales-oriented objectives (8)   Budgeting objectives related to sales effects such as increasing sales volume.

sales promotion (1)   Marketing activities that provide extra value or incentives to the sales force, distributors, or the ultimate consumer and can stimulate immediate sales.

sales promotion trap (17)   A spiral that results when a number of competitors extensively use promotions. One firm uses sales promotions to differentiate its product or service and other competitors copy the strategy, resulting in no differential advantage and a loss of profit margins to all.

salient beliefs (4)   Beliefs concerning specific attributes or consequences that are activated and form the basis of an attitude.

sampling (17)   A variety of procedures whereby consumers are given some quantity of a product for no charge to induce trial.

schedules of reinforcement (4)   The schedule by which a behavioral response is rewarded.

script (11)   A written version of the commercial that provides a detailed description of its video and audio content.

selective attention (4)   A perceptual process in which consumers choose to attend to some stimuli and not others.

selective binding (14)   A computerized production process that allows the creation of hundreds of copies of a magazine in one continuous sequence.

selective comprehension (4)   The perceptual process whereby consumers interpret information based on their own attitudes, beliefs, motives, and experiences.

selective demand advertising (2)   Advertising that focuses on stimulating demand for a specific manufacturer's product or brand.

selective exposure (4)   A process whereby consumers choose whether or not to make themselves available to media and message information.

selective learning (6)   The process whereby consumers seek information that supports the choice made and avoid information that fails to bolster the wisdom of a purchase decision.

selective perception (4)   The perceptual process involving the filtering or screening of exposure, attention, comprehension, and retention.

selective retention (4)   The perceptual process whereby consumers remember some information but not all.

selectivity (14)   The ability of a medium to reach a specific target audience.

self-liquidating premiums (17)   Premiums that require the consumer to pay some or all of the cost of the premium plus handling and mailing costs.

self-paced media (7)   Media that viewers and/or readers can control their exposure time to, allowing them to process information at their own rate.

self-regulation (23)   The practice by the advertising industry of regulating and controlling advertising to avoid interference by outside agencies such as the government.

semiotics (6)   The study of the nature of meaning.

shaping (4)   The reinforcement of successive acts that lead to a desired behavior pattern or response.

showing (15)   The percentage of supplicated audience exposed to an outdoor poster daily.

similarity (7)   The supposed resemblance between the source and the receiver of a message.

situational determinants (4)   Influences originating from the specific situation in which consumers are to use the product or brand.

single-source tracking (20)   A research method designed to track the behaviors of consumers from the television set to the supermarket checkout counter.

sleeper effect (7)   A phenomenon in which the persuasiveness of a message increases over time.

social class (4)   Relatively homogeneous divisions of society into which people are grouped based on similar lifestyles, values, norms, interests, and behaviors.

social style model (21)   A model that suggests businesspersons' "social styles" will influence how they react on the job.

source (6)   The sender—person, group, or organization—of the message.

source bolsters (6)   Favorable cognitive thoughts generated toward the source of a message.

source derogations (6)   Negative thoughts generated about the source of a communication.

source power (7)   The power of a source as a result of his or her ability to administer rewards and/or punishments to the receiver.

specialty advertising (15)   An advertising, sales promotion, and motivational communications medium that employs useful articles of merchandise imprinted with an advertiser's name, message, or logo.

split runs (14)   Two or more versions of a print ad are printed in alternate copies of a particular issue of a magazine.

split run test (20)   An advertising effectiveness measure in which different versions of an ad are run in alternate copies of the same newspaper and/or magazine.

split 30s (13)   30-second TV spots in which the advertiser promotes two different products with two different messages during a 30-second commercial.

sponsorship (13)   When the advertiser assumes responsibility for the production and usually the content of the program as well as the advertising that appears within it.

spot advertising (13)   Commercials shown on local television stations, with the negotiation and purchase of time being made directly from the individual stations.

standard advertising unit (SAU) (14)   A standard developed in the newspaper industry to make newspaper purchasing rates more comparable to other media that sell space and time in standard units.

standard learning model (6)   Progression by the consumers through a learn-feel-do hierarchical response.

station reps (13)   Individuals who act as sales representatives for a number of local stations and represent them in dealings with national advertisers.

storyboard (10)   A series of drawings used to present the visual plan or layout of a proposed commercial.

strategic marketing plan (2)   The planning framework for specific marketing activities.

subcultures (4)   Smaller groups within a culture that possess similar beliefs, values, norms, and patterns of behavior that differentiate them from the larger cultural mainstream.

subheads (11)   Secondary headlines in a print ad.

subliminal perception (4)   The ability of an individual to perceive a stimulus below the level of conscious awareness.

superagencies (3)   Large external agencies that offer integrated marketing communications on a worldwide basis.

superstations (13)   Independent local stations that send their signals via satellite to cable operators that, in turn, make them available to subscribers (WWOR, WPIX, WGN, WSBK, WTBS).

support advertising (16)   A form of direct marketing in which the ad is designed to support other forms of advertising appearing in other media.

support argument (6)   Consumers' thoughts that support or affirm the claims being made by a message.

support media (15)   Those media used to support or reinforce messages sent to target markets through other more "dominant" and/or more traditional media.

sweeps periods (12)   The times of year in which television audience measures are taken (February, May, July, and November).

sweepstakes (17)   A promotion whereby consumers submit their names for consideration in the drawing or selection of prizes and winners are determined purely by chance. Sweepstakes cannot require a proof of purchase as a condition for entry.

syndicated programs (13)   Shows sold or distributed to local stations.

target marketing (5)   The process of identifying the specific needs of segments, selecting one or more of these segments as a target, and developing marketing programs directed to each.

target ratings points (TRPs) (12)   The number of persons in the primary target audience that the media buy will reach—and the number of times.

team approach (18)   A method of measuring the effectiveness of public relations programs whereby evaluators are actually involved in the campaign.

teaser advertising (11)   An ad designed to create curiosity and build excitement and interest in a product or brand without showing it.

tele-media (16)   The use of telephone and voice information services (800, 900, 976 numbers) to market, advertise, promote, entertain, and inform.

television network (13)   The provider of news and pro-gramming to a series of affiliated local television stations.

terminal posters (15)   Floor displays, island showcases, electronic signs, and other forms of advertisements that appear in train or subway stations, airline terminals, etc.

testing bias (20)   A bias that occurs in advertising effectiveness measures because respondents know they are being tested and thus alter their responses.

tests of comprehension and reaction (20)   Advertising effectiveness tests that are designed to assess whether the ad conveyed the desired meaning and is not reacted to negatively.

theater testing (20)   An advertising effectiveness pretest in which consumers view ads in a theater setting and evaluate these ads on a variety of dimensions.

top-down approaches (9)   Budgeting approaches in which the budgetary amount is established at the executive level and monies are passed down to the various departments.

total audience/readership (14)   A combination of the total number of primary and pass-along readers multiplied by the circulation of an average issue of a magazine.

tracking studies (20)   Advertising effectiveness measures designed to assess the effects of advertising on awareness, recall, interest, and attitudes toward the ad as well as purchase intentions.

trade advertising (2)   Advertising targeted to wholesalers and retailers.

trademark (2)   An identifying name, symbol, or other device that gives a company the legal and exclusive rights to use.

trade-oriented sales promotion (17)   A sales promotion designed to motivate distributors and retailers to carry a product and make an extra effort to promote or "push" it to their customers.

trade regulation rules (TRRs) (23)   Industrywide rules that define unfair practices before they occur. Used by the Federal Trade Commission to regulate advertising and promotion.

trade show (17)   A type of exhibition or forum where manufacturers can display their products to current as well as prospective buyers.

transformational advertising (11)   An ad that associates the experience of using the advertised brand with a unique set of psychological characteristics that would not typically be associated with the brand experience to the same degree without exposure to the advertisement.

transit advertising (15)   Advertising targeted to target audiences exposed to commercial transportation facilities, including buses, taxis, trains, elevators, trolleys, airplanes, and subways.

trustworthiness (7)   The honesty, integrity, and believability of the source of a communication.

two-sided message (7)   A message in which both good and bad points about a product or claim are presented.

two-step approach (16)   A direct-marketing strategy in which the first effort is designed to screen or qualify potential buyers, while the second effort has the responsibility of generating the response.

undifferentiated marketing (5)   A strategy in which market segment differences are ignored and one product or service is offered to the entire market.

unduplicated reach (12)   The number of persons reached once with a media exposure.

unique selling proposition (10)   An advertising strategy that focuses on a product or service attribute that is distinctive to a particular brand and offers an important benefit to the customer.

up-front market (13)   A buying period that takes place prior to the upcoming television season when the networks sell a large part of their commercial time.

values and lifestyles program (**VALS**) (5)   Stanford Research Institute's method for applying lifestyle segmentation.

vehicle option source effect (20)   The differential impact the advertising exposure will have on the same audience member if the exposure occurs in one media option rather than another.

vertical cooperative advertising (17)   A cooperative arrangement under which a manufacturer pays for a portion of the advertising a retailer runs to promote the manufacturer's product and its availability in the retailer's place of business.

video advertising (15)   Advertisements appearing in movie theaters and on videotapes.

videotext (16)   An information retrieval service that occurs through one's personal computer.

voice-over (11)   Action on the screen in a commercial that is narrated or described by a narrator who is not visible.

want (4)   A felt need shaped by a person's knowledge, culture, and personality.

waste coverage (12)   A situation where the coverage of the media exceeds the target audience.

Wheeler-Lea Amendment (23)   An act of Congress passed in 1938 that amended section 5 of the FTC Act to read that unfair methods of competition in commerce and unfair or deceptive acts or practices in commerce are declared unlawful.

word-of-mouth communications (6)   Social channels of communication such as friends, neighbors, associates, co-workers, or family members.

Yellow Pages advertising (15)   Advertisements that appear in the various Yellow Pages type phone directories.

Z

zapping (13)   The use of a remote control device to change channels and switch away from commercials.

zipping (13)   Fast-forwarding through commercials during the playback of a program previously recorded on a VCR.

Endnotes

chapter 1

1. Thomas R. King, "Spending on Ads Expected to Rise Only 4.6% in '91," *The Wall Street Journal,* December 11, 1990, p. B1.
2. "Survey of World Advertising Expenditures: Twenty Fourth Edition" (New York: Starch INRA Hooper & The Roper Organization, 1991).
3. Martin Fleming, "Media Spending in the 1990s," *American Demographics,* September 1991, pp. 48–53.
4. "AMA Board Approves New Marketing Definition," *Marketing News,* March 1, 1985, p. 1.
5. Richard P. Bagozzi, "Marketing as Exchange," *Journal of Marketing* 39 (October 1975), pp. 32–39.
6. John Fitzgerald, "Integrated Communications," *Advertising Age,* February 15, 1988, p. 18.
7. Michael L. Ray, *Advertising and Communication Management*

(Englewood Cliffs, N.J.: Prentice Hall, 1982).
8. Ralph S. Alexander, ed., *Marketing Definitions* (Chicago: American Marketing Association, 1965), p. 9.
9. "Trends in Media," research report by Television Bureau of Advertising, New York, July 1991.
10. Peter H. Farquar, "Managing Brand Equity," *Journal of Advertising Research,* August–September 1990, pp. RC7–11.
11. Janet Meyers and Laurie Freeman, "Marketers Police TV Commercial Costs," *Advertising Age,* April 3, 1989, p. 51.
12. "Trends in Media," research report by Television Bureau of Advertising, New York, July 1991.
13. *Donnelley Marketing Fourteenth Annual Survey of Promotional Practices* (Stamford, Conn: Donnelley Marketing, 1992).

14. David Kiley, "Scott Throws in Advertising Towel," *Adweek's Marketing Week,* March 7, 1988, p. 1.
15. Judann Dagnoli, "Sorry Charlie, Heinz Puts Promos First," *Advertising Age,* March 30, 1992, p. 3.
16. H. Frazier Moore and Bertrand R. Canfield, *Public Relations: Principles, Cases, and Problems,* 7th ed. (Homewood, Ill.: Richard D. Irwin, 1977), p. 5.
17. Art Kleiner, "The Public Relations Coup," *Adweek's Marketing Week,* January 16, 1989, pp. 20–23.
18. Laboratory of Advertising Performance Study no. 8052–4, McGraw-Hill Research, 1990.
19. Anne B. Fisher, "Spiffing Up the Corporate Image," *Fortune,* July 21, 1986, pp. 68–72.

chapter 2

1. Janice Castro, "Rock and Roll," *Time,* August 19, 1991, pp. 42–44.
2. "Mountain Bikes Just Keep on Climbing," *Business Week,* December 21, 1990, p. 60.
3. "Marketing: The New Priority," *Business Week,* November 21, 1983, pp. 96–106.
4. "What Happened To Advertising?" *Business Week,* September 23, 1991, pp. 66–72.
5. Judann Dagnoli, "Campbell Ups Ad $," *Advertising Age,* July 1, 1991, p. 1.
6. "Time to Rebuild Brand Muscle," *Advertising Age,* September 23, 1991, p. 20.
7. J. Paul Peter and Jerry C. Olson, *Consumer Behavior* (Homewood, Ill.: Richard D. Irwin, 1987), p. 505.
8. Michael R. Solomon, "The Role of Products as Social Stimuli: A Symbolic Interactionism Perspective," *Journal of Consumer Research,* December 1983, pp. 319–29.
9. Peter H. Farquhar, "Managing Brand Equity," *Journal of Advertising Research* 30, no. 4, August/September 1990.

10. "What's in a Name? Less and Less," *Business Week,* July 8, 1991, pp. 66–67.
11. Farquhar, "Managing Brand Equity."
12. Al Ries and Jack Trout, *Positioning: The Battle for Your Mind* (New York: McGraw-Hill, 1982).
13. Kenneth E. Runyon and David W. Stewart, *Consumer Behavior* (Columbus, Ohio: Merrill, 1987).
14. Elliot Young, "Judging a Product by Its Wrapper," *Progressive Grocer,* July 1985, pp. 10–11.
15. Peter and Olson, *Consumer Behavior,* p. 571.
16. David J. Curry, "Measuring Price and Quality Competition," *Journal of Marketing* 49 (Spring 1985), pp. 106–17.
17. Paul W. Farris and David J. Reibstein, "How Prices, Ad Expenditures and Profits Are Linked," *Harvard Business Review,* November–December 1979, pp. 173–84.
18. Philip Kotler, *Marketing Management,* 7th ed. (Englewood Cliffs, N.J.: Prentice Hall, 1991), p. 508.
19. Francine Schwadel, "Retailers Broaden Their Ad Campaigns to Promote Image

as Well as Products," *The Wall Street Journal,* June 8, 1988, p. 28.
20. Peter Francese, "A Symphony of Demographic Change," *Advertising Age,* November 9, 1988, pp. 130, 132.
21. J. J. Burnett and A. J. Bush, "Profiling the Yuppies," *Journal of Advertising Research,* April–May 1986, pp. 27–36.
22. Raymond Serafin, "BMW Puts $30M behind Ads to Drive away Yuppie Image," *Advertising Age,* June 24, 1991, pp. 3, 62.
23. Christy Fisher, "Wooing Boomers' Babies," *Advertising Age,* July 22, 1991, pp. 3, 30.
24. Katie Fitzergerald, "Sears Offers KidVantage," *Advertising Age,* July 22, 1991, p. 30.
25. Gary Levin "Boomers Leave a Challenge," *Advertising Age,* July 8, 1991, pp. 1, 14.
26. "Europe Cooks up a Cereal Brawl," *Fortune,* June 3, 1991, pp. 175–78.
27. "The Year 2000: A Demographic Profile of Consumer Market," *Marketing News,* May 25, 1984, pp. 8–10.

28. "Last Year It Was Yuppies—This Year It's Their Parents," *Business Week,* March 10, 1986, p. 68.
29. Lisa Fried, "Modern Maturity: When Having It All Is Too Much," *Folio,* June 1, 1991, p. 16.
30. U.S. Bureau of the Census, *Current Population Reports,* Series P-60, no. 196 (Washington D.C.: Government Printing Office, 1989).
31. U.S. Bureau of the Census, *Current Population Reports,* Series P-60, no. 161 (Washington D.C.: Government Printing Office, 1989).
32. "Working Women More Attractive—Y&R," *Advertising Age,* January 11, 1982, p. 76.

33. "The Numbers," *Mediaweek,* July 15, 1991, p. 18.
34. Pauline Yoshihashi, "Why More Ads Aren't Targeting Asians," *The Wall Street Journal,* July 20, 1989, p. B1.
35. Ibid.
36. Alecia Swasy, "Changing Times," *The Wall Street Journal,* March 22, 1991, p. B6.
37. "Home Alone—with $660 Billion," *Business Week,* July 29, 1991, pp. 76–77.
38. See "Business Guide to Demographic Products and Services," *American Demographics,* June 1985, pp. 23–33.
39. R. Craig Endicott, "P&G Spends $2.28 billion, Surges to Head of Top 100,"

Advertising Age, September 25, 1991, p. 1.
40. "What Happened to Advertising?"
41. Eric Hallreisen, "Volkswagen Offers Consumer Protection," *Adweek's Marketing Week,* February 3, 1992, p. 5.
42. Judann Dagnoli, "Recession's Bleak Legacy," *Advertising Age,* July 29, 1991, p. 1.
43. "1990 Nielsen Report on Television," Nielsen Media Research, 1990.
44. L. Freeman and Judann Dagnoli, "Green Concerns Influence Buying," *Advertising Age,* July 30, 1990, p. 19.

chapter 3

1. Barry Brown, "P&G Hires 10 Shops," *Advertising Age,* October 21, 1991, p. 38.
2. Thomas J. Cosse and John E. Swan, "Strategic Marketing Planning by Product Managers—Room for Improvement?" *Journal of Marketing* 47 (Summer 1983), pp. 92–102.
3. Alison Fahey, "Lintas Wins Kodak Prize," *Advertising Age,* June 24, 1991, p.l; and John McManus, "Clean Sweep," *Mediaweek,* April 15, 1991, p.l.
4. Victor P. Buell, *Organizing for Marketing/Advertising Success* (New York: Association of National Advertisers, 1982).
5. "The Marketing Revolution at Procter and Gamble," *Business Week,* July 25, 1988, p. 72.
6. Bruce Horovitz, "Some Companies Say the Best Ad Agency Is No Ad Agency at All," *Los Angeles Times,* July 19, 1989, Sec. IV, p. 5.

7. "Do Your Ads Need a Super Agency?" *Fortune,* April 27, 1987, p. 81.
8. "Media Costs '89: Easy Does It," *Marketing & Media Decisions,* August 1988, pp. 32–34.
9. "Achenbaum Puts His Cards on the Table," *Advertising Age,* May 9, 1988, p. 3.
10. Laurie Peterson, "Pursuing Results in the Age of Accountability," *Adweek's Marketing Week,* November 19, 1990, pp. 20–22.
11. Nancy Giges, "Reviewing the Review: Borden Likes System of Agency Evaluation," *Advertising Age,* April 18, 1977, p. 3.
12. Peter Doyle, Marcel Corstiens, and Paul Michell, "Signals of Vulnerability in Agency-Client Relations," *Journal of Marketing* 44 (Fall 1980), pp. 18–23; and Daniel B. Wackman, Charles Salmon, and Caryn C. Salmon, "Developing an Advertising Agency-Client Relationship," *Journal of*

Advertising Research 26, no. 6 (December 1986/January 1987), pp. 21–29.
13. Cathy Taylor, "Client Conflicts Can Whipsaw Even Small Agencies," *Adweek,* August 6, 1990, p. 40.
14. William Abrams, "Big Contest for Ad Accounts Forces Agencies to Go All Out," *The Wall Street Journal,* November 18, 1982, p. 33; and "Big Agencies Starting to Call for End to Costly Free Pitches," *The Wall Street Journal,* February 22, 1989, p. B7.
15. "A Cure for What Ails Advertising?" *Fortune,* December 16, 1991, pp. 119–22.
16. Scott Hume, "New Ideas, Old Barriers," *Advertising Age,* July 22, 1991, p. 6.
17. "Ad Firms Falter on One-Stop Shopping," *The Wall Street Journal,* December 1, 1988, p. 81; and "Do Your Ads Need a Superagency?"
18. "A Cure For What Ails Advertising?" p. 122.

chapter 4

1. Russell W. Belk, "Possessions and the Extended Self," *Journal of Consumer Research,* September 1988, pp. 139–68.
2. Eric N. Berkowitz, Roger A. Kerin, Steven W. Hartley, and William Rudelius, *Marketing,* 3rd ed. (Homewood, Ill.: Richard D. Irwin, 1992), p. 14.
3. A. H. Maslow, "Higher' and 'Lower' Needs," *Journal of Psychology* 25 (1948), pp. 433–36.
4. Morton Deutsch and Robert M. Krauss, *Theories in Social Psychology* (New York: Basic Books, 1965).
5. Jagdish N. Sheth, "The Role of Motivation Research in Consumer Psychology" (Faculty Working Paper, University of Illinois, Champaign, Ill., 1974); Bill Abrams, "Charles of the Ritz Discovers What Women Want,"

The Wall Street Journal, August 20, 1981, p. 29; and Ernest Dichter, *Getting Motivated* (New York: Pergamon Press, 1979).
6. For an excellent discussion of memory and consumer behavior, see James R. Bettman, "Memory Factors in Consumer Choice: A Review," *Journal of Marketing* 43 (Spring 1979), pp. 37–53.
7. Gilbert Harrell, *Consumer Behavior* (San Diego: Harcourt Brace Jovanovich, 1986), p. 66.
8. Raymond A. Bauer and Stephen A. Greyser, *Advertising in America: The Consumer View* (Boston: Harvard Business School, 1968).
9. Neal Santelmann, "Color That Yells 'Buy Me,'" *Forbes,* May 2, 1988, p. 110.

10. J. Paul Peter and Jerry C. Olson, *Consumer Behavior,* 2nd ed. (Homewood, Ill.: Richard D. Irwin, 1990), p. 73.
11. Gordon W. Allport, "Attitudes," in *Handbook of Social Psychology,* ed. C. M. Murchison (Winchester, Mass.: Clark University Press, 1935), p. 810.
12. Robert B. Zajonc and Hazel Markus, "Affective and Cognitive Factors in Preferences," *Journal of Consumer Research* 9 (1982), pp. 123–31.
13. Alvin Achenbaum, "Advertising Doesn't Manipulate Consumers," *Journal of Advertising Research,* April 2, 1970, pp. 3–13.
14. William D. Wells, "Attitudes and Behavior: Lessons from the Needham Lifestyle Study," *Journal of Advertising Research,* February–March 1985,

40–44; and Icek Ajzen and Martin Fishbein, "Attitude-Behavior Relations: A Theoretical Analysis and Review of Empirical Research," *Psychological Bulletin,* September 1977, pp. 888–918.

15. For a good review of multiattribute models see William L. Wilkie and Edgar A. Pessemier, "Issues in Marketing's Use of Multiattribute Models," *Journal of Marketing Research* 10 (November 1983), 428–41.

16. Joel B. Cohen, Paul W. Minniard, and Peter R. Dickson, "Information Integration: An Information Processing Perspective," in *Advances in Consumer Research,* vol. 7, ed. Jerry C. Olson (Ann Arbor: Association for Consumer Research, 1980), pp. 161–70.

17. N. K. Malhorta, "Multi-Stage Information Processing Behavior," *Journal of the Academy of Marketing Science,* Winter 1982, pp. 54–71.

18. Peter and Olson, *Consumer Behavior,* p. 182.

19. Peter L. Wright, "Consumer Choice Strategies: Simplifying vs Optimizing," *Journal of Marketing Research* 11 (1975), pp. 60–67.

20. Peter L. Wright and Fredric Barbour, "The Relevance of Decision Process Models in Structuring Persuasive Messages," *Communications Research.* July 1975, pp. 246–59.

21. James R. Bettman and Michel A. Zins, "Constructive Processes in Consumer Choice," *Journal of Consumer Research* 4 (1977) pp. 75–85.

22. James F. Engel, "The Psychological Consequences of a Major Purchase Decision," in *Marketing in Transition,* ed. William S. Decker (Chicago: American Marketing Association, 1963), pp. 462–75.

23. John A. Howard and Jagdish N. Sheth, *The Theory of Consumer Behavior* (New York: John Wiley & Sons, 1969).

24. Leon G. Schiffman and Leslie Lazar Kannuk, *Consumer Behavior,* 4th ed. (Englewood Cliffs, N.J.: Prentice Hall, 1991), p. 192.

25. I. P. Pavlov, *The Work of the Digestive Glands.* 2nd ed., trans. W. N. Thompson (London: Griffin, 1910).

26. Gerald J. Gorn, "The Effects of Music in Advertising on Choice: A Classical Conditioning Approach," *Journal of Marketing* 46 (Winter 1982), pp. 94–101.

27. Brian C. Deslauries and Peter B. Everett, The Effects of Intermittent and Continuous Token Reinforcement on Bus Ridership," *Journal of Applied Psychology* 62 (August 1977), pp. 369–75.

28. Michael L. Rothschild and William C. Caidis, "Behavioral Learning Theory: Its Relevance to Marketing and Promotions," *Journal of Marketing*

Research 45, no. 2 (Spring 1981), pp. 70–78.

29. David E. Rumelhart, *Introduction to Human Information Processing* (New York: John Wiley & Sons, 1977).

30. Rom J. Markin, Jr., *Consumer Behavior: A Cognitive Orientation* (New York: Macmillan, 1974), p. 239.

31. For an excellent discussion of social class and consumer behavior, see Richard P. Coleman, "The Continuing Significance of Social Class to Marketing," *Journal of Consumer Research* 10, no. 3 (December 1983), pp. 265–80.

32. Lyman E. Ostlund, *Role Theory and Group Dynamics in Consumer Behavior: Theoretical Sources,* ed. Scott Ward and Thomas S. Robertson (Englewood Cliffs, N.J.: Prentice Hall, 1973), pp. 230–75.

33. James Stafford and Benton Coca-nougher, "Reference Group Theory," in *Perspective in Consumer Behavior,* ed. H. H. Kassarjian and T. S. Robertson (Glenview, Ill.: Scott, Foresman, 1981), pp. 329–43.

34. Jagdish N. Sheth, "A Theory of Family Buying Decisions," in *Models of Buying Behavior,* ed. Jagdish N. Sheth (New York: Harper & Row, 1974), pp. 17–33.

35. Russell Belk, "Situational Variables and Consumer Behavior," *Journal of Consumer Research,* December 1975, pp. 157–64.

chapter 5

1. Eric N. Berkowitz, Roger A. Kerin, and William Rudelius, *Marketing,* 2nd ed. (Homewood, Ill.: Richard D. Irwin, 1989).

2. *9 Nations News* 4, no. 3 (October 1991).

3. *The 9 Nations of USA Weekend* 2, no. 9 (1990).

4. *The 9 Nations of USA Weekend* 2, no. 12 (1990).

5. Robert Rueff, "Demographics Won't Find the Bulls Eye," *Advertising Age,* February 4, 1991, p. 20.

6. Edward M. Tauber, "Research on Food Consumption Values Finds Four Market Segments: Good Taste Still Tops," *Marketing News,* May 15, 1981, p. 17; Rebecca C. Quarles, "Shopping Centers

Use Fashion Lifestyle Research to Make Marketing Decisions," *Marketing News,* January 22, 1982, p. 18; and "Our Autos, Ourselves," *Consumer Reports,* June 1985, p. 375.

7. Judith Graham, "New VALS 2 Takes Psychological Route," *Advertising Age,* February 13, 1989, p. 24.

8. Victor J. Cook and William A. Mindak, "A Search for Constants: The 'Heavy User' Revisited," *Journal of Consumer Marketing* 1, no. 4 (Spring 1984), p. 80.

9. *Ayer's Dictionary of Advertising Terms* (Philadelphia: Ayer Press, 1976).

10. David A. Aaker and John G. Myers, *Advertising Management,* 3rd ed.

(Englewood Cliffs, N.J.: Prentice Hall, 1987), p. 125.

11. Jack Trout and Al Ries, "Positioning Cuts through Chaos in the Marketplace," *Advertising Age,* May 1, 1972, pp. 51–53.

12. Ibid.

13. David A. Aaker and J. Gary Shansby, "Positioning Your Product," *Business Horizons,* May–June 1982, pp. 56–62.

14. Aaker and Myers, *Advertising Management.*

15. Trout and Ries, "Positioning Cuts."

16. Trapped between the Up and Down Escalators," August 26, 1991, p. 49.

17. Aaker and Myers, *Advertising Management.*

chapter 6

1. Wilbur Schram, *The Process and Effects of Mass Communication* (Urbana: University of Illinois Press, 1955).

2. Ibid.

3. Joseph Ransdell, "Some Leading Ideas of Pierce's Semiotic," *Semiotica* 19, (1977), pp. 157–78.

4. Ronald Alsop, "Agencies Scrutinize Their Ads for Psychological Symbolism," *The Wall Street Journal,* June 11, 1987, p. 25.

5. For an excellent article on the application of semiotics to consumer behavior and advertising, see David G. Mick, "Consumer Research and

Semiotics: Exploring the Morphology of Signs, Symbols, and Significance," *Journal of Consumer Research* 13, no. 2 (September 1986), pp. 196–213.

6. Barry L. Bayus, "Word of Mouth: The Indirect Effect of Marketing Efforts," *Journal of Advertising Research,* June–July 1985, pp. 31–39.

7. Quote by Gorden S. Bower in *Fortune,* October 14, 1985, p. 11.

8. Thomas V. Bonoma and Leonard C. Felder, "Nonverbal Communication in Marketing: Toward Communicational Analysis," *Journal of Marketing Research,* May 1977, pp. 169–80.

9. Harold D. Laswell, *Power and Personality* (New York: W. W. Norton, 1948), pp. 37–51.

10. Jacob Jacoby and Wayne D. Hoyer, "Viewer Miscomprehension of Televised Communication: Selected Findings," *Journal of Marketing,* Fall 1982, pp. 12–26; idem, "The Comprehension and Miscomprehension of Print Communications: An Investigation of Mass Media Magazines" (Advertising Education Foundation study, New York, 1987).

11. E. K. Strong, *The Psychology of Selling* (New York: McGraw-Hill, 1925), p. 9.

12. Robert J. Lavidge and Gary A. Steiner, "A Model for Predictive Measurements of Advertising Effectiveness," *Journal of Marketing* 24 (October 1961), pp. 59–62.

13. A summary review of problems with the hierarchy of effects model is offered by Kristin S. Palda, "The Hypothesis of a Hierarchy of Effects: A Partial Evaluation," *Journal of Marketing Research* 3 (February 1966), pp. 13–24. For a good discussion of the historical development of the hierarchy of effects, see Thomas E. Barry, "The Development of the Hierarchy of Effects: An Historical Perspective," in *Current Issues & Research in Advertising* 10, no. 2 (1987), pp. 251–96.

14. Everett M. Rogers, *Diffusion of Innovations* (New York: Free Press, 1962), pp. 79–86.

15. William J. McGuire, "An Information Processing Model of Advertising Effectiveness," in *Behavioral and Management Science in Marketing,* ed. Harry J. Davis and Alvin J. Silk (New York: Ronald Press, 1978), pp. 156–80.

16. Michael L. Ray, "Communication and the Hierarchy of Effects," in *New Models for Mass Communication Research,* ed. P. Clarke (Beverly Hills, Calif.: Sage Publications, 1973), pp. 147–75.

17. Herbert E. Krugman, "The Impact of Television Advertising: Learning without Involvement," *Public Opinion Quarterly* 29 (Fall 1965), pp. 349–56.

18. Harry W. McMahan, "Do Your Ads Have VIP?" *Advertising Age,* July 14, 1980, pp. 50–51.

19. Robert E. Smith and William R. Swinyard, "Information Response Models: An Integrated Approach," *Journal of Marketing* 46, no. 2 (Winter 1982), pp. 81–93.

20. Ibid., p. 90.

21. Ibid., p. 86.

22. Harold H. Kassarjian, "Low Involvement: A Second Look," *Advances in Consumer Research* 8 (1981), pp. 31–34; also see Anthony G. Greenwald and Clark Leavitt, "Audience Involvement in Advertising: Four Levels," *Journal of Consumer Research* 11, no. 1, (June 1984), pp. 581–92.

23. Judith L. Zaichkowsky, "Conceptualizing Involvement," *Journal of Advertising* 15, no. 2 (1986), pp. 4–14.

24. Richard Vaughn, "How Advertising Works: A Planning Model," *Journal of Advertising Research* 20, no. 5 (October 1980), pp. 27–33.

25. Idem, "How Advertising Works: A Planning Model Revisited," *Journal of Advertising Research* 26, no. 1 (February–March 1986), pp. 57–66.

26. John R. Rossiter, Larry Percy, and Robert J. Donovan, "A Better Advertising Planning Grid," *Journal of Advertising Research* (October/November 1991), pp. 11–21.

27. Jerry C. Olson, Daniel R. Toy, and Philip A. Dover, "Mediating Effects of Cognitive Responses to Advertising on Cognitive Structure," in *Advances in Consumer Research,* Vol. V, ed. H. Keith Hunt (Ann Arbor: Association for Consumer Research, 1978), pp. 5:72–78.

28. Anthony A. Greenwald, "Cognitive Learning, Cognitive Response to Persuasion and Attitude Change," in *Psychological Foundations of Attitudes,* ed. A. G. Greenwald, T. C. Brock, and T. W. Ostrom (New York: Academic Press, 1968); and Peter L. Wright, "The Cognitive Processes Mediating Acceptance of Advertising," *Journal of Marketing Research* 10 (February 1973), pp. 53–62.

29. Idem, "Message Evoked Thoughts, Persuasion Research Using Thought Verbalizations," *Journal of Consumer Research* 7, no. 2 (September 1980), pp. 151–75.

30. Scott B. Mackenzie, Richard J. Lutz, and George E. Belch, "The Role of Attitude toward the Ad as a Mediator of Advertising Effectiveness: A Test of Competing Explanations," *Journal of Marketing Research* 23 (May 1986), pp. 130–43; and Rajeev Batra and Michael L. Ray, "Affective Responses Mediating Acceptance of Advertising," *Journal of Consumer Research* 13 (September 1986), pp. 234–49.

31. Ronald Alsop, "TV Ads That Are Likeable Get Plus Rating for Persuasiveness," *The Wall Street Journal,* February 20, 1986, p. 23.

32. Andrew A. Mitchell and Jerry C. Olson, "Are Product Attribute Beliefs the Only Mediator of Advertising Effects on Brand Attitude?" *Journal of Marketing Research* 18 (August 1981), pp. 318–32.

33. Julie Edell and Marian C. Burke, "The Power of Feelings in Understanding Advertising Effects," *Journal of Consumer Research* 14 (December 1987), pp. 421–33.

34. Richard E. Petty and John T. Cacioppo, "Central and Peripheral Routes to Persuasion: Application to Advertising," in *Advertising and Consumer Psychology,* ed. Larry Percy and Arch Woodside (Lexington, Mass.: Lexington Books, 1983), pp. 3–23.

35. David A. Aaker, Rajeev Batra, and John G. Myers, *Advertising Management,* 4th ed. (Englewood Cliffs, N.J.: Prentice Hall, 1992).

36. Richard E. Petty, John T. Cacioppo, and David Schumann, "Central and Peripheral Routes to Advertising Effectiveness: The Moderating Role of Involvement," *Journal of Consumer Research* 10 (September 1983), pp. 135–46.

chapter 7

1. William J. McGuire, "An Information Processing Model of Advertising Effectiveness," in *Behavioral and Management Science in Marketing,* ed. Harry J. Davis and Alvin J. Silk (New York: Ronald Press, 1978), pp. 156–80.

2. Herbert C. Kelman, "Processes of Opinion Change," *Public Opinion Quarterly* 25 (Spring 1961), pp. 57–78.

3. William J. McGuire, "The Nature of Attitudes and Attitude Change," in *Handbook of Social Psychology,* 2nd ed., ed. G. Lindzey and E. Aronson (Cambridge, Mass.: Addison-Wesley, 1969), pp. 135–214.

4. "Business Celebrities," *Business Week,* June 23, 1986, pp. 100–107.

5. Roger Kevin and Thomas E. Barry, "The CEO Spokesperson in Consumer

Advertising: An Experimental Investigation," in *Current Issues in Research in Advertising,* ed. J. H. Leigh and C. R. Martin (Ann Arbor: University of Michigan, 1981), pp. 135–48; J. Poindexter, "Voices of Authority," *Psychology Today,* August 1983.

6. A. Eagly and S. Chaiken, "An Attribution Analysis of the Effect of Communicator Characteristics on Opinion Change," *Journal of Personality and Social Psychology* 32 (1975), pp. 136–44.

7. For a review of these studies, see Brian Sternthal, Lynn Phillips, and Ruby Dholakia, "The Persuasive Effect of Source Credibility: A Situational Analysis," *Public Opinion Quarterly* 42 (Fall 1978), pp. 285–314.

8. Brian Sternthal, Ruby Dholakia, and Clark Leavitt, "The Persuasive Effects of Source Credibility: Tests of Cognitive Response," *Journal of Consumer Research* 4, no. 4 (March 1978), pp. 252–60; and Robert R. Harmon and Kenneth A. Coney, "The Persuasive Effects of Source Credibility in Buy and Lease Situations," *Journal of Marketing Research* 19 (May 1982), pp. 255–60.

9. For a review, see Noel Capon and James Hulbert, "The Sleeper Effect: An Awakening," *Public Opinion Quarterly* 37 (1973), pp. 333–58.

10. Darlene B. Hannah and Brian Sternthal, "Detecting and Explaining the Sleeper Effect," *Journal of Consumer Research* 11, no. 2 (September 1984), pp. 632–42.

11. H. C. Triandis, *Attitudes and Attitude Change* (New York: John Wiley & Sons, 1971).

12. J. Mills and J. Jellison, "Effect on Opinion Change Similarity between the Communicator and the Audience He Addresses," *Journal of Personality and Social Psychology* 9, no. 2 (1969), pp. 153–56.

13. Arch G. Woodside and J. William Davenport, Jr., "The Effect of Salesman Simlarity and Expertise on Consumer Purchasing Behavior," *Journal of Marketing Research* 11 (May 1974), pp. 198–202; and Paul Busch and David T. Wilson, "An Experimental Analysis of a Salesman's Expert and Referent Bases of Social Power in the Buyer-Seller Dyad," *Journal of Marketing Research* 13 (February 1976), pp. 3–11.

14. Aliza Laufer, "Hot Selling Properties," *Backstage,* June 5, 1987, p. 1; and Patricia Winters, "Pepsi to Use Jackson in 4-Part Spot," *Advertising Age,* September 14, 1987, p. 1.

15. Bruce Horowitz, "The Future of Advertising," *Los Angeles Times,* October 6, 1991, pp. D1, 18.

16. Bruce Horowitz, "Mazda Drops Garner to Try New Route in Commercials," *Los Angeles Times,* February 10, 1989, pt. IV, p. 1.

17. John C. Mowen and Stephen W. Brown, "On Explaining and Predicting the Effectiveness of Celebrity Endorsers," in *Advances in Consumer Research* 8 (Ann Arbor: Association for Consumer Research, 1981), pp. 437–41.

18. "It Seemed Like a Good Idea at the Time," *Forbes,* February 28, 1987, p. 98.

19. Ibid.

20. Charles Atkin and M. Block, "Effectiveness of Celebrity Endorsers," *Journal of Advertising Research,* 23, no. 1 (February—March 1983), pp. 57–61.

21. Alix M. Freedman, "Marriages between Celebrity Spokesmen and Their Firms Can Be Risky Venture," *The Wall Street Journal,* January 22, 1988, p. 23.

22. James R. Schiffman, "PepsiCo Cans TV Ads with Madonna, Pointing Up Risks of Using Superstars," *The Wall Street Journal,* April 5, 1989, p. B-11.

23. Bruce Horowitz, "It May Be Hard to Swallow Some Endorsements," *Los Angeles Times,* February, 11, 1992, p. D1.

24. J. Forkan, "Product Matchup Key to Effective Star Presentations," *Advertising Age,* October 6, 1980, p. 42; and Michael A. Kamins, "An Investigation into the "Match-up" Hypothesis in Celebrity Advertising," *Journal of Advertising* 19, no. 1 (1990), pp. 4–13.

25. Roobina Ohanian, "The Impact of Celebrity Spokespersons' Image on Consumers' Intention to Purchase," *Journal of Advertising Research,* February–March 1991, pp. 46–54.

26. Pat Sloan, "Nuprin's Smash Hit," *Advertising Age,* October 14, 1991, p. 3.

27. Grant McCracken, "Who Is the Celebrity Endorser? Cultural Foundations of the Endorsement Process," *Journal of Consumer Research* 16, no. 3 (December 1989), pp. 310–21.

28. Ibid., p. 315.

29. "HIV Revelation Tests Magic's Ad Appeal," *Advertising Age,* November 11, 1991, p. 2.

30. For an excellent review of these studies, see W. B. Joseph, "The Credibility of Physically Attractive Communicators," *Journal of Advertising* 11, no. 3 (1982), pp. 13–23.

31. M. J. Baker and Gilbert A. Churchill, Jr., "The Impact of Physically Attractive Models on Advertising Evaluations," *Journal of Marketing Research* 14 (November 1977), pp. 538–55.

32. Robert W. Chestnut, C. C. La Chance, and A. Lubitz, "The Decorative Female Model: Sexual Stimuli and the Recognition of the Advertisements," *Journal of Advertising* 6 (Fall 1977), pp. 11–14; and Leonard N. Reid and Lawrence C. Soley, "Decorative Models and Readership of Magazine Ads," *Journal of Advertising Research* 23, no. 2 (April–May 1983), pp. 27–32.

33. "Why P & G Wants a Mellower Image," *Business Week,* June 7, 1982, p. 60.

34. Herbert E. Krugman, "On Application of Learning Theory to TV Copy Testing," *Public Opinion Quarterly* 26 (1962), pp. 626–39.

35. C. I. Hovland and W. Mandell, "An Experimental Comparison of Conclusion Drawing by the Communicator and by the Audience," *Journal of Abnormal and Social Psychology* 47 (July 1952), pp. 581–88.

36. Allan G. Sawyer and Daniel J. Howard, "Effects of Omitting Conclusions in Advertisements to Involved and Uninvolved Audiences," *Journal of Marketing Research* 28 (November 1991), pp. 467–74.

37. Paul Chance, "Ads without Answers Make Brain Itch," *Psychology Today* 9 (1975), p. 78.

38. Robert E. Settle and Linda L. Golden, "Attribution Theory and Advertiser Credibility," *Journal of Marketing Research* 11 (May 1974), pp. 181–85; and Edmund J. Faison, "Effectiveness of One-Sided and Two-Sided Mass Communications in Advertising," *Public Opinion Quarterly* 25 (Fall 1961), pp. 468–69.

39. Alan G. Sawyer, "The Effects of Repetition of Refutational and Supportive Advertising Appeals," *Journal of Marketing Research* 10 (February 1973), pp. 23–37; and George J. Szybillo and Richard Heslin, "Resistance to Persuasion: Inoculation Theory in a Marketing Context," *Journal of Marketing Research* 10 (November 1973), pp. 396–403.

40. Andrew A. Mitchell, "The Effect of Verbal and Visual Components of Advertisements on Brand Attitudes and Attitude toward the Advertisement," *Journal of Consumer Research* 13 (June 1986), pp. 12–24; and Julie A. Edell and Richard Staelin, "The Information Processing of Pictures in Advertisements,"

Journal of Consumer Research 10, no. 1 (June 1983), pp. 45–60; Elizabeth C. Hirschmann, "The Effects of Verbal and Pictorial Advertising Stimuli on Aesthetic, Utilitarian and Familiarity Perceptions," *Journal of Advertising* 15, no. 2 (1986), pp. 27–34.

41. Jolita Kisielius and Brain Sternthal, "Detecting and Explaining Vividness Effects in Attitudinal Judgments," *Journal of Marketing Research* 21, no. 1 (1984), pp. 54–64.

42. H. Rao Unnava and Robert E. Burnkrant, "An Imagery-Processing View of the Role of Pictures in Print Advertisements," *Journal of Marketing Research* 28, (May 1991), pp. 226–31.

43. William L. Wilkie and Paul W. Farris, "Comparative Advertising: Problems and Potential," *Journal of Marketing* 39 (1975), pp. 7–15.

44. Janet Neiman, "The Trouble with Comparative Ads," *Adweek,* January 12, 1987, pp. BR4–5.

45. For a review of comparative advertising studies see Cornelia Pechmann and David W. Stewart, "Development of a Contingency Model of Comparative Advertising" (Working Paper, Graduate School of Management, University of California, Irvine, 1988).

46. "Emotion a Powerful Tool for Advertisers," *Advertising Age,* July 8, 1985, p. 28.

47. Bill Abrams, "If Logic Doesn't Sell, Try a Little Tug on the Heartstrings," *The Wall Street Journal,* April 8, 1982, p. 27.

48. Morris B. Holbrook and Rajeev Batra, "Assessing the Role of Emotions as Mediators of Consumer Responses to Advertising," *Journal of Consumer Research* 14, no. 3 (December 1987), pp. 404–420; and Julie A. Edell and Marian Chapman Burke, "The Power of Feelings in Understanding Advertising Effects," *Journal of Consumer Research* 14, no. 3 (December 1987), pp. 421–33.

49. Michael L. Ray and William L. Wilkie, "Fear: The Potential of an Appeal Neglected by Marketing," *Journal of Marketing* 34 (January 1970), pp. 54–62.

50. Brian Sternthal and C. Samuel Craig, "Fear Appeals Revisited and Revised," *Journal of Consumer Research* 1 (December 1974), pp. 22–34.

51. C. Samuel Craig and Brian Sternthal, For a discussion of the use of humor in advertising, see "Humor in Advertising," *Journal of Marketing* 37 (October 1973), pp. 12–18.

52. Harold C. Cash and W. J. E. Crissy, "Comparison of Advertising and Selling," *The Salesman's Role in Marketing, The Psychology of Selling* 12 (1965), pp. 56–75.

53. Marshall McLuhan, *Understanding Media: The Extensions of Man* (New York: McGraw-Hill, 1966).

54. Marvin E. Goldberg and Gerald J. Gorn, "Happy and Sad TV Programs: How They Affect Reactions to Commercials," *Journal of Consumer Research* 14, no. 3 (December 1987), pp. 387–403.

55. Peter J. Boyle, "Chrysler Pulls Ads from Amerika," *New York Times,* January 28, 1987, p. C26.

56. "GF, Coke Tell Why They Shun TV News," *Advertising Age,* January 28, 1980, p. 39.

57. Peter H. Webb, "Consumer Initial Processing in a Difficult Media Environment," *Journal of Consumer Research* 6, no. 3 (December 1979), pp. 225–36.

68. For a review of marketing communications studies involving source, message, channel, and receiver factors, see George E. Belch, Michael A. Belch, and Angelina Villarreal, "Effects of Advertising Communications: Review of Research," in *Research in Marketing* (Greenwich, CT: JAI Press, 1987), 9: 59–117.

chapter 8

1. Kenneth R. Sheets, "Infiniti's Art of Pacific Persuasion," *U.S. News & World Report,* November 13, 1989, p. 67.

2. Ibid.

3. Robert A. Kriegel, "How to Choose the Right Communications Objectives," *Business Marketing,* April 1986, pp. 94–106.

4. James Risen, "Poor Infiniti Sales Cheer Firm's Luxury Car Rivals," *Los Angeles Times,* April 12, 1990, pp. D1, 5.

5. Joseph B. White, "New Ads Give a Boost to the Olds Image But Don't Help the Old Sales Woes Much," *The Wall Street Journal,* June 19, 1989, p. B1.

6. Donald S. Tull, "The Carry-over Effect of Advertising," *Journal of Marketing,* April 1965, pp. 46–53.

7. Darral G. Clarke, "Econometric Measurement of the Duration of Advertising Effect on Sales," *Journal of Marketing Research* 23 (November 1976), pp. 345–57.

8. Philip Kotler, *Marketing Decision Making: A Model Building Approach* (New York: Holt, Rinehart and Winston, 1971), chap. 5.

9. For a more detailed discussion of this, see William M. Weilbacher, *Advertising,* 2nd ed. (New York: Macmillan, 1984), p. 112.

10. Courtland I. Bovee and William F. Arens, *Advertising,* 3rd ed. (Homewood, Ill.: Richard D. Irwin, 1989).

11. Russell H. Colley, *Defining Advertising Goals for Measured Advertising Results* (New York: Association of National Advertisers, 1961).

12. Ibid., p. 21.

13. Don E. Shultz, Dennis Martin, and William Brown, *Strategic Advertising Campaigns,* 2nd ed. (Lincolnwood, Ill.: Crain Books, 1984).

14. Scott Hume, "McDonald's Heavy in Print for Nutrition," *Advertising Age,* January 19, 1987, p. 2.

15. Michael L. Ray, "Consumer Initial Processing: Definitions, Issues, Applications," in *Buyer/Consumer Information Processing,* ed. G. David Hughes (Chapel Hill: University of North Carolina Press, 1974); and David A. Aaker and John G. Myers, *Advertising Management,* 2nd ed. (Englewood Cliffs, N.J.: Prentice Hall, 1982), pp. 122–23.

16. Sandra Ernst Moriarty, "Beyond the Hierarchy of Effects: A Conceptual Framework," in *Current Issues and Research in Advertising,* ed. Claude R. Martin, Jr., and James H. Leigh (Ann Arbor: University of Michigan, 1983), pp. 45–55.

17. Aaker and Myers, *Advertising Management.*

18. Thomas S. Robertson, *Innovative Behavior and Communication* (New York: Holt, Rinehart and Winston, 1971).

19. Richard Vaughn, "How Advertising Works: A Planning Model," *Journal of Advertising Research* 20, no. 5 (October 1980), p. 29.

20. A. W. Wicker, "Attitudes vs. Action: The Relationship of Verbal and Overt Behavioral Responses to Attitude Objects," *Journal of Social Issues* 25, no. 4 (1969), pp. 41–78; and Icek Ajzen and Martin Fishbein, "Attitude-Behavior Relations: A Theoretical Analysis and Review of Empirical Research," *Psychological Bulletin,* September 1977, pp. 888–918.

21. Icek Ajzen and Martin Fishbein, *Understanding Attitudes and Predicting Social Behavior* (Englewood Cliffs, N.J.: Prentice Hall, 1980).

22. Alvin A. Achenbaum, "Advertising Doesn't Manipulate Consumers,"

Journal of Advertising Research 12 (April 1972), pp. 3–13.

23. Kristian S. Palda, "The Hypothesis of a Hierarchy of Effects: A Partial Evaluation," *Journal of Marketing Research* 3 (February 1966), pp. 13–24.

chapter 9

1. Robert L. Steiner, "The Paradox of Increasing Returns to Advertising," *Journal of Advertising Research,* February–March 1987, pp. 45–53.
2. Frank M. Bass, "A Simultaneous Equation Regression Study of Advertising and Sales of Cigarettes," *Journal of Marketing Research* 6, no. 3 (August 1969), p. 291.
3. David A. Aaker and James M. Carman, "Are You Overadvertising?" *Journal of Advertising Research* 22, no. 4 (August–September 1982), pp. 57–70.
4. Julian A. Simon and Johan Arndt, "The Shape of the Advertising Response Function," *Journal of Advertising Research* 20, no. 4 (1980), pp. 11–28.
5. Paul B. Luchsinger, Vernan S. Mullen, and Paul T. Jannuzzo, "How Many Advertising Dollars Are Enough?," *Media Decisions* 12 (1977), p. 59.
6. Paul W. Farris, "Determinants of Advertising Intensity: A Review of the Marketing Literature" (Report no. 77–109, Marketing Science Institute, Cambridge, Mass., 1977).

chapter 10

1. Ron Alsop, "Don Rickles, Devilish Kid Brings Dull Carpet Ads to Life," *The Wall Street Journal,* July 9, 1987, p. 31.
2. Bill Abrams, "What Do Effie, Clio, Addy, Andy and Ace Have in Common?" *The Wall Street Journal,* July 16, 1983, p. 1; Jennifer Pendleton, "Awards—Creatives Defend Pursuit of Prizes," *Advertising Age,* April 25, 1988, p. 1; and David Herzbrun, "The Awards Awards," *Advertising Age,* May 2, 1988, p. 18.
3. David Mars, "Organizational Climate for Creativity" (Occasional Paper no. 4, Creative Education Foundation, Buffalo, 1969).
4. Emily T. Smith, "Are You Creative?" *Business Week,* September 30, 1985, p. 81–82.
5. Elizabeth C. Hirschman, "Role-Based Models of Advertising Creation and Production," *Journal of Advertising* 18, no. 4 (1989), pp. 42–53.
6. Ibid., p. 51.
7. Ronald Alsop, "TV Ads That Are Likeable Get Plus Rating For Persuasiveness," *The Wall Street Journal,* February 20, 1986, p. 23; and Cyndee Miller, "Study Says 'Likability'

24. Steven W. Hartley and Charles H. Patti, "Evaluating Business-to-Business Advertising: A Comparison of Objectives and Results," *Journal of Advertising Research* 28 (April–May 1988), pp. 21–27.

7. Melvin E. Salveson, "Management's Criteria for Advertising Effectiveness" (Proceedings 5th Annual Conference, Advertising Research Foundation, New York, 1959), p. 25.
8. Robert Settle and Pamela Alreck, "Positive Moves for Negative Times," *Marketing Communications,* January 1988, pp. 19–23.
9. James O. Peckham, "Can We Relate Advertising Dollars to Market Share Objectives?" in *How Much to Spend for Advertising,* ed. M. A. McNiven (New York: Association of National Advertisers, 1969), p. 30.
10. "Marketers Fuel Promotion Budgets," *Marketing and Media Decisions,* September 1984, p. 130.
11. Ibid.
12. John P. Jones, "Ad Spending: Maintaining Market Share," *Harvard Business Review,* January–February 1990, pp. 38–42; and James C. Schroer, "Ad Spending: Growing

Surfaces as Measure of TV Ad Success," *Marketing News,* January 7, 1991, pp. 6, 14.
8. For an interesting discussion on the embellishment of advertising messages, see William M. Weilbacher, *Advertising,* 2nd ed. (New York: Macmillan, 1984), pp. 180–82.
9. David Ogilvy, *Confessions of an Advertising Man* (New York: Atheneum Publishers, 1963); and Hanley Norins, *The Compleat Copywriter* (New York: McGraw-Hill, 1966).
10. Hank Sneiden, *Advertising Pure and Simple* (New York: ANACOM, 1977).
11. Ronald Alsop, "Advertisers Take a Dim View of Sincerest Form of Flattery," *The Wall Street Journal,* September 24, 1987, p. 29.
12. Quoted in Valerie H. Free, "Absolut Original," *Marketing Insights,* Summer 1991, p. 65.
13. Cathy Taylor, "Risk Takers: Wieden & Kennedy," *Adweek's Marketing Week,* March 23, 1992, pp. 26, 27.
14. Frank Barron, *Creative Person and Creative Process* (New York: Holt, Rinehart and Winston, 1969).

25. Ibid., p. 25.
26. Study cited in Robert F. Lauterborn, "How to Know If Your Advertising Is Working," *Journal of Advertising Research* 25 (February–March 1985), pp. RC 9–11.

Market Share," *Harvard Business Review,* January–February 1990, pp. 44–48.
13. Randall S. Brown, "Estimating Advantages to Large Scale Advertising," *Review of Economics and Statistics* 60 (August 1978), pp. 428–437.
14. Kent M. Lancaster, "Are There Scale Economies in Advertising?" *Journal of Business* 59, no. 3 (1986), pp. 509–526.
15. Johan Arndt and Julian Simon, "Advertising and Economies of Scale: Critical Comments on the Evidence," *Journal of Industrial Economics* 32, no. 2 (December 1983), pp. 229–41; and Aaker and Carman, "Are You Overadvertising?"
16. George S. Low and Jakki J. Mohr, "The Budget Allocation between Advertising and Sales Promotion: Understanding the Decision Process," *1991 AMA Educators' Proceedings, Chicago, Ill.:* Summer 1991, pp. 448–57.

15. James Webb Young, *A Technique for Producing Ideas,* 3rd ed. (Chicago: Crain Books, 1975), p. 42.
16. Graham Wallas, *The Art of Thought* (New York: Harcourt, Brace and World, 1926).
17. Sandra E. Moriarty, *Creative Advertising: Theory and Practice* (Englewood Cliffs, N.J.: Prentice Hall, 1986).
18. Joanne Lipman and Joann S. Lublin, "Mideast TV News Is Deterring Sponsors," *The Wall Street Journal,* January 18, 1991, p. B1; and "Marketers Slash Ads as War Erupts," *Advertising Age,* January 21, 1991, pp. 1, 54.
19. E.E. Norris, "Seek Out the Consumer's Problem," *Advertising Age,* March 17, 1975, pp. 43–44.
20. Joseph M. Winski, "Research + 'Creative Leap' = Award-Winning Ads," *Advertising Age,* September 24, 1990, p. 24.
21. William D. Wells, Clark Leavitt, and Maureen McConville, "A Reaction Profile for Commercials," *Journal of Advertising Research* 11 (December 1971), pp. 11–17.

22. A. Jerome Jeweler, *Creative Strategy in Advertising* (Belmont, Calif.: Wadsworth, 1981).
23. John O'Toole, *The Trouble with Advertising,* 2nd ed. (New York: Random House, 1985), p. 131.
24. David Ogilvy, *Ogilvy on Advertising* (New York: Crown, 1983), p. 16.
25. Rosser Reeves, *Reality in Advertising* (New York: Knopf, 1961), pp. 47, 48.

26. Bill Abrams, "Ad Constraints Could Persist Even If the FTC Loosens Up," *The Wall Street Journal,* December 10, 1981, p. 33.
27. Alecia Swasy, "How Innovation at P&G Restored Luster to Washed-Up Pert and Made It No. 1," *The Wall Street Journal,* December 6, 1990, p. B1.
28. Ogilvy, *Confessions.*

29. Martin Mayer, *Madison Avenue, U.S.A.* (New York: Pocket Books, 1958).
30. Jack Trout and Al Ries, "The Positioning Era Cometh," *Advertising Age,* April 24, 1972, pp. 35–38; May 1, 1972, pp. 51–54; May 8, 1972, pp. 114–16.
31. David A. Aaker and John G. Myers, *Advertising Management,* 3rd ed. (Englewood Cliffs, N.J.: Prentice Hall, 1987).

chapter 11

1. Sandra E. Moriarty, *Creative Advertising: Theory and Practice,* 2nd ed. (Englewood Cliffs, N.J.: Prentice Hall, 1991), p. 76.
2. William M. Weilbacher, *Advertising,* 2nd ed. (New York: MacMillan, 1984), p. 197.
3. William Wells, John Burnett, and Sandra Moriarty, *Advertising* (Englewood Cliffs, N.J.: Prentice Hall, 1989), p. 330.
4. For a review of research on the effect of mood states on consumer behavior, see Meryl Paula Gardner, "Mood States and Consumer Behavior: A Critical Review," *Journal of Consumer Research* 12, no. 3 (December 1985), pp. 281–300.
5. Cathy Madison, "Researchers Work Advertising into an Emotional State," *Adweek,* November 5, 1990. p. 30.
6. Christopher P. Puto and William D. Wells, "Informational and Transformational Advertising: The Different Effects of Time," in *Advances in Consumer Research,* vol. 11, ed. Thomas C. Kinnear (Ann Arbor: Association for Consumer Research, 1984), p. 638.
7. Ibid.
8. Bill Abrams, "If Logic Doesn't Sell, Try a Tug on the Heartstrings," *The*

Wall Street Journal, April 8, 1982, p. 27.
9. David Ogilvy and Joel Raphaelson, "Research on Advertising Techniques That Work and Don't Work," *Harvard Business Review,* July–August 1982, p. 18.
10. Hal Riney, "Emotion in Advertising," *Viewpoint: By, for and about Ogilvy and Mather* 1 (New York: Ogilvy and Mather, 1981), pp. 5–13.
11. Jacqueline Mitchell, "New Jeep to Roll Out with 'Teaser' Ads," *The Wall Street Journal,* February 6, 1992, p. B7.
12. Martin Mayer, *Madison Avenue, U.S.A.* (New York: Pocket Books, 1958), p. 64.
13. Alecia Swasy, "P&G Tries Bolder Ads—With Caution," *The Wall Street Journal,* May 7, 1990, pp. B1, 7.
14. Lynn Coleman, "Advertisers Put Fear into the Hearts of Their Prospects," *Marketing News,* August 15, 1988, p. 1.
15. Sandra E. Moriarty, *Creative Advertising,* p. 77.
16. Courtland L. Bovee and William F. Arens, *Contemporary Advertising,* 4th ed. (Homewood, Ill.: Richard D. Irwin, Inc., 1992), p. 292.
17. W. Keith Hafer and Gordon E. White, *Advertising Writing,* 3rd ed.

(St. Paul, Minn.: West Publishing, 1989), p. 98.
18. "How Much Should a Commercial Cost?" *Marketing Communications,* June 1983, p. 41.
19. Linda M. Scott, "Understanding Jingles and Needledrop: A Rhetorical Approach to Music in Advertising," *Journal of Consumer Research* 17, no. 2 (September 1990), pp. 223–36.
20. Ibid., p. 223.
21. Russell I. Haley, Jack Richardson, and Beth Baldwin, "The Effects of Nonverbal Communications in Television Advertising," *Journal of Advertising Research* 24, no. 4, pp. 11–18.
22. Gerald J. Gorn, "The Effects of Music in Advertising on Choice Behavior: A Classical Conditioning Approach," *Journal of Marketing* 46 (Winter 1982), pp. 94–100.
23. Alecia Swasy, "P&G Tries Bolder Ads."
24. Eva Pomice, "Madison Avenue's Blind Spot," *U.S. News & World Report,* October 3, 1988, p. 49.
25. Bruce Horowitz, "TV Spots for Light Bulbs, Diet Pepsi This Year's Big Clio Award Winners," *Los Angeles Times,* June 21, 1988, part IV, p. 6.

chapter 12

1. "MasterCard Targets Youth with $10–million Campaign," *Mediaweek,* March 16, 1992, p. 4.
2. Michael J. Naples, *Effective Frequency: The Relationship between Frequency and Advertising Effectiveness* (New York: Association of National Advertisers, 1979).
3. Joseph W. Ostrow, "Setting Frequency Levels: An Art or a Science?"

Market and Media Decisions, 1987, p. 19.
4. David Berger, "How Much to Spend" (Foote, Cone & Belding Internal Report), in Michael L. Rothschild, *Advertising* (Lexington, Mass.: D. C. Heath, 1987), p. 468.
5. David W. Olson, "Real World Measures of Advertising Effectiveness for New

Products" (Speech to the 26th Annual Conference of the Advertising Research Foundation, New York, March 18, 1980).
6. Naples, *Effective Frequency.*
7. Joseph W. Ostrow, "What Level Frequency?" *Advertising Age,* November 1981, pp. 13–18.
8. Ibid.

chapter 13

1. *Radio Marketing Guide and Fact Book for Advertisers* (New York: Radio Advertising Bureau, Inc., 1992).
2. "Trends in Television" (New York: Television Bureau of Advertising, Inc., July 1991), p. 7.

3. *Radio Marketing Guide and Fact Book for Advertisers* (New York: Radio Advertising Bureau, Inc., 1992).
4. *Trends in Media* (New York: Television Bureau of Advertising July 1991).
5. *Trends in Media.*

6. R. Craig Endicott, "P&G Spends $2.28 Billion, Surges to Head of Top 100," *Advertising Age,* September 25, 1991, pp. 1, 72.
7. Dennis Kneale, "Zapping of TV Ads Appears Pervasive," *The Wall Street Journal,* April 25, 1988, p. 27.

8. Janet Meyers and Laurie Freeman, "Marketers Police TV Commercial Costs," *Advertising Age,* April 3, 1989, p. 51.
9. Robert Parcher, "15-Second TV Commercials Appear to Work 'Quite Well,'" *Marketing News,* January 3, 1986, p. 1.
10. Wayne Walley, "Popularity of :15s Falls," *Advertising Age,* January 14, 1991, pp. 1, 41.
11. Joe Mandese, "ABC Whittles Clutter by :15 per Night," *Advertising Age,* April 13, 1992, p. 4.
12. Mary Connors, "Catching TV Viewers in the Act of Being Themselves," *Adweek,* March 9, 1987, p. 30.
13. Dennis Kneale, "Zapping of TV Ads Appears Pervasive."
14. Carrie Heeter and Bradley S. Greenberg, "Profiling the Zappers," *Journal of Advertising Research,* April–May 1985, pp. 9–12; and Patricia Orsini, "Zapping: A Man's World," *Spring Television Report: Adweek's Marketing Week,* April 8, 1991, p. 3.
15. Ernest F. Larkin, "Consumer Perceptions of the Media and Their Advertising Content," *Journal of Advertising* 8 (1979), pp. 5–7.
16. Adapted from Charles H. Patti and Charles F. Frazier, *Advertising* (New York: Dryden Press, 1988).
17. "Zeroing in with a Network Buy," *Marketing & Media Decisions,* February 1987, p. 31.
18. "Marketing's New Look," *Business Week,* January 26, 1987, pp. 64–69.

19. Mary Lou Carnevale, "FCC Gives Last Chance for Objections in Bitter Fight on TV Syndication Rule," *The Wall Street Journal,* March 18, 1991, p. B6.
20. John Lippman, "Too Costly for Prime Time," *Los Angeles Times,* March 22, 1992, pp. D1, 8.
21. Eric Schmuckler, "Playing the Network Game," *Adweek's Marketing Week,* January 20, 1992, pp. 17–27.
22. *Report on Television 1990, Nielsen Media Research* (New York: A. C. Nielsen Co., 1990).
23. Christine Larson, "On the Spot." *Cable Television Special Report: Adweek,* April 6, 1992.
24. Ibid.
25. John Lippman, "Merchants Begin to Shift Their Ad Focus to Cable TV," *Los Angeles Times,* February 3, 1992, pp. D1, 2.
26. Stephen Battaglio, "The Rise and Stall," *Cable Television Special Report: Adweek,* April 6, 1992, pp. 10–12.
27. John Lippman, "MTV Will Split into 3 Cable Channels," *Los Angeles Times,* July 31, 1991, pp. D1, 3.
28. Adam Snyder, "The Revolt Against Cable," *Adweek's Marketing Week,* November 18, 1991, pp. 16–18.
29. Kevin Goldman, "TV Affiliates of 3 Networks Turn to CNN," *The Wall Street Journal,* January 21, 1991, p. B1.
30. "Sports on TV: Cable Is the Team to Watch," *Business Week,* August 22, 1988, pp. 66–69.
31. William Smith, "ESPN's New Game Plan," *Marketing & Media Decisions,* March 1989, p. 26.

32. Daozheng Lu and David A. Kiewit, "Passive Peoplemeters: A First Step," *Journal of Advertising Research,* June–July/1987, pp. 9–14.
33. Erik Larson, "Watching Americans Watch TV," *Atlantic Monthly,* March 1992, pp. 66–80.
34. Joanne Lipman, "Single-Source Ad Research Heralds Detailed Look at Household Habits," *The Wall Street Journal,* February 16, 1988, p. 35.
35. Quote by William Staklein, head of Radio Advertising Bureau, cited in: "More Firms Tune into Radio to Stretch Their Ad Budgets," *The Wall Street Journal,* July 17, 1986, p. 27.
36. *Radio Marketing Guide and Fact Book.*
37. "More Firms Tune into Radio."
38. *Radio Marketing Guide and Fact Book.*
39. Verne Gay, "Image Transfer: Radio Ads Make Aural History," *Advertising Age,* January 24, 1985, p. 1.
40. Stephen Battaglio, "Radio," *Adweek,* September 11, 1989, p. 184.
41. "Broadcast Beat," *Marketing & Media Decisions,* July 1988, pp. 143–44.
42. Bob Davis, "U.S. Looks into Global Radio Network Using Satellites," *The Wall Street Journal,* June 26, 1990, p. B1.
43. Robert J. Coen, "How Bad a Year for Ads Was '91? Almost the Worst," *Advertising Age,* May 4, 1992, pp. 3, 51.
44. John Lippman, "Merchants Begin to Shift Their Ad Focus to Cable TV."

chapter 14

1. *The Magazine Handbook* (New York: Magazine Publishers Association, 1991), no. 59; and Fred Plaff, "Trading Up," *Marketing & Media Decisions,* August 1988, pp. 77–83.
2. Herbert E. Krugman, "The Measurement of Advertising Involvement," *Public Opinion Quarterly* 30 (Winter 1966–67), pp. 583–96.
3. *The Magazine Handbook.*
4. Robert J. Coen, "U.S. Advertising Volume," report prepared by McCann-Erickson Worldwide 1992.
5. Sue Knapp, "New Directions for the Business Press," *Business Marketing,* September 1991, pp. 32–36.
6. Jerry Schlosberg, "The Glittering City Magazines," *American Demographics,* July 1986, pp. 22–25.
7. *Magazine Audiences 2* (New York: Mediamark Research Inc., Spring 1982).
8. Ibid.

9. Steve Fajen, "Numbers Aren't Everything." *Media Decisions* 10 (June 1975), pp. 65–69.
10. *A Study of Media Involvement* 6 (New York: Magazine Publishers of America, April 1991).
11. Ibid.
12. Amy Alson, "Making Ends Meet," *Marketing & Media Decisions,* August 1988, pp. 67–75.
13. *The Magazine Handbook.*
14. Garfield Ricketts, "The ABCs of ABC Statements," *Marketing & Media Decisions,* November 1988, p. 84.
15. Study cited in Jim Surmanek, *Media Planning: A Practical Guide* (Lincolnwood, Ill.: Crain Books, 1985).
16. Cahners Publishing Company, "How Advertising Readership Is Influenced by Ad Size," (Cahners Advertising Research Report no. 110.1); and McGraw-Hill Research, "Larger Advertisements Get Higher Readership," LAP Report no. 3102.

17. McGraw-Hill Research, "Effect of Size, Color and Position Number of Responses to Recruitment Advertising," LAP Report no. 3116.
18. *The Magazine Handbook,* p. 23.
19. Eric Garland, "The Road to Recovery," *Adweek Special Report: Consumer Magazines,* February 17, 1992, pp. 4, 5.
20. Victor F. Zonana, "Hard-Pressed Magazines Push for New Image," *Los Angeles Times,* April 7, 1991, pp. D1, 10
21. Lorne Manly, "No Gains, No Pain," *Adweek Special Report: Consumer Magazines,* February 17, 1992, p. 27.
22. Evan Smith, "Cross Magazine Ad Buys Appear to Be Catching On," *Mediaweek,* March 23, 1991, p. 5.
23. Joe Mandese, "Strong Roots for Cross-Media," *Advertising Age,* October 6, 1991, pp. 34, 35.
24. Scott Donaton, "The Personal Touch," *Advertising Age,* October 6, 1991, p. 22.

25. Junu Bryan Kim, "Cracking the Barrier of Two Dimensions," *Advertising Age,* October 6, 1991, pp. 32, 34.
26. Robert J. Coen, "U.S. Advertising Volume."
27. *Key Facts 1991: Newspapers, Advertising & Marketing* (New York: Newspaper Advertising Bureau, 1991).
28. Tamara Goldman, "Big Spenders Develop Newspaper Strategies," *Marketing Communications,* June 1988, pp. 24–29.
29. Survey by Newspaper Advertising Bureau, October 1988.

30. "Newspapers Cut National Ad Rate," *Advertising Age,* June 8, 1987, p. 1.
31. Survey reported in *NewsInc.,* May–June 1989, p. 81.
32. Amy Alson, "The Search for National Ad Dollars," *Marketing & Media Decisions,* February 1989, pp. 29–31.
33. Robert J. Coen, "U.S. Advertising Volume."
34. Thomas B. Rosentiel, "Newspapers Fear Being Bypassed by Advertisers," *Los Angeles Times,* April 27, 1989, pt. IV., p. 1.
35. Lisa Benenson, "The Data Chase," *Adweek Special Report: The*

Newspaper Business, May 4, 1992, pp. 6–7.
36. Ibid.
37. Dan Cray, Tom Weisend, Michael J. McDermott, Pat Hinsberg, and Meryl Davids, "Making Change," *Newspapers: Special Supplement to Adweek's Marketing Week,* May 6, 1991, pp. 6–13.
38. Ibid.
39. Daniel Pearl, "Newspapers Strive to Win Back Women," *The Wall Street Journal,* May 4, 1992, pp. B1, 12.
40. Thomas B. Rosentiel, "Newspapers Courting the MTV Generation," *Los Angeles Times,* July 31, 1991, p. A5.

chapter 15

1. Scotty Dupree, "Billboard's Top Ten," *Mediaweek,* April 8, 1991, pp. 26–30.
2. "Outdoor Advertising: Special Report," *Advertising Age,* December 12, 1985, p. 20.
3. John Medearis, "Ads on Wheels Run into Flak," *Los Angeles Times,* July 11, 1984, part IV, p. 2.
4. David Kalish, "Supermarket Sweepstakes," *Marketing & Media Decisions,* November 1988, p. 34.
5. Adam Snyder, "Outdoor Forecast: Sunny, Some Clouds," *Adweek's Marketing Week,* July 8, 1991, p. 18–19.
6. Laurie Freeman and Alison Fahey, "Package Goods Ride with Transit," *Advertising Age,* April 23, 1990, p. 28.
7. *Advertisers Take the City Bus to Work* (New York: Winston Network, 1988), p. 13.
8. *Transit Fact Book* (New York: American Public Transit Association, 1990).
9. *Preference Building: The Dynamic World of Specialty Advertising* (Irving, Tex.: Specialty Advertising Association, 1988).
10. Specialty Advertising Association, 1992.

11. George L. Herpel and Steve Slack, *Specialty Advertising: New Dimensions in Creative Marketing* (Irving, Tex.: Specialty Advertising Association, 1983), pp. 76, 79–80.
12. Ibid., p. 78.
13. Ibid., p. 75.
14. Alan D. Fletcher, *Target Marketing through the Yellow Pages* (Troy, Mich.: Yellow Pages Publishers Association, 1991) p. 2.
15. Carol Hall, "Branding the Yellow Pages," *Marketing & Media Decisions,* April 1989, p. 59.
16. Ibid., p. 3.
17. Ibid.
18. Ibid., p. 5.
19. Ibid.
20. Ibid., p. 8.
21. Scott Hume, "Consumers Pan Ads on Video Movies," *Advertising Age,* May 28, 1990, p. 8.
22. Joanne Lipman and Kathleen A. Hughes, "Disney Prohibits Ads in Theaters Showing Its Movies," *The Wall Street Journal,* February 9, 1990, p. B1.
23. "1991 Is 3rd Best B.O. Year; Tix Sales Fall," *Daily Variety,* January 16, 1992, p. 10.

24. Betsy Baurer, "New Quick Flicks: Ads at the Movies," *USA Today,* March 13, 1986, p. D1.
25. Ibid.
26. Michael A. Belch and Don Sciglimpaglia, "Viewers' Evaluations of Cinema Advertising" (Proceedings of the American Institute for Decision Sciences, March 1979).
27. "Hershey Befriends Extra-terrestrial," *Advertising Age,* July 19, 1982, p. 1.
28. "1991 Is Third-Best B.O. Year; Tix Sales Fall," *Daily Variety,* January 16, 1992, p. 10.
29. Colin Leinster, "A Tale of Mice and Lens," *Fortune,* September 28, 1987, p. 8.
30. "Consumer Products Become Movie Stars," *The Wall Street Journal,* February 29, 1988, p. 23.
30. Ibid.
32. Jennifer Lawrence, "In-Flight Gets above Turbulence," *Advertising Age,* August 19, 1991, p. 32.
33. Ibid.
34. Joann S. Lublin, "In-Flight TV Commercials Are Booming," *The Wall Street Journal,* September 19, 1990, p. B6.

chapter 16

1. Stan Rapp and Thomas I. Collins, *Maximarketing* (New York: McGraw-Hill, 1987).
2. P. D. Bennett ed., *Dictionary of Marketing Terms* (Chicago: American Marketing Association, 1988), p. 58.
3. Direct Marketing Association, 1992.
4. MasterCard, International, 1992.
5. Jagdish N. Sheth, "Marketing Megatrends" *Journal of Consumer Marketing* 1, no. 1 (June 1983), pp. 5–13.
6. *Statistical Abstracts of the U.S.* (Washington, D.C.: U.S. Bureau of Labor Statistics, 1991).
7. Joanne Cleaver, "Consumers at Home with Shopping," *Advertising Age,* January 18, 1988, pp. S16–18.

8. Herbert Kanzenstein and William S. Sachs, *Direct Marketing,* 2nd ed. (New York: Macmillan Publishing Co., 1992).
9. *Direct Marketing Magazine,* January 1992.
10. Cleveland Horton, "Porsche 300,0000: The New Elite," *Advertising Age,* February 5, 1990, p. 8.
11. *Discount Store News,* January 6, 1992, p. 63.
12. Richard Zoglin, "It's Amazing! Call Now!" *TIME,* June 17, 1991, p. 71.
13. *Marketing News,* January 20, 1992, p. 6.
14. "Last Minute News," *Advertising Age,* January 6, 1992, p. 8.
15. Cleveland Horton, "Porsche 300,000."
16. Connie Lauerman, "Hypetech," *Chicago Tribune Magazine,* November 24, 1991, pp. 20–24.

17. Tom Eisenhart, "Tele-media: Marketing's New Dimension," *Business Marketing,* February 1991, pp. 50–53.
18. "Prodigy Signs New Advertisers," *Adweek's Marketing Week,* September 9, 1991, p. 8; and David Kiley, "Prodigy Offers 'USA Today' Classified Ads," *Adweek's Marketing Week,* April 22, 1991, p. 9.
19. Michael J. Major, "Videotex Never Really Left, But It's Not All Here," *Advertising Age,* November 12, 1990, p. 2.
20. Direct Selling Association, 1992.
21. "Half of All Junk Mail Gets Read, Firm Says," *Los Angeles Times,* April 17, 1990, p. D6.

chapter 17

1. Louis J. Haugh, "Defining and Redefining," *Advertising Age,* February 14, 1983, p. m-44.
2. Scott A. Nielsen, John Quelch, and Caroline Henderson, "Consumer Promotions and the Acceleration of Product Purchases," in *Research on Sales Promotion: Collected Papers,* ed. Katherine E. Jocz (Cambridge, Mass.: Marketing Science Institute, 1984).
3. Joe Mandese and Scott Donaton, "Media, Promotion Gap to Narrow," *Advertising Age,* June 29, 1992, p. 16.
4. *Donnelley Marketing 14th Annual Survey of Promotional Practices* (Stamford, Conn.: Donnelley Marketing, 1992).
5. *The Wall Street Journal Centennial Survey,* cited in Ron Alsop, "Brand Loyalty Is Rarely Blind Loyalty," *The Wall Street Journal,* October 19, 1989, p. B1.
6. Todd Johnson, NPD Research Inc., "Declining Brand Loyalty Trends: Fact or Fiction?" (Paper presented at the Fourth Annual AMA Marketing Research Conference, October 5, 1983).
7. Bob Schmitz and Keith Jones, "The New Retailer/Marketer: Friend or Foe?" in *Looking at the Retail Kaleidoscope, Forum IX* (Stamford, Conn.: Donnelley Marketing, 1988).
8. Scott Hume, "Coupons Score with Consumers," *Advertising Age,* February 15, 1988, p. 40.
9. Robert B. Settle and Pamela L. Alreck, "Hyperchoice in the Marketplace," *Marketing Communications,* May 1988, p. 15.
10. Study cited in Julie Liesse, "Brands in Trouble," *Advertising Age,* December 2, 1991, p. 16.
11. Leigh McAlister, "A Model of Consumer Behavior," *Marketing Communications,* April 1987, p. 27.
12. Ruth M. McMath, "Winning the Space Wars," *Marketing Communications,* May 1988, pp. 55–58.
13. Lynn G. Coleman, "Marketers Advised to Go Regional," *Marketing News,* May 8, 1989, p. 1; and Lisa Petrison, "Aiming the Pitch at the Corner Store," *Adweek's Marketing Week—Promote,* September 21, 1987, p. 6.
14. *Donnelley Marketing 14th Annual Survey of Promotional Practices.*
15. "What Happened to Advertising," *Business Week,* September 23, 1991, pp. 66–72.
16. Richard Gibson, "How Products Check Out Helps Determine Pay," *The Wall Street Journal.* August 1, 1991, p. B1.
17. Nielsen Clearing House, *NCH Reporter,* no. 1 (1983).
18. *The Magazine Handbook, Number 59* (New York: Magazine Publishers of America, 1991).

19. Judann Dagnoli, "Jordan Hits Ad Execs for Damaging Brands," *Advertising Age,* November 4, 1991, p. 47.
20. Study cited in "What Happened to Advertising."
21. R. M. Prentice, "How to Split Your Marketing Funds between Advertising and Promotion Dollars," *Advertising Age,* January 10, 1977, pp. 41–42, 44.
22. Quote by Vincent Sottosanti, president of Council of Sales Promotion Agencies, in "Promotions That Build Brand Image," *Marketing Communications,* April 1988, p. 54.
23. Jeffrey K. McElenea and Michael J. Enzer, "Building Brand Franchises," *Marketing Communications,* April 1986, pp. 42–64.
24. Ibid.
25. *Donnelley Marketing 14th Annual Survey of Promotional Practices.*
26. Reference cited in John P. Rossiter and Larry Percy, *Advertising and Promotion Management* (New York: McGraw-Hill, 1987), p. 360.
27. *National Study of Consumer Attitudes: The State of the Economy and Its Effect on Coupon Usage* (Chicago: NCH Promotional Services, 1992).
28. Ibid.
29. N. Giges, "GF Trims Its Use of Coupons," *Advertising Age,* December 7, 1981, p. 22.
30. Amy E. Gross, "Curing the Misredemption Malady," *Adweek's Promote,* May 1, 1989, p. 32.
31. Julie Liesse Erickson, "FSI Boom to Go Bust?" *Advertising Age,* May 1, 1989, pp. 1, 82.
32. Survey by Oxtoby-Smith, Inc., cited in "Many Consumers View Rebates as a Bother," *The Wall Street Journal,* April 13, 1989, p. B1.
33. William R. Dean, "Irresistible but Not Free of Problems," *Advertising Age,* October 6, 1980, pp. S1–S12.
34. William A. Robinson, "What Are Promos' Weak and Strong Points?" *Advertising Age,* April 7, 1980, p. 54.
35. "Sweepstakes Fever," *Forbes,* October 3, 1988, pp. 164–66.
36. Quote by Richard Kane, president of Marden-Kane Sweepstakes Consulting firm, cited in "Catching Consumers with Sweepstakes," *Fortune,* February 8, 1982, p. 87.
37. Example from William A. Robinson, "Best Promotions of 1986–1987," *Marketing Communications,* October 1987, p. 43.
38. "Catching Consumers."
39. Russell D. Bowman, *Couponing and Rebates: Profits on the Dotted Line* (New York: Lebhar-Friedman Books, 1980).

40. "Many Consumers View Rebates."
41. Peter Tat, William A. Cunningham III, and Emin Babakus, "Consumer Perceptions of Rebates," *Journal of Advertising Research,* August–September 1988, pp. 45–50.
42. Martha Graves, "Mail-in Rebates Stirring, Shopper, Retailer Backlash," *Los Angeles Times,* January 11, 1989, Part IV, p. 1.
43. Edward A. Blair and E. Laird Landon, "The Effects of Reference Prices in Retail Advertisements," *Journal of Marketing* 45, no. 2 (Spring 1981), pp. 61–69.
44. "Nothing Sells Like Sports," *Business Week,* August 31, 1987, pp. 48–53.
45. Laurie Freeman, "P&G Has Event-ful Plans," *Advertising Age,* June 22, 1987, p. 41.
46. Shav Glick, "Takeovers, Mergers Take Their Toll, Too," *Los Angeles Times,* March 27, 1989, pt. III, p. 14.
47. Ronald Alsop, "Laundry Soap and Pantyhose Hitch a Ride on Racing Cars," *The Wall Street Journal,* December 13, 1987, p. 21.
48. Scott Hume, "Sponsorship Up 18%," *Advertising Age,* March 23, 1992, p. 4.
49. Judann Dagnoli, "Sorry Charlie, Heinz Puts Promos First," *Advertising Age,* March 30, 1992, p. 3.
50. "Want Shelf Space at the Supermarket? Ante Up," *Business Week,* August 7, 1989, pp. 60–61.
51. Ibid.
52. Tom Steinhagen, "Space Management Shapes Up with Planograms," *Marketing News,* November 12, 1990, p. 7.
53. Cynthia Rigg, "Hard Times Means Growth for Co-op Ads," *Advertising Age,* November 12, 1990, p. 24.
54. Ibid.
55. Don Sunoo and Lynn Y. S. Lin, "Sales Effect of Advertising and Promotion," *Journal of Advertising Research* 18, no. 5 (October 1978), p. 37.
56. Edwin L. Artzt, "The Lifeblood of Brands," *Advertising Age,* November 4, 1991, p. 32.
57. "Everyone Is Bellying Up to this Bar," *Business Week,* January 27, 1992, p. 84.
58. Benson P. Shapiro, "Improved Distribution with Your Promotional Mix," *Harvard Business Review,* March–April 1977, p. 116; and Roger A. Strang, "Sales Promotion—Fast Growth, Faulty Management," *Harvard Business Review,* July–August 1976, p. 119.
59. Quote by Thomas E. Hamilton, director of Sales Promotion

Service—William Esty Advertising, cited in Felix Kessler, "The Costly Couponing Craze," *Fortune,* June 9, 1986, p. 84.

60. Alan G. Sawyer and Peter H. Dickson, "Psychological Perspectives on Consumer Response to Sales Promotion," in *Research on Sales Promotion: Collected Papers,* ed.

Katherine E. Jocz (Cambridge, Mass.: Marketing Science Institute, 1984).

61. William E. Myers, "Trying to Get Out of the Discounting Box," *Adweek,* November 11, 1985, p. 2.

62. Leigh McAlister, "Managing the Dynamics of Promotional Change," in *Looking at the Retail Kaleidoscope,*

Forum IX (Stamford, Conn.: Donnelley Marketing, April 1988).

63. "Promotions Blemish Cosmetic Industry," *Advertising Age,* May 10, 1984, pp. 22–23, 26.

64. "Triple-Mileage Plans: How High a Price?" *The Wall Street Journal,* January 28, 1988, p. 17.

chapter 18

1. Raymond Simon, *Public Relations, Concept and Practices,* 2nd ed. (Columbus, Ohio: Grid Publishing, 1980), p. 8.

2. William N. Curry, "PR Isn't Marketing," *Advertising Age,* December 18, 1991, p. 18.

3. Philip Kotler and William Mindak, "Marketing and Public Relations," *Journal of Marketing* 42 (October 1978), pp. 13–20.

4. Simon, *Public Relations,* p. 164.

5. Bob Donath, "Corporate Communications," *Industrial Marketing,* July 1980, pp. 53–57.

6. Scott M. Cutlip, Allen H. Center, and Glenn M. Broom, *Effective Public Relations,* 6th ed. (Englewood Cliffs, N.J.: Prentice Hall, 1985), p. 200.

7. John E. Marston, *Modern Public Relations* (New York: McGraw-Hill, 1979).

8. Joe Agnew, "Marketers Find the Antidrug Campaign Addictive," *Marketing News,* October 9, 1987, p. 12.

9. Raymond Serafin, "Cars Squeeze Mileage from Awards," *Advertising Age,* June 4, 1990, p. 36.

10. Raymond Simon, *Public Relations, Concepts and Practices,* 3rd ed. (New York: John Wiley & Sons, 1984), p. 291.

11. Harold Mendelsohn, "Some Reasons Why Information Campaigns Can Succeed," *Public Opinion Quarterly,* Spring 1973, p. 55.

12. Raymond Serafin, "Cars Squeeze Mileage."

13. Alice Z. Cuneo, "Visa Ad Is Packing Them In at Fog City," *Advertising Age,* November 19, 1990, p. 21.

14. Neil Cole, "How Scandal Helped No Excuses Sell Jeans," *Adweek,* January 16, 1989, pp. 52–53.

15. Gary Levin, "PR Gives New Life to Rejected TV Ads," *Advertising Age,* October 8, 1990, p. 76.

16. Joseph Bruillard, "Timely Messages," *Advertising Age,* August 29, 1983, p. M-30.

17. Jaye S. Niefeld, "Corporate Advertising," *Industrial Marketing,* July 1980, pp. 64–74.

18. Tom Garbett, "What Companies Project to Public," *Advertising Age,* July 6, 1981, p. 51.

19. Francis Houghton, "How Ads Can Sell More Than Products," *Nations Business,* March 1984, pp. 61–62.

20. Bob Seeter, "AMA Hopes New Ads Will Cure Image Problem," *Los Angeles Times,* August 14, 1991, p. A-5.

21. *Adweek,* June 16, 1986, p. 39.

22. Laura Bird, "LISOC Curbs 'Backdoor' Tie-Ins," *Adweek's Marketing Week,* April 8, 1991, p. 4.

23. Ed Zotti, "An Expert Weighs the Prose and Yawns," *Advertising Age,* January 24, 1983, p. M-11.

24. Prakash Sethi, *Advertising and Large Corporations* (Lexington, Mass.: Lexington Books, 1977), pp. 7–8.

25. Janet Myers, "JWT Anti-Japan Ad Is a Bomb," *Advertising Age,* April 2, 1990, p. 4.

26. Niefeld, "Corporate Advertising," p. 64.

27. Donath, "Corporate Communications," p. 52.

28. Ibid., p. 53.

29. Ibid., p. 52.

chapter 19

1. Carl G. Stevens and David P. Keane, "How to Become a Better Sales Manager: Give Salespeople How to Not Rah Rah," *Marketing News,* May 30, 1980, p. 1.

2. Tom Wotruba and Edwin K. Simpson, *Sales Management* (Boston: Kent Publishing, 1989).

3. *Carr Reports* No. 542.2D (Newton, Mass.: Cahners Publishing Co., 1992).

4. Thomas R. Wotruba, "The Evolution of Personal Selling," *Journal of Personal*

Selling & Sales Management 11, no. 3 (Summer 1991), pp. 1–12.

5. *Carr Reports* No.542.D (Newton, Mass.: Cahners Publishing Co., 1992).

6. Thayer C. Taylor, "A Letup in the Rise of Sales Call Costs," *Sales & Marketing Management,* February 25, 1980, p. 24.

7. Theodore Levitt, "Communications and Industrial Selling," *Journal of Marketing* 31 (April 1967), pp. 15–21.

8. John E. Morrill, "Industrial Advertising Pays Off," *Harvard Business Review,* March–April 1970, p. 4.

9. "Salespeople Contact Fewer Than 10% of Purchase Decision-Makers over a Two-Month Period," McGraw-Hill LAP Report no. 1029.3 (New York: McGraw-Hill, 1987).

10. Rolph E. Anderson, Joseph F. Hair, and Alan J. Bush, *Professional Sales Management* (New York: McGraw-Hill, 1988).

chapter 20

1. "Pepsi: Memorable Ads, Forgettable Sales," *Business Week,* October 21, 1991, p. 36.

2. Bruce Horowitz, "TV Ads That Public Will Never See," *Los Angeles Times,* August 3, 1988, p. 1.

3. "McGraw-Hill Lap Report," no. 3151 (New York: McGraw-Hill, Inc., 1988); and Alan D. Fletcher, *Target Marketing through the Yellow Pages* (Troy, Mich.: Yellow Pages Publishers Association, 1991), p. 23.

4. Personal interview with Jay Khoulos, president of World Communications, Inc., 1988.

5. David A. Aaker and John G. Myers, *Advertising Management,* 3rd ed. (Englewood Cliffs, N.J.: Prentice Hall, 1987), p. 474.

6. Joel N. Axelrod, "Induced Moods and Attitudes toward Products," *Journal of Advertising Research* 3 (June 1963), pp. 19–24; and Lauren E. Crane, How Product, Appeal, and Program Affect

Attitudes toward Commercials," *Journal of Advertising Research* 4 (March 1964), p. 15.

7. Robert Settle, "Marketing in Tight Times," *Marketing Communications* 13, no. 1 (January 1988), pp. 19–23.

8. "21 Ad Agencies Endorse Copy Testing Principles," *Marketing News* 15, no. 17 (February 19, 1982), p. 1.

9. Ibid.

10. John M. Caffyn, "Telepex Testing of TV Commercials," *Journal of*

Advertising Research 5, no. 2 (June 1965), pp. 29–37; Thomas J. Reynolds and Charles Gengler, "A Strategic Framework for Assessing Advertising: The Animatic vs. Finished Issue," *Journal of Advertising Research*, October– November 1991, pp. 61–71; and Nigel A. Brown and Ronald Gatty, "Rough V Finished TV Commercials in Telepex Tests," *Journal of Advertising Research* 7, no. 4 (December 1967), p. 21.

11. Charles H. Sandage, Vernon Fryburger, and Kim Rotzoll, *Advertising Theory and Practice,* 10th ed. (Homewood, Ill.: Richard D. Irwin, 1979).

12. Lymund E. Ostlund, "Advertising Copy Testing: A Review of Current Practices, Problems and Prospects," *Current Issues and Research in Advertising,* 1978, pp. 87–105.

13. Jack B. Haskins, "Factual Recall as a Measure of Advertising Effectiveness," *Journal of Advertising Research* 4, no. 1 (March 1964), pp. 2–7.

14. Paul J. Watson and Robert J. Gatchel, "Autonomic Measures of Advertising,"

Journal of Advertising Research 19 (June 1979), pp. 15–26.

15. Flemming Hansen, "Hemispheric Lateralization: Implications for Understanding Consumer Behavior," *Journal of Consumer Research* 8 (1988), pp. 23–36.

16. Hubert A. Zielske, "Does Day-After Recall Penalize 'Feeling Ads'?" *Journal of Advertising Research* 22, no. 1 (1982), pp. 19–22.

17. Terry Haller, "Day After Recall to Persist Despite JWT Study; Other Criteria Looming," *Marketing News,* May 18, 1979, p. 4.

18. Dave Kruegel, "Television Advertising Effectiveness and Research Innovations," *Journal of Consumer Marketing* 5, no. 3 (Summer 1988), pp. 43–52.

19. Gary Levin, "Tracing Ads' Impact," *Advertising Age,* November 12, 1990, p. 49.

20. Jeffrey L. Seglin, "The New Era of Ad Measurement," *Adweek's Marketing Week,* January 23, 1988, p. 24.

21. James F. Donius, "Marketing Tracking: A Strategic Reassessment and Planning Tool," *Journal of Advertising Research* 25, no. 1 (February–March 1985), pp. 15–19.

22. Russell I. Haley and Allan L. Baldinger, "The ARF Copy Research Validity Project," *Journal of Advertising Research,* April–May 1991, pp. 11–32.

23. "Journeying Deeper into the Minds of Shoppers," *Business Week,* February 4, 1991, p. 85.

24. David W. Schumann, Jennifer Grayson, Johanna Ault, Kerri Hargrove, Lois Hollingsworth, Russell Ruelle, and Sharon Seguin, "The Effectiveness of Shopping Cart Signage: Perceptual Measures Tell a Different Story," *Journal of Advertising Research,* February–March 1991, pp. 17–22.

25. June Bryan Kim, "Research Makes Ski Run Easier," *Advertising Age,* August 18, 1991, p. 30.

26. Scott Hume, "Sports Sponsorship Value Measured," *Advertising Age,* August 6, 1990, p. 22.

chapter 21

1. Business Professional Advertising Association, 1992.

2. Yolanda Brugaletta, "What Business-to-Business Advertisers Can Learn from Consumer Advertisers," *Journal of Advertising Research* 25, no. 3 (June–July 1985), pp. 8–9.

3. Anderson & Lembke, Inc., Stamford, Conn., 1985 sales promotion literature.

4. Tom Eisenhart, "How to Really Excite Your Prospects," *Business Marketing,* July 1988, pp. 44–55.

5. Business Professional Advertising Association, 1992.

6. *Carr Reports,* Newton, Mass.: Cahners Publishing Co., 1991.

7. Tom Eisenhart, "What's Right, What's Wrong with Each Medium,"

Business Marketing, April 1990, pp. 40–47.

8. National Telemarketing Association, 1992.

9. Trade Show Bureau, 1992.

10. *Cahners Advertising Research Report,* No. 510.1A, 1990.

11. *1986 Starmark Report, Business Marketing,* p. 17.

12. *1986 Starmark Report,* p. 17.

chapter 22

1. "PM on Right Track Overseas," *Advertising Age,* November 21, 1988, p. 37.

2. Ira Teinowitz, "Coors Looks Abroad," *Advertising Age,* January 6, 1992, p. 4.

3. Christoper Knowlton, "Europe Cooks up a Cereal Brawl," *Fortune,* June 3, 1991, pp. 175–78.

4. "They're All Screaming for Häagen-Dazs," *Business Week,* October 14, 1991, p. 121.

5. Brian Dumaine, "Japan's Next Push into U.S. Markets," *Fortune,* September 26, 1988, pp. 135–42; and David Killburn, "Kao Angles Its Way onto the U.S. Stage," *Advertising Age,* April 10, 1989, p. 54.

6. *Survey of World Advertising Expenditures: Twenty-Fourth Edition* (New York: Starch INRA Hooper & The Roper Organization, 1991).

7. Vern Terpstra, *International Marketing,* 4th ed. (New York: Holt, Rinehart and Winston–Dryden Press, 1987), p. 427.

8. *Survey of World Advertising Expenditures.*

9. "We Are the World," *Adweek's Superbrands 1990,* pp. 61–68.

10. Shawn Tully, "Nestlé Shows How to Gobble Markets," *Fortune,* January 16, 1989, pp. 74–78.

11. "World of Change," *Adweek's Superbrands 1991,* pp. 34–41.

12. For an excellent discussion of various elements of Japanese culture such as language and its implications for promotion, see John F. Sherry, Jr., and Eduardo G. Camargo, "May Your Life Be Marvelous: English Language Labelling and the Semiotics of Japanese Promotion," *Journal of Consumer Research* 14 (September 1987), pp. 174–88.

13. Barbara Mueller, "Reflections on Culture: An Analysis of Japanese and American Advertising Appeals," *Journal of Advertising Research,* June–July 1987, pp. 51–59.

14. Barbara Mueller, "Standardization vs. Specialization: An Examination of Westernization in Japanese Advertising," *Journal of Advertising Research,* January–February 1992, pp. 15–24.

15. Marian Katz, "No Women, No Alcohol, Learn Saudi Taboos Before

Placing Ads," *International Advertiser,* February 1986, pp. 11–12.

16. Dean M. Peebles and John K. Ryans, *Management of International Advertising* (Newton, Mass.: Allyn and Bacon, 1984).

17. Geoffrey Lee Martin, "Tobacco Sponsors Fear Aussie TKO," *Advertising Age,* April 27, 1992, p. I–8.

18. Laurel Wentz, "Local Laws Keep International Marketers Hopping," *Advertising Age,* July 11, 1985, p. 20.

19. David Bartel and Laurel Wentz, "Danes Phase in TV Spots," *Advertising Age,* November 23, 1987, p. 65.

20. Marian Katz, "No Women, No Alcohol."

21. Derek Turner, "Coke Pops Brazilian Comparative Ad," *Advertising Age,* September 9, 1991, p. 24.

22. J. Craig Andrews, Steven Lysonski, and Srinivas Durvasula, "Understanding Cross-Cultural Student Perceptions of Advertising in General: Implications for Advertising Educators and Practitioners," *Journal of Advertising* 20, no. 2 (June 1991), pp. 15–28.

23. J. J. Boddewyn and Iris Mohr, "International Advertisers Face Government Hurdles," *Marketing News,* May 8, 1987, pp. 21–22.

24. Ron Alsop, "Countries' Different Ad Rules Are Problem for Global Firms," *The Wall Street Journal,* September 17, 1984, p. 33.

25. Robert D. Buzzell, "Can You Standardize Multinational Marketing?" *Harvard Business Review,* November–December 1968, pp. 102–13; and Ralph Z. Sorenson and Ulrich E. Wiechmann, "How Multinationals View Marketing," *Harvard Business Review,* May–June 1975, p. 38.

26. Theodore Levitt, "The Globalization of Markets," *Harvard Business Review,* May–June 1983, pp. 92–102; and Theodore Levitt, *The Marketing Imagination* (New York: Free Press, 1986).

27. Anne B. Fisher, "The Ad Biz Gloms onto Global," *Fortune,* November 12, 1984, p. 78.

28. Keith Reinhard and W. E. Phillips, "Global Marketing: Experts Look at Both Sides," *Advertising Age,* April 15, 1988, p. 47; and Anthony Rutigliano, "The Debate Goes On: Global vs. Local Advertising," *Management Review,* June 1986, pp. 27–31.

29. Michael J. McCarthy, "Coke to Use 'Can't Beat the Feeling' as World-Wide Marketing Theme," *The Wall Street Journal,* December 12, 1988, p. B5.

30. Michael J. McCarthy, "Coca-Cola Plans a New Slogan for Coke Classic," *The Wall Street Journal,* May 12, 1992, pp. B1, 5.

31. Example from speech by Eugene H. Kummel, chairman emeritus, McCann-Erickson Worldwide, and Koji Oshita, president and CEO, McCann-Erickson, Hakuhodo, Japan, in San Diego, California, October 19, 1988.

32. Joanne Lipman, "Marketers Turn Sour on Global Sales Pitch," *The Wall Street Journal,* May 12, 1988, p. 1.

33. Joseph M. Winski and Laurel Wentz, "Parker Pens: What Went Wrong?" *Advertising Age,* June 2, 1986, p. 1.

34. Laurie Freeman, "Colgate Axes Global Ads, Thinks Local," *Advertising Age,* November 26, 1990, pp. 1, 59.

35. Joanne Lipman, "Marketers Turn Sour."

36. Criteria cited by Edward Meyer, CEO, Grey Advertising, in Rebecca Fannin, "What Agencies Really Think of Global Theory," *Marketing & Media Decisions,* December 1984, p. 74.

37. Marcy Magiera, "Nike Takes Global Steps," *Advertising Age,* January 14, 1991, pp. 1, 46.

38. Quote cited in Keith Reinhard and W. E. Phillips, "Global Marketing," p. 47.

39. Rebecca Fannin, "What Agencies Really Think," p. 75.

40. Gary Levin, "Ads Going Global," *Advertising Age,* July 22, 1991, pp. 4, 42.

41. Robert E. Hite and Cynthia L. Fraser, "International Advertising Strategies of Multinational Corporations," *Journal of Advertising Research,* August–September 1988, pp. 9–17.

42. Ali Kanso, "International Advertising Strategies: Global Commitment to Local Vision," *Journal of Advertising Research,* January–February 1992, pp. 10–14.

43. Sherri Shamoon, "Centralized International Advertising," *International Advertiser,* September 1986, pp. 35–36.

44. Gary Levin, "Ogilvy under WPP Wing," *Advertising Age,* May 22, 1989, pp. 1, 72.

45. Vern Terpstra, *International Marketing;* and Dean M. Peebles and John K. Ryans, *Management of International Advertising.*

46. Doris Walsh, "Demographics for Advertisers," *International Advertiser,* June 1986, p. 47.

47. John D. Furniss, "Germany Leads the Way in Special Audience Research," *International Advertiser,* October 1985, p. 30.

48. Nancy Giges, "Europeans Buy Outside Goods, but Like Local Ads,"

Advertising Age International, April 27, 1992, pp. I–1, 26.

49. Joseph T. Plummer, "The Role of Copy Research in Multinational Advertising," *Journal of Advertising Research,* October–November 1986, p. 15.

50. Ron Alsop, "Efficacy of Global Ad Projects Is Questioned in Firm's Survey," *The Wall Street Journal,* September 13, 1984, p. 31.

51. Rebecca Fannin, "What Agencies Really Think."

52. "They're All Screaming for Häagen-Dazs."

53. David Bartel and Laurel Wentz, "Danes Phase in TV Spots."

54. Sheila Tefft, "India Advertising Flourishes," *Advertising Age,* December 7, 1987, p. 52.

55. James H. Rosenfield, "The Explosion of Worldwide Media," *Marketing Communications,* September 1987, p. 65.

56. Laurel Wentz, "All Eyes on Europe TV Time," *Advertising Age,* May 23, 1988, p. 71.

57. Elena Bowes, "British Sky TV Picks Up Pace," *Advertising Age International,* April 27, 1992, p. I–18.

58. Laurel Wentz, "TV Nationalism Clouds Sky Gains," *Advertising Age,* December 1, 1987, p. 56.

59. Laurel Wentz, "All Eyes on Europe TV Time."

60. Alison Fahey, "Pepsi's Concerts vs. Coke's Games," *Advertising Age,* February 10, 1992, p. 47.

61. Kamran Kashani and John A. Quelch, "Can Sales Promotion Go Global?" *Business Horizons,* May–June 1990, pp. 37–43.

62. "What You Should Know about Advertising in Japan," *Advertising World,* April 1985, pp. 18, 42.

63. Kamran Kashani and John A. Quelch, "Can Sales Promotion Go Global?"

64. "Foreign Ads Go Further with PR," *International Advertiser,* December 1986, p. 30.

65. Shawn Tully, "Nestlé Shows How."

chapter 23

1. Cyndee Miller, "Proposed Alcohol Ad Restrictions Cause Big Brew-haha," *Marketing News,* February 13, 1989, p. 2.

2. Alex M. Freedman, "Koop Urges Alcoholic-Beverage Curbs, Including Ad Restrictions and Tax Rise," *The Wall Street Journal,* June 1, 1989, p. B6.

3. Priscilla A. LaBarbera, "Analyzing and Advancing the State of the Art of Advertising Self-Regulation," *Journal of Advertising* 9, no. 4 (1980), p. 30.

4. John F. Archer, "Advertising of Professional Fees: Does the Consumer

Have a Right to Know?" *South Dakota Law Review* 21 (Spring 1976), p. 330.

5. *Bates v. State of Arizona,* 97 S.Ct. 2691. 45 *U.S. Law Week* 4895 (1977).

6. "Lawyers Learn the Hard Sell—And Companies Shudder," *Business Week,* June 10, 1985, p. 70.

7. Bruce H. Allen, Richard A. Wright, and Louis E. Raho, "Physicians and Advertising," *Journal of Health Care Marketing* 5 (Fall 1985), pp. 39–49.

8. Robert E. Hite and Cynthia Fraser, "Meta-Analyses of Attitudes toward Advertising by Professionals," *Journal*

of Marketing 52, no. 3 (July 1988), pp. 95–105.

9. "NAD Slaps Kellogg over Special K Ads," *Advertising Age,* March 21, 1988, p. 70.

10. Gary M. Armstrong and Julie L. Ozanne, "An Evaluation of NAD/NARB Purpose and Performance," *Journal of Advertising* 12, no. 3 (1983), pp. 15–26.

11. Dorothy Cohen, "The FTC's Advertising Substantiation Program," *Journal of Marketing* 44, no. 1 (Winter 1980), pp. 26–35.

12. Lynda M. Maddox and Eric J. Zanot, "The Suspension of the National Association of Broadcasters' Code and Its Effects on the Regulation of Advertising," *Journalism Quarterly* 61 (Summer 1984), pp. 125–30, 156.
13. Eric Zanot, "Unseen But Effective Advertising Regulation: The Clearance Process," *Journal of Advertising* 14, no. 4 (1985), p. 48.
14. Steven W. Colford, "Speed Up the NAD, Industry Unit Told," *Advertising Age,* May 1, 1989, p. 3.
15. *FTC v. Raladam Co.*, 258, U.S. 643 (1931).
16. Edward Cox, R. Fellmeth, and J. Schultz, *The Consumer and the Federal Trade Commission* (Washington, D.C.: American Bar Association, 1969); and American Bar Association, *Report of the American Bar Association to Study the Federal Trade Commission* (Washington, D.C.: The Association, 1969).
17. Ivan L. Preston, *The Great American Blow-Up: Puffery in Advertising and Selling* (Madison: University of Wisconsin Press, 1975), p. 3.
18. Isabella C. M. Cunningham and William H. Cunningham, "Standards for Advertising Regulation," *Journal of Marketing* 41 (October 1977), pp. 91–97; and Herbert J. Rotfeld and Kim B. Rotzell, "Is Advertising Puffery Believed?" *Journal of Advertising* 9, no. 3 (1980), pp. 16–20.
19. Herbert J. Rotfeld and Kim B. Rotzell, "Puffery vs. Fact Claims—Really Different?" in *Current Issues and Research in Advertising*, ed. James H. Leigh and Claude R. Martin, Jr. (Ann Arbor: University of Michigan, 1981), pp. 85–104.
20. Ivan Preston, *The Great American Blow-Up.*

21. Federal Trade Commission, "Policy Statement on Deception," 45 ATRR 689 (October 27, 1983), at 690.
22. Gary T. Ford and John E. Calfee, "Recent Developments in FTC Policy on Deception," *Journal of Marketing* 50, no. 3 (July 1986), pp. 86–87.
23. Ray O. Werner, ed. "Legal Developments in Marketing," *Journal of Marketing* 56 (January 1992), p. 102.
24. Dorothy Cohen, "The FTC's Advertising Substantiation Program."
25. *Trade Regulation Reporter,* Par. 20,056 at 22,033, 1970–1973 Transfer Binder, Federal Trade Commission, July 1972.
26. William L. Wilkie, Dennis L. McNeill, and Michael B. Mazis, "Marketing's 'Scarlet Letter': The Theory and Practice of Corrective Advertising," *Journal of Marketing* 48 (Spring 1984), pp. 11–31.
27. Steven W. Colford, "ABA Panel Backs FTC over States," *Advertising Age,* April 10, 1989, p. 1.
28. Jeanne Saddler, "FTC's New Case-by-Case Policy Irks Those Favoring Broader Tack," *The Wall Street Journal,* July 3, 1985, p. 17.
29. "Deceptive Ads: The FTC's Lassez-Faire Approach Is Backfiring," *Business Week,* December 2, 1985, p. 136.
30. Steven Colford, "ABA Panel."
31. Bill Abrams, "Ad Constraints Could Persist Even If the FTC Loosens Up," *The Wall Street Journal,* December 10, 1981, p. 33.
32. William M. Bulkeley, "False Claims in Ads Carry a New Price," *The Wall Street Journal,* March 15, 1990, pp. B1,5.
33. Steven W. Colford, "$12 Million Bite," *Advertising Age,* December 2, 1991, p. 4.

34. Bruce P. Keller, "How Do You Spell Relief? Private Regulation of Advertising under Section 43(a) of the Lanham Act," *Trademark Reporter* 75 (1986), p. 227.
35. Bruce Buchanan and Doron Goldman, "Us vs. Them: The Minefield of Comparative Ads," *Harvard Business Review,* May–June 1989, pp. 38–50.
36. "Deceptive Ads."
37. Robert Johnson, "3 States Charge McDonald's Ads on Its Foods' Nutrition Are Deceptive," *The Wall Street Journal,* April 27, 1987, p. 14.
38. Jennifer Lawrence, "State Ad Rules Face Showdown," *Advertising Age,* November 28, 1988, p. 4.
39. "Ally in Plax Settlement," *The Wall Street Journal,* February 12, 1991, p. B4.
40. Steven Colford, "ABA Panel."
41. S. J. Diamond, "New Director Putting Vigor Back into FTC," *Los Angeles Times,* March 29, 1991, pp. D1,4.
42. Federal Trade Commission, "Trade Regulation Rule: Games of Chance in the Food Retailing and Gasoline Industries," 16 CFR, Part 419 (1982).
43. Steven W. Colford, "Top Kid TV Offender: Premiums," *Advertising Age,* April 29, 1991, p. 52.
44. Federal Trade Commission, "Guides for Advertising Allowances and Other Merchandising Payments and Services," 16 CFR, Part 240 (1983).
45. Federal Trade Commission, "Trade Regulation Rule: Use of Negative Option Plans by Sellers in Commerce," 16 CFR, Part 42 (1982).
46. For a more thorough discussion of legal aspects of sales promotion and mail order practices, see Louis W. Stern and Thomas L. Eovaldi, *Legal Aspects of Marketing Strategy* (Englewood Cliffs, N.J.: Prentice Hall, 1984).

chapter 24

1. Robert L. Heilbroner, "Demand for the Supply Side," *New York Review of Books* 38 (June 11, 1981), p. 40.
2. Eric N. Berkowitz et al., *Marketing*, 2nd ed. (Homewood, Ill.: Richard D. Irwin, 1992), p. 90.
3. J. Edward Russo, Barbara L. Metcalf, and Debra Stephens, "Identifying Misleading Advertising," *Journal of Consumer Research* 8 (September 1981), pp. 119–31.
4. Fara Warner, "What Happened to the Truth?" *Adweek's Marketing Week,* October 28, 1991, pp. 4–5.
5. Quote cited in Alex M. Freedman, "FTC Alleges Campbell Ad Is Deceptive," *The Wall Street Journal,* January 27, 1989, pp. B1, 4.
6. Shelby D. Hunt, "Informational vs. Persuasive Advertising: An Appraisal,"

Journal of Advertising, Summer 1976, pp. 5–8.
7. Study cited in Ron Alsop, "Advertisers Find the Climate Less Hostile outside the U.S.," *The Wall Street Journal,* December 10, 1987, p. 29.
8. "More Stations Accepting Condom Spots," *Broadcasting,* February 23, 1987, p. 41.
9. Bruce Horowitz "Trojan Gets a Condom Ad on Network TV," *Los Angeles Times,* November 19, 1991, pp. D1, 6.
10. David A. Aaker and Donald E. Bruzzone, "Causes of Irritation in Advertising," *Journal of Marketing* 5 (Spring 1985), pp. 47–57.
11. Stephen A. Greyser, "Irritation in Advertising," *Journal of Advertising Research* 13 (February 1973), pp. 3–10.

12. Ron Alsop, "Personal Product Ads Abound as Public Gets More Tolerant," *The Wall Street Journal,* April 14, 1986, p. 19.
13. Joanne Lipman, "Censored Scenes: Why You Rarely See Some Things in Television Ads," *The Wall Street Journal,* August 17, 1987, p. 17.
14. "Maidenform Is Going Braless in Its Sexy New Ad Campaign," *The Wall Street Journal,* April 23, 1987, p. 31.
15. Thomas R. King, "Maidenform Ads Focus on Stereotypes," *The Wall Street Journal,* December 10, 1990, p. B1.
16. Bruce Horowitz, "Sex in Ads: It Can Even Sell Detergent," *Los Angeles Times,* July 8, 1987, p. 1.
17. Andrew Sullivan, "Flogging Underwear: The New Raunchiness of American Advertising," *The New Republic,* January 18, 1988, pp. 20–24.

18. Laurie P. Cohen, "Sex in Ads Becomes Less Explicit as Firms Turn to Romantic Images," *The Wall Street Journal,* February 11, 1988, p. 25.

19. Rita Weisskoff, "Current Trends in Children's Advertising," *Journal of Advertising Research* 25, no.1 (1985), pp. RC 12–14.

20. Scott Ward, Daniel B. Wackman, and Ellen Wartella, *How Children Learn to Buy: The Development of Consumer Information Processing Skills* (Beverly Hills, Calif.: Sage, 1979).

21. Thomas S. Robertson and John R. Rossiter, "Children and Commercial Persuasion: An Attribution Theory Analysis," *Journal of Consumer Research* 1, no. 1 (June 1974), pp. 13–20; and Scott Ward and Daniel B. Wackman, "Children's Information Processing of Television Advertising," in *New Models for Communications Research,* ed. G. Kline and P. Clark (Beverly Hills, Calif.: Sage, 1974), pp. 81–119.

22. Merrie Brucks, Gary M. Armstrong, and Marvin E. Goldberg, "Children's Use of Cognitive Defenses against Television Advertising: A Cognitive Response Approach," *Journal of Consumer Research* 14, no. 4 (March 1988), pp. 471–82.

23. For a discussion on consumer socialization, see Scott Ward, "Consumer Socialization," *Journal of Consumer Research* 1, no. 2 (September 1974), pp. 1–14.

24. *FTC Staff Report on Advertising to Children* (Washington, D.C.: Government Printing Office, 1978).

25. Ben M. Enis, Dale R. Spencer, and Don R. Webb, "Television Advertising and Children: Regulatory vs. Competitive Perspectives," *Journal of Advertising* 9, no. 1 (1980), pp. 19–25.

26. Daniel B. Wackman, Scott Ward, and Emily Wartella, "Comments on FTC Staff Report," *Public Policy Issues in Marketing,* 1979, pp. 81–97.

27. Ronald Alsop, "Watchdogs Zealously Censor Advertising Targeted to Kids," *The Wall Street Journal,* September 5, 1985, p. 35.

28. Robert E. Hite and Randy Eck, "Advertising to Children: Attitudes of Business vs. Consumers," *Journal of Advertising Research,* October–November 1987, pp. 40–53.

29. Ronald Berman, *Advertising and Social Change* (Beverly Hills, Calif.: Sage, 1981), p. 13.

30. John K. Galbraith, *The New Industrial State* (Boston: Houghton Mifflin, 1967), cited in Richard W. Pollay, "The Distorted Mirror: Reflections on the Unintended Consequences of Advertising," *Journal of Marketing,* August 1986, p. 25.

31. Raymond A. Bauer and Stephen A. Greyser, "The Dialogue That Never Happens," *Harvard Business Review,* January–February 1969, pp. 122–28.

32. Morris B. Holbrook, "Mirror Mirror on the Wall, What's Unfair in the Reflections on Advertising," *Journal of Marketing* 5 (July 1987), pp. 95–103; and Theodore Levitt, "The Morality of Advertising," *Harvard Business Review,* July–August 1970, pp 84–92.

33. Stephen Fox, *The Mirror Makers: A History of American Advertising and Its Creators* (New York: Morrow, 1984), p. 330.

34. Richard W. Pollay, "The Distorted Mirror: Reflections on the Unintended Consequences of Advertising," *Journal of Marketing* 50 (April 1986), p. 33.

35. Jules Backman, "Is Advertising Wasteful?" *Journal of Marketing* 32 (January 1968), pp. 2–8.

36. Shelby Hunt, "Informational."

37. Ibid., p. 6.

38. Alice E. Courtney and Thomas W. Whipple, "Sex Stereotyping in America: An Annotated Bibliography," *Marketing Science Institute,* Report no. 80–100, February 1980, p. v.

39. "Women's Image in Ads Changing, But Shape Isn't," *Marketing News,* February 15, 1988, p. 6.

40. Joanne Lipman, "Farewell, At Last to Bimbo Campaigns," *The Wall Street Journal,* January 31, 1992, p. B2.

41. Helen Czepic and J. Steven Kelly, "Analyzing Hispanic Roles in Advertising," in *Current Issues and Research in Advertising,* ed. James H. Leigh and Claude Martin (Ann Arbor: University of Michigan, 1983), pp. 219–40; R. F. Busch, Allan S. Resnik, and Bruce L. Stern, "A Content Analysis of the Portrayal of Black Models in Magazine Advertising," in *American Marketing Association Proceedings: Marketing in the 1980s,* ed. Richard P. Bagozzi (Chicago: AMA, 1980); and R. F. Busch, Allan S. Resnik, and Bruce L. Stern, "There Are More Blacks in TV Commercials," *Journal of Advertising Research* 17 (1977), pp. 21–25.

42. James Stearns, Lynette S. Unger, and Steven G. Luebkeman, "The Portrayal of Blacks in Magazine and Television Advertising," in *AMA Educator's Proceedings,* ed. Susan P. Douglas and Michael R. Solomon (Chicago: American Marketing Association, 1987).

43. Robert E. Wilkes and Humberto Valencia, "Hispanics and Blacks in Television Commercials," *Journal of Advertising* 18, no. 1 (1989), pp. 19–26.

44. Thomas H. Stevenson, "How Are Blacks Portrayed in Business Ads?"

Industrial Marketing Management 20 (1991), pp. 193–99.

45. Robert Mack, "Tapping into the Hispanic Market," *Marketing Communications,* March 1988, pp. 54–61.

46. Janet Guyon, "Do Publications Avoid Anti-Cigarette Stories to Protect Ad Dollars?" *The Wall Street Journal,* November 22, 1982, pp. 1, 20; Elizabeth M. Whelan, "When *Newsweek* and *Time* Filtered Cigarette Copy," *The Wall Street Journal,* November 1, 1984, p. 3; and "RJR Swears Off Sootchi and Nabisco Is in a Sweat," *Business Week,* April 18, 1988, p. 36.

47. Judith Graham, "'Roe' Advertisers Risk Boycotts," *Advertising Age,* May 15, 1989, p. 2.

48. For a discussion of ethics in advertising, see John Crichton, "Morals and Ethics in Advertising," in *Ethics, Morality & the Media,* ed. Lee Thayer (New York: Hastings House, 1980), pp. 105–15.

49. For a discussion of monopolies in the cereal industry, see Paul N. Bloom, "The Cereal Industry: Monopolists or Super Marketers?" *MSU Business Topics,* Summer 1978, pp. 41–49.

50. Lester G. Telser, "Advertising and Competition," *Journal of Political Economy,* December 1964, pp. 537–62.

51. Robert D. Buzzell, Bradley T. Gale, and Ralph G. M. Sultan, "Market Share—A Key to Profitability," *Harvard Business Review,* January–February 1975, pp. 97–106.

52. Robert D. Buzzell and Paul W. Farris, "Advertising Cost in Consumer Goods Industries," *Marketing Science Institute,* Report no. 76–111, August 1976; and Paul W. Farris and David J. Reibstein, "How Prices, Ad Expenditures, and Profits Are Linked," *Harvard Business Review,* November–December 1979, pp. 173–84.

53. Paul W. Farris and Mark S. Albion, "The Impact of Advertising on the Price of Consumer Products," *Journal of Marketing* 44, no. 3 (Summer 1980), pp. 17–35.

54. Ibid., p. 19.

55. Lee Benham, "The Effect of Advertising on the Price of Eyeglasses," *Journal of Law and Economics* 15 (October 1972), pp. 337–52.

56. Robert L. Steiner, "Does Advertising Lower Consumer Price?" *Journal of Marketing* 37, no. 4 (October 1973), pp. 19–26.

57. Paul Farris and Mark Albion, "The Impact," p. 30.

58. James M. Ferguson, "Comments on the Impact of Advertising on the Price of Consumer Products," *Journal of Marketing* 46, no. 1 (Winter 1982), pp. 102–5.

Credits and Acknowledgments

chapter 1

Opening photo and Exhibit 1–1 Energizer bunny: courtesy Eveready Battery Co., Inc.

Promotional Perspective 1–1 Pepsi around the world: courtesy Pepsi-Cola Company.

Exhibit 1–2 March of Dimes: courtesy March of Dimes Birth Defects Foundation.

Exhibit 1–3 Vanderbilt perfume: reprinted by permission of Cosmair, Inc., New York, N.Y.

Exhibit 1–5 (a) Marlboro: reprinted by permission of Philip Morris, Incorporated; (b) dancing raisins: California Raisin Advisory Board.

Exhibit 1–6 Lite beer: used by permission of Miller Brewing Company.

Promotional Perspective 1–2 1984 Apple storyboard: copyright Apple Computer, Inc. 1984.

Exhibit 1–7 Soloflex: © Soloflex Inc.

Exhibit 1–8 Brawny: reprinted with permission of the James River Corporation.

Exhibit 1–9 State Farm: reprinted with permission of State Farm Insurance Companies.

Exhibit 1–10 Model: adapted from Michael L. Ray, "A Decision Sequence Analysis of Developments in Marketing Communications," *Journal of Marketing* 37 (January 1973), p. 31.

Exhibit 1–11 Coors: used by permission of Adolph Coors Company.

Exhibit 1–13 San Diego Zoo and Wild Animal Park: courtesy San Diego Zoo and Wild Animal Park.

chapter 2

Opening photo and Exhibit 2–1 Smartfoods: courtesy Frito-Lay, Inc.

Exhibit 2–2 Marketing and promotions process: adapted from Fred C. Allvine, *Marketing* (San Diego: Harcourt Brace Jovanovich, 1987).

Exhibit 2–3 Bike: courtesy Schwinn Bicycle Company.

Promotional Perspective 2–1 Pepsi audition storyboard: reprinted with permission of Pepsi-Cola.

Exhibit 2–4 Tires: courtesy Michelin Tire Corporation.

Exhibit 2–5 Guess? jeans: Art director, Paul Marciano; photographer, Ellen Von Unwerth.

Exhibit 2–6 Michelob: courtesy Anheuser-Busch, Inc.

Exhibit 2–7 P&G Crest: courtesy The Procter & Gamble Company.

Promotional Perspective 2–2 Pepsi logos: courtesy PepsiCo.

Exhibit 2–9 Godiva: used by permission of Godiva Chocolatier, Inc.

Exhibit 2–10 Yonex golf clubs: courtesy Mendelsohn/Zien Advertising, Los Angeles.

Exhibit 2–11 Ames Tool: Ames Lawn & Garden Tools, Parkersburg, W.Va.

Exhibit 2–12 Jell-O: © General Foods Corporation.

Exhibit 2–13 Leading advertisers: reprinted with permission from ADVERTISING AGE, September 25, 1991. Copyright Crain Communications, Inc. All rights reserved.

Exhibits 2–14, 2–15 Broadway sale ads: courtesy The Broadway.

Exhibit 2–16 Soup: courtesy Campbell Soup Company.

Exhibit 2–17 Beef: courtesy Beef Industry Council.

Promotional Perspective 2–3 Pork: courtesy Pork Industry Council.

Exhibit 2–18 Copiers: Ricoh Corporation/Gigante Vaz & Partners Advertising, Inc.

Exhibit 2–19 (a) McGraw-Hill: reproduced with permission from McGraw-Hill, Inc.; (b) Viadent toothpaste: courtesy VICOM FCB.

Promotional Perspective 2–4 Levi Dockers: DOCKERS and LEVI'S are registered trademarks of LEVI STRAUSS & CO.

Exhibit 2–21 (a) Choice Hotels: courtesy Choice Hotels International; (b) *Modern Maturity:* courtesy Modern Maturity.

Exhibit 2–22 Magazine cover: reprinted with permission from *Working Woman* Magazine. Copyright © 1992 by Working Woman Magazine.

Exhibit 2–23 Visa Olympic: © Visa U.S.A. Inc. 1991. All rights reserved. Reproduced with permission of Visa U.S.A. Inc.

Exhibit 2–24 Recession: Reproduced with permission of Volkswagen United States, Inc.

Exhibit 2–25 Stouffers: © 1992 Stouffer Food Corporation.

Exhibit 2–26 Evian: courtesy Evian Waters of France, Inc.

chapter 3

Agency ad: courtesy J. Walter Thompson, North America.

Exhibit 3–2 *Soap Opera Digest:* Sheila Auscander, Soap Opera Digest Magazine/Jane Kosstrin, DOUBLESPACE.

Exhibit 3–5 P&G organization: reprinted from ADVERTISING AGE, October 19, 1987. Copyright Crain Communications, Inc. All rights reserved.

Exhibit 3–6 P&G competing brands: copyright © Patricia M. Doty 1992.

Exhibit 3–8 Benetton: courtesy Benetton Cosmetics Corporation/photo: Toscani.

Exhibit 3–9 Top U.S. agencies: reprinted with permission from ADVERTISING AGE, March 25, 1991. Copyright Crain Communications, Inc. All rights reserved.

Exhibit 3–10 Top world agencies: reprinted with permission from ADVERTISING AGE, March 25, 1991. Copyright Crain Communications, Inc. All rights reserved.

Exhibit 3–11 Phillips-Ramsey: courtesy Phillips-Ramsey.

Exhibit 3–12 Full-service agency: adapted from American Association of Advertising Agencies.

Exhibit 3–13 *Adweek* ad: reprinted with permission of AD WEEK.

Exhibit 3–15 Clients not paying 15 percent: Julie Liesse, "Quaker Guarantees Agency Pay," *Advertising Age,* October 28, 1991, p. 4; "A Word from the Sponsor: Get Results—Or Else," *Business Week,* July 4, 1988, p. 66; and "More Companies Offer Their Ad Agencies Bonus Plans That Reward Superior Work," *The Wall Street Journal,* July 26, 1988, p. 29.

Exhibit 3–16 Report card: Borden, Inc.

Tumbleweeds cartoon: reprinted with special permission of NAS, Inc.

Exhibit 3–18 Franklin Associates: courtesy Franklin-Stoorza Advertising.

Promotional Perspective 3–2 Subaru: courtesy Subaru of America.

Exhibit 3–19 Don Jagoda: courtesy Don Jagoda Associates, Inc.

Exhibit 3–20 Dallas Focus: courtesy DeWesse & DeWesse, Arlington, Texas.

Exhibit 3–21 Leo Burnett: United Airlines/Leo Burnett Co., Inc.

chapter 4

Taco Bell: © 1990 Taco Bell Corporation.
Exhibit 4–1 Hyundai: courtesy Hyundai Motor America.
Exhibit 4–2 Mazda: copyright 1991 Mazda Motor of America, Inc.; used by permission; Sean Thonson, photographer.
Promotional Perspective 4–1 Frito-Lay: courtesy Frito-Lay, Inc.
Exhibit 4–4 Toothbrush: courtesy Oral-B Laboratories.
Exhibit 4–5 Fax: courtesy Panasonic.
Exhibit 4–7 Soup: used by permission of Campbell Soup Co./Backer Spielvogel Bates, Inc.
Exhibit 4–8 Volvo: courtesy Volvo Cars of North America, Inc.
Promotional Perspective 4–2: reprinted by permission of *The Wall Street Journal*, © 1988 Dow Jones & Company, Inc. All rights reserved worldwide.
Exhibit 4–10 (a) Calvin Klein: used by permission of Calvin Klein; (b) After Six: courtesy After Six Inc.
Ethical Perspective 4–1 Subliminal perception: © American Association of Advertising Agencies.
Exhibit 4–11 Boring stereo: © American Association of Advertising Agencies.
Exhibit 4–13 Jewelry: courtesy Swarovski Jewelry U.S. Ltd.—SAVVY Brand.
Exhibit 4–14 Audi: courtesy Audi of America, Inc.
Exhibit 4–15 Camera: courtesy Nikon Inc.
Exhibit 4–16 Tennis balls: courtesy Penn Athletic Products.
Exhibit 4–17 Listerine: courtesy Warner-Lambert Company.
Exhibit 4–18 Ski bindings: courtesy Geze Sport Products Inc./Michael Furman, photographer; Richard Parker, art director; Michael Erickson, copywriter.
Exhibit 4–19 Ultra 270: courtesy Wilson Sporting Goods Company.
Exhibit 4–20 Budweiser ad: courtesy Anheuser-Busch Companies.
Exhibit 4–21 Faithful or fickle: reprinted by permission of *The Wall Street Journal*, © 1989 Dow Jones & Company, Inc. All rights reserved worldwide.
Exhibit 4–22 Ford: courtesy Ford Motor Co.
Promotional Perspective 4–3 Wheaties: used with the permission of General Mills, Inc.
Exhibit 4–23 Printer: courtesy Epson America Inc.
Exhibit 4–25 Mountain Dew: courtesy Pepsi-Cola Company.
Exhibit 4–27 Dixie bathroom cups: reprinted with permission of the James River Corporation.
Exhibit 4–28 Shaping procedures: reprinted with permission from the JOURNAL OF MARKETING RESEARCH 45, published by the American Marketing Association, by Michael L. Rothschild and William C. Gaidis, Spring 1981.
Exhibit 4–31 *Upscale* magazine: courtesy UPSCALE MAGAZINE.
Exhibit 4–32 Insurance: courtesy Chubb Group Insurance Companies.
Exhibit 4–33 (a) Air Force: courtesy United States Air Force; (b) Children's Defense Fund: courtesy Children's Defense Fund.

chapter 5

Eldorado: courtesy Cadillac Motor Car Division, General Motors Corp.
Exhibit 5–2 Coke products: Coca-Cola, diet Coke, and Sprite are trademarks of The Coca-Cola Company and are used with permission.
Exhibit 5–3 Beer market: Beverage Industry/Annual Manual 1991/1992.
Exhibit 5–4 Bases for segmentation: Eric N. Berkowitz, Roger A. Kerin, Steven W. Hartley, and William Rudelius, *Marketing* (Homewood, Ill.: Richard D. Irwin, 1992), pp. 203, 207.
Exhibit 5–5 9 nations of *USA Weekend:* adapted from *The 9 Nations of USA Weekend* (Roper Organization) 1, no. 7 (1987).
Exhibit 5–6 Blue Cross: courtesy Blue Cross of California.

Exhibit 5–7 Secret deodorant: © The Procter & Gamble Company. Used with permission.
Exhibit 5–8 Billboard: DOCKERS and LEVI'S are registered trademarks of Levi Strauss & Co.
Exhibit 5–9 VALS 2: SRI International.
Exhibit 5–10 Product users: Victor J. Cook and William A. Mindak, "A Search for Constants: The 'Heavy User' Revisited!," *Journal of Consumer Marketing* 1, no. 4 (Spring 1984), p. 80.
Exhibit 5–11 Rembrandt toothpaste: courtesy Den-Mat Corporation/Eisaman, Johns & Laws Advertising.
Exhibit 5–12 Microvision market segments: courtesy Equifax National Decision Systems.
Exhibit 5–13 Dewar's and Royal Bank of Scotland: courtesy Schenley Industries, Inc.
Exhibit 5–14 Above the Rim: courtesy Reebok.
Exhibit 5–15 (a) Timex: courtesy Timex; (b) Gucci: courtesy Gucci Timepieces.
Exhibit 5–16 Hewlett-Packard: reprinted with permission of Hewlett-Packard Company.
Exhibit 5–17 Acura: courtesy Acura Division, American Honda Motor Co., Inc.
Exhibit 5–18 (a) Discman CD: courtesy Sony Corporation; (b) Oneida: courtesy Oneida Ltd. All rights reserved.
Exhibit 5–19 (a) New Balance shoes: courtesy New Balance Athletic Shoe, Inc.; (b) Nike shoes: used by permission of Pete Stone Photography and NIKE, Inc.
Exhibit 5–20 WD-40: used by permission of WD-40 Company.
Exhibit 5–21 Yogurt: courtesy America's Dairy Farmers, National Dairy Board.
Exhibit 5–22 273 perfume: ad reprinted courtesy of FRED HAYMAN Beverly Hills.
Exhibit 5–23 Advil: courtesy Whitehall Laboratories/Young & Rubicam Advertising Agency.
Exhibit 5–24 Cultural symbols: courtesy the Museum of Modern Mythology.
Exhibit 5–25 *Rolling Stone:* copyright by Straight Arrow Publishers, Inc., 1992. All rights reserved. Reprinted by permission.
Exhibit 5–26 Pontiac map and ad: the case was written by Peter Langenhorst, under the supervision of Prof. William E. Fulmer, The Darden Graduate School of Business Administration, University of Virginia; copyright The Darden Graduate School Sponsors, 1987.

chapter 6

Acura: courtesy Acura Division, American Honda Motor Co., Inc.
Exhibit 6–2 Motorola: courtesy Motorola.
Exhibit 6–3 Lee Trevino: courtesy Motorola Cellular Telephones.
Exhibit 6–4 Perfume: courtesy Estee Lauder.
Exhibit 6–5 Snuggle: courtesy Lever Brothers Company.
Promotional Perspective 6–2 IVAC: courtesy IVAC Corporation.
Exhibit 6–6 Response model: (a) E. K. Strong, *The Psychology of Selling* (New York: McGraw-Hill, 1925), p. 9; (b) Robert J. Lavidge and Gary A. Steiner, "A Model for Predictive Measurements of Advertising Effectiveness," *Journal of Marketing*, October 1961, p. 61; (c) Everett M. Rogers, *Diffusion of Innovations* (New York: Free Press, 1962), pp. 79–86; (d) William J. McGuire, "An Information Processing Model of Advertising Effectiveness," in *Behavioral and Management Science in Marketing*, ed. Harry L. Davis and Alvin J. Silk (New York: Ronald/Wiley, 1978), pp. 156–80; and Philip Kotler, *Marketing Management*, 5th ed. (Englewood Cliffs, N.J.: Prentice Hall, 1984), p. 612.
Promotional Perspective 6–3 Macintosh: copyright 1984 Apple Computer Company.
Exhibit 6–7 Feedback in response hierarchy: William J. McGuire, "An Information-Processing Model of Advertising Effectiveness." In *Behavioral and Management Science in Marketing*, ed. H. I. Davis and A. J. Silk (New York: Ronald/Wiley, 1978), p. 161.
Exhibit 6–8 Mitsubishi: courtesy Mitsubishi Electronics America, Inc.

Exhibit 6–9 Alaska Airlines: courtesy Alaska Airlines; photographer, Steve Bonini.

Exhibit 6–10 Alternative response hierarchies chart: reprinted with permission from ATTITUDE RESEARCH PLAYS FOR HIGH STAKES, edited by John C. Maloney and Bernard Silverman, "An Appraisal of Low-Involvement Consumer Information Processing," by F. S. DeBruicker, published by the American Marketing Association, 1979.

Exhibit 6–11 Morris: courtesy Heinz Pet Products/Leo Burnett U.S.A.

Exhibit 6–12 Integrated information: reprinted with permission from the JOURNAL OF ADVERTISING 46, published by the American Marketing Association, Robert E. Smith et al., Winter 1982.

Exhibit 6–13 Conceptualizing involvement: Judith L. Zaichkowsky, "Conceptualizing Involvement." *Journal of Advertising* 15, no. 2 (1986), p. 6.

Exhibit 6–14 FCB grid: Richard Vaughn, "How Advertising Works: A Planning Model," *Journal of Advertising Research* 20, no. 5 (October 1980), p. 31.

Exhibit 6–15 Lady Stetson: courtesy Lady Stetson.

Exhibit 6–16 GE kitchen: reproduced with permission of the copyright owner, General Electric Company.

Exhibit 6–17 Cognitive response model: adapted from Richard J. Lutz, Scott B. MacKenzie, and George E. Belch, "Attitude toward the Ad as a Mediator of Advertising Effectiveness," in *Advances in Consumer Research X* (Ann Arbor: Mich.: Association for Consumer Research, 1983), p. 532.

Exhibit 6–18 Ultra Tide: © The Procter & Gamble Company. Used with permission.

Exhibit 6–19 ELM model: David A. Aaker and John C. Myers, *Advertising Management*, 3rd ed. (Engelwood Cliffs, N.J.: Prentice Hall, 1987), p. 251.

Exhibit 6–20 Canon Rebel: Michael O'Neil photo.

chapter 7

Cliff Robertson: courtesy AT&T Advertising.

Exhibit 7–1 MCI friends and family: courtesy MCI.

Exhibit 7–2 Persuasion matrix: William J. McGuire, "An Information-Processing Model of Advertising Effectiveness," In *Behavioral and Management Science in Marketing,* ed. Harry L. Davis and Alvin J. Silk (New York: Ronald/Wiley Press, 1978), pp. 156–80.

Exhibit 7–4 Wilfred Brimley: reprinted with permission of The Quaker Oats Company.

Exhibit 7–6 Chuck Yeager: courtesy A.C. Delco Corporation.

Exhibit 7–7 Iacocca: courtesy Chrysler Corporation.

Promotional Perspective 7–1 Frank Perdue: courtesy Perdue Farms Incorporated.

Exhibit 7–8 Michael Jordan: reprinted with permission of The Quaker Oats Company.

Exhibit 7–9 Lee Trevino: used with permission of Spalding Sports Worldwide.

Exhibit 7–10 (a) Jimmy Connors: courtesy Bristol-Myers Products; (b) Nolan Ryan: courtesy Duracell International Inc.

Exhibit 7–11: Chart: reprinted with permission from the JOURNAL OF CONSUMER RESEARCH, December 1989, "Who Is the Celebrity Endorser? Cultural Foundation of the Celebrity Endorser," by Grant McCracken, p. 15. © 1989 by the University of Chicago.

Promotional Perspective 7–2 1991 promoters: Joanne Lipman, "Celebrity Pitchmen Are Popular Again," *The Wall Street Journal,* September 4, 1991, p. B5.

Crock cartoon: reprinted with special permission of NAS, Inc.

Exhibit 7–12 Charles Bronson: courtesy Ad Council.

Promotional Perspective 7–3 Benson & Hedges: reprinted by permission of Philip Morris Incorporated.

Exhibit 7–14 Rice cakes: reprinted with permission of The Quaker Oats Company.

Exhibit 7–15 Ortega salsa: Ortega is a registered trademark of Nabisco, Inc. Advertisement reproduced with permission of Nabisco.

Exhibit 7–16 IVAC: courtesy IVAC Corporation.

Exhibit 7–17 California Slim: courtesy California Slim, Inc.

Exhibit 7–18 Suisse Mocha: © General Foods Corporation.

Exhibit 7–19 "Faces": courtesy BBDO Inc. and Partnership for a Drug-Free America.

Exhibit 7–20 Fear levels and message acceptance: Michael L. Ray and William L. Wilkie, "Fear: The Potential of an Appeal Neglected by Marketing," *Journal of Marketing* 34 (January 1970), pp. 54–62.

Exhibit 7–21 Alaska Airlines: courtesy Alaska Airlines.

Exhibit 7–22 Humor: Thomas J. Madden and Marc C. Weinberger, "Humor in Advertising: A Practitioner View." *Journal of Advertising Research* 24, no. 4 (August–September 1984), pp. 23–26.

Exhibit 7–23 Attila the Mac: Apple, the Apple logo, and "The Power to Be Your Best" are registered trademarks of Apple Computer, Inc.

Exhibit 7–24 Olympic promotional: reproduced with permission of U.S. Postal Service.

chapter 8

Infiniti ad: Infiniti Division, Nissan Motor Corporation in USA; photography by Greta Carlstrom ©.

Exhibits 8–1 and 8–2 Infiniti ads: Infiniti Division, Nissan Motor Corporation in USA.

Exhibit 8–3 Dow Chemical: courtesy The Dow Chemical Company.

Exhibit 8–4 Roche research: courtesy Hoffmann-LaRoche Inc.

Exhibit 8–5 Del Monte: reprinted with permission of Del Monte Foods.

Exhibit 8–7 Oldsmobile: courtesy Oldsmobile Division, General Motors Corporation.

Exhibit 8–8 Radar detector: courtesy Cincinnati Microwave.

Exhibit 8–9 Sale: courtesy The Broadway.

Exhibit 8–10 RCA: courtesy RCA Brand, Thomson Consumer Electronics.

Promotional Perspective 8–1 Avia shoes: courtesy Avia.

Exhibit 8–11 Effect of advertising: Robert J. Lavidge and Gary A. Steiner, *Journal of Marketing* 25 (1961), pp. 59–62.

Exhibit 8–13 Checklist: Russell H. Colley, *Defining Advertising Goals for Measured Advertising Results* (New York: Association of National Advertisers, 1961), pp. 62–68.

Exhibit 8–14 Sonance: © Sonance, a Division of Dana Innovations, Kevin W. Topp, art director.

Exhibit 8–15 Hush Puppies: courtesy Fallon McElligott.

Exhibit 8–16 Modified hierarchy: Richard Vaughn, "How Advertising Works: A Planning Model," *Journal of Advertising Research* 20, no. 5 (October 1980), p. 29.

chapter 9

Graphic: © Peter Angelo Simon/The Stock Market.

AAAA recession ad: © American Association of Advertising Agencies.

Exhibit 9–2 Lockheed: courtesy Lockheed Corporation.

Exhibit 9–4 Factors influencing budgets: Paul W. Farris, "Determinants of Advertising Intensity: A Review of the Marketing Literature" (Report no. 77–109, Marketing Science Institute, Cambridge, Massachusetts, 1977).

Exhibit 9–5 RPS: courtesy RPS.

Exhibit 9–6 Importance of budget factors: Herbert Zeltner, "Strategy, Creative Shaping Ad Budgets," *Advertising Age,* January 20, 1986, p. 2.

Exhibit 9–9 Ratios: *Business Marketing,* November, 1991, pp. 111–13.

Exhibit 9–10 Diconix printer: reprinted courtesy Eastman Kodak Company.

Exhibit 9-11 Acura: courtesy Acura Division, American Honda Motor Co., Inc.

Exhibit 9-12 Methods used by consumer advertisers: Kent M. Lancaster and Judith Stern, "Computer Based Advertising Budgeting Practices of Leading U.S. Advertisers," *Journal of Advertising* 12, no. 4 (1983), p. 6.

Exhibit 9-14 Share of advertising/sales relationships: James O. Peckham, *The Wheel of Marketing* (Chicago: A. C. Nielsen Company, 1975).

Exhibit 9-16 Edible advertising: courtesy Gift Service, Inc.

Exhibit 9-17 SOV effect and ad spending chart: James C. Schroer, "Ad Spending: Growing Market Share," *Harvard Business Review,* January–February 1990, p. 48.

chapter 10

Alka Seltzer: courtesy Consumer Healthcare Products, Miles, Inc.

Levy's rye bread: © 1967 Arnold Foods Company, Inc.

Exhibit 10-1 Hallmark: courtesy Hallmark Cards/creative, Leo Burnett U.S.A.; photography, Ken Reid.

Exhibit 10-2 Dupont storyboards: courtesy Dupont Flooring Systems.

Promotional Perspective 10-2 Absolut Vodka: created by Carillon Importers, Ltd., and TBWA Advertising.

Exhibit 10-4 Subaru: courtesy Subaru of America.

Exhibit 10-5 MPA Research newsletter: courtesy Magazine Publishers of America.

Exhibit 10-6 Southwestern Bell: courtesy Southwestern Bell.

Promotional Perspective 10-3 USPS: reproduced with permission of U.S. Postal Service.

Exhibit 10-8 San Diego Bank: used by permission of San Diego Trust & Savings Bank.

Exhibit 10-10 Hathaway man: courtesy Hathaway.

Exhibit 10-12 Nike: courtesy Nike, Inc.

Exhibit 10-13 Mobil 1: reprinted with permission of Mobil Corporation.

Exhibit 10-14 Shampoo: © Patricia M. Doty 1992.

Exhibit 10-15 (a) Lawman jeans: courtesy Lawman Jeans; (b) The Baron: courtesy Evyan Perfumes, New York, NY 10016.

Exhibit 10-16 Raisin Bran: courtesy Kellogg's.

Ethical Perspective 10-1 Benetton: The United Colors of Benetton Spring/Summer, 1992 Advertising campaign; concept, D. Toscani.

chapter 11

Nike montage: courtesy Nike, Inc.

1991 best commercials: Video Storyboard Tests, Inc.

Exhibit 11-1 Goodyear Aquatred: courtesy Goodyear Tire and Rubber Company.

Exhibit 11-2 Jaguar: reprinted courtesy Jaguar Cars, Inc.

Exhibit 11-3 UPS: courtesy United Parcel Service.

Exhibit 11-4 American Airlines: courtesy American Airlines.

Exhibit 11-5 Sharp: courtesy Sharp Electronics Corporation.

Promotional Perspective 11-1 Storyboard: courtesy San Diego Trust & Savings.

Exhibit 11-7 Saab: courtesy Saab-Scania of America, Inc.

Exhibit 11-8 Hershey's ad: courtesy Hershey Foods Corporation. AMERICAN BEAUTY, HERSHEY'S and HERSHEY'S KISSES are trademarks of Hershey Foods Corporation.

Exhibit 11-9 Jeep Cherokee: courtesy Chrysler Corporation.

Exhibit 11-10 Puritan Oil: © The Procter & Gamble Company. Used with permission.

Exhibit 11-11 Castrol GTX: courtesy Castrol, Inc.

Exhibit 11-12 IVAC CRIS: courtesy IVAC Corporation.

Exhibit 11-13 Acura: courtesy Acura Division, American Honda Motor Co., Inc.

Exhibit 11-14 LaserJet: reprinted with permission of Hewlett-Packard Company.

Exhibit 11-15 AT&T: courtesy AT&T Advertising Dept.

Exhibit 11-16 Spuds MacKenzie: courtesy Anheuser-Busch, Inc.

Exhibit 11-17 Travelers Cheques: courtesy American Express Co.

Exhibit 11-18 Audemars Piguet: courtesy Victor Norman & Partners, Inc.

Exhibit 11-19 Children's Defense Fund: courtesy Children's Defense Fund.

Exhibit 11-20 Delta Air Lines: courtesy Delta Air Lines, Inc.

Exhibit 11-21 International Coffees: © General Foods Corp.; used by permission of Young & Rubicam.

Exhibit 11-22 Sanka ad: © General Foods Corporation.

Exhibit 11-23 Art gallery: courtesy American Honda Motor Co., Inc.

Global Perspective 11-1 Taster's Choice: courtesy Nestlé Beverage Company.

Exhibit 11-24 Electronic media production: adapted from *What Every Account Representative Should Know about Television Commercial Production,* 1989. Adapted by permission of the American Association of Advertising Agencies, Inc.; and S. Watson Dunn, Arnold M. Barban, Dean M. Krugran, and Leonard R. Reid, *Advertising: Its Role in Modern Marketing,* 7th ed. (Hinsdale, Ill.: The Dryden Press, 1990), p. 348.

Exhibit 11-25 Phillips: courtesy Phillips Lighting Company.

chapter 12

Universal Card: courtesy AT&T Universal Card Services Corp.

Sensor: courtesy The Gillette Company.

Exhibit 12-1 Advertiser expenditures chart: copyright 1992 by Leading National Advertisers, Inc., Publishers Information Bureau, Inc., and The Arbitron Company.

Exhibit 12-2 Developing media plan: adapted from Jack Z. Sissors and E. Reynolds Petray, *Advertising Media Planning* (Chicago: Crain Books, 1976).

Exhibit 12-4 Cola users: Simmons Market Research Bureau: 1991 Study of Media and Markets.

Exhibit 12-5 Lipstick/gloss users: Mediamark Research, Spring 1992.

Exhibit 12-8 Multimedia services: © copyright 1989 by Arbitron Ratings Company, Leading National Advertisers, Inc., Publishers Information Bureau, Inc., and Media Records, Inc.

Exhibit 12-9 BPI: *Sales & Marketing Management,* August 7, 1989.

Exhibit 12-12 Using BDI and CDI indexes: adapted from Jack C. Sissors and Lincoln Bumba, *Advertising Media Planning,* 3rd. ed. (Lincolnwood, Ill.: NTC Business Books, 1989), p. 155.

Exhibit 12-15 Aerobics traits: Simmons Market Research Bureau: 1991 Study of Media and Markets.

Exhibit 12-18 Who watches ads?: December–January Ratings in New York Market, R.D. Percy & Co.

Exhibit 12-20 Reach for network TRPs: Foote, Cone & Belding, *TV Reach/Frequency Reference Manual* (New York, 1985), p. 4.

Exhibit 12-21 Effects of reach and frequency: adapted from Michael J. Naples, *Effective Frequency: The Relationship between Frequency and Advertising Effectiveness* (New York: Association of National Advertisers, 1979).

Exhibit 12-22 Effective reach graph: data "Effective Exposure: A New Way of Evaluating Media," New York City, Feb. 3, 1977; Michael J. Naples, *Effective Frequency: The Relationship between Frequency and Advertising Effectiveness* (New York: Association of National Advertisers, Inc., 1979), p. 59.

Exhibit 12-23 Frequency level factors: Joseph W. Ostrow, "Setting Frequency Levels: An Art or a Science?" *Marketing and Media Decisions,* 1987, pp. 9–11.

Exhibit 12-28 BAR/LNA: © Copyright 1992 The Arbitron Company and Leading National Advertising, Inc.

Exhibit 12-29 Reach and frequency analyses: San Diego Trust & Savings Bank.

chapter 13

Bud Bowl photos: courtesy Anheuser-Busch.

Exhibit 13-1 TV ownership: *Report on Television-Nielsen Media Research* (New York City: A.C. Nielsen, 1992).

Exhibit 13-2 Acura: courtesy Acura Division, American Honda Motor Co., Inc.

Exhibit 13-3 Top TV advertisers: reprinted with permission from ADVERTISING AGE, September 25, 1991. Copyright Crain Communications, Inc. All Rights Reserved.

Exhibit 13-4 MTV: © 1992 MTV Networks. All rights reserved.

Exhibit 13-5 TV commercials length: Television Advertising Bureau from Arbitron.

Exhibit 13-6 Hershey: courtesy Hershey Foods Corporation.

Exhibit 13-7 Cost of TV commercials: reprinted with permission from ADVERTISING AGE, September 19, 1991. Copyright Crain Communications, Inc. All Rights Reserved.

Exhibit 13-8 WGN-TV: courtesy WGN-TV.

Exhibit 13-9 Syndicated TV programs: *Mediaweek,* March 11, 1991, p. 7.

Exhibit 13-10 Children's programming: *Upfront '91: A Guide to Advertiser Supported Syndication* (New York: Advertiser Syndicated Television Association, 1991), p. 35.

Exhibit 13-12 Cable networks: "*1992 Cable TV Facts,*" Cable-television Advertising Bureau, 1992.

Exhibit 13-13 Cable advertising revenues: Cable Television Special Report, *Adweek,* April 6, 1992, p. 30.

Exhibit 13-14 Nickelodeon: © 1992 MTV Networks. All rights reserved.

Global Perspective 13-1 MTV: © 1992 MTV Networks. All rights reserved. Photo by Fred/Alan, Inc.

Exhibit 13-15 Cable TV: courtesy National Cable Television Association.

Exhibit 13-16 Group W Sports Marketing ad: courtesy Group W Sports Marketing.

Exhibit 13-17 Households using TV: *Report on Television 1989,* Nielsen Media Research (Northbrook, Ill.: A. C. Nielsen Co., 1989).

Exhibit 13-18 People meter photo: courtesy A.C. Nielsen Co.

Exhibit 13-19 Arbitron ADI page: The Arbitron Company.

Exhibit 13-20 TV market sizes: *Cablecasting Yearbook.*

Exhibit 13-21 Radio revenue growth: Radio Advertising Bureau, RADIO MARKETING GUIDE AND FACT BOOK, 1992, p. 21.

Exhibit 13-22 Radio station formats: reprinted from THE M STREET JOURNAL, 1992.

Exhibit 13-23 Radio users: Radio Advertising Bureau, RADIO MARKETING GUIDE AND FACT BOOK, 1992, p. 39.

Exhibit 13-24 Molson radio script: courtesy Martlet Importing Co.

Exhibit 13-26 Radio rate card: The Arbitron Company.

Exhibit 13-27 Arbitron radio ratings: The Arbitron Company.

chapter 14

Life After College magazine: courtesy Life After College and Cosmopolitan Magazine.

Exhibit 14-2 Top magazines: Audit Bureau of Circulations' FAS-FAX report for six months ended December 31, 1991.

Exhibit 14-3 *Runner's World* magazine: courtesy Runner's World Magazine.

Exhibit 14-4 *Beef* magazine: courtesy BEEF, Webb Division, Intertec Publishing Corp.

Exhibit 14-5 *Newsweek 50+* edition: Newsweek Magazine.

Exhibit 14-6 *San Diego* magazine: courtesy San Diego Magazine.

Exhibit 14-7 Geographic editions map: courtesy Newsweek Magazine.

Exhibit 14-8 Honeywell and Transamerica pop-ups: courtesy Honeywell, Inc., and Transamerican Corporation.

Exhibit 14-9 Gatorade scorecard: reprinted with permission of The Quaker Oats Company.

Ethical Perspective 14-1 Cutty Sark ad: courtesy Cutty Sark Scots Whisky.

Exhibit 14-10 Personal and business travel: *A Study of Media Involvement* (New York: Magazine Publishers Association, April 1991), p. 21.

Exhibit 14-11 Top magazines: *Adweek Special Report: Consumer Magazines,* February 17, 1992, p. 26.

Exhibit 14-12 Audit Bureau of Circulations statement: courtesy Audit Bureau of Circulations.

Exhibit 14-13 Magazine demographics: "The Readers of San Diego Magazine—1989," By Don Bowdren Associates.

Exhibit 14-14 Space rates: *Newsweek* 1992 Rates & Data.

Exhibit 14-15 Petersen: courtesy Petersen Publishing Company.

Exhibit 14-16 *Parenting* magazine: reprinted with permission of *Parenting* Magazine.

Exhibit 14-17 Mazda: © 1991 Mazda Motor of America, Inc.; used by permission.

Exhibit 14-18 High-tech costs: reprinted with permission from ADVERTISING AGE, October 6, 1991. Copyright Crain Communications Inc. All Rights Reserved.

Exhibit 14-19 *USA Today* logo: courtesy USA TODAY, Gannett Company Inc.

Promotional Perspective 14-1 *The National:* used by permission of *THE NATIONAL Sports Daily.*

Exhibit 14-20 Hispanic paper: courtesy HispaniMedia.

Exhibit 14-21 *Daily Aztec* paper: courtesy The Daily Aztec.

Exhibit 14-22 Sunday magazine: courtesy Los Angeles Times.

Promotional Perspective 14-2 Merrill Lynch: courtesy Merrill Lynch & Co., Inc.

Exhibit 14-23 Zone editions: Courtesy Los Angeles Times.

Exhibit 14-24 Newspapers read: Simmons Market Research Bureau, *1990 Study of Media & Markets.* This table appeared in "Key Facts 1991," Newspaper Advertising Bureau.

Exhibit 14-25 Union-Tribune market studies: courtesy Union-Tribune Publishing Company.

Exhibit 14-26 Jaguar island: courtesy Jaguar Cars Inc.

Exhibit 14-27 Advertising rates: courtesy The Columbus Dispatch.

Exhibit 14-28 Standard advertising units: courtesy Newspaper Advertising Bureau, Inc.

Exhibit 14-29 Network of City Business Journals: Frank Della Sala, marketing manager—The Network of City Business Journals; Jim Aylward, creative director—Barkley & Evergreen Advertising; Powell Michael, art director—Barkley & Evergreen Advertising.

Exhibit 14-30 *Los Angeles Times:* courtesy Los Angeles Times.

chapter 15

BINGO promotion: courtesy Creative Entertainment Services, Inc.

Summer partnerships: reprinted with permission from ADVERTISING AGE, April 15, 1991. Copyright Crain Communications, Inc. All Rights Reserved.

Exhibit 15-1 Out-of-home billings: reprinted with permission from ADVERTISING AGE Outdoor Services. Copyright Crain Communications, Inc. All Rights Reserved.

Exhibit 15-2 Top outdoor spenders: reprinted with permission from ADVERTISING AGE, April 1, 1991. Copyright Crain Communications, Inc. All Rights Reserved.

Exhibit 15-3 Gorilla Tropics: courtesy San Diego Zoo.

Exhibit 15-4 Tropicana inflatable: Tropicana, Pure Premium & REP. of Girl Device are trademarks of Tropicana Products, Inc. Used in this text by permission.

Ethical Perspective 15-1 Litter removal: courtesy *San Diego Business Journal.*

Exhibit 15-5 Aerial advertising: courtesy National Aerial Advertising, Inc., Wayne Mansfield, president.

Exhibit 15-6 Mobile boards: courtesy Mobile Billboards, Inc.

Exhibit 15-7 In-store media options: "Alternative Media," MEDIAWEEK, February 17, 1992, p. 34.

Exhibit 15-8 Campbell billboard on ski lift: copyright 1989 Ken Kerbs. All rights reserved.

Promotional Perspective 15-1 VideOcart ad: courtesy VideOcart, Inc.

Exhibit 15-9 Rate tables: courtesy Gannett Outdoor Groups.

Exhibit 15–10 Ticket holder: courtesy United Airlines, AT&T/Young & Rubicam.

Exhibit 15–11 Transit posters: courtesy Transportation Displays Incorporated.

Exhibit 15–12 Terminal poster: courtesy Gannett Transit.

Exhibit 15–13 Specialty advertising items: Specialty Advertising Association International.

Exhibit 15–14 Yellow Pages: courtesy Bell Atlantic Directory Services, Bell Atlantic Corporation.

Exhibit 15–15 How people feel about video ads: reprinted with permission from ADVERTISING AGE, May 28, 1990. Copyright Crain Communications, Inc. All Rights Reserved.

Exhibit 15–16 Justin Boots/*City Slickers* ad: courtesy Creative Entertainment Services, Inc.

Exhibit 15–17 CPM for motion picture advertising: *Hollywood Reporter,* July 21, 1992; and Creative Entertainment Services, Inc.; Burbank, CA, 1992.

chapter 16

●**candidates** (right) © Chromosohm/Sohm/The Stock Market (left) © Photri/The Stock Market

Video campaigns: *Adweek's Marketing Week,* "The High-Tech Election."

Exhibit 16–1 Direct marketing chart: Direct Marketing magazine, 224 Seventh St., Garden City, NY 11530-5771.

Exhibit 16–3 Lexus: courtesy LEXUS; photographer, Doug Taub.

Exhibit 16–4 Data collection activity: reprinted with permission from ADVERTISING AGE, December 13, 1991. Copyright Crain Communications, Inc. All Rights Reserved.

Exhibit 16–5 Lists available: courtesy Alvia B. Zeller, Mailing Lists.

Exhibit 16–6 Mail/phone orders: © 1991 by Simmons Market Research Bureau, Inc. All rights reserved.

Exhibit 16–7 Porsche ad: courtesy Porsche Cars North America/Heiman & Associates.

Exhibit 16–8 Catalog shopping: Carla Lazzareschi, "It's in the Mail," *Los Angeles Times,* March 21, 1992, pp. D1–D2.

Exhibit 16–9 Catalogs: courtesy Calyx & Corolla—The Forest Flower Catalog, 1-800-800-7788; Lands' End, Inc.; Chadwick's of Boston; and Tweeds, Inc., Edgewater, N.J.

Exhibit 16–10 USA Sport: courtesy Sport Optics International.

Exhibit 16–11 Dreyfus: courtesy Dreyfus.

Exhibit 16–12 Telemarketing boom: reprinted by permission of THE WALL STREET JOURNAL, © 1991 Dow Jones & Company, Inc. All Rights Reserved Worldwide.

Exhibit 16–13 900 calls categories: reprinted with permission from ADVERTISING AGE, February 17, 1992. Copyright Crain Communications, Inc. All Rights Reserved.

Exhibit 16–14 How videotext works: courtesy The Times Mirror Company, Los Angeles, CA.

Exhibit 16–15 Marketers choose videotext: Videotex America—Gateway—Times Mirror Corporation, 1985, p. 7.

Exhibit 16–16 Tupperware: courtesy Tupperware.

Exhibit 16–17 Cadillac: used by permission of Cadillac Motor Car Division.

chapter 17

Chicken of the Sea: courtesy Van Camp Seafood Co.

Exhibit 17–1 Kix T-shirt offer: TOTAL and KIX are registered trademarks of General Mills, Inc. Advertisements and promotional materials are used with permission of General Mills, Inc.

Exhibit 17–2 Zee towels: courtesy James River Corporation.

Exhibit 17–4 Promotions: ADWEEK'S MARKETING WEEK, April 13, 1992, p. 26.

Global Perspectives 17–1 Diaper wipes: reprinted with permission of Nice-Pak Products, Inc.

Exhibit 17–5 Local promotions: courtesy Pizza Hut, Inc.

Exhibit 17–6 Data bases: Donnelley Marketing, Inc.

Exhibit 17–7 Welch's: courtesy Welch's.

Exhibit 17–8 China: courtesy Colgate-Palmolive Company.

Exhibit 17–9 (a) Arm & Hammer: The ARM & HAMMER® name and logo are registered trademarks of Church & Dwight Co., Inc.; (b) Toro: courtesy The Toro Company.

Exhibit 17–10 Pepsi Challenge: reprinted with permission of Pepsi-Cola Co.

Exhibit 17–11 Consumer promotions: *Donnelley Marketing 11th Annual Survey of Promotional Practices* (Stamford, Conn.: Donnelley Marketing, 1991).

Exhibit 17–12 Sampling methods: Donnelley Marketing, Inc.

Exhibit 17–13 (a) FAB: used by permission of Colgate-Palmolive Company; (b) ArmorAll: courtesy ArmorAll Products Corporation.

Exhibit 17–14 Coupon distribution: *Coupon Distribution and Redemption Patterns* (Chicago: NCH Promotional Services, 1992).

Exhibit 17–15 Ralph's coupons: courtesy Ralph's Grocery Co.

Exhibit 17–16 Coupon redemption: David J. Reibstein and Phyllis A. Traver, "Factors Affecting Coupon Redemption Rates," *Journal of Marketing* 46 (Fall 1982), p. 104.

Exhibit 17–17 Coupon redemption costs: James F. Engel, Martin R. Warshaw, and Thomas C. Kinnear, *Promotional Strategy,* 7th ed. (Homewood, Ill.: Richard D. Irwin, Inc., 1991), p. 553.

Exhibit 17–18 Grocery coupon redemption: *Coupon Distribution and Redemption Patterns, 1991 International Edition* (Chicago: NCH Promotional Services, 1991), p. 25.

Exhibit 17–19 Eggo coupon: Eggo®, Common Sense®, and Kellogg's are registered trademarks of Kellogg Company. All rights reserved.

Promotional Perspective 17–1 Catalina Marketing coupon: courtesy Catalina Marketing Corporation.

Exhibit 17–20 Colgate/Life promotion: used by permission of The Quaker Oats Company.

Exhibit 17–21 Michelob: courtesy Anheuser-Busch, Inc.

Exhibit 17–22 British Airways: courtesy British Airways.

Exhibit 17–23 Quaker Oats: used by permission of The Quaker Oats Company.

Exhibit 17–24 Minute Maid: Minute Maid Orange juice is a registered trademark of The Coca-Cola Company. Used with permission.

Exhibit 17–25 ArmorAll package: courtesy ArmorAll Products Corporation.

Exhibit 17–26 Ban: courtesy Bristol-Myers Company.

Exhibit 17–27 Event sponsorships: reprinted with permission from ADVERTISING AGE, March 23, 1992. Copyright Crain Communications, Inc. All Rights Reserved.

Exhibits 17–28 and 17–29 Chicken of the Sea: courtesy Van Camp Seafood Co.

Exhibit 17–31 WD-40: used by permission of WD-40 Company.

Exhibit 17–32 Ski Summit Colorado ad: courtesy Ski the Summit Colorado—Arapahoe Basin, Breckenridge, Copper Mountain & Keystone.

Exhibit 17–33 Ad: courtesy E. I. DuPont de Nemours & Company and Metal-Cladding, Inc.

Exhibit 17–34 Ad: courtesy DuPont Flooring Systems.

Exhibit 17–35 Interaction of advertising & sales promotions: Don Sunoo and Lynn Y. S. Lin, "Sales Effects of Promotion and Advertising," *Journal of Advertising Research* 18, no. 5 (October 1978), p. 37.

Exhibit 17–36 Lever 2000: courtesy Lever Brothers Company.

Exhibit 17–37 Role of promotions agency: Russ Bowman, "The Envelope, Please," *Marketing & Media Decisions,* April 1988, p. 130.

Exhibit 17–38 Sales promotion dilemma: Michael L. Rothschild, *Marketing Communications* (Lexington, Mass.: D. C. Heath, 1987), p. 436.

chapter 18

American Express: courtesy American Express.

Exhibit 18–1 Uses of marketing and PR: reprinted with permission from the JOURNAL OF MARKETING 42, published by the American Marketing Association, by Philip Kotler and William Mindak, October 1978.

Exhibit 18–2 Exxon: courtesy Exxon Corporation.

Exhibit 18–3 Times Mirror ad rates: Times Mirror Company, Los Angeles, CA.

Exhibit 18–4 Evaluating marketing PR plans: reprinted with permission from MARKETING NEWS, published by the American Marketing Association, by Hugh W. Ryan, March 13, 1989.

Exhibit 18–5 Newsletter: courtesy Hershey Foods Corporation.

Exhibit 18–6 Annual report: courtesy Mycogen Corporation.

Exhibit 18–7 Chevron: courtesy Chevron Corporation.

Exhibit 18–8 SDGE outreach program: San Diego Gas & Electric Company.

Exhibit 18–9 SD KGTV channel 10: courtesy KGTV.

Exhibit 18–10 *Link* Yellow Pages: courtesy Yellow Pages Publishers Association.

Exhibit 18–11 Getting PR story told: reprinted with permission from MARKETING NEWS, published by the American Marketing Association, October 9, 1987.

Exhibit 18–13 *Wall Street Journal* ad: Copyright 1991, Dow Jones & Company, Publisher of *The Wall Street Journal*. All Rights Reserved.

Exhibit 18–14 Measuring PR effectiveness: reprinted with permission from MARKETING NEWS, published by the American Marketing Association, by Katharine Gaine, November 6, 1987.

Ethical Perspective 18–1 Chart: Robert Burns, *Los Angeles Times*.

Exhibit 18–15 Tree Top: used by permission of Tree Top, Inc.

Exhibit 18–16 No Excuses jeans: courtesy New Retail Concepts, Inc.

Exhibit 18–17 Publicity tracking model: reprinted by permission of Ketchum Communications, Inc.

Exhibit 18–18 Allstate: courtesy Allstate Insurance Company.

Exhibit 18–19 NBC Olympics: courtesy NBC Sports.

Exhibit 18–20 1992 Olympics sponsors: Laura Bird, "USOC Curbs 'Backdoor' Tie-Ins," ADWEEK'S MARKETING WEEK, April 8, 1991, p. 4.

Exhibit 18–21 Deloitte & Touche: courtesy Deloitte & Touche.

Exhibit 18–22 Reputation attributes: "The Eight Key Attributes of Reputation," FORTUNE, February 10, 1992, p. 42.

Exhibit 18–23 (a) Mobil Heroes: reprinted with permission of Mobil Corporation; (b) USCEA nuclear energy: this advertisement provided courtesy the U.S. Council for Energy Awareness, Washington, D.C.

Exhibit 18–24 Advocacy ads: courtesy AT&T Advertising.

chapter 19

Hotel employees: courtesy ITT Sheraton Corporation.

Exhibit 19–1 Importance of promotion mix: adapted from Table 9 in Gene R. Laczniak and Robert F. Lusch, "Environment and Strategy in 1995: A Survey of High-Level Executives," *Journal of Business and Industrial Marketing* 2 (Winter 1987), pp. 16–17.

Exhibit 19–2 Sales force in communications mix: David W. Cravens, Gerald E. Hills, and Robert B. Woodruff, *Marketing Decision Making: Concepts and Strategy* (Homewood Ill.: Richard D. Irwin, 1987), p. 546. Reprinted by permission of Richard D. Irwin, Inc.

Exhibit 19–3 Evolution of selling: Thomas R. Wotruba, "The Evolution of Personal Selling," *Journal of Personal Selling and Sales Management* XI, no. 3 (Summer 1991), pp. 1–12.

Exhibit 19–4 Costs per sales call: *Cahners Advertising Research Report* No. 542.2D (Newton, MA: Cahners Publishing Co., 1992).

Exhibit 19–5 Costs to close sales calls: *Cahners Advertising Research Report* No. 542.5C (Newton, MA: Cahners Publishing Co., 1992).

Exhibit 19–7 Giltspur: courtesy Giltspur, Inc./Haddon Advertising.

Promotional Perspective 19–1 How salespeople spend day: adapted from William A. O'Connell and William Keenan, Jr.,

"The Shape of Things to Come," p. 39. Reprinted by permission of SALES & MARKETING MANAGEMENT. Copyright: January 1990.

Exhibit 19–8 Gordon Publications: courtesy Gordon Publications, Inc.

Exhibit 19–9 M/A/R/C: The Richards Group, Dallas, TX.

Exhibit 19–10 Growth of telemarketing: Kate Bertrand, "The Inside Story," *Business Marketing*, September 1987, p. 62.

Exhibit 19–11 Evaluating sales force: Ralph E. Anderson, Joseph F. Hair, and Alan J. Bush, *Professional Sales Management* (New York: McGraw Hill, 1988), p. 519.

chapter 20

Photodeck faces: courtesy BBDO New York: An Agency of the BBDO Worldwide Network.

Exhibit 20–1 After recall: courtesy Chiat/Day/Mojo Inc. Advertising.

Exhibit 20–2 Test methods: adapted from the classification schema utilized by Ivan Ross at the University of Minnesota, in Engel, Warshaw, and Kinnear, *Promotional Strategy,* 6th ed. (Homewood, Ill.: Richard D. Irwin, 1991), p. 504.

Exhibit 20–3 Copy research findings: Benjamin Lipstein and James P. Neelankavil, "Television Advertising Copy Research: A Critical Review of the State of the Art," *Journal of Advertising Research* 24, no. 2 (April–May 1984), p. 21.

Exhibit 20–4 Positioning advertising copy testing: reprinted with permission from MARKETING NEWS, published by the American Marketing Association, February 19, 1982.

Exhibit 20–7 Rough testing terms: "Burke Rough Commercial Recall Testing," Burke Market Research.

Exhibit 20–15, Keds Starch Scored ad: courtesy Starch INRA Hooper.

Exhibit 20–18 Single-source tracking: Dave Kruegel, "Television Advertising Effectiveness and Research Innovation," *Journal of Consumer Marketing* 5, no. 3 (Summer 1988), p. 45; also David Kiley, "Information Resources Wires the Drugstores," *Adweek's Marketing Week,* May 27, 1991, p. 34.

Exhibit 20–19 Make-or-break tracking studies: adapted from Fred Cuba, "Fourteen Things That Make or Break Tracking Studies," *Journal of Advertising Research* 25, no. 1 (February–March 1985), pp. 21–23.

chapter 21

Mass Mutual baseball promos: courtesy Mass Mutual Life Ins. Co.

Exhibit 21–2 Brock: courtesy Brock Control Systems.

Exhibit 21–3 Rating ad agencies: *Starmark Report I*, 1988, p. 7. Reprinted with permission from Business Marketing Magazine. Copyright Crain Communications, Inc.

Exhibit 21–4 Marketers' complaints: *Starmark Report I*, 1988, p. 7. Reprinted with permission from Business Marketing Magazine. Copyright Crain Communications, Inc.

Exhibit 21–5 Transitions: courtesy Transitions Comfort Lenses.

Exhibit 21–6 Nomadic Instand: courtesy Nomadic Display.

Exhibit 21–7 Tektronix: courtesy Tektronix, Inc.

Exhibit 21–8 Promotion allocation: Business/Professional Advertising Association, 1992.

Exhibit 21–9 Top business publications advertisers: *Business Marketing,* October 1991, p. 12.

Exhibit 21–10 Using TV in business advertising: Jeffrey Kaumeyer, "When Should Business/Industrial Advertising Use Broadcast TV?" *Business Marketing,* April 1985, pp. 106–15. Reprinted with permission from Business Marketing Magazine. Copyright Crain Communications, Inc.

Exhibit 21–11 Copiers: courtesy Ricoh Corporation/Gigante Vaz & Partners Advertising, Inc.

Exhibit 21–12 Telemarketing applications: *Business Marketing,* September 1987, p. 70. Reprinted with permission from Business Marketing Magazine. Copyright Crain Communications, Inc.

Exhibit 21–13 Impact Exhibits: courtesy Impact Exhibits, Inc.

Exhibit 21–14 Norwegian Cruise Line: courtesy Norwegian Cruise Line.

Exhibit 21–15 Marketers emphasize PR: *Starmark Report 1,* 1988, p. 12. Reprinted with permission from Business Marketing Magazine. Copyright Crain Communications, Inc.

Exhibit 21–17 Research studies: *Starmark Report I,* 1988, p. 10. Reprinted with permission from Business Marketing Magazine. Copyright Crain Communications, Inc.

Exhibit 21–18 Effectiveness measures: adapted from *Advertising Research* (New York: Business Professional Advertising Association, 1983), pp. 37–60.

Exhibit 21–19 Copy Chasers criteria: *Business Marketing,* January 1989, p. 75. Reprinted with permission from Business Marketing Magazine. Copyright Crain Communications, Inc.

chapter 22

Russian ad: courtesy Merrill Lynch & Co., Inc.

Exhibit 22–1 Seiko: courtesy Seiko Corporation of America.

Exhibit 22–2 McDonald's in Japan: © Tom Wagner/SABA.

Exhibit 22–3 French WD-40: used by permission of WD-40 Company.

Exhibit 22–4 Top advertisers outside U.S.: reprinted with permission from ADVERTISING AGE, October 28, 1991. Copyright Crain Communications, Inc. All Rights Reserved.

Exhibit 22–6 Advertising expenditures: "Twenty-Second Survey of World Advertising Expenditures," Starch INRA Hooper, Inc., in cooperation with International Advertising Association, 1991.

Exhibit 22–7 Nestlé: courtesy Nestlé.

Exhibit 22–8: Heineken: courtesy Heineken Breweries.

Exhibit 22–9 Deodorant consumption: reprinted with permission from ADVERTISING AGE, April 29, 1992. Copyright Crain Communications, Inc. All Rights Reserved.

Exhibit 22–10 Advertising to Japanese: Milton Pierce, "Direct Response in Japan," *Direct Marketing,* November 1986, p. 160.

Exhibit 22–11 Coca-Cola and Coca-Cola Light are registered trademarks of The Coca-Cola Company. Permission granted by The Coca-Cola Company.

Global Perspective 22–1 Country restrictions: courtesy NCH Promotional Services.

Exhibit 22–12 Coca-Cola and Coca-Cola Light are registered trademarks of The Coca-Cola Company. Permission granted by The Coca-Cola Company.

Global Perspective 22–2 Sensor: courtesy The Gillette Company.

Exhibit 22–13 Foreign Nescafe ads: courtesy Nestlé.

Exhibit 22–14 Russian Colgate: courtesy The Colgate-Palmolive Company.

Exhibit 22–15 Saatchi & Saatchi: courtesy Saatchi & Saatchi Advertising Wordwide.

Exhibit 22–16 Singapore Airways: courtesy Singapore Airways.

Exhibit 22–17 Xerox: courtesy Xerox Corporation.

Exhibit 22–18 Lintas: courtesy Lintas Worldwide.

Exhibit 22–19 Criteria to select agency: adapted from Vern Terpstra, *International Marketing,* 4th ed. (New York: Dryden Press, 1987), pp. 432–33.

Exhibit 22–20 NCH: courtesy NCH Promotional Services.

Exhibit 22–21 Purchase habits & brand loyalty: reprinted with permission from AD AGE INTERNATIONAL, April 27, 1992. Copyright Crain Communications, Inc. All Rights Reserved.

Exhibit 22–22 British Häagen-Dazs ad: courtesy Häagen-Dazs.

Exhibit 22–23 *Cosmo:* courtesy Cosmopolitan Magazine.

Global Perspective 22–3 Coupon redemption: NCH Promotional Services, 1991.

Exhibit 22–24 Countries allowing promotions: reprinted with permission from ADVERTISING AGE, August 7, 1989. Copyright Crain Communications, Inc. All Rights Reserved.

Exhibit 22–25 Influence and roles in sales promotion: Kamran Kashani and John A. Quelch, "Can Sales Promotion Go Global," p. 40. Reprinted from BUSINESS HORIZONS (May/June 1990). Copyright 1990 by the Foundation for the School of Business at Indiana University. Used with permission.

chapter 23

Courtroom: Comstock Inc.

Exhibit 23–1 Kinney & Lange ad: published with permission of Kinney & Lange, P.A., Suite 1500, 625 Fourth Avenue South, Minneapolis, Minnesota, 55415; (612) 339-1863, a law firm practicing advertising, communications, entertainment, copyright, trademark, and patent law.

Exhibit 22–2 Wine Institute Code: courtesy the Wine Institute.

Exhibit 22–3 Jacoby Meyers: Jamko Advertising (in-house agency for Jacoby & Meyers Law Offices).

Exhibit 23–4 Sources of NAD cases: *NAD Case Reports,* National Advertising Division, Council of Better Business Bureaus 21, no. 11 (January 20, 1992), p. 58.

Exhibit 23–5 Steps in NAD/NARB review: Council of Better Business Bureaus, Inc., National Advertising Division/National Advertising Review Board Procedures, November 1, 1991.

Exhibit 23–6 AAAA code: © American Association of Advertising Agencies, Inc.

Exhibit 23–7 Kid advertising guidelines: "Double Standard for Kids' TV Ads," *The Wall Street Journal,* June 10, 1988, p. 25.

Exhibit 23–8 FTC organization: Office of the Federal Register National Archives and Records Administration. *The United States Government Manual 1989/90.*

Exhibit 23–9 FTC complaints process: Gary Armstrong and Julie Ozanne, "An Evaluation of NAD/NARB Purpose and Performance," *Journal of Advertising* 12, no. 3 (1983), p. 24. Reprinted with permission.

Exhibit 23–10 Corrective advertising: reprinted with permission from the JOURNAL OF MARKETING 48, published by the American Marketing Association, by William W. Wilkie, Dennis L. McNeill, and Michael B. Mazis, Spring 1984.

Exhibit 23–11 Conclusions on corrective advertising: William L. Wilkie, Dennis L. McNeill, and Michael B. Mazis, "Marketing's 'Scarlet Letter': The Theory and Practice of Corrective Advertising," *Journal of Marketing* 48 (Spring 1984), p. 26.

Exhibit 23–12 Great Earth Teas: © 1992 Wildcraft® Herbs, Santa Cruz, CA 95060.

Exhibit 23–13 Direct-selling code: courtesy the Direct Selling Association.

chapter 24

Sports complex: © Joe Sohm/Chromosohm 1990/The Stock Market

Exhibit 24–1 Anheuser-Busch: reprinted with permission of Anheuser-Busch.

Exhibit 24–2 Calvin Klein perfume: used by permission of Calvin Klein.

Exhibit 24–3 AAF principles: courtesy the American Advertising Federation.

Exhibit 24–4 Lifestyles condoms: courtesy Ansell Inc.

Exhibit 24–5 Corbin Berenson for Maidenform: agency, Levine, Huntley, Schmidt & Beaver; creative, Rochelle Klein, Michael Vitiello; director, Mark Coppos, Coppos Films.

Exhibit 24–6 Maidenform storyboard: agency, Levine, Huntley, Schmidt & Beaver; creative, Rochelle Klein, Michael Vitiello; director, Mark Coppos, Coppos Films.

Exhibit 24–7 Travel Fox ad: courtesy Travel Fox, Inc.

Ethical Perspective 24–1 Calvin Klein: used by permission of Calvin Klein.

Exhibit 24–8 Children's advertising: Children's Advertising Review Unit. *Self-Regulatory Guidelines for Children's Advertising,* 3rd ed., 1988, National Advertising Division, Council of Better Business Bureaus, Inc., pp. 4–5.

Exhibit 24–9 Rolls-Royce: reprinted by permission of Rolls-Royce Motor Cars, Inc.

Exhibit 24–10 Ad Council: © American Association of Advertising Agencies.

Ethical Perspective 24–2 NaturaLawn: courtesy NaturaLawn of America, Inc.

Exhibit 24–11 AAAA ad: © American Association of Advertising Agencies.

Exhibit 24−12 Nike: Courtesy Nike, Inc.

Exhibit 24−13 Doll: Shani® ad is used with the permission of Mattel, Inc.

Exhibit 24−14 AAAA save money ad: © American Association of Advertising Agencies.

Exhibit 24−15 AAAA John Scully ad: © American Association of Advertising Agencies.

Exhibit 24−16 Hyundai: courtesy Hyundai Motor America.

Exhibit 24−17 Product differentiation: reprinted with permission from the JOURNAL OF MARKETING 44, published by the American Marketing Association, by Paul W. Farris and Mark S. Albion, Summer 1980.

Exhibit 24−18 AAAA simple lesson: American Association of Advertising Agencies.

Exhibit 24−19 Advertising's role in economy: reprinted with permission from the JOURNAL OF MARKETING, published by the American Marketing Association, by Paul W. Farris and Mark S. Albion, Summer 1980.

Exhibit 24−20 Leo Burnett speech: used with permission of Leo Burnett Company, Inc.

Name/Company/Brand Index

Subject Index